BLUES LYRIC POETRY

GARLAND REFERENCE LIBRARY
OF THE HUMANITIES
(VOL. 361)

BLUES LYRIC POETRY
An Anthology

Michael Taft

GARLAND PUBLISHING, INC. • NEW YORK & LONDON
1983

This volume is associated with a series of contextual
concordances published by Garland under the general
editorship of Michael J. Preston, Director of The Center
for Computer Research in the Humanities, University of
Colorado at Boulder.

Library of Congress Cataloging in Publication Data

Taft, Michael.
  Blues lyric poetry.

  (Garland reference library of the humanities ; v. 361)
  Bibliography: p.
  Discography: p.
  Includes index.
  1. American poetry—Afro-American authors.   2. American
poetry—20th century.   3. Blues(Songs, etc.)—Texts.
4. Afro-American songs—Texts.   I. Title.   II. Series.
PS591.N4T34   1983   811'.52'08089073   82-48266
ISBN 0-8240-9235-X

Printed on acid-free, 250-year-life paper
Manufactured in the United States of America

For Terry Preston

CONTENTS

PREFACE

This computer-generated anthology serves two main purposes. First, it is a companion piece to *Blues Lyric Poetry: A Concordance* (Taft, *Blues*), and thus gives the user of that concordance the complete poetic context for every word, phrase, or line in which he is interested. Second, this anthology makes available to the reader a large and varied selection of blues lyrics which have either never appeared in print before, or which are scattered among smaller anthologies and blues studies. All of the texts transcribed here are from the 1920 to 1942 period—the race record era—and comprise over two thousand commercially recorded songs sung by over three hundred and fifty singers. Other than the fact that all these singers were black and sang the blues, there are few other common factors in their make-up: their backgrounds, repertoires, styles, and reasons for recording vary greatly. Thus, this anthology includes both country and urban, both male and female, both "downhome" (to use Titon's term) and vaudeville singers. Among those represented here are singers who recorded only one or two songs and those who recorded over a hundred; those who sang accompanied only by their own guitar or piano, and those who were a part of a string band, jug band, or jazz band. As a whole, this anthology is an exploration of the blues lyric and, more specifically, the blues couplet, which defines this lyric form.

The blues, as a form of folk and popular song, demands a clear definition, since the word "blues" itself has generally been used to cover a wide range of both musical and lyric forms. Since this work concentrates upon the lyrics rather than the music of the song form, my inclusion or exclusion of texts in this anthology was based on lyric poetic criteria. Indeed there are both etic and emic reasons for defining the blues primarily as poetry and only secondarily as music. Charles Keil (51) and John Szwed (222) have both seen the blues as primarily a poetic form, and ex-blues singer Rubin Lacy agrees: "the blues is not sung for the tune. It's sung for the words mostly. A real blues singer sings a blues for the words" (Evans 13). Thus, the definition often given of the blues as an eight-, twelve-, or sixteen-bar form of song is not relevant to this study. In fact, this criterion has been overused and overstated in the discussion of the blues form, since the blues rarely conforms to a tight metric structure. Early in the history of blues scholarship, Odum and Johnson discovered this disjoint relationship between blues lyrics and blues music (291), and more recently, Jean Wagner has examined the same phenomenon: "a more or less indefinite number of unaccentuated syllables can be put between the stresses, which makes a blues verse quite lengthy, so that it can be represented typographically in two lines of equal or unequal length" (from *Les poètes nègres des Etats-Unis*, translated in Jahn 167).

To define the structure of the blues stanza is to define the blues itself. As Newman I.

White wrote, "the stanza, and not the song, is the only true unit" in the blues ("White Man" 207), and most scholars since his time have tended to agree with this general premise (for example, see Charters 4, Ferris 34, and Hyman 306). But what is the nature of the blues stanza? Again, since the beginnings of blues scholarship, there has been general agreement that the structure of the stanza is a couplet with the first line repeated twice; but this definition is somewhat off the mark. Niles (2) and White (*American* 387–88) were among the first to recognize that the repetiton of lines is variable in the blues, although the commonest stanzaic form is the one described above. This three-line form is so common, in fact, that even if it is not the best criterion for definition, it is very much the trademark of the blues. Thus, blues singer Leonard Caston's definition is no different from the definitions of most blues scholars:

> In the blues they'd be making these recordings, you're playing the twelve-bar blues, you have to do these things in order for maybe whomsoever listen to this particular thing wouldn't hear it the first thing you said. So you would repeat it so you make sure you get the first thing. And so they would add the rhyming thing at the end. So this would make you do your first line two times and your rhyme would come after. Well this got to be the thing where people listening would expect that; so they still do. So in order to get things across they would do it. (Titon, ed. 24)

Virtually all scholars and singers agree that the lines in the blues stanza should rhyme, although the exact nature of the blues rhyme is more complex than it first appears (see Taft, "Willie" for an extended discussion of this subject). But there is another major stanzaic criterion which, if more subtle, is nevertheless as important as rhyme in defining the blues: the caesura which separates each line into two half-lines. Odum and Johnson were perhaps the first to describe this caesura (267) and three years later, Milton Metfessel actually timed the duration of these half-line breaks in hundredths of a second:

> Take me back daddy [.62] try me one mo' time [.47]
> Ef I doan do to suit you [.29] I'll break my back-bone tryin' (109–10)

More recently Jeff Todd Titon has explored the nature of the caesura from a musicological point of view (Titon 142–43).

The most general definition of the blues stanza, then, is that it is a rhymed couplet in which each line is divided by a caesura. Perhaps one final characteristic is that in most cases there is no enjambment from one line to the next in the stanza; that is, each line is end-stopped. Oster compared the blues stanza to the heroic couplet (70), but of course the blues couplet lacks the strong metrical demand of the heroic couplet. In terms of theme or content of the stanza, perhaps the only generalization to be made is that the blues couplet is a secular rather than a sacred form of poetry and that it describes everyday life. The predominant theme is love and indeed the blues can be described as love poetry or erotic poetry, although some songs (and certainly many individual couplets) are concerned with drink, poverty, war, dancing, eating, horse racing, and countless other common subjects.

What are some of the variations upon this basic blues couplet? The most common type of variation is in the number of repetitions of either the first, the last, or both lines in the couplet. If we represent the basic blues couplet as AA, we can readily see the kinds of repetitions which occur in the blues. As already mentioned, the most common form of repetition is 2AA:

> I'm flying to South Carolina : I got to get there this time
> I'm flying to South Carolina : I got to get there this time
> Women in Dallas Texas : is about to make me lose my mind (JefB 67)

However, the simple, unembellished AA couplet is also quite frequent:

> Good Lord good Lord : send me an angel down
> Can't spare you no angel : will spare you a teasing brown (McTW 33)

It is the first line of the couplet which is most often repeated, but not necessarily just twice. Note the following 3AA form:

> If you want a good woman : get one long and tall
> If you want a good woman : get one long and tall
> If you want a good woman : get one long and tall
> When she go to loving : she make a panther squall (Barn 2)

But the second line of the couplet is also capable of being repeated, as in this A2A example:

> I tell you girls : and I'm going to tell you now
> If you don't want me : please don't dog me around
> If you don't want me : please don't dog me around (Wilk 4)

A singer might opt for a 2A2A stanza, but more commonly, he chose to repeat the entire couplet twice in a 2(AA) structure:

> Well I solemnly swear : Lord I raise my right hand
> That I'm going to get me a woman : you get you another man
> I solemnly swear : Lord I raise my right hand
> That I'm going to get me a woman babe : you get you another man (Hous 2)

Theoretically any combination of repetitions is possible—4AA, 2A3A, 3(AA), 2(2AA), etc.—but the above forms account for nearly all the variations in repetition found in this corpus of the blues.

However, a large number of blues songs employ a type of variation which is not based on repetition; rather these couplets are embellished with a refrain. The refrain may be a short tag-line or a multi-line verse, but it does not have to conform to the blues couplet structure in any way. Note the following examples:

> You say you done quit me : now what should I do
> Can't make up my mind : to love no one but you
>   (refrain): I don't like that
>   No I don't
>   I don't like that
>   No I don't
>   You know it kill me dead
>   I don't like that (Bare 5)

> Look here woman : making me mad
> Done bringing me something : somebody done had
>   (refrain): Carry it right back home
>   I don't want it no more (BelE 5)

Both examples might be represented as AAr couplets, but a more complex stanzaic form combines both repetition and a refrain. Note the following 2AAr couplet:

> I went down in the alley : trying to sell my coke today
> I went down in the alley : trying to sell my coke today
> And a woman run out and hollered : scared my mule away
>   (refrain): She wanted to boodlie-bum-bum
>   She hollered boodlie-bum-bum
>   Oh boodlie-bum boodlie-bum boodlie-bum-bum (CovB 2)

To add further complexity to blues poetry, the refrain itself might also take the stanzaic form of the blues couplet. Thus, the following two examples represent AAr:AA and AAr:2AA stanzaic forms, respectively:

> Early one morning : just about half past three
> You done something : that's really worrying me
>   (refrain): Come on baby : take a little walk with me
>   Back to the same old place : where we long to be (Lock 2)

> I got a gal : she got a Rolls Royce
> She didn't get it all : by using her voice
>   (refrain): I'm wild about my tuni : only thing I crave
>   I'm wild about my tuni : only thing I crave
>   Well sweet patuni : going to carry me to my grave (BakW 8)

Just as the refrain might manifest itself in a number of different forms which bear little or no resemblance to the structure of the blues couplet, the couplet itself may become a refrain, chorus, or blues-like interjection in a basically non-blues song. This phenomenon most often occurs in the songs of female vaudeville singers which, though blues-like in many ways, do not conform to the poetic criteria of the blues. In the following song by Trixie Smith, the first stanza exhibits a non-blues ABAB structure; the second stanza is ABBA; and the third stanza, although AA in structure, has no caesuras in its lines. Only the last two stanzas are blues couplets:

> Now some folks long to have a-plenty money
> Some will want their wine and song
> But all I want is my sweet loving honey
> I cry about him all night long
>
> Once I had a dear sweet daddy but I didn't treat him right
> So he left town
> With Mandy Brown
> That is why I'm blue tonight
>
> So I'm leaving here today
> When I find him he will say
>
> Please come back and love me like you used to do : I think about you every day
> You reap just what you sow in the sweet bye and bye : and be sorry that you went away
>
> Oh baby I'm crazy : almost dead
> I wish I had you here : to hold my aching head (SmiT 14)

In this song there is a definite instrumental and vocal break as Smith shifts into a blues texture. The last line of the third stanza, "When I find him he will say," acts as an introduction to the blues stanzas which follow. Titon has pointed out that such semi-blues were typical Tin Pan Alley, vaudeville songs in which the composers consciously embedded the blues form within a larger framework and often marked the blues section of the song "tempo di blues" on the published sheet music (Titon xvi).

In addition to repetitions, refrains, and "embedding," there were some stylistic devices which singers employed to vary the structure of the individual line or to make one repetition of the line different from the next. Perhaps the most common device of this sort is what might be termed "staggering," in which the singer would repeat parts of a line or a half-line in an incremental fashion. Note the following 3AA couplet:

> When you hear me walking : turn your lamp down, turn your lamp down, lamp down low
> When you hear me walking : turn your lamp down low
> When you hear me walking : turn your lamp down low
> Then turn it so : your man'll never know (Gran 1)

On rare occasions, the singer might sing only a partial blues stanza; that is, there would be no rhyming line to complete the couplet. These partial stanzas could take any number of forms, depending upon the repetitions and refrains which the singer used: A, 2A, 3A, Ar, 2Ar:AA, and so on. In theory, these partial stanzas should not be considered blues couplets at all, but they generally occur within the context of a song where the other stanzas conform to the texture of blues poetry. Rather than being "embedded" non-blues stanzas in a blues song, these stanzas seem to be "implied couplets" in which the singer and listener agree to break the rules in a song. Perhaps indicative of the fact that these half-couplets are a part of the blues poetic form is that they occur, not in the vaudeville compositions, but rather in the more conservative, downhome blues.

The combinations possible within the confines of the simple stanza are many. Add to this the possible combinations of stanzaic types within the same song and the varieties inherent to the texture of the blues become truly astounding. However, the blues singers were rather conservative; many possible combinations never appear in the blues. This conservative tendency is especially clear when one considers that perhaps 80 percent of all blues songs follow the classic 2AA pattern.

Both this anthology and the concordance grew out of a detailed study of the structural and formulaic properties of the half-line and line in the blues couplet (Taft, "Lyrics"). As a reflection of this type of analysis, I have stripped down the transcriptions of these blues texts to their basic couplets. Thus, all repetitions, all refrains which do not conform to the blues couplet structure, and all non-blues stanzas in the vaudeville songs, as well as any spoken interjections or other extrastanzaic elements in the songs have been left out of these transcriptions. Where a refrain does conform to blues couplet structure, I have transcribed it, but only once, no matter how many times that refrain occurs in the song. I transcribed staggered lines only if there was no unstaggered repetition of that line in the stanza.

Admittedly, such transcriptions are not as useful as full verbatim texts, but the choice of stripped-down songs was necessary for the type of computerized study from which these works grew. Thus, as stated at the beginning of the preface, this anthology is more a study of the blues couplet than the blues song. If there is a rationale beyond expediency for this choice of transcription, it is that the blues is an extremely fluid song form; indeed, as pointed out by several recent scholars, the blues is a prime example of formulaic poetry in which neither lines nor half-lines nor stanzas are set, invariable structures (see Barnie, both articles, Taft, "Lyrics," and Titon 178–93). In effect, there is one great blues song from which all the actual blues texts arose. Thus, the floating couplet is the essence of blues poetry and all else is embellishment upon this form.

Of course these texts are stripped down in other ways. I have not attempted musical transcriptions of the tunes, even though the entire song form is an amalgamation of music and poetry. Nor have I attempted to account for stress patterns, intensity of speech, voice quality (such as falsetto), elision, duration, or emphasis in the singing. Indeed no transcription gives a complete version of a text; there must always be compromises based on expediency, clarity, and the intended purpose of the transcription. For the complete version of a text, the reader must listen to the recording; and even then the performance is incomplete, since the actions of the singer in the recording studio were not recorded along with his music and words. However, for every text in this anthology there is relatively easy access to the recording, since all the songs transcribed are available on one or more reissue, long-playing albums (see the Discography). Ideally, the reader can listen to the songs with this anthology in hand and make notes on the transcriptions in order to fill in the gaps inherent in these stripped-down versions.

The method of transcription was the same for all texts in this book. The album was first recorded onto tape and then the tape was played on a transcribing machine, so that difficult passages could be replayed any number of times, speeded up or slowed down, in order to acquire the most accurate transcriptions possible. I used other people's transcriptions only after attempting my own version of a song and then only to verify or clear up those passages which were either questionable or impossible to decipher. There were, of course, many occasions when I could not be sure of what the singer was singing or when I had no idea whatsoever. Worn and scratchy recordings, unfamiliar dialects, dated speech, the slurring of sung words, the interference of the music, and my own idiosyncratic conceptions of the blues lyric all contributed to the inaccuracies in this anthology. As well, since I did these transcriptions over a six-year period (1971–1977) in a fairly random fashion as I acquired more and more albums, my ability to understand the words became increasingly sophisticated as time went on. Unfortunately, this means that my earlier transcriptions are probably less accurate than my later ones.

Where I have been unable to decipher a passage, I have placed three question marks (???), as in the following example:

> And nobody shake it : like papa ??? can (Glov 1)

This symbol in no way indicates the length of the untranscribable passage, but on occasion I have modified the symbol if I think that I hear a word-ending or syllable:

> I'm down in the bottom : ???ing for Johnny Rye (LedB 5)

In total, there are 469 undecipherable passages out of approximately 20,000 lines of poetry. However, there are many more questionable passages; that is, some passages which I have transcribed can only be called educated guesses at what is being sung, either because of the peculiar wording of the passage or the almost inaudible nature of that part of the song. These passages are enclosed in asterisks (*. . .*) in the following manner:

> Now my mama dead : so is my daddy too
> *Should I caught the wire* : trying to get along with you (But1S 3)

Although I have not transcribed repetitions of lines, neither did I make composites of the repetitions. Rather, I generally chose the first singing of a repeated line, or if that line was staggered or in some sense incomplete, I chose the second or third repetition of the line for my transcription. In many cases, however, the repetitions of a line are not exact duplicates of one another—yet another kind of variation in blues poetry. Often a singer would change or leave out exclamations or evocative elements from one repetition to the next (for example, *oh* or *mama*), change verb tenses, alter adverbial or adjectival modifications, or replace a noun with a pronoun. In all such cases in which the change in the repetitions seemed substantive—that is, where a part of the sentence structure or vocabulary was radically changed—I have noted these alterations in the transcription. For example, note the following 2AA stanza:

> Nice to meet strangers : just to come and spend the day
> Awful nice to meet strangers : just to come and spend the day
> But that old-timey rider : can drive your blues away (GibC 11)

Here the word *awful* is inserted in the repetition of the first line. In the transcription, this line appears as "[Awful] nice to meet strangers : just to come and spend the day."

Where a word or phrase is exchanged for another in a repetition, both appear within brackets. Note the following example:

> Tell me what time : do the trains come through your town
> I want to know what time : do the trains come through your town
> I want to laugh and talk : with a long-haired teasing brown (JefB 5)

This variation is transcribed as "[Tell me, I want to know] what time : do the trains come through your town."

There is another variation, however, which is not reflected in these transcriptions. Although in most cases the caesura occurs at a convenient syntactic point in the line—between clauses, before a prepositional phrase, or after a nominal phrase—singers did not always follow this rule. The contingencies of the tune or simply artistic innovation sometimes place the caesura in other parts of the line; indeed sometimes the singer dispensed with the caesura altogether, usually in the second line of the couplet. In all cases, however, I have placed the symbol for the caesura, the colon (:), at the traditional syntactic point in the line, regardless of where the caesura actually falls. Again, this feature of the transcription is a reflection of the structural analysis for which this work was originally intended (Taft, "Lyrics"). In that analysis, I found that each syntactically coherent half-line corresponded to a potential formula in the poetry. By standardizing the placement of the caesura, these formulaic half-lines could be better visualized in the anthology and, more importantly, in the concordance. Thus, although in the great majority of cases the colon corresponds to where the caesura actually occurs, this symbol should be seen as a half-line marker or "ideal" caesura marker. There are a few cases in the corpus in which the singer seemed to substitute a musical break for either the first or second half-line; in these cases, the line either begins or ends with a colon.

Perhaps the most difficult decision to make in transcribing texts concerns dialect and pronunciation. How far should the transcriber go in trying to preserve the phonetic qualities of the singer? In earlier scholarship, blues transcribers tried to be faithful to the dialect (note Metfessel's attempt above), but these efforts usually resulted in transcriptions which were difficult to read, highly inaccurate, and rather insulting to the singer. What might be termed the "Uncle Remus" school of transcribing is a poor substitute for accurate phonetic transcription. But phonetic transcriptions are very difficult to read and, despite their firm bases in linguistics, they are still open to different interpretations by different readers.

For these reasons I have made no attempt to transcribe the singers' pronunciations of words. For example, regardless of whether the word *going* is pronounced *goin'*, *goan*, or *gwine*, I have always transcribed it as *going*. However, I have not changed or standardized dialect words, morphemes, or syntactic features which are peculiar to a singer's speech. Thus, *I's*, *a-crying*, *you be done lost your wife*, *drownded*, and other nonstandard forms remain unaltered in these transcriptions. But there is an area between pronunciation and other dialect features which called for arbitrary decisions. For example, what should be done with nonstandard contractions such as *'cause* and *'fore*? In the case of *'cause*, I standardized all forms of the word to *because*, since such a contraction was not always easily distinguishable from its full form in the singing: the initial *be-* often seemed an unvoiced phonetic element rather than an absent element. The contraction *'fore*, however, seems to have a separate and distinct usage from *before* in the blues, especially when part of the phrase *'fore day creep*; therefore, I have retained this contraction in the transcriptions. Similarly, should *gal* be treated as a phonetic variation on *girl* or as a word in its own right? Because of its frequency and its rhyming qualities, I have chosen to retain *gal* as a separate word from *girl*. In all, I have tried to apply common sense to all such transcription problems.

I have avoided virtually all punctuation in these transcriptions, since periods at the ends of lines, semi-colons, commas, and quotation marks seemed unnecessary and often arbitrary. Although this might lead to certain ambiguities in the texts, I prefer that the reader supply his own sense of punctuation to these songs. This feature of the texts is also an outgrowth of the specific analysis and use of these songs in my earlier work (Taft, "Lyrics"); my aim was to produce clear, uncluttered texts.

The blues songs in this anthology are arranged according to singer and, under each singer, according to the chronological order of dates of recording and sequences in the recording sessions. At the beginning of every text is certain contextual information, as in the following example:

AleT   1   Alexander, Texas
                         title: Long Lonesome Day Blues
                         place and date: New York, 11 Aug. 1927
                         record numbers: (81213–A) OK–8511 Rt RL–315

At the far left is an abbreviation for the singer's name which is necessary for references to and from the concordance. All abbreviations correspond exactly to the alphabetical order of singers as listed in Godrich and Dixon, and each abbreviation has been fashioned so that further singers from the race record era can be inserted, with their abbreviations, into their correct alphabetical order. (Because this anthology is also in computer storage, further names and songs can be added to those printed in this anthology.)

Following this abbreviation is the number of the song—in this case, song number 1 out of 19 songs by Alexander in this anthology—and the name of the singer. Where a song is attributed to a group in Godrich and Dixon, such as the Memphis Jug Band, I have listed the text under the name of the lead vocalist for the group, again as cited in Godrich and Dixon. In a few cases, the lead vocalist is not known; such texts have been placed under UnkA which stands for "unknown artist." In order to retrieve all songs sung by a band or group, refer to the Cross-Reference List of Groups. Where a singer does not appear in Godrich and Dixon under his own name but under the name of a group or another singer, this information appears in parentheses after the singer's name. For example, see BigB 20 Big Bill (State Street Boys).

On the next line is the title of the song as given in Godrich and Dixon. Where Godrich and Dixon give more than one title for a song, I have noted only the first title which they list. Information on place and date of recording also comes from Godrich and Dixon, unless more accurate information was available from record notes.

The line marked "record numbers" contains four pieces of information. First, the matrix or master number of the recording is given in parentheses. This number pinpoints the location and sequence in the daily recording sessions of the record companies and is important in identifying the relationship of the song to the entire output of the race record era. In the above example, the master number is 81213. Within the parentheses following this number is the take number or letter which indicates which version of the song sung in the recording studio has been transcribed. Thus, A1eT 1 was the first (and perhaps only) version of the song recorded by Alexander. Note however that JorL 1 and JorL 2 are different versions of the same song sung by Luke Jordan and recorded in succession; they have the same master number, 39819, but different take numbers, 1 and 2. All master and take numbers are from Godrich and Dixon unless more accurate information was available from record notes (as was the case with JorL 1).

The next information on this line is the original catalogue number for the 78 rpm recording of the text. The letters before the dash are an abbreviation for the record company or label on which the song was recorded (see Abbreviations for Race Record Labels) and the alphanumeric designation after the dash is the catalogue number. Customers and store owners used this number for ordering records and the record companies kept track of their inventories through this numbering system. Because nearly all of the race records were two-sided discs, two songs share the same catalogue number. See Aker 1 and Aker 2 for an example of a shared catalogue number on the Vocalion label, Vo–1442. Where a song was issued on two or more race record labels, I have indicated only the first label and catalogue number listed in Godrich and Dixon. In some cases, the recording was never issued but remained a test pressing or a master in the possession of the record company. Where such songs have been recorded on more recent long-playing albums, their catalogue number is replaced by the word "unissued." See JorL 1 for an example. Again, Godrich and Dixon has been the major source for this information.

The final information on this line is the label and catalogue number of the long-playing album from which the song was transcribed. The label either appears as a separate two or three-letter abbreviation followed by an alphanumeric catalogue designation, or, where the catalogue designation contains no letters, as an abbreviation attached by a dash to the catalogue number. Thus, in the example above, Rt is the label, Roots, and RL–315 is the catalogue number for the album. Under Aker 1, however, the more simple OJL–2 refers to the Origin Jazz Library label, record number 2. For the code to long-playing album abbreviations, see the Discography and Abbreviations for Long-Playing Album Labels. Although some of these songs have been reissued on more than one album, the designated album is the one from which the song was transcribed.

The song couplets themselves are transcribed in the order in which they were sung. Where a blues couplet refrain appears throughout a song, its first appearance is noted in the text (for example, coming after the first AA couplet) and further repetitions have not been transcribed. However, if each repetition of the refrain shows substantive changes, each of these altered refrains has been transcribed. Note that in some instances the line numbers skip; see ThoH 7 for one example. These skips indicate that the singer has sung a half-couplet stanza (A, 2A, Ar, etc.), and the missing line number refers to the missing or implied second line of the couplet. Thus, in all songs, the odd numbers always refer to the first line of the couplet and the even numbers always refer to the second line in the couplet.

In a few instances, a blues song is sung by two singers, each singing alternating stanzas or even sometimes alternating lines within the couplets. Following the general format of the anthology, those lines and stanzas sung by one singer are listed under her name, while those of the other singer are listed under his name. For example, note that JohLo 10 and SpiV 7 are different parts of the same song.

The final section of this anthology is a line-concordance index to the titles of the songs. Because of the fluid nature of blues titles, a simple alphabetical listing of titles seemed a less-than-useful exercise. However, one of the advantages of a computer-generated anthology is that different text-reordering programs can be applied to the corpus with relative ease. Thus, a more useful index of titles is the one presented: a concordance which lists every word in the titles in alphabetical order and lists every instance of every word by the alphabetical and numerical order of the singer and song. For instance, if one wishes to know which songs have the word *jail* in their title, one simply looks up the word in the concordance-index. There one sees the head-word *JAIL* followed by the number of occurrences of the word among the two thousand song titles—in this case, eight. Reading down the list, one finds every instance in the same order as one would find if one laboriously read through the entire anthology: first Bare 3, then CollS 1, then EvanJ 1, and so on. In order to save space, some insubstantive words such as *a*, *and*, and *the* have not been searched.

I am in debt to a number of people and institutions. I thank Neil V. Rosenberg for lending me records from his collection and for giving me his advice over the years. I also thank the Archives of Traditional Music at Indiana University for allowing me access to their record collection; and thanks as well to Frank Gillis, Director of the Archives for his encouragement and help. The computing centres at Memorial University of Newfoundland and the University of Saskatchewan have been most cooperative, and I thank them. My greatest debt is to Dr. Michael J. Preston, Director of the Center for Computer Research in the Humanities at the University of Colorado at Boulder, a good friend and colleague, who kept me on track and who played an essential part in the alchemy which turned a jumble of transcriptions into an anthology.

REFERENCES

Barnie, John. "Formulaic Lines and Stanzas in the Country Blues." *Ethnomusicology* 22 (1978), 457–73.

——————. "Oral Formulas in the Country Blues." *Southern Folklore Quarterly* 42 (1978), 39–52.

Charters, Samuel B. "An Introduction." In *Country Blues Songbook*. Ed. Stefan Grossman, Stephen Calt, and Hal Grossman. New York: Oak, 1973, 4–6.

Evans, David. "The Rev. Rubin Lacy—Part 4." *Blues Unlimited* 43 (1967), 13–14.

Ferris, William R., Jr. *Blues from the Delta*. London: Studio Vista, 1970.

Godrich, John, and Robert M.W. Dixon. *Blues & Gospel Records 1902–1942*. Rev. ed. London: Storyville, 1969.

Hyman, Stanley Edgar. "Negro Literature and Folk Tradition." *Partisan Review* (1958). Rpt. *The Promised End: Essays and Reviews 1942–1962*. By Stanley Edgar Hyman. Cleveland and New York: World, 1963, 295–315.

Jahn, Jahnheinz. *A History of Neo-African Literature*. Trans. Oliver Coburn and Ursula Lehrburger. London: Faber and Faber, 1968.

Keil, Charles. *Urban Blues*. Chicago: Univ. of Chicago Press, 1966.

Metfessel, Milton. *Phonophotography in Folk Music*. Chapel Hill: Univ. of North Carolina Press, 1928.

Niles, Abbe. "Introduction." In *Blues: An Anthology*. By W.C. Handy. New York: Boni, 1926, 1–40.

Odum, Howard W., and Guy B. Johnson. *The Negro and His Songs*. Chapel Hill: Univ. of North Carolina Press, 1925.

Oster, Harry. *Living Country Blues*. Detroit: Folklore Associates, 1969.

Szwed, John F. "Afro-American Musical Adaptation." In *Afro-American Anthropology: Contemporary Perspectives*. Ed. Norman E. Whitten, Jr. and John F. Szwed. New York: The Free Press; London: Collier-Macmillan, 1970, 219–27.

Taft, Michael. *Blues Lyric Poetry: A Concordance*. New York: Garland, forthcoming.

——————. "The Lyrics of Race Record Blues, 1920–1942: A Semantic Approach to the Structural Analysis of a Formulaic System." Diss. Memorial Univ. of Newfoundland, 1977.

——————. "Willie McTell's Rules of Rhyme: A Brief Excursion into Blues Phonetics." *Southern Folklore Quarterly* 42 (1978), 53–71.

Titon, Jeff Todd. *Early Downhome Blues: A Musical and Cultural Analysis.* Urbana: Univ. of Illinois Press, 1977.

——————, ed. *From Blues to Pop: The Autobiography of Leonard "Baby Doo" Caston.* JEMF Special Series, no. 4. Los Angeles: John Edwards Memorial Foundation, 1974.

White, Newman I. *American Negro Folk-Songs.* 1928; rpt. Hatboro, Pa.: Folklore Associates, 1965.

——————. "The White Man in the Woodpile: Some Influences on Negro Secular Folk-Songs." *American Speech* 4 (1928–29), 207–15.

DISCOGRAPHY

This discography lists all long-playing albums from which the texts were taken. All albums are twelve-inch, 33⅓ rpm phonodiscs. Unless otherwise noted, each citation refers to one, double-sided phonodisc. Albums are listed alphabetically according to label and numerically according to catalogue number. Where place and date of recording are noted on the album, this information is included in the listing.

Ace of Hearts
    AH-77 *The Harlem Hamfats.* London, 1964.
    AH-158 *Out Came the Blues: Vol. 2.* London, 1967.
Biograph
    BLP-12000 *Blind Lemon Jefferson, 1926–1929.* New York.
    BLP-12001 *Blues the World Forgot: Ma Rainey and Her Georgia Jazz Band, 1924–28.* New York.
    BLP-12003 *Bootleg Rum Dum Blues: Blind Blake, 1926–1930.* New York.
    BLP-12004 *Ramblin' Mind Blues: Ramblin' Thomas, 1928.* New York.
    BLP-12013 *Early Leadbelly, 1935–1940: Narrated by Woody Guthrie.* New York, 1969.
    BLP-12015 *Master of the Blues: Blind Lemon Jefferson, Vol. 2: 1926–1929.* New York, 1969.
    BLP-12022 *Ethel Waters, "Oh Daddy."* New York.
    BLP-12023 *Search Warrant Blues: Blind Blake, 1926–1932.* New York.
    BLP-12029 *Skip James: King of the Delta Blues Singers, 1928–1964.* Canaan, N.Y.
    BLP-12031 *No Dough Blues, Vol. 3: Blind Blake, 1926–1929.* Canaan, N.Y.
    BLP-12037 *Rope Stretchin' Blues: Blind Blake, Vol. 4, 1926–31.* Canaan, N.Y., 1972.
    BLP-12041 *Mississippi & Beale Street Sheiks, 1927–1932.* Canaan, N.Y., 1972.
    BLP-12042 *Papa Charlie Jackson, 1925–1928.* Canaan, N.Y., 1972.
    BLP-C4 *Mississippi John Hurt, 1928: His First Recordings.* Canaan, N.Y., 1972.
    BLP-C6 *Mr. Armstrong Plays the Blues: Featuring Louis Armstrong, 1925–1927.* Canaan, N.Y., 1973.
    BLP-C9 *Leroy Carr: Singin' the Blues, 1934.* Canaan, N.Y., 1972.
Blues Classics
    BC-1 *Blues Classics by Memphis Minnie.*
    BC-2 *Blues Classics by the Jug, Jook and Washboard Bands.* Berkeley.
    BC-3 *Blues Classics by Sonny Boy Williamson.*
    BC-4 *Peetie Wheatstraw and Kokomo Arnold.*
    BC-5 *Country Blues Classics, Volume 1.*
    BC-6 *Country Blues Classics, Volume 2.*
    BC-7 *Country Blues Classics, Volume 3.*
    BC-10 *Blues Classics by Washboard Sam.*

BC-11 *Blind Boy Fuller with Sonny Terry and Bull City Red.*
BC-13 *Memphis Minnie, Vol. 2: With Kansas Joe, 1930–31.* Berkeley.
BC-14 *Country Blues Classics, Volume 4.* Berkeley.
BC-20 *Blues Classics by Sonny Boy Williamson, Volume 2.* Berkeley.
BC-21 *Big Joe Williams and Sonny Boy Williamson.* Berkeley.
Brunswick
Br-87.504 *Bad Luck Blues: Une anthologie du blues.* Paris
BYG
529.073 *Ida Cox.* Archive of Jazz, Vol. 23. France
529.078 *Gertrude "Ma" Rainey.* Archive of Jazz, Vol. 28. France.
Collector's Classics
CC-3 *The Male Blues Singers, Vol. 1.*
CC-25 *Kokomo Arnold.* Masters of the Blues, Vol. 4.
CC-29 *Trixie Smith.* Masters of the Blues, Vol. 5.
CC-30 *Lonnie Johnson.* Masters of the Blues, Vol. 6.
CC-32 *Louis Armstrong: The Blues Singers.* Masters of the Blues, Vol. 8.
CC-33 *Little Brother Montgomery.* Masters of the Blues, Vol. 9.
CC-36 *Barbecue Bob.* Masters of the Blues, Vol. 10.
CC-37 *Gut Bucket Trombone: Ike Rodgers.* Masters of the Blues, Vol. 11.
Columbia
C-30034 *Robert Johnson: King of the Delta Blues Singers, Volume II.*
C-30035 *Leadbelly.*
C-30036 *Bukka White: Parchman Farm.* New York.
C-30496 *Blues Before Sunrise: Leroy Carr, Piano and Vocal.* New York.
CL-855 *The Bessie Smith Story, Vol. I.*
CL-856 *The Bessie Smith Story, Vol. II.*
CL-857 *The Bessie Smith Story, Vol. III.*
CL-858 *The Bessie Smith Story, Vol. IV.*
CL-1654 *Robert Johnson: King of the Delta Blues Singers.*
Coral
CP-58 *Out Came the Blues.* London, 1970.
Flyright
LP-103 *Goin' Away Walking: Various Artists.* Weybridge, U.K.
Folkways
FA-2951 *Anthology of American Folk Music: Volume One: Ballads.* New York, 1952. 2 phonodiscs.
FA-2953 *Anthology of American Folk Music: Volume Three: Songs.* New York, 1952. 2 phonodiscs.
FJ-2801 *Jazz, Vol. 1: South.* New York, 1950.
FJ-2802 *Jazz, Vol. 2: The Blues.* New York, 1950.
Herwin
H-201 *Sic 'Em Dogs on Me, 1927 to 1939.* Glen Cove, N.Y.
H-205 *Fillin' in Blues, 1928–1930.* Glen Cove, N.Y.
H-208 *Cannon's Jug Stompers.* New York, 1973. 2 phonodiscs.
Historical Records
HLP-1 *Rare Blues of the Twenties, No. 1.* New York, 1966.
HLP-2 *Rare Blues of the Twenties.* Jersey City, N.J.
HLP-4 *Rare Blues, 1927–1935.* Jersey City, N.J.
HLP-5 *Rare Blues, 1927–1930.* Jersey City, N.J.
HLP-15 *Pot Hound Blues, 1923–1930.* Jersey City, N.J.
HLP-17 *They Sang the Blues, Vol. 1 (1927–1929).* Jersey City, N.J.
HLP-21 *Anna Bell, Katherine Henderson, Laura Bryant. Acc. by Clarence Williams' Orchestra, 1928–1929.* Jersey City, N.J.
HLP-22 *They Sang the Blues, 1927–1934.* Jersey City, N.J.

HLP-31 *Masters of the Blues, 1928–1940*. Jersey City, N.J., 1969.
HLP-32 *I'm Wild About My Lovin', 1928–1930*. Jersey City, N.J., 1969.
HLP-8002 *Early Country Music*. Jersey City.

Joker
SM-3098 *Great Blues Singers*. La storia del jazz. Milano, 1971.
SM-3104 *The Jug Bands: Memphis Jug Band 1929–1934*. La storia del jazz. Milano, 1971.

Mamlish
S-3802 *Mississippi Bottom Blues*.
S-3803 *Low Down Memphis Barrelhouse Blues (1928–1935)*. New York.
S-3804 *Stop and Listen Blues: The Mississippi Sheiks*. New York.

Melodeon
MLP-7324 *The Party Blues*. Washington, D.C.

Milestone
MLP-2001 *The Immortal Ma Rainey*. New York, 1966.
MLP-2004 *The Immortal Blind Lemon Jefferson*. New York, 1967.
MLP-2007 *Blind Lemon Jefferson, Volume Two*. New York, 1968.
MLP-2013 *Black Snake Moan: Blind Lemon Jefferson*. New York, 1970.
MLP-2018 *Pitchin' Boogie: A Second Collection of Boogie Woogie Rarities*. New York, 1971.

Origin Jazz Library
OJL-2 *Really! The Country Blues*. New York.
OJL-3 *Henry Thomas Sings the Texas Blues*.
OJL-4 *The Great Jug Bands*. Berkeley.
OJL-5 *The Mississippi Blues 1927–1940*. Berkeley.
OJL-6 *The Country Girls*. Berkeley.
OJL-8 *Country Blues Encores 1927–1935*. Berkeley.
OJL-10 *Crying Sam Collins and His Git-Fiddle*.
OJL-11 *The Mississippi Blues No. 2: The Delta, 1929–32*. Berkeley.
OJL-14 *Alabama Country, 1927–31*. Berkeley.
OJL-15 *Rugged Piano Classics, 1927–1939*. Berkeley.
OJL-17 *The Mississippi Blues, No. 3: Transition, 1926–1937*. Berkeley.
OJL-18 *Let's Go Riding*. Berkeley.
OJL-19 *More of That Jug Band Sound, 1927–1939*. Berkeley.
OJL-20 *The Blues in St. Louis, 1929–1937*. Berkeley.
OJL-21 *The Blues in Memphis, 1927–39*. Berkeley.

Paltram
PL-101 *The Early Recordings of Memphis Minnie and Kansas Joe (1929–1936)*.

RBF Records
RF-1 *The Country Blues*. New York, 1959.
RF-6 *The Jug Bands*. New York, 1963.
RF-8 *Sleepy John Estes, 1929–1940*. New York, 1964.
RF-9 *The Country Blues: Volume Two*. New York, 1964.
RF-11 *Blues Rediscoveries*. New York, 1966.
RF-12 *Piano Blues*. New York, 1966.
RF-14 *Blues Roots/Mississippi*. New York, 1966.
RF-15 *The Atlanta Blues*. New York, 1966.
RF-16 *Blues Roots/Chicago: The 1930's*. New York, 1967.
RF-202 *The Rural Blues: A Study of the Vocal and Instrumental Resources*. New York, 1964.
 2 phonodiscs.

RCA, RCA International
730.581 *Memphis Slim (1940–1941)*. Black & White, Vol. 10. France.
INT-1085 *Think You Need a Shot: Walter Davis*. London, 1970.
INT-1087 *Big Joe Williams: Crawlin' King Snake*. London, 1970.

INT-1088 *Sonny Boy Williamson: Bluebird Blues.* London, 1970.

INT-1175 *Travellin' This Lonesome Road: A Victor/Bluebird Anthology.* London, 1970.

INT-1177 *You Got to Reap What You Sow: Jazz Gillum.* London, 1970.

LPV-518 *Bluebird Blues.* Vintage Series. New York, 1965.

LPV-574 *Lil Green: Romance in the Dark.* Vintage Series. New York, 1971.

LPV-577 *Feeling Lowdown: Washboard Sam.* Vintage Series. New York, 1971.

Riverside

RLP-12-125 *Blind Lemon Jefferson: Classic Folk-Blues by Blind Lemon Jefferson.* Jazz Archive Series. New York.

RM-8803 *Georgia Tom and Friends.* Classic Jazz Masters. New York.

RM-8819 *Mr. Sykes Blues, 1929–1932.* Classic Jazz Masters. New York.

Roots

RL-301 *Blind Lemon Jefferson: Volume 1.*

RL-305 *"Cross Cut Saw Blues": Tommy McClennan (1939–1941).*

RL-306 *Blind Lemon Jefferson: Volume 2.*

RL-307 *The Memphis Area, 1927–1932.*

RL-308 *Frank Stokes with Dan Sane and Will Batts (1927–1929).*

RL-310 *Missouri and Tennessee (1924–1937).*

RL-311 *Harmonicas, Washboards, Fiddles, Jugs (1927–1933).*

RL-312 *Texas Country Music, Vol. 1 (1928–1936).*

RL-313 *"Down South" (Louisiana–Mississippi–Alabama–Florida).*

RL-314 *Mississippi Blues, Vol. 3 (1928–1942).*

RL-315 *Texas Country Music, Vol. 2 (1927–1937).*

RL-316 *The Country Fiddlers.*

RL-317 *Lucille Bogan and Walter Roland (1930–1935).*

RL-318 *The East Coast States (Georgia–Carolinas–Virginia) (1927–1940).*

RL-319 *Up and Down the Mississippi (1926–1940).*

RL-321 *Great Harmonica Players (1927–1940): Volume 2.*

RL-322 *Memphis Jug Band Volume 1: 1927–1929.*

RL-323 *Memphis Blues (1927–1939).*

RL-324 *King of the Georgia Blues Singers: Blind Willie McTell (1929–1935).*

RL-325 *Alabama Country Blues (1924–1933).*

RL-326 *The East Coast States: Vol. 2 (1924–1938).*

RL-327 *Texas Country Music Vol. 3 (1927–1937).*

RL-329 *Memphis Blues (1927–1939), Vol. 2.*

RL-330 *The Famous 1928 Tommy Johnson–Ishman Bracey Session.*

RL-333 *Kings of Memphis Town (1927–1930).*

RL-334 *Country Blues Obscurities, Vol. 1 (1926–1936).*

RL-335 *Texas & Louisiana Country (1927–1932).*

RL-337 *Memphis Jug Band: Volume 2 (1927–1934).*

RL-340 *Country Blues Obscurities, Vol. 2 (1927–1936).*

Saydisc

SDR-163 *Kokomo Arnold.* Matchbox Blues Series. Badminton, U.K., 1969.

SDR-191 *Volume One: Peetie Wheatstraw: The Devil's Son-In-Law, 1930–36.* Matchbox Blues Series. Badminton, U.K.

SDR-192 *Volume Two: Peetie Wheatstraw: The High Sheriff from Hell.* Matchbox Blues Series. Badminton, U.K.

Spivey

LP-2001 *The Victoria Spivey Recorded Legacy of the Blues.* New York.

Swaggie

S-1219 *The Blues of Sleepy John Estes: Volume One.* The Jazz Makers. Victoria, Australia.

S-1220 *The Blues of Sleepy John Estes: Volume Two.* The Jazz Makers. Victoria, Australia.

S-1225 *The Blues of Lonnie Johnson.* The Jazz Makers. Victoria, Australia, 1969.
S-1240 *Blues Singers: Jazz Sounds of the 20's.* The Jazz Makers. Victoria, Australia, 1962.
S-1276 *Eddie Lang and Lonnie Johnson: Volume Two.* The Jazz Makers. Victoria, Australia, 1970.

VJM
VLP-15 *Clara Smith: Volume One.* London, 1967.
VLP-16 *Clara Smith: Volume Two.* London, 1968.
VLP-17 *Clara Smith: Volume Three.* London, 1969.
VLP-23 *Maggie Jones: Volume One, 1924–5.* London, 1969.
VLP-25 *Maggie Jones: Volume Two, 1925–6.* London, 1969.
VLP-40 *Hard Luck Blues.* London, 1972.

Yazoo, Blezona
L-1001 *Mississippi Blues, 1927–1941.* New York.
L-1002 *Ten Years in Memphis, 1927–1937.* New York.
L-1003 *St. Louis Town, 1929–1937.* New York.
L-1004 *Tex-Arkana–Louisiana Country, 1927–1932.* New York.
L-1005 *Blind Willie McTell: The Early Years (1927–1933).* New York.
L-1006 *Alabama Blues, 1927–1931.* New York.
L-1007 *Jackson Blues, 1928–1938.* New York.
L-1008 *Frank Stoke's Dream, 1927–1931 (The Memphis Blues).* New York.
L-1009 *Mississippi Moaners, 1927–42.* New York.
L-1010 *Buddy Boy Hawkins & His Buddies.* New York.
L-1011 *The Young Big Bill Broonzy, 1928–1935.* New York
L-1012 *The Georgia Blues, 1927–1933.* New York.
L-1014 *Bo Carter: Greatest Hits, 1930–1940.* New York.
L-1015 *Favorite Country Blues-Guitar Duets (1929–1937).* New York.
L-1016 *Guitar Wizards (1926–1935).* New York.
L-1017 *Bessie Jackson & Walter Roland (1927–1935).* New York.
L-1018 *Going Away Blues (1926–1935).* New York.
L-1019 *Scrapper Blackwell (1928–1934).* New York.
L-1020 *Charley Patton: Founder of the Delta Blues.* New York. 2 phonodiscs.
L-1021 *Memphis Jamboree, 1927–1936.* New York.
L-1025 *Cripple Clarence Lofton & Walter Davis.* New York.
L-1026 *Bottleneck Blues Guitar Classics, 1926–1937.* New York.
L-1027 *Clifford Gibson: Beat You Doing It.* New York.
L-1028 *Barrelhouse Blues, 1927–1936.* New York.
L-1029 *Papa Charlie Jackson: Fat Mouth, 1924–1929.* New York.
L-1030 *St. Louis Blues, 1929–1935: The Depression.* New York.
L-1031 *"Funny Papa" Smith: The Original Howling Wolf, 1930–1931.* New York.
L-1032 *Blues from the Western States, 1927–1949.* New York.
L-1033 *Roosevelt Sykes: The Country Blues Piano Ace, 1929–1932.* New York.
L-1034 *Bo Carter, 1931–1940.* New York.
L-1035 *Big Bill Broonzy, 1928–1935: Do That Guitar Rag.* New York.
L-1036 *Leroy Carr & Scrapper Blackwell: Naptown Blues, 1929–1934.* New York.
L-1037 *Blind Willie McTell, 1927–1935.* New York.
L-1038 *Lonesome Road Blues: 15 Years in the Mississippi Delta, 1926–1941.* New York.
L-1039 *Tampa Red: Bottleneck Guitar, 1928–1937.* New York.
L-1041 *Georgia Tom Dorsey, 1928–1932: Come on Mama Do That Dance.* New York.

ABBREVIATIONS FOR RACE RECORD LABELS

Ajax	*Ajax*	Me	*Melotone*
ARC	*American Record Company*	OK	*Okeh*
Ba	*Banner*	Or	*Oriole*
BB	*Bluebird*	Pat	*Pathe-Actualle*
BP	*Black Patti*	Pe	*Perfect*
Br	*Brunswick*	Pm	*Paramount*
BS	*Black Swan*	QRS	*QRS*
Ch	*Champion*	Spt	*Supertone*
Co	*Columbia*	Vi	*Victor*
De	*Decca*	Vo	*Vocalion*
Ge	*Gennett*		

ABBREVIATIONS FOR LONG-PLAYING ALBUM LABELS

AH	*Ace of Hearts*	Mel	*Melodeon*
BC	*Blues Classics*	Mil	*Milestone*
Bio	*Biograph*	OJL	*Origin Jazz Library*
Br	*Brunswick*	Pal	*Paltram*
BYG	*BYG*	RBF	*RBF Records*
CC	*Collector's Classics*	RCA	*RCA, RCA International*
Co	*Columbia*	Riv	*Riverside*
Cor	*Coral*	Rt	*Roots*
Fly	*Flyright*	Say	*Saydisc*
Fwy	*Folkways*	Spi	*Spivey*
Her	*Herwin*	Sw	*Swaggie*
His	*Historical Records*	VJM	*VJM*
Jo	*Joker*	Yz	*Yazoo, Belzona*
Mam	*Mamlish*		

CROSS-REFERENCE LIST FOR GROUPS

Birmingham Jug Band, *see* UnkA 7, UnkA 8, UnkA 9, UnkA 10.

Butterbeans and Susie, *see* EdwJ 1, EdwJ 2, EdwS 1, EdwS 2.

Cannon's Jug Stompers, *see* LewN 1, LewN 2, LewN 3, ThpA 1, WooH 1, WooH 2, WooH 3, WooH 4, WooH 5.

Dallas Jamboree Jug Band, *see* DaviC 1.

Famous Hokum Boys, *see* BigB 3.

Frenchy's String Band, *see* JonCo 2.

Harlem Hamfats, *see* McCoJ 20, McCoJ 21, McCoJ 22, McCoJ 23, McCoJ 24, McCoJ 25, McCoJ 26, MoraH 1.

The Hokum Boys, *see* RobB 1, RobB 2.

T. C. Johnson Groups, *see* HayeN 1, NelsT 1.

Kansas City Blues Strummers, *see* UnkA 1.

Memphis Jug Band, *see* BlacM 1, BlacM 2, BlacM 3, Burs 1, ClayJ 1, ClayJ 2, ClayJ 3, HarZ 1, HarZ 2, MemM 6, MemM 7, Nick 1, Nick 2, Nick 3, Nick 4, Nick 5, Nick 6, Nick 7, Nick 8, Nick 9, PooJ 1, PooJ 2, Rame 1, Rame 2, Rame 3, Shad 1, Shad 2, Shad 3, Shad 4, Shad 5, Shad 6, Shad 7, Shad 8, Shad 9, Shad 10, Shad 11, Shad 12, Shad 13, Shad 14, Shad 15, Shad 16, Shad 17, Shad 18, Shad 19, Shad 20, Shad 21, Stev 1, Stev 2, Stev 5, Stev 6, Stev 7, Stev 8, UnkA 2, UnkA 4, Weld 1, Weld 2, Weld 3, Weld 6.

Mississippi Sheiks, *see* ChatB 11, ChatL 1, ChatL 2, ChatL 3, Vinc 2, Vinc 3, Vinc 4, Vinc 5, Vinc 6, Vinc 7, Vinc 8, Vinc 9, Vinc 10, Vinc 11, Vinc 12, Vinc 13, Vinc 14, Vinc 15, Vinc 16, Vinc 17, Vinc 18, Vinc 19, Vinc 20.

Shreveport Home Wreckers, *see* Scha 1, Scha 2.

Smith and Harper, *see* SmiA 1.

State Street Boys, *see* BigB 20.

An Anthology of
Blues Lyric Poetry

Aker   1   Akers, Garfield

        title: Cottonfield Blues--Part 1
        place and date: Memphis, c. 23 Sept. 1929
        record numbers: (M-201-) Vo-1442 OJL-2

1   I said look a-here mama : what in the world are you
      trying to do
2   You want to make me love you : you going to break my
      heart in two
3   I said you don't want me : what made you want to lie
4   Now the day you quit me fair brown : baby that's the
      day you die
5   I'd rather see you dead : buried in some cypress
      grove
6   Than to hear some gossip mama : that she had done
      you so
7   It was early one morning : just about the break of
      day
8   And along brownskin coming : man and drove me away
9   Lord my baby quit me : she done set my trunk
      outdoors
10 That put the poor boy wandering : Lord along the
      road
11 I said trouble here mama : and trouble everywhere
      you go
12 And it's trouble here mama : baby good gal I don't
      know

Aker   2   Akers, Garfield

        title: Cottonfield Blues--Part 2
        place and date: Memphis, c. 23 Sept. 1929
        record numbers: (M-202-) Vo-1442 OJL-2

1   I got something I'm going to tell you : mama keep it
      all to yourself
2   Don't you tell your mama : don't you tell nobody
      else
3   I'm going to write you a letter : I'm going to mail
      it in the air
4   Then I know you going to catch it : babe in this
      world somewhere
5   I'm going to write you a letter : I'm going to mail
      it in the sky
6   Mama I know you going to catch it : when the wind
      blows on the line
7   Ooh : mama I don't know what to do
8   I knows you'll go : leave me all lowdown and blue
9   Ooh : that's the last word you said
10 And I just can't remember : babe last old words you
      said

Aker   3   Akers, Garfield

        title: Dough Roller Blues
        place and date: Memphis, c. 21 Feb. 1930
        record numbers: (MEM-776-) Vo-1481 OJL-11

1   And I rolled and I tumbled : and I cried the whole
      night long
2   And I rose this morning : and I didn't know right
      from wrong
3   Have you ever woke up : and found your dough-roller
      gone
4   Then you wring your hands : and you cry the whole
      day long
5   And I told my woman : just before I left your town
6   Don't you let nobody : tear the barrelhouse down
7   And I fold my arms : and I begin to walk away
8   I said that's all right sweet mama : your trouble's
      going to come some day

Aker   4   Akers, Garfield

        title: Jumpin' and Shoutin' Blues
        place and date: Memphis, c. 21 Feb. 1930
        record numbers: (MEM-777-A) Vo-1481 OJL-8

1   Lord I know my baby : sure going to jump and shout
2   When the train get here : I come a-rolling out
3   Lord I tell you it wasn't no need : of mama trying
      to be so kind
4   Ah you know you don't love me : you ain't got me on
      your mind
5   Mmm : you ain't got me on your mind
6   And it's what is the need : of baby trying to be so
      kind
7   Mmm : tried to treat her right
8   But you started with another man : and stayed out
      every day and night
9   Says I ain't going down : this big road by myself
10 If I can't get you mama : I'm going to get somebody
      else
11 Mmm : what you want your babe to do
12 Says I know it's something : gal it ain't no use

AleT   1   Alexander, Texas

        title: Long Lonesome Day Blues
        place and date: New York, 11 Aug. 1927
        record numbers: (81213-A) OK-8511 Rt RL-315

1   Yes today has been : a long old lonesome day
2   Lord it seem like tomorrow : going to be the same
      old way
3   Oh tell me pretty mama : how you want your rolling
      done
4   Don't want to do : just like my old-time rider done
5   Don't a woman act funny : she's going to put you
      down
6   She *jumped in the bay* : with a case of ???
7   Woman *use the jelly* : I like those old-time ???

AleT   2   Alexander, Texas

        title: Corn-Bread Blues
        place and date: New York, 12 Aug. 1927
        record numbers: (81223-A) OK-8511 Rt RL-315

1   I've got a brownskin woman : she lives up on that
      hill
2   Lord the fool trying to quit me : man but I love her
      still
3   She was a *broad back middy* : and a gambling
      stomping whore
4   She got a new way of getting down : have to get low
      as a toad
5   Some of [these, you] women : I just can't understand
6   They cook corn bread for their husbands : and
      biscuits for their men

AleT   3   Alexander, Texas

        title: Section Gang Blues
        place and date: New York, 12 Aug. 1927
        record numbers: (81224-B) OK-8498 Rt RL-312

1   I been working on the section : *section* thirty-two
2   I'll get a dollar and a quarter : I won't have to
      work hard as you
3   Oh nigger licked molasses : and the white man licked
      them too
4   I wonder what in the world : is the Mexican going to
      do
5   Oh captain captain : what's the matter with you
6   If you got any Battle Ax : please sir give me a chew
7   Water boy water boy : bring your water around
8   If you ain't got no water : set your bucket down

3

AleT   3   Alexander, Texas

  9   Oh captain captain : what time of day
10   Oh he looked at me : and he walked away

AleT   4   Alexander, Texas

    title: Levee Camp Moan Blues
    place and date: New York, 12 Aug. 1927
    record numbers: (81225-B) OK-8498 RBF RF-9

  1   Lord they accused me of murder : I haven't harmed a
     man
  2   Oh they accused me of forgery : I can't write my
     name
  3   Oh I went all around : that whole corral
  4   Lord I couldn't find a mule : with his shoulder well
  5   Oh I worked old Maude : and I worked old Belle
  6   Lord I couldn't find a mule : Maggie with his
     shoulder well
  7   Mmm : mmm
  8   Mmm : Lord that morning bell
  9   Lord she went up the country : and but she's on my
     mind
11   Oh if she don't come on the big boat : she better
     not land

AleT   5   Alexander, Texas

    title: Yellow Girl Blues
    place and date: San Antonio, 9 Mar. 1928
    record numbers: (400442-B) OK-8801 His HLP-31

  1   Some of these women : I just can't understand
  2   They run around here : with one another's man
  3   Oh black woman evil : brownskin evil too
  4   Going to get me a yellow woman : see what she will
     do
  5   Going to get me a heaven : heaven kingdom of my own
  6   So these brownskin women : can cluster around my
     throne

AleT   6   Alexander, Texas

    title: No More Woman Blues
    place and date: San Antonio, 9 Mar. 1928
    record numbers: (400446-A) OK-8624 Rt RL-312

  1   Lord she won't pick cotton : girl won't pick no corn
  2   Baby I don't see why : you want to hang around me so
     long
  3   And it's one two three four : five six seven eight
     nine
  4   When I count them blues : the men and women is mine
  5   Lord if I get lucky : mama in this world again
  6   I ain't going to fool with no more women : and a
     mighty few men
  7   Mmm : mmm
  8   Lord I walked all last night : and all last night
     before

AleT   7   Alexander, Texas

    title: Sittin' on a Log
    place and date: San Antonio, 10 Mar. 1928
    record numbers: (400454-B) OK-8624 Rt RL-312

  1   I was sitting on a log : just like a doggone dog
  2   That's the mean old woman : come and crossed my
     heart
  3   Says I went to the church : and they called on me to
     pray
  4   I fell down on my knees : and forgot just what to
     say
  5   Oh Lordy mama : what am I to do

AleT   7   Alexander, Texas

  6   I'm going to stay right here : wait on something new

AleT   8   Alexander, Texas

    title: Work Ox Blues
    place and date: New York, 15 Nov. 1928
    record numbers: (401330-A) OK-8658 Sw S-1276

  1   Mama I ain't going to be : your old work ox no more
  2   You done fooled around woman : let your ox get gored
  3   She will get up early in the morning : just awhile
     before day
  4   Then cook your breakfast : man rush you away
  5   Come in daddy : know my ox is gone
  6   You can never tell : when your ox is coming back
     home
  7   You can never tell : what the double-crossing women
     will do
  8   Says they will have your buddy : then play fake on
     you

AleT   9   Alexander, Texas

    title: The Risin' Sun
    place and date: New York, 15 Nov. 1928
    record numbers: (401331-A) OK-8673 Sw S-1276

  1   My woman got something : just like the rising sun
  2   You can never tell : when that work is done
  3   It's no use to worrying : about the days being long
  4   Neither worry about your rolling : because it's sure
     going on
  5   She got something round : and it look just like a
     bat
  6   Sometime I wonder : what in the hell is that

AleT   10   Alexander, Texas

    title: I Am Calling Blues
    place and date: New York, 20 Nov. 1928
    record numbers: (401349-A) OK-8801 His HLP-31

  1   Listen here woman : I'm calling on your name
  2   You got me in trouble : and you say you ain't to
     blame
  3   Don't you never drive : a stranger from your door
  4   He may be your best friend : mama says you don't
     know
  5   My woman got something : and I ain't ashamed
  6   When I love my woman : it puts me in a strain

AleT   11   Alexander, Texas

    title: Double Crossing Blues
    place and date: San Antonio, 15 June 1929
    record numbers: (402639-B) OK-8745 Yz L-1032

  1   Some men like dogging : I just declare I don't
  2   Babe if you think I'm same your mistreating men : I
     declare I won't
  3   Let's stop our foolishness : and try to settle down
  4   Says I [always] [wants, likes] a woman : that do not
     run around
  5   I used to have a woman : good as any in this town
  6   She had so many men : she kept me always crying

AleT 12   Alexander, Texas

      title: Ninety-Eight Degree Blues
      place and date: San Antonio, 15 June 1929
      record numbers: (402640-A) OK-8705 Yz L-1004

1 I'm going to get up in the morning : do like Buddy
    Brown
2 I'm going to eat my breakfast : man and lay back
    down
3 When a man get hairy : know he needs a shave
4 When a woman get musty : you know she needs to bathe
5 I've got something to tell you : make the hair rise
    on your head
6 Got a new way of loving a woman : make the springs
    screech on her bed
7 If you don't believe I love you : look what a fool
    I've been
8 Woman if you don't believe I love you : ah look what
    a shape I'm in
9 I says I love my baby : better than I do myself
10 If she don't love me : she won't love nobody else

AleT 13   Alexander, Texas

      title: Water Bound Blues
      place and date: San Antonio, 15 June 1929
      record numbers: (402642-A) OK-8785 Rt RL-327

1 Now my home's on the water : spending awhile on land
2 I was trying to find a woman : that ain't got no man
3 Says I used to have a friend : by the name of Sam
4 Says we was ragged and dirty : some called us a
    tramp
5 Says I stole my woman : from my friend they call him
    Sam
6 Says that scoundrel got lucky : stoled her back
    again
7 I was raised on the desert : born in a lion's den
8 Says my chief occupation : taking *musky* men women
9 Says I never had a woman : couldn't get her back
    again
10 Says I traveled over this country : every kind of
    man

AleT 14   Alexander, Texas

      title: Awful Moaning Blues--Part 1
      place and date: San Antonio, 15 June 1929
      record numbers: (402643-B) OK-8731 Rt RL-327

1 I been moaning moaning : ever since you been gone
2 Going to find a new way of moaning : bring my woman
    back home
3 Says I went back home : and I looked up side the
    wall
4 Says I could not find : my woman's clothes at all

AleT 15   Alexander, Texas

      title: Awful Moaning Blues--Part 2
      place and date: San Antonio, 15 June 1929
      record numbers: (402644-B) OK-8731 Rt RL-327

1 Mmm : mmm
2 I been moaning woman : ever since you been gone
3 Says I went back home : and I looked up on the shelf
4 Says I'm getting mighty tired : sleeping by myself
5 Says I went back home : and I walked up and down the
    hall
6 Says I spied another mule : pawing in my stall
7 Says I moaned early in the morning : moaned late
    late at night
8 I was trying to moan to your satisfaction : till I
    treat my woman right
9 Mmm : mmm

AleT 15   Alexander, Texas

10 Says I'm going to moan going to moan : till I treat
    my baby right

AleT 16   Alexander, Texas

      title: When You Get to Thinking
      place and date: San Antonio, 27 Nov. 1929
      record numbers: (403359-B) OK-8764 Fly LP-103

1 A married woman : best woman ever been born
2 Only trouble you have : is trying to keep her at
    home
3 My woman left me this morning : but I blame myself
4 That backbiting man taken my woman : now he's going
    to the west
5 I can't sleep at night : when I lay down to take my
    rest
6 Say the woman I love Lord : she is my partner's maid

AleT 17   Alexander, Texas

      title: Seen Better Days
      place and date: San Antonio, 9 June 1930
      record numbers: (404112-B) OK-8890 Rt RL-316

1 I seen better days : when times wasn't so hard
2 Says my woman got mad : and drove me out of her yard
3 I wonder what can the matter : with poor Betsy Mae
4 Lord she got mad : and drove poor me away
5 Says I wonder what's the matter : with my
    troublesome mind
6 Says I must be thinking : about my woman I left
    behind
7 My woman she got something : works like sleeping
    pills
8 It takes all of my time : to try to keep my backbone
    still
9 That's why I can't keep from thinking : times I used
    to have
10 Sometime I think : Lord I declare I declare

AleT 18   Alexander, Texas

      title: Frost Texas Tornado Blues
      place and date: San Antonio, 9 June 1930
      record numbers: (404117-B) OK-8890 Rt RL-316

1 I was sitting looking : way out across the world
2 Said the wind had things switching : almost in a
    twirl
3 Says I been a good fellow : just good as I can be
4 Says it's Lord have mercy : Lord have mercy on me
5 Mmm : mmm
6 Says I been a good fellow : just as good as a man
    could be
7 Some *lost their baby* : was blowing for two three
    miles around
8 When they come to their right mind : they come on
    back to town
9 Said rooster was crowing cows was lowing : never
    heard such a noise before
10 Does it seem like hell was broke out : in this place
    below

AleT 19   Alexander, Texas

      title: Easy Rider Blues
      place and date: Fort Worth, 30 Sept. 1934
      record numbers: (FW-1138) Vo-02856 Yz L-1010

1 Says I wonder where : my easy rider gone
2 She's a easy rider : but she do right not so long
3 Some give her a nickel : some give her a lousy dime

AleT 19   Alexander, Texas

4   She's a easy rider : but she do right all sometime
5   I wonder what's the matter : you ain't got no
    settled mind
6   Says I got a little woman : ??? behind
7   Say it's in the morning : so late in the night
8   When she's loving you man : she loves you just right
9   I say every time : that evening sun go down
10 We gets in the bed : and we stay there a great long
    time
11 It takes midnight *watch* : the early rising sun
12 I looked out the window : says here my baby comes
13 What you going to do mama : when your thing give out
14 I'm going to telephone you : *we all* jump and shout
15 I ain't going to tell no story : tell you no doggone
    lie
16 Say when you get to loving : man I near about die

Amos 1   Amos, Blind Joe

        title: C and O Blues
        place and date: probably Chicago, c. July 1927
        record numbers: (   ) Vo-1116 OJL-17

1   Did you ever wake up : between midnight and day
2   And felt for your rider : she done eased away
3   Fourteen long years : C and O run by my door
4   My fair brown told me this morning : she didn't want
    me no more
5   If you don't want me baby : what makes you wine and
    cry
6   You put that thing on me mama : and let a black
    child die
7   Which a-way which a-way : did the C and O leave your
    town
8   She's gone west baby : *Capital* Creek Junction
    bound
9   My mama told me baby : two long years ago
10 If you fool with that little woman : you'll have
    nowhere to go
11 Want all of you men : to clearly understand
12 Take a Alabama woman : sure going to quit you for
    another man
13 I love you baby : tell the whole round world I do
14 I love you baby : don't care what you do

Ande 1   Anderson, . . . (Walter Taylor)

        title: Thirty-Eight and Plus
        place and date: Richmond, Ind., 14 Feb. 1930
        record numbers: (16266-B) Ge-7157 Fwy FJ-2801

1   I woke up this morning : about half past four
2   Told my girl : I couldn't use her no more
3   Look here pretty mama : what you done done
4   You done made me love you : now your man done come
5   Say God made a woman : he made her mighty funny
6   Ring around her mouth : is just as sweet as any
    honey
7   Say I got a key : shine like gold
8   The women all tell me : satisfied their soul
9   ??? : treat me right
10 ??? *women* : ??? *side*
11 Going away pretty mama : won't be back till fall
12 If I don't get back then : I won't be back at all
13 Said a monkey and a baboon : setting in the grass
14 One said no : and the other said yes

AndeJ 1   Anderson, Jelly Roll

        title: Free Woman Blues
        place and date: Chicago or Richmond, Ind.,
         19 Apr. 1927
        record numbers: (12718-B) Ge-6135 Rt RL-340

1   Six bits ain't no dollar : six months ain't no long
    time

AndeJ 1   Anderson, Jelly Roll

2   If you want to come to your baby : you can see me
    any time
3   Take me for your prisoner : let that one I love go
    free
4   Six months in the workhouse : sure ain't hard for me
5   If you take me back baby : I'll let you be my boss
6   Let you do anything : but nail me on the cross
7   Baby baby baby : I got all my clothes out on pawn
8   I'm going to wake up one morning : and have all my
    glad rags gone

AndeJ 2   Anderson, Jelly Roll

        title: I. C. Blues
        place and date: Chicago or Richmond, Ind.,
         19 Apr. 1927
        record numbers: (12722) Ge-6135 His HLP-22

1   Trouble trouble : ever since I been a man
2   Seems like me and trouble : is just running hand and
    hand
3   I've had trouble in Rock Island : also on the old S
    T
4   But I seem so miscontented : every time I ride the
    big I C
5   Very next time I ride the I C : that long whistle
    blow
6   I'm going to hop right on : won't even stop to pack
    my clothes
7   When that I C train : goes hurrying around that
    lonesome bend
8   I'll be back to see my baby : but the Lord only
    knows when

ArnK 1   Arnold, Kokomo

        title: Rainy Night Blues
        place and date: Memphis, 17 May 1930
        record numbers: (59938-2) Vi-23268 Yz L-1012

1   Now it was early one morning mama : I was on my way
    to school
2   Lord that's when I got the notion : to break my
    mama's rule
3   Oh the blues : falling like showers of rain
4   I tell you once in a while moment : think I hear my
    baby call my name
5   Lord I cried last night mama : then I cried the
    whole night long
6   Going to do right mama : then I won't have to cry no
    more
7   Lord I don't feel welcome : pretty mama no place I
    go
8   Because the little woman I love mama : has a-drove
    me from her door

ArnK 2   Arnold, Kokomo

        title: Milk Cow Blues
        place and date: Chicago, 10 Sept. 1934
        record numbers: (C-9428-B) De-7026 BC-4

1   Hollering good morning : I said blues how do you do
2   Fell mighty well this morning : can't get along with
    you
3   I cannot do right baby : when you won't do right
    yourself
4   Lord if my good gal quits me : well I don't want
    nobody else

ArnK   2   Arnold, Kokomo

5   Now you can read out your handbook : preach out your Bible
6   Fall down on your knees and pray : the good Lord to help you
7   Because you going to need : you going to need my help some day
8   Mama if you can't quit your sinning : please quit your lowdown ways
9   Says I woke up this morning : and I looked outdoors
10 Says I know my mamlish milkcow pretty mama : Lord by the way she lows
11 Lord if you see my milkcow buddy : I said please drive her home
12 Says I ain't had no milk and butter mama : Lord since my cow been gone
13 Says my blues fell this morning : and my love come falling down
14 Says I'll be your lowdown dog mama : but please don't dog me around
15 Takes a rocking chair to rock mama : a rubber ball to roll
16 Take a little teasing brown mama : just to pacify my soul
17 Lord I don't feel welcome : eee no place I go
18 Lord the little woman I love mama : have done drove me from her door

ArnK   3   Arnold, Kokomo

    title: Old Original Kokomo Blues
    place and date: Chicago, 10 Sept. 1934
    record numbers: (C-9429-B) De-7026 BC-4

1   Now one and one is two mama : two and two is four
2   Mess around here pretty mama : you know we got to go
3   Crying oh : baby don't you want to go
4   Back to the *living light* city : to sweet old Kokomo
5   Now four and one is five mama : five and one is six
6   You mess around here pretty mama : you going to get me tricked
7   Now six and one is seven mama : seven and one is eight
8   You mess around here pretty mama : you going to make me late
9   Says I told you mama : when you first fell across my bed
10 You been drinking your bad whiskey : and talking all out your head
11 I don't drink because I'm dry mama : don't drink because I'm blue
12 The reason I drink pretty mama : I can't get along with you
13 Now eight and one is nine mama : nine and one is ten
14 You mess around here pretty mama : I'm going to take you in
15 Now ten and one is eleven mama : eleven and one is twelve
16 You mess around here pretty mama : you going to catch you a lot of hell

ArnK   4   Arnold, Kokomo

    title: Old Black Cat Blues
    place and date: Chicago, 15 Jan. 1935
    record numbers: (C-9653-A) De-7050 CC-25

1   I believe : that I got those black cat blues
2   Lord if I win on Friday : please Saturday night I'm sure to lose
3   Yes the black cat blues mama : ain't nothing but a doggone heart disease
4   Said I was broke and disgusted : I didn't have no money for Christmas Eve

ArnK   4   Arnold, Kokomo

5   Yes this black cat blues mama : don't mean no one nar' no good
6   Said all my friends done forgot me : everybody's down on me in my neighborhood
7   Lord some folks said blues and trouble nothing : but evil running across your mind
8   When you get to setting down thinking : about the black gal treated you so nice and kind
9   Oh if the black cat blues was money : I would be rich as Henry Ford
10 Lord if the black cat blues don't leave me mama : Lord I've got to get further down the road

ArnK   5   Arnold, Kokomo

    title: Sissy Man Blues
    place and date: Chicago, 15 Jan. 1935
    record numbers: (C-9654-A) De-7050 CC-25

1   I believe : I believe I'll go back home
2   Lord acknowledge to my good gal mama : Lord that I have done you wrong
3   Now I'm going to ring up China yeah man : see can I find my good gal over there
4   Says the Good Book tells me : that I got a good gal in this world some where
5   Oh and the church bells is toning yeah man : on one Sunday morning
6   Hollering some old dirty deacon : I mean rung that bell stole my gal and gone
7   Lord if you can't send me no woman : please send me some sissy man
8   Lord I woke up this morning : with my Port China tickets in my hand
9   I'm going to sing these blues mama yeah man : and I'm going to lay them upon your shelf
10 Lord you going to hear these blues again mama : well you sure got to sing them yourself

ArnK   6   Arnold, Kokomo

    title: Front Door Blues
    place and date: Chicago, 15 Jan. 1935
    record numbers: (C-9655-A) De-7156 BC-4

1   Says I knocked on my front door mama : my good gal wouldn't seem to let me in
2   Says it must be another rounder : laying up with my old black hen
3   Says it thunders and lightnings : and the rain begins to fall
4   Says it must've be another mule : mama kicking in my stall
5   Says I'm going to buy me a thirty-two twenty mama : with a long six inch barrel
6   Says I'm going to kill that mule : then I'm sure going kill my gal
7   Then I'm going to Caruthersville mama : just to take that right-hand road
8   Says I never quit walking : till I walked up in my mama's door
9   Says I'll be sad and I'll be lonesome : worried I'll be blue
10 Says I'm tired : of being worried with you

ArnK   7   Arnold, Kokomo

    title: Back Door Blues
    place and date: Chicago, 15 Jan. 1935
    record numbers: (C-9656-A) De-7156 CC-25

1   Says the blues come down the alley : headed up to my back door

2   Says I had the blues today mama : just like I never
     had before
3   Blues and trouble : have been my best friends
4   I says when my blues leave me : my trouble just
     walked in
5   Now some folks says blues is trouble : nothing but
     evil running across your mind
6   Lord when you setting down thinking about someone :
     have treated you so nice and kind
7   Said you roll and you tumble : till it almost make
     you blind
8   When you get to thinking about your good gal : well
     you almost to lose your mind
9   I said when you start walking : your mind running
     every way
10   If you think about that old black woman : Lord that
     led you off astray

ArnK   8   Arnold, Kokomo

     title: The Twelves
     place and date: Chicago, 18 Jan. 1935
     record numbers: (C-9671-A) De-7083 Say SDR-163

1   Says I want everybody : fall in line
2   Shake your shimmy : like I'm shaking mine
3   You shake your shimmy : shake it fast
4   If you can't shake your shimmy : shake your yas yas
     yas
5   Says *I am* with your mama : out across the field
6   Slipping and a-sliding : just like an automobile
7   I hollered at your mama : I told her to wait
8   She slipped away from me : just like a Cadillac
     Eight
9   Say I like your mama : sister too
10   I did like your papa : but your papa wouldn't do
11   I met your papa : around the corner the other day
12   I soon found out : that he was funny that a-way
13   Says I went out yonder : New Orleans
14   The wildcat jumped : on the sewing machine
15   The sewing machine : sewed so fast
16   Sewed ninety-nine stitches : up his yas yas yas
17   Says God made Adam : made him stout
18   He wasn't satisfied : until he made him a snout
19   He made him a snout : just as long as a rail
20   He wasn't satisfied : until he made him a tail
21   He made him a tail : just to fan the flies
22   He wasn't satisfied : until he made him some eyes
23   He made him some eyes : just to look on the grass
24   He wasn't satisfied : then he made his yas yas yas
25   He made his yas yas yas : so he couldn't get a trick
26   He wasn't satisfied : until he made him sick
27   He made him sick : and then made him well
28   You know by that : the big boy's coughing in hell

ArnK   9   Arnold, Kokomo

     title: Slop Jar Blues
     place and date: Chicago, 5 Feb. 1935
     record numbers: (C-9776-A) De-7092 Say SDR-163

1   Says I feel just like mama : throwing my slop jar in
     your face
2   Said you done lost your mind : and let that old
     out-minder take my place
3   Now I could cut your throat mama : and drink your
     blood like wine
4   Because you's a dirty old buzzard : and you sure
     done lost your mind
5   Mama here I am : right out in the cold again
6   Says the woman that I'm loving : got brains just
     like a turkey hen
7   Says I'd rather be a catfish : down in the Gulf of
     Mexico

8   Than to hear the woman that I'm loving : say sweet
     papa I got to go
9   Then I cried : till my pillow got soaking wet
10   Says I walked all the way up Beale Street : I bowed
     my head at every old gal I met

ArnK   10   Arnold, Kokomo

     title: Black Annie
     place and date: Chicago, 5 Feb. 1935
     record numbers: (C-9777-A) De-7092 Say SDR-163

1   Well I stood on the corner mama : and I looked two
     blocks and a half
2   Lord I never seed Black Annie : but I sure God heard
     her laugh
3   Then I went down the alley : with my gatling gun in
     my hand
4   Just to kill my woman : for loving another man
5   Now it's trouble trouble : I been had it all my days
6   Well it seems like trouble : going to follow me to
     my grave
7   Now my love is just like water : you can turn it off
     and on
8   Now when you think I'm loving you mama : well I done
     turned you off and gone
9   Now I'm going to set my picture : Lord up on your
     shelf
10   Lord if you don't live with me mama : well you ain't
     going to live with nobody else

ArnK   11   Arnold, Kokomo

     title: Southern Railroad Blues
     place and date: Chicago, 18 Apr. 1935
     record numbers: (C-9921-A) De-7139 Say SDR-163

1   Says my gal she caught the Southern : and the
     fireman he rang the bell
2   And the engineer he left the station : just like a
     bat up out of hell
3   Said I waved my hand : she didn't even look around
4   Said and I felt like dropping : right down on the
     ground
5   Mama here I am : down on my bended knees
6   Says I'm crying to the good Lord : send me back my
     good gal if you please
7   Said now I got a notion : to leave this lonesome
     town
8   Says my gal she caught the Southern : and I know she
     done put me down
9   Now my old bones is aching : and my hair is turning
     grey
10   Said I'm going back home mama : and I'm going back
     there to stay

ArnK   12   Arnold, Kokomo

     title: Busy Bootin'
     place and date: Chicago, 18 Apr. 1935
     record numbers: (C-9923-A) De-7139 Say SDR-163

1   Busy booting : and you can't come in
2   Come back tomorrow night : and try it again
3   I met your mama : in the alley way
4   She's catching hunkies : both night and day
5   Don't you remember : last Friday night
6   You go out in the street : and you want to fight
7   Keep talking : about your neighbor next door
8   I caught her boogie-woogying : down on the floor
9   Don't you remember : when my door was locked
10   I had your mama : on the chopping block
11   Pretty mama : I'm telling you
12   I'm sick and tired : of the way you do

ArnK   12   Arnold, Kokomo

    13   Stop knocking : on my windowpane
    14   You tell what you see : don't you call my name

ArnK   13   Arnold, Kokomo

            title: Let Your Money Talk
            place and date: Chicago, 18 Apr. 1935
            record numbers: (C-9924-) De-7191 BC-4

    1   Let your money talk let your money talk : let your
            money talk let your money talk
    2   If you feel like riding : and don't want to walk
    3   Now you look so neat and you look so neat : and you
            talk so sweet you talk so sweet
    4   Now you can't get by no matter how you try : on your
            dead beat
    5   Let your money talk let your money talk : so we can
            hear so we can hear
    6   If you ain't coming back tell me right now : leave a
            dime for beer
    7   Let your money talk let your money talk : put it in
            my hand put it in my hand
    8   If you like your cool kind beer pretty mama : we can
            rush the can
    9   If you go to the butcher if you go to the butcher :
            to get you sausage grind your sausage grind
    10   If he can't get it in the front door : he don't want
            it behind
    11   You want your ashes hauled you want your ashes
            hauled : and ain't got no man ain't got no man
    12   Just lay it on the wood pretty mama : I do the best
            I can
    13   If you want to boogie-woogie if you want to
            boogie-woogie : and haven't got the price haven't
            got the price
    14   Just let the landlady know man : and she will put it
            on ice
    15   And now if you can't see if you can't see : if you
            deaf and dumb you deaf and dumb
    16   Don't stand around looking cute : and on a bum

ArnK   14   Arnold, Kokomo

            title: Policy Wheel Blues
            place and date: Chicago, 15 July 1935
            record numbers: (90158-A) De-7147 CC-25

    1   Now while you playing policy buddy : play four
            eleven and forty-four
    2   When you get your money : then pack your bags and go
    3   Crying oh : look what that [policy wheel,
            coal-field, greyhound] have done to me
    4   Says it done took all my money : and but it still
            won't let me be
    5   Now while you playing policy : play four eighteen
            and fifty-six
    6   You can pile up your black money : because you sure
            going to get it fixed
    7   Now when you change your numbers : play thirteen
            thirty-two and fifty-one
    8   But be careful buddy : because you might have to run
    9   Now while you playing policy buddy : play five nine
            and fifty-nine
    10   But be careful buddy : because you might lose your
            mind
    11   Now *ask you to* about gambling : play eleven
            seventeen and sixty-one
    12   If they don't give you your money : go buy you a
            gatling gun
    13   Now if you wake up in the morning : ain't got
            nothing on your mind
    14   Play that old country number : that you call three
            sixty-nine
    15   Now you can break out your windows : and look down
            at your glass

ArnK   14   Arnold, Kokomo

    16   Think you going to get my money mama : that's your
            yas yas yas

ArnK   15   Arnold, Kokomo

            title: Stop Look and Listen
            place and date: Chicago, 23 July 1935
            record numbers: (90201-A) De-7181 BC-4

    1   Oh stop and listen : hear those bells a-tone
    2   I found my faro : lying on a cooling board
    3   Says today has been : a long old lonesome day
    4   Seems like tomorrow : mama going to be the same old
            way
    5   Now don't your house look lonesome : when a hearse
            roll in front of your door
    6   I found my faro : lying on a cooling board
    7   Says and it smokes like lightning : and it *faro*
            shine like gold
    8   I wouldn't have seen her : not to save nobody's soul
    9   Lord then I ain't going down : that big road by
            myself
    10   If I don't carry you : mama I'm going to carry
            somebody else
    11   And I followed my faro : to the new burying ground
    12   Watch the pallbearers : when they lay my faro down

ArnK   16   Arnold, Kokomo

            title: Big Leg Mama
            place and date: Chicago, 11 Sept. 1935
            record numbers: (90314-A) De-7116 Say SDR-163

    1   Now it's mama mama mama : please keep your big legs
            down
    2   So I can stop old John Russell : Lord from hanging
            around
    3   Says I load coal in the morning : and I cut corn
            late at night
    4   When I come on home : and you and John Russell sure
            don't treat me right
    5   Says I hate like the devil : to declare war in my
            happy home
    6   Says I loaned you my money : and then you stole my
            gal and gone
    7   Now you going to hear thunder and lightning : from
            the end of my pistol barrel
    8   Says you stole my money : then you turned around and
            took my gal
    9   Now my *old back* is a-breaking : and my lights is
            a-burning low
    10   When I load this carload of coal captain : I sure
            ain't going load no more

ArnK   17   Arnold, Kokomo

            title: Milk Cow Blues--No. 4
            place and date: Chicago, 11 Sept. 1935
            record numbers: (90316-A) De-7163 CC-25

    1   I can't get my milk in the morning : I can't get my
            cream no more
    2   And I want somebody to come here : help me get this
            bull from my door
    3   Says I went out to my barn this morning : he didn't
            have one word to say
    4   He was laying down by my heifer's side : please on a
            pile of hay
    5   Then I walked away : and I hung my head and cried
    6   Says I feel so lonesome : I ain't got my heifer by
            my side
    7   Now there's nothing that I could do : for that old
            bull has tea-rolled me

ArnK   17   Arnold, Kokomo

8   When I get myself another heifer : I'm going to move
    back to Tennessee
9   Says I'm still in love with my milkcow : I just
    can't stand the way she do
10 I don't mind her drinking her whiskey : but please
    don't ballyhoo

ArnK   18   Arnold, Kokomo

        title: I'll Be Up Some Day
        place and date: New York, 18 Feb. 1936
        record numbers: (60515-) De-7172 Say SDR-163

1   Says I've been traveling mama : all by myself
2   When I had you baby : you thought I had somebody
    else
3   But that's all right mama : I'll be up some day
4   And just like you did me baby : I'm going to do you
    the same old way
5   Says I asked my baby : to take me back once more
6   She said you ain't got no money : sweet papa there
    is the door
7   Said now I ain't got no money : and no place to go
8   I asked you for a little small favor : and you drove
    me from your door
9   Now I've got a little sweet woman : that I can call
    my own
10 I want your *turning-gate* women : to please leave
    me alone
11 Ever since you been gone mama : I've been about to
    lose my mind
12 But I got another little sweet woman : and I don't
    want your three sixty-nine

ArnK   19   Arnold, Kokomo

        title: Shake That Thing
        place and date: Chicago, 9 July 1936
        record numbers: (90795-A) De-7212 CC-25

1   Says down in Georgia : where the dance is new
2   Ain't nothing to it : because it's easy to do
3   Now the old folks started it : and the young folks
    too
4   Old folks teaching the young ones : what to do
5   Said grandpa Johnson : grabbed sister Kate
6   Shook her like he shaking : jelly on a plate
7   Says old Uncle Jack : he is a jellyroll king
8   He got a hump in his back : just from shaking that
    thing
9   Says now I sees it : just a little funny swing
10 You don't need no lesson : to shake that thing

ArnK   20   Arnold, Kokomo

        title: Mister Charlie
        place and date: Chicago, 24 Oct. 1936
        record numbers: (90958-A) De-7261 CC-25

1   Why shouldn't I take a chance mama : when good luck
    comes along
2   Seems like everybody's down on me : always
    somebody's doing me wrong
3   Says I can't live for loving : but I just can't help
    myself
4   Now the little woman I'm loving quit me : well I
    sure don't want nobody else
5   Oh Mr Charlie : why don't you leave my gal alone
6   Well you keep on kicking her : you bound to break up
    my happy home
7   And it was early this morning : I was walking down
    the avenue
8   Says I had a good spirit : thought I was strolling
    along with you

ArnK   20   Arnold, Kokomo

9   Says I turned around : and I wrung my hands and
    cried
10 Says I felt so lonesome : I didn't have my baby by
    my side

ArnK   21   Arnold, Kokomo

        title: Long and Tall
        place and date: Chicago, 12 Jan. 1937
        record numbers: (91070-A) De-7306 CC-25

1   Says I love you mama : but you don't even care for
    me
2   Because you a long tall woman : and I sure God ain't
    going to let you be
3   Now she's long and she's tall : shaped just like a
    cannonball
4   Says I found that woman : where the Southern cross
    the Yellow Dog
5   Then I heard the church bells toning : way out on
    Dago Hill
6   Then my heart struck sorrow : I guess you know just
    how I feel
7   Says now tell me mama : what make you do me like you
    do
8   Now some day you going to want me : and I swear and
    I won't want you
9   Some people crave high yellow : please give me my
    black and brown
10 Now if you mess with me mama : I'm sure going to
    turn your damper down

ArnK   22   Arnold, Kokomo

        title: Salty Dog
        place and date: Chicago, 12 Jan. 1937
        record numbers: (91070-A) De-7267 Rt RL-318

1   Now just one thing : that worry my mind
2   All of these womens : ain't none of them mine
3   Scaredest I ever been : in my life
4   Old Uncle Bud liked to caught me : kissing his wife
5   Now big fish little fish : playing in the water
6   Come on back here man : and give me my quarter
7   Just like looking for a needle : in a bed of sand
8   Just try to find a woman : ain't got no man
9   Says God made a woman : and he made her mighty funny
10 The lips around her mouth : just sweet as any honey
11 Old Uncle Bud : he's a man like this
12 He saves his money : and use his fist

ArnK   23   Arnold, Kokomo

        title: Wild Water Blues
        place and date: Chicago, 12 Mar. 1937
        record numbers: (91134-A) De-7285 Cor CP-58

1   I woke up this morning : I couldn't even get out of
    my door
2   Said this wild water got me covered : and I ain't
    got no place to go
3   Now I hear my mama crying : but I just can't help
    myself
4   Now this wild water keep on rising : I got to get
    help from someone else
5   Now good morning Mr wild water : why did you stop in
    my front door
6   Says you reaches from Cairo : clean down to the Gulf
    of Mexico
7   Now don't you hear your mother crying : weeping and
    moaning all night long
8   Because old man wild water done been here : took her
    best friends and gone

ArnK   23   Arnold, Kokomo

9 Now look a-here Mr wild water : why do you treat me
   so doggone mean
10 Says you took my house out of Cairo : carried it
   down in New Orleans

ArnK   24   Arnold, Kokomo

        title: Laugh and Grin Blues
        place and date: Chicago, 12 Mar. 1937
        record numbers: (91135-A) De-7285 CC-25

1 Now when you happy mama : everybody smiles with you
2 Just as soon as you feel down-hearted: the whole
   round world turns blue
3 Now when the sun is shining : everybody's happy as
   can be
4 Just as soon as it start to raining : you quiver
   just like a leaf on a tree
5 Now I got something to tell you mama : and I really
   want you to understand
6 Every man you see wearing britches : he sure God
   ain't no monkey-man
7 Now when I had plenty money : everybody want to be
   my friend
8 Just as soon as I got ragged and hungry : now they
   all wants to laugh and grin
9 Now I'm going to tell all you people : when I get on
   my feet again
10 Says you need not ask for no small favors : just go
   ahead laugh and grin

ArnK   25   Arnold, Kokomo

        title: Mean Old Twister
        place and date: Chicago, 30 Mar. 1937
        record numbers: (91161-A) De-7347 BC-4

1 Now this dark cloud is rising : and it's thundering
   all around
2 Look like something bad is going to happen : you
   better lower your airplane down
3 Now that mean old twister's coming : poor people
   running every which a-way
4 Everybody's got to wonder : what's the matter with
   this cruel world today
5 Now my mama told me : when I was only five months
   old
6 If you obey your preacher : the good Lord is going
   to bless your soul
7 Now the daylight is failing : and the moon begin to
   rise
8 I'm just down here weeping and moaning : right by my
   mama's side
9 Now I'm going home : I done did all in this world
   that I could
10 Says I got everybody happy : around here in my
   neighborhood

ArnK   26   Arnold, Kokomo

        title: Red Beans and Rice
        place and date: Chicago, 30 Mar. 1937
        record numbers: (91162-A) De-7347 BC-4

1 When I was down in Georgia : I was doing mighty well
2 Since I been here in Chicago : I been catching a
   plenty hell
3 Says I'm going down to the station : ain't going to
   take no one's advice
4 Says I'm going back to Georgia : where I can get my
   red beans and rice
5 Now these Chicago women : have give me such a hard
   way to go

ArnK   26   Arnold, Kokomo

6 Says they done took all my black money : and they
   got me running from door to door
7 Now I been setting here looking : way down that
   lonesome road
8 Says I'm raggedy and I'm hungry : and I ain't got no
   place to go
9 Now I been rolling : I been rolling from sun to sun
10 Says I got where I can't get no loving : not until
   my payday comes

ArnK   27   Arnold, Kokomo

        title: Set Down Gal
        place and date: Chicago, 30 Mar. 1937
        record numbers: (91166-A) De-7361 OJL-20

1 Said I ain't no preacher : I'm just a bachelor man
2 Some of these days mama : you bound to understand
3 Now set down gal : stop your crazy ways
4 Got trouble in the land : you're going to need my
   help some day
5 Now when I want it : I want it awful bad
6 If I don't get it : you know it's going to make me
   mad
7 Said I asked my mama : to not to be so rough
8 She ain't the type : to keep on strutting her stuff
9 Says I asked my baby : not to be so mean
10 She acts like a woman : from down in New Orleans
11 Now come on baby : stop this up and down
12 Don't like to catch you : start to messing around

ArnK   28   Arnold, Kokomo

        title: Big Ship Blues
        place and date: Chicago, 30 Mar. 1937
        record numbers: (91167-A) De-7361 Say SDR-163

1 Now this big ship was a-rocking : and my body's
   filled with aches and pains
2 Now if I get across the Atlantic Ocean : good people
   I will not live to Spain
3 Now the big tide is rising : you better lower your
   anchors down
4 Now if we don't make the circle : we never will get
   back to New York town
5 Now why don't you people quit laughing : I feel
   mighty sad in my mind
6 Said this big fog go to rising : and a cyclone is
   right behind
7 Now I feels bad : nobody seems to want to go my way
8 Says this big ship going to leaking : right between
   midnight and day
9 Now I see something shining : daylight is breaking
   all around
10 Soon as we make a few more lurches : I will be right
   back in New York town

ArnK   29   Arnold, Kokomo

        title: Buddie Brown Blues
        place and date: Chicago, 23 Oct. 1937
        record numbers: (91299-A) De-7449 CC-25

1 Captain rung the bell this morning : just at the
   break of day
2 Said now it's time for you to go rolling : buddy why
   don't you be on your way
3 Mama you can cook my breakfast : great God don't you
   burn my bread
4 Do and I'm going to take my black hand razor : I'm
   going to cut you on your doggone head
5 Now my captain done called me : Lord and I got to go
6 Because he's on his old black stallion : and he's
   riding from door to door

ArnK 29   Arnold, Kokomo

7   Now I will be so glad : when my payday comes
8   Says I'm getting so tired mama : rolling from sun to
    sun
9   Now I'm going to get up in the morning : do just
    like old Buddy Brown
10 Says I'm going to eat my breakfast : please and lay
    back down

ArnK 30   Arnold, Kokomo

        title: Rocky Road Blues
        place and date: Chicago, 23 Oct. 1937
        record numbers: (91300-A) De-7449 CC-25

1   Now my road is rocky : but it won't be rocky long
2   Says I been catching the devil : ever since my good
    gal been gone
3   Says my mama told me : Lord when I was quite a child
4   Son you must always remember : Lord that you was
    born to die
5   Now I got so many wagons : till I done cut that good
    road down
6   Because the little woman that I been loving : said
    she do not even want me around
7   Says she won't write me no letter : she won't send
    me no telegram
8   She just a hard-headed woman : and she don't even
    give a damn
9   Now I'm going to smoke my reefer : drink my good
    champagne and wine
10 Say I ain't going to let these hard-headed women :
    make me lose my mind

ArnK 31   Arnold, Kokomo

        title: Head Cuttin' Blues
        place and date: Chicago, 3 Nov. 1937
        record numbers: (91331-A) De-7417 BC-4

1   I believe to my soul : there's a black cat sleeping
    under my bed
2   Every time I get drunk : my woman wants to cut my
    head
3   She keeps me running : ducking and dodging all night
    long
4   Every time I get drunk : I don't mean to treat
    nobody wrong
5   Now listen here mama : I ain't going to do it no
    more
6   When I get full of my good whiskey : you got me
    running from door to door
7   Now I'm leaving you mama : Lord and it won't be long
8   Now if you don't believe I'm leaving : please count
    the days I'm gone
9   Now just as sure as a freight train : rolls up in
    the yard
10 Says I'm going to go far : take two dollars to send
    me a postal card

ArnK 32   Arnold, Kokomo

        title: Broke Man Blues
        place and date: Chicago, 3 Nov. 1937
        record numbers: (91332-A) De-7417 CC-25

1   Well I dreamed last night now : that my old shack
    was falling down
2   And when I woke up this morning : my poor head was
    going round and round
3   Now I'm going to be a robber and a cheater : I'm
    going to take that to be my game
4   And when I make my black money : I'm going on back
    home to Mary Jane

ArnK 32   Arnold, Kokomo

5   Now when I was a schoolboy : I would not take no
    one's advice
6   Now I'm just a broke man : nobody seems to want to
    treat me right
7   Now my poor heart is aching : and I really don't
    know what to do
8   Says I got a strong notion : coming right on back
    home to you
9   Now I'm going to close conversation : and I have no
    more to say
10 And a since I been a broke man : nobody seems to
    want to go my way

ArnK 33   Arnold, Kokomo

        title: Back on the Job
        place and date: Chicago, 3 Nov. 1937
        record numbers: (91333-A) De-7390 Say SDR-163

1   Some of these days you're going to miss me : mama
    Lord when I'm gone
2   Now just go ahead and forget it : and try to carry
    my good works on
3   Now I'm going away mama : but I'll be back some day
    soon
4   Just don't lose your head : let no lowdown rounder
    have my room
5   Mama here I am : right back on the job again
6   Says I've had no loving : Lord since God knows when
7   Now you acted bad : and you don't obey my rules
8   Because I'm back home again : I'm going to take you
    to a brand new school
9   Now listen here mama : go ahead and set down and be
    yourself
10 But the next time I go strolling : just try to find
    you someone else

ArnK 34   Arnold, Kokomo

        title: Your Ways and Actions
        place and date: New York, 11 May 1938
        record numbers: (67344-A) De-7510 Say SDR-163

1   Now your ways and your actions : speaks almost as
    loud as words
2   Because your dreamy eyes told me something : Lord
    that I never heard
3   Now you know that you love me : mama why don't you
    tell me so
4   Because you always hanging around : knocking on my
    door
5   Every time I see you baby : my flesh begin to crawl
6   Says why don't you be good : but my mule is kicking
    in your stall
7   How can I miss you : mama Lord when I got dead aim
8   Says I feel so different : till this old world don't
    look the same
9   Now there's nothing that I can do : I did all in
    this world that I could
10 Now she's gone and left me : she didn't mean me no
    good

ArnK 35   Arnold, Kokomo

        title: Tired of Runnin' from Door to Door
        place and date: New York, 11 May 1938
        record numbers: (67346) De-7464 Say SDR-163

1   I'm getting so tired : of running from town to town
2   For when I wake up in the morning : my head is going
    around and around
3   Some of these days : Lord and it won't be long
4   Says I'm going to run lucky : and find me a happy
    home

ArnK   35   Arnold, Kokomo

5   Now I'm going to keep on traveling : till *such
    another* comes my way
6   Says my woman get a chance to see me : not until the
    sunshiny day
7   Now I been waiting for tomorrow : look like tomorrow
    ain't going never come
8   Every day seems like Monday : just at the rising sun
9   Now my poor heart is aching : and my head can't rest
    no more
10 Says I'm getting so tired : of running from door to
    door

ArnK   36   Arnold, Kokomo

    title: My Well Is Dry
    place and date: New York, 11 May 1938
    record numbers: (63748-A) De-7540 CC-25

1   Says I never missed my water : not until my well
    went dry
2   Says I never missed sweet Annie : not until she said
    goodbye
3   Hey Lord sweet mama : tell me when you're coming
    back again
4   Says I ain't had none of your loving : Lord since
    God knows when
5   Now the mailman he passed : but he did not leave no
    news
6   Says he left me standing here : with the doggone
    aching-heart blues
7   Well I ain't going to be no fool man : I'm going to
    hold up my head and walk
8   Says my woman get a chance to see me : but they all
    hear me when I talk
9   Says I holler in the morning : I begin to moan late
    at night
10 Says I got a hard-hearted woman : and she don't know
    how to treat me right

ArnK   37   Arnold, Kokomo

    title: Midnight Blues
    place and date: New York, 11 May 1938
    record numbers: (63750-A) De-7510 Say SDR-163

1   In the morning : right between midnight and day
2   I'm going to pack my suitcase : and start to drift
    away
3   My gal she got ways : just like a snake in the grass
4   If I don't leave here soon : my life won't never
    last
5   It's so hard : to get right up and change your mind
6   When someone that you love : has been left behind
7   Sooner or later : one of us has got to walk away
8   She says I don't mind you going : but please don't
    go away to stay
9   Now I don't care baby : if the wind don't never
    change
10 If your coming don't bring sunshine : it sure God
    will bring rain

ArnK   38   Arnold, Kokomo

    title: Bad Luck Blues
    place and date: New York, 12 May 1938
    record numbers: (63753-A) De-7540 CC-25

1   Now there's trouble trouble : I been having all my
    days
2   Now it seems like troubles : going to put me in my
    lonesome grave
3   Now my woman she got ways : just like a wildcat in
    the woods

ArnK   38   Arnold, Kokomo

4   She always raising hell and disturbance : right here
    in my neighborhood
5   I'm scared to stay here : scared to leave this old
    bad-luck town
6   So when I wake up every morning : my head is going
    round and round
7   Now listen here people : I don't want no one's
    advice
8   I done changed my way of living : going to find
    someone to treat me right
9   I'm going to tell everybody : what bad luck I've had
    in my life
10 I'd kill my sister and my brother : not a woman
    break my line

ArnK   39   Arnold, Kokomo

    title: Kid Man Blues
    place and date: New York, 12 May 1938
    record numbers: (63754-A) De-7464 Say SDR-163

1   Now my [old] heart is ticking : just like a clock up
    on the wall
2   Says I tried to be good : but my woman treats me
    like a dog
3   Now I've got my name written : right on my right arm
4   Every time I want to leave : I know she's got to
    come back home
5   Now you said that you loved me : what make you treat
    me so unkind
6   You just old hard-headed woman : but I believe you
    about to lose your mind
7   Now you can tell your kid-man : he needn't take it
    so doggone hard
8   Because if he messes with me : going to crack him
    right on his nog
9   Now that's all I got to say mama : I ain't going to
    let you worry my mind
10 When I go away to leave you : I will stop by to see
    you sometime

BaiK   1   Bailey, Kid

    title: Mississippi Bottom Blues
    place and date: New York, 12 May 1938
    record numbers: (M-209/10) Br-7114 OJL-5

1   Way down in Mississippi : where I was bred and born
2   Reason : that will forever be my native home
3   And my poor mother's old : Lord and her hair is
    turning grey
4   I know it would break her heart : if she found I was
    barrelhousing this way
5   And I'm going to where : now the water drink like
    wine
6   Where I can be drunk there : and staggering all the
    time
7   And it ain't but the one thing now : Lord that
    worries my mind
8   That's a house full of women Lord : none in there is
    mine
9   And my friend passed me : and she never said a word
10 Nothing I had did : but was something she had heard

BaiK   2   Bailey, Kid

    title: Rowdy Blues
    place and date: Memphis, c. 25 Sept. 1929
    record numbers: (M-211) Br-7114 OJL-5

1   Ain't going to marry : neither settle down
2   I'm going to stay right here : till they tear this
    barrelhouse down
3   And I love you babe : and I tell the world I do

BaiK   2   Bailey, Kid

```
 4   I don't love nobody : whole in this round world but
       you
 5   Ain't no use of weeping : ain't no need of crying
 6   For you've got a home : just as long as I got mine
 7   Is you ever been lucky now : woke up cold in hand
 8   I would call that now : nothing but a monkey-man
 9   And I love you baby : you so nice and brown
10   Because you put it up solid : so it won't come down
11   Did you get that letter now : mailed in your back
       yard
12   It's a sad word to say : but the best of friends
       have to part
```

BakW   1   Baker, Willie

title: Mama, Don't Rush Me Blues
place and date: Memphis, c. 25 Sept. 1929
record numbers: (14666) Ge-6766 His HLP-22

```
 1   Paid my room rent last night : half past ten
 2   Take my gal to the door : but she wouldn't go in
 3   I take a gal for a ride : she tried to get rough
 4   *How* I been in your doorway : strutting my stuff
 5   Ain't these women funny : about the way they do
 6   Start to loving a man : then go to dogging you
 7   I buy you a cigarette : and I buy you snuff
 8   I know doggone well now : when I get enough
 9   Now make someone : to tell you *loves* every day
10   I know that's enough : to let you have your way
11   Mama you been just like : says a farmer's mule
12   Longer I live with you : harder you is to rule
13   I told my wife : if you want me to wait
14   You better stop your sister : from doing her *gait*
```

BakW   2   Baker, Willie

title: No No Blues
place and date: Richmond, Ind., 9 Jan. 1929
record numbers: (14667) Ge-6766 BC-5

```
 1   I woke up this morning : my good gal was gone
 2   Stood by my bedside : and I hung my head and hung my
       head and moaned
 3   I walked down the street : I couldn't be satisfied
 4   I had the no no blues : I couldn't keep from I
       couldn't keep from crying
 5   It ain't none of my business : but it sure ain't
       right
 6   Take another man's gal : walk the streets all walk
       the streets all night
 7   Take a mighty *pricky* woman : to treat her good man
       wrong
 8   Take a mighty mean man : take another man's take
       another man's home
 9   I'm a stranger here : I just blowed in your town
10   If I ask for a favor : don't turn me don't turn me
       down
11   I'm long and tall : like a cannonball
12   Take a long tall man : make a good gal make a good
       gal squall
13   If I mistreat you : I don't mean no harm
14   Because I'm a motherless child : don't know right
       from don't know right from wrong
15   I ain't no gambler : and I don't play no pool
16   I'm a rambling roller : jelly-baking jelly-baking
       fool
17   She's low and squatty : right down on the ground
18   She's a lightweighted mama : so I can bear so I can
       bear down
19   I'm a stranger here : I come in on the train
20   I long to hear : some good gal call my good gal call
       my name
```

BakW   3   Baker, Willie

title: Weak-Minded Blues
place and date: Richmond, Ind., 10 Jan. 1929
record numbers: (14668) Spt-9427 Yz L-1012

```
 1   I wonder : will a matchbox hold my dirty clothes
 2   I haven't got so many : but I got so far to go
 3   Women all singing the blues : I can't raise my right
       hand
 4   What make a woman have them blues : well you know
       somebody's got her man
 5   The blues is something : woman I ain't never had
 6   Just get your *best friend's good man* : and do the
       best you can
 7   A weak-minded woman : will let a rounder tear her
       down
 8   And when she get in trouble : that rounder can't be
       found
 9   She got up last night : she crawled around my bed
10   Going love you long time daddy : I guess I will see
       you dead
11   Woman take the blues : she going to buy her a paper
       and read
12   Man take them blues : he going to catch a train and
       leave
13   My gal got a mouth : like a lighthouse on the sea
14   Every time she smiles : she throws that light on me
```

BakW   4   Baker, Willie

title: Bad Luck Moan
place and date: Richmond, Ind., 10 Jan. 1929
record numbers: (14892) Ge-6812 Rt RL-326

```
 1   Bad luck in my bed : bad luck's in my home
 2   That's the reason why : singing this bad-luck moan
 3   I got a gal : though she's a little bit up in years
 4   But she sure knows how : how to shift her gears
 5   Some like pigmeat : but hogmeat's what I crave
 6   I believe : this sure going to carry me to my grave
 7   Mmm : mama come to my rescue
 8   I'm feeling so bad : till I don't know what to do
 9   Well the chinch has moved in : all in my room
10   Somebody better come here : pretty doggone soon
```

BakW   5   Baker, Willie

title: Crooked Woman Blues
place and date: Richmond, Ind., 11 Mar. 1929
record numbers: (14894-A) Ge-6846 Yz L-1012

```
 1   When a man gets down : the trouble lasts always
 2   Your gal will leave you : and be gone for days and
       days
 3   Tell all you women : how to make a happy home
 4   Keep you a workingman : and leave those sweet boys
       alone
 5   There's coming a time : these women won't need no
       men
 6   Their body washed up : and money'll come rolling in
 7   When you think : your women always running hand to
       hand
 8   You can bet your bottom dollar : one's got the other
       one's man
 9   On one Monday morning : on my way to school
10   That's the Monday morning : I broke my mama's rule
```

BakW   6   Baker, Willie

title: Rag Baby
place and date: Richmond, Ind., 11 Mar. 1929
record numbers: (14895-B) Ge-6846 Her H-201

```
 1   Yonder she goes : with a broom in her hand
 2   Sweep me off : for another man
```

BakW   7   Baker, Willie

    title: Weak-Minded Blues
    place and date: Richmond, Ind., 11 Mar. 1929
    record numbers: (14896) Ge-6751 Her H-201

1 I wonder : will a matchbox mama hold my dirty
   clothes
2 I ain't got so many : but I got so far to go
3 Women all singing the blues : I ain't raise my right
   hand
4 What make a woman have them blues : when she knows
   somebody's got her man
5 The blues is something : woman I ain't never had
6 Just get your *best friend's good man* : and do the
   best you can
7 A weak-minded woman : will let a rounder tear her
   down
8 And when she get in trouble : that rounder can't be
   found
9 She got up last night : she crawled around my bed
10 Going love you long time daddy : guess I will see
   you dead
11 Woman take the blues : she going to buy her a paper
   and read
12 Man take them blues : he going to catch a train and
   leave
13 My gal got a mouth : like a lighthouse on the sea
14 Every time she smiles : she throws that light on me

BakW   8   Baker, Willie

    title: Sweet Patunia Blues
    place and date: Richmond, Ind., 11 Mar. 1929
    record numbers: (14897) Ge-6751 His HLP-22

1 I got a gal : she got a Rolls Royce
2 She didn't get it all : by using her voice
3 I'm wild about my tuni : only thing I crave
4 Well sweet patuni : going to carry me to my grave
5 Every time : my gal walk down the street
6 All the boys holler : ain't tuni sweet
7 I got a gal : she lives up on the hill
8 You can't get her tuni : she got automobile
9 Well I woke up this morning : half past four
10 A long tall gal : rapping at my door
11 She was singing sweet patuni : only thing I crave
12 Well sweet patuni : going to carry me to my grave
13 If all these tuni : was brought to a test
14 A long tall gal : can *break* it the best
15 Telling all you men : I been well blessed
16 If I get what I want : you can have the rest

Bare   1   Barefoot Bill

    title: My Crime Blues
    place and date: Richmond, Ind., 11 Mar. 1929
    record numbers: (149352-2) Co-14510-D OJL-14

1 I got the blues for my baby : she got the blues for
   I say me
2 But I can't see my baby : and she can't see me
3 I'm going to be condemned : early tomorrow I say
   morn
4 But I am not guilty : because I ain't done nobody
   wrong
5 My crime my crime : I really can't understand
6 They got me accused of murder : and I never harmed a
   man
7 Will you please come down : on my trial day
8 So when I be condemned : you can wipe my tears away
9 They ain't no need to cry : no need to weep and moan
10 Just try to get somebody : to go on my bond
11 It's going to be weeping : I begin to moan
12 Said I'm a poor boy here : I sure ain't got no home
13 The jury found me guilty : the judge say listen here

Bare   1   Barefoot Bill

14 It ain't no fine for you : get ready for the
   electric chair

Bare   2   Barefoot Bill

    title: Snigglin' Blues
    place and date: Atlanta, 4 Nov. 1929
    record numbers: (149353-2) Co-14510-D Yz L-1006

1 I done everything : a poor ??? man can do
2 Well mama *done leaving* : taken no ??? on you
3 I said you get blue mama : honey you can dance
4 But papa done got you : you've had your last chance
5 You going to miss me : baby when I'm gone
6 Won't be no need : a-sing this lonesome song
7 I give you all my money : I was cold in hand
8 And you spent all my money : on your other man
9 When you in my presence : mama you giggles and
   laughs
10 And tell me so many ??? : that I have no need no
   cash

Bare   3   Barefoot Bill

    title: Big Rock Jail
    place and date: Atlanta, 4 Nov. 1929
    record numbers: (149356-2) Co-14481-D Rt RL-313

1 Said high sheriff been here : got my girl and gone
2 I said isn't it lonely : since I'm all alone
3 Well listen Mr : what have my baby done
4 I just want to know : if she done anybody wrong
5 They took her on down : to that big rock jail
6 And her crime was so evil : nobody will go her bail
7 You took your gun : made her raise her hand
8 And you went wrong : because she ain't never harmed
   a man
9 My babe in jail : I can't get no news
10 I don't get nothing : but the mean old high sheriff
   blues

Bare   4   Barefoot Bill

    title: From Now On
    place and date: Atlanta, 4 Nov. 1929
    record numbers: (149357-2) Co-14481-D OJL-14

1 Oh you used to told me : you could drive me like a
   cow
2 But now you can't drive me : because you don't know
   how
3 From now on mama : I tell you just like that
4 If you hit my dog : sure going to kick your cat
5 From now on mama : I ain't going to have no rule
6 I'm going to get hard-headed : and act just like a
   doggone mule
7 From now on mama : you going to do what I say
8 You must understand : you can't have your ways
9 From now on mama : this way you got of doing
10 Sugar you better stop that : Lord it's sure going to
   be your ruin
11 From now on mama : starting from this very day
12 I'm going to get someone : who can drive my blues
   away
13 I want her to drive them off : so they won't come
   back no more
14 From now on mama : I said I'm going to let you go

Bare   5   Barefoot Bill (Pillie Bolling)

     title: I Don't Like That
     place and date: Atlanta, 19 Apr. 1930
     record numbers: (150301-1) Co-14544-D Rt RL-325

1 I saw you doing something : don't do it no more
2 Because if I catch you : baby walking slow
3 *Lord* took another man : *right across my face*
4 Then told me : that the one had took my place
5 You say you done quit me : now what should I do
6 Can't make up my mind : to love no one but you
7 Now you take him for your sweet : take me to be a
   slave
8 You better see the undertaker : get someone to dig
   your grave
9 You say your suitcase is packed : your trunks done
   gone
10 Better stop your bus : and bring it right back home
11 I knocked on your door : and I *quit quit quit*
12 Begged till daybreak : and I ain't got none yet

Bare   6   Barefoot Bill (Pillie Bolling)

     title: She's Got a Nice Line
     place and date: Atlanta, 19 Apr. 1930
     record numbers: (150302-1) Co-14544-D Rt RL-325

1 Big girl I love : live on Eighteenth Street
2 She got a new line : for every man she meets
3 To let her tell it : she ain't got no man
4 But she hangs around here : always raising sand
5 One day ??? : we're riding along
6 I asked her how about it : and she walked back home
7 She don't do this : she don't do that
8 Rub your hand down her back : she act like a cat
9 She ain't low and squatty : she ain't long and slim
10 Only way you'll get it : have to grab your lemon
11 *It ain't right* : and I don't have fun
12 This girl I love : won't give me none
13 I want it right now : please tell me can I get it
14 I better not catch : nobody else with it

Bare   7   Barefoot Bill

     title: Squabblin' Blues
     place and date: Atlanta, 20 Apr. 1930
     record numbers: (150303-2) Co-14526-D OJL-14

1 My baby done quit me : talked all over town
2 And I'm too good a man : for to let that talk go
   around
3 Take the shoes I bought her : bare foots on the I
   say ground
4 One these days : Jack Frost said he sure going to
   tear you down
5 Now Mr Mr : please spare my life
6 I got four little children : I got one *bald-*headed
   wife
7 If I should die : in the state of Arkansas
8 I want you to send my body : home to my
   mother-in-law
9 Said if she don't want it : baby give it to my ma
10 Said if my ma don't want it : baby give it to my pa
11 Said if my pa don't want it : baby give it to Abby
   Lee
12 Said if Abby don't want it : say give it to my
   used-to-be
13 Said if she don't want it : baby cast it in the sea
14 Then these squabbling women in Greenville : will
   quabbling over me
   rried : with these blues no I say

                      T did

Bare   8   Barefoot Bill

     title: Barefoot Bill's Hard Luck Blues
     place and date: Atlanta, 20 Apr. 1930
     record numbers: (150304-1) Co-14561-D Rt RL-325

1 Baby I been working : all this blasted year
2 I want to go home : ain't got no shoes to wear
3 The times so hard : can't get no work to do
4 And my hard luck mama : because I ain't got no shoes
5 I'm going to sit right down : hang my head and cry
6 I feel just like : I could lay right down and die
7 Sugar I will never : be contented here
8 I am so barefooted : ain't got no shoes to wear
9 My coat all busted : my pants all full of holes
10 Barefooted hungry and raggedy : doggone my hard-luck
   soul

Bare   9   Barefoot Bill

     title: One More Time
     place and date: Atlanta, 20 Apr. 1930
     record numbers: (150305-1) Co-14561-D Rt RL-325

1 I can't sleep no more : can't get her off my mind
2 Know I wants to see my baby : man only one more time
3 I treated her wrong : before she left my home
4 I guess I'm not her daddy : and she would not have
   been gone
5 I didn't know I loved my baby : till she packed her
   trunk to leave
6 I telephoned the undertaker : just come and bury me
   please
7 Might get a black cat bone : going to bring my baby
   back home
8 Lord and if that don't do it : might be one more
   rounder gone

Bare   10   Barefoot Bill

     title: Bad Boy
     place and date: Atlanta, 20 Apr. 1930
     record numbers: (150306-2) Co-14526-D CC-3

1 I been a bad bad boy : didn't treat nobody right
2 They want to give me thirty-five years : some want
   to turn out my light
3 Judge please don't kill me : I won't be bad no more
4 And I will listen to anybody : something I ain't
   never done before
5 I'm sitting here in prison : with my black cap on
6 I want to speak to all you fast fellows : that you
   are in the wrong
7 Well I'm so sorry : every day that I was born
8 But God remember this : even when I'm gone
9 When they get you in jail : with your back turned to
   the wall
10 I ain't going to sing no more : baby that is all

Barn   1   Barner, Wiley

     title: My Gal Treats Me Mean
     place and date: Birmingham, Ala., c. 15 Aug. 1927
     record numbers: (GEX-803) Ge-6261 OJL-14

1 Take your picture : make it in a frame
2 When you're gone : I'll see you just the same
3 Believe to my soul : my girl got a black cat bone
4 Treat me mean : and I won't let her alone
5 See that spider : climbing up the wall
6 Hunt some place : to get his ashes hauled
7 Treat my slippers : with some *hog eye* lard
8 Hear me tipping : towards my good gal's yard
9 Mama mama : please let me alone
10 In the corner : can get what I want

Barn   2   Barner, Wiley

      title: If You Want a Good Woman--Get One Long
          and Tall
      place and date: Birmingham, Ala., c. 15 Aug.
          1927
      record numbers: (GEX-804-A) Ge-6261 Rt RL-313

1   If you want a good woman : go to the Larkin Dam
2   You want to ruin your woman : take her to Birmingham
3   Have you ever waked up babe : between midnight and
      day
4   Turn over and grab the pillow : where you great gal
      used to lay
5   If you want a good woman : get one long and tall
6   When she go to loving : she make a panther squall
7   I'm motherless and fatherless : sister and
      brotherless too
9   I wake up this morning : blues all around my bed
10 Well I had a high fever : going up to my head

Batt   1   Batts, Will

      title: Country Woman
      place and date: New York, 1 Aug. 1933
      record numbers: (13718-1) Vo-02531 Rt RL-329

1   I'm got two women in the country : I'm got two women
      stays in town
2   Reason I consider it so careful : because men don't
      dog me around
3   They may be brownskin woman : with Georgia hair long
      as my own
4   They can do the best playing poker : you sure done
      lost your home
5   I don't want no jealous-hearted woman : who tries
      making up my bed
6   And she puts *straw* in your mattress : makes you
      wish you was dead

Batt   2   Batts, Will

      title: Highway No. 61 Blues
      place and date: New York, 3 Aug. 1933
      record numbers: (13729-1) Vo-02531 Yz L-1021

1   I'm going to leave here walking : going down Number
      Sixty-One
2   If I find my baby : we are going to have some fun
3   I walked Sixty-One Highway : till I gives out in my
      knees
4   *Every time* that M and O : when she came on that
      Santa Fe
5   That Sixty-One Highway : longest road I ever knowed
6   It runs to Atlanta Georgia : clean to the Gulf of
      Mexico
7   I'm going home : get my Bible and set down and read
8   I'm going to ask the good Lord : give me back my
      baby if he please

BaxJ   1   Baxter, Jim (Andrew and Jim Baxter)

      title: Bamalong Blues
      place and date: Charlotte, N.C., 9 Aug. 1927
      record numbers: (39784-2) Vi-20962 Rt RL-318

1   Who's going to be : in the second bamalong
3   Been to the nation : and I just got back
4   Didn't get no money : but I'll go to *there*
5   If you didn't want me : don't you dog me around
6   I didn't come here : to be nobody's dog
7   Just as sure as the sun : sets in the golden west
8   I got the one : that I love the best

BaxJ   2   Baxter, Jim (Andrew and Jim Baxter)

      title: K. C. Railroad Blues
      place and date: Charlotte, N.C., 9 Aug. 1927
      record numbers: (39785-1) Vi-20962 Rt RL-326

1   Thought I heard : old K C when it blowed
2   She blowed like : it never blowed before
3   Oh it's coming a time : when a woman won't need no
      man
4   Honey I love : God knows I do
5   Sister : give me that long-distance phone
6   I'm going to talk : to that brown of mine

Beam   1   Beaman, Lottie

      title: Wayward Girl Blues
      place and date: Richmond, Ind., c. Aug. 1928
      record numbers: (14161-A) Ge-6607 OJL-6

1   I've got the blues : on my mother's knee
2   And I know : she's got the blues for me
3   I've been thinking all day : thinking of the past
4   And I'm thinking : of my mother last
5   I received a letter : what do you suppose it read
6   Said come home : your poor old mother's dead
7   Said I grabbed a train : I went home a-flying
8   She wasn't dead : but she was slowly dying
9   Said run here daughter : fall down on your knees
10 Won't you song : Nearer My God to Thee
11 Fell down on my knees : I begin to moan
12 Yes dear mother : I'll try to sing that song
13 The tears rolled out : like a black shower of rain
14 Goodbye mother : I won't see you again
15 Then I scampered away : with fear in my heart
16 I had no mother : here to take my part

Beam   2   Beaman, Lottie

      title: Rolling Log Blues
      place and date: Richmond, Ind., c. Aug. 1928
      record numbers: (14162) Ge-6624 OJL-6

1   I been drifting and rolling : along the road
2   Looking : for my room and board
3   Like a log : I've been jammed on the bank
4   So hungry : I grew lean and lank
5   Get me a pick and shovel : dig down in the ground
6   Going to keep on digging : till the blues come down
7   I've got the blues : for my sweet man in jail
8   Now the judge : won't let me go his bail
9   I've been rolling and drifting : from shore to shore
10 Going to fix it : so I won't have to drift no more

Beam   3   Beaman, Lottie

      title: Goin' Away Blues
      place and date: Richmond, Ind., c. Aug. 1928
      record numbers: (14163-A) Ge-6624 OJL-6

1   I'm going away : it won't be long
2   I know you'll miss me : from singing this lonesome
      song
3   I'm going away : mmm I won't be long
4   And then you know : you must have done me wrong
5   My daddy got ways : like a baby child
6   Those doggone ways : are driving me wild
7   Those doggone ways : are driving me wild
8   And that is why : you never see poor Lottie smile
9   My heart aches so : I can't be satisfied
10 I believe : I'll take a train and ride
11 I believe : I'll take a train and ride
12 Because I miss my cruel daddy : from my side
13 I've got Cadillac ways : got some super ideas
14 I can't see : what brought me here
15 I can't see : what brought me here

17

Beam   3   Beaman, Lottie

16   It must have been : this new canned city beer
17   I'm lame and blind : can't hardly see
18   My doggone daddy : turned his back on me
19   Because I'm lame : I can't hardly see
20   I ain't got nobody : to really comfort me

Beam   4   Beaman, Lottie

        title: Going Away Blues
        place and date: Kansas City, early Nov. 1929
        record numbers: (KC-604-) Br-7147 Yz L-1018

1   I'm going away : it won't be long
2   I know you'll miss me : from singing this lonesome
        song
3   I'm going away : it won't be long
4   And then you know : you must have done me wrong
5   My daddy got ways : like a baby child
6   Those doggone ways : are driving me wild
7   Those doggone ways : are driving me wild
8   And that is why : you never see poor Lottie smile
9   My heart aches so : I can't be satisfied
10   I believe : I'll take a train and ride
11   I believe : I'll take a train and ride
12   Because I miss my cruel daddy : from my side
13   I've got Cadillac ways : got some super ideas
14   I can't see : what brought me here
15   I can't see : what brought me here
16   It must have been : this new canned city beer
17   I'm lame and blind : can't hardly see
18   My doggone daddy : turned his back on me
19   I'm lame : I can't hardly see
20   I ain't got nobody : to really comfort me

Beam   5   Beaman, Lottie

        title: Rollin' Log Blues
        place and date: Kansas City, early Nov. 1929
        record numbers: (KC-605-) Br-7147 Yz L-1018

1   I been rolling and drifting : along the road
2   Just looking : for my room and board
3   Like a log : I've been jammed on the bank
4   So hungry : I grew lean and lank
5   Get me a pick and shovel : dig down in the ground
6   Going to keep on digging : till the blues come down
7   I've got the blues : for my sweet man in jail
8   And the judge : won't let me go his bail
9   I've been rolling and drifting : along the road
10   Going to fix it : I won't have to drift no more

BelA   1   Bell, Anna

        title: Hopeless Blues
        place and date: Long Island City, c. Sept. 1928
        record numbers: (171-A) QRS-R7007 His HLP-21

1   Is it hopeless : when I lost my best friend
2   Lord in my *doorbox* : is a call to him
3   Lowdown mean and hopeless : is just the way I feel
4   I can see from now on : all *luck flee* from me
5   Love sure have : made a fool out of me
6   Since my daddy left me : I'm hopeless as can be
7   ??? : I sure can't find
8   Ooh : I can't get this daddy off my mind
9   Lonesome for you in my heart : way down in my ???ee
10   I want somebody to help me : if you ??? please

BelA   2   Bell, Anna

        title: Every Woman Blues
        place and date: Long Island City, c. Sept. 1928
        record numbers: (172-A) QRS-R7007 His HLP-21

1   I love my daddy : better than I love myself
2   And I love *them* more : swear he can't be *less*
3   Get away from my window : stop knocking on my door
4   I got a brand new papa : I can't use you no more
5   If you see me stealing : please don't tell on me
6   I'm just stealing from my regular : back to my
        used-to-be
7   I ain't good-looking : I don't dress so fine
8   I'm just a big fat mama : I'm just taking my time
9   Have you ever seen sweet potatoes : growing on a
        vine
10   If you take a peep in my back yard : better take a
        look at mine

BelA   3   Bell, Anna

        title: Shake It, Black Bottom
        place and date: Long Island City, c. Sept. 1928
        record numbers: (175-) QRS-R7009 His HLP-21

1   There's a certain girl : name is Suley Brown
2   She win a big fortune : shaking him down
3   Every time he shake it : makes you feel young
4   I could see him shake it : the whole night long
5   Oh don't be ashamed : to shake it so
6   Shake it : till they say ???
7   If you be in a gym : and want to reduce
8   Oh shake it yourself gals : put it on a juice
9   You can shake : just like it would shake a tree
10   The way you shake it : it's pleasing me
11   Just let me tell you : a thing or two
12   A plenty of people shake it : but not like you
13   Oh shake it : you know just what I mean
14   You are what I call : real shaking scene
15   Let me see you shake it : once more again
16   I spent all my money : to ??? that thing

BelA   4   Bell, Anna

        title: I Don't Care Who Gets What I Don't Want
        place and date: Long Island City, c. Sept. 1928
        record numbers: (176-A) QRS R7009 His HLP-21

1   If that were me : and me was it
2   I was so glad : to get rid of it
3   I can use a man : when it amuses me
4   Because a happy man : I never did meet
5   At first you think : that he is great
6   But you will find out : that always ain't
7   One time : he could put it on strong
8   But I think : those days now gone

BelE   1   Bell, Ed

        title: Mamlish Blues
        place and date: Chicago, c. Sept. 1927
        record numbers: (4816-3) Pm-12524 OJL-14

1   Used to be my sugar : you ain't sweet no more
2   Because you mistreated me : and you threwed me from
        your door
3   Mama my cot's ready : keep it for myself
4   Mama I done got tired : of sleeping by myself
5   Mama didn't like me : papa give me ways
6   That's the very reason : I'm a wandering child today
7   Talk about your sure love : just ought to meet mine
8   She ain't so good-looking : but she do just fine
9   She stood on the corner : *see she going to steal
        that* man
10   And a blind man see her : dumb man call her name

BelE   1   Bell, Ed

11 Dumb man asked her : who your [man, regular] can be
12 And the blind man looked at you : sure look good to
    me

BelE   2   Bell, Ed

        title: Ham Bone Blues
        place and date: Chicago, c. Sept. 1927
        record numbers: (4817-3) Pm-12524 OJL-14

1   Jellyroll jellyroll : jellyroll is so hard to find
2   Ain't a baker in town : can bake a sweet jellyroll
    like mine
3   I got to go to Cincinnati : just to have my hambone
    boiled
4   Womens in Alabama : going to let my hambone spoil
5   Well she's mine and she's yours : and she's somebody
    else's too
6   Don't you mention about rolling : because she'll
    play her trick on you
7   That's the way that's the way : these barefooted
    soul'll do
8   They will get your money : and they'll have a man on
    you
9   You come home at night : she got a towel on her head
10 Don't you mention about rolling : because she swear
    she nearly dead
11 Jellyroll jellyroll : well you see what you went and
    done
12 You done had my grandpa : now you got his youngest
    son
13 I'm getting tired of walking : I believe I'll fly
    awhile
14 I'm getting tired of women : telling me their lies
15 I wonder : what made grandpa hey love your grandma
    so
16 She got the same jellyroll : she had forty years ago

BelE   3   Bell, Ed

        title: Mean Conductor Blues
        place and date: Chicago, c. Sept. 1927
        record numbers: (4820-1) Pm-12546 Yz L-1006

1   That same train : same engineer
2   Took my woman away Lord : left me standing here
3   My girl caught a passenger : I caught the mamlish
    blinds
4   Hey you can't quit me : ain't no need a-trying
5   Hey Mr conductor : let a broke man ride your blinds
6   You better buy you a ticket : know this train ain't
    mine
7   I just want to blind it : from this half-good town
8   When she blows for the crossing : I'm going ease it
    on
9   I pray to the Lord : that Southern would wreck
10 *Till they* kill that fireman : break that
    engineer's neck
11 I stand here : looking up at the rising sun
12 Some train don't run : why be some walking done

BelE   4   Bell, Ed

        title: Frisco Whistle Blues
        place and date: Chicago, c. Sept. 1927
        record numbers: (4822-1) Pm-12546 OJL-14

1   Well I saw the Frisco : when she left the yard
2   When that train pull out babe : it nearly broke my
    heart
3   They's two trains running : none of them going my
    way
4   I'm going to leave here walking : on this very day

BelE   4   Bell, Ed

5   Well there's one thing I don't like : about the
    railroad track
6   They'll take your rider : never bring her back
7   Honey where were you babe : when the Frisco left the
    yard
8   I was on the corner : police had me barred

BelE   5   Bell, Ed

        title: Carry It Right Back Home
        place and date: Atlanta, 4 Dec. 1930
        record numbers: (151037-2) Co-14595-D Rt RL-325

1   Look here woman : making me mad
2   Done bringing me something : somebody done had
3   Let me tell you : what these women do
4   Go out and get something : bring it home to you
5   Now you need not think : because you look cute
6   I've got to put up : with the way you do
7   The woman I love : she's long and tall
8   When she grab you and shake you : you bound to fall
9   Now bring this thing : down to a test
10 A long tall man : you know's the best
11 A short stubble man : go bumpty bump
12 Because he ain't got the movements : in his hump
13 Know what you been doing : by the whiff of your jaw
14 *My* ??? : ???
15 You need not come here : you ain't not get none of
    mine
16 You left a man on the doorstep : hollering and
    crying

BelE   6   Bell, Ed

        title: She's a Fool Gal
        place and date: Atlanta, 4 Dec. 1930
        record numbers: (151038-2) Co-14595-D Rt RL-325

1   Now you need not think : because you're black
2   I'm going to beg you : to take me back
3   No you need not think : because I look green
4   I ain't never been : down in New Orleans
5   I went down the road : that smoky road
6   Like to brought me back : on a cooling board
7   See that woman : all dressed in red
8   Cause a man : to kill you dead
9   You see that woman : all dressed in blue
10 You can't put up : with the way she do
11 See that woman : all dressed in white
12 She get your five dollars : she won't treat you
    right
13 Run to town : hurry back
14 Buddy got a girl : I really like
15 See that woman : all dressed in dark
16 Things will look better : in the Washington Park
17 You need not think : because you look sweet
18 You can make : a fool of me
19 Every time : I go to town
20 Meet my gal : hanging around
21 Girl I love : ain't no fool
22 Big as an elephant : strong as a mule

BennW   1   Bennett, Will

        title: Railroad Bill
        place and date: Knoxville, Tenn., c. Sept. 1930
        record numbers: (K-127-) Vo-1464 OJL-18

1   Railroad Bill : ought to be killed
2   Never worked : and he never will
3   Railroad Bill : done took my wife
4   Threatened to kill me : that he would take my life
5   Going up the mountain : take my stand
6   Forty-one derringer : in my right and left hand

19

BennW 1   Bennett, Will

7   Going up the mountain : going out west
8   Forty-one derringer : sticking in my breast
9   Buy me a gun : just as long as my arm
10 Kill everybody : ever done me wrong
11 Buy me a gun : with a shiny barrel
12 Kill somebody : about my good-looking gal
13 Got a thirty-eight special : on a forty-four frame
14 How in the world can I miss him : when I've got dead aim
15 When I went to the doctor : asked him what the matter could be
16 Said if you don't stop drinking son : it'll kill you dead
17 Going to drink my liquor : drink it and win
18 Doctor said it will kill me : but he never said when
19 If the river was brandy : and I was a duck
20 I'd sink to the bottom : and I'd never come up
21 Honey honey : do you think of me
22 Times have caught me : living on pork and beans
23 Son you talk about your honey : you ought to see mine
24 She's humpbacked bow-legged : crippled and blind
25 Honey honey : do you think I'm a fool
26 Think I'm going to quit you : while the weather is cool
27 Honey honey : quit your worrying me
28 It's going through the world : in my heart disease
29 Going up the mountain : *do everything*
30 Go through the world : ???

BennW 2   Bennett, Will

    title: Real Estate Blues
    place and date: Knoxville, Tenn., c. Sept. 1930
    record numbers: (K-128-) Vo-1464 Rt RL-334

1   All I want is a new pair of shoes : that is all I pray
2   Some old place I can go : to lay my weary head
3   ??? *dissatisfied* : any old place to be
4   For any old where I hangs my hat : is home sweet home to me
5   I don't need no real estate : and neither no ??? *long*
6   All I want is a place to stay : I can call my home
7   I say goodbye hard luck hello joy : here I come for tea
8   For I didn't bring nothing to this old world : and I can't carry nothing away

BigB 1   Big Bill

    title: Down in the Basement Blues
    place and date: Chicago, c. Oct. 1928
    record numbers: (20922-1) Pm-12707 Yz L-1035

1   Down to the depot mama Lord : I looked up on the board
2   Lord I asked the ticket agent : how long the southbound train been gone
3   Got my ticket Lord Lord : conductor can I ride
4   Lord I want to *get to* that basement : I'll be satisfied
5   Sweety in the basement mama Lord : sweet as she can be
6   Lord she is low and she is squatty : she's all right with me
7   Down to the railroad mama Lord : and I looked up at the sun
8   Lord if the train don't come : there's going to be some walking done
9   Don't want no woman Lord Lord : *declare I'll stay at home*
10 Because she will hide in the bushes : she is hard to find

BigB 2   Big Bill

    title: Starvation Blues
    place and date: Chicago, c. Oct. 1928
    record numbers: (20923-2) Pm-12707 Yz L-1011

1   Starvation in my kitchen : rent sign's on my door
2   And if my luck don't change : I can't stay at my home no more
3   And I got up this morning : just about the dawn of day
4   Mean I ain't got no job : I ain't got no place to stay
5   Lord I walked to a store : I ain't got a dime
6   When I asked for a darn neckbone : the clerk don't pay me no mind
7   Lord Lord : mama some old rainy day
8   Mean my luck going to change : and I going to be treated this a-way

BigB 3   Big Bill (Famous Hokum Boys)

    title: Eagle Riding Papa
    place and date: New York, 9 Apr. 1930
    record numbers: (9595-1) Ba-0712 Yz L-1011

1   Listen everybody : from near and far
2   You want to know : just who we are
3   Now if you like : the way we play
4   Listen boy : we'll try to stay
5   We'll make you loose : we'll make you tight
6   Make you shake it : till broad daylight
7   I would never do brag : never do boast
8   Played this tune : from coast to coast
9   Now if you like this tune : think it's fine
10 Set right down : and drop a line
11 Sometime : we're down your way
12 We'll drop in : and spend the day
13 Now some want to know : just what you got
14 Got good okra man : serve it hot
15 Now we ain't good-looking : and we don't dress fine
16 The way we whip it : it's a hanging crime
17 If you see me stealing : don't tell on me
18 Just stealing : back to my used-to-be
19 We never have one gal : at a time
20 Always have : seven eight or nine

BigB 4   Big Bill

    title: Grandma's Farm
    place and date: New York, 9 Apr. 1930
    record numbers: (9600-1) Pe-187 Yz L-1035

1   Got up this morning : with the same thing on my mind
2   And the girl I'm loving : but she don't pay me no mind
3   Lord my girl caught the train : and she left me a mule to ride
4   When the train turn the corner : got a note my black mule died
5   Just as sure as the grape vine : grows all around that stump
6   Said I want you and I need you : mama to be my sugar lump
7   Just as sure as the rabbit : mama plays on your grandma's farm
8   Said I done got tired : of that stuff you been carrying on
9   Now you see me coming : now mama heist your window high
10 But you know I'm going to leave you : girl I know you're going to grieve and cry
11 I've got so many wagons : it done run my good road down
12 And I got so many women : till the men don't want me around

BigB   5   Big Bill

    title: Skoodle Do Do
    place and date: New York, 9 Apr. 1930
    record numbers: (9601-2) Pe-157 Yz L-1011

1 Got up this morning : about half past four
2 Somebody's knocking : on my back door
3 Some of these mornings : mama it won't be long
4 You going to call me baby : and I'll be gone
5 Your right foot in mama : your left one out
6 Your time baby : and move your body about
7 Get me a picket : off of my back fence
8 Whop you on your head : until you learn some sense

BigB   6   Big Bill

    title: I Can't Be Satisfied
    place and date: Richmond, Ind., 2 May 1930
    record numbers: (16569) Ge-7230 Yz L-1011

1 Now listen here my baby : tell you what I want you
   to do
2 Want you treat me mama : like I do you
3 Because I can't be satisfied : and I can't be
   satisfied
4 And I can't mistreat her : not to please nobody's
   mind
5 Now I love my sweety : tell you the reason why
6 My baby got something : to satisfy my mind
7 Lord starvation's in my kitchen : rent sign's on my
   door
8 Good girl told me : she can't use me no more
9 I'm leaking at the heart : bleeding at the nose
10 Good girl told me : she can't use me no more
11 Got on my high-cut stockings : low cut shoes
12 Mama and I ain't ??? : ??? sure can use
13 Now look a-here boys : ain't this rich
14 I got to pay my wife : for everything I get

BigB   7   Big Bill

    title: Skoodle Do Do
    place and date: Richmond, Ind., 2 May 1930
    record numbers: (16573) Ge-7210 Yz L-1035

1 I got up this morning : mama about half past four
2 Somebody was knocking : on my back door
3 Some of these mornings : mama it won't be long
4 You going to call me babe : and I'll be gone
5 Down in Mississippi mama : doing very well
6 Now I went up north with you ma : I ain't doing so
   well
7 Get me a picket : off of my back fence
8 Whop you on the head : until you learn some sense

BigB   8   Big Bill (Jane Lucas)

    title: Pussy Cat Blues
    place and date: New York, 15 Sept. 1930
    record numbers: (10031-2) Ba-32138 Yz L-1035

1 Pussy cat pussy cat : where have you been so long
2 Lord the mouse done been here : packed his grip and
   gone
3 Pussy cat pussy cat : why don't you stay at home
4 You sleep all day : run up the alley all night long

BigB   9   Big Bill

    title: The Banker's Blues
    place and date: Richmond, Ind., 19 Nov. 1930
    record numbers: (17281) Ch-16327 Yz L-1011

1 If you got money in the bank : don't let your woman
   draw it out
2 Because she'll spend your money : then she will
   throw you out
3 Oh Lord Lord Lord : crying Lord Lordy Lord
4 Said I used to be your regular : now I've got to be
   your dog
5 You were the cause got me broke : how can you be so
   mean
6 Say you taken all my money : give it to your no-good
   man
7 Said I have had money : but now I'm cold in hand
8 Says and the woman that I'm loving : living with
   another man
9 Says I know my baby : she sure going to jump and
   shout
10 When I get down to the bank : and draw my money out

BigB   10   Big Bill

    title: Big Bill Blues
    place and date: Richmond, Ind., 9 Feb. 1932
    record numbers: (18385) Ch-16400 Yz L-1035

1 Lord my hair is a-rising : my flesh begin to crawl
2 I had a dream last night babe : another mule in my
   doggone stall
3 And it's some people said : these Big Bill blues
   ain't bad
4 Lord it must not have been : them Big Bill blues I
   had
5 Lord I wonder what's the matter : Papa Bill can't
   get no mail
6 Lord the post office must be on fire : and the
   mailman must undoubtedly be in jail
7 I can't be your wagon : cinch I ain't going to be
   your mule
8 I ain't going to fix up your black *tarnation* : I
   ain't going to be your doggone fool

BigB   11   Big Bill

    title: Mr. Conductor Man
    place and date: Richmond, Ind., 9 Feb. 1932
    record numbers: (18392) Ch-16426 Yz L-1035

1 I got up this morning : hear the train whistle blow
2 Lord I thought about my baby : I sure did want to go
3 Lord I grabbed up my suitcase : I *dropped it on the
   floor*
4 I could see the conductor : he waving his hands to
   go
5 I said Mr conductor man : I want to talk to you
6 I want to ride your train : from here to Bugaloo
7 I'm leaving this morning : man I ain't got my fare
8 But I will shovel coal in your engine : till your
   train get me there
9 Crying please Mr conductor man : please take my last
   thin dime
10 Lord I got a woman in Bugaloo waiting : man I can't
   lose no time
11 When the bell started ringing : conductor hollered
   all aboard
12 Lord I picked up my suitcase : start walking down
   the road
13 I'm leaving this morning : I sure don't want to go
14 Lord and the woman I been loving : she don't want me
   no more

        title: Worrying You Off My Mind--Part 1
        place and date: New York, 29 Mar. 1932
        record numbers: (16606-?) Ba-32559 Yz L-1035

1   I made a long day : walking along and crying
2   I lost my baby : can't be satisfied
3   When you get in trouble : haven't got a friend
4   Just take it easy : they'll need your help again
5   Now ain't it hard : to live alone
6   Just as hard to be married : and break up your home
7   But that's all right : that's all right for you
8   You need me some morning : when I won't need you
9   When I was down : lost my wife and my friend
10 When I got my money : they all come back again
11 Well money and pretty women : running hand in hand
12 When they raising a squabble : taking some woman's
    man

        title: Bull Cow Blues
        place and date: New York, 29 Mar. 1932
        record numbers: (11610-2) Ba-32653 Yz L-1035

1   If you got a good bullcow : better feed him every
    day
2   Because may come along some young cow : and tow your
    bull away
3   Leave you bull in a pasture : where there ain't no
    grass
4   But you women all thought you loved me : look like
    every minute going to be my last
5   Oh babe : don't mean your bull no good
6   Why don't you rub your bullcow and pet him : tell
    him what you want your bull to do
7   Babe your bull got a horn mama : as long as your
    right arm
8   Lord if you play with my horn baby : make you break
    up your happy home
9   Babe you may be beautiful : you got to die some day
10 So you well as to give me some of your loving :
    before you pass away
11 I got four feet to walk on : tail to shake if it's
    all night long
12 Lord at daybreak call me baby : you'll find your
    bullcow gone

        title: How You Want It Done?
        place and date: New York, 29 Mar. 1932
        record numbers: (11611-2) Ba-32436 Yz L-1011

1   Why don't you tell me loving mama : how you want
    your rolling done
2   Lord I'll give you satisfaction : now if it's all
    night long
3   Lord I got up this morning : just about the break of
    day
4   Lord I'm thinking about my baby : Lord the one that
    went away
5   Lord I got me a little old brownskin : just as sweet
    as she can be
6   Lord she low and she squatty : but she's all right
    with me
7   Now you can put me in the alley : my gal is name is
    Sally
8   You wake me up in the morning : mama I still got
    that old habit
9   Won't you tell me : how you want it done
10 Lord I'll give you satisfaction : now if it's all
    night long
11 Lord it's some of these old mornings : Lordy know it
    won't be long

12 Lord I know you going to call me : baby Lord and
    I'll be gone

        title: Long Tall Mama
        place and date: New York, 30 Mar. 1932
        record numbers: (11617-1) Ba-33085 Yz L-1011

1   Got a long tall mama : she stands about seven feet
    nine
2   And when she get to loving : holler papa won't you
    take your time
3   Oh when she start to loving : she sure can do her
    stuff
4   And she squeezing so tight : holler mama Lordy
    that's enough
5   Got a brand new movement : one that she calls her
    own
6   And when she start to kissing : make a poor man
    leave his home
7   And she do a little of this : and mama and she do a
    little of that
8   And when she put on full steam : make a freight
    train jump a track
9   Said she's long and tall : and half as sweet as she
    can be
10 To satisfy that woman : takes more than a bumblebee

        title: Mississippi River Blues
        place and date: Chicago, 23 Mar. 1934
        record numbers: (80395-1) Ba-32670 Yz L-1011

1   Mississippi River : is so long deep and wide
2   I can't see my good gal : standing on that other
    side
3   I was crying and I called : I could not make my baby
    hear
4   Lord I'm going to get me a boat mama : paddle on
    down from here
5   Ain't it hard to love someone : when they are so far
    from you
6   Lord I'm going to get me a boat : and paddle this
    old river through
7   I went down to the landing : to see if any boats was
    there
8   And the ferryman told me : could not find no boats
    nowhere
9   The big boat is up the river : a-turning around and
    around
10 Lord I'm going to get me a good girl : or jump
    overboard and drown

        title: C and A Blues
        place and date: Chicago, 20 June 1935
        record numbers: (C-1020-B) ARC-5-12-65 Yz L-1035

1   It's a little train leaving out of here : they call
    the C and A
2   Going to take me home baby : I'm going home to stay
3   Because I'm leaving in the morning : Lord on that C
    and A
4   Babe I'm going back to St Louis : I'm going there to
    stay
5   Now my baby got unruly : she left from home
6   What she going to come back and say : when she find
    her daddy gone
7   My woman walks around : with her mouth poked out
8   She won't tell nobody : what it's all about
9   Now pack up my clothes : shove into your door

BigB   17   Big Bill

10 I'm leaving this morning mama : I won't be back no
    more
11 Now it's C for Chicago : A for Arkan
12 Why did I leave you baby : because I'm tired of
    taking you dogging

BigB   18   Big Bill

        title: Keep Your Hands Off Her
        place and date: Chicago, 31 Oct. 1935
        record numbers: (96230-1) BB B6188 RBF RF-16

1   Boy she strictly tailor-made : boy she ain't no
    hand-me-down
2   Catch you messing with her boy : I sure shoot you
    down
3   She got them little bitty hands : them great big
    legs
4   She sure looks good : because everybody says it
5   She got them real dark eyes : now real curly hair
6   Big Bill is going to follow : that woman everywhere
7   You can look her up : and you can look her down
8   She got a heaven boy : ain't never been found
9   Ah watch her boy : as she pass by
10 Because the day I catch you with her : boy that's
    the day you're going to die

BigB   19   Big Bill

        title: Good Liquor Gonna Carry Me Down
        place and date: Chicago, 31 Oct. 1935
        record numbers: (96232-1) BB B6230 Yz L-1011

1   Now I know a little girl : about sixteen years old
2   She said Bill stop drinking : and I will satisfy
    your soul
3   Now my woman told me : about fifteen years ago
4   Bill you going to drink one of these mornings : and
    you'll never drink no more
5   Now I wake up in the morning : holding a bottle
    tight
6   When I lay down at night : mama just a gallon out of
    sight
7   Yes I went to the doctor : with my head in my hand
8   The doctor said Big Bill : I think I'll have to give
    you monkey glands
9   Now my woman told me to stop drinking : and come on
    home
10 Said if you don't Big Bill : some other man will
    carry your business on

BigB   20   Big Bill (State Street Boys)

        title: Rustlin' Man
        place and date: Chicago, 9 Dec. 1935
        record numbers: (C-890-3) ARC unissued Rt RL-316

1   I'm a rustling man : I rustle night and day
2   Just as soon as I get my money : I won't have to
    rustle this a-way
3   A rustling man : have a hard time in this town
4   Because when you get broke and down baby : your
    friends all turn you down
5   I am a rustling man : I go from town to town
6   I believe I will get married : married Lord and
    settle down
7   I've traveled and traveled : mama I mean this whole
    world through
8   I haven't found nothing : boy for a poor rustling
    man to do

BigB   21   Big Bill

        title: I've Got to Dig You
        place and date: Chicago, 17 Apr. 1940
        record numbers: (WC-3034-A) Vo-05563 RBF RF-16

1   Going to tell you women : and it goes for the men
2   Don't fool with me : because you sure can't win
3   You's all right baby : but your line's too short
4   Give me back my hat and shoes : now baby I bought
5   You may be fat : woman slim or tall
6   I've got something gal : that can kick in your stall
7   I asked my wife : where she had been all night
8   She said what you car : long as I treat you right
9   Going to tell you baby : like the farmer told his
    potato
10 I'm going to plant you now woman : but I will dig
    you later

BigB   22   Big Bill

        title: When I Had Money
        place and date: Chicago, 17 Apr. 1940
        record numbers: (WC-3036-A) Vo-05563 RBF RF-16

1   I listened to my baby : when she was telling me her
    dreams
2   Lord everything now : baby would be peaches and
    cream
3   I had money on the horses : money on one two three
4   Now my water got muddy : and my horse run into a
    stream
5   Now when I had money : I had friends and a real good
    home
6   Lord I done lost my money : babe my friends and home
    is gone
7   Lord my mother tried : Lord to make me do right
8   Lord I would stay drunk all day : baby and I
    wouldn't come home at night
9   Lord if I had a-listened to my mother : Lord what
    she say
10 Lord I would not have been here no : baby laying in
    this old hospital bed

BigB   23   Big Bill

        title: Key to the Highway
        place and date: Chicago, 2 May 1941
        record numbers: (C-3745-1) OK-06242 RBF RF-1

1   I've got the key to the highway : and I'm booked out
    and bound to go
2   I'm going to leave here running : because walking is
    most too slow
3   I'm going down on Florida : now where I'm better
    known
4   Because woman you don't do nothing : drive a good
    man away from home
5   Now when the moon peeps over the mountain : I'll be
    on my way
6   Now I'm going to walk this old highway : until the
    break of day
7   Run here sweet mama : run and help me with this
    heavy load
8   I'm due in West Texas : and I got to get on the road
9   I'm going to West Texas : I'm going down behind the
    sun
10 I'm going to ask the good Lord : what evil have I
    done

23

BirB   1   Bird, Billy

          title: Mill Man Blues
          place and date: Atlanta, 29 Oct. 1928
          record numbers: (147323-2) Co-14381-D Yz L-1016

1   Yond comes a woman : with a peck of corn on her back
2   I'm going to stick around here : and I'm going to
    try and keep her from carrying it back
3   Now lady I ain't no mill man : just a mill man's son
4   But I can do your grinding : till the mill man comes
5   I want you to tell me pretty lady : how you want
    your grinding done
6   Said I want it fixed up baby : just like your daddy
    done
7   Said : I ain't going to talk no more
8   Since you told how you want it fixed baby : just
    like my daddy done
9   Many nights I rambled : and I hid out the whole
    night long
10 Trying to teach my woman : how to do right from
    wrong
11 Now mmm : mmm
12 Said I'm worried now baby : won't be worried long

BirB   2   Bird, Billy

          title: Alabama Blues--Part 1
          place and date: Atlanta, 29 Oct. 1928
          record numbers: (147325-1) Co-14418-D His HLP-5

1   Now T for Texas : and T for Tennessee
2   I'm not after your woman : man she's after me
3   And I went up on a mountain : and I looked down a
    little old hole
4   And I seen two monkeys : doing the sweet jellyroll
5   Now look here baby : look what you've done done
6   You done made me like you : now your man's done come
7   And I went up on a mountain : and I looked down in
    the sea
8   And I seen two monkeys : playing around after me

BirB   3   Bird, Billy

          title: Alabama Blues--Part 2
          place and date: Atlanta, 29 Oct. 1928
          record numbers: (147326-1) Co-14418-D His HLP-5

1   I went up on a mountain : just to see what I could
    see
2   And I seen two monkey-women : climbing up a tree
3   I want you women : to strictly understand
4   When my mother raised me : she didn't raise no
    monkey-man
5   Now one two three : four five six
6   I'm going to Chattanooga : get my hambone fixed
7   Said I went up to my girl's house : and I tipped
    right through the hall
8   I looked in through the keyhole : there's another
    nigger in my stall

Bird   1   Bird, John (Mae Glover)

          title: Gas Man Blues
          place and date: Richmond, Ind., 29 July 1929
          record numbers: (15396-A) Ge-7040 Yz L-1009

2   Oh yes pretty mama : have no money to pay
4   Better get you a wood-chopper : to back up in your
    stall
6   You better go the the doctor : get you a seasick
    pill
8   I've been in pretty mama : and I won't be back no
    more
10 If I call around pretty mama : will you let me park

Bird   1   Bird, John (Mae Glover)

12 ???-hearted woman : that man got nothing that he
    wants fixed
14 I can't help you woman : gasman got no jellyroll
16 I can't help it pretty mama : the gasman don't take
    no chance

BlaAB   1   Black Boy Shine

          title: Sugarland Blues
          place and date: San Antonio, 20 Nov. 1936
          record numbers: (SA-2551-1) Vo-03417 BC-7

1   You never have nothing : long as you live in
    Sugarland
2   Because you working for a woman : and a sweetback
    man
3   I dump sugar all day : clean until broad daylight
4   I done everything for that woman : still she don't
    treat me right
5   I'm going to stop working baby : get yourself
    another man
6   Because I've got another woman : you'll have to do
    the best you can
7   I work for you in the winter : I work for you in the
    ice and snow
8   And baby you told me : you didn't want me no more
9   It done come summertime : and I ain't going to work
    no more
10 Because I've got another woman : baby and I'm going
    to let you go

BlaAI   1   Black Ivory King

          title: The Flying Crow
          place and date: Chicago, 15 Feb. 1937
          record numbers: (61795-A) De-7307 BC-5

1   Flying Crow leave Port Arthur : why they come in
    Shreveport to change their crew
2   They'll take water in Texarkana : and for Ashtown
    they'll keep on through
3   Twenty-five minutes from evening : for a cup of
    coffee and a slice of cake
4   Flying Crow is heading for Kansas City : and boy she
    just won't wait
5   Yon she gone she gone : with a red and green light
    behind
6   Well now the red mean trouble : and the green means
    a rambling mind
7   Well I hate to hear : that old fireman when he tones
    the bell

BlaAL   1   Black, Lewis

          title: Rock Island Blues
          place and date: Memphis, 10 Dec. 1927
          record numbers: (145361-3) Co-14429-D His HLP-5

1   See the train : weaving up and down the track
2   Said I won't be dead : just ain't coming back
3   When you see a train mama : come weaving up and down
    the line
4   Said I'm bound to get a letter : from that cheating
    brown of mine
5   Well I'm going away mama : won't be back till fall
6   And if I get kind of lucky : won't be back at all
7   I'm going to write a letter : mail it in the air
8   I'm going to find this gal : she's in the world
    somewhere
9   Don't you see mama : see what you done done
10 You made me love you : now your man done come
11 Mmm : I won't be here long
12 In a few more days : up the road I'm going
13 Said I'm going away mama : make it lonesome here

BlaAL 1   Black, Lewis

15 I said mmm : what you got on your mind
18 I got a mind to ramble : mind to leave this town

BlaAL 2   Black, Lewis

        title: Gravel Camp Blues
        place and date: Memphis, 10 Dec. 1927
        record numbers: (145366-2) Co-14291-D Fly LP-103

 1 I'm going away tomorrow mama : going out on the cue
 2 And if I find anything : coming back after you
 3 It's soon one morning : I heard a panther squall
 4 Tell your mama caught the local : you catch the
       Cannonball
 5 Tell you my man caught the local : I caught on
       behind
 6 Say now you can't leave me : 'tain't no need of
       crying
 7 Mmm pretty mama : ain't going to be here long
 8 You : and you treated me wrong
 9 When I leave from here : going out on the O
10 I don't find no log camp : I'll find a gravel camp
       sure
11 Mmm what's the matter here
12 Ain't nothing going on wrong : but mama I don't care
13 Mmm : don't need you nohow
14 When I had you black gal : you didn't have nobody
       nohow

BlaAL 3   Black, Lewis

        title: Corn Liquor Blues
        place and date: Memphis, 10 Dec. 1927
        record numbers: (145367-2) Co-14291-D Rt RL-327

 1 Hey hey hey : corn liquor in my bones
 3 Now hurry up here you gals : and get me a barrel
 4 I'm going to make corn liquor : for to tickle you
       gals
 5 I went home last night : about half past four
 6 I seen corn liquor : running out my back door
 7 And it's mmm mama : what's the matter now
 9 Now pick me up mama : put me in your bed
10 Corn liquor : is going all through your sweet
       daddy's head
11 Now mama when I die : I want you to bury me deep
12 I want you to put corn liquor : at my head and feet
13 I want you to put one bottle : in my hand
14 So I can drink my way : to the Promised Land
15 Oh Lord mama when I die : I want you to bury me low
16 So these corn liquor gals : know I ain't coming here
       no more
17 Now mama ashes to ashes : and dust to dust
18 Corn liquor daddy : done *push his first*
19 Now if anybody ask you : who composed this song
20 Tell them it's corn liquor daddy : he's been here
       and gone
21 Mmm : corn liquor on my mind
22 If you catch me out drinking : I'm not drinking just
       to keep from crying

Blacm 1   Blackman, Tewee (Memphis Jug Band)

        title: K. C. Moan
        place and date: Memphis, 4 Oct. 1929
        record numbers: (56346-1) Vi-V38558 Rt RL-337

 1 I thought I heard that K C : when she blowed
 2 And she blowed : like my woman's on board
 3 When I get back : on that K C road
 4 Going to love my baby : like I never loved before

Blacm 2   Blackman, Tewee (Memphis Jug Band)

        title: K. C. Moan
        place and date: Memphis, 4 Oct. 1929
        record numbers: (56346-2) Vi V38558 Fwy FA-2953

 1 I thought I heard : that K C when she blowed
 2 And she blowed like : my woman's on board
 3 When I get back : on that K C road
 4 Going to love my baby : like I never loved before

Blacm 3   Blackman, Tewee (Memphis Jug Band)

        title: I Whipped My Woman With a Single Tree
        place and date: Memphis, 4 Oct. 1929
        record numbers: (56347-2) Vi-V38578 Rt RL-311

 1 I said my woman : had a falling out
 2 People in town : want to know what it was all about
 3 Yes I whipped my woman : with a singletree
 4 You ought a-heard her hollering : don't you murder
       me
 5 Yes I went to the Gypsy : to get my fortune told
 6 The Gypsy told me something : I didn't want no one
       to know
 7 Yes I went to my back door : and that ??? was locked
 8 I went to that front door : you know the ??? was
       locked
 9 Now don't you wish : your easy roller was little and
       cute like mine
10 Every time she walks : she leaves a lot behind

Blacw 1   Blackwell, Francis Scrapper

        title: Kokomo Blues
        place and date: Indianapolis, c. June 1928
        record numbers: (IND-624-) Vo-1192 Yz L-1019

 1 Mmm : baby don't you want to go
 2 Pack your little suitcase : papa's going to Kokomo
 3 Mmm : baby where you been so long
 4 I can tell mama : there's something going on wrong
 5 Mmm : baby you don't know you don't know
 6 Papa's already : going back to Kokomo
 7 And me and my baby : had a falling out last night
 8 ??? : my babe won't treat me right
 9 Mmm : baby what's the matter now
10 Trying to quit your daddy : baby but you don't know
       how
11 And I'll sing this verse : baby I can't sing no more
12 My train is ready : and I'm going to Kokomo

Blacw 2   Blackwell, Francis Scrapper

        title: Penal Farm Blues
        place and date: Indianapolis, c. June 1928
        record numbers: (IND-625-) Vo-1192 Yz L-1019

 1 Early one morning : on my way to the penal farm
 2 Baby all I've done : ain't done nothing wrong
 3 Loaded in the *dog* wagon : and down the road we go
 4 Oh baby : oh baby you don't know
 5 Into the office : then to the bathhouse below
 6 And with a light shower : baby we change our clothes
 7 All last night : baby it seemed so long
 8 All I've done : I ain't done nothing wrong
 9 I'll tell you people : the penal farm is a lonesome
       place
10 And no one there : to smile up in your face
11 Oh baby baby : it won't be so long now
12 Before your daddy : he will be coming home
13 Oh baby baby : won't you come after me
14 My time is up : and penal farm has set me free

Blacw   3   Blackwell, Francis Scrapper

      title: Trouble Blues--Part 1
      place and date: Chicago, c. 17 Aug. 1928
      record numbers: (C-2229-) Vo-1213 Yz L-1019

1 When trouble starts : it stops at my front door
2 I've had more trouble : than ever in my life before
3 I wonder why : troubles keeps on worrying me
4 I'd just soon have my body : baby buried in the sea
5 I had trouble this morning : mailman didn't leave no
    mail
6 I can't see my baby : she's all locked up in jail
7 When trouble starts : it lasted so long
8 Look like everything happened : and everything goes
    wrong
9 Tell me baby : what trouble have done to me
10 Come and got my regular : then took my used-to-be

Blacw   4   Blackwell, Francis Scrapper

      title: Trouble Blues--Part 2
      place and date: Chicago, c. 17 Aug. 1928
      record numbers: (C-2230-) Vo-1213 Yz L-1019

1 I can get my money : but trouble won't let it stay
2 Trouble gets on me : and my money gets away
3 I wonder why : trouble keeps on worrying me
4 I'd just soon : have my body baby buried in the sea
5 Trouble in the morning : noon and night
6 Seemed like I'm treated : every way but right
7 When trouble gets on me : it never ends
8 I get out of one thing : and back into something
    else again
9 Nobody knows : the trouble I do see
10 Nobody knows : but the good Lord and me

Blacw   5   Blackwell, Francis Scrapper

      title: Rambling Blues
      place and date: Richmond, Ind., 24 Nov. 1931
      record numbers: (18216) Ch-16370 BC-6

1 I woke up this morning : with rambling on my mind
2 And I lit out to walking : just to pass away the
    time
3 I rambled all night long : and I'm rambling again
    today
4 All I need is someone : drive my blues away
5 Come here baby : and let me be your man
6 I may not suit you : but I'll do the best I can

Blacw   6   Blackwell, Francis Scrapper

      title: Blue Day Blues
      place and date: Richmond, Ind., 24 Nov. 1931
      record numbers: (18217-A) Ch-16452 Yz L-1019

1 One day I sit thinking : when the rain pour down
    outside
2 And the more I thought : the more I began to cry
3 Today has been : a long old lonesome day
4 And it looks like tomorrow : going to be the same
    old way
5 My days seem lonesome : and my nights they are so
    long
6 I'll be mighty glad : when them old blue days are
    gone

Blacw   7   Blackwell, Francis Scrapper

      title: Down South Blues
      place and date: Richmond, Ind., 24 Nov. 1931
      record numbers: (18218-A) Ch-16452 Yz L-1019

1 I'm just sitting here thinking : of dear old sunny
    Tennessee
2 And wondering if my baby : is waiting there for me
3 I'm going : where the Monon crosses the L and N
4 And catch me a freight train : and go back home
    again
5 I'm going back south : where it's warm the whole
    year round
6 I'll be so glad : when my train pulls up in town

Blacw   8   Blackwell, Francis Scrapper

      title: Hard Time Blues
      place and date: Richmond, Ind., 24 Nov. 1931
      record numbers: (18220) Ch-16361 Yz L-1019

1 I'm going down to the river : just to see the water
    run
2 And to think about my troubles : and where all my
    money's gone
3 Times has got so hard : that I cannot find a job
4 And every morning : the rent man grabs on my
    doorknob
5 I'm getting so ragged : I ain't got no decent
    clothes
6 I ain't got nobody : ain't got nowhere to go
7 Now I'm worried : ain't no telling what I'm going to
    do
8 My friends don't know me : and I can't get a dime or
    two
9 Soon as hard time strike me : my baby puts me out
10 Now guess you know : what these hard time is all
    about

Blacw   9   Blackwell, Francis Scrapper

      title: Back Door Blues
      place and date: Richmond, Ind., 24 Nov. 1931
      record numbers: (18221) Ch-16361 Yz L-1019

1 I left my baby : standing in the back door crying
2 Begging and pleading : don't you leave this time
3 Oh the sun's going to shine : in my back door some
    day
4 I wish I had somebody : to drive my blues away
5 Blues and trouble : both running hand in hand
6 If you ain't never had the blues : you just can't
    understand
7 You can always tell : when your woman's got another
    man
8 She will take your bad treatments : and do the best
    she can

Blacw 10   Blackwell, Francis Scrapper

      title: No Good Woman Blues
      place and date: Chicago, 7 July 1935
      record numbers: (90082-A) Ch-50049 Cor CP-58

1 I got a no-good woman : and she sure don't mean me
    no good
2 I hope there ain't another woman like her : in
    nobody's neighborhood
3 She leaves every morning : come back at the break of
    day
4 And when she comes in the morning : she ain't got a
    word to say
5 Every time I look at that woman : she's got a frown
    on her face

Blacw 10   Blackwell, Francis Scrapper

6 I believe that woman : done let my best friend take
   my place
7 Every evening : do you stop by my door
8 But since he's got my woman : she don't stop there
   no more
9 She's just a no-good woman : and I took her to be my
   friend
10 But she's taught me a lesson : about no-good women
   and men

Blak   1   Blake, Blind

     title: Early Morning Blues
     place and date: Chicago, c. Sept. 1926
     record numbers: (3057-1) Pm-12387 Bio BLP-12031

1 Early this morning : my baby made me sore
2 I'm going away to leave you : ain't coming back no
   more
3 Tell me pretty mama : where did you stay last night
4 It ain't none of your business : daddy since I treat
   you right
5 When you see me sleeping : baby don't you think I'm
   drunk
6 I got one eye on my pistol : and the other on your
   trunk
7 I love you pretty mama : believe me it ain't no lie
8 The day you dare to quit me : baby that's the day
   you die

Blak   2   Blake, Blind

     title: Early Morning Blues
     place and date: Chicago, c. Sept. 1926
     record numbers: (3057-2) Pm-12387 Bio BLP-12037

1 Early this morning : my baby made me sore
2 I'm going away to leave you : ain't coming back no
   more
3 Tell me pretty mama : where did you stay last night
4 It ain't none of your business : daddy since I treat
   you right
5 When you see me sleeping : baby don't you think I'm
   drunk
6 I got one eye on my pistol : and the other on your
   trunk
7 Love you pretty mama : believe me it ain't no lie
8 The day you try to quit me : baby that's the day you
   die

Blak   3   Blake, Blind

     title: Too Tight
     place and date: Chicago, c. Sept. 1926
     record numbers: (3059-2) Pm-12431 Bio BLP-12031

1   Grab your gal : fall in line
2   While I play : this rag of mine
3   Too tight : won't behave
4   Too tight : make you rave
5   Too tight : won't jump
6   Too tight : can't just once
7   Too tight : make you cry
8   Too tight : you want to die
9   Too tight : won't quit
10 Too tight : I'm singing it
11 Too tight : I'll confess
12 Too tight : it's a mess
13 Too tight : you hear me sing
14 Too tight : to shake that thing

Blak   4   Blake, Blind

     title: Blake's Worried Blues
     place and date: Chicago, c. Sept. 1926
     record numbers: (3060-2) Pm-12442 Bio BLP-12023

1 I woke up this morning : worried in my mind
2 Thinking about : that girl I left behind
3 I'm worried now : I won't be worried long
4 The brownie I love : makes me sing this song
5 If the blues don't kill me : they will drill me
   through and through
6 Woman I love : don't know what to do
7 There's one thing in this world : I cannot
   understand
8 That's a bow-legged woman : crazy about a cross-eyed
   man

Blak   5   Blake, Blind

     title: Come On Boys Let's Do that Messin' Around
     place and date: Chicago, c. Sept. 1926
     record numbers: (3061-2) Pm-12413 Bio BLP-12003

1 I'm feeling blue : lowdown as I can be
2 Come on gals : run and kiss poor me
3 I'm going downtown : to spread the news
4 My gal quit me : and I ain't got the blues
5 Come on gals : bob it up and down
6 But don't let me catch you : messing around

Blak   6   Blake, Blind

     title: Tampa Bound
     place and date: Chicago, c. Sept. 1926
     record numbers: (3062-2) Pm-12442 Bio BLP-12023

1 I'm going back to Tampa : to that girl I left behind
2 I'm going back to Tampa : just to kill my worried
   mind
3 Did you ever lie down at night : thinking about your
   brown
4 You commence rolling and tumbling : I guess I'm
   Tampa bound
5 The bridge washed out : the wire's all down
6 My gal is in the flood : and I'm Tampa bound
7 I got up this morning : put on my walking shoes
8 I'm going back to Tampa : just to kill my lowdown
   blues

Blak   7   Blake, Blind

     title: Stonewall Street Blues
     place and date: Chicago, c. Oct. 1926
     record numbers: (3081-1) Pm-12431 Bio BLP-12031

1 Hey hey hey hey : hey hey hey hey
2 My Stonewall Street gal : makes me feel this a-way
3 You call me in the morning : you call me late at
   night
4 You swear that you love me : but you know you don't
   treat me right
5 I got the blues so bad : can feel them with my
   natural hand
6 I been your dog : ever since I been your man
7 I'm going to grab me a freight train : ride until it
   stops
8 I ain't going to stay around here : and be your
   stumbling block

Blak   8   Blake, Blind

        title: Black Dog Blues
        place and date: Chicago, c. Apr. 1927
        record numbers: (4362-1) Pm-12464 Bio BLP-12003

1   Let me tell you mama : what my black dog done done
      to me
2   He chased me from my regular : now he's after my
      used-to-be
3   Black dog black dog : you caused me to weep and moan
4   You caused me : to leave my sweet old happy home
5   Black dog black dog : you forever on my mind
6   If you only let me : see my baby one more time
7   So long black dog : I'm quitting you on the fly
8   Because you got the nerve : to leave my good woman
      to cry

Blak   9   Blake, Blind

        title: One Time Blues
        place and date: Chicago, c. Apr. 1927
        record numbers: (4363-2) Pm-12479 Bio BLP-12037

1   Ah : the rising sun going down
2   I ain't got nobody : since my baby's blowed this
      town
3   Ah : mama love me one more time
4   You give me a little chance : maybe you will change
      your mind
5   I done called you : till I almost lost my mind
6   I ain't going call no more : good man is hard to
      find
7   Ah : mama who can your regular be
8   I ain't got no regular : baby please take me
9   Take me : mama I'll tell you what I'll do
10 I'll get up every morning : work hard all day for
      you

Blak   10   Blake, Blind

        title: Bad Feeling Blues
        place and date: Chicago, c. May 1927
        record numbers: (4443-1) Pm-12497 Bio BLP-12003

1   I got the bad feeling blues : keeps me worried all
      the time
2   I can't get along : with that high brown gal of mine
3   Look a-here mama : you done throwed your papa down
4   I wouldn't hate it so bad : but the news all over
      town
5   Look a-here mama : what you want me to do
6   I work all the time : bring my money home to you
7   Lord Lord : your papa done going to stay
8   I never thought : you would treat your daddy this
      a-way
9   I got the bad feeling blues : keeps me so lowdown
10 I'm going to pack my grip : leave this lonesome town

Blak   11   Blake, Blind

        title: Brownskin Mama Blues
        place and date: Chicago, c. Oct. 1927
        record numbers: (20106-2) Pm-12606-2 Bio BLP-12003

1   Brownskin mama : what in the world you want me to do
2   You keep my poor heart aching : I'm blue through and
      through
3   I helped you when you were down : and could not help
      yourself
4   Now I'm down : you want to help somebody else
5   You can go : do anything that you want to do
6   Some day you want me : mama and I won't want you
7   You treat me lowdown and dirty : baby that's all you
      do
8   But some old rainy day : it's coming home to you

Blak   11   Blake, Blind

9   My mind's all churned up : that's why I'm all
      confused
10 That's the reason why : I'm moaning these brownskin
      mama blues

Blak   12   Blake, Blind

        title: Hard Road Blues
        place and date: Chicago, c. Oct. 1927
        record numbers: (20107-2) Pm-12583 Bio BLP-12031

1   Keep on walking and walking : talking to myself
2   Gal I love : with somebody's else
3   I got the hard road blues : walking on down the line
4   Maybe some day : my gal must change her mind
5   It's a hard hard road : when your baby done throwed
      you down
6   Going to keep on walking : from town to town
7   It's been a long long time : since I seen my baby's
      face
8   And I don't see her joker : stand to my place
9   I'm going to find my baby : don't say she can't be
      found
10 Going to walk this hard hard road : until my
      mustache drags the ground

Blak   13   Blake, Blind

        title: Hey Hey Daddy Blues
        place and date: Chicago, c. Oct. 1927
        record numbers: (20108-1) Pm-12606 Bio BLP-12003

1   Hey hey : your daddy's feeling blue
2   I'm worried all the time : can't keep you off my
      mind
3   Hey hey : love you till the day you die
4   Nobody but me : you know the reason why
5   Hey hey : your daddy lonesome for you
6   I ain't going to tell no lie : your daddy's about to
      die
7   Hey hey : I'm lonesome night and day
8   I told you what I said : don't you drive the blues
      away

Blak   14   Blake, Blind

        title: You Gonna Quit Me Blues
        place and date: Chicago, c. Oct. 1927
        record numbers: (20110-1) Pm-12597 Yz L-1016

1   You going to quit me baby : good as I been to you
3   Give you my money honey : to buy your shoes and
      clothes
5   You going to quit me baby : put me out-of-doors
7   Six months on the chain-gang : believe me 'tain't no
      fun
9   The day you quit me baby : that's the day you die
11 Jailhouse ain't no place baby : believe me 'tain't
      no lie

Blak   15   Blake, Blind

        title: Wabash Rag
        place and date: Chicago, c. Nov. 1927
        record numbers: (20154-2) Pm-12597 Yz L-1016

1   Down south : on Wabash Street
2   Everybody : you chance to meet
3   They're doing it : night and day
4   See : if it will drive your blues away
5   Every little kid : that you meet
6   In the alley : in the street
7   Grab me mama : hold me tight

Blak   15   Blake, Blind

    8 Let's mess around : the rest of the night
    9 Throw your hands : way up high
   10 Grab me mama : make me cry
   11 People come : from miles around
   12 Get on Wabash : break them down

Blak   16   Blake, Blind

        title: Doggin' Me Mama Blues
        place and date: Chicago, c. Apr. 1928
        record numbers: (20517-3) Pm-12673 Bio BLP-12037

    1 There's no need of you dogging me : mama I ain't
       done nothing to you
    2 If you keep on dogging me : no telling what I'll do
    3 You dog me in the morning : mama you dog me late at
       night
    4 If you keep on dogging daddy : I sure ain't going to
       treat you right

Blak   17   Blake, Blind

        title: Goodbye Mama Moan
        place and date: Chicago, c. May 1928
        record numbers: (20541-1) Pm-12634 Bio BLP-12037

    1 For years and years : I been your hard-working mule
    2 I may be crazy : but I ain't no doggone fool
    3 You used to be sugar : but you ain't sweet no more
    4 Better keep your other man : from hanging around my
       door
    5 You used to be kind : now you begun to change
    6 You treat me : like an old dog got the mange
    7 Goodbye mama : you ain't the same no more
    8 Don't come back : but treat me like you did before

Blak   18   Blake, Blind

        title: No Dough Blues
        place and date: Chicago, c. May 1928
        record numbers: (20559-1) Pm-12723 Bio BLP-12031

    1 It's a hard hard time now : good man can't get no
       dough
    2 All I do for my baby : don't satisfy her no more
    3 I ain't got no job : now you going to put me down
    4 You going to quit me baby : for a hard-working clown
    5 Time is so hard now : maybe things will change some
       day
    6 And when I get a job : maybe you will change your
       way
    7 Don't quit me baby : because I can't find no work to
       do
    8 Because all the dirt you done for me : it's coming
       back home to you
    9 I used to be a joker : now I'm going to make a
       change
   10 I'm going to get me a job : keep coal in your cold
       kitchen range

Blak   19   Blake, Blind

        title: Bootleg Rum Dum Blues
        place and date: Chicago, c. May 1928
        record numbers: (20566-1) Pm-12695 Bio BLP-12003

    1 I love my whiskey : crazy about it as I can be
    2 But my new bootlegger : well he's about to poison me
    3 Took one drink last night : and it made me go stone
       blind
    4 Got to run away : leave my sweet mama behind
    5 Sometime one drink : make me act like a doggone fool

Blak   19   Blake, Blind

    6 But two or three drinks : make me kick like a
       doggone mule
    7 Mama mama : don't treat your papa mean no more
    8 Get full of my bootleg whiskey : make you fly
       through the door
    9 I'm a good man when I'm sober : but Lord Lord when
       I'm drunk
   10 If you see me reeling : mama go hide in your trunk

Blak   20   Blake, Blind

        title: Panther Squall Blues
        place and date: Chicago, c. May 1928
        record numbers: (20582-2) Pm-12723 Yz L-1016

    1 I got a sweet mama : she ain't low at all
    2 She got the kind of loving : will make a panther
       squall
    3 She got Elgin movements : and a twenty-year
       guarantee
    4 I bet you my last dollar : she don't put them jinx
       on me

Blak   21   Blake, Blind

        title: Walkin' Across the Country
        place and date: Chicago, c. Sept. 1928
        record numbers: (20868-2) Pm-12754 Bio BLP-12031

    1 Walking walking : talking to myself
    2 Wondering if I die : would my baby love somebody
       else
    3 Sighing and crying : broke down with the blues
    4 My clothes are worn out : holes all in my shoes
    5 Walking across the country : trying to get a stake
    6 Because my baby : want every cent I make
    7 Tired and hungry : I've been walking many days
    8 Wondering : if my baby would stop her hateful ways
    9 Walking across the country : with my head bowed down
   10 A woman can still make a man : act like a clown

Blak   22   Blake, Blind

        title: Search Warrant Blues
        place and date: Chicago, c. Sept. 1928
        record numbers: (20871-3) Pm-12737 Bio BLP-12023

    1 Mr police captain : listen to my plea
    2 I want to make my baby : come back home to me
    3 Give me a search warrant : and a great big hound
    4 I'm going to find my baby : if I have to track her
       down
    5 I know where she's at : but her man won't let me in
    6 All I want is a search warrant : and a bottle of gin
    7 I'm going to get running drunk : and go into that
       place
    8 And that backbiting man : better not show his face
    9 I love my baby : but she treat me so unkind
   10 If she thinks she can quit me : she really have lost
       her mind

Blak   23   Blake, Blind

        title: Notoriety Woman Blues
        place and date: Chicago, c. Sept. 1928
        record numbers: (20875-2) Pm-12754 Bio BLP-12031

    1 I got a notoriety woman : she about to drive me wild
    2 Beside that woman : sits ever meek and mild
    3 That woman is like a tiger : got ways like a bear
    4 Carries a gun in her pocket : a dagger in her hair
    5 To keep her quiet : I knocked her teeth out her
       mouth

6 That notoriety woman : is known all over the South
7 I can't get along with her : and I can't leave her alone
8 Because she knows just how to make me : come back home
9 She likes to fight : she likes to break them down
10 Everybody knows : when my notoriety woman come to town

Blak   24   Blake, Blind

       title: Low Down Loving Gal
       place and date: Chicago, c. Sept. 1928
       record numbers: (20887-5) Pm-12695 Bio BLP-12003

1 Listen folks : to my moan
2 I'm going to tell you : about Sally Jones
3 I'm a man : play one gal
4 And that's : my loving Sal
5 She stepped out : I could see
6 He tried : to two-time me
7 So I thought : that I'd found out
8 What this man : all about
9 He was tall : he was thin
10 Drinks ??? : but *sips her* gin
11 Thought I'd catch her : when I walked in
12 Find her : loving my brother Jim
13 He pulled out a gun : said she was through
14 I'm going : to Chicago you
15 He started to shoot : the gun wouldn't go
16 I said that's all : I want to know
17 We got married : had a baby lamb
18 But that baby : looked like her iceman
19 When the rooster saw the eggs : and they was red
20 He walked across the road : and knocked the peacock dead
21 She's gone away : boys and I'm glad
22 Making : another poor fool sad
23 Six men are in jail : faces to the wall
24 But that gal : was the cause of it all

Blak   25   Blake, Blind

       title: Poker Woman Blues
       place and date: Richmond, Ind., 20 July 1929
       record numbers: (15248-A) Pm-12810 Bio BLP-12023

1 I love to gamble : and gambling's all I do
2 And when I lose : it never makes me blue
3 I gambled away my money : and I gambled away my shack
4 Same way I lost it : same way I'll get it back
5 I won a woman : in a poker game
6 I lost her too : win another one just the same
7 Sometime I'm rich : sometime I ain't got a cent
8 But I've had a good time : everywhere I went
9 Got a new mama : ain't going to gamble her away
10 Going to keep her with me : each and every day

Blak   26   Blake, Blind

       title: Doing a Stretch
       place and date: Richmond, Ind., 20 July 1929
       record numbers: (15249-A) Pm-12810 Bio BLP-12023

1 I had a fall : five to twenty-one
2 When I get back : we going to have some fun
3 Baby baby : tell me the true facts
4 Will you be waiting : when I get back
5 I told the warden : you pay my fine
6 It didn't seem : that he paid me no mind
7 The good things you have done : I can't forget
8 If you quit me baby : it will be my death
9 I love you baby : whole heart and soul

10 Stand by me : until I get my parole
11 Be careful baby : while I'm gone
12 You can't be good : I'll be gone too long
13 Going away : and how happy I will be
14 I know : still love me

Blak   27   Blake, Blind

       title: Fightin' the Jug
       place and date: Richmond, Ind., 20 July 1929
       record numbers: (15250) Pm-12863 Bio BLP-12037

1 Went home last night : my baby won't let me in
2 She made me mad : and I've got in my gin
3 I been drunk so long : dizzy all the time
4 And I found out : whiskey ain't no friend of me
5 When I die : folks without a doubt
6 You won't have to do nothing : but pour me out
7 I can't sleep : and I can't eat a thing
8 The woman I love : has driven me to drink
9 I'm deep down in a hole : somebody else is up
10 Getting sick and tired : of fighting that jug

Blak   28   Blake, Blind

       title: Hookworm Blues
       place and date: Richmond, Ind., 20 July 1929
       record numbers: (15251-A) Pm-12794 Bio BLP-12031

1 Hookworm in your body : and your food don't do you no good
2 Same way with a rounder : come in a nice neighborhood
3 Dirty old hookworm : got into my room
4 Causes me to walk : groan and moan
5 Man like a hookworm : got a hold to my baby
6 He got to *point it fast* : people and I don't mean maybe
7 Never can tell : what a hookworm man will do
8 Take your baby : and make her stop loving you
9 I'm going to leave my baby : and let her have her way
10 She want me back some day : when he throws her down
11 Mmm : mmm
12 Her man like a hookworm : taking a hold to my babe

Blak   29   Blake, Blind

       title: Diddie Wa Diddie
       place and date: Richmond, Ind., 17 Aug. 1929
       record numbers: (15459-A) Pm-12888 Mel MLP-7324

1 There's : a great big mystery
2 And it surely : is worrying me
3 The little girl : about four feet four
4 Come on papa : and give me some more
5 I went out : and walked around
6 Somebody yelled : said look who's in town
7 Went to church : put my hat on the seat
8 Lady sat on it : said daddy you sure is sweet
9 I said sister : I'll soon be gone
10 Just give me that thing : you setting on
11 Then I got : put out of church
12 Because I talk : about diddie wa diddie too much

Blak   30   Blake, Blind

       title: Too Tight Blues No. 2
       place and date: Richmond, Ind., 17 Aug. 1929
       record numbers: (15460) Pm-12824 Bio BLP-12037

1 Got my gal : took a chance
2 We went : to a midnight dance

Blak   30   Blake, Blind

    3   Too tight : it's a mess
    4   Too tight : it's the best
    5   Too tight : it's a wow
    6   Too tight : I'll show you how
    7   Too tight : stepping out
    8   Too tight : hear me shout
    9   Too tight : it's hot stuff
   10   Too tight : can't get enough
   11   Too tight : it's too bad
   12   Too tight :
   13   Too tight : sick in bed
   14   Too tight : went to my head

Blak   31   Blake, Blind

        title: Police Dog Blues
        place and date: Richmond, Ind., 17 Aug. 1929
        record numbers: (15463) Pm-12888 Yz L-1012

    1   All my life : I been a traveling man
    2   Staying alone : and doing the best I can
    3   I shipped my trunk : down to Tennessee
    4   Hard to tell : about a man like me
    5   I met a gal : I couldn't get her off my mind
    6   She passed me up : says she didn't like my kind
    7   I'm scared to bother : around her house at night
    8   Got a police dog : craving for a fight
    9   His name is rambler : and when he gets a chance
   10   He leaves his mark : on everybody's pants
   11   Guess I'll travel : I guess I'll let her be
   12   Before she sics : her police dog on me

Blak   32   Blake, Blind

        title: Georgia Bound
        place and date: Richmond, Ind., 17 Aug. 1929
        record numbers: (15466) Pm-12824 Bio BLP-12037

    1   Packing my duffle : going to leave this town
    2   And I'm going to hustle : to catch that train
            southbound
    3   I got the Georgia blues : for the plow and the hoe
    4   Walked out of my shoes : over this ice and snow
    5   Tune up the fiddle : dust the cat and bow
    6   Put on the griddle : and open the cabin door
    7   I thought I was going : to the northland to stay
    8   South is on my mind : my blues won't go away
    9   Potatoes in the ashes : possum on the stove
   10   You can have the hash : but please leave me the claw
   11   Chicken on the roof : and melons on the vine
   12   I'll be glad : to get back to that Georgia gal of
            mine

Blak   33   Blake, Blind

        title: Playing Policy Blues
        place and date: Grafton, Wis., c. Dec. 1930
        record numbers: (L-647-1) Pm-13035 Bio BLP-12003

    1   Numbers numbers : about to drive me wild
    2   Thinking about the money : that I should have had
    3   I dreamed last night : the woman I love was dead
    4   If I had played the dead row : I would come out
            ahead
    5   I act like a fool : and played on three six nine
    6   Lost my money : and that gal of mine
    7   I played on clearing house : couldn't make a grade
    8   Lord think of the money : that I should have made
    9   I begged my baby : let me in her door
   10   Wanted to put my twenty-five fifty seventy-five : in
            her seven seventeen twenty-four
   11   I want fifteen fifty : and see if it won
   12   I'm going to keep playing policy : till some good
            luck comes

Blak   34   Blake, Blind

        title: Righteous Blues
        place and date: Grafton, Wis., c. Dec. 1930
        record numbers: (L-648-1) Pm-13035 Bio BLP-12003

    1   Listen everybody : I'm going to sing a song
    2   It won't be dirty : and it won't be long
    3   When you want some whiskey : right off the *stove*
    4   Go over : and see Miss Stella Gold
    5   The gals from the alley : slipping all around
    6   Telling everybody : they're leaving town
    7   I got a yellow gal : and a brown named Mame
    8   But the best I've ever had : was the old Crow Jane
    9   Met a funny fellow : he didn't like girls
   10   Painted his face : and with his hair all curls
   11   I'm staying with a woman : about fifty-two
   12   I thought she was too old : I'm telling you

Blak   35   Blake, Blind

        title: Rope Stretchin' Blues--Part 1
        place and date: Grafton, Wis., c. Oct. 1931
        record numbers: (L-1099-2) Pm-13103 Bio
            BLP-12037

    1   I caught a stranger in my house : and I busted his
            head with a club
    2   I lay him out cold : with his heels in a tub
    3   I seen the sheriff coming : and I jumped for the
            door
    4   But I jumped too late : the sheriff had done jumped
            before
    5   They buried a man Thursday : just two short days you
            see
    6   And it makes me wonder : what they going to do to me
    7   I killed a man : and that's the how and how
    8   I'm sitting here wondering : if a woman's worth it
            now
    9   Mmm : rope stretching all day long
   10   In just a few more days : I won't be able to sing my
            song

Blak   36   Blake, Blind

        title: Rope Stretchin' Blues--Part 2
        place and date: Grafton, Wis., c. Oct. 1931
        record numbers: (L-1101-2) Pm-13103 Bio
            BLP-12037

    1   Don't trust no woman : who mistreats her man
    2   When you think she's in your kitchen cooking : she's
            got a stranger by the hand
    3   Ain't no need of you chasing women : brother if you
            really haven't got the cash
    4   Other men get all the chicken : and all you get is
            hash
    5   I have a lot of woman : but I sure don't want one
            now
    6   She always milks me dry : better than you ever milk
            a cow
    7   Mmm : rope stretching all day long
    8   I'm singing now mama : because it won't be long
    9   It wouldn't be so bad : if the rope would just get
            slack
   10   I wouldn't mind at all : but I just got a crick in
            my back
   11   When it's all over mama : and you're all alone by my
            side
   12   Just keep the flies from buzzing by me : and then I
            will be satisfied

Blak   37   Blake, Blind

        title: Depression's Gone from Me Blues
        place and date: Grafton, Wis., c. June 1932
        record numbers: (L-1476-2) Pm-13137 Bio
        BLP-12023

1   All last winter : and all last fall
2   I didn't have nobody : to worry me at all
3   No need running : holding out your hand
4   I can get a woman : same as you can a man
5   When I first met you : you had your diamonds on
6   Since I done left you : you've got them all in pawn
7   No need a-running : hollering and crying
8   I'll take you back baby : if you was dying
9   Come on daddy : and tell me one more time
10 When I left : I didn't have my right mind
11 Ain't no need of sitting : with my head hung down
12 Your black man : ought to get on out of town

BliN   1   Blind Norris

        title: Sundown Blues
        place and date: Chicago, 18 Feb. 1937
        record numbers: (61850-A) De-7290 BC-6

1   I was standing in my back door : looking at the
    evening sun go down
2   I was standing there wondering : if my woman was in
    this town
3   She left me this morning : she carried away all my
    clothes
4   I'm going to find that woman : I don't care where
    she goes
5   She sobbed when she told me : I just could not
    change my mind
6   I was loving that woman : I know she was quitting me
    all the time
7   Honey I went to the fortuneteller : asked her where
    had my baby gone
8   She left me this morning : I hadn't done nothing
    wrong

BliP   1   Blind Percy

        title: Coal River Blues
        place and date: Chicago, c. Oct. 1927
        record numbers: (20138-2) Pm-12584 Yz L-1010

1   Going up Coal River : coming down no more
2   Going to leave your town pretty baby : stop knocking
    on your back door
3   Across deep water : ain't no skiffs around
4   The ??? won't bring ??? : just let her sink on down
5   My mama told me baby : my papa told me too
6   Never let a fat little woman : going have no place
    to *spoon*
7   Don't want no woman : got hair like horse's mane
8   Woman's so doggone evil : want every woman's man
9   Ooh : broke down in tears today
10 I got the blues so bad pretty mama : I can't *gee*
    away

BliP   2   Blind Percy

        title: Fourteenth Street Blues
        place and date: Chicago, c. Nov. 1927
        record numbers: (20180-2) Pm-12584 Rt RL-327

1   Fourteenth Street women : don't mean no man no good
2   Go out and get full of liquor : wake the whole
    neighborhood
3   Let me tell you mama : like the Dago told the Jew
4   If you don't want me : it's cinch I don't want you
5   There's two kind of nations : I sure can't
    understand

BliP   2   Blind Percy

6   That's Chinese women : and a doggone Dago man
7   I was born in Texas : I raised in Tennessee
8   You *missed a real brownie* : when you picked all
    over me
9   I feel like jumping : through the keyhole in your
    door
10 Told me this morning : you didn't want me no more
11 I feel like snapping : my big gun in your face
12 Had the nerve to tell me : another man's got my
    place

BogL   1   Bogan, Lucille

        title: Sweet Patunia
        place and date: Chicago, c. Mar. 1927
        record numbers: (4309-1) Pm-12459 Yz L-1017

1   Let me tell you : what sweet patuni do
2   It take your money : and stay all night for you
3   Well I'm wild about my tuni : the only thing I crave
4   Sweet patuni : is going to follow me to my grave
5   I went up on the mountain : looked down in the deep
    blue sea
6   A big fat man : was trying to play with me
7   If I could holler : like a mountain jack
8   Go out on the mountain : call sweet patuni back
9   Sweet patuni man : I can't understand
10 He got ways like a barber : he's a full-blown man

BogL   2   Bogan, Lucille

        title: Levee Blues
        place and date: Chicago, c. Mar. 1927
        record numbers: (4324-1) Pm-12459 Yz L-1017

1   Down in the levee : Camp Number Nine
2   You can pass my house : honey you can hear me cry
3   I never had no blues : *sure am* ???
4   I'm going to leave this camp : you *can go starry*
    here
5   I ain't found no doctor : ain't no doctor in this
    whole round world
6   Just to cure the blues : the blues of the leveecamp
    girl

BogL   3   Bogan, Lucille

        title: Jim Tampa Blues
        place and date: Chicago, c. July 1927
        record numbers: (4672-2) Pm-12504 Yz L-1017

1   Hey Jim Tampa : you treat your women so mean
2   You treat your *townie* : like a woman you ain't
    never seen
3   Womens all know my name : call him Mr Tampa Long
4   He made so much money : women when the weather was
    warm
5   My man's got five women : I can call them by their
    natural names
6   And all them are cheaters : sounds just the same
7   It must be a black cat bone : jomo can't work that
    hard
8   Every time I wake up : Jim Tampa's in my yard
9   I can stand right here : five miles down the road
10 Give a gander the way : Jim Tampa used to go

title: Coffee Grindin' Blues
place and date: Chicago, 10 May 1929
record numbers: (C-3461-) Br-7083 His HLP-15

1 It ain't nobody in town : can grind their coffee like mine
3 I drink so much coffee : till I grind it in my sleep
4 And when you get like that : you know it can't be beat
5 It's so doggone good : that it made made me bite my tongue
6 Going to keep it for my daddy : ain't going to give nobody none
7 I ain't ever loved it : this a-way before
8 And I hope to the Lord : I won't love it anymore
9 I got so now : that I can't control my mind
10 I go to bed blue : and I get up crying
11 It's so doggone good : it made me talk out of my head
12 And it's better to me : than any I ever had
13 Now I grind my coffee : till it's two and three dollars a pound
14 And there ain't no more : cheap like mine in town
15 It's so doggone good : till it make you bite your tongue
16 And I'm a coffee-grinding mama : won't you let me grind you some

title: Pot Hound Blues
place and date: Chicago, 10 May 1929
record numbers: (C-3462-) Br-7083 His HLP-15

1 You must bring me a job : or money from anywhere
2 Because I can get your kind of loving : in the streets just anywhere
3 You come home every day : looking for your stew and beans
4 And you have got more nerve : than any pot hound I've ever seen
5 Now you take your money : and you have your fun
6 You don't have nothing : when house rent comes
7 And I'm through : cooking you stew and beans
8 And you can eat more neckbones : than any man I've ever seen
9 Now if you want me baby : you got to make your *for sure* down
10 And you got to put your money : down where I got mine
11 Now you laying up in my bed : between my two white sheets
12 I can't see or smell nothing : but your doggone feet
13 And I'm through : trying to make a man of you
14 And if you can't bring a job : don't you look for your daily stew
15 I worked hard from Monday : until late Saturday night
16 And you's a dirty mistreater : you ain't treating me right
17 And I'm through : cooking you stew and beans
18 And you's a dirty pot hound : dirtier than any man I seen

title: My Georgia Grind
place and date: Chicago, c. 1 Feb. 1930
record numbers: (C-5347-) Br unissued Rt RL-317

1 Look here papa : I don't mean no harm
2 Come get some Georgia grind : to carry the good work on
3 The thing I do : it's mighty fine
4 And the mens pays their ??? : all the time

5 When you got to doing it : it's a one-way strand
6 Got to do my Georgia grind : like a natural man
7 All you got to do : is to fall in line
8 Put your right hand up : and your left one behind
9 If you want to learn : you got to pay
10 Because I ain't going to give : my Georgia grind away
11 If you do it once : you'll do it twice
12 And it's mighty fine I tell you : if you do it right
13 I'm talking about my Georgia : I do mean grind
14 And if something bothers you baby : it will satisfy your worried mind
15 Some likes it slow : some likes it fast
16 But I like my Georgia grind : at half and half
17 Come past my house : and hear me cry
18 Big *bad* daddy : won't you take your time
19 I'm going back to Georgia : where I can have my fun
20 Going down in Georgia : where I get my good grinding done

title: They Ain't Walking No More
place and date: Chicago, late Mar. 1930
record numbers: (C-5549-) Br-7163 Yz L-1017

1 Sometimes I'm up : sometimes I'm down
2 I can't make my living : around this town
3 Because tricks ain't working : tricks ain't working no more
4 And I got to make my living : don't care where I go
5 I need shoes on my feet : clothes on my back
6 Get tired of walking these streets : all dressed in black
7 Because tricks ain't working : tricks ain't working no more
8 And I see four or five good tricks : standing in front of my door
9 Please have mercy : bad luck's on my head
10 Four or five good tricks : is all the money I need
11 Because tricks ain't working : tricks ain't working no more
12 And I can't get a break : don't care where I go
13 I got a store on the corner : selling stuff cheap
14 I got a market across the street : where I sell my meat
15 This way of living : sure is hard
16 Ducking and dodging : the Cadillac squad
17 Because tricks ain't working : tricks ain't working no more
18 And if you think I'm lying : follow me to the door

title: Sloppy Drunk Blues
place and date: Chicago, late Mar. 1930
record numbers: (C-5562-A) Br-7210 Rt RL-317

1 I'd rather be sloppy drunk : than anything I know
2 And another half a pint : will see me go
3 I love my moonshine whiskey : better than I do my man
4 You can have your beer and your bottle : give me my cool kind can
5 I'd rather be sloppy drunk : sitting in the can
6 Than to be at home : rolling with my man
7 Mmm : bring me another two-bit pint
8 Because I got my habits on : I'm going to wreck this joint
9 I been on this sloppy drunk : for a solid year
10 And when I can't get my whiskey : bring me my cool can beer
11 My good man quit me : for somebody else
12 And I'm sloppy drunk : drinking by myself

BogL   9   Bogan, Lucille

      title: Alley Boogie
      place and date: Chicago, late Mar. 1930
      record numbers: (C-5563-A) Br-7210 Rt RL-317

1 I'm doing something now : I ain't never done before
2 Going to do it this time : ain't going to do it no
    more
3 My alley boogie: only thing I choose
4 And it's the only thing I do : to drown away by
    blues
5 I boogie all night : all the night before
6 When I woke up this morning : I want to boogie some
    more
7 Old alley boogie : only thing I crave
8 I can do my alley boogie : so many different ways
9 I got a bed in my bedroom : a pallet on my floor
10 Got to do the alley boogie : everywhere I go
11 Because I'm wild about my boogie : only thing I
    crave
12 Good alley boogie : will carry me to my grave
13 Mama loves my boogie : papa loves it too
14 And it runs in my family : that's all I like to do
15 I'm wild about my boogie : only thing I crave
16 I'm going to do my boogie : the rest of my days
17 Papa got a watch : mama got a ring
18 Sister got a hump : from really boogying that thing
19 I'm wild about my boogie : only thing I choose
20 Now she got to do the boogie : to buy her alley baby
    some shoes
21 Now I done sung this song : until I quit
22 And there ain't nobody : ??? no alley boogie yet
23 And I'm wild about my boogie : only thing I crave
24 I been doing my alley boogie : I been boogying all
    of my days

BogL   10   Bogan, Lucille

      title: Black Angel Blues
      place and date: Chicago, c. mid Dec. 1930
      record numbers: (C-6847-A) Br-7186 His HLP-15

1 I got a sweet black angel : I like the way he spread
    his wings
2 And I'm crazy about him : he spreads so much joy in
    everything
3 If I ask him for a dime : he gives me a ten dollar
    bill
4 Yes he does everything : to keep my wants filled
5 If my black angel would leave me : I believe that I
    would die
6 And if I see him looking at another woman : I just
    scream and cry
7 I love my black angel : and I want him by myself
8 Lord I don't want him spreading his wings : over no
    one else
9 Womens don't bother my black angel : don't bother
    him in any way
10 I'll serve ninety-nine years in jail : most any day
11 I'm wild about my black angel : I like the way he
    spread his wings
12 He's got a new way of getting goose : and he sure
    can shake that thing

BogL   11   Bogan, Lucille

      title: Tricks Ain't Working No More
      place and date: Chicago, c. mid Dec. 1930
      record numbers: (C-6848-A) Br-7186 His HLP-15

1 Times is done got hard : money's done got scarce
2 Stealing and robbing : is going to take place
3 Because tricks ain't working : tricks ain't working
    no more
4 And I'm going to rob somebody : if I don't make me
    some dough

BogL   11   Bogan, Lucille

5 I'm going to do just like a blind man : stand and
    beg for change
6 Until these arresting officers : change my tricking
    name
7 Because tricks ain't working : tricks ain't working
    no more
8 And I've got to make my living : don't care where I
    go
9 I'm going to learn these working tricks : what it's
    all about
10 I'm going to get them in my house : and ain't going
    to let them out
11 Because tricks ain't working : tricks ain't working
    no more
12 And I can't make no money : don't care where I go
13 I got up this morning : with the rising sun
14 Been working all day : and I ain't caught a one
15 Because tricks ain't working : tricks ain't working
    no more
16 And I can't make a dime : don't care where I go
17 I got up this morning : feeling tough
18 I've got to call in my tricks : in the rough rough
    rough
19 Because tricks ain't working : tricks ain't working
    no more
20 And I've got to change my luck : if I have to move
    next door

BogL   12   Bogan, Lucille

      title: T N and O Blues
      place and date: New York, 17 July 1933
      record numbers: (13549-1) Ba-32845 Rt RL-317

1 The train I ride : is eighteen coaches long
2 And the man that I love : done been here and gone
3 I hate to hear : that T and N O blow
4 Puts my mind on the wander : makes me want to go
5 Going to beat the train to the crossing : going to
    burn the trestle down
6 That's the onliest way : I can keep my man in town
7 He's a railroad man : and he sure do love to ride
8 If he don't ride that T and N O : he sure ain't
    satisfied
9 Going to fall down on my knees : pray to the Lord
    above
10 Please send me back : the only man I love

BogL   13   Bogan, Lucille

      title: Baking Powder Blues
      place and date: New York, 17 July 1933
      record numbers: (13569-1) Ba-33059 Yz L-1017

1 Got up this morning : by the rising sun
2 Didn't have no whiskey : I tried to buy me some
3 I use my Skeet and Garret : *feed* it everywhere
4 Lord I like them baking powder blues : and I sure
    don't care
5 Dice jumped to hustle Lord : I swear my money don't
    lose
6 I got to win tonight : and buy this baking powder
    man some shoes
7 Play them blues boy : and don't play them so slow
8 Because I'm going to give you some more money : and
    I'm going to give it to you sure

BogL   14   Bogan, Lucille

>   title: You Got to Die Some Day
>   place and date: New York, 30 July 1934
>   record numbers: (15477-2) ARC-6-04-63 Rt RL-317

1   You may be beautiful : but baby you got to die some
    day
2   And you going to reap what you sow : for treating me
    this a-way
3   When the sun rose this morning : I was laying in my
    floor crying
4   And I've done got tired : of being dogged all the
    time
5   Tell me baby : what fault do you find in me
6   You don't treat me : like I'm no human being
7   Love hides all faults : make you do things you don't
    want to do
8   When you love someone : and that someone don't love
    you

BogL   15   Bogan, Lucille

>   title: Lonesome Midnight Blues
>   place and date: New York, 30 July 1934
>   record numbers: (15478-2) ARC-6-04-63 Rt RL-317

1   I'm lonesome I'm lonesome : and I got them lonesome
    midnight blues
2   And I'm blue to my heart : my man I hate to lose
3   Blues and trouble : have overtaken me
4   And I've got those midnight blues : blue as I can be
5   Late last night : when my clock was striking three
6   My daddy was leaving : and the blues had me

BogL   16   Bogan, Lucille

>   title: My Man Is Boogan Me
>   place and date: New York, 31 July 1934
>   record numbers: (15487-2) Ba-33375 Rt RL-317

1   Just one thing : I want my man to know
2   I ain't going to be : his lowdown dog no more
3   He gets up every morning : and before he goes
4   Say he don't want me to put my head : out of my
    front door
5   He won't buy me no shoes : he won't buy me no
    clothes
6   And he's got so lowdown : he wants to put me
    outdoors
7   I ain't got no coal : I ain't got no wood
8   And you know by that : that man don't mean me no
    good
9   I ain't got no flour : I ain't got no lard
10 And he knows doggone well : the times is done got
    hard

BogL   17   Bogan, Lucille

>   title: Pig Iron Sally
>   place and date: New York, 31 July 1934
>   record numbers: (15490-2) Ba-33375 Rt RL-317

1   Some folks say black is evil : but I will tell the
    world they're wrong
2   Because I'm a sealskin brown : and I been evil ever
    since I been born
3   I a-scared to trust a rabbit : and I won't even
    trust a squirrel
4   And I won't bat my eyes : because I might lose sight
    on this whole round world
5   I've got a head like a freight train : and I walk
    just like a grizzly bear
6   And I use my Skeet and Garret : and I keep my ???
    everywhere

BogL   17   Bogan, Lucille

7   They call me Pig Iron Sally because I live in Slag
    Iron Alley : and I'm evil and mean as I can be
8   And I ain't going to let nobody : put that doggone
    thing on me
9   I ain't nothing but a mistreater : baby and it ain't
    no joke
10 And if you don't believe I'm dirty : you can watch
    my bogus stroke

BogL   18   Bogan, Lucille

>   title: I Hate that Train Called the M. and O.
>   place and date: New York, 31 July 1934
>   record numbers: (15491-1) ARC-6-02-04 OJL-6

1   I hate that train : that they all call the M and O
2   It took my baby away : and he ain't coming back to
    me no more
3   When he was leaving : I couldn't hear nothing but
    that whistle blow
4   And the man at the throttle : Lord he wasn't coming
    back no more
5   He had his head in the window : that man the drivers
    roll
6   They are going away baby : and doggone your bad-luck
    soul
7   Now I'm so worried : and I'm so full of gloom
8   And deep down in my heart : ain't nothing but a
    lover's ruin
9   I was sorry : I was sorry sorry to my heart
10 To see that M and O train : and me and my daddy part

BogL   19   Bogan, Lucille

>   title: Tired as I Can Be
>   place and date: New York, 1 Aug. 1934
>   record numbers: (15505-1) Ba-33313 His HLP-4

1   I worked all the winter : and I worked all the fall
2   I got to wait until spring : to get my ashes hauled
3   And now I'm tired : tired as I can be
4   And I'm going back home : where these blues don't
    worry me
5   I'm a free-hearted woman : I let you spend my dough
6   And you never did win : you kept on asking for more
7   And now I'm tired : I ain't going to do it no more
8   And when I leave you this time : you won't know
    where I go
9   My house rent's due : they done put me outdoors
10 And here you riding around here : in a V-Eight Ford
11 I done got tired : of your lowdown dirty ways
12 And your sisters say you been dirty : dirty all your
    days
13 I never will forget : when the times was good
14 I caught you standing out yonder : in the piney
    woods
15 And now I'm tired : tired as I can be
16 And I'm going back south : to my used-to-be

BogL   20   Bogan, Lucille

>   title: Sweet Man, Sweet Man
>   place and date: New York, 1 Aug. 1934
>   record numbers: (15506-2) Ba-33149 Rt RL-317

1   Sweet man sweet man : what makes you candy taste so
    hard
2   And I would come to see you : but your woman is got
    me barred
3   He caught the Frisco he caught the Frisco : and I
    just can't keep from crying
4   And if he don't come back : I will lose my worried
    mind

35

BogL 20   Bogan, Lucille

5 He is a rambler he is a rambler : and he is never
   satisfied
6 And I know he was a rambler : when he caught that
   train to ride
7 I'm going to find him I'm going to find him : with
   my smoking forty-five
8 Because you know I love that man : he so hard to
   find
9 He's gone he's gone : and he's forever on my mind
10 And I want to see my man : because because he's so
   good and kind

BogL 21   Bogan, Lucille

      title: Reckless Woman
      place and date: New York, 1 Aug. 1934
      record numbers: (15507-2) Ba-33313 His HLP-4

1 A woman gets tired : of one man all the time
2 And don't care what you give her : you can't change
   her rambling mind
3 Don't never think : you got a whole woman by
   yourself
4 Because there never was a woman : didn't love
   somebody else
5 I ain't never loved : just one man in my life
6 Because this kind of love I got : I can love the
   same way twice
7 Some womens like two men : some womens they like
   three
8 But I like as many men : I see is good to me

BogL 22   Bogan, Lucille

      title: Down in Boogie Alley
      place and date: New York, 1 Aug. 1934
      record numbers: (15508-2) Ba-33149 Rt RL-317

1 Way down in Boogie Alley : ain't nothing but skulls
   and bones
2 And when I get drunk : who's going to take me home
3 I'm going to stop my man : from running around
4 Because down in Boogie Alley : is where he can be
   found
5 He goes down in Boogie Alley : house number three
6 And when he gets down there : the womens won't let
   him come to see me
7 I went down in Boogie Alley : with my razor in my
   hand
8 And the blues struck : I brought back my man
9 If you go in Boogie Alley : you better take you
   forty-four
10 The womens will get your man down there : and they
   won't let him go

BogL 23   Bogan, Lucille

      title: Barbecue Bess
      place and date: New York, 6 Mar. 1935
      record numbers: (16984-1) Ba-33475 Yz L-1017

1 When you come to my house : come down behind the
   jail
2 I got a sign on my door : barbecue for sale
3 I'm talking about my barbecue : only thing I crave
4 And that good-doing meat : going to [carry, take] me
   to my grave
5 I'm selling it cheap : because I got good stuff
6 And if you try one time : you can't get enough
7 I'm talking about barbecue : only thing I sell
8 And if you want my meat : you can come to my house
   at twelve
9 Now some like it hot : some like it cold
10 Some take it : any way it's sold

BogL 23   Bogan, Lucille

11 Some people wants it : some people don't
12 If you buy my barbecue : it just won't don't don't
   don't
13 Some people wants to know : the regular price
14 Fifty-five cents : you can get some twice
15 And I'm talking about my barbecue : only thing I
   sell
16 And you can get my meat : any night at twelve

BogL 24   Bogan, Lucille

      title: Jump Steady Daddy
      place and date: New York, 7 Mar. 1935
      record numbers: (16993-2) ARC-5-12-58 Yz L-1017

1 Jump steady daddy : please take your time
2 You got a year and a day : to satisfy my mind
3 Love me daddy : love me all the time
4 And if you love me like I tell you : you'll be the
   jump-steady man of mine
5 Jump-steady got to jumping : jumping in the room
6 And I got crazy about him : because he could strut
   his stuff
7 Now when jump-steady starts to jumping : he does it
   slow
8 He goes from the top : down to the floor
9 Ooh : just can't let him go
10 Because he jumps better : than any man that I know
11 He don't work on no rock pile : he don't tote no
   slag
12 And the way he jumps steady : it's just too bad

BogL 25   Bogan, Lucille

      title: Man Stealer Blues
      place and date: New York, 7 Mar. 1935
      record numbers: (16997-2) ARC-35-09-13 Rt RL-317

1 I went to bed last night : and the blues wouldn't
   let me rest
2 Because I ain't been used : to sleeping by myself
3 Oh blues oh blues : blues don't you see
4 You are carrying me down : blues you trying kill
   poor me
5 Now blues and trouble : go walk hand in hand
6 I never had these blues : until my best friend loved
   my man
7 She may have loved him one time : but that one man
   she can't hold
8 Because it's ??? *in Texas* : that I could sell fast
   jellyroll
9 He puts his arms around me : like the ring around
   the good Lord's sun
10 Said he ain't had no woman to love him : Lord like I
   done

BogL 26   Bogan, Lucille

      title: Stew Meat Blues
      place and date: New York, 8 Mar. 1935
      record numbers: (17013-1) Ba-33448 Rt RL-317

1 A man say I had something : look like new
2 He want me to trade a *cam* : for some of my stew
3 Say he's going up the river : tried to sell his sack
4 He would pay me for my stuff : when the boat get
   back
5 I got good stew : and it's got to be sold
6 The price ain't high : I want to get you told
7 Go on up the river : man and sell your sack
8 It will be stew meat here : baby when the boat get
   back
9 Now look here man : what you want me to do
10 Give you my stew meat : and credit you too

BogL   26   Bogan, Lucille

11   I credit one man : it was to my sorrow
12   It's cash today : credit tomorrow
13   Now it's ashes to ashes : dust to dust
14   You try my stuff one time : you can't get enough

BogL   27   Bogan, Lucille

         title: Skin Game Blues
         place and date: New York, 8 Mar. 1935
         record numbers: (17014-1) Ba-33448 Rt RL-317

1   Good morning skin game : hollering skin game please
       last
2   I done staked my man to win : and I hope my money
       will pass
3   He done pawned my house : he got my life at stake
4   And I got to get it back : with that money he gamble
       and make
5   He never lost no money : until he drew that black
       queen of spades
6   And my man was in need of begging : he was in hard
       luck that very day
7   When he come back to me : got a dollar two
8   I want him to go back to that skin game : and see
       what he can do
9   If my man : he could only win my money back
10   I would take a walk downtown : buy me a brand new
       pair of shoes and hat

Bond   1   Bonds, Son

         title: Weary Worried Blues
         place and date: Chicago, 6 Sept. 1934
         record numbers: (C-9403-A) Ch-50064 RBF RF-9

1   I'm worried now babe : I won't be worried long
2   Now when we is all going together : it's got to be
       carried on
3   Now did you get that letter : baby that I wrote to
       you
4   Oh you sitting in the shade baby : I declare you
       just won't do
5   Now I say once ain't forever : say but two time
       ain't for twice
6   Now when you get a good woman : you just won't treat
       her right
7   Mmm : Lord Lord Lord Lord Lord
8   Now if I can't be your regular mama : I sure ain't
       going to be your dog

Bond   2   Bonds, Son (Sleepy John Estes)

         title: Black Gal Swing
         place and date: Chicago, 24 Sept. 1941
         record numbers: (064918-) BB-B8852 BC-7

1   Now a yellow gal rides in an automobile : a
       brownskin gal rides the same
2   A black gal *will tell you* an old hay wagon : she's
       getting by just the same
3   A yellow gal drinks good old whiskey : a brownskin
       gal drinks the same
4   But a black gal drinks shoe polish : she's getting
       drunk just the same
5   A yellow gal will bite you she will pop you with a
       stick : a brownskin gal bites the same
6   But a black gal get a rusty razor and run you all
       over town : and you know that woman raises hell
       just the same
7   Now a yellow gal will kiss you she will kiss you
       awful sweet : a brownskin gal do the same
8   But a black gal spit bacca juice *shoo* snuff all on
       your lips : oh loving you just the same

Bond   3   Bonds, Son

         title: 80 Highway Blues
         place and date: Chicago, 24 Sept. 1941
         record numbers: (064921-1) BB-B8927 BC-7

1   Sitting down here thinking : yes babe I believe I
       better go
2   You know I believe I'll go down : that long long old
       dusty road
3   Now that Eighty Highway : is the longest highway
       that I know
4   Running all the way from Frisco Texas : *right
       cross* the Atlantic on the other *water course*
5   That church bell was beginning to tone : yes some
       other good gambler's gone
6   You know I wouldn't hate it so bad : but that Eighty
       Highway so long
7   You women fuss and argue with your good man : when
       you know you don't do right yourself
8   You know when I look for you at night : way down on
       Eighty Highway with someone else
9   Yes if you get in trouble : call on a *car* about
       forty-five
10   Baby now I just open up my chifforobe : and you'll
       see where my dollar lies

BoyG   1   Boyd, Georgia

         title: Never Mind Blues
         place and date: Chicago, 2 Aug. 1933
         record numbers: (76835-1) BB-B5573 Yz L-1030

1   Never mind : honey never mind
2   Never mind : there's time to shine
3   You said you loved me : you know you told a lie
4   Oh never mind : never mind
5   I'm just a good woman : baby gone astray
6   Drinking charcoal liquor : throwing myself away
7   But never mind : there's time to shine
8   Spread your heart : babe just like mine

Brac   1   Bracey, Ishman

         title: Saturday Blues
         place and date: Memphis, 4 Feb. 1928
         record numbers: (41842-1) Vi-21349 OJL-8

1   Now you tell me mama : do you think that's right
2   You with your kid all day : and run to me at night
3   Now my regular woman : totes my pocket change
4   And my sometime woman : wants to do the same
5   And you better not let : my regular catch you here
7   Because it ain't no telling : what she might do
8   Now she might cut you : and she might shoot you too
9   Now she's the meanest woman : that I've ever seen
10   And when I asked for water : give me gasoline
11   Now if you want your woman : to look like the rest
12   You buy her high brown powder : and Farmer's Skin
       Success
13   Now I got four or five puppies : and got one shaggy
       hound
14   It takes all them dogs : to run my woman down

Brac   2   Bracey, Ishman

         title: Left Alone Blues
         place and date: Memphis, 4 Feb. 1928
         record numbers: (41843-2) Vi-21349 Rt RL-330

1   I said the woman I'm loving : caught the train and
       gone
2   Got the lowdown feeling : I sure won't be here long
3   Now I went to the station : fold my arms and moan
4   Asked the operator : how long my rider been gone
5   Let me tell you : what that dirty train will do

6   Take your last rider Lord : blow black smoke on you
7   Ain't got no special : got no trifling kind
8   Ain't got nobody mama : *she has rock the ship*
9   Lord take me rider : take me to your hand
10 Let me in your darkest corner woman : hide me from
    your man
11 You don't want me rider : please don't dog me around
12 Just like you found me : you took and threw me down
13 Ask you to forgive me : darling if you please
14 Mama sure as I told you : I fall down on my knees

Brac   3   Bracey, Ishman

        title: Leavin' Town Blues
        place and date: Memphis, 31 Aug. 1928
        record numbers: (45458-?) Vi-V38560(?) Rt RL-330

1   Now I tell you mama : now I'm sure going to leave
    this town
2   Because I been in trouble : ever since I set my
    suitcase down
3   Now you don't believe I'm leaving : just watch the
    train I'm on
4   And you don't believe I'm lucky : just count the
    days I'm gone
5   Now I ain't going to be : your teasing brown no more
6   Sugar the way you do me : you make my blood run cold
7   Now before I stay here mama : and be treated this
    a-way
8   Now I'll let some freight train : *throw me in the
    sea*
9   Mmm Lord oh Lord oh : oh Lord oh Lord oh Lord
10 Now the woman I'm loving : she treat me like a mangy
    dog
11 Now look a-yonder sugar : where the rising sun done
    gone
12 I can't live over here mama : a long way from my
    home

Brac   4   Bracey, Ishman

        title: My Brown Mama Blues
        place and date: Memphis, 31 Aug. 1928
        record numbers: (45459-?) Vi-21691(?) Rt RL-330

1   Won't you tell me mama mama : what have I said *or
    done*
2   For you treat me : like my sugar just ain't *hard*
3   Mama mama mama : you sure can worry me
4   *I ain't seen* none of my best woman : since my
    old-time used-to-be
5   Now you see my rider now : I'll tell you what I'll
    do
6   I'll rob and steal : and I'll bring it home to you
7   See [how] the sun went down mama : left it so
    lonesome here
9   Mama this lonesome place : don't seem like home to
    me
12 Lord it's soon in the morning : going to believe
    I'll leaving here

Brac   5   Bracey, Ishman

        title: Trouble-Hearted Blues
        place and date: Memphis, 31 Aug. 1928
        record numbers: (45460-1) Vi-21691 Yz L-1007

1   Down so long : down don't worry me
3   Don't believe I'm sinking : believe what a hole I'm
    in
4   You don't believe I loved you : think what a fool I
    been
5   Went to the graveyard : fell down on my knees
6   I said Lord have mercy : on this lonesome place

7   Went to the graveyard : peeped in my rider's face
8   Says I love you rider Lord : just can't take your
    place
9   Thousands of people mmm : around the burying ground
10 Just to see the ??? : let my rider down
11 Felt so sorry mmm : till they let her down
12 Lord my heart felt sorry : tears come rolling down
13 Tell me mama : what's the matter now
14 Trying to quit your daddy Lord : and you don't know
    how
15 Tell me mama : on your worried mind
16 If I don't get no better mama : believe I'm going
    I'm going

Brac   6   Bracey, Ishman

        title: Trouble-Hearted Blues
        place and date: Memphis, 31 Aug. 1928
        record numbers: (45460-2) Vi-RCX7167 Rt RL-330

1   I've been down so long : down don't worry me
3   Don't believe I'm sinking : believe what a hole I'm
    in
4   You don't believe I love you Lord : think what a
    fool I been
5   Went to the graveyard : fell down on my knees
6   Hollered Lord have mercy : on this lonesome place
7   Thousands of people : round the burying ground
8   Just to see the ??? : let my rider down
9   Felt so sorry : till they let her down
10 Lord my heart struck sorrow : tears come rolling
    down
11 Love you mama : till the sea go dry
12 Lord I love you rider Lord : till the day you die
13 Anybody ask you : who wrote this worried song
14 Tell them you don't know the writer : he'd rather
    had his happy song

Brac   7   Bracey, Ishman

        title: The Four Day Blues
        place and date: Memphis, 31 Aug. 1928
        record numbers: (45461-2) Vi-V38560 Yz L-1007

1   Woke up this morning : mama was treating me night
    and day
2   I reached for my sugar : and the fool had stoled
    away
3   Worried now mama : but I shan't be very long
4   Mama this the way I be treated : be on the county
    farm
5   Wouldn't treat a dog : babe like you treat me
7   Woke up soon this morning : with my face up to the
    ground
8   I didn't have no sugar : not to pick up in my arms
9   Mama that's all right : sugar that's all right for
    you
10 Now you know you got me : just the way you do

Brac   8   Bracey, Ishman

        title: Woman Woman Blues
        place and date: Grafton, Wis., c. Mar. 1930
        record numbers: (L-239-2) Pm-12970 OJL-2

1   Woman woman woman woman : Lord what in the world you
    trying to do
2   Baby the way you treat me : break my heart in two
3   I got a woman good little woman : she got coal-black
    curly hair
4   Now every time she smiles Lord : kindness everywhere
5   I got a woman good little woman : she ain't a thing
    but a *courtesy*

Brac   8   Bracey, Ishman

6   *Takes a* little redheaded woman : and I'll keep you
     company
7   Treat me like ??? little baby : want you turn me
     around and around
8   Babe when you love me : good Lord take me around and
     around
9   Now these blues blues ain't nothing : Lord but a
     doggone hungry feel
10 Got no money in your pocket : to get a decent meal
11 And I went went to the depot : Lord I read up on the
     board
12 Babe if you see me catch you there : ???
13 Now I got to send send down soon : for my old-time
     used-to-be
14 Lord I felt so hard : till the blues crept up on me

Brac   9   Bracey, Ishman

        title: Suitcase Full of Blues
        place and date: Grafton, Wis., c. Mar. 1930
        record numbers: (L-240-1) Pm-12970 Her H-201

1   Hand me down my suitcase : *reach* my walking cane
2   *Know* my mother *treat me* : catch that morning
     train
3   Well I thought I'd write : but I believe I'll
     telephone
5   Now if you catch me stealing : please don't tell on
     me
6   Because I'm stealing : to my doggone used-to-be
7   I woke up this morning : had the blues all around my
     bed
8   I couldn't help but to think : about what my good
     gal said
9   Now I got a heart full of trouble : and a suitcase
     full of blues
10 I never seen no trouble : babe till I *stopped* with
     you
11 I'm going to leave here walking Lord : and talking
     to myself
12 I'm going to take my baby : or carry somebody else
13 It's hard it's hard : it's hard *to get out of this*
     town
14 *Get* another ??? : ???

Brac   10   Bracey, Ishman

        title: Bust Up Blues
        place and date: Grafton, Wis., c. Mar. 1930
        record numbers: (L-241-2) Pm-13038 Her H-205

1   Woke up this morning : couldn't even walk in my
     shoes
2   My baby just quit me : she left me with the bust up
     blues
3   When you see two women : running hand in hand for
     long
4   Bet your B V Ds : something is going on wrong
5   Bought you a yo-yo dress : *full packed in* ???
6   Now that's the thanks you give me : you left me with
     those bust up blues

Brac   11   Bracey, Ishman

        title: Pay Me No Mind
        place and date: Grafton, Wis., c. Mar. 1930
        record numbers: (L-242-2) Pm-13038 Yz L-1007

1   Have you woke up in the morning : *you weep and
     moan*
2   Your best girl quit you : left you all alone
3   Got a brownskin woman : just about as I need
4   And the reason I say so : she so sweet to me
5   When she rub my head : she make my fever rise

Brac   11   Bracey, Ishman

6   When she rub my ??? : she's improved my appetite
7   Now I had me a woman : didn't mean me no good
8   Now I got me another woman : best in the
     neighborhood

BracM   1   Bracey, Mississippi

        title: You Scolded Me and Drove Me from Your Door
        place and date: Jackson, Miss., 17 Mar. 1930
        record numbers: (404764-B) OK-8904 OJL-17

1   You scold me faro now : drove all from your door
2   Well the Good Book say : you got to reap just what
     you sow
3   There was ice and snow now : laying outside your
     door
4   Your good old man rolled for you : at times when he
     was not able to go
5   I can't sleep for dreaming now : I can't stay woke
     for crying
6   I was thinking about : that little old brown of mine
7   Now I'm worried now : but I won't be worried long
8   It takes a worried woman now : sing a worried song
9   Now you got a bad husband now : baby that'll be all
     right
10 Said I'll dodge your husband : like a rabbit dodge a
     dog at night
11 I'll be so glad : when my buddy dead and gone
12 Know my buddy got something now : Lord I'd like to
     own

BracM   2   Bracey, Mississippi

        title: Cherry Ball
        place and date: Jackson, Miss., 17 Mar. 1930
        record numbers: (404765-B) OK-8867 Yz L-1038

1   I'm going to give my baby : no more cherry ball
2   Don't you let her get drunk Lord : and she'll
     lower her ???
3   She used to be mine : but look who's got her now
4   Well he sure can't keep her : she don't mean no good
     nohow
5   You see me coming now : put your man outdoors
6   You know I ain't no stranger baby : I been here
     before
7   Sun rose this morning : I was laying out on my floor
8   No sweet woman to love me : I didn't have no place
     to go
9   Said the sun going down now : black dark caught me
     here
10 Ain't got nobody to love me : nobody to feel my care

BracM   3   Bracey, Mississippi

        title: Stered Gal
        place and date: Jackson, Miss., 17 Mar. 1930
        record numbers: (404766-B) OK-8867 Yz L-1038

1   She wouldn't if she could : and she wouldn't do it
     at all
2   Grab another man : and went across the hall
3   Grabbed my gal : around the waist
4   Told me you better hurry : and you better make haste
5   Run around the house : took me a peep through the
     crack
6   See my baby : at a dirty act
7   Just as well : make it up in your mind
8   Ain't mush *chitlin* : but stir it in the house

BracM   4   Bracey, Mississippi

        title: I'll Overcome Some Day
        place and date: Jackson, Miss., 17 Mar. 1930
        record numbers: (404767-B) OK-8904 OJL-17

 1 Worked all the summer : and all the fall
 2 Now I've got to take Christmas now : in my overalls
 3 Going up the country : won't be back till fall
 4 Times get no better : I won't be back at all
 5 You treat me : like didn't know my name
 6 You mistreated me now : for another man
 7 My baby quit me : didn't say a word
 8 Was on account : of something that she heard
 9 When I had money : I had a friend
10 Ain't got no money : I ain't ain't got no friend
11 Take one more drink : make me tell it all
12 Somebody : stole my little all-in-all

BradT   1   Bradley, Tommie

        title: Adam and Eve
        place and date: Richmond, Ind., 27 Sept. 1930
        record numbers: (17084) Ch-16149 OJL-19

 1 Because Adam said to Eve : *you been cute so cute*
 2 You wouldn't give me none : of that forbidden fruit
 3 They had one is named Cabel : one is named Ain
 4 You know by that : they must have shook that thing

BradT   2   Bradley, Tommie

        title: Pack Up Your Trunk Blues
        place and date: Richmond, Ind., 27 Oct. 1930
        record numbers: (17206) Ch-16149 Yz L-1019

 1 Everybody here baby : seem to have a jolly time
 2 Lord there nobody knows : what's on my troubled mind
 3 Lord but I may be the youngest : Lord take my advice
 4 And don't never let : the same woman quit you twice
 5 Don't let your woman know you love her : you do you
       have done wrong
 6 She'll *commence* ??? : pack up her clothes and gone
 7 When you catch you a freight train baby : bounded
       for Santa Fe
 8 That's when I done found out baby : this ain't no
       place for me
 9 Because I did everything mama : tried to make you
       kind
10 Now seem everything everything you do : it is to
       worry my mind

BradT   3   Bradley, Tommie

        title: Please Don't Act that Way
        place and date: Richmond, Ind., 17 July 1931
        record numbers: (17884) Ch-16339 Mam S-3802

 1 Sometimes I wonder : I want to go back home
 2 Because my baby : have left me all alone
 3 The clothes look lonesome : hanging out on the line
 4 You can tell by that : I've got rambling on my mind
 5 And I said Lord : baby don't act that way
 6 Baby when I leave you : I'm going away to stay
 7 I said Lord : what you want me to do
 8 I took all my money : and I brought it home to you

BradT   4   Bradley, Tommie

        title: Four Day Blues
        place and date: Richmond, Ind., 17 July 1931
        record numbers: (17886-A) Ch-16339 OJL-19

 1 Lord it's early this morning : Lord about four
       o'clock

BradT   4   Bradley, Tommie

 2 There was something in my bedroom : began to reel
       and rock
 3 Lord have you ever been accused baby : [when you]
       ain't done nothing wrong
 4 Lord that's a heart filled with squalor: Lord just
       sure as you born
 5 Lord but you can't be [mine, my baby] : and someone
       else's too
 6 There can no one get you baby : Lord until I get
       through
 7 Oh you can always tell : when a when a woman loves a
       man
 8 Lord she'll take bad treatment : and she'll do the
       best thing she can

BradT   5   Bradley, Tommie

        title: Window Pane Blues
        place and date: Richmond, Ind., 16 Jan. 1932
        record numbers: (18326) Ch-16696 BC-5

 1 Lord when I got up this morning : snow was on my
       windowpane
 2 I couldn't even see my baby : couldn't even hear her
       name
 3 Lord and my baby is leaving : crying won't make her
       stay
 4 Lord if crying would do : now I'd cry myself away
 5 Lord and my room looked so lonesome : since my baby
       been gone
 6 Lord I ain't got nobody : that I can call my own
 7 Baby but you didn't come to see me : mama when I had
       felt alone
 8 *If it had been love with you* baby : I wouldn't
       have been dead and gone
 9 And you a no-good woman : you don't mean a man no
       good
10 Lord and if I don't love you : I would not if I
       could

Bras   1   Brasswell, Frank (Big Bill)

        title: Guitar Rag
        place and date: Richmond, Ind., 2 May 1930
        record numbers: (16580-A) Ge unissued Yz L-1035

 1 I long to hear that : old guitar rag
 2 Whenever I hear it : I do that guitar drag
 3 Play that thing : old guitar for me
 4 Take me back : to my home in Tennessee

BrowB   1   Brown, Bessie

        title: Nobody But My Baby Is Getting My Love
        place and date: New York, c. early Sept. 1926
        record numbers: (6813-?) Ba-1859 VJM VLP-40

 1 Now some folks say : that love is blind
 2 But I'm one gal : who knows her mind
 3 Now one hot papa : is enough
 4 Because I don't believe : in that two-time stuff

BrowI   1   Brown, Hi Henry

        title: Titanic Blues
        place and date: New York, 14 Mar. 1932
        record numbers: (11476-A) Vo-1728 Yz L-1030

 1 Early one morning : just about four o'clock
 2 When the old Titanic : begin to reel and rock
 3 Smith took his glasses : and walked out to the front
 4 And he spied the iceberg a-coming : oh Lord had to
       bump

BrowI 1   Brown, Hi Henry

    5 Some was drinking : some was playing cards
    6 Some was in the corner : praying to their God
    7 Little children cried mama : mama what shall we do
    8 Captain Smith said children : I'll take care of you
    9 Titanic sinking : in the deep blue sea
   10 And the band all playing : Nearer My God to Thee

BrowI 2   Brown, Hi Henry

      title: Preacher Blues
      place and date: New York, 14 Mar. 1932
      record numbers: (11477-A) Vo-1728 Yz L-1030

    1 If you want to hear : preacher curse
    2 Take his bread sweet mama : and save him the crust
    3 Preacher in the pulpit : Bible in his hand
    4 Sister in the corner : crying there's my man
    5 Preacher comes to your house : you ask him to rest
       his hat
    6 Next thing he want to know : sister where your
       husband at
    7 Come in here elder : and shut my door
    8 Want you to preach [for me] the same text : you did
       night before
    9 See that preacher : walking down the street
   10 Fixing to meddle : with every sister he meets
   11 Preacher preacher : you nice and kind
   12 Better not catch you : at that house of mine

BrowI 3   Brown, Hi Henry

      title: Nut Factory Blues
      place and date: New York, 17 Mar. 1932
      record numbers: (11506-A) Vo-1692 Yz L-1003

    1 Jellyroll keep working : just about Sixteenth Street
    2 Well they got a nut factory : where the women do
       meet
    3 Got a nut factory : where they work so hard
    4 Well it's all over the country : husbands ain't got
       no job
    5 Saturday evening : when they draw their pay
    6 Well they don't draw nothing : if husbands don't
       draw them away
    7 Some draw checks babe : some draw nothing at all
    8 When they don't draw nothing : their husbands bust
       them in the jaw
    9 Down on Franklin Avenue : jellybeans standing to and
       fro
   10 Well you hear one jellybean ask the other one :
       which way did the good girl go

BrowI 4   Brown, Hi Henry

      title: Skin Man
      place and date: New York, 17 Mar. 1932
      record numbers: (11509-A) Vo-1692 Yz L-1003

    1 Skin man's hollering : passing right by my door
    2 Well he's hollering skin : everywhere he goes
    3 Some begs a nickel : some some begs a dime
    4 Some begs the jelly : to that teasing brown of mine
    5 Well it's skins oh skins : skin skin skin skin
    6 I'm going away old skin : but I'm coming back again
    7 Let me tell you : what the skin mens'll do
    8 Well they sell your wife skins : and take her away
       from you

BrowR 1   Brown, Richard Rabbit

      title: James Alley Blues
      place and date: New Orleans, 11 Mar. 1927
      record numbers: (38000-1) Vi-20578 Yz L-1032

    1 Times ain't now : nothing like they used to be
    2 And I'm tell you all the truth : ooh take it for me
    3 I done seen better days : but I'm putting up with
       these
    4 I could have a much better time : but these girls
       now is so hard to please
    5 Because I was born in the country : she thinks I'm
       easy to rule
    6 She tried to hitch me to a wagon : she want to drive
       me like a mule
    7 You know I bought the groceries : and I paid the
       rent
    8 She tried to make me wash her clothes : but I got
       good common sense
    9 I said if you don't want me : why don't you tell me
       so
   10 Because it ain't like a man : that ain't got nowhere
       to go
   11 I'll give you sugar for sugar : let you get salt for
       salt
   12 And if you can't get along with me : well it's you
       own fault
   13 Now wanted me to love you : and you treated me mean
   14 You might *give a thought* : on my nightly dream
   15 Sometime I think : that you too sweet to die
   16 Then another time I think : you ought to be buried
       alive

BrowV 1   Brown, Willie

      title: M and O Blues
      place and date: Grafton, Wis., 28 May 1930
      record numbers: (L-413-2) Pm-13090 OJL-5

    1 Now when I leave here : I'm going to catch that M
       and O
    2 I'm going way down south : where I ain't never been
       before
    3 Once I had a notion : Lord and I believe I will
    4 I'm going to build me a mansion : out on Decatur
       Hill
    5 Now it's all of you men : ought to be ashamed of
       yourself
    6 Going around here swearing before God : you got a
       poor woman by yourself
    7 I started to kill my woman : till she laid down
       across the bed
    8 And she looked so ambitious : till I took back
       everything I said
    9 And I asked her how about it : Lord and she said all
       right
   10 But she never showed up : at the shack last night

BrowV 2   Brown, Willie

      title: Future Blues
      place and date: Grafton, Wis., 28 May 1930
      record numbers: (L-418-2) Pm-13090 OJL-5

    1 Can't tell my future : and I can't tell my past
    2 Lord it seems like every minute : sure going to be
       my last
    3 Oh a minute seems like hours : and hour seems like
       days
    4 And it seems like my woman : ought to stop her
       lowdown ways
    5 Oh that woman I love now : she's five feet from the
       ground
    6 And she's tailor-made : and ain't no hand-me-down
    7 I say that I've got a woman : Lord and she lightning
       when she smiles

BrowV   2   Brown, Willie

   8   Five feet and four inches : and she's just good
         hugging size
   9   I know you see that picture : now up on your
         mother's shelf
  10   Well you know by that : I'm getting tired of
         sleeping by myself
  11   And it's T for Texas now : and it's T for Tennessee
  12   Lord bless that woman : that put that thing on me

BryL   1   Bryant, Laura

         title: Dentist Chair Blues--Part 1
         place and date: Long Island City, c. Jan. 1929
         record numbers: (322-A) QRS-R7055 His HLP-21

   1   I'm having so much trouble : with those tooth ache
         blues
   2   It's got me floor-walking : and wearing out my shoes
   3   I need a quick-filling dentist : because I'm mean
         and cross
   4   At night I'm hot with fever : and I just roll and
         toss
   5   When I went to my dentist : he put me in his chair
   6   It's a long pointed sharp something : don't make me
         pull my hair
   7   He shot a burning something : into my cavity
   8   Cocaine or soothing liquid : to ease my pain for me

BryL   2   Bryant, Laura

         title: Dentist Chair Blues--Part 2
         place and date: Long Island City, c. Jan. 1929
         record numbers: (323-A) QRS-R7055 His HLP-21

   1   I told him : he was grinding into my roots too deep
   2   Sure was a rough old dentist : he made me moan and
         weep
   3   He kept right on *a-progging* : until I lost my head
   4   Right now I can't remember : the many things he did
   5   And when he lay me way back : my senses left me fast
   6   Before I hardly knew it : he flooded me with gas
   7   I woke up weak and dizzy : he told me that I would
   8   But all my pain had left me : he really done me good

Bunn   1   Bunn, Teddy

         title: It's Sweet Like So
         place and date: New York, 7 Apr. 1930
         record numbers: (59739-1) Vi-V38592 His HLP-5

   1   Three pickaninnies : eating sugar-cane
   2   Each one turned to the other : and said
   3   *Must have made it good* : chicken in a pot
   4   *Butter like melting* : on the front
   5   Like a lollipop : with sugar tip
   6   Wild about : my baby's lips
   7   Grandma baked grandpa : some jellyroll
   8   Ate it : and *said oh oh* my soul
   9   *Went to my gal* : *on a Saturday night*
  10   *Dinner* : suits her appetite
  11   The blackest berry : the sweetest juice
  12   *Black hair* : *for my prejudice*

Bunn   2   Bunn, Teddy

         title: Pattin' Dat Cat
         place and date: New York, 7 Apr. 1930
         record numbers: (59740-1) Vi-V38592 His HLP-5

   1   Martha's sitting : on up that fence
   2   Yowling : like she didn't have no sense
   3   Blackbird cheeping : in a tree
   4   Said to the redbird : skeedle-um-skee

Bunn   2   Bunn, Teddy

   5   Aunt Louise : she bought blue goose cheese
   6   When she start shaking : it's *long loose please*
   7   White little June bug : big fat duck
   8   Come on ducky : let us try our luck
   9   Jenny Mae : brother Sam
  10   If you want to be : a good-time man
  11   The night I saw : little Mickey Mouse
  12   Sashaying : all around the house

Burs   1   Burse, Charlie (Memphis Jug Band)

         title: Tappin' that Thing
         place and date: Richmond, Ind., 3 Aug. 1932
         record numbers: (18648) Ch-16654 Rt RL-307

   1   Say excuse me mama : I don't mean no harm
   2   Just come here : to sing this little song
   3   Say my brown's got a wrist watch : and I got a ring
   4   Bought that jewel : just tapping that thing
   5   I been down in Memphis : been down in New Orleans
   6   The way we tap it : boys it's most *obscene*
   7   Now I bought a brand new car : it really wouldn't
         quit
   8   I gave it to my baby : like to had a fit
   9   Now look here baby : always having *soup*
  10   *Got no rest : over my dead loot*

Burs   2   Burse, Charlie

         title: I Got Good Taters
         place and date: Richmond, Ind., 3 Aug. 1932
         record numbers: (18650) Ch-16481 Rt RL-337

   1   I got a house : way up on the hill
   2   I got potatoes : and *they want* ???
   3   I've got a patch : sitting in the back
   4   ??? *potatoes* : and it's tight like that
   5   People in the kitchen : trying to ???
   6   I've got potatoes : ???
   7   I don't need no wife : don't need no home
   8   Hang my potatoes : in a little brown ???
   9   Potatoes on the simmer : potatoes on the boil
  10   I've got potatoes : boys it won't stop at all
  11   ??? good as ??? : ??? good as ???
  12   I've got potatoes : Lord they ought to ???

Burs   3   Burse, Charlie

         title: Boodie Bum Bum
         place and date: Chicago, 7 Nov. 1934
         record numbers: (C-792-1) OK-8956 Jo SM-3104

   1   Oh tell me baby : where did you stay last night
   2   For you come in this morning : sun was shining
         bright
   3   Oh the black cat told the white one : let's go
         across town and clown
   4   And the white cat told the black one : you better
         set your black self down
   5   Tell me baby : where did you get your sugar from
   6   I haven't had no boodle-bum : since you been gone
   7   Now it was old lady *Diana* : was sitting on the
         rock
   8   Along flew a bumblebee : and raised a great big knot
   9   Tell me bumblebee : when did you fly from home
  10   Oh you ain't done no stinging : on the boodie-bum
  11   You know the baby kitten jumped up : oh and began to
         wine
  12   You know he didn't know the racket : but he had the
         same thing on his mind
  13   Tell me baby sister : where did you get your sugar
         from
  14   Oh you don't know the racket : you ought to go back
         home

42

Burs   3   Burse, Charlie

15 Oh tell me mama : what's the matter now
16 You don't know how to boodle-bum-bum : I know you
    didn't do it nohow

But1S 1   Butler, Sam

        title: Some Screamed High Yellow
        place and date: Chicago, c. Oct. 1926
        record numbers: (2677-2) Pm-12423 Yz L-1016

1   I didn't *roll in here* : *till Lord sometime* last
    night
2   I had to *ask* ??? : ??? *today*
3   I think I'll ramble : *rambling* on my mind
4   I ain't got no right to leave : ain't got no right
    to change my mind
5   Oh did you dream lucky : and wake up cold in hand
6   And you want to see some good gal : ain't got no man
7   Sometime I think I will : then I think that I won't
8   Sometime I think that I love her : then I think that
    I don't
9   Some screaming high yellow : I scream black or brown
10 For high yellow may mistreat you : but black won't
    turn you down
11 Mama I got a notion : honey and I believe I will
12 Catch a long jumping Judy : go on across the hill

But1S 2   Butler, Sam

        title: You Can't Keep No Brown
        place and date: Chicago, c. Oct. 1926
        record numbers: (2678-2) Pm-12389 Yz L-1026

1   Now I woke up this morning mama : blues all around
    my bed
2   Thinking about the kinds words : that my mama had
    said
3   Now my mama's dead : so is my daddy too
4   That's the reason I tried to hard : to get along
    with you
5   Now where there ain't no loving : ain't no getting
    along
6   Because you'll have more trouble : honey than all
    the day is long
7   So many days : I stoled away and cried
8   Poor boy has been mistreated : now I can't be
    satisfied
9   Now I'm going to write a letter : mail it in the air
10 Because the March wind blows : it blows news
    everywhere
11 Because I'm going up the country : won't be very
    long
12 Good gal : you can count the days I'm gone
13 I often tell my honey : don't have to fight
14 The gal that gets you : has got to try to treat you
    right
15 I'm crazy about my Jane : tell the world that I am
16 Because I'm going : got to sing long-distance blues
17 Now you get way back : you get to ball the jack
18 You begin to fuss : and get your rider back
19 I want to see my Jane : tell the world that I do
20 Because I'm going I'm going : to sing long-distance
    blues

But1S 3   Butler, Sam

        title: Poor Boy Blues
        place and date: Chicago, c. Oct. 1926
        record numbers: (   ) Vo-1057 Yz L-1016

1   I woke up this morning : blues all around my bed
2   Thinking about that wire : that my brown had sent
3   Lord I'm poor boy here : long ways from home
4   Ain't got nowhere : not to lay my head

But1S 3   Butler, Sam

5   Cold frosty ground : was my bed last night
6   Thinking about the wire : that my baby had sent
7   But my mama told me : Sam come down fast
8   Whiskey and women : will bother your learning bad
9   Now my mama dead : so is my daddy too
10 *Should I caught the wire* : trying to get along
    with you
11 So many days : I stoled away and cried
12 Poor boy's in the streets : can't be satisfied
13 Going write a letter : mailed it in the air
14 *Mail it by the window : love yous* everywhere
15 Lord Lord : ain't going to moan no more

But1S 4   Butler, Sam

        title: Jefferson County Blues
        place and date: Chicago, c. Oct. 1926
        record numbers: (   ) Vo-1057 Yz L-1016

1   If you wants your man : keep him out of Birmingham
2   Because the red-hot mama : drives your dollar down
3   I thought I'd send her : *but I'd leave it* at home
4   *Oh she showed a lot of farmers : boys how to right
    from wrong*
5   If you want your brown : better stay aside
6   I said on that train : you gone off of my mind
7   My road seem rocky : so the people do say
8   But I'm a ??? driver : lucky to find my way
9   Hot mama : sit down on my knee
10 *I got to walk them down the city : how you got it
    up for me*
11 *I said being in Alabama : meanest place I know*
12 Because I'm going up the country : mama how bad *I
    feel*

Byrd   1   Byrd, John

        title: Billy Goat Blues
        place and date: Grafton, Wis., c. Apr. 1930
        record numbers: (L-289-2) Pm-12997 Yz L-1001

1   Lord that Harlem goat mama : sure was feeling fine
2   *I went ??? search light* : up and down that long
    line
3   Now she grabbed that stick : and she broke that
    Harlem's back
4   And she tied old Harlem : to the railroad track
5   Lord the fast mail train : honey was coach and nine
6   And that Harlem goat : she was serving time
7   Lord *he gave her a shirt : it was a shirt of pink*
8   He caught that red shirt mama : trying to flag a
    train
9   He said when I die : don't bury me at all
10 Just pickle my body : up in alcohol
11 Lord I love my goat : better than I love myself
12 I'm going to kill my goat : I'm going kill somebody
    else
13 Lord it was early in the morning : about the break
    of day
14 With my head on a pillow : where my goat Lord used
    to lay

Byrd   2   Byrd, John

        title: Old Timbrook Blues
        place and date: Grafton, Wis., c. Apr. 1930
        record numbers: (L-291-1) Pm-12997 OJL-8

2   Old Timbrook was a black horse : black as any crow
3   Had a white ring around his forepaw : white as any
    snow
4   Yes old Timbrook he come darting : like a bullet
    from a gun

Byrd   2   Byrd, John

5   And old Molly she come creeping : like a criminal to
    be hung
6   Johnny Walker Johnny Walker : Johnny Walker my dear
    son
7   Hold tight rein on Timbrook : so that horse can run
8   Oh the cuckoo was a fine bird : hollers when he fly
9   But he never hollers cuckoo : till the fourth day of
    July
10 Oh the race track it was dusty : and the wind was
    high
11 Well you couldn't see old Timbrook : as he come
    darting by
12 Oh the children they did holler : and the old folks
    squalled
13 But old Timbrook he beat Molly : to the hole in the
    wall
14 I love my race horse : likes to have my fun
15 Old Mrs went to the race track : and lost all her
    mon'

Cali   1   Calicott, Joe

        title: Fare Thee Well Blues
        place and date: Memphis, c. 21 Feb. 1930
        record numbers: (MEM-778-) Br-7166 OJL-11

1   Told me late last fall : you never had no man at all
2   Well you got more men : than a two-ton truck can
    haul
3   Told me to my face : that a good man in my place
5   Told me it was early last spring : when the birds
    began to sing
6   Well it's the last chance : kid to be around here
    with me
7   I told you early last June : when the flowers began
    to bloom
8   You can't do no better : another good girl can take
    your room
9   Go and heist your window : let your curtain down
10 Well you can't tell : there may be some joker around
11 Go and put on your nightgown : baby let's we go lie
    down
12 Well it's the last chance : shaking in bed with you

Cali   2 .   Calicott, Joe

        title: Traveling Mama Blues
        place and date: Memphis, c. 21 Feb. 1930
        record numbers: (MEM-779-) Br-7166 Yz L-1009

1   Well a short-legged mama : trying to carry your
    daddy by
2   Said I want to let you know : I growed most too high
3   When you see your rider : out in the road
4   Said she's telling all her friends : that's a
    nineteen thirty Ford
5   Now she doing things : that you don't never know
7   Oh stop and listen : at the *one-note* how she blow
8   Said you sell anyone parts : make the motor go
9   Walk with my good girl in the daytime : walk with
    her at night
10 Said I taught my kitchen *teller* : how to treat a
    good man right
11 Way you doing me mama : says its out of sight
12 Said anything a kid-man do : well it bes all right
13 I'm going to *jack* me a picket : from my yard back
    fence
14 I'm going to start a-whooping : learn the good girl
    some sense
15 Well I do and I do : do and I do love you
16 Said *nothing funny* : in a state about you

Call   1   Calloway, Blanche

        title: Lazy Woman's Blues
        place and date: Chicago, 9 Nov. 1925
        record numbers: (9458-A) OK-8279 CC-32

1   A lot of these women: too lazy to put up with none
    of good man's dirt
2   But they ain't too lazy : to count his money
    Saturday night
3   I know a lazy woman : put ten dollars in a telephone
4   Just to tell her sweet man : her monkey-man is out
    and gone
5   When a woman's too lazy : to try and bake an apple
    pie
6   She's too lazy to live : and she's too darn lazy to
    die
7   I know you lazy women are going to *pan me* : when
    you hear this song
8   But the truth *is* ??? : and I surely have to carry
    it on

Call   2   Calloway, Blanche

        title: Lonesome Lovesick
        place and date: Chicago, 9 Nov. 1925
        record numbers: (9459-A) OK-8279 CC-32

1   Lonesome lovesick blues will make you feel so lonely
    : when you're left all alone
2   Dying for some loving : and the one you love has
    gone
3   Deep down in my heart : I'm feeling blue
4   Lonesome and lovesick : baby just for you
5   When I'm alone : I moan the whole night through
6   I want some loving : no one but you will do
7   My heart is aching : breaking for some news
8   My heart is aching : gee I'm all confused

CamB   1   Campbell, Bob

        title: Dice's Blues
        place and date: New York, 30 July 1934
        record numbers: (15483-1) Vo-02830 Rt RL-340

1   I said dices oh dices : please don't you three on me
2   I'm just as broke and hungry : as any gambler can be
3   My buddy played the jack : when he give me that
    hard-luck queen
4   He was one of the luckiest at cards : that a gambler
    have ever seen
5   Jack of diamonds jack of diamonds : will turn your
    money green
6   It's the luckiest card : that a gambler have ever
    seen
7   I went to gamble in Cuba : I went to gamble in Spain
8   Say my woman told me last night : she did not want
    no gambling man
9   I said run here baby : sit on your daddy's knee
10 Say I just want to show you honey : just what
    gambling have done for me

CamB   2   Campbell, Bob

        title: Shotgun Blues
        place and date: New York, 30 July 1934
        record numbers: (15484-1) Vo-02830 Rt RL-340

1   Get me a shotgun : and use it in the woods
2   I would fix you this way : that you wouldn't do no
    man no good
3   Started to kill her : and she fell down on my bed
4   Before *ten* this morning : you had me talking out
    my head
5   Don't the moon look pretty : shining down from that
    willow tree

CamB   2   Campbell, Bob

6   I can see my baby : and she can't see me
7   Some of these menfolks : look just like my
     sure-to-be
8   If you mistreat my woman : I'm going to make you
     jump in the deep blue sea
9   Say run here woman : and see what you done done
10   You done started me to loving you : and now your
     other man done come

CamB   3   Campbell, Bob

     title: Starvation Farm Blues
     place and date: New York, 1 Aug. 1934
     record numbers: (15503-2) Vo-02798 Fly LP-103

1   Well I'm going to Detroit : get myself a job
2   I'm tired of laying around here : working on the
     starvation farm
3   Yeah I'm going down there and get me a job : working
     in Mr Ford's place
4   Say that woman told me last night : that you cannot
     even stand Mr Ford's ways
5   Say I got me a little [low, bitty] woman : five
     [foot, feet] from the ground
6   She five foot standing : and she four feet lying
     down
7   Say I know my dog : baby if I hear him bark
8   And I know my woman : if I feel her in the dark
9   Say you better stop your woman : from smiling in my
     face
10   Woman if you keep on a-smiling : I'm sure going to
     take your place

CamC   1   Campbell, Charlie

     title: Goin' Away Blues
     place and date: Birmingham, Ala. 25 Mar. 1937
     record numbers: (B-32-2) Vo-03571 Fly LP-103

1   One of these mornings : it won't be long
2   You going to look for me baby : and I will be gone
3   Lord I'm going to leave here walking : Lord I'm
     going away
4   But I may be back to see you : one cold rainy day
5   She tried to make me think : she is true to me
6   But she just as crooked : as she can be
7   I spent her money : she spent mine
8   She used to spend my dollars : just like she spent
     my dimes
9   That's all right : *bad luck pass on*
10   I'd love to go home any time : and catch another
     mule in my stall
11   I don't want no woman : that wears a number nine
12   I wake up in the morning : I can't tell her shoes
     from mine

CamG   1   Campbell, Gene

     title: Wandering Blues
     place and date: Chicago, c. May 1930
     record numbers: (C-5701-A) Br-7170 His HLP-2

1   Every night : I wander all by myself
2   Thinking about the woman I love : loving someone
     else
3   Boo hoo : I just can't keep from crying
4   I'm worried about my baby : she's on my mind
5   Sometimes I wonder : do she think of me
6   And again I wonder : if I will ever be free
7   I'm telling all you women : what's on my mind
8   I never loved one woman : no more at a time
9   Boo hoo : I wring my hands and cry
10   I'm thinking about the loving : that I let go by

CamG   1   Campbell, Gene

11   Since you been gone baby : I haven't been a bit of
     good
12   Because I never get the loving : that I really
     should

CamG   2   Campbell, Gene

     title: Robbin' and Stealin' Blues
     place and date: Chicago, c. May 1930
     record numbers: (C-5704-B) Br-7170 His HLP-2

1   My baby ain't good-looking : and she don't dress
     fine
2   But she gives me money : all of the time
3   She goes out at night : just like she's on wheels
4   And then I know : she's going out to rob and steal
5   I lay in my bed : my baby brings me my meals
6   What good is a woman : if she don't rob and steal
7   I used to live with a woman : they called her *Tilty
     Til*
8   I soon got rid of her : she couldn't rob and steal
9   I know : how you hungry hustlers feel
10   Your woman don't know how to rob : she is too
     doggone scared to steal

Cann   1   Cannon, Gus

     title: Poor Boy, Long Ways from Home
     place and date: Chicago, c. Nov. 1927
     record numbers: (20144-2) Pm-12571 Yz L-1002

1   Been a poor boy : a long way from home
3   ??? : no money to bear my fine
5   Lord I guess : I'll have to catch that *Frisco out*
7   And if that don't do : I'm going to try the woods
     awhile
9   I cried hello Central : give me your long-distance
     phone
11   I cried please ma'am : give me thirteen forty-nine

Cann   2   Cannon, Gus

     title: Heart Breakin' Blues
     place and date: Memphis, 9 Sept. 1928
     record numbers: (47001-2) Vi-V38523 OJL-4

1   Well I'm going downtown baby : won't be gone so long
2   Say I'm tired and worried : about to sing this song
3   And I stay at home baby : you don't treat me right
4   The best time I have girl : when you's out of my
     sight
5   Said give me back the wig I bought you : let your
     head go bald
6   But when I first met you babe : you didn't have no
     hair at all

Cann   3   Cannon, Gus

     title: Feather Bed
     place and date: Memphis, 9 Sept. 1928
     record numbers: (47002-2) Vi-V38515 Fwy FA-2953

1   I went downtown : didn't mean no harm
2   Police grabbed me : right by my arm
3   Soon I began to kick : I began to rear
4   They like to throw *me* : in the air
5   Now ??? : was in the stand
6   Had them law books : in his hand
7   *Evil Bridges* : and Moses Brown
8   Am going across the street ??? : going to town

45

Cann   4   Cannon, Gus

        title: Last Chance Blues
        place and date: Chicago, c. 12 Sept. 1929
        record numbers: (C-4337-) Br-7138 His HLP-15

1   I said hey mama : I'll give you your last chance
2   You do the world a service : but you want to wear my
    pants
3   I said hey : what's the matter now
4   You just a trifling woman : don't mean me no good
    nohow
5   I give you my money : but that don't do no good
6   I begun ??? *to worry* : that's just what I should

CarrL   1   Carr, Leroy

        title: Naptown Blues
        place and date: Chicago, 17 June 1929
        record numbers: (C-3267-) Vo-1400 Yz L-1036

1   Nobody knows old Naptown : baby like I do
2   If you will stop and listen : I will tell you a
    thing or two
3   When you get lonesome : and want to have some fun
4   You just grab a train : and try old Naptown some
5   When you get to Naptown : the blues won't last very
    long
6   Because they have their pleasure : and they sure do
    carry on
7   I would rather be in Naptown : than any place I know
8   I can get me a ticket : and stop by the *Walter*
    show
9   I'm going back to Naptown : baby don't you want to
    go
10 Because there ain't nobody : knows old Naptown like
    I know

CarrL   2   Carr, Leroy

        title: Gettin' All Wet
        place and date: Chicago, 13 Aug. 1929
        record numbers: (C-4034-) Vo-1423 Yz L-1036

1   Woke up my baby : come my love
2   Unlock the door : the sky's above
3   Are leaking : on your bed
4   Papa's in the rain : getting all wet
5   Getting all wet : getting all wet
6   And if I die : you will regret
7   Papa had : no place to go
8   You got a nice warm room : and so
9   Share it with papa : don't forget
10 Papa's in the rain : getting all wet
11 This rain ain't healthy : I've been told
12 Hear me cough : catching cold
13 Ain't no telling : what I'll get
14 Papa's in the rain : getting all wet
15 Papa's got : no coat at all
16 You got a raincoat : in your hall
17 This suit I told you : was too small
18 You nappy head : you knew it all
19 It lets me stand : but I can't sit
20 Papa's in the rain : getting all wet
21 Papa must eat : or he will die
22 You got pork chops: you got pie
23 Graveyard : is such a lonely place
24 Don't want dirt : thrown in my face
25 Pity old papa : and don't forget
26 Papa's in the rain : getting all wet

CarrL   3   Carr, Leroy

        title: Papa Wants a Cookie
        place and date: Chicago, 2 Jan. 1930
        record numbers: (C-5070-) Vo-1561 Yz L-1036

1   Mama's baking cookies : out in the kitchen
2   Papa smells the cookies : and his nose starts to
    itching
3   Papa tried to steal one : like he did before
4   But mama's got the lock : on the kitchen door
5   Papa says to mama : come a little closer
6   Mama looks at papa : says oh oh no sir
7   Papa turns around : starts to go away
8   Comes right back : when she hear him say
9   Papa says to mama : you a real nice-looker
10 You turn on the heat : like a fireless cooker
11 Come a little closer : in your papa's arms
12 Another little kiss : wouldn't do us any harm
13 Papa comes home : when his work is over
14 Mama says to papa : you sure ain't clover
15 Guess what I cooked : for you today
16 Mama just smiles : when she hear papa say

CarrL   4   Carr, Leroy

        title: Memphis Town
        place and date: Chicago, 2 Jan. 1930
        record numbers: (C-5071-) Vo-1527 Yz L-1036

1   Went to the station : to get me a train
2   Going to climb on board : and ride again
3   Just climb aboard : and ride around
4   I might get off : at Memphis town
5   Shovel in the coal : see the wheels go around
6   Everybody's going : down to Memphis town
7   I said conductor : where the trains all going
8   I want to go see : that gal of mine
9   He answered me : with a railroad frown
10 All trains going : to Memphis town
11 I said what's doing : down old Memphis way
12 The trains all going : there today
13 The trainman said : there's a jubilee
14 And Memphis is town : that's only place for me
15 I said to the station man : where's my train
16 He said I never knowed : you own the train
17 I said you better answer : or I'll smack you down
18 He said all trains going : to Memphis town
19 Goodbye folks : I'm on my way
20 See you : on some other day
21 Got my ticket : here's my train
22 Going down to Memphis : see my gal again

CarrL   5   Carr, Leroy

        title: Sloppy Drunk Blues
        place and date: Chicago, 19 Sept. 1930
        record numbers: (C-6086-B) Vo-1541 Yz L-1015

1   I'd rather be sloppy drunk : than anything I know
2   And another half a pint : mama will see me go
3   I love my moonshine whiskey : better than a filly
    loves her mare
4   You can take your pretty bucks : give me my cool
    kind can
5   I'd rather be sloppy drunk : sitting in the can
6   Than to be out in the streets : running from the man
7   Mmm : bring me another two-bit pint
8   Because I got my habits on : and I'm going to wreck
    this joint
9   My gal trying quit me : for somebody else
10 Now I'm sloppy drunk mama : sleeping all by myself

CarrL   6   Carr, Leroy

        title: Four Day Rider
        place and date: Chicago, 19 Sept. 1930
        record numbers: (C-6090-A) Vo-1574 Yz L-1036

1   I'm a 'fore-day rider mama : riding all night long
2   Anywhere I come mama : I sing my worried song
3   Now I'm going to leave you mama : we can't get along
4   Going to let you go mama : and sing my worried song
5   I won't carry nobody mama : I'm riding by myself
6   Because the 'fore-day blues : don't worry nobody
    else
7   And I rode to make you happy baby : rode all night
    and day
8   You brought me these blues mama : seems like they're
    going to stay

CarrL   7   Carr, Leroy

        title: Alabama Woman Blues
        place and date: Chicago, 19 Sept. 1930
        record numbers: (C-6091-B) Vo-1549 RBF RF-1

1   Did you ever go down : on the Mobile and K C line
2   I just want to ask you : did you ever see that girl
    of mine
3   I rode the Central : and I hustled the L and N
4   The Alabama women : they live like section men
5   Don't cry baby : your papa will be home some day
6   I've been away baby : but I did not go to stay
7   Don't the clouds look lonesome : across the deep
    blue sea
8   Don't my gal look good : when she's coming after me

CarrL   8   Carr, Leroy

        title: Low Down Dog Blues
        place and date: Chicago, c. 20 Jan. 1931
        record numbers: (C-7215-A) Vo-1605 Yz L-1036

1   I ain't going to be : your lowdown dog no more
2   You don't want me baby : down the road I'll go
3   Now I work hard mama : and I brought you home my pay
4   You say you ain't going to miss me : when I'm gone
    away
5   Ooo : ooo wee
6   It's a lowdown shame : the way you treat poor me
7   My home ain't here : I ain't compelled to stay
8   It's your time now : but it'll be mine some sweet
    day
9   And I ain't going to be : your lowdown dog no more
10 The train is at the station : my mind's made up to
    go

CarrL   9   Carr, Leroy

        title: New How Long How Long Blues--Part 2
        place and date: Chicago, c. 20 Jan. 1931
        record numbers: (C-7221-A) Vo-1585 RBF RF-202

1   I'm going to the country : put my watch in pawn
2   I don't want it to tell me : that you've been gone
3   I had some tough luck lately : I got locked up in
    jail
4   I sat and called you baby : to come and go my bail
5   I'm going down to Georgia : then up to Tennessee
6   So look me over baby : this is the last you'll see
    of me
7   The last time I tried to love you : you were so very
    cold
8   I thought that I was standing : holding the North
    Pole
9   I can look and see the greenback : growing on that
    hill
10 But I ain't seen the greenback : on a dollar bill

CarrL   9   Carr, Leroy

11 I haven't any money : for a ticket on the train
12 But I will ride the rods baby : to be with you again

CarrL   10   Carr, Leroy

        title: What More Can I Do?
        place and date: Chicago, c. 20 Jan. 1931
        record numbers: (C-7222-A) Vo-1651 Yz L-1036

1   I come to your house : and knock upon your door
2   You had the nerve to tell me : you didn't want me no
    more
3   After all I've done : what more can I do
4   I gave you my love : and tried to get along with you
5   I fed you when you were hungry : took you in when
    you was outdoors
6   I give you my money : and even bought your clothes
7   I tried to treat you right : you would not pay that
    no mind
8   There ain't no more I can do : there ain't no needs
    in trying
9   I know you won't miss me : after I am gone
10 But always remember : that you treated your daddy
    wrong
11 Now I'm going to leave you : and do the best I can
12 Because you don't want me : there must be some other
    man

CarrL   11   Carr, Leroy

        title: Papa Wants to Knock a Jug
        place and date: Chicago, c. 20 Jan. 1931
        record numbers: (C-7223-A) Vo-1651 Yz L-1036

1   I saw your mama : in Kansas City
2   The way she was looking : was a doggone pity
3   Feet on the ground : clothes wasn't clean
4   Dirtiest old stuff : I ever seen
5   Now I got a gal : she is big as a bull
6   She never stops drinking : till her belly gets full
7   Gets full of liquor : and tries to sing
8   Tight like that : and shake that thing
9   I ask her about it : she said before long
10 Let's get together : because your water's on
11 Let's get started : be long gone
12 Let's get together : what you waiting on
13 I saw you mama : way last spring
14 Eyeballs shining : like a diamond ring
15 Staggered down the street : hollering and a-fussing
16 I tried to stop her : and I got a good cussing
17 I saw your mama : your papa too
18 What they was doing : just won't do
19 I slipped up on them : and took one look
20 What they was doing : wasn't in the book
21 If you want some loving : you want it cheap
22 Go down on Ellsworth : about the middle of the week
23 Show them girls a quarter : they won't let you go
24 It's four or five times : and then some more

CarrL   12   Carr, Leroy

        title: I Keep the Blues
        place and date: New York, 15 Mar. 1932
        record numbers: (11497-A) Vo-1709 Yz L-1036

1   About four this morning : blues come in my door
2   Please Mr blues : don't come here no more
3   I keep the blues all night : and the whole day
    through
4   I'm so full of blues : I don't know what to do
5   Well something has got to be done : to get these
    blues off my mind
6   I believe I'll get drunk : and stay drunk all the
    time

CarrL 12   Carr, Leroy

7   Well I'm going to leave you : I ain't going to sing
    no more
8   Because I'm full of blue : and I have got to go

CarrL 13   Carr, Leroy

       title: Midnight Hour Blues
       place and date: New York, 16 Mar. 1932
       record numbers: (11499-A) Vo-1703 Co C-30496

1   In the wee midnight hours : long before the break of
    day
2   When the blues creep up on you : and carry your mind
    away
3   While I lay in my bed : and cannot go to sleep
4   While my heart's in trouble : and my mind is
    thinking deep
5   My mind was running : back to days of long ago
6   And the one I love : I don't see her anymore
7   Blues why do you worry me : why do you stay so long
8   You come to me yesterday : been with me all night
    long
9   I've been so worried : I didn't know what to do
10 So I guess that's why : I've had these midnight hour
    blues

CarrL 14   Carr, Leroy

       title: Mean Mistreater Mama
       place and date: St. Louis, 20 Feb. 1934
       record numbers: (SL-1-?) Vo-02657 Co C-30496

1   You're a mean mistreating mama : and you don't mean
    me no good
2   And I don't blame you baby : I'd be the same way if
    I could
3   You say you're going to leave me : well you say you
    going away
4   That's all right baby : maybe you'll come back home
    some day
5   Now you're a mean mistreater : and you mistreats me
    all the time
6   Now I tried to love you : swear but you won't pay
    that no mind
7   Can you remember mama : in the morning I knocked
    upon your door
8   You had the nerve to tell me : that you didn't want
    me no more
9   Ain't it lonesome : sleeping all by yourself
10 When the one that you love : is loving someone else

CarrL 15   Carr, Leroy

       title: Hurry Down Sunshine
       place and date: St. Louis, 20 Feb. 1934
       record numbers: (SL-4-3) Vo-02741 Co C-30496

1   Hurry down sunshine : see what tomorrow brings
2   May bring drops of sorrow : and it may bring drops
    of rain
3   Now I love my baby : but [she, my baby] don't love
    me
4   When I get in trouble : she is the last one that I
    see
5   Going down on the bottom : back to the Lone Star
    State
6   Stand back pretty mama : I don't want you to make me
    wait
7   So long people and sweethearts : I'll soon be on my
    way
8   Now I'm leaving this lonesome old town : now I may
    come back some day
9   Now I never got worried : until the fireman rang his
    bell

CarrL 15   Carr, Leroy

10 Two keen long whistles : bid me long farewell

CarrL 16   Carr, Leroy

       title: Corn Licker Blues
       place and date: St. Louis, 20 Feb. 1934
       record numbers: (SL-5-3) Vo-02741 Co C-30496

1   Now I love my good corn liquor : and I really mean I
    do
2   Now I don't care who knows it : and I really mean
    that too
3   Now I've been drinking my good corn liquor : I mean
    don't no one get rough
4   Now I try to treat everybody right : but I mean
    don't start no stuff
5   Give me another half a pint : [and, then] maybe I'll
    go home
6   The reason why I'm getting drunk today : I swear my
    baby's gone
7   Some folks like their alcohol : but give me my corn
    I believe all the time
8   Reason why I love it so well : it's so soothing to
    my mind
9   So give me some more corn liquor : if I get drunk
    [just please, please just] take me home
10 I ain't going to bother nobody : just let the good
    times baby roll on

CarrL 17   Carr, Leroy

       title: Hold Them Puppies
       place and date: St. Louis, 20 Feb. 1934
       record numbers: (SL-6-3) Vo-02751 Yz L-1036

1   Nights so lonesome : and the days so long
2   Ain't had no loving : since you been gone
3   If you see my baby : tell her to hurry home
4   Ain't had no mmm : since she has been gone
5   You put the puppies on my mama : you drove me crazy
    too
6   You done made me love you : what can I do
7   Won't you tell my baby : to hurry back to me
8   She's got the best old mmm : I ever did see
9   Won't you tell my baby : to hurry back to me
10 She got the best old loving : that I ever did see
11 You can pull your dress babe : up above your knees
12 You can strut your stuff babe : but don't mess with
    me
13 You going to leave me you going to leave me : you
    going to leave me blue
14 I want some of your loving : don't care what you do

CarrL 18   Carr, Leroy

       title: Shady Lane Blues
       place and date: St. Louis, 20 Feb. 1934
       record numbers: (SL-7-3) Vo-02762 Co C-30496

1   Now I've got a girl : she lives down in in Shady
    Lane
2   I love that girl : but I'm scared to call her name
3   It's going to be one of these mornings : swear and
    it won't be long
4   I'm going to catch the first thing smoking : and
    down the road I'm going
5   Where I long ain't here baby : it's way out in the
    west
6   In the Smoky Mountains : where the eagle builds his
    nest
7   Did you ever love a girl : a girl you hate to lose
8   Don't lose your temper : when you've been drinking
    booze

CarrL 19   Carr, Leroy

    title: Blues Before Sunrise
    place and date: St. Louis, 21 Feb. 1934
    record numbers: (SL-12-1) Vo-02657 Co C-30496

1   I had the blues before sunrise : with tears standing
    in my eyes
2   It's such a miserable feeling : a feeling I do
    despise
3   Seems like everybody : everybody's down on me
4   I'm going to cast my troubles : down in the deep
    blue sea
5   Today have been : such a long old lonesome day
6   I've been sitting here thinking : with my mind a
    million miles away
7   Blues starts a-rolling : and it stops at my front
    door
8   I'm going to change my way of living : ain't going
    to worry no more
9   Now I love my baby : but my baby won't behave
10 I'm going to buy me a hard-shooting pistol : and put
    her in her grave

CarrL 20   Carr, Leroy

    title: Take a Walk Around the Corner
    place and date: New York, 14 Aug. 1934
    record numbers: (15604-) Vo-02986 Co C-30496

1   Believe I'll take me a walk : around the corner by
    myself
2   And if I can't find my baby : I don't want nobody
    else
3   She went out last night : and she didn't even say
    goodbye
4   How come she left me : Lord I really don't know why
5   Now I'm going out this morning : my forty-five in my
    hand
6   Now I'm going to kill my woman : for loving another
    man
7   Then I'm going to the judge : and I'm going to fall
    down on my knees
8   Ask him please fair judge : have mercy on me please
9   Judge I done killed my woman : because she treated
    me so unkind
10 Treated me so unkind : till I swear I lost my mind
11 Well it's please please please : don't send me to
    the electric chair
12 Just give me my time : and I'll try to do it
    anywhere
13 When I'm dead and gone : and six feet in the ground
14 You can only say : there's a good man has gone down
15 Oh it looks mighty cloudy : and I believe it's going
    to rain
16 I just love to hear : my baby call my name

CarrL 21   Carr, Leroy

    title: My Woman's Gone Wrong
    place and date: New York, 14 Aug. 1934
    record numbers: (15626-1) Vo-02950 Co C-30496

1   Now I woke up this morning : my woman was standing
    over me
2   She had a big forty-five : and she was mad as she
    could be
3   Now I prayed to my baby : and to the Lord above
4   Now I said honey please don't shoot me : baby you
    the only woman I love
5   She seen me with a woman : standing at her front
    gate
6   Now I tried my best to dodge her : but I was just a
    little too late
7   Now and it's please please please darling : honey
    please don't take my life

CarrL 21   Carr, Leroy

8   Because you got me all wrong baby : honey that was
    another man's wife

CarrL 22   Carr, Leroy

    title: Southbound Blues
    place and date: New York, 14 Aug. 1934
    record numbers: (15627-2) Vo-03107 Co C-30496

1   No need to ask me : why I'm packing my clothes
2   I'm going to leave you mama : and I really don't
    care who knows
3   Now I used to love you : but now I'm getting tired
    of your kind
4   I'm going down south : just to see what I can find
5   Now I may miss you : but I don't think I will
6   I'm going to get me a new woman : to love me till I
    get my fill
7   You mistreated me mama : you would not treat me nice
    and sweet
8   So I'm going down south : shake this dust of this
    town off my feet

CarrL 23   Carr, Leroy

    title: Barrel House Woman
    place and date: New York, 14 Aug. 1934
    record numbers: (15628-2) Vo-02791 Co C-30496

1   My woman so lowdown : she barrelhouse all the time
2   She's low and squatty : but I love that girl of mine
3   When she gets up in the morning : she starts to
    drink her corn
4   Every time I think of that woman : I wished I had
    never been born
5   She struts around all day : she barrelhouses the
    whole night through
6   But when she loves me : I forget that I ever was
    blue
7   I wish that I could cure : her barrelhousing ways
8   And is I stay with her : I'll barrelhouse some day
    myself
9   Now I love my woman : swear that she won't act right
10 Gets her head full of whiskey : and wants to start a
    fight

CarrL 24   Carr, Leroy

    title: Barrel House Woman No. 2
    place and date: New York, 15 Aug. 1934
    record numbers: (15633-2) Vo-02820 Yz L-1019

1   Well this barrelhouse woman : what makes you so mean
2   Well you the meanest old woman : baby that I ever
    seen
3   You stay drunk all night : and the whole day long
4   Sometimes I begin to wonder : what in the world is
    going on wrong
5   Now I've told you once : ain't going to tell you no
    more
6   Now the next time you get drunk : right out my door
    you'll go
7   Now I'm going to get real mean baby : I swear I
    won't act right
8   Next time I catch you drunk : baby we going to have
    a fight
9   I don't want no barrelhouse woman : messing around
    with me
10 If you got to get drunk baby : mama please just let
    me be

CarrL 25   Carr, Leroy

> title: I Believe I'll Make a Change
> place and date: New York, 16 Aug. 1934
> record numbers: (15645-2) Vo-02820 Co C-30496

1 Now I believe : I believe I'll go back home
2 Because this life I'm living : won't let me stay here long
3 His wife is gone : but she was all right with me
4 He would give her ninety-four dollars : and she would give me ninety-three
5 I believe : I believe I'll make a change
6 Going to turn off this gas stove : I'm bound for a brand new range

CarrL 26   Carr, Leroy

> title: Bo Bo Stomp
> place and date: New York, 16 Aug. 1934
> record numbers: (15649-1) Vo-02969 Co C-30496

1   Come on boy : let's go down on Tenth Street
2   Some of the prettiest women down there : that you ever did meet
3   Now down on Smith Street : where you get your rocking rye
4   Boy that's what I'm talking about : and I ain't talking no lie
5   Now I'm got a gal : she's so sweet
6   Sweetest little gal : that I ever did meet
7   Every time I see my woman : walking down the street
8   Boy great big legs : and that little bitty feet
9   Now give me whiskey : you can give him gin
10 I'm going away baby : but I'll be back again
11 Now down on Tenth Street : boy it's a terrible mess
12 Boy we can have more fun down there : than any place I guess
13 Now I like my bucketful of beer : and I like my gin
14 Boy I ain't coming back here no more : with a *very win*
15 You hear me talking to you : you hear me talking fast
16 Boy you liable to slip up : and fall on your yas yas yas

CarrL 27   Carr, Leroy

> title: Big Four Blues
> place and date: New York, 14 Dec. 1934
> record numbers: (16416-1) Vo-03349 Co C-30496

1   Big Four blowed this morning : at the break of day
2   And it sounds so lonesome : because it taken my baby away
3   Big Four Big Four : won't you please turn your train around
4   Because here I sit all down and out : with my head hung down
5   I tried to be as good to that woman : as one man could be
6   And I mean it's a shame : the way she went and left poor me
7   Yes I'm down and out : ain't got no money to ride no train
8   But I'm going to find my good gal : and bring her back home again
9   Please Mr brakeman : won't you let a poor man ride your blinds
10 I'm just trying to make it : back to that gal who is worrying my mind

CarrL 28   Carr, Leroy

> title: Hard Hearted Papa
> place and date: New York, 14 Dec. 1934
> record numbers: (16417-2) Vo unissued Bio BLP-C9

1   I'm a hard-hearted papa : there's nothing pleases me
2   I've had to be good long enough : now I'm going to be mean as I can be
3   I don't even like what I drink : my food don't taste right at all
4   And a lowdown no-good woman : is the cause of it all
5   When I tried to be soft and easy : people would not let me be
6   Now I'm just as mean and hateful : swear as I can be
7   I spent all of my money : showing my friends a great big time
8   Now they laugh and grin at me : because I ain't got a lousy dime
9   So I'm a hard-hearted papa : I've done changed my ways
10 And I think they will stay changed : for the rest of my days

CarrL 29   Carr, Leroy

> title: You Left Me Crying
> place and date: New York, 14 Dec. 1934
> record numbers: (16418-2) Vo unissued Bio BLP-C9

1   You left me crying baby : please come back to me
2   And you know I've done all baby : I've been as good as I could be
3   Why did you go : and leave me cold in hand
4   I know what it's all about : it was on account of your other man
5   Now I can't sleep at night : there's rocks all in my bed
6   Because I ain't got you pretty mama : to hold my aching head
7   I'm going to buy me a shiny pistol : I'm coming after you
8   I ain't going to let you : treat me just like you do
9   So watch your step mama : you know what you've done
10 If you don't come back to me : hot spring water won't help you none

CarrL 30   Carr, Leroy

> title: Broken-Hearted Man
> place and date: New York, 14 Dec. 1934
> record numbers: (16425-1) Vo unissued Bio BLP-C9

1   Minutes seem like hours : and hours seem like years
2   Since I've had these blues : I just can't keep from shedding tears
3   I'm going to tell everybody : what my good gal done to me one day
4   She put me out and broke my heart : just to pass the time away
5   Now I ain't got no money : and I ain't got nowhere to stay
6   But that's all right baby : if you want to turn me away
7   You know I work hard baby : and I brung you home my check
8   Now I ain't never loved no woman : like I loved you yet

CarrL 31   Carr, Leroy

    title: Evil-Hearted Woman
    place and date: New York, 14 Dec. 1934
    record numbers: (16426-1) Vo unissued Bio BLP-C9

1 You evil-hearted woman : you got a heart like a stone
2 You don't mean me no good : so I leave you alone
3 You used to be sweet : but you ain't sweet no more
4 You want to leave me alone : and stay away from my door
5 You're just like a rattler : you always ready to bite
6 So I'm going to get me a good woman : who will treat me right
7 Yes you're evil : just as evil as you can be
8 I don't want you to cook for me no more : because you might poison me
9 So be on your way evil-hearted woman : and stay away from my door
10 I done took your foolishness long enough : and I don't want you no more

CarrL 32   Carr, Leroy

    title: Good Woman Blues
    place and date: New York, 14 Dec. 1934
    record numbers: (16427-1) Vo-03296 Yz L-1019

1 Women if you got a good man : give him three good meals every day
2 If you don't : some other woman is going to tow your man away
3 I've got so many women : that I don't care when one dies
4 I don't even weep : I don't even cry
5 Some men crave high yellow : but give me black or brown
6 Because I can't tell the difference : when the sun goes down
7 Blacker the berry : sweeter is the juice
8 I got a good black woman : and I ain't going to turn her loose
9 They say black is evil : and they don't mean you no good
10 But I would not quit my black woman : baby if I could
11 I've got a good black gal : I've got a good black gal
12 She's my buddy : and I swear she is my pal

CarrL 33   Carr, Leroy

    title: Hustler's Blues
    place and date: New York, 14 Dec. 1934
    record numbers: (16428-1) Vo-03034 Co C-30496

1 Whiskey is my habit : good women is all I crave
2 And I don't believe in two things : will carry me to my grave
3 I'm going to Louisiana : where I can drink and have my fun
4 I can't stay here much longer : because my time has just about come
5 When you see me leaving baby : don't you wear no black
6 You see your loving daddy : walking down some lonesome railroad track
7 When I was a hustler : I'm in my prime
8 I would drink good whiskey : and gamble all the time

CarrL 34   Carr, Leroy

    title: Eleven Twenty-Nine Blues
    place and date: New York, 14 Dec. 1934
    record numbers: (16429-1) Vo-03157 Bio BLP-C9

1 She ain't good-looking : but the good gal do go clean
2 And I'm crazy about my baby : though she is so mean
3 My gal got arrested : and they put her in the county jail
4 They fined her eleven twenty-nine : and they even allowed her no bail
5 Now I'm going to see that judge : and talk to him myself
6 Tell him that he sent my gal to the county road : and left me by myself
7 Now I never felt so sorry : till the people walked down the lane
8 And my heart struck sorrow : when they called my good gal's name
9 And I heard the jailor say hello : prisoners all fall in line
10 I'm also talking about that long-chain woman : that got eleven twenty-nine
11 I've got the blues so bad : that I just can't rest
12 I'm going to ask that jailor : can I do my good gal's time myself

CarrL 35   Carr, Leroy

    title: You've Got Me Grieving
    place and date: New York, 14 Dec. 1934
    record numbers: (16430-2) Vo-03349 Bio BLP-C9

1 Now you got me grieving mama : over nobody else but you
2 Yes you got me grieving mama : I really mean that's true
3 I'm not going to worry : in my life no more
4 If you want to leave me : you can go
5 Now you got me grieving mama : over nobody else but you
6 Yes you got me grieving mama : I love no one else but you
7 I woke up this morning : didn't find you there
8 Wondering what man : had his hand running down through your hair down there
9 But I'm not going to cry : I'm not going to sigh
10 You going to leave me : bye bye bye

CarrL 36   Carr, Leroy

    title: Bread Baker
    place and date: New York, 17 Dec. 1934
    record numbers: (16432-1) Vo-03296 Yz L-1036

1 She's got a bed in her bedroom : it shines like a morning star
2 When it starts to rocking : it looks just like a Cadillac car
3 Baby baby baby : you had better get your back yard cleaned
4 Because you *better* cook the best old corn bread : a poor man ever seen
5 Get your red ripe tomato : and your T-bone steak
6 And if you fix it like I like it : I will get you a new V-Eight
7 I like it early in the morning : I've got to have it late at night
8 I don't want you to fix it : if you don't fix it right
9 I smell your cabbage burning : baby turn your good bread around
10 Because in your kitchen baby : it's where the good stuff can be found

CarrL 37   Carr, Leroy

        title: Tight Time Blues
        place and date: New York, 17 Dec. 1934
        record numbers: (16433-1) Vo-03034 Bio BLP-C9

1   Times is done got so tight : so I'm going to rob and
    steal
2   It's done got so tight : a man can't get a decent
    meal
3   I ain't got no shoes : and I ain't got no clothes
4   The house rent man : has done put my things outdoors
5   It was thundering out and lightning : oh Lord how it
    did rain
6   But somehow : I'm going to get even with that house
    rent man
7   I've done got evil : and I've done got mean
8   And when I start to stealing : I'm going to pick the
    rounders clean

CarrL 38   Carr, Leroy

        title: Longing for My Sugar
        place and date: New York, 17 Dec. 1934
        record numbers: (16434-1) Vo-02875 Yz L-1036

1   I'm longing for my sugar : and I don't want no one
    else
2   And I don't miss her so much : until I'm all by
    myself
3   Now I knowed when I quit her : I was doing wrong
4   Now I've got trouble on my mind : it's trying to get
    her back home
5   I'm going to pay the boss : and get my check-card
    today
6   And give it to my sugar : if she'll come back home
    to stay
7   Fussing and fighting : ain't no way to get along
8   This done caused me a world of trouble : and broke
    up my happy home
9   I can't work in the daytime : I can't sleep a wink
    at night
10 Thinking the woman that I love : ain't been treated
    right

CarrL 39   Carr, Leroy

        title: Shinin' Pistol
        place and date: New York, 17 Dec. 1934
        record numbers: (16438-1) Vo-03067 Co C-30496

1   I'm going to get me a brand new [shiny] pistol :
    with a long shiny barrel
2   I'm going to ramble this town over : until I find my
    girl
3   I'm going to go to the station : and try to find her
    there
4   And if the Lord has not got her : she's in this
    world somewhere
5   She left me with a head full of trouble : and a head
    full of misery
6   And now she's got me crying : baby please come back
    home to me
7   My mother told me : don't you weep don't you moan
8   Because son there'll be women here : when you dead
    and gone
9   When I get through rambling : and looking this whole
    world through
10 I won't be dead with trouble : you know I died to
    lose

CarrL 40   Carr, Leroy

        title: It's Too Short
        place and date: New York, 17 Dec. 1934
        record numbers: (16440-1) Vo-02875 Co C-30496

1   Now I'm down and out : ain't got no friends around
2   I'm going from door to door : everybody turns me
    down
3   Now my woman treats me : [just] like I'm a
    motherless child
4   She's always squabbling : she don't give me a ???
    smile*
5   Now here I am people : out in the ice and snow
6   My clothes all in pawn : ain't got nowhere to go
7   She said she liked my music : but my tune's too
    short
8   But if she gets long winded player : she's sure to
    get caught
9   Now babe I can't help it : if I can't play long
10 I'm just a little skinny fellow : and a player is
    strong

CarrL 41   Carr, Leroy

        title: Suicide Blues
        place and date: New York, 17 Dec. 1934
        record numbers: (16442-1) Vo unissued Bio BLP-C9

1   If somebody finds me : when I'm dead and gone
2   Say I did self-murder : I died with my boots on
3   Took me a Smith and Wesson : and blew out my brains
4   I didn't take no poison : I couldn't stand the
    strain
5   No I ain't no coward : and I'll tell you why
6   I was just tired of living : but wasn't afraid to
    die
7   Take me to the graveyard : put me in the ground
8   Please write on my tombstone : my woman threw me
    down
9   In my farewell letter : someone's sure to find
10 Goodbye old cruel world : I'm glad I left you behind

CartG 1   Carter, George

        title: Rising River Blues
        place and date: Chicago, c. Feb. 1929
        record numbers: (21153-2) Pm-12750 Yz L-1012

1   Rising river blues : running by my door
2   They running sweet mama : like they have not run
    before
3   I got to move in the alley : I ain't allowed on your
    street
4   These rising river blues : sure have got me beat
5   Come here sweet mama : let me speak my mind
6   *If you need to talk* : take a long long time

CartG 2   Carter, George

        title: Hot Jelly Roll Blues
        place and date: Chicago, c. Feb. 1929
        record numbers: (21154-2) Pm-12750 Yz L-1012

1   Jellyroll jellyroll : you can eat it on the fence
2   If you don't go get it : you ain't got no sense
3   Talking about my jelly : about my sweet jellyroll
4   When you take my jelly : mama can't keep you at home
5   Can make a blind man see : a lame man walk
6   It make a deaf woman hear : and a little baby talk
7   Now tell all you people : what jellyroll done done
8   Made grandma : marry her youngest grandson
9   Jellyroll is a thing : a man won't do without
10 He'll ??? *things* ??? : if the people *put him out*
11 I went up on the mountain : looked down in the sea
12 A good-looking woman : winked her eye at me

CartG 2   Carter, George

13 If you don't believe : my jellyroll will do
14 You can ask anybody : on Auburn Avenue

CartM 1   Carter, Margaret

        title: I Want Plenty of Grease in My Frying Pan
        place and date: New York, Aug. 1926
        record numbers: (107041) Pat-7511 His HLP-15

1   You know I use plenty grease : every day
2   But I ain't did no frying : while you was away
3   My frying pan was on the stove : getting hot
4   I said sweet papa : put some grease in my pot

CartS 1   Carter, Spider

        title: Don't Leave Me Blues
        place and date: Chicago, c. 8 Nov. 1930
        record numbers: (C-6165-) Br-7188 Rt RL-340

1   Don't leave me *don't you* babe : all my clothes in
       pawn
2   I mistreated you baby : and I know I was wrong
3   I gave you all my love : still you were unsatisfied
4   But my love for you baby : is all gone and died
5   ??? baby : you can't have this town
6   I'm leaving here baby : *feel no urge of backing
       down*
7   When I call you babe : you refuse to come
8   Hot spring waters : they won't help you none
9   Some day baby : when I'm dead and gone
10 You're going to hear : this old lonesome song

ChatB 1   Chatman, Bo

        title: I'm an Old Bumble Bee
        place and date: Jackson, Miss., 15 Dec. 1930
        record numbers: (404720-B) OK-8852 RBF RF-9

1   I am an old bumblebee : a stinger just as long as my
       arm
2   I stings every good-looking woman now : everywhere I
       goes along
3   Says as I fly around now : I makes a beautiful song
4   And everywhere I sting a good-looking woman : says
       I'll sure find me a home
5   Now I'm an old bumblebee : just dropped in your town
6   It ain't none of these women : turn this old
       bumblebee down
7   They crying come here bumblebee : you know you know
       your stuff
8   And you sting you old bumblebee : your old stinger
       just long enough
9   Mmm : what's going become of me
10 Every time I need stinging now : I get those
       long-stinger bumblebees
11 Says when I get to stinging them : I sting just like
       I should
12 And they all crying old bumblebee : you know it
       hurts so good

ChatB 2   Chatman, Bo

        title: Ram Rod Daddy
        place and date: New York, 4 June 1931
        record numbers: (404926-A) OK-8897 His HLP-5

1   I'm a ramrodding daddy : I stays up on Main Street
2   I keeps my gun loaded : for every good-looking woman
       I meet
3   I'm a ramrodding daddy : Lord my rod is long and
       slim

ChatB 2   Chatman, Bo

4   And every time I load a gun for a woman : you know
       it's too tight Jim
5   I'm a ramrodding daddy : I rams as I walk along
6   Every time I use my ramrod : I surely will win a
       home
7   I want all you women : you better bear this in mind
8   A good ramrodding daddy : these days is hard to find
9   When I get to use my ramrod : I sure Lord take my
       time
10 It ain't no other ramrodding daddy : can put his
       load below where I put mine

ChatB 3   Chatman, Bo

        title: The Law Gonna Step on You
        place and date: New York, 5 June 1931
        record numbers: (404935-A) OK unissued Yz L-1034

1   I done told you told you : I told you too
2   Quit having liquor : and gambling too
3   A-look a-here baby : you [going, traveling] too fast
4   The law going to step : on your yas yas yas
5   Now you can twist you can twist : you can step on
       its tail
6   You going to need somebody : to go your bail
7   Now you may think : that they doing you wrong
8   But they'll send you : to the county farm
9   Now if you want : to leave from home
10 Walk around : with a bottle of corn
11 Now I told you told you : like a friend
12 You better draw : your business in

ChatB 4   Chatman, Bo

        title: Ants in My Pants
        place and date: New York, 5 June 1931
        record numbers: (404938-B) OK-8897 His HLP-5

1   It makes no difference : baby where you go
2   I got something : want you to know
3   Every time I come : and feel your arms
4   It makes my feeling : just get all wrong
5   It is tomorrow : it's early or late
6   I want you baby : give me a date
7   You's a red-hot mama : meat shakes on the bone
8   Thinks about your loving : baby when you gone
9   Every time : meet you on the street
10 A funny feeling : my head to my feet
11 But your arms around me : baby like you should
12 I'm telling you baby : your loving is good
13 I'm going to hug you : baby good and tight
14 Now love me baby : like you done last night

ChatB 5   Chatman, Bo

        title: I Want You To Know
        place and date: Atlanta, 25 Oct. 1931
        record numbers: (405025-1) OK-8935 Yz L-1014

1   Baby I want you to know : babe I want you to know
2   That way you been doing : Lord baby don't you do it
       no more
3   Babe I want you to know : honey I want you to know
4   That the way you been giving : Lord baby don't you
       give it no more
5   Because I'm a stranger here : just dropped in your
       town
6   Ain't none of these women : Lord turn me down
7   They want you to understand : honey want you to
       understand
8   I don't mean you no more good : now please get you
       another man

53

ChatB   6   Chatman, Bo

       title: Bo Carter Special
       place and date: San Antonio, 26 Mar. 1934
       record numbers: (82611-1) BB-B5489 Yz L-1034

1   Bo Carter is a man : broadcasts all over this land
2   And he takes women from their men : Lord just any
    old place he lands
3   When I get to use my broadcaster : it goes all
    around and around
4   And when the women receiving you : they'll sure to
    put their men all down
5   When you turn your radio light on baby : you look
    right in Bo Carter's face
6   But you neither not worry : I'm going to surely
    broadcast for you some day
7   The men can always tell : when Bo Carter has hit
    this land
8   Says the women they all start : says a-really
    mistreating all their men
9   They give their women their money : they really buy
    them the clothes
10 But to that broadcasting Bo Carter : their women
    they are bound to go

ChatB   7   Chatman, Bo

       title: Beans
       place and date: San Antonio, 26 Mar. 1934
       record numbers: (82612-1) BB-B5629 Yz L-1014

1   I don't want no more navy beans : boys I don't want
    no more
2   I don't want no more navy beans : they're about to
    make my stomach sore
3   I ate them last night : and the night before
4   When I got through : I couldn't shut my door
5   I don't want no more pinto beans : boys I don't want
    no more
6   I don't want no more pinto beans : they about to
    make my stomach sore
7   I ate them last night : and the night before
8   When I got through : I had to scrub my floor
9   I don't want none of them *favor* beans : boys I
    don't want no more
10 I don't want none of them *favor* beans : they about
    to make my stomach sore
11 I ate them last night : and the night before
12 Get in the luck : I ain't going to eat no more
13 I don't want none of them *quinto* beans : boys I
    don't want no more
14 I don't want none of them *quinto* beans : they
    about to make my stomach sore
15 I ate them last night : and the night before
16 Run to the little house in the back : couldn't shut
    the door

ChatB   8   Chatman, Bo

       title: Tellin' You 'Bout It
       place and date: San Antonio, 26 Mar. 1934
       record numbers: (82616-1) BB-B5629 Yz L-1014

1   When a man gets the blues : he sure will run around
2   And when a woman gets the blues : she try to put her
    sweety down
3   Let me tell you one thing : man don't you never do
4   Don't you never let your woman : know her bad ways
    is worrying you
5   Listen here sweet babe : one thing I want you to
    know
6   If I don't do to suit you : I'm really going to let
    you go
7   One more thing : I really want you to understand
8   If I don't love to suit you : you can get you
    another man

ChatB   8   Chatman, Bo

9   You can call me dirty : or any old thing you please
10 But some day baby : you really need my little aid

ChatB   9   Chatman, Bo

       title: Sales Tax
       place and date: San Antonio, 27 Mar. 1934
       record numbers: (82635-1) BB-B5453 Yz L-1014

1   These times now : ain't suiting me
2   *Account it* : costing a dollar three
3   Old Aunt Martha : live behind the jail
4   A sign on the wall : saying liquor for sale
5   I never seen : the likes since I been born
6   The women got the sales tax : on the South End home
7   You used to buy it : for a dollar round
8   Now sales tax is on it : all over town
9   I'm as loving : as a woman can be
10 The stuff I've got : will cost you a dollar and
    three
11 Now you may take me : to be a fool
12 Everything is sold : by the government rule

ChatB   10   Chatman, Bo

       title: Let Me Roll Your Lemon
       place and date: New Orleans, 19 Jan. 1935
       record numbers: (87624-1) BB-B5861 Yz L-1034

1   Now listen here sweet baby : I never have been down
2   But I can roll your lemon better : than any man in
    this town
3   Baby please let me roll your lemon : and squeeze it
    the whole night long
4   Oh let me squeeze and roll your lemon : oh baby
    until your good juice come
5   There's some say your juice is sour : baby can't you
    see
6   But your juice baby : is plenty sweet enough for me
7   Now I just squeeze your lemon : baby one time
8   I believe it'll give me ease : baby all up in my
    mind
9   Says I come down last night : half past ten
10 I want to roll your lemon baby : soon as I got in
11 Says I woke up this morning : half past four
12 I want to roll your lemon baby : just before I go

ChatB   11   Chatman, Bo (Mississippi Sheiks)

       title: Howlin' Tom Cat Blues
       place and date: San Antonio, 27 Mar. 1934
       record numbers: (82630-1) BB-5536 Yz L-1034

1   Now don't you hear me mama : I'm begging at your
    door
2   Now I'm begging now mama : don't treat me this way
    no more
3   Says I'm here begging mama : down on my bended knees
4   I'm begging now mama : don't treat me this way no
    more if you please
5   Says [can't, don't] you hear me mama : rapping on
    your back door
6   But if I get what I want mama : I won't rap no more
7   Now don't you hear me mama : howling at your door
8   But if you give me what I want mama : you won't hear
    me rap no more
9   Now listen here mama : treat me in a lowdown way
10 But if I get what I want mama : you'll see me walk
    away
11 I'm at your door howling : like an old tomcat
12 But most any man now : will howl about something
    like that

ChatB 12   Chatman, Bo

    title: I Get the Blues
    place and date: New Orleans, 20 Feb. 1936
    record numbers: (99235-1) BB-B6589 Yz L-1034

1 Now listen here sweet baby : please listen to me
2 I know that your loving : is the best that I ever
   seen
3 Now listen here sweet baby : I really can't
   understand
4 Thinking about your loving : mixed with some other
   man

ChatB 13   Chatman, Bo

    title: Rolling Blues
    place and date: New Orleans, 20 Feb. 1936
    record numbers: (99237-1) BB-B6373 Yz L-1034

1 Now listen here women : I want you to know
2 I've got a new woman : just to roll my dough
3 She roll me every morning : she roll me every night
4 She never like to roll me : unless she roll me just
   right
5 Now listen here baby : I want you to know
6 It's no other woman : can do my rolling like you
7 She shook me this morning : at half past one
8 Oh wake up daddy : rolling must go on
9 She shook me again : at half past two
10 Oh wake up daddy : rolling ain't near through
11 She don't roll it too high : or either too low
12 She roll it good and easy : and it ain't too slow

ChatB 14   Chatman, Bo

    title: All Around Man
    place and date: New Orleans, 20 Feb. 1936
    record numbers: (99238-1) BB-B6295 Mel MLP-7324

1 Now I ain't no butcher : no butcher's son
2 I can do your cutting : until the butcher man comes
3 Now I ain't no plumber : no plumber's son
4 I can do your screwing : till the plumber man comes
5 Now I ain't no miller : no miller's son
6 I can do your grinding : till the miller-man comes
7 Now I ain't no milkman : no milkman's son
8 I can pull your titties : till the milkman comes
9 Now I ain't no spring-man : no spring-man's son
10 I can bounce your springs : till the spring-man
   comes
11 Now I ain't no auger-man : no auger-man's son
12 I can bore your hole : till the auger-man comes

ChatB 15   Chatman, Bo

    title: Dinner Blues
    place and date: New Orleans, 20 Feb. 1936
    record numbers: (99242-1) BB-B6407 Yz L-1014

1 I asked my good girl : to feed me some
2 She said wait : until my dinner get on
3 Dinner got on : and she fed me some
4 Now you know : we're carrying the good work on
5 I asked the good girl : to give me some
6 She said wait : until my dinner get on
7 Dinner got on : and she give me some
8 Now you know : we're carrying the good work on
9 I asked the good girl : to squeeze me some
10 She said wait : until my dinner get on
11 Dinner got on : and she squeezed me some
12 Now you know : we're carrying the good work on
13 I asked the good girl : to kiss me some
14 She said wait : until my dinner get on
15 Dinner got on : and she kissed me some
16 Now you know : we're carrying the good work on

ChatB 15   Chatman, Bo

17 I asked the good girl : to love me some
18 She said wait : until my dinner get on
19 Dinner got on : and then she love me some
20 Now you know : we're carrying the good work on

ChatB 16   Chatman, Bo

    title: Cigarette Blues
    place and date: New Orleans, 20 Feb. 1936
    record numbers: (99244-1) BB-B6295 RBF RF-14

1 Says now come over here sweet baby : because I'm all
   alone
2 Haven't got nobody : just to carry my smoking on
3 Won't you just draw on my cigarette : smoke it the
   whole night long
4 Just draw on my cigarette baby : until you make my
   good ashes come
5 Now I got to go up the country : just to get my
   cigarette boiled
6 The women around this place : going to let my
   cigarette spoil
7 I come over here sweet baby : just to get my ashes
   hauled
8 Lord the women at the other place : going to let my
   ashes spoil
9 Here's one thing I want you to know : before you
   leave from home
10 My cigarette ain't too big : and you know it ain't
   too long

ChatB 17   Chatman, Bo

    title: Pussy Cat Blues
    place and date: New Orleans, 15 Oct. 1936
    record numbers: (02613-1) BB-B6735 Yz L-1034

1 Oh pussy cat pussy cat : where you been so long
2 Says I been around *the curve* : see could I find
   old Tom
3 Says pussy cat pussy cat : you couldn't not wait
4 You's afraid : old Tommy's going to make you late
5 Oh pussy cat pussy cat : what you whine all night
6 Says ain't old Tommy : doing you just right
7 Says the old cats and the kittens : is sitting in
   the sun
8 Says the old cats coughed : and the kittens all run
9 Says the little bitty kittens : come out the door
   a-saying
10 Baby I hear mama coughing : it's bound to be a *ben*
11 She dug a hole : with her right hand
12 And she buried her *corky* : down in the sand
13 Old Tom and old pussy cat : playing seven up
14 Old pussy turned the joker : and picked the money up
15 They had a mighty fight : and not much of a race
16 Old Tommy scratched pussy : in a dangerous place
17 Says the little bitty kittens : says papa Uncle Bud
18 Says all around your mouth : is something like mud

ChatB 18   Chatman, Bo

    title: The Ins and Outs of My Girl
    place and date: New Orleans, 15 Oct. 1936
    record numbers: (02614-1) BB-B7213 Yz L-1014

1 Says my baby got something : I don't know what it is
2 I mean every time she love me: and you know I can't
   be still
3 She got something : like a stingaree
4 She can stand in Melford : man and put the check on
   me
5 What she got : is really surprise
6 I mean what she got man : surely will hypnotize
7 She told me things : that was a fact

ChatB 18   Chatman, Bo

  8 She said man if you ever love me : you surely will
      trot along back
  9 She got something : that I really do love
 10 It ain't in her stockings : and you know it's just
      above
 11 I told her things : that I wanted her to und
 12 Says I want you to come : and do my loving in my own
      home

ChatB 19   Chatman, Bo

     title: Bo Carter's Advice
     place and date: New Orleans, 15 Oct. 1936
     record numbers: (02616-1) BB-B7073 Yz L-1014

  1 Now listen here men : what Bo Carter say for you to
      do
  2 Says don't you never let none of these old trifling
      women : man never worry you
  3 I mean they'll keep you worried : they'll bother you
      all the time
  4 Says they'll take some other man and leave you :
      after you give them your last dime
  5 I mean they'll fuss and squabble : man the whole
      night through
  6 Just let you know they want some other man now : go
      in the bed in the place of you
  7 Says when you say you going to leave them : they'll
      beg you the whole night long
  8 Says they'll tell you that they're going to do
      better : they'll swear they going to stay home
  9 Now just listen here men : want you take Bo Carter's
      advice
 10 Just learn to live a bachelor : then you play safe
      the first

ChatB 20   Chatman, Bo

     title: Double Up in a Knot
     place and date: New Orleans, 15 Oct. 1936
     record numbers: (02617-1) BB-B6659 Yz L-1034

  1 Go down the river : there's something new
  2 It ain't nothing to it : it ain't hard to do
  3 Now listen here baby : this is coming to a test
  4 We going to see : who can double in a knot the best
  5 Now listen here baby : this ain't no fun
  6 Double in a knot : you'll always get my mon'
  7 Say you double in a knot : is the way
  8 You can't make no money : laying straight these days
  9 You can double in a knot : or you can let it be
 10 You want to : hold your man you see
 11 Now listen here baby : bear this in mind
 12 You double in a knot right : you'll always have a
      dime
 13 Says the women these days : trying to learn
      something new
 14 See if they can : take your man from you

ChatB 21   Chatman, Bo

     title: Your Biscuits Are Big Enough for Me
     place and date: New Orleans, 15 Oct. 1936
     record numbers: (02619-1) BB-B8159 Yz L-1014

  1 Baby don't put no more baking powder : in your bread
      you see
  2 Because you [two] biscuits : is plenty tall enough
      for me
  3 Baby I don't want no more sugar : in your jellyroll
      you see
  4 Because your jellyroll : is plenty sweet enough for
      me

ChatB 21   Chatman, Bo

  5 Some men like lunch meat : and some they likes old
      tongue
  6 Some men don't care for biscuits : they like the
      doggone big fat bun
  7 Says some men you know they're straight : some
      crooked as a barrel of snakes
  8 Some men don't like bun and biscuits : like the
      doggone flat batter cake

ChatB 22   Chatman, Bo

     title: Sue Cow
     place and date: New Orleans, 15 Oct. 1936
     record numbers: (02624-1) BB-B6695 OJL-18

  1 Little boy little boy : who made your britches
  2 Oh mama cut them out : daddy runned the stitches
  3 Little girl little girl : who made your dress
  4 Hey mama cut it out : and daddy done the rest
  5 Soo cow : don't you buck your eye
  6 I got to have the milk today : to make me a pie
  7 Soo cow : won't you back your leg
  8 I got to have that milk today : to make my bread

ChatB 23   Chatman, Bo

     title: Shake 'Em On Down
     place and date: San Antonio, 22 Oct. 1938
     record numbers: (027869-1) BB-B7927 Yz L-1034

  1 Say you laying around here sweet baby : your face
      full of frowns
  2 Must I keep dealing : must I shuck them on down
  3 Baby must I keep dealing : or must I shuck them on
      down
  4 Baby I done quit dealing : I got to shuck them on
      down
  5 Now here's one thing sweet baby : I really want you
      to know
  6 You can push you can pull : don't you tear my
      clothes
  7 Now there's two big cars : rolling side and side
  8 You got my good girl : guess you satisfied
  9 Now there's a big T for Texas : T for Tennessee
 10 T for the girl : she didn't care for me
 11 Says I went up to the station : looks up on the
      board
 12 There's a good time here : better one around the
      road

ChatB 24   Chatman, Bo

     title: Who's Been Here?
     place and date: San Antonio, 22 Oct. 1938
     record numbers: (027873-1) BB-B7927 Yz L-1014

  1 Baby who been here : since your daddy been gone
  2 Says he must have been a preacher daddy : had a long
      coat on
  3 Baby who been here : since you daddy been gone
  4 I don't know who the man was daddy : had a derby on
  5 Baby who been here : since you daddy been gone
  6 Says he must have been a jellybean : had long shoes
      on
  7 Baby preacher's on the pulpit : just trying to save
      souls
  8 And his daughter's out on the highway corner :
      selling sweet jellyroll
  9 And the preacher's in the pulpit : jumping up and
      down
 10 And the sisters back in the amen corner : their
      southern bound

ChatB 25   Chatman, Bo

      title: Let's Get Drunk Again
      place and date: San Antonio, 22 Oct. 1938
      record numbers: (027876-1) BB-B8045 Yz L-1014

1 Baby I got the whiskey : and you got the gin
2 Let's both baby drink : and get drunk again
3 Hey whiskey : uh what you say gin
4 Let's both baby drink : and get drunk again
5 It don't make me no difference : how drunk you may
   be
6 Since you don't hold back baby : honey in loving me
7 Hey I got the washboard : and you got the tub
8 Let's put them together : baby and we'll
   rub-a-dub-dub
9 Hey washboard : what you say tub
10 Let's put them together : baby and we'll
   rub-a-dub-dub
11 It don't make me no difference : how tired you may
   be
12 Since you don't hold back baby : honey in rubbing
   with me

ChatB 26   Chatman, Bo

      title: Some Day
      place and date: San Antonio, 22 Oct. 1938
      record numbers: (027877-1) BB-B8147 Yz L-1034

1 Baby I say you going to need : my little help some
   old lonesome day
2 But it will be too late sweet baby : your daddy will
   be gone away
3 But I mean that's all right now baby : honey now
   that's all right for you
4 You got me here in all this lowdown trouble : baby
   and this lowdown way that you do

ChatB 27   Chatman, Bo

      title: Old Devil
      place and date: San Antonio, 22 Oct. 1938
      record numbers: (027878-1) BB-B8093 Yz L-1007

1 Go back old devil : and look up on your shelf
2 And get you soap and water : and bathe your dirty
   self
3 I beat my baby : man with a rope and a line
4 : until she went stone blind
5 Some lowdown scoundrel : been fishing in my pond
6 Catching all my game fish : and grinding up their
   bones
7 What you want with a woman : man and she can't rob
   and steal
8 You don't need no man baby : don't know you in the
   dark when he feel

ChatB 28   Chatman, Bo

      title: Country Fool
      place and date: San Antonio, 22 Oct. 1938
      record numbers: (027879-1) BB-B8122 Yz L-1014

1 I says he's a country man : but that fool done moved
   to town
2 He really done sold his cotton : and now he's
   walking around
3 He's got the women : all calling him their old sugar
   pie
4 But now that country fool is broke : and they
   calling him the old country guy
5 He really wore a hole : in the bottom of his last
   pair of shoes
6 And his pants behind is hollering : I got those
   raggedy-holey blues

ChatB 28   Chatman, Bo

7 He's got to rob and steal : don't he got to leave
   out of this man's town
8 Know he'll say going back to the country : going to
   sow some more cotton seed down

ChatB 29   Chatman, Bo

      title: Arrangement for Me--Blues
      place and date: Atlanta, 12 Feb. 1940
      record numbers: (047647-1) BB-B8397 Yz L-1014

1 Baby I'll split your kindling : you know I'll bellow
   your fire
2 I will pack your water : from the boggy bayou
3 Hey now tell me sweet baby : who may your manager be
4 Before many more questions : won't you please make
   arrangements for me
5 Your hair so doggone curly : and your eyes ain't
   blue
6 That's why sweet baby : I'm making a fool about you
7 Says I ain't good-looking : baby I don't dress fine
8 When you come to loving : I'll pacify your mind
9 Here's another little thing baby : want you to bear
   in mind
10 When I get my pay check: I give you my last dime
11 I wished I was like a little fish : in the deep blue
   sea
12 So a woman like you : could take a little fish at me

ChatB 30   Chatman, Bo

      title: My Baby
      place and date: Atlanta, 12 Feb. 1940
      record numbers: (047652-1) BB-B8495 Yz L-1034

1 I taken my baby : to the candy stand
2 She got stuck : on the candy man
3 I taken my baby : to the candy stand
4 She got a fool : about the candy man
5 I taken my baby : to the peanut stand
6 She got a fool : about the old [nut, peanut] man
7 I taken my baby : to the banana stand
8 She got a fool : about the banana man
9 I taken my baby : to the whiskey stand
10 She fell on her face : about the whiskey man
11 I taken my baby : to the whiskey stand
12 She fell out : about the whiskey man
13 I taken my baby : to the money stand
14 She fell on her face : about the moneyman

ChatB 31   Chatman, Bo

      title: Policy Blues
      place and date: Atlanta, 12 Feb. 1940
      record numbers: (047653-1) BB-B8495 Yz L-1034

1 Hey I wonder : where is that policy right man [at]
   now
2 I done lose all my money shooting craps : and I
   can't win no money nohow
3 I'm going to put my last dime : on the twenty thirty
   and the little old ten
4 Because they tell me that's my baby's initial : and
   it ought bring my money back home again
5 I'm going to play them straight across : man you
   know [I'm playing, I got] them straight down
6 Now policy man my number's done come out : bring me
   twenty-seven dollars on around
7 I'm going to put a four bit piece : back on the
   twenty thirty and the little old ten
8 And if them numbers come out man : it'll bring my
   money back right again
9 Policy man if my numbers come out : don't fool
   around on the street

ChatB 31   Chatman, Bo

10 Just cut across on St Lawrence Avenue : and bring my
    money on home to me

ChatB 32   Chatman, Bo

    title: Honey
    place and date: Atlanta, 12 Feb. 1940
    record numbers: (047657-1) BB-B8555 Yz L-1034

1 Now it don't make no difference sweet little old
   honey : a-how you trying to carry on
2 A-what you trying to do to me honey : I happen to
   have it in my bag
3 Now it don't make a bit of difference with me honey
   : things you trying To do to me
4 A-what you trying to do to me honey : I happen to
   have it in my bag
5 Now you may go honey you may go : you may stray all
   alone
6 But one of these days now little old sweet honey :
   you'll be out of house and home
7 Now you trying to do little dirty things honey : and
   keep it out of your daddy's sight
8 You fool right around now little old honey : and let
   me catch you dead to the right

ChatL 1   Chatman, Lonnie (Mississippi Sheiks)

    title: It's a Pain to Me
    place and date: Grafton, Wis., c. July 1932
    record numbers: (L-1545-2) Pm-13143 Bio
    BLP-12041

1 I've had a funny feeling : all day and all night
2 Somehow here : I don't be treated just right
3 I ain't going to stay here today : if I have to walk
4 Ever since I been here : it's been the whole town's
   talk
5 I don't seem happy no more : I done got it bad
6 Thinking of the money : that I once have had
7 Now when you lose your money : don't lose your mind
8 If you lose your good girl : there's no use a-crying
9 I've had so much trouble : I've take it for my name
10 If you ever have trouble : man I want you to do the
   same
11 You will think : you left trouble all behind
12 Get well away from home : then it will roll across
   your mind

ChatL 2   Chatman, Lonnie (Mississippi Sheiks)

    title: New Sittin' On Top of the World
    place and date: Grafton, Wis., c. July 1932
    record numbers: (L-1556-2) Pm-13134 Bio
    BLP-12041

1 Made a date today : early or late
2 My baby got movements : like a old Cadillac Eight
3 I go away : I won't stay long
4 Thinking about that sweet thing : I've left at home
5 My baby loves me : tried to treat me right
6 Gives me her loving : both day and night
7 My baby says one thing : I know it is true
8 Can't have another man : and be good to you
9 Up in Chicago : long way from home
10 Wanted somebody else : carry my loving on
11 I'm going home : if I had a lock and key
12 To keep these men : from stealing my loving from me

ChatL 3   Chatman, Lonnie (Mississippi Sheiks)

    title: Please Baby
    place and date: Grafton, Wis., c. July 1932
    record numbers: (L-1562-2) Pm-13153 Bio
    BLP-12041

1 Please baby please baby : won't you come back to
   your daddy one more time
2 You know baby you know baby : when I get my money
   will give you my last dime
3 When you left me babe : you left me feeling so blue
4 You know babe : I didn't love no one but you
5 I'm so blue baby I'm so blue baby : I can't sleep
   for drinking hardly talk for crying
6 You know baby you know baby : you are always forever
   on my mind
7 You know baby : I can't sleep at night
8 I go to take my meals : and can't eat a bite

ChatP 1   Chatman, Peter

    title: Beer Drinking Woman
    place and date: Chicago, 30 Oct. 1940
    record numbers: (053590-1) BB-B8584 RCA-730.581

1 I walked into a beer tavern : to give a girl a nice
   time
2 I had forty-five dollars when I entered : when I
   left I had one dime
3 Wasn't that a beer-drinking woman : don't you know
   man don't you know
4 She was a beer-drinking woman : I don't want to see
   her no more
5 When I spent down to my last dime : she said darling
   I know you're not through
6 I told her yes baby doll : and the diploma belongs
   to you
7 She'd often say excuse me a minute : I've got to
   step around here
8 And every time she'd come back : she'd say daddy buy
   me another quart of beer
9 I said got to step off baby : are there anything if
   she like
10 She said daddy I'll keep this table : if you promise
   me you'll be back
11 I said I'm sorry baby : but I only have one more
   dime
12 She said daddy buy me a small bottle of beer : so I
   can concentrate my mind

ChatP 2   Chatman, Peter

    title: You Don't Mean Me No Good
    place and date: Chicago, 30 Oct. 1940
    record numbers: (053591-1) BB-B8615 RCA-730.581

1 I got wise to you baby : after so many years
2 Once you had me worried : always shedding tears
3 But no : all over now
4 I just found out baby : you don't mean no good nohow
5 I tried to make things happy : so we could live a
   happy life
6 But darling after all I done : you wouldn't treat me
   right
7 People used to ask you was I your husband : you
   would gladly tell them no
8 Every time we'd get home : you said daddy I love you
   so
9 Now you want to come back baby : since you realized
   yourself
10 That I would treat you better : anybody else

ChatP   3   Chatman, Peter

      title: Grinder Man Blues
      place and date: Chicago, 30 Oct. 1940
      record numbers: (053592-1) BB-B8584 RCA-730.581

1 My name is Memphis Slim : they call me the grinder man
2 If you be my customer : I'll let you have it on a easy plan
3 I do my ramming at midnight : and I don't be seen in the day
4 When everything is quiet and easy : Mr grinder can have his way
5 I got so many customers : it takes me a week to get around
6 But you need not be uneasy baby : Mr grinder won't let you down
7 If you want to see me baby : you better see me while you can
8 Because I'm a very busy fellow : you know they call me the grinder man

ChatP   4   Chatman, Peter

      title: Empty Room Blues
      place and date: Chicago, 30 Oct. 1940
      record numbers: (053593-1) BB-B8615 RCA-730.581

1 My room was empty : and my woman was gone
2 I didn't have a nickel : and all my clothes in pawn
3 I asked my next-door neighbor : which a-way did my baby go
4 She said she left for the border : down in old Mexico
5 I find a note on the floor : it almost send me off in a trance
6 She said it's nothing that you done : I'm just leaving in advance
7 It's so hard when a woman leave you : and she leave you on a *goon*
8 You come home feeling very happy : and find only a empty room

ChatP   5   Chatman, Peter

      title: I See My Great Mistake
      place and date: Chicago, 30 Oct. 1940
      record numbers: (053595-1) BB-B8645 RCA-730.581

1 I've got something to tell you baby : don't let it break your heart
2 So long together : now we've got to part
3 Because I'm tired : of fattening frogs for snakes
4 After these long many years : believe I just see my great mistake
5 You told me that you loved me : say you love me all your life
6 I caught you around the corner : telling that same lie twice
7 Once I used to love you : I couldn't help myself
8 Found out : you given your love baby to somebody else
9 Now listen little girl : you don't worry my mind anymore
10 Found out you acting funny : I'm sure going to let you go

ChatP   6   Chatman, Peter

      title: Old Taylor
      place and date: Chicago, 1 Apr. 1941
      record numbers: (059497-1) BB-B8903 RCA-730.581

1 Now I love to sing : that good old Taylor blues
2 When we want a drink : I swear we just can't lose

ChatP   6   Chatman, Peter

3 Now you see [Mr Melrose, that man] : standing in the floor
4 He going to give us a little drink : just before he go

ChatP   7   Chatman, Peter

      title: I Believe I'll Settle Down
      place and date: Chicago, 1 Apr. 1941
      record numbers: (059498-1) BB-B8903 RCA-730.581

1 I believe I'll marry : I believe I'll settle down
2 Lord I'm tired of being a rambler : my last trip of running around
3 Lord I wonder : will she ever call my name
4 Now if she don't love me no more : peoples ain't that a crying shame
5 They tell me marriage is a sweet life : I believe I'll try it myself
6 Lord I wonder : will she ever think of me
7 I'm sitting with my head bended down : and tears falling on my knee

ChatP   8   Chatman, Peter

      title: Jasper's Gal
      place and date: Chicago, 1 Apr. 1941
      record numbers: (059499-1) BB-B8749 RCA-730.581

1 How he's got a gal : she's shaped like a hog
2 Her voice remind me : of an awful dog
3 Her hair look just like : a chinchilla coat
4 You get close up on her : she smells just like a goat
5 You know she's smelling : got B O all the time
6 And she thinks soap and water : is a doggone crime
7 Now her ears are so long : her nose so flat
8 Her head so big : she can't wear no hat
9 Now her dogs are swollen : and she got one eye
10 She looks like a wreck : that happened last July
11 She's a ugly : got B O all the time
12 And she thinks soap and water : is a doggone crime
13 Now she must have been : her mother's only child
14 She should be a gorilla : because she sure is wild
15 Got ways like a monkey : as sly as a fox
16 She should be in a chain-gang : breaking up rocks
17 Now she got legs like a needle : she ain't got no chin
18 She's a beautiful woman : for the shape she's in
19 Her feet look like swings : way out on a limb
20 That's why : her mother put her off on him
21 Because she's buggish : she's got B O all the time
22 And she thinks soap and water : is a doggone crime

ChatP   9   Chatman, Peter

      title: You Got to Help Me Some
      place and date: Chicago, 1 Apr. 1941
      record numbers: (064000-1) BB-B8834 RCA-730.581

1 Now you may be sweet little woman : as an apple on a tree
2 Don't want no woman : to *lay* up and depend on me
3 Now if I'm the Pullman porter girl : you got to be the maid
4 So when every Saturday comes : we both can get paid
5 Now when I go to bed little girl : and lay beside of you
6 Now if I shake the cover : please try to shake it too
7 Now there's no such thing : as man and wife nowadays
8 We'll just call partners : so you cannot get sold for slaves

ChatP 10   Chatman, Peter

> title: Two of a Kind
> place and date: Chicago, 1 Apr. 1941
> record numbers: (064001-1) BB-B8749 RCA-730.581

1 Woman you been having your way : and you don't want
   to see me have mine
2 So there's no getting along : we're just two of the
   same old kind
3 I tried to make things happy : and your life I tried
   to let you enjoy
4 But you tell me you your mother's baby girl : do you
   realize I'm my mother's baby boy
5 Around home you was just a spoiled one : and what
   you said it had to be
6 But do you know that's the same old story : little
   girl really go for me
7 Since we are just two babies : darling why can't we
   agree
8 I'll talk baby-talk to you : if you'll talk
   baby-talk to me

ChatP 11   Chatman, Peter

> title: Maybe I'll Loan You a Dime
> place and date: Chicago, 1 Apr. 1941
> record numbers: (064003-1) BB-B8784 RCA-730.581

1 Now once I lived a life : of a millionaire
2 I was spending plenty of money : and I didn't bit
   more care
3 I was taking my boy friend out : for a good time
4 Buying him champaign whiskey : and sometime wine
5 But somehow or other : Lord my money ran low
6 Well well and I couldn't find a friend : I declare
   nowhere I go
7 Now if I ever get hold : to a dollar again
8 People I'm going to squeeze on to it : until the
   eagle grins
9 Now you got to be *deep* born blind : and cannot see
10 Both legs cut off : above your knee
11 All this must happen : and then I must agree
12 And then I said maybe boy friend : you can borrow a
   dime from me
13 Now you must not have : a tooth in your head
14 Get a letter from home : some of your folks is dead
15 Bring me the Titanic : that sailed the sea

ChatP 12   Chatman, Peter

> title: Me, Myself, and I
> place and date: Chicago, 1 Apr. 1941
> record numbers: (064004-1) BB-B8784 RCA-730.581

1 Everybody wants to know : how do Memphis slim get by
2 Well but it ain't but three in my family : that's me
   myself and I
3 Now my mother she told me : son just don't lead a
   doggone mule
4 She said son have good manners : learn to paddle
   your own canoe
5 Even my woman she asked me : daddy do you really
   love me
6 I said maybe some day baby : but now my love is just
   for three
7 She said daddy who is it please : with tears
   standing in her eye
8 I said baby at this particular time : it's just me
   myself and I

ChatP 13   Chatman, Peter

> title: Whiskey and Gin Blues
> place and date: Chicago, 4 Dec. 1941
> record numbers: (070434-1) BB-B8945 RCA-730.581

1 I've been out all day : drinking both whiskey and
   gin
2 Now if you catch me sober : please make me drunk
   again
3 I'm not drinking because I'm thirsty : neither
   because I'm blue
4 I've just got to stay drunk woman : to try to get
   along with you
5 Whiskey make me stagger and stumble : fall down and
   scar my chin
6 I know you ain't no good Mr whiskey : but I got to
   try you again
7 I'm drunk Monday Tuesday and Wednesday : Thursday
   Friday and Saturday too
8 I'm supposed to get drunk on a Sunday : as I have
   nothing else to do
9 Good whiskey good whiskey : is all in the world I
   crave
10 I'm going to drink good whiskey : the rest of my
   doggone days

ChatP 14   Chatman, Peter

> title: You Gonna Worry Too
> place and date: Chicago, 4 Dec. 1941
> record numbers: (070435-1) BB-B8945 RCA-730.581

1 I'm down now baby : I'll be up some day
2 And I won't have to put up : with your evil ways
3 But there's a day coming baby : you going to worry
   too
4 Lord and I won't have to put up : with the lowdown
   way you do
5 You know I done : woman all in this world I could
6 But I found out baby : you didn't mean no good
7 You know I loved you : babe you breaking my heart
8 It hurts me so bad : for us to part
9 Now I'm not going to worry : my sweet life no more
10 You been making your tip woman : I'm going to let
   you go
11 So bye bye babe : if you call it gone
12 I know it's going to worry me : but it won't last
   long

ChatP 15   Chatman, Peter

> title: Caught the Old Coon at Last
> place and date: Chicago, 4 Dec. 1941
> record numbers: (070437-1) BB-B8974 RCA-730.581

1 Here I am : head over heels in love again
2 Besides the woman was my mother : and that's where
   love begins
3 I used to be a playboy : I played out both night and
   day
4 But since I met Miss *Lamar* : she have made me
   change my ways
5 Oh yes woman : you've caught the old coon at last
6 But I just hope I'll be happy with my future : as I
   am with my present and past
7 Now I love the life I'm living : and I'm living the
   life I love
8 Woman I don't believe I could be any happier : if I
   were living in heaven above

ChatP 16   Chatman, Peter

    title: Lend Me Your Love
    place and date: Chicago, 4 Dec. 1941
    record numbers: (070439-1) BB-B9028 RCA-730.581

1 Now lend me your love : baby please lend me your
   love
2 I know you hear me keep moaning : just like Noah's
   dove
3 You got a mortgage on my love : you know there
   really is no doubt
4 But some day I'm going to find another woman : is
   going to buy your love mortgage out

Chur   1   Church, Blind Clyde

    title: Number Nine Blues
    place and date: Memphis, 30 Sept. 1929
    record numbers: (56307) Vi-23271 Rt RL-329

1 Down on Number Nine : where the M and M men go
2 Every day : to have a real good time
3 If you want some fun : and a real nice time
4 You better join the boys and girls : down on old
   Number Nine
5 Do that dance : they call the bedspring *pop*
6 You can shut your eyes : begin reel and rock
7 All you've got to do : is take your time
8 Drink good whiskey : gin and wine

Chur   2   Church, Blind Clyde

    title: Pneumatic Blues
    place and date: Memphis, 30 Sept. 1929
    record numbers: (56308) Vi-23271 Rt RL-329

1 You can go to the ocean : you can go to the deep
   blue sea
2 But you can't find nobody : going to treat you like
   poor me
3 You can spend my money : you can pawn my *sicking*
   clothes
4 Catch you stooping : I'm going to let your meat
   outdoors
5 Well the sun's going down : mama you know what you
   promised me
6 Midnight supper : and my 'fore-day tea
7 Leaving your town : mama and I sure don't want to go
8 But to keep down trouble : mama guess I better go

ClaL   1   Clark, Lonnie

    title: Broke Down Engine
    place and date: Richmond, Ind., 21 Sept. 1929
    record numbers: (15660) Pm-12871 Rt RL-340

1 If you ever been down mama : you know just how I
   feel
2 Just like a broke down engine : ain't got no driving
   wheel
3 Easy mama : somebody knocking at my door
4 It may be my yellow woman : mama you sure don't know
5 I love you pretty mama : I tell the world I do
6 I'm going to love you mama : till my dreams come
   true
7 If you want me to love you mama : have to do like
   Jesse James
8 Go out on some railroad track : and rob your daddy a
   passenger train

ClaL   2   Clark, Lonnie

    title: Down in Tennessee
    place and date: Richmond, Ind., 21 Sept. 1929
    record numbers: (15661) Pm-12871 Rt RL-340

1 I'm worried today mama : but I won't be worried long
2 I'm going to catch me a freight train : and I'm
   going to be long long gone
3 My woman got a bed mama : shine just like the
   morning star
4 When me and her get to laying in it : it ride like a
   Cadillac car
5 I'm going back south mama : way down in Tennessee
6 Know the woman I love : she sure was good to me
7 I cried last night mama : and I cried the night
   before
8 I ain't going to let you mistreat me mama : so I
   won't have to cry no more

ClayJ   1   Clayton, Jennie (Memphis Jug Band)

    title: I Packed My Suitcase, Started to the
    Train
    place and date: Atlanta, 19 Oct. 1927
    record numbers: (40312-1) Vi-21412 Rt RL-311

1 It is up to you baby : do anything that you want to
   do
2 *So long as I can get ??? : get back out of you*
3 You ought to be grateful daddy : ???
4 You are three times seven : you know just what you
   want to do

ClayJ   2   Clayton, Jennie (Memphis Jug Band)

    title: State of Tennessee Blues
    place and date: Atlanta, 19 Oct. 1927
    record numbers: (40313-2) Vi-21185 Rt RL-322

1 I'm worried now : and I won't be worried long
2 If he don't come to see me : you can count the days
   I'm gone
3 Some sweet day : I say it's after a while
4 You having a good time now : but your troubles will
   be after a while
5 When I leave this town : don't pin black crepe on my
   door
6 I won't be dead baby : but I ain't coming back here
   no more
7 I want all of you women : to strictly understand
8 If you don't want no trouble : please don't you
   worry my man

ClayJ   3   Clayton, Jennie (Memphis Jug Band)

    title: Bob Lee Junior Blues
    place and date: Atlanta, 19 Oct. 1927
    record numbers: (40314-2) Vi-21412 Fwy FA-2953

1 I can't sleep for dreaming : and I can't stay awake
   for crying
2 Cried the man I love : said he's traveling on the
   line
3 If my man could holler : like the Bob Lee Junior
   blows
4 I would follow my daddy : most everywhere he goes
5 And I asked the conductor : to let me ride the
   blinds
6 He said buy you a ticket : you know this train ain't
   mine
7 Oh I hate the train : that carried my man away
8 But the same train carried him : going to bring him
   back some day

61

Clev   1   Cleveland, Big Boy

        title: Goin' to Leave You Blues
        place and date: Chicago or Richmond, Ind.,
            12 Apr. 1927
        record numbers: (12700) Ge-6108 His HLP-22

1   The train I ride : burn no coal at all
2   But the *doggone engine* : pull my *Texas haul*
3   I'm going away : to wear you off my mind
4   Keep me worried : bothered all the time
5   I hate to see : the evening sun go down
6   Make me feel : that I'm on my last go-round
7   My mama told me : papa told me too
8   Don't you let no woman : make a fatmouth out of you
9   I'm leaving here : crying won't make me stay
10 The more you cry : the further I'm going away
12 Train's down here : track's all out of line

ColeJ   1   Cole, James

        title: Mistreated the Only Friend You Had
        place and date: Richmond, Ind., 16 Jan. 1932
        record numbers: (18324) Ch-16718 Rt RL-311

1   Mistreat me baby : mistreat your only friend
2   Mistreat me baby : sure going to do it again
3   I'm going to the river : sit right on the ground
4   If the blues overtake me : jump overboard and drown
5   Going to buy a shotgun : long as I am tall
6   I'm going to shoot my baby : just to see her fall

ColeK   1   Cole, Kid

        title: Hard Hearted Mama Blues
        place and date: Chicago, c. June 1928
        record numbers: (C-1997-1) Vo-1187 Rt RL-313

1   Oh now it's loving : really really wor-worrying me
2   And that cruel-hearted loving : it's going to be the
        death of me
3   Prison : sure don't want to make it my home
4   I'm a good-hearted poor boy : just a long way from
        home
5   Tell me cruel-hearted mama : what's on your
        hard-hearted mind
6   Say you keep me in trouble : so worried and bothered
        all the time
7   And I love my little baby : tell you just how I know
8   I will work rob and steal for her : baby in the
        frosty snow
9   And it's blues : woke me for my telephone
10 I got a long-distance call from my baby : daddy I
        ain't coming back home
11 The two women I'm loving : they keep bothering my
        heart
12 That's one in Cincinnati : my Waco wife that broke
        my heart
13 Tell me cruel-hearted mama : what you want your
        daddy to do
14 I'd rather see you murder me : baby and to leave me
        too
15 And I'm going away : little baby crying it won't be
        long
16 Said take your Bible pretty mama : and read the days
        your daddy's gone

ColeK   2   Cole, Kid

        title: Niagara Fall Blues
        place and date: Chicago, c. June 1928
        record numbers: (C-1998-1) Vo-1187 Rt RL-313

1   I got the Niagara Falls blues : pretty mama keeps
        a-worrying you

ColeK   2   Cole, Kid

2   And those Niagara Falls blues pretty mama : going to
        be the death of you
3   I walked down my pantry : I walked back up my hall
4   I stuck my head over the transom : another mule was
        in my stall
5   I got the blues so bad : that it hurts my tongue to
        talk
6   I got the blues so bad : that it hurts my baby's
        feet to walk
7   Now it's run to your window : heist your shade up
        high
8   It's stick your head out the window : see the
        worried blues pass by
9   I looked down the lonesome road pretty mama : far as
        I could see
10 Another man had my wife : and I swear the Niagara
        blues had me
11 I got the blues in a bottle : got the rattlesnake in
        my hand
12 How can I live in this world babe : my baby with
        another man
13 Now it's run here sweet mama : I'm [about to,
        certainly going to] get you told
14 You ain't the onliest woman in Cincinnati : got such
        a loving jellyroll
15 And I woke up this morning : my pillow slip wringing
        wet
16 I looked around for my baby : daddy I can't use you
        yet

ColFB   1   Coleman, Bob

        title: Sing Song Blues
        place and date: Richmond, Ind., 7 June 1929
        record numbers: (15167) Pm-12791 Rt RL-340

1   If you ever been down mama : you know just how [I, a
        prisoner] feel
2   I ain't got nobody on the outside : *to play in the
        field*
3   And I laid in prison : my face turned to the wall
4   Says a no-good crow-jane woman : was the cause of it
        all
5   And it's a many old day : I drop my weary head and
        cry
6   I did not have no blues : but little mama just
        wasn't satisfied
7   It's pull on your race horse : bet on your derby too
8   I ain't got nobody in this world : will do love me
        true
9   And I locked in the death cell : and drop my weary
        head and cried
10 I told the sing sing prison board : this ain't like
        being outside
11 And if if hadn't been for you little mama : I
        wouldn't not been here
12 I drinking wine and whiskey : mama and your
        home-brewed beer

ColFJ   1   Coleman, Jaybird

        title: Man Trouble Blues
        place and date: Birmingham, Ala., c. 3 Aug. 1927
        record numbers: (GEX-771) Ge-6245 OJL-8

1   When a man gets in trouble : every woman throws him
        down
3   I'm so worried : don't know what to do
4   I waked up this morning : mama feeling sad and blue
5   Because my woman had done quit me : didn't have
        nowhere to go
7   Hey hey : hey hey hey
8   When I'm in my good whiskey : this is the way I sing
        my blues

ColFJ 2   Coleman, Jaybird

    title: No More Good Water
    place and date: Birmingham, Ala., c. 11 Aug.
    1927
    record numbers: (GEX-800) Ge-6276 OJL-14

1 Says there's no more good water : because this pond
   is dry
3 I walked down to the river : then turned around and
   run
5 If the fishes in the water had my blues : they'd die
7 Got a head full of foolishness : my baby got a
   rambling mind
9 Hey pretty mama : tell me what have you done

ColFJ 3   Coleman, Jaybird

    title: Mistreatin' Mama
    place and date: Birmingham, Ala., c. 11 Aug.
    1927
    record numbers: (GEX-801-A) BP-8052 OJL-14

1 I done told you mama : ain't going to tell you no
   more
3 Now the blues so worrisome mama : between midnight
   and day
4 Now the blues done caused my woman : hon' to run
   away
6 Lord I can't *let its* continue : don't care what I
   do

ColFJ 4   Coleman, Jaybird

    title: Save Your Money--Let These Women Go
    place and date: Birmingham, Ala., c. 11 Aug.
    1927
    record numbers: (GEX-802-B) BP-8052 Rt RL-313

1 Mama told me : six long weeks ago
2 Son you save your money : just to buy your clothes
3 Buy your clothes : let these women go
5 Hey hey mama : what is going on wrong
6 Spend my woman's money : mama and she won't come
7 Can't rest contented : don't care where I go
9 You're a mean mama : whispering in your ear

ColFJ 5   Coleman, Jaybird

    title: Coffee Grinder Blues
    place and date: Atlanta, 22 Apr. 1930
    record numbers: (150360-2) Co-14534-D Yz L-1006

1 I'm going to grind my coffee : two or three dollars
   a pound
2 Ain't a man in this town : can grind this coffee
   like mine
3 It done got so good : that it make you bite your
   tongue
4 I'm a coffee-grinding fool : now let me grind you
   some

ColFJ 6   Coleman, Jaybird

    title: Man Trouble Blues
    place and date: Atlanta, 22 Apr. 1930
    record numbers: (150631-1) Co-14534-D Rt RL-313

1 Trouble worried trouble : I been having all my days
3 When a man gets in trouble : every woman throws him
   down
5 I woke up Lord this morning : *things are worrying
   on a-* poor me
7 Then I went upstairs : fell down across my bed

ColFJ 6   Coleman, Jaybird

8 Now my baby has a-quit me : talked all out of my
   head

ColFL 1   Coleman, Lonnie

    title: Old Rock Island Blues
    place and date: Atlanta, 12 Apr. 1929
    record numbers: (148258-2) Co-14440-D RBF RF-15

1   I've got the Rock Island blues : waiting for the
    Rock Island train
2   I took the Rock Island train : and take a Rock
    Island ride somewhere
3   I've got a free transportation : looking for the
    train to ride
4   I need to ride the Rock Island : *just riding to
    satisfy*
5   If you ever been down : you know just how I feel
6   I'm going away : *I come* to get on board
7   Leaving : hang crepe on your door
8   I've got the rickets and the rackets : and my baby's
    got the Mobile blues
9   I've got the Rock Island blues : and I don't know
    what to do
10 One thing about these women : I cannot understand
11 All wear short dresses : trying to fool a workingman
12 Baby if anyone should ask you : who composed this
    song
13 Just tell Lonnie Coleman : done been to your town
    and gone

ColFL 2   Coleman, Lonnie

    title: Wild About My Loving
    place and date: Atlanta, 12 Apr. 1929
    record numbers: (148259-2) Co-14440-D Rt RL-318

1   Wild about my loving : *crazy deeds* I have my fun
2   And if you want me to love you : don't pretend you
    never done
3   I ain't rough : I don't bite
4   ??? *womens* : don't you treat me right
5   Baby come right in : coming right at me
6   I can *catch those* ??? : ??? *at the Santa Fe*
7   You know I been out east : been out west
8   Hard to tell : which mamas love the best
9   *Turkey's for some* : ??? *France*
10 Where the men in Texas going : it seems just the
    same
11 Now there's two things about : I just can't
    understand
12 A *cawdy-cawdy* husband : ??? *scrubby* man
13 Well I'm going out the country : and I can't carry
    you
14 Nothing up the country : monkey-man can do

CollC 1   Collins, Chasey

    title: Walking Blues
    place and date: Chicago, 31 Oct. 1935
    record numbers: (96248-1) BB-B6261 Rt RL-316

1 You can mistreat me here : but you can't when I go
   home
2 I got somebody there : will make you leave me alone
3 Walk on : walk on little girl walk on
4 Say you going to keep on walking : till you lose
   your happy home
5 And you know you didn't love me : you fell across my
   bed
6 Full of your moonshine whiskey : mama talking all
   out of you head
7 Say I walked around to my window : and I peeped
   right through my blinds

CollC   1   Collins, Chasey

8   I seen another darky : trying to change my woman's
    mind

CollC   2   Collins, Chasey

        title: Atlanta Blues
        place and date: Chicago, 31 Oct. 1935
        record numbers: (96249-1) BB-B6187 BC-6

1   When I find a town : that will satisfy my mind
2   Tell you that's where I'll be : for a great long
    time
3   When I get to Atlanta : walk on Decatur Street
4   I'm going to shimmy-shee-wobble : with every fair
    brown I meet
5   I got a woman named Miss Hattie : she lives on
    Fourteenth Street
6   Oh the way that woman love me : I swear she can't be
    beat
7   I done spent all of my money : my bank account run
    low
8   My woman had the nerve to tell me : daddy aren't you
    spending slow
9   Says my mama's dead : and my daddy's in the mines
10 And I'm a motherless child : and I just can't keep
    from crying

CollS   1   Collins, Sam

        title: The Jail House Blues
        place and date: Richmond, Ind., c. 23 Apr. 1927
        record numbers: (12736) Ge-6167 OJL-2

1   When I was lying in jail : with my back turned to
    the wall
2   I could lay down and dream : I could hear my good
    gal squall
3   Lord she brought me coffee : and she brought me tea
4   Fell dead on the floor : with the jailhouse key
5   I'm going down to the courthouse : see the judge and
    the chief police
6   My good gal fell dead : now I sure can't see no
    peace
7   I'll tell you what I'll do : and I sure God ain't
    going to tell no lie
8   I believe I'll lay down : take morphine and die

CollS   2   Collins, Sam

        title: Devil in the Lion's Den
        place and date: Richmond, Ind., c. 23 Apr. 1927
        record numbers: (12737-A) Ge-6181 OJL-10

1   Now my mama's dead : and my papa can't be found
2   I ain't got nobody : throw my arms around
3   Yonder comes the devil : going to set this town on
    fire
4   Now when the chance comes up : I'm going to bid this
    town goodbye
5   I got ways like the devil : slipping around your
    gate
6   So I can find me a good gal : or won't have to take
    no *hate*
7   Let me tell you mama : what you said last night
8   Lay down on my bedside : try to treat me right
9   Lord I'm going up the country : but crying won't
    make me stay
10 More you cry : the farer I'll ride away

CollS   3   Collins, Sam

        title: Yellow Dog Blues
        place and date: Richmond, Ind., c. 23 Apr. 1927
        record numbers: (12738) Ge-6146 OJL-10

1   Easy mama : don't fade away
2   I'm going : where the Drummond cross the Yellow Dog
3   Lord I'm freezing here : with *you a-fighting all
    around the hall*
4   And I felt so rotten : and I didn't want to ride no
    train
5   I want to ride the Yellow Dog : where way out in the
    ???
6   I sat deep in my saddle : and I don't *remember the
    name*
7   Sat deep in my saddle Lord : and I ??? *name*
8   Just as sure as the train : leaves the rounded curve

CollS   4   Collins, Sam

        title: Loving Lady Blues
        place and date: Richmond, Ind., c. 23 Apr. 1927
        record numbers: (12739) Ge-6146 OJL-10

1   I never felt so worried : till I found the loving
    lady blues
3   I can't sleep for dreaming : I can't eat for crying
4   I lay down last night : with that gal all on my mind
5   I got nineteen bird dogs : got one floppy-eared
    hound
6   It just take those twenty : run my fair brown down
7   I got a good gal in town : but she don't treat me
    right
8   I feel like going to the cemetery : laying right
    down and die
9   Feel like going to the cemetery : laying right down
    and die
10 For I done got worried : with that gal of mine

CollS   5   Collins, Sam

        title: Riverside Blues
        place and date: Richmond, Ind., c. 23 Apr. 1927
        record numbers: (12740) Ge-6167 OJL-10

1   I went down to the river : just thirty-one days and
    nights
2   I'm looking for my good gal : come back and treat me
    right
3   I ain't got me nobody : carry my troubles to
4   I tell you peoples : I don't know what to do
5   Just as sure as your train : Lord backs up in your
    yard
6   I'm going to see my baby : if I have to ride the
    rods
7   I went away last summer : got back in the fall
8   My mind had a-changed : I wouldn't have come back at
    all
9   You can press my jumper : iron my overalls
10 I'm going to the station : meet the Cannonball

CollS   6   Collins, Sam

        title: Hesitation Blues
        place and date: Richmond, Ind., c. 17 Sept. 1927
        record numbers: (13033) Ge-6379 OJL-10

1   She has the hesitating stockings : the hesitating
    shoes
2   *The rich and the poor* : got the hesitating blues
3   How long now : will I have to wait
4   Can I get you now : honey have to hesitate
5   I can learn ??? : not to ball the jack
6   I can beat anybody : getting the good gal back
7   And I got a gal : who loves to roll

CollS 6   Collins, Sam

8   ??? : right by her door
9   Around the curve : and around the bend
10   Yonder comes : that engineer
11   *Rifle's* on the *stage* : my *coffee's* in the
     cool
12   My little gal's : from Illinois
13   I'm not so good-looking : got no curly hair
14   Have a woman : take me anywhere

CollS 7   Collins, Sam

     title: Midnight Special Blues
     place and date: Richmond, Ind., c. 17 Sept. 1927
     record numbers: (13035) Ge-6307 OJL-10

1   When you get up in the morning : when the ding-dong
     rings
2   You make it to the station : see the same old thing
3   Ain't nothing on the table : but the pots and the
     pans
4   Say anything about it : have supper with the man
5   Yonder come the little Nora : how do you know
6   I know by the apron : and the dress she wear
7   ??? on her shoulder : piece of paper in her hand
8   Looking for some sergeant : to release some man

CollS 8   Collins, Sam

     title: It Won't Be Long
     place and date: Richmond, Ind., c. 17 Sept. 1927
     record numbers: (13049-A) Ge-6379 OJL-10

1   I aim to take my gun : ??? in your face
2   Going to let some graveyard : be your resting place
3   You going to miss me when I'm gone : honey and it
     won't be long
4   When you think I'm going : I'm standing right here
     with your *wally* on
5   When I'm gone : don't you grieve after me
6   Don't you forget : how I went away

CollS 9   Collins, Sam

     title: Do That Thing
     place and date: Richmond, Ind., c. 17 Sept. 1927
     record numbers: (13050-A) Ge-6307 OJL-10

1   She's long and tall : and wears a diamond ring
2   But she can beat anybody : at doing that thing
3   You go through the *barrel* : and you ride like a
     tiger
4   You throws your backbone : clean out of sight

CollS 10   Collins, Sam

     title: Lonesome Road Blues
     place and date: New York, 8 Oct. 1931
     record numbers: (10836-1) Ba-32669 Yz L-1038

1   You did cause me to weep : you did cause me to moan
2   You did cause me : to leave my home
3   I cried last night : and the night before
4   And I swore : not to cry no more
5   In eighteen hundred : and ninety-nine
6   He got killed on that streetcar line
7   They took him down : that smoky road
8   Brought him back : on that cooling board
9   Says run here mama : and fall in your daddy's breast
10   These blues : going to let me rest

CollS 11   Collins, Sam

     title: New Salty Dog
     place and date: New York, 8 Oct. 1931
     record numbers: (10837-1) Ba-32311 OJL-10

1   Said come in here : and you shut that door
2   He got shot : with a forty-four
3   I got a brand new pistol : and a box of balls
4   Going to shoot that woman : just to see her fall
5   You ??? *those stitches* : in the ???
6   He dug those potatoes : with the pocketknife
7   I'm going to town : hurry back
8   I'm going to show your people : how to ball the jack
9   She got good jelly : she sells it hot
10   I know here's something : that a man can't buy
11   Twenty-five cents : is the regular price
12   There's fifty cents : you can buy her twice
13   She pulls her dress : up above her knees
14   She shakes her shimmy : to who she please

CollS 12   Collins, Sam

     title: Slow Mama Slow
     place and date: New York, 8 Oct. 1931
     record numbers: (10839-2) Ba-32311 OJL-10

1   Take your time kind mama : I'm going to do it just
     as slow as I can
2   I might start shimmying : don't let nobody in
3   Make your bed up higher : and turn your lamp way low
4   I'm going to hug and kiss you : ain't coming here no
     more
5   Make your lamp up higher : and turn your lamp around
6   Look out your back door : see me leave this town

CollS 13   Collins, Sam

     title: I'm Sitting on Top of the World
     place and date: New York, 8 Oct. 1931
     record numbers: (10842-2) Ba-32395 OJL-10

1   The day you left me : you throwed me down
2   You didn't hurt me so bad babe : talk over town
3   Because I'm broke : I'm down and out
4   You ever quit me : and put me out
5   Went to the nation : and the territory'
6   Going to catch me the first train : I've got to go
7   You press my jumper : my overalls
8   Went to the station : meet the Cannonball
9   I'd rather ride : this ??? line
10   To be uneasy : be treated right
11   I give my money : and a diamond ring
12   Now come her partner : beat me shaking that thing
13   The day you left me : won't wear no black
14   I write you a letter : come sneaking back

CollS 14   Collins, Sam

     title: My Road Is Rough and Rocky
     place and date: New York, c. Oct. 1931
     record numbers: (   ) unknown Yz L-1038

1   You don't believe I'm traveling : on the road
     somewhere
2   Get your book : and count come and count the days
     I'm gone
3   You can go to *Moosefall* : find me there
4   Yes if I drink smoky : find me on the road somewhere
5   You can talk about your brick house : but you ought
     to see mine
6   It ain't so pretty : but it ??? fine
7   I got up this morning : looked at the rising sun
8   Can't nobody run me : like them bloodhounds done
9   I got up in my stockings : tipping across the floor
10   Scared the bloodhounds : are rapping upon my door

CollS 14   Collins, Sam

11   Now chickens on my back : and there's the hounds on
     my track
12   I dropped my head : and I couldn't stop to look back
13   I could hear those pistol balls : zooming by my head
14   I believe to my soul : they going to kill me dead
15   I got up this morning : just about the break of day
16   I could hear *a bunch of* bloodhounds : a-coming
     down my way
17   I got up this morning : fell down across my bed
18   I could hear something pushing : all around my head

CookR   1   Cooksey, Robert (Bobby Leecan)

     title: Dollar Blues
     place and date: New York, c. 21 Mar. 1927
     record numbers: (E-22051) Br-7007 Rt RL-321

1   My woman woke up this morning : dollar in her hand
2   Two bits for the monkey : six bits for her man

CookR   2   Cooksey, Robert (Bobby Leecan)

     title: Hock My Shoes
     place and date: New York, c. 21 Mar. 1927
     record numbers: (E-22059) Br-7007 Rt RL-321

1   I hocked everything : from my hat down to my shoes
2   So now sweet mama : got those doggone hockshop blues

CovB   1   Covington, Blind Bogus Ben

     title: It's a Fight Like That
     place and date: Chicago, c. 9 Oct. 1928
     record numbers: (C-4630-) Br-7121 Rt RL-325

1   Now right is right : wrong is wrong
2   Ain't no harm : to sing a little song
3   Uncle Bud went home : just like they said
4   Stuck a match : caught a man in his bed
5   If I go home : about half past ten
6   Put the key in the hole : and can't get in
7   Now Lucy came home : with a big excuse
8   She left there tight : but she come back loose
9   I had a little kitty : I called her mine
10   Way in the night : I could hear her cry
11   We shoot a little dice : bound to have a little fun
12   Law walked up : and away we run
13   I asked the lady for a drink : this is what she said
14   I don't have the white : but I have the red
15   Some folks hates it : call it a sin
16   You see women : give money to men

CovB   2   Covington, Blind Bogus Ben

     title: Boodle-De-Bum Bum
     place and date: Chicago, c. 9 Oct. 1928
     record numbers: (C-4631-) Br-7121 Rt RL-325

1   I went down in the alley : trying to sell my coke
     today
2   And a woman run out and hollered : scared my mule
     away
3   I went with iceman Jackson : he sold me ice and coke
4   But he blowed in all his money : buying sweet
     jellyroll
5   We stopped on Eighteenth and Federal : just two
     blocks west of State
6   And when he got up under that ??? : well he would
     not wait
7   She said money don't excite me : and that we all
     know well
8   But Jackson showed her fifty dollars : and she
     almost fell

CovB   2   Covington, Blind Bogus Ben

9   She had wind like the greyhound : and she sure could
     run
10   And Jackson got down like a reindeer : and he runned
     her some

CoxI   1   Cox, Ida

     title: Ida Cox's Lawdy, Lawdy Blues
     place and date: Chicago, July 1923
     record numbers: (1488-?) Pm-12064 BYG-529073

1   Tell me pretty daddy : what's the matter now
2   Are you trying to quit me : and you don't know how
3   I'd rather be dead : buried in the sea
4   Than to have the man I love : say he don't want me
5   Lord Lord : Lordy Lordy Lord
6   Oh the man I love : treats me like a dog
7   I'd rather see : my coffin come rolling in my door
8   Than to hear the man I love : say I don't want you
     no more

CoxI   2   Cox, Ida

     title: Wild Women Don't Have the Blues
     place and date: Chicago, c. Aug. 1924
     record numbers: (1842-?) Pm-12228 Jo SM-3098

1   I hear these women raving : about their monkey-man
2   About their trifling husbands : and their no-good
     friends
3   These poor women sit around : all day and moan
4   Wondering why : their wandering papa don't come home
5   Now when you got a man : don't never be on the
     square
6   Because if you do : he'll have a woman everywhere
7   I never was known : to treat no one man right
8   I keep them working hard : both day and night
9   I've got a different system : and a way of my own
10   When my man starts kicking : I let him find another
     home
11   I get full of good liquor : walk the streets all
     night
12   Go home and put my man out : if he don't act right
13   You never get nothing : by being an angel child
14   You better change your ways : and get me awhile
15   I want to tell you something : I wouldn't tell you a
     lie
16   Wild women are the only kind : that do ???

CoxI   3   Cox, Ida

     title: Misery Blues
     place and date: New York, late Jan. 1925
     record numbers: (1999-?) Pm-12258 BYG-529073

1   Early this morning : when everything was still
2   My daddy said he was leaving : though it's against
     my will
3   He said I'm leaving mama : and your crying won't
     make me stay
4   The more you cry : the further I'm going away
5   A man is like a car : that you have to overhaul
6   Keep him three or four weeks : and you can't get
     along at all
7   I gave him everything : from a diamond on down
8   The next thing I give him : will be six feet of
     ground

CoxI   4   Cox, Ida

        title: Blue Kentucky Blues
        place and date: New York, late Jan. 1925
        record numbers: (2003-2) Pm-12258 BYG-529073

1   You can always tell : when your best man don't want
        you around
2   He will come home at night : turn the bed upside
        down
3   My heart's full of sorrow : tears come rolling down
4   Because my baby : was Kentucky bound
5   The pale moon shines : down on the mountain still
6   Way down in old Kentucky : mid those high blue hills
7   Shine on old moon : harvest moon shine on
8   Because old moon you'll be shining : when I'm dead
        and gone
9   I'm going to tell my mama : when I go back home
10 Tell her the folks up here : won't let my Kentucky
        man alone

CoxI   5   Cox, Ida

        title: Long Distance Blues
        place and date: Chicago, Aug. 1925
        record numbers: (2243-?) Pm-12307 BYG-529073

1   Hello Central : give me long-distance please
2   I'm begging with tears in my eyes : and down on my
        bended knees
3   Hello Central : give me Mr Henry Brown
4   What you say you were calling : a storm has blown
        the wires down
5   Listen long-distance : can you send a telegram
6   Do this please : before I fall down *left in a jam*
7   You just tell him : he better hurry home
8   Because I'm tired : of making all these nights alone

CoxI   6   Cox, Ida

        title: Southern Woman's Blues
        place and date: Chicago, Aug. 1925
        record numbers: (2244-?) Pm-12298 Jo SM-3098

1   Takes a southern woman : to sing this southern song
2   Lord I'm worried now : but I won't be worried long
3   When I was downtown : I wouldn't take no one's
        advice
4   But I ain't going to let : that same bee sting me
        twice
5   Because I'm going back : where the weather suits my
        clothes
6   Down where there ain't no snow : and the chilly
        winds never blow
7   I don't want no northerner : no northern black or
        brown
8   Southern men will stick by you : when the northern
        men can't be found
9   You ever been south : you know just what I mean
10 Southern men are all the same : from Kentucky to New
        Orleans
11 I'm going back south : where I can get my hambone
        boiled
12 These northern men : are about to let my poor
        hambone spoil

CoxI   7   Cox, Ida

        title: Lonesome Blues
        place and date: Chicago, Aug. 1925
        record numbers: (2246-1) Pm-12307 BYG-529073

1   The blues came down my alley : and stopped right at
        my door
2   They made me feel : like I've never felt before
3   I'm a good-hearted woman : never done nobody wrong

CoxI   7   Cox, Ida

4   But the better I treat my daddy : the worse we get
        along
5   If you don't want me daddy : please tell me what to
        do
6   I've never loved nobody daddy : like I'm loving you
7   I've got ten little puppies : twelve little shaggy
        hound
8   It takes all twenty-two : to run my good man down

CoxI   8   Cox, Ida

        title: Coffin Blues
        place and date: Chicago, Sept. 1925
        record numbers: (2293-1) Pm-12318 BYG-529073

1   Daddy oh daddy : won't you answer me please
2   All day I stood by your coffin : trying to give my
        poor heart ease
3   I rubbed my hands over your head : and whispered in
        your ear
4   And I wonder if you know : that your mama's near
5   You told me that you loved me : and I believed what
        you said
6   And I wished that I could fall : here across your
        coffin dead
7   When I left the undertakers : I couldn't help but
        cry
8   And it hurts me so bad : to tell the man I love
        goodbye

CoxI   9   Cox, Ida

        title: Rambling Blues
        place and date: Chicago, Sept. 1925
        record numbers: (2294-?) Pm-12318 BYG-529073

1   Early this morning : the blues come walking in my
        room
2   I said blues please tell me : what are you doing
        here so soon
3   He looked at me and smiled : but yet they refused to
        say
4   I asked him again : and they turned and walked away
5   The first thing they told you : your man you're
        going to lose
6   At first I didn't believe it : but I found that it
        was true
7   Blues oh blues : you know you been here before
8   The last time you were here : you made me cry and
        walk the floor

CoxI   10   Cox, Ida

        title: Worn Down Daddy Blues
        place and date: Chicago, c. Aug. 1928
        record numbers: (20766-1) Pm-12704 BYG-529073

1   The time has come : for us to part
2   I ain't going to cry : it won't break my heart
3   Because I'm through with you : and I hope you don't
        feel hurt
5   You are like an old horseshoe : that's had its day
6   You're like an old shoe : I must throw away
7   You're like an old ship : that sprung a leak
8   You ain't young no more : and your loving is weak
9   You ain't got no money : you're down and broke
10 You're just an old has-been : like a worn out joke

67

CoxI 11   Cox, Ida

        title: You Stole My Man
        place and date: Chicago, c. Aug. 1928
        record numbers: (20768-1) Pm-12704 BYG-529073

 1 Old pal old pal : you stole my man away
 2 But that's all right : I'll get him back some day
 3 You stole my man : between midnight and day
 4 And if I catch you old pal : I sure will make you
      pay
 5 Why should you : have a daddy of your own
 6 Old pal old pal : you better let my man alone
 7 Old pal you said : two friends could understand
 8 But that's no sign : we should take each other's man

CrawR 1   Crawford, Rosetta

        title: My Man Jumped Salty on Me
        place and date: New York, 1 Feb. 1939
        record numbers: (64972-A) De-7567 Cor CP-58

 1 Going down to the river : take a rope and a rock
 2 Tie it around my neck : and jump off the dock
 3 Ain't no one : can change my mind
 4 I've been mistreated : and I don't mind dying
 5 Going to get me some poison : kill myself
 6 Because the man I love : has put me on the shelf
 7 If he didn't want me : he didn't have to lie
 8 The day I see him : that's the day he'll die
 9 Baby : you don't know my mind
10 When you see me laughing : I'm laughing just to keep
      from crying
11 A crooked man's worse : than crooked dice
12 With dice you lose your money : with your man you
      lose your life
13 I'm going to get me a razor : and a gun
14 Cut him if he stands still : shoot him if he runs

Crud   1   Crudup, Arthur Big Boy

        title: Black Pony Blues
        place and date: Chicago, 11 Sept. 1941
        record numbers: (064873-1) BB-B8896 RCA LPV-518

 1 I got a coal-black mare : but Lord how that horse
      can run
 2 Yes she win every race : man you don't see how it's
      done
 3 I give her three gold teeth : I put earings in her
      ears
 4 There ain't no use a-worrying : I do swear the stuff
      is here
 5 I cut her mane : I put streamline shoes on her feet
 6 Ain't a horse in the country : I do swear my horse
      can't beat
 7 Say she foxtrot and pace : and I rode that horse
      today
 8 Yeah when morning comes : she had never broke her
      gait
 9 She going to the race track at midnight : and I rode
      her all night long
10 Yeah when morning come : she had never changed her
      weight
11 She's a coal-black mare : she's got long black curly
      mane
12 Well I'll follow that horse : man in any land

Crud   2   Crudup, Arthur Big Boy

        title: Death Valley Blues
        place and date: Chicago, 11 Sept. 1941
        record numbers: (064874-1) BB-B8858 RCA LPV-518

 1 I went down in Death Valley : among the tombstones
      and dry bones

Crud   2   Crudup, Arthur Big Boy

 2 That's where poor me will be : Lord when I'm dead
      and gone
 3 Now if I should die : I should die before my time
 4 I want you to bury my body : down by that Frisco
      line
 5 Now bury me mama : low down in the sand
 6 Now bury me mama : where I won't bother your next
      old man
 7 Oh bye bye baby : I said goodbye
 8 Death Valley is my home : mama I want to die
 9 Tell all the women : please come dressed in red
10 They going down Sixty-One Highway : that's where the
      poor boy he fell dead
11 Wear your patent leather slippers : mama put out
      your morning gown
12 You going to follow poor Crudup : down to his
      burying ground

Crud   3   Crudup, Arthur Big Boy

        title: If I Get Lucky
        place and date: Chicago, 11 Sept. 1941
        record numbers: (064876-1) BB-B8858 RBF RF-202

 1 That's all right mama : that's all right for you
 2 Treat me lowdown and dirty : any old way you do
 3 I've been worried all night mama : now worried again
      today
 4 Because the woman I love : done throwed me away
 5 Babe I wouldn't have been here : if it had not been
      for you
 6 *Down in* Chicago : you treat me like you do
 7 I'm leaving town mama : just to wear you off my mind
 8 Now you treat me lowdown and dirty : I believe I'll
      lose my mind
 9 If I get lucky mama : with my train fare home
10 I'm going back to Mississippi : Lord now where I
      belong

Crud   4   Crudup, Arthur Big Boy

        title: Mean Old 'Frisco Blues
        place and date: Chicago, 15 Apr. 1942
        record numbers: (070863-1) BB-34-0704 RBF RF-202

 1 Well that mean old old Frisco : and that lowdown
      Santa Fe
 2 Done took my babe away : Lord and blowed back at me
 3 Yes my mama told me : papa told me too
 4 Son every woman scream in your face : Lord she ain't
      no friend to you
 5 Lord I wonder : do she ever think of me
 6 Well I wonder I wonder : will my babe come back to
      me
 7 Yes I'm standing and looking : watching that
      Southern whistle blow
 8 Well she didn't catch that Southern : Lord now where
      did the woman go
 9 Lord I ain't got no : special rider here
10 I might leave : because I don't feel welcome here

Curr   1   Curry, Ben

        title: Fat Mouth Blues
        place and date: Grafton, Wis., c. Jan. 1932
        record numbers: (L-1236-2) Pm-13118 Rt RL-325

 1 Do anything mama : tell the truth don't mean no lie
 2 I have so many hard-working women : tell you men I
      don't mean no jive
 3 Now she's *making* her jelly : and she will not give
      it away
 4 She's going to save it for *Sally* : he will be home
      today

Curr   1   Curry, Ben

    5   Some of these funny women : just like driving an
        automobile
    6   You have to step on the gas : to make them climb the
        hill
    7   Never mind never mind baby : I got my eyes on you
    8   Some of these days mama : you going to do like I
        want you to

Dadd   1   Daddy Stovepipe

            title: Sundown Blues
            place and date: Richmond, Ind., 10 Mar. 1924
            record numbers: (11861-A) Ge-5459 Rt RL-325

    1   Mama I woke up this morning : mama had the sundown
        blues
    2   And my fair brown told me : I refuse to go
    3   Mama I had so much chicken : mama cackles in my
        sleep
    4   You don't like my potatoes mama : oh don't you plow
        so deep
    5   I got nineteen fair browns : said I want you all to
        know
    6   Mama if you want to see me : mama I'll let the
        nineteen go
    7   Now you see my little fair brown : tell her to bring
        me meat
    8   When the wintertime gets here : I'll wear the B V Ds

Dadd   2   Daddy Stovepipe

            title: Stove Pipe Blues
            place and date: Richmond, Ind., 10 Mar. 1924
            record numbers: (11862-A) Ge-5459 Rt RL-325

    1   When you get down to Memphis : won't find me there
    2   Just lightning and smoking : on the road somewhere
    3   I was born in Texas : raised in Tennessee
    4   Good Lord oh when you get to Memphis : won't find me
        there
    5   Well they call me Daddy Stove Pipe : turn your
        damper down
    6   Good Lord now when you get to Memphis : won't find
        me there

Dadd   3   Daddy Stovepipe

            title: Tuxedo Blues
            place and date: Birmingham, Ala., c. 13 July
                1927
            record numbers: (GEX-730-A) Ge-6212 OJL-14

    1   I don't want no sugar : stirred up in my rice
    2   That long *short* yellow : gives me my appetite
    3   Mama toot your whistle : you can't blow your horn
    4   Your little bow-legged daddy : left you all alone
    5   Mama I don't like chicken : neither no piece of cake
    6   Takes a big fat fan-belt : drive a Cadillac Eight
    7   When you get through to Bessemer : almost to
        Birmingham
    8   When you love your daddy : give me your right hand

DanJ   1   Daniels, Julius

            title: My Mama Was a Sailor
            place and date: Atlanta, 19 Feb. 1927
            record numbers: (37931-2) Vi-20658 Rt RL-326

    1   My mama was a sailor : she love the ocean life
    2   She ride top and bottom : sometime on the side
    3   Said I'm going to China : honey what you want me to
        bring you back
    4   Said a bobtailed coat : and a *hot ??? China* hat

DanJ   1   Daniels, Julius

    5   Lord I told Mr Russell : don't you broke my plow
    6   Says he got bull-headed : and broke it off anyhow
    7   Standing on the corner : talking with my brown
    8   Up stepped this policeman : take both of us down
    9   Honey where was you : when thirty blows was sound
   10   Standing on the corner : teasing with my brown
   11   Lord a lowdown fireman : dirty engineer
   12   Say they took my brown : left me standing here
   13   All you jealous men : better keep your women tied
   14   If they flag my train : I'm sure going to let them
        ride
   15   If anybody asks you : who composed this song
   16   Tell them Julius Daniels : done been here and gone

DanJ   2   Daniels, Julius

            title: Ninety-Nine Year Blues
            place and date: Atlanta, 19 Feb. 1927
            record numbers: (37932-2) Vi unissued Fwy
                FA-2953

    1   I'm take me my pistol : three rounds of ball
    2   Going kill everybody : *broke the poor boy law*
    3   On a Monday I was arrested : on a Tuesday I was
        tried
    4   Judge found me guilty : and I hung my head and cried
    5   Judge : what'll be my fine
    6   Says a pick and a shovel : way down *Joe Brown's*
        coal mine
    7   Be light on me judge : I ain't been here before
    8   Give you ninety-nine years : don't come back here no
        more

Darb   1   Darby, Blind

            title: Lawdy Lawdy Worried Blues
            place and date: Richmond, Ind., 7 Sept. 1929
            record numbers: (15566) Pm-12828 Yz L-1003

    1   : what's on your worried mind
    2   You keep your poor man worried : and bothered all
        the time
    3   Lord Lordy : Lord Lord Lord Lord
    4   I'm a poor boy : been treated just like a dog
    5   Got a new way baby : spelling Memphis Tennessee
    6   Double T M double E : double T double X Y Z
    7   Baby baby : what makes you treat me so
    8   I've done all : that a poor boy could do
    9   I helped you baby : when your kinfolks turned you
        down
   10   Now you loving someone else baby : and you done left
        this town
   11   Look a-here baby : what more you want me to do
   12   I sacrificed my mother : just to get along long with
        you
   13   Ever lay down laughing : and wake up hollering and
        crying
   14   And you think about the woman : you treated so nice
        and kind
   15   Take me back baby : try poor me one more time
   16   I'll bet you hundred dollar : that I will change
        your mind
   17   When you got money : your friends will hear your
        plea
   18   When you ain't got no money : then you have to come
        home to me
   19   Take my woman : I won't get mad with you
   20   For she's three times seven : and she knows what she
        wants to do
   21   Woke up this morning : and I was half most dead
   22   I was bone-down weary : a low and ache aching head
   23   Baby baby : won't you forgive me please
   24   You're the only woman : can give my poor poor heart
        ease

Darb   2   Darby, Blind

        title: Deceiving Blues
        place and date: Chicago, 29 Sept. 1931
        record numbers: (67583-1) Vi-23311 OJL-20

1   You deceived me babe : about the things I did not
    want you to do
2   Now I've lost confidence in you : because you won't
    be true
3   I regarded you : like I were your baby child
4   But when it comes to find out : you was misusing me
    all the while
5   But me and my baby : we going to make everything all
    right
6   And if we don't tomorrow : we will tomorrow night
7   Beef to me baby : me and pork chops do not agree
8   I love you : but I don't like the way that you are
    jiving me
9   I'll work up to you : or you'll slip back [down] to
    me some day
10 And you going to be sorry : that you done me this
    a-way

Darb   3   Darby, Blind

        title: Built Right on the Ground
        place and date: Chicago, 29 Sept. 1931
        record numbers: (67584-1) Vi-23311 Yz L-1003

1   I never cried : till my babe got on the train
2   And the tears went down : great God like drops of
    rain
3   Now let me tell you : what that mean old train will
    do
4   It will take your woman : and blow the smoke at you
5   And it's oh my baby : don't treat me good no more
6   And I ain't got no babe : ain't got nowhere to go
7   And this woman I'm loving : don't pay me no mind
8   And she keeps me worried : and bothered all the time
9   I believe I believe : I'll stop my barrelhouse ways
10 For I feel myself : sinking every day
11 And it's oh my baby : don't act right no more
12 And I can't feel welcome : babe nowhere I go
13 If whiskey don't kill me : I'm doomed to lose my
    mind
14 For I'm worried and bothered : and drinking all the
    time
15 Farewell farewell : I bid this world goodbye
16 Little babe done quit me : and I'll give on up to
    die

DaveC   1   Davenport, Charles Cow Cow

        title: I Ain't No Ice Man
        place and date: New York, 8 May 1938
        record numbers: (63764-A) De-7462 AH-158

1   I ain't no iceman : I ain't no iceman's son
2   But I can keep you cool : until the iceman comes
3   I ain't no wood chopper : I ain't no wood chopper's
    son
4   But babe I can chop your kindling : until the wood
    chopper comes
5   Baby I ain't no stove man : I ain't no stove man's
    son
6   But I can keep you heated up : babe until the stove
    man comes
7   Baby I ain't no butcher : and I ain't no butcher's
    son
8   But I can furnish you plenty of meat : baby until
    the butcher comes
9   I ain't no milkman : I ain't no milkman's son
10 But I can furnish you plenty of cream : baby until
    that milkman comes

DaveJ   1   Davenport, Jed

        title: Save Me Some
        place and date: Memphis, 20 Oct. 1930
        record numbers: (MEM-774) Vo-1513 OJL-19

1   Work now mama : both night and day
2   Make my money : bring it all away
3   Liquor sure : is a craving sin
4   Steal it from the white folks : now and then
5   Up to my lips : then down to my toes
6   That's the way : ??? ten gallons goes
7   Went to the doctor : and the doctor said
8   Don't stop drinking : going to kill you dead
9   Mama told me : papa told me too
10 Doing that stuff : will be the death of you

DaviC   1   Davis, Carl (Dallas Jamboree Jug Band)

        title: Elm Street Woman Blues
        place and date: Dallas, 20 Sept. 1935
        record numbers: (DAL-103-) Vo-03092 BC-2

1   Now if you're ever in Dallas boy : please visit old
    Elm Street
2   You can see the snuff-sniffing women : like a police
    on his beat
3   Lordy I'm so glad I'm so glad : police is back on
    the beat
4   So he can stop them women : from begging every man
    they meet
5   Lord I ain't going to marry : ain't going to settle
    down
6   I'm going to hang around Dallas Texas : and run old
    pigmeat down
7   Now if you ever come to Dallas : yes and get put in
    jail
8   Yes sweet papa Charlie Chicken : he will pay your
    bail
9   I'm going to tell you something mama : every word is
    true
10 Lord I'm crazy about my pork and beans : wild about
    my good beef stew

DaviM   1   Davis, Madlyn

        title: It's Red Hot
        place and date: Chicago, c. Oct. 1928
        record numbers: (20908-?) Pm-12703 Yz L-1039

1   Now you talk about rags : boys but you ought to hear
    mine
2   My red-hot shaker : plays it all the time
3   It's called : the red-hot shaker rag
4   It's the best rag : that I ever had
5   Now you can talk about pepper : boys but it ain't
    hot
6   You ought to hear my boys : making up their plot
7   Let's play : the red-hot shaker's rag
8   Now blow it boys : you know it's just too bad

DaviM   2   Davis, Madlyn

        title: Too Black Bad
        place and date: Chicago, c. Oct. 1928
        record numbers: (20909-?) Pm-12703 Yz L-1039

1   I'd rather be in the *cripty* river : floating like
    a log
2   Than to stay around here : be treated like a dog
3   Now all the little children : playing around in a
    ring
4   Playing hooky from school : just to rag that thing
5   Now it's some folks says : a preacher won't steal
6   But I caught a preacher : in the potato field
7   Now one had the sack : the other had the hoe

DaviM   2   Davis, Madlyn

  8   If that ain't stealing : boys I'd like to know
  9   Here come my father : with his gun
10   You ought to see : them preachers run

DaviW   1   Davis, Walter

    title: M. and O. Blues
    place and date: Cincinnati, 12 June 1930
    record numbers: (62907-2) Vi-V38618 RCA INT-1085

  1   My baby's gone : and she won't come back no more
  2   Oh she left me this morning : and she caught that M
     and O
  3   Listen here people : I've done everything that I
     could
  4   But she's gone and left me : she didn't mean me no
     good
  5   There is one thing baby : I just can't understand
     myself
  6   When the gal I love quit me : I don't want nobody
     else
  7   But that's all right babe : I can't stand the way
     you do
  8   You are running me crazy : and it's going to worry
     you
  9   When she left me she bought a ticket : just as long
     as she was tall
10   She didn't know how much I loved her : or else she
     wouldn't have left at all

DaviW   2   Davis, Walter

    title: That Stuff You Sell Ain't No Good
    place and date: Louisville, 10 June 1931
    record numbers: (69416-2) Vi-V23282 RCA INT-1085

  1   That stuff you sell : ain't no good
  2   Smell just like : old rotten burnt wood
  3   That stuff you sell : ain't no wine
  4   One thing about it : you serve it so kind
  5   The stuff you sell : ain't no booze
  6   One thing about it : mama give you the blues
  7   The stuff you sell : in a jug
  8   You don't give me some : I'm going to raise a bug
  9   I know you're sick : can't get well
10   When you sell any more : it take God to tell
11   You can go down on the corner : Market and Tenth
12   Get that stuff : for fifty cents
13   That stuff you sell : ain't so good
14   I wouldn't buy none of that : even if I could

DaviW   3   Davis, Walter

    title: Howling Wind Blues
    place and date: Chicago, 29 Sept. 31
    record numbers: (67579-1) Vi-V23308 RCA INT-1085

  1   The north wind has begin howling : [and, but] the
     skies are pretty and blue
  2   And winter is coming : wonder what the poor people
     are going to do
  3   People talk about the time : that they never have
     seen before
  4   But hard times : is knocking on everybody's door
  5   Poor people are like prisoners : but they just ain't
     got on a ball and chain
  6   But the way they are faring : I do swear it's all
     the same
  7   There ain't no need to worry : times will bring
     about a change
  8   And if it don't : I swear it will always be the same

DaviW   4   Davis, Walter

    title: M. and O. Blues No. 3
    place and date: Dallas, 10 Feb. 1932
    record numbers: (70676-1) Vi-V23333 RBF RF-12

  1   I'm a railroad man : and I love that M and O
  2   And when I leave this time : I ain't coming back no
     more
  3   Now don't the moon look pretty : shining down
     through the trees
  4   I can see my baby : but I swear that she can't see
     me
  5   I'm in a world of trouble : and I believe I've got
     to go
  6   I'm going to leave here people : going to catch that
     M and O

DaviW   5   Davis, Walter

    title: L and N Blues
    place and date: Chicago, 2 Aug. 1933
    record numbers: (76802-1) BB-B5143 RCA INT-1085

  1   The L and N is a fast train : also that I N C N
  2   If I ever leave Chicago : going to ride that
     Sunshine Special again
  3   L and N L and N : bring my baby back to me
  4   You keep me bound down in trouble : just as long as
     I can be
  5   Don't your house look lonesome : when the one that
     you love is gone
  6   And you ain't got nobody : just to keep a happy home
  7   I wonder will my baby : ever come back to me again
  8   When she left me good people : she rode that L and N

DaviW   6   Davis, Walter

    title: Sloppy Drunk Again
    place and date: Chicago, 25 Feb. 1935
    record numbers: (85479-1) BB-B5879 OJL-20

  1   My gal done quit me : found somebody else
  2   And now I'm tired : of sleeping by myself
  3   I love my moonshine whiskey : and I love my cherry
     wine
  4   Sloppy drunk : about to lose my mind
  5   I'm going to get sloppy drunk : tell everything I
     know
  6   Another half a pint : mama will see me *Joe*
  7   Ooo : ooo wee
  8   Wonder what will : what will become of me
  9   Water when I'm thirsty : whiskey when I'm dry
10   A brownskin woman : tell her when I come to die

DaviW   7   Davis, Walter

    title: Travelin' this Lonesome Road
    place and date: Chicago, 25 Feb. 1935
    record numbers: (85480-1) BB-B5982 RCA INT-1175

  1   I am traveling this lonesome road : if I never get
     back no more
  2   I have something to tell you : people just before I
     go
  3   Take care of my wife and my children : I hope to
     come back home some day
  4   The racket that I am now in : Lord it make *white
     slavery*
  5   I'm going to rob and I'm going to hijack : until I
     get satisfied
  6   And if the freight train leaves me : Lord I got a
     mule to ride
  7   I thinking about the times : when I was laying in my
     mother's arms
  8   She always told me : son don't you do nothing wrong

9 But people before I will stand to see : my good
   woman go down
10 I will pack my suitcase : while I hunt from town to
   town

DaviW   8   Davis, Walter

     title: Sad and Lonesome Blues
     place and date: Chicago, 25 Feb. 1935
     record numbers: (85481-1) BB-B5982 RCA INT-1175

1 I was sad and lonesome : when I walked into my
   baby's door
2 And here's the words she told me : I can't use you
   no more
3 I folded up my arms : and I slowly walked away
4 That's all right baby : you going to need my help
   some day
5 Oh Lord : oh Lord oh Lord oh Lord
6 Don't you remember the day : you treated me like a
   lowdown dirty dog
7 Some day I'm going to see you : when you down and
   out just like myself
8 Mama just as I have told you : some day you going to
   need my help
9 So goodbye : I ain't got no more to say
10 I did not think : you would treat me this a-way

DaviW   9   Davis, Walter

     title: Minute Man Blues--Part 1
     place and date: Chicago, 25 Feb. 1935
     record numbers: (85482-1) BB-B5965 RCA INT-1085

1 Every since every since : I [first] left my mother's
   door
2 I don't have the good times people : that I have had
   in my life so long
3 So in believe I will go : right down I Paris
   Tennessee
4 Because this life that I'm living : Lord it's bad
   luck *here* ???
5 Going to write and tell my mother : to look for me
   on my way
6 I'm going back home people : Lord and I'm going back
   there to stay
7 And if you see my black angel : please don't tell
   her the way I've gone
8 Tell her there ain't no need to worry : neither cry
   or weep and moan
9 I'll try to travel if I want to : but I believe I
   will go by *mail*
10 I've got a V-Eight Ford now sweet mama : Lord you
   know I'm a minuteman

DaviW 10   Davis, Walter

     title: Minute Man Blues--Part 2
     place and date: Chicago, 25 Feb. 1935
     record numbers: (85483-1) BB-B5965 RCA INT-1085

1 My tires ain't going to fail me : and my motor it is
   good and strong
2 I have a V-Eight Ford now sweet mama : Lord and you
   know it won't be long
3 All I want is my thirty-two twenty : hanging by my
   side
4 I will pour in the high-powered gasoline : and see
   how fast we can ride
5 I'm going to make traintime and over : and I ain't
   going to be one minute late
6 I'm going to hold it around ninety miles : and I
   ain't going to break my gait

7 Won't you listen to my V-Eight motor : won't you
   listen to how my motor hums
8 This minuteman is on that lonesome highway : and I
   swear it won't be long

DaviW 11   Davis, Walter

     title: Sweet Sixteen
     place and date: Chicago, 25 Feb. 1935
     record numbers: (85484-1) BB-B5931 RCA INT-1085

1 Uncle Bert thought : he had *his daughter* trained
2 She's out there : shaking that little old thing
3 Shaking her *rumble* : just like she shake her
   strike
4 She say run into me baby : and make me break my back
5 She got a crankshaft motion : she got a cross-town
   swing
6 She got *the regular* : doing that thing
7 She's out there : looking like a sugar lump
8 She say want to *pum-pitty* : got to make me drunk
9 *I'm burn that* chicken : *and down handcuff*
10 Come on here darling : let's go and talk
11 *Aunt Dinah got a preacher* : *roll* above her knee
12 And she strutting her stuff : to who she please

DaviW 12   Davis, Walter

     title: Root Man Blues
     place and date: Chicago, 28 July 1935
     record numbers: (91430-1) BB-B6040 RCA INT-1085

1 Mama here come your root man : open the door and let
   him in
2 It is just about time : you using some of your good
   roots again
3 You face is getting bumpy : and your skin looks
   awful bad
4 I believe my root do you more good mama : than any
   herbs that you ever had
5 There is one thing baby : you want the root all by
   yourself
6 But you know I'm a doctor mama : I got to give it to
   somebody else
7 The root that I'm selling : from it you can get lots
   of juice
8 And when I'm giving it to you mama : you don't want
   to turn your doctor loose
9 I was doctoring on a woman : she said Lord I can't
   see how can it be
10 She say go away from here doctor : you got too much
   root for me

DaviW 13   Davis, Walter

     title: I Can Tell By the Way You Smell
     place and date: Chicago, 28 July 1935
     record numbers: (91433-1) BB-B6059 Yz L-1025

1 You hair all wrinkled : and you full of sweat
2 Your underskirt : is wringing wet
3 You show your linen : to any man
4 And that's something mama : that I just can't stand
5 Here you come in here walking : just like a goose
6 You look like : somebody just turned you loose
7 Run here mama : just look at sis
8 She got her hand in her toodle-um : up to her wrist
9 Mama and papa's in the back yard : trying to *call
   up Knot Hill*
10 Papa ain't ready : so help me God
11 He got the motion : and she got the swing
12 Just look at papa out there : on that thing

DaviW 14   Davis, Walter

    title: Santa Claus
    place and date: Chicago, 28 July 1935
    record numbers: (91434-1) BB-B6125 Yz L-1025

1 Santy Claus : won't you please hear my lonesome plea
2 I don't want nothing for Christmas : but my baby
   back to me
3 You know I loved you baby : that is why we could not
   get along
4 But some day you going to be sorry : that you ever
   done me wrong
5 Oh Lord it's near Christmas time : and I want to see
   Santa Claus
6 If you don't bring my baby : swear I'll break all
   the laws
7 Santy Claus Santy Claus Santy Claus : I'm down on my
   bended knees
8 I don't want nothing for Christmas : but my baby
   back to me

DaviW 15   Davis, Walter

    title: Moonlight Is My Spread
    place and date: Chicago, 31 Oct. 1935
    record numbers: (96234-1) BB-B6167 RCA INT-1085

1 The blue sky is my blanket : and the moonlight is my
   spread
2 The rock is my pillow : that is where I rest my head
3 A ghost and a night owl : they come to see me
   sometime
4 And a Gypsy women : she comes and reads my mind
5 The woman that I was loving : she did not mean me no
   good
6 She give me so much trouble : I had to move back in
   the woods
7 I am friendless and I'm lonesome : people you would
   be the same old way
8 If the woman that you were loving : would mistreat
   you both night and day

DaviW 16   Davis, Walter

    title: Ashes in My Whiskey
    place and date: Chicago, 31 Oct. 1935
    record numbers: (96237-1) BB-B6201 RCA INT-1085

1 They put ashes in my whiskey : they put strychnine
   in my glass
2 Lord I went out car-riding with them : and they
   carried me too fast
3 She put [castor oil, black drops] in my coffee :
   with that [black drops, castor oil] in my tea
4 Lord she's the meanest old woman : that a man most
   ever seen
5 I believe I believe : that they trying to carry me
   down
6 Lord the way they are feeding me : that they don't
   want me around
7 She carries a razor in her pocket : with them frowns
   all in her face
8 Lord I believe some other good joker : trying to
   root me out of my place

DaviW 17   Davis, Walter

    title: Jacksonville--Part 2
    place and date: Chicago, 3 Apr. 1936
    record numbers: (100338-1) BB-B6468 Yz L-1025

1 I'm going to write you a letter : my wife and I
   ain't going to do right no more
2 I know the way you treat me baby : Lord you did not
   want me no more

DaviW 17   Davis, Walter

3 What I've got on my mind : ain't nobody in this
   world can tell
4 And if I never see you no more baby : Lord I sure do
   wish you well
5 Now I'm having bad luck : and bad luck I can't
   understand
6 Got me out here scuffling mama : trying to make it
   if I can
7 Baby baby : I ain't going to worry with you no more
8 Lord I'm going down the country : let you have Mr
   so-and-so

DaviW 18   Davis, Walter

    title: Think You Need a Shot
    place and date: Chicago, 3 Apr. 1936
    record numbers: (100339-1) BB-B6498 RCA INT-1085

1 You got bad blood mama : I believe you need a shot
2 Now turn over here mama : let me see what else you
   got
3 I doctors on women : I don't fool around with men
4 All right take it easy here mama : whilst I stick my
   needle in
5 Lord your ways is so loving : and your skin is nice
   and soft
6 Lord if you keep on drunk mama : you going to make
   me break my needle off
7 Lord my needle is in you baby : and you seem to feel
   all right
8 And when your medicine go to coming down : I want
   you to hug me tight
9 Yeah your medicine come now baby : put your [foot,
   leg] up side the wall
10 I don't want to waste none of it mama : I want you
   to have it all

DaviW 19   Davis, Walter

    title: Let Me in Your Saddle
    place and date: Chicago, 21 July 1939
    record numbers: (040511-1) BB-B8282 RCA INT-1085

1 You is built for speed : and fast just like twenty
   grand
2 I would give more for you now : than a farmer would
   for land
3 I'm a well-trained jockey : won't you please ma'am
   let me ride
4 I may not give a ride like you old jockey : but I'll
   try to make you satisfied
5 If you let me get in your saddle : and just try me
   one time
6 Lord I may can do something : baby that might change
   your mind
7 Twenty grand is the fastest race horse : that ever
   run around a track
8 And if you let me get in your saddle mama : I may
   ride the way you like
9 Just let me get in your saddle baby : I ain't going
   to never do no wrong
10 I'm a good jockey rider : and I don't stay there too
   long

DaviW 20   Davis, Walter

    title: Call Your Name
    place and date: Chicago, 21 July 1939
    record numbers: (040523-1) BB-B8470 Yz L-1025

1 Have you ever been low in spirits : mama and you
   didn't know what was on your mind
2 Lord it hurts you so bad sometimes : Lord you can't
   keep from crying

DaviW 20   Davis, Walter

3   The house where you were living : it don't [even]
    look right no more
4   And you can't find no consolation : nowhere in the
    world you go
5   Then you wonder what did you ever do : to make your
    poor heart ache and pain
6   Lord it hurts you so bad : to hear somebody call Mr
    so-and-so's name
7   I looked for you Sunday morning : till Monday in the
    afternoon
8   But I hope you'll be here Tuesday morning : hope you
    will be here Tuesday morning soon
9   If I don't never see you no more : please drop me a
    post card
10 Lord you know the way that you left me : mama it
    almost broke my heart

DaviW 21   Davis, Walter

        title: Can't See Your Face
        place and date: Chicago, 12 July 1940
        record numbers: (049320-1) BB-B8600 Yz L-1025

1   Your picture has faded : mama that hangs up on the
    wall
2   It's been hanging there so long : I can't see your
    face at all
3   Even my old house seems haunted : mama and there
    ain't nobody around
4   Sometime it seem like at night : that the old house
    is falling down
5   I can hear my back door slamming : [seem like] I can
    hear a little baby crying
6   Lord I wonder baby : have you got me on your mind
7   My old clock is [still] ticking : that hangs up on
    the wall
8   But now you gone and left me : and I can't see your
    face at all

DaviW 22   Davis, Walter

        title: Please Don't Mistreat Me
        place and date: Chicago, 12 July 1940
        record numbers: (049323-1) BB-B8664 Yz L-1025

1   Please don't mistreat me : if you don't want me
    around
2   Lord don't be mad with me baby : because your good
    man have left this town
3   You say you don't [even] love me : you don't even
    love yourself
4   I know there ain't a room in your heart for me :
    mama you loving someone else
5   I got myself a mama : she always keep me feeling
    blue
6   Lord she act just like the weather : and I don't
    know what she is going to do
7   If I really loved you baby : I would not tell you no
    lies
8   Lord I wouldn't say hard things to you mama : to
    make you hang your head and cry

DaviW 23   Davis, Walter

        title: Why Shouldn't I Be Blue
        place and date: Chicago, 12 July 1940
        record numbers: (049325-1) BB-B8737 Yz L-1025

1   Mama why should I be worried : and why should I be
    so blue
2   Lord it's all on account : of all on account of you
3   How can I sleep and keep from worrying : how can I
    laugh and keep from crying

DaviW 23   Davis, Walter

4   Lord every time I turn my back : you always doing
    something to change my mind
5   I just flutters when I see you : like a little bird
    up in his nest
6   Lord sometime I think I love you : sometime I think
    I love my little gal the best
7   I can't keep from worrying : Lord I can't keep from
    telling you lies
8   Lord I would do all right with you baby : but you
    know you try to be too wise

DaviW 24   Davis, Walter

        title: The Only Woman
        place and date: Chicago, 21 Mar. 1941
        record numbers: (053975-1) BB-B8773 RCA INT-1085

1   Now this was my sad story : I never will forget the
    day
2   It was in the year of nineteen thirty-five : on the
    twenty-sixth day of May
3   As I walked into my bedroom : crowd all gathered
    around
4   They was standing seemed to be in mourning : with
    their heads all hanging down
5   In the midst there stood a doctor : he was standing
    gazing on
6   The only woman in the world that I ever loved :
    she's gone she's gone
7   Now I'm left here all alone : all in this great big
    world alone
8   That's the end of my happy days : and I can't have
    no more happy home
9   On the bed there laid a letter : said be as good as
    you can be
10 Lord I'm sorry you couldn't be here now : to have
    the last few words with me

DaviW 25   Davis, Walter

        title: New Come Back Baby
        place and date: Chicago, 21 Mar. 1941
        record numbers: (053979-1) BB-B8833 RCA INT-1085

1   Now you must have a heart : like a rock in the sea
2   I been begging you baby : babe please don't leave
3   My nights are getting lonely : my days are getting
    long
4   Now tell me baby : I did not do no wrong
5   I don't want to hurt your feelings : either make you
    mad
6   I love you : better than anything I ever had
7   I like you baby : I like to see you smile
8   But I like to please you : every once in a while

DaviW 26   Davis, Walter

        title: Don't You Want to Go
        place and date: Chicago, 5 Dec. 1941
        record numbers: (070448-1) BB-B9027 RCA INT-1085

1   I heard somebody calling me : papa don't you want to
    go
2   Mama dee-da-da calling me : papa so-and-so
3   Down in the land of California : sweet home Chicago
4   I begged you all night baby : all the night before
5   If I ever did you wrong : I won't do that no more
6   All last night baby : I tried to talk to you
7   But you told me : there was nothing I could do
8   I been good to you baby : did everything that I
    could
9   Now you want to leave me : don't mean me no good
10 Oh babe oh baby : down on my bended knees
11 Begging you now baby : don't leave me please

DaviW 26   Davis, Walter

12 Oh babe oh baby : don't leave me now
13 All alone by myself baby : won't be satisfied

DaviW 27   Davis, Walter

        title: Just Want to Talk Awhile
        place and date: Chicago, 5 Dec. 1941
        record numbers: (070451-1) BB unissued RCA
            INT-1085

1   Now I walked over to the table : and I picked up my
        telephone
2   But the line was busy : or if it ain't nobody home
3   Give me long long-distance : I wonder what's wrong
        with my line
4   Lord I just want to talk awhile : to that little old
        girl of mine
5   All right operator : maybe it ain't nobody home
6   But I'm sitting here wondering : why is my baby gone
7   I'm calling long-distance : and I wonder where could
        she be
8   Lord I wonder is she listening : and won't even
        answer me

DayT   1   Day, Texas Bill

        title: Goin' Back to My Baby
        place and date: Dallas, 4 Dec. 1929
        record numbers: (149512-1) Co-14494-D Rt RL-327

1   I woke up this morning moaning : with the worried
        blues on my mind
2   I was thinking about someone : who were left behind
3   It's oh Lord Lord : please get him off of my mind
4   I can't eat for dreaming : and I can't rest for
        crying
5   I'm going back to my baby : going to knock on my
        baby's door
6   I'm going to ask my pretty mama : baby can't you use
        me no more
7   Baby : can I lay down here till day
8   I'm a poor boy : and I got nowhere to stay
9   Love is like water : it turns off and on
10 When you think you got a good girl : Lord she done
        turn off and gone

DayT   2   Day, Texas Bill

        title: Elm Street Blues
        place and date: Dallas, 5 Dec. 1929
        record numbers: (149538-2) Co-14514-D Fly LP-103

1   Elm Street painted in brass : Main Street painted in
        gold
2   I got a good girl live on East Commerce : I wouldn't
        mistreat her to save nobody's soul
3   Hey Billiken : these Elm Street women don't mean you
        no good
4   When your back is turned : they with every man in
        the neighborhood
5   These Elm Street women : Billiken they don't mean
        you no good
6   If you want to make a good woman : have to get on
        Hospital Avenue

DayT   3   Day, Texas Bill

        title: Billiken's Weary Blues
        place and date: Dallas, 5 Dec. 1929
        record numbers: (149539-2) Co-14514-D Rt RL-335

1   Don't the moon look pretty : shining through the
        trees

DayT   3   Day, Texas Bill

2   Don't your house look lonesome : when your good girl
        is fixing to leave
3   Down on my knees this morning : I prayed to the good
        Lord above
4   Please let me live one more time : with the good
        girl that I love
5   I'm going to get me a wire : stretched across the
        deep blue sea
6   So when my good girl gets worried : she can sit down
        and talk to me

DayW   1   Day, Will

        title: Central Avenue Blues
        place and date: New Orleans, 25 Apr. 1928
        record numbers: (146186-2) Co-14318-D Yz L-1010

1   I'm going to build me a little mansion : on Central
        Avenue
2   So I can stick my head out the window : and see what
        my wicked women will do
3   Lord I got a pretty mama : lives on Central Avenue
4   Lord if that woman left and quit me *now* : what in
        the world that I would do
5   I pray to heaven Lord : I seen my pretty mama up
        there
6   She had one foot loose : and *curled up with the
        air*
7   Good girl used to live here : don't live here no
        more
8   Left here early this morning : carried all of her
        clothes
9   Boy I'd *better see my good girl* : leave me in this
        town
10 I'd beat the train to the *crossroads* : and I'd
        burn the depot down
11 Lord pretty mama I wonder : what you trying to do
12 *She make it trying* to run with me : and my buddy
        too
13 I'm going to West Texas : Lord I'm going to stay
14 Some little brownskin woman : *stepping* in my way

DayW   2   Day, Will

        title: Sunrise Blues
        place and date: New Orleans, 25 Apr. 1928
        record numbers: (146191-2) Co-14318-D Yz L-1032

1   Well the sun rose this morning : and laid down on my
        floor
2   When I ended my dreams : it was all around my door
3   Good morning blues : what makes you come so soon
4   Here early this morning : *crying ???* soon
5   Now blues and trouble : boys what a nagging ache
6   These old women now baby : running from man to man
7   Just tell me pretty mama : what you trying to do
8   You didn't do no more : than I looked for you to do
9   You leave me laughing : some day you come back
        crying
10 You been gone so long darling : wear you off of my
        mind
11 Lord Lord : Lord Lordy Lord Lord
12 The girl I loving : treat me like a dog
13 My heart's in trouble : mind's in misery
14 Got the blues so bad : I really can't hardly see

Dean   1   Dean, Joe

        title: I'm So Glad I'm Twenty-One Years Old
            Today
        place and date: Chicago, c. 7 Aug. 1930
        record numbers: (C-5991-) Vo-1544 Yz L-1028

1   Well I'm so glad : I'm twenty-one years old today

Dean   1   Dean, Joe

  2   Lord I'm so glad : my baby can't treat me that a-way
  3   Oh babe : what you want poor me to do
  4   Driving a coal wagon babe : give all my money to you
  5   Oh babe : don't play me for no fool
  6   Lord I ain't no plumber : and I ain't nobody's stool
  7   I send it to the river : river to the deep blue sea
  8   Now your monkey ways babe : don't take no effect on
      me
  9   Oh babe : don't make no fool of me
 10   Lord I'm three time seven : baby why can't you see
 11   That's why I'm so glad : I'm twenty-one years old
      today
 12   Lord I'm three times seven : I'm going to have my
      way

DelaM   1   Delaney, Mattie

        title: Down the Big Road Blues
        place and date: Memphis, c. 21 Feb. 1930
        record numbers: (MEM-785-) Vo-1480 Yz L-1009

  1   I can't go down : that big road by myself
  2   If I can't carry you : I carry someone else
  3   I asked him how about it : and he said all right
  4   I asked him how long : and he said all night
  5   I asked him how about it : said he didn't know how
  6   But I will do you mama : like a calf will do a cow
  7   I'm a traveling woman : I got a traveling mind
  8   If you don't take me back daddy : sure going to lose
      your mind
  9   My mother said : six months before I was born
 10   She was going to have a good child : wouldn't never
      stay at home
 11   I feel like crying : ain't got no tears to spare
 12   I had a happy home : and I wouldn't stay there

DelaM   2   Delaney, Mattie

        title: Tallahatchie River Blues
        place and date: Memphis, c. 21 Feb. 1930
        record numbers: (MEM-786-) Vo-1480 Yz L-1001

  1   Tallahatchie River rising : Lord it's mighty bad
  2   Some peoples on the Tallahatchie : done lost
      everything they had
  3   Some people in the Delta : wondering what to do
  4   They don't build some levees : I don't know what
      become of you
  5   High water rising : get me troubled in mind
  6   I got to go : and leave my daddy behind
  7   Lord this water rising : and I sure can't swim
  8   But if it keeps on rising : sure going to follow him
  9   Going pack my suitcase : go back to Tennessee
 10   But this Tallahatchie River : done got the best of
      me

DickP   1   Dickson, Pearl

        title: Twelve Pound Daddy
        place and date: Memphis, 12 Dec. 1927
        record numbers: (145370-3) Co-14286-D Yz L-1008

  1   Mmm : hey hey hey hey
  2   Now the man I love : treats me like a dog
  3   I've got a twelve pound daddy : and eight pound one
      too
  4   And if my twelve pound one won't come : my eight
      pound one will do
  5   I'm going to build me a castle : out of ice and snow
  6   So when my blues come around : I can freeze them
      from my door
  7   Oh pretty daddy : will you please tell me what to do
  8   I will do anything : baby to satisfy you
  9   And it's one thing baby : that I can't understand

DickP   1   Dickson, Pearl

 10   If you are *loving* me : I don't want no partnership
      man

DickP   2   Dickson, Pearl

        title: Little Rock Blues
        place and date: Memphis, 12 Dec. 1927
        record numbers: (145371-2) Co-14286-D OJL-6

  1   I started to heaven : but I changed my mind
  2   But I'm going to Little Rock : where I can have
      better time
  3   Yes when I go to Little Rock : I can go three days
      without
  4   I tell people there : it's a wonderful town
  5   This is the place : where I have long to be
  6   Because where I come from : the mens have mistreated
      poor me
  7   Oh I don't know why : they treat me so lowdown and
      cruel
  8   And if you don't want me baby : you don't have to
      use me as no fool

DickT   1   Dickson, Tom

        title: Death Bell Blues
        place and date: Memphis, 27 Feb. 1928
        record numbers: (400355-B) OK-8590 Yz L-1002

  1   Hey hey : death bells in my ear
  2   It 'tain't going to be long : before they going to
      ring me away from here
  3   I lay down last night all night : and the night
      before
  4   Going back home to mama : won't have to lay down no
      more
  5   I'm a stranger here : they're sending out in the sea
  6   I'm broke and hungry : not a bite to eat
  7   Going to stand right here : catch the first old gal
      I see
  8   I'm going to beg her to take me : see what she make
      of me
  9   I'm going to ask my rider : would she set my trunk
      outdoors
 10   I don't mean quitting you : but I got another place
      to go
 11   The woman I had : these men must have had her
      foiled
 12   She loved me all this summer : but she put me out
      this fall
 13   I began to study : and the wind begin to blow
 14   I couldn't figure no place : for a man like me to go
 15   My mama's dead : my papa's across the sea
 16   That leaves no one : to love and care for me

DickT   2   Dickson, Tom

        title: Happy Blues
        place and date: Memphis, 27 Feb. 1928
        record numbers: (400359-B) OK-8590 Yz L-1002

  1   Just as happy : woman as I can be
  2   Because the woman I'm loving : is going back to
      Kankakee
  3   Woman I'm loving : done mistreated me
  4   For another new morning : going to need your friend
      again
  5   Treat me : like someone you never seen
  7   Blues ain't nothing : good man on your mind
  8   Well it keep you worried : bothered all the time
  9   When you see me : with my head hung down
 10   I ain't got the blues : but another gal on my mind
 11   I'm going away baby : to see what could do
 12   I done all I could : can't get along with you

DickT 2   Dickson, Tom

13 I went to the station : I looked up on the board
14 Well my train ain't here : but it's somewhere on the
   go

DickT 3   Dickson, Tom

    title: Labor Blues
    place and date: Memphis, 27 Feb. 1928
    record numbers: (400360-A) OK-8570 Yz L-1008

1 Said good morning captain : said good morning shine
2 'Tain't nothing the matter : captain but I just
   ain't going
3 I don't mind working : captain from sun to sun
4 But I want my money : captain when payday come
5 Work me all this summer : and you started on this
   fall
6 Now I've got to take Christmas : in my overalls
7 If you good men : want to keep her out of town at
   night
8 Just feed her little pork chops : suits her appetite
9 Lord it 'tain't no telling : what a Mississippi gal
   will do
10 She will get your money : then *poor gam* at you
11 It's one pretty mama : going to need a friend again
12 You can sing this song : when you want me to be your
   friend
13 Hey tell me woman : where did you stay last night
14 For your shoes unfastened : and your skirt don't fit
   you right

Dool 1   Dooley, Simmie (Pink Anderson)

    title: Gonna Tip Out Tonight
    place and date: Atlanta, 14 Apr. 1928
    record numbers: (146067-1) Co-14436-D OJL-18

1 I says go on girl : don't sing them blues to me
2 Because I'm sweet : as any man can be
3 She even told me : to my face
4 That any old rounder : sure can take my place
5 Said I'm getting tired : of your lowdown ways
6 I'm going back : to my babe today
7 So come on girl : honey you can't bluff
8 I'm going to tip out tonight : and I'm going to
   strut my stuff

DorsT 1   Dorsey, Thomas A.

    title: Grievin' Me Blues
    place and date: Chicago, c. 6 Sept. 1928
    record numbers: (   ) Vo-1216 His HLP-1

1 I went down on the corner : with my money in my hand
2 To kill my woman : about loving another man
3 You see it's grieving me : oh it's grieving me
4 Going to pack my grip : beat it back to Tennessee
5 I'm so sad and lonely : love has been refused
6 Can't have no loving : but I still have the blues
7 They call me pretty papa : swellest man in town
8 Women all screaming about me : but I can't give up
   my brown
9 Daddy's got the washboard : mama's got the tub
10 Sister's got the liquor : and brother's got the jug
11 My water pipe's all rusted : water's running cold
12 Someone's in the basement : trying to find the hole

DorsT 2   Dorsey, Thomas A.

    title: Broke Man's Blues
    place and date: Richmond, Ind., 8 July 1929
    record numbers: (15306-A) Ge-7008 Riv RM-8803

1 Just another evening : wasted away
2 Spending and a-lending : and it left me broke today
3 Run here pretty mama : sit down on your daddy's knee
4 I'll tell you : how these women made a perfect fool
   of me
5 I wasted lots of money : went out every night
6 My pals done all forsake me : and the times is
   getting tight
7 I'm feeling like an outcast : looking like a tramp
8 Can't price a post card : can't even buy a stamp
9 Ah you used to call me papa : you used to call me
   dunce
10 You used to call me daddy : and you used to love me
   once
11 Some folks need the ice : some folks need the snow
12 If I could get you back : mama I wouldn't need
   nothing more

DorsT 3   Dorsey, Thomas A.

    title: Pig Meat Blues
    place and date: Richmond, Ind., 8 July 1929
    record numbers: (15310) Ge-7008 Riv RM-8803

1 You may be little : you may have a tender snoot
2 But I know what you is mama : when you start to root
3 You go before the butcher : try to put on your stunt
4 He can stick a knife in you : and you won't even
   grunt
5 I see you got your squeal : you got your snoot
6 Still you got your grunt : but you done lost your
   root
7 Oh mama : you may have your snoot
8 Still you got your grunt : but you done lost your
   root

DorsT 4   Dorsey, Thomas A.

    title: Second-Hand Woman Blues
    place and date: Richmond, Ind., 5 Feb. 1930
    record numbers: (16221) Ge-7130 Riv RM-8803

1 All dolled up : looking keen
2 Like a girlie : in her teens
3 Strutting : down the avenue
4 Making eyes : and flirting too
5 Now the other night : when I phoned
6 You had another : in your home
7 Parts of me : big and fat
8 Can't blame nobody : for that
9 I want your love : I can't refuse
10 But I don't want it : if it's ever been used
11 Some is tall : some is cute
12 Some is sweet : and some is true
13 I don't mean : to speak so bold
14 Can't use it : if it's forty years old

DorsT 5   Dorsey, Thomas A.

    title: Maybe It's the Blues
    place and date: Richmond, Ind., 5 Feb. 1930
    record numbers: (16222) Ge-7190 Riv RM-8803

1 Something pounding : in my breast
2 When I lay down : to take my rest
3 Horrid nightmares : scary dreams
4 Then the blues : steps on the scene
5 Oh maybe it's the blues : that keeps me worried all
   the time

DorsT 5   Dorsey, Thomas A.

6   If I could lose these weary blues : that's on my
    mind
7   Happiness that comes around : but never comes to
    stay
8   If I only had someone : just to drive my tears away

DorsT 6   Dorsey, Thomas A.

      title: Levee Bound Blues
      place and date: Richmond, Ind., 5 Feb. 1930
      record numbers: (16224) Ch-16682 Riv RM-8803

1   I had a brown in my town : sweet as any gal could be
2   I loved my gal with all my might : she didn't love
    nobody but me
3   The other night : a man named Willie come and stole
    my gal away
4   Now I'm feeling down and out : and I've got the
    blues today
5   Say if you see my gal : don't you tell her what I've
    done
6   I got the blues : I going to sing them all night
    long
7   Now folks if you see my gal : tell her that I'm gone
8   Feel like riding : if it takes me all night long
9   Now back to the levee I'm bound : I'm through with
    high yellows and browns
10 Now I'm going to the levee : because my gal done
    turned me down
11 Now say folks if you see my gal : tell her that I'm
    gone
12 I feel like leaving : if it takes me all night long

DorsT 7   Dorsey, Thomas A.

      title: Gee, But It's Hard
      place and date: Richmond, Ind., 5 Feb. 1930
      record numbers: (16225) Ch-16682 Riv RM-8803

1   Take me back sweet mama : try me one more time
2   If I don't satisfy you : I'll break my backbone
    trying
3   You lay in your bed : with your face to the wall
4   Thinking if you die : would that end it all

DorsT 8   Dorsey, Thomas A. (Jane Lucas)

      title: Terrible Operation Blues
      place and date: New York, 17 Sept. 1930
      record numbers: (10048-2) Or-8033 Yz L-1035

1   Get up on the table : pull off that gown
2   Raise up that right leg : let the left one down
3   Pull off them stockings : that silk underwear
4   The doctor's got to cut you mama : Lord knows where
5   Got two or three tumors : shaped like a cube
6   Two or three leaks : in your inner tube
7   Bring on that ether : bring on that gas
8   The doctor's got to cut you mama : yas yas yas
9   Four monkey wrenches : and a two-horse shay
10 Pair of old britches : and a bale of hay
11 Your ribs was kind of loose : they moved about
12 If I hadn't've sewed you up : everything would fell
    out
13 I put in new tubes : hide the exhaust
14 I went into your hood : and cleaned your spark plugs
    off
15 Your body's kind of weak : now don't be hard
16 From now on be careful : with them connection rods
17 Now your body's kind of weak : don't be hard
18 Go kind of easy : with them connection rods

DorsT 9   Dorsey, Thomas A. (Jane Lucas)

      title: Terrible Operation Blues
      place and date: Richmond, Ind., 19 Nov. 1930
      record numbers: (17276-B) Ch-16171 Riv RM-8803

1   Get up on this table : pull off that gown
2   Raise up that right leg : let that left one down
3   Pull off them stocking : that silk underwear
4   The doctor's got to cut you : mama don't know where
5   You got two or three tumors : shape like a cube
6   Two or three leaks : in your inner tube
7   Bring on that ether : bring on that gas
8   The doctor's got to cut you mama : yas yas yas
9   Four monkey wrenches : two-horse shay
10 Pair of old britches : and a bale of hay
11 Your ribs was kind of loosened : they moved about
12 If I hadn't sewed you up : everything would fell out
13 I put in new tubes : tightened up the exhaust
14 Went into your hood : and cleaned your spark plugs
    off
15 Your body's kind of weak : don't be hard
16 From now on you be careful : with them there
    connection rods

DorsT 10   Dorsey, Thomas A. (Jane Lucas)

      title: Where Did You Stay Last Night?
      place and date: Richmond, Ind., 19 Nov. 1930
      record numbers: (17277-A) Ch-16171 Riv RM-8803

1   Tell me pretty mama : where'd you stay last night
2   Shoes ain't buttoned : and you don't smell right
3   Now you all drawed up : you look half drunk
4   Your hair ain't combed : and you smell like a skunk
5   Train's in the depot : boxcar's on the track
6   My gal come home : with a tie across her back

DorsT 11   Dorsey, Thomas A. (Jane Lucas)

      title: Fix It
      place and date: Richmond, Ind., 19 Nov. 1930
      record numbers: (17278-A) Ch-16215 Riv RM-8803

1   Now when I fix it lady : sure will be mighty good
2   I fixed so many of them : all over this neighborhood

DorsT 12   Dorsey, Thomas A.

      title: Been Mistreated Blues
      place and date: Richmond, Ind., 20 Nov. 1930
      record numbers: (17290) Ch-16237 Riv RM-8803

1   I had a sweet woman : she done turned sour on me
2   I had a good woman : but the men wouldn't let her be
3   I had a new way of loving : but I done lost my
    stroke
4   I had a new gal : I lost her when I got broke
5   Now I'm a real kind fellow folks : and that ain't so
    bad
6   But I just ain't got them things : I once have had
7   I got my mind all made up : and I'm going to leave
    this town
8   I'm a-going so far : till the women can't run me
    down
9   Now I had a speak-easy: but the police come and
    closed it down
10 Now it sure is a hard thing : to sell booze around
    this town
11 I got a woman down in Florida : got two up in
    Tennessee
12 Got one in Indiana : keeps on pulling after me
13 Now the angels keep singing : the moon shines down
    at night
14 But the good Lord knows : that the women don't treat
    me right

DorsT 13   Dorsey, Thomas A. (Jane Lucas)

      title: Come On In
      place and date: Grafton, Wis., c. Jan. 1931
      record numbers: (L-719-2) Pm-13104 Riv RM-8803

1 Oh set right down : and let's have some fun
2 My wife's gone out : on a all-night run
3 Oh take this : take some of that
4 Take anything : in the doggone flat
5 I'll fry some meat : cook some bread
6 You get sleepy : there's a great big bed
7 Oh take this liquor : drink this wine
8 Let's get drunk : and have one good time
9 Take off your shirt : hang it on the chair
10 Take off your socks : and give your feet some air
11 I'm drunk and disorderly : I don't care
12 If you want to : you can pull off your underwear

DorsT 14   Dorsey, Thomas A.

      title: If You Want Me to Love You
      place and date: New York, 5 Feb. 1932
      record numbers: (11242-A) Vo-1682 Yz L-1039

1 Now if you want me to love you : here's what you got
   to do
2 You want me to love you mama : and make [me, you]
   love [you, me] too
3 I got to have my loving : when my habit get on
4 Start at nine in the evening : and love me all night
   long
5 You got to get up early in the morning : fix your
   lunch
6 And get out early : with that scuffling bunch
7 If I wake up at night : and I wants to eat
8 It's up to you : to get me some of that western meat
9 You got to take all your money : throw it against
   the wall
10 You take what sticks : and I'll take what falls
11 Take a butcher knife : cut off your head
12 Send me a telegram : that your heart is dead

Doyl 1   Doyle, Little Buddy

      title: Hard Scufflin' Blues
      place and date: Memphis, 1 July 1939
      record numbers: (MEM-17-1) OK-05771 Rt RL-329

1 Scuffling have got so hard : seem like I can't even
   make a dime
2 I must a-have the wrong woman : seem like can't save
   money all the time
3 I never want another women : that don't do nothing
   but hang around ???
4 She will ??? to your weakness : she will keep you
   with a turned-down hand
5 Life have gotten miserable : seem like no more
   happiness to be made
6 But life is really too short : to be worried about
   them old no-good ways
7 Good Book trying to tell us : where there's a will
   there's a way
8 But it seem like the *many ways draining* out of me
   : more and more every day

Doyl 2   Doyle, Little Buddy

      title: Grief Will Kill You
      place and date: Memphis, 1 July 1939
      record numbers: (MEM-18-1) Vo-05111 Rt RL-319

1 Lord grief will kill you : it will get you down to
   skin and bones
2 And that devil *brother be upstairs* now : Lord
   after you are dead and gone

Doyl 2   Doyle, Little Buddy

3 I once grieved so hard : until I wake up weeping in
   my sleep
4 But after you continue this life boys : you'll be
   living down in some graveyard deep
5 Women now about nowadays they don't want to love
   nobody : and don't worry about the man behind the
   left
6 Boys you better watch them women : because they're
   just slipping up the kingdom's steps

Doyl 3   Doyle, Little Buddy

      title: Renewed Love Blues
      place and date: Memphis, 14 July 1939
      record numbers: (MEM-152-1) OK-05771 Rt RL-329

1 Now baby let's stop our foolishness : and try to
   renew love over again
2 Because I can't stay here in this world *after* : in
   this condition my poor heart's in
3 Now baby I'm going to make you this promise : I make
   our home happy for you in every way
4 But I want you to take care of my money baby : and
   please don't give my belongings away
5 Now baby you know I love you : now why can't we get
   along
6 Maybe some day you will consider baby : Lord and
   acknowledge that you have done wrong

Doyl 4   Doyle, Little Buddy

      title: Bad in Mind Blues
      place and date: Memphis, 14 July 1939
      record numbers: (MEM-153-1) Vo-05111 Rt RL-319

1 Boys I ain't doing no good : this slow death is
   killing me
2 Every time *you going out swinging* : I'm just as
   blue as I can be
3 My mind in such a condition : until I hardly know
   the days in the week
4 Baby you give me plenty trouble : but some day you
   bound to see
5 When I'm sleeping deep down in my grave : don't let
   no high *flat flappers* worry you
6 You can just step out in any yard : that old jimson
   weed will sure ??? you
7 Now boys you can be cute with your woman : and see
   won't she do you dirty *ass*
8 She'll forever keep you working : working with your
   coffin on your back

East 1   Easton, Amos

      title: No Woman No Nickel
      place and date: Grafton, Wis., c. Oct. 1931
      record numbers: (L-1120-3) Pm-13109 Yz L-1012

1 I'm cold in hand : can't get nothing here
2 I'm hungry as a hound : I can't travel nowhere
3 I can't help but worry : how my good friend done
4 Spent my money by the dollar : now won't give me
   nickel one
5 Mama told me : times and times again
6 Anybody laughs in my face : just can't be my friend
7 Lord look down on poor me : pity my worried cares
8 Help me to rise once more : I'm going to change my
   free-hearted ways
9 Just give me one friend : to keep me from feeling so
   sad
10 Lord you know I want a friend : like the one that
   Adam had

East   2   Easton, Amos

      title: I'm Waitin' On You
      place and date: New York, 16 Mar. 1932
      record numbers: (11503-A) Vo-1719 His HLP-31

1 Come here pretty mama : come here right now
2 I've been waiting on you so long : till I'm burning down
3 I'm waiting on you : I'm waiting on you
4 I'm waiting on you baby : tell me what you going to do
5 I know a good woman well : something going on wrong
6 You ain't never kept me waiting : this lonesome long
7 I wait all last night : all the night before
8 If I have to wait tonight : I'm going to pack my trunk and go
9 If you don't want me baby : just leave me alone
10 I can get another woman : to carry your business on
11 If you meant : to treat me right
12 You wouldn't keep me waiting : all day and night
13 That's all right baby : if you don't want me no more
14 There many more women : just rearing to go

East   3   Easton, Amos

      title: Green Country Gal
      place and date: New York, 23 Aug. 1936
      record numbers: (61241-A) De-7440 AH-158

1 Now I talked and I talked : now I ain't got no more to say
2 Hand me down my jumper : and I'll be on my lonesome way
3 I tried everything baby : don't nothing do no good
4 I can't blame you honey : I'd be the same way if I could
5 You came here from the country : just as green as green could be
6 Now you're a wise city city : and you dodge all over me
7 Well I ain't got no more to say : and I ain't going to chase you around
8 Some day I'll be running : with the biggest shots in town

EdwF   1   Edwards, Frank

      title: Terraplane Blues
      place and date: Chicago, 28 May 1941
      record numbers: (C-3811-1) OK-06393 BC-6

1 I saying I sad and lonesome : Lord what I'm going to do
2 Say I'm going buy me a terraplane : I swear and a V-Eight too
3 Well I'm going to put them both there together : put them out on the road
4 Paint both show mama : got a heavy load
5 Now I saying I sad and lonesome : Lord what I'm going to do
6 Say I'm going to step on that accelerator : till that gas come through
7 Say my gal just quit me now man : pulled in another lane
8 Didn't want to come back : till I bought that airplane
9 Crying please Frank : please let me ride with you
10 Say I got room for two or three more : I swear and you too
11 Says stop now Frank : let's get a sack of flour
12 How can I stop this airplane : making ninety mile an hour
13 Crying please Frank : please let me ride with you
14 Say I can *peel off* that accelerator : and that gas come through

EdwF   2   Edwards, Frank

      title: We Got to Get Together
      place and date: Chicago, 28 May 1941
      record numbers: (C-3812-1) OK-06393 BC-6

1 Hitler cutting the world : gotten disturbed
2 Uncle Sam better decide : and gotten blood in his eye
3 You got to get together : you got to get together
4 Got to closen up together : join one hand in hand
5 Mussolini jumped back : up in the sack
6 Hitler kicked him out : so he couldn't get back
7 Uncle Sam called the men down : name by name
8 He ain't together : but they ready just the same
9 Uncle Sam need a champ : ???
10 A well trained man : when you leave camp ???
11 Well left my woman : standing in the door
12 Crying Lord they mustn't let him : please don't go

EdwJ   1   Edwards, Joe (Butterbeans and Susie)

      title: Construction Gang
      place and date: New York, 12 Sept. 1924
      record numbers: (72817-B) OK-8163 Sw S-1240

1 Now there is something : you say that you expect
2 Now come and tell me what it is : that I neglect
3 Come and tell your papa : what you want me to do
4 Now just before : I got from you
5 Get up every morning : at half past three
6 Ease out to your job : without disturbing me
7 Now when you come back : you must have plenty of jack
8 Because any *??? still* : really hurts your papa's back
9 I want you to work hard : for me and my brother
10 I want you to come back from work : looking just like first one thing and then another

EdwJ   2   Edwards, Joe (Butterbeans and Susie)

      title: He Likes It Slow
      place and date: Chicago, 18 June 1926
      record numbers: (9750-A) OK-8355 Sw S-1240

2 Says I never like to hurry : I just take my time

EdwS   1   Edwards, Susie (Butterbeans and Susie)

      title: Construction Gang
      place and date: New York, 12 Sept. 1924
      record numbers: (72817-B) OK-8163 Sw S-1240

1 Now here's all I ask of you : kind man
2 I want an answer : I can understand
3 How you get up every morning : at half past three
4 Bring the coal and kindling : make a fire for me
5 Cook your own breakfast : fix your lunch
6 Get your pick and shovel : work with that construction bunch
7 *Seven eighty-three* : without neglect
8 So you bring me all your money : when they pay your check

EdwS   2   Edwards, Susie (Butterbeans and Susie)

      title: He Likes It Slow
      place and date: Chicago, 18 June 1926
      record numbers: (9750-A) OK-8355 Sw S-1240

1 He likes it slow : when he goes to *play*
2 He likes it slow : when he goes to pray
3 When he calls : he never brings no news
4 Always got : them slow-down blues

EdwS   2   Edwards, Susie (Butterbeans and Susie)

5   Just like a snail : that man of mine

EdwT   1   Edwards, Big Boy Teddy

        title: Louise
        place and date: Chicago, 14 June 1934
        record numbers: (80608-1) BB-B5826 CC-3

1   Standing on the corner : *all ??? man*
2   Police come along : take me by his hand
3   Led me down : to the county jail
4   Looking for my Louise : to come and go my bail
5   Now the judge have sentenced me : out on the county
        road
6   On a horse : there's a man he rode
7   He count me in the morning : count me through the
        day
8   Count me every hour : see if I'd run away
9   It was early in the evening : sun was going down
10 Seen a lady coming : all dressed in brown
11 Looked in her face : and I looked down in her hands
12 Was Louise coming : coming to get her man

Este   1   Estes, Sleepy John

        title: The Girl I Love, She Got Long Curly Hair
        place and date: Memphis, 24 Sept. 1929
        record numbers: (55581-1) Vi-V38549 RBF RF-8

1   Now I'm going to Brownsville : take that right-hand
        road
2   Lord I ain't going to stop walking : till I get in
        sweet mama's door
3   Now the girl I'm loving : she got this great long
        curly hair
4   And her mama and her papa : they sure don't allow me
        there
5   If you catch my jumper : hanging outside your wall
6   Now you know by that babe : I need my ashes hauled
7   Now what you going to do babe : your dough-roller
        gone
8   Go in your kitchen : Lord and cook until she come
        home

Este   2   Estes, Sleepy John

        title: Broken-Hearted, Ragged and Dirty Too
        place and date: Memphis, 26 Sept. 1929
        record numbers: (55531-3) Vi-V38582 Rt RL-307

1   Now I'm broken-hearted : ragged and dirty too
2   And if I clean up pretty mama : may I stay all night
        with you
3   Now if I can't come in mama : then I'll sit out on
        your porch
4   Lord I will leave so soon : that your man he won't
        never know
5   Now I went to my window : but I couldn't see through
        my blinds
6   I heard the bedsprings popping : and I believe I
        heard my baby crying
7   Lord how can I feel misery : Lord and feel like you
8   I have a woman in Brownsville : and she *doing the
        coochie-coo*
9   Now I'm going to Chicago : trying to ???
10 You know I'm bound to ??? : ???

Este   3   Estes, Sleepy John

        title: Diving Duck Blues
        place and date: Memphis, 26 Sept. 1929
        record numbers: (55596-2) Vi-V38549 RBF RF-8

1   Now if the river was whiskey : and I was a diving
        duck
2   I would dive on the bottom : never would come up
3   Don't never take a married woman : to be your friend
4   She will get all your money : give it to her other
        man
5   Now a married woman : always been my crave
6   Now a married woman : going to carry me to my grave
7   Now ain't it hard : to love someone else *dame*
8   You can't get her when you want her : have to use
        her when you can
9   Now the sun's going to shine : in my back door some
        day
10 Now the wind's going to rise : going to blow my
        blues away
11 Now went to the railroad : and looked up at the sun
12 If the train don't hurry : going to be some walking
        done

Este   4   Estes, Sleepy John

        title: Black Mattie Blues
        place and date: Memphis, 2 Oct. 1929
        record numbers: (56335-1) Vi-V38582 Rt RL-307

1   Oh Black Mattie : where did you stay last night
2   With your hair all tangled : clothes ain't fitting
        you right
3   Now when I had money : hello sugar pie
4   Now I'm spending all my money : goodbye country guy
5   Lord my eyes are sorrow : tears come a-rolling down
6   Now you know by that babe : fixed to leave your town
7   Now life ain't worth living : if you ain't with the
        one you love
9   Now you three times seven : you know what you want
        to do
10 Now the day that you quit me : I won't be mad with
        you

Este   5   Estes, Sleepy John

        title: Milk Cow Blues
        place and date: Memphis, 13 May 1930
        record numbers: (59918-) Vi-V38614 RBF RF-202

1   Now asked sweet mama : let me be her kid
2   She said I might go buggy : and I couldn't keep it
        hid
3   Well she looked at me : she begin to smile
4   Says I thought I would use you : for my man awhile
5   Now went upstairs : to pack my leaving trunk
6   I never saw no whiskey : the blues done made me
        sloppy drunk
7   Now some say they *dream* : some say they was ???
8   But it's a slow consumption : killing you by degrees

Este   6   Estes, Sleepy John

        title: Street Car Blues
        place and date: Memphis, 13 May 1930
        record numbers: (59919-) Vi-V38614 RBF RF-8

1   Now I know the people : is on the wander everywhere
2   Because they heard of poor John : was going around
        electric car
3   Now catch it Smith and Park Lord : ride it down to
        Summer Street
4   Lord I'm going to ease it down in Roebust : catch my
        baby out on a midnight creep

5 Lord the reason why baby : I I been so long writing
   to you
6 Because I been studying so hard : Lord how to sing
   these blues
7 Lord I lost my papa : and my dear mama too
8 Lord I'm going to quit my bad way of living : and
   visit the Sunday school

Este   7   Estes, Sleepy John

   title: Watcha Doin'?
   place and date: Memphis, 21 May 1930
   record numbers: (59967-) Vi-V38628 Rt RL-323

1 I married my baby : married her for myself
2 Then if I don't keep her : don't want nobody else
3 Now depot agent : don't tell me no lie
4 Did my baby stop here : did she keep in going
5 Now I hate to hear : Illinois Central blow
6 When my shoes get tickled : makes me want to go
7 When a man's out working : know he's doing what's
   right
8 Some old lowdown rascal : trying to steal his wife
9 Now I got up this morning : couldn't make no time
10 I didn't have no blues : messed all up in mind
11 Now take me baby : I'll be mean no more
12 You can get all my loving : let that black snake go
13 Get up in the morning : grey towel around your head
14 Ask her cook your breakfast : but she never did

Este   8   Estes, Sleepy John

   title: Poor John Blues
   place and date: Memphis, 21 May 1930
   record numbers: (59968-) Vi-V38628 Rt RL-323

1 Now I'd rather be dead : sleep in an old hollow log
2 And to be here baby : and you doing me like a dog
3 Now : what you want poor John to do
4 Lord I done everything : tried to get along with you
5 Now the woman I'm loving : she got one teeth solid
   gold
6 Lord that's been the onliest woman : got a mortgage
   on my soul
7 Now sure as the grass : on Texas earth grow green
8 Lord I ain't crazy : about nobody I ever seen

Este   9   Estes, Sleepy John

   title: Stack O' Dollars
   place and date: Memphis, 30 May 1930
   record numbers: (62547-2) Vi-23397 Rt RL-307

1 Stack of dollars : just as long as I am tall
2 If you be my woman : you can have them all
3 And I heard a rumbling : way down in the ground
4 Must have been somebody : slowly jumping down
5 You see see two women : they walking hand by hand
6 They just thinking of something Lord : how to fool
   some man
7 And I went on the mountain : I looked down in the
   sea
8 Niggers had my woman : Lord and the blues had me
9 Baby done quit me : ain't said a mumbling word
10 It weren't nothing that she knowed Lord : just
   something that she heard

   title: My Black Gal Blues
   place and date: Memphis, 30 May 1930
   record numbers: (62548-2) Vi-23397 Rt RL-307

1 Black gal she took meth : gave my brown *to her*
   death
2 If I hadn't've had my pistol : think I would run
   myself
3 When you see me coming : heist your window high
4 When you see me leaving : hang your head and cry
5 Now if I just had a-listened : what my mama said
6 I would have been at home Lord : in my faro's bed
7 Got a man on your man : kid-man on your kid
8 Lord she done got so buggy : don't try to keep it
   hid
9 Now I got up this morning : blues all around my bed
10 I turned back my *chivver* : blues all in my bed

Este   11   Estes, Sleepy John

   title: Down South Blues
   place and date: Chicago, 9 July 1935
   record numbers: (90094-A) Ch-50001 Sw S-1219

1 Now I'm going down south : and I'll stay until
   winter is gone
2 Time that wintertime is gone : I might come back
   home
3 Now I get up every morning : and I walk to Third and
   Field
4 And I'm just standing and I'm wondering : Lord just
   how to make a meal
5 Now the peoples in Memphis : they are walking the
   streets up and down
6 And you know the time is hard : peoples is starving
   all over town
7 Now I once have been a lover : baby back in my young
   days
8 But now baby was so mean : she done drove all my
   love away
9 Now I've got a girl in Brownsville : she lives down
   on *Buliphant* Lane
10 But my gal so mean : I'm scared to call her name

Este   12   Estes, Sleepy John

   title: Stop That Thing
   place and date: Chicago, 9 July 1935
   record numbers: (90095-A) Ch-50001 Sw S-1219

1 Now mama killed a chicken : and thought it was a
   duck
2 Put him on the table : with his legs straight up
3 ??? : with your cup and glass
4 Catch the liquor : just to make me laugh
5 Now I went upstairs to sleep a little bit : went
   back to sleep a little more
6 The old bed fell down : had to sleep on the floor
7 Old Aunt Dinah : walking down the street
8 When she walk : she begin to creep
9 Skin on her head : just as tight as a drum
10 A little song : called deedle dee dum
11 One could beat it : and one could sing
12 One tell you : why don't you do that thing
13 Now a bow-legged rooster : and a knock-kneed hen
14 Both run together : but they ain't no kin
15 Now the monkey and the baboon : sitting on the fence
16 The monkey told the baboon : you got no sense

Este 13   Estes, Sleepy John

    title: Someday Baby Blues
    place and date: Chicago, 9 July 1935
    record numbers: (90096-A) Ch-50068 Br-87.504

1 I don't care how long you gone : I won't care how
     long you stay
2 But that good kind treatment : bring you back home
     some day
3 Now if that wind : that chilly old breeze
4 Come blowing : through your B V Ds
5 If you don't quit betting : boys them dice won't
     pass
6 It's going to send you a-home : on your yas yas yas
7 It ain't but the one thing : that give a man the
     blues
8 He ain't got no bottom : in his last pair of shoes
9 I telled all the people : in your neighborhood
10 You's a no-good woman : you don't mean no good

Este 14   Estes, Sleepy John

    title: Who's Been Tellin' You Buddy Brown Blues
    place and date: Chicago, 9 July 1935
    record numbers: (90097-A) Ch-50068 Sw S-1219

1 Baby who : I mean who been telling you
2 Babe whosoever told you : they did not tell you true
3 Now have you ever tried loving : and you can't get
     it out of your mind
4 And if you could find someone : to treat you loving
     and kind
5 Now you used to be sweet : but I can't name you
     sweet no more
6 Because every time I come to your house : some man
     hanging around your door
7 Now I'm going to get up in the morning : and I'm
     going to do like Buddy Brown
8 Know I'm going to eat my breakfast : I believe I'll
     lay back down
9 Now I know my dog : [anywhere, wherever] I hear him
     bark
10 Know I can tell my little woman : if I feel her in
     the dark

Este 15   Estes, Sleepy John

    title: Married Woman Blues
    place and date: Chicago, 17 July 1935
    record numbers: (90175-A) Ch-50048 OJL-21

1 Now don't never take : a married woman to be your
     friend
2 She will get all your money : to her same man back
     again
3 Now my sweet woman : she always *doing my cleans*
4 Now my little woman : won't help me sell my greens
5 Now I looked down the railroad : till my eyes got
     green and sore
6 If you don't stop tomorrow : then ??? will be my
     goal
7 Now it must've be traintime : I hear the whistle
     blow
8 Now it blow just like : it ain't going to blow no
     more
9 Now just as sure as the grass : on the ground grow
     green
10 I ain't crazy faro : woman that I ever seen

Este 16   Estes, Sleepy John

    title: Drop Down Mama
    place and date: Chicago, 17 July 1935
    record numbers: (90176-A) Ch-50048 OJL-21

1 Now drop down baby : let your ??? be
2 I know : just what you trying to pull on me
3 Well mama you don't allow me : to fool around all
     night long
4 Now I may look like I'm crazy : poor John do know
     right from wrong
5 Go away from my window : quit scratching on my
     screen
6 You were badly mistreated : I know just what you
     mean
7 Some of these womens : sure do make me *charged*
8 Have a handful of give-me : a mouthful of
     much-obliged
9 Woman I'm loving : wants *me sell this gold*
10 That's the onliest woman : a mortgage on my soul
11 See me coming : put your men outdoors
12 You know I ain't no stranger : done been here before

Este 17   Estes, Sleepy John

    title: Government Money
    place and date: New York, 2 Aug. 1935
    record numbers: (62461-A) De-7414 Sw S-1219

1 Now on the farm : they all have joined the
     government loan
2 Now the government give you three years chance : and
     you could have something of your own
3 Now the government furnish you a milkcow : a rooster
     and some portion of hen
4 You know long through the spring : then you can have
     some money to spend
5 Now the women used to [count, holler] on the bonus :
     but they are [hollering, counting] on the *rent*
     check now
6 You know I didn't go to the army : but I am using
     this government money anyhow
7 Now the governor he fought : for the plant of plenty
     corn and wheat
8 You know long through the winter : you can have
     something to eat

Este 18   Estes, Sleepy John

    title: I Wanta Tear It All the Time
    place and date: New York, 2 Aug. 1935
    record numbers: (62462-A) De-7342 Sw S-1219

1 Tear it long : tear it wide
2 Can tear it down : to my sides
3 Tear it for the young : tear it for the old
4 I can tear it : just dry long so
5 Tear it on the street : tear it on the shore
6 Know by that : I want to tear it some more
7 Tear it in the yard : tear it at the gate
8 Know by that : I can tear it of late
9 Tear it for Mae : tear it for Joe
10 You know by that : I want to tear it some more
11 Tear it in the morning : late at night
12 You know by that : I didn't tear it just right

Este 19   Estes, Sleepy John

    title: Vernita Blues
    place and date: New York, 2 Aug. 1935
    record numbers: (62463-A) De-7342 Cor CP-58

1 Vernita : honey what do you want me to do
2 Now I've done everything : but I can't get along
     with you

Este 19   Estes, Sleepy John

3 Now if you see Vernita : tell her hurry home
4 Had no loving : since she been gone
5 Vernita : baby where did you stay last night
6 Now you come home this morning : babe the moon was
   shining bright
7 Now I met Alberta : way out across the sea
8 Now she didn't write no letter : and she didn't care
   for me
9 Vernita : could anything I do to change your mind
10 Now I could come to love you : if you would treat me
   nice and kind

Este 20   Estes, Sleepy John

     title: I Ain't Gonna Be Worried No More
     place and date: New York, 2 Aug. 1935
     record numbers: (62464-A) De-7414 Sw S-1219

1 You know I worried last night : all night before
2 You know by that : I won't be worried no more
3 I was worried for you : I was worried for me
4 You know by that : I'm going to let it be
5 Now look here baby : see what you done done
6 Made me love you : now your man done come
7 Now my baby doing something : that I never could
   stand
8 I believe she's running : with a cooncan game
9 Now I bought some slippers : I bought some socks
10 Come home last night : had the back door locked

Este 21   Estes, Sleepy John

     title: Floating Bridge
     place and date: New York, 2 Aug. 1935
     record numbers: (62465-A) De-7442 RBF RF-8

1 Now I never will forget : that floating bridge
2 Tell me five minutes time : under water I was hid
3 When I was going down : I throwed up my hands
4 Please : take me on dry land
5 Now they carried me in the house : and they laid me
   across the bank
6 About a gallon and a half of muddy water : I had
   drank
7 They dried me off : and they laid me in the bed
8 Couldn't hear nothing : but muddy water running
   through my head
9 Now my mother often taught me : quit playing a bum
10 Go somewhere : settle down and make a crop
11 Now the people standing on the bridge : screaming
   and crying
12 Lord have mercy : where we going

Este 22   Estes, Sleepy John

     title: Need More Blues
     place and date: New York, 2 Aug. 1935
     record numbers: (62466-A) De-7365 RBF RF-8

1 Need-more : it has hung a-many men
2 And that's the reason : I believe I'll make a change
3 Now something to tell you : keep it to yourself
4 Don't tell your sister : don't tell nobody else
5 Now bought some gloves : bought you some socks
6 I believe poor John : he needs a box
7 Now look a-here baby : see what you done done
8 Done made me love you : now your man done come
9 Now take me back : won't do you mean no more
10 Get all my loving : you let Mr so-and-so go

Este 23   Estes, Sleepy John

     title: Jack and Jill Blues
     place and date: New York, 3 Aug. 1935
     record numbers: (62479-A) De-7365 RBF RF-8

1 Now the sun going to shine : in my back door some
   day
2 Now the wind going to rise : blow my blues away
3 Now sure as the stars : shine in the world above
4 You know life is too short : to worry about the one
   you love
5 Now I ain't got no woman : ain't got no *child to
   school*
6 Reason I'm hanging around here : sticking here dry
   long so
7 Now you never have told me : how you want your
   rolling done
8 Now I believe you must a-want me : to roll from sun
   to sun
9 Now it was late last night : when everything was
   still
10 Now me and my baby : was playing old Jack and Jill

Este 24   Estes, Sleepy John

     title: Poor Man's Friend
     place and date: New York, 3 Aug. 1935
     record numbers: (62480-A) De-7442 RBF RF-11

1 Well well when you see *lindy women* : I want you to
   throw your wives in the van
2 Well well probably next spring : hey I'm going to
   rig up my T Model again
3 Well well the T Model Ford : I say is the poor man's
   friend
4 Well well it will get you there : hey well when your
   money is spent
5 Well well one thing about the T Model : you don't
   have to shift no gears
6 Well well just let down the brake and feed the gas :
   hey and the stuff is here
7 Well well a V-Eight Ford : and it done took to style
8 Well well they raised it all the way from ninety :
   hey down to a hundred miles
9 Well well somebody : they done stole my wine on the
   road
10 Well well it's find somebody : hey got a T Model
   Ford

Este 25   Estes, Sleepy John

     title: Hobo Jungle Blues
     place and date: New York, 3 Aug. 1935
     record numbers: (62481-A) De-7354 Sw S-1219

1 Now when I left Chicago : I left on that G and M
2 Then if I reach my home : I'll be changed all on
   that L and N
3 Now I came in all in that Main West : and I putted
   down at Chicago Heights
4 Now you know it didn't hobo John none : and that's
   where I stayed all night
5 Now if you hobo in Brownsville : you better not be
   peeping out
6 Now Mr Whitten will get you : and Mr Guy will wear
   you out
7 Now out east of Brownsville : about four miles from
   town
8 Now if you ain't got your fare : that's where they
   will let you down

Este 26   Estes, Sleepy John

    title: Airplane Blues
    place and date: New York, 3 Aug. 1935
    record numbers: (62482-A) De-7354 Sw S-1219

1 I'm going to get in my airplane I'm going to get in
   my airplane : I'm going to ride all over I'm going
   to ride all over your town
2 Then if I spy the woman I'm loving : poor John going
   to let this air poor John going to let this
   airplane down
3 Here's my hand here's my hand : you can lead me
   where you want you can lead me where you want me
   to go
4 Then if you lead me wrong this time : you won't lead
   me no and you won't lead me no more
5 I know my baby I know my baby : and she's bound to
   jump and she's bound to jump and shout
6 Now when she gets over to Atlanta : I done rolled
   them few I done rolled them few days out
7 You three times seven you three times seven : you
   ought to know what you want you ought to know what
   you want to do
8 Now the day that you quit me : and I won't be mad
   with I won't be mad with you
9 Just the day before Christmas just the day before
   Christmas : let me bring your present let me bring
   your present tonight
10 Now I will be your Santa Claus : even if my whiskers
   even if my whiskers is white

Este 27   Estes, Sleepy John

    title: Everybody Oughta Make a Change
    place and date: New York, 22 Apr. 1938
    record numbers: (63647-A) De-7571 RBF RF-8

1 Now change in the ocean : change in the deep blue
   sea
2 Take me back baby : you'll find some change in me
3 Everybody : they ought to change sometime
4 Because it's soon or late : we have to go down in
   that old lonesome ground
5 Now change my money : change my honey
6 I change baby : just to keep from being funny
7 Now change my pants : change my shirt
8 I change baby : to get shed of the dirt
9 Now change home : I change town
10 I change baby : all the way around
11 Now change walk : I change talk
12 I change baby : just to keep from being balked

Este 28   Estes, Sleepy John

    title: Liquor Store Blues
    place and date: New York, 22 Apr. 1938
    record numbers: (63648-A) De-7491 RBF RF-11

1 Now if you're ever on *Fourth Street* : I'll tell
   you what to do
2 Let Mr Peter Adams : get acquainted with you
3 Well you won't have to go : well you won't have to
   go
4 You can get what you want to : right here in my
   liquor store
5 He got a little whiskey : he got a little gin
6 All you got to do : is step in the back end
7 I met Mr Peter : down on Monroe Street
8 Come to Fourth Street : right around with me
9 He got some on his floor : he got some on his shelf
10 All you got to do : is just to help yourself
11 Mr Peter Albert : the discount man
12 You ask him for a favor : he won't make you ashamed

Este 29   Estes, Sleepy John

    title: Easin' Back to Tennessee
    place and date: New York, 22 Apr. 1938
    record numbers: (63649-A) De-7516 Sw S-1220

1 Now woke up this morning : couldn't hardly see
2 Snow on the ground : about eight foot deep
3 Lord have mercy : baby what become of me
4 You know I feel just like easing : back down into
   Tennessee
5 Now call William in the office : want to see you
   alone
6 I can't do nothing : with this white stuff on
7 Now I'm on the South Side : my buddy on the east
8 I don't know : whether he got any place to sleep
9 Say car can't go : margin too slick
10 Probably might slip back : off in a ditch
11 Now twenty-two twenty-four : West *Hubbard* Avenue
12 That's where you get : my nineteen and thirty-two

Este 30   Estes, Sleepy John

    title: Fire Department Blues
    place and date: New York, 22 Apr. 1938
    record numbers: (63650-A) De-7571 Sw S-1220

1 Now go call the fire department : for my house is
   burning down
2 You know that must be little Martha Hardin : because
   it's on the north side of town
3 I said the people is running : and I wonder who
   could it be
4 You know that must be little Martha Hardin : I saw
   them turn down on Wilson Street
5 When you see the chief : boys please clear the
   street
6 Because you know he's going down : save little
   Martha Hardin's house for me
7 She's a hard-working woman : you know her salary is
   very small
8 Then when she pay up her house rent : that don't
   leave anything for insurance at all
9 Now I wrote little Martha a letter : five days it
   returned back to me
10 You know little Martha Hardin's house done burnt
   down : she done moved on Bathurst Street

Este 31   Estes, Sleepy John

    title: Clean Up at Home
    place and date: New York, 22 Apr. 1938
    record numbers: (63651-B) De-7516 Sw S-1220

1 I washed my clothes : I hanged them by the fire
2 Get up in the morning : they be finally dry
3 I went to the ??? : trying to make me a dime
4 Say go away boy : clean up and get on some time
5 Five cent cap : and ten cent suit
6 Then you all think : I'm trying to act cute
7 I done something : that you can't do
8 Go down on State Street : get a one potful stew
9 I played for the colored : I play for the white
10 All you got to do : act kind of nice

Este 32   Estes, Sleepy John

    title: New Someday Blues
    place and date: New York, 22 Apr. 1938
    record numbers: (63652-A) De-7473 RBF RF-8

1 When trouble first started : down in my front door
2 Seems like I had more trouble : in my life before
3 Now trouble in the morning : trouble late at night
4 Seems like I'm treated : every way but right

Este   32   Estes, Sleepy John

5 Now you got a little woman : she won't treat you
       right
6 Feed you in the day : go out with some man at night
7 I wonder what's the matter : can't get no mail
8 Had a dream last night : black cat crossed my trail
9 I know my baby : tell you how I know
10 By the great long hair : same little dress she wore
11 Now look a-here baby : see what you done done
12 You done made me love you : now your man done come

Este   33   Estes, Sleepy John

       title: Brownsville Blues
       place and date: New York, 22 Apr. 1938
       record numbers: (63653-A) De-7473 RBF RF-8

1 Now I can straighten your wires : you know poor
       Vasser can grind your valves
2 Man when I turn your motor loose : and it sure will
       split the air
3 Now Vasser can line your wheels : you know poor
       Vasser can tune your horn
4 Then when he set it out on the highway : you can
       hear your motor hum
5 Now my generator is bad : and you know my lights
       done stopped
6 And I reckon I'd better take it over to Durhamville
       : and I'm going to stop at Vasser Williams' shop
7 Now I were raised in Lauderdale County : you know I
       was schooled on Winfield Lane
8 Then what I made of myself : I declare it was a
       crying shame
9 Now Brownsville is my home : and you know I ain't
       going to throwed it down
10 Because I'm acquainted with John Law : and they
       won't let me down

Este   34   Estes, Sleepy John

       title: Special Agent
       place and date: New York, 22 Apr. 1938
       record numbers: (63654-A) De-7491 RBF RF-1

1 Now when I left for Richmond : the weather was kind
       of cool
2 Said boy you all be careful : probably you might
       catch the flu
3 Now I *swung that manifest* : I went down in the
       three rail *box*
4 Now I couldn't hear the special agent : when he come
       tipping over *soft*
5 Now some special agents up the country : sure is
       hard on a man
6 Now they will put him off when he hungry : and won't
       even let him ride no train
7 Now I was setting down in Centralia : and I sure was
       feeling bad
8 Now they wouldn't let me ride no fast train : they
       put me off on a doggone *drag*
9 Now special agent special agent : put me off close
       to some town
10 Now I got to do some recording : and I ought to be
       recording right now

Este   35   Estes, Sleepy John

       title: Mailman Blues
       place and date: Chicago, 4 June 1940
       record numbers: (93004-A) De-7789 Sw S-1220

1 Mailman : please stop by my box today
2 You know I'm looking for a letter from my baby : you
       know I want to hear from her right away

Este   35   Estes, Sleepy John

3 Reason I ain't been getting no mail : you know I
       done found out what it's all about
4 You know the mailman been getting drunk : he been
       leaving my mail at somebody else's house
5 Now I been waiting on the mailman : he usually come
       around about eleven o'clock
6 Now I guess he must have had car trouble : or either
       the road must be blocked
7 Mailman : please don't you lose your head
8 You know I'm looking for a letter from my babe :
       some of my people might be dead

Este   36   Estes, Sleepy John

       title: Time Is Drawing Near
       place and date: Chicago, 4 June 1940
       record numbers: (93005-A) De-7789 Sw S-1220

1 Now it used to be the time : be getting two bucks a
       day
2 But now we getting fifty cents : *running down*
       proper pay
3 Time : time is drawing near
4 Now can't you see : more and more every year
5 Now I remember back in time : before we got grown
6 Be damned : to let sundown catch a ??? on
7 Now my mother used to say : the sign will be
8 We couldn't tell summer from winter : no more by the
       birds and of the trees
9 Now it used to be the time : get a corn crop in
       March
10 But now we can't get one in June : and neither July
11 Now you'd go to the church : just to work for soul
12 But now we go : to buy one another's clothes

Este   37   Estes, Sleepy John

       title: Mary Come On Home
       place and date: Chicago, 4 June 1940
       record numbers: (93006-A) De-7814 Sw S-1220

1 Stopped little Mary : across the creek
2 Soon as I got her : somebody took her from me
3 Love little Mary : always will
4 Once in town : she liked to got me killed
5 Took little Mary : down to Tipton *bell*
6 All the time she was out : she was raising hell
7 Down in *Lake* County : in that gumbo mud
8 Where the mosquito bills : keep a-biting through her
       tub
9 You get to *Stanford* : and look all around
10 Ask anybody : little Mary in town

Este   38   Estes, Sleepy John

       title: Jailhouse Blues
       place and date: Chicago, 4 June 1940
       record numbers: (93007-A) De-7814 RBF RF-8

1 Now I was sitting in jail : with my eyes all full of
       tears
2 You know I'm glad I didn't get lifetime : boys and I
       escaped the electric chair
3 Now I consulted lawyers : and I know darn well I was
       wrong
4 You know I couldn't get a white man in Brownsville :
       yes to even say they would go my bond
5 Now the sheriff he arrest me : and he march me
       around front of the circuit court
6 You know I knowed the thing was getting kind of
       squally : I heard the city judge when he set up
       his court
7 Now no more stewball : yes and neither no more white
       rice

Este   38   Estes, Sleepy John

8   Now you ought need not feel uneasy : you won't have
    to take this workhouse advice

Este   39   Estes, Sleepy John

        title: Tell Me About It
        place and date: Chicago, 4 June 1940
        record numbers: (93008-A) De-7766 Sw S-1220

1   *Some* was good : some said mean
2   All these *cotton nip* : ain't got no tea
3   Ever in Brownsville : go into nineteen
4   Old *Tim Lepson* : *get stoned on gin*
5   Tommy so tall : *no shine* low
6   Everybody in Brownsville : say he got a-plenty of
    dough
7   He *rattle his field* : get *a ??? rule*
8   Ask for a little money : he say boys share the mule
9   *Stone* live in country : Mr ??? live in town
10 Soon that morning : Mr ??? hit that black line
11 ??? on the ??? : ??? on the truck
12 *Men say why* : *and hog people's stuff*

Este   40   Estes, Sleepy John

        title: Drop Down
        place and date: Chicago, 4 June 1940
        record numbers: (93009-A) De-7766 Sw S-1220

1   My old lady coming : down the line
2   She was low in front : she was bouncy behind
3   I believe I'll drop down : I don't feel welcome here
4   Now I'm going to get me a woman : for the brand new
    coming year
5   Went to the barber shop : to get me a shine
6   Say go away darky : to that door around the line
7   Now an old lady : had a jug of wine
8   Say go away son : you can't play the *lion*
9   Look here baby : see what you done done
10 You made me love you : now your man done come
11 Way down yonder : in the old West End
12 Women out there : look like sex of men

Este   41   Estes, Sleepy John

        title: You Shouldn't Do That
        place and date: Chicago, 24 Sept. 1941
        record numbers: (064916-1) BB-B8915 BC-7

1   Don't a man do wrong : till a man make hisself at
    home
2   He may come back : catch his head while you lay on
3   Men goes and gambles : lose all his change
4   He come back home : his little wife has to bear the
    blame
5   Don't a man act funny : when a single woman ease in
    town
6   He stay out all night : he throw his home girl down
7   I knowed you never loved me : when you fell down on
    my knees
8   You had been drinking that old moonshine : trying to
    jive poor me
9   I won't play marbles : on my baby's marble ground
10 I won't be worried with the ??? : I'm going to move
    out to the edge of town

Este   42   Estes, Sleepy John

        title: Lawyer Clark Blues
        place and date: Chicago, 24 Sept. 1941
        record numbers: (064924-1) BB-B8871 RCA LPV-518

1   Now got offices in town : resident out on *Sentry*
    Road
2   He got a nice little lake : right inside the grove
3   But you know I like Mr Clark : yes he really is my
    friend
4   He say if I just stay out of the [grave, graveyard]
    : he see that I won't go to the pen
5   Now Mr Clark is a lawyer : his youngest brother is
    too
6   When the battles get hot : he tell him just what to
    do
7   Now he lawyers for the rich : he lawyers for the
    poor
8   He don't try to rob nobody : just bring *along to
    the store*
9   Now once I got in trouble : you know I was going to
    take a ride
10 He didn't let it reach the courthouse : he kept it
    on the outside
11 Now Mr Clark is a good lawyer : he good as I ever
    seen
12 He the first man that proved : that water run
    upstream

Este   43   Estes, Sleepy John

        title: Little Laura Blues
        place and date: Chicago, 24 Sept. 1941
        record numbers: (064925-1) BB-B8871 RCA LPV-518

1   Little Laura was a gal : she was sixteen
2   Her *dammy dam* won't listen : to her dream
3   Little Laura was a dreamer : dream those disturbing
    dreams
4   She's the dreamingest gal : dreamingest gal I ever
    seen
5   Now she dreamed : she was going with the man next
    door
6   She dreamed : she was kissing his oh oh oh
7   She dreamed : she was riding in some man's
    automobile
8   She's the dreamingest gal : dreamingest gal I ever
    seen
9   Now she dreamed : she was sitting in the grass by
    the mill
10 She dreamed : she had taken me from the gal on the
    hill
11 Little Laura was a dreamer : most all of the dreams
    forecast
12 She's the dreamingest gal : dreamingest gal I ever
    seen
13 Now she dreamed : I was hugging her close to my
    breast
14 She told Jimmy that much of the dream : but she
    wouldn't tell the rest
15 Now she dreamed about love : from kissing on down
16 She's the dreamingest gal : for miles around
17 Little Laura was a dreamer : most all of her dreams
    come true
18 She had dream all about loving : and she know just
    what to do

Este   44   Estes, Sleepy John

        title: Working Man Blues
        place and date: Chicago, 24 Sept. 1941
        record numbers: (064926-1) BB-B8950 RBF RF-8

1   Now you done spent all my nineteen forty rent :
    woman you done worked on my substitute

Este 44   Estes, Sleepy John

2 Then if you don't reach that nineteen forty-one :
   ooh babe what in the world you going to do
3 Now you ought to cut off so many trucks and tractors
   : white folks you ought to work more mules and men
4 Then you know that would make : ooh boy money get
   thick again
5 Now when a man gets to gambling : you know he's
   turning his stocks into feed
6 He say he going to sell his corn and buy gas : ooh
   boys pour it in the automobile
7 Now I been studying I been wondering : what makes a
   man turn the ground over in the wintertime
8 You know let the snow and rain rot the grass : ooh
   boys that make fertilizer for the ground
9 Now the government give us a school in Brownsville :
   boy you know I think that's very nice
10 You know the children can go in the daytime : ooh
   boys and the old folks have it at night

EvanJ   1   Evans, Joe

     title: New Huntsville Jail
     place and date: New York, 20 May 1931
     record numbers: (10651-2) Or-8080 His HLP-8002

1 Write me a letter : and send it by mail
2 I want you to tell my dear old mother : I'm in the
   New Huntsville jail
3 I want you to tell her beans is tough : and the meat
   is so fat
4 I want you to tell my dear old mother : it's hard
   for me to eat that
5 If I had a-listened : what my mother said
6 I might have been rolling : somewheres in a folding
   bed
7 But I fooled around : with my long *harred*
8 Now I'm laying here in this New Huntsville jail :
   and I'm almost dead
9 Ashes to ashes : and dust to dust
10 And if God don't have me : you know the devil must
11 As I lay down in my cell at night : I tries so hard
   to take my rest
12 Cockroaches and chinches : begin to crawl over my
   breast

EvanJ   2   Evans, Joe

     title: Sitting on Top of the World
     place and date: New York, 21 May 1931
     record numbers: (10659-1) Ba-32211 His HLP-8002

1 Worked all the summer : and all the fall
2 Just trying to find : my little all and all
3 Was in the spring : one summer day
4 Just when she left me : she's gone to stay
5 Needn't come here running : holding up your hands
6 I can get me a woman : quick as you can a man
7 It have been days : I didn't know your name
8 Why should I worry : and cry in vain
9 Going down to the station : down in the yard
10 Going to catch me a freight train : when times got
   hard
11 The lonesome days : have done gone by
12 Why should you beg me : and say goodbye

EvanJ   3   Evans, Joe

     title: Down in Black Bottom
     place and date: New York, 21 May 1931
     record numbers: (10664-1) Or-8083 Yz L-1015

1 You go down Black Bottom : put your money in your
   shoe

EvanJ   3   Evans, Joe

2 Because the Black Bottom women gal : ain't going to
   do nothing but take it away from you
3 They don't care nothing : about what in the world
   they do
4 They'd sooner take that money : out of the bottom of
   your shoe
5 They'll take your money : and they'll take your
   clothes
6 And one of them tell the police next morning :
   partner ???
7 Now run here mama : and run here quick
8 Just take a look out here in the back yard : just
   look at sis
9 Come in here sis : you dirty little thing
10 Out there trying to be something : and you don't
   know how
11 I got me a woman : she lives way down in Tennessee
12 Just big as black and greasy : great God as greasy
   can be
13 Her head is nappy : and her feet done got long
14 Take God to tell : who she been waiting on

EvanJ   4   Evans, Joe

     title: Shook It This Morning Blues
     place and date: New York, 21 May 1931
     record numbers: (10665-2) Or-8083 Yz L-1015

1 Now I shook it this morning : baby until late last
   night
2 And when I come in twelve o'clock : ??? shake it up
   right
3 Said now if I could holler : just like a mountain
   jack
4 I would crawl up on some mountain : holler for that
   woman back
5 Two kind of people : baby I can't understand
6 A bow-legged woman : likes a knock-kneed man
7 Now when you see two women : running hand in hand
8 You can bet your life : one's got the other's man
9 ??? *upped* and come here : caught me in a barrel
10 I ain't even got no friends : even got no gal
11 I got a rock for my pillow : treetop for my bed
12 I ain't got nowheres : to lay my weary head

Ezel   1   Ezell, Will

     title: Pitchin' Boogie
     place and date: Richmond, Ind., 20 Sept. 1929
     record numbers: (15650) Pm-12855 Mil MLP-2018

1 Now look here girl : put on your best dress
2 We going to see : who can do the boogie-woogie the
   best
3 Now look over : where them girls got them dress of
   green
4 I swear to God : this boogie too mean
5 Get a half pint of moonshine : two or three bottles
   of beer
6 I believe : I'll pitch the boogie right here
7 Get all your moonshine : get all your beer
8 Close the door : ain't going to let nobody up here

FloN   1   Florence, Nellie

     title: Jacksonville Blues
     place and date: Atlanta, 21 Apr. 1928
     record numbers: (146174-1) Co-14342-D OJL-6

1 Let me be your wiggler : until your wobbler come
2 If she beats me wiggling : she got to wobble some
3 Women crying danger : but I ain't raising my hand
4 I got a way of loving : they just can't understand
5 Men they call me oven : they say that I'm red-hot

FloN   1   Florence, Nellie

   6   They say I got something : the other gals ain't got
   7   I can strut my pudding : spread my grease with ease
   8   Because I know my onions : that's why I always
         please
   9   Wild about coffee : but I'm crazy about China tea
  10   But this sugar daddy : is sweet enough for me
  11   One John in the city : one lives up on the hill
  12   But the man I'm loving : lives down in Jacksonville

FloN   2   Florence, Nellie

         title: Midnight Weeping Blues
         place and date: Atlanta, 21 Apr. 1928
         record numbers: (146175-2) Co-14342-D OJL-6

   1   I moaned I moaned : I cried the whole night long
   2   I was wondering : where in the world my man done
         gone
   3   I'd rather be dead : in some lonesome place
   4   Than for my man : keeps treating me this a-way
   5   When you see two of you women : going hand in hand
   6   You can judge by that : they got one of the other
         one's man
   7   I went to the Gypsy : to get my fortune told
   8   *Said the evil* is hard luck : doggone your
         hard-luck soul
   9   I said Lord Lord : something going on wrong
  10   Because the man I love : done been here and gone
  11   I turned around : and two of them Gypsies I told
  12   Say Nellie needs a man : most anywhere you go
  13   I went to my bedside : hung my head and cried
  14   Got a letter from my man : that my man had died
  15   I hung my head : and I cried the whole night long
  16   Said I'm right upset : and I've got those weeping
         blues

FosD   1   Foster, Dessa

         title: Tell It to the Judge No. 1
         place and date: Chicago, c. 28 Jan. 1931
         record numbers: (C-7238-A) Me-M12117 Yz L-1031

   1   I'm telling you this morning : I'm tired of you
         searching my house
   2   I have a notion this morning : beating you up and
         throwing you out
   3   The hell with the search warrant : go look and see
         what you can find
   4   You ain't never found no liquor : and you searched
         my house two or three times
   5   Give me a break : don't make me pay no fine
   6   That judge is going to lick me : because I been here
         so many times

FosD   2   Foster, Dessa

         title: Tell It to the Judge No. 2
         place and date: Chicago, c. 28 Jan. 1931
         record numbers: (C-7239-?) Me-M12117 Yz L-1031

   1   I'm guilty kind old judge : please treat me nice and
         kind
   2   For I'll stay home and try my best : to get money to
         pay my fine
   3   I never seen : a judge as mean as you before
   4   Sending me a poor woman : and letting everybody else
         go
   5   You can do as you please : thirty days won't make me
         cry
   6   When I come back I'm going to gamble : and sell
         moonshine all my life

FoxJ   1   Fox, John D.

         title: The Worried Man Blues
         place and date: Richmond, Ind., 14 Dec. 1927
         record numbers: (GEX-1011-A) Ge-6352 OJL-10

   1   On a Sunday morning : just about half past four
   2   My babe took my hand : said daddy I can't use you no
         more
   3   Lord I may get better : babe I can't get well
   4   I'm going back to my used-to-be : and baby it's
         country farewell
   5   Lord I'm worried now : but I won't be worried long
   6   It takes a man like me : to carry this worried song
   7   Baby I've been worried so long : that worrying don't
         bother me
   8   But ain't nobody here babe : to take pity on poor me
   9   I've got a good girl : and I've got a lazy friend
  10   And if I tell about her : he always tell me where
         she been
  11   I always will have trouble : until I'm dead and gone
  12   If you will love me mama : you'd never treat me
         wrong

FoxJ   2   Fox, John D.

         title: The Moanin' Blues
         place and date: Richmond, Ind., 15 Dec. 1927
         record numbers: (GEX-1019-A) Ge-6352 Rt RL-334

   1   And I got a letter from my baby : and it said that
         she was dying
   2   I have to catch this mail train : I'm going back
         home flying
   3   Now when I came in your town babe : I didn't come
         here to stay long
   4   Now *do you believe that I gone back to her people*
         : but my baby knowed that I was gone
   5   Lordy Lordy : Lordy Lordy Lord
   6   The only little girl that I love : she treats me
         like a dog
   7   I'm going to leave you baby : your crying won't make
         me stay
   8   But it's just like I told you : you're going to need
         my help some day
   9   Mama I'm the same man : you just only changed your
         ways
  10   ??? *has beaten* mama : you're going to be sorry
         some day

FulB   1   Fuller, Blind Boy

         title: I'm a Rattlesnakin' Daddy
         place and date: New York, 23 July 1935
         record numbers: (17862-2) ARC-6-01-56 BC-11

   1   I woke up this morning : about half past four
   2   Somebody knocking : on my back door
   3   Yes he rattle this morning : about half past three
   4   Half past four : he want to rattle some more
   5   I got a range in my kitchen : bake bread nice and
         brown
   6   Get my rattlesnake daddy : turn my damper upside
         down
   7   I can rattle to the left : rattle to the right
   8   My woman said I believe my rattlesnake daddy : can
         rattle all night
   9   I rattle every morning : till late at night
  10   Reason why : my rattlesnake mama don't allow me out
         of her sight
  11   Now the old folks rattling : the young ones too
  12   Ain't nobody rattle : just like the way I do
  13   Yes I rattled this morning : about half past ten
  14   Half past nine : I'm going to rattle again

FulB 2 Fuller, Blind Boy

title: Rag, Mama, Rag
place and date: New York, 25 July 1935
record numbers: (17863-2) ARC-35-10-32 BC-6

1 Says I'm going up to town : hat in my hand
2 Looking for a woman : ain't got no man
3 Just as well be looking : for a needle in the sand
4 Looking for a woman : ain't got no man
5 Says I wouldn't have thought : my baby treat me so
6 Let another man : stayed at my back door
7 Mind mama : what you sow
8 You got to reap : just what you sow
9 Now if you get you one woman : you better get you
   two
10 One for your buddy : other one for you
11 I's got me a wife : and a sweetheart too
12 Wife don't love me : my sweetheart do
13 Cried my gal hollered murder : I ain't raised my
   hand
14 Pistol in my pocket : blackjack in my hand
15 Took my gal : under willow tree
16 Ought to hear her hollering : don't murder me

FulB 3 Fuller, Blind Boy

title: Stealing Bo-Hog
place and date: New York, 7 Sept. 1937
record numbers: (21627-2) ARC-8-01-65 BC-11

1 I'm not an elephant baby : my snout is large and
   round
2 Come to see me mama : when your love some down
3 If you see my pigmeat mama : tell her to hurry home
4 Says some lowdown bo-hog woman : have take my
   sow-pig from home
5 Yes the reason why I like pigmeat : you know it's
   nice and sweet
6 My gal she got something : sure is hard to beat
7 Yes she's large in the body : she's neat in the
   waist
8 My gal she got something : I know you would like to
   taste
9 Say you get away from my window : don't knock at my
   door
10 I got me a pigmeat woman : don't need sowbelly no
   more

FulB 4 Fuller, Blind Boy

title: Bye Bye Baby Blues
place and date: New York, 15 Dec. 1937
record numbers: (22156-1) Vo-04843 RBF RF-9

1 Which a-way which a-way : do that Blood Red River
   run
2 Run from my window : to that rising sun
3 Now that jumper says loader : please send me six
   foot of clay
4 Because that Blood Red River mama : is rising six
   foot a day
5 Go down to the camp : and tell my brother Bill
6 The woman he's loving : is sure going to get him
   killed
7 Now the reason why these men here : they sure don't
   draw no more
8 Right from the long table : back to that commissary
   door
9 Now I love to hear : that M and O whistle blow
10 I'm in a world of trouble God knows : and I got to
   go
11 Now I got two women : and I don't know one apart
12 There's one in my bosom : t'other one in my heart

FulB 5 Fuller, Blind Boy

title: Pistol Snapper Blues
place and date: New York, 5 Apr. 1938
record numbers: (22674-1) Vo-04106 BC-11

1 I can tell my dog : anywhere I hear him bark
2 I can tell my rider : if I feel her in the dark
3 You's a cold-blooded murderer : when you want me out
   your way
4 Says that's all right mama : you going need my help
   some day
5 And you say you going to put me : woman down in my
   lonesome grave
6 Say you must remember : I once have been your slave
7 And I feel like snapping : my pistol in your face
8 Let some brownskin woman : be here to take your
   place
9 Now you know you didn't want me : when you lied down
   across my bed
10 Drinking your moonshine whiskey mama : talking all
   out your head
11 Now give me the money baby : I'll catch that train
   and go
12 You don't have to kill me : because you don't want
   me no more
13 Now if you see my rider : tell her I said bring it
   home
14 I ain't had no loving : since my gal been gone
15 It's two kind of people in the world : that I can't
   stand
16 That's a lying woman : and a monkey-man

FulB 6 Fuller, Blind Boy

title: Piccolo Rag
place and date: New York, 5 Apr. 1938
record numbers: (22677-1) OK-06437 BC-11

1 You talk about loving : that sure is *hit*
2 You got me to loving : and it just won't quit
3 Says when I'm on a farm : I hollering whoa haw gee
4 My gal's uptown : hollering who wants me
5 Every night I come home : you got your lips painted
   red
6 Then come on daddy : let's go to bed
7 Got great big legs : and a little bitty feet
8 Something about you : is sweet sweet sweet
9 You think : you the best-looking gal in town
10 You do that loving : let it go round and round

FulB 7 Fuller, Blind Boy

title: Big House Bound
place and date: possibly Columbia, S.C., 29 Oct.
   1938
record numbers: (SC-25-1) Vo-04897 BC-11

1 I never will forget the day : they transferred me to
   the county jail
2 I had shot the woman I love : ain't got no one to
   come go my bail
3 Then I sent for my friend : please spare the rod
4 Then my friend sent me word : Lord the job was too
   doggone hard
5 I got friend who's got money : please tell him come
   go my bail
6 And my friend sent me word : had no business in the
   county jail
7 Then I felt all right : till the judge turned around
   and frowned
8 Well I'm sorry for you buddy : but you on your last
   go-round
9 I says mmm : ain't got nobody now
10 Well I got nobody : Lord come and go my bail
12 I says mmm : I mean come and go my bail

90

FulB   8   Fuller, Blind Boy

    title: You've Got Something There
    place and date: Memphis, 12 July 1939
    record numbers: (MEM-102-1) Vo-05083 BC-11

1 The day I went uptown : caught you looking well
2 She fell down : her mouth flew open like a country
    well
3 Now if you go out : stay all night
4 ??? : *about a* fuss and fight
5 She's built up a little : and I stay around
6 She can look up : long as you can look down
7 Get out now boys : and let me shut the door
8 I got to *cup them* : before I go
9 Going to tell you boys : just to call you my pals
10 A mighty bad sign : to advertise your gals

FulB   9   Fuller, Blind Boy

    title: Step It Up and Go
    place and date: New York, 5 Mar. 1940
    record numbers: (26592-A) Vo-05476 BC-11

1 Had a little girl : she was little and low
2 Used to love me : but she don't no more
3 Got a little girl : she stays upstairs
4 Try to make a living : by putting on airs
5 Front door shut : back one too
6 Blinds pulled down : what you going to do
7 Now I got a little gal : whose name was ball
8 Give her a little bit : and she took it all
9 Me and my baby : walking down the street
10 Dealing everybody : but the chief of police
11 See my woman : tell her to hurry home
12 Ain't had no loving : since she been gone
13 I'll sing this verse : ain't going to sing no more
14 Hear my gal call me : and I got to go

FulB   10   Fuller, Blind Boy

    title: Somebody's Been Talkin'
    place and date: New York, 6 Mar. 1940
    record numbers: (26599-A) Vo-05527 Rt RL-318

1 I hate to see : that rising sun go down
2 It makes me believe : my woman got me on my last
    go-round
3 She used to be mine : but look who got her now
4 She didn't mean me no good : God knows I couldn't
    keep her nohow
5 Said hear me mama : who in the world been telling
    you
6 You don't even treat me : nothing like you used to
    do
7 Said it may be a week : and it could be a month or
    two
8 But when I get lucky gal : I'm coming right back to
    you
9 Said a woman I love : she rolled all over the bed
10 She got the kind of loving : make me talk out of my
    head
11 She got coal-black eyes : she got long black curly
    hair
12 My baby got something : to lead me most anywhere
13 I hate to see : that rising sun go down
14 Lord I got a notion : my woman done and left this
    town

FulB   11   Fuller, Blind Boy

    title: Three Ball Blues
    place and date: New York, 6 Mar. 1940
    record numbers: (26600-A) Vo-05440 BC-11

1 I was walking around the streets : hear somebody
    call me and I can't stop
2 Yeah I was broke and I was hungry : on my way to the
    pawnshop
3 Says I went to the pawnshop : great God with my
    shoes in my hand
4 Says give me a loan Mr pawnshop man : and help me if
    you can
5 Says I called up in Burlington : ask my bossman to
    help me if he please
6 Says please hurry up and do something : great God
    I'm about to freeze
7 He wrote me and told me : just be sure it's one and
    two and three
8 Yeah that pawnshop something : great God that come
    falling down on poor me
9 Says I'm about to lose my home : I've done and lost
    my car
10 Yeah I'm going down to the pawnshop : see can I pawn
    my guitar
11 Says I asked that pawnshop man : what the three
    balls doing hanging on that wall
12 Says it's two to one buddy : you don't get your
    things back out of here at all

FulB   12   Fuller, Blind Boy

    title: Good Feeling Blues
    place and date: New York, 7 Mar. 1940
    record numbers: (26616-A) OK-06231 BC-11

1 You got a little woman : she won't treat you right
2 Leave in the day : and go back nights
3 When I called this morning : about half past one
4 Wake up baby : loving has just begun
5 Said I know my little woman : going to change her
    mind
6 When she walks : she reels and rocks behind
7 Says I told my baby : about half past two
8 Wake up mama : loving ain't half through
9 Says my woman she quit me : keep me worried and blue
10 Take me in your arms and love me : like you used to
    do
11 Then I called her this morning : about half past ten
12 Wake up mama : loving is just began

FulB   13   Fuller, Blind Boy

    title: Crooked Woman Blues
    place and date: New York, 7 Mar. 1940
    record numbers: (26619-A) Vo-05527 Rt RL-318

1 You can always tell : when your woman don't want you
    around
2 She will put you in jail : six feet in the ground
3 Yeah locked up in jail : and I just can't help
    myself
4 Yeah when I get out : I'm going to find me someone
    else
5 Yeah I don't believe no woman : in the whole round
    world do right
6 She act like an angel in the daytime : crooked as
    the devil at night
7 Said I got the blues : been had them all day long
8 And when I get my pistol : I won't have them long
9 Yeah I know my woman : tell you how I know
10 By the great long hair : and the same little dress
    she wore

FulB 14   Fuller, Blind Boy

    title: Bus Rider Blues
    place and date: Chicago, 19 June 1940
    record numbers: (WC-3139-A) OK-05933 BC-11

1   Going to catch that old Greyhound : going to ride
    from town going to ride from town to town
2   Then I will find my little woman : don't think she
    can't be don't think she can't be found
3   Now Mr redcap porter : won't you help me with my
    heavy won't you help me with my heavy load
4   Say now my woman she done and quit me : she's far on
    down the she's far on down the road
5   Then I know my little woman : she bound to love she
    bound to love me some
6   When she throws her arms around poor me : like the
    circle around a like the circle around the sun
7   It's the day before Christmas : let me bring your
    presents let me bring your presents tonight
8   Then I will be your Santy Claus : says even if my
    whiskers says even if my whiskers ain't white

FulB 15   Fuller, Blind Boy

    title: You Got to Have Your Dollar
    place and date: Chicago, 19 June 1940
    record numbers: (WC-3140-A) OK-05712 His HLP-31

1   When I had money : I had women and friends for miles
    around
2   Yeah now I'm broke : women and friends they can't be
    found
3   Says I'm talking about a dollar : I mean a dollar
    bill
4   And I just got your dollar : you sure can get your
    order filled
5   Said if I could only read : read my little woman's
    mind
6   Then I wouldn't be here worrying : and stayed blue
    all the time
7   My baby keep me guessing : about things I want to
    know
8   Yes she got me doing things : that I never did
    before

FulB 16   Fuller, Blind Boy

    title: Thousand Women Blues
    place and date: Chicago, 19 June 1940
    record numbers: (WC-3142-A) OK-05657 RBF RF-202

1   I ain't never loved : but a thousand women in my
    life
3   Now the love I have for you woman : God knows it
    sure is strong
4   Then if you love me now woman : then you won't do
    nothing wrong
5   Now my woman please don't worry : baby while I'm out
    of your town
6   Now the love I have for you mama : God knows it
    can't be turned around
7   Now my little woman : I said she's sweet as she can
    be
8   Every time I kiss her : send a cold chill run over
    me

Gait 1   Gaither, Bill

    title: Georgia Barrel House
    place and date: Chicago, 12 June 1940
    record numbers: (WC-3104-A) OK-05714 His HLP-31

1   I know you from Georgia : but you are all right with
    me
2   And if you love me : I wonder what can it be

Gait 1   Gaither, Bill

3   You was once a good girl : and I had faith in you
4   But when you started to drinking : Lord that's too
    bad to do
5   Drinking won't help you none : crying won't do no
    good
6   Before day in the morning : I'll be done left your
    neighborhood
7   I'm going to drink one of these nights : and tell my
    sober thoughts
8   You know what I mean : give me back everything I
    bought

GibB 1   Gibson, Cleo

    title: I've Got Ford Movements in My Hips
    place and date: Atlanta, 14 Mar. 1929
    record numbers: (402311) OK-8700 Sw S-1240

1   I've got Ford engine movements in my hips : ten
    thousand miles guarantee
2   A Ford is a car everybody wants to ride : jump in
    you will see
3   You can all have the Rolls Royal : your Packard and
    Studs
4   Take a Ford engine boys : to do your stuff

GibB 2   Gibson, Cleo

    title: Nothing But the Blues
    place and date: Atlanta, 14 Mar. 1929
    record numbers: (402312) OK-8700 Sw S-1240

1   I'm so blue : just as blue as I can be
2   Because every day : is a cloudy day for me
3   I went to the depot : and looked up on the board
4   Oh I asked the operator : how long that train been
    gone
5   Oh it left here this evening : just about five
    o'clock
6   Oh that must have been the train : that my good man
    caught
7   Oh what makes my grandpa : love my grandma so
8   She's got the same old jelly : she had forty years
    ago
9   I'm going to Washington : to get my hambone boiled
10   Because these mens in Atlanta : about to let my
    hambone spoil

GibC 1   Gibson, Clifford

    title: Beat You Doing It
    place and date: Long Island City, c. June 1929
    record numbers: (482-A) QRS-R7087 Yz L-1027

1   I've have the blues about my money : had the blues
    because I'm feeling bad
2   But when my sweet woman quit me : them was the worst
    blues I ever had
3   You can ever so much money : and friends of
    different kinds
4   But to find someone to love you : I swear they're
    hard to find
5   If you should find someone to love you : someone to
    treat you right
6   You must be kind and loving : and don't run around
    at night
7   Because a woman's very funny : she wants you around
    her all the time
8   And find you's been gone : some old rounder might
    change her mind
9   Don't you never believe : your woman thinks too much
    of you
10   Because there's always been some good man : to beat
    you doing what you're trying to do

GibC   2   Gibson, Clifford

    title: Whiskey Moan Blues
    place and date: Long Island City, c. June 1929
    record numbers: (483-A) QRS-R7087 Yz L-1006

1 I been drinking and gambling : barrelhousing all my days
2 But I found someone to love me : I'm going to change my ways
3 I've always heard it : but now I know it's true
4 If you mistreat a good woman : she'll turn her back on you
5 If your woman loves you : she'll stand by you to the end
6 Nobody can steal your place : you can leave her with a bunch of men
7 If you get a jealous-hearted woman : be careful what you do
8 Because there's always somebody : tell her lies on you
9 Whiskey has been my pleasure : good-time places I've always found
10 But it's been so different now : since I have fell down

GibC   3   Gibson, Clifford

    title: Tired of Being Mistreated Part 1
    place and date: Long Island City, c. June 1929
    record numbers: (484-A) QRS-R7079 Yz L-1027

1 Ain't going to cut no kindling : ain't going to pack no coal
2 I wouldn't spend a nickel : not to save your soul
3 Because I'm tired of being mistreated : and the way you do
4 Want you to tell everybody : that I'm down on you
5 You taken my money : you left me cold in hand
6 I'm going to black your eye : you can tell your man
7 You can go tell the parson : you can tell Chief O'Brien
8 Before I take you back : I'd rather serve some time
9 You fooled me once : you fooled me twice
10 You fooled me just enough : for me to take your life
11 You left me this morning : you stayed away all day
12 You must've found something : to keep you away
13 A nickel for some sugar : a dime for some rice
14 I'm going to crucify my woman : I'm going to *take her life*

GibC   4   Gibson, Clifford

    title: Tired of Being Mistreated Part 2
    place and date: Long Island City, c. June 1929
    record numbers: (485-A) QRS-R7079 Yz L-1006

1 You might be brownskin : I might be black
2 But what I want baby : you really like
3 Girl I'm tired of being mistreated : and the way you do
4 Want you tell everybody : that I'm down on you
5 I got the money : to buy a house and lot
6 But what I want baby : you really haven't got
7 *Nice little partner* : ???
8 When I get you home : I'm going to curl your hair
9 I'm not short : I'm long and tall
10 I've just got what it takes : to make you crawl
11 Go out with me baby : in a brand new car
12 Taking a ride woman : you won't have to walk so far
13 I had two wives : I want one more
14 Come in here baby : let us lock the door

GibC   5   Gibson, Clifford

    title: Stop Your Rambling
    place and date: Long Island City, c. June 1929
    record numbers: (486-A) QRS-R7083 Yz L-1027

1 Baby stop your way of rambling : stay at home with me sometime
2 Because this way you going every night : will soon start me with a rambling mind
3 I don't mind you going : please don't stay the whole night long
4 Because you made me love you baby : and I miss you when you go
5 Oh it seems so different : you don't care for me no more
6 But some day baby : you're going to reap just what you sow

GibC   6   Gibson, Clifford

    title: Sunshine Moan
    place and date: Long Island City, c. June 1929
    record numbers: (478-A) QRS-R7083 Yz L-1027

1 Oh tell me baby : how can it be
2 You will give everybody : but you won't give me
3 Ooh baby : the sun begins to shine
4 Bought you a brand new dress : now you won't pay me no mind
5 You can spend my money : but you got to stay at home with me
6 Got to give me lots of loving : and keep my company

GibC   7   Gibson, Clifford (Roosevelt Sykes)

    title: I'm Tired of Being Mistreated
    place and date: New York, 14 June 1929
    record numbers: (402459-B) OK-8742 Yz L-1027

1 Ain't going to cut no kindling : ain't going to buy no corn
2 I wouldn't spend a quarter : not to save your soul
3 Because I'm tired of being mistreated : tired of the way you do
4 Want you to tell everybody : that I'm down on you
5 You fooled me once : you fooled me twice
6 You fooled me just enough : for me to take your life
7 You taken my money : you left me cold in hand
8 I'm going to black your eyes : you can go tell your man
9 You can go tell the sergeant : you can tell Chief O'Brien
10 But before I take it back : I'd rather serve some time
11 Now you left me this morning : you stayed away all day
12 You must have found something : to keep you away

GibC   8   Gibson, Clifford

    title: Ice and Snow Blues
    place and date: New York, 26 Nov. 1929
    record numbers: (57173-2) Vi-V38562 Yz L-1027

1 I'm going to build me a castle : out of ice and snow
2 So I can freeze these barefooted women : away from around my door
3 Just because you were a cheater : I won't give up the game
4 It don't break my heart to win : when I lose I feel the same
5 I'm going I'm going : my face you'll never see
6 But you can kiss my picture : and think the world of me

93

GibC   8   Gibson, Clifford

  7 You accuse me of women : brought your men right
     before my face
  8 After all your mistreating : no one can take your
     place

GibC   9   Gibson, Clifford

      title: Don't Put That Thing On Me
      place and date: New York, 26 Nov. 1929
      record numbers: (57174-2) Vi-V38572 Yz L-1006

  1 Don't care what you say : don't care what you do
  2 You sure can't quit your woman : and if she put that
     thing on you
  3 She put that thing on you : she puts it on you right
  4 You can't eat when you get hungry partner : you
     can't sleep at night
  5 I asked a married woman : to let me be her kid
  6 She said she's afraid she'd put that thing on me :
     and I couldn't keep it hid
  7 My woman quit me : got her another man
  8 And the way she had that thing on me : I couldn't
     raise my hand
  9 Now from my experience : I give you your advice
 10 If you got a good woman partner : you'd better treat
     her right

GibC   10   Gibson, Clifford

      title: Drayman Blues
      place and date: New York, 26 Nov. 1929
      record numbers: (57175-2) Vi-V38562 Yz L-1027

  1 Mr drayman Mr drayman : back your truck up to my
     door
  2 Take my trunk down to the station : take it never
     here no more
  3 I'm in bad luck now : going to catch me somebody's
     train
  4 Take this whole world through : my luck will be
     bound to change
  5 Bad luck wakes me every morning : trouble follows me
     all night long
  6 If I see this ain't no place for me : I'm going back
     where I belong
  7 I just received a letter : baby won't you please
     come home
  8 Say the days seem so lonesome : and the nights so
     long

GibC   11   Gibson, Clifford

      title: Old Time Rider
      place and date: New York, 26 Nov. 1929
      record numbers: (57176-2) Vi-23255 Yz L-1027

  1 Believe I'll take : my old-timey rider back
  2 Because she got a way of loving : that her daddy
     likes
  3 [Awful] nice to meet strangers : just to come and
     spend the day
  4 But that old-timey rider : can drive your blues away
  5 Did you ever wake up in the morning : and find your
     rider gone
  6 I know just how it feels : that's why I composed
     this song
  7 I went to the doctor : for my misery
  8 Said it's nothing but the blues : bearing down on me
  9 And I asked the doctor : [was there] anything that
     he could do
 10 Says I can't do nothing : till that woman come back
     to you

GibC   12   Gibson, Clifford

      title: Bad Luck Dice
      place and date: New York, 10 Dec. 1929
      record numbers: (57753-) Vi-V38590 Yz L-1027

  1 I believe I'll try : them bad-luck dice again
  2 If I keep on a-trying : I'll be bound to win
  3 Every man tries to gamble : must have a losing day
  4 So he shouldn't get evil : and throw my dice away
  5 Sometimes I believe : my woman's bad luck to me
  6 Because every time I start to gamble : I can't throw
     a thing but a three
  7 I lost all I had : everything I had to lose
  8 Even lost the one I love : but I swear I can't lose
     with you
  9 Nine and five my weakness : ten and four keeps me
     all in pawn
 10 But if I ever get lucky : I swear I'll have my
     diamonds on

GibC   13   Gibson, Clifford

      title: Levee Camp Moan
      place and date: New York, 10 Dec. 1929
      record numbers: (57754-2) Vi-V38577 Yz L-1027

  1 I am sorry : that I can't take you
  2 You don't know how to gamble : nothing else for you
     to do
  3 It's not because I love you : but it's just because
     I've been with you so long
  4 And I know you bound to miss me : baby when I'm gone
  5 Blues have mercy : have mercy on poor me
  6 Oh it might be my fault : please have my sympathy
  7 Baby if you never : never never no more
  8 If you never no more see me : you'll miss me when I
     go
  9 Mmm baby : believe I will go back home
 10 Going back to the one I love : and acknowledge that
     I done wrong

GibC   14   Gibson, Clifford

      title: Hard-Headed Blues
      place and date: New York, 10 Dec. 1929
      record numbers: (57755-2) Vi-V38577 Yz L-1027

  1 A hard-headed woman : just like a bulldog without a
     chain
  2 She won't never listen to what you say : and that
     will leave your heart in pain
  3 I've fooled with women : till I lost everything I
     own
  4 It was a married woman : cause me to lose my home
  5 A woman's so deceitful : but she's so loving and
     kind
  6 You can pack up your trunk to move : but you will
     change your mind
  7 You told me you loved me : told my boy friend too
  8 And I would not have been here : if it don't been
     for you
  9 When a dumb man tries to gamble : he expects to lose
 10 When you got a hard-headed woman : you bound to have
     the blues

GibC   15   Gibson, Clifford

      title: Blues Without a Dime
      place and date: New York, 10 Dec. 1929
      record numbers: (57756-) Vi-V38590 Yz L-1027

  1 Bad luck and trouble : and the blues without a dime
  2 When a man's got money : the blues don't cross his
     mind
  3 Always try : to keep a dollar in your hand

GibC   15   Gibson, Clifford

  4   When you ain't got no money : your woman get another
      man
  5   Don't never allow your woman : to talk no baby-talk
      to you
  6   You can tell by that : they got something in their
      heads to do
  7   I don't want no woman : if she ain't got a railroad
      man
  8   Because every day's like Sunday : I mean she's
      always got a dollar in her hand

GibC   16   Gibson, Clifford

      title: Keep Your Windows Pinned
      place and date: New York, 10 Dec. 1929
      record numbers: (57757) Vi-V38612 Yz L-1006

  1   Keep your back door locked : baby keeps your windows
      pinned
  2   If your husband should knock : tell him you're
      cooking and he can't come in
  3   You ought to buy you a bulldog : to watch us whilst
      we sleep
  4   So he can see your husband : if he makes a 'fore-day
      creep
  5   Wake up baby : please don't be so still
  6   Unless you fixing a good way : to get your daddy
      killed
  7   What's that baby : pecking on your windowpane
  8   Say the stars is shining : I know it can't be rain
  9   The big star's falling : I know it can't be long
      before day
 10   And I think it's time for me : to make my get-away

GibC   17   Gibson, Clifford

      title: Jive Me Blues
      place and date: New York, 10 Dec. 1929
      record numbers: (57758-1) Vi-V38572 Yz L-1027

  1   You can jive me baby : but I don't believe a thing
      you say
  2   You just a confidencing woman : and wants to have
      your way
  3   You can spend my money baby : you can get my loving
      too
  4   I'll do most anything : just to get along with you
  5   I lay down on my pillow : I rolled from side to side
  6   I didn't have no blues : I just was not satisfied
  7   When you see me coming : my head all hanging down
  8   It's that my sweet woman done quit me : the news all
      over town
  9   My suitcase is packed : my trunk's already gone
 10   You can tell by that : I won't be here long

GibC   18   Gibson, Clifford

      title: Brooklyn Blues
      place and date: New York, 10 Dec. 1929
      record numbers: (57759-1) Vi-23255 Yz L-1027

  1   Since we been apart : ??? seems strange to me
  2   We been together all these years : and now we can't
      agree
  3   Somebody must have told you : something to worry
      your mind
  4   But you should stop your way of living : and stay at
      home sometime
  5   All my past life : I found till today
  6   I've been trying to listen : to everything you say
  7   If you call that leaving : make the best out of life
      you can
  8   But you must always remember : your daddy has been
      your friend

GibC   18   Gibson, Clifford

  9   Some of these mornings : you going to long for me
 10   You going to want me baby : just for company

GibC   19   Gibson, Clifford

      title: Society Blues
      place and date: New York, 10 Dec. 1929
      record numbers: (57760-) Vi-38612 Yz L-1027

  1   When I was society : the women would not let me be
  2   Now I'm wild and reckless : and nobody cares for me
  3   Some people like religion : some like to rob and
      steal
  4   But I like to play with my yellow women : and my
      whiskey right from the still
  5   Cigarettes is my pleasure : and whiskey I do crave
  6   And some long tall and slender : to follow me to my
      grave
  7   I want to tell you something : happened to me one
      day
  8   It was a little brownskin woman : stole my heart
      away

GibC   20   Gibson, Clifford

      title: She Rolls It Slow
      place and date: Louisville, 9 June 1931
      record numbers: (69405-) Vi-23290 RCA INT-1175

  1   I got a little woman : but I swear she treats me
      mean
  2   Well she can bake good jellyroll : and she's so nice
      and clean
  3   She don't make no charges : she don't set no price
  4   But if you roll it once : you want to roll it twice
  5   Now the best doctor in my town : says he never heard
      tell of such
  6   Little bitty woman : could roll that jellyroll so
      much
  7   She roll it for Uncle Bill : he like to lost his
      mind
  8   He want her to keep rolling it : all the time
  9   Oh she mix up her jelly : she rolls it over slow
 10   Gets it all together : then she mix it in her dough

Gill   1   Gillum, Bill Jazz

      title: You're Laughing Now
      place and date: Aurora, Ill., 16 June 1938
      record numbers: (020822-) BB-B7769 RCA INT-1177

  1   Said I work for you baby : I treat you like a baby
      child
  2   Well you laughing at me now mama : you'll be crying
      after a while
  3   Says I give you my money : you treat me like a tramp
  4   I got holes in my shoes : and my feet is getting
      damp
  5   Oh babe : you oughtn't be so doggone wise
  6   Well you laughing at me now mama : you'll be crying
      after a while
  7   Says you three time seven : and you knows what you
      want to do
  8   Sometimes you going to think : about the good things
      I used to do
  9   You laughed and laughed : until you put my clothes
      in a pile
 10   Well you laughing at me now mama : you'll be crying
      after a while
 11   Says I tried so hard : to get along with you
 12   But somehow I couldn't please you : no way I do
 13   You laughed and said : honey I was driving you wild
 14   Well you laughing at me now mama : you'll be crying
      after a while

Gill   2   Gillum, Bill Jazz

        title: I'm Gonna Get It
        place and date: Aurora, Ill., 16 June 1938
        record numbers: (020823-) BB-B7769 RCA INT-1177

 1 Say the holdup man : says don't act tough
 2 Give me your money : I'll treat you rough
 3 Now the little dog : started in to run
 4 The big dog said : pup you just begun
 5 Now I'm going downtown : to see Lizzie Brown
 6 She got the best jellyroll : that is in town
 7 Yes there's one thing : I'm pleased to say
 8 A short-legged woman : can go a long long way
 9 I've got what it takes : I am no child
10 Makes no mistake : yes I'm running wild

Gill   3   Gillum, Bill Jazz

        title: Let Her Go
        place and date: Aurora, Ill., 16 Dec. 1938
        record numbers: (030823-) BB-B8027 RCA INT-1177

 1 I have never been worried : like I'm worried today
 2 Said my baby is going to leave me : and she's going
    away to stay
 3 When you get to thinking : about your gal
 4 Says you baby is going to leave you : and taken dime
    you have
 5 I work all day : I wrestle all night
 6 I did not think my baby : would go out and stay all
    night

Gill   4   Gillum, Bill Jazz

        title: She Won't Treat Me Kind
        place and date: Aurora, Ill., 16 Dec. 1938
        record numbers: (030826-) BB-B8106 RCA INT-1177

 1 Well I worry I worry : I worries all the time
 2 For the gal I love : she just won't treat me kind
 3 I just worry : worry all the time
 4 Yes I worry : because she won't treat me kind
 5 I just lay down on my bed : I smoke cigarettes all
    night
 6 Just thinking about my gal : because she ain't doing
    me right
 7 Says I woke up this morning : feeling so bad
 8 Thinking about the good times : that I once have had
 9 I'm going to pack my suitcase : and down the road
    I'll go
10 Because the good times I used to have : I can't have
    no more

Gill   5   Gillum, Bill Jazz

        title: I'll Get Along Somehow
        place and date: Aurora, Ill., 16 Dec. 1938
        record numbers: (030827-) BB-B8106 RCA INT-1177

 1 I'm going to leave here : walking too
 2 Just on account : of the way you do
 3 Now you told me : that wouldn't do
 4 It may be me : it may be you
 5 I have been walking : for nights and days
 6 Thinking about the words baby : that you have said
 7 I give you my money : you wouldn't play fair
 8 You taken my money : and gave me the air

Gill   6   Gillum, Bill Jazz

        title: Got to Reap What You Sow
        place and date: Chicago, 17 May 1939
        record numbers: (034810-) BB-B8287 RCA INT-1177

 1 I woke up this morning : Lord and my baby was gone
 2 I didn't have no sweet woman : just to hold me in
    her arms
 3 Yes I'm a poor poor boy : and a great long way from
    home
 4 I ain't got nobody : just to teach me right from
    wrong
 5 I'm bound down in trouble : and you know just how I
    feel
 6 Like a broke down engine : without a driving wheel
 7 That's why I'm leaving : I ain't got no place to go
 8 Because the Good Book says : you going to reap just
    what you sow

Gill   7   Gillum, Bill Jazz

        title: Keyhole Blues
        place and date: Chicago, 17 May 1939
        record numbers: (034813-) BB-B8221 RCA INT-1177

 1 Well I followed my woman : to a place she didn't
    want me to be
 2 And I seed something : that I did not want to see
 3 Well I seen my friend : give her a bottle of booze
 4 And then what hurt me : she started pulling off her
    shoes
 5 Says I was in a place : that I did not want to be
 6 And I seen something : that I did not want to see
 7 I said to myself : what you think of that
 8 I seen on the wall : they hung their coat and hat
 9 And then I begin to wonder : what to think of this
10 And then I saw them : begin to hug and kiss
11 She was with my friend : instead of being with me
12 And I seen something : that I did not want to see

Gill   8   Gillum, Bill Jazz

        title: Key to the Highway
        place and date: Chicago, 9 May 1940
        record numbers: (044972-) BB-B8529 RBF RF-16

 1 I got the key to the highway : billed out and ready
    to go
 2 I'm going to leave here running : because walking is
    most too slow
 3 I'm going back to the border : where I'm better
    known
 4 Because you haven't done nothing : but drove a good
    man away from home
 5 Give me one more kiss mama : just before I go
 6 Because when I'm leaving here : I won't be back no
    more
 7 When the moon creep over the mountain : honey I'll
    be on my way
 8 I'm going to walk this highway : until the break of
    day
 9 Well it's so long so long baby : I must say goodbye
10 I'm going to roam this highway : until the day I die

Gill   9   Gillum, Bill Jazz

        title: Riley Springs Blues
        place and date: Chicago, 4 July 1941
        record numbers: (064737-) BB-B8846 RCA INT-1177

 1 I ain't going down : to Riley Springs no more
 2 When I was there : you drove me from your door
 3 You don't know : how you treated me
 4 You used to love me : and went back to your
    used-to-be

Gill   9   Gillum, Bill Jazz

 5 Riley Springs : is a place to go
 6 But you done me so bad : I won't be back no more
 7 You don't care : what become of me
 8 All you care : is to give your poor heart ease
 9 See now : what you done to me
10 You broke my heart : and left me in misery

Gill   10   Gillum, Bill Jazz

        title: I Got Somebody Else
        place and date: Chicago, 4 July 1941
        record numbers: (064739-) BB-B8816 RCA INT-1177

 1 Now you didn't want me : when I was treating you
       nice and kind
 2 Now it's too late baby : I have changed my mind
 3 You won't act right : when I tried to do right
       myself
 4 Now it's no no baby : I've got somebody else
 5 It ain't no need : you calling me on my telephone
 6 It's too bad baby : you have broke up your happy
       home
 7 Now I am through : going from door to door
 8 For what you done : I don't want you no more
 9 Now what you done : you done it to yourself
10 When I wanted you : you wanted someone else

Gill   11   Gillum, Bill Jazz

        title: It Looks Bad for You
        place and date: Chicago, 4 July 1941
        record numbers: (064741-) BB-B8816 RCA INT-1177

 1 I tried to get you : to stop raising sand
 2 Before they put you : back in the can
 3 Oh baby : it looks bad for you
 4 Now you hear me talking : I've done all I'm going to
       do
 5 I tried to love you : a long time ago
 6 I love you : until you drove me from your door
 7 Now love is mighty : rest on either hand
 8 I know you don't love : when you keep on raising
       sand
 9 I tried to tell you : but you wouldn't understand
10 Now I'm leaving you : cold in hand
11 I tried to tell you baby : just before you go
12 Don't you looking : for me no more

Gill   12   Gillum, Bill Jazz

        title: Me and My Buddy
        place and date: Chicago, 4 July 1941
        record numbers: (064742-) BB-B8872 RCA INT-1177

 1 Me and my buddy : I mean he is my friend
 2 We can drink more whiskey : ooo well well than a
       thousand men
 3 My buddy my buddy : was a dear old friend of mine
 4 When I didn't have the price of whiskey : ooo well
       well my buddy had it all the time
 5 When I was in trouble : with my hands and feet both
       tied
 6 I didn't have to look for my buddy : ooo well well
       he's right there by my side
 7 I know me and my buddy : never will have no falling
       out
 8 Because we got wise to women : ooo well well we
       knows what it's all about

Gill   13   Gillum, Bill Jazz

        title: It's All Over Now
        place and date: Chicago, 5 Dec. 1941
        record numbers: (070440-) BB-B8975 RCA INT-1177

 1 When I had you baby : you wouldn't act right
 2 You with your man honey : staying out every night
 3 It was a time : you broke my heart
 4 That's when I found out : that I and you had to part
 5 It's come a day : it won't be long
 6 You will be sorry : that you drove me away from home
 7 When I was in trouble : had my ups and downs
 8 I looked for you baby : you could not be found

Gill   14   Gillum, Bill Jazz

        title: One Letter Home
        place and date: Chicago, 5 Dec. 1941
        record numbers: (070443-) BB-B8943 RCA INT-1177

 1 I believe I'll write : just one more letter home
 2 I'm going to ask my baby : what's been going on
       wrong
 3 I'm going to tell my baby : baby I will be home
 4 You better make some arrangements : because it
       a-won't be very long
 5 I'm going to ask my baby : baby is that your friend
 6 She said now don't you worry : you just walk on in
 7 Now I have acknowledged : baby that I have done you
       wrong
 8 Now tell me what is the reason : that a-we can't get
       along

Gill   15   Gillum, Bill Jazz

        title: You Drink Too Much Whiskey
        place and date: Chicago, 5 Dec. 1941
        record numbers: (070445-) BB-B9004 RCA INT-1177

 1 The graveyard is lonely : you better put brakes on
       yourself
 2 Because that's just where you're going : if I catch
       you with anyone else
 3 It's a hard pill to swallow : when the neighbors all
       bring you the news
 4 They say you drinks in the alley : on corners or any
       place you choose
 5 If you don't treat me no better : I ain't going to
       be your man no more
 6 I love you it's true : but I will have to let you go
 7 If you don't want to tell your mother : that you
       soon will be coming home
 8 You better cut out you late hours : and let other
       mens alone
 9 You drinks way too much whiskey : you ain't got no
       stopping point
10 And as soon as all the taverns close : you then head
       for some moonshine joint

Gill   16   Gillum, Bill Jazz

        title: I'm Gonna Leave You on the Outskirts of
           Town
        place and date: Chicago, 30 July 1942
        record numbers: (074648-) BB-B9042 RCA INT-1177

 1 I'm going to leave you baby : out here on the
       outskirts of town
 2 I brought you out here mama : and you won't stop
       fooling around
 3 I've cut out my iceman : I bought me a frigidaire
 4 Now you let the serviceman : take you everywhere
 5 I'm going to leave you baby : out here on the
       outskirts of town

Gill 16   Gillum, Bill Jazz

    6   I ain't going to stand nobody : ooo always hanging
        around
    7   I brought my own groceries : I brought them every
        day
    8   Now you letting the grocery boy : lay up in the hay
    9   I see you wiggling and giggling : when I'm mad as I
        can be
   10   Now we got seven children : ain't none of them look
        like me

Gill 17   Gillum, Bill Jazz

        title: Woke Up Cold in Hand
        place and date: Chicago, 30 July 1942
        record numbers: (074651-) BB-B9042 RCA INT-1177

    1   Since the hard time is got me : I've been running
        from door to door
    2   I ain't got no bed to sleep in : I've got to sleep
        down on the doggone floor
    3   Well it's hard times here : and it's hard times
        everywhere I go
    4   I've got to make me some money : so I won't have
        these hard-luck blues no more
    5   You know I used to get me a dollar : before I could
        catch my breath
    6   But now I ain't got me a dime : unless I toss my
        poor self to death
    7   Have you ever dreamed you were lucky : and then woke
        up cold in hand
    8   Well you dreamed you had a dollar : and your woman's
        got another man

Glaz 1   Glaze, Ruby (Blind Willie McTell)

        title: Rollin' Mama Blues
        place and date: Atlanta, 22 Feb. 1932
        record numbers: (71603-) Vi-23328 Rt RL-324

    1   Now tell me baby : how do you want your loving done
    3   Oh roll me on my belly baby : feed me with your
        chocolate drop
    5   Want you to roll me baby : like the baker rolls his
        dough
    7   Oh reel and rock me baby : honey if it's all night
        long
    9   Won't you come back baby : you get me all confused

Glaz 2   Glaze, Ruby (Blind Willie McTell)

        title: Lonesome Day Blues
        place and date: Atlanta, 22 Feb. 1932
        record numbers: (71604-1) Vi-23353 RCA LPV-518

    1   You can go : you can stay
    2   But you'll come home : some old lonesome day
    3   Some day baby : some old lonesome day
    4   I'm coming home to my baby : some old lonesome day
    5   The Mississippi River : so deep and wide
    6   I can't see my good man : on the other side
    7   I was born in Georgia : but I hangs around Tennessee
    8   I've got a man here in Georgia : partner he's crazy
        about me
    9   Where were you baby : when that L and N left the
        shed
   10   You was standing in your back door : with a hung
        down head

Glov 1   Glover, Mae

        title: Shake It Daddy
        place and date: Richmond, Ind., 29 July 1929
        record numbers: (15392) Ge-6964 OJL-6

    1   You used to be sweet milk : but you done turned sour
        on me
    2   If you want me to love you : you hum like a honeybee
    3   Now the old folks shake it : young folks too
    4   Ain't nobody shake it : like my daddy do
    5   Lord the way he shakes it : will make me lose my
        appetite
    6   And nobody shake it : like papa ??? can
    7   Because the way you shake it : will make me lose my
        appetite
    8   Because the way you shake it : will make me do
        things right

Glov 2   Glover, Mae

        title: Pig Meat Mama
        place and date: Richmond, Ind., 29 July 1929
        record numbers: (15393) Ge-6948 Rt RL-319

    1   I'm a pigmeat mama : pigmeat's all I crave
    2   Pigmeat's going to carry me : carry me to my grave
    3   Some women like their pork chops: some women like
        their wine
    4   But I'm a pigmeat mama : give it to me all the time
    5   I got pigmeat in Texas : pigmeat in Tennessee
    6   My pigmeat in Virginia : Lord is wild about me
    7   Tell all you women : what you better do
    8   You better lay off my pigmeat : or it won't be good
        for you
    9   Pigmeat for breakfast : pigmeat when I'm in bed
   10   If I don't get my pigmeat : Lord I'd rather be dead

Glov 3   Glover, Mae

        title: I Ain't Giving Nobody None
        place and date: Richmond, Ind., 29 July 1929
        record numbers: (15395-A) Ge-6948 Her H-201

    1   My man left me : he left me feeling bad
    2   He's the best *kind fellow* : that I ever had
    3   I'm going to send you a ticket : hoping you will
        come
    4   Come back home : nevermore to roam
    5   If you come back home baby : tell you what I'll do
    6   I'll *teach* my kid-man : how to live true to you
    7   Since you been gone papa : listen what I've done
    8   I've made a lot of money: but I ain't give nobody
        none
    9   I'll wash you clothes in the morning : bake
        jellyroll at night
   10   When you come home : that'll be so doggone nice
   11   I drink so much coffee : the grounds are in my
        wheeze
   12   I don't care how I do it : doggone heart disease

Glov 4   Glover, Mae

        title: Gas Man Blues
        place and date: Richmond, Ind., 29 July 1929
        record numbers: (15396-A) Ge-7040 Yz L-1009

    1   Mr gasman : please don't turn off my gas today
    3   But the wind is blowing : and the snow begins to
        fall
    5   But Mr gasman : these cold winds will really give me
        a chill
    7   Mr gasman come into my parlor : I want to ask you to
        close the door
    9   Mr gasman : will you please come around after dark

Glov   4   Glover, Mae

11   Are you coming in Mr gasman : I want to tell you
     something right quick
13   I want to get you early : and *beat some head cold*
15   Mr gasman : you got that old hot bankroll right over
     there in your pants

Gran   1   Grant, Bobby

        title: Nappy Head Blues
        place and date: Chicago, c. Dec. 1927
        record numbers: (20204-3) Pm-12595 Yz L-1001

1   When you hear me walking : turn your lamp down low
2   Then turn it so : your man'll never know
3   Going to buy me a bed : and it shine like a morning
     sun
4   When I get to bed : it rock like a Cadillac car
5   Your head is nappy : your feet so mamlish long
6   And you move like a turkey : coming through the
     mamlish corn
7   I done told you I loved you : what more can I do
8   And you must a-want me : to lay down and die for you

Gran   2   Grant, Bobby

        title: Lonesome Atlanta Blues
        place and date: Chicago, c. Dec. 1927
        record numbers: (20212-2) Pm-12595 Yz L-1009

1   I'm so lonesome : I'm so lonesome and I'm so blue
2   I'm so sad and lonesome : mama I don't know what to
     do
3   When you have a feeling : that I sure gal don't want
     no more
4   You just might as well leave her : even if it hurts
     you so
5   I'm going to walk down that dirt road : till
     somebody lets me ride
6   If I can't find my baby : I'll run away and hide
7   I'm going back to Atlanta : down on Decatur Street
8   If I can't find my baby : I'll be so kind to meet

Grav   1   Graves, Blind Roosevelt

        title: New York Blues
        place and date: Richmond, Ind., 20 Sept. 1929
        record numbers: (15640-A) Pm-12820 His HLP-15

1   I got a brown in New York : what I am afraid
2   If I *just tell her* in her face baby : *that will*
     ???

GreLi   1   Green, Lil

        title: Just Rockin'
        place and date: Chicago, 9 May 1940
        record numbers: (044975-1) BB-B8464 RCA LPV-574

1   Rocking : rocking myself to sleep
2   Watching my baby : make that midnight creep
3   I'm rocking : rocking my worries away
4   What worries me now : worries me every day
5   Rocking : rocking on down the road
6   I'm rocking in places : I never rocked before
7   Rocking : rocking my blues away
8   I'm going to rock right here : until the break of
     day

GreLi   2   Green, Lil

        title: What Have I Done?
        place and date: Chicago, 9 May 1940
        record numbers: (044976-1) BB-B8524 RCA LPV-574

1   Listen babe : tell me the truth
2   Please tell me babe : what you going to do
3   I love you babe : always treated you kind
4   But your ways and actions : make me lose my mind
5   I took you in babe : right off the block
6   You was beat and raggedy : as a mop
7   You going to be sorry : you treated me this way
8   You going to want me babe : I'll be far away
9   Goodbye babe : I'm leaving you
10   You haven't did babe : what you should do

GreLi   3   Green, Lil

        title: Give Your Mama One Smile
        place and date: Chicago, 21 Jan. 1941
        record numbers: (059150-1) BB-B8640 RCA LPV-574

1   I love you baby : ain't going to tell you no lie
2   Always want you : by my side
3   Come on baby : let's talk awhile
4   You know I love you : don't you realize
5   I'll do anything : just to be with you
6   Say anything darling : don't say we're through
7   I love you baby : and you know that's true
8   What make you do your little mama : like you do
9   I don't care what they say : I don't care what they
     do
10   I'll do anything : in the world for you
11   Put your arms around me : hold me tight
12   And love your mama baby : love your mama right

GreLi   4   Green, Lil

        title: My Mellow Man
        place and date: Chicago, 21 Jan. 1941
        record numbers: (059151-1) BB-B8640 RCA LPV-574

1   Mmm : oh my mellow man
2   Can't nobody thrill me : like my mellow man can
3   He don't stand on no corners : he don't rob and
     steal
4   Come home to me : each day to get his meal
5   Now he ain't no organ grinder : he just nice and
     sweet
6   I love that man : from his head down to his feet
7   My man is so mellow : they call him spongy boy
8   But that ain't his name : his name is plain Leroy

GreLi   5   Green, Lil

        title: Knockin' Myself Out
        place and date: Chicago, 21 Jan. 1941
        record numbers: (059152-1) BB-B8659 RCA LPV-574

1   Listen girls and boys : I've got one stick
2   Give me a match : and let me take a whiff quick
3   I started blowing my gauge : and I was having my fun
4   I spied the police : and I started to run
5   But the very moment : I looked around
6   My mind fell ill : throwed that gauge on the ground
7   I used to didn't blow gauge : drink nothing of the
     kind
8   But my man quit me : and that changed my mind
9   I know to blow this jive : it's a sin and a shame
10   But it's the only thing : ease my heart about my man

GreLi 6   Green, Lil

    title: Why Don't You Do Right?
    place and date: Chicago, 23 Apr. 1941
    record numbers: (064130-1) BB-B8714 RCA LPV-574

 1 You had plenty of money : in nineteen twenty-two
 2 But you let other women : make a fool of you
 3 Why don't you do right : like some other men do
 4 Get out of here : and get me some money too
 5 You sitting down wondering : what it's all about
 6 If you ain't got no money : they going to put you
      out
 7 If you had prepared : twenty years ago
 8 You wouldn't have been drifting : from door to door
 9 I fell for your jiving : I took you in
10 Now all you got to offer me : is a drink of gin

GreLi 7   Green, Lil

    title: Love Me
    place and date: Chicago, 23 Apr. 1941
    record numbers: (064131-1) BB-B8714 RCA LPV-574

 1 I tried hard : a long time
 2 To get you : to change your mind
 3 You want to know : what it's all about
 4 If you love me : you will soon find out
 5 I work : hard for you
 6 Now tell me daddy : what you going to do
 7 When I see you : walking down the street
 8 I get the thrill : from my head to my feet
 9 It's no use : for us to fuss and fight
10 We should love some : every night

GreLi 8   Green, Lil

    title: What's the Matter with Love?
    place and date: Chicago, 23 Apr. 1941
    record numbers: (064133-1) BB-B8754 RCA LPV-574

 1 You got me : feeling sad
 2 The worst feeling : I ever had

GreLi 9   Green, Lil

    title: Country Boy Blues
    place and date: Chicago, 23 Apr. 1941
    record numbers: (064134-1) BB-B8754 RCA LPV-574

 1 I got a man : a real handsome one
 2 He ain't no loafer : he's just a little old country
      boy
 3 I love him : if he is a little old country boy
 4 Yes I love him : because he fills my heart with joy
 5 Some people say he is lazy : but I know that is a
      lie
 6 For three years he been doing my work : and I'm
      perfectly satisfied
 7 I know he will [learn to] love me : when he gets to
      be a man
 8 Because I'm always going to feed him : right from my
      hand
 9 Now people all want to know : why do I follow my man
10 There's no need to explain : because they really
      wouldn't understand

GreLi 10   Green, Lil

    title: How Can I Go On?
    place and date: Chicago, 23 Apr. 1941
    record numbers: (064135-1) BB-B8790 RCA LPV-574

 1 I'm so sorry you heard : I don't know what to do
 2 I'm sorry for the time : I made you blue

GreLi 11   Green, Lil

    title: If I Didn't Love You
    place and date: Chicago, 23 Apr. 1941
    record numbers: (064728-1) BB-B8865 RCA LPV-574

 1 Baby what's the matter : why don't you be yourself
 2 If I didn't love you : I'd get somebody else
 3 But you are so dull and rotten : you think everybody
      like yourself
 4 If I didn't love you : I'd get somebody else
 5 Because I love you baby : and I want you for myself
 6 If I didn't love you : I would get somebody else
 7 The way you been doing : you know it's wrong
 8 How do you expect : for us to get along
 9 Now maybe some day baby : you'd know for yourself
10 If I didn't love you : I'd get somebody else

GreLi 12   Green, Lil

    title: If I'm a Fool
    place and date: Chicago, 21 Jan. 1942
    record numbers: (070802-1) BB-B8985 RCA LPV-574

 1 You say I'm a fool : and everyone knows
 2 They wondering why : I don't let you go
 3 Everybody tells me : what he do
 4 But still : I don't believe it's true
 5 You say : he don't treat me right
 6 But he say he love me : both day and night
 7 I'm telling you : right from the start
 8 I don't intend : for us to part
 9 This is all : I have done my best
10 I love him : and darn the rest

GreLi 13   Green, Lil

    title: I'm Wasting My Time on You
    place and date: Chicago, 21 Jan. 1942
    record numbers: (070803-1) BB-B9010 RCA LPV-574

 1 I'm so down-hearted : feeling sad
 2 Baby you left me : sick in bed
 3 Mama and papa told me : when I left my home
 4 I would have to face : the world alone
 5 I keep knocking : but they won't let me in
 6 Because you in there with your new love : drinking
      your gin
 7 I'm so down-hearted : no place to go
 8 Out in the rain : hail sleet and snow
 9 I'm so down-hearted : everywhere I go
10 Hard luck and trouble : meets me at the door

Gros   1   Gross, Helen

    title: Hard Luck Blues
    place and date: New York, c. May 1924
    record numbers: (31564-1) Ajax-17037 VJM VLP-40

 1 My man done quit me : he done throwed me down
 2 I'm sad : because he didn't call around
 3 Did you ever lay down : and dream the whole night
      long
 4 Dream about your man : and all your ??? *is gone*

Gros   2   Gross, Helen

    title: Strange Man
    place and date: New York, c. July 1924
    record numbers: (31590-1) Ajax-17050 VJM VLP-40

 1 Last night I went out alone : I was lonesome as
      could be
 2 How I longed to find someone : to keep my company
 3 Strange man strange man : let me come close to you

Gros   2   Gross, Helen

4   I'm feeling lonely : won't you tell me what to do
5   I'm looking for someone to love : who can your good
    gal be
6   I ain't got nobody : and you sure look good to me

Hann   1   Hannah, George

     title: Freakish Man Blues
     place and date: Grafton, Wis., c. Oct. 1930
     record numbers: (L-562-1) Pm-13024 Mil MLP-2018

1   Call me a freakish man : what more was there to do
2   Just because she said I was strange : that did not
    make it true
3   I sent her to the mill : to have her coffee ground
4   Because my wheel was broke : and my grinder could
    not be found
5   You mix ink with water : bound to turn it black
6   You run around with funny people : you get a streak
    of it up your back
7   There was a time when I was alone : my freakish ways
    to see
8   But they're so common now : you get one every day in
    the week
9   Had a strange feeling this morning : I swear I've
    had it all day
10 I'll wake up one of these mornings : that feeling
    will be here to stay

Hard   1   Hardin, Lane

     title: California Desert Blues
     place and date: Chicago, 28 July 1935
     record numbers: (91450-1) BB-B6242 Rt RL-319

1   Now I was just sitting here wondering : where I
    would go get some ease
2   Now I'm going back to California : so I can do just
    as I please
3   Crossing that old desert mama : just like breaking
    the Hindenburg Line
4   Now if you get ditched off on that freight train :
    you know that will be the end of the line
5   Oh yes I know I know : oh yes I know
6   Now the train's at the station : in my mind I'm made
    up to go
7   When I reach old Los Angeles California : you ought
    to hear me jump and shout
8   Now the people in Los Angeles : they didn't know
    what it's all about

HarM   1   Harris, Magnolia

     title: Mama's Quittin' and Leavin'--Part 1
     place and date: Chicago, c. late Dec. 1930
     record numbers: (C-7100-) Me-M12077 Yz L-1031

1   I feel bluer this morning : than I ever felt before
2   I'm changing friends and men : and I won't be blue
    no more
3   I know you 'buke and dog me : baby with your
    forty-five
4   And I couldn't do nothing : but wring my hands and
    cry
5   Know you trying to be mean babe : and use me as a
    child
6   But it's going to hurt you to your heart : when I
    leave you for a while

HarM   2   Harris, Magnolia

     title: Mama's Quittin' and Leavin'--Part 2
     place and date: Chicago, c. late Dec. 1930
     record numbers: (C-7101-) Me-M12077 Yz L-1031

1   I'm tired of being scolded : when I know I'm doing
    to best I can
2   To keep from being your dog daddy : I will get me a
    brand new man
3   No use of getting on your knees : because I can't
    use you no more
4   I been your dog long enough : so this morning I'll
    have to go
5   You know all this time : thinking you was all mine
6   And I come to find : you was worse all the time
7   And I didn't say one sentence : till six months
    after you left
8   I'll give you one more chance : to make a man out of
    yourself

HarO   1   Harris, Otis

     title: Waking Blues
     place and date: Dallas, 8 Dec. 1928
     record numbers: (147608-1) Co-14428-D Fly LP-103

1   Did you ever wake up with the blues : and didn't
    have no place to go
2   And you couldn't do nothing : but just walk from
    door to door
3   It was late last night mama : and I hear you cry out
    in bed
4   I went *over rolled* my baby : and she talked all
    out of her head
5   If you don't like my loving : what make you keep on
    worrying me
6   Why don't you get you some other man : oh mama and
    just let me be
7   Good morning Mr blues : Mr blues I come to talk with
    you
8   Mr blues ain't doing nothing : and I would like to
    get a job from you

HarO   2   Harris, Otis

     title: You'll Like My Loving
     place and date: Dallas, 8 Dec. 1928
     record numbers: (147609-2) Co-14428-D Yz L-1032

1   I know you like my loving : I can tell from the way
    you wine
2   Let you taste my jelly : you just worries me all the
    time
3   I told you pretty mama : I have the best jelly in
    your town
4   Bet you got a little taste : you just keep on
    hanging around
5   I swim deep pretty mama : just like a catfish loaded
    down
6   And every time you see me : you wants to fall down
    on the ground
7   When me and my baby start to loving : we wants to
    fight like cats and dogs
8   But before it's over with : we hollering Lord oh
    Lordy Lord

HarW   1   Harris, William

     title: I'm Leavin' Town
     place and date: Birmingham, Ala., c. 18 July
     1927
     record numbers: (GEX-743-B) Ge-6306 Yz L-1001

1   Yeah mean mama : where you stay last night

HarW   1   Harris, William

2   Oh your hair all wrinkled : and your clothes ain't
     fitting you right
3   Got up this morning : and I could not keep from
     crying
4   Thinking about my rider : she done put me down
5   The sun going to shine : in my back door some day
6   I know my woman : going to come my way some day
7   When I get drunk : well I don't want to drink no
     more
9   Listen here : what my dear old mother says
10   These women and whiskey : going to get my child
     astray
11   Easy mama : no good bearing down

HarW   2   Harris, William

        title: Bull Frog Blues
        place and date: Richmond, Ind., 10 Oct. 1928
        record numbers: (14318) Ge-6661 OJL-5

1   Have you ever woke up : with them bullfrogs on your
     mind
3   It's going to rain today mama : sun shine in your
     back door
4   I'm going to tell you this time mama : I ain't going
     to tell you no I ain't going to tell you no I mean
     more
5   I'm going to tell you this time mama : ain't going
     to tell you no more
6   I'm going to leave you partner : and I won't be back
     here no more
7   I left you standing here : in your back door crying
8   I got the bullfrog blues : and I can't be satisfied
9   Have you ever dreamed lucky : woke up cold in hand
11   I'm going to tell you : what a Chinaman told a Jew
12   You don't likee me : well I sure God don't like you
13   Look a-here partner : see what you done to me
15   The sun going to shine : in my back door some day

HarW   3   Harris, William

        title: Hot Time Blues
        place and date: Richmond, Ind., 10 Oct. 1928
        record numbers: (14323) Ge-6707 OJL-5

1   Say it makes no difference : what mama don't allow
2   We going to have a good time : right anyhow
3   Well come on daddy : what do you say
4   Just give me a kiss : that very same way
5   Well I'm just going to tell you : this one time
6   Mama this ain't nothing : but to worry your mind
7   Well it's take me back : try me again
8   Says I may do better : than what I once have been
9   Oh come on daddy : this ain't no joke
10   If you got a good cigarette : just give me a smoke
11   Take me back : and try me again
12   Says we'll do better : than what we used to
13   Well if you don't like my peaches : don't shake my
     tree
14   Gal stay out of my orchard : and let my peaches be
15   Well I tell you buddy : this is a natural fact
16   Whenever you quit me : I ain't going to take you
     back

HarX   1   Harris, Willie

        title: Lonesome Midnight Dream
        place and date: Chicago, c. mid Mar. 1930
        record numbers: (C-5551-) Br-7149 Rt RL-340

1   If you just listen closely : tell you just what I
     mean
2   I want to tell you : all about my lonesome midnight
     dream

HarX   1   Harris, Willie

3   Something was troubling me last night baby : I swear
     it was very mean
4   All night long in my sleep : I felt like I wanted to
     scream
5   I would lie down on my bed : I just rolled from side
     to side
6   Feel like the girl that I love : have just lay down
     and died
7   And I called the undertaker : and the hearse came
     driving slow
8   Made me feel so sorry : to see my baby go
9   Lord I heard a mighty rumbling : just about the dawn
     of day
10   It was only the wagon : coming to carry my baby away
11   When I woke up this morning : folks I just started
     to scream
12   Why when I came to find out : that it was just a
     lonesome midnight dream

HarY   1   Harrison, Smoky

        title: Hop Head Blues
        place and date: Grafton, Wis., c. Dec. 1929
        record numbers: (L-79-1) Pm-12920 Rt RL-340

1   Lord I remember : what my big fat mama said
2   She so big and fat : got to put ashes all in my bed
3   Now I got rocks all in my pillow : gravel all in my
     bed
4   I got morphine in my belly : cocaine in my head
5   Now if you go : have to bring my good clothes on
     back
6   I says go on home mama : you gots: *ruses* all in
     your back
7   Says I been to Montana : been all over Tennessee
8   Says now tell me what's the reason you get tired of
     here : baby I been really homesick about you
9   So true so true Lord : mama so true
10   Says I seen you leaving last night : baby by the
     light of the moon
11   Got three great big bulldogs Lord : to watch you
     while you sleep
12   To keep papa's little gold *watch-key* : from doing
     that 'fore-day creep

HarY   2   Harrison, Smoky

        title: Iggly Oggly Blues
        place and date: Grafton, Wis., c. Dec. 1929
        record numbers: (L-80-1) Pm-12920 Rt RL-340

1   So soon this morning mama : you were knocking on my
     door
2   Babe you knock : just like you never knocked before
3   I'm going to tell my baby : what the Chinaman told
     the Jew
4   Baby no iggly-oggly me mama : sister no iggly-oggly
     you
5   I got eighty in New York : I got ninety in Tupalo
6   No need to smile mama : don't believe I want no more
7   Says so cold in China baby : those birds can't
     hardly sing
8   Says they don't do nothing : but fly in *frosty*
     wings
9   My gal's got a new way : Lord spelling Tennessee
10   Double S double E : double I double A double L
11   Lord I'm going I'm going mama Lord : I'm I'm going
     so far away
12   Says I'm going too far baby : that you can't hear me
     say

HarZ   1   Hart, Hattie (Memphis Jug Band)

        title: Memphis Yo Yo Blues
        place and date: Memphis, 4 Oct. 1929
        record numbers: (56345-2) Vi-V38558 Rt RL-322

1   I woke up this morning : feeling sad and blue
2   Couldn't find my yo-yo : didn't know what to do
3   I hurried downtown : called my daddy on the phone
4   He said don't cry mama : daddy will bring your yo-yo
     home
5   If you don't believe I can yo-yo : watch me wind my
     string
6   Come home daddy : and make the yo-yo sing
7   Bring your yo-yo : wind the string around my thumb
8   I'm an old milkcow : to make the yo-yo mum
9   If your daddy can't yo-yo : you better learn him how
10   Listen women : I don't mean to start no row

HarZ   2   Hart, Hattie (Memphis Jug Band)

        title: Oh Ambulance Man
        place and date: Memphis, 17 May 1930
        record numbers: (59932-2) Vi-V38605 Mel MLP-7324

1   Hey daddy hey daddy : don't let me cry in vain
2   You see I'm wounded wounded and bleeding : can't you
     ease my pain
3   Hearts is aching day is breaking : listen to me pray
4   See it's snowing cold wind is blowing : so please be
     on your way
5   Mr ambulance man : I can't stay still to save my
     soul
6   And you ought to be careful : how you handle my
     jellyroll

HarZ   3   Hart, Hattie

        title: I Let My Daddy Do That
        place and date: New York, 13 Sept. 1934
        record numbers: (15899-) Vo-02855 Mam S-3803

1   Says people call me Mama Treetop : because I'm
     slender and tall
2   But when I get ready : to get my ashes hauled
3   I got a range in my kitchen : I've got a strict rule
4   When it gets too hot : I want my oven just cool
5   You can drink my liquor : where my clothes
6   But when it comes time : for spending my dough
7   You can milk my cow : use the cream
8   But when it comes to loving me : that will be in a
     dream
9   You can crank my car : shift my gear
10   But when any easy riding : goes on here

HarZ   4   Hart, Hattie

        title: Coldest Stuff in Town
        place and date: New York, 14 Sept. 1934
        record numbers: (15952-) Vo-02821 Yz L-1021

1   When I go out singing : I goes out all alone
2   I got a new way of singing : makes a good woman lose
     her home
3   Singing is my trade : I don't have to lie
4   If you feel my stinger : you want to until you die
5   It was soon this morning : I heard my doorbell ring
6   I thought slim was working : and he wasn't doing a
     doggone thing

Hawk   1   Hawkins, Walter Buddy Boy

        title: Shaggy Dog Blues
        place and date: Chicago, c. Apr. 1927
        record numbers: (4415-) Pm-12489 Rt RL-319

1   I'm going up on a mountain : I'm going to do just
     like a hog
2   Because the women around here : just treat a good
     man like a dog
3   I say I'd rather be shaggy : mama just like a dog
4   Than to hear my little jet-black woman : say Buddy
     Boy she don't need me no more
5   When you see two [jet-black, old black] women :
     standing and talking so long
6   Bet your life : there's something going on wrong
7   My mama told me : my papa told me too
8   Son these women around here : just *they pretty
     want* you

Hawk   2   Hawkins, Walter Buddy Boy

        title: Number Three Blues
        place and date: Chicago, c. Apr. 1927
        record numbers: (4416-2) Pm-12475 Yz L-1010

1   I lost all my money : I got nowhere to go
2   I believe to my soul : I'm about to lose my brown
3   All you women get mad : because I won't twa twa twa
4   All you women get mad at buddy boy : because I won't
     dee da da da
5   I say I *flied when I was four* mama : be careful
     in years gone by
6   I couldn't do anything partner : but fold my little
     arms and cry
7   I said here come Number Three : with her headlights
     turned down
8   I believe to my soul : *she* is Alabama bound
9   Apples on my table : peaches on my chair
10   I got to stay there : to eat them all by myself

Hawk   3   Hawkins, Walter Buddy Boy

        title: Jailhouse Fire Blues
        place and date: Chicago, c. Apr. 1927
        record numbers: (4419-2) Pm-12489 Rt RL-319

1   Hey Mr jailor : don't sleep so sound
2   Jailhouse on fire : ??? burning down
3   I say the woman I love : she in the jailhouse now
4   But please Mr jailor : she got to get out of there
     somehow
5   Mmm : my woman in trouble now
6   I said but one of these good mornings : I'm bound to
     get her out of jail
7   When I get my little cell-block key : I'm going to
     be country bound
8   *And hey* Mr jailor : I hope the jailhouse burns
     down

Hawk   4   Hawkins, Walter Buddy Boy

        title: Snatch It Back Blues
        place and date: Chicago, c. Apr. 1927
        record numbers: (4420-2) Pm-12475 Yz L-1010

1   I'm going to lay my head : down on some railroad
     track
2   Boy when that train come along : I'm going to snatch
     it back
3   Tell me brownskin mama : where did you stay last
     night
4   With your hair all down : your face is never washed
5   I say I love you pretty mama : I don't care what you
     do
6   You go to your black man mama : I'll stick to my gal

7   I say if you don't [need your black woman, want me
     mama] : you [don't have to, ain't got to] turn
     your head and stall
8   Because I can get more jet-black women : than
     a-seven freight trains can haul
9   I got ooo : twa twa twa twa twa twa twa
10   Ooo : ooo

Hawk   5   Hawkins, Walter Buddy Boy

          title: Awful Fix Blues
          place and date: Chicago, c. Sept. 1927
          record numbers: (20034-1) Pm-12539 Yz L-1004

1   Hey mama : tell me what have I done
2   I just seem like you trying : to beat your loving
     self on down
3   You going to wake up one of these mornings : mama
     baby and I'll be gone
4   And you may not never : mama see me in your town no
     more
5   Lord I'm a stranger [to you, in here] brownskin :
     mama I just blowed in your town
6   And if I ask you for a favor : mama please now don't
     turn me down
7   If you get one old woman : you better get you five
     or six
8   So if that one happen to quit you : it won't leave
     you in a awful fix
9   When I had you little black woman : I tried to do
     the best I could
10   Now your little daddy's gone : now who you going to
     get to chop your wood

Hawk   6   Hawkins, Walter Buddy Boy

          title: How Come Mama Blues
          place and date: Richmond, Ind., 14 June 1929
          record numbers: (15213) Pm-12802 Yz L-1010

1   How come you do me like you do baby : how come you
     do me like you do
2   How come you try to make me feel so blue : mama you
     know I ain't done nothing unto you
3   Now you know you left poor me at seven : come back
     at eight
4   You got another big fat man : slam up to my gate
5   You know you hug and kissed him : said daddy you
     sure is fat
6   I stuck my head out the window : man and hollered
     who in the world is that
7   I bought a pistol : I bought it today
8   Now I got the undertaker with me : just to haul you
     away
9   You know you kept on talking : about that you want
     to get my goat
10   I had a brand new razor woman : just to slit your
     throat
11   A nickel is a nickel : a dime is a dime
12   A woman get tired of one man : all the time
13   You try to give these women : everything they need
14   You have to make them : one of your G B V Ds

Hawk   7   Hawkins, Walter Buddy Boy

          title: Voice Throwin' Blues
          place and date: Richmond, Ind., 14 June 1929
          record numbers: (15219) Pm-12802 Yz L-1010

1   Come in at dawn : stay out late
2   If I call you : don't you hesitate
3   Tell me how long : does I have to wait
4   Can I get you now honey : or must I hesitate
5   I ain't no miller : no miller's son

6   Can be your miller : till your miller come
7   I might think it's funny : ???
8   Make me mad : think ???
9   *Ain't yellow evil* : ??? *too*
10   The reason fair brown : I don't need you
11   Mama told me : daddy told me too
12   *Womens* ??? : and it'll be end of you
13   I ain't no doctor : doctor's son
14   Ease your pain : till your doctor come
15   I don't want no sugar : in my tea
16   The woman I got : sweet enough for me

HayeN   1   Hayes, Nap (T. C. Johnson Groups)

          title: Violin Blues
          place and date: Memphis, 15 Feb. 1928
          record numbers: (400239-A) OK-8708 Rt RL-316

1   Ooh : my baby don't treat me good no more
2   When I was sick and down : she drove me from her
     door
3   I just found out : why my baby treats me so unkind
4   When she go to bed every night : she tells
     everything what's on her mind

HendB   1   Henderson, Bertha

          title: Lead Hearted Blues
          place and date: Chicago, c. May 1928
          record numbers: (20560-2) Pm-12655 Bio BLP-12037

1   Baby baby : I am so lonesome for you
2   Can't wear you off my mind : don't care what I do
3   When I wake up in the morning : my heart it feels
     like lead
4   When I go to bed at midnight : sometimes I wish I
     was dead
5   You told me baby : before you left my door
6   Some day I'd be sorry : that I told you to go
7   Lord Lord : can't rest no place I go
8   Blues is driving me crazy : must be reaping what I
     sow

HendB   2   Henderson, Bertha

          title: Let Your Love Come Down
          place and date: Chicago, c. May 1928
          record numbers: (20562-2) Pm-12655 Bio BLP-12037

1   Let's get our gauge up papa : let our love come down
2   Get leaping drunk : and leave this lowdown town
3   Go down on the levee : where the water's high
4   Let our love come down : till the *cleared outside*
5   Hey hey my daddy : he's so nice and brown
6   We going to get our gauge up : let our love come
     down
7   If you quit me daddy : I'm going to leave this town
8   Can't get my gauge up : and let my love come down

HendK   1   Henderson, Katherine

          title: West End Blues
          place and date: Long Island City, c. Sept. 1928
          record numbers: (235-A) QRS-R7024 His HLP-21

1   I'm full of mean evil feeling : and I'm full of gin
2   I'm on my way to the West End : and there's where
     troubles will begin
3   They're going to see some shooting : like they've
     never seen before
4   I mean my man and my best friend : won't cheat in
     West End anymore

HendK   1   Henderson, Katherine

    5   I got a mean evil feeling : you going to hear bad
        news
    6   I'm on my way to the West End : to lose those ugly
        old West End blues

HendK   2   Henderson, Katherine

        title: St. Louis Blues
        place and date: Long Island City, c. Sept. 1928
        record numbers: (236-A) QRS-R7024 His HLP-21

    1   I hate to see : that evening sun go down
    2   Because my daddy : he's done left this town
    3   Feeling tomorrow : just like I feel today
    4   I'm going to pack up my grip : and make my get-away
    5   Oh St Louis women : with their diamond rings
    6   Just pull their men around : by their apron strings
    7   If it weren't for *mortar* : and for store-bought
        hair
    8   Why the man I love : would not have gone nowhere

HendK   3   Henderson, Katherine

        title: Have You Ever Felt That Way?
        place and date: Long Island City, c. Oct. 1928
        record numbers: (257-A) QRS-7023 His HLP-21

    1   You're walking around : no one in sight
    2   Wondering : where your baby is tonight
    3   You're feeling forlorn : you've got the blues
    4   Night and day : you sing those weary tunes
    5   You so down-hearted : you don't know what to do
    6   You ain't got nobody : to tell your troubles to
    7   You're walking for miles : no place to go
    8   You're talking to yourself : Lord but you don't know

HendK   4   Henderson, Katherine

        title: Mushy Love
        place and date: Long Island City, c. Nov. 1928
        record numbers: (274-A) QRS-7054 His HLP-21

    1   Pick me up : don't let me go
    2   Hold me hold me : whisper something sweet and low
    3   Call me lovey : lovey-do
    4   Something sweet : to drive away the blues
    5   Then hold me tight : with all your might
    6   And swear : that you will treat me right
    7   Oh love me : like a caveman does
    8   Because everybody's crazy : about mushy love

HendR   1   Henderson, Rosa

        title: Get It Fixed
        place and date: New York, c. Apr. 1925
        record numbers: (   ) Vo-1177 His HLP-15

    1   Papa papa : let me tell to you
    2   Daddy daddy : here's what you must do
    3   When you come around : sweet precious turtledove
    4   Better come here ready : if you want to win my love
    5   Don't come around : telling me a lot of lies
    6   Because a lying man : I do despise
    7   Papa papa : better do your stuff
    8   Daddy daddy : but don't be too rough
    9   Mama want some loving kisses : right away
   10   Want them when I want them : come on honey don't
        delay
   11   Don't make me think : you've got a lot of dough
   12   If you ain't got nothing : please tell me so

HenrH   1   Henry, Hound Head

        title: Low Down Hound Blues
        place and date: Chicago, 17 Oct. 1928
        record numbers: (C-2451-) Vo-1288 His HLP-2

    1   Now run here pretty mama : tell papa where you been
        so long
    2   Say you come in here mama : with your clothes on
        wrong
    3   Says a brownskin gal : make a mule kick his stable
        down
    4   But a right black gal : make a rabbit move his
        family to town
    5   Says I went to my gal last night : papa knocked on
        her door
    6   She said is that you Mr Houndhead : mama can't use
        you no more
    7   Now woke up this morning : my gal had the worried
        blues
    8   I looked over in the corner : my poor grandma *what*
        had them too

HenrH   2   Henry, Hound Head

        title: My Silver Dollar Mama
        place and date: Chicago, 17 Oct. 1928
        record numbers: (C-2452-) Vo-1288 His HLP-2

    1   The gal I love : she lives on a silver dollar
    2   Every time she leaves me : I declare I'm bound to
        holler
    3   I don't care who you are : I don't care where you
        been
    4   Woman on the dollar : that's my best friend
    5   Said she knock and kick me : treat me like a lowdown
        dirty dog
    6   So I got a pocket full of dollars : huh so you see I
        ain't on the hog
    7   I got a gal in Alabama : gal in Tennessee
    8   But the gal on the dollar : that's the sweetest baby
        for me

HenrL   1   Henry, Lena

        title: Low Down Despondent Blues
        place and date: New York, 22 Aug. 1924
        record numbers: (13596) Vo-14873 His HLP-15

    1   I feel worried : I feel sad
    2   I lost the best friend : I ever had
    3   Don't care about living : don't want to die
    4   That's the reason : that I hang my head and cry
    5   My man quit me this morning : about the break of day
    6   And he told me : he was going away to stay
    7   He packed his grip up : didn't even say goodbye
    8   When I think of how he left me : I can't help but
        cry

HicR   1   Hicks, Robert

        title: Barbecue Blues
        place and date: Atlanta, 25 Mar. 1927
        record numbers: (143757-1) Co-14205-D CC-36

    1   Woke up this morning gal : 'twixt midnight and day
    2   With my hand around my pillow : where my brownie
        used to lay
    3   I know I ain't good-looking : teeth don't shine like
        pearls
    4   So glad : good looks don't take you through this
        world
    5   Going to starch my jumper mama : iron my overalls
    6   My brown done quit me : God knows she had it all
    7   I'm going to tell you now gal : like Gypsy told the
        Jew

HicR   1   Hicks, Robert

8   If you don't want me : it's a cinch I don't want you
9   Did you ever dream lucky : wake up cold in hand
10   That's a mighty true sign : your brown got some
     other man
11   My mama told me : papa told me too
12   Some brownskin woman : going to be the death of you

HicR   2   Hicks, Robert

        title: Cloudy Sky Blues
        place and date: Atlanta, 25 Mar. 1927
        record numbers: (143758-2) Co-14205-D CC-36

1   It seems cloudy brown : I believe it's going to rain
2   Going back to my regular : because she got
     everything
3   Hey hey mama : mama that ain't no way to do
4   You trying to quit me : mama you know I been good to
     you
5   Hello Central : give me long long-distant phone
6   I want to hear : from my sweet mama back home
7   When your brown [gets, acts] funny : everything you
     do she gets off
8   You can hunt you another home : because she don't
     want you no more

HicR   3   Hicks, Robert

        title: Poor Boy a Long Ways from Home
        place and date: New York, 16 June 1927
        record numbers: (144281-2) Co-14246-D Rt RL-326

1   I'm a poor boy : I'm a long way from home
2   I'm a poor boy : ain't got nowhere to go
3   Ain't got nowhere : to lay my worried head
4   Sometime : I'd sooner to be dead
5   Please tell me : what you going to do
7   I left my brown : standing in the door
8   What you reckon she said : you're not obliged to go
9   I'm a poor boy : stood on the road and cried
10   I didn't have no blues : just couldn't be satisfied
11   Now give me : long-distance phone
12   I want to hear : from my sweet mama back home
13   I said to her : ring six four nine
14   I want to hear : from that bobcat gal of mine

HicR   4   Hicks, Robert

        title: Easy Rider Don't Deny My Name
        place and date: New York, 16 June 1927
        record numbers: (144282-3) Co-14231-D RBF RF-15

1   Going up to town : what you want me to bring you
     back
2   Oh just anything : you think your baby like
3   Honey honey : you sweet as a plum
4   Baby you throw your arms around me : let's have some
     fun
5   Going up to town : with my hat in my hand
6   I'm looking for the woman : ain't got no man
7   Mama mama : just look at sis
8   Standing on the corner : trying to do the twist
9   Come here sis : you old stinking sow
10   You trying to be a woman : and you don't know how
11   Ain't but two things : I just like
12   That's salting the dog : and balling the Jack
13   Wears them in the summer : and she wears them in the
     fall
14   Some folks : they don't wear them at all
15   Honey honey : I'm going to tell you the truth
16   The day you quit me : that's the day you die

HicR   5   Hicks, Robert

        title: Motherless Chile Blues
        place and date: Atlanta, 5 Nov. 1927
        record numbers: (145134-1) Co-14299-D RBF RF-15

1   If I mistreat you gal : I sure don't mean no harm
2   I'm a motherless child : and I don't know right from
     wrong
3   Please tell me pretty mama : honey where you stayed
     last night
4   You didn't come home : till the sun was shining
     bright
5   I have to go so far : to get my hambone boiled
6   These Atlanta women : going to let my hambone spoil
7   I done done more for you : than your daddy ever done
8   I give you my jelly : he ain't give you none
9   When you see two women : always running hand in hand
10   You can bet your bottom dollar : one's got the other
     one's man
11   I'm going to the river : get me a *dang* old rocking
     chair
12   If the blues overtake me : going to rock on away
     from here

HicR   6   Hicks, Robert

        title: Crooked Woman Blues
        place and date: Atlanta, 10 Nov. 1927
        record numbers: (145198-1) Co-14280-D CC-36

1   Oh the way my wife treats me : it sure is a sin
2   Stayed out all night long : before day come creeping
     in
3   Then I wanted to know : honey where have you been
4   She couldn't say nothing : but it'll never happen
     again
5   I think sweet mama : I'll have to let you go
6   So pack up all your clothes : you can't sleep here
     no more
7   It's bad to have a crooked woman : she'll keep you
     living in sin
8   Then all she will say : it'll never happen again
9   Now if I had a-listened : to my mama's rule
10   I wouldn't have been singing : these crooked woman
     blues
11   I'm going to sing this verse : and I ain't going to
     sing no more
12   I got them blues : and I'm sure Lord got to go

HicR   7   Hicks, Robert

        title: 'Fo Day Creep
        place and date: Atlanta, 10 Nov. 1927
        record numbers: (145199-1) Co-14280-D CC-36

1   You passed my door brown : you won't even look in
2   You passed : just like a whirlwind
3   You can pass me up : try to ignore me too
4   You like you ignore me : somebody's going to ignore
     you
5   I lied down last night : I couldn't even sleep
6   I thinking about that gal : might make that
     'fore-day creep
7   It's a lowdown fireman : dirty engineer
8   Done took my gal : and left me standing here
9   Then I asked the brakeman : let me ride your blinds
10   Say I'm sorry buddy : but you know this train ain't
     mine
11   Some people are happy : and some are burdened down
12   Some are *so ???ing* : some are so lowdown

HicR   8   Hicks, Robert

        title: Blind Pig Blues
        place and date: Atlanta, 13 Apr. 1928
        record numbers: (146050-1) Co-14372-D CC-36

 1 Let me in please Charlie : no one here but me
 2 I'm speaking easy : give me a pint of stingaree
 3 Pour me out some white mule : pour me out some sandy
     rye
 4 I don't want no bug juice : that old stuff is too
     darn high
 5 Oh liquor liquor liquor : give me liquor until I die
 6 And I'm always happy : when I've got my liquor nigh
 7 I'm kind of worried : got something on my mind
 8 That's why I drink my whiskey : make my faro wait
     behind
 9 Blind pig blind pig : sure glad you can't see
10 For if you could : it would be too tight for me
11 I'm slipping slipping slipping : trying to dodge
     United States law
12 I'm loaded down with bootleg : like to make them
     yammies bawl

HicR   9   Hicks, Robert

        title: Chocolate to the Bone
        place and date: Atlanta, 13 Apr. 1928
        record numbers: (146054-?) Co-14331-D CC-36

 1 So glad I'm brownskin : chocolate to the bone
 2 And I've got what it takes : to make a monkey-man
     leave his home
 3 Black man is evil : yellow is so lowdown
 4 I walk into these houses : just to see these black
     men frown
 5 I'm just like Miss Lilliam : I mean Miss Lynn you
     see
 6 She said a brownskin man : is just all right with me
 7 Yellow man won't quit : black man just won't hey
 8 But a pigmeat mama crazy : about brownskin baby ways
 9 I got a yellow mama : always got a pleasant smile
10 But that brownskin gal : with her coal-black dreamy
     eyes

HicR   10   Hicks, Robert

        title: Hurry and Bring It Back Home
        place and date: Atlanta, 13 Apr. 1928
        record numbers: (146055-2) Co-14372-D CC-36

 1 I got them blues : and I can't be satisfied
 2 Got them so bad : I could just lay down and die
 3 Woke up this morning : my clock was striking four
 4 Someone started knocking : knocking on my door
 5 I went to see : what the noise was all about
 6 Someone told me : your brown done left this town
 7 On a Monday morning : first thing sad news
 8 Listen here professor : play for me those blues
 9 Now mama mama : hurry bring it on back to me
10 You were so crazy : for ever leaving me
11 Now haven't I done : everything you asked me to
12 You know by that : I don't love no one but you
13 Listen here sweet mama : I'm going to tell you a
     natural fact
14 You got what I want : so hurry bring it back

HicR   11   Hicks, Robert

        title: Ease It to Me Blues
        place and date: Atlanta, 21 Apr. 1928
        record numbers: (146173-2) Co-14614-D BC-7

 1 Some people want to have plenty of money : some want
     their wine and song

HicR   11   Hicks, Robert

 2 All I crave is my sweet mama : that I dreams about
     all night long
 3 Once I had a dear sweet mama : I didn't treat her
     right
 4 She left this town with a teasing brown : and her
     name was Mandy White
 5 I'm leaving town : today
 6 When I find that gal : this what I'm going to say
 7 You can have my money : all I want is the facts
 8 I ain't got no time to lose : I got to hurry on back
 9 When I find that aggravated papa : who tried to
     two-time me
10 I know I serve a great long sentence : in the
     penitentiary
11 I'm going to buy me a gun : airplane and a submarine
12 I'm going to kill everybody : ever treat me mean

HicR   12   Hicks, Robert

        title: She's Gone Blues
        place and date: Atlanta, 26 Oct. 1928
        record numbers: (147306-1) Co-14461-D RBF RF-15

 1 When you were down : sick down on your bed
 2 Know bobby brought you your medicine : also brought
     you bread
 3 You is up today : looking good again
 4 I knocked on your door : wouldn't even let me in
 5 But the sun going to shine : once more in my back
     door
 6 It's true I love you sweet mama : but you can't
     mistreat me no more
 7 I was standing at the terminal : arms fold up and
     cried
 8 Crying I wonder what train : taking that brown of
     mine
 9 And I run to the telephone : took the receiver down
10 I said hello Central : give me Doctor Brown
11 My baby looks for me : at any old hour at night
12 No matter when I go there : she's never turning off
     her light
13 Mmm : Lord Lord Lord
14 You womens in Atlanta : treat your men like your dog
15 Before this time brown : maybe another year
16 I'll be up the country : drinking that cool can beer

HicR   13   Hicks, Robert

        title: California Blues
        place and date: Atlanta, 18 Apr. 1929
        record numbers: (148358-2) Co-14573-D CC-36

 1 How long how long : how long my train been gone
 2 Been gone long enough : to take you to your good gal
     home
 3 Tell my wild women in California : where I so long
     to be
 4 Wild women and whiskey : can make a fool out of me
 5 They can lead me like a little airedale : that's
     only seven weeks old
 6 They can lead me to the water : shake my head no no
     no
 7 The longest train I ever rode : was seventy-nine
     coaches long
 8 But if the man had a-seed me : around the mountain
     I'd have been gone
 9 I was on my way to California : where I so long to
     be
10 Honey I'm from Missouri : you have to *side* me

107

HicR 14   Hicks, Robert

        title: Black Skunk Blues
        place and date: Atlanta, 18 Apr. 1929
        record numbers: (148360-2) Co-14573-D CC-36

1   I caught a pretty little animal : it was striped
    black and white
2   What it done to me : spoiled me the rest of my life
3   I thought it was a squirrel : I took him into my
    camp
4   When I put him down : all my clothes was damp
5   All the people around me : they give me plenty of
    air
6   It was so doggone strong : I sniffled it everywhere
7   I never smelled a smell : that smelled so doggone
    bad
8   It was the worst old smell : baby I ever had
9   I jumped into the water : I scrubbed scrubbed
    scrubbed scrubbed
10 But I smelled stronger : baby the harder I rubbed
11 It was a doggone polecat : and he [sure] ain't no
    friend of mine
12 He as pretty as a white dog : but he ain't worth a
    doggone dime

HicR 15   Hicks, Robert

        title: Freeze to Me Mama
        place and date: Atlanta, 3 Nov. 1929
        record numbers: (149345-2) Co-14507-D CC-36

1   Said come along mama : give me a hug
2   You got the world : I got the stopper and the jug
3   Gals all call me : big bad Pete
4   But they crazy : about this little pigmeat
5   Skinny gal in the summer : may be all right
6   But a fat gal in the winter : just too tight
7   My gal she's easy : some say she's slow
8   There's things about her : you don't know
9   Listen to me : please listen to my song
10 Take it slow and easy : you bound to get along
11 Me and my gal : was side by side
12 She said daddy : I would like to ride

HicR 16   Hicks, Robert

        title: Me and My Whiskey
        place and date: Atlanta, 3 Nov. 1929
        record numbers: (149346-2) Co-14507-D CC-36

1   When I'm in my whiskey : I don't care what I say
2   Because me and my whiskey : we going to have our way
3   Please tell me mama : what kind of loving you crave
4   I got the *kind that know about* : seven different
    ways
5   I'm down in Atlanta : where the womens they all know
    me
6   I'm going up to Detroit : give me you gal you ain't
    seen
7   Don't you never : want new loving sometimes
8   They moves it a little different : but it's all the
    same old kind
9   Don't let your gal fix you : like my gal fixed me
10 She made me love her : now she's way down in
    Tennessee
11 Wild women out west : where I so long to be
12 Wild women and whiskey : can make a fool out of me

HicR 17   Hicks, Robert

        title: unnamed title
        place and date: Atlanta, 3 Nov. 1929
        record numbers: (149347-1) Co unissued Yz L-1012

1   Let me be your little dog : until your big hound
    comes
2   I can do more howling : than your big dog ever done
3   Look over your role books : see if you got my baby's
    name
4   She's acting funny : and I she don't seem the same
5   Take care of the baby : because she'll a broad some
    day
6   And if I'm not too busy : I'll be stopping by your
    way
7   I feel like falling : from the treetop to the ground
8   My girl got a mean joker : and a-he don't allow me
    around
9   I go there early in the morning : and I'll go there
    late at night
10 She used to be my sugar : now he ain't treating her
    right
11 You got to love your baby : so she'll stay home at
    night
12 And if you don't love her : she sure ain't going to
    treat you right
13 You can't love me baby : and love my brother too
14 Because that's that's something : it will never do

HicR 18   Hicks, Robert

        title: Yo-Yo Blues No. 2
        place and date: Atlanta, 17 Apr. 1930
        record numbers: (150269-2) Co-14523-D CC-3

1   Hey Mr conductor : let me ride your train
2   I want to play your yo play your yo : play your
    yo-yo again
3   You don't let me on : I'm going to ride the blinds
4   You wants to yo-yo Bob : but you know this train you
    know this train ain't mine
5   I know a man : his age was fifty-four
6   Oh he didn't do nothing : but play with his yo play
    with his yo-yo
7   I like to yo-yo : yes both night and day
8   Some folks say it's hard work : but me it's famous
    me it's famous play
9   You may be blue : and way down in the depths
10 Go play your yo-yo : your yo-yo your little yo-yo
    will help
11 When you hear them yelling : up and down the hall
12 Don't get uneasy : they's playing yo-yo playing
    yo-yo that's all
13 I got a gal : she sure is big and fat
14 Let's yo-yo Bob : because it's tight because it's
    tight like that
15 I'm just a traveler : I've got to leave this squat
16 You want to yo-yo mama : call on Barbecue call on
    Barbecue Bob

HicR 19   Hicks, Robert

        title: We Sure Got Hard Times Now
        place and date: Atlanta, 18 Apr. 1930
        record numbers: (150273-1) Co-14558-D CC-36

1   Got a song to sing you : and it's no excuse
2   And as sure as the devil : I believe he's got
    a-loose
3   [When] you want a drink of liquor : you think it's
    awful nice
4   You put your hand in your pocket : and you ain't got
    the price
5   You hear about a job : now you is on your way
6   Twenty mens after the same job : all in the same old
    day

HicR   19   Hicks, Robert

7   Hard times hard times : we [sure] got hard times now
8   Just drink and think about it : we got hard times
     now
9   You start in mooching : but your mooching been in
     vain
10 Be careful with yourself : you'll get a ball and
     chain
11 Lord and bacon : gone to a dollar a pound
12 Cotton have started to selling : but it keeps going
     down and down
13 Just before election : you was talking about how you
     was going to vote
14 And after election was over : your head's down like
     a billygoat

HicR   20   Hicks, Robert

        title: The Spider and the Fly
        place and date: Atlanta, 23 Apr. 1930
        record numbers: (150365-2) Co-14558-D CC-36

1   Up said the spider : to the little fly one day
2   Won't you come around : let's pass the time away
3   Come into my parlor : said the spider to the fly
4   You won't have to do no hollering : I love you until
     you die
5   My mama told me be careful : wherever I flew
6   Spider's will try to tempt you : and be *baby*
7   I think it would be a treat : just for you and I
8   To order in some quince meat : and get all ???fied
9   Come into my parlor : said the spider to the fly
10 I'll give you loving : loving until you die

HicR   21   Hicks, Robert

        title: Atlanta Moan
        place and date: Atlanta, 5 Dec. 1930
        record numbers: (151054-2) Co-14591-D Yz L-1026

1   Oh nobody knows : Atlanta like I do
2   But the reason I know it : I traveled it through and
     through
3   If you got a good woman : here's the lesson I'll
     give to you
4   Don't you take her to Atlanta : the men will take
     her away from you
5   Lord they taken my woman : hurt me to the bone
6   That's the reason why : you hear me cry and moan
7   I taken one woman : believe me I am through
8   Just for what you do : it coming home to you
9   Oh don't you hear : that steamboat whistle blow
10 And it blows just like : it never blowed before
11 That's all right baby : about how you run around
12 But you had to face sorrow : when Bob gets back in
     town
13 If you take my woman : I won't get mad with you
14 Like you take her from me : somebody sure take her
     from you

HicR   22   Hicks, Robert

        title: Doin' the Scraunch
        place and date: Atlanta, 5 Dec. 1930
        record numbers: (151056-2) Co-14591-D CC-36

1   Down in Dixie : there's a dance that's new
2   Ain't much to it : it is easy to do
3   You wiggle and you wobble : and you move it around
4   Ball the jack : and you go to town
5   I know a gal : by name of Lizzie Brown
6   She do that scraunch : she's the best in town
7   She steps so fast : and she steps so light
8   Find her doing that scraunch : on a Saturday night
9   My little gal : know what scraunching means

HicR   22   Hicks, Robert

10 Showed her once : now she's a scraunching queen
11 Grandma and grandpa : at the age of eighty-three
12 They's the best scraunchers : you ever see
13 Standing on the levee : in New Orleans
14 Find the best scraunchers : the world ever seen
15 Got the right step : you move it just right
16 You do that scraunch : and it's just too tight
17 I've got a gal : by the name of Blind Lemon Mack
18 She do that scraunch : it's good like that

HilB   1   Hill, Bertha Chippie

        title: Low Land Blues
        place and date: Chicago, 9 Nov. 1925
        record numbers: (9456-A) OK-8273 Bio BLP-C6

1   I ain't going to marry : ain't going to settle down
2   I'll keep on drinking : keep on running around
3   The mouse got the measles : the dog's got the
     whooping cough
4   Doggone any man : lets a woman be his boss
5   The womens don't like me : because I speak my mind
6   But the men call mama : because I take my time
7   I ain't good-looking : and I ain't long and tall
8   Don't believe I'm a donkey : put me in a stall

HilB   2   Hill, Bertha Chippie

        title: Kid Man Blues
        place and date: Chicago, 9 Nov. 1925
        record numbers: (9457-A) OK-8273 Bio BLP-C6

1   Papa papa : something's going on wrong
2   If I catch you stealing : regret the day you's born
3   When daddy gets his razor : babies in the cradle
     moan
4   Because they lost their mama : he's got them all
     alone
5   Nobody knows : what the sheik will do
6   They'll spend all their money : leave you sad and
     blue
7   I'm going to quit my kid-man : I like my used-to-be
8   My kid-man don't want nobody : to talk to me

HilB   3   Hill, Bertha Chippie

        title: Pleadin' for the Blues
        place and date: Chicago, 23 Nov. 1926
        record numbers: (9949-A) OK-8420 Sw S-1240

1   I'm not crying : pleading at your feet
2   Sent for you baby : you treat me kind and sweet
3   Baby I'd rather work : than to play
4   But if you treat me mean : I'll have to run away
5   I left my mother : why can't I leave you
6   I will leave anybody : that treats me like you do

HilB   4   Hill, Bertha Chippie

        title: Pratt City Blues
        place and date: Chicago, 23 Nov. 1926
        record numbers: (9950-A) OK-8420 Sw S-1240

1   Pratt City : is where I was born
2   If you get to there : you can get your water on
3   Get full of high-powered liquor : it's bound to make
     him scream
4   Going back to Pratt City : if it takes *nice and
     mean*
5   You walk Sandusky : keep your head hung down
6   Don't worry hot papa : I'm *driftrack* bound

HilB 5   Hill, Bertha Chippie

        title: Lovesick Blues
        place and date: Chicago, 26 Nov. 1926
        record numbers: (9971-A) OK-8453 CC-32

1 Lonesome lovesick blues will make you feel so lonely
   : when you're left all alone
2 Dying for some loving : and the one you love has
   gone
3 Deep down in my heart : I'm feeling blue
4 Lonesome and lovesick : baby just for you
5 When I am alone : I moan the whole night through
6 I want some loving : no one but you will do
7 My heart is aching : breaking for some news
8 My heart is aching : gee I'm all confused

HilB 6   Hill, Bertha Chippie

        title: Lonesome Weary Blues
        place and date: Chicago, 26 Nov. 1926
        record numbers: (9972-A) OK-8453 CC-32

1 When I'm alone : I long to see my used-to-be
2 Because he's the only one : to ??? for me
3 I was down with a rock : rock by the deep blue sea
4 So I could roll : these lonesome lowdown blues from
   me
5 I'm lonesome mama : and I know it's true
6 Way my heart aches : you'd be lonesome mama too
8 If I ever lose these blues : never be worried again

HilK 1   Hill, King Solomon

        title: Whoopee Blues
        place and date: Grafton, Wis., c. Jan. 1932
        record numbers: (L-1252-1) Pm-13116 Rt RL-335

1 Baby you been gone all day : that you may make
   whoopee all night
2 If I going to take my razor and cut your late hours
   : you wouldn't think I be serving you right
3 Undertaker been here and gone : I give him your
   height and size
4 You'll be making whoopee with the devil : in hell
   tomorrow night
5 Oh you done made me love you : now got me for your
   slave
6 From now on you'll be making whoopee : baby in your
   lonesome grave
7 Devil got ninety thousand women : he just need one
   more
8 He's on the mountain calling for you : women broke
   down surely must go
9 Next time you go out : carry your black suit along
10 Coffin going to be your present : hell going to be
   your brand new home
11 Cuckoo was howling : sun was almost down
12 Then I got to go through Death Valley : there ain't
   a house for twenty-five miles around

HilK 2   Hill, King Solomon

        title: Whoopee Blues
        place and date: Grafton, Wis., c. Jan. 1932
        record numbers: (L-1252-2) Pm-13116 Yz L-1026

1 Honey you been gone all day : that you may make
   whoopee all night
2 I'm going to take my razor and cut your late hours :
   you wouldn't think I be serving you right
3 Undertaker been here and gone : I give him your
   heightth and size
4 You'll be making whoopee with the devil : in hell
   tomorrow night

HilK 2   Hill, King Solomon

5 You done made me love you : now you got me for your
   slave
6 From now on you'll be making whoopee : baby in your
   lonesome grave
7 Baby next time you go out : carry your black suit
   along
8 Coffin going to be your present : hell going to be
   your brand new home
9 I say the devil got ninety thousand women : he just
   need one more
10 He's on the mountain calling for you : baby broke
   down surely must go
11 Cuckoo was howling : sun was almost down
12 Then I got to go through Death Valley : there ain't
   a house for twenty-five miles around
13 My poor feet is so tired : Lord help me some way
14 Then I got three hundred miles to go : traveling
   through the mud and clay

HilK 3   Hill, King Solomon

        title: Down on My Bended Knee
        place and date: Grafton, Wis., c. Jan. 1932
        record numbers: (L-1253-2) Pm-13116 Yz L-1032

1 Ella Ella : down on my bended knees
2 I'm worried about my baby : bring her back to me
3 You know I love my baby : that's why we can't get
   along
4 Looks like everything I do : something going on
   wrong
5 I can see the sun a-shining : leaves shaking on the
   tree
6 I got a letter from my dona : my babe sung a song to
   me
7 Mmm : hear my lonesome plea
8 I'm worried about my baby : down on my bended knee

HilK 4   Hill, King Solomon

        title: The Gone Dead Train
        place and date: Grafton, Wis., c. Jan. 1932
        record numbers: (L-1254-2) Pm-13129 Yz L-1004

1 Lord I'm going way down : Lord I'm going to try to
   leave here today
2 Tell me that's a mean old fireman : and that train
   is just that way
3 Got to get on that train : I said I'd even brought
   my trunk
4 Boys if you have been running around in this world :
   this train will wreck your mind
5 Lord I once was a hobo : I crossed so many *points*
6 But I decided to pull down for a fast life : and
   take it as it comes
7 There's so many people : have gone down today
8 And these fast trains north and south : have settled
   their lives in clay
9 I said look here engineer : can I ride your train
10 He said look you ought to know this train ain't mine
   : and you asking me in vain
11 Said if you go to the Western Union : you might get
   a chance
12 You might to wire to some of your people : and your
   fare will be sent right here
13 I want to go home : and this train is done gone dead
14 I done lost my wife and my three little children :
   and my mother's sick in bed
15 Mmm please : help me win my fare
16 Because I'm a traveling man : boys I can't stay here

110

HilK   5   Hill, King Solomon

        title: Tell Me Baby
        place and date: Grafton, Wis., c. Jan. 1932
        record numbers: (L-1258-2) Pm-13129 Yz L-1004

1   Now tell me baby : what time your ??? leave
2   I'm going pack my suitcase : beat it back to
    Tennessee
3   I wrung my hands and cried : ???
4   Now tell me baby : what time your ??? leave
5   Nickel is a nickel : dime is a dime
6   Wish I had a loving mama : love me all the time
7   Nickel is a nickel : dime is a dime
8   Got a house full of children : and ain't nary one
    mine
9   Babe I can't see : honey to save my life
10 Why we can't get along : oh just like man and wife
11 I say mama told me : papa told me too
12 All these Winston women : going to be the ruin of
    you

HilR   1   Hill, Robert

        title: I Had a Gal for the Last Fifteen Years
        place and date: New Orleans, 15 Oct. 1936
        record numbers: (02603-1) BB-B6741 His HLP-31

1   When the rooster gets to worrying : he brings it to
    the hen
2   Ought to be on tiptoe : of you know *wouldn't let
    in*
3   Well the ground hog even gets it : puts it in his
    hole
4   So my woman's got to get it : doggone her soul
5   Well the bee gets the honey : puts it in his comb
6   If he kick out : of his own sweet home
7   Tired of buying pork chops : to grease your fat lips
8   You got to find another place : for to park your
    rotsy hips

HilSy   1   Hill, Sammy

        title: Cryin' for the Blues
        place and date: Dallas, 9 Aug. 1929
        record numbers: (55319) Vi-V38588 Yz L-1004

1   Did you ever wake up in the morning baby : same
    thing all on your mind
2   Something keep you bothered mama : honey worried all
    the time
3   When I was just a little boy sweet mama : on my way
    to school
4   Met an old *dark-kissing* brown boy : made me break
    my teacher's rule
5   Mmm : mmm
6   I ain't got no sweet mama : teach me right from
    wrong
7   My mama got a hen great God Lord : lays nineteen
    eggs a day
8   He layed so many eggs : my baby ??? away
9   Lord : am I right or wrong
10 I ain't got no sweet mama : Lord to rock me in her
    arms
11 Now take your black daddy : wrap him all in your
    arms
12 Sweet mama I haven't my right mind baby : Lord since
    you been gone

HilSy   2   Hill, Sammy

        title: Needin' My Woman Blues
        place and date: Dallas, 9 Aug. 1929
        record numbers: (55320) Vi-V38588 Yz L-1004

1   My baby's gone : please don't wait till day

HilSy   2   Hill, Sammy

2   I'm sorry I wasn't at home mama : just my babe
    hadn't've stayed
3   Well I went back home great God : sit in my back
    kitchen door
4   I just want to tell my mama : I mustn't see my baby
    anymore
5   Well I went out mama : and I begin to prayer and
    moan
6   I want to be good Lord Lord : send me my babe back
    home
7   Once I heard a knocking : on my back kitchen door
8   It's knock like my sweet mama : boys she been here
    before
9   Babe : honey what am I to do
10 Don't you want your sweet man mama : honey lie down
    and die for you
11 But I feel so sad baby : honey and I'm lonesome too
12 Ain't nothing in this world boys : Lord for your
    black man to do

Hite   1   Hite, Mattie

        title: Graveyard Dream Blues
        place and date: New York, c. mid Nov. 1923
        record numbers: (70413) Pat-032014 VJM VLP-40

1   Blues on my mind : blues all around my head
2   Had a dream last night : that the man I love was
    dead
3   Went to the graveyard : fell down on my knees
4   And I asked the gravedigger : to give me back my
    good man please
5   The gravedigger : looked me in the eye
6   Says I'm sorry lady : but your man has said his last
    goodbye
7   I wrung my hands : and I wanted to scream
8   But when I woke up : I found it was only a dream

Hite   2   Hite, Mattie

        title: Mason-Dixon Blues
        place and date: New York, c. mid Nov. 1923
        record numbers: (70414) Pat-032014 VJM VLP-40

1   Way down : below the Mason-Dixon line
2   That's where I'm going : just to ease my mind
3   Want to see my folks : I miss them so
4   I bought my ticket : and I'm bound to go
5   Won't I be glad : when my train pulls in
6   See my mammy : and my Uncle Ben
7   This northern country : it make you choose
8   But it will never cure : the Mason-Dixon blues

Hogg   1   Hogg, Andrew

        title: Family Trouble Blues
        place and date: Chicago, 18 Feb. 1937
        record numbers: (61856-A) De-7303 Rt RL-315

1   Well now I have a woman : I try to treat her right
2   Well now she will get drunk : ooo well well and fuss
    and fight all night
3   I love that woman : I done the best I could
4   Well now she proved to me : ooo well well that she
    didn't mean me no good
5   There's a day coming : I believe I'll make a change
6   Well now the way she treat me : ooo well well a
    lowdown dirty shame
7   I wonder what's the matter : that I can't sleep at
    night
8   Well something in my family : ooo well well you know
    ain't going on right
9   That's all right baby : *sorry* you drove me away

Hogg   1   Hogg, Andrew

10 Well now you don't think : ooo well well that you
    need my help some day
11 My woman she told me : nineteen and thirty-four
12 Well now you have a new man : ooo well well she
    can't use me no more

HollT   1   Hollins, Tony

        title: Stamp Blues
        place and date: Chicago, 3 June 1941
        record numbers: (C-3843-1) OK-06351 BC-5

1   Well I woke up this morning : half past four
2   Met a big crowd : at the ??? store
3   Well I'm a country man : never go to town
4   The women in Chicago : trying to jive me around
5   Well if you ever in Chicago : and the times get hard
6   Take a little walk : out on South Park
7   Well the womens up here : play me to be a fool
8   Think I'm the boy : ain't never been schooled
9   Well now I got cheer : I had good luck
10 The woman I love : she keeps me up
11 Well I woke up this morning : half past two
12 Streets was crowded : and I couldn't get through

Hous   1   House, Son

        title: My Black Mama--Part 1
        place and date: Grafton, Wis., 28 May 1930
        record numbers: (L-408-2) Pm-13042 OJL-2

1   Well black mama : what's the matter with you today
2   Ain't satisfactory : don't care what I do
3   Hey mama : what's the matter with you
4   Baby it ain't satisfactory : baby I don't care what
    I do
5   You say a brownskin woman : will make a rabbit move
    to town
6   Say a [jet, real] black woman : will make a mule
    kick his stable down
7   Yeah it ain't no heaven now : and it ain't no
    burning hell
8   Said I where I'm going when I die : can't nobody
    tell
9   Well my black mama's face : shine like the sun
10 Oh lipstick and powder : sure won't help her none
11 Well if you see my milkcow : tell her to hurry home
12 I ain't had no milk : since that cow been gone
13 Well I'm going to the race track : to see my pony
    run
14 He ain't the best in the world : but he's a running
    son of a gun
15 Oh Lord have mercy : on my wicked soul
16 I wouldn't mistreat you baby : for my weight in gold

Hous   2   House, Son

        title: My Black Mama--Part 2
        place and date: Grafton, Wis., 28 May 1930
        record numbers: (L-409-2) Pm-13042 OJL-2

1   Well I solemnly swear : Lord I raise my right hand
2   That I'm going to get me a woman : you get you
    another man
3   I got a letter this morning : how do you reckon it
    read
4   Oh hurry hurry : gal you love is dead
5   I grabbed my suitcase : I took on up the road
6   I got there : she was laying on the cooling board
7   Well I walked up close : I looked down in her face
8   Good old gal : got to lay there till Judgment Day
9   Oh my woman's so black : she stays apart of this
    town
10 Can't nothing go : when the poor gal is around

Hous   2   House, Son

11 Oh some people tell me : the worried blues ain't bad
12 It's the worst old feeling : that I ever had
13 Mmm I fold my arms : and I walked away
14 That's all right mama : your troubles will come some
    day

Hous   3   House, Son

        title: Preachin' the Blues--Part 1
        place and date: Grafton, Wis., 28 May 1930
        record numbers: (L-410-1) Pm-13013 OJL-5

1   Oh I'm going to get me religion : I'm going to join
    the Baptist Church
2   I'm going to be a Baptist preacher : and I sure
    won't have to work
3   Oh I'm going to preach these blues now : and I want
    everybody to shout
4   I'm going to do like a prisoner : I'm going to roll
    my time on out
5   Oh up in my room : I bowed down to pray
6   Say the blues come along : and they drove my spirit
    away
7   Oh and I had religion : Lord this very day
8   But the womens and whiskey : well they would not let
    me pray
9   Oh I wish I had me : a heaven of my own
10 Then I'd give all my women : a long long happy home
11 Yeah I love my baby : just like I love myself
12 Well if she don't have me : she won't have nobody
    else

Hous   4   House, Son

        title: Preachin' the Blues--Part 2
        place and date: Grafton, Wis., 28 May 1930
        record numbers: (L-411-1) Pm-13013 OJL-5

1   Hey I'm going to fold my arms : I'm going to kneel
    down in prayer
2   When I get up : I'm going to see if my preaching
    suit a man's ear
3   Now I met the blues this morning : walking just like
    a man
4   I said good morning blues : now give me your right
    hand
5   Now it ain't nothing now baby : Lord that's going to
    worry my mind
6   Oh I'm satisfied : I got the longest line
7   Oh I got to stay on the job : I ain't got no time to
    lose
8   I swear to God : I got to preach these gospel blues
9   Oh I'm going to preach these blues : and choose my
    seat and sit down
10 When the spirit comes sisters : I want you to jump
    straight up and down

Hous   5   House, Son

        title: Dry Spell Blues--Part 1
        place and date: Grafton, Wis., 28 May 1930
        record numbers: (L-425-4) Pm-12990 OJL-11

1   The dry spell blues have fallen : drive me from door
    to door
2   The dry spell blues : have put everybody on the
    killing flood
3   Now the people down south : sure won't have no home
4   Because the dry spell : have parched all this cotton
    and corn
5   Hard luck's on everybody : and many people are blue
6   Now besides the shower : ain't got no help for you
7   Lord I fold my arms : and I walked away
8   Just like I tell you : somebody's got to pay

Hous   5   House, Son

9 Pork chops forty-five cents a pound : cotton is only
   ten
10 I can't keep no woman : no no nowhere I been
11 So dry : old boll weevil turned up his toes and died
12 Now ain't nothing to do : bootleg moonshine and rye

Hous   6   House, Son

   title: Dry Spell Blues--Part 2
   place and date: Grafton, Wis., 28 May 1930
   record numbers: (L-426-2) Pm-12990 OJL-11

1 It have been so dry : you can make a powderhouse out
   of the world
2 Then all the moneymen : like a rattlesnake in his
   coil
3 I done throwed up my hands : Lord and solemnly swore
4 There ain't no need of me changing towns : it's a
   drought everywhere I go
5 It's a dry old spell : everywhere I been
6 I believe to my soul : this old world is about to
   end
7 Well I stood in my back yard : wrung my hands and
   screamed
8 And I couldn't see nothing : couldn't see nothing
   green
9 Oh Lord : have mercy if you please
10 Let your rain come down : and give our poor hearts
   ease
11 These blues these blues : is worthwhile to be heard
12 For it's very likely : bound to rain somewhere

Howe   1   Howell, Peg Leg

   title: Coal Man Blues
   place and date: Atlanta, 8 Nov. 1926
   record numbers: (143116-2) Co-14194-D RBF RF-202

1 Woke up this morning : about five o'clock
2 Get me some eggs : and a nice pork chop
3 Cheap cigar : and a magazine
4 Had to run through the street : to catch the
   five-fifteen
5 Let me tell you something : that I seen
6 Coalman got run over : by the five-fifteen
7 Cut off his arms : and it cracked his ribs
8 Did the poor man die : no the poor man lived
9 Let me tell you something : that I know
10 Coalman got run over : by the five forty-four
11 Cut off his arms : and it crunched his head
12 The poor man died : no the poor man lived
13 I ain't got : but a little bit left
14 If you don't come and get it : I'm going to burn it
   myself
15 Get the wood in the stove : and the match in your
   hand
16 You run to the door : and stop the *dirty* coalman
17 Sell it to the rich : and I sell it to the poor
18 Sell it to the nice brown : a-standing in the door
19 Furnish you wood : furnish you coal
20 Make you love me : doggone your soul
21 I got your water : got you gas
22 You treat me mama : says that's your last
23 Let me tell you mama : what's the matter now
24 You don't want me : take me anyhow
25 Sweet mama sweet mama : what's on your mind
26 Say you can't quit me : no need of trying
27 I'm going up the country : don't you want to go
28 Leaving here : ain't coming back no more
29 Me and my rider : and two or three more
30 We're going up the country : don't you want to go
31 Went down the road : feeling bad
32 I feel so worried : that I ever had
33 Don't believe I'm leaving : count the day I'm gone

Howe   2   Howell, Peg Leg

   title: Tishamingo Blues
   place and date: Atlanta, 8 Nov. 1926
   record numbers: (143117-1) Co-14194-D RBF RF-9

1 I'm going to Tishamingo : because I'm sad today
2 Say the woman I love : she done drove me away
3 I'm going to Tishamingo : to have my hambone boiled
4 These Atlanta women : done let my hambone spoil
5 I woke up this morning : between midnight and day
6 I felt for my rider : she done walked away
7 Can't you always tell : when your good gal going to
   treat you mean
8 You meals is unregular : you house ain't never clean
9 You can always tell : that something going on wrong
10 When you come in : your rider she's out and gone
11 Say when she come in : she got a rag tied around her
   head
12 You speak about loving : she swear she's almost dead
13 Sweet mama : what's on your loving mind
14 You can't quit me : 'tain't no need of trying
15 I got a loving faro : she's long and tall like me
16 I love my brownskin : don't care where she be

Howe   3   Howell, Peg Leg

   title: Too Tight Blues
   place and date: Atlanta, 1 Nov. 1927
   record numbers: (145062-1) Co-14298-D Rt RL-316

1 Grab your gal : fall in line
2 While I play : this rag of mine
3 Too tight : it won't *don*
4 Too tight : it'll make you warm
5 Too tight : ain't it a shame
6 Too tight : shaking that thing
7 Too tight : hear me cry
8 Too tight : just don't die
9 Too tight : ???
10 Too tight : he tried to pull it back out
11 Too tight : give it the gate
12 Too tight : let's don't wait
13 Too tight : you hear me say
14 Too tight : it make us afraid

Howe   4   Howell, Peg Leg

   title: Doin' Wrong
   place and date: Atlanta, 9 Nov. 1927
   record numbers: (145184-2) Co-14473-D RBF RF-11

1 Take me sweet mama : allow me one more show
2 I swear to the Lord : that I won't do wrong no more
3 I don't love no woman : if she ain't got baby ways
4 I'm crazy about my loving : it's always been my
   crave
5 I hung my head : I cried just like a child
6 Said the way I'm treated mama : I sure ain't
   satisfied
7 If you ever go to Memphis : stop by Jessie's hall
8 You'll see my picture : hanging on the wall
9 I got the blues so bad : mama my poor heart is sore
10 Can't rest contented : nowhere I go
11 Take me mama : please don't throw me down
12 I'm going to pack my suitcase : I'm going to blow
   this town

Howe   5   Howell, Peg Leg

   title: Skin Game Blues
   place and date: Atlanta, 9 Nov. 1927
   record numbers: (145185-2) Co-14473-D RBF RF-202

1 When I ??? game last night : thought I'd have some
   fun

2 Lost all the money that I had baby : pawned my
   special gun
3 Says I gambled all over Missouri : gambled all
   through Spain
4 Police come to arrest me babe : and they did not
   know my name
5 Gambled all over Missouri : gambled through
   Tennessee
6 Soon as I reach old Georgia : the niggers carried a
   handcuff to me

Howe   6   Howell, Peg Leg

    title: Please Ma'am
    place and date: Atlanta, 20 Apr. 1928
    record numbers: (146159-2) Co-14356-D RBF RF-15

1 Been begging you : all night long
2 I'll acknowledge : I done wrong
3 Begging you : down on my knees
4 Begging you : babe if you please

Howe   7   Howell, Peg Leg

    title: Low Down Rounder Blues
    place and date: Atlanta, 20 Apr. 1928
    record numbers: (146161-1) Co-14320-D RBF RF-1

1 Just a worried old rounder : with a troublesome mind
2 All bundled up from hardship : fate to me have been
   unkind
3 I wouldn't listen to my mother : wouldn't listen to
   my dad
4 And by my reckless living : I've put myself in bad
5 I ain't trusting nobody : I'm afraid of myself
6 I've been too lowdown : life have put me on the
   shelf
7 My friends have turned against me : smiling in my
   face
8 Since I been so disobedient : I must travel in
   disgrace
9 I cannot shun the devil : he stay right by my side
10 There is no way to cheat him : I'm so dissatisfied
11 Ain't nobody wants me : they wouldn't be in my shoes
12 I feel so disgusted : I've got them lowdown rounder
   blues

Howe   8   Howell, Peg Leg

    title: Ball and Chain Blues
    place and date: Atlanta, 13 Apr. 1929
    record numbers: (148270-2) Co-14535-D Rt RL-318

1 I'm laying in jail : my back turned to the wall
2 Says a Georgia woman : was the cause of it all
3 They arrested me : carried me before the judge
4 Say the judge wouldn't like me : and he say a
   mumbling word
5 I asked the judge : what might be my fine
6 Get a pick and shovel : dig down in the mine
7 I told the judge : I ain't been here before
8 If you give me light sentence : I won't come here no
   more
9 Mr judge Mr judge : please don't break so hard
10 I always been a poor boy : never hurt no John
11 So the next day : they carried the poor boy away
12 Said the next day : I *led* a ball and chain
13 Take the stripes off my back : chains from around my
   legs
14 This ball and chain : about to kill me dead

    title: Away from Home
    place and date: Atlanta, 13 Apr. 1929
    record numbers: (148273-2) Co-14535-D Rt RL-318

1 Standing in the station : waiting for my train
2 I was outdoors : sleeping in the rain
3 My mama's sick : papa's dead and gone
4 Didn't have no loving pillow : to lay head on
5 Thousand miles : baby away from home
6 My mama's sick : my papa's dead and gone
7 I asked the operator : how long the train been gone
8 Your train been gone : ever since this morn
9 Said the train I ride : it's eighteen coaches long
10 I'm a poor boy : I'm a long ways from my home
11 I'm a poor boy : ain't got nowhere to stay
12 Says everybody : sure done throwed me away
13 I'm down in Cincinnati : baby on the hog
14 I'm drinking muddy water : sleep in a hollow log

Hull   1   Hull, Papa Harvey

    title: Gang of Brownskin Women
    place and date: Chicago, c. 8 Apr. 1927
    record numbers: (12689) Ge-6122 Yz L-1001

1 Got a gang of brownskin sweet women : got a gang of
   high yellows too
2 I got so many womens : I don't know what to do
3 Got a Monday Monday girl : she works it on Broad and
   Main
4 Got a Tuesday one *there : to issue* my spending
   change
5 Got a Wednesday Wednesday girl : she works it on
   Broadway Square
6 Got a Thursday one : take me each and everywhere
7 Got a Friday Friday girl : she brings me a bottle of
   beer
8 Got a Saturday one : well she better not catch me
   here
9 Now gang around girls and boys : explain my sonnet
   to you
10 Wear those patent leather slippers : mama don't
   made dad blue
11 Well I love my sweet baby : I tell this world I do
12 And I hope some day : she'll learn to love daddy too
13 Got a gang of brownskin sweet women : got a gang of
   high yellows too
14 And I hope some day : she'll learn to love daddy too

Hull   2   Hull, Papa Harvey

    title: France Blues
    place and date: Chicago, c. 8 Apr. 1927
    record numbers: (12690) Ge-6106 OJL-2

1 Have you ever took a trip : baby on the Mobile Line
2 That's the road to ride baby : ease your troubling
   mind
3 Well I got a letter baby : this is the way it read
4 Come home come home baby : because your love is dead
5 Well I packed my suitcase : bundled up my clothes
6 When I got there : she was laying on the cooling
   board
7 Well I took my baby : to the burying ground
8 You ought to heard me hollering : when they let her
   down
9 Well there's two black horses : standing on the
   burying ground
10 When I turned around : these big tears run on down
11 When you go to heaven : going to babe going to stop
   by France
12 Going to stop by there : just to give these girls a
   chance
13 Baby when I die : don't bury daddy at all
14 Well pickle daddy's bones : baby in alcohol

Hull   2   Hull, Papa Harvey

15 Well the boat's up the river : baby and she won't
       come down
16 Well I believe to my soul : baby boat is water bound
17 Baby when I die : put daddy's picture in a frame
18 So where daddy's going : you can see him just the
       same
19 Hello heaven : daddy want to give you a telephone
20 So you can talk to your daddy :any time when he's
       gone

Hull   3   Hull, Papa Harvey

       title: Two Little Tommies Blues
       place and date: Chicago, c. 8 Apr. 1927
       record numbers: (12691) Ge-6122 Yz L-1009

1   Got two little Tommies : can't hardly tell them
       apart
2   One is my lover : the other in my heart
3   Got two little Tommies : they is black and brown
4   One lives in the country : the other lives in town
5   When you see me coming : put your man outdoors
6   Well I ain't no stranger : I been here before
7   When you see me coming : bake your biscuits brown
8   Put your meat in the cupboard : turn your damper
       down
9   When you see me leaving : hang your head and cry
11 Got a mind to ramble : ain't going to settle down
12 Going to move to the city : tear these girls on down
13 Can you tell me : how far Jackson to back home

Hull   4   Hull, Papa Harvey

       title: Don't You Leave Me Here
       place and date: Chicago, c. 8 Apr. 1927
       record numbers: (12692) Ge-6106 OJL-8

1   Boat's up the river : running side by side
2   Well you got my loving sweet babe : guess you're
       satisfied
3   Don't you leave me here : don't you leave me here
4   Well I don't mind you going sweet loving babe :
       leave a dollar for beer
5   How long how long : had the train been gone
7   Katy Adams got ways : just like a man
8   Because she steals a woman sweet loving babe :
       everywhere she lands
9   Can you tell me how long : Jackson to McComb
10 Well it's fifteen miles sweet loving babe : Memphis
       to my home

Hull   5   Hull, Papa Harvey

       title: Mama You Don't Know How
       place and date: Chicago, c. May 1927
       record numbers: (   ) BP-8030 Her H-201

1   Ooh : I ain't got no mama now
2   Going to be another *war* : don't need no mama nohow
3   Lord it was late last night mama : everything was
       still
4   Here to meet my sweet baby : *he's* around the hill
5   Lord I'd rather be dead mama : mouldering in the
       clay
6   Seeing my sweet baby : treated this a-way
7   Ooh : mama you don't know how
8   Got another sweet baby : know she's taking it now
9   Going to sing this verse mama : ain't going to sing
       no more
10 Because the landlady's liquor : Lord it's coming too
       slow

Hurt   1   Hurt, Mississippi John

       title: Nobody's Dirty Business
       place and date: Memphis, 14 Feb. 1928
       record numbers: (400223-B) OK-8560 Bio BLP-C4

1   Some of these mornings : going to wake up crazy
2   Going to grab me a gun : kill my baby
3   Some of these mornings : going to wake up boozy
4   Going to grab my gun : going to kill old Suzie
5   Going back : to Pensicola
6   Going to buy my babe : a money *moler*
7   Babe babe : did you get that letter
8   Oh you take me back : I'll treat you better

Hurt   2   Hurt, Mississippi John

       title: Ain't No Tellin'
       place and date: New York, 21 Dec. 1928
       record numbers: (401471-A) OK-8759 Bio BLP-C4

1   Don't you let : my good girl catch you here
3   She might shoot you : may cut you and stab you too
4   'Tain't no telling : what she might do
5   I'm up the country : where the cold sleet and snow
6   Ain't no telling : how much further I may go
7   Eat my breakfast here : my dinner in Tennessee
8   I told you I was coming : baby won't you look for me
9   The way I'm sleeping : my back and shoulders tired
10 Going to turn over : try it on this side

Hurt   3   Hurt, Mississippi John

       title: Avalon Blues
       place and date: New York, 21 Dec. 1928
       record numbers: (401473-B) OK-8759 Bio BLP-C4

1   I been in New York this morning : just about half
       past nine
2   Thought of my mama in Avalon : couldn't hardly keep
       from crying
3   Avalon my home town : always on my mind
4   Pretty mama's in Avalon : want me there all the time
5   When the train left Avalon : throwing kisses and
       waving at me
6   Says come back daddy : stay right here with me
7   Avalon's a small town : have no great big range
8   Pretty mama's in Avalon : sure will spend your
       change
9   New York's a good town : but it's not for mine
10 Going back to Avalon : stay there with pretty mama
       all the time

Hurt   4   Hurt, Mississippi John

       title: Big Leg Blues
       place and date: New York, 21 Dec. 1928
       record numbers: (401474-A) OK unissued Bio
       BLP-C4

1   Raise up baby : get your big leg off of mine
2   It's so heavy : made a good man change his mind
3   I asked you baby : come and hold my head
4   Send me away : said you'd rather see me dead
5   I'm going I'm going : crying won't make me stay
6   The more you cry : further you drive me away
7   Some crave high yellow : I like black and brown
8   Black won't quit you : brown won't lay you down
9   It was late at midnight : moon shine bright like day
10 I seen you faro : going up the right of way

Hurt   5   Hurt, Mississippi John

    title: Candy Man Blues
    place and date: New York, 28 Dec. 1928
    record numbers: (401483-B) OK-8654 Bio BLP-C4

1 Want all you ladies : all gather around
2 That good sweet candy man's : in town
3 He got a stick of candy : just nine inch long
4 He sells as fast : a hog can chew his corn
5 All heard : what sister Johnson said
6 She always takes : a candy stick to bed
7 Don't stand close : to the candy man
8 He'll leave a big candy stick : in your hand
9 He sold some candy : to sister bad
10 The very next day : she took all he had
11 If you try his candy : good friend of mine
12 You sure will want it : for a long long time
13 His stick candy : don't melt away
14 It just gets better : so the ladies say

Hurt   6   Hurt, Mississippi John

    title: Got the Blues Can't Be Satisfied
    place and date: New York, 28 Dec. 1928
    record numbers: (401484-B) OK-8724 Bio BLP-C4

1 Got the blues : can't be satisfied
2 Keep the blues : I'll catch that train and ride
3 Whiskey straight : will drive the blues away
4 That be the case : I want a quart today
5 Bought my gal : a great big diamond ring
6 Come right back home : and caught her shaking that thing
7 I said baby : what makes you act this a-way
8 Said I won't miss a thing : she gives away
9 Took my gun : and I broke the barrel down
10 Put my baby : six feet under the ground
11 I cut that joker : so long deep and wide
12 You got the blues : and still ain't satisfied

Hurt   7   Hurt, Mississippi John

    title: Blue Harvest Blues
    place and date: New York, 28 Dec. 1928
    record numbers: (401487-A) OK-8692 Bio BLP-C4

1 Standing on the mountain : far as I can see
2 Dark clouds above me : clouds all around poor me
3 Feeling low and weary : Lord I've got a trouble in mind
4 Everything that gets me : everybody's so unkind
5 Harvest time's coming : and will catch me unprepared
6 Haven't made a dollar : bad luck is all I've had
7 Lord how can I bear it : Lord what will the harvest bring
8 Putting up all my money : and I isn't got a doggone thing
9 I'm a weary traveler : roaming around from place to place
10 If I don't find something : this will end me in disgrace
11 Ain't got no mother : father left me long ago
12 I'm just like an orphan : where my folks is I don't know
13 Blues around my shoulder : blues are all around my head
14 With my heavy burden : Lord I wished I was dead

JackC   1   Jackson, Papa Charlie

    title: Papa's Lawdy Lawdy Blues
    place and date: Chicago, c. Aug. 1924
    record numbers: (1850-1) Pm-12219 RBF RF-9

1 I love my baby : and my baby do love me

JackC   1   Jackson, Papa Charlie

3 Get away from my window : honey babe get away from my door
5 Honey babe honey babe : why don't you tell me what you're going to do
7 I ain't crazy about no yellow : I ain't no fool about no brown
8 Because you can't tell the difference : mama when the sun goes down
10 I got a wife got a girl : and I'm fooling on the outside too

JackC   2   Jackson, Papa Charlie

    title: Airy Man Blues
    place and date: Chicago, c. Aug. 1924
    record numbers: (1851-2) Pm-12219 Yz L-1029

1 Now *look here Mr* ??? : *says you take a good drop*
2 ??? : he done broke your heart
3 Put you out : told you to go
4 You never come back : to her house no more
5 Now just trying : to throw it down
6 You know : you the foolishest man in town
7 Keep on talking : *to the will*
8 Says you'll never : get to ??? *Bill*
9 Well you can bring a lot of wood: you can bring in my clothes
10 You can iron my shirts : you can bless my soul

JackC   3   Jackson, Papa Charlie

    title: Salty Dog Blues
    place and date: Chicago, c. Sept. 1924
    record numbers: (1893-?) Pm-12236 Yz L-1029

1 Says it ain't but the one thing : that grieve my mind
2 All these women : and none is mine
3 Says a little fish big fish : swimming in the water
4 Come on back here man : and give me my quarter
5 It's like hunting for a needle : in a bed of sand
6 Trying to find a woman : haven't got no man
7 Three barrels of your whiskey : four barrels of gin
8 Says I have a papa home : and you can't come in
9 Says God made a woman : and he made her mighty funny
10 Kiss her on the mouth : just sweet as any honey
11 Now who in the *ham* : *and the confoundation*
12 Been sowing them potatoes : on my plantation
13 Now the scariest I ever been : in my life
14 Uncle ??? caught me : kissing his wife
15 Now if this was a coffeepot : and that was a spout
16 I'll be the *worst* boy : to pour the coffee out

JackC   4   Jackson, Papa Charlie

    title: The Cats Got the Measles
    place and date: Chicago, c. Jan. 1925
    record numbers: (10019-3) Pm-12259 Bio BLP-12042

1 Now the cat's got the measles : dog's got the whooping cough
2 Doggone a man : let a woman be his boss
3 Now I ain't no devil : crawl in a lion's den
4 But my chief occupation : taking women from their monkey-men
5 Says I ain't good-looking : my teeth don't shine like pearls
6 But I've got something babe : to carry me through this big darn world
7 Now I think I heard a rumbling : deep down in the ground
8 Well it must have been the devil : chaining my good gal down

JackC   4   Jackson, Papa Charlie

    9 Now the men don't like me : just because I speak my
       mind
   10 But the women cry papa : just because I take my time

JackC   5   Jackson, Papa Charlie

       title: I Got What It Takes
          But It Breaks My Heart to Give It Away
       place and date: Chicago, c. Jan. 1925
       record numbers: (10020-3) Pm-12259 Bio BLP-12042

    1 I saved it up : since the Lord knows when
    2 I ain't saved a thing : because of any of you men
    3 I've had it so long : I hate to lose it
    4 Because ever gets broke : I'll be able to use it
    5 Now when you're laying in jail : with your head in
       your arms
    6 And then you realize : your sweet mama's gone

JackC   6   Jackson, Papa Charlie

       title: Shave Em Dry
       place and date: Chicago, c. Feb. 1925
       record numbers: (10042-?) Pm-12264 Yz L-1029

    1 Now here's one thing : can't understand
    2 Why a bow-legged woman : likes a knock-kneed man
    3 *Times* way downtown : spread the news
    4 State Street women : wearing broken shoes
    5 Now I'm going away : to wear you off my mind
    6 You keep me broken-hearted : mama all the time
    7 Now here's one thing : I can't understand
    8 A good-looking woman : likes a workingman
    9 Now I don't see how : you *honky* women can *pace*
   10 Shimmy all day : without a bite to eat
   11 Now if it wasn't for the powder : store-bought hair
   12 State Street women : couldn't go nowhere
   13 Now I went to the show : the other night
   14 The people on State Street : trying to fight
   15 I ain't crazy about my brown : or about my brown
   16 You can't tell the difference : when the sun go down
   17 When you see two women : running hand by hand
   18 You bet your bottom dollar : she's got the other
       one's man
   19 Now run here mama : stay back in my home
   20 If your man catch you : I don't mean no harm

JackC   7   Jackson, Papa Charlie

       title: Coffee Pot Blues
       place and date: Chicago, c. Feb. 1925
       record numbers: (10043-?) Pm-12264 Yz L-1029

    1 You can always tell : when your good gal don't want
       to be seen
    2 Because your meals ain't ready : the house is never
       clean
    3 Just like hunting for a needle : buried in a bed of
       sand
    4 That is to find a woman : haven't got no man
    5 Three barrels of whiskey : mama four barrels of gin
    6 She said the *headknots* at home : daddy and you
       can't in
    7 It was early one morning : just at the close of four
    8 When Dolly Smith : knocked on Evelyn's door
    9 She jumped up sweet babe : tipped on across the
       floor
   10 Hollering long tall daddy : don't you knock no more
   11 It was in the loving kitchen : where they made the
       plot
   12 For to poison her father and her mother : in the
       coffeepot
   13 Then they carried the remains : throwed it out in
       the *shore*

JackC   7   Jackson, Papa Charlie

   14 Killed fifteen chickens : ???
   15 Policeman said to Freddie : what do you know about
       this
   16 Says I guess : you'll have to go arrest poor Dolly
       Smith
   17 Then they carried poor dolly : put her behind the
       bar
   18 Give him thirty-nine days : mama and that ain't all
   19 Poor evelyn's in jail : with her back turned to the
       wall
   20 Hollering cool kind daddy : you know you the cause
       it all
   21 I'm going to sing this time : ain't going to sing no
       more
   22 Because my throat's got dry : swear my tonsil's sore

JackC   8   Jackson, Papa Charlie

       title: Shake That Thing
       place and date: Chicago, c. May 1925
       record numbers: (2120-?) Pm-12281 Yz L-1029

    1 Now down in Georgia : they got a dance that's new
    2 There ain't nothing to it : it is easy to do
    3 Now it ain't no Charleston : ain't no buck and wing
    4 All you got to do : is to shake that thing
    5 Now the old folks like it : the young folks too
    6 The old folks showing : the young folks how to do
    7 Now get back to me : and ???
    8 Let your mammy ??? you : just *all to do*
    9 I was walking downtown : and stumbled and fell
   10 My mouth jumped open : like a country well
   11 Now grandpa Johnson : grabbed sister Kate
   12 He shook her : just like you shake the *jelly from
       the wheat*
   13 Now old Uncle Jack : the jellyroll king
   14 He just got back : from shaking that thing
   15 Now old Uncle Moe : he's sick in bed
   16 The doctor says : he's almost dead
   17 Now the folks in Georgia : they done got wild
   18 The *hobo* ??? : ???

JackC   9   Jackson, Papa Charlie

       title: The Faking Blues
       place and date: Chicago, c. May 1925
       record numbers: (2121-?) Pm-12281 Yz L-1029

    1 I got plenty of whiskey : put them up on the shelf
    2 But I'm getting sick and tired : of doing ??? by my
       faking self
    3 Now tell me pretty mama : tell me please don't lie
    4 Can your sweet papa stop by here : or must I pass on
       by
    5 I got the faking blues : going to sing them anywhere
       I please
    6 That's the reason why : give my poor heart some ease
    7 Lord I'm going away mama : believe me it ain't stall
    8 Because I can get more women : than a passenger can
       haul
    9 Lord I'm going to the nation : buy me an Indian
       squaw
   10 I'm going to raise me a family : got me an Indian ma
   11 I got the faking blues : sing them anywhere I go
   12 Tell you the reason I sing them : my sweet mama
       don't love me no more
   13 Lord I went to the river : looking for a place to
       set down
   14 I thought about my faking jellyroll : come on back
       to town

JackC 10   Jackson, Papa Charlie

        title: I'm Alabama Bound
        place and date: Chicago, c. May 1925
        record numbers: (2144-2) Pm-12289 Yz L-1029

1   Stood on the corner : feet got soaking wet
2   I was hollering and crying to every brown : to hell
     I'm at
3   I'm Alabama bound : I'm Alabama bound
4   Then if you want me to love you babe : you got to
     leave this town
5   When the rooster crowed : the hen looked around
6   Said if you want me to love you babe : you got to
     run me down
7   Look here pretty mama : who can your regular be
8   Says the reason I'm *blacking out stalling* babe :
     you been so good to me
9   There's a preacher in the pulpit : Bible in his hand
10   And the sisters was back in the amen corner :
     hollering that's my man
11   Now the boat's up the river : can't be floated down
12   But she's *way on south* now darling babe : Alabama
     bound
13   Just like a beefsteak beefsteak : ain't got no bone
14   Then if a man like a good brownskin woman now babe :
     he ain't got no home
15   Elder Green's in town : and he's going around
16   And he's telling all the sisters and the brothers he
     meets : he's Alabama bound
17   Now don't you leave me here : don't you leave me
     here
18   Just before you and your partner get ready to go :
     leave a dime for beer

JackC 11   Jackson, Papa Charlie

        title: Drop that Sack
        place and date: Chicago, c. May 1925
        record numbers: (2145-1) Pm-12289 Yz L-1029

1   Now I got a gal : works in the yard
2   She brings me meat : she brings me lard
3   Only thing : that keep me barred
4   People she works for : don't allow me in the yard
5   Going to tell you one thing : it's a natural fact
6   Want you to come on home : and drop that sack
7   Now I got a gal : she lives on the hill
8   Took our corn : to the sugar mill
9   Still I know : I wouldn't take no salt
10   I'll grind your corn : into sweet jellyroll
11   I asked for one : she brought me two
12   Down to the crap game : me and you
13   Got two dollars : my point was nine
14   Police come a-running : and the *chips* went flying
15   Said I went to the Gypsy : to get me a hand
16   See my gal walking : with another man
17   I said you may go : you'll come back
18   If you ever come back : you got to drop that sack

JackC 12   Jackson, Papa Charlie

        title: Hot Papa Blues
        place and date: Chicago, c. Aug. 1925
        record numbers: (2207-2) Pm-12305 Bio BLP-12042

1   I ain't good-looking : and I don't dress cute
2   But I just want to *break* : some good man's
     opportune
3   I ain't no race horse : I ain't built for speed
4   But I got everything : that a race horse papa needs
5   You may fall from the mountain : down in the deep
     blue sea
6   You ain't done no falling : till you fall in love
     with me
7   I ain't no coalman : ain't no coalman's son
8   But I can keep you warm : until your coalman comes

JackC 12   Jackson, Papa Charlie

9   Won't you tell me pretty mama : I won't have to wait
10   Will I be your regular : or did I come too late
11   I may look green : but I ain't no clown
12   I'm just a red-hot papa : just blowed in your town

JackC 13   Jackson, Papa Charlie

        title: Take Me Back Blues
        place and date: Chicago, c. Aug. 1925
        record numbers: (2208-2) Pm-12296 Bio BLP-12042

1   Take me back baby : you know I don't know my mind
2   For when I'm mistreating you : I'm loving you all
     the time
3   I walked the streets all day : hung my head and
     cried
4   I laid awake all night : trying to make myself
     satisfied
5   There's one thing honey : I want you to understand
6   That's your time ain't long : if I catch you with
     another man
7   You ain't good-looking : and you don't dress fine
8   But there ain't no reason : let some other man read
     my sign
9   Going down to the river : honey don't you wear no
     black
10   Because when you think I'm gone : I'll come creeping
     back
11   If you don't want me : why don't you tell me why
12   Because you flirting with the undertaker : I mean it
     ain't no lie

JackC 14   Jackson, Papa Charlie

        title: Mama, Don't You Think I Know?
        place and date: Chicago, c. Aug. 1925
        record numbers: (2224-2) Pm-12305 Bio BLP-12042

1   Got a knock-kneed mama : down in Tennessee
2   She's short and squatty : she's all right with me
3   Now knock-kneed mama : what you going to cook
     tonight
4   Whatever you cook : just cook it right
5   You got a face like a washboard : and a mouth like a
     tub
6   Teach my mama : that washboard rub
7   Now some people say : chitlings are good to eat
8   I'll never eat chitlings : long as hog got feet
9   Takes a long-tailed monkey : a short-tailed dog
10   To do that dance : they call the falling off the log
11   Now the monkey told the elephant : if he's not drunk
12   I know you're sober : you got the tail in front
13   Now the monkey told the elephant : you may be
     drinking wine
14   You can't switch your tail : like I switch mine

JackC 15   Jackson, Papa Charlie

        title: Maxwell Street Blues
        place and date: Chicago, c. Sept. 1925
        record numbers: (2288-2) Pm-12320 Bio BLP-12042

1   I was walking down Morgan : stopped on Maxwell
     Street
2   I asked the desk sergeant ??? police force : my gal
     ain't off of the street
3   I couldn't talk to the desk sergeant : tell him
     when and where it took place
4   Because I knew my mama : got arrested on Maxwell
     Street
5   Lord I'm talking about the wagon : talking about the
     ??? car too
6   Because Maxwell Street's so crowded on a Sunday :
     you can hardly pass through

JackC 15   Jackson, Papa Charlie

  7 There's Maxwell Street Market : got Water Street
     Market too
  8 If you ain't got no money : the women got nothing
     for you to do
  9 I got the Maxwell Street blues : mama and it just
     won't pay
 10 Because the Maxwell Street women : going to carry me
     to my grave
 11 I live six twenty-four Maxwell : mama and I'm
     talking about you
 12 Because I swear I don't walk : said Buly Buly Buly
     how do you

JackC 16   Jackson, Papa Charlie

     title: All I Want Is a Spoonful
     place and date: Chicago, c. Sept. 1925
     record numbers: (2298-1) Pm-12320 Bio BLP-12042

  1 I told you once : this makes twice
  2 That's the last time : don't you boil them rice
  3 You can brown your gravy : fry your steak
  4 Sweet mama : don't make no mistake
  5 Just sure as the winter : follows the fall
  6 There ain't no one woman : got it all
  7 You can meet a woman : that you can't understand
  8 Must be looking for you : or a monkey-man
  9 Now cool kind mama : says you needn't've stalled
 10 Throw it out the window : I'll catch it before it
     falls
 11 I got the blues so bad : I couldn't sleep last night
 12 My cool kind mama : want to fuss and fight
 13 Now I'm so glad : that dog can talk
 14 I can't teach him : to take a morning's walk
 15 Now if you don't believe : that I can run mighty
     fast
 16 Ask that man : that run me last

JackC 17   Jackson, Papa Charlie

     title: Texas Blues
     place and date: Chicago, c. Dec. 1925
     record numbers: (11031-?) Pm-12335 Yz L-1029

  1 I'm Texas bound : I got a freight train on my mind
  2 If you miss me on the local : look for me on the
     gine
  3 My suitcase is packed : my trunk's already home
  4 Said you can know by that : your sweet papa's going
     to be gone
  5 Just look around the corner : see that passenger
     train
  6 Be a long long time : before you see my face again
  7 Takes a good old fireman : a cool kind engineer
  8 Now to pull that train : take me away from here
  9 I'm Texas bound : got no time to lose
 10 Because my sweet mama quit me : left me with the
     Texas blues

JackC 18   Jackson, Papa Charlie

     title: Butter and Egg Man Blues
     place and date: Chicago, c. Feb. 1926
     record numbers: (11069-1) Pm-12358 Bio BLP-12042

  1 Everybody in town : got a butter and egg man but me
  2 Tell me please : Lord because I can't see
  3 Come here mama : sit down on your papa's knee
  4 I'm just a butter and egg man : you can easy get
     along with me
  5 Why don't you take me pretty mama : make something
     out of poor me
  6 I'm just a butter and egg man : just as soft as I
     can be

JackC 18   Jackson, Papa Charlie

  7 Well it's butter and eggs butter and eggs : butter
     and eggs is all you crave
  8 When you die : put butter and eggs on your grave
  9 Why don't you take me pretty mama : let you treat me
     as you do
 10 Because my weakness is pretty women : keep me with
     the butter and egg blues

JackC 19   Jackson, Papa Charlie

     title: Up the Way Bound
     place and date: Chicago, c. May 1926
     record numbers: (2547-1) Pm-12375 Yz L-1029

  1 My baby done quit me : and talk's all over town
  2 I'm too good a man : to let that talk go around
  3 I'm leaving today : going to leave this southern
     town
  4 Because my baby caught a plane : that was up the way
     bound
  5 I feel like jumping : from a treetop to the ground
  6 To get a flying start : and run my baby down
  7 I'm reeling and rocking : Lord howling like a hound
  8 If brownskin's the best : I'll *play a teasing
     brown*
  9 Oh feel like a dirty : feel like a dat dat dat
 10 Doesn't somebody know : where my baby at
 11 I'm going to grab me a train : beat it on up the
     line
 12 I'm going to ride : until I find that good-goody
     woman of mine

JackC 20   Jackson, Papa Charlie

     title: Your Baby Ain't Sweet Like Mine
     place and date: Chicago, c. Aug. 1926
     record numbers: (2613-4) Pm-12383 Yz L-1029

  1 Everybody's talking : about the *gren??? day*
  2 I got one : with the sweetest ways
  3 Your baby : can roll her jelly fine
  4 Nobody's baby : can roll it like mine
  5 Your baby : ain't sweet like mine
  6 She bake her jellyroll : all the time
  7 And when I'm feeling : lonesome and blue
  8 My baby : know just what to do
  9 Never has a baby : put me outdoor
 10 She even buys me : all my clothes
 11 I don't want to brag : just want to put you in line
 12 Your baby : ain't sweet like mine

JackC 21   Jackson, Papa Charlie

     title: Fat Mouth Blues
     place and date: Chicago, c. Jan. 1927
     record numbers: (2769-3) Pm-12422 Yz L-1029

  1 Tell me tell me : please has anybody seen my brown
  2 She used to love me : till old fatmouth blew in town
  3 She's a long tall woman : with coal-black curly hair
  4 With one gold tooth : then you'll know her anywhere
  5 She used to be mine : but the fatmouth has got her
     now
  6 That's a dirty mistreater : didn't mean me no good
     nohow
  7 I'm going to love you mama : till my whiskers pass
     the ground
  8 When you die : I'm going to keep on hanging around
  9 I bought all her clothes : I bought her a diamond
     ring
 10 Then along come a fatmouth : keep me shaking that
     thing

JackC 22   Jackson, Papa Charlie

      title: She Belongs to Me Blues
      place and date: Chicago, c. Mar. 1927
      record numbers: (4243-1) Pm-12461 Yz L-1029

1 It was early one morning : just about the break of
   day
2 Says I thought I heard : my sweet baby say
3 You can read a newspaper : you can't read a person's
   mind
4 But when you think she's loving you : dropping you
   all the time
5 Now baby you can tell me : just what are you to do
6 Now I believe I'll go back : to my old-time
   used-to-be
7 She's long and she's tall : she's shaped just like a
   willow tree
8 And the reason I love her : says she belongs to me

JackC 23   Jackson, Papa Charlie

      title: Coal Man Blues
      place and date: Chicago, c. Mar. 1927
      record numbers: (4244-2) Pm-12461 Bio BLP-12042

1 I get up early in the morning : sweet mama and I
   comb and curry my horse
2 Because I don't want nobody : not to *see my pause*
3 Then I goed up to the coal pile : get me a friend to
   buy some coal
4 Then I get on my wagon : *then I'm a coal-traveling
   snow*
5 *I ought to tell how much* for coal : thirty-five
   cents a bag
6 And if you want to know my name : just look around
   on my sack
7 I got on my wagon : trying my best to sell my coal
8 My baby's back home : serving my jellyroll
9 Now a lot of your women : ought to be put in jail
10 Some standing on the corner : trying to get
   themselves in jail

JackC 24   Jackson, Papa Charlie

      title: Skoodle Um Skoo
      place and date: Chicago, c. July 1927
      record numbers: (4670-1) Pm-12501 Bio BLP-12042

1 Now I got a lady : by the name of Sue
2 She'd like to know : just what to do
3 Now when you what it : I agree
4 Don't forget : to ask for me
5 Now she's a woman : hard to beat
6 All you got to do is dance : and stay on your feet
7 Now you ain't good-looking : you don't dress cute
8 You got to keep a papa : for your personal use
9 Now January February : and March too
10 The women come along : and showed her just what to
   do
11 Now a woman needn't think : she got a man by herself
12 A man needn't think : he got a woman by himself
13 Now tain't but one thing : that grieve my mind
14 All these brownskins : none of them mine

JackC 25   Jackson, Papa Charlie

      title: Sheik of Desplaines Street
      place and date: Chicago, c. July 1927
      record numbers: (4671-2) Pm-12501 Bio BLP-12042

1 I know a man : he's on our street
2 He don't do nothing : but eat and sleep
3 Now he's a man : that I would love to meet
4 He's always dressed up : and out in the street
5 Now he don't drink whiskey : nothing sweet

JackC 25   Jackson, Papa Charlie

6 When it comes to pretty women : he sure loves to
   meet
7 *I'm hot as the devil* : *I walk about the street*
8 All that ??? : to the sweet man's *feet*
9 Now he's a man : has a *copper* good to eat
10 He always looks good : from his head to his feet
11 Now when he walks into a place : and takes his seat
12 His ways and actions : is hard to beat

JackC 26   Jackson, Papa Charlie

      title: Ash Tray Blues
      place and date: Chicago, c. May 1928
      record numbers: (20604-2) Pm-12660 Bio BLP-12042

1 I ain't talking to one : I ain't talking to two
2 I'm talking to the captain : and the whole doggone
   crew
3 Yes she smokes the cigarettes : throws ashes in the
   tray
4 She's a good woman : she likes to have her way
5 I'm going away : won't be long
6 You look for me : I'll be gone

JackC 27   Jackson, Papa Charlie

      title: Jungle Man Blues
      place and date: Chicago, c. Dec. 1928
      record numbers: (21045-2) Pm-12721 Bio BLP-12042

1 Ain't nothing in the jungle : that's any better than
   me
2 I'm the baddest man : ever came from Tennessee
3 I slept with a panther : until just about the break
   of day
4 I grabbed the wildcat in the collar : and asked the
   tiger what he had to say
5 I wear a scorpion for my watch fob : a rattlesnake
   for my chain
6 I scares a gorilla : and make him change his big
   ugly name
7 I make a *sea tick* catch a freight train : I make a
   flea grab the mail
8 I make a jumbo elephant : grab an airplane and sail
9 I was traveling in a rowboat : drifting out in the
   sea
10 I made a sea lion cub come back : and shake glad
   hands with me
11 Way down in the forest : there's where I long to be
12 Because ain't nothing in the jungle : that's any
   better than me

JackC 28   Jackson, Papa Charlie

      title: Baby Please Loan Me Your Heart
      place and date: Chicago, c. Jan. 1929
      record numbers: (21081-2) Pm-12736 Yz L-1029

1 Now you know baby : you know it's true
2 I don't love : no one but you
3 I'm going to tell you : just before we start
4 All I want you to do : is to lone me your heart
5 I'm going to ask you : now baby before you start
6 All you got to do : is to lone me your heart

JackJ 1   Jackson, Jim

      title: Bootlegging Blues
      place and date: Memphis, 14 Feb. 1928
      record numbers: (41904-2) Vi-21268 Rt RL-323

1 This corn liquor ??? : there's plenty more to be
   made

JackJ   1   Jackson, Jim

2   Just get a job at one of these stills : and you
    surely will be paid
3   I tell you it's a mighty risk to run : and a mighty
    chance to take
4   To spend your money : for the corn that the
    bootlegger makes
5   When the bootlegger goes to his still : get ready to
    make his stuff
6   He got his concentrated lye : cocaine and his snuff
7   I went home the other night : I swore I wouldn't
    drink no more
8   Until saloons come back with bottle and *bondy* : in
    the days of long ago
9   But I see that will never be : so I just got drunk
    again
10 I haven't nothing so long as corn liquor lasts : and
    I got no money to spend

JackJ   2   Jackson, Jim

    title: I'm Wild About My Lovin'
    place and date: Memphis, 27 Aug. 1928
    record numbers: (45416-1) Vi-V38505 His HLP-32

1   I'm going to tell the sergeant : *he the* chief of
    police
2   The women around here : won't let me see no peace
3   Because I'm wild about my loving : and I like to
    have my fun
4   You want to be a girl of mine baby : bring me
    whiskey when you come
5   Hello Central : what's the matter with your line
6   I want to talk : to that high brown of mine
7   I don't want no sugar : stirred up in my tea
8   Because the girl I want : is sweet enough for me
9   I ain't no iceman : no iceman's son
10 But I can keep you cool : till the iceman comes
11 I ain't no fireman : and no fireman's son
12 But I can keep you warm : until the fireman comes
13 I'm going to tell you people : to listen to this
    song
14 I'm going to see my gal : and it won't be long

JackJ   3   Jackson, Jim

    title: This Mornin' She Was Gone
    place and date: Memphis, 27 Aug. 1928
    record numbers: (45417-1) Vi-V38003 His HLP-32

1   Oh how she loved to dance : that old grizzly bear
2   I guess she's gone to Frisco : to dance it there
3   Always a sign : everybody know you through
4   The more you do for people : the less they think of
    you

JackJ   4   Jackson, Jim

    title: This Mornin' She Was Gone
    place and date: Memphis, 27 Aug. 1928
    record numbers: (45417-2) Vi-V38003 His HLP-5

1   Oh how she loved to dance : that old grizzly bear
2   I guess she's gone to Frisco : to dance it there
3   It's always a sign : everybody knows it's true
4   The more you do for people : the less they they
    think of you

JackJ   5   Jackson, Jim

    title: Hesitation Blues
    place and date: Memphis, c. Feb. 1930
    record numbers: (MEM-804-) Vo-1477 Her H-205

1   Hello Central : what's the matter with your line
2   I want to talk : to that high brown of mine
3   I'm going to the river : with a rope and a rock
4   And the way you treat me : I'm going to jump over
    the dock
5   Tell me how long : will I have to wait
6   Can I get you now : or must I hesitate
7   I'm got something to tell you : and I know it ain't
    good news
8   Because a hesitating woman : give me the hesitation
    blues
9   I'm going to tell the sergeant : and the see the
    chief police
10 Because the women around here : won't let me see no
    peace
11 I've got a girl in Memphis : she's all right
12 But the girl in Cincinnati : is just too tight
13 I'm got a girl in Cairo : loves me I know
14 But the gal in Louisville : has got the best
    clothes
15 My mother says I'm wicked : daddy says I'm wild
16 I know I ain't good-looking : but some woman's angel
    child
17 I'll sing you these verses : and it didn't take long
18 If you want to hear any more : you'll have to buy
    this song

JackJ   6   Jackson, Jim

    title: St. Louis Blues
    place and date: Memphis, c. Feb. 1930
    record numbers: (MEM-805-) Vo-1477 Yz L-1003

1   Well I hates to see : that evening sun go down
2   Because it makes me think : about my last go-round
3   It I'm feeling tomorrow : a-like I feel today
4   I'm going to pack my suitcase : and make my long
    get-away
5   Because the St Louis woman : she wears a diamond
    ring
6   She leads a man around : by her apron string
7   If it wasn't for powder : and this store-bought hair
8   Oh the girl I love : wouldn't go nowhere
9   A redheaded woman : make a freight train jump the
    track
10 And a black-headed girl : will make a preacher ball
    the jack

JamF   1   James, Frank

    title: Poor Coal Passer
    place and date: Chicago, 21 Dec. 1936
    record numbers: (01893-1) BB-B7116 Yz L-1015

1   I'm a poor coal loader : I'm in the mine
2   Slave for my woman : till I'm almost blind
3   I work so hard : from dawn to dusk
4   Can't find a woman : that I can trust
5   I work so : from six to six
6   Kid-man wait : to get his business fixed
7   I work every day : in the mine
8   Come home at night : you got my best friend crying
9   The food you cook : a hound dog sick
10 Woman I swear : you's a no-good chick

121

JamJ   1   James, Jesse

        title: Sweet Patuni
        place and date: Chicago, 3 June 1936
        record numbers: (90760-) De unissued Yz L-1028

1   Ah wake up mama : wake up and don't sleep so sound
2   Give me what you promised me : before you lay down
3   I said get my tuni : only thing I love
4   Make you weep like a willow : sling snot like a turtledove
5   Now I've got a gal : and the kid live out on the hill
6   She got good doing : serve to the one she may will
7   She got good tuni : I'm a fool about my yam yam yam
8   Get my yam yam yam : I'm going back to Alabam'
9   Now come in here baby : and sit down in my lap
10 Sit one side : I forgot to tell you I had the
11 Clap your hands Charlie : Charlie where's you been so long
12 I been down in Tennessee : and I couldn't stay there very long
13 I got a job in the freight house : trying to learn how to truck
14 A box fell on me this morning : like to bust one of my
15 Nuthouse for crazy folks : folks got sense don't go there
16 And all the friends I had : done shook hands and left there
17 I got a gal : and the kid playing deaf and dumb
18 But the movements in her hip : will make a dead man
19 Come on out my window : don't knock on my door
20 And I told you two or three times : don't want you no more
21 Now run in here baby : because I done got kind of sick
22 It ain't nothing ailing my stomach : it's something wrong with my
23 Dixieland was a camp in Georgia : you can't stay there very long
24 All the friends I had : done shook hands and gone
25 Now here's a verse : I don't want a soul to miss
26 I been taking charity grub : I've got to go outside
27 Shut your mouth boy : four boys can't talk at once
28 And I done told you two or three times : I don't want no junk

JamJ   2   James, Jesse

        title: Southern Casey Jones
        place and date: Chicago, 3 June 1936
        record numbers: (90761-A) De-7213 AH-158

1   I heard the people say : Casey Jones can't run
2   I'm going to tell you : what the poor boy done
3   Left Cincinnati : about half past nine
4   Got to Newport News : before dinner time
5   Now Casey Jones said : before he died
6   He fixed the road : so a bum could ride
7   And if he ride : he have to ride the rod
8   Rest his heart : in the hand of God
9   Now little girl says : mama is that a fact
10 Papa got killed : on the I C track
11 Yes yes honey : but hold your breath
12 Get that money : from your daddy's death
13 When the news reached town : Casey Jones was dead
14 Women went home : and *had it* out in red
15 Slipping and sliding : all across the streets
16 With their loose mother hubbard : and their stocking feet
17 Now Casey Jones : went from place to place
18 Another train hit his train : right in the face
19 People got off : but Casey Jones stayed on
20 Natural policeman : but he dead and gone
21 Here come the biggest boy : coming right from school
22 Hollering and crying : like a doggone fool
23 Look here mama : is our papa dead

24 Womens going home : and *had it* out in red
25 *Low cut* shoes : and their evening gowns
26 Following papa : to the burying ground
27 Now tell the truth mama : he say is that a fact
28 Papa got killed : on the I C track
29 Quit crying boy : don't do that
30 You got another daddy : on the same damn track

JamJ   3   James, Jesse

        title: Lonesome Day Blues
        place and date: Chicago, 3 June 1936
        record numbers: (90762-A) De-7213 AH-158

1   Lord today has been : a long lonesome day
2   You hear me talking to you : did you hear what I say
3   Lord today has been : a long old lonesome day
4   And now my rider : eee Lord will be the same old way
5   I've been to the nation : around the territor'
6   You hear me talking to you : you got to reap what you sow
7   I've been all through the nation : and around the territor'
8   But I found no heaven on earth : Lord nowhere I go
9   I'm going to the big house : and I don't even care
10 Don't you hear me talking to you : I'm scolding to my dear
11 I'm going in the morning : and I don't even care
12 I might get four or five years : Lord I might get the chair
13 Oh stop and listen : see tomorrow bring
14 You hear me talking to you : start to playing
15 You better stop now and listen : and see what tomorrow brings
16 It might bring you sunshine : Lord and it may bring rain
17 Some got six months : some got a solid year
18 You hear me talking to you : buddy what made you stop by here
19 Some of them got six months partner : and some got a solid year
20 But I believe my partner : Lord got a lifetime here

JamS   1   James, Skip

        title: Devil Got My Woman
        place and date: Grafton, Wis., c. Feb. 1931
        record numbers: (L-746-1) Pm-13088 Bio BLP-12029

1   I'd rather be the devil : to be that woman's man
3   Oh nothing but the devil : changed my baby's mind
5   I laid down last night : tried to take my rest
6   My mind got to rambling : like the wild geese from the west
7   The woman I love Lord : stoled her from my best friend
8   But he got lucky : stoled her back again

JamS   2   James, Skip

        title: Cypress Grove Blues
        place and date: Grafton, Wis., c. Feb. 1931
        record numbers: (L-747-2) Pm-13088 Bio BLP-12029

1   I would rather be buried : in some cypress grove
2   To have some woman : Lord I can't control
3   And I'm going away now : I'm going away to stay
4   That'll be all right pretty mama : you going to need my help some day
5   Well the sun going down : and you know what you promised me
6   And what's the matter : baby I can't see
7   I would rather be dead : and six feet in my grave
8   To be way up here honey : treated this a-way

JamS 2   James, Skip

```
 9  Well the old people told me : baby but I never did
      know
10  The Good Book declares : we got to reap just what we
      sow
11  When your knee bones aching : and your body cold
12  Well you just getting ready : honey for the cypress
      grove
```

JamS 3   James, Skip

title: Cherry Ball Blues
place and date: Grafton, Wis., c. Feb. 1931
record numbers: (L-748-2) Pm-13065 Bio BLP-12029

```
 1  I love my cherry ball : better than I love myself
 2  She gets so she don't love me : she won't love
      nobody else
 3  Cherry ball quit me : she quit me in a calm good way
 4  Lordy what to take to get her : I carries it every
      day
 5  Sure as that spider : hanging on the wall
 6  I warned little old cherry ball : she was *falling
      out cold*
 7  I'll catch the Southern : and she'll take the Santa
      Fe
 8  I'm going to ride and ramble : till cherry come back
      to me
```

JamS 4   James, Skip

title: Hard Time Killin' Floor Blues
place and date: Grafton, Wis., c. Feb. 1931
record numbers: (L-752-2) Pm-13065 Bio BLP-12029

```
 1  Hard times here : everywhere you go
 2  Times is harder : than ever been before
 3  Well the people are drifting : from door to door
 4  Can't find no heaven : I don't care where they go
 5  Let me tell you people : just before I go
 6  These hard times will kill you : just dry long so
 7  When you hear me singing : my so lonesome song
 8  These hard times : can last us so very long
 9  If I ever get off : this killing floor
10  I'll never : get down this low no more
11  If you say you had money : you better be sure
12  Because these hard times will drive you : from door
      to door
13  Sing this song : and I ain't going to sing no more
14  Hard times will drive you : from door to door
```

JamS 5   James, Skip

title: Special Rider Blues
place and date: Grafton, Wis., c. Feb. 1931
record numbers: (L-760-2) Pm-13098 Yz L-1001

```
 1  I ain't got no : special rider here
 2  Ain't got nobody : nobody feel my care
 3  I woke up this morning : looked at the special
      rising sun
 4  I prayed to the Lord : my special rider would come
 5  I'm going tell you something : to ease your trouble
      in mind
 6  *Them whiskey women* : *give* trouble all the time
 7  Now *honey* : what more can I do
 8  Hear you done call : the easy rider special blues
```

JamS 6   James, Skip

title: Little Cow and Calf Is Gonna Die Blues
place and date: Grafton, Wis., c. Feb. 1931
record numbers: (L-763-1) Pm-13085 Bio BLP-12029

```
 1  Hey hey hey hey : hey hey hey hey hey
 2  And every cow's calf man : honey he was born to die
 3  I going to take my heifer : ???
 4  If you see my rider : tell her carry on carry on
 5  I wring my hands : baby and I want to scream
 6  And I woke up : I found out it was all a dream
 7  Hey hey hey : I ain't going to be here long
 8  That's the reason why you hear me : sing my old
      lonesome song
 9  Hey hey hey hey : hey hey hey hey hey
10  And every cow's calf : honey got to lay down and die
11  I walked the levee : I just walked end to end
12  I just want to find : my cow again
13  I'm stealing I'm stealing : back to my used-to-be
14  Hey pretty mama : please don't tell on me
```

JamS 7   James, Skip

title: 22-20 Blues
place and date: Grafton, Wis., c. Feb. 1931
record numbers: (L-765-1) Pm-13066 Bio BLP-12029

```
 1  If I send for my baby : and she don't come
 2  All the doctors in West *Conton* : they won't help
      her none
 3  And if she gets unruly : and she don't want to do
 4  Take my thirty-two twenty : I cut her half in two
 5  You talk about your forty-four forty : buddy it'll
      do very well
 6  But my twenty-two twenty : Lord is a burning hell
 7  Now that thirty-eight special : buddy it's most too
      light
 8  But my twenty-two twenty : make the *camp* go right
 9  Hey hey hey : and I can't take my rest
10  And my forty-four : laying up and down my breast
```

JamS 8   James, Skip

title: If You Haven't Got Any Hay Get on Down
  the Road
place and date: Grafton, Wis., c. Feb. 1931
record numbers: (L-766-1) Pm-13066 Bio BLP-12029

```
 1  If you haven't any hay : get on down the road
 2  Get your habit in your hand mama : Lord Lord get on
      down the road
 3  I'm going I'm going : coming here no more
 4  If I go to Louisiana mama : Lord Lord they'll hang
      me sure
 5  If you haven't any hay : get on down the road
 6  I'm going I'm going : coming back no more
 7  Hitch up my buggy : saddle up my black mare
 8  You'll find me riding : mama Lord Lord in this world
      somewhere
```

JaxF 1   Jaxon, Frankie Half Pint

title: It's Heated
place and date: Chicago, 11 June 1929
record numbers: (C-3585-) Vo-1539 Yz L-1039

```
 1  Folks I'm going to tell you : about a brand new song
 2  I'm going to beat some dirt : and it won't take long
 3  Well they cool it on State Street : warm it down the
      line
 4  You ought to hear the frogs on Durban : singing and
      crying
 5  Now the folks down east : are crying Lord Lord Lord
 6  Gang in the west : say the cops is so hard
 7  Well I went down to Michigan : came up Grant
```

JaxF   1   Jaxon, Frankie Half Pint

8   Saw the sweetbacks and the strutters : all raising
    sand
9   I went to a good-time flat : last Saturday night
10 The cops knocked on the door : everybody made their
    flight
11 I met myself a good gal : she said she was fifty-one
12 She started to loving and squeezing : I thought she
    say son you just begun
13 Now a yellow gal is like a frigid zone : brownskin's
    about the same
14 You want some good loving : get yourself an old Crow
    Jane
15 Now I ain't no janitor : no fireman's son
16 But I can keep your boiler hot : till the
    superintendent come

JaxF   2   Jaxon, Frankie Half Pint (Tampa Red)

        title: Come On, Mama, Do That Dance
        place and date: Chicago, 27 June 1929
        record numbers: (   ) Vo-1420 Yz L-1039

1   Come on and let me know : who you are
2   Do that dance : called the *don't be long*
3   Do the Mississippi : and the Mobile Bay
4   Turn right around : go the other way
5   Put your hands on your hips : and let your mind move
    on
6   Holler like you did : the first day you was born
7   Do the black snake wriggle : and the frog hop
8   Take it to the attic : if it gets too hot
9   Now old sister Sue : *got* heavy a load
10 She likes to do it : because she got kind of cold
11 *Hatsie Gray* : and old friend Lou
12 Some day : this thing's going to happen to you

JaxF   3   Jaxon, Frankie Half Pint (Tampa Red)

        title: She Can Love So Good
        place and date: Chicago, c. mid Aug. 1930
        record numbers: (C-6079-A) Vo-1540 Mel MLP-7324

1   I've got a gal : she's low and squatty
2   I mean boys : she'll suit anybody
3   Last night : she loved me for a while
4   You could hear me holler : mmm for a while
5   Sometimes she makes me sneeze : sometimes she makes
    me cough
6   Lord you ought to see her : when she starting me off
7   Last night : while I was sound asleep
8   I felt a funny feeling : from my head to my feet
9   She was born in Kentucky : raised in Tennessee
10 Came all the way from Dixie : to put that thing on
    me

JaxF   4   Jaxon, Frankie Half Pint

        title: Callin' Corrine
        place and date: New York, 19 May 1939
        record numbers: (65608-A) De-7619 AH-158

1   Ain't you getting tired : of [trying to cheat,
    cheating] on your papa hon'
2   Corrine : you the meanest gal I ever seen
3   Corrine : she just about five feet tall
4   She sleeps in the kitchen : one foot in the hall
5   I've got a corrine in Texas : sure can bring me down
6   Got a corrine in Harlem : make a rabbit hug a hound

JefB   1   Jefferson, Blind Lemon

        title: Got the Blues
        place and date: Chicago, c. Mar. 1926
        record numbers: (2471-1) Pm-12354 Bio BLP-12000

1   I walked from Dallas : I walked to Wichita Falls
2   After I lost my sugar : I wasn't going to walk at
    all
3   Women see you coming : they go get their rocking
    chair
4   I want to fools this man : and make out he's welcome
    here
5   So cold in China : this voice can't hardly sing
6   You didn't make me mad : till you broke my diamond
    ring
7   I'm going to grab my sugar : papa don't care what
    you do
8   I know my baby : she's going to jump and shout
9   When she gets a letter from Lemon : I wrote her two
    days out
10 Tell me what's the matter : [papa Lemon, I] can't
    get no mail
11 Mama said last night : don't let a black cat cross
    your trail
12 I got up this morning : the blues all around my bed
13 Went in to eat my breakfast : and the blues all in
    my bread

JefB   2   Jefferson, Blind Lemon

        title: Long Lonesome Blues
        place and date: Chicago, c. Mar. 1926
        record numbers: (2472-2) Pm-12354 Bio BLP-12000

1   Well the blues come to Texas : loping like a mule
2   You take a high brown woman : man she's hard to fool
3   You can't never tell : what a woman's got on her
    mind
4   You might think she's crazy about you : but she
    leaving you all the time
5   Ain't so good-looking : your teeth don't shine like
    pearls
6   But that nice disposition : carry a woman all
    through the world
7   I'm going to the river : going to carry my rocking
    chair
8   Going to ask that gal for a ??? : *how* the worried
    blues left here
9   I think I heard : my good gal call my name
10 She couldn't call so loud : but she calls so nice
    and plain
11 I was raised in Texas : schooled in Tennessee
12 High-stepper you can't make : no fatmouth out of me
13 Can't a woman act funny : quit you for another man
14 Can't go look down the street : but she's always
    raising sand

JefB   3   Jefferson, Blind Lemon

        title: Booster Blues
        place and date: Chicago, c. Mar. 1926
        record numbers: (2474-1) Pm-12347 Bio BLP-12000

1   My right foot itches : something going on wrong
2   My right foot itching me : and I just can't stay
    here long
3   I thought I'd write : but it's the best to telephone
4   For that fast mail train : can carry your sugar so
    far from home
5   Girl I can't live right : ain't going to try no more
6   This woman's left town : and she ain't coming back
    no more
7   I went to the depot : and I set my suitcase down
8   I thought about my baby : and tears come rolling
    down
9   I said ticket agent : how long your train been gone

JefB   3   Jefferson, Blind Lemon

10 Say yon go the train : that this fair brown left
    here on
11 I couldn't buy [me] no ticket : but I walked on to
    the door
12 Well my baby left town : she ain't coming here no
    more
13 I got up this morning : my sure-enough on my mind
14 I had to raise a conversation with the landlady : to
    keep from crying
15 Excuse me woman : I won't say that no more
16 I'm fixing to leave town : and hang crepe on your
    door

JefB   4   Jefferson, Blind Lemon

        title: Dry Southern Blues
        place and date: Chicago, c. Mar. 1926
        record numbers: (2475-1) Pm-12347 Bio BLP-12000

1   Well my mind leads me : to take a trip down south
2   Take a trip down south : *it's tough to spend my
    round*
3   A train left the depot : with a red and blue light
    behind
4   Well the blue light's the blues : the red light's
    the worried mind
5   I hate to tell you : it ain't nobody there
6   If a man stay here : he stay most anywhere
7   I got up this morning : rambling for my shoes
8   The little woman : sung me a song of her worried
    blues
9   Uncle Sam wasn't no woman : but didn't he grab your
    man
10 Tell me them good-looking womens : is on the border
    raising sand
11 Well women on the border : drinking out of the water
    trough
12 I wish uncle Sam would hurry up : and pay these
    soldiers off
13 I can't drink coffee : and the woman won't make no
    tea
14 I believe to my soul : sweet mama going to hoodoo me
15 I asked the girl did she love me : she said Lemon I
    don't know how
16 Caught me *commentating* : yes I love you *sky high*
17 She has feet like a monkey : head like a teddy bear
18 And a mouthful of lip : I guarantee it's everywhere
19 I got a girl in Cuba : I got a girl in Spain
20 I got a brown yonder in Dallas : I's afraid to call
    her name

JefB   5   Jefferson, Blind Lemon

        title: Black Horse Blues
        place and date: Chicago, c. May 1926
        record numbers: (2543-1) Pm-12367 Mil MLP-2004

1   [Tell me, I want to know] what time : do the trains
    come through your town
2   I want to laugh and talk : with a long-haired
    teasing brown
3   One goes south at eight : and it's one goes north at
    nine
4   I got to have a good talk : with that long-haired
    brown of mine
5   Go and get my black horse : and saddle up my grey
    mare
6   I'm going home to my good gal : she's in the world
    somewhere
7   I can't count the times : that I'm so unsatisfied
8   Sugar the blues ain't on me : but things ain't going
    on right

JefB   6   Jefferson, Blind Lemon

        title: Corinna Blues
        place and date: Chicago, c. May 1926
        record numbers: (2544-2) Pm-12367 Mil MLP-2004

1   See see rider : you see what you done done
2   Made me love you : and now your friend is come
3   A great tall engine : and a little small engineer
4   Carried the woman away Lord : and left me standing
    here
5   If I had a-listened : to my second mind
6   I don't believe I'd a-been here : wringing my hands
    and crying
7   Ain't no more good 'taters : the frost have killed
    the vine
8   The blues ain't nothing : but a good woman on your
    mind
9   I done told you woman : I been telling your partner
    too
10 You're three times seven : and you know what you
    want to do
11 If you see Corinna : tell her to hurry home
12 I ain't had no true love : since Corinna been gone

JefB   7   Jefferson, Blind Lemon

        title: Chock House Blues
        place and date: Chicago, c. May or June 1926
        record numbers: (2558-2) Pm-12373 Mil MLP-2007

1   So many wagons : they have cut that good road down
2   And the girl I love : her mama don't want me around
3   Baby I can't drink whiskey : but I'm a fool about my
    homemade wine
4   Ain't no sense in leaving Dallas : they makes it
    there all the time
5   These here women want these men : to act like some
    boxer dog
6   Grab a pick and shovel : and roll from sun to sun
7   I got a girl for Monday Tuesday : Wednesday Thursday
    Friday too
8   I'm going to sweeten up on Saturday : what are the
    women through the week going to do
9   Don't look for me on Sunday : I want to take pigmeat
    to Sunday school
10 She's a fine looking fair brown : but she ain't
    never learned Lemon's rule

JefB   8   Jefferson, Blind Lemon

        title: Beggin' Back
        place and date: Chicago, c. Aug. 1926
        record numbers: (3016-4) Pm-12394 Bio BLP-12000

1   Listen here mama : I'll be good
2   Drink your wine : cut your wood
3   When I had you : you wouldn't do
4   Now I got another : and I don't want you
5   Every evening : half past eight
6   *Hobbling along* : *with my gait*
7   Working in the spring : *sleeping in the sand*
8   Got to get that fifty dollars : that I wish I had
9   You may think : because you're black
10 I'm going to beg you : to take me back
11 I went a-walking : down the line
12 To see if this woman : changed her mind
13 She turned around : two or three times
14 Take you back : in the wintertime

JefB   9   Jefferson, Blind Lemon

    title: Old Rounders Blues
    place and date: Chicago, c. Aug. 1926
    record numbers: (3018-?) Pm-12394 Rt RL-306

1 I ain't going to marry : ain't going to [be no
   settling, settle] down
2 I'm going to stay like I am : going to ride from
   town to town
3 There's a house over yonder : painted all over green
4 Going to find these young women : that a man most
   ever seen
5 I'm going to run to town : talk with that chief of
   police
6 Tell him my good gal has quit me : and I can't live
   in no peace
7 My home's in Oklahoma : I ain't got no business here
8 I'm just stopping around : to have a drink of a
   little drink of beer
9 I went home last night : fell down on my bed
10 I got to dreaming so : I was talking all out of my
   head

JefB   10   Jefferson, Blind Lemon

    title: Stocking Feet Blues
    place and date: Chicago, c. Oct. 1926
    record numbers: (3066-1) Pm-12407 Mil MLP-2013

1 Somebody : just keep on calling me
2 She got hair : like a mermaid on the sea
3 Make me down a pallet : on your floor
4 Make it ??? and easy : make it down by your door
5 I can't stay away : I done cried the whole night
   long
6 The good woman I love : she done packed her trunk
   and gone
7 Don't mistreat me : because I'm young and wild
8 Sister you ought to remember : that you once was a
   child
9 I don't feel welcome : and I don't care where I go
10 The woman I love : she drove me from her door
11 Said fair brown : where did you stay last night
12 Your hair's all down : and you know you ain't
   talking right
13 I'm a stranger here : just come in on the train
14 Won't some good man : tell me some woman's name

JefB   11   Jefferson, Blind Lemon

    title: That Black Snake Moan
    place and date: Chicago, c. Oct. 1926
    record numbers: (3067-2) Pm-12407 Mil MLP-2013

1 Oh : ain't got no mama now
2 She told me late last night : you don't need no mama
   nohow
3 Mmm : black snake crawling in my room
4 Some pretty mama : better come and get this black
   snake soon
5 Oh that must've been a bedbug : baby a chinch can't
   bite that hard
6 Asked my sugar for fifty cents : she said Lemon
   ain't a dime in the yard
7 Mama that's all right : mama that's all right for
   you
8 Mama that's all right : most any old way you do
9 Mmm : what's the matter now
10 Sugar what's the matter : don't like no black snake
   nohow
11 Mmm : wonder where my black snake gone
12 Black snake mama : done run my darling home

JefB   12   Jefferson, Blind Lemon

    title: Wartime Blues
    place and date: Chicago, c. Oct. 1926
    record numbers: (3070-1) Pm-12425 Rt RL-301

1 What you going to do : when they send your man to
   war
2 I'm going to drink muddy water : go sleep in a
   hollow log
3 Ain't got nobody : I'm all here by myself
4 Well these women don't care : but the men don't need
   me here
5 Well I'm going to the river : going to walk it up
   and down
6 If I don't find *fourteen* : I'm going to jump
   overboard and drown
7 If I could shine my light : like a headlight on some
   train
8 I would shine my light : in Corinna's brain
9 Well they tell me that southbound train : had a
   wreck last night
10 You little section foreman : ain't treating your
   railroad right
11 Well the girl I love : is the one I crave to see
12 Well she's living in Memphis : and the fool won't
   write to me
13 Now tell me woman : what have I said and done
14 You treat me : like my trouble have just begun

JefB   13   Jefferson, Blind Lemon

    title: Broke and Hungry
    place and date: Chicago, c. Oct. 1926
    record numbers: (3076-?) Pm-12443 Mil MLP-2007

1 I am broke and hungry : ragged and dirty too
2 Mama if I clean up : can I go home with you
3 I am motherless fatherless : sister and brotherless
   too
4 Reason I'm trying so hard : to make the trip with
   you
5 You miss me woman : count the days I'm gone
6 I'm going away : to build me a railroad of my own
7 I feel like jumping : through the keyhole in your
   door
8 If you jump this time baby : you won't jump no more
9 I believe : my good gal have found my black cat bone
10 I can leave here Sunday morning : Monday morning I'm
   sitting around home
11 I want to show you women : what careless love have
   done
12 Caused a man like me : steal way away from home
13 Girl if you don't want me : why don't you let me
   know
14 So I can leave at once : and hunt me somewhere else
   to go

JefB   14   Jefferson, Blind Lemon

    title: Shuckin' Sugar
    place and date: Chicago, c. Oct. 1926
    record numbers: (3077-2) Pm-12454 Mil MLP-2007

1 I've got your picture : and I'm going to put it in a
   frame
2 And then if you leave town : we can find you just
   the same
3 Now if you don't love me : please don't dog me
   around
4 If you dog me around : I know you put me down
5 I know my baby : thinks the world and all of me
6 Every time she smiles : she shines her light on me
7 Oh I said fair brown : something's going on wrong
8 This here woman I love : she's done been here and
   gone
9 Oh listen fair brown : don't you want to go

JefB   14   Jefferson, Blind Lemon

10 Going to take you across the water : where that
      brownskin man can't go
11 Lord I'm worried here : worried everywhere
12 Now I just started home : and I'll not be worried
      there
13 Lord I'm tired of being married : tired of this
      settling down
14 I only want to stay like I am : and slip from town
      to town

JefB   15   Jefferson, Blind Lemon

       title: Booger Rooger Blues
       place and date: Chicago, c. Oct. 1926
       record numbers: (3088-2) Pm-12425 Bio BLP-12015

1 I drived to the station : woman I bid you all adieu
2 Tell me : you always got a fatmouth following you
3 Now my baby quit me : and she done throwed me down
4 I wouldn't hate it so bad : but that talk is all
      over town
5 She's a long tall woman : she got relatives in
      Arkansas
6 She ain't so good-looking : but boys them dimples is
      going to draw
7 I cried all night : and all that night before
8 Know it's the best to get single : then you won't
      have to cry no more
9 I got ten little puppies : I got twelve little
      shaggy hounds
10 Well it just takes them twenty-two dogs : to run my
      good gal down
11 I got a girl in *North Clifton* : *hollering for a
      good long-legged man* too
12 I may live in Magnolia Texas : what them Mill City
      women going to do
13 Some joker learned my baby : how to shift gears on a
      Cadillac Eight
14 If you ever shift that habit : now I can't keep my
      business straight

JefB   16   Jefferson, Blind Lemon

       title: Rabbit Foot Blues
       place and date: Chicago, c. Oct. 1926
       record numbers: (3089-1) Pm-12454 Mil MLP-2004

1 Blues jumped a rabbit : run him one solid mile
2 This rabbit sat down : cried like a natural child
3 Well it seem like you hungry : honey come and lunch
      with me
4 I want to stop these married-looking women : from
      worrying me
5 I have Uneeda biscuits here : and a half a pint of
      gin
6 The gin is mighty fine : them biscuits are a little
      too thin
7 [Baby tell me something, I want to know] : about
      those meatless and wheatless days
8 This not being my home : I don't think I could stay
9 I cried for flour and meat : I declare it was gone
10 Keep a-feeding me corn bread : I just can't stick
      around long
11 Got an airplane baby : now I'm going to get a
      submarine
12 Going to get that Kaiser : and we'll be seldom seen
13 Mmm hitch me to your buggy mama : drive me like a
      mule
14 Reason I'm going home with you sugar : I ain't much
      hard to be fooled

JefB   17   Jefferson, Blind Lemon

       title: Bad Luck Blues
       place and date: Chicago, c. Oct. 1926
       record numbers: (3090-2) Pm-12443 Mil MLP-2007

1 I want to go home : and I ain't got sufficient
      clothes
3 I bet my money : and I lost it Lord it's dough
4 I'll never bet : on this old trey game no more
5 Oh my ??? *gambler's* gone : why don't you quit
      crying
6 That joker stole off : with that long-haired brown
      of mine
7 Sister you catch the Katy : I'll catch that Santa Fe
8 When you get to Denver : pretty mama look around for
      me
9 The woman I love : why she's five feet from the
      ground
10 She's a tailor-made woman : she ain't no
      hand-me-down
11 I ain't seen my sugar : in two long weeks today
12 Girl it's been so long : seems like my heart going
      to break
13 I'm going to run across town : catch that southbound
      Santa Fe
14 Be on my way : to what you call loving Tennessee

JefB   18   Jefferson, Blind Lemon

       title: Black Snake Moan
       place and date: Chicago, 14 Mar. 1927
       record numbers: (80523-B) OK-8455 Fwy FJ-2802

1 Hey : ain't got no mama now
2 She told me late last night : you don't need no mama
      nohow
3 Mmm : black snake crawling in my room
4 And some pretty mama : had better come and get this
      black snake soon
5 Oh that must have been a bedbug : you know a chinch
      can't bite that hard
6 Asked my baby for fifty cents : she said Lemon ain't
      a dime in the yard
7 Mama that's all right : mama that's all right for
      you
8 Said baby that's all right : most any old way you do
9 Mmm : what's the matter now
10 Tell me what's the matter baby : I don't like no
      black snake nohow
11 Well : wonder where's that black snake gone
12 Lord that black snake mama : done run my darling
      home

JefB   19   Jefferson, Blind Lemon

       title: Match Box Blues
       place and date: Chicago, 14 Mar. 1927
       record numbers: (80524-B) OK-8455 RBF RF-1

1 I'm going to the river : going to walk down by the
      sea
2 I got those tadpoles and minnows : arguing over me
3 Sitting here wondering : would a matchbox hold my
      clothes
4 I ain't got so many matches : but I got so far to go
5 Lord mama : who may your manager be
6 He asked so many questions : can you make
      arrangements for me
7 I got a brown across town : she crochet all the time
8 Baby if you don't quit crocheting : you going lose
      your mind
9 I wouldn't mind marrying : but I can't stand
      settling down
10 I'm going to act like a preacher : so I can ride
      from town to town
11 I'm leaving town : crying won't make me stay

JefB   19   Jefferson, Blind Lemon

12 Baby the more you cry : the further you drive me
    away

JefB   20   Jefferson, Blind Lemon

        title: Easy Rider Blues
        place and date: Chicago, c. Apr. 1927
        record numbers: (4423-2) Pm-12474 Mil MLP-2004

1   Now tell me : where my easy rider's gone
2   Now easy riding woman : always in the wrong
3   Well easy rider : died on the road
4   I'm a poor blind man : ain't got nowhere to go
5   It's going to be the time : that a woman don't need
    no man
6   Then baby shut your mouth : and don't be raising
    sand
7   The train I ride : don't burn no coal at all
8   The coal I'm burning : everybody says it's
    cannonballs
9   I mean I went to the depot : and set my suitcase
    down
10 The blues overtake me : and tears come rolling down
11 The woman I love : she must be out of town
12 She left me this morning : with a face that's full
    of frowns
13 I got a gal across town : she crochets all the time
14 Baby if you don't quit crocheting : you going to
    lose your mind
15 Said fair brown : what's the matter now
16 You turn your back to quit me : woman and you don't
    know how

JefB   21   Jefferson, Blind Lemon

        title: Match Box Blues
        place and date: Chicago, c. Apr. 1927
        record numbers: (4424-2) Pm-12474 Mil MLP-2004

1   I'm sitting here wondering : will a matchbox hold my
    clothes
2   I ain't got so many matches : but I got so far to go
3   Brown across town : going to be my teddy bear
4   Put that thing on me : and I'll follow you
    everywhere
5   I say a peg leg woman : just can't hardly get her
    dough
6   I left one in Lakeport last night : and I'm selling
    jellyroll
7   I don't see why : these women treat me so mean
8   Sometimes I think : a good man these women ain't
    never seen
9   Well I got up this morning : with my [sure-enough,
    same thing] on my mind
10 The woman I love : she keeps a good man worried all
    the time
11 Now tell me mama : who may your manager be
12 I asked so many questions : can't you make
    arrangements for me

JefB   22   Jefferson, Blind Lemon

        title: Match Box Blues
        place and date: Chicago, c. Apr. 1927
        record numbers: (4446-4) Pm-12474 Bio BLP-12000

1   I'm sitting here wondering : will a matchbox hold my
    clothes
2   I ain't got so many matches : but I got so far to go
3   I said fair brown : who may your manager be
4   He asked so many questions : can't you make
    arrangements for me
5   I got a girl across town : she crochets all the time

JefB   22   Jefferson, Blind Lemon

6   Sugar the blues ain't on me : but things ain't going
    on right
7   Mama if you don't quit crocheting : you going to
    lose your mind
8   I can't count the times : I stoled away and cried
9   If you want your [lover, baby] : you better pin him
    to your side
10 If she flag my train : papa Lemon's going to let her
    ride
11 Ain't seen my good gal : in three long weeks today
12 Lord it's been so long : seems like my heart going
    to break
13 Excuse me mama : for knocking on your door
14 If my mind don't change : I'll never knock here no
    more

JefB   23   Jefferson, Blind Lemon

        title: Rising High Water Blues
        place and date: Chicago, c. May 1927
        record numbers: (4491-5) Pm-12487 Mil MLP-2007

1   Backwater rising : southern people can't make no
    time
2   And I can't get no hearing : from that Memphis gal
    of mine
3   Water all in Arkansas : people screaming in
    Tennessee
4   If I don't leave Memphis : black water been all over
    poor me
5   People since it's raining : it has been for nights
    and days
6   Thousand people stands on the hill : looking down
    where they used to stay
7   Children stand there screaming : mama we ain't got
    no home
8   Papa says to children : black water left us all
    alone
9   Backwater rising : come in my windows and doors
10 I leave with a prayer in my heart : backwater won't
    rise no more

JefB   24   Jefferson, Blind Lemon

        title: Right of Way Blues
        place and date: Chicago, c. May 1927
        record numbers: (4515-2) Pm-12510 Rt RL-301

1   I hate to hear : my good gal call my name
2   She don't call so loud : but she call so nice and
    plain
3   Lord the train I ride : eighteen coaches long
4   And the girl I love : she's just now leaving home
5   Well a high brown girl : loves to ride away
    somewhere
6   If a man is worthy : she would make you a
    millionaire
7   Don't never drive : a stranger away from your door
8   It could be your best friend : mama you don't know
9   Don't tell no stories : please don't tell no lies
10 Did my gal stop here : Lord did the mama keep on by
11 Oh if you don't love me : pretty mama don't run no
    stall
12 There's a whole lots of women : *just ran through
    your brown's hall*

JefB   25   Jefferson, Blind Lemon

        title: Teddy Bear Blues
        place and date: Chicago, c. June 1927
        record numbers: (4567-2) Pm-12487 Mil MLP-2007

1   I'm going to make friends : with the fish in the
    deep blue sea

JefB 25   Jefferson, Blind Lemon

2 And stop the Chicago women : from arguing over me
3 Come here pretty mama : going to take you far across
   the pond
4 I'm going to make my stop in Italy : where the
   monkey-man don't belong
5 These women in Chicago : they like their fashions
   and forms
6 But these women from Nashville : swear they just
   won't be here long
7 I said fair brown : let me be your teddy bear
8 Tie a string on my neck : and I'll follow everywhere

JefB 26   Jefferson, Blind Lemon

     title: Black Snake Dream Blues
     place and date: Chicago, c. June 1927
     record numbers: (4577-2) Pm-12510 Bio BLP-12015

1 Black snake is deceitful : crawling in all in my bed
2 I had a dream last night : black snake is killed my
   baby dead
3 Hey hey mama : black [snake's lying, snake is] all
   in my hall
4 And if you quit me mama : you can't see that black
   snake at all
5 Listen here mama : black snake is wearing my clothes
6 And I told you about it : and you put my trunk
   outdoors
7 Take me back mama : I [won't, can't] be bad no more
8 And you can get my loving : if you let that black
   snake go
9 Black snake crawl out : he said he don't mean no
   harm
10 But I'm getting tired of that black snake : lying in
   my baby's arms

JefB 27   Jefferson, Blind Lemon

     title: Struck Sorrow Blues
     place and date: Chicago, c. Sept. 1927
     record numbers: (20039-2) Pm-12541 Rt RL-335

1 I'm going away : now don't you want to go
2 I'm going to stop at a place : I haven't never been
   before
3 I ain't got no watch : I ain't got no *China spoon*
4 Reason I'm hanging around here : man I'm sticking
   here dry long so
5 If you got a sweet woman : you better love her while
   you can
6 For your heart strike sorrow : when I come back to
   town again
7 I lie down last night : rolled from side to side
8 Say that the blues ain't on me : but things ain't
   going on right
9 I drink so much whiskey : I travel in my sleep
10 For that brown across town : I declare she is
   worrying me
11 I believe I'll sing this song : ain't going to sing
   no more
12 Going to leave town : and hang crepe on your door

JefB 28   Jefferson, Blind Lemon

     title: Rambler Blues
     place and date: Chicago, c. Sept. 1927
     record numbers: (20040-2) Pm-12541 Bio BLP-12015

1 Well the train's ??? : track's all out of line
2 And I commence to how I want to : catch that Number
   Nine
3 I'm worried and bothered : don't know what to do
4 Reason I'm worried and bothered : it's all on
   account of you

JefB 28   Jefferson, Blind Lemon

5 When I left home : I left my baby crying
6 She keeps me worried : and bothered in the mind
7 Now don't your house look lonesome : when your baby
   pack up and leave
8 You may drink your moonshine : but baby your heart
   ain't free
9 If you take my rider : I can't get mad with you
10 Just like you taken mine : I'll take someone else's
   too
11 I got a girl in Texas : I got a brown in Tennessee
12 Lord but that brown in Chicago : have put that jinx
   bug on me

JefB 29   Jefferson, Blind Lemon

     title: Chinch Bug Blues
     place and date: Chicago, c. Oct. 1927
     record numbers: (20064-1) Pm-12551 Bio BLP-12015

1 I never feel uneasy : I know how you love your
   tricks
2 You leave town the spate of ten days : you got your
   business well fixed
3 I wonder if the chinches bite in Beaumont : bite
   like they do in Beale Street town
4 The first night I stayed in Memphis : chinch bugs
   turned my bed around
5 I had to get sinful with the bedbugs : to keep the
   chinches from taking my life
6 Because the chinches got my number : wrote a letter
   to my wife
7 My wife caught me easing : way across that Richland
   Road
8 The next time I go to slip out : I ain't going to
   leave on the light anymore
9 My wife has quit me : and my best pigmeat gal has
   too
10 All of ??? *Lord* : here with the chinch bug blues

JefB 30   Jefferson, Blind Lemon

     title: Deceitful Brownskin Woman
     place and date: Chicago, c. Oct. 1927
     record numbers: (20065-2) Pm-12551 Bio BLP-12015

1 There's a brown across town : and she's taller as a
   sycamore tree
2 That's the gal'd walk through the rain and snow :
   for to ease that thing on me
3 Brownskin girl is deceitful : till she gets you all
   worn down
4 She get all your pocket change : she going drive you
   from her town
5 Went home last night : found a note in my
   brownskin's door
6 Daddy *stay long* has got your room : man you can't
   live here no more
7 I [begun to walk, commenced walking] : walked till
   my feet got soaking wet
8 Trying to find good home mama : man I ain't found
   none yet
9 Well the sun's going to shine : in my back door some
   day
10 Ah it's one more drink : going to drive these blues
   away
11 Lord it's heavy-hipped mama : and the meat shakes on
   the bone
12 Every time it shakes : it's a sign my baby's home

JefB   31   Jefferson, Blind Lemon

        title: Sunshine Special
        place and date: Chicago, c. Oct. 1927
        record numbers: (20066-?) Pm-12593 Mil MLP-2007

1   Burn the railroad down : so that Sunshine Special
    can't run
2   I got a gang of women : man they ride from sun to
    sun
3   Same old fireman : going to keep this same old
    engineer
4   So that Sunshine Special : is going to run me on
    away from here
5   Going to leave on the Sunshine Special : going in on
    the Santa Fe
6   Going to *set up and stop* that Katy : because it's
    taking my brown from me
7   Going to ride that kansas Texas : right on to San
    Antone
8   Somebody's been trying to fire your engines : man
    ever since you been gone
9   Cotton Belt is a slow train : also that I and C N
10 If I leave Texas anymore : going to leave on that L
    and N

JefB   32   Jefferson, Blind Lemon

        title: Lonesome House Blues
        place and date: Chicago, c. Oct. 1927
        record numbers: (20076-2) Pm-12593 Mil MLP-2007

1   I had a dream last night : all about my gal
2   You can tell by that : sweet papa ain't been so well
3   I'm going away mama : just to wear you off my mind
4   So if I live in Chicago : murder's going to be my
    crime
5   This house is lonesome : my baby left me all alone
6   If your heart ain't rock : sugar it must be marble
    stone
7   I got the blues so bad : it hurts my feet to walk
8   It has settled on my brain : and it hurts my tongue
    to talk

JefB   33   Jefferson, Blind Lemon

        title: Blind Lemon's Penitentiary Blues
        place and date: Chicago, c. Feb. 1928
        record numbers: (20363-2) Pm-12666 Mil MLP-2013

1   Take Fort Worth for your dressing : and Dallas all
    for your sal
2   So you want to go to the state penitentiary : go to
    Grossbeck for your trial
3   I hung around Grossbeck : I work in hard showers of
    rain
4   I never felt the least bit uneasy : till I caught
    that penitentiary bound train
5   I used to be a drunkard : rowdy everywhere I go
6   If ever I get out of this trouble I'm in : man I
    won't be rowdy no more
7   Boys don't be bad : please don't crowd your mind
8   If you get in trouble in Grossbeck : they going to
    send you to penitentiary flying
9   I want you to stop and study : don't take nobody's
    life
10 They got walls at the state penitentiary : you can't
    jump man as hard as you try

JefB   34   Jefferson, Blind Lemon

        title: 'Lectric Chair Blues
        place and date: Chicago, c. Feb. 1928
        record numbers: (20364-2) Pm-12608 Bio BLP-12015

1   I walked to the jail with my partner : asked him how
    come he's here
2   I had a *ruckus* with my family : they going to send
    me to the electric chair
3   I wonder why they electrocute a man : *if he ???
    line*
4   Because the current's much stronger : *when they
    send it straight out on the line*
5   *I said to the electrocutor* : *awful lousy crime*
6   And my baby asked the judge : was he going to
    electrocute that man of mine
7   Going to get me a taxi : to take me away from here
8   I don't know but one thing in this world : could
    keep me *married* to the electric chair
9   I feel like jumping in the ocean : I feel like
    jumping in the deep blue sea
10 There wasn't no blood left in my heart : and they
    brought my electrocuted daddy to me

JefB   35   Jefferson, Blind Lemon

        title: Lemon's Worried Blues
        place and date: Chicago, c. Feb. 1928
        record numbers: (20375-3) Pm-12622 Mil MLP-2004

1   I'm going to tell you why : I got Lemon's lowdown
    worried blues
2   I left my meal ticket down at ??? : my pot of
    chitlings boiling a little past noon
3   Lord I'm worried here : worried everywhere I go
4   I worried my rider so late last night : she had a
    mule wagon backed up to my door
5   I woke up this morning : took a walk till the break
    of day
6   I asked for a woman to marry me : and I just made my
    get-away
7   I woke up this morning : woke up about half past ten
8   Ease my head in the window : she's singing Lemon's
    worried blues again
9   Worried so bad : can't tell my stockings from my
    shoes
10 I lay down last night : with Lemon's lowdown worried
    blues
11 Lord what makes that [banty] rooster : he keeps
    crowing for the dawn of day
12 His man better watch his footsteps for the hen : now
    doggone his ways

JefB   36   Jefferson, Blind Lemon

        title: Mean Jumper Blues
        place and date: Chicago, c. Feb. 1928
        record numbers: (20380-2) Pm-12631 Mil MLP-2007

1   I feel like jumping : through the keyhole in your
    door
2   If you jump this time baby : you won't jump no more
3   I feel like falling : from treetops to the ground
4   My rider's got a mean jumper : and he don't allow me
    around
5   I go there early in the morning : and I goes there
    late at night
6   Don't care how late I goes there : he hasn't ever
    turned down his light
7   I believe he's looking for me : he's up all hours at
    night
8   She used to be my rider : and he ain't treating her
    right
9   I met this jumper one morning : he was out on the
    out edge of town

JefB   36   Jefferson, Blind Lemon

10 I had to talk and plead : for to keep him from
    blowing me down

JefB   37   Jefferson, Blind Lemon

        title: Balky Mule Blues
        place and date: Chicago, c. Feb. 1928
        record numbers: (20381-3) Pm-12631 Mil MLP-2007

1   I got up this morning : sure was feeling fine
2   I heard a rap at the door : must be that bad cat
    woman of mine
3   She was fussing she was fighting : and acting like a
    doggone fool
4   And hemming and a-hawing : and acting just like a
    balky mule
5   Bad cat ain't no wildcat : and he's going to stay
    home at night
6   But when it comes to squabbling : he sure can
    scratch and bite
7   I got up this morning : I was easing across this
    floor
8   Now my bad cat's leaving me : ain't going to catch
    my mice no more
9   I was standing on the corner : when they brought me
    the bad cat news
10 Now here come my bad cat mama : to run me away with
    them bad cat blues

JefB   38   Jefferson, Blind Lemon

        title: Change My Luck Blues
        place and date: Chicago, c. Feb. 1928
        record numbers: (20387-2) Pm-12639 Mil MLP-2007

1   Hey hey mama : that rider's done and gone
2   I just can't see : what in the world is you waiting
    on
3   I've got another mama : she ain't long and up tall
4   But to tell you the truth man : she is as soft as a
    butterball
5   She got Elgin movements : from her head down to her
    toe
6   And she can break in on a dollar : man most anywhere
    she goes
7   She was my best mama : but she wouldn't treat me
    right
8   She wouldn't do nothing : but barrelhouse all night
    long
9   I'm going to get me a mama : I mean with lots of
    bucks
10 I'm going to be gone mama : so I can change my luck

JefB   39   Jefferson, Blind Lemon

        title: Prison Cell Blues
        place and date: Chicago, c. Feb. 1928
        record numbers: (20388-2) Pm-12622 Mil MLP-2004

1   Getting tired of sleeping : in this lowdown lonesome
    cell
2   Lord I wouldn't't've been here : if it hadn't't've been
    for Nell
3   Lay awake at night : and just can't eat a bite
4   Used to be my rider : but she just won't treat me
    right
5   Got a red-eyed captain : and a squabbling boss
6   Got a mad dog sergeant : honey and he won't knock
    off
7   I asked the government : to knock some days off my
    time
8   Well the way I'm treated : I'm about to lose my mind
9   I wrote to the governor : please turn me a-loose

JefB   39   Jefferson, Blind Lemon

10 Since I didn't get no answer : I know it ain't no
    use
11 I hate to turn over : and find my rider gone
12 Walked across my floor : Lordy how I moan
13 Lord I wouldn't't've been here : if it hadn't't've been
    for Nell
14 I'm getting tired of sleeping : in this lowdown
    lonesome cell

JefB   40   Jefferson, Blind Lemon

        title: Long Lastin' Lovin'
        place and date: Chicago, c. Feb. 1928
        record numbers: (20407-2) Pm-12666 Mil MLP-2013

1   I wonder why : my partner sitting around looking sad
2   I mean the woman if she quit me : it's going to be
    too black bad
3   She's a fair made woman : and she's cunning as a
    squirrel
4   When she starts to loving : man it's out the world
5   Oh she's a dark brownskin : we always call her
    chocolate drop
6   If the fool starts a-loving : man it just won't stop
7   When I first met the woman : I says I hadn't made no
    hit
8   She got this old-fashioned loving : man it just
    won't quit
9   I met her at a *sociable* : she acts just like a
    crook
10 Lord when she starts to loving : man it ain't in the
    book

JefB   41   Jefferson, Blind Lemon

        title: Piney Woods Money Mama
        place and date: Chicago, c. Mar. 1928
        record numbers: (20408-2) Pm-12650 Mil MLP-2004

1   Lord heavy-hipped mama : she done moved to the piney
    wood
2   She's a high-stepping mama : and she don't mean no
    man no good
3   She got ways like the devil : and hair like a Indian
    squaw
4   She been trying two years : to get me to be her
    son-in-law
5   Big mama : own everything in her neighborhood
6   But when she made the money : is when she lived in
    the piney wood
7   Blues in my kitchen : blues in my dining room
8   And some nice young fair brown : had better come
    here soon
9   Well the cook's in the kitchen : picking and fussing
    over turnip greens
10 White folks in the parlor playing cards : and
    they're serving their cake and tea
11 My baby loves my baby : like a cow loves to chew her
    cud
12 But that fool just off and left me : she done moved
    to the piney wood

JefB   42   Jefferson, Blind Lemon

        title: Low Down Mojo Blues
        place and date: Chicago, c. June 1928
        record numbers: (20636-1) Pm-12650 Mil MLP-2004

1   I love my baby : better than a farmer likes his
    Jersey cow
2   Been trying to quit my baby for two years : and man
    I don't know how
3   When I was young : on my big-foot way to school

JefB   42   Jefferson, Blind Lemon

4   I met a nice-looking brownskin : made me lose my
      mammy's rule
5   My rider's got a mojo : and she won't let me see
6   Every time I start to loving : she ease that thing
      on me
7   She's got to fool her daddy : she's got to keep that
      mojo hid
8   But papa's got something : for to find that mojo
      with
9   She got four speeds forward : and she don't never
      stall
10 The way she bumps over the hill : it would make a
      panther squall

JefB   43   Jefferson, Blind Lemon

      title: Competition Bed Blues
      place and date: Chicago, c. July 1928
      record numbers: (20749-2) Pm-12728 Rt RL-306

1   Competition worrying me : you been having a
      competition with me
2   *Big foot* stops at every man's door : and he's
      always in his midnight creep
3   I have a loving brown : I did never miss it *till
      her gone*
4   I found a ??? competition : he better not get in
      town
5   I passed my partner's house : I stopped in to comb
      my head
6   Who should I find : but my gal making up my
      partner's bed
7   I'm going to wreck my mind : competition going
      between me and my friend
8   It hurt me so : I thought we'd be pals till the end
9   It makes a man feel bad : when competition ???
10 Now there's so much competition : I believe I'll
      leave your town

JefB   44   Jefferson, Blind Lemon

      title: Sad News Blues
      place and date: Chicago, c. July 1928
      record numbers: (20772-2) Pm-12728 Rt RL-306

1   I got a letter : I got a letter here in my hand
2   My brown wrote to tell me sad news : she got a brand
      new man
3   I'm a long long way from home : I ain't got no
      lover in town
4   I'm going to get that *B and M* to Baltimore boy : I
      heard my baby *is there*
5   I was drinking all night [long] : got up this
      morning sloppy drunk
6   I would pack my things : but somebody done stole my
      trunk
7   I went uptown last night : I tried drinking hard to
      ease my pain
8   But you ain't got no money : so don't come back here
      again
9   It's sad news : when your baby's ???ing on you
10 Even though you been kind : there's nothing that you
      can do

JefB   45   Jefferson, Blind Lemon

      title: How Long How Long
      place and date: Chicago, c. July 1928
      record numbers: (20788-1) Pm-12685 Bio BLP-12015

1   Standing at the station : watch my baby leave town
2   I feel disgusted : no peace can be found
3   Now you can hear the whistles blowing : but I just
      can't see no train

JefB   45   Jefferson, Blind Lemon

4   Way down in my heart : got a lot of aches and pains
5   Sometime I feel disgusted : and I feel so blue
6   I hardly know what in this world baby : a good man
      can do
7   If I could holler : just like a mountain jack
8   I'd go up on the mountain : and call my baby back
9   Some day you're going to be sorry : you ever done me
      wrong
10 It'll be too late darling : your man will be gone
11 My mind goes to wondering : I feel so bad
12 Thinking about the trouble : a good man always have

JefB   46   Jefferson, Blind Lemon

      title: Lock Step Blues
      place and date: Chicago, c. Aug. 1928
      record numbers: (20815-2) Pm-12679 Mil MLP-2004

1   I used to take my feet : in a midnight tramp
2   Now they got me : doing a different kind of dance
3   I couldn't keep away from [wild, bad] women : bad
      [liquor, whiskey] cards and dice
4   Now I'm doing the lock-step baby : things ain't
      going so nice
5   It don't matter to me : whether it sunshine snow or
      rains
6   Because I can't go gay cutting : and carry a ball
      and chain
7   Mean old jailor : taking away my dancing shoes
8   I can't strut my stuff : when I got those lock-step
      blues
9   Big rats in my cell : keeps me woke all night
10 My woman done turned me down : and I don't think
      that's right
11 Every morning : I walk down that big long hall
12 I'm screaming for my mama : can't make no time at
      all

JefB   47   Jefferson, Blind Lemon

      title: Hangman's Blues
      place and date: Chicago, c. Aug. 1928
      record numbers: (20816-2) Pm-12679 Mil MLP-2004

1   Hangman's rope : it's so tough and strong
2   They got to hang me : because I done something wrong
3   I want to tell you : the gallows Lord is a fearful
      sight
4   Hang me in the morning : and cut me down at night
5   Well the mean old hangman : he went and tightened up
      that noose
6   Lord I'm so scared : I am trembling in my shoes
7   [Jury, jurymen] heard my case : and it said my hand
      was red
8   And the judge is telling me : be hanging till I'm
      dead
9   The crowd around the courthouse : and the time is
      growing fast
10 Soon a good-for-nothing killer : is going to breathe
      his last
11 Lord I'm almost dying : gasping for my breath
12 And that trifling woman staying : until I breaks my
      neck

JefB   48   Jefferson, Blind Lemon

      title: Christmas Eve Blues
      place and date: Chicago, c. Aug. 1928
      record numbers: (20818-2) Pm-12692 Bio BLP-12000

1   Now it's the day before Christmas : mama won't you
      hear me moan
2   If you take me back baby : I'll give you anything
      you need

132

JefB 48   Jefferson, Blind Lemon

3   I had a good chance : baby give me just one more
4   I will change the way I'm loving : like you never
    have been before
5   I know I did do wrong : I'm just as sorry as I can
    be
6   It's the day before Christmas : mama come back to me
7   Mama don't turn me down : on this Christmas Eve
8   I cried about you so hard : done wetted my whole
    coat sleeve
9   It's the day before Christmas : let me bring [me]
    your present tonight
10 I'm going to be your Santa Claus : even if my
    whiskers ain't white

JefB 49   Jefferson, Blind Lemon

      title: Happy New Year Blues
      place and date: Chicago, c. Aug. 1928
      record numbers: (20819-2) Pm-12692 Bio BLP-12000

1   I'm thinking about the year : of nineteen and
    twenty-nine
2   New year caught me with *marked money* : man I was
    doing just fine
3   I was lying down with my baby : we had one small
    quart of gin
4   That old doorbell kept ringing : I wouldn't leave
    nobody come in
5   The whistle was blowing for New Year : around twelve
    o'clock at night
6   I lied down on there with my baby : until the good
    Lord brought daylight
7   Early one New Year morning : I was walking down by
    the hill
8   Every man likes his liquor : when he gets it fresh
    from the still
9   I hate to drink all new year : for this whiskey they
    making is too strong
10 Because when I take two or three drinks : I'll be
    drunk the whole year long

JefB 50   Jefferson, Blind Lemon

      title: Maltese Cat Blues
      place and date: Chicago, c. Aug. 1928
      record numbers: (20820-1) Pm-12712 Bio BLP-12015

1   Rats is mean in my kitchen : and I lost my Maltese
    cat
2   I'm going to make things right with my good gal :
    man and it's tight like that
3   I'm going to start walking : walk the shoes clean
    off of my feet
4   Just thinking about my mama : and man that woman
    sure is sweet
5   I ain't got no suitcase : I don't have a one bottle
    of gin
6   I've got to stay drunk to keep warm : because my
    clothes is so thin
7   Long lonesome train : come passing me a-flying
8   I was thinking about my mama : and I didn't pay that
    train no mind
9   When you get a-home : buy a Maltese cat
10 And a good strong brownskin : man it's tight like
    that

JefB 51   Jefferson, Blind Lemon

      title: D B Blues
      place and date: Chicago, c. Aug. 1928
      record numbers: (20821-1) Pm-12712 Bio BLP-12015

1   Who is that coming : hey with a motor so strong

JefB 51   Jefferson, Blind Lemon

2   That's Lemon in his D B : people think he's got his
    girl out on
3   Going to get out of my four-cylinder Dodge : I want
    to get me a Super Six
4   I'm always around the ladies : and I like to have my
    business fixed
5   I'm crazy about a Packard : but my baby only rates a
    Ford
6   A Packard is too expensive : Ford will take you
    where you want to go
7   Come here brownskin : listen to my motor roar
8   Because my Super Six sufficient : to take you where
    you want to go
9   I never did like no horses : I never could stand no
    steel
10 Ever since I was old enough to catch a brown : give
    me the automobile

JefB 52   Jefferson, Blind Lemon

      title: Eagle Eyed Mama
      place and date: Chicago, c. Jan. 1929
      record numbers: (21095-3) Pm-12739 Rt RL-301

1   My woman got eyes like an eagle : and she watching
    me all the time
2   The way she follow me around : Lordy it's going to
    be a crime
3   Watching me all through the day : watching me all
    through the night
4   Keeps her eagle eyes on me : till the good Lord
    brings daylight
5   Mmm : papa Lemon's feeling so blue
6   Eagle-eyed mama's worrying me : what am I going to
    do
7   Dog in my back yard : oh Lordy how he can howl
8   I'm trying to quit that eagle-eyed woman : man and I
    don't know how
9   My eagle-eyed woman : is got ways I can't explain
10 If I ever leave her : I must be going insane

JefB 53   Jefferson, Blind Lemon

      title: Dynamite Blues
      place and date: Chicago, c. Jan. 1929
      record numbers: (21096-1) Pm-12739 Rt RL-301

1   I feel like tramping : from the *great big corral*
2   Because the woman I love : says she don't want me
    nohow
3   She swore that she loved me : but I know that she
    doing me wrong
4   I'm going to start something man : and I tell you it
    won't be long
5   The way I feel now : I could get a keg of dynamite
6   Put it all in her window : and blow her up late at
    night
7   I just swallowed some fire : take a drink of
    gasoline
8   Throw it up all over that woman : and let her go off
    and scream
9   I'm going to get in a cannon : and let them blow me
    out to sea
10 Going down with the whales : and the mermaids make
    love to me

JefB 54   Jefferson, Blind Lemon

      title: Oil Well Blues
      place and date: Chicago, c. Mar. 1929
      record numbers: (21197-1) Pm-12771 Riv RLP-12-12

1   There ain't nothing mama : no use ???

133

JefB   54   Jefferson, Blind Lemon

2   There's a long distance well : and it's blowing oil
    that's all
3   Ain't nothing to hurt you : it ain't nothing that's
    bad
4   It's the first oil well : that *your* ??? ever had
5   I'm a long distance driller : and I work every
    country through
6   Going to stop working : if I bring in this well for
    you
7   I'm a mean old well driller : and I been a driller
    since I been a man
8   Ain't going to stop drilling : till I strikes that
    Woodburn sand
9   I got a [mean] reputation : and they call me
    Drilling Sam
10 When I starts to drilling : you hear women hollering
    too black bad

JefB   55   Jefferson, Blind Lemon

        title: Tin Cup Blues
        place and date: Chicago, c. Mar. 1929
        record numbers: (21198-1) Pm-12756 Mil MLP-2013

1   I was down and I cried : *my pillowcase was on the
    line*
2   Ain't it tough to see a man : go to *wreck and
    almost fall and die*
3   I stood on the corner : and almost bust my head
4   I couldn't earn enough money : to buy me a loaf of
    bread
5   Baby times is so hard : I almost call it tough
6   I can't earn money to buy no bread : and you know I
    can't buy my snuff
7   My gal's a housemaid : and she earns a dollar a week
8   And I'm so hungry on payday : I can't hardly speak
9   Now gather around me people : let me tell you a true
    fact
10 That tough luck has sunk me : and the rats is
    creeping in my hat

JefB   56   Jefferson, Blind Lemon

        title: Empty House Blues
        place and date: Chicago, c. Mar. 1929
        record numbers: (21200-1) Pm-12946 Rt RL-335

1   The furniture man : he done been here and gone
2   Taking all my furniture : didn't left nothing for me
    to sit down on
3   Well it's tough to be alone : when I got to have my
    biscuits browned
4   Most of these women I know : cooking ??? *down for
    down*
5   I loved my baby in the morning : Lord loved her late
    at night
6   I miss that midnight loving : and you know I ain't
    treated right
7   I feel so disgusted : and I hate to be alone
8   I'm getting some other man's loving : when I ought
    to be getting my own
9   My love is like a storm : what blowed the walls all
    down
10 Soon as you get some of my loving : they can't keep
    you out of town

JefB   57   Jefferson, Blind Lemon

        title: Saturday Night Spender Blues
        place and date: Chicago, c. Mar. 1929
        record numbers: (21201-2) Pm-12771 Rt RL-335

1   Every Saturday : go to work in a doggone place

JefB   57   Jefferson, Blind Lemon

2   *With food in my craw* : I goes there for *spending
    place*
3   I find six or seven women : and a whole lots of fun
4   Then we go out and break them down : honey till
    early morn
5   I don't mind no men friends : but I am afraid of my
    grandma's child
6   I like me a-plenty of women : but man I like them
    wild
7   All during the week : I work hard and I really save
8   But on a Saturday night : I can get all the loving I
    crave
9   Now I can't have the times : like I once have had
10 My regular found out I was a Saturday night spender
    : and it sure did make her mad

JefB   58   Jefferson, Blind Lemon

        title: That Black Snake Moan No 2
        place and date: Chicago, c. Mar. 1929
        record numbers: (21202-1) Pm-12756 Mil MLP-2013

1   Mmm : going to run that black snake down
2   I ain't seen my mama : since black snake taken her
    away from town
3   Mmm : black snake is so hard to find
4   I am worried about my mama : I can't keep her off my
    mind
5   Oh : better find my mama soon
6   I woke up this morning : black snake was making
    easy ruckus in my room
7   Black snake is evil : black snake is all I see
8   I woke up this morning : black snake was moving in
    on me
9   Mmm : black snake was hanging around
10 He occupied my livingroom : and broke my *fairybook*
    down

JefB   59   Jefferson, Blind Lemon

        title: Peach Orchard Mama
        place and date: Chicago, c. Aug. 1929
        record numbers: (21400-2) Pm-12801 Riv RLP-12-12

1   Peach orchard mama : you swore nobody'd pick your
    fruit but me
2   I found three kid-men : shaking down your peaches
    tree
3   One man bought your groceries : another joker paid
    your rent
4   While I work in your orchard : and giving you every
    cent
5   Went to the police station : begged the police to
    put me in jail
6   I didn't want to kill you mama : but I hate to see
    your peaches tree fail
7   Peach orchard mama : don't treat your papa so mean
8   Chase out all those kid-men : and let me keep your
    orchard clean
9   Peach orchard mama : don't turn your papa down
10 Because when I gets mad : I acts just like a clown

JefB   60   Jefferson, Blind Lemon

        title: Big Night Blues
        place and date: Chicago, c. Aug. 1929
        record numbers: (21402-2) Pm-12801 Riv RLP-12-12

1   My feets is so cold : can't hardly wear my shoes
2   Out last night with wild women : and it give me the
    big night blues
3   I grabbed my baby : I danced till the clock struck
    twelve

JefB 60   Jefferson, Blind Lemon

4 I had to wrestle so hard with my good gal : I just
   ain't feeling so well
5 I'm going back to that party : get with them wild
   women again
6 Well I ain't going to leave my home : till I order
   me a quart of gin
7 Wild women like their liquor : their gin and their
   rocking rye
8 My gal wouldn't let me go home last night : wouldn't
   tell me the reason why
9 Turned my face to the wall : and my baby made an
   awful moan
10 Well I needs my daddy : because my clock is run down
   at home

JefB 61   Jefferson, Blind Lemon

        title: Bed Springs Blues
        place and date: Richmond, Ind., 24 Sept. 1929
        record numbers: (15664) Pm-12872 Mel MLP-7324

1 Got something to tell you : make the hair rise on
   your head
2 Got a new way of getting down : make the springs
   tremble on your bed
3 My gal got a new way of trembling down : make a
   crazy man leave his home
4 When she grabs you and turns you loose : makes the
   flesh tremble on your bones
5 Well my gal got something at home : that I sure do
   like
6 That's the long folding bed : with the cover all
   right back
7 Don't blame me mama : for talking out my head
8 I'm worried about the movements you got : and those
   springs trembling on your bed

JefB 62   Jefferson, Blind Lemon

        title: Yo Yo Blues
        place and date: Richmond, Ind., 24 Sept. 1929
        record numbers: (15665) Pm-12872 Bio BLP-12000

1 I want to yo-yo : but I broke my yo-yo string
2 I believe my baby's going crazy losing her mind :
   Lord the woman is going insane
3 Don't a man feel bad : when he can't yo-yo no more
4 Broke my yo-yo string last night : and I can't come
   home no more
5 My sugar got ways : partner I can't understand
6 Leave me all in my bed : go yo-yo with some other
   man
7 I love me yo-yo : better than anything I know
8 I'm feeling funny and foolish : I can't shake that
   thing no more

JefB 63   Jefferson, Blind Lemon

        title: Mosquito Moan
        place and date: Richmond, Ind., 24 Sept. 1929
        record numbers: (15666) Pm-12899 Mil MLP-2013

1 Lamp sits in my kitchen : mosquitoes all around my
   screen
2 I'm about all ready to get a mosquito bomb : I'll be
   seldom seen
3 [I'm going to, I believe I'll] keep on the Pinto :
   drive on back to Brandyville
4 Oh mosquitoes so bad in this man's town : keep me
   away from my whiskey still
5 I love my whiskey : better than some people like to
   eat
6 Mosquitoes bother me so : I can't hardly stay on my
   feet

JefB 63   Jefferson, Blind Lemon

7 I bought a spray last night : and I sprayed all over
   my house
8 Mosquitoes all around my door : won't leave nobody
   come out
9 Mosquitoes all around me : mosquitoes are everywhere
   I go
10 No matter where I go : well they sticks their bills
   in me
11 I wouldn't say a gabber-nipper : these
   gabber-nippers bite too hard
12 I stepped back in my kitchen : and they springing up
   in my back yard

JefB 64   Jefferson, Blind Lemon

        title: Southern Woman Blues
        place and date: Richmond, Ind., 24 Sept. 1929
        record numbers: (15667) Pm-12899 Mil MLP-2013

1 Way down south : you ought to see the women shimmy
   and shake
2 Their new way of wiggle : make a weak man break his
   neck
3 You fed me greens : and I mean that they really can
   cook
4 Make me a jellyroll : and I mean it's out the book
5 I was down south : where all my whiskey cook
6 Just looking at them women : makes me want to get my
   gauge stuck
7 Southern women : man [they're, they sure is] hard to
   beat
8 Ain't so easy to get along with : but Lord so sweet
9 I'm going down south : and I believe I'll take my
   hook
10 I'm going to fish in southern women : I declare it's
   out the book
11 Me and my sugar : *something I did hold*
12 I won't go to fishing : mama I done broke my pole

JefB 65   Jefferson, Blind Lemon

        title: Bakershop Blues
        place and date: Richmond, Ind., 24 Sept. 1929
        record numbers: (15668) Pm-12852 Mil MLP-2013

1 I'm standing in front of the bakershop : and I'm
   feeling lowdown in mind
2 Hungry as could be : looking at all cakes of kind
3 Girl in the bakershop : she hollered papa don't look
   so sad
4 Come and try some of my cake : and you won't feel so
   bad
5 *And with* sweet rolls in the window : honey and
   light bread cold
6 I want to buy me some cake : but I had shot dice and
   lost my roll
7 I'm crazy about my light bread : and my pigmeat on
   the side
8 If I had a piece of your jellyroll : honey I'd be
   satisfied
9 I want to know if your jellyroll fresh : I want to
   know if your jellyroll's stale
10 I'm going to haul off and buy me some : if I have to
   break her loose in jail
11 It's hard to be broke : and so hungry you about to
   drop
12 If I don't get a break soon : I'll fall dead front
   of this bakershop

135

JefB   66   Jefferson, Blind Lemon

        title: Pneumonia Blues
        place and date: Richmond, Ind., 24 Sept. 1929
        record numbers: (15669) Pm-12880 Mil MLP-2013

1   I'm aching all over : believe I got the pneumonia
    this time
2   And it's all on account of : that lowdown gal of
    mine
3   Slinking around the corner : running up alleys too
4   Watching my woman : trying to see what she going to
    do
5   Stood down in the street : one cold dark stormy
    night
6   Trying to see : if my good gal going to make it home
    all right
7   [I believe she's, she must have] found something :
    that probably made her fall
8   I stood out in the cold all night : and she didn't
    come home at all
9   Wear B V Ds in the winter : traveling around in the
    rain
10 Last time : my baby give me this pneumonia pain
11 Now when I die : bury me in a Stetson hat
12 Tell my good gal I'm going : but I'm still
    a-standing pat

JefB   67   Jefferson, Blind Lemon

        title: Long Distance Moan
        place and date: Richmond, Ind., 24 Sept. 1929
        record numbers: (15670-A) Pm-12852 Mil MLP-2013

1   I'm flying to South Carolina : I got to go there
    this time
2   Women in Dallas Texas : is about to make me lose my
    mind
3   Long distance long distance : will you please give
    me a credit call
4   Want to talk to my gal in South Carolina : who looks
    like a Indian squaw
5   Just want to ask my baby : what in the world is she
    been doing
6   Give your loving to another joker : and it's sure
    going to be my ruin
7   Hey long distance : I can't help but moan
8   My baby's voice sound so sweet : oh I'm going to
    break this telephone
9   You don't know you love your rider : till she is so
    far from you
10 You can get long distance moan : and you don't care
    what you do
11 I think I will use ??? poison : to get my brownie
    off my mind
12 This long distance moan : about to worry me to death
    this time

JefB   68   Jefferson, Blind Lemon

        title: That Crawlin' Baby Blues
        place and date: Richmond, Ind., 24 Sept. 1929
        record numbers: (15671) Pm-12880 Mil MLP-2013

1   Well the baby crawling : on up to his mama's knee
2   He's crying about his sweet milk : and she won't
    feed him just that cream
3   Crawled from the fireplace : and he stopped in the
    middle of the floor
4   Said mama ain't that your second daddy : standing
    back there in the door
5   Well she grabbed my baby and spanked him : I tried
    to make her leave him alone
6   I tried my best to stop her : and she said that baby
    ain't none of mine
7   Some woman rocks the cradle : and I declare she
    rules her home

JefB   68   Jefferson, Blind Lemon

8   Many man rocks some other man's baby : and the fool
    thinks he's rocking his own
9   It was late last night : when I liked to crawl in
    baby's room
10 My woman threw my clothes outdoors : and now I got
    those crawling baby blues

JefB   69   Jefferson, Blind Lemon

        title: Fence Breakin' Yellin' Blues
        place and date: Richmond, Ind., 24 Sept. 1929
        record numbers: (15672) Pm-12921 Bio BLP-12015

1   Here comes two women : I liked to drove them wild
2   Well you drinking bad liquor : you'll be overtaken
    after a while
3   He must be desperated : I don't know nothing else it
    could be
4   Standing on the corner didn't mean no harm : the boy
    made a dash at me
5   Made a break at me : groped for my pocketknife
6   One had me cooling off : while the other one talked
    about taking my wife
7   And when I went for my gun : you ought to see them
    yelling breaking that fence
8   I first thought they was crazy : but I found out
    they didn't have no sense
9   You can take my money : I mean you can wear my best
    clothes
10 Lemon won't kill no quicker : if you bother with my
    jellyroll
11 Some people like their sugar : I'm a fool about my
    China tea
12 You can have all this world : but leave my honeycomb
    home with me

JefB   70   Jefferson, Blind Lemon

        title: Cat Man Blues
        place and date: Richmond, Ind., 24 Sept. 1929
        record numbers: (15673) Pm-12921 Bio BLP-12015

1   Cat man cat man : stay away from my house at night
2   Prowling around my back door when I'm gone : you
    know that ain't right
3   When I come home last night I heard a noise : asked
    my wife what was that
4   She said don't be so suspicious : that wasn't a
    thing but a cat
5   I've been all over the world : I've taken all kinds
    of chance
6   I've never seen a cat : come home in a pair of pants
7   I'm tired of this jellyroll man : come to my home
    when I'm out
8   Know it's the cause of my woman : boys is *necking*
    about
9   Reason I call him cat man : he don't [come, go]
    around in the day
10 Come around at midnight : steals my cream when I'm
    away
11 Tell me a cat got nine lives : honey and I believe
    that's true
12 If the cat man is got nine lives : he going to need
    them when I get through

JefB   71   Jefferson, Blind Lemon

        title: Bootin' Me 'Bout
        place and date: Richmond, Ind., 24 Sept. 1929
        record numbers: (15675) Pm-12946 Mil MLP-2004

1   I got a brownskin mama : she built right to the
    ground

JefB 71   Jefferson, Blind Lemon

2   When I goes to her house : old man starts to booting
    me around
3   Now you mustn't blame his gal : it's nailed up to
    his door
4   Don't want to go near no man : pretty soon she'll be
    too old
5   Hey here Mr : you must be losing your mind
6   Everybody's got to have : a little bit of loving
    sometime
7   Her father told me : better not to come back no more
8   If I catch you here : I'm going to boot you through
    the door
9   I love my little brownskin : she's so young and
    green
10 The old man's the bootingest thing : that I most
    ever seen
11 I got to find me a scheme : to get my gal all to
    herself
12 Because I'm a fool about that woman : don't want
    nobody else

JohAl 1   Johnson, Alec

        title: Miss Meal Cramp Blues
        place and date: Atlanta, 2 Nov. 1928
        record numbers: (147379-2) Co-14446-D CC-3

1   Lord I'm broke and hungry : and my money's all gone
2   Weather is summer : I've got to travel on
3   All my crops a failure : couldn't raise a doggone
    thing
4   I'm just like a beggar : hear these lonesome blues I
    sing
5   If I steal a pork chop : Lord I believe I'll pass
    away
6   I ain't had a square meal : in many doggone days
7   I'm so broke and hungry : I could eat a kangaroo
8   I feel just like stealing : there's nothing else to
    do
9   Won't somebody help me : with a little bite to eat
10 Don't care what you give me : I'd eat even chicken
    meat
11 Standing on the roadside : with a great big sign it
    read
12 Say Uneeda biscuits : ??? near dropped dead
13 My body feels so weary : because I got the miss-meal
    cramp
14 Right now I could eat more : than a whole carload of
    tramps

JohAl 2   Johnson, Alec

        title: Next Week Sometime
        place and date: Atlanta, 2 Nov. 1928
        record numbers: (147382-2) Co-14416-D CC-3

1   I went out last night I got drunk : I was in whiskey
    up to my head
2   A young lady she walked up to me : and this is what
    she said
3   I told her to give me time : and let me think
4   And I'd tell her : exactly when to buy that
    expensive drink
5   I went to see a fortuneteller : just to have my
    fortune told
6   She says young man you are partly rich : you're
    worth a great big pot of gold
7   I got myself a pick and shovel : I reached twelve
    that night
8   When I got there : I do declare I spied a form all
    dressed in white
9   Now me and this haunt : run breast and breast
10 He says look here brother : when are you going to
    rest

JohBi 1   Johnson, Billiken

        title: Sun Beam Blues
        place and date: Dallas, 3 Dec. 1927
        record numbers: (145322-1) Co-14293-D Rt RL-335

1   Sunbeam's on time : I ain't got my fare
2   And if I start walking : Sunbeam will beat me there
3   Don't need an airplane : steamboat or submarine
4   But if I miss the Sunbeam : I will be seldom seen

JohBi 2   Johnson, Billiken

        title: Interurban Blues
        place and date: Dallas, 3 Dec. 1927
        record numbers: (145323-2) Co-14293-D Rt RL-335

1   Standing here a-wondering : will that car pass my
    way
2   I'm going back to my baby : going back there to stay
3   I know my baby : is bound to love me some
4   She throws her arms around me : like the circle
    around the sun

JohBi 3   Johnson, Billiken

        title: Frisco Blues
        place and date: Dallas, 8 Dec. 1928
        record numbers: (147606-2) Co-14405-D Rt RL-312

1   I told the ticket agent : don't let your window down
2   I'm sick and blue : but I'm Frisco bound
3   Well a mean old fireman : a cruel old engineer
4   That would leave big fat Billiken : *walking along
    out there*

JohBi 4   Johnson, Billiken

        title: Wild Jack Blues
        place and date: Dallas, 8 Dec. 1928
        record numbers: (147607-2) Co-14405-D Rt RL-315

1   Wild jack on the mountain : and he brays the whole
    day long
2   Going to find me some lumber : build that old jack a
    home
3   I'm going to build a stable : as long as he is tall
4   So I can hear my wild jack : every time he calls
5   You ought to see : this big black jack of mine
6   He can eat more corn : than I feel like frying
7   This big black jack : got mane just like a horse
8   Going to keep my wild jack : lock him in my stall
9   He's a big bad jack : and you can hear him all over
    town
10 Going to keep my wild jack : if I have to chain him
    down

JohBu 1   Johnson, Buster

        title: Undertaker Blues
        place and date: Richmond, Ind., 16 Jan. 1932
        record numbers: (18323) Ch-16718 OJL-2

1   Mr undertaker Mr undertaker : drop your hammer and
    saw
2   You take my baby to the cemetery : and don't bring
    her back no more
3   I'm going take my females : hang them on a single
    line
4   I'm going to count one two three four five : six
    seven eight and nine
5   Well I went to the graveyard : kneeled down by my
    baby to talk
6   I have to leave you to heaven : *oh my baby's do no
    wrong*

JohE   1   Johnson, Edith North

      title: Nickel's Worth of Liver Blues
      place and date: Richmond, Ind., 7 Sept. 1929
      record numbers: (15558-A) Pm-12823 CC-37

1   Bring me a nickel's worth of liver : a dime's worth
   of stew
2   Feed everybody : on ??? Avenue
3   Got a man upside one downside : one across the
   street
4   Got your eyes wide open : but you're sound asleep
5   Bring me a nickel's worth of liver : a dime's worth
   of grease
6   ??? my man : he called all the police
7   Listen papa : don't give me none of your head
8   Keep on fooling : you'll be filled full of lead
9   When you see me worried : I'm thinking about my
   burnt liver
10 I'll kill you about him : and my hand won't even
   quiver

JohE   2   Johnson, Edith North

      title: Good Chib Blues
      place and date: Richmond, Ind., 7 Sept. 1929
      record numbers: (15559) Pm-12864 CC-37

1   Ooh : tomorrow I may be far away
2   Don't try to dog me honey : sweet talk can't make me
   stay
3   Now if you get loaded baby : and think you want to
   go
4   Remember baby : you ain't no better than the man I
   had before
5   When I get drunk I'm evil : I don't know what to do
6   If I get my good chib : can get something good from
   you
7   Now the man I love : he's just about the heightth of
   me
8   I'm five foot two : Lord and that sweet man's five
   foot three

JohE   3   Johnson, Edith North

      title: Can't Make Another Day
      place and date: Richmond, Ind., 7 Sept. 1929
      record numbers: (15560) Pm-12864 Riv RM-8819

1   All this world's against me : I believe my baby is
   too
2   Ah my baby's against me : Lord I can tell by the way
   he do
3   Now the man I love : Lord he don't mean me no good
4   Takes all his good jelly : around all the whole
   neighborhood
5   Now if I was a Gypsy : Lord and I could read your
   mind
6   Then I wouldn't have to wonder : where you spend all
   your time

JohE   4   Johnson, Edith North

      title: Honeydripper Blues
      place and date: Richmond, Ind., 7 Sept. 1929
      record numbers: (15561) Pm-12823 Mil MLP-2018

1   I wake up every morning : with the rising sun
2   Oh thinking about my honeydripper : and all the
   wrongs he done
3   Oh he treats me mean : [only, just] comes to see me
   sometime
4   But the way he spreads his honey : Lord it makes me
   think I'll lose my mind
5   Oh because I'm brown : Lord he wants to drive me
   away

JohE   4   Johnson, Edith North

6   He knows he's a good honeydripper : Lord and I want
   him every day
7   Lord the man I love : oh Lord he really made me fall
8   Oh the way he drips his honey : Lord he won my heart
   that's all
9   Oh sometimes I feel so lonesome : Lord I don't know
   where to go
10 When my love comes down babe : I'll need you more
   than you'll ever know
11 Because he's a real sweet man : and I [want to lease
   him, got to sign him up] for ninety-nine years
12 That's what it takes to ease my mind : and stop all
   my tears

JohEb   1   Johnson, Elizabeth

      title: Be My Kid Blues
      place and date: New York, 30 Oct. 1928
      record numbers: (401279-B) OK-8789 Her H-201

1   If you be my kid : I'll be your teddy bear
2   I'll get in your pocket : and follow you everywhere
3   When you see me coming : heist your window high
4   See me leaving : hand your head and cry
6   It's raining here : storming on the sea
7   I'm leaving here : but I sure don't want to go
8   *Thieving* man : don't want me no more
9   I'm going to town : I'm going to buy me a bed
10 Sleep with my man : if it kills me dead

JohEb   2   Johnson, Elizabeth

      title: Sobbin' Woman Blues
      place and date: New York, 30 Oct. 1928
      record numbers: (401280-?) OK-8789 Her H-201

1   Oh I ain't got : no easy rider now
2   The man I love : sure done turned me down
3   He treats me : like I'm some old body's dog
4   I ain't no dog : please don't dog me around
5   Oh your time now : be mine after a while
6   Give me my fare : I sure will leave this town
7   I'm going home : I ain't been home in so long
8   Going back to Georgia : if I don't stay long
9   Wonder what's the matter : I can't get no mail
10 Believe to my soul : they got my man in jail
11 Going to buy me a pistol : with a great long shiny
   barrel
12 When I'm dead : give it to my faro
13 Get your one man : you sure better get you two
14 Ain't no telling : what these men will do
15 I'm going away : just to wear you off my mind
16 Keep me worried : bothered all the time

JohJa   1   Johnson, James Stump

      title: Barrel of Whiskey Blues
      place and date: Dallas, 10 Feb. 1932
      record numbers: (70680-1) Vi-23327 Yz L-1033

1   I ain't going to marry : and I ain't going to settle
   down
2   I'm going to do like a pimp : I'm going to walk all
   around this town
3   Goodbye whiskey : sure don't worry me
4   I can get just as drunk : as any drunken man can be
5   My baby's gone : she didn't tell me because
6   If she don't come back : I am going to starve
7   Ever since : my baby's been gone away
8   I've been raggedy and dirty : haven't got no place
   to stay
9   My old gal : came into town last night
10 She didn't have no money : but she was too tight

JohJa 1   Johnson, James Stump

11 Me and my gal : are going to make everything all
     right
12 If we don't today : we will tomorrow night

JohJo 1   Johnson, Joe (Memphis Minnie)

      title: I'm Going Back Home
      place and date: Memphis, 26 May 1930
      record numbers: (59992-) Vi-23352 His HLP-32

1   Oh mercy dear : you cause my heart
2   *Sad and long* : *with how to win my part*
3   I learn to love you : most all the rest
4   You're leaving me : wrecking happiness
5   I'll count the hours : *living when alone*
6   Think of you : when you back home
7   My lonesome heart : will shake with fear
8   The very hour : that you call my name
9   Minnie every hour : is a living fear
10 For I'm not at ease : with anyone else
11 I'll hunger long : for you evermore
12 I'm asking you dear : please don't go
13 Going to tell you this : ain't going to tell no lie
14 Day you leave me : that's the day you die

JohJo 2   Johnson, Joe (Memphis Minnie)

      title: Don't Want No Woman
      place and date: Memphis, 26 May 1930
      record numbers: (62539-) Vi-23313 Pal PL-101

1   Don't want no woman : have to give my money to
3   I tried hard baby : did the very best I could
5   I'm going to the mountain : hold up my right hand
7   The girl I love : sings like a turtledove
9   That's the way baby : you have *things* to do

JohK 1   Johnson, Ki Ki

      title: Lady, Your Clock Ain't Right
      place and date: Long Island City, c. Aug. 1928
      record numbers: (   ) QRS-R7003 His HLP-17

1   Every man that comes to see you : in this
     neighborhood
2   Keeps on buzzing to each other : that your clock
     ain't no good
3   Now your clock don't set : where it used to set
     before
4   It used to be on the *centre* : close to your back
     door

JohK 2   Johnson, Ki Ki

      title: Wrong Woman Blues
      place and date: Long Island City, c. Aug. 1928
      record numbers: (   ) QRS-R7003 His HLP-17

1   I was lying down dreaming : when the blues eased up
     on me
2   I was feeling so blue : down-hearted as could be
3   A brownskin gal : makes a bulldog bark with pain
4   And a bow-legged mama : make a snail catch a
     passenger train
5   Now you can always tell : when your woman treats you
     mean
6   I say your meals are never ready : and your house
     ain't never clean
7   She will come downstairs : a towel was tied around
     her head
8   You'll ask her for loving : she'll swear she's
     almost dead

JohLe 1   Johnson, Lem

      title: Candy Blues
      place and date: New York, 19 May 1942
      record numbers: (70761-A) De-7895 Br-87.504

1   I left my baby : standing in the doorway crying
2   She said daddy you've got a home : just as long as I
     got mine
3   My mama told me : papa told me too
4   Some day son : candy's going to be the death of you
5   Now it's chocolate candy : till my dying day
6   The same old candy : is going to carry me away
7   I've got one good woman : trying to make it four
8   When one pretty woman quits me : I'll have three
     more

JohLi 1   Johnson, Lil

      title: Never Let Your Left Hand Know
         What Your Right Hand Do
      place and date: Chicago, 23 Apr. 1929
      record numbers: (C-3355-) Vo-1299 His HLP-2

1   I had the blues last night : I've got them again
     today
2   My man told me : he was going away
3   Trouble trouble : is all I can see
4   Look like my man : has turned his back on me
5   Just let me tell you : what your friends will do
6   Grin in your face : and then they'll talk about you
7   Me and my girl friend : went out for a little run
8   When she seen my man : she told him what I had done
9   Bring me a pint of whiskey : and a bottle of beer
10 If I get drunk : I sure don't care
11 Take me back baby : try me one more time
12 I do everything : to satisfy your mind
13 Listen people : to what I'm telling you
14 Don't let your left hand : know what your right hand
     do

JohLi 2   Johnson, Lil

      title: You'll Never Miss Your Jelly
         Till Your Jelly Rollers Gone
      place and date: Chicago, 23 Apr. 1929
      record numbers: (C-3356-) Vo-1299 His HLP-2

1   I woke up this morning : with the blues all around
     my bed
2   I felt just like : somebody in my family was dead
3   I began to moan : and I began to cry
4   My sweet man went away : you know the reason why
5   If you don't like my sweet potato : what made you
     dig so deep
6   You in my potato field : three or four times a week
7   Whooping I've been whooping : whooping all night
     long
8   Whooping I've been whooping : ever since my man been
     gone
9   My dog got the rabbit : the rabbit fell down on his
     knees
10 He looked up at the dog : he say won't you have
     mercy on me please
11 Just as sure : as you hear me sing this song
12 You never miss your jelly : till your jellyroller's
     gone

JohLi 3   Johnson, Lil

      title: House Rent Scuffle
      place and date: Chicago, c. 29 June 1929
      record numbers: (C-3749-) Vo-1410 Yz L-1039

1   Play that thing : play that thing just right
2   We got to scuffle : that house rent tonight

139

JohLi 3   Johnson, Lil

  3 My house rent's due : my gas going up to ten
  4 I wouldn't have no lights : but the lightman
    couldn't get in

JohLo 1   Johnson, Lonnie

     title: Mr. Johnson's Blues
     place and date: St. Louis, 4 Nov. 1925
     record numbers: (9435-A) OK-8253 CC-30

  1 I want all you people : to listen to my song
  2 Remember me : after the days I'm gone

JohLo 2   Johnson, Lonnie

     title: Falling Rain Blues
     place and date: St. Louis, 4 Nov. 1925
     record numbers: (9436-A) OK-8253 CC-30

  1 The storm is rising : the rains begin to fall
  2 I'm all alone by myself : no one to love me at all
  3 My blues at midnight : and don't leave me until day
  4 I've got no sweet woman : to drive my blues away
  5 Blues : falling like showers of rain
  6 Every once in a while : think I hear my baby call my
    name

JohLo 3   Johnson, Lonnie

     title: Sweet Woman You Can't Go Wrong
     place and date: New York, 5 Aug. 1927
     record numbers: (81189-B) OK-8512 CC-30

  1 I'm lonesome as I can be : baby please come home to
    me
  2 Because you know I love you : and how come we can't
    agree
  3 You been gone the whole night long : I believe to my
    soul something going on wrong
  4 But there will come a day : and I know you will be
    glad to say
  5 I tried to please your mind : and you keep me
    worried all the time
  6 You will either run me crazy : or I'll lose my mind
  7 You know you don't treat me right : when you stay
    out both day and night
  8 And I must stop you now : because you got to
    consider somehow
  9 You know I love you now : and I love you all along
 10 Although you my sweet woman : and I mean you can't
    go wrong

JohLo 4   Johnson, Lonnie

     title: St. Louis Cyclone Blues
     place and date: New York, 3 Oct. 1927
     record numbers: (81503-B) OK-8512 CC-30

  1 I was sitting in my kitchen : looking way out across
    the sky
  2 I thought the world was ending : I started to cry
  3 The wind was howling : the buildings begin to fall
  4 I seen that mean old twister coming : just like a
    cannonball
  5 The world was black as midnight : I never heard such
    a noise before
  6 Sound like a million lions : when they turn loose
    their roar
  7 Poor people was screaming : and running every which
    a-way
  8 I fell down on my knees : I started in to pray
  9 The shack where we was living : she reel and rock
    but never fell

JohLo 4   Johnson, Lonnie

 10 How the cyclone spared us : nobody but the Lord can
    tell

JohLo 5   Johnson, Lonnie

     title: Life Saver Blues
     place and date: New York, 9 Nov. 1927
     record numbers: (81801-B) OK-8557 CC-30

  1 It's raining and storming on the sea : we're miles
    and miles from shore
  2 The way the waves is rocking this ship : we won't
    see home no more
  3 The wind is so strong : turning this old ship round
    and round
  4 Something tells me : won't be long before we're
    sinking down
  5 The captain say get your lifesavers : fasten them
    around your waist
  6 Because we're sinking down : and the lifeboat is
    your safest place
  7 Uncle Sam's ship was coming : painted in red white
    and blue
  8 We say we live in New York City : red white and blue
    brought us all the way through

JohLo 6   Johnson, Lonnie

     title: Blue Ghost Blues
     place and date: New York, 9 Nov. 1927
     record numbers: (81802-B) OK-8557 CC-30

  1 Mmm : I feel myself sinking down
  2 My body is freezing : I feel something cold creeping
    around
  3 My windows is rattling : my doorknob turning round
    and round
  4 This haunted house blues is killing me : I feel
    myself sinking down
  5 I been fastened in this haunted house : six long
    months today
  6 The blue ghost has got the house surrounded : Lord
    and I can't get away
  7 They got shotguns and pistols : standing all around
    my door
  8 They haunt me all night long : so I can't sleep no
    more
  9 The blue ghost haunts me all night : the nightmare
    ride me all night long
 10 They worry me so in this haunted house : I wish I
    was dead and gone

JohLo 7   Johnson, Lonnie

     title: Low Land Moan
     place and date: Chicago, 12 Dec. 1927
     record numbers: (82043-A) OK-8677 CC-30

  1 I went down to the levee : and [over, out] to the
    freight house yard
  2 They paid a dollar an hour : but the work was too
    long and hard
  3 Have pigtails in my pantry : neckbones on my shelf
  4 I ain't got none to give you : I got just enough for
    myself
  5 I'm going to buy me a shotgun : long as I am tall
  6 I'm going to shoot my woman : just to see her fall
  7 Over yonder's the river : yonder is your big lake
  8 At your house rent party : you made your last
    mistake
  9 I chew my bacca : and I spit my juice
 10 I tried to love you so hard : but I found out
    there's no use

JohLo 8   Johnson, Lonnie

    title: I'm So Tired of Living All Alone
    place and date: San Antonio, 9 Mar. 1928
    record numbers: (400447-B) OK-8677 CC-30

1 Although we are drifting : so far apart
2 My arms may be empty : have not give up in my heart
3 Although we are drifting : so far apart
4 My arms may be empty : but never down in my heart

JohLo 9   Johnson, Lonnie

    title: Way Down That Lonesome Road
    place and date: San Antonio, 13 Mar. 1928
    record numbers: (400490-A) OK-8574 CC-30

1 Look down look down : that long old lonesome road
2 And look up to the good Lord : just before you go
3 That's a long that's a long : a long old tiresome
   road
4 You'll find troubles and worries : that you never
   found before
5 Then look back look back : and see what you're
   leaving all alone
6 To grieve and worry : after the days you gone
7 Then your days begin dreary : down that long old
   lonesome road
8 And you want the Lord have mercy : how much more
   further I've got to go
9 That's a long old road : a long road that has no end
10 Then the blues will make you think : about all your
   right-hand friends

JohLo 10   Johnson, Lonnie (Victoria Spivey)

    title: New Black Snake Blues--Part 1
    place and date: New York, 13 Oct. 1928
    record numbers: (401222-A) OK-8626 Spi LP-2001

1 Something keep a-moaning : I don't know what it is
3 When my right eye winks : on my knees I begin to
   crawl
4 It will be hell to tell the captain : if I catch
   another man kicking in my stall
5 There's no use a-worrying : baby about the days
   being long
6 The black snake is got the dough : you can't roll
   him from home

JohLo 11   Johnson, Lonnie

    title: When You Fall For Someone That's Not Your
    Own
    place and date: New York, 16 Nov. 1928
    record numbers: (401336-B) OK-8635 CC-30

1 They tell me blues and trouble : walk hand in hand
2 But you ain't had no trouble : till your woman falls
   for some no-good man
3 A married woman will swear : she'll love you all her
   life
4 And meet her other man around the corner : and tell
   the same lie twice
5 You tell me you've had troubles : and worry all your
   life
6 Man but you ain't had no trouble : till you fall for
   another man's wife
7 Then if you get a woman of your own : and make her
   happy night and day
8 There will be some no-good man she'll fall for :
   pretty soon she'll go away
9 When it begin raining : and you're looking through
   your windowpane
10 And crazy about another man's wife : it's enough to
   drive you insane

JohLo 11   Johnson, Lonnie

11 But a married woman : is the sweetest woman ever was
   born
12 Only thing that hurts you : she have to go home
   sometime

JohLo 12   Johnson, Lonnie

    title: Baby Please Don't Leave Me No More
    place and date: New York, 11 June 1929
    record numbers: (402441-A) OK-8754 CC-30

1 I been lonesome all day : I've been grieving all
   night long
2 Baby please hear my plea : why don't you come back
   home
3 How many times : have I cried all night long
4 You know I must love you baby : when I beg you to
   come back home
5 I'll get a job in the coal yard : work in the rain
   and snow
6 All I ask you baby : please don't leave me no more

JohLo 13   Johnson, Lonnie

    title: Sam, You're Just a Rat
    place and date: New York, 9 Feb. 1932
    record numbers: (405141-A) OK-8937 Yz L-1028

1 Sam you say you my friend : but your ways I just
   don't like
2 Soon as I leave my home : you trying to bite me in
   my back
3 Now Sam you not my friend : and my home you better
   stop hanging around
4 Because I've paid for your coffin : and I mean that
   you graveyard bound
5 Sam if you want a woman go get one : and let my wife
   alone
6 Because if I ever catch you with my wife : you hell
   bound sure as I'm born
7 Sam a real man can live happy : but no-good men like
   you
8 You trying to wreck my family : and some other man's
   family too
9 Sam I thought you was my friend : I thought you just
   was swell
10 So I'm going to give you a vacation : that's a
   round-trip ticket to hell

JohLo 14   Johnson, Lonnie

    title: I'm Nuts About that Gal
    place and date: New York, 12 Aug. 1932
    record numbers: (152259-2) OK-8946 CC-30

1 Now she ain't good-looking : she don't dress fine
2 The way that gal can love : change any man's mind
3 Now she bake good jellyroll : she bakes it nice and
   hot
4 It never fails : to touch the spot
5 If I was sentenced to be hung : and this ain't no
   lie
6 If I could just see my baby : I would be willing to
   die
7 Now my gal is built : long and tall
8 Lord when she starts to loving : I can't help from
   to fall
9 She likes her music soft : when the lights are low
10 When she starts to kiss me : does me good down in my
   toes
11 When I met my gal : she was dumb as dumb could be
12 But I believe to my soul : she put that thing on me

JohLo 15   Johnson, Lonnie

        title: Racketeers Blues
        place and date: New York, 12 Aug. 1932
        record numbers: (152260-2) OK-8946 CC-30

1   If you got over fifteen grand : better split it
    ninety-nine different ways
2   Because the racketeers : got no certain place to dig
    your grave
3   When they demand your money : you got to give it up
    with a smile
4   And if you refuse : they'll read about you in a
    short little while
5   When the gang is out to get you : it don't do no
    good to run
6   It's true you can dodge the law : but you can't
    dodge them slugs out the machine gun
7   You [slave, work] hard for your money : just to give
    it to some other one
8   And if you refuse : the answer will be from a
    racketeer's gun
9   When the gang is out to get you : they'll follow you
    everywhere
10 You can even move to West Hell : doggone if they
    don't find you there

JohLo 16   Johnson, Lonnie

        title: Man Killing Broad
        place and date: Chicago, 8 Nov. 1937
        record numbers: (91339-A) De-7445 Sw S-1225

1   You've got a hatchet under your pillow baby : you
    got ice pick in your hand
2   The best thing you better do : is find you another
    man
3   You've got a shotgun in the corner : blackjack under
    your bed
4   But you'll never catch me asleep : I know you wants
    to whip my head
5   You put lice all in my gravy : black potash in my
    tea
6   But I fed it to your man baby : instead of me
7   That's the very reason why : you been so mean to me
8   Trying to steal my life : to have your old
    used-to-be

JohLo 17   Johnson, Lonnie

        title: Hard Time Ain't Gone No Where
        place and date: Chicago, 8 Nov. 1937
        record numbers: (91340-A) De-7388 Sw S-1225

1   People is [raving, hollering] about hard times :
    tell me what it's all about
2   Hard times don't worry me : I was broke when it
    first started out
3   Friends it could be worser : you don't seem to
    understand
4   Some is crying with a sack of gold under each arm :
    and a loaf of bread in each hand
5   If you're a single man : you better drink and have
    your fun
6   Because when that lovebug bites you : then your
    worries ain't never done
7   People raving about hard times : I don't know why
    they should
8   If some people was like me : they didn't have no
    money when times was good

JohLo 18   Johnson, Lonnie

        title: Flood Water Blues
        place and date: Chicago, 8 Nov. 1937
        record numbers: (91341-A) De-7397 Sw S-1225

1   It's been snowing forty days and nights : lakes and
    rivers begin to freeze
2   Some places through my old home town : water's up
    above my knees
3   Storm begin rising : and the sun begin sinking down
4   I says mother and dad pack your trunk : we ain't
    safe here in this town
5   When it lightning my mind gets frightened : my
    nerves begin weaken down
6   And the shack where we was living : begin moving
    around
7   Women and children were screaming : saying mama
    where must we go
8   The flood water have broke the levee : and we ain't
    safe here no more

JohLo 19   Johnson, Lonnie

        title: It Ain't What You Usta Be
        place and date: Chicago, 8 Nov. 1937
        record numbers: (91342-A) De-7427 Sw S-1225

1   You see it ain't what you used to be baby : it's
    what you are today
2   You see your good looks didn't hold your man : a
    little black gal's loving stole your man away
3   I've got a woman now that I love : better than I
    love myself
4   She treats me so cold sometimes : I think she got
    somebody else

JohLo 20   Johnson, Lonnie

        title: Something Fishy
        place and date: Chicago, 8 Nov. 1937
        record numbers: (91345-A) De-7388 Sw S-1225

1   You arms don't feel the same : your lips is icebox
    cold
2   It's a mean black snake : is making his morning
    stroll
3   You know : you once was the sweetest woman I ever
    found
4   But since you been running out with your girl friend
    : you just a plain old everyday clown

JohLo 21   Johnson, Lonnie

        title: I'm Nuts Over You
        place and date: Chicago, 8 Nov. 1937
        record numbers: (91346-A) De-7397 Sw S-1225

1   If love is a crime then I'm guilty : but there's
    nothing I can do
2   After all the good women in this world : why did I
    have to fall in love with you

JohLo 22   Johnson, Lonnie

        title: Friendless and Blue
        place and date: New York, 31 Mar. 1938
        record numbers: (63517-A) De-7487 Sw S-1225

1   Don't the world seem lonely : when you got to battle
    it all by yourself
2   Even the one you love : turn their back on you for
    someone else
3   My mother and dad left me : when I was too small to
    help myself

JohLo 22   Johnson, Lonnie

4 And my sisters and brothers : drove me away to
     somebody else
5 I'm motherless and I'm fatherless : I'm almost
     friendless too
6 Seems the world is down on you : know knows what to
     do
7 Rocks was my pillow : and the cold ground was my bed
8 The blue skies was my blanket : and the moonlight
     was my spread

JohLo 23   Johnson, Lonnie

    title: Devil's Got the Blues
    place and date: New York, 31 Mar. 1938
    record numbers: (63518-A) De-7487 Sw S-1225

1 Good morning blues : where have you been so long
2 I just stopped by to leave you enough of worries :
     to last you while I'm gone
3 My brains is cloudy : my soul is upside down
4 When I get that lowdown feeling : I know the blues
     must be somewhere close around
5 The blues is like the devil : it comes on you like a
     spell
6 Blues will leave your heart full of trouble : and
     your poor mind full of hell
7 Some people say that's no blues : but that story's
     old and stale
8 The blues will drive you to drink and murder : and
     spend the rest of your life in jail
9 The blues and the devil : is your closest friend
10 The blues will leave you with murder in your mind :
     that's when the devil out of hell steps in

JohLo 24   Johnson, Lonnie

    title: I Ain't Gonna Be Your Fool
    place and date: New York, 31 Mar. 1938
    record numbers: (63519-A) De-7509 Sw S-1225

1 I work all day long for you : until the sun go down
2 And you take all my money and drink it up : and come
     home and wants to fuss and clown
3 It hurts to love a person : that don't belong to you
4 Because when they find out that you really love them
     : and they don't care what they do
5 They'll take your heart and they'll use it : like a
     football on a football ground
6 And when they get through playing with your heart :
     and they'll start dragging you all around

JohLo 25   Johnson, Lonnie

    title: Mr. Johnson Swing
    place and date: New York, 31 Mar. 1938
    record numbers: (63520-A) De-7509 Sw S-1225

1 Want all of you people to listen : while my guitar
     sings
2 If you ain't got that rhythm : it don't mean a thing
3 Some people thinks I'm dead : because I've been gone
     so long
4 I just stop to see : would you miss me from singing
     these lonesome songs
5 I want all you people to listen : while I swing this
     song
6 If you were born with that rhythm : honest you can't
     never go wrong

JohLo 26   Johnson, Lonnie

    title: New Falling Rain Blues
    place and date: New York, 31 Mar. 1938
    record numbers: (63521-A) De-7461 Sw S-1225

1 Storm is rising : and the rain begin to fall
2 Trouble is breaking down my window : blues breaking
     down my door
3 My blues started at sunrise : and rides me all
     through the day
4 It takes the sweet woman I love : to drive these
     blues away
5 Come into my arms sweet woman : and please explain
     yourself to me
6 Tell me who do you really want : or do you still
     want your used-to-be
7 Because sometimes you with me : baby then again you
     gone
8 If you want your used-to-be : then you better let me
     alone
9 Blues : falling like showers of rain
10 Every once in a while : I can hear my baby call my
     name

JohLo 27   Johnson, Lonnie

    title: Laplegged Drunk Again
    place and date: New York, 31 Mar. 1938
    record numbers: (63522-A) De-7537 Sw S-1225

1 I've been drinking all night long : I've started
     again today
2 I been trying my best : to drink these worried blues
     away
3 Some people drinks to hide their [worries and]
     troubles : but that don't mean a thing
4 When you think your troubles are gone : and you find
     yourself drunk again
5 Friends I drink to keep from worrying : I smile to
     keep from crying
6 That's why I cover my troubles : so the public don't
     know what's on my mind
7 I said I was through with love : both whiskey wine
     and gin
8 You know when I found myself : I was lap-legged
     drunk again
9 Love will make a-many man drink and gamble : and
     stay out all night long
10 Love will drive you to many places : sometimes where
     you don't belong

JohLo 28   Johnson, Lonnie

    title: Blue Ghost Blues
    place and date: New York, 31 Mar. 1938
    record numbers: (63523-A) De-7537 AH-158

1 Mmm : something cold is creeping around
2 Blue ghost has got me : I feel myself sinking down
3 Black cat and an owl : come to keep me company
4 They understands my troubles : mmm and sympathize
     with me
5 I been in this haunted house : for three long years
     today
6 Blue ghost has got my shack surrounded : oh Lord and
     I can't get away
7 I feel cold arms around me : and ice lips upon my
     cheek
8 My lover is dead : how plainly plainly I can hear
     her speak
9 My windows begin rattling : and my doorknob is
     turning around and around
10 My lover's ghost has got me : and I know my time
     won't be long

JohLo 29   Johnson, Lonnie

    title: South Bound Backwater
    place and date: New York, 31 Mar. 1938
    record numbers: (63524-A) De-7461 Sw S-1225

1 It's been snowing forty days : and the ground is
   covered with snow
2 I'm snow-bound in my cabin : and ice up around my
   door
3 I woke up this morning : couldn't even get out my
   door
4 I was snowbound in my cabin : had water seeping up
   through my floor
5 Snow begin melting : and the rain begin to fall
6 The backwaters done broke the levee : and I can't
   stay here no more
7 Rowed my boat : just about four miles across the
   pond
8 Backwater done wrecked my cabin : and there's no
   place that I can call my home

JohLo 30   Johnson, Lonnie

    title: Crowin' Rooster Blues
    place and date: Chicago, 7 Feb. 1941
    record numbers: (059205-1) BB-B8804 RCA LPV-518

1 What makes the rooster : crow every morning before
   day
2 To let the pimps know : that the workingman is on
   his way
3 We're up before sunrise : slaving sixteen hours a
   day
4 We pay our house rent and grocery bills : and the
   pimps get the rest of our pay
5 Men can't you see : you can't keep a whole woman by
   yourself
6 If your best friend can't get your woman : he'll
   frame her for somebody else
7 Something about some women : that I never could
   understand
8 They're not satisfied with a good husband : they
   want some other woman's man

JohLs 1   Johnson, Louise

    title: All Night Long Blues
    place and date: Grafton, Wis., 28 May 1930
    record numbers: (L-398-1) Pm-12992 OJL-11

1 I woke up this morning : blues all around my bed
2 I never had no good man : I mean to ease my aching
   head
3 Well : pretty near all night long
4 Well I swear before God : the man I'm loving is
   doing wrong
5 Well I'm going away : swear the time ain't long
6 If you don't believe I'm leaving daddy : count them
   days I'm gone
7 You done caused me to weep baby : and I swear you
   done caused me to moan
8 Well you know by that rider : that I ain't going to
   be here long
9 Well : what evil have I done
10 Well it must be something : my man have heard before
   he gone
11 Lord I'm going to get drunk : and I'm going to walk
   the streets all night
12 Because the man that I'm loving : I swear he sure
   don't treat me right

JohLs 2   Johnson, Louise

    title: Long Way from Home
    place and date: Grafton, Wis., 28 May 1930
    record numbers: (L-399-2) Pm-12992 OJL-11

1 Lord I woke up this morning : blues all around my
   bed
2 I never had no good man : I mean to ease my worried
   head
3 Now now now now now : I cried like a newborn child
4 Lord even when I was a baby : I wasn't satisfied
5 Well I'm going I'm going : daddy to wear you off my
   mind
6 Because you keeps me worried baby : and troubled all
   the time
7 I said Lord have mercy : I mean Lord have mercy on
   me
8 I said Lord have mercy : mercy's all I need
9 Lord ??? : and I fell down on my knees
10 Well I done cried I cried : Lord have mercy on me

JohLs 3   Johnson, Louise

    title: On the Wall
    place and date: Grafton, Wis., 28 May 1930
    record numbers: (L-419-1) Pm-13008 Yz L-1028

1 Well I'm going to Memphis : come to stop at
   Cincinnat'
2 I'm going to tell you women : how to treat a man
3 I said now you ain't good-looking : and you don't
   dress fine
4 That kind of treatment : make me ??? you most any
   old time
5 Well I'm going to Memphis : stop at *Satches* hall
6 Going to tell you women : how to cock it on the wall
7 Now you can snatch it you can break it : you can
   hang it on the wall
8 Throw it out the window : see if you catch it before
   it fall
9 Well I'm going to leave here :

JohLs 4   Johnson, Louise

    title: By the Moon and Stars
    place and date: Grafton, Wis., 28 May 1930
    record numbers: (L-420-2) Pm-13008 Mil MLP-2018

1 ??? : I saw the moon go down
2 And I swear my man must be somewhere : turning
   around and around
3 I say the big star are falling : it don't be long
   before day
4 The moon *want* my baby : ??? mighty far away
5 I'm going to wake up : between midnight and day
6 You going to ??? *my need* baby : and I swear I'll
   be gone away
7 Now won't you come here baby : sit down on my knee
8 Now I just want to tell you : black man how you have
   treated me

JohM 1   Johnson, Margaret

    title: If I Let You Get Away With It Once
    You'll Do It All of the Time
    place and date: New York, 19 Oct. 1923
    record numbers: (71972-B) OK-8107 Sw S-1240

1 You said you's going to leave me : but I don't care
2 You thought the way I treated you : wasn't fair
3 You went and told somebody : you thought I wouldn't
   do
4 But if you think you'll get away with it : I'll sing
   this verse to you

JohM   1   Johnson, Margaret

5   Because if I let you get away with it once : you'll
    do it all the time
6   Now if you think I'm going crazy about you : you'd
    better change your mind
7   You promised me once : you wouldn't cheat anymore
8   But had a dozen keys : to fit my back door
9   You crept away : to see a movie show today
10 But when you came home : you didn't know the name of
    the play

JohM   2   Johnson, Margaret

    title: When a 'Gator Holler, Folk Say
      It's a Sign of Rain
    place and date: New York, 20 Oct. 1926
    record numbers: (36846-1) Vi-20333 Fwy FJ-2801

1   Blow whistle : my stomach say it's eating time
2   My appetite is worth a million : and just got a
    measly dime
3   It's Saturday night : and I'm higher than a Georgia
    pine
4   One more drink of corn : and I'll leave my Georgia
    mind
5   When a gator holler : folks say it's a sign of rain
6   The weather's getting cloudy Lord : how these
    birdies sing

JohMa   1   Johnson, Mary

    title: Barrel House Flat Blues
    place and date: Grafton, Wis., c. Feb. 1930
    record numbers: (L-176-2) Pm-12996 CC-37

1   I got a barrelhouse flat in *Eastport* : and one I
    St Louis too
2   But my barrelhouse flat in *Eastport* : really get
    my ???
3   I'm going to build me a barrelhouse flat : way out
    on Dago Hill
4   Where I can get my beer and whiskey : and it's fresh
    from the still
5   I got a barrelhouse flat in Chicago : it's fifteen
    stories high
6   I get all of these high yellows : and play these
    crazy dice
7   Those ??? like my good whiskey : and they drink my
    cherry wine
8   If you women want a good time : stop by this
    barrelhouse flat of mine

JohMa   2   Johnson, Mary

    title: Key to the Mountain Blues
    place and date: Grafton, Wis., c. Feb. 1930
    record numbers: (L-177-3) Pm-12996 Jo SM-3098

1   My man's in the mountain : and I've got the mountain
    key
2   If you want to see my man : you got to come to me
3   Mmm he was my man : before you women ever knew his
    name
4   And you know by that : you got to see me just the
    same
5   If you women wants a good man : find one of your own
6   For this man is my man : I want you women to leave
    my man alone
7   Now I have no place : for you women you see
8   Oh my man's in the mountain : and I've got the
    mountain key

JohMa   3   Johnson, Mary

    title: Rattlesnake Blues
    place and date: Richmond, Ind., 22 Sept. 1932
    record numbers: (18791) Ch-16570 Riv RM-8819

1   Rattlesnake treating papa : what makes you treat
    your mama so mean
2   You know that your mama loves you : that's why you
    treat me like you do
3   You treats me like a rattlesnake : crawling on the
    ground
4   The better I try to treat you : the more you throw
    your mama down
5   Ah that's all right : daddy that's all right for you
6   Some day you'll want poor Mary : and she'll be
    somewhere from you
7   Oh rattlesnake crawling daddy : you know you doing
    me wrong
8   I'm looking for you baby : and you crawling around
    some other person's home
9   You dog me all in the morning : and dog me late at
    night
10 And I can tell by that : you ain't treating your
    mama right

JohMa   4   Johnson, Mary

    title: Mary Johnson Blues
    place and date: Richmond, Ind., 22 Sept. 1932
    record numbers: (18792) Ch-16570 Riv RM-8819

1   I once was a married woman : sorry the day I ever
    was
2   I was a young girl at home : and I did not know the
    world
3   I'd rather be an old maid : than to be worried and
    blue each and every day
4   Because these worrisome old men : will cause your
    head to turn white and grey
5   Babe you caused me to leave my happy home : and you
    caused me to weep and moan
6   That is why babe : this bad luck's taking place
    today
7   I was just sitting here thinking : baby just a
    minute ago
8   I once was a married woman : sorry the day I ever
    was

JohR   1   Johnson, Robert

    title: Kind Hearted Woman Blues
    place and date: San Antonio, 23 Nov. 1936
    record numbers: (SA-2580-1) ARC unissued
      Co CL-1654

1   I got a kind-hearted woman : do anything in this
    world for me
2   But these evil-hearted women : man they will not let
    me be
3   I love my baby : my baby don't love me
4   But I really love that woman : can't stand to leave
    her be
5   Now ain't but the one thing : makes Mr Johnson drink
6   That's worry about how you treat me baby : I begin
    to think
7   Oh babe : my life don't feel the same
8   You breaks my heart : when you call Mr so-and-so's
    name
9   She's a kind-hearted woman : she studies evil all
    the time
10 You have to kill me : just to have it on your mind

JohR   2   Johnson, Robert

    title: Kind Hearted Woman Blues
    place and date: San Antonio, 23 Nov. 1936
    record numbers: (SA-2580-2) ARC-7-03-56 Co
    C-30034

1   I got a kind-hearted mama : do anything in this
    world for me
2   But these evil-hearted women : man they will not let
    me be
3   I love my baby : and my baby don't love me
4   I really love that woman : can't stand to leave her
    be
5   Now it ain't but one thing : make Mr Johnson drink
6   I get worried about how you treat me baby : I begin
    to think
7   Oh babe : my life don't feel the same
8   You breaks my heart : when you call Mr so-and-so's
    name
9   She's a kind-hearted [mama, woman] : [but she]
    studies evil all the time
10 You have to kill me baby : just to have it on your
    mind
11 Some day some day : I will shake your hand goodbye
12 I can't give any more of my loving : because I just
    ain't satisfied

JohR   3   Johnson, Robert

    title: I Believe I'll Dust My Broom
    place and date: San Antonio, 23 Nov. 1936
    record numbers: (SA-2581-1) ARC-7-04-81 Co
    C-30034

1   I'm going to get up in the morning : I believe I'll
    dust my broom
2   Because then the black man you been loving : girl
    friend can get my room
3   I'm going to write a letter : telephone every town I
    know
4   If I can't find her in West Selma : she must be in
    East Monroe I know
5   I don't want no woman : wants every downtown man she
    meet
6   She's a no-good dony : they shouldn't allow her on
    the street
7   I believe : I believe I'll go back home
8   If you mistreat me here babe : but you can't when I
    go home
9   I'm going to call up China : see is my good girl
    over there
10 If I can't find her on Philippines Island : she must
    be in Ethiopia somewhere

JohR   4   Johnson, Robert

    title: Sweet Home Chicago
    place and date: San Antonio, 23 Nov. 1936
    record numbers: (SA-2582-) Vo-03601 OJL-17

1   Ooh : baby don't you want to go
2   Back to the land of California : to my sweet home
    Chicago
3   Now one and one is two : three and two is four
4   I'm heavy loaded baby : I'm booked I've got to go
5   Now two and two is four : four and two is six
6   You going to keep on monkeying around here *pin boy*
    : you going to get your ??? in a fix
7   Now six and two is eight : eight and two is ten
8   His wife get tricky one time : she sure going to do
    it again
9   I'm going to California : *some passing in my byway*
10 Somebody will tell me : that you need my help some
    day

JohR   5   Johnson, Robert

    title: Ramblin' On My Mind
    place and date: San Antonio, 23 Nov. 1936
    record numbers: (SA-2583-1) ARC-7-05-81 Co
    C-30034

1   I got rambling : I got rambling [all] on my mind
2   Hate to leave my baby : but she treats me so unkind
3   Running down to the station : catch [that old, the]
    first mail train I see
4   I got the blues about Miss so-and-so : and the child
    got the blues about me
5   And I'm leaving this morning : with my arms folded
    up and crying
6   I hate to leave my baby : but she treats me so
    unkind
7   I got mean things : I got mean things [all] on my
    mind
8   I got to leave my baby : but she treats me so unkind

JohR   6   Johnson, Robert

    title: Ramblin' On My Mind
    place and date: San Antonio, 23 Nov. 1936
    record numbers: (SA-2583-2) ARC-7-05-81 Co
    CL-1654

1   I got rambling : I got rambling [all] on my mind
2   Hate to leave my baby : but she treats me so unkind
3   Running down to the station : catch [that old, the]
    first mail train I see
4   I got the blues about Miss so-and-so : and the child
    got the blues about me
5   And I'm leaving this morning : with my arms folded
    up and crying
6   I hate to leave my baby : but she treats me so
    unkind
7   I got mean things : I got mean things [all] on my
    mind
8   I got to leave my baby : but she treats me so unkind

JohR   7   Johnson, Robert

    title: When You Get a Good Friend
    place and date: San Antonio, 23 Nov. 1936
    record numbers: (SA-2584-1) ARC unissued Co
    CL-1654

1   When you got a good friend : have her stay right by
    your side
2   Give her all of your spare time : love and treat her
    right
3   I mistreated my baby : [but, and] I can't see no
    reason why
4   Any time I think about it : I just wring my hands
    and cry
5   Wonder could I ever apologize : or will she
    fisty-fight with me
6   She's a brownskin woman : just as sweet as a girl
    friend can be
7   Baby *do you think it mmm* : oh I may be right or
    wrong
8   Got you a close friend baby : then your enemies
    can't do you no harm

JohR   8   Johnson, Robert

    title: Come On in My Kitchen
    place and date: San Antonio, 23 Nov. 1936
    record numbers: (SA-2585-1) ARC unissued Co
    CL-1654

1   Mmm : mmm
2   You better come on in my kitchen : well it's going
    to be raining outdoors

JohR   8   Johnson, Robert

3   The woman I love : took from my best friend
4   Some joker got lucky : stoled her back again
5   Oh oh she's gone : I know she won't come back
6   I taken her last nickel : out of her nation sack
7   When a woman gets in trouble : everybody throws her
    down
8   Looking for her good friends : none can be found
9   And the time coming : it's going to be so
10 You can't make the winter babe : just dry long so

JohR   9   Johnson, Robert

    title: Terraplane Blues
    place and date: San Antonio, 23 Nov. 1936
    record numbers: (SA-2586-1) ARC-7-03-56 Co
    CL-1654

1   Well I feel so lonesome : you hear me when I moan
2   Who's been driving my terraplane for you : since
    I've been gone
3   I said I flashed your lights mama : your horn won't
    even blow
4   Got a short in this connection : hoo well babe and
    it's way down below
5   I'm going heist your hood mama : I'm bound to check
    your oil
6   I got a woman that I'm loving : way down in Arkansas
7   Now you know the coils ain't even buzzing : little
    generator won't get the spark
8   Motor's in a bad condition : you got to have these
    batteries charged
9   I'm crying please : please don't do me wrong
10 Who's been driving my terraplane : now for you since
    I've been gone
11 Mr highwayman : please don't block the road
12 Because she's registering a cold one hundred : and
    I'm booked till I got to go
13 Eee : you can hear me weep and moan
14 Who's been driving my terraplane now for you : since
    I've been gone
15 I'm going to get deep down in this connection : keep
    on tangling with your wires
16 And when I mash down on your little starter : then
    your spark plug will give me fire

JohR   10   Johnson, Robert

    title: Phonograph Blues
    place and date: San Antonio, 23 Nov. 1936
    record numbers: (SA-2587-2) ARC unissued Co
    C-30034

1   Yeah but she got a phonograph : but it won't say a
    lonesome word
2   What evil have I done : what evil has the poor girl
    heard
3   Yeah but I love my phonograph : but she have broke
    my winding chain
4   And you've taken my loving : and given it to your
    other man
5   Now we played it on the sofa now : we played it side
    the wall
6   My needles have got rusty baby : it will now play at
    all
7   Yeah but if I go crazy : baby I will lose my mind
8   I can bring your clothes back home : and try me one
    more time

JohR   11   Johnson, Robert

    title: 32-20 Blues
    place and date: San Antonio, 26 Nov. 1936
    record numbers: (SA-2616-1) ARC-7-04-60 Co
    CL-1654

1   If I send for my baby : and she don't come
2   All the doctors in [Hot Springs, Westmount] : sure
    can't help her none
3   And if she gets unruly : things she don't want to do
4   Take my thirty-two twenty : and I can cut her half
    in two
5   She got a thirty-eight special : but I believe it's
    most too light
6   I got a thirty-two twenty : got to make the camps
    all right
7   I'm going to shoot my pistol : going to shoot my
    gatling gun
8   You made me love you : now your man done come
9   Ooh : baby where you stay last night
10 You got your hair all tangled : and you ain't
    talking right
11 Her thirty-eight special boys : it do very well
12 I got a thirty-two twenty : now it's a burning hell
13 Hey hey : baby where you stay last night
14 You didn't come home : till the sun was shining
    bright
15 Ooh : boys I just can't take my rest
16 With this thirty-two twenty : laying up and down my
    breast

JohR   12   Johnson, Robert

    title: They're Red Hot
    place and date: San Antonio, 27 Nov. 1936
    record numbers: (SA-2627-1) ARC-7-07-57 Co
    C-30034

1   I got a girl : said she's long and tall
2   She sleeps in the kitchen : with her feets in the
    hall
3   She got two for a nickel : got four for a dime
4   It's worth paying more : but they ain't none of mine
5   I got a letter : from my girl in the room
6   Now she got something good : she got to bring it
    home soon
7   The billygoat backed : in the bumblebee's nest
8   Ever since that : he can't take his rest
9   I'm going to hump in your back : going to put your
    kidneys to sleep
10 I due to break away your liver : and tear your heart
    to piece
11 You know grandma left me : now grandpa too
12 Well I wonder what in the world : we children going
    to do
13 Me and my baby : bought a V-Eight Ford
14 Well they ride that thing : all on the running board
15 You know the monkey now the baboon : playing in the
    grass
16 Well the monkey said to *fatto* : *good luck gas*

JohR   13   Johnson, Robert

    title: Dead Shrimp Blues
    place and date: San Antonio, 27 Nov. 1936
    record numbers: (SA-2628-2) ARC-7-04-81 Co
    C-30034

1   I woke up this morning : and all my shrimps was dead
    and gone
2   I was thinking about you baby : will you hear me
    weep and moan
3   I got dead shrimps here : someone is fishing in my
    pond
4   I've sold you my best bait baby : and I can't do
    that no more

147

JohR 13   Johnson, Robert

5 Everything I do baby : you got your mouth stuck out
6 Hole where I used to fish : you got me forced out
7 I got dead shrimps here : someone's fishing in my
   pond
8 Catching my goggle-eyed perches : and they
   barbecuing the bones
9 Now you taken my shrimp baby : you know you turned
   me down
10 I couldn't do nothing : until I got myself unwound

JohR 14   Johnson, Robert

        title: Cross Road Blues
        place and date: San Antonio, 27 Nov. 1936
        record numbers: (SA-2629-2) ARC unissued Co
        CL-1654

1 I went to the crossroads : fell down on my knees
2 Asked the Lord above have mercy : save poor Bob if
   you please
3 Mmm standing at the crossroads : I tried to flag a
   ride
4 Didn't nobody seem to know me : everybody passed me
   by
5 Mmm the sun going down boys : not going to catch me
   here
6 I haven't got no loving sweet woman : but not to
   feel my care
7 You can run you can run : tell my friend boy Willie
   Brown
8 Lord that I'm standing at the crossroad baby : I
   believe I'm sinking down

JohR 15   Johnson, Robert

        title: Walkin' Blues
        place and date: San Antonio, 27 Nov. 1936
        record numbers: (SA-2630-1) Vo-03601 Co CL-1654

1 I woke up this morning : feeling around for my shoes
2 Know by that : I got these old walking blues
3 Lord I feel like blowing : my poor lonesome horn
4 Got up this morning : my little Berniece was gone
5 Lord I feel like blow : my lonesome horn
6 Well I got up this morning : all I had was gone
7 Well leaving this morning : if I have to oh ride the
   blinds
8 I feel mistreated : and I don't mind dying
9 Leaving this morning : I have to ride the blinds
10 Babe I been mistreated : baby and I don't mind dying
11 Well some people tell me : that the worried blues
   ain't bad
12 Worst old feeling : I most ever had
13 She's got Elgin movements : from her head down to
   her toes
14 Break in on a dollar : most anywhere she goes

JohR 16   Johnson, Robert

        title: Last Fair Deal Gone Down
        place and date: San Antonio, 27 Nov. 1936
        record numbers: (SA-2631-1) ARC-7-04-60 Co
        CL-1654

1 If you cry about a nickel : you die about a dime
2 She wouldn't cry : but the money ain't mine

JohR 17   Johnson, Robert

        title: Preachin' Blues
        place and date: San Antonio, 27 Nov. 1936
        record numbers: (SA-2632-1) ARC-7-04-60 Co
        C-30034

1 I got up this morning : the blues walking like a man
2 Worried blues : give me your right hand
3 Blues grabbed mama's child : and it tore me all
   upside down
4 Travel on poor Bob : just can't turn you around
5 The blues : is a lowdown shaking chill
6 You ain't never had them : I hope you never will
7 Well the blues : is a aching old heart disease
8 Like consumption : killing me by degrees
9 Now if it's starting a-raining : I'm going to drive
   my blues away
10 Going to the ??? : stay out there all day

JohR 18   Johnson, Robert

        title: Preachin' Blues
        place and date: San Antonio, 27 Nov. 1936
        record numbers: (SA-2632-2) ARC-7-04-60 Co
        C-30034

1 I got up this morning : the blues walking like a man
2 Worried blues : give me your right hand
3 Blues grabbed mama's child : and it tore me all
   upside down
4 Travel on poor Bob : just can't turn you around
5 The blues : is a lowdown shaking chill
6 You ain't never had them : I hope you never will
7 Well the blues : is a aching old heart disease
8 Like consumption : killing me by degrees
9 Now if it's starting a-raining : I'm going to drive
   my blues away
10 Going to the ??? : stay out there all day

JohR 19   Johnson, Robert

        title: If I Had Possession Over Judgment Day
        place and date: San Antonio, 27 Nov. 1936
        record numbers: (SA-2633-1) ARC unissued Co
        CL-1654

1 If I had possession : over Judgment Day
2 Lord the little woman I'm loving : wouldn't have no
   right to pray
3 I went to the mountain : look as far as my eyes
   could see
4 Saw where the man got my woman : and lonesome blues
   got me
5 And I rolled and I tumbled : and I cried the whole
   night long
6 When I woke up this morning : my biscuit-roller's
   gone
7 Had to fold my arms : and I slowly walked away
8 I said in my mind : your trouble going to come some
   day
9 Now run here baby : set down on my knee
10 I want to tell you : all about the way they treated
   me

JohR 20   Johnson, Robert

        title: Stone in My Passway
        place and date: Dallas, 19 June 1937
        record numbers: (DAL-377-2) ARC-7-12-67 Co
        CL-1654

1 I got stones in my passway : and my road seem dark
   as night
2 I have pains in my heart : they have taken my
   appetite

148

JohR 20   Johnson, Robert

3 I have a bird to whistle : and I have a bird to sing
4 I got a woman that I'm loving : boy but she don't
   mean a thing
5 My innocence betrayed me : have overtaken poor Bob
   at last
6 And that's one thing certain : they have stones all
   in my pass
7 Now you trying to take my life : and all my loving
   too
8 You laid a passway for me : now what are you trying
   to do
9 I'm crying please : please let us be friends
10 And when you hear me howling in my passway rider :
   please open your door and let me in
11 I got three legs to truck on : boys please don't
   block my road
12 I been feeling ashamed about my rider : babe I'm
   booked and I got to go

JohR 21   Johnson, Robert

     title: I'm a Steady Rollin Man
     place and date: Dallas, 19 June 1937
     record numbers: (DAL-378-) ARC-7-12-67 OJL-17

1 I'm a steady rolling man : I roll both night and day
2 But I haven't got no sweet woman : mmm boys to be
   rolling this a-way
3 I'm the man that rolls : when icicles hanging on the
   tree
4 And now you hear me howling : baby mmm down on my
   bended knee
5 I am a hard-working man : have been for many years I
   know
6 And some cream puff's using my money : ooo well well
   babe but that'll never be no more
7 You can't give your sweet woman : everything she
   wants in one time
8 Well boys she get rambling in her brain : mmm some
   other man on her mind

JohR 22   Johnson, Robert

     title: From Four Until Late
     place and date: Dallas, 19 June 1937
     record numbers: (DAL-379-1) ARC-7-09-56 Co
     C-30034

1 From four until late : I was wringing my hands and
   crying
2 I believe to my soul : that your daddy's going fall
   down
3 From Memphis to Norfolk : is a thirty-six hour's
   ride
4 A man is like a prisoner : and he's never satisfied
5 A woman is like a dresser : with a man always
   rambling through its drawers
6 It caused so many men : wear an apron overall
7 From four until late : she give us a no-good
   bunching clown
8 Now she won't do nothing : but tear a good man's
   reputation down
9 When I leave this town : I'm going to bid you fare
   farewell
10 And when I return again : you'll have a great long
   story to tell

JohR 23   Johnson, Robert

     title: Hell Hound on My Trail
     place and date: Dallas, 20 June 1937
     record numbers: (DAL-394-2) ARC-7-09-56 Co
     CL-1654

1 I've got to keep moving : blues falling down like
   hail
2 And the days keep on worrying me : there's a
   hellhound on my trail
3 If today was Christmas Eve : and tomorrow was
   Christmas Day
4 All I would need my little sweet rider : just to
   pass the time away
5 You sprinkled hot-foot powder : mmm around my door
6 It keeps me with a rambling mind rider : every old
   place I go
7 I can tell the wind is rising : the leaves trembling
   on the trees
8 All I need my little sweet woman : and to keep my
   company

JohR 24   Johnson, Robert

     title: Little Queen of Spades
     place and date: Dallas, 20 June 1937
     record numbers: (DAL-395-?) Vo-04108 Co C-30034

1 Mmm she is a little queen of spades : and the men
   will not let her be
2 Every time she makes a spread : a cold chill runs
   all over me
3 Well I'm going to get me a gambling woman : the last
   thing that I do
4 A man don't need a woman : ooo fair brown he got to
   give all of his money to
5 And everybody say she got a mojo : [because she,
   baby you] been using that stuff
6 She got a way trimmering down : ooo well babe and I
   mean it's most too tough
7 Well well little girl says I'm the king : fair brown
   and you is the queen
8 Let's we put our heads together : ooo fair brown
   then we can make our money green

JohR 25   Johnson, Robert

     title: Little Queen of Spades
     place and date: Dallas, 20 June 1937
     record numbers: (DAL-395-?) Vo-04108 His HLP-31

1 Now she is a little queen of spades : and the men
   will not let her be
2 Every time she makes a spread : ooo fair brown cold
   chills just runs all over me
3 I'm going to get me a gambling woman : if the last
   thing that I do
4 Well a man don't need a woman : ooo fair brown that
   he got to give all his money to
5 Everybody says she got a mojo : [because, now] she's
   been using that stuff
6 Says she got a way of trimming it down : ooo fair
   brown and I mean it's most too tough
7 Now little girl say I'm the king : baby and you is
   the queen
8 Let's us put our heads together : ooo fair brown
   then we can make our money green

JohR 26   Johnson, Robert

    title: Malted Milk
    place and date: Dallas, 20 June 1937
    record numbers: (DAL-396-1) ARC-7-10-65 Co
    C-30034

1 I keep drinking malted milk : trying to drink my
   blues away
2 Baby you just as welcome to my loving : as the
   flowers is in may
3 Malted milk malted milk : keep rushing to my head
4 And I have a funny funny feeling : that I'm talking
   all out my head
5 Baby fix me one more drink : and hug your daddy one
   more time
6 Keep on spilling my malted milk mama : until I
   change my mind
7 My doorknob keeps on turning : it must be spooks
   around my bed
8 I have a warm old feeling : and the hair rising on
   my head

JohR 27   Johnson, Robert

    title: Drunken Hearted Man
    place and date: Dallas, 20 June 1937
    record numbers: (DAL-397-1) ARC unissued Co
    C-30034

1 I'm a [poor] drunken-hearted man : my life seems so
   misery
2 And if I could only change my way of living : it
   would mean so much to me
3 I've been drunk and I've been driven : ever since I
   left my mother's home
4 And I can't see the reason why : that I can't leave
   these no-good womens alone
5 My poor father died and left me : and my mother done
   the best that she could
6 Every man loves that game you call love : but it
   don't mean no man no good
7 I'm a poor drunken-hearted man : and sin was the
   cause of it all
8 But the day you get weak for no-good women : that's
   the day that you surely fall

JohR 28   Johnson, Robert

    title: Drunken Hearted Man
    place and date: Dallas, 20 June 1937
    record numbers: (DAL-397-2) ARC unissued Rt
    RL-314

1 I'm a [poor] drunken-hearted man : my life seems so
   misery
2 And if I could only change my way of living : it
   would mean so much to me
3 I've been dogged and I've been driven : ever since I
   left my mother's home
4 And I can't see the reason why : that I can't leave
   these no-good womens alone
5 My poor father died and left me : and my mother done
   the best that she could
6 Every man loves that game you call love : but it
   don't mean no man no good
7 I'm the poor drunken-hearted man : and sin was the
   cause of it all
8 But the way you get weak for no-good women : that's
   the day that you surely fall

JohR 29   Johnson, Robert

    title: Me and the Devil Blues
    place and date: Dallas, 20 June 1937
    record numbers: (DAL-398-2) ARC unissued Co
    CL-1654

1 Early this morning : when you knocked upon my door
2 And I said hello Satan : I believe it's time to go
3 Me and the devil : was walking side by side
4 I'm going to beat my woman : until I get satisfied
5 She said you knows the way : that I always dog her
   around
6 It must've be that old evil spirit : so deep down in
   the ground
7 You may bury my body : down by the highway side
8 So my old evil spirit : can get a Greyhound bus and
   ride

JohR 30   Johnson, Robert

    title: Stop Breakin' Down Blues
    place and date: Dallas, 20 June 1937
    record numbers: (DAL-399-1) Vo-04002 Co C-30034

1 Every time I'm walking : down the street
2 Some pretty mama : starts breaking down with me
3 Stop breaking down : yeah stop breaking down
4 The stuff I got about you breaking down : ooo it
   will make you lose your mind
5 I can't walk the streets : nor com- *compelate* my
   mind
6 Some no-good woman : she starts breaking down
7 Now you Saturday night women : you love to ape and
   clown
8 You won't do nothing : but tear a good man's
   reputation down
9 Now I gave my baby now : the ninety-nine degree
10 She jumped up : and throwed a pistol down on me
11 I can't start walking : down the street
12 When some pretty mama : starts breaking down on me

JohR 31   Johnson, Robert

    title: Traveling Riverside Blues
    place and date: Dallas, 20 June 1937
    record numbers: (DAL-400-2) ARC unissued Co
    CL-1654

1 If your man gets personal : want to have your fun
2 Just come on back to Friar's Point mama : and
   barrelhouse all night long
3 I've got womens in Vicksburg : clean on into
   Tennessee
4 But my Friar's point rider now : hops all over me
5 I ain't going to state no color : but her front
   teeth crowned with gold
6 She got a mortgage on my body : and a lien on my
   soul
7 Lord I'm going to Rosedale : going to take my rider
   by my side
8 We can still barrelhouse baby : because it's on the
   riverside

JohR 32   Johnson, Robert

    title: Honeymoon Blues
    place and date: Dallas, 20 June 1937
    record numbers: (DAL-401-) Vo-04002 Co C-30034

1 Betty Mae Betty Mae : you shall be my wife some day
2 I wants a little sweet girl : that will do anything
   that I say
3 Betty Mae you is my heart-strings : you is my
   destiny

JohR   32   Johnson, Robert

4   And you rode across my mind : baby each and every
    day
5   Little girl little girl : my life seems so misery
6   Baby I guess it must be love now : ooo Lord that's
    taken effect on me
7   Some day I will return : with a marriage license in
    my hand
8   I'm going to take you for a honeymoon : in some long
    long distant land

JohR   33   Johnson, Robert

        title: Love in Vain
        place and date: Dallas, 20 June 1937
        record numbers: (DAL-402-?) Vo-04630 Co C-30034

1   And I followed her to the station : with a suitcase
    in my hand
2   Well it's hard to tell it's hard to tell : when all
    your love's in vain
3   When the train rolled up to the station : I looked
    her in the eye
4   Well I was lonesome I felt so lonesome : and I could
    not help but cry
5   The train it left the station : with two lights on
    behind
6   Well the blue light was my blues : and the red light
    was my mind

JohR   34   Johnson, Robert

        title: Love in Vain
        place and date: Dallas, 20 June 1937
        record numbers: (DAL-402-?) Vo-04630 His HLP-31

1   I followed her to the station : with my suitcase in
    my hand
2   Well it's hard to tell it's hard to tell : when all
    your love's in vain
3   When the train rolled up to the station : and I
    looked her in the eye
4   Well I felt so lonesome I was lonesome : and I could
    not help but cry
5   When the train it left the station : with two lights
    on behind
6   Well the blue light was my blues : and the red light
    was my mind

JohR   35   Johnson, Robert

        title: Milkcow's Calf Blues
        place and date: Dallas, 20 June 1937
        record numbers: (DAL-403-2) ARC-7-10-65 Yz
        L-1026

1   Tell me milkcow : what on earth is wrong with you
2   Well well you have a new calf : ooo and your milk is
    turning blue
3   Your calf is hungry : and I believe he needs a suck
4   Well now but your milk is turning blue : ooo and I
    believe he's out of luck
5   Now I feel like milking : and my cow won't come
6   I feel like churning : and my milk won't turn
7   I'm crying please : please don't do me wrong
8   You can give right milk and butter now baby : who
    will stay at home
9   My milkcow been rambling : ooo wee for miles around
10 She been suckling some other bullcow : ooo Lord in a
    strange man's town

JohR   36   Johnson, Robert

        title: Milkcow's Calf Blues
        place and date: Dallas, 20 June 1937
        record numbers: (DAL-403-3) ARC unissued Co
        CL-1654

1   Tell me milkcow : what on earth is wrong with you
2   Now you have a little new calf : ooo and your milk
    is turning blue
3   Now your calf is hungry : I believe he needs a suck
4   But your milk is turning blue : ooo I believe he's
    out of luck
5   Now I feel like milking : and my cow won't come
6   I feel like churning : and my milk won't turn
7   I'm crying please : please don't do me wrong
8   If you see my milkcow baby now : please drive her
    home
9   My milkcow been rambling : ooo wee for miles around
10 Now she been suckling some other man's bullcow : ooo
    in a strange man's town

JohT   1   Johnson, T. C.

        title: J. C. Johnson's Blues
        place and date: Memphis, 16 Feb. 1928
        record numbers: (400250-B) OK-8838 Rt RL-316

1   I was born in the state : of old Arkansas
2   Where they don't allow : no Mississippi women there
    at all
3   I'm going I'm going : back to my old home to stay
4   And you'll find me : hanging around the levee both
    night and day
5   Then after I walk the levee : from end to end
6   I'll go to Sweet Mama Alley : go and get my hooch
    and gin
7   I've tried old jelly : and old *loosha* too
8   But me and my gin house liquor : well we sure can do
9   I don't see why : white folks don't have no blues
10 They got all kinds of money : and brownskin women
    too
11 When you go to Vicksburg : please ask for old
    dripper king
12 For he's the bootlegging fellow : your *turkey* sure
    can swing

JohTo   1   Johnson, Tommy

        title: Cool Drink of Water Blues
        place and date: Memphis, 3 Feb. 1928
        record numbers: (41836-2) Vi-21279 OJL-8

1   I asked for water : and she gave me gasoline
3   Crying Lord I wonder : will I ever get back home
5   I went to the depot : looked up on the board
6   I asked the conductor : how long has this eastbound
    train been gone
7   It done taken your faro : blowed its smoke on you
9   Lord I asked the conductor : could I ride the blinds
10 Son buy your ticket buy your ticket : because the
    train ain't none of mine

JohTo   2   Johnson, Tommy

        title: Big Road Blues
        place and date: Memphis, 3 Feb. 1928
        record numbers: (41837-2) Vi-21279 Rt RL-330

1   Crying I ain't going down : this big road by myself
2   If I don't carry you : going to carry somebody else
3   Crying sun going to shine : in my back door some day
4   And the wind going to change : going to blow my
    blues away
5   What makes you do me : like you do do do

151

JohTo 2   Johnson, Tommy

6 Now you think you going to do me : like you done
   poor Cherry Red
7 Taken the poor boy's money now : sure Lord won't
   take mine

JohTo 3   Johnson, Tommy

      title: Bye-Bye Blues
      place and date: Memphis, 4 Feb. 1928
      record numbers: (41838-1) Vi-21409 Yz L-1007

1 Crying by-and-by : baby by-and-by
3 Says Good Book tell you : reap just what you sow
4 Going to reap it now : or baby reap it by-and-by
5 Well I'm going away : won't be back till fall
6 If I meet my good gal : then baby won't be back at
   all
7 Well it's two trains running : running side by side
8 You got my woman : babe I know you're satisfied

JohTo 4   Johnson, Tommy

      title: Maggie Campbell Blues
      place and date: Memphis, 4 Feb. 1928
      record numbers: (41839-2) Vi-21409 Rt RL-330

1 Mmm who's that yonder : coming down the road
2 Well it looks like Maggie : baby but she walks too
   slow
3 Mmm sun going to shine : in my back door some day
4 And the wind going to change : going to blow my
   blues away
5 Mmm see see rider : see what you done done
6 You done made me love you : now you're trying to put
   me down
7 Well I'm going away Lord : won't be back till fall
8 And if I meet my good gal : well I won't be back at
   all

JohTo 5   Johnson, Tommy

      title: Canned Heat Blues
      place and date: Memphis, 31 Aug. 1928
      record numbers: (45462-2) Vi-V38535 His HLP-31

1 Crying canned heat mama : sure Lord killing me
2 Takes alcorub : to take these canned heat blues
3 Crying mama mama mama : you know canned heat killing
   me
4 Canned heat don't kill me : crying babe I'll never
   die
5 I woke up up this morning : with canned heat on my
   mind
7 I woked up up this morning : crying canned heat
   around my bed
8 Run here somebody : take these canned heat blues
9 Crying mama mama mama : crying canned heat killing
   me
10 Believe to my soul : Lord it going to kill me dead

JohTo 6   Johnson, Tommy

      title: Lonesome Home Blues
      place and date: Memphis, 31 Aug. 1928
      record numbers: (45463-1) Vi unissued His HLP-31

1 Won't you wash my jumper : starch my overalls
2 I'm going to find my woman : says she's in the world
   somewhere
3 Well it's good to you mama : sure Lord killing me
5 I wonder : do my rider think of [poor] me
6 Lord if she did : she would sure Lord feel my care
7 I woke up this morning : said my morning prayers

JohTo 6   Johnson, Tommy

9 I ain't got no woman : speak in my behalf

JohTo 7   Johnson, Tommy

      title: Lonesome Home Blues
      place and date: Memphis, 31 Aug. 1928
      record numbers: (45463-2) Vi unissued His HLP-31

1 Won't you wash my jumper : starch my overalls
2 I'm going to find my woman : says she's in this
   world somewhere
3 I wonder : do my good girl think of me
4 Crying if she did : she would sure Lord feel my care
5 Honey it's good to you : mama sure Lord killing me
7 I woke up this morning : said my morning prayers
8 I ain't got no woman : to speak in my behalf

JohTo 8   Johnson, Tommy

      title: Big Fat Mama Blues
      place and date: Memphis, 31 Aug. 1928
      record numbers: (45465-1) Vi-38535 Rt RL-330

1 Crying big fat mama : meat shaking on her bones
2 Time the meat shake : it's a sign a woman lose her
   home
3 Mmm going away mama : won't be back till fall
4 Big fat mama : with the meat shaking on her bones
5 Mmm no need to holler : I got to murmur low
6 Big fat mama : Lord meat shake on her bones
7 Mmm time meat shake : it's sign a fatmouth lose his
   home
9 Mmm what's the matter rider : where did you stay
   last night
10 Hair all down baby : and you won't treat me right
12 Mmm big fat mama : meat shaking on her bones

JohTo 9   Johnson, Tommy

      title: Lonesome Home Blues
      place and date: Grafton, Wis., c. Jan. 1930
      record numbers: (L-230-2) Pm-13000 Yz L-1007

1 Lonesome place : don't seem like it's home to me
3 Lord I woke up this morning : blues all around my
   bed
4 Had the blues so bad mama : till I couldn't raise up
   my head
5 If you want to live easy : pack your clothes with
   mine
7 Mmm soon one morning : blues come falling down
8 Well they fell so heavy : that it caused my heart to
   moan
9 Well I'm going back home : going to fall down on my
   knees
10 Says I'll acknowledge now pretty baby : that I
   treated you mean

JohTo 10   Johnson, Tommy

      title: Black Mare Blues
      place and date: Grafton, Wis., c. Jan. 1930
      record numbers: (L-245-2) Pm-13000 Yz L-1007

1 Hitch up my buggy : saddle up my black mare
2 Find my woman : because she's out in the world
   somewhere
3 Aah if I call you : and you will fail to come
4 If I call you mama : going to sure Lord call your
   name
5 I been drinking all night gal : did the night before
6 Been drunk baby : and I ain't got sober yet
7 Mmm : I ain't going to tell you no more

152

JohTo 10   Johnson, Tommy

8   Told you last night mama : what I did the night
    before
10 Says you going to have : a rounder for your own

JonAn 1   Jones, Anna

    title: Trixie Blues
    place and date: New York, c. June 1923
    record numbers: (1473-1) Pm-12052 His HLP-15

1   Woke up this morning : blues all around my bed
2   I didn't have my daddy : to hold my aching head
3   I know the blues ain't nothing : but a woman wants
    to see her man
4   Because every time my man leaves me : Lord knows I
    feel so bad
5   You can never tell : what's on a brownskin man's
    mind
6   He'll be hugging and kissing you : and quit you all
    the time

JonB 1   Jones, Bo

    title: Back Door Blues
    place and date: Dallas, c. Nov. 1929
    record numbers: (DAL-460-) Vo-1452 Rt RL-327

1   Early one morning : I set down in my door
2   Lord I sitting here wondering : where in the world
    can a good man go
3   I hear my rider hollering : way up on the hill
4   Said I know it's my rider : she got a voice like a
    whippoorwill
5   I'm going to get you a ticket : going to take you on
    away from here
6   Lord if you never come back : Lord I will never care
7   I'm going to write my name : up on my baby's back
    door
8   So she can see my name : if she never see me no more

JonB 2   Jones, Bo

    title: Leavenworth Prison Blues
    place and date: Dallas, c. Nov. 1929
    record numbers: (DAL-461-) Vo-1452 Rt RL-327

1   I ain't got no money : nobody won't loan me none
2   Said I heard my rider was dead : and I sure want to
    get back home
3   If I had good luck Lord : like I once have had
4   Says I won't have to worry : about the trouble I had
5   I went to the graveyard : looked in my baby's face
6   Says I love you rider : but I can't take your place
7   The little boy's hollering extra : people did you
    read the news
8   Says I done killed my rider : and I got them
    Leavenworth blues

JonCo 1   Jones, Coley

    title: Sweet Mama Blues
    place and date: Dallas, 6 Dec. 1925
    record numbers: (145344-3) Co-14290-D Rt RL-312

1   I tried to love you : way back on my young days
2   You were so evil-hearted : throwed all my good love
    away
3   Mmm : what's the matter now
4   But now you want to quit me : and you don't know how
5   I'm going down to the river : take me a rocking
    chair
6   If the blues overtake me : rock away from there

JonCo 2   Jones, Coley (Frenchy's String Band)

    title: Texas and Pacific Blues
    place and date: Dallas, 5 Dec. 1928
    record numbers: (147566-1) Co-14387-D His HLP-17

1   That mean T P [railroad, railway] : sure has done me
    wrong
2   It let that Sunshine Special : carry my good gal
    from home
3   The blues : come down like showers of rain
4   I couldn't see nothing : but smoke from that train
5   Every time I hear : that Sunshine Special blow
6   It makes me : want to pack up all my clothes and go

JonCo 3   Jones, Coley

    title: Drunkard's Special
    place and date: Dallas, 6 Dec. 1929
    record numbers: (149558-2) Co-14489-D Fwy
    FA-2951

1   First night that I went home : drunk as I could be
2   There's another mule in the stable : where my mule
    ought to be
3   Come here honey : explain yourself to me
4   How come another mule in the stable : where my mule
    ought to be
5   Oh crazy oh silly : can't you plainly see
6   That's nothing but a milkcow : where your mule ought
    to be
7   I've traveled this world over : million times or
    more
8   Saddle on a milkcow's back : I've never seen before
9   Second night when I got home : as drunk as I could
    be
10 There's another coat on the coat rack : where my
    coat ought to be
11 Come here honey : explain this thing to me
12 How come another coat on the coat rack : where my
    coat ought to be
13 Oh crazy oh silly : can't you plainly see
14 Nothing but a bed quilt : where your coat ought to
    be
15 I've traveled this world over : million times or
    more
16 Pockets in a bed quilt : I've never seen before
17 The third night when I went home : drunk as I could
    be
18 There's another head on the pillow : where my head
    ought to be
19 Come here honey come here : explain this thing to me
20 How come another head on the pillow : where my head
    ought to be
21 Oh crazy oh silly : can't you plainly see
22 That's nothing but a cabbage head : that your
    grandma sent to me
23 I've traveled this world over : million times or
    more
24 Hair on a cabbage head : I've never seen before

JonCo 4   Jones, Coley

    title: The Elder's He's My Man
    place and date: Dallas, 6 Dec. 1929
    record numbers: (149559-2) Co-14489-D Rt RL-315

1   I washes hard : both day and night
2   Catch you arguing with that fellow : you going to
    have a miserable fight
3   Ashes to ashes : dust to dust
4   The police don't get you : now the undertaker must

153

JonE   1   Jones, Elijah

    title: Katy Fly
    place and date: Aurora, Ill., 13 Mar. 1938
    record numbers: (020120-1) BB-B7616 RCA INT-1175

1 I was standing at the station : wondering what train
    boys must I ride
2 Lord I'm on my way down in Louisiana : I believe
    I'll wait here for the Katy Fly
3 My woman left me this morning : left me wondering
    all to myself
4 Lord she said she didn't love me no more boys :
    wonder do she love anybody else
5 Ain't but the two old roads : boys I did not want to
    ride
6 Lordy that Southern Pacific now boys : and you know
    the Katy Fly
7 I got the railroad blues bad : I got the boxcars on
    my running mind
8 Now every time I get to studying about my sweet
    woman : boys I can hardly keep from crying

JonE   2   Jones, Elijah

    title: Mean Actin' Mama
    place and date: Aurora, Ill., 13 Mar. 1938
    record numbers: (020124-1) BB-B7616 RCA INT-1175

1 Now I can remember my baby : it was late one Friday
    night
2 Now you know you mistreat me woman : you know you
    didn't do me right
3 I walked and I walked baby : I walked to see you
    both night and day
4 Oh now you know I give you my money baby : womans
    and I lets you have your doggone way
5 Farewell baby : you going to need my help again
6 Now you said that you didn't knowed that I was
    coming baby : you wouldn't have even let me in
7 Now the troubles that I'm having : woman you was the
    cause of it all
8 Now you even had me down walking baby : I could
    hardly but crawl along

JonJ   1   Jones, Jake

    title: Monkeyin' Around
    place and date: Dallas, c. Oct. 1929
    record numbers: (DAL-473-) Br-7130 His HLP-2

1 I'm going to buy me a pistol : hang it up side the
    wall
2 I'm going to stop that jellybean : from kicking in
    my stall
3 I got a long tall woman : she don't do nothing but
    run around
4 Every time I leave : she don't do nothing but mess
    around
5 My woman's got a new way of loving : a monkey-man
    can't catch on
6 When he knows anything : she done got his dollar and
    gone

JonJ   2   Jones, Jake

    title: Southern Sea Blues
    place and date: Dallas, c. Oct. 1929
    record numbers: (DAL-474-) Br-7130 His HLP-2

1 I was shipwrecked on the ocean : throwed off on the
    southern sea
2 When you get to Chicago : pretty mama please
    remember me
3 I was standing beside the ocean : looking across on
    the other side

JonJ   2   Jones, Jake

4 My woman got little bitty legs : but man what a
    noble thigh
5 I went down to the ocean : just to get a permanent
    wave
6 My woman got a new way of loving : man and it won't
    behave
7 When it storms on the ocean : you cannot see the sky
8 If I don't love you pretty mama : I will pray to die

JonL   1   Jones, Little Hat

    title: New Two Sixteen Blues
    place and date: San Antonio, 15 June 1929
    record numbers: (402647-A) OK-8712 His HLP-32

1 I got a woman in Dallas : got one in San Antone too
2 I pick this one in San Antone : I don't know what
    this poor girl in Dallas going to do
3 She got nine gold teeth people : all that wavy hair
4 And if you ever come in San Antone : you going to
    find my sweet woman there
5 I never mistreated my baby : boy but I do wrong
    myself
6 For if I be mean to my woman : she will really quit
    and take someone else
7 Mmm baby : oh don't you think I know
8 Said I want to make an end of her people : and shake
    hands and go
9 I went to bed last night : I rolled from side to
    side
10 Honey I didn't have no blues really : but things
    wasn't going on right
11 I want someone to tell me : oh what Lord have mercy
    means
12 So if it means anything : well Lord have mercy on me
13 I'm going back to Dallas : oh don't you want to go
14 Honey I'm going to stop in towns : I believe that I
    haven't never been before

JonL   2   Jones, Little Hat

    title: Two String Blues
    place and date: San Antonio, 15 June 1929
    record numbers: (402648-A) OK-8712 His HLP-32

1 I said listen baby : honey I can't move no more
2 Oh these blues crawling up my windows : and
    traveling up under my door
3 Some womens weeps like a willow : some only sack of
    dough
4 But your life in misery : the minute that you ain't
    with the woman you love
5 Mmm : mmm
6 Lord it's something telling me : keeps on troubling
    me
7 Will you please tell the judge : don't have a trial
    till June
8 Because I got a working baby : let me see what my
    woman can do
9 People here she come in the evening : honey hundred
    in her hand
10 She had done robbed some fatmouth : who really
    looking for her man
11 Tell me sweet baby : honey what's on your mind
12 You keep a poor man troubled : really looking
    down-hearted all the time
13 Mmm baby : honey don't you think I know
14 Said I wouldn't make a man love her : if he wouldn't
    shake hands and go
15 Lord I'm going to Louisiana : going to get me a
    hoodoo hand
16 I'm going to stop my woman : and fix it so she can't
    have another man

JonL   3   Jones, Little Hat

title: Rolled From Side to Side Blues
place and date: San Antonio, 21 June 1929
record numbers: (402698-A) OK-8794 Yz L-1010

1   Mr Ferris Mr Ferris : let your womenfolks go
2   I done trying to get my sweet woman : like Mr Ferris
    got his girl
3   Mmm : baby don't you think I know
4   Pretty woman like a man : love him people and shake
    hands and go
5   No you never take a woman : speaking about to be
    your friend
6   Oh she get all of your money : then look what a hole
    you're in
7   I went to bed last night : keep a-rolling from side
    to side
8   I didn't have no blues : understand that things
    wasn't going right
9   When you catch me sleeping : baby don't you think
    I'm drunk
10 I's a-got one on the dresser : keep the other one on
    your trunk
11 Tell me sweet baby : all what's on your mind
12 You keep a poor man troubled : really looking
    down-hearted all the time

JonL   4   Jones, Little Hat

title: Hurry Blues
place and date: San Antonio, 21 June 1929
record numbers: (402699-A) OK-8735 Yz L-1010

1   I know this eagle's on a dollar : other side In God
    We Trust
2   Well a woman loves a man : but I know this dollar's
    first
3   Have you ever loved a woman : man that didn't love
    you
4   Then you have the worried blues : to bother you the
    whole night through
5   Well I'm going sweet baby : honey don't you want to
    go
6   Well I may stop in town : where I haven't never been
    before
7   Sometime you hear me singing : Nearer My God To Thee
8   Then again you hear me singing : sweet Atlanta blues
    to you

JonL   5   Jones, Little Hat

title: Little Hat Blues
place and date: San Antonio, 21 June 1929
record numbers: (402700-A) OK-8794 Yz L-1032

1   Oh the train pass by : oh with my sweet baby inside
2   And when I looked up and seen her : couldn't help
    but hang my head and cry
3   She gets her water at *Fairman* : coal at *Shabama
    Mines*
4   And I wouldn't let everybody ride : but people you
    know the train ain't mine
5   I said good morning conductor : oh please let a
    broke man ride
6   Because I want to see my sweet woman : just one more
    time before she get on
7   Said I'm tired of hearing me singing : Our Father
    Kingdom Come
8   Another year you hear me moaning : Lord let Thy will
    be done

JonL   6   Jones, Little Hat

title: Corpus Blues
place and date: San Antonio, 21 June 1929
record numbers: (402701-B) OK-8735 Rt RL-315

1   I remember one time people : oh it is in nineteen
    and twenty-four
2   Something happened that year : that I never want to
    see no more
3   I remember one time : oh it is in nineteen
    twenty-one
4   They say I got to watch my sweet woman : she's
    running from sun to sun
5   I thought : that my woman oh was treating me right
6   But oh when I went down to call for her : she didn't
    do nothing but fuss and fight
7   I never earned nothing : oh so much to hurt me so
8   Oh when I was talking to my babe that morning : and
    she told me that I didn't ???
9   Mmm : baby what's on your mind
10 Oh you want to be mean to me woman : give me a good
    word all the time

JonL   7   Jones, Little Hat

title: Bye Bye Baby Blues
place and date: San Antonio, 14 June 1930
record numbers: (404198-B) OK-8815 Yz L-1004

1   Well I'm leaving sweet baby : can't carry you
2   Well I'm leaving sweet baby : don't you want to go
3   Well I tried to love a sweet mama : but she couldn't
    understand
4   But I know she realized the trouble : since she met
    another man

JonL   8   Jones, Little Hat

title: Cross the Water Blues
place and date: San Antonio, 14 June 1930
record numbers: (404199-B) OK-8829 Yz L-1032

1   I say you got a sweet woman : man which you just
    don't understand
2   The man needs to take you women : and move across
    the no man's land
3   Mmm : ain't going to [sing, blow] no more
4   Blues done called up my woman : and traveled her and
    brought her up to my door
5   I want you to take me on with you baby : let you
    ease me down across your bed
6   I want you talk baby-talk to me : and then suck my
    tongue cherry red

JonL   9   Jones, Little Hat

title: Cherry Street Blues
place and date: San Antonio, 14 June 1930
record numbers: (404300-A) OK-8829 Yz L-1032

1   Just as sure as the train come in San Antone : then
    ease up in the yard
2   It's going to take two dollars and a quarter : I
    declare to send me a postal card
3   Mmm baby : oh honey what's on your mind
4   Because you really keeps me troubled : and I think
    about you all the time
5   I'm going to move to the bottom : camp out on the
    ground
6   Every morning I'll call my woman : to see have my
    coat found
7   I got a woman in San Antone : I declare that is
    sweet to me
8   Because the people don't know she's here : but she
    lives on Cherry Street

JonL   9   Jones, Little Hat

 9 Mmm : Lord Lord Lordy Lord
10 I want Eddie Duncan : listen to be my brother-in-law
11 Well I'll tell you men something : know you ain't
    going to think it's so

JonM   1   Jones, Maggie

        title: Four Flushing Papa
        place and date: New York, 14 Oct. 1924
        record numbers: (140104-2) Co-14044-D VJM VLP-23

 1 Four-flushing papa : what kind of man is you
 2 Four-flushing papa : you thrill me through and
    through
 3 I've never been crazy : about men
 4 Who ain't done no strutting : since the Lord knows
    when
 5 Four-flushing papa : what have you done to me
 6 Because when you leave me : I'm blue as blue can be
 7 Now when I get a payday : I don't have no plans
 8 Keep a quarter for myself : have to give to my man
 9 Now when I get a payday : right to you I go
10 You take it all papa : because it's all yours

JonM   2   Jones, Maggie

        title: Jealous Mama Blues
        place and date: New York, 14 Oct. 1924
        record numbers: (140105-1) Co-14044-D VJM VLP-23

 1 I got the blues : blue as blue can be
 2 Because these no-good gals : trying to backbite me
 3 Now these backbiters : don't live long I'm told
 4 So you'd better watch out : doggone your bad-luck
    soul
 5 Just let your conscience : be your safety guide
 6 *Anything wrong* with me : *is a mitten to a side*
 7 It's one more thing : I can't understand
 8 Why these trifling gals : run after a good gal's man
 9 Take my advice : and please don't lose your head
10 If you take my man : sure going to wake up dead

JonM   3   Jones, Maggie

        title: Box Car Blues
        place and date: New York, 13 Nov. 1924
        record numbers: (140134-3) Co-14047-D VJM VLP-23

 1 Every time : I see a railroad track
 2 Feel like riding : feel like going back
 3 Catch a train : that's headed for the South
 4 Going back south : to get smacked in the mouth
 5 Got a man : way down old Texas way
 6 Going to meet him : ain't got time to stay
 7 Got the boxcar blues : feel like a tramp
 8 Going to be down : in a Texas camp
 9 Told the engineer : to drive them down
10 Broke and hungry : tired of tramping around
11 Boxcar boxcar : don't you carry two
12 Ride me ride me : sooth my boxcar blues

JonM   4   Jones, Maggie

        title: Western Union Blues
        place and date: New York, 13 Nov. 1924
        record numbers: (140135-3) Co-14047-D VJM VLP-23

 1 Western Union : send this telegram
 2 To my man : way down in Birmingham
 3 ??? : please don't play today
 4 So disgusted : got no place to stay
 5 Send me car fare : want to come back home
 6 When I get back : never will I roam

JonM   4   Jones, Maggie

 7 Am I hungry : I ain't nothing but
 8 Stomach's empty : think my throat is stuck

JonM   5   Jones, Maggie

        title: Poor House Blues
        place and date: New York, 9 Dec. 1924
        record numbers: (140171-2) Co-14050-D VJM VLP-23

 1 The road to hardship : leads right to the poorhouse
    door
 2 I'm going there : and ain't coming back no more
 3 Poorhouse poorhouse : open wide your poorhouse gate
 4 I'm down and out : now I know it's too late
 5 Spent my money : spent it on my so-called friends
 6 And now I'm broke : that's where their friendship
    ends
 7 Here's the wagon : it's come to take me away
 8 In the poorhouse : I'll be till Judgment Day

JonM   6   Jones, Maggie

        title: Anybody Here Want to Try My Cabbage
        place and date: New York, 10 Dec. 1924
        record numbers: (140174-2) Co-14063-D VJM VLP-23

 1 Anybody here want to try my cabbage : just step this
    way
 2 Anybody here like to buy good cabbage : just holler
    hey
 3 There's no sweeter cabbage : anywhere in town
 4 You can have it boiled : until it's nice and brown
 5 Gave some to the parson : and he shook with glee
 6 He took up collection : gave it all to me
 7 Gave it to a corn doctor : to fix my feet
 8 Every time he sees me : he wants to eat
 9 Gave some to the jailor : who turned the key on me
10 When I got through feeding him : he said gal you're
    free

JonM   7   Jones, Maggie

        title: Thunderstorm Blues
        place and date: New York, 10 Dec. 1924
        record numbers: (140175-2) Co-14050-D VJM VLP-23

 1 Hear the thunder rumbling : see the lightning flash
 2 Devil is a-groaning : listen to that crash
 3 The trees are breaking : shaking all around
 4 The wind is howling : hear that wicked sound
 5 Gee I'm frightened : nearly scared to death
 6 That's why I'm hiding : I'm all out of breath
 7 My man's cruel : left me all alone
 8 In the darkness : I just weep and moan
 9 The storm is raging : I know what I'll do
10 I'll start in praying : till the storm is through

JonM   8   Jones, Maggie

        title: If I Lose, Let Me Lose
        place and date: New York, 17 Dec. 1924
        record numbers: (140187-1) Co-14059-D VJM VLP-23

 1 I got on : my walking shoes
 2 I'm going to walk : away my blues
 3 He stays out late : every night
 4 Comes back home : and wants to fight
 5 Whiskey : and trifling men
 6 In the jail : would be my end

JonM   9   Jones, Maggie

        title: Screamin' the Blues
        place and date: New York, 17 Dec. 1924
        record numbers: (140188-1) Co-14055-D VJM VLP-23

1   Talk about blues : you ought to hear mine
2   The man I love : keeps me worried all the time
3   One thing I hate : I can't have my way
4   The man that mistreat me : should be buried today
5   The better I treat him : the worse he treats me
6   I'm going to keep a good man : wherever he can be
7   You can always call : your good man's hand
8   Just let him know : that you got another man

JonM   10   Jones, Maggie

        title: Good Time Flat Blues
        place and date: New York, 17 Dec. 1924
        record numbers: (140191-2) Co-14055-D VJM VLP-23

1   Can't sell no whiskey : I can't sell no gin
3   Ain't got no money : to buy my winter coat
4   Can't save a dollar : to save my doggone soul
5   I can't keep open : I'm going to close the shack
7   The chief of police : done tore my playhouse down
8   No use in grieving : I'm going to leave this town

JonM   11   Jones, Maggie

        title: You May Go, But You'll Come Back Some Day
        place and date: New York, 18 Dec. 1924
        record numbers: (140192-2) Co-14063-D VJM VLP-23

1   Now you may go : but you'll come back some day
2   And you'll be sorry : that you went away
3   When you think of my good loving : that's the time
        you'll find
4   That none of your flip-floppers : going to satisfy
        your mind
5   You miss my love and kisses : and you wish you back
        home
6   But someone else : will be picking on your chicken
        bones
7   I've got another daddy : and he's sweet as can be
8   And what I like about him : he just idolize me
9   You might back up in your stable : when the snow
        begins to fall
10 But you'll find another mule : just kicking in your
        stall

JonM   12   Jones, Maggie

        title: Early Every Morn'
        place and date: New York, 18 Dec. 1924
        record numbers: (140193-2) Co-14059-D VJM VLP-23

1   Everybody in this world : got something that they
        crave
2   And when they get just what they want : then you see
        them rave
3   Poor folks crave fine clothes and money : rich folks
        crave the gold
4   But what I crave is loving : that will satisfy my
        soul
5   And when he kisses me : Lordy knows
6   A funny feeling : goes from my head to my toes

JonM   13   Jones, Maggie

        title: Dangerous Blues
        place and date: New York, 1 Apr. 1925
        record numbers: (140489-3) Co-14070-D VJM VLP-23

1   I'm like a red-hot stove : I'm burning down

JonM   13   Jones, Maggie

2   And the *moon is* ??? : in this man's town
3   I'm low and ornery : don't care what I do
4   Feel like cutting my man : half in two
5   A hornets' nest : don't mean a thing to me
6   I been stung so much : I'm up a tree
7   Now dynamite : ain't got a chance you see
8   I'm red-hot : and dangerous as can be

JonM   14   Jones, Maggie

        title: Suicide Blues
        place and date: New York, 1 Apr. 1925
        record numbers: (140490-3) Co-14070-D VJM VLP-23

1   If somebody finds me : when I'm dead and gone
2   Say I did self-murder : I died with my boots on
3   Took a Smith and Wesson : and blew out my brain
4   Didn't take no poison : I couldn't stand the strain
5   No I ain't no coward : and I'll tell you why
6   I was tired of living : but wasn't scared to die
7   Take me to the graveyard : put me in the ground
8   Please write on my tombstone : my daddy threw me
        down
9   In my farewell letter : someone's sure to find
10 So goodbye old cold world : I'm glad you're left
        behind

JonM   15   Jones, Maggie

        title: Undertaker's Blues
        place and date: New York, 16 Apr. 1925
        record numbers: (140533-2) Co-14092-D VJM VLP-23

1   Six pallbearers : take his to his last go-round
2   Going to place him : 'neath six feet of ground
3   Cemetery : sure is one old lonesome place
4   When you're dead : they throw dirt in your face
5   Yes I loved him : but he trifled with my heart
6   Had to shoot him : because he was too smart
7   Went gay-cutting : with another sealskin brown
8   Rambled : till the butcher cut him down

JonM   16   Jones, Maggie

        title: North Bound Blues
        place and date: New York, 16 Apr. 1925
        record numbers: (140534-2) Co-14092-D VJM VLP-23

1   Going north child : where I can be free
2   Where there's no hardships : like in Tennessee
3   Going where : they don't have Jim Crow laws
4   Don't have to work there : like in Arkansas
5   When I cross : the Mason-Dixon Line
6   Goodbye old *gallion* : mama's going a-flying
7   Going to daddy : got no time to lose
8   *So I won't be alone* : can hear my northbound blues

JonM   17   Jones, Maggie

        title: Mamma
        place and date: New York, 5 May 1925
        record numbers: (140584-1) Co-14074-D VJM VLP-25

1   Don't know what to do with myself : at night
2   Don't know anyone : that will treat me right
3   Listen I don't mean maybe : but you know
4   Take it from me : and don't you call my bluff
5   Need the kind of loving : that will make my heart
        beat
6   The sort that will thrill me : from my head to my
        feet

157

JonM 18   Jones, Maggie

    title: I'm a Back Bitin' Mama
    place and date: New York, 17 Sept. 1925
    record numbers: (140951-4) Co-14127-D VJM VLP-25

1 I'm a backbiting mama : looking for a cheating man
2 When you start double-crossing : you play right into
   my hand
3 If you stay out all night : and come home at four
4 You'll get back in time : to see me unlock my door
5 You can tell the world : I ain't no fool
6 I learned backbiting : when I went to school

JonM 19   Jones, Maggie

    title: Dallas Blues
    place and date: New York, 17 Sept. 1925
    record numbers: (140952-3) Co-14114-D VJM VLP-25

1 I've got the Dallas blues : and the Main Street
   heart disease
2 Buzzing around my head : like a swarm of little
   honeybees
3 I'm going to put myself : on a Santa Fe and go
4 To that Texas town : where you never see the ice and
   snow
5 I wonder : if my sweet baby will wait for me
6 Maybe someone else : ???

JonM 20   Jones, Maggie

    title: Never Drive a Beggar from Your Door
    place and date: New York, 18 Sept. 1925
    record numbers: (140965-3) Co-14127-D VJM VLP-25

1 If you see a blind man : on the street
2 Just remember : that he's got to eat
3 You can't live : in this big world alone
4 You might have : the finest kind of home
5 No one ever knows: what the future has in store
6 Never drive : a beggar from your door

JonM 21   Jones, Maggie

    title: Single Woman's Blues
    place and date: New York, 29 Sept. 1925
    record numbers: (141056-1) Co-14102-D VJM VLP-25

1 I don't feel welcome : I'm going to blow
2 Your ways and actions : really ails me so
3 Crying and weeping : won't do me no good
4 I'm a lonesome mama : need someone to chop my wood
5 I'm going to keep on going : till I find a mate
6 Then I will quit wandering : before it's too late

JonM 22   Jones, Maggie

    title: Never Tell a Woman Friend
    place and date: New York, 29 Sept. 1925
    record numbers: (141057-2) Co-14102-D VJM VLP-25

1 If you start telling her : he's got the stuff
2 She will walk right in : and make your home life
   tough
3 If your good man can please you : don't tell a soul
4 Just keep him well supplied : with down-home
   jellyroll
5 If he's got a little something : not like the rest
6 Just keep him busy : he will never leave your nest
7 He beats you *then* and loves you : pay that no mind
8 Because what you got must suit him : that's the
   surest sign

JonM 23   Jones, Maggie

    title: The Man I Love Is Oh So Good
    place and date: New York, 7 May 1926
    record numbers: (142165-3) Co-14243-D VJM VLP-25

1 The man I love : is oh so good to me
2 I'm just crazy : want the world to see
3 Buys me clothes : like I never had
4 *Now all* : it used to be *the mad*
5 I have to pinch myself : to see if I'm awake
6 Meals with him : all taste like wedding cake

JonM 24   Jones, Maggie

    title: I'm a Real Kind Mama
    place and date: New York, 7 May 1926
    record numbers: (142167-?) Co-14139-D VJM VLP-25

1 I'm a real kind mama : looking for a loving man
2 I ain't got nobody : who will come and claim my hand
3 Now all I want : is all your love
4 At morning noon and night : that's all I'm thinking
   of

JorC 1   Jordan, Charley

    title: Stack O' Dollars Blues
    place and date: Chicago, c. mid June 1930
    record numbers: (C-5834-) Vo-1557 Yz L-1018

1 Now it's too late to holler baby : too late to weep
   and moan
2 Too late to holler great God : when that stack of
   dollars done gone
3 Well it's mama mama mama : what that you got in that
   grip
4 That's nothing but a stack of dollars : you babe
   going to take a little trip
5 I'm sitting on a stack of dollars : just as high as
   I am tall
6 If you be my little old baby : you sure can have
   them all
7 Well it's baby baby : I tell you what I will do
8 I will give you stack of dollars : just to make one
   more night with you
9 You can mistreat me baby : do anything you want to
   do
10 Some day you going to want me : but your baby won't
   want you
11 Now I'm going to sing this verse baby : and I ain't
   going to sing no more
12 For that stack of dollars is worrying me : Lord and
   I got to go

JorC 2   Jordan, Charley

    title: Keep It Clean
    place and date: Chicago, c. mid June 1930
    record numbers: (C-5836-) Vo-1511 Yz L-1030

1 I went to the river : couldn't get across
2 I jumped on your papa : because I thought he was a
   horse
3 Up she jumped : down she fell
4 Her mouth flew open : like a mussel shell
5 You sister was a teddy : your daddy was a bear
6 Put the muzzle on your mama : because she had bad
   hair
7 If you want to hear : that elephant laugh
8 Take him down to the river : and wash his yas yas
   yas
9 If you want to go to heaven : when you D I E
10 You got to put on your collar : and your T I E
11 If you want to get the rabbits : out the L O G
12 You got to put on the stump : like a D O G

158

13   Run here doctor : run here fast
14   See what's the matter : with his yas yas yas

title: Big Four Blues
place and date: Chicago, c. mid June 1930
record numbers: (C-5837-) Vo-1511 Yz L-1030

1   And that Big Four the Big Four : is a mean old train
     to ride
2   She took my babe away : and left me dissatisfied
3   Baby is all I want mama : just one more crack at you
4   If I can't make you love me : then I don't care what
     you do
5   Please hold my head baby : and let my whiskey run
     down
6   Lord I catch that Big Four : and beat it on back to
     town
7   When I asked that woman : Lord to let me be her kid
8   She say you might get buggish : Lord you won't keep
     it hid
9   I've got the blues for my baby : my babe got the
     blues for me
10   For she went and caught that Big Four : she beat it
     back to Tennessee
11   Just a few more days : and a few more nights ain't
     long
12   You going to reach for your boiler : and your plate
     will be gone

title: Raidin' Squad Blues
place and date: Chicago, c. mid June 1930
record numbers: (C-5840-) Vo-1528 Yz L-1030

1   It's too late too late : too late too late too late
2   Here we are on our way to the holdover : and we
     cannot hesitate
3   Mmm : these boards is killing me
4   Say I know I am a criminal : but I always want to be
     free
5   Oh no : these raids is killing me
6   *See that woman* about it baby : Lord it's down in
     Tennessee
7   Mmm : these raids is killing me
8   I got the raiding squad blues : the holdover is
     killing poor me
9   When the raid began : the people began to squall
10   The sergeant said ain't no need a-squalling : the
     captain said to bring you all
11   When I had money : my friends all ganged around
12   Now I'm in this raid : my friends have all thrown me
     down

title: Hunkie Tunkie Blues
place and date: Chicago, c. mid June 1930
record numbers: (C-5841-) Vo-1528 Yz L-1003

1   Baby I'm going uptown : tell the chief police
2   My woman quit me : I can't see no peace
3   She keep me worried : bothered all the time
5   Well I love you woman : love your husband too
6   I have to love your husband : to get to be with you
7   Because he don't allow : no man around his house
9   My mama told me : my papa too
10   Don't let no woman : be the death of you
11   She don't allow me : to stay out all night long
13   What you going to do : when they tear your
     barrelhouse down
14   Going to pack my suitcase : hunt some other town

15   Well they say everybody talking : about your
     honky-tonky blues
17   Well they say everybody talking : about your
     honky-tonky baby
18   You ought to see : that curly-headed monkey-head
19   Head is curly : baby and bushy too

title: Gasoline Blues
place and date: Chicago, 19 Sept. 1930
record numbers: (C-6164-) Vo-1551 Yz L-1030

1   You can always tell baby : when your woman going to
     treat you mean
2   If you ask for a glass of water : she give you a
     glass of gasoline
3   Some of these women : they sure to be ashamed
4   Babe they go out and take money : from a man walking
     with a walking cane
5   What makes you blow up baby : every time I speak to
     you
6   You make me think : that you full of gasoline too
7   I've got the trickiest woman : that you ever seen
8   Whenever she get mad : she blows up just like
     gasoline
9   Won't you let me tell you partner : what the
     gasoline women will do
10   They will stay out all night long : then come home
     and blow up on you
11   Hey baby : you just full of gas as you can be
12   Because when you get drunk : you come home and blow
     up on me
13   Some of these gasoline women : I just can't
     understand
14   They'll cook *make one* for their husband : they'll
     chicken for their man

title: Keep It Clean--No. 2
place and date: Chicago, 17 Mar. 1931
record numbers: (VO-141-) Vo-1611 Yz L-1003

1   I runned to the river : runned so fast
2   And you couldn't see nothing : but that yas yas yas
3   If you want to hear : that elephant grunt
4   You take him down to the river : and then wash his
     trunk
5   Up he jumped : down he fell
6   His trap flew open : like a mussel shell
7   If you keep it dirty : and I keep it clean
8   You don't know : what keeping it dirty means
9   I will tell you one thing : and I mean it
10   It sure will take soap and water : for to keep it
     clean
11   The terriblest sight : that I ever seen
12   Was a cook cooking victuals : and his hands wasn't
     clean
13   You got a head like a mouse : mouth like a goat
14   Every time you see me : you looking for some soap

title: You Run and Tell Your Daddy
place and date: Chicago, 17 Mar. 1931
record numbers: (VO-143-) Vo-1611 Yz L-1003

1   Well it's everything I tell you : you run and tell
     your daddy-law
3   I ain't going to tell you nothing else : because you
     done run and tell your daddy-law
5   And it's everything I give you : you give it to your
     daddy-law

JorC   8   Jordan, Charley

7   Hey my doggy jumped a rabbit : and he run him for a
    solid mile
8   When he seen he couldn't catch him : so he cried
    just like a natural child
9   Yeah your sister was a teddy : your daddy was a
    great big bear
10 Put a rope around my neck : you can lead me anywhere
11 When I asked that woman : to let me be her kid
12 She say you might get mawkish : baby you won't keep
    it hid

JorC   9   Jordan, Charley

        title: Tight Haired Mama Blues
        place and date: Chicago, 17 Mar. 1931
        record numbers: (VO-144) Vo-1645 OJL-20

1   Here come my tight-haired woman : I can tell by the
    way she walks
2   But I know she be shaking that thing : because I can
    tell by the way she talks
3   I don't want no tight-haired woman : to cook no meat
    for me
4   Because she's so tight-haired and evil : I'm scared
    she might poison poor me
5   Now your hair ain't curly : know your teeth ain't
    neither pearls
6   If the men were asking for hair : you would have a
    hard time in this world
7   Babe you know I did more for you : than the good
    Lord ever done
8   You know I bought you some hair : because he sure
    didn't give you none
9   Now if you got good hair : you want to keep it
    looking neat
10 Just go down to the ten-cents store : get you a
    nickel worth of ???
11 I will tell you girls one thing : you know it really
    is true
12 Baby now you got good hair : but you bought bought
    this from the Jew

JorC   10   Jordan, Charley

        title: I Couldn't Stay Here
        place and date: New York, 10 Apr. 1936
        record numbers: (18980-) ARC-6-09-61 Yz L-1021

1   I went home last night baby : found my good gal
    there
2   I'm going to leave you baby : traveling everywhere
3   I said ain't it hard to leave you : hoo Lord going
    to travel everywhere
4   I had a good home mama : Lord but I couldn't stay
    there
5   I was down in jail baby : I went down on my knees
6   Been so good to you honey : *good meat* for me
7   I said hoo I'm going to leave you : hoo Lord
    traveling everywhere
8   I had a good home baby : Lord but I wouldn't stay
    there
9   Have you ever been down baby : way down in Polack
    Town
10 She slashing and she twisting : till she turned my
    damper down
11 Won't you tell me baby : who can your good man be
12 I woke up this morning baby : with a hex all over me
13 I can do more for you : than the good Lord ever done
14 I can buy you foresight baby : when the Lord ain't
    give you none

JorC   11   Jordan, Charley

        title: Got Your Water On
        place and date: New York, 10 Apr. 1936
        record numbers: (18982-2) ARC-6-06-61 Rt RL-310

1   I met my gal this morning : long long way from home
2   Ain't no use drinking good baby : said I ain't got
    your water on
3   I'd rather be dead baby : buried in the deep blue
    sea
4   Than to be so far from home baby : people making a
    fool of me
5   Lord my girl got something : sure Lord worries me
6   I woke up soon this morning : had that thing all
    over me
7   Now I got something to tell you : make your hair
    rise on your head
8   I got a-this old Elgin movement : make the springs
    tremble all on your bed

JorC   12   Jordan, Charley

        title: Don't Put Your Dirty Hands on Me
        place and date: New York, 10 Apr. 1936
        record numbers: (18983-1) ARC-6-06-61 Rt RL-310

1   If you put your dirty black hands on me : I'm going
    to put you back in jail
2   Put so many crimes against you loving baby : take a
    millionaire to go your bail
3   I was walking down Main Street : looking for a zoo
4   ??? *you trying to make* : *would make a ??? of* you
5   Tell me pretty mama : where have you been
6   Don't like whiskey : and you're drunk again
7   And I'm going downtown : going to spread the news
8   A big-feet woman : wearing *broken* shoes
9   Now if I get lucky : get a bottle of gin
10 *Pull a number of* women : *to their* mighty few men

JorL   1   Jordan, Luke

        title: Church Bells Blues
        place and date: Charlotte, N.C., 16 Aug. 1927
        record numbers: (39819-1) Vi unissued RCA
            INT-1175

1   Children's in the pulpit : mama trying to learn the
    Psalms
2   Now the lowdown dirty deacon : done stole my gal and
    gone
3   Woke up this morning : the family had the weary
    blues
4   Now *must've* peep over in the corner : poor
    grandmammy had them too
5   I did more for you woman : good Lordy ever done
6   Went downtown and bought you good hair : and the
    Lord hadn't give you none
7   You better stop your gal : from from tickling under
    my chin
8   You going to run over some of these mornings : papa
    swear you can't get in

JorL   2   Jordan, Luke

        title: Church Bells Blues
        place and date: Charlotte, N.C., 16 Aug. 1927
        record numbers: (39819-2) Vi-21076 RBF RF-9

1   Children's in the pulpit : mama trying to learn the
    Psalms
2   Now that lowdown dirty deacon : done stole my gal
    and gone
3   Woke up this morning : the family had the weary
    blues

4   Poked my head over in the corner : poor grandmammy
    had them too
5   I did more for you woman : than the good Lord had
    ever done
6   Went out town bought you good hair : and the Lord
    hadn't give you none
7   You don't like your daddy : you got no right to
    carrying a stole
8   Hand me back that wig I bought you : mama let your
    doggone head go bald
9   But then I promised the good Lord : partner not to
    dig no coal
10 I'm going to hang around the country : and try to
    sell some jellyroll
11 Some men is crave for yellow women : some men like
    the teasing brown
12 I'm a stranger in town mama : figuring on going the
    whole way down
13 She squawk about my supper : she kicked me outdoors
14 She had a nerve to ask me : would a matchbox hold my
    clothes

JorL   3   Jordan, Luke

     title: Cocaine Blues
     place and date: Charlotte, N.C., 16 Aug. 1927
     record numbers: (39821-2) Vi-21076 Rt RL-326

1   I'm going gal : don't you take me for no fool
2   I'm not going to quit you pretty mama : whilst the
    weather's cool
3   Around your back door : says honey I'm going to
    creep
4   As long as : you make your two and a half a week
5   Now I got a girl : she works in the white folk's
    yard
6   She brings me meat : I can swear she brings me lard
7   Now Barnum Bailey Circus : came to town
8   They had a *stepper* : looking good and brown
9   They didn't know : it was against the law
10 But the monkey stopped : at a ??? drugstore
11 Stepped around the corner : just a minute too late
12 Another one sitting there : *to kick back eight*
13 Say come on sister : with her nose all *spoiled*
14 The doctor's gone : going to sell no more
15 Now there's twenty-two men came to my house : it was
    last Sunday morn
16 They asked me was my wife at home : and I told she
    has long been gone
17 He backed his wagon up to my door : took everything
    I had
18 He carried it back to the furniture store : and I
    swear that I did feel sad
19 Saying coke's for horses : not women or men
20 The doctors say it'll kill you : but they didn't say
    when

JorL   4   Jordan, Luke

     title: My Gal's Done Quit Me
     place and date: New York, 18 Nov. 1929
     record numbers: (57703-1) Vi-V38564 Rt RL-318

1   Well a-my gal had quit me : the talks all over town
2   She left me a note laying on the kitchen table :
    saying daddy I'm Alabama bound
3   I went running to the station : wringing my hands
    and crying
4   Crying come back pretty mama : God sakes don't go
    this time
5   I done bought my ticket : daddy I'm compelled to
    ride
6   Say you done know when you had me : man you couldn't
    be satisfied

7   Then she showed me a ticket : just as long as my
    right arm
8   Have to be riding it so long : I expect you dead and
    gone
9   I had the railroad blues : I didn't have the
    railroad fare
10 Say my shoes hold up : I mean to walk the distance
    there
11 I woke up this morning : with traveling on my mind
12 Kept a-feeling my pocket : and I didn't have a lousy
    dime

KelE   1   Kelly, Eddie

     title: Poole County Blues
     place and date: Charlotte, N.C., 6 Aug. 1937
     record numbers: (013023-1) BB-B7204 RBF RF-9

1   There's nobody know : Polk County like I do
2   Because I traveled Polk County : mama through and
    through
3   Well woke up this morning : and I feeling bad
4   I thinking about good times : that I used to have
5   Say if I'd listened : what my mama said
6   I'd be at home : in my folding bed
7   Don't your house look lonesome : when your best
    buddy's gone
8   You turn over on your pillow : then you cry right on
9   Ooh : mama what's the matter now
10 You make me think : I'll break my heart in that
    house
11 Say look a-here baby : I'm going to tell the truth
12 I don't love nobody : honey else but you
13 I'm going away mama : and it won't be long
14 You sure going to miss me : just as sure as you born
15 I'm going to sing this old song : ain't going to
    sing no more
16 I'm going to sing this old song : everywhere I go

KelE   2   Kelly, Eddie

     title: Shim Shamming
     place and date: Charlotte, N.C., 6 Aug. 1937
     record numbers: (013026-1) BB-B7148 BC-2

1   Said I don't care : what mama don't allow
2   Going to strut my stuff : old anyhow
3   Said I don't care : what mama don't allow
4   Going to eat my watermelon : anyhow
5   Said I don't care : what mama don't allow
6   Going to play our washboard : any old how
7   Said I don't care : what mama don't allow
8   Going to play that trombone : anyhow
9   Said we don't care : what mama don't allow
10 He going to do his stuff : old anyhow
11 Said I don't care : what mama don't allow
12 Going to *eeya-eeya* : anyhow

KelJ   1   Kelly, Jack

     title: Highway No. 61 Blues
     place and date: New York, 1 Aug. 1933
     record numbers: (13712-1) Ba-32844 Rt RL-316

1   I'm going to leave here walking : I'm going down
    Number Sixty-One
2   And if I find my baby : you know we going to have
    some fun
3   I walked Sixty-One Highway : and I give down in my
    knees
4   I looking for my babe on Indian Ocean : but she come
    on that China sea
5   That Sixty-One Highway : longest highway that I ever
    knowed

KelJ   1   Kelly, Jack

6   It reach from Atlanta Georgia : clean down to the
     Gulf of Mexico
7   Now I'm going home : get my Bible and sit down and
     read
8   I'm going to ask the good Lord : to give me back my
     baby if you please

KelJ   2   Kelly, Jack

     title: Highway No. 61 Blues No. 2
     place and date: New York, 1 Aug. 1933
     record numbers: (13713) Ba-32934 Rt RL-329

1   I can hear the hell dog ringing : and the people all
     a-crying
2   I mean all up and down : I say that old Sixty-One
     Line
3   The man that built the Sixty-One flat-top : he's
     just as true as a *fox*
4   You can ride or walk across it : and you can't even
     hear a knock
5   That flat-top flat-top : is the prettiest thing I
     ever seen
6   ??? : and it takes me *Water* Street
7   I am in dear love with Sixty-One : I say it from my
     heart
8   That is the reason I am so *love with it* :
     Sixty-One has give me a new start

KelJ   3   Kelly, Jack

     title: Red Ripe Tomatoes
     place and date: New York, 1 Aug. 1933
     record numbers: (13714-2) Ba-32844 OJL-4

1   I've got a thirty-two twenty : shoots just like a
     forty-five
2   I can walk that old Green River levee : babe I won't
     have to hide
3   I ain't going to sell it : too good to give away
4   I'm going to save it for me and my baby : and snatch
     her some rainy day
5   Now red ripe tomatoes : don't forget your T-bone
     steak
6   Well when you get ready to go fishing : *put* ??? on
     that heart you take
7   Well Mr Charlie : you had better watch your men
8   They are going through the bushes : and they are
     going in

KelJ   4   Kelly, Jack

     title: Believe I'll Go Back Home
     place and date: New York, 1 Aug. 1933
     record numbers: (13715-2) Me-M12812 Rt RL-311

1   I believe I believe : I believe I'll go back home
2   I'm going down to tell my baby : that I have done
     her wrong
3   St Louis is on afire : Chicago is burning down
4   I'm so sick and tired : that my baby keeps on
     cooling down
5   Babe please forgive me : I know that I've done you
     wrong
6   I'm going to get down on my knees : I want my little
     old baby back home
7   It's the same old fireman : same old engineer
8   And it took my baby : and it left me standing here

KelJ   5   Kelly, Jack

     title: Ko-ko-mo Blues
     place and date: New York, 1 Aug. 1933
     record numbers: (13721-2) Me-M12812 Rt RL-311

1   Now my first love is in Texas : my [next one,
     second] lives in Kokomo
2   I'm going to catch me a freight train : and I'm
     going on down the road
3   I said don't ever drive a stranger : from your door
4   May be your sister or brother : say you don't never
     know
5   I have got a brother : and his name is Dan
6   The women all say : he sure can sing
7   Dan Sane Dan Sane : where have you been so long
8   And you know : that you have I say done me wrong

KelJ   6   Kelly, Jack

     title: Cold Iron Bed
     place and date: New York, 1 Aug. 1933
     record numbers: (13722-) Ba-32934 OJL-4

1   Baby take me upstairs : baby won't you lay me down
     in your cool iron bed
2   If I don't get no better : I want you to come and
     rub my head
3   You're a no good wheat : the cow is going to mow you
     down
4   And if I want to ??? : I'll run you wheat out of
     town
5   Ever since ever since : my poor mother been dead
6   The rocks have been my pillow : and the cold ground
     have been my bed
7   Baby : I'll make everything all right
8   If I don't see you tomorrow : I'll see you tomorrow
     night

KelJ   7   Kelly, Jack

     title: Betty Sue Blues
     place and date: Memphis, 14 July 1939
     record numbers: (MEM-143-1) Vo unissued OJL-19

1   Betty Sue Betty Sue : is the sweetest girl I know
2   Well you caused me to walk from Chicago : clear to
     the Gulf of Mexico
3   Now Betty Sue got ways : like a horse that it get
     wild
4   Every time she struggles : I swears it's out the
     world
5   Betty Sue the big boat's up the river : on a *bank*
     of sand
6   If it don't [change the, strike that deep] water :
     swear it won't land
7   Now look a-here Sue : what you trying to do
8   Giving away my luggage : and trying to love me too

KelJ   8   Kelly, Jack

     title: Flower Blues
     place and date: Memphis, 14 July 1939
     record numbers: (MEM-144-1) Vo unissued OJL-21

1   I'd rather see the flowers : growing on top of my
     baby's grave
2   Than to see some other man : smiling smiling in my
     baby's face
3   Here I am here I am : setting in that chair with
     folded arms
4   Well it seems like all good times : I mean this
     whole world have gone
5   I've got a ??? to glory : papa he's done throwed me
     away

KelJ   8   Kelly, Jack

6 But you had a lowdown dirty heart : to baby to
   mistreat me this a-way
7 If you take me back baby : I'll tell you just what
   I'll do
8 I will work hard and I'll slave : babe I'll bring
   that money back home to you

KelJ   9   Kelly, Jack

       title: Men Fooler Blues
       place and date: Memphis, 14 July 1939
       record numbers: (MEM-151-) Vo-05312 OJL-19

1 I had a girl : give her everything I had
2 Well my friend took her from me : and it surely was
   too bad
3 Now I'm going to kill her : if I should happen to
   live
4 I'm going to take something from her : Lord that I
   really can give
5 I've got another woman : man she's so bony and lean
6 Well she's got something : Lord I ain't never seen
7 She's got a little bitty foot now : Lord and got
   them great big thighs
8 Well she's got something on the under : weep just
   like a *pool hall eye*

KidS   1   Kid Stormy Weather

       title: Short Hair Blues
       place and date: Jackson, Miss., 17 Oct. 1935
       record numbers: (JAX-179-2) Vo-03145 BC-7

1   That's all right baby : Lord that's all right for
    you
2   Now it's all right baby : Lord about the way you do
3   The blues came down my alley : rolling up into my
    back door
4   I got the blues this morning : Lord Lord like I
    never had before
5   Mama you remember the time : babe I made you like it
    and how
6   But the thing you trying to do : babe somebody doing
    it now
7   Go on back old gal : you know you can't make me
    change
8   Because your hair is so short : swear to God I can
    smell your *brand*
9   Way way down babe : way down in old Polack Town
10 Dirty roaches and the chinches : done tore my little
    gin house down

King   1   King David

       title: What's That Tastes Like Gravy
       place and date: Atlanta, 11 Dec. 1930
       record numbers: (404664-A) OK-8913 RBF RF-6

1 Says she killed a chicken : and she cook him down
   low
2 Said cook that chicken : a sweet jellyroll
3 Said they cooked that possum : and they cook him
   down low
4 And the grease come running : from his jo jo jo
5 Said she *sound so loo : sound so soo*
6 *Sound* just like : she couldn't *blow*
7 Great life for sure : when time was tough
8 I was laying coal yard : strutting my stuff

King   2   King David

       title: Rising Sun Blues
       place and date: Atlanta, 11 Dec. 1930
       record numbers: (404665-A) OK-8913 RBF RF-6

1 Woke up this morning : look at the rising sun
2 I thought about my good gal : who done gone along
3 I ain't never loved : and I hope I never will
4 Why love is proposition : sure get a good man killed
5 I got twelve little puppies : ten big shaggy hounds
6 It takes all twenty-two : to run my brownskin down

King   3   King David

       title: Sweet Potato Blues
       place and date: Atlanta, 11 Dec. 1930
       record numbers: (404666-B) OK-8901 Rt RL-311

1   There ain't no more potatoes : the frost done killed
    the vine
2   Ain't no more good times : with that girl of mine
3   I ain't never loved Lord : I hopes I never will
4   A loving proposition : sure get a good man killed
5   I got twelve little puppies : ten big shaggy hounds
6   Take the whole twenty-two : to run my brownskin down
7   My brownie caught a passenger : left me a mule to
    ride
8   When the train pulled out : the mule lay down and
    die
9   There's one thing certain : I sure can't understand
10 She could feed the ??? *pigmeat* : corn bread for
    her man

King   4   King David

       title: I Can Deal Worry
       place and date: Atlanta, 11 Dec. 1930
       record numbers: (404668-A) OK-8901 Rt RL-311

1 I'm worried now Lord : I won't be worried long
2 It takes a worried man Lord : to sing a worried song
3 Take me mama : try me one more time
4 I don't do better : kill myself a-trying
5 Just as sure as the birds : fly in the sky above
6 Say you know pretty mama : you ain't with the man
   you love
7 Well I cooked her breakfast : brought it to her bed
8 Say she taking one bite : threw the teacup at my
   head

Kyle   1   Kyle, Charlie

       title: Kyle's Worried Blues
       place and date: Memphis, 1 Sept. 1928
       record numbers: (45468-2) Vi-21707 Yz L-1018

1   I'm worried now : but I won't be worried long
2   It takes a worried man : to sing this worried song
3   I'm going away : baby and it won't be long
4   You mistreat me : I'm going to leave my happy home
5   I'm going to the river : sit down on the ground
6   If the blues overtake me : I'll jump overboard and
    drown
7   I woke up this morning : those blues were on my mind
8   I was so down-hearted : I couldn't do nothing but
    cry
9   When you see me leaving : baby don't you cry
10 If you mistreat me again : baby you will surely die
11 Lord I'm going away : honey I cannot stay
12 I can't be down-hearted : mistreated this a-way
13 Lord I went up on a mountain : peeped in a little
    hole
14 I saw two little monkeys : doing the monkey
    jellyroll

Lacy   1   Lacy, Rubin

       title: Mississippi Jail House Groan
       place and date: Chicago, Mar. 1928
       record numbers: (20419-2) Pm-12629 OJL-8

1   Eee laying in jail now : with my back turned to the
     wall
3   And she brought me coffee : and she brought me tea
4   She brought me everything : now but that lowdown
     jailhouse key
5   Mmm : mmm
6   I promised not to holler now : now mama now hey hey
     hey
7   I looked at my mama : and I hung my head and cried
8   If my woman kills me now : Lord I'll pray to die

Lacy   2   Lacy, Rubin

       title: Ham Hound Crave
       place and date: Chicago, Mar. 1928
       record numbers: (20420-3) Pm-12629 Yz L-1009

1   You can read my letter : now you sure don't know my
     mind
2   When you think I'm loving you : I'm leaving all the
     time
3   I ain't got nobody now : I'm all here by myself
5   Let me be your sometime now : till your always comes
6   And I'll do more for you now : your always ever done
7   Mama got a hambone : I wonder can I get it boiled
8   Because these Chicago women now : about to let my
     hambone spoil
9   The dirty deacon : has taken my gal and gone
10 And all the children now : papa trying to sing my
     song
11 Let me be your rocker : till your straight chair
     comes
12 And I rock you easier : you straight chair ever done

Lask   1   Lasky, Louie

       title: How You Want Your Rollin' Done
       place and date: Chicago, 2 Apr. 1935
       record numbers: (C-915-C) Vo-02955 Her H-201

1   Now tell me mama : just how you want your rolling
     done
2   And just as long as you like it : if it takes the
     whole night long
3   Now gal got teeth : like the lighthouse on the sea
4   And every time she smiles : she throws her loving
     light on me
5   Now my rider got something : and I don't know just
     what it is
6   And every time she wiggles and wobbles : papa can't
     keep his black stuff still
7   Now I can get religion : baby most any day
8   But the dice and these women : I swear they won't
     let me pray
9   Now if you steal my rider : I won't get mad with you
10 Because she's three time seven : and she knows just
     exactly what to do

Lask   2   Lasky, Louie

       title: Teasin' Brown Blues
       place and date: Chicago, 2 Apr. 1935
       record numbers: (C-945-B) Vo-02955 Her H-201

1   Oh mama : I dream about you night and day
2   I had my hand on some this morning : and I swear I
     let it get away
3   I love you mama : and I'll tell the world I do
4   Because can't nobody treat me : honey like my rider
     do

Lask   2   Lasky, Louie

5   You don't have to cook me no chicken : because your
     plain old neckbone will do
6   I'm going to buy you some blackeyed peas : mama and
     try to get along with you
7   I'm crazy about the way you do it : I'm talking
     about your jellyroll
8   Because I know you got something : will send
     salvation to your soul
9   She got hair like Gloria Swanson : and she walk just
     like Priscilla Deane
10 Because she's the prettiest woman : old Louie ever
     seen
11 I'm going to ask the good Lord : to send me an angel
     down
12 But she ain't not a good one : I'm going to cling on
     to my teasing brown

Ledb   1   Ledbetter, Huddie

       title: Roberta--Part 1
       place and date: New York, 23 Jan. 1935
       record numbers: (16683-) ARC unissued Co
       C-30035

1   Oh Roberta : honey where you been so long
2   You done been across the country : a-with my long
     clothes on
3   Oh Roberta : sit down on my knee
4   Got a lot to tell you : a-that's been worrying me
5   Way up the river : far as I can see
6   Lord I thought I spied : my old-time used-to-be
7   Lord I thought I spied : my old-time used-to-be
8   And it was nothing : honey but a cypress tree
9   Honey I'm down on the river : sitting out on the
     ground
10 Well I'll stay right here Lord : until Roberta come
     down

Ledb   2   Ledbetter, Huddie

       title: Roberta--Part 2
       place and date: New York, 23 Jan. 1935
       record numbers: (16684-) ARC unissued Co
       C-30035

1   Oh Roberta : what in the world you mean
2   Honey the way you treat me : beats all I ever seen
3   Lord I'm going to the station : going to tell the
     chief of police
4   Roberta done quit me : and I can't see no peace
5   She's a brownskin woman : got black wavy hair
6   And I can describe her : oh partner most anywhere
7   Tell me Roberta : what's the matter with you
8   This man ain't got nobody : to take his troubles to

Ledb   3   Ledbetter, Huddie

       title: Packin' Trunk Blues
       place and date: New York, 23 Jan. 1935
       record numbers: (16685-1) Ba-33359 Rt RL-315

1   I'm sitting down here wondering : would a matchbox
     hold my clothes
2   I don't want to be bothered : with no suitcase on my
     road
3   Now what would you do : when your baby packing up
     her trunk
4   You get half a gallon of whiskey : you get on your
     big drunk

Ledb   4   Ledbetter, Huddie

        title: C. C. Rider
        place and date: New York, 23 Jan. 1935
        record numbers: (16686-) ARC unissued Co
        C-30035

1   See see rider : see what you done done
2   You made me love you : now your man done come
3   I was looking right at her : when the sun went down
4   She was standing in the kitchen : in her morning
     gown
5   Let me be your sidetrack : till your mainline comes

Ledb   5   Ledbetter, Huddie

        title: Honey, I'm All Out and Down
        place and date: New York, 23 Jan. 1935
        record numbers: (16688-2) Ba-33359 Rt RL-315

1   I'm broke baby : and I ain't got a dime
2   Every good man : gets in hard luck sometimes
3   I'm going to tell my woman : like the Dago told the
     Jew
4   You don't want me : now honey I don't want you
5   Oh the women in the levee : *Charlie because it's
     most* payday
6   The men on the levee : hollering don't you move your
     knee
7   Oh the women on the levee : honey hollering whoa gee
8   The men on the levee : hollering don't you murder me
9   I'm down in the bottom : ???ing for Johnny Rye
10   Wouldn't mind a jug : honey on the mule's behind
11   Yes a brownskin woman : make a preacher lay his
     Bible down
12   A jet-black woman : make a rabbit hug a hound

Ledb   6   Ledbetter, Huddie

        title: New Black Snake Moan
        place and date: New York, 23 Jan. 1935
        record numbers: (16691-2) Ba-33360 Co C-30035

1   Ooh : I ain't got no mammy now
2   She told me late last night : you didn't need no
     mammy nohow
3   Ooh : black snake crawling in my room
4   Better tell somebody : better come and get this old
     black snake soon
5   Oh must have been a bedbug : because a chinch
     couldn't bite me that hard
6   Asked my sugar for fifty cents : said Leadbelly
     ain't a child in the yard
7   Honey that's all right : that's all right for you
8   Darling that's all right : most any old way you do
9   Mmm : oh honey what's the matter now
10   Darling tell me what's the matter : don't like no
     black snake nohow
11   Well : wonder where that black snake gone
12   That old black snake mama : done run my darling home

Ledb   7   Ledbetter, Huddie

        title: Alberta
        place and date: New York, 23 Jan. 1935
        record numbers: (16692-) ARC unissued Co
        C-30035

1   Oh Alberta oh Alberta : don't you hear me calling
     you
2   If Alberta hear your calling : what you want Alberta
     to do
3   I woke up this morning I woke up this morning : with
     the blues right there around my bed
4   Went to eat my breakfast : and the blues all in my
     bread

Ledb   7   Ledbetter, Huddie

5   I lay down last night I lay down last night : I was
     turning from side to side
6   And I was not sick : but I was just dissatisfied
7   I called for you yesterday I called for you
     yesterday : honey and here you come ??? *day*
8   Had you mouth wide open : and you don't know what to
     say
9   Please Alberta please Alberta : tell me what in the
     world you mean
10   Honey the way you treats me : beats all I ever seen
11   What makes an old woman what makes an old woman :
     she go crazy about a right young man
12   Because she know she can take him : and raise him to
     hang

Ledb   8   Ledbetter, Huddie

        title: Baby, Don't You Love Me No More?
        place and date: New York, 24 Jan. 1935
        record numbers: (16693-) ARC unissued Co
        C-30035

1   Mmm : baby why you have to go
2   Oh you ain't love me baby : you used to love me so
3   Mmm : when you left you broke my heart
4   You said you love me baby : and we would never part
5   Mmm : baby your papa ain't a fool
6   There's nothing wrong baby : sweet mama turning cool
7   Mmm : baby what are you going to do
8   You say you love me baby : but now you say you are
     through
9   Mmm : baby ain't you coming back
10   Got money baby : going to use it as I like

Ledb   9   Ledbetter, Huddie

        title: Death Letter Blues--Part 1
        place and date: New York, 24 Jan. 1935
        record numbers: (16695-1) ARC unissued Bio
        BLP-12013

1   Yes she wrote me a letter : what you reckon it read
2   Come home big papa : your loving baby's dead
3   Yes I went to the depot : caught a train a-flying
4   When I walked in Lord : she was slowly dying
5   My mama said howdy : papa said goodbye
6   Poor boy couldn't do nothing : but hang his head and
     cry
7   He went to the bedside : looked down in her face
8   I love you pretty mama : just can't take your place

Ledb   10   Ledbetter, Huddie

        title: Death Letter Blues--Part 2
        place and date: New York, 24 Jan. 1935
        record numbers: (16696-1) ARC unissued Bio
        BLP-12013

1   So many high *gate* buggies : were a-standing around
2   Waiting to take my baby : to the burying ground
3   Yes you taken my baby : to the burying ground
4   You didn't break my heart Lord : till you laid her
     down
5   Yes he went to the headboard : fell down on his
     knees
6   If you speak one word babe : you can give my heart
     some ease
7   You don't miss your water : till your well go dry
8   You don't miss pretty mama : till you shake your
     hand goodbye
9   Don't your house look lonesome : when your woman is
     gone
10   Don't you feel mistreated : but you won't let on

165

Ledb   11   Ledbetter, Huddie

        title: Kansas City Papa
        place and date: New York, 24 Jan. 1935
        record numbers: (16697-1) ARC unissued Bio
        BLP-12013

 1 I'm going to Kansas City : I'm going to lower my
    line
 2 I get in Kansas City : I be hard to find
 3 Women in Kansas City Lord : doing the turkey trot
 4 The women in Louisiana Lord : doing the eagle rock
 5 The funniest thing : that I ever seen
 6 The tomcat stitching : on a sewing machine
 7 The funniest thing : that I ever did see
 8 A polecat climbing : up a 'simmon tree
 9 You keep on talking : till you make me think
10 You daddy was a bulldog : your mammy was a mink
11 You keep on talking : till you make me mad
12 I tell you about the troubles : that your sister had

Ledb   12   Ledbetter, Huddie

        title: Red River Blues
        place and date: New York, 24 Jan. 1935
        record numbers: (16704-) ARC unissued Co
        C-30035

 1 Tell me which a-way : do the Red River run
 2 I suppose : they run oh run sun to sun
 3 Lord it's some boats sail : run from sun to sun
 4 Way down in Louisiana : oh where the work all done
 5 Tell me pretty mama : which a-way you going
 6 If you can't tell me : that going to be your ruin
 7 I got up this morning : hung all around my brown
 8 Because she told me : which a-way the Red River was
    a-running down
 9 Would you take a poor ??? : *or a slave* like me
10 I love my baby : you going to let me be

Ledb   13   Ledbetter, Huddie

        title: My Friend Blind Lemon
        place and date: New York, 5 Feb. 1935
        record numbers: (16807-) ARC unissued Co
        C-30035

 1 Dreamed last night : and all that night before
 2 Heard my baby : knocking on my door
 3 Crying babe : have I ever done you wrong
 5 You's a long time coming : daddy but you welcome
    here

Ledb   14   Ledbetter, Huddie

        title: Mr. Hughe's Town
        place and date: New York, 5 Feb. 1935
        record numbers: (16808-) ARC unissued Co
        C-30035

 1 My mama told me : my sister too
 2 Women in Shreveport son : going to be the death of
    you
 3 I told my mama : mama you don't know
 4 Women in Shreveport kill me : why don't you let me
    go
 5 Told my mama : fell on my knees
 6 Crying oh Lordy mama : will you forgive me please
 7 I got a woman : living on Stony Hill
 8 She been sitting down : gambling with Buffalo Bill
 9 Been sitting down : gambling with Buffalo Bill
10 *You chance it once* baby : you ain't done got
    killed
11 Anybody should ask you : who composed this song
12 Tell them : Huddie Ledbetter's done been here and
    gone

Ledb   15   Ledbetter, Huddie

        title: Shorty George
        place and date: New York, 5 Feb. 1935
        record numbers: (16814-2) ARC unissued Bio
        BLP-12013

 1 Well Shorty George : ain't no friend of mine
 2 He keeps a-taking all the women : keep all the men
    behind
 3 Lord I went to my captain : and the man he don't
    care
 4 I'm going to take my woman : bring her right back
    here
 5 I want to tell you captain : it's a dirty shame
 6 Shorty George got my woman : left me all in vain
 7 Yes I went to the station : looked up on the sign
 8 Lord the train she ride : you marked up on time
 9 Well I can't do nothing : hon' but wave my hands
10 Got me a lifetime sentence : down in Sugarland
11 Lordy some has got six months : some got two and
    three years
12 But it's so many good men : got lifetime here
13 And Shorty George : traveling through the land
14 He don't take your woman : take some woman's man
15 Got something to tell you : don't let it make you
    mad
16 I ain't got long down here : honey you heard I had

Ledb   16   Ledbetter, Huddie

        title: Match Box Blues
        place and date: New York, 5 Feb. 1935
        record numbers: (168??-) ARC unissued Co
        C-30035

 1 Sitting down here wondering : would a matchbox hold
    my clothes
 2 I don't want to be bothered : with no big trunk on
    my road
 3 Now what would you do : when your baby packing up
    her trunk
 4 Get you half a gallon of whiskey : and get on you a
    big drunk
 5 Lord : have mercy on me

Ledb   17   Ledbetter, Huddie

        title: Yellow Jacket
        place and date: New York, 23 Mar. 1935
        record numbers: (17179-1) ARC unissued Bio
        BLP-12013

 1 Yellow jacket yellow jacket : you sting me once more
 2 You can sting me once more : and then I've got to go
 3 You stung me this morning : stung me till I was sore
 4 You can sting me one more time : please don't sting
    me no more
 5 You can buzz yellow jacket : buzz all around my face
 6 I don't want no other yellow jacket : to just take
    your place
 7 You can go downtown : can buzz all around
 8 But if I catch you stinging : believe I'll pull your
    nest all on down

Ledb   18   Ledbetter, Huddie

        title: T. B. Woman Blues
        place and date: New York, 23 Mar. 1935
        record numbers: (17180-1) ARC unissued Bio
        BLP-12013

 1 It's too late too late : too late too late too late
 2 I'm on my way to Denver : and mama must I hesitate
 3 T B's all right to have : if your friend didn't
    treat you so lowdown

166

Ledb   18   Ledbetter, Huddie

4 Don't you ask them for no favor : they even stop
     a-coming around
5 Mmm : this T B is killing me
6 I'm a-like a prisoner : I'm always a-working the
     street
7 When I was on my feet : couldn't even walk down the
     street
8 I want my body buried : in the deep blue sea
9 Mmm : mmm
10 I got tuberculosis : consumption is killing me

Ledb   19   Ledbetter, Huddie

      title: Pig Meat Papa
      place and date: New York, 23 Mar. 1935
      record numbers: (17181-2) ARC-6-04-55 His HLP-4

1 Just look a-here mama : don't treat pigmeat the way
     you do
2 Your baby's pigmeat : as anybody in the neighborhood
3 If you don't believe it's pigmeat : come in and you
     won't regret
4 I got something about this pigmeat : sweet mama I
     ain't told you yet
5 I was born and raised in the country : mama but I'm
     staying in town
6 If you don't believe this pigmeat : mama from my
     head on down
7 You can take me to the mountain : there will be
     pigmeat there
8 You take a boat to China : *they'll catch us*
     anywhere
9 Ooh : and *catch us* anywhere
10 Take a boat to China : then it's *catch us* anywhere

Ledb   20   Ledbetter, Huddie

      title: Bull Cow
      place and date: New York, 23 Mar. 1935
      record numbers: (17182-) ARC unissued Co
         C-30035

1 If you got you a bullcow : *feed her morning grass*
2 Because when them heifers come around : eat your yas
     yas yas
3 If you got you a bullcow : *feed her in the grove*
4 Because when them heifers leave him : you know he's
     going to rove
5 Oh oh oh : hey hey hey hey
6 But you know good and well baby : *might be a heifer
     calf*
7 If you got you a bullcow : lead her with a long line
8 Because when them heifers leave him : you know they
     on his mind
9 Oh bullcow : where you been so long
10 I been all out in the country : with my big bell on

LeeB   1   Lee, Bertha

      title: Mind Reader Blues
      place and date: New York, 31 Jan. 1934
      record numbers: (14736-1) Vo-02650 OJL-17

1 Baby I can see : just what's on your mind
2 You got a long black woman : with a gold teeth in
     her face
3 I'll take a long look : right smack down in your
     mind
4 And I don't see but one woman : rambling up and down
     the line
5 Don't kid your mama : you ain't fooling nobody but
     yourself
6 And when I see on your mind : you would not have no
     friend

LeeB   1   Lee, Bertha

7 I remember the day : when I was living at Lula town
8 My man did so many wrong things : that I had to
     leave the town
9 I'm by the riverside : my man caught the transfer
     boat
10 And the last time I seed him : he had done gone way
     up the road
11 Well I'm worried now : and I won't be worried long

LeeX   1   Leecan, Bobby

      title: Macon Georgia Cut-Out
      place and date: New York, c. June 1927
      record numbers: (   ) Pat-7533 His HLP-17

1 Now if you want to learn this dance : don't do it in
     a *pout*
2 Put both feet together : and do the Macon cutout
3 You need not to worry : neither think
4 Just tell the waiter man : to bring on a drink
5 Now you grab your girl : you hold her tight
6 You do it in one position : all night
7 Ease up daddy : you been a good old scout
8 You made a hit with your mama : now you can't lose
     out
9 Now back in eighteen hundred : and sixty-two
10 Folks mess around : but they didn't know what to do
11 Old Uncle Mose : he was the jellyroll king
12 He get to flat-foot shuffling : call it everything
13 Old *Rufus* Pete : he was very slow
14 All the women loved him : and give him their dough
15 Now take it easy mama : and be a good scout
16 If you want to do this dance : Macon cutout

LeeX   2   Leecan, Bobby

      title: Nobody Knows You When You're Down and Out
      place and date: New York, c. June 1927
      record numbers: (   ) Pat-7533 His HLP-17

1 Now I went downtown : along Broadway
2 Looked up at a sign : that said no free meals today
3 Walked right in : I took a seat
4 Waiter looked at me and said : hey brother pay up
     before you eat
5 I was raggedy : thirsty too
6 *Last* all my money : was won from two-by-two
7 In my pocket : I didn't have a cent
8 Sashay down the street : to where I went
9 In your pockets : you ain't ain't got a dime
10 Look all over town : not a friend you can find
11 As soon as your money : grows treetop tall
12 Bill Jack and Harry : will give you a call
13 Now listen now brother : this ain't no doubt
14 Nobody wants you : when you're down and out
15 Now I was singing : them lonesome kind of blues
16 I thought I'd play some numbers : like most colored
     people do
17 I put my money down : on old twenty-two
18 I didn't play no believing : I thought that would do
19 As soon as I saw : that I had won
20 The man *brought over* eleven : instead of
     twenty-one
21 A friend walked up to me : the very next day
22 He said he lost on that number : the very same way

LewAr   1   Lewis, Archie

      title: Miss Handy Hanks
      place and date: Richmond, Ind., 30 Mar. 1933
      record numbers: (19107) Ch-16677 Rt RL-334

1 I got spreading mustard : from north to south
2 Seeds taste good : right in your mouth

LewF   1   Lewis, Furry

        title: Jellyroll
        place and date: probably New York, 28 May 1927
        record numbers: (   ) Vo-1115 RBF RF-11

1   I went to the Gypsy : get my fortune told
2   Lord the Gypsy told me : boy you got a jellyroll
3   Ain't nobody in town : cook a jellyroll like mine
5   I was first on Main Street : Lord and I started down
     Beale
6   Looking for my girl : Lord that we all call Lucille
7   I know you don't want me : why don't you tell me so
8   Then you won't be bothered : with me around your
     house no more
9   Lord my good girl quit me : my kid done put me down
10   I wouldn't hurt so bad : but the doggone news across
     town
11   We got a new way of spelling : Memphis Tennessee
12   Double M double E : Lord A Y Lord Z
13   Ooh : my gal done quit me now
14   I'm going to the river : I'm going to jump overboard
     and drown

LewF   2   Lewis, Furry

        title: Mr. Furry's Blues
        place and date: probably New York, 28 May 1927
        record numbers: (   ) Vo-1115 Rt RL-323

1   I wish I had : my poor heart in my hand
2   I'd show you women : how to treat a man
3   I'm going I'm going : your crying won't make me stay
4   For the more you cry : further you drive me away
5   You know you didn't want me : you oughtn't've made
     no stall
6   There's plenty more women : ???
7   If the river was whiskey : I'd stay drunk all the
     time
8   So a woman like you : could not worry my mind
9   Some of these mornings : baby listen to what I say
10   I'm going away to leave you : it will be too late to
     pray

LewF   3   Lewis, Furry

        title: Sweet Papa Moan
        place and date: probably New York, 28 May 1927
        record numbers: (   ) Vo-1116 RBF RF-11

1   Ooh : what am I going to do now
2   Because the girl I love : she don't treat me right
3   Baby : what do you want [me, your papa] to do
4   Beg borrow and steal : bring it all home to you
5   Say the sun's going to shine : in my back door some
     day
6   Lord the wind's going to blow : blow my blues away
7   Hey : wonder where the I C train
8   Babe I'll go to my woman : you go to your man
9   Ooh : I'd rather be dead and in my grave
10   Than be here in the world : baby and be your slave

LewF   4   Lewis, Furry

        title: Good Looking Girl Blues
        place and date: probably New York, c. late Oct.
        1927
        record numbers: (   ) Vo-1132 Rt RL-329

1   Don't you wish : your good girl was long and tall
     like mine
2   Lord she ain't good-looking : but I think she takes
     her time
3   Said my good girl said : she didn't want me no more
4   But she don't mind *dancing* : Lord everywhere I go
5   Lord the train I ride : is sixteen coaches long

LewF   4   Lewis, Furry

6   And she don't *allow* nothing : but chocolate to the
     bone
7   I'm worried now : been worried all day long
8   Babe I'm going to be worried : until the day I'm
     gone
9   Lord there's some say yellow : but give me my black
     and brown
10   When your high brown quit you : your black will run
     you down
11   I want to see want to see : the girl I'm *for
     painted about*
12   I be so glad : I sure can't help but shout

LewF   5   Lewis, Furry

        title: Big Chief Blues
        place and date: probably New York, c. late Oct.
        1927
        record numbers: (   ) Vo-1133 Yz L-1002

1   I'm going away baby : take me seven long months to
     ride
2   January February : March April May June July
3   I was three years old : when my poor mother died
4   If you mistreat me : mistreat a motherless child
5   I dreamt last night : the whole round world was mine
6   Wasn't nothing at all : but my good girl jumping
     down
7   She put carbolic in my coffee : turpentine in my tea
8   Strychnine in my biscuits : Lord but she didn't hurt
     me
9   Baby when I marry : going to marry an Indian squaw
10   Big chief Lord : be my daddy-in-law

LewF   6   Lewis, Furry

        title: Falling Down Blues
        place and date: probably New York, c. late Oct.
        1927
        record numbers: (   ) Vo-1133 OJL-21

1   I got the blues so bad : it hurts my feet to walk
2   I wouldn't hurt so bad : but it hurt my tongue to
     talk
3   Mama I feel like jumping : through the keyhole in
     your door
4   I can jump so easy : your man will never know
5   Some people say : worried blues ain't tough
6   If they don't kill you : hell you mighty rough
7   Hitch up my buggy : please saddle up my black mare
8   I'm going to find my woman : on the road somewhere
9   She caught the rumbling : I caught the falling down
10   If I ever see her : I never turn around

LewF   7   Lewis, Furry

        title: Mean Old Bedbug Blues
        place and date: probably New York, c. late Oct.
        1927
        record numbers: (   ) Vo-1134 Rt RL-333

1   Man those bedbugs sure is evil : he sure don't mean
     me no good
2   He thinks I'm a woodpecker : and he taken me for a
     chunk of wood
3   When I lay down at night : and I wonder how can a
     poor man sleep
4   When one holding your hand : while the other one
     eating your feet
5   Bedbugs big as a jackass : he will bite you and
     stand and grin
6   *Think you pull the bedbug apart* : come back and
     bite you again

LewF   7   Lewis, Furry

7   Someone moaning in the corner : Lord I tried so hard
    to see
8   It was a mother bedbug : Lord praying for some more
    to eat
9   I have to sit up all night long : my feet can't
    touch the floor
10 Because the mean old bedbug : told me I can't live
    there no more

LewF   8   Lewis, Furry

    title: Why Don't You Come Home Blues
    place and date: probably New York, c. late Oct.
    1927
    record numbers: (   ) Vo-1134 Rt RL-333

1   Sarah Lee : why don't you come home
2   I ain't had no loving : gal since you been gone
3   My mama told me : when I was a child
4   Good time now : trouble after a while
5   If I had a-listened : to what my mother said
6   I wouldn't be in here : treated this a-way
7   I'd rather see my coffin : roll in front of my door
8   Than to hear my good gal : say I don't want you no
    more
9   I dreamt last night : the world was caving in
10 Wasn't nothing at all : my girl coming home again
11 I feel like jumping : from the treetop to the ground
12 The girl I love : she sure done put me down
13 I wished I had a-died : babe when I was young
14 I would not have : this *here red suit on*

LewF   9   Lewis, Furry

    title: Furry's Blues
    place and date: Memphis, 28 Aug. 1928
    record numbers: (45424-1) Vi-V38519 Rt RL-333

1   I believe I'll buy me : a graveyard of my own
2   I'm going to kill everybody : that have done me
    wrong
3   If you want to go to Nashville : man and ain't got
    no fare
4   Cut your good girl's throat : and the judge will
    send you there
5   I'm going to get my pistol : forty rounds of ball
6   I'm going to shoot my woman : just to see her fall
7   I'd rather hear the screws : on my coffin sound
8   Than to hear my good girl : says I'm jumping down
9   Get my pencil and paper : I'm going to sit right
    down
10 I'm going to write me a letter : back to Youngstown
11 This ain't my home : I ain't got no right to stay
12 This ain't my home : must be my stopping place
13 When I left my home : you would not let me be
14 Wouldn't rest contented : till I come to Tennessee

LewF   10   Lewis, Furry

    title: I Will Turn Your Money Green
    place and date: Memphis, 28 Aug. 1928
    record numbers: (45425-2) Vi-V38506 Yz L-1008

1   When I was in Missouri : would not let me be
2   Wouldn't rest content : till I came to Tennessee
3   If you follow me baby : I'll turn your money green
4   I show you more money : Rockerfeller ever seen
5   If the river was whiskey : baby and I was a duck
6   I'd dive to the bottom : Lord and I'd never come up
7   Lord the woman I hate : I see her every day
8   But the woman I love : she's so far away
9   Talk about *sweetheart* : I declare I'm a honest man
10 Give my woman so many dollars : it broke her apron
    string

LewF   10   Lewis, Furry

11 All she give me was trouble : I'm troubled all the
    time
12 I been troubled so long : trouble don't worry my
    mind
13 I been down so long : it seem like up to me
14 Woman I love : she done quit poor me
15 What's the need of me hollering : what's the need of
    me crying
16 Woman I love : she don't pay me no mind

LewF   11   Lewis, Furry

    title: Mistreatin' Mama
    place and date: Memphis, 28 Aug. 1928
    record numbers: (45428-2) Vi-V38519 Rt RL-323

1   If your heart ain't iron : it must be marble stone
2   For you're a mistreating mama : baby as sure as you
    born
3   I can tell from a little : just what a whole lot
    means
4   You treat me just like : somebody you ain't never
    seen
5   I got a woman in Cuba : got a woman in Spain
6   I got a woman in Chicago : I'm scared to call her
    name
7   I got nineteen women : and all I wants one more
8   If the one more suit me : I'm going to let the
    nineteen go
9   I could have religion : Lord this very day
10 But the womens and whiskey : Lord won't let me pray
11 I can sit right here : and look on Jackson Avenue
12 I can see everything : that my good woman do
13 Sometime I believe I will : sometime I believe I
    won't
14 Sometime I believe I do : sometime I believe I don't

LewF   12   Lewis, Furry

    title: Dry Land Blues
    place and date: Memphis, 28 Aug. 1928
    record numbers: (45429-1) Vi-23345 Yz L-1021

1   I can look through muddy water baby : and spy dry
    land
2   If you don't want me honey : let's take and in hand
3   I'm going so far : I can't hear your rooster crow
4   This is my last time : ever knocking at your door
5   You won't cook me no dinner : baby you won't iron me
    no clothes
6   You won't do nothing : but walk the *Horn Lake* Road
7   Man if you love your woman : better mess it in her
    cup
8   So if she have not quit you boy : won't leave you in
    tough luck
9   Now you can take my woman : but you ain't done
    nothing smart
10 For I got more than one woman : playing in my back
    yard
11 Windstorm come : and it blowed my house away
12 I'm a good old boy : but I ain't got nowhere to stay
13 And it's trouble here : and it's trouble everywhere
14 So much trouble : floating in the air
15 What you going to do : when your trouble get like
    mine

LewF   13   Lewis, Furry

    title: Judge Harsh Blues
    place and date: Memphis, 28 Aug. 1928
    record numbers: (45433-2) Vi-V38506 Yz L-1008

1   Good morning judge : what may be my fine
2   Fifty dollars : and eleven twenty-nine

LewF 13   Lewis, Furry

3   They arrest me for murder : I ain't never harmed a
        man
4   Women hollered murder : and I ain't raised my hand
5   I ain't got nobody : get me out on bond
6   I would not mind : but I ain't done nothing wrong
7   Please Judge Harsh : make it light as you possibly
        can
8   I ain't done no work : judge in I don't know when
9   My woman come a-running : with a hundred dollars in
        her hand
10 Crying judge : please spare my man
11 One hundred dollars won't do : better run and get
        you three
12 I can keep you man : from penitentiary
13 Because I'm arrested baby : please don't grieve and
        moan
14 Penitentiary : seems just like my home
15 People all hollering : about what in the world they
        will do
16 Lots of people had justice : and been in
        penitentiary too

LewF 14   Lewis, Furry

        title: Black Gypsy Blues
        place and date: Memphis, 22 Sept. 1929
        record numbers: (M-185-) Vo-1547 Yz L-1008

1   My woman must be a black Gypsy : she knows every
        place I go
2   She met me this morning : with a brand new
        forty-four
3   When you used to be my Gypsy : done just so and so
4   Now I got another baby : I can't use you no more
5   Eagle rock me mama : *Sally long me too*
6   Ain't nobody in town : can eagle rock like you
7   My woman got a mouth : like a lighthouse in the sea
8   Every time she smiles : she shine her light on me
9   Had the blues all of twenty-eight : started again in
        twenty-nine
10 They tell me the New York Central : is a
        nickel-plated line
11 Lord I asked for cabbage : she brought me turnip
        greens
12 I asked her for water : and she brought me gasoline

LewF 15   Lewis, Furry

        title: Creeper's Blues
        place and date: Memphis, 22 Sept. 1929
        record numbers: (M-186-) Vo-1547 Yz L-1008

1   I woke up this morning : and I looked up against the
        wall
2   Roaches and the bedbugs : playing a game of ball
3   Score was twenty to nothing : the roaches was ahead
4   Roaches got to fighting : and kicked me out of bed
5   Bedbugs so bad : pull the pillow from under my head
6   They got a Winchester rifle : and try to kill me
        dead
7   When I woke up this morning : I looked down on the
        floor
8   Bedbug had been in my pocket : and pulled out all my
        dough
9   Mama get your hatchet : kill the fly on your baby's
        head
10 Mama get your hatchet : and run here to my bed
11 Please bedbugs : please I done begged you twice
12 You done taken all my money : and now you want to
        take my life

LewN 1   Lewis, Noah (Gus Cannon)

        title: Viola Lee Blues
        place and date: Memphis, 20 Sept. 1928
        record numbers: (47066-?) Vi-V38523 OJL-21

1   The judge he repeat it : the clerk he wrote it down
2   If you *mistreat your* ??? : you must be *Nashville*
        bound
3   Some got six months : some got one solid year
4   But me and my buddy : both got lifetimes here
5   Fix my supper : let me go to bed
6   I been drinking white lightning : it gone to my head

LewN 2   Lewis, Noah (Gus Cannon)

        title: Going to Germany
        place and date: Memphis, 1 Oct. 1929
        record numbers: (56318-2) Vi-V38585 OJL-4

1   I'm going to Germa : I'll be back some old day
3   Please tell me mama : what more can I do
4   Done all I knowed : I can't get along with you
5   Go away from my window : stop knocking on my door
6   I got another woman : can't use you no more
7   When you's in trouble : I worked and paid your fine
8   Now I'm in trouble : you don't pay me no mind

LewN 3   Lewis, Noah (Gus Cannon)

        title: Pretty Mama Blues
        place and date: Memphis, 3 Oct. 1929
        record numbers: (56342-2) Vi-V38585 RCA INT-1175

1   Hey pretty mama : can I get a job with you
2   I ain't got no money : I can't get no work to do
3   The woman I love : she weighs a thousand and four
4   I don't care : if she weighed a thousand more
5   I wrote her a letter : I mailed it in the air
6   You may know by that : I got a friend somewhere
7   I ain't never loved : but four womens in my life
8   That was my mama my sister : sweetheart and my wife

LewN 4   Lewis, Noah

        title: Ticket Agent Blues
        place and date: Memphis, 26 Nov. 1930
        record numbers: (64736-) BB-B5675 OJL-4

1   Ticket agent : please raise your window high
2   So I will know my train : when it's passing by
3   Depot agent : please turn your depot around
4   My woman done quit me now : going to leave your town

LewN 5   Lewis, Noah

        title: New Minglewood Blues
        place and date: Memphis, 26 Nov. 1930
        record numbers: (64737-2) Vi-23266 OJL-4

1   I was born in the desert : I was raised in the
        lion's den
2   Said my regular occupation : taking women from their
        men
3   When you come to Memphis : please stop by Minglewood
4   Says there's womens in the camp : don't mean no man
        no good

LewN   6   Lewis, Noah

    title: Bad Luck's My Buddy
    place and date: Memphis, 26 Nov. 1930
    record numbers: (64739-) Vi-23266 Rt RL-307

1 And it's trouble here : it's trouble in the air
2 Says I want to go home : but I know it's trouble
   there
3 I'm going home : going to tell my brother will
4 Said that old woman he's got : is sure going to get
   him killed
5 Bad luck is my buddy : and trouble is my friend
6 I been in trouble : ever since here I been

Linc   1   Lincoln, Charley

    title: Jealous Hearted Blues
    place and date: Atlanta, 4 Nov. 1927
    record numbers: (145103-2) Co-14305-D RBF RF-9

1 You can have my money : all I own
2 For God's sake : leave my gal alone
3 I got a range in my kitchen : bakes nice and brown
4 All I need : someone to turn my damper down
5 Take a rocking chair to rock : take a rubber ball to
   roll
6 Take a gal I love : satisfy my soul
7 I know the mens don't like me : because I speak my
   mind
8 All the women crazy about me : because I takes my
   time
9 I left my wife and baby : sitting on the doorstep
   crying
10 I got a house full of children : and there ain't
   nar' one mine
11 I says I got love : if I could have it in your home
12 I can keep it turned off : or I can turn it on
13 Says hello Central : give me two three nine
14 *What takes : to get a day's help for mine*
15 Oh some folks say : that them blues ain't bad
16 That must not have been : ??? blues I had
17 I says I can't help mama : what you do
18 You can tell the world : I got those jealous-hearted
   blues
19 I said stop still mama : and let me give you my
   advice
20 If I catch you with a man : going to be too tight

Linc   2   Lincoln, Charley

    title: Hard Luck Blues
    place and date: Atlanta, 4 Nov. 1927
    record numbers: (145104-2) Co-14272-D His HLP-4

1 Two kind of people in this world mama : babe that I
   sure can't stand
2 That's a two-faced woman : baby and a monkey-man
3 Just as sure as a sparrow mama : babe flying in the
   air
4 I got a loving sweet mama : in this world somewhere
5 Said the blues in my body : I said making towards my
   head
6 I believe to my soul : mama them blues going to kill
   me dead
7 I ain't going to grieve mama : I sure ain't going to
   cry no more
8 Going to take my best friend's gal : said the one
   that lives next door
9 She's a married woman : but she says she likes me
10 Hate to bite my friend : somebody been biting me
11 Said I used to have money : but said now I'm cold in
   hand
12 Said I used to have a good gal : but now she's got
   another man
13 Talk about hard luck babe : sure done fell on me

Linc   2   Lincoln, Charley

14 Says my brother stole a *ham sand* : the police has
   locked up me

Linc   3   Lincoln, Charley

    title: Mojoe Blues
    place and date: Atlanta, 4 Nov. 1927
    record numbers: (145105-3) Co-14475-D RBF RF-15

1 Oh the mojo blues mama : crawling across the floor
2 Some hard-luck rascal : done told me I ain't here no
   more
3 I'm leaving here mama : babe crying won't make me
   stay
4 Honey the more you cry : further I'm going away
5 Aw she went to a hoodoo : she went there all alone
6 Because every time I leave her : I have to hurry
   back home
7 Said I love you sweet mama : but I sure ain't no
   fool about you
8 I can get another kid gal : just like I got you
9 When I leave here : you can pin crepe over my door
10 Said I won't be dead : just ain't coming here no
   more
11 Some people tell me : honey them blues ain't bad
12 That must not been : them lowdown things I had

Linc   4   Lincoln, Charley

    title: My Wife Drove Me From the Door
    place and date: Atlanta, 4 Nov. 1927
    record numbers: (145106-1) Co-14305-D RBF RF-202

1 When I came home this morning : my wife she met me
   at the door
2 Go away sweet daddy : said I can't use you no more
3 Hey hey mama : baby what the matter now
4 Say you trying to quit me : honey and you don't know
   how
5 Well it ain't no love : sure ain't no getting along
6 Said my brown treat me so mean : that I don't know
   right from wrong
7 Come back baby : papa ain't mad with you
8 Says I do just like : mama babe that I used to do
9 Take me back baby : try me just one more time
10 If I don't do to suit you honey : I'll break my
   backbone trying
11 I know the mens don't like me : because that I speak
   my mind
12 But the women crazy about me : because that I take
   my time

Linc   5   Lincoln, Charley

    title: Country Breakdown
    place and date: Atlanta, 4 Nov. 1927
    record numbers: (145107-1) Co-14475-D RBF RF-15

1 I'm leaving here mama : crying won't make me stay
2 Oh the more you cry babe : the farther I'm going
   away
3 Soon as I get sober : I'll make me drunk again
4 Said I'm going to leave the chicken : said I'm going
   back to the hen
5 Did you ever wake up : 'twixt night and day
6 Had your arm around your pillow : where your good
   gal used to lay
7 I believe to my soul : my brown's got a stingaree
8 When I woke up this morning : say she was stinging
   poor me
9 Don't want no dollar mama : I sure can't use no half
10 Say I got a brown : says I can hear her laugh

Linc   6   Lincoln, Charley

        title: Chain Gang Trouble
        place and date: Atlanta, 4 Nov. 1927
        record numbers: (145108-2) Co-14272-D His HLP-4

1   I asked my captain : for the time of day
2   Say : he throwed his watch away
3   If I listened at my mother : in farther day
4   I never : would have been here today
5   If I ever get back home : oh baby to stay
6   I never : be treated this a-way
7   How long how long : how long how long
8   How long : before I can go home
9   I rise with the blues : and I work with the blues
10 Nothing I can get : but bad news

Linc   7   Lincoln, Charley

        title: Doodle Hole Blues
        place and date: Atlanta, 18 Apr. 1930
        record numbers: (150275-2) Co-14550-D Yz L-1012

1   I'm a little bit worried : getting kind of old
2   Like to take my straw : go play in the doodle hole
3   Do the doodle doodle do : oh doing the doodle doodle
    do
4   I like to take my straw : go play in that doodle
    hole
5   First time you try to doodle : take my advice
6   Put a little spit on your straw : you can do so nice
7   I knowed a little girl : who was very very nice
8   She got to doodle once : and she want it twice
9   Sometime a little doodle : pretty hard to get
10 Keep on twisting : you will find it
11 All you girls get together : with your straw in your
    hand
12 Try to get to doodle : now just see if you can
13 Keep twisting and twisting : around the hole
14 Everybody like to doodle : both young and old
15 I knowed a man once : who got a-on the doodle track
16 He doodled so much : he got a hump in his back
17 It sound mighty funny : but it sure is nice
18 Get this doodle : it's sure worth the price

Lint   1   Linthecome, Joe

        title: Pretty Mama Blues
        place and date: Richmond, Ind., 20 Nov. 1929
        record numbers: (15906-A) Ge-7131 Rt RL-326

1   Listen here pretty mama : what's on your worried
    mind
2   How come you treat me : so unkind
3   If you don't want me mama : why don't you tell me so
4   I can beat an ??? : getting down the road
5   Mama mama : why don't you treat me right
6   Now your papa's loving you : both day and night
7   I'm not so good-looking : I don't dress [so] fine
8   I'm just a plain daddy : and I takes my time
9   I was raised in the mountains : way down in
    Tennessee
10 If you don't like my peaches : don't you shake my
    tree
11 The train's in the station : the crew has climbed
    aboard
12 I'm going to grab that train : travel far down the
    road

List   1   Liston, Virginia

        title: Rolls-Royce Papa
        place and date: New York, 29 May 1926
        record numbers: (   ) Vo-1032 His HLP-1

1   Daddy I'll drop you in my garage : and that's no
    doubt
2   I'm going to wipe your windshield : cut your
    taillight out
3   Your carburettor's rusty : this I really mean
4   Your gas tank's empty : won't hold gasoline
5   Your windshield is broken : it ain't worth a cent
6   Your steering wheel is wobbly : your piston rod is
    bent
7   Your fender's all broken : your wheels ain't tight
8   And I know doggone well : your spark plugs ain't
    hitting right

LitS   1   Little Son Joe

        title: Black Cat Swing
        place and date: Chicago, 12 Dec. 1941
        record numbers: (C-4098-1) OK-06707 BC-1

1   Yes you is one black rat : some day I'll find your
    trail
2   Then I'll hide my shoes : somewhere here in your
    shirt-tail
3   Yes I've taken you downtown : paid your doctor bill
4   Now I'm in a little trouble : and you trying to get
    me killed
5   Says he sneaked in my kitchen : eat up all the bread
6   Soon as I left home : start to cutting up in my bed
7   He *must dance* in the basement : was seen in my
    bedroom
8   Trapped in ??? : I'm going to catch him some day
    soon

Lock   1   Lockwood, Robert

        title: Little Boy Blue
        place and date: Chicago, 30 July 1941
        record numbers: (064640-) BB-B8820 BC-7

1   Little boy blues : please come blow your horn
2   My baby she gone and left me : she left me all alone
3   Now the sheep is in the meadow : and the cows is in
    the corn
4   I've got a girl in Chicago : she loves to hear me
    blow my lonesome horn
5   I'm going to take my whip and whip her : I'm going
    to whip her down to the ground
6   I'm going to take dirk and stab her : then I'm you
    know I'm going to turn it around and around
7   Now I've rambled and I've rambled : until I broke my
    poor self down
8   I believe to my soul : that the little girl is out
    of town

Lock   2   Lockwood, Robert

        title: Take a Little Walk with Me
        place and date: Chicago, 30 July 1941
        record numbers: (064641-) BB-B8820 Yz L-1038

1   Come on baby : please take a walk with me
2   Back to the same old place : where we long to be
3   Come on baby : take a little walk with me
4   Back to the same old place : Memphis Tennessee
5   Early one morning : just about half past three
6   You done something : that's really worrying me
7   Let's take a walk : out on the old avenue
8   I have got something : for you to do
9   Come on baby : now we going to walk so slow

Lock   2   Lockwood, Robert

10 Until every time you see me: you want to walk some
    more

LofC   1   Lofton, Cripple Clarence

        title: Monkey Man Blues
        place and date: Chicago, 2 Apr. 1935
        record numbers: (C-948-A) Vo-02951 Yz L-1015

1   Some of these old days mama : some of these old sad
    lonely nights
2   You will look for your good daddy : and he'll be
    getting his *half-day right*
3   Because I leave town mama : don't count the days I'm
    gone
4   Just count them days baby : that you tried to do
    your daddy wrong
5   I been doing the same thing baby : ever since
    nineteen and twelve
6   I been breaking down with you dizzy mares : seem
    like you want me to dig a country well
7   I would be your monkey-man mama : just can't climb
    no coconut tree
8   I breaks down with you dizzy mares : but I don't get
    on my happy black knees
9   Some day you going to need me mama : swear when I
    won't need you
10 Because when I try to love you right baby : seems
    like my loving won't do

LofC   2   Lofton, Cripple Clarence

        title: Brown Skin Girls
        place and date: Chicago, 18 July 1935
        record numbers: (C-1074-A) ARC-6-11-66 Yz L-1025

1   Got a gang of brownskin womens : bunch of high
    yellows too
2   I got so many brownskins : I don't know what to do
3   I love all of my loving women : I tell this world I
    do
4   I hope some day : that they learn to love their
    daddy too
5   Got a Monday Monday girl : she works on Broadway
    Main
6   I've got a Tuesday girl : that *mama is* spending
    change
7   Wednesday girl : drinks a bottle of beer
8   I've got a Thursday one : that she better not catch
    me here
9   Friday Friday girl : she love those teddy bears
10 I've got a Saturday girl : takes me each and
    everywhere
11 It's run here boys and girls : let *me papa* send a
    word to you
12 She wears a bearcat skin : she got a suit of navy
    blues

LofC   3   Lofton, Cripple Clarence

        title: I Don't Know
        place and date: probably Chicago, c. 1936-1938
        record numbers: (   ) private record Yz L-1025

1   Got to sit around : for a while
2   Shook his *juicy rib* : down his aisle
3   There's a lady : but her name is Lou
4   Shook that thing : till she caught the flu
5   Getting sick and tired : of the way you do
6   Time mama : I'm going to poison you
7   Sprinkle gopher-dust : around your bed
8   Wake up some morning : find your own self dead
9   Shake it and break it Lord : you can hang it on the
    wall

LofC   3   Lofton, Cripple Clarence

10 Out the window : catch it before it fall
11 Stop awhile : shimmy if it's all night long
12 ??? things : is got your habits on

LofC   4   Lofton, Cripple Clarence

        title: Change My Mind Blues
        place and date: probably Chicago, c. 1936-1938
        record numbers: (   ) private record Yz L-1025

1   If I change my mind Jane : I'll change my mind once
    again
2   I have mistaken my life : people and I can't get
    back again
3   Sometimes I wonder : what make you treat me so mean
4   Good as I have been to you darling : now I can't get
    the things I need

LofC   5   Lofton, Cripple Clarence

        title: Streamline Train
        place and date: probably Chicago, c. 1936-1938
        record numbers: (   ) private record Yz L-1025

1   Streamline train : back train to front
2   That that train : took my baby on
3   Yes I'm leaving you in the morning : leaving on that
    streamline train
4   One thing I could tell you : get your mind off that
    thing
5   Trains rolled for New York : half past four
6   Four o'clock that morning : I was thinking on my
    baby *door*
7   She says come in loving daddy : where have you done
    been so long
8   I ain't had my great loving : since my streamline
    been gone
9   Train rolled to Birmingham : half past six
10 Half five that morning : I trying to get it fixed
11 I'm going out to West ??? : I'm going to marry me an
    Indian squaw
12 Stay with them Indian chiefs : be my father-in-law
13 Baby I'm leaving you in the morning : leaving on
    that streamline train
14 One thing I can tell you : get your mind off that
    man

LofW   1   Lofton, Willie

        title: Jake Leg Blues
        place and date: Chicago, 24 Aug. 1934
        record numbers: (C-9386-A) De-7076 Rt RL-314

1   I say jake leg jake leg jake leg : tell me what in
    the world you going to do
2   I say you done drunk so much jake oh Lord : till it
    done give him the *lemon leg*
3   I say I know the jake leg oh Lord : just as far as I
    can hear the poor boy walk
4   I say the people drink their jake on the rush : now
    oh Lord they even throw their bottle away
6   But the jake leg ??? oh Lord : that keep them coming
    every day
7   Mmm mama mama mama mama mama Lord children keep on
    crying : wonder what in the world poor daddy going
    to do
8   I say he done drunk so much jake oh Lord : till it
    done give him the *lemon leg*
9   Mama mama mama mama crying out and say oh Lord :
    there's nothing in the world poor daddy can do
10 Because he done drunk so much jake oh Lord : till
    they got the *lemon leg* too

173

LofW   2   Lofton, Willie

        title: My Mean Baby Blues
        place and date: Chicago, 24 Aug. 1934
        record numbers: (C-9387-A) De-7076 Rt RL-314

1 When my baby left me : she didn't even say goodbye
2 When I turned my back : she packed her clothes on
   the sly
3 You can read my letter : but you sure can't read my
   mind
4 You see me laughing honey : just to keep from crying
5 Some of the meanest people : the poor boy most ever
   seen
6 You ask for water : they give you gasoline
7 I used to try to love you baby : a-loving you *in
   crime*
8 Some day you going to want to love the poor boy :
   and I'll be done changed my mind

LofW   3   Lofton, Willie

        title: Dark Road Blues
        place and date: Chicago, 1 Nov. 1935
        record numbers: (96257-) BB-B6229 Yz L-1007

1 Crying I ain't going down : that dark road by myself
2 Crying if I don't carry you : carry somebody else
3 Crying who that yonder : coming up the road
4 Crying that look like my faro : but she walk too
   slow
5 Crying won't let you do me : like you did poor shine
6 Crying you taken the poor boy's money : going to
   have to kill me before you take mine
7 Crying smokes like lightning : shine like faro gold
8 Crying I wouldn't get in trouble : to save nobody's
   soul
9 Crying I spied a spider : climbing up the wall
10 Crying I asked the spider : did he want his ashes
   hauled
11 Crying I ain't going to marry : ain't going to
   settle down
12 Crying I'm a-stay right here : till my mustache
   dragged the ground
13 Crying where was you : when the Frisco left the yard
14 Crying I was standing right there : police had me
   barred

Luca   1   Lucas, Jane

        title: Pussy Cat Blues
        place and date: New York, 15 Sept. 1930
        record numbers: (10031-2) Ba-32138 Yz L-1035

1 You can play with my pussy : but please don't dog it
   around
2 If you going to mistreat it : no pussy will be found
3 Soon as I get sober : going to get drunk again
4 If I can't get no liquor : drink that good garden
   gin
5 If you got a good pussy : folks don't give it away
6 The rats may overtake you : need your pussy cat some
   day

Luca   2   Lucas, Jane

        title: Where Did You Stay Last Night?
        place and date: Richmond, Ind., 19 Nov. 1930
        record numbers: (17277-A) Ch-16171 Riv RM-8803

1 You can talk about me going : push me to the wall
2 Check up on my loving : but you sure can't get it
   all

Luca   3   Lucas, Jane

        title: Fix It
        place and date: Richmond, Ind., 19 Nov. 1930
        record numbers: (17278-A) Ch-16215 Riv RM-8803

1 Mr oh Mr : can't you fix this thing for me
2 I'd give anything to fix it : I don't care what it
   be
3 Mr won't you fix it : what makes you wait so long
4 If you don't want to fix it : tell me and I'll be
   moving on
5 You got tools Mr : everybody say your work is fine
6 So don't have no part missing : I want you to work
   all night

Luca   4   Lucas, Jane

        title: Double Trouble Blues
        place and date: Richmond, Ind., 19 Nov. 1930
        record numbers: (17285) Ch-16289 Yz L-1035

1 When you get in trouble : you can always tell who's
   your friend
2 If you ask him for any money : say I ain't got none
   to lend
3 Trouble wake me in the morning : put me to bed late
   at night
4 Now if I get out of trouble : going to start living
   right
5 Trouble trouble : I've been having it all my days
6 Old trouble killed my sister : got me one foot in my
   grave
7 Sometime I wonder : what am I going to do
8 Sometime I'm happy : most every time I am blue

Luca   5   Lucas, Jane

        title: Leave My Man Alone
        place and date: Richmond, Ind., 19 Nov. 1930
        record numbers: (17286) Ch-16289 Yz L-1035

1 Didn't get this man : for nobody else
2 I got this man : all for myself
3 Call my man : on the telephone
4 He was so sad : I wasn't at home
5 He got plenty of money : ain't no *junk*
6 He got one-way pocket : because he's going to come
   out
7 You ain't good-looking : you ain't fair
8 Look like you could find you : a man somewhere
9 Had my man : long enough
10 He ought to be tired : of that old stuff
11 I let you stay here : in my house
12 You took my man : you dirty louse
13 If I catch you : in my bed
14 Mama I'm going to : kill you dead

McCl   1   McClennan, Tommy

        title: Brown Skin Girl
        place and date: Chicago, 22 Nov. 1939
        record numbers: (044243-1) BB-B8444 RCA LPV-518

1 Now I got a brownskin [girl, woman] : with her front
   tooth crowned with gold
2 She got a lien on my body : and a mortgage on my
   soul
3 Now friend don't never let your good girl : fix you
   like this woman got me
4 Got me stone crazy about her : as a doggone fool can
   be
5 Now I ain't going to tell nobody : baby about the
   way you do
6 Say you always keep : some some fatmouth following
   you

McCl   1   McClennan, Tommy

7   Now I told you once now baby now : ain't going to
    tell you no more
8   Next time I have to tell you : I'm sure going to let
    you go
9   Now when you get you one of them faulty women : she
    won't do the truck
10 Get you a two-by-four : and I swear you can strut
    your stuff
11 Mmm : baby that's all I want
12 Just a little bit of loving : and then you can be
    gone

McCl   2   McClennan, Tommy

        title: Baby, Don't You Want to Go?
        place and date: Chicago, 22 Nov. 1939
        record numbers: (044245-) BB-B8408 Rt RL-305

1   Mmm : baby don't you want to go
2   To that land of California : sweet old Chicago
3   Now did you get that letter : dropped in your back
    yard
4   Wants to come to see you : your best man got me
    barred
5   Now I don't drink because I'm dry : or drink because
    I'm blue
6   The reason I drink pretty mama : now I can't get
    along with you
7   Now look a-here baby : don't have to take no more
8   You can get my loving : if you just let him go
9   Now my my mama told me : papa started to cry
10 Son you're too young a man : to have the women at
    your side
11 She cried look a-here baby : I know you want to go
12 To that land of California : sweet old Chicago

McCl   3   McClennan, Tommy

        title: New Highway No. 51
        place and date: Chicago, 10 May 1940
        record numbers: (044986-) BB-B8499 RBF RF-202

1   Highway Fifty : runs right by my baby's door
2   Now if I don't get the girl I'm loving : ain't going
    down Highway Fifty-One no more
3   Now if I should die : [just] before my time do come
4   I want you to please bury my body : out on Highway
    Fifty-One
5   Now yon come that Greyhound : with his tongue
    sticking out on the side
6   If you buy your ticket : swear 'fore God that man'll
    let you ride
7   My baby didn't have one five dollars : baby and I
    owned me a V-Eight Ford
8   If I ever meet that Greyhound bus : on that Highway
    Fifty-One road
9   Now any time you get lonesome : and you wants to
    have some fun
10 Come out to little Tommy's cabin : he lives on
    Highway Fifty-One

McCl   4   McClennan, Tommy

        title: She's Just Good Huggin' Size
        place and date: Chicago, 10 May 1940
        record numbers: (044987-) BB-B8605 Rt RL-305

1   Oh my baby : just about good hugging size
2   Lord and if anybody wants to take her : I believe to
    my soul I'd die
3   Lord I tried to give the little woman : everything
    that she tell me she needs
4   But she will hold a conversation : with every
    lowdown dirty man she meets

McCl   4   McClennan, Tommy

5   That little woman she won't wash : now now she won't
    even iron my clothes
6   She won't do nothing I tell her : but she done bake
    me jellyroll
7   Now I ain't going to tell you babe : about the way
    you do
8   But I swear the way you do : it keeps on worrying me
9   Now I used to have a woman : now now she's [just] as
    good as any in this [white man's] town
10 But I caught her two-timing me : and I swear I turn
    her damper down

McCl   5   McClennan, Tommy

        title: My Little Girl
        place and date: Chicago, 10 May 1940
        record numbers: (044988-) BB-B8605 Rt RL-305

1   I say my little girl : just as sweet as she can be
2   And every time she kisses me : cold chill run all
    over me
3   Now baby don't you worry : just because I'm out of
    town
4   All my love I have for you darling : swear it can't
    be turned around
5   Now you hurt my feelings : babe but [I swear] I
    wouldn't let on
6   I believe it's some dirty deacon : is done been here
    and gone
7   Now I love you baby : don't care what you do
8   But the way you doing : I swear it's coming back
    home to you

McCl   6   McClennan, Tommy

        title: My Baby's Doggin' Me
        place and date: Chicago, 10 May 1940
        record numbers: (044991-) BB-B8545 Rt RL-305

1   Now she dog me every morning : she dog me late at
    night
2   She keep on a-dogging me : till I going to make
    everything all right
3   Now look a-here mama : tell me where you stay last
    night
4   She said ain't none of your business : you know you
    don't treat me right
5   Now I done told you once pretty mama : ain't going
    to tell you no more
6   You can get all my loving : if you just let him go
7   I say look a-here babe : I'm getting tired of the
    way you're dogging me
8   Because I like pretty mama : better than any woman
    that I ever seen
9   Mmm : my baby's dogging me
10 I love that little old woman : better than any woman
    that I ever seen

McCl   7   McClennan, Tommy

        title: She's a Good Looking Mama
        place and date: Chicago, 10 May 1940
        record numbers: (044992-) BB-B8545 Rt RL-305

1   She's a good-looking woman : teeth don't even shine
    like pearls
2   But that old good disposition that woman got : I do
    swear it will carry her all through the world
3   Now please don't never let your good girl : treat
    you like this here woman got me
4   She got me stone crazy about her : as a good-looking
    woman can be
5   Now you know that I love you baby : and that's why
    we can't get along

McCl   7   McClennan, Tommy

6   But some day you're going to be sorry : that you
     ever did your daddy wrong
7   Now some day you're going to want me back : baby now
     now and you going to acknowledge that you did
     wrong
8   But it's going to be too late pretty mama : your
     daddy will be gone
9   Ooh : Lord Lord Lordy Lord
10   Sure I love you sweet mama : but I sure ain't going
     to be your dog

McCl   8   McClennan, Tommy

        title: Whiskey Head Man
        place and date: Chicago, 12 Dec. 1940
        record numbers: (053736-) BB-B8760 RBF RF-14

1   Now he's a whiskey-headed man : and he stays drunk
     all the time
2   Just as sure if he don't stop drinking : I believe
     he's going to lose his mind
3   Now every time I see this man : he's at some whiskey
     joint
4   Trying to catch a big bet : so he can get him one
     more half a pint
5   Now every time I see this man : he's standing on the
     street
6   Laughing grinning talking : with most every man he
     meets
7   Now every time I see this man : he at some whiskey
     joint
8   Sniffing around the back door : begging one more
     half a pint

McCl   9   McClennan, Tommy

        title: New Sugar Mama
        place and date: Chicago, 12 Dec. 1940
        record numbers: (053737-) BB-B8760 Rt RL-305

1   Sugar mama sugar mama : won't you please come back
     to me
2   Bring me that granulated sugar : sugar mama to
     relieve my misery
3   Now my coffee's sweet in the morning : you know I'm
     crazy about [that, my] tea at night
4   Don't get my sugar three times a day : great Lord I
     don't feel right
5   Now you been bragging about your whiskey : now now
     you've been bragging all over town
6   The bootlegger won't sell enough sugar to make
     whiskey : don't even sell but about four or five
     pounds
7   Now sugar mama sugar mama : [won't you] please come
     [on] back to me
8   Bring me that granulated sugar : that all it take to
     ease my misery
9   Now sugar mama sugar mama : you know you been gone
     all day long
10   You been doing something with my sugar : ooo Lord
     now I know it was wrong
11   Now sugar mama sugar mama : now won't you please
     come on back to me
12   You know I don't like nothing but my sugar : and
     that's what it takes to ease my misery

McCl   10   McClennan, Tommy

        title: Down to Skin and Bones
        place and date: Chicago, 12 Dec. 1940
        record numbers: (053738-) BB-B8725 Rt RL-305

1   I say my little woman : got me down to skin and bone

McCl   10   McClennan, Tommy

2   She done got me to the place : I hate to see my baby
     leave home
3   Now she leave me every morning : she don't come home
     till night
4   She know I know she doing something : oh Lord but
     she know it ain't right
5   Don't think because I love you : I'm going to be
     your dog
6   I'll drink muddy water : and I'll lives in a hollow
     log
7   Mmm : gal I don't know why I should
8   Because you go with every man : mmm in anybody's
     neighborhood

McCl   11   McClennan, Tommy

        title: Katy Mae Blues
        place and date: Chicago, 12 Dec. 1940
        record numbers: (053739-1) BB-B8689 Rt RL-305

1   Katy Mae's a good-looking woman now : but she stays
     out all night long
2   Katy Mae be doing something : oh Lord well you know
     is wrong
3   You know I love you Katy Mae : and that's why we
     can't get along
4   Some day you going to be sorry : that you ever done
     poor Tommy wrong
5   I give you all my loving : Katy Mae what more can a
     poor man do
6   You's a sweet little girl : but I swear you won't be
     true
7   Now how can I do right : now baby you won't do right
     yourself
8   Before you love me baby : you wants to love somebody
     else
9   Now Katy Mae she won't wash : now she won't starch
     [and iron] my clothes
10   Katy Mae won't do nothing : oh but walk the road

McCl   12   McClennan, Tommy

        title: Love with a Feeling
        place and date: Chicago, 12 Dec. 1940
        record numbers: (053740-1) BB-B8689 Rt RL-305

1   If you're going to have a woman : love her with a
     thrill
2   And if you don't love her : some other man will
3   Now no woman no woman : *ever but halfway stuffed*
4   Because when you turn her loose : be sure she got
     enough
5   Now you know 'Berta : you ain't doing me right
6   And when you come home : we'll go to fuss and fight
7   Mmm mama told me : papa started to cry
8   The way you got doing babe : won't take your life

McCl   13   McClennan, Tommy

        title: Drop Down Mama
        place and date: Chicago, 12 Dec. 1940
        record numbers: (053741-1) BB-B8704 Rt RL-305

1   Drop down mama : let daddy see
2   You got something : really worry me
3   Now my mama she don't allow me : stay out the whole
     night long
4   Because you may be a *model* : and you may be
     treated wrong
5   Now my baby got ways soon in the morning : just like
     a squirrel
6   Get up every morning : grabbing them *covers* on the
     world

McCl 13   McClennan, Tommy

7   Now when you get your women : and she act funny in
    every way
8   Just D B all right : she'll be home some day
9   I'm going to write you a letter soon in the morning
    : mail it in the air
10 You can tell by that : babe I got a somewhere
11 Now if you get you a woman : now now treat her nice
    in every way
12 Because when you get to Chicago : these women
    walking around here any day

McCl 14   McClennan, Tommy

    title: Black Minnie
    place and date: Chicago, 12 Dec. 1940
    record numbers: (053742-1) BB-B8704 Rt RL-305

1   Black Minnie Black Minnie : you know you ain't doing
    me right
2   But the day you quit me Black Minnie : I swear
    that's the day you die
3   Black Minnie you know I love you : and I love you
    for myself
4   And I'd rather be with you Black Minnie : than to be
    with anyone else
5   I give my money Black Minnie : and everything that
    you told me you need
6   And one time done come and caught me : baby with my
    B V Ds
7   Now Black Minnie Black Minnie : I'm going to take
    you one more time
8   And if you don't suit me : I'm going to try to *fade
    the line*
9   Black Minnie Black Minnie : what in the world are
    you trying to do
10 I believe trying to love me Black Minnie : and my
    partner too
11 Now Black Minnie Black Minnie : you know you don't
    mean me no good
12 Because you going with the man : that lives right
    above my neighborhood
13 Black Minnie Black Minnie : girl you stays in the
    dark
14 And your no-good way : I ain't going to never give
    you my last dime
15 Black Minnie Black Minnie : I'm going to try you one
    more time
16 And if you don't do : I'm going to break your neck
    a-trying

McCl 15   McClennan, Tommy

    title: Elsie Blues
    place and date: Chicago, 12 Dec. 1940
    record numbers: (053743-) BB-B8725 Rt RL-305

1   Elsie : is sweetest girl I know
2   If you didn't love me Elsie : why didn't you tell me
    so
3   Now I followed Elsie : right to the jumping-off
    ground
4   But I never felt sorry : till they let my baby down
5   Now I followed my baby Lord : long days and long
    nights
6   I followed my baby : till I see she wasn't going to
    treat me right
7   You can misuse me here now now : but you can't when
    I go home
8   Elsie I got somebody there : will really make you
    leave me alone
9   Now I give you all my loving : Elsie what more can a
    poor man do
10 You a sweet little girl : Elsie but I swear you
    won't be true

McCl 15   McClennan, Tommy

11 Now you can't have me Elsie : now now and my partner
    too
12 Because your no-good way baby : oh baby that won't
    do
13 Now I followed you to them dance now : and you jook
    jook all the time
14 You jook jook so : that I wouldn't pay you no mind
15 You if you don't quit jooking baby : that's going to
    be all right
16 If your good man don't see you : I'll try to see you
    tomorrow night

McCl 16   McClennan, Tommy

    title: Cross Cut Saw Blues
    place and date: Chicago, 15 Sept. 1941
    record numbers: (064885-) BB-B8897 Rt RL-305

1   Now I'm a crosscut saw : drive me across your log
2   Baby I cut your wood so easy : you can't help but
    say hot dog
3   They call me wood-cutting Sam : call me wood-cutting
    Bill
4   But the woman I did the wood-cutting for : she wants
    me back again
5   I got a double-bladed ax : and it sure cuts good
6   But try my crosscut saw : it's evil to the wood
7   Now look a-here mama : you stay last night
8   Said ain't none of your business : you don't do me
    right
9   Now when you go to fishing : now don't forget the
    pole
10 You you's a good girl : but you ain't been out long

McCl 17   McClennan, Tommy

    title: You Can't Read My Mind
    place and date: Chicago, 15 Sept. 1941
    record numbers: (064887-) BB-B8897 Rt RL-305

1   I say my good-looking woman : honey she lives up on
    that hill
2   She been trying to quit poor Tommy : oh Lord but I
    love her still
3   She walks the street [late at, every] night : she
    won't treat nobody right
4   Oh she drinks her moonshine whiskey : but me and her
    will make everything all right
5   I say if you quit Mr Butler : we will make
    everything all right
6   If I can't see you today : we may get together
    tomorrow night
7   Now you can read my letter : oh but you can't read
    my mind
8   Sometime you think I'm crazy about you : I'm liable
    to be quitting you all the time
9   Now that's all right babe : what you did [last, one]
    Sunday night
10 If I hadn't been in my whiskey too : it's liable to
    cause our fussing and fight

McCl 18   McClennan, Tommy

    title: Deep Blue Sea Blues
    place and date: Chicago, 15 Sept. 1941
    record numbers: (064889-) BB-B9005 Rt RL-313

1   I'm going babe I'm going : and crying won't make me
    stay
2   Because the more you cry now now baby : the further
    you drive me away
3   Now I wished that I was a bullfrog : swimming in the
    deep blue sea

McCl   18   McClennan, Tommy

4   Lord I would have all these good-looking women now
      now now : fishing after me
5   Now I went to my baby's house : and I sat down on
      her steps
6   She said walk on in now now Tommy : my husband just
      now left
7   Now it ain't none of none of my business : babe but
      you know I know it ain't right
8   Hit your kid-man all day long : and play sick on
      your husband at night
9   Now Lord oh Lord : baby hear me blow the blues
10 Don't got nobody now now now : give me my last pair
      of shoes

McCl   19   McClennan, Tommy

        title: I'm a Guitar King
        place and date: Chicago, 15 Sept. 1941
        record numbers: (064890-) BB-B8957 RBF RF-1

1   I'm a guitar king : singing the blues everywhere I
      go
2   I'm going to sing these blues : till I get back in
      territory'
3   Now my mama told me : son you most too old
4   Oh don't forget : you got a soul
5   But that ain't none of your business : keep it to
      yourself
6   Don't you tell your kid-man : please don't tell
      nobody else
7   Now I went to my baby's house : knocked upon her
      door
8   She had the nerve to tell me : that she didn't want
      me no more
9   I say that's all right babe : [most any, any old]
      way you do
10 If you mistreat poor Tommy : I swear it's coming
      back home to you
11 It's a crying pity : lowdown dirty shame
12 Crazy about a married woman : afraid to call her
      name

McCl   20   McClennan, Tommy

        title: It's a Cryin' Pity
        place and date: Chicago, 15 Sept. 1941
        record numbers: (064891-) BB-B9005 Rt RL-305

1   It's a crying pity : a lowdown dirty shame
2   Crazy about a no-good woman : scared to call her
      name
3   Now where were you babe : when I knocked upon your
      door
4   You hadn't never tell poor Tommy : that you couldn't
      use me no more
5   But that's all right babe : got to reap [just] what
      you sow
6   But don't forget that night : I knocked upon you
      door
7   Now I done some last winter : don't expect to do it
      no more
8   Quit the best woman I had : and I have drove her
      from my door
9   But forgive me baby : won't do wrong no more
10 You can get all my loving : but you got to let that
      black man go
11 Now I love you baby : I don't see why I should
12 Because you going with the man : that lives right in
      my neighborhood

McCl   21   McClennan, Tommy

        title: Mozelle Blues
        place and date: Chicago, 20 Feb. 1942
        record numbers: (074100-) BB-B9015 Rt RL-314

1   Mozelle : why we can't get along
2   Because you know you always doing something : baby
      when you know it's wrong
3   Mozelle you know you been rambling : rambling all
      night long
4   Yeah I know you been doing something : yeah Mozelle
      well you know is wrong
5   Mozelle you know you [like, love] your whiskey :
      don't forget I [likes, love] mine too
6   But I'll get my whiskey so strong : I'll forget
      about you
7   Mozelle : I love you for myself
8   Every time I hear somebody speaking about you : I
      will beat you in the *B W O L*

McCl   22   McClennan, Tommy

        title: Mr. So and So Blues
        place and date: Chicago, 20 Feb. 1942
        record numbers: (074102-) BB-B9015 Rt RL-314

1   Babe I feel so worried : yeah and I feel so low
2   Because I believe you been out : with Mr so-and-so
3   Now baby I ??? : please get out of my face
4   Because I got myself a brand new woman : yeah girl
      to take your place
5   Ooo babe : you know that sure ain't right
6   *You're off having a binge* : you don't come home at
      all at night

McCl   23   McClennan, Tommy

        title: Bluebird Blues
        place and date: Chicago, 20 Feb. 1942
        record numbers: (074107-) BB-B9037 RCA LPV-518

1   Bluebird bluebird : please fly down south for me
2   If you don't find me on the M and O : you'll find me
      somewhere on that Santa Fe
3   Bluebird when you get in Jackson : don't tell nobody
      I'm home
4   Tell them I'm going back to Kansas City : that's
      where poor Tommy belong
5   Oh babe : you is on my mind
6   I hope to see you some of these days : you know I
      sure ain't lying
7   Now bluebird you get to Jackson : out on China
      Street
8   Tell them Tommy's too bad : go away girl you know I
      got the blues about me
9   Oh babe : please your Tommy be all right
10 If I can't see you today : it'll be all right
      tomorrow night

McCli 1   McClintock, Lil

        title: Furniture Man
        place and date: Atlanta, 4 Dec. 1930
        record numbers: (151016-2) Co-14575-D Rt RL-318

1   Well a-this piano : and everything
2   Mr Cooper had it written down : under my name

178

McClu   1   McClure, Matthew

       title: Prisoner's Blues
       place and date: Richmond, Ind., 22 Sept. 1932
       record numbers: (18798) Ch-18514 Riv RM-8819

1   Did you ever get in trouble : and they take you down
    to jail
2   You didn't have a friend : to come and go your bail
3   When you got a lot of money: you've got friends for
    miles around
4   But any time that you're broke : your good friends
    they can't be found
5   When I lost all my money : no one would loan me a
    dime
6   I could hear them all saying : he ain't no friend of
    mine
7   It's tough when you're broke friends : you can't
    even get a dime
8   If you even go a-begging : everyone will turn you
    down
9   I'm going back to prison : don't know what else to
    do
10   That's the only thing I know : to cure a prisoner's
    blues

McCoC   1   McCoy, Charlie

       title: Last Time Blues
       place and date: Memphis, c. 22 Sept. 1929
       record numbers: (M-176-) Br-7141 Yz L-1001

1   Babe just as sure as a blackbird : flies in the
    skies above
2   Bet your life ain't worth living babe : if you ain't
    with the one you love
3   My baby tried to do me : like the tadpole do the
    trout
4   That's getting me out in the deep water baby : then
    she walks on out
5   Mmm good Lordy : send me an angel down
6   Son I can't spare you no angel : but I'll send you a
    teasing brown
7   I don't think : no woman in this whole round world
    do right
8   If they be good all day : they will do wrong at
    night
9   Baby you know it may be my last time : rider you
    sure don't know
10   It may be my last time baby : knocking on your door

McCoC   2   McCoy, Charlie

       title: That Lonesome Train Took My Baby Away
       place and date: Jackson, Miss., 15 Dec. 1930
       record numbers: (404726-A) OK-8863 RBF RF-14

1   Woke up this morning : found something wrong
2   My loving babe : had caught that train and gone
3   Now won't you starch my jumper : iron my overalls
4   I'm going to ride that train : that they call the
    Cannonball
5   Mr depot agent : close your depot down
6   The woman I'm loving : she's fixing to blow this
    town
7   Now that mean old fireman : that cruel old engineer
8   Going to take my baby : and leave me lonesome here
9   It ain't no telling : what that train won't do
10   It'll take your baby : and run right over you
11   Now that engineer man : ought to be ashamed of
    himself
12   Take women from their husbands : babies from their
    mother's breast
13   I walked down the track : when the stars refused to
    shine
14   Looked like every minute : I was going to lose my
    mind

McCoC   2   McCoy, Charlie

15   Now my knees was weak : my footsteps was all I heard
16   Looked like every minute : I was stepping in another
    world

McCoJ   1   McCoy, Joe

       title: That Will Be Alright
       place and date: New York, 18 June 1929
       record numbers: (148708-3) Co-14439-D Yz L-1021

1   Well look here mama : see what you done done
2   Took all my money : put me on a bum
3   ??? : go to your knees
4   Try and bum jelly : to who you please
5   Going to buy me a dog : tired and old
6   Keep these men : from my jellyroll
7   I'm crazy about your loving : don't see why she can
8   Saw them going : with another man
9   Now you talk about jelly : you ought to see mine
10   Sharing her jelly : all over town
11   I had a good *cake* : *now sweet as mama's shelf*
12   *Now she gone to town : with somebody else*
13   I'm going to build me a house : out on the sea
14   So these women : come see poor me
15   Me and my brother : went around the bend
16   Heard my gal : putting *cider* in

McCoJ   2   McCoy, Joe (Memphis Minnie)

       title: Goin' Back to Texas
       place and date: New York, 18 June 1929
       record numbers: (148709-2) Co-14455-D OJL-21

1   Oh mercy dear : you caused my heart
2   It really is wrong : that we must part
3   You learned I love you : *mores* all the rest
4   Your leaving me : breaks my happiness
5   I'll count the hours : lover when I'm gone
6   Think of you : wish you back home
7   My lonesome heart : will shake with fear
8   The very hour : I call your name
9   Every hour : ???
10   Not at ease : with anyone else
11   I'll *haunt the line* : for you I know
12   I'm asking you dear : please don't go
13   Oh honey babe : mama *ray*
14   *Glory be* : I see that thing

McCoJ   3   McCoy, Joe

       title: When the Levee Breaks
       place and date: New York, 18 June 1929
       record numbers: (148711-1) Co-14439-D BC-1

1   If it keeps on raining : levee's going to break
2   And the water going to come : and we'll have no
    place to stay
3   Well all last night : I sat on the levee and moaned
4   Thinking about my baby : and my happy home
5   If it keeps on raining : levee's going to break
6   And all these people : have no place to stay
7   Now look here mama : what am I to do
8   I ain't got nobody : tell my troubles to
9   I worked on the levee : mama both night and day
10   I ain't got nobody : to keep the water away
11   On crying won't help you : praying won't do no good
12   When the levee break : mom you got to move
13
14   I worked on the levee : mama both night and day
15   When the levee break : mom you got to move
16   I worked on the levee : mama both night and day
17   Say worked so hard : keep the water away
18   I had a woman : she wouldn't do for me
19   I'm going back : to my used-to-be

McCoJ   3   McCoy, Joe

20 Old mean old levee : cause me to weep and moan
21 Cause me to leave my baby : and my happy home

McCoJ   4   McCoy, Joe

         title: I'm Wild About My Stuff
         place and date: Chicago, c. early June 1930
         record numbers: (C-5820-A) Vo-1570 His HLP-32

 1 All of my chicken : is dressed mighty fine
 2 Can't get my chicken : take dressing from mine
 3 Went to the henhouse : looked on the roof
 4 Looking for my stuff : but it was no use
 5 Take a boa constrictor : and a lemon stick
 6 Wouldn't mind going : but my mama's sick
 7 You can toot your whistle : you can ring your bell
 8 Know you been waddling : by the way you smell
 9 Good stuff good stuff : is hard to find
10 Kill my daddy : run my mama blind
11 Now I'm going girls : don't flirt after me
12 Got good stuff : and it's all I need
13 Listen boys : don't mean no harm
14 Go ahead on : let my stuff alone
15 Now somebody ask you : who sung this song
16 Kansas Joe : been here and gone

McCoJ   5   McCoy, Joe

         title: My Mary Blues
         place and date: Chicago, c. early June 1930
         record numbers: (C-5830-) Vo-1576 Pal PL-101

 1 Early one morning : *my mind* ???
 2 Was thinking about my Mary : didn't have no place to
        stay
 3 Now tell me Mary : where did you stay last night
 4 Come home this morning : the sun was shining bright
 5 I met my Mary : way across the sea
 6 She wouldn't write me no letter : she didn't care
        for me
 7 You see my Mary : tell her to hurry home
 8 Haven't been long loving : honey since you been gone
 9 I love my Mary : tell the whole round world I do
10 I want some real good loving : why don't your heart
        be true
11 Goodbye Mary : goodbye and it's fare you well
12 That's when I get back home : can't anyone tell

McCoJ   6   McCoy, Joe

         title: Cherry Ball Blues
         place and date: Chicago, c. mid June 1930
         record numbers: (C-5864-A) Vo-1535 Pal PL-101

 1 Ain't going to give you : no more cherry ball
 2 Well you might get mad now : show your Santa Claus
 3 Rocks and gravel : ??? road
 4 Takes a get-along woman : satisfy my soul
 5 See you dead now : in some cedar grove
 6 Than to see some man now : bothering with your
        clothes
 7 Ain't no driver : but the driver's son
 8 I can do your driving : till that driver comes

McCoJ   7   McCoy, Joe

         title: Botherin' that Thing
         place and date: Chicago, c. mid June 1930
         record numbers: (C-5865-A) Vo-1570 His HLP-32

 1 I went to my window : my window was *cracked*
 2 Went to my door : my door was locked
 3 Old lady diamond : setting on a rock

McCoJ   7   McCoy, Joe

 4 Raising her hand : trying to *change* that knot
 5 My old lady : ought to be ashamed
 6 She kept the watch : and give me the change
 7 Mama got the washboard : papa got the tub
 8 Brother got mad : because they wouldn't let him rub
 9 Drive up to the station : to catch that train
10 Got there too late : from bothering that thing
11 Went to the doctor : the doctor said
12 Bothering that thing : is going to kill you dead

McCoJ   8   McCoy, Joe

         title: Pile Drivin' Blues
         place and date: Chicago, c. 14 July 1930
         record numbers: (C-6012-) Vo-1612 Yz L-1002

 1 Drove so many piles : my hammer's all worn out
 2 That's when I do my driving : they began to jump and
        shout
 3 Want all you people : just to understand
 4 That's when I do my driving : drive just like a man
 5 When I was young : driving was my crave
 6 You drove me so hard : drove me to my grave
 7 Get you a hammer : you can drive all the time
 8 You have broke my hammer : my hammer's out of line

McCoJ   9   McCoy, Joe

         title: I Called You This Morning
         place and date: Chicago, c. 14 July 1930
         record numbers: (C-6013-) Vo-1631 BC-13

 1 I called you this morning : about half past one
 2 Told me : that you just got on
 3 I called you this morning : about half past two
 4 Told me : that you just got through
 5 I called you this morning : about half past three
 6 Told me : that you couldn't use me
 7 I called you this morning : about half past four
 8 Told me : that you didn't want me no more
 9 I called you this morning : about half past five
10 You turned over : cried like a child
11 I called you this morning : about half past six
12 You told me : that it was out of fix

McCoJ 10   McCoy, Joe

         title: Beat It Right
         place and date: Chicago, c. 31 Jan. 1931
         record numbers: (C-7246-) Vo-1643 Pal PL-101

 1 Some got both queens : some got both kings
 2 I got both aces : I know I got the best hand
 3 Oh I can beat it : I can beat it tonight
 4 I can beat it baby : got something to beat it right
 5 Now it's dark and cloudy : don't need no light
 6 You want me to beat it : you got to move it just
        right
 7 Oh I can beat it : I can beat it tonight
 8 I can beat it baby : got something to beat it with
 9 Now listen girl : don't be afraid
10 I hits every nail : right on the head
11 Now the men don't like me : because I speak my mind
12 The women like me : because I can beat it all the
        time
13 Now all you women : love to fuss and fight
14 Come on around : now let us beat it up tight
15 Now listen folks : don't mean no harm
16 I got to go : and beat my way back home
17 Well I went to the doctor : to get me a piece of
        advice
18 Keep on beating it : it's going to take your life

McCoJ 11   McCoy, Joe

    title: Preachers Blues
    place and date: Chicago, c. 31 Jan. 1931
    record numbers: (C-7247-) Vo-1643 BC-13

1 Some folks say : a preacher won't steal
2 I caught three : in my cornfield
3 One had a yellow : one had a brown
4 Looked over by the mill : one was getting down
5 Now some folks say : that a preacher won't steal
6 But he will do more stealing : than I can get
   regular meals
7 I went to my house : about half past ten
8 Looked on my bed : where the preacher had been
9 He will eat your chicken : he will eat your pie
10 He will lead your wife out : on the sly
11 I been trying so hard : trying to save my life
12 To keep that preacher : from my wife
13 I went out last night : came in late
14 I found out : where he had made his date
15 I done told you once : done told you twice
16 ??? over that preacher : you be done lost your wife

McCoJ 12   McCoy, Joe

    title: Shake Mattie
    place and date: Chicago, c. Feb. 1931
    record numbers: (VO-109-A) Vo-1668 Mam S-3803

1 Shake shake Mattie : shake rattle and roll
2 I can't get enough now : satisfy my soul
3 Old shaking Mattie : meat shake on the bone
4 Every time she shakes them : poor man's dollar gone
5 Old shaking Mattie : and shaking Sue
6 I can't get by now : at the way they do
7 Old *gate-foot* Mattie : and *gate-foot bright*
8 They meets at the levee : every Saturday night
9 Well the bell rung for *dinner* : as I been *bad*
10 If you ask her about it : have to reckon with her
   man
11 Yonder come old Mattie : with a paper in her hand
12 Going to the sergeant : trying to free her man
13 Yonder come old Mattie : how in the world you know
14 I know old Mattie : by the dress she wore

McCoJ 13   McCoy, Joe

    title: My Wash Woman's Gone
    place and date: Chicago, c. Feb. 1931
    record numbers: (VO-110-A) Vo-1668 Yz L-1026

1 My baby's *deaf-toweled* : can't hardly hear
2 Such fussing and fighting : this whole round year
3 Now my baby's gone : left my clothes in the tub
4 I ain't got no washwoman : *mean* nobody can rub
5 I got up this morning : said my morning prayers
6 Didn't have nobody : to speak in my behalf
7 I got an old tub now : so deep and wide
8 Keep me rubbing : from side to side
9 Well I got an old lady now : wash mighty clean
10 When she go to rub : she rub so mean
11 I feel like falling down : on bended knees
12 Cried Lord have mercy : if you please

McCoJ 14   McCoy, Joe

    title: Joliet Bound
    place and date: New York, 3 Feb. 1932
    record numbers: (11220-A) Vo-1686 Yz L-1021

1 Now those police coming : with his ball and chain
2 And they accusing me of murder : never harmed a man
3 Now some got six months : some got one solid year
4 Now me and my buddy : got a lifetime here
5 Now the judge he pleaded : clerk he wrote it down

McCoJ 14   McCoy, Joe

6 Now I hear my last jail sentence now : must be
   Joliet bound
7 Now cook my supper : let me go to bed
8 I've been drinking white lightning : and it's gone
   to my head
9 Now go and hurt me baby : do anything you want to do
10 Some day you going to want it : and then I won't
   want you
11 Now those police shifted : those pistol in my side
12 Now if you run big boy now : ??? bound to die
13 When they had my trial : you could not be found
14 Now I done got on that dock : and I'm Joliet bound

McCoJ 15   McCoy, Joe

    title: Someday I'll Be in the Clay
    place and date: Chicago, 13 Aug. 1932
    record numbers: (C-9290) De-7008 Rt RL-329

1 I dropped my baby off : among my friends
2 First thing I know : she done had turned me in
3 But some day : I'll be in the clay
4 And I won't be long here : to be treated this a-way
5 When I was a man : I tried to prove a friend
6 First thing I know : you had four or five men
7 There come a time : I can't say no more
8 I'll be a-hearsing : out my door
9 But when I'm gone : don't cry over me
10 Just think about : your used-to-be
11 Now I can't stay : but fare you well
12 If I ain't gone to heaven : you know I gone to hell

McCoJ 16   McCoy, Joe

    title: Evil Devil Woman Blues
    place and date: Chicago, 16 Aug. 1934
    record numbers: (C-9299-A) De-7822 BC-5

1 I'd rather be the devil : be that woman's man
2 Because she was evil : wouldn't work hand in hand
3 On she's all right now : she's all right with me
4 But the devil is evil : evil as he can be
5 I tried : to be nice and kind
6 Oh she was evil : would not change her mind
7 I'll cut your wood baby : and I'll build your fire
8 I'll bring you water : through that muddy bayou
9 I'll give my money : to buy your shoes and clothes
10 But you was evil : throwed me out-of-doors
11 But that's all right baby : it's coming home to you
12 I tried to be : tried to be a man to you

McCoJ 17   McCoy, Joe

    title: Going Back Home
    place and date: Chicago, 16 Aug. 1934
    record numbers: (C-9300-A) De-7087 Yz L-1007

1 Lord wonder : will I ever get back home
2 Crying how long : you going to keep me away from
   home
3 I walked and I wandered : crying the whole night
   long
4 Crying wonder : will I ever get back home
5 I went to the station : looked up on the board
6 Crying is it possible : will I ever get back home
7 So long I traveled : the *way side and more*
8 Crying wonder : will I ever get back home
9 You may never never : see me anymore
10 But you will never forget the day : I knocked upon
   your door

McCoJ 18   McCoy, Joe (Memphis Minnie)

    title: You Got to Move--Part 1
    place and date: Chicago, 24 Aug. 1934
    record numbers: (C-9380-) De-7038 BC-1

1 Say little girl : can I spend the night
2 Wife and I : just had a fight
3 I've got to move : out of the neighborhood
4 For the woman I love : don't mean me no good
5 Babe it ain't no use : you talking about no money
    tonight
6 Pay for everything : tomorrow night
7 If you can take it baby : it'll be all right
8 Pay you off : right here tonight
9 When I had her : she lived on Easy Street
10 Now she's begging : every man she meets

McCoJ 19   McCoy, Joe

    title: Something Gonna Happen to You
    place and date: Chicago, 1 Nov. 1935
    record numbers: (96262-) BB-B6260 Yz L-1021

1 I'm going to ask my buddy now : how come he shares
2 Going to fool around : ???
3 Crying something bad now : sure is going to happen
    to you
4 That's when I done everything : that a poor boy
    could do
5 I'm have bought me a pistol : shotgun and some
    shells
6 Start some stuff : to show them raise some hell
7 Yes you talked about me : all through the
    neighborhood
8 Told everybody : that I was no good
9 Yes you called on the old law : and he brought his
    ball and chain
10 Accused me of murder : I never harmed a man
11 Yes my mother she told me : my daddy sat down and he
    cried
12 Some day son : you got to lay down and die
13 There'll be one of these mornings : you going to
    jump and shout
14 Open the jailhouse door : and you come walking out
15 I used to have so many women : I didn't know what
    Lord
16 Used to gang around me : like the ants on a bug

McCoJ 20   McCoy, Joe (Harlem Hamfats)

    title: Oh Red
    place and date: Chicago, 18 Apr. 1936
    record numbers: (90691-A) De-7182 AH-77

1 Oh Red : wish you were dead
2 I'm sick and tired : rubbing my baby's head
3 Oh Red : what you going to do
4 I'm sick and tired : chastizing you
5 Oh Red : baby's in jail
6 She ain't got nobody : come and go her bail
7 Oh Red : she's outdoors
8 She ain't got nowhere : carry her dirty clothes
9 Oh Red : she's all right
10 And we ain't going to fuss : and we ain't going to
    fight
11 Oh Red : all over now
12 You didn't have no right : raise no hell nohow

McCoJ 21   McCoy, Joe (Harlem Hamfats)

    title: What You Gonna Do?
    place and date: Chicago, 2 July 1936
    record numbers: (90782-A) De-7205 AH-77

1 What you going to do : when they put you in jail
    again
2 Do like I would do : get out if you can
3 What you going to do : when they put you outdoors
    again
4 Do like I would do : get back if you can
5 What you going to do : when you lose your money
    again
6 Do like I would do : win it back if you can
7 What you going to do : when you lose your baby again
8 Do like I would do : win her back if you can
9 What you going to do : when she put the dog on you
10 Do like I would do : get loose if you can
11 What you going to do : when she close the door in
    your face
12 Do like I would do : open it if you can

McCoJ 22   McCoy, Joe (Harlem Hamfats)

    title: Southern Blues
    place and date: Chicago, 2 Oct. 1936
    record numbers: (90913-A) De-7229 AH-77

1 Blues jumped the monkey : and run him for a solid
    mile
2 And the poor fellow lie down : cried like a natural
    child
3 Blues is something : I just can't understand
4 And when they gets on me : talk like a natural man

McCoJ 23   McCoy, Joe (Harlem Hamfats)

    title: The Garbage Man
    place and date: Chicago, 2 Oct. 1936
    record numbers: (90914-A) De-7229 AH-77

1 Stick out your can : here comes the garbage man
2 Ain't nobody : stick it out like you can

McCoJ 24   McCoy, Joe (Harlem Hamfats)

    title: My Daddy Was a Movin' Man
    place and date: Chicago, 22 Oct. 1936
    record numbers: (90949-A) De-7251 AH-77

1 I want to do : like my daddy done
2 He loved women : from sun to sun
3 My daddy : was a loving man
4 And he make them like it : everywhere he land
5 When he start to loving : they cry for more
6 Even laid the woman : lived next door
7 Had twenty women : that I know
8 Each one told me : he sure could go
9 The only thing : he didn't do good
10 Was make his women : lay it on wood

McCoJ 25   McCoy, Joe (Harlem Hamfats)

    title: We Gonna Pitch a Boogie Woogie
    place and date: Chicago, 13 Nov. 1936
    record numbers: (90982-A) De-7326 AH-77

1 We drinking whiskey : champagne and wine
2 Want you to know : your woman from mine
3 We're going to pitch boogie-woogie : going to have a
    ball tonight
4 And we ain't going to fuss : and we ain't going to
    fight
5 That's your woman : pin her to your side

McCoJ 25   McCoy, Joe (Harlem Hamfats)

6   She flag my train : I'm going to give her a ride
7   Everybody's talking : know what it's all about
8   Your man started some stuff : we're going to put him
    out
9   I'm taking one : to ninety-nine
10 Don't be careful : you're liable to lose your mind
11 Ain't no use : your gal being afraid
12 He'll pay you off : if you use your head
13 Pull your dresses : above your knees
14 Sell your stuff : to who you please

McCoJ 26   McCoy, Joe (Harlem Hamfats)

        title: Hallelujah Joe Ain't Preachin' No More
        place and date: Chicago, 14 Jan. 1937
        record numbers: (91074-A) De-7299 AH-77

1   Everybody thought : he was through
2   And he made a little song : about what you going to
    do
3   All the sisters and brothers thought : he was dead
4   Then he wrote a little song : by the name of Oh Red
5   He made a little trip : down to New Orleans
6   And he wrote that song : weed-smoker's dreams
7   Everybody knew : his preaching was grand
8   Then he wrote another blues : about move your hand

McCoR 1   McCoy, Robert Lee

        title: Tough Luck
        place and date: Aurora, Ill., 5 May 1937
        record numbers: (07655-1) BB-B7115 Rt RL-321

1   Now got in tough luck : all my people dead and gone
2   And I haven't got any money : no place to call my
    home
3   When a man gets in tough luck : nobody wants him
    around
4   If he haven't got any money : there is no friend to
    be found
5   When a man got lots of money : he'll have friend at
    every house
6   But if he haven't got any money : he'll be treated
    like a cat with a mouse
7   Now when I got in tough luck : my pigmeat didn't
    treat me right
8   But why should I worry about the pigmeat : sleeping
    with an old hog every night
9   So when I get out of this tough luck : I'm going to
    leave your home
10 Because you treats me mean : you know you done me
    wrong

McCoR 2   McCoy, Robert Lee

        title: Friar's Point Blues
        place and date: Chicago, 5 June 1940
        record numbers: (93037-A) De-7819 Rt RL-319

1   Babe I know that you love me : you won't treat me
    right
2   If you do good in the day : you'll go and do wrong
    at night
3   Still I ain't going to worry : and I ain't going to
    raise no sand
4   I'm going back to Friar's Point : down in sweet old
    Dixieland
5   You can love me in the morning : you can love me
    late at night
6   You don't have to worry : I'm going to treat you
    right
7   Still I ain't going to worry : and I ain't going to
    raise no sand
8   Yes I'm going away : way down in Dixieland

McCoR 2   McCoy, Robert Lee

9   Every time you kiss me : you make my love come down
10 Sometimes I believe : you the sweetest girl in town
11 Still I ain't going to worry : and I ain't going to
    raise no sand
12 Yes I'm going to leave you : going down to Dixieland
13 Babe I know you love me : you won't treat me right
14 All you want to do : is fuss and fight

McCoW 1   McCoy, William

        title: Central Tracks Blues
        place and date: Dallas, 8 Dec. 1928
        record numbers: (147611-1) Co-14453-D Yz L-1018

1   Mmm : what's the matter now
2   Well you're trying to quit your daddy mama : and you
    don't know how
3   If you don't want me : hey [please] don't dog me
    around
4   Oh just hand me my suitcase : I'll leave your Dallas
    town

McFa   1   McFadden, Charlie Specks

        title: People People Blues
        place and date: Grafton, Wis., c. Feb. 1930
        record numbers: (L-154-1) Pm-12928 Riv RM-8819

1   People people : you don't know my mind
2   I'm sitting here thinking : about the girls that I
    left behind
3   Blues and trouble : have been my best friends
4   When my blues leave me : my trouble just begins
5   Blues come down the alley : backing up to my door
6   I've got the blues today : like I never had before
7   Take me back mama : you know that I have been true
8   ??? *me* ??? : is the same thing that I've done for
    you
9   Left my baby : standing in the back door crying
10 You got a home : just as long as I've got mine

McFa   2   McFadden, Charlie Specks

        title: Groceries on the Shelf
        place and date: Grafton, Wis., c. Feb. 1930
        record numbers: (L-155-1) Pm-12928 Riv RM-8819

1   My name is Piggly Wiggly : I've got groceries on my
    shelf
2   Getting mighty tired : making these nights all by
    myself
3   My mama told me : my papa told me too
4   Don't let these Cadillac women : make no flat tire
    out of you
5   If I had a-listened : to what my mama said
6   Wouldn't have had such a hard time : in this world
    today
7   I don't want no woman : wants to rove these streets
    night and day
8   A woman like that : always wants to have her way
9   I'm leaving you now mama : baby baby bye bye
10 Going to miss your daddy : cuddling by your cozy
    side

McFaB 1   MacFarland, Barrel House Buck

        title: I Got to Go Blues
        place and date: Chicago, 20 Aug. 1934
        record numbers: (C-9321-) De-7013 OJL-20

1   I got to go : got to leave my baby be
2   And I love my woman : but my woman do not care for
    me

McFaB   1   MacFarland, Barrel House Buck

3   Baby : baby what more can I do
4   I done everything : cannot get along with you
5   Oh yes : babe oh yes oh yes I know
6   You don't want me woman : do like a *Mrs so-and-so*
7   My God : babe my God my God my God
8   I've got enough of you woman : I won't want to be
       your dog
9   Nero : make me a soldier with a cross
10   My babe quit me : then I know my soul is lost
11   Baby : baby why don't you answer me
12   I been a ??? fellow : babe I don't intend to be
13   Sometime : my woman too sweet to die
14   And again I believe : ought to be buried alive
15   Oh : babe it hurts me to my heart
16   But the Good Book says : that the best of friends
       must part
17   Because I'm black : I was born black 'fore my birth
18   And the women do tell me : I'm the sweetest black
       man on earth
19   And : baby what's the matter now
20   I'll always remember : you don't mean me no good
       nohow
21   Oh : baby what's the matter you
22   You worry me woman : babe I don't know what to do

MackA   1   Mack, Alura

         title: West End Blues
         place and date: Richmond, Ind., 1 Mar. 1929
         record numbers: (14847) Ge-6813 His HLP-4

1   I've got that *mainliner* feeling ooo : I'm full of
       gin
2   I'm on my way to the West End : and that's where the
       trouble will begin
3   Want to see some shooting : like there never has
       been before
4   I mean my man and my best friend : will never see
       the West End anymore

MackA   2   Mack, Alura

         title: Wicked Daddy Blues
         place and date: Richmond, Ind., 1 Mar. 1929
         record numbers: (14848) Ge-6797 His HLP-4

1   I feel awfully : sad and blue
2   Won't somebody : please tell me what to do
3   My daddy left me : other day
4   Couldn't be surprised : I was a poison snake
5   Wicked daddy : I'll no longer be your slave
6   Wicked daddy : now I'm going to put you in your
       grave
7   I loved your pigmeat : so nice and so sweet
8   And your loving ways : brother was hard to beat
9   Now wicked daddy : you treat your mama cruel and
       rough
10   I ain't *your rough* : and I sure know when I've had
       enough
11   Oh wicked daddy : get out of my life
12   Because you won't *smother* me : another night
13   All of these mornings : how my poor heart aches
14   Wicked daddy all you do : is take and take

McMu   1   McMullen, Fred

         title: Wait and Listen
         place and date: New York, 16 Jan. 1933
         record numbers: (12913-1) Ba-32690 Yz L-1012

1   Well you can't wait and listen : hear me when I cry
2   When you hear me crying : know there's something
       wrong

McMu   1   McMullen, Fred

3   Well you can't wait and listen : *yeah there Willie
       Mae*
4   *When it's through* baby : *something* churches tone
5   Well he dug her grave : with a long-handled silver
       spade
6   Well he let her down : with a great long leather
       line
7   Well I followed my baby : to the burying ground
8   What make it so sad eee baby : had done let her down
9   Mmm smoke like lightning : church bells shine like
       gold
10   *But with searching* I cry mama : see my baby laying
       on the bed

McMu   2   McMullen, Fred

         title: De Kalb Chain Blues
         place and date: New York, 18 Jan. 1933
         record numbers: (12936-) Ba-32784 BC-5

1   And I'll tell all you people : that ain't no place
       to go
2   Where they treat you cruel : dog you from morning
       till night
3   Well they beat me and they search me : forty-five in
       my side
4   ??? : mama working all day long
5   Take these rings and chains : from all around my
       legs
6   Well I believe to the Lord : these going to kill me
       dead

Macon   1   Macon, Ed

         title: Wringing that Thing
         place and date: Atlanta, 12 Mar. 1929
         record numbers: (402289-A) OK-8676 Mel MLP-7324

1   Now listen here folks : we don't mean no harm
2   Don't get mad : we going to sing a little song
3   There was a little black rooster : met a little
       brown hen
4   Made a date at the barn : about half past ten
5   I had a little woman : lived out Peach Tree Road
6   Made more money : than John Henry Ford
7   And the rooster crowed : and the hen looked around
8   The bum-bum-biddly : going to carry you to town
9   Now mama had a little dog : name was Ball
10   Give him a lick : and he want it all
11   Old Bill came in : about half past ten
12   Key in the hole : but he couldn't get in
13   Aunt Jane and Uncle Bud : ???
14   ??? : ???
15   If you see my girl : hurry home
16   Had no breakfast : she been gone

McPB   1   McPhail, Black Bottom

         title: Down in Black Bottom
         place and date: New York, 17 Mar. 1932
         record numbers: (11512-A) Vo-1721 Yz L-1019

1   Now down in Black Bottom : that is so they say
2   They drink good moonshine : and stay drunk all day
3   Yes I went down in Black Bottom : I didn't go to
       stay down there long
4   Police brought me out : by my right arm
5   Now go down in Black Bottom : and you don't know the
       rules
6   Black Bottom women : will try to make a fool out of
       you
7   I'm crazy about Black Bottom : mmm so they say
8   That's where they drink good moonshine : and stay
       drunk all day

184

McPB   1   McPhail, Black Bottom

9   If you go down in Black Bottom : put your money in your shoes
10   Don't them Black Bottom women : will give your pop the blues
11   Now if you go down in Black Bottom : put your money down in your britches
12   For them womens going to rob you : now you dirty mmm bitches
13   Now if anybody asks you : who composed this song
14   Tell them the Black Bottom Buddy : done been here and gone

McPB   2   McPhail, Black Bottom

title: My Dream Blues
place and date: New York, 17 Mar. 1932
record numbers: (11513-A) Vo-1690 Yz L-1019

1   I'm going to tell all you people : my dream I had one week ago
2   I dreamed my baby was leaving me : and I was begging her please don't go
3   But whensoever you have a dream : always take you dream the other way
4   For now I've been mistreated : and I'm leaving town this very day
5   I'd rather be up on a mountain : or down in the deep blue sea
6   Than to be right here baby : treated like you treat poor me
7   Lord I cried last night : and I cried the night before
8   But there's one thing I hope : I won't have to cry no more
9   Now if you don't want me baby : why don't you tell me so
10   Then I can sleep at night : and won't have to dream no more

McPB   3   McPhail, Black Bottom

title: Whiskey Man Blues
place and date: New York, 17 Mar. 1932
record numbers: (11514-A) Vo-1721 Yz L-1019

1   Well I drink so much whiskey : till they call me whiskey man
2   Lord I get drunk every morning : with a whiskey bottle in my hand
3   Lord my baby treats me mean : she keeps me worried all the time
4   And if I didn't drink my whiskey : I believe I would lose my mind
5   When I drink my whiskey : I don't mistreat my friend
6   I am sober now : but I'm going to get drunk again
7   Lord whiskey whiskey : it don't mean me no good
8   And I would stop drinking whiskey : baby if I only could
9   Lord Lord : whiskey is killing me
10   And why I can't stop drinking whiskey : Lord Lord I just can't see
11   My baby put me out : I'm just going from hand to hand
12   And I drink so much whiskey : till they call me whiskey man

McTW   1   McTell, Blind Willie

title: Writin' Paper Blues
place and date: Atlanta, 18 Oct. 1927
record numbers: (40308-1) Vi-21474 Yz L-1005

1   I wrote you a letter mama : put it in your front yard

McTW   1   McTell, Blind Willie

2   I would love to come to see you : but your good mens got me barred
3   Oh you wrote me a letter : to come back to Newport News
4   To leave the town : and don't spread the news
5   I wrote you a letter mama : sent you a telegram
6   Not to meet me in Memphis : but meet me in Birmingham
7   Mmm : hear my weep and moan
8   Now don't you hear me pleading : hear my grieve and groan
9   Now if I could get me : one more drink of booze
10   I guess it would ease : these old writing paper blues
11   I caught a freight train special : and my mama caught a passenger behind
12   Because you can't quit me papa : there's no need in trying

McTW   2   McTell, Blind Willie

title: Stole Rider Blues
place and date: Atlanta, 18 Oct. 1927
record numbers: (40309-2) Vi-21124 Yz L-1037

1   I'm going to grab me a train : ride the lonesome rail
2   Liquor stole my baby: she's in the lonesome jail
3   He took my mama : ??? her to the town of *Rome*
4   Now she's screaming and crying : papa let your mama come back home
5   I stole my good gal : from my bosom friend
6   That fool got lucky : he stoled her back again
7   That little woman I love : got a mouth chock full of good gold
8   Every time you hug and kiss me : it make my blood run cold
9   When you see two women : running hand in hand
10   Bet you my last dollar : one done stole the other one's man
11   I'm leaving town : please don't spread the news
12   That why : I've got these old stole rider blues

McTW   3   McTell, Blind Willie

title: Mama, 'Tain't Long Fo' Day
place and date: Atlanta, 18 Oct. 1927
record numbers: (40310-1) Vi-21474 Yz L-1005

1   Wake up mama : don't you sleep so hard
2   For these old blues : walking all over your yard
3   I've got these blues : means I'm not satisfied
4   That's the reason why : I stole away and cried
5   Blues grabbed me at midnight : didn't turn me loose till day
6   I didn't have no mama : drive these blues away
7   The big star falling : mama it ain't long 'fore day
8   Maybe : the sunshine'll drive these blues away

McTW   4   McTell, Blind Willie

title: Mr. McTell Got the Blues
place and date: Atlanta, 18 Oct. 1927
record numbers: (40311-?) Vi unissued RCA INT-1175

1   I'm leaving town : baby going to leave my home
2   I'm going : where honey I'm better known
3   I walk these blocks : I got to buy me some shoes
4   That's the reason why : Mr McTell got the blues
5   Got drunk last night : mama and the night before
6   And if luck don't change : Mr McTell won't get drunk no more
7   Cigarettes is my ruin : whiskey is my crave

McTW   4   McTell, Blind Willie

8 Some of these nice-looking women : going to take me
   to my grave

McTW   5   McTell, Blind Willie

       title: Three Women Blues
       place and date: Atlanta, 17 Oct. 1928
       record numbers: (47185-2) Vi-V38001 Yz L-1005

1 Got three womens : yellow brown and black
2 It'll take the Governor of Georgia : to judge one of
   these women I like
3 One for in the morning : one for late at night
4 I got one for noontime : to treat your old daddy
   right
5 These blues at midnight : they don't leave me till
   day
6 I didn't have none of my three women : to drive
   those blues away
7 One is a Memphis yellow : the other is a Savannah
   brown
8 One is a Statesboro darkskin : she'll really turn
   your damper down
9 Now if I had a-listened : to what my three women
   said
10 I'd a-been home sleeping : in a doggone feather bed

McTW   6   McTell, Blind Willie

       title: Statesboro Blues
       place and date: Atlanta, 17 Oct. 1928
       record numbers: (47187-3) Vi-V38001 Yz L-1005

1 Wake up mama : turn your lamp down low
2 Have you got the nerve : to drive papa McTell from
   your door
3 My mother died and left me reckless : my daddy died
   and left me wild wild wild
4 Know I'm not good-looking : but I'm some sweet
   woman's angel child
5 She's a mighty mean woman : do me this a-way
6 When I leave this time : pretty mama I'm going away
   to stay
7 I once loved a woman : better than even I'd ever
   seen
8 Treated me like I was a doggone king : and she was a
   doggone queen
9 Going up the country : mama don't you want to go
10 May take me a fair brown : may take one or two more
11 Big Eighty left Savannah : Lord it did not stop
12 You ought to see that colored fireman : when he got
   them boiler hot
13 You can reach over in the corner mama : and hand me
   my traveling shoes
14 You know by that : I've got them Statesboro blues
15 We woke up this morning : we had them Statesboro
   blues
16 I looked over in the corner : grandma and grandpa
   had them too

McTW   7   McTell, Blind Willie

       title: Atlanta Strut
       place and date: Atlanta, 30 Oct. 1929
       record numbers: (149299-2) Co-14657-D Yz L-1037

1 Went up on Kinnesaw Mountain : gave my horn a blow
2 Prettiest girl in Atlanta : come stepping up to my
   door
3 Hug me and she kissed me : called me sugar lump
4 Throwed them sweet arms around me : like a grape
   vine around a stump

McTW   8   McTell, Blind Willie

       title: Travelin' Blues
       place and date: Atlanta, 30 Oct. 1929
       record numbers: (149300-1) Co-14484-D Yz L-1005

1 Mr engineer : let a [poor] man ride the blind
2 Said I wouldn't mind it fellow : but you know this
   train ain't mine
3 You's a cruel fireman : lowdown engineer
4 I'm trying to hobo my way : and you leave me
   standing here
5 Get up fellow : ride all around the world
6 Poor boy : you ain't got no girl
7 I love you Emery : I love you true
8 I love you Emerald : tell the world I do

McTW   9   McTell, Blind Willie

       title: Come On Around to My House Mama
       place and date: Atlanta, 30 Oct. 1929
       record numbers: (149302-2) Co-14484-D Rt RL-324

1 Come on around to my house mama : ain't nobody there
   but me
2 Call me a hot-shot liar and a cheater : because I'm
   from Tennessee
3 Take it easy : don't get rough
4 Just want to tell you : that I knows my stuff
5 Come on around to my house mama : ain't nobody there
   but me
6 That's why you hear me [screaming and crying,
   moaning] : going back to Tennessee
7 Can't read and write : can't spell my name
8 I can really drive : your man's heart insane
9 I love my corn : and I love my booze
10 I'll really give : your man the blues
11 Pull down your windows : and lock up your blinds
12 I'll tell you something : that will change your mind
13 Went to the door : door was locked
14 Think my baby : done changed the lock
15 Wake up in the morning : about half past three
16 Think my baby : done quit poor me

McTW   10   McTell, Blind Willie

       title: Kind Mama
       place and date: Atlanta, 31 Oct. 1929
       record numbers: (149319-2) Co-14657-D Yz L-1037

1 She's a real kind mama : looking for another man
2 She ain't got nobody [in town] : [here] to hold her
   hand
3 Way down yonder : on Cripple Creek
4 Men all grow : over sixteen feet
5 Would go to bed : but it ain't no use
6 They pile up on the bed : like chickens on a roost
7 Rooster chewed tobacco : and the hen did the snuff
8 Bet he can't shimmy : but he struts his stuff
9 See that fellow : with that derby on
10 Looks good to me : just as sure as you're born
11 Tell you the truth : and it's a natural fact
12 *Could've built a road* : without being that black
13 See that fellow : that's standing right there
14 He don't live here : but he lives somewhere
15 *Got a batch of* hair : right around his mouth
16 He like he swallowed a mule : and left his tail
   hanging out
17 Wake up in the morning : at half past three
18 Think pretty mama : done fell on me
19 Soon in the morning : at half past four
20 Hot-shot rider : rapping at her door
21 Went to the door : and the door was locked
22 Think my baby : trying to eagle rock

McTW 11   McTell, Blind Willie

title: Drive Away Blues
place and date: Atlanta, 26 Nov. 1929
record numbers: (56599-1) Vi-V38580 Yz L-1005

1 I believe that if I had my sweet woman's heart : in
   my hand in my hand
2 I believe I could teach her : how to treat a real
   good man
3 I drink so much whiskey : I can't hardly talk
4 Well it's done addled on my brain : people I can't
   hardly walk
5 How my poor heart weeped and worried : baby when you
   drove me away
6 It was crying for poor boy McTell : some old rainy
   day
7 Climbing on the Lookout Mountain : look dived in
   Niagara Falls
8 Seem like to me : I can hear my Atlanta mama call
9 Don't [fret, grieve] and worry : and don't [grieve,
   fret] after me
10 Don't you scream and cry : because I'm going back to
   Tennessee
11 Can't read and write : can't even spell my name
12 You drove me away : and drove my heart insane

McTW 12   McTell, Blind Willie

title: Love-Changing Blues
place and date: Atlanta, 29 Nov. 1929
record numbers: (56635-1) Vi-V38580 Yz L-1005

1 My love don't change : there's going to be some
   stealing done
2 And if I backbite you : I don't mean no harm
3 What do you want with a woman : when she won't do
   nothing she say
4 What do you want with a rooster : when he won't crow
   'fore day
5 If my love don't change : there's going to be some
   riding done
6 And if I take you woman : I just be made my run
7 Going in one of these alleys : get me [some
   lonesome, a quart of this] booze
8 My woman done left me : I got these love-changing
   blues

McTW 13   McTell, Blind Willie

title: Talking to Myself
place and date: Atlanta, 17 Apr. 1930
record numbers: (150257-2) Co-14551-D Yz L-1005

1 Good Lord good Lord : send me an angel down
2 Can't spare you no angel : but I'll swear I'll send
   you a teasing brown
3 That new way of loving : mama it must be best
4 These here Georgia women : just won't let Mr Samuel
   rest
5 There was a crowd out on the corner : wondered who
   could it be
6 It weren't a thing : but the women trying to get to
   me
7 I even went down to the depot : with my suitcase in
   my hand
8 Crowd of womens all crying : Mr Samuel won't you be
   my man
9 My mama she told me : when I was a boy playing
   mumblepeg
10 Don't drink no black cow's milk : don't you eat no
   black hen's eggs
11 Black man give you a dollar : mama he won't think it
   nothing strange
12 A yellow man'll give you a dollar : but he'll want
   back ninety-five cents change

McTW 13   McTell, Blind Willie

13 You may call me a cheater : pretty boy I'll real
   treat you
14 But if you'll allow me a chance : I'll gnaw your
   backbone half in two
15 I took a trip out on the ocean : walked the sand of
   the deep blue sea
16 I found a crab with a shrimp : trying to do the
   shimmy-shee
17 I want to tell you something mama : seem mighty
   doggone strange
18 You done mess around gal : and made me break my
   yo-yo string
19 Honey I ain't going to be : your old work ox no more
20 You done mess around baby : and let your doggone ox
   get poor
21 My mama she got a mojo : believe she trying to keep
   it hid
22 Papa Samuel got something : to find that mojo with
23 I even heard a rumbling : deep down in the ground
24 It weren't a thing : but the women trying to run me
   down

McTW 14   McTell, Blind Willie

title: Razor Ball
place and date: Atlanta, 17 Apr. 1930
record numbers: (150258-2) Co-14551-D Yz L-1037

1 Down in Atlanta at the razor ball : even at the
   razor ball
2 Sluefoot Mose and cross-eyed Joe : didn't go in at
   all
3 Big crap game in the hall : started in to fight
4 Joe got drunk that wasn't all : went and turn out
   the lights
5 And that *matcher* Charlie : shot his automatic
   twins
6 Charlie grabbed his girl : and he *crow forked* in
7 Playing baseball and football : and don't get enough
8 Playing baseball and football : and strutting the
   stuff
9 Mighty big chief : shot his automatic twin
10 The high sheriff took the couple : and double-cross
   ten
11 Put you lights on calico : and fight it for game
12 Put me at the head of the list : and don't forget to
   call my name

McTW 15   McTell, Blind Willie

title: Southern Can Is Mine
place and date: Atlanta, 23 Oct. 1931
record numbers: (151904-1) Co-14632-D Yz L-1005

1 Now look here mama : let me tell you this
2 Now if you wants to get crooked : I'm going to give
   you my fist
3 You might read from Revelation : back to Genesee
4 You get crooked : your southern can belong to me
5 If you go uptown : have me arrested and have me put
   in jail
6 Some hot-shot got money : come in and go my bail
7 Soon as I get out : kiss the ground
8 Your southern can : worth two dollar half a pound
9 You might take it from the South : you might carry
   it up north
10 But understand you can't rule : and either be my
   boss
11 Take it from the east : hide it in the west
12 When I get it mama : your can will see no rest
13 Well ashes to ashes mama : and sand to sand
14 Every time I hit you : you think I got a dozen hands
15 Hit you first : through that barbed wire fence
16 Every time I hit you : you say I got no sense
17 Get me a brick : out of my back yard

18 Give you the devil : if you act kind of hard
19 Now if I catch you mama : down in the heart of town
20 Take me a brand new brick : and tear your can on
    down
21 You may be deathbed sick : and mama and graveyard
    bound
22 Make your can : moan like a hound
23 Sit here and study : with your eyes all red
24 What I said : kicked your grandma dead
25 Oh you got to stop your balking : and raising the
    deuce
26 I'll grab you mama : and turn you every way but
    loose
27 You might twiggle like a tadpole : let it jump like
    a frog
28 But every time I hit it : you going to holler God
    dog

McTW   16   McTell, Blind Willie

    title: Broke Down Engine Blues
    place and date: Atlanta, 23 Oct. 1931
    record numbers: (151905-1) Co-14632-D Yz L-1005

1   Feel like a broke down engine : ain't got no
    driving-wheel
2   You ever been down and lonesome : you know how a
    poor man feels
3   I've been shooting craps and gambling : mama and I
    done got broke
4   I done pawned my pistol : mama and my best clothes
    in soak
5   I went down to my praying ground : and fell on
    bended knees
6   I ain't crying for no religion : Lordy give me back
    my good gal please
7   If you give me my baby : Lord I won't worry you no
    more
8   You ain't got to put it in my house : Lordy only
    leave it to my door
9   Don't you hear me baby : rapping on your door
10 Can I get off *snake living* and tapping : playing
    tip light across your floor
11 Feel like a broke down engine : ain't got no drivers
    at all
12 What makes me love my woman : she can really do the
    Georgia crawl
13 Feel like a broke down engine : ain't got no
    weather-the-bell
14 If you's a real hot mama : drive away daddy's
    weeping spell

McTW   17   McTell, Blind Willie

    title: Stomp Down Rider
    place and date: Atlanta, 23 Oct. 1931
    record numbers: (405002-1) OK-8936 Yz L-1005

1   When I first met you mama : you were so nice and
    kind
2   You done got reckless : and change your mind
3   When I was down south baby : I was with my broad
4   I'm here in Atlanta : treated like a dog
5   Now if you don't want me baby : don't you dog me
    around
6   My home ain't here : and I can leave your town
7   Now if you don't want me : baby give me your right
    hand
8   I'll go back to my woman : you go back to your man
9   I even give you my money : *I admire*
10 I done all for you : that you require
11 Even hold your head : when you're feeling sad
12 Sing and dance for you : when you're sad
13 You done come in this morning : you won't tell me
    where you been

14 You got strange living : going back again
15 I'm walking around baby : with my head hung low
16 Look here mama : I ain't going to do right no more
17 I'm going to take me a trip : up on the mountain top
18 Come back and show you : how to eagle rock

McTW   18   McTell, Blind Willie

    title: Scarey Day Blues
    place and date: Atlanta, 23 Oct. 1931
    record numbers: (405003-1) OK-8936 Yz L-1037

1   I wants to wait around here baby : until your fried
    rice get done
2   Because I think I got a nickel : I wants to buy me
    one
3   I wonder could I find a woman : to do like my last
    rider done
4   She kept it all for her daddy : she didn't give
    nobody none
5   Said my baby got a bed : it shines like a morning
    star
6   And when I crawls in the middle : it rides me like a
    Cadillac car
7   My good gal got a mojo : she's trying to keep it hid
8   But Georgia Bill got something : to find that mojo
    with
9   I said she got that mojo : and she won't let me see
10 And every time I start to love her : she's tried to
    put them jinx on me
11 Well she shakes it like the Central : she wobbles
    like the L and N
12 Well she's a hot-shot mama : and I'm scared to tell
    her where I been
13 Said my baby got something : she won't tell her
    daddy what it is
14 But when I crawls in my bed : I just can't keep my
    black stuff still
15 Well I done got reckless : and I broke my mama's
    rule
16 I been wandering around Georgia : with these doggone
    scary day blues

McTW   19   McTell, Blind Willie

    title: Georgia Rag
    place and date: Atlanta, 31 Oct. 1931
    record numbers: (405085-1) OK-8924 Yz L-1005

1   Down on Atlanta : on Harris Street
2   That's where the boys and gals : do meet
3   Out in the alley : in the street
4   Every little kid : that you meet
5   Buzz all around : like a bee
6   Shake it : like a ship on the sea
7   Came all the way : from Paris France
8   Come into Atlanta : to get a chance
9   Grab your mama : and hold her tight
10 Let's mess around : the rest of the night
11 Grip your head : way up high
12 Grab your daddy : and make him cry
13 People come : from miles around
14 Get in Dark Town : to break them down
15 Down in dark town : night and day
16 Trying to dance : them blues away
17 Go all the way back : to Newport News
18 Singing : these doggone Atlanta blues

McTW 20   McTell, Blind Willie

   title: Rollin' Mama Blues
   place and date: Atlanta, 22 Feb. 1932
   record numbers: (71603-) Vi-23328 Rt RL-324

2 I want you to start in the morning baby : and roll
   me with the setting of the sun
4 I want you to keep it all for your daddy : and don't
   give nobody none
6 And if you get some of my loving : you won't want
   your rider no more
8 You don't have to worry about your loving : I'm a
   deep-sea diver and I don't go wrong
10 That's why I'm singing : these barrelhouse woman
   blues

McTW 21   McTell, Blind Willie

   title: Searching the Desert for the Blues
   place and date: Atlanta, 22 Feb. 1932
   record numbers: (71606-1) Vi-23353 RCA LPV-518

1 You may search the ocean : you might go across the
   deep blue sea
2 But mama you'll never find : another hot-shot like
   me
3 I followed my baby : from the station to the train
4 And the blues came down : like doggone showers of
   rain
5 I left her at the station : wringing her hands and
   crying
6 I told her she had a home : just as long as I got
   mine
7 I've got two women : and you can't tell them apart
8 I got one in my bosom : the other one in my heart
9 The one in my bosom : she's in Tennessee
10 And the one in my heart : don't even give a darn for
   me
11 I used to say a married woman : was the sweetest
   woman ever was born
12 But I've changed that thing : you better let married
   women alone
13 Take my advice : let these married women be
14 Because their husbands'll grab you : and beat you
   ragged as a cedar tree
15 When a woman say she love you : about as good as she
   do herself
16 I don't pay her no attention : tell that same lie to
   somebody else
17 I really don't believe : no woman in the whole round
   world do right
18 Act like an angel in the daytime : ??? at night
19 I'm going pretty mama : please don't break this rule
20 That's why : I'm searching these deserts for the
   blues
21 I'm going pretty mama : searching these deserts now
22 That's why : I'm walking my baby home anyhow

McTW 22   McTell, Blind Willie

   title: Warm It Up to Me
   place and date: New York, 14 Sept. 1933
   record numbers: (14008-2) Vo-02595 Yz L-1005

1 Take a little trip : up on a mountain top
2 Show the Florida women : how to eagle rock
3 Tell you like the *bana* : told the *king of sal*
4 Get another man : I got another gal
5 Now if you don't believe : I can warm you right
6 Take me to your house : and let me stay all night
7 When you see me mama : standing in the door
8 Papa wound up : saying mama won't go
9 Don't be no *resting* : don't be no late
10 Don't let these women : leave your heart insane
11 Now look here boy : don't get rough
12 These here women : they really knows their stuff

McTW 22   McTell, Blind Willie

13 I want you to set on a Cadillac : sit on a Ford
14 You do that strutting : on the running board
15 Don't be no rat : and don't be no fool
16 Don't let these here women : break your rule
17 Now look here boy : if you going to be my friend
18 Let's go drink : moonshine again
19 Now take it easy : late at night
20 One of these here women : ain't going to treat you
   right

McTW 23   McTell, Blind Willie

   title: It's a Good Little Thing
   place and date: New York, 14 Sept. 1933
   record numbers: (14010-1) Vo-02622 Yz L-1037

1 Look a-here mama : just a word or two
2 Said I get you : to let's go loo loo
3 Look here mama : just don't stop
4 I ain't going to be : your other man's stumbling
   block
5 Wait just a minute : let's get this right
6 We're going go a-looing : till broad daylight
7 Going to Savannah : make some jack
8 Hold that cat : till I get back
9 What is that mama : you got in that sack
10 It's got hair on it : and I believe it's a cat
11 Well it looks pretty much : like Santy Claus
12 Best little something : I ever saw
13 Look here mama : just like a log
14 She gets kissing : like a shaggy dog

McTW 24   McTell, Blind Willie

   title: Savannah Mama
   place and date: New York, 18 Sept. 1933
   record numbers: (14035-1) Vo-02568 Yz L-1005

1 Mmm : Lordy Lordy Lord
2 Say the woman I love : treats me just like a dog
3 I love you baby : but your ways I just can't stand
4 Say you walked away and left me : good gal with
   another man
5 Going back to Savannah mama : and sign my initial
   down
6 Atlanta mens all hate me : and the women don't want
   me around
7 Going back to Savannah baby : and write my initial
   on the wall
8 Because these North Georgia women : don't mean me no
   good at all
9 Mmm : babe ain't it hard ain't it hard ain't it hard
10 Says I'd like to love you baby : but your good men
   got me barred

McTW 25   McTell, Blind Willie

   title: Broke Down Engine
   place and date: New York, 18 Sept. 1933
   record numbers: (14036-2) Vo-02577 RBF RF-15

1 Feel like a broke down engine : mama ain't got no
   driving-wheel
2 You ever been down and lonesome : you know just how
   Willie McTell feels
3 I been shooting craps and gambling : good gal and I
   done got broke
4 I done pawned my thirty-two special : good gal and
   my clothes in soak
5 I even went to my praying ground : dropped down on
   bended knees
6 I ain't crying for no religion : Lordy give me back
   my good gal please

189

McTW 25   McTell, Blind Willie

7   If you give me my baby : Lord I won't worry you no
    more
8   You ain't got to put her in my house : but Lordy
    only lead her to my door
9   Don't you hear [me, your daddy] baby : knocking on
    your door
10 Can I get off *sneak living and tapping* : playing
    tip light across your floor

McTW 26   McTell, Blind Willie

    title: My Baby's Gone
    place and date: New York, 18 Sept. 1933
    record numbers: (14038-2) Vo-02668 Yz L-1037

1   My baby's gone : and I'm almost in my grave
2   But for your love : good gal I will be you slave
3   My baby left me : says she didn't mean me no good
4   And that's the reason why : I'm moving on back to
    the woods
5   My baby left me : she didn't even say goodbye
6   Says I'm drinking real good whiskey : that's the
    reason I did not *inquire why*
7   My baby's gone : says I ain't even worried at all
8   Before she even left me : says she riding that
    Cannonball
9   Mmm : Lordy Lordy Lordy Lord
10 Says my good gal she's gone : she didn't mean me no
    good at all

McTW 27   McTell, Blind Willie

    title: Death Cell Blues
    place and date: New York, 19 Sept. 1933
    record numbers: (14049-1) Vo-02577 RBF RF-15

1   Mmm : chained down in this dark cell by myself
2   And my gal she skipped : guess she got somebody else
3   Well they've got me accused for murder : and I
    haven't even harmed a man
4   Oh they got me charged with burgling : and I haven't
    even raised my hand
5   Mmm : the judge won't give me no fine
6   Ain't but one thing could release me : and that's
    old father time
7   Goodbye : oh here comes the jailor with the key
8   I'll have to cry farewell to freedom : I want none
    of your women to pity me
9   I'll have to give you my number : five nine
    ninety-four
10 Because I'll be there forever : I'll have no other
    place to go
11 They got me accused for forging : and I can't even
    write my name
12 And my eyes *filled on this* : my baby left my poor
    heart in pain
13 Mmm : Lordy Lordy Lord
14 Inside my breast felt lonely : my baby left my heart
    in pain

McTW 28   McTell, Blind Willie

    title: B and O Blues No. 2
    place and date: New York, 21 Sept. 1933
    record numbers: (14066-1) Vo-02568 Yz L-1037

1   I'm going to grab me a train : I'm going back to
    Baltimore
2   I'm going to find my baby : because she rode that B
    and O
3   I'm going to act like a rambler : and I can't stay
    home no more
4   Because the gal I love : she rode that B and O

McTW 28   McTell, Blind Willie

5   She says daddy I'm leaving : and I can't come back
    no more
6   And if she don't come back : I'm going down in Ohio
7   I never would have thought : that my baby would
    treat me so
8   Oh she broke my heart : when she grabbed that B and
    O
9   Now she wants to come back : and I can't use that
    child no more
10 Because I got another hot mama : and she lives in
    Baltimore

McTW 29   McTell, Blind Willie

    title: Weary Hearted Blues
    place and date: New York, 21 Sept. 1933
    record numbers: (14067-1) Vo-02568 Rt RL-324

1   Look a-here pretty mama : I'll tell you what I'll do
2   I'll make these lonesome dollars : and bring them
    all home to you
3   Now I'm weary : weary-hearted and blue
4   And that's why I'm crying : these weary-hearted
    blues
5   I'll give you my money : and baby I *admire*
6   I does all for you mama : you require
7   I even hold your head : when you are feeling bad
8   I sing and dance for you : mama when you sad
9   I want to tell all you men : nice and kind
10 You lose your best woman : don't you fool with mine
11 Now a white man go to the river : take him a seat
    and sit down
12 The blues overtake him : he jump overboard and drown
13 Now a colored man go to the river : take him a seat
    and sit down
14 If he takes the blues : he come on back to town
15 I wants all you men : to let my good gal alone
16 I'll give her a dollar in the street : and I'll give
    her two at home

McTW 30   McTell, Blind Willie

    title: Southern Can Mama
    place and date: New York, 21 Sept. 1933
    record numbers: (14069-2) Vo-02622 Yz L-1037

1   Now look a-here mama : let me explain you this
2   You wants to get crooked : I'll even give you my
    fist
3   Read from Revelation : back to Genesee
4   You get crooked : your southern can belongs to me
5   You might go uptown : and have me arrested and have
    me put in jail
6   Some hot-shot got money : come in and go my bail
7   Soon as I get out : kiss the ground
8   Your southern can : worth two dollars and a half a
    pound
9   You might take it from the South : you might carry
    it up north
10 Understand you can't rule : and either be my boss
11 Take it from the east : hide it in the west
12 When I get it mama : your can won't see no rest
13 Ashes to ashes : and sand to sand
14 Every time I strikes you : you know I got a dozen
    hands
15 Give you a punch : through that barbed wire fence
16 Every time I hit you : you know I ain't got no sense
17 Look here women : don't get hard
18 I'll get me a brick : and use it out of my back yard
19 If I catch you mama : down in the heart of town
20 Take a brand new brick : and tear your can on down
21 You may be deathbed sickness : graveyard bound
22 I'll make your can moan : like a graveyard hound
23 You got to stop balking : and raising the deuce

24 I'll grab you woman : and turn you every way but loose

   title: Runnin' Me Crazy
   place and date: New York, 21 Sept. 1933
   record numbers: (14070-1) Vo-02595 Rt RL-324

1   Says I'm almost crazy : and I'm all here by myself
2   All these women about to run me crazy : Lord she's got someone else
3   Lord she's about to run me crazy : these reckless women are worrying me
4   She don't have to treat me so bad : because she lives in Tennessee
5   Lord you'll either run me crazy woman : or either make me lose my mind
6   Because you keep me worried : and troubled all the time
7   Lord these womens will run you crazy : they'll drive your heart insane
8   They'll spend all your money : turn around and run you insane
9   Well she spent all my money : and then she drove me outdoors
10 And I was almost crazy : because I had nowhere to go
11 Lord if you got a reckless woman : man don't never let her break your rule
12 And when you know anything : you'd be almost crazy with the blues

   title: Bell Street Blues
   place and date: Chicago, 23 Apr. 1935
   record numbers: (C-9946-A) De-7078 Rt RL-324

1   I live down in Bell Street Alley : just as drunk as I can be
2   Seem like them Bell Street Crow Janes : have done got rough with me
3   I drink so much Bell Street whiskey : they won't sell [McTell, poor boy] no more
4   I've got the *cavenglass* boys : playing all around my door
5   This Bell Street whiskey : make you sleep all in your clothes
6   And when you wake up next morning : feel like you done laid outdoors
7   You can get booze down on Bell Street : for two bits and half a *throw*
8   They'll make you *send* out your mother and father : to just break down the jailhouse door
9   Walked in my room : the other night
10 Man come in : he want to fight
11 Took my gun : my right hand
12 ??? : I don't want to kill no man
13 When I said that : he rapped me across my head
14 The first shot I fired : then the man fell dead
15 Bell street whiskey : drove me to the county jail
16 Got me laying back here on my bunk : nobody in the world to go my bail

   title: Ticket Agent Blues
   place and date: Chicago, 25 Apr. 1935
   record numbers: (C-9954-A) De-7078 Yz L-1037

1   Good Lord good Lord : send me an angel down
2   Can't spare you no angel : will spare you a teasing brown

3   That new way of loving : swear to God it must be best
4   Because these Georgia women : won't let Willie McTell rest
5   There was a crowd down on the corner : and I wondered who could it be
6   Weren't a thing : but the women boy trying to get to me
7   I went down to the shed : put my suitcase in my hand
8   Crowd of women run crying : that McTell be my man
9   Ticket agent ticket agent : which a-way has my woman gone
10 Say describe your woman : and I'll tell you what road she's on
11 She's a long tall mama : five and a half from the ground
12 She's a tailor-made mama : and she ain't no hand-me-down
13 Mama if you ride the Southern : I'll ride the Santa Fe
14 When you get in Memphis : pretty mama look around for me
15 You can't never tell : what a double-crossing woman will do
16 They'll tip out with your buddy : and come home play sick on you
17 I got two women : you can't tell them apart
18 I got one in my bosom : the other one's in my heart
19 Now the one in my bosom : she's in Tennessee
20 And the one in my heart : don't even give a darn for me
21 I used to say a married woman : was the sweetest woman ever was born
22 I changed that thing : you better let married women alone
23 Take my advice : let all married womens be
24 Because their husbands will grab you : and beat you ragged with a cedar tree
25 Now love ain't nothing : single women loving married men
26 It will do for a while : but it will jam you after a end
27 When a woman says she loves you : about as good as she do herself
28 Don't pay her no attention : tell the same lie to somebody else
29 She'll tell you that she love you : and love you all her life
30 She'll have a man on the corner : and tell that same lie twice
31 My baby she got a mojo : I believe she trying to keep it hid
32 Mctell got something : to find that mojo with
33 I want to tell you pretty mama : exactly who I am
34 When I walk out the front door : I hear that back door slam

   title: Cold Winter Day
   place and date: Chicago, 25 Apr. 1935
   record numbers: (C-9956-A) De-7810 Yz L-1037

1   I did everything baby : that I could do
2   Fell on my knees : mama get along with you
3   I give you my money baby : my last dime
4   Soon as you got up mama : you changed your mind
5   I gave you my money mama : buy you shoes and clothes
6   Soon as you got bid change : you put me outdoors
7   I took you mama : your shoes were thin
8   No man wanted you : no one took you in
9   When I took you mama : *feet'll* on the ground
10 Ain't no man baby : wanted you around
11 Took your breakfast : brought it to your bed
12 Took my comb baby : combed your head
13 Make no difference mama : take your lock and key

McTW   34   McTell, Blind Willie

14 Too many women : want a man like me
15 Going away mama : it won't be long
16 I know you'll miss me : the days I'm gone
17 I took you mama : treated you nice and kind
18 Soon as you got on your feet : you wouldn't pay me
    no mind

McTW   35   McTell, Blind Willie

        title: Your Time to Worry
        place and date: Chicago, 25 Apr. 1935
        record numbers: (C-9957-A) De-7117 Rt RL-324

1   I done told you mama : right from the start
2   I ain't going to let no one woman : break my heart
3   Your time to worry : my time to be alone
4   Your reckless disposition : done drove your good man
    away from home
5   I told you in my days : things I do
6   Go out and work hard : and bring my money home to
    you
7   You drink your whiskey : run around
8   Get out in the street : and act like a sand-foot
    clown
9   Went out with you baby : trying to treat you right
10 I drinking whiskey woman : and drunk all night
11 Need not come here pleading : holding up your hands
12 I got myself a woman : you better get yourself a man
13 Leave me alone baby : best you can do
14 I would have been a murderer : if I'd a-fooled
    around with you
15 Now go ahead baby : leave me alone
16 Mess around with you : the chain-gang will be my
    home

Mann   1   Manning, Leola

        title: The Blues Is All Wrong
        place and date: Knoxville, Tenn., c. Apr. 1930
        record numbers: (K-8089-) Vo-1529 Yz L-1015

1   *Feel like voting* : fall in line
2   While I sing : this song of mine
3   This song's all right : if you thinks it's wrong
4   It's all right : it's a ??? song
5   This song's all right : it just won't jump
6   It's all right : it just won't
7   This song brings joy : to our *cry*
8   We're baptized : with fire
9   This song's *composed* : the blues too tight
10 Got the blues tune : but the words all right
11 This song's all right : it just won't quit
12 It's all right : we're singing it
13 You can talks about me : treat me mean
14 You got the *train* : ???

MartC 1   Martin, Carl

        title: Farewell to You Baby
        place and date: Chicago, 8 Jan. 1935
        record numbers: (C-877-1) OK-8961 Yz L-1016

1   I'm leaving you baby : just because you won't be
    true
2   Oh you don't love me : after all I done for you
3   You know I worked hard all winter : when the snow
    was on the ground
4   You mistreated me then baby : Eli wouldn't throw you
    down
5   You made a mistake baby : after you made your vow
6   But your mistake-making : is all over now
7   You going to miss [your daddy, me] : some old
    lonesome day
8   And you going to be sorry : you did me this way

MartC 1   Martin, Carl

9   Now I'm leaving you [baby] : with my clothes in my
    hand
10 Farewell to you baby : get yourself a monkey-man

MartC 2   Martin, Carl

        title: Badly Mistreated Man
        place and date: Chicago, 8 Jan. 1935
        record numbers: (C-881-2) OK-8961 Yz L-1016

1   I worked hard baby : I worked hard every day
2   I even turned over in your hand : every cent of my
    pay
3   I been done so dirty : treated so lowdown mean
4   You've even accused me of women : that I ain't never
    seen
5   People what's the use of loving : when I can't see
    why I should
6   Especially when you got a woman : and she don't mean
    you no good
7   I woke up this morning : got on a stroll
8   Met my baby : got her told
9   Look a-here baby : you thinking wrong
10 Let your papa help you : to sing this song
11 I grabbed my coat and hat : down the road I'll start
12 Before I'd worry : I'd rather part
13 I wouldn't work : for no human being
14 Neither no woman : that I ever seen
15 Eighteen hundred : ninety years
16 All of my women : sit in rocking chairs
17 But ever since : nineteen and twenty-three
18 All of my women : been working for me
19 I got a mind : never work no more
20 I've been badly mistreated : I've been drove from
    door to door

MartC 3   Martin, Carl

        title: Good Morning, Judge
        place and date: Chicago, 8 Jan. 1935
        record numbers: (C-882-) Vo-03047 OJL-18

1   They arrested my baby : accused her of selling moon
2   Judge they found whiskey : but it wasn't even in her
    room
3   Now good morning judge : judge how do you do
4   I just came here : to have a few words with you
5   Please kind judge : listen to my plea
6   And let my baby : go back home with me

MartC 4   Martin, Carl

        title: Joe Louis Blues
        place and date: Chicago, 4 Sept. 1935
        record numbers: (90293-A) De-7114 Yz L-1016

1   Now listen all you prize fighters : who don't want
    to meet defeat
2   Take a tip from me : stay off Joe Louis' beat
3   Now he won all his fights : twenty-three or four
4   And left twenty of his opponents : lying on the
    floor
5   They all tried to win : but the test was too hard
6   When he laid the hambone : *couple jumped out for
    it*
7   Listen all you prize fighters : don't play him too
    cheap
8   If he lands with either hand : he'll sure put you to
    the seat
9   Now he packs dynamite in his left : he carries a
    punching right
10 He's the one will make you balky : or as high as a
    kite

MartC 4   Martin, Carl

11 He charges on his opponents : from the beginning of
    the gong
12 He batters them into submission : then they all sing
    a song
13 I bet on the Brown Bomber : for he knows his stuff
14 And lays it on his opponents : until he get enough
15 Now he's a natural born fighter : who likes to fight
    them all
16 The bigger they come : he says the harder they fall
17 That terrific left : boys is all he needs
18 But that six-inch right : come with lightning speed
19 Listen all you prize fighters : don't play him too
    cheap
20 Take a tip from me : stay off Joe Louis' beat

MartC 5   Martin, Carl

        title: Let's Have a New Deal
        place and date: Chicago, 4 Sept. 1935
        record numbers: (90294-A) De-7114 BC-14

1 Now everybody's crying : let's have a new deal
2 Relief station's closing down : I know just how you
   feel
3 Everybody's crying : let's have a new deal
4 Because I've got to make a living : if I have to rob
   and steal
5 Now I'm getting mighty tired : of sitting around
6 I ain't making a dime : just wearing my shoe soles
   down
7 I ain't making a dime : just wearing my shoe soles
   down
8 Now I woke up this morning : doggone my soul
9 My flour barrel was empty : swear I didn't have no
   coal
10 We're going to dance : till *another* sun
11 Now you go to your wicket : put in your complaint
12 Eight time out of ten : you know they'll say I can't
13 They don't want to give you no dough : won't hardly
   pay your rent
14 Now it ain't costing them : one doggone cent
15 Now I ain't made a dime : since they closed down the
   mill
16 I'm sitting right here : waiting on that brand new
   deal

MartD 1   Martin, Daisy

        title: Feelin' Blue
        place and date: New York, c. late July 1923
        record numbers: (5237-1) Ba-1262 VJM VLP-40

1 Does anybody : does anybody feel like me
2 Now if they do : I know the feeling is sad as can be
3 Now I'm going home : to take a snooze
4 Try to wear away : a thing they call the feeling
   blues
5 I'm tired of fooling around : with one who don't
   love me
6 If I ever find a way to leave him : if we cannot
   agree

MartD 2   Martin, Daisy

        title: What You Was You Used to Be
        place and date: New York, c. late July 1923
        record numbers: (5238-1) Ba-1262 VJM VLP-40

1 Because what you was you used to be : but you ain't
   no more
2 I'm giving you your dispossess : welcome's off the
   door
3 Be on your way : you got yourself in wrong
4 You'll get flat feet : from standing too long

MartD 2   Martin, Daisy

5 Let this be a lesson : now that I have left you flat
6 There's someone sitting pretty : in the place where
   you once sat
7 You ought to see him do his stuff : my latest loving
   man
8 Because where you left off : is just the place where
   he began
9 You said you craved a gal with speed : that's why I
   wouldn't do
10 But now the gal you left behind : is way ahead of
   you
11 But what you was you used to be : but you ain't no
   more
12 Just make your exit *smiling please* : there's no
   use getting sore
13 You ran away : and left me on the shelf
14 Keep right on running : go chase yourself

MartS 1   Martin, Sara

        title: Blind Man Blues
        place and date: New York, c. 1 Aug. 1923
        record numbers: (71711-B) OK-8090 Sw S-1240

1 I ain't going to marry : I ain't going to settle
   down
2 I'm going to stay down here : and swing these men
   around
3 Just when you think : that your loving man is true
4 Then he's your man my man : somebody else's too
5 Oh big fat woman : with the meat shaking on her
   bones
6 Every time she shimmies : a skinny woman leaves her
   home

MartS 2   Martin, Sara

        title: Death Sting Me Blues
        place and date: Long Island City, Nov. 1928
        record numbers: (278-A) QRS-R7042 BYG-529073

1 I want all you women : to listen to my tale of woe
2 I've got consumption of the heart : I feel myself
   sinking low
3 Oh my heart is aching : and the blues are all around
   my *loo*
4 Blues is like the devil : they'll have me hell bound
   too
5 Blues you made me roll and tumble : you made me weep
   and sigh
6 Made me use cocaine and whiskey: but you wouldn't
   let me die
7 Blues blues blues : why did you bring trouble to me
8 Oh death please sting me : and take me out of my
   misery

MartS 3   Martin, Sara

        title: Mistreating Man Blues
        place and date: Long Island City, Dec. 1928
        record numbers: (306) QRS-R7042 BYG-529073

1 I've got the blues : since I made up my mind
2 I want to stop loving you : because you mistreat me
   all the time
3 Oh this game called love : I played it on the square
4 But you think : a good woman can be found anywhere
5 You never meant me no good : you've always had your
   way
6 But things can't go on forever : they are bound to
   change some day
7 So now I'm leaving you : some day you'll understand
8 *That's why* I can't go on : loving a mistreating
   man

MasM   1   Mason, Moses

        title: Molly Man
        place and date: Chicago, c. Jan. 1928
        record numbers: (20283-2) Pm-12605 OJL-8

1   Molly man's coming : I hear his voice
2   He's got hot tamales : and it's just my choice
3   Come on boys : and don't wait too long
4   All my 'males : soon will be gone
5   I can judge : by the way you act
6   Somebody around here : had on a cotton-picking track
7   Feeling tired : shoulder's getting sore
8   If you see 'male : you're going to take some more
9   Two for a nickel : four for a dime
10 Thirty cents a dozen : and you'll sure eat fine
11 Good times have come in : don't you see the signs
12 Cotton bolls are open : you can make a-many dimes
13 I can judge : by the way you walk
14 You going to carry : half a dozen off
15 If my holler boys : trouble your mind
16 You had to come running : with a dime
17 Good times have come in : don't you see the signs
18 White folks standing around here : spending a-many
        dimes
19 'Males so hot : it burns my hand
20 Says I can't hardly get them : out of my can

MasM   2   Mason, Moses

        title: Shrimp Man
        place and date: Chicago, c. Jan. 1928
        record numbers: (20302-3) Pm-12605 Rt RL-325

1   Shrimp is the thing : you love best
2   *Ring them nice : and they'll* ???
3   Here is my shrimp : fifty cents a quart
4   Ask me for a gallon : two dollars is all
5   Have my shrimp : both done and raw
6   Have my shrimp hot : they are ready to go
7   Have my shrimp : I'm selling them fast
8   When I see you coming : you make me laugh
9   If you going to bed : you can call
10 I'll poke them through the window : that is all
11 If your heart feel troubled : you can call
12 I'll make *change selling* : that is all
13 Selling your shrimp : don't sell them so high
14 Want to buy it cold : so I can make up a pie
15 Selling my shrimp : don't mean no harm
16 My shrimp sick : it don't make no alarm
17 Selling my shrimp : won't be here long
18 I'm going to holler : but I'm going home

MemM   1   Memphis Minnie

        title: Goin' Back to Texas
        place and date: New York, 18 June 1929
        record numbers: (148709-2) Co-14455-D OJL-21

1   When I lived in Texas : doing very well
2   You can ??? telling : I'm catching hell
3   I'm going I'm going : crying won't make me stay
4   The more you cry : the further it drive me away
5   I've got something to tell you : know it's going to
        break your heart
6   We been together a good while : but now we got to
        part
7   When I had you : that wouldn't do
8   Now I've got another man : and I can't use you
9   You ought to have told me that : two or three weeks
        ago
10 Lord when you heard : you might've thought you
        wasn't going to get broke
11 I don't mind going : to say goodbye
12 ??? : I'm *stopping* to die

MemM   2   Memphis Minnie

        title: 'Frisco Town
        place and date: New York, 18 June 1929
        record numbers: (148710-2) Co-14455-D Yz L-1008

1   That old Frisco train : left a mile a minute
2   Well it's that old coach : I'm going to sit right in
        it
3   You can toot your whistle : you can ring your bell
4   Well I know you been worried : by the way you smell
5   Oh there's a boa constrictor : and a lemon stick
6   I don't mind being with you : but my mama's sick
7   I would tell you what's the matter : but I done got
        scared
8   Got to wait now : until we go to bed
9   If you was sick : I wouldn't worry you
10 I wouldn't want you to do something : that you
        couldn't do
11 Well if you want it you can get it : and I ain't mad
12 If you tell me this is something : that you ain't
        never had
13 Look a-here you get mad : every time I call your
        name
14 I ain't never told you : that you couldn't get that
        thing
15 I woke up this morning : about half past five
16 My baby turned over : cried just like a child
17 I got something to tell you : I don't want to make
        you mad
18 I got something for you : make you feel glad
19 Look a-here look a-here : what you want me to do
20 Give you my jelly : then I die for you
21 I got something to tell you : going to break your
        heart
22 We been together so far : we got to get ???

MemM   3   Memphis Minnie

        title: I'm Talking About You
        place and date: Memphis, 20 Feb. 1930
        record numbers: (MEM-772-A) Vo-1476 Pal PL-101

1   You can quit me : do anything you want to do
2   Some day you'll want me : and I won't want you
3   You's a man : running from hand to hand
4   You can get you a woman : I got another man
5   You will mistreat me : and you won't do right
6   You can take it on back : where you had it last
        night
7   Well you can't be mine : and somebody else's too
8   I ain't going to stand : that way you do
9   Know you is a married man : and you got a wife
10 You keep a-running around here : you'll lose your
        life
11 That that you had for me : the other night
12 You can turn it around : and bring it home tonight
13 When I was at home : I was with my man
14 Now you got me here : from hand to hand
15 Ain't no need you walking around : with your mouth
        poked out
16 That is something : just wasn't *cut it* out
17 You know when I met you : from house to house
18 I know some of your women : had put you out
19 It wouldn't been so bad : but you didn't have a dime
20 And I wouldn't mind helping you : you no man of mine
21 Well look a-here : what you expect for me to do
22 Want me to be your mammy : and your doctor too

MemM   4   Memphis Minnie

        title: Bumble Bee
        place and date: Memphis, 20 Feb. 1930
        record numbers: (MEM-773-) Vo-1476 His HLP-2

1   Bumblebee bumblebee : where is you been so long

MemM   4   Memphis Minnie

2   You stung me this morning : I been reckless all day
     long
3   I met my bumblebee this morning : as it flying in
     the door
4   And the way he stung me : he made me cry for more
5   Mmm : don't stay so long from me
6   You's my bumblebee : you got something that I really
     need
7   I'm going to build me a bungalow : just for me and
     my bumblebee
8   Then I won't worry : I will have all the honey I
     need
9   He makes my honey : evil John makes my corn
10   It's all I want now : my bumblebee just to stay at
     home

MemM   5   Memphis Minnie

        title: I'm Going Back Home
        place and date: Memphis, 26 May 1930
        record numbers: (59992-) Vi-23352 His HLP-32

1   When I was home : I was resting at ease
2   Now you got me here : you trying to mistreat me
3   I got something to tell you : know it's going to
     break your heart
4   We been together a good while : but now we got to
     part
5   I done told you once : I done told you twice
6   If you don't mind : you will lose your life
7   You ought to told me that : two or three weeks ago
8   Know when you had your money : thought that you
     wouldn't get broke

MemM   6   Memphis Minnie (Memphis Jug Band)

        title: Bumble Bee Blues
        place and date: Memphis, 26 May 1930
        record numbers: (59993-2) Vi-V38599 BC-7

1   Bumblebee bumblebee : won't you please come back to
     me
2   Because your best old stinger : than any bumblebee
     that I ever see
3   He come in this morning : I been working for him all
     day long
4   Lord he come in to the place : hate to see my
     bumblebee leave home
5   You're my bumblebee : and you know your stuff
6   Oh sting me bumblebee : until I get enough
7   Mmm : stinger go in my right arm
8   He stung me this morning : I been look for him all
     day long
9   Sometimes he makes me happy : then sometimes he
     makes me cry
10   He had me to the place : where I wish to God that I
     could die

MemM   7   Memphis Minnie (Memphis Jug Band)

        title: Meningitis Blues
        place and date: Memphis, 26 May 1930
        record numbers: (59994-) Vi-23421 Rt RL-337

1   I come home one Saturday night : pull off my clothes
     and lie down
2   And that morning just about the break of day : the
     meningitis began to creep around
3   My head and neck was paining me : seem like my back
     going to break in two
4   I hurried to the neighbors that morning : I didn't
     know what in the world to do
5   My companion take me to the doctor : doctor please
     tell me my wife's complaint

MemM   7   Memphis Minnie (Memphis Jug Band)

6   Doctor looked down on me and shook his head : said I
     wouldn't mind telling you son but I can't
7   He taken me down to the city hospital : the clock
     was striking ten
8   I imagine my companion say : I don't believe I'll
     see your smiling face again
9   Then the nurses all began to stand around me : the
     doctors had done me out
10   Every time I would have a potion : I would have a
     foaming at the mouth
11   Mmm : the meningitis killing me
12   I'm spinning I'm spinning baby : my head is nearly
     down in to my knees

MemM   8   Memphis Minnie

        title: Don't Want No Woman
        place and date: Memphis, 29 May 1930
        record numbers: (62539-) Vi-23313 Pal PL-101

2   You's a worthless ??? man : I'll take it all away
     from you
4   Yes but you don't treat me : honey papa like you
     should
6   Yes I'm going somewhere : try to find me another man
8   But I got nothing to worry about now : because I got
     the man I love
10   Well I'm a good-hearted woman : just trying to get
     along with you

MemM   9   Memphis Minnie

        title: Georgia Skin
        place and date: Memphis, 29 May 1930
        record numbers: (62540-) Vi-23352 His HLP-32

1   The reason I like the game : the game they call
     Georgia skin
2   Because when you fall : you can really pick out
     again
3   When you lose your money : please don't lose your
     mind
4   Because each and every gambler : gets in hard luck
     sometimes
5   I had a man : he gambled all the time
6   He played the dice so in vain : until he liked to
     lose his mind
7   Mmm : give me Georgia skin
8   Because the womens can play : well so as the men

MemM   10   Memphis Minnie

        title: Memphis Minnie-Jitis Blues
        place and date: Chicago, c. early June 1930
        record numbers: (C-5822-) Vo-1588 BC-13

1   Mmm : the meningitis killing me
2   I'm feeling upended baby : my head is nearly down to
     my knees
3   I coming home one Saturday night : pull my clothes
     off and I lie down
4   And next morning just about day : the meningitis
     begin to creep around
5   My head and neck was paining me : seem like my back
     going to break in two
6   Lord I had such a mood that morning : I didn't know
     what in the world to do
7   My companion take me to the doctor : doctor please
     tell me my worst complaint
8   The doctor looked down at me and shook his head :
     said I wouldn't mind telling you son but I can't
9   You take around to the city hospital : just as quick
     quick as you possibly can

10   Think about the condition you in now : you never
      will get her back home alive again
11   You roam around to the city hospital : the clock was
      striking ten
12   I heard my ??? companion say : I will see your
      smiling face again

MemM 11   Memphis Minnie

     title: Plymouth Rock Blues
     place and date: Chicago, c. early June 1930
     record numbers: (C-5831-) Vo-1631 BC-13

1   I got so many chickens : can't tell my roosters from
    my hens
2   I got to go back now : and look them all over again
3   I found my rooster this morning : by looking at his
    comb
4   You can look out now pullets : this won't be long
5   My hens are cackling : I can't find no eggs
6   You ain't got no excuse now pullets : ain't nothing
    in your way
7   I might take these old hens : I going down to the
    doctor's shop
8   I don't see what's the matter with them : they won't
    never *cluck*
9   I done told you one time papa : I don't want my
    chicken mixed
10   Shoo chicken shoo : I don't want no banties on my
     yard
11   I don't want them banties : mixed up with my
     Plymouth Rocks

MemM 12   Memphis Minnie

     title: New Dirty Dozens
     place and date: Chicago, 1 July 1930
     record numbers: (C-5894-) Vo-1618 BC-13

1   I don't want them banties : mixed up with my
    dominics
2   Come all you folks : and start to walk
3   I'm fixing to start : my dozen talk
4   What you thinking about : ain't on my mind
5   That stuff you got : isn't ??? kind
6   Some of you womens : ought to be in the can
7   Out on the corner : stopping every man
8   Now the soap is a nickel : and the towel is three
9   I'm pigmeat *peppy* : now who wants me
10   Now the funniest thing : I ever seen
11   Tomcat jumping : on a sewing machine
12   Sewing machine : run so fast
13   Sewed ninety-nine stitches : in his yas yas yas
14   I'm going to tell you : all about old man Bill
15   He can't see : but he sure can smell
16   Fish man pass here : the other day
17   I done hear him : pretty mama I'm going your way
18   Your auntie and your uncle : and your ma and pa
19   They all got drunk : and showed their Santa Claus

MemM 13   Memphis Minnie

     title: New Bumble Bee
     place and date: Chicago, 1 July 1930
     record numbers: (C-5895-) Vo-1618 BC-13

1   I got a bumblebee : don't sting nobody but me
2   And I tell the world : he got all the stinger I need
3   And he makes better honey : any bumblebee I ever
    seen
4   And when he makes it : Lord how he makes me scream
5   He get to flying and buzzing : stinging everybody he
    meets
6   Lord I wonder why : my bumblebee want to mistreat me

7   Mmm : where my bumblebee gone
8   I been looking for him : my bumblebee's so long so
    long
9   My bumblebee got ways : just like a natural man
10   He stinging somebody : everywhere he lands

MemM 14   Memphis Minnie

     title: I'm Talking About You--No. 2
     place and date: Chicago, c. 14 July 1930
     record numbers: (C-6010-A) Vo-1556 His HLP-2

1   You up and quit me : do anything you want to do
2   Some day you'll want me : and I won't want you
3   You ever saw a man : running from hand to hand
4   You can get your woman : I got another man
5   You will mistreat me : and you won't do right
6   You can take it all back : where you had it last
    night
7   Well you can't be mine : and somebody else's too
8   I ain't going to stand : that way you do
9   Know you's a married man : and you got a wife
10   You keep a-running around here : you'll lose your
     life
11   That that you had for me : the other night
12   You can turn it around : and bring it home tonight
13   When I was at home : I was with my man
14   Now you got me here : from hand to hand
15   Ain't no need you walking around : with your mouth
     poked out
16   Daddy has something : just to cut it out
17   You know when I met you : from house to house
18   I know some of your women : had cut you out
19   It wouldn't a-been so bad : but you didn't have a
     dime
20   But I wouldn't mind helping : you no man of mine
21   Well look a-here : what you expect for me to do
22   Want me to be your mammy : and your doctor too

MemM 15   Memphis Minnie

     title: I Called You This Morning
     place and date: Chicago, c. 14 July 1930
     record numbers: (C-6013-) Vo-1631 BC-13

1   I got something to tell you : hope I don't make you
    mad
2   I got something for you : that you never had
3   I got something to tell you : I hope I don't break
    your heart
4   We been together a good while : but now we got to
    part
5   I went to your house : I fell down on the floor
6   You done something to me : wouldn't do it no more
7   I want you to hug me baby : hug and squeeze me good
    and tight
8   I been trying to hard : now can't you save my life
9   I got something to tell you : just before you go
10   Yes you going to leave your mama : standing in this
     door

MemM 16   Memphis Minnie

     title: Grandpa and Grandma Blues
     place and date: Chicago, 9 Sept. 1930
     record numbers: (C-6082-) Vo-1601 OJL-4

1   Grandma got something : make grandpa break his pipe
2   And grandpa got something : keep grandma awake all
    night
3   Grandma grandma : please don't sleep so long
4   Grandpa ain't smoked his pipe : grandma since you
    been gone
5   Here comes grandpa : staring up and down the road

MemM   16   Memphis Minnie

6   With that pipe in his hand : he'll find you
    everywhere you go
7   Grandma grandma : why don't you stay at home
8   That's why you and grandpa : grandma can't get along
9   Grandma grandma : what makes you love grandpa so
10 He's got the same pipe now : he had forty years ago
11 Grandpa swears : he won't get drunk no more
12 Because he broke his pipe : he had forty years ago

MemM   17   Memphis Minnie

        title: Garage Fire Blues
        place and date: Chicago, 9 Sept. 1930
        record numbers: (C-6083-) Vo-1601 Rt RL-307

1   My house on fire : where's that fire wagon now
2   Ain't but the one thing : I don't want my garage to
    burn down
3   I got a Hudson Super Six : I got me *a little old*
    Cadillac Eight
4   I woke up this morning : my Cadillac standing at my
    back gate
5   Hop on boys : I got the best chauffeur in town
6   He said Hudson Super Six : my Cadillac didn't burn
    down
7   Oh Lord Lord : wonder where is my chauffeur now
8   Got my Cadillac Eight : done Cadillaced out of town
9   I tell the whole round world : I ain't going to walk
    no more
10 I got a Cadillac Eight : take me anywhere I want to
    go

MemM   18   Memphis Minnie

        title: What's the Matter with the Mill?
        place and date: Chicago, c. 15 Oct. 1930
        record numbers: (C-6442-) Vo-1550 BC-13

1   Well I had a little corn : I put it in a sack
2   Started to the mill : and come right back
3   Well the people keep a-talking : all over town
4   Telling me : that the mill had broken down
5   Now listen here folks : I don't want no stuff
6   You can't bring me my meal : bring me the husk
7   Well my papa said try : my brothers too
8   They both been to the mill : they can't get nothing
    for two
9   Now listen here folks : I want you all to bear this
    in mind
10 If you're going to the mill : you get to there
    crying

MemM   19   Memphis Minnie

        title: North Memphis Blues
        place and date: Chicago, c. 15 Oct. 1930
        record numbers: (C-6443-) Vo-1550 BC-13

1   I tell all you people : you can rest at ease
2   You won't have to worry about cooking : go to North
    Memphis Cafe and eat
3   I tell all of you people : you can rest at ease
4   Because the North Memphis Cafe : got everything that
    you really need
5   I don't buy no wood : even buy no coal
6   I go to North Memphis Cafe : and eat and don't be
    outdoors
7   I will tell you all something : I won't change like
    the wind
8   If you go to North Memphis Cafe to eat : you'll go
    back again
9   Now listen to me good people : I don't aim to make
    you mad

MemM   19   Memphis Minnie

10 You go to North Memphis Cafe : get something you
    never had

MemM   20   Memphis Minnie

        title: I Don't Want that Junk Outa You
        place and date: Chicago, c. 30 Jan. 1931
        record numbers: (VO-111-A) Vo-1678 Yz L-1008

1   I give you my money : and I ain't ashamed
2   Now you got me here : and I'm scared to call your
    name
3   I stood on the corner : looking for you all night
    long
4   You know baby : you been doing me wrong
5   And I ain't going to put up : at the way you do
6   You can't be mine : and somebody else's too
7   I ??? : till I done got tired
8   *Oh joyful* : much obliged
9   Now look here baby : what you take me to be
10 Walking around with this low-life : in front of me
11 And you got ways : I sure don't like
12 You give me money : just to take it back
13 Now look here baby : I don't want to make you mad
14 I give you everything : in the world I had
15 You come here baby : set down on my knee
16 I do anything : to give your poor heart ease

MemM   21   Memphis Minnie

        title: Crazy Cryin' Blues
        place and date: Chicago, c. 30 Jan. 1931
        record numbers: (VO-112-A) Vo-1678 BC-13

1   I been going crazy : I just can't help myself
2   Because the man I'm loving : he loving someone else
3   I was locked outdoors : huddled myself all night
    long and cried
4   I'm going crazy : crazy as I can be
5   I got up this morning : I made a fire in my stove
6   And made up my bread : and stuck my pan outdoors
7   I'm crazy I'm crazy : just can't help myself
8   I'm just as crazy crazy : as a poor girl can be

MemM   22   Memphis Minnie

        title: Soo Cow Soo
        place and date: Chicago, 25 Mar. 1931
        record numbers: (VO-151-A) Vo-1658 Yz L-1021

1   If you see my cow : tell her hurry home
2   I ain't had no sweet milk : since she been gone
3   If you see my cow : drive her to the barn
4   I ain't had nothing to drink : since she been gone
5   My cow little aches : she can't get no water
6   She got a little calf : say you might've heard her
    holler
7   I'm taking my cow : can of beer
8   Never stopped a-jumping : till she finds good ???
9   I got up this morning : I went outdoors
10 I'd know my cow : by the way she lows
11 I give her corn : I give her wheat
12 I'd give anything : that the poor cow needs

MemM   23   Memphis Minnie

        title: After While Blues
        place and date: Chicago, 25 Mar. 1931
        record numbers: (VO-152-A) Vo-1658 BC-13

1   I walked around this world : ???
2   You ought to heard them holler : say I've the whole
    round world

197

MemM   23   Memphis Minnie

3   I want you to let them know : ???
4   You ain't my partner : because the times have done
      got hard
5   I want you : like a monkey up a tree
6   Using them coconuts : ??? some of them on me
7   ??? : ???
8   Don't you worry : because you got the *goodest
      thing*
9   I got a man I love : better than myself
10 *No one can take him* : I wouldn't want nobody else

MemM   24   Memphis Minnie

        title: Where Is My Good Man
        place and date: New York, 3 Feb. 1932
        record numbers: (11216-A) Vo-1698 OJL-6

1   Lord I wonder : where is my good man at
2   He left here this morning : didn't carry nothing but
      his hat
3   He left his suit : hanging all on the rack
4   He left here this morning : didn't carry nothing but
      his hat
5   If only : could get my good man back
6   He left here this morning : didn't carry nothing but
      his hat

MemM   25   Memphis Minnie

        title: Ain't No Use Trying to Tell On Me
        place and date: New York, 27 Oct. 1933
        record numbers: (152537-2) Co unissued Yz L-1021

1   Just as sure as this paper : sticks aside the wall
2   I'm going somewhere : and have my ashes hauled
3   Because I remember last winter : when the weather
      was cold
4   You's out on the corner : trying to sell jellyroll
5   I was sitting in my kitchen : just as quiet as a
      lamb
6   I wasn't too quiet : to hear my back door slam
7   I want you tell me : how come you do like you do do
      do
8   You know I love you : ain't done a thing to you
9   When I want it I wants it : and I wants it bad
10 You don't give it to me : want to make me mad

MemM   26   Memphis Minnie

        title: Stinging Snake Blues
        place and date: Chicago, 25 Mar. 1934
        record numbers: (CP-1069-1) Vo-02711 Pal PL-101

1   This house is full of stinging snakes : crawling all
      in my bed
2   I can't rest at night : from them crawling all under
      my head
3   I got up this morning : one stung me on my leg
4   I can't sleep at night : because he keeps me awake
5   Mmm : wonder where is my stinging snake gone
6   I can't see no peace : since my stinging snake left
      the home
7   I've got a stinging snake : I love sometime better
      than I do myself
8   If the Lord was to take him : I wouldn't be stung by
      nobody else
9   Mmm : where is my stinging snake now
10 I believe to my soul : that my stinging snake trying
      to put me down

MemM   27   Memphis Minnie

        title: Drunken Barrelhouse Blues
        place and date: Chicago, 25 Mar. 1934
        record numbers: (CP-1070-1) Vo-02711 Yz L-1021

1   If you listen to me good people : I'll tell you what
      it's all about
2   We have that good Dr Cheer: and it just come now
3   Eight o'clock in the morning : don't say one
      mumbling word
4   I can tell you all about it : and I ain't going to
      tell you nothing I heard
5   Hey I believe I'll get drunk : tear this old
      barrelhouse down
6   Because I ain't got no money : but I can hobo out of
      town
7   Give me one more drink : drink of that *bottling
      burn*
8   And I will tell everything : just as soon as I get
      back home
9   Give me a draught of beer : if not a drink of gin
10 I feel myself getting sober : I want to get back
      drunk again

MemM   28   Memphis Minnie

        title: You Got to Move--Part I
        place and date: Chicago, 24 Aug. 1934
        record numbers: (C-9380-) De-7038 BC-1

1   Look here baby : you ain't got to go
2   I've got my *first time* : to drive you from my door
3   You ain't got to move : out this neighborhood
4   Because I tell the world : I mean you only good
5   I have a brand new bed : a brand new stool
6   Come back baby : you ain't got to move
7   Well you don't have to worry : about something to
      eat
8   I made a-plenty money : all last week

MemM   29   Memphis Minnie

        title: Chickasaw Train Blues
        place and date: Chicago, 24 Aug. 1934
        record numbers: (C-9382-) De-7019 Cor CP-58

1   I might tell everybody : what that Chickasaw have
      done done for me
2   She done stole my man away : and blowed back dark
      smoke on me
3   Ain't no woman : like to ride that Chickasaw
4   Because everywhere she stops : she's stealing some
      woman's good man off
5   I told the depot agent this morning : I don't think
      you treat me right
6   He done sold my man a ticket : and know that
      Chickasaw is leaving town tonight
7   I walking down the railroad track : that Chickasaw
      even wouldn't let me ride the blinds
8   And she start picking up man : all up and down the
      line
9   Mmm : Chickasaw don't pay no woman no mind
10 And she start picking up men : all up and down this
      line

MemM   30   Memphis Minnie

        title: Squat It
        place and date: Chicago, 10 Sept. 1934
        record numbers: (C-9426-A) De-7146 Rt RL-329

1   I've got a man : works on the railroad track
2   The reason he keeps his job : he can squat it in the
      sack
3   He's not so good-looking : he don't dress so fine

4 But when he does his squatting : he really takes his
   time
5 Now I want you to go ahead on girls : and leave him
   alone
6 That's the very reason : scared to trust him at home
7 That's the man : he's scared to call his name
8 Because when he go to squatting : it's a crying
   shame
9 He not so short : he not so tall
10 But when he's doing the squatting : you might a-hear
   me squall

MemM 31   Memphis Minnie

       title: Dirty Mother For You
       place and date: Chicago, 10 Jan. 1935
       record numbers: (C-9641-A) De-7048 Pal PL-101

1 I ain't no doctor : but I'm the doctor wife
2 You better come to me : if you want to save your
   life
3 He's a dirty mother for you : he don't mean no good
4 He got drunk this morning : tore up the neighborhood
5 I want you to come here baby : come here quick
6 You done give me something : about to make me sick
7 I went down to the station : talk to the judge
8 He said don't bring me : none of that doggone crap
   you heard
9 I went down to the office : fell out on the floor
10 He done something to me now : he won't do no more
11 Now won't you look here baby : what you done done
12 You done *spread* my *liver* : now you done *broke
   the rungs*

MemM 32   Memphis Minnie

       title: You Can't Give It Away
       place and date: Chicago, 10 Jan. 1935
       record numbers: (C-9644-A) De-7048 Pal PL-101

1 What is that : you going around here trying to sell
2 It ain't good to eat : you know it ain't good to
   smell
3 The first time I met you : you had the meat in your
   hand
4 Going to give it : to some woman's man
5 You got something you can't sell : and you can't
   give away
6 You just as well to take it : on back where you stay
7 And don't let me catch you : trying to give it to my
   man
8 If you do : *I'm ??? to pin a* doggone can
9 Look a-here black girl : why don't you get off the
   line
10 What you trying to sell : ain't nobody buying

MemM 33   Memphis Minnie

       title: Reachin' Pete
       place and date: Chicago, 27 May 1935
       record numbers: (90018-) De-7102 Mam S-3803

1 When you go to Helena : stop on Cherry Street
2 And just ask anybody : to show you Reaching Pete
3 He's the tallest man : walks on Cherry Street
4 And the baddest copper : ever walked that beat
5 He met me one sunny morning : just about the break
   of day
6 I was drinking my moonshine : he made me throw my
   knife away
7 Well he taken my partner : down to the jail
8 After he locked her up : he turned and went her bail
9 Reaching Pete's all right : but his buddy *overzeal*
10 Every time he meet you : he's ready for plenty hell

       title: He's in the Ring
       place and date: Chicago, 22 Aug. 1935
       record numbers: (C-1099-B) Vo-03046 Pal PL-101

1 Hey all you peoples going out tonight : just going
   to see Joe Louis fight
2 And if you ain't got no money : have to go tomorrow
   night
3 Crying he even carried a mean left : and he carried
   a mean right
4 And if he hits you with either one : same as a
   charge from a dynamite
5 I'm going to tell all of you prize fighters : don't
   play Joe for no fool
6 If he hits you with that left duke : same as a kick
   from a Texas mule
7 Joe Louis is a two-fist fighter : and he stands six
   feet tall
8 And the bigger they come : he say the harder they
   fall
9 Boys if I only had ten hundred dollars : I'd a-laid
   it up on my shelf
10 I'd bet anybody pass my house : that one round Joe
   would knock him out
11 I wouldn't even pay my house rent : I wouldn't buy
   me nothing to eat
12 Joe Louis would take a chance with them : I would
   put you on your feet

MemM 35   Memphis Minnie

       title: Black Cat Blues
       place and date: Chicago, 27 May 1936
       record numbers: (C-1386-1) Vo-03581 Pal PL-101

1 I got a big black cat : sitting in my back door
2 He catches every rat : run across my floor
3 If it wasn't for that cat : I wouldn't know what I
   would do
4 Rats cutting up : all of my clothes and shoes
5 I been had this old cat now : for three or four
   years
6 Still nobody want him : till I brought him here
7 Before I got that cat : rats had holes all in my
   walls
8 Since I brought her home : you can't find no holes
   at all
9 You have seen a lots of cats : and you going to see
   a lots of more
10 I got one-eyed cats : everywhere I go

MemM 36   Memphis Minnie

       title: Man You Won't Give Me No Money
       place and date: Chicago, 27 May 1936
       record numbers: (C-1388-2) Vo-03474 BC-1

1 Man you won't give me no money : you won't buy me no
   clothes to wear
2 Want to take me off in France : and know I ain't got
   no business over there
3 Tell me men : what do you expect for us poor women
   to do
4 Work and give you all our money : and be used like a
   doggone tool
5 I'm so glad : that I ain't nobody's fool
6 If I keep every dime of my money : sure got to come
   under my rule
7 Know when you was a schoolboy : when you was going
   to school
8 You know if you take my money : you be done broke
   your teacher's rule
9 I don't mind trying to help you : please don't play
   me for no fool

MemM   36   Memphis Minnie

10   Don't forget these last words : you sure got to come
     under my rule

MemM   37   Memphis Minnie

          title: Moonshine
          place and date: Chicago, 12 Nov. 1936
          record numbers: (C-1670-1) Vo-03894 BC-1

1   I got to leave this town : I'm got to go before the
     sun go down
2   Because I done got tired : of these coppers running
     me around
3   I stayed in jail last night : and all last night
     before
4   I would have been there now : if my daddy hadn't've
     sprung the door
5   I been in so much of trouble : that's why I'm got to
     go
6   But when I get out this time : I won't sell
     moonshine no more
7   I done packed my trunk : and done shipped it on down
     the road
8   Now I won't be bothered : with these big fat bulls
     no more
9   Just keep me a-moving : going from door to door
10   I done made up in my mind : not to sell moonshine no
     more

MemM   38   Memphis Minnie

          title: It's Hard to Be Mistreated
          place and date: Chicago, 12 Nov. 1936
          record numbers: (C-1671-1) Vo-03474 BC-1

1   Well it's hard to be mistreated : when you ain't
     done nothing wrong
2   And you caught your lover-man : when you can't keep
     him at home
3   Now I'm going to get myself a single man : and leave
     these married mens alone
4   They ain't nothing but a wad of trouble : when they
     laying up in your arms
5   I need someone to love me : but someone to call my
     own
6   I'm tired of loving these married men : can say I
     know their wives got them and gone
7   Well I'm getting so tired : staying home all by
     myself
8   And every man I fall in love with : he loving
     someone else
9   But I tried to be nice : tried to be nice and kind
10   But every man I love : don't seem like he want to
     pay me no mind

MemM   39   Memphis Minnie

          title: My Baby Don't Want Me No More
          place and date: Chicago, 17 June 1937
          record numbers: (C-1936-1) Vo-03894 BC-1

1   I don't believe : my baby wants me no more
2   Well if he did : he would take me everywhere he goes
3   Asked my daddy last night : please take me to the
     show
4   Said I wouldn't mind carrying you : but your daddy
     ain't got no dough
5   Well you say you going away to leave me : going back
     down the road
6   Well I just want to find out : now which a-way must
     I go
7   If you catch that midnight train : I might ride that
     midnight train too

MemM   39   Memphis Minnie

8   Well I could still be riding : I don't have to be
     with you
9   Mmm : look what you done made me do
10   Done left my good man : all on account of you

MemM   40   Memphis Minnie

          title: Lonesome Shark Blues
          place and date: Chicago, 27 June 1940
          record numbers: (WC-3166-A) OK-05728 BC-1

1   Out across the hill : I built a lonesome shack
2   So when my good man quit me : I won't have to beg
     him back
3   In the southeast corner : that's where I'll put my
     cool iron bed
4   So when he puts me out : have some place to lay my
     head
5   Found my groceries and my stove : where they are
     selling cheap
6   So when he stops feeding me : have some place to
     cook and eat
7   Time I get me a sweetheart : and a ??? machine
8   So when we part : be hard to find a ??? *bean*

MemM   41   Memphis Minnie

          title: Nothin in Rambling
          place and date: Chicago, 27 June 1940
          record numbers: (WC-3167-A) OK-05670 BC-1

1   I's born in Louisiana : I raised in Algiers
2   And everywhere I been : the peoples all say
3   Ain't nothing in rambling : either running around
4   Well I believe I'll marry : ooo Lord and settle down
5   I first left home : I stopped in Tennessee
6   The peoples all begging : come and stay with me
7   Because ain't nothing in rambling : either running
     around
8   Well I believe I'll get me a good man : ooo Lord and
     settle down
9   I walked through the alley : with my hand in my coat
10   The police start to shoot me : thought it something
     I stole
11   The peoples on the highway : is walking and crying
12   Some is starving : some is dying
13   You may go to Hollywood : and try to get on the
     screen
14   But I'm going to stay right here : and eat these old
     charity beans

MemM   42   Memphis Minnie

          title: Boy Friend Blues
          place and date: Chicago, 27 June 1940
          record numbers: (WC-3168-A) OK-05670 BC-1

1   I'm alone : traveling by myself
2   If I don't find the one I love : I don't want nobody
     else
3   I was down : down one old lonesome road
4   I didn't have me no baby : couldn't find no place to
     go
5   Mmm : people wonder where could my baby be
6   It don't make me no difference : just seem so
     lonesome here to me
7   I can't feel happy : nowhere in the world I be
8   If I don't find my baby : you going to have some
     trouble out of me
9   Boy friend boy friend : where in the world can you
     be
10   Ever since you been gone : you sure is worrying me

MemM   43   Memphis Minnie

        title: It's Hard to Please My Man
        place and date: Chicago, 27 June 1940
        record numbers: (WC-3170-A) OK-05728 BC-1

1 You keep me thinking : and wondering all the time
2 Oh people it's so hard : to please that man of mine
3 I combs his hair : I washes his feet
4 And when I think that works : he's out strolling the
   street
5 Last night he started an argument : he dared poor me
   to grunt
6 Then taken my last dollar : to make his girl friend
   drunk
7 I ain't going to give you my money : and don't know
   what it's all about
8 Soon as I get cold in hand : you be ready to kick me
   out

MemM   44   Memphis Minnie

        title: In My Girlish Days
        place and date: Chicago, 21 May 1941
        record numbers: (C-3764-1) OK-06410 BC-1

1 Late hours at night : trying to play my hand
2 Through my window : out stepped a man
3 My mama cried : papa did too
4 Oh daughter : look what a shame on you
5 I flagged a train : didn't have a dime
6 Tried to run away : from that home of mine
7 I hit the highway : caught me a truck
8 Nineteen and seventeen : when the world was tough
9 All of my playmates : is not surprised
10 I had to travel : before I got wise

MemM   45   Memphis Minnie

        title: Me and My Chauffeur Blues
        place and date: Chicago, 21 May 1941
        record numbers: (C-3765-1) OK-06788 BC-1

1 Won't you be my chauffeur : I want someone to drive
   me I want someone to drive me downtown
2 Baby drives so easy : I can't turn him around
3 But I don't want him : to be riding these girls to
   be riding these girls around
4 You know I'm going to steal me a pistol : shoot my
   chauffeur down
5 Well I must buy him : a brand new V-Eight a brand
   new V-Eight Ford
6 And he won't need no passengers : I will be his load
7 Going to let my chauffeur : drive me around the
   drive me around the world
8 Then he can be my little boy : yes I'll feed him
   good

MileL   1   Miles, Lizzie

        title: Shootin' Star Blues
        place and date: New York, 4 Jan. 1928
        record numbers: (7708-2) Ba-7025 VJM VLP-40

1 I done crossed my fingers : and counted up to
   twenty-three
2 I seen a star falling : that means bad luck done
   fell on me
3 A black cat bone's a-boiling : I put it on at half
   past twelve
4 I'll tie it in a sack : and walk off talking to
   myself
5 A shooting star means evil : ain't never seen that
   thing to fail
6 I'll either spend a month in jail : or I'm sure to
   lose my job

MileL   1   Miles, Lizzie

7 Now I ain't superstitious : don't believe in not a
   sign I know
8 But when my right hand itches : I know I'll get some
   money sure
9 I let a black cat cross me : I walked right through
   a funeral line
10 But when the stars are shooting : I know bad luck is
   in that sign

MillL   1   Miller, Lillian

        title: Dead Drunk Blues
        place and date: Richmond, Ind., c. 3 May 1928
        record numbers: (13718-A) Ge-6518 OJL-6

1 You knowed I was drunk : when I lay down across your
   bed
2 All the whiskey I drank : it's gone right to my head
3 Oh give me Houston : that's the place I crave
4 So when I'm dry : I can get whiskey ??? *made*
5 Whiskey whiskey : is some folk's downfall
6 But if I don't get whiskey : I ain't no good at all
7 When I was in Houston : drunk most every day
8 I drank so much whiskey : I thought I'd pass away
9 Have you ever been drunk : and slept in all your
   clothes
10 And when you wake up : feel like you want a dose
11 I'm going to get drunk : daddy just one more time
12 Because when I'm drunk : nothing don't worry my mind

MillS   1   Miller, Sodarisa

        title: Sunshine Special
        place and date: Chicago, c. Apr. 1925
        record numbers: (2092-?) Pm-12276 Mil MLP-2018

1 Sunshine Special : shine down on me
2 I ain't going home till morning : ???
3 I've had the blues all my life : I think that's long
   enough
4 I'm going out all night : ??? going to strut my
   stuff
5 *Take your good girl* : *take your hands away*
6 It's the way you *crow* mama : just awhile before
   day
7 I say Sunshine Special : throw your light down on me
8 I'm going home to my regular : drunk as I can be
9 What my mama told me : ???
10 ??? : my ruination ???

MissM   1   Mississippi Moaner

        title: Mississippi Moan
        place and date: Jackson, Miss., 20 Oct. 1935
        record numbers: (JAX-201-1) Vo-03166 Yz L-1009

1 Hey : something going on wrong
2 Lord when I come in : find my *good gal* gone
3 Lord I wish she come here : right down on her head
4 And might be a few questions : she swore sure *kill
   her dead*
5 And you treat me good : Lord will bless your soul
6 If you treat me bad : mama to hell you surely go
7 But I'm on my way back : to that lonesome hill
8 Because that's where I can look down : where the
   stack man used to live
9 I said mama : what become of me
10 Every time I leave home : some of my follies follow
   me
11 Some of my former deeds mama : cause me to leave my
   old home
12 Lord I tried and tried : and I just can't let her go

MissM 2   Mississippi Moaner

       title: It's Cold in China Blues
       place and date: Jackson, Miss., 20 Oct. 1935
       record numbers: (JAX-202-1) Vo-03166 OJL-8

1 So cold in China : birds can't hardly sing
2 You didn't make me mad : till you broke my diamond
    ring
3 Take me mama : won't be bad no more
4 You can get my loving : if you let that old black
    snake go
5 Black snake crawling : crawling in my room
6 Some high brown woman : better come and get this
    here black snake soon
7 Hey mama : what have I said and done
8 Folks tell me your loving : baby sure going to be my
    ruin
9 Crying eee : your daddy do love you
10 You's a high-stepping mama : and I don't care what
     you do
11 I was a little boy : on my way to school
12 Met a high brown woman : and she broke my mammy's
     rule
13 Mama said I'm reckless : daddy said I'm young and
     wild
14 Quit being so reckless : be my baby child

MontE 1   Montgomery, Eurreal Little Brother

       title: The Woman I Love Blues
       place and date: New Orleans, 10 Aug. 1935
       record numbers: (94418-1) BB-B6140 CC-35

1 The woman I love : she only sixteen years of age
2 And she's a full-grown woman : but she just got
    childish ways
3 She got a head full of diamonds : and a mouth chock
    full of gold
4 And every time she smiles : Lord it makes my blood
    run cold
5 And she's low and she's squatty : and made right to
    the ground
6 And she's tailor-made : Lord and ain't no
    hand-me-down
7 And the woman I love : Lord she do not pay me no
    mind
8 And the one I hate : I see her all the time
9 And the woman I love : she's gone far away
10 And the one I hate : at the house every day

MontE 2   Montgomery, Eurreal Little Brother

       title: Pleading Blues
       place and date: New Orleans, 10 Aug. 1935
       record numbers: (94419-1) BB-B6140 CC-35

1 Folks you don't know : how worried must I be
2 Nobody knows : but the good Lord and me
3 Lord Lord : now won't you hear my plea
4 Now I want you to stop my gal : from mistreating me
5 Lord Lord : now I ain't got a friend
6 Now one gal is in jail : and the other one is in the
    pen

MontE 3   Montgomery, Eurreal Little Brother

       title: Vicksburg Blues No. 2
       place and date: New Orleans, 10 Aug. 1935
       record numbers: (94420-1) BB-B6072 Yz L-1028

1 I've been worrying all day mama : and could hardly
    sleep last night
2 I had the blues for Vicksburg Mississippi : and
    couldn't be satisfied

MontE 3   Montgomery, Eurreal Little Brother

3 *Now if ever they find me the ship at* : where I
    long to be
4 I've got a good gal pretty mama : waiting there for
    me
5 Now there's nothing I can do mama : oh no more I can
    say
6 All I know I do in Vicksburg : Lord is *paraday*

MontE 4   Montgomery, Eurreal Little Brother

       title: Mama You Don't Mean Me No Good
       place and date: New Orleans, 10 Aug. 1935
       record numbers: (94421-1) BB-B6072 CC-35

1 I love you mama : but you don't mean me no good
2 I done everything for you : sweet mama that I could
3 I brought you clothes : and diamond rings
4 Give you all my money : and everything
5 If you don't want me mama : now let your daddy be
6 *For me* I may find someone : that cares for me
7 I ain't no doctor : I can't ease your pain
8 Ain't no brakeman : I can't take your train
9 You know sweet : I'm a good-looking brown
10 What it takes to please : I'm going to carry that
     around

MontE 5   Montgomery, Eurreal Little Brother

       title: The First Time I Met You
       place and date: New Orleans, 16 Oct. 1936
       record numbers: (02642-1) BB-B6766 RBF RF-12

1 The first time I met the blues mama : they came
    walking through the wood
2 They stopped at my house first mama : and done me
    all the harm they could
3 Now my blues got at me : Lord and run me from tree
    to tree
4 You should have heard me begging : Mr blues don't
    murder me
5 Good morning blues : what are you doing here so soon
6 You bes with me every morning : Lordy every night
    and noon
7 The blues came down the alley : mama and stopped
    right at my door
8 They give me more hard luck and trouble : than I
    ever had before

MontE 6   Montgomery, Eurreal Little Brother

       title: Vicksburg Blues--Part 3
       place and date: New Orleans, 16 Oct. 1936
       record numbers: (02645-1) BB-B6697 CC-35

1 Had a cool loving mama : and they call her Jesse P
2 And she's the sweetest woman : has ever walked down
    Mulberry Street
3 Now she's a kind loving baby : and give the men a
    thrill
4 Now the reason I love her : she live in Vicksburg on
    the hill
5 And I love her I love her : and I always will
6 The reason I really love her : I think of Vicksburg
    on the hill

MontE 7   Montgomery, Eurreal Little Brother

       title: Out West Blues
       place and date: New Orleans, 16 Oct. 1936
       record numbers: (02649-1) BB-B6916 CC-35

1 I were laying upstairs mama : trying to take my rest

MontE 7   Montgomery, Eurreal Little Brother

2 And a notion struck me : Lord I believe I'll go out
   west
3 Now I'm going out west mama : Lord and I can't take
   you
4 Because it's nothing out there mama : that a woman
   like you can do
5 Just as soon : as a train mama makes up in the yard
6 And I'm out westbound : that's if the bulls don't
   have me barred

MontE 8   Montgomery, Eurreal Little Brother

   title: Leaving Town Blues
   place and date: New Orleans, 16 Oct. 1936
   record numbers: (02650-1) BB-B6916 CC-35

1 Now I'm leaving town baby : because you know you
   treats me wrong
2 You go out at night and get full of bad whiskey :
   and stay out the whole night long
3 And I tried everything mama in this world : to get
   along with you
4 Now and you know I love you : that's why you treat
   me like the way you do
5 And I'm going I'm going : mama and your crying won't
   make me stay
6 And the more you cry mama : the farther that you
   drive me away
7 Now when I leave this time mama : you can pin crepe
   on my door
8 And I won't be dead : baby but I ain't coming here
   no more

MontE 9   Montgomery, Eurreal Little Brother

   title: West Texas Blues
   place and date: New Orleans, 16 Oct. 1936
   record numbers: (02651-1) BB-B7178 CC-35

1 I got a letter from Texas : how do you reckon it
   read
2 It said hurry home brother : for the one you love is
   dead
3 And I went to the station : but the train had gone
4 I got to thinking about my baby : and I started
   walking on
5 And I walked up on a stranger : I told him I was in
   so much misery
6 He said you'll never start to Texas : you better
   take the T and T
7 And he dropped me off in Texas : in a little place
   they call San Antone
8 And you can't really imagine : how you hear those
   wild ox moan

MontE 10   Montgomery, Eurreal Little Brother

   title: Never Go Wrong Blues
   place and date: New Orleans, 16 Oct. 1936
   record numbers: (02652-1) BB-B6825 CC-35

1 Now boys I once had a good woman : but I really did
   not treat her right
2 And I would do everything evil : and everything I
   could for spite
3 I would go out at night : and get full of bucket gin
4 And she would be absolutely hospital bound : if she
   ever even asked me where I had been
5 Now I'm sorry that I mistreated her : just as sorry
   as a man can be
6 Now it seem like the more that I do for her : it is
   the less she care for me
7 Now boys if you got a good woman : treat her kind in
   every way

MontE 10   Montgomery, Eurreal Little Brother

8 Because a real good woman : can't be found every day

MontE 11   Montgomery, Eurreal Little Brother

   title: Mistreatin' Woman Blues
   place and date: New Orleans, 16 Oct. 1936
   record numbers: (02654-1) BB-B7178 CC-35

1 Boys have you ever had a woman : and she didn't mean
   you no good
2 And you trust her with your hide : and she treat it
   just like a piece of wood
3 And you will turn your back on everybody : baby you
   will really worry you best friend
4 On account of a no-good woman : and then she loving
   other men
5 Then you will sit right down and worry : about a
   friend that you could gain
6 After you have forsaken everybody : it will be on
   account of another dame
7 Now boys don't never let : no woman treat you nice
   and kind
8 Because she's only been *you* : I can tell *you
   about the* mine

MooA   1   Moore, Whistlin' Alex

   title: West Texas Woman
   place and date: Dallas, 5 Dec. 1929
   record numbers: (149531-2) Co-14496-D His HLP-32

1 I met a woman in West Texas : she had been left by
   herself all alone
2 I spied her looking ??? *cross* me : where I wasn't
   even known
3 She fell for me a raggedy stranger : standing in the
   drizzling rain
4 She said daddy I'll follow you : though you don't
   know my name
5 We snuggled closely together : muddy water around
   our feet
6 No place to call home : wet hungry and no place to
   eat
7 She said I care for you daddy : but I love no man
   better than I do myself
8 But I have a mind to care : a heart to love like
   anyone else
9 The wolves howled at midnight : wild ox moaned till
   day
10 The man in the moon looked down on us : but had
   nothing to say

MooA   2   Moore, Whistlin' Alex

   title: It Wouldn't Be So Hard
   place and date: Dallas, 6 Dec. 1929
   record numbers: (149562-2) Co-14496-D His HLP-32

1 I get up early every morning : to toil the whole day
   through
2 Baby it wouldn't be so hard : if I was getting up
   from beside of you
3 I'm so lonesome without you baby : I can't be
   satisfied
4 Aren't you a little lonesome for me too : so we can
   both be pacified
5 Your hugs are so shocking : your eyes tell me yes
6 And you don't *store* it to me : that's what makes
   my happiness
7 I'm not lying baby : you were always really mine
8 And if I don't see you soon : I'll sure be found
   crying
9 Right back to Dallas : I got to be on my way

MooA   2   Moore, Whistlin' Alex

10   I'm going to let that Texas Special : drop me in
      southern U S A
11   Right or wrong : I must be with my little southern
      Chocktaw
12   I don't know that she loves me : but still she calls
      me her southpaw

MooAl   1   Moore, Alice

      title: Black and Evil Blues
      place and date: Richmond, Ind., 16 Aug. 1929
      record numbers: (15447) Pm-12819 CC-37

1   I'm black and I'm evil : and I did not make myself
2   If my man don't have me : he won't have nobody else
3   I've got to buy me a bulldog : he'll watch me while
     I sleep
4   Because I'm so black and evil : that I might make a
     midnight creep
5   I believe to my soul : the Lord has got a curse on
     me
6   Because every man I get : a no-good woman steals him
     from me
7   *Even as* I lay down at night : behind you lies an
     empty space
8   And you wish on every *no-good* star : *bring here
     your baby to me*

MooAl   2   Moore, Alice

      title: Prison Blues
      place and date: Richmond, Ind., 16 Aug. 1929
      record numbers: (15448) Pm-12868 CC-37

1   Oh the judge he sentenced me : and the clerk he
     wrote it down
2   My man *sat and stared before you babe* : that you
     are county farm bound
3   Oh six months in *jail* : and a month on the county
     farm
4   If my man hadn't a-been in the *jug* : he would help
     with my bond
5   I worked hard on the county farm : tried to forget
     my man
6   And some day he's going to be sorry : he treated me
     this a-way
7   I've got to build me a scaffold : just to hang
     myself
8   Because the man I'm loving : I don't care where he
     follow me ???

MooAl   3   Moore, Alice

      title: My Man Blues
      place and date: Richmond, Ind., 16 Aug. 1929
      record numbers: (15449-A) Pm-12868 CC-37

1   My man my man : treats me so lowdown
2   Anything I do : he like to leave his mind
3   I love my man : but he loves somebody else
4   I think I'm a big fool : he'll keep on wearing my
     ???
5   *Ever get ready for* lay down : and think about your
     man at night
6   And you will get to twisting and turning : and you
     couldn't lay just right
7   My babe turned to me : with tears running down his
     face
8   Says I'm sorry for you woman : another woman has
     taken your place

MooAl   4   Moore, Alice

      title: Broadway St. Woman Blues
      place and date: Richmond, Ind., 16 Aug. 1929
      record numbers: (15452) Pm-12819 CC-37

1   I was standing on the corner : just between Broadway
     and Main
2   A cop walked up : and he *laughed ??? me my name*
3   ??? : my name was *little known* myself
4   I'm a good-time woman : and I sure don't have to ???
5   He says I'll take you to the station : and see what
     you will do
6   *I'll make him despise you* : and he *lay* ???
7   Oh he took me to the judge : with my head hanging
     low
8   And the judge said hold you head up : for you are
     bound to go

MooAl   5   Moore, Alice

      title: Lonesome Dream Blues
      place and date: Grafton, Wis., c. Feb. 1930
      record numbers: (L-170-2) Pm-13107 CC-37

1   I had a dream last night : babe I can't understand
2   I had a dream I saw some woman : *thieving* with my
     man
3   I tried to be good : but he would not let me be
4   Now he is leaving : just to spite me
5   Now you got all my money : still you ain't satisfied
6   And now you got another woman : going to catch the
     train and ride
7   You may go babe : you may have your way
8   But when you think of your loving : I know that you
     cannot behave

MooAl   6   Moore, Alice

      title: Kid Man Blues
      place and date: Grafton, Wis., c. Feb. 1930
      record numbers: (L-171-2) Pm-13107 CC-37

1   Baby when I was all down and out : you just could
     not be found
2   Now I have someone to care for me : don't want you
     hanging around
3   I have got a regular man here : Lord the good
     kid-man's downtown
4   I can't quit my regular : and I won't throw my
     kid-man down
5   Lord I quit my kid-man : because I caught him in a
     lie
6   And all I can hear now : is his moaning his mournful
     cry
7   Yes he told a little gal : looking in the deep blue
     sea
8   I am ??? : so don't bring your blues to me

MooAl   7   Moore, Alice

      title: Black Evil Blues
      place and date: Chicago, 18 Aug. 1934
      record numbers: (C-9317-A) De-7028 OJL-20

1   And I'm black and I'm evil : and I did not make
     myself
2   If my babe don't have me : he won't have nobody
     there
3   Going to buy me a bulldog : to watch me while I
     sleep
4   Because I'm so black and evil : that I might make a
     midnight creep
5   I believe to my soul : the Lord have got a curse on
     me

MooAl 7   Moore, Alice

6 Because every *meat* that I gain : a no-good woman
   steals him from me
7 Did you ever lay down at night : behind you lies an
   empty space
8 You will turn over and hug a pillow : where your
   daddy used to die

MooM 1   Moore, Monette

     title: Black Hearse Blues
     place and date: New York, c. Jan. 1925
     record numbers: (31777) Ajax-17093 VJM VLP-40

1 Old death wagon : don't you dare stop at my door
2 You took my first three daddies : you can't have
   number four
3 Smallpox got my first man : booze killed number two
4 I wore out the last one : but with this one I ain't
   through
5 Slow down *bone archer* : call your *cold cart* back
6 My daddy's engine running : on my *double track*
7 Black hearse ain't no use : you sure can't have my
   man
8 I'm just using him up : on the old ???

MooM 2   Moore, Monette

     title: Scandal Blues
     place and date: New York, c. Jan. 1925
     record numbers: (31779) Ajax-17093 VJM VLP-40

1 Spreading lies and gossip : surely is one shameful
   sin
2 I hope when winter comes : they steal coal from her
   bin
3 Scandal : is just a nice fancy name for dirt
4 I'll *spy* some woman : lying *mouse* just in her
   skirt
5 The buzzard : surely one lowdown rotten bird
6 But when folks smell scandal : how they fly to
   spread the word
7 Next time : I hear that mean ornery lowdown talk
8 I'll put coals in someone's shoes : to make warts
   when they walk

MooP 1   Moore, Kid Prince

     title: Bug Juice Blues
     place and date: New York, 8 Apr. 1936
     record numbers: (18971-2) ARC-6-09-56 Rt RL-340

1 Love my bug juice : just as crazy about it as I can
   be
2 *My late bug juice vane* : Lord I'm afraid he's
   going to pour it on me
3 Took one drink last night : and it made me go stone
   blind
4 Thought I'd run away : but I had to take my time
5 Sometime : a drink make me act just like a doggone
   fool
6 Two three drinks : make me kick like a doggone mule
7 Good man when I'm sober : tiger when I'm drunk
8 ??? : mama I'm going to hide in your trunk

MooP 2   Moore, Kid Prince

     title: Honey Dripping Papa
     place and date: New York, 11 Apr. 1936
     record numbers: (18999-2) ARC-6-09-56 Rt RL-340

1 'Tain't none of my business : but it sure ain't
   right
2 Take another man's woman : play honeydrip all night

MooP 2   Moore, Kid Prince

3 I'm a stranger : I just come in your town
4 I want some honeydrip : please don't turn me down
5 If I mistreat you mama : I sure don't mean no harm
6 I'm a honeydripping papa : I don't know right from
   wrong
7 I got me a mama : she's so big and fat
8 She hurt her honeydrip prince : because I know it's
   tight like that
9 Don't play honeydrip : way down in no cell
10 She's a sweet loving mama : I know she's going to
   raise a little hell
11 Went up on a mountain : looked down in the deep blue
   sea
12 Big fat woman : tried to flirt with me
13 If I could holler : like that mountain jack
14 I'd go up on the mountain : call my baby back

MooR 1   Moore, Rosie Mae

     title: Staggering Blues
     place and date: Memphis, 3 Feb. 1928
     record numbers: (41830-2) Vi-21280 Rt RL-310

1 Because you see me staggering : baby don't you think
   I'm drunk
2 For I'm going away to leave you : I'm coming back no
   more
3 Can't you tell me pretty papa : where did you stay
   last night
4 He said it's none of your business : mama so I treat
   you right
5 Because you see me staggering : daddy don't you
   think I'm drunk
6 I got my eye on my shotgun : the other one is on
   your trunk
7 Well I love you Mr Charlie : honey God knows I do
8 But the day you try to quit me : brother that's the
   day you die

MooR 2   Moore, Rosie Mae

     title: Ha-Ha Blues
     place and date: Memphis, 3 Feb. 1928
     record numbers: (41831-1) Vi-21280 Her H-201

1 Go on old man : don't sing those blues to me
2 I'm about as blue : as any girl can be
3 You even told me : right to my face
4 That you had another woman : to shimmy in my place
5 I'm getting tired : of your dirty ways
6 I'm going back : to my baby again
7 So *crying to me* : don't mean you can't bluff
8 Papa I'm slipping out tonight : I'm going ha ha ha
9 *All you men* : you may go your way
10 I'm sick and tired : of your dirty ways

MooR 3   Moore, Rosie Mae

     title: School Girl Blues
     place and date: Memphis, 3 Feb. 1928
     record numbers: (41832-2) Vi-21408 OJL-17

1 Now tell me little daddy : what you got on your
   worried mind
2 Tell your little mama your troubles : swear I'll
   tell you mine
3 I'll just ??? your carriage : and I'll check your
   line
4 I just come to tell you : another man is got your
   child
5 It's hard to love a man : when you know you really
   love
6 Lord I can't quit him : and I sure can't let him
   alone

205

MooR   3   Moore, Rosie Mae

7 Lord early one morning : girls on my way to school
8 Lord that brownskin man : caused me not to obey my
   poor mother's rule

MooR   4   Moore, Rosie Mae

      title: Stranger Blues
      place and date: Memphis, 3 Feb. 1928
      record numbers: (41833-2) Vi-21408 OJL-6

1 If I feel tomorrow : like I feel today
2 Before I stand to be mistreated : girls I'll take
   morphine and die
3 Lord my daddy got something : that's a brand new
   thing to me
4 I just want to tell you : it's sure been good to me
5 I'm poor old stranger girls : and I just rolled in
   your town
6 Lord I just come here : to ease my troubled mind
7 Lord I'm so heart-broken girls : I cannot cry at all
8 Well if I finds my man girls : I'm going to nail him
   to the wall
9 I'm poor old stranger girls : and I just rolled in
   your town
10 Lord I find my man : I'm going to nail him to the
   wall

MooR   5   Moore, Rosie Mae

      title: Mad Dog Blues
      place and date: New Orleans, c. Dec. 1928
      record numbers: (NOR-760) Br-7049 Rt RL-329

1 Read my search warrant lady : I'm just looking for
   my man
2 I got my razor in my bosom : and my pistol in my
   hand
3 I'm just like a mad dog : I snaps at everything I
   meet
4 But if I find my man : he sure is going to be my
   meat
5 I'm going to cut him with my razor : I'm going to
   use my pistol too
6 Now they can call the undertaker : to put your last
   clean shirt on you
7 I'm going to kill my man : then I'm going to kill
   myself
8 I'd rather we both to be dead : than to see him with
   someone else

MooW   1   Moore, William

      title: One Way Gal
      place and date: Chicago, c. Jan. 1928
      record numbers: (20309-1) Pm-12648 OJL-8

1 There's one thing I like : about that gal of mine
2 She treats me right : and loves me all the time
3 Sometimes I'm broke : and blue as I can be
4 But still my baby : she looks after me
5 She walked in the rain : till her feet got soaking
   wet
6 And these are the words : she said to every man she
   met
7 Mr change a dollar : and give me one lousy dime
8 So I can feed : this hungry man of mine
9 She took me over : to a cabaret
10 I ate and drank : and then I went away
11 This gal of mine : she's one way all the time
12 She takes the blues away : and satisfies my mind

MooW   2   Moore, William

      title: Midnight Blues
      place and date: Chicago, c. Jan. 1928
      record numbers: (20312-2) Pm-12636 Rt RL-340

1 Some people say : that the midnight blues ain't bad
2 Well it must not have been : those midnight blues I
   had
3 Tell me fair brownie : where did you stay last night
4 Your hair's all down : and your clothes ain't
   fitting you right
5 Oh run here mama : run and tell me now
6 Says do you love your papa : anyhow
7 When you see two women : going together so long
8 You can bet your life : that there's something going
   on wrong
9 I'm going to buy me a pistol : as long as my right
   arm
10 Going to carry it in my pocket : and make you stay
   at home

MoraH 1   Morand, Herb (Harlem Hamfats)

      title: Root Hog or Die
      place and date: New York, 6 Oct. 1937
      record numbers: (62661-A) De-7439 AH-77

1 I pawned my watch : and my clothes and diamond ring
2 Now you will have to stop : shaking shaking that old
   thing

MossB 1   Moss, Buddy

      title: Daddy Don't Care
      place and date: New York, 16 Jan. 1933
      record numbers: (12908-1) Ba-33106 RBF RF-15

1 She goes out Lord : and stays all day
2 Got another woman : to take her place
3 I got a gal : says she's long and tall
4 Way she keep loving : says Lord Lord Lord
5 I got a gal : says she's named Sally Right
6 Says way she keep a-loving : says *it's* just too
   tight
7 She stays out : all night long
8 She's going to come home : and find me gone
9 She stays out : both day and night
10 Said I know my babe : she ain't treating me right

MossB 2   Moss, Buddy

      title: Hard Road Blues
      place and date: New York, 19 Jan. 1933
      record numbers: (12946-1) Ba-33106 RBF RF-15

1 Walking down the hard road : done wore the soles off
   of my shoes
2 My soles are ragged : I got those hard road blues
3 Have you ever laid down at night : thinking about
   your brown
4 And get the hard road blues : and ramble from town
   to town
5 Reason why I start : why I lowdown
6 My gal done quit me : I got to leave this town
7 I'm going to put some wheels : on my *broken* shoes
8 Going to roll back to my baby : to get rid of these
   hard road blues
9 I lay down last night : a thousand things on my mind
10 Going to walk these hard roads : just to cure my
   lowdown mind
11 Come here baby : give me your right hand
12 Walking these hard roads : going to drive me insane

MossB   3   Moss, Buddy

        title: Gravy Server
        place and date: New York, 21 Aug. 1935
        record numbers: (17981-) ARC-6-11-56 Rt RL-318

1   I've got a woman : she's sweet as she could be
2   She long tall woman : she's all right with me
3   Lord I love my woman : she treats me nice and kind
4   All admit she got something : to ease my worried
    mind
5   I'm going to ask my woman : will she be my wife
6   I would believe she could boil water : make it suit
    my appetite
7   Say the way she fries my steak : peoples I'm
    satisfied
8   And the way she serves her gravy : man you'd be
    surprised
9   Say she serves me in the morning : she serves me
    late at night
10 Said and everything she serves me : she serves it to
    me right

NelsR   1   Nelson, Romeo

        title: Gettin' Dirty Just Shakin' that Thing
        place and date: Chicago, 9 Oct. 1929
        record numbers: (C-4629-) Vo-1447 OJL-15

1   Now sister fooled brother man : and brother *moved
    down*
2   The broad catch you signifying : you breaking her
    down
3   Now mama : just poisoned you
4   Sick and tired : of the way you do
5   Spread the *goo-goo* dust : around your bed
6   In the morning : find your own self dead
7   I know a sister : called Miss Lou
8   Shook so : she had the German flu
9   Another sister : somebody call Miss Boone
10 Shook so : you couldn't stay in her room
11 Say mama cooked some cabbage : didn't have no meat
12 Had to throw them : on Thirty-Fifth Street
13 Old folk : go run and get your glass
14 Catching the juice : from the too black bad
15 Say mama killed a chicken : and she thought it was a
    duck
16 Put him on the table : with his heel cocked up
17 I had a mama : that spoke like this
18 Shake your shoulder : shake your wig

NelsR   2   Nelson, Romeo

        title: Dyin' Rider Blues
        place and date: Chicago, 26 Nov. 1929
        record numbers: (C-4752-) Vo-1494 RBF RF-12

1   I got a letter from my rider : what do you reckon it
    read
2   Say hurry home papa : rider's almost dead
3   And I walked slowly : looked down in the rider's bed
4   These are the words : that rider's said
5   You haven't kissed me papa : like you done before
6   I got a ??? : I just about have to go
7   And I walked back : looking down in rider's face
8   These are the words : rider heard me say
9   And now goodbye mama : I'll meet you some old day
10 The way I been treated : I sure will pass away

NelsS   1   Nelson, Sonny Boy

        title: Street Walkin'
        place and date: New Orleans, 15 Oct. 1936
        record numbers: (02600-1) BB-B6672 Yz L-1038

1   Nobody knows : streetwalking women like I do

NelsS   1   Nelson, Sonny Boy

2   She'll keep you up all night long : then will spend
    your money too
3   She'll come home every morning : with a rag tied on
    her head
4   And if you speak about loving man : she'll swear
    that she's almost dead
5   She won't cook you no breakfast : clothes ain't
    never clean
6   But she can spend more money : than any woman that
    you ever seen
7   Sometimes she will say : baby I love you so
8   Then again she will tell you : to pack your clothes
    and go

NelsT   1   Nelson, Blue Coat Tom (T. C. Johnson Groups)

        title: Blue Coat Blues
        place and date: Memphis, 17 Feb. 1928
        record numbers: (400258-B) OK-8838 Rt RL-316

1   Hey baby : see what you have done
2   You went made me love you : now your man did come
3   I'm going away baby : to wear you off my mind
4   For you keeps me worried : a-bothered all the time
5   I woke up here this morning : feeling bad
6   I was dreaming about sweet mama : the time once I've
    had
7   Hey late last night : when everything was still
8   And I found my Georgie : a-way behind some hill
9   Now gal got something : I don't know what it is
10 But on every time she touches me : my mind can't be
    still
11 *Down down alley* : and heist your window high
12 ??? : when he go easing by
13 I'm going down south : to have my fortune told
14 For I believe : some dirty rascal stole my jellyroll

Newb   1   Newbern, Hambone Willie

        title: She Could Toodle-Oo
        place and date: Atlanta, 13 Mar. 1929
        record numbers: (402295-A) OK-8740 Rt RL-323

1   Her mama phoned the doctor : says come here quick
2   Says I believe I got to have my daughter :
    check-a-check checked
3   Well the doctor came : says I never seen such
4   Your daughter got the fever : she toodle-oo too much
5   Toodle-oo in the summer : in the fall
6   Got so cold : she couldn't toodle-oo at all
7   Her mama's in the kitchen : cooking in a stew
8   Me around the house : just a toodle-oodle-oo
9   Well she went to leave me : *rat* stuck to her shoe
10 Fell down : and broke her little toodle-oodle-oo

Newb   2   Newbern, Hambone Willie

        title: Nobody Knows
        place and date: Atlanta, 13 Mar. 1929
        record numbers: (402296-B) OK-8679 Rt RL-307

1   There was one old brother : by the name of Mose
2   He got so happy : bull of *barley the claw*
3   There was one old sister : by the name of *Yoon*
4   Shame to tell you brother : what that sister was
    doing
5   There was one old sister : lived down on Vance
6   Said I'd have been her shimmy partner : Lord if I
    had a chance
7   There was one old sister : named sister Green
8   Jumped up and done the shimmy Lord : you ain't never
    seen
9   She pulled off her slipper : and then one sock
10 Got way back : and done the double eagle rock

Newb   3   Newbern, Hambone Willie

      title: Shelby County Workhouse Blues
      place and date: Atlanta, 13 Mar. 1929
      record numbers: (402297-B) OK-8740 RBF RF-202

1   I left old Memphis Tennessee : on my way back to
    [dear old] *Maltree*
2   I ??? my baby : if this ???
3   Says I phoned my *room* : I didn't have but one word
    to say
4   Cast my eyes to the Lord : say you please have mercy
    on poor me
5   Well I left old *Maltree* : [on my way back, going
    back] to Memphis Tennessee
6   No sooner I got at the bus station Lord : police he
    arrested me
7   Lord the police arrest me : carried me before the
    judge
8   Well the lawyers talk so fast : didn't have time to
    say not nary word
9   Well the lawyer pleaded: and the judge he done wrote
    it down
10 Says I'll give you ten days buddy : out in little
    old Shelby town
11 And they stood me up : *tied me around the peg*
12 Guard said to the trustee : said put the shackles
    still around his leg
13 Mmm : Lordy Lordy Lord
14 Lord the guards done treat me : like I was a lowdown
    dog

Newb   4   Newbern, Hambone Willie

      title: Hambone Willie's Dreamy-Eyed Woman's
           Blues
      place and date: Atlanta, 14 Mar. 1929
      record numbers: (402305-B) OK-8693 OJL-17

1   I've got a dreamy-eyed woman : lives down on Cherry
    Street
2   And she laughs and talks : with every brownskin old
    man she meets
3   Says I told her last night : and all night before
4   Say if you don't quit so much running : you can't be
    mine no more
5   Put both hands on her hips : and these is the words
    she said
6   Said big boy I couldn't miss you : if the good Lord
    told me you was dead
7   I'm going to leave here walking : chances I may ride
8   For I got the blues baby : and I can't be satisfied
9   Honey mmm : baby what more can I do
10 Want me to cut my throat : baby trying to get along
    with you

Newb   5   Newbern, Hambone Willie

      title: Roll and Tumble Blues
      place and date: Atlanta, 14 Mar. 1929
      record numbers: (402306-B) OK-8679 OJL-17

1   And I rolled and I tumbled : and I cried the whole
    night long
2   And I rosed this morning mama : and I didn't know
    right from wrong
3   Did you ever wake up : and find your dough-roller
    gone
4   And you wrings your hands : and you cry the whole
    day long
5   And I told my woman Lord : [just] before I left her
    town
6   Don't she let nobody : tear her barrelhouse down
7   And I fold my arms Lord : and I [slowly] walked away
8   Says that's all right sweet mama : your trouble
    going to come some day

Nick   1   Nickerson, Charlie Bozo (Memphis Jug Band)

      title: Everybody's Talking About Sadie Green
      place and date: Memphis, 12 May 1930
      record numbers: (59917-2) Vi-V38599 Jo SM-3104

1   Down in Memphis : Tennessee
2   There's a gal : sweet as she can be
3   She's not too thin : not too fat
4   But everything about her : is tight like that
5   She wears her dresses : above her knees
6   Lets folks say : what they please
7   She lets you ride her : in your car
8   But won't let you : ride her too far
9   She don't dress shabby : and wears a tam
10 Legs look as nice : as Georgia ham
11 She uses powder : uses paint
12 It makes her look : like what she ain't
13 She spends it : so they say
14 Because : she won't give nothing away
15 When she dances : she don't move her head
16 But moves everything else : instead
17 Man you can believe it : or not
18 Some day : I'll see what Sadie's got

Nick   2   Nickerson, Charlie Bozo (Memphis Jug Band)

      title: Cave Man Blues
      place and date: Memphis, 21 May 1930
      record numbers: (59962-2) Vi-V38605 Mel MLP-7324

1   Mr caveman : doggone your caving soul
2   You better quit your bad habits : digging in every
    dark hole
3   You cave so much : till you can't keep it hid
4   You going to get in the wrong cave : like Floyd
    Collins did
5   You won't go to the barber : you won't even shave
6   You know a clean-face man : don't go in no cave
7   I'm going in the cave : at the sounding of the drums
8   And I'll dig and dig : till my good gal comes

Nick   3   Nickerson, Charlie Bozo (Memphis Jug Band)

      title: It Won't Act Right
      place and date: Memphis, 21 May 1930
      record numbers: (59964-2) Vi-V38620 Jo SM-3104

1   I take my gal out : to a dance one night
2   She would've did the shimmy : but her dress was too
    tight
3   I would play my fiddle : but I ain't got no bow
4   It have worn off : I can't use it no more
5   I went uptown : to see old lady Moore
6   The bed fell down : I bumped my head on the floor
7   I had a little dog : ???
8   I leant him to my gal : to keep her company
9   Around that chicken coop : the *fool* ???
10 My baby tried to pull off : my derby ???
11 She bit my rooster : bit him to the bone
12 I told her : to let my thing alone

Nick   4   Nickerson, Charlie Bozo (Memphis Jug Band)

      title: Going Back to Memphis
      place and date: Memphis, 5 June 1930
      record numbers: (62583-) Vi-23310 Jo SM-3104

1   I'm leaving here mama : don't you want to go
2   Because I'm sick and tired : of all this ice and
    snow
3   When I get back to Memphis : you can bet I'll stay
4   And I ain't going to leave : until that Judgment Day
5   I love old Memphis : the place where I was born
6   Wear my buck??? shoes : and drink my pint of corn
7   I wrote my gal a letter : way down in Tennessee

Nick   4   Nickerson, Charlie Bozo (Memphis Jug Band)

8 Because I was up here hungry : hurry up and ??? to
   me
9 I'm going to walk and walk : until I walk out of my
   shoes
10 Because I've got what they call : *the new living
   here* blues

Nick   5   Nickerson, Charlie Bozo (Memphis Jug Band)

        title: Got a Letter from My Darlin'
        place and date: Memphis, 26 Nov. 1930
        record numbers: (64731-) Vi-23267 Rt RL-337

1 I got a letter from my darling : said hurry home
2 I got a letter from my darling : said how long you
   been gone
3 She's little and neat : all nice so sweet
4 Great big legs : and ??? feet
5 She got great big eyes : rosy cheeks
6 Now buddy : you know she must be a peach
7 I'm coming home mama : if I have to ???
8 I'm coming home mama : if I have to ride the rods
9 You know you're as sweet : as a candy doll
10 You know : you didn't have another man in my stall
11 I got a letter from my darling : said hurry home
12 I got a letter from my darling : didn't have a
   single dime
13 I'm going in the morning : ain't going to lose no
   time
14 *Easy kind of* walk : *reel and* rock behind

Nick   6   Nickerson, Charlie Bozo (Memphis Jug Band)

        title: You May Leave But This Will Bring You
        Back
        place and date: Memphis, 26 Nov. 1930
        record numbers: (64733-) Vi-23267 Rt RL-337

1 My father was a jockey : learned me to ride behind
2 You know by that : I got a job any time
3 I walked around the corner : to the peanut stand
4 My gal got stuck : on the peanut man
5 You quit me pretty mama : because you couldn't be my
   boss
6 But a rolling stone : don't gather no moss
7 Just a nickel's worth of meal : a dime's worth of
   lard
8 Will feed every dame : in *Jack Burse* yard

Nick   7   Nickerson, Charlie Bozo (Memphis Jug Band)

        title: Move that Thing
        place and date: Memphis, 28 Nov. 1930
        record numbers: (64740-2) Vi-23274 Rt RL-323

1 Last night : my gal went to bed
2 She put a pistol : under my head
3 I got a gal : *pass the* ??? out of my place
4 The mules backed up : in my face
5 A horse and a flea : and two little mice
6 Was down in the cellar : shooting dice
7 Says the horse he slipped : fell on the flea
8 The flea said police : the horse on me
9 Said the little red rooster : to the little red hen
10 You haven't laid an egg : since I don't know when

Nick   8   Nickerson, Charlie Bozo (Memphis Jug Band)

        title: Round and Round
        place and date: Memphis, 26 Nov. 1930
        record numbers: (64732-) Vi-23256 Jo SM-3104

1 My gal's got something : that I surely like

Nick   8   Nickerson, Charlie Bozo (Memphis Jug Band)

2 Every time she hugs me : it nearly breaks my back
3 Preacher in the pulpit : bobbing up and down
4 Sisters in the amen corner : singing let's go round
   and round
5 I got a gal : got movements like a cannonball
6 You women better be careful : you won't have no man
   at all
7 This winter you women better shimmy : and shimmy
   right fast
8 If they miss *airy* movement : it sure is their last

Nick   9   Nickerson, Charlie Bozo (Memphis Jug Band)

        title: You Got Me Rollin'
        place and date: Memphis, 28 Nov. 1930
        record numbers: (64741-2) Vi-23274 Rt RL-323

1 You got me rolling mama : I don't know how come
2 You want me to roll : from sun to sun
3 I rolled in the summer : I rolled in the fall
4 Winter's here : you don't want no rolling at all
5 If I had swings : and a carpet bag
6 I know by that : I'd get my baby back
7 Squeeze me : till I get as little as a gnat
8 Mama : then I'll bite like a cat

Nobl   1   Noble, George

        title: The Seminole Blues
        place and date: Chicago, 11 Feb. 1935
        record numbers: (C-897-2) ARC-7-06-75 Yz L-1028

1 And I came up this morning : baby don't you want to
   go
2 She said ain't nothing I could say : *and Mary fact
   started home* and gone
3 I got a rambling woman : she got a rambling mind
4 I buy her a ticket : let her ease on down the line
5 I think I heard that old Seminole : yeah baby when
   she blows
6 I got a note about my baby : she was way down the
   road
7 Lord I asked Mr conductor : won't you please help
   her with her load
8 Because the way that she treated me : every day
   nobody knows
9 Lord she treat me like a hog : treated me like a dog
10 She treated me like a bear one morning : and then ah
   just like a log
11 Don't nobody know : how she mistreated me
12 Lord I got a-traveling on the mind : *anyone thing
   I'll be dying*

Oden   1   Oden, Jimmy

        title: I Have Made Up My Mind
        place and date: Richmond, Ind., 22 Sept. 1932
        record numbers: (18795) Ch-16540 Riv RM-8819

1 I have made up my mind : to explain to you in every
   way
2 Today I am leaving : and I'm going away to stay
3 And another thing baby : you don't worry me no more
4 Because I can get a woman like you : anywhere I go
5 I have made up my mind : baby to tell you the truth
6 I'm explaining all I know how : and nothing more can
   I do
7 I don't love you no more : and I don't see where I
   can
8 I've got a woman in ??? : so you can find you
   another man

Oden   2   Oden, Jimmy

        title: Sitting Down Thinking Blues
        place and date: Richmond, Ind., 22 Sept. 1932
        record numbers: (18796) Ch-16540 Riv RM-8819

 1 Just sitting down thinking : drinking my trouble
        through
 2 What in the world : makes me feel so blue
 3 I don't want to leave you : want to give you another
        break
 4 And just to see : what kind of woman you make
 5 Says you was off of whiskey : but you won't leave it
        alone
 6 And the next drink I see you with : babe you done
        lost your home
 7 Listen here little girl : love for you is true
 8 But if you don't stop drinking : I don't know what
        I'll do with you
 9 Why do you worry : when your daddy cares for you
10 And if I don't love you : I wouldn't care what you
        do

Oden   3   Oden, Jimmy

        title: Going Down Slow
        place and date: Chicago, 11 Nov. 1941
        record numbers: (070409-1) BB-B8889 RBF RF-16

 1 I have had my fun : if I don't get well no more
 2 My health is failing me : and I'm going down slow
 3 Please write my mother : tell her the shape I'm in
 4 Tell her to pray for me : forgive me for my sin
 5 Tell her don't send no doctor : doctor can't do no
        good
 6 It's all my fault : didn't do things I should
 7 On the next train south : look for my clothes home
 8 If you don't see my body : all you can do is moan
 9 Mother please don't worry : this is all in my prayer
10 Just say your son is gone : I'm out in this world
        somewhere

OweG   1   Owens, Big Boy George

        title: Kentucky Blues
        place and date: Richmond, Ind., Oct. 1926
        record numbers: (12571) Ge-6006 Yz L-1018

 1 I'm worried today : Lord and I'm worried in mind
 2 Be worried : honey be worried all the time
 3 What will you do : when your good friend throws you
        down
 4 Going to catch me a plane : babe going to leave your
        town
 5 Many days : I sit down weep and cry
 6 That's why : I'm dying to be by your side
 7 Some of these mornings : babe and it won't be long
 8 Going to call my name : darling and I'll be gone
 9 I woke up this morning : baby and feeling bad

OweG   2   Owens, Big Boy George

        title: The Coon Crap Game
        place and date: Richmond, Ind., Oct. 1926
        record numbers: (12579) Ge-6006 Rt RL-334

 1 Well I went down to a coon crap game : *although it*
        went against my will
 2 The ??? won all the money I had : except a greenback
        dollar bill
 3 When I went down to see my girl : well the hour was
        about nine
 4 I ??? : but I got there just in time
 5 Well I went down to ??? Street : where the ???
        fine
 6 Well I heard the ??? : ??? be no friend of mine

OweM   1   Owens, Marshall

        title: Texas Blues
        place and date: Grafton, Wis., c. Jan. 1932
        record numbers: (L-1238-2) Pm-13117 Yz L-1006

 1 I'm going back to Texas : hear that wild ox moan
 2 Lord that is why : you hear me yell this moan
 3 Some day you going to be sorry : honey you done me
        wrong
 4 *Honey babe that's all right* : honey and I'll be
        gone
 5 Oh baby baby : you don't know my mind
 6 When you think I'm loving you : *I'm in the bed* all
        the time
 7 Oh I woke up this morning : honey about the break of
        day
 8 I hugging the pillow : where my fair brown did lay

OweM   2   Owens, Marshall

        title: Try Me One More Time
        place and date: Grafton, Wis., c. Jan. 1932
        record numbers: (L-1240-1) Pm-13117 Yz L-1006

 1 Woke up this morning : get my shoes
 2 I love a woman : that I can't give it to
 3 Woke up this morning : to get my coat
 4 My brown knocking : on a-my back door
 5 Woke up this morning : to get my tie
 6 *I can't get you women* : *because you* let me die
 7 Woke up this morning : about the break of day
 8 Hugging the pillow : where that fair brown lay
 9 Mama told me : daddy told me too
10 You got to *live in your place* : ??? you

Palm   1   Palmer, Sylvester

        title: Broke Man Blues
        place and date: Chicago, 15 Nov. 1929
        record numbers: (403305-B) Co-14524-D RBF RF-12

 1 I know just how baby : Lord a broke man feels
 2 Says there is no one baby: that will do him a real
        good deal
 3 I been broke all day baby : did not have a lousy
        dime
 4 But I'll be all right baby : I swear some other time
 5 Lord I don't feel welcome : mama in St Louis no more
 6 Because I have no friends : baby and no place to go
 7 I'm going to leave this town baby : and I swear I
        ain't coming back no more
 8 I've been treated so bad : I can't be happy no more
 9 I've lost all my money : baby and everything I had
        too
10 That's why you hear me crying : mama these broke man
        blues
11 Mmm : I ain't got to sing it no more
12 Because I been broke baby : and I got these broke
        man blues

Patt   1   Patton, Charley

        title: Mississippi Bo Weavil Blues
        place and date: Richmond, Ind., 14 June 1929
        record numbers: (15211) Pm-12805 Yz L-1020

 1 It's a little boll weevil : she's moving in the air
 2 You can plant your cotton : and you won't get half a
        cent
 3 Boll weevil boll weevil : where's your little home
 4 A-Louisiana and Texas : is where I's bred and born
 5 Well I saw the boll weevil : Lord a-circle Lordy in
        the air
 6 The next time I seen him : Lord he had his family
        there

Patt   1   Patton, Charley

  7 Boll weevil left Texas : Lord he bid me fare you well
  8 I'm going down to Mississippi : going to give Louisiana hell
  9 Boll weevil and his wife : went and sit down on the hill
10 Boll weevil told his wife : let's take this forty in
11 Boll weevil told his wife : I believe I may go north
12 Let's leave Louisiana : and go to Arkansas
13 Boll weevil told the farmer : that I ain't going to treat you fair
14 Took all the blossoms : and leave you an empty square
15 Boll weevil boll weevil : where your little home
16 Most anywhere : they raise cotton and corn
17 Boll weevil boll weevil : call that treating me fair
18 Next time I seen you : you have your family there

Patt   2   Patton, Charley

title: Screamin' and Hollerin' Blues
place and date: Richmond, Ind., 14 June 1929
record numbers: (15214) Pm-12805 Yz L-1020

  1 Jackson on a high hill mama : Natchez just below
  2 I ever get back home : I won't be back no more
  3 Oh my mama's getting old : her head is turning grey
  4 Don't you know it'll break her heart : know I'm living this a-way
  5 I woke up this morning : jinx all around my bed
  6 Turned my face to the wall : and I didn't have a word to say
  7 No use a-hollering : no use screaming and crying
  8 For you know you got a home : mama long as I got mine
  9 Hey Lord have mercy : on my wicked soul
10 I wouldn't mistreat you : baby for my weight in gold
11 Oh I'm going away baby : don't you want to go
12 Take God to tell : when I'll be back here anymore

Patt   3   Patton, Charley

title: Down the Dirt Road Blues
place and date: Richmond, Ind., 14 June 1929
record numbers: (15215) Pm-12854 Yz L-1020

  1 I'm going away : to the one I know
  2 I'm worried now : but I won't be worried long
  3 My rider got something : she trying to keep it hid
  4 Lord I got something : to find that something with
  5 I feel like chopping : chips flying everywhere
  6 I've been to the nation : Lord but I couldn't stay there
  7 Some people say : them overseas blues ain't bad
  8 It must not have been : them overseas blues I had
  9 Every day : seem like murder here
10 I'm going to leave tomorrow : I know you don't didn't want me here
11 Can't go down : this dark road by myself
12 I don't carry my rider : going to carry me someone's else

Patt   4   Patton, Charley

title: Pony Blues
place and date: Richmond, Ind., 14 June 1929
record numbers: (15216) Pm-12792 Yz L-1020

  1 You can catch my pony : saddle up my black mare
  2 I'm going to find a rider : baby in the world somewhere
  3 Hello Central : what's the matter with your line
  4 Come a storm last night : tore the wires down
  5 Got a brand new Shetland : man already trained

Patt   4   Patton, Charley

  6 Just get in the saddle : tighten up on your reins
  7 And a brownskin woman : like something fit to eat
  8 But a jet-black woman : don't put your hand on me
  9 Took my baby : to meet the morning train
10 And the blues come down baby : like showers of rain
11 I got something to tell you : when I gets a chance
12 I don't want to marry : just want to be your man

Patt   5   Patton, Charley

title: Banty Rooster Blues
place and date: Richmond, Ind., 14 June 1929
record numbers: (15217) Pm-12792 Yz L-1020

  1 I'm going to buy me a banty : put him in my back door
  2 Lord he sees a stranger coming : he'll flap his wings and crow
  3 What you want with a rooster : he won't crow 'fore day
  4 What you want with a man : when he won't do nothing he say
  5 What you want with a hen : won't cackle when she lay
  6 What you want with a woman : when she won't do nothing I say
  7 Oh take my picture : hang it up in Jackson's wall
  8 Anybody ask you what about it : tell them that's all that's all
  9 My hook's in the water : and my cork's on top
10 How can I lose Lord : with the help I got
11 I know my dog : anywhere I hear him bark
12 I can tell my rider : if I feel her in the dark

Patt   6   Patton, Charley

title: It Won't Be Long
place and date: Richmond, Ind., 14 June 1929
record numbers: (15220) Pm-12854 Yz L-1020

  1 I believe sweet mama : going to do like she say
  2 Going to cook my supper : Lord put me in her bed
  3 You ever go to Memphis : stop by Minglewood
  4 You Memphis women : don't mean no man no good
  5 She's got a man on her man : got a kid on her kid
  6 Done got so bold : Lord won't keep it hid
  7 Ah all right : ain't going to be here long
  9 I believe sweet mama : sure was kind to me
10 She's up at night : like a police on his beat
11 I'll tell you something : keep it to yourself
12 Please don't tell your husband : Lord and no one else
13 [She's, got] a long tall woman : tall like a cherry tree
14 She gets up before day : and she puts that thing on me

Patt   7   Patton, Charley

title: Pea Vine Blues
place and date: Richmond, Ind., 14 June 1929
record numbers: (15221-A) Pm-12877 Yz L-1001

  1 I think I heard : the Pea Vine when she blowed
  2 Blowed just like : my rider getting on board
  3 You're living single : Lord you know I ain't going to stay
  4 I'm going up the country : mama in a few more days
  5 Yes you know it you know it : you know you done done me wrong
  7 Yes I cried last night : and I ain't going to cry no more
  8 But the Good Book tell us : you got to reap just what you sow

211

Patt   7   Patton, Charley

9   Stop your way of living : and you won't have to cry
      no more
11   I think I heard : the Pea Vine when she blowed
12   She blowed just like : she wasn't going to blow no
      more

Patt   8   Patton, Charley

      title: Tom Rushen Blues
      place and date: Richmond, Ind., 14 June 1929
      record numbers: (15222-A) Pm-12877 Yz L-1020

1   I lay down last night : hoping I would have my peace
2   But when I woke up : Tom Rushen was shaking me
3   When you get in trouble : there's no use of
      screaming and crying
4   Tom Rushen will take you : back to Cleveland
      a-flying
5   It was late one night : Holloway was gone to bed
6   Mr Day brought the whiskey : taken from under
      Holloway's head
7   It take boozy booze : Lord to carry me through
8   Thirty days seem like years in the jailhouse : where
      there is no booze
9   I got up this morning : Tom Day was standing around
10   If he lose his office now : he's running from town
      to town
11   [Let me, I'm going to] tell you folksies : just how
      he treated me
12   Ah he brought me here : and I was drunk as I could
      be

Patt   9   Patton, Charley

      title: Going to Move to Alabama
      place and date: Grafton, Wis., c. late Nov. 1929
      record numbers: (L-37-1) Pm-13014 Yz L-1020

1   Aah : she's long and tall
2   *The way she do the boogie* : makes a panther squall
3   I'm going to show you common women : how I feel
4   Going to get me another woman : before I leave
5   Say mama got the washboard : my sister got the tub
6   My brother got the whiskey : mama got the jug
7   Well these evil women : sure make me tight
8   Got a handful of give-me : mouthful of much-obliged
9   Well I got a woman : she's long and tall
10   But when she wiggles : she makes a panther squall
11   Say mama and papa : going to work
12   Left my sister standing : at the watering trough
13   My mama told me :
14   Never love a woman : like she can't love you
15   I got up this morning : my hat in my hand
16   Didn't have no other brown : didn't have no man

Patt   10   Patton, Charley

      title: Devil Sent the Rain
      place and date: Grafton, Wis., c. late Nov. 1929
      record numbers: (L-40-1) Pm-13040 Yz L-1009

1   Good Lord send the sunshine : devil he send the rain
2   I will be here tomorrow : on the morning train
3   You don't know : sure don't know my mind
4   I don't show you my ticket : and you don't know
      where I'm going
5   Followed sweet mama : to the burying ground
6   I didn't know that I loved her : till they laid her
      down
7   I been to the ocean : peeped down the deep blue sea
8   I didn't see nobody : looked like my sweet mama to
      me
9   One of these mornings : you know it won't be long

Patt   10   Patton, Charley

10   You going to be mistreated : and I'll have to leave
      you home
11   I'm going away : mama don't you want to go

Patt   11   Patton, Charley

      title: Green River Blues
      place and date: Grafton, Wis., c. late Nov. 1929
      record numbers: (L-44-3) Pm-12972 Yz L-1020

1   I went up Green River : rolling like a log
3   Think I heard : that Marion whistle blow
4   And it blew just like : my baby getting on board
5   I'm going : where the Southern cross the Dog
7   Some people say : the Green River blues ain't bad
8   Then it must not have been : them Green River blues
      I had
9   It was late one evening : everything was still
10   I could see my baby : upon a lonesome hill
11   How long : evening train been gone
12   Yes I'm worried now : but I won't be worried long
13   I'm going away : to make it lonesome here

Patt   12   Patton, Charley

      title: Hammer Blues
      place and date: Grafton, Wis., c. late Nov. 1929
      record numbers: (L-47-2) Pm-12998 Yz L-1020

1   Going to buy me a hammock : carry it underneath
      through the trees
2   So when the wind blow : the leaves may fall on me
3   Go on baby : you can have your way
4   Sister : every dog sure must have his day
5   They got me in shackles : I'm wearing my ball and
      chain
6   And they got me ready : for that Parchman train
7   I went to the depot : I looked up at the board
8   And the train had left : went steaming on up the
      road
9   I was way up Red River : calling all night long
10   I think I heard : the Bob Lee boat when she moaned

Patt   13   Patton, Charley

      title: When Your Way Gets Dark
      place and date: Grafton, Wis., c. late Nov. 1929
      record numbers: (L-49-1) Pm-12998 Yz L-1020

1   When your way gets dark : baby turn your lights up
      high
2   When you see my man : Lordy he come easing by
3   I take my baby : seven forty-five
5   Trouble baby : trying to blow me down
6   It wouldn't hurt so bad : but the news all over this
      town
7   I love my baby : and I tell the world I do
8   What made me love her : you'll come and love her too
9   Yeah some day baby : well and it won't be long
10   She calling me baby : and I'll be gone
11   I'm going away baby : don't you want to go

Patt   14   Patton, Charley

      title: Heart Like Railroad Steel
      place and date: Grafton, Wis., c. late Nov. 1929
      record numbers: (L-50-1) Pm-12953 Her H-201

1   My babe's got a heart : like a piece of railroad
      steel
2   If I leave you this morning : don't say dad how do
      you feel

Patt   14   Patton, Charley

    3   I will leave her at the crossing : when the train
         pass by
    4   She blowed for the crossing : then she started to
         fly
    5   I got up this morning : something after five
    6   And the morning sun Lord : was beginning to rise
    7   Cut your wood : baby I will make your fire
    8   I will tote you water : from the boggy bayou
    9   If your woman mistreat you : *better off in your
         lap*
   10   I didn't find me nobody : did not have a man

Patt   15   Patton, Charley

         title: High Water Everywhere--Part I
         place and date: Grafton, Wis., c. early Dec.
         1929
         record numbers: (L-59-1) Pm-12909 Yz L-1020

    1   The backwater done rose all around Sumner : drove
         [me, poor Charley] down the line
    2   Well I tell the world : the water done struck
         through this town
    3   Lord the whole round country : Lord creek water is
         overflowed
    4   I would go to the hill country : but they got me
         barred
    5   Now the water now mama : done struck Charlotte town
    6   Well I'm going to Vicksburg : before I have mine
    7   Lord the water done [rushed, raised] : all over that
         old Jackson Road
    8   I'm going back to the hilly country : won't be
         worried no more

Patt   16   Patton, Charley

         title: High Water Everywhere--Part II
         place and date: Grafton, Wis., c. early Dec.
         1929
         record numbers: (L-60-2) Pm-12909 Yz L-1020

    1   The water was rising : up in my friend's door
    2   The man said to his womenfolk : Lord we'd better go
    3   The water was [rising, rolling] : got up in my bed
    4   I thought I would take a trip Lord : out on the big
         ice slab

Patt   17   Patton, Charley

         title: Rattlesnake Blues
         place and date: Grafton, Wis., c. early Dec.
         1929
         record numbers: (L-63-2) Pm-12924 Yz L-1020

    1   I say I'm just like a rattlesnake baby : I say in
         the middle of his coil
    2   I ain't going to have no hard time : mama rolling
         through this world
    3   When I leave here mama : I'm going further down the
         road
    4   So if I meet him up there : I'm going back to the
         Gulf of Mexico
    5   I'm going to shake glad hands mama : I say Lord with
         your loving boy
    6   Fixing to eat my supper : in Shelby Illinois
    7   Vicksburg on a high hill : and Louisiana Lord it's
         just below
    8   If I get back there : I ain't going to never be bad
         no more
    9   And my baby's got a heart : like a piece of railroad
         steel
   10   If I leave here this morning : never say daddy how
         do you feel

Patt   18   Patton, Charley

         title: Mean Black Moan
         place and date: Grafton, Wis., c. early Dec.
         1929
         record numbers: (L-77-1) Pm-12953 Yz L-1001

    1   It's a mean black moan : and it's lying front of my
         door
    2   When I leave Chicago : Lord I ain't coming back no
         more
    3   Ninety men were laid off : at the railroad shop
    4   And the strike in Chicago : Lordy Lord it just won't
         stop
    5   I'm tired of mean black moans : friends lying front
         of my door
    6   But when I leave Chicago Lord : I ain't coming back
         here no more
    7   There are a hundred men Lordy : [standing] all
         around my bed
    8   I wish somebody : might be able to kill the black
         moan dead
    9   Every morning : Lord rent man is at my door
   10   And my man hasn't worked Lord : in two or three
         weeks or more
   11   It's all I can do Lord : ah fight for my life
   12   But when the strike is over : Lord I will be all
         right

Patt   19   Patton, Charley

         title: Dry Well Blues
         place and date: Grafton, Wis., c. 28 May 1930
         record numbers: (L-429-2) Pm-13070 Yz L-1020

    1   When I was living at Lula : I was living there at
         ease
    2   Lord the drought come in cold autumn : parched up
         all the trees
    3   Oh today over in Lula : we'll bid that town goodbye
    4   Well when it come to another day : Lord the Lula
         well was gone dry
    5   Lord the citizens around Lula : all doing very well
    6   Lord they all got together : and they done bored a
         well
    7   I ain't got no money : and I sure ain't got no home
    8   The old weather done come in : and parched all the
         cotton and corn
    9   Oh look down the country : Lord it'll make you cry
   10   Most everybody : Lord had a watering bayou
   11   Lord the Lula women Lord : ??? up and down
   12   Lord you ought to been there : Lord see the womens
         all leaving town

Patt   20   Patton, Charley

         title: Moon Going Down
         place and date: Grafton, Wis., c. 28 May 1930
         record numbers: (L-432-1) Pm-13014 Yz L-1020

    1   Oh the moon is going down : baby sun's about to
         shine
    2   Rosetta Henry told me Lord : I don't want you
         hanging around
    3   Oh well where were you now baby : Clarksdale mill
         burned down
    4   I was way down Sunflower : with my face all full of
         frowns
    5   There's a house over yonder : painted all over green
    6   Some of the finest young women : Lord a man most
         ever seen
    7   Lord I think I heard : that Helena whistle Helena
         whistle Helena whistle blow
    8   Lord I ain't going to stop walking : till I get in
         my rider's door
    9   Oh the smokestack is black : and the bell it shine
         like gold

213

Patt   20   Patton, Charley

10 Lord I ain't going to walk here : baby around no
    more
11 I was out at night : when I heard the loco blow
12 I got to see my rider : where she's getting her
    dough

Patt   21   Patton, Charley

      title: Bird Nest Bound
      place and date: Grafton, Wis., c. 28 May 1930
      record numbers: (L-433-1) Pm-13070 Yz L-1020

1   Come on mama : out to the edge of town
2   I know where there's a bird nest : built down on the
    ground
3   If I was a bird mama : I would build a nest in the
    heart of town
4   So when the town get lonesome : I'd be bird nest
    bound
5   Hard luck is at your front door : blues are in your
    room
6   Trouble is at your back door : what is going to
    become of you
7   Sometimes I say I need you : then again I don't
8   Sometimes I think I'll quit you : then again I won't
9   Oh I remember one morning : standing in my baby's
    door
10 Look a-here papa Charley : I don't want you no more
11 Take me home sweet home : baby to that shining star
12 You don't need no telling : mama take me in your car

Patt   22   Patton, Charley

      title: Jersey Bull Blues
      place and date: New York, 30 Jan. 1934
      record numbers: (14723-) Vo-02782 Mam S-3802

1   If you got a good bullcow : you ought to keep your
    bull bull at home
2   Say may come along a young heifer : and just tow
    your bull from home
3   Oh my bull's in the pasture babe : Lord where
    there's no grass
4   I swear every minute : it seems like it's going to
    be my last
5   And my bull got a horn : long as my arm
7   I've an old five pound ax : and I'll cut two
    different ways
8   And I cut my little woman : both night and day
9   I've an old five pound ax : and I just dropped in
    your town
10 I got women now behind me : just try that old ax on
    down
11 And I remember one morning : between midnight and
    day
12 I were way upstairs : throwing myself away

Patt   23   Patton, Charley

      title: High Sheriff Blues
      place and date: New York, 30 Jan. 1934
      record numbers: (14725-2) Vo-02680 Yz L-1020

1   When the trial was in Belzoni : it ain't no use to
    screaming and cry
2   Mr Webb will take you : back to Belzoni jail
    a-flying
3   Let me tell you folks : just how he treated me
4   And he put me in the cellar : it was dark as it
    could be
5   It's late one evening : Mr Purvis was standing
    around
6   Mr Purvis told Mr Webb : to let poor Charley down
7   It takes boozy booze : Lord to carry me through

Patt   23   Patton, Charley

8   Thirty days seem like years in a jailhouse : where
    there is no booze
9   I got up one morning : feeling mighty bad
10 And it must not have been : them Belzoni jail I had
11 When I was in prison : it ain't no use to scream and
    cry
12 Mr Purvis on his mansion : he don't pay no mind

Patt   24   Patton, Charley

      title: Stone Pony Blues
      place and date: New York, 30 Jan. 1934
      record numbers: (14727-1) Vo-02680 Yz L-1020

1   I got me a stone pony : and I don't ride Shetland no
    more
2   You can find my stone pony : hooked to my rider's
    door
3   Vicksburg's my pony : Greenville is my grey mare
4   You can find my stone pony : down in Lula town
    somewhere
5   And I got me a stone pony : don't ride Shetland no
    more
6   And I can't feel welcome : rider nowhere I go
7   Vicksburg's on a high hill : and Natchez just below
8   And I can't feel welcome : rider nowhere I go
9   Well I didn't come here : steal nobody's brown
10 I just stopped by here : well to keep you from
    stealing mine
11 Hello Central : what's the matter with your line
12 Come a storm at night : and tore the wire down

Patt   25   Patton, Charley

      title: 34 Blues
      place and date: New York, 31 Jan. 1934
      record numbers: (14739-1) Vo-02651 Yz L-1020

1   I ain't going to tell nobody : thirty-four have done
    for me
2   Took my roll Lord : I was broke as I could be
3   They run me from Will Dockery's : ???
4   Ah one of them told papa Charley : I don't want you
    hanging around my job no more
5   Well look down the country : it almost make you cry
6   Women and children : flagging freight trains for
    rides
7   Carmen got a little Six Buick : big Six Chevrolet
    car
8   And it don't do nothing : but follow behind
    Holloway's farmer's plow
9   And it may bring sorrow : Lord and it may bring
    tears
10 Oh Lord oh Lord : let me see your brand new year

Patt   26   Patton, Charley

      title: Love My Stuff
      place and date: New York, 31 Jan. 1934
      record numbers: (14746-) Vo-02782 Mam S-3802

1   I love my stuff babe : I want to give it *a hop*
2   And my rider's got the ??? shivers : swear it just
    won't stop
3   Oh I know she want it hard babe : sure don't want it
    chawed
4   It would break my heart : if *the ??? need* no more
5   And I keeps on telling my rider : well she was
    shivering down
6   Lord that jelly-baking strut : will make a
    monkey-man leave his town
7   Oh the light burning dim : ??? *terrible near*
8   It must a-be the devil : inside this barrel of gin

214

Patt   26   Patton, Charley

    9   Oh I'm going to leave Mississippi now babe : before
        it be too late
   10   It may be like Twenty-Seven Highway : swear it just
        won't wait
   11   Oh I once had a notion : Lord I believe I will
   12   I'm going to go to the river : and stop at Dago Hill

Patt   27   Patton, Charley

        title: Revenue Man Blues
        place and date: New York, 31 Jan. 1934
        record numbers: (14747-) Vo-02931 Yz L-1020

    1   Aw the revenue man is riding : boy you'd better look
        out
    2   If he halts you don't stop : you will likely be
        knocked out
    3   Well I don't love salt water : well she always wants
        a drink
    4   If they see you with a bottle : they will almost
        break your neck
    5   Aw take me home : to Lord that shining star
    6   She don't need no telling : daddy will take you in
        his car
    7   Aw come one mama : let us go to the edge of town
    8   I know where there's a bird nest : built down on the
        ground
    9   Aw I wake up every morning : now with the jinx all
        around my bed
   10   I have been a good provider : but I believe I've
        been misled

Patt   28   Patton, Charley

        title: Poor Me
        place and date: New York, 1 Feb. 1934
        record numbers: (14757-1) Vo-02651 Yz L-1020

    1   You may go : you may stay
    2   But she'll come back : some sweet day
    3   Don't the moon look pretty : shining down through
        the tree
    4   I can see Bertha Lee : Lord but she can't see me

PerkG   1   Perkins, Gertrude

        title: No Easy Rider Blues
        place and date: Dallas, 6 Dec. 1927
        record numbers: (145340-1) Co-14313-D Fwy
        FJ-2802

    1   I walked all night : got a few more miles to go
    2   Before the sun rises : I'll be at my rider's door
    3   *Blackland farms* : ???
    4   If I don't find my rider : I'm going to walk on
        across the way
    5   Hey : hey
    6   For my own easy rider : for he ain't no secondhand
        man
    7   The man I love : I know he's out of town
    8   And when I find him : he better not be messing
        around
    9   If the man across town : may get my rider's place
   10   *But he will stay where he set : and search hard in
        his face*
   11   No easy rider : hey hey hey
   12   When you ain't here to love me : I'll simply hey hey

Pett   1   Petties, Arthur

        title: Two Time Blues
        place and date: Memphis, 14 Feb. 1928
        record numbers: (41906-2) Vi-21282 Yz L-1007

    1   A two-timing woman : don't want no one man
    2   *You allow her Lord* : take some poor girl's man
    3   When the blues is trailing you : you don't know what
        to do
    4   Go back to the one you love now : the blues will
        soon leave you
    5   You trying act right : girl will not let you
    6   Heart full of sorrow now : blues are all riding you
    7   A two-timing woman : keep you on that killing floor
    8   How can I love : when she's always in the road
    9   Once little lad I want to talk to you : don't be
        feeling sad
   10   Better get you a new girl : or one you once have had
   11   Well well well well : I ain't going to stay here
        long

Pett   2   Petties, Arthur

        title: Out on Santa Fe--Blues
        place and date: Memphis, 14 Feb. 1928
        record numbers: (41907-2) Vi-21282 Rt RL-314

    1   The little woman in the cellar : the boss upstairs
    2   I'm going from hand to hand : and a woman going from
        man to man
    3   Don't let a woman know you love her : if you do you
        have done wrong
    4   You come in from your work now : she got her clothes
        and gone
    5   Then you catch you a freight train : going out on
        the Santa Fe
    6   I can't stay here now : this ain't the place for me
    7   Your mama tell you to travel : *it ain't* everywhere
    8   *When you're there* you going to stay now : you
        can't stay nowhere
    9   I can tell the day mama : I seen my baby's face
   10   She started me to loving her : then treat me this
        a-way
   11   You had all you want now : now please let me alone
   12   *It won't be love you* : back up this road I'm going

Pett   3   Petties, Arthur

        title: Good Boy Blues
        place and date: Chicago, c. 2 July 1930
        record numbers: (C-5921-B) Br-7182 Yz L-1038

    1   When you's a good fellow : they'll always leave you
        alone
    2   When you's a bad fellow : the jail will be your home
    3   Canned heat ain't no good boy : keep you with *sin*
        ??? on your mind
    4   Jailhouse doors open : then you got a rambling mind
    5   You sit and you wondering : you looking through your
        mind
    6   You don't want no more canned heat : when the judge
        give you your time
    7   Wake up every morning : when everything look blue
    8   Go see the one you love : the blues will soon leave
        you
    9   Walking all night long : walking from place to place
   10   I was wandering and walking : to see my baby's face

PetW   1   Petway, Robert

    title: Catfish Blues
    place and date: Chicago, 28 Mar. 1941
    record numbers: (059476-1) BB-B8838 Yz L-1038

1   Well I lay down down last night : well I tried to
    take my rest
2   Notion struck me last night baby : I believe I take
    a stroll out west
3   Well if I were a catfish mama : I said swimming deep
    down in the deep blue sea
4   All these gals now sweet mama : I said now setting
    out hooks for me
5   Well I went down yeah down to the churchhouse : yes
    well they called on me to pray
6   Got on my knees now mama : I didn't know not not a
    word to say
7   Somebody write write me a letter baby : I'm going to
    write it just you see
8   See if my baby my baby : do she thinking of little
    old thing of me

PetW   2   Petway, Robert

    title: Bertha Lee Blues
    place and date: Chicago, 20 Feb. 1942
    record numbers: (074108-1) BB-B9008 RBF RF-14

1   Bertha Lee : you sure have been good to me
2   You been good Bertha Lee : as you's intend to be
3   Bertha Lee : honey please don't you stray from home
4   If you do Bertha Lee : something sure is going on
    wrong
5   Bertha Lee : won't you come back home to me
6   If you don't Bertha Lee : oh babe I sure can't sleep
7   Look a-here now Bertha Lee : I don't want you to run
    around
8   If you do Bertha Lee : please lay my money down

PetW   3   Petway, Robert

    title: My Baby Left Me
    place and date: Chicago, 20 Feb. 1942
    record numbers: (074114-1) BB-B9036 Rt RL-314

1   My baby left me this morning : she did not even
    shake my hand
2   It's because you know partner : she got her another
    man
3   Lord I'm going down south : where the weather sure
    do suit my clothes
4   Well my baby said look daddy : I do swear to God you
    sure don't know
5   Oh Lord baby : please don't you fool me no more
6   You told me last night black gal : meet you at the
    honey next door
7   That's all right baby : I'll see you just the same
8   I'm getting tired now baby : that you trying to call
    my name
9   I been down south so long : know it sure don't worry
    my mind
10   I'm going to leave in the morning now partner : with
    that little sweety sure God on my mind

PetW   4   Petway, Robert

    title: Cotton Pickin' Blues
    place and date: Chicago, 20 Feb. 1942
    record numbers: (074115-1) BB-B9036 Rt RL-314

1   She's a cotton-picking woman : Lord she does it all
    the time
2   If you don't stop picking cotton now baby : I
    believe you sure going to lose you mind

PetW   4   Petway, Robert

3   She picked so much cotton : she even don't know
    where to go
4   She'll even moan now sweet mama : honey she's going
    from door to door
5   She's a cotton-picking woman : I swear she pick
    cotton all the time
6   If you don't stop picking now baby : I believe you
    going to lose your mind
7   I'm so far from my home : well I can't tell right
    from wrong
8   Now my baby last night mama : oh well she said now
    black man I'm going
9   How long : on my bended knees
10   Pick so much cotton now partner : will you forgive
    me if you please

Pick   1   Pickett, Charlie

    title: Crazy 'Bout My Black Gal
    place and date: New York, 2 Aug. 1937
    record numbers: (62467-A) De-7762 Rt RL-310

1   Now tell me little black gal : what are you going to
    do
2   Taking my money black gal : give it all to you
3   Now I'm so crazy about my black gal : I'm just as
    wild as I can be
4   Now I'm so crazy about my black gal : she ought to
    be a fool about me
5   Now me and my black gal : had a fight last night
6   Will you let me tell you : what it was all about
7   Now tell me little black gal : where did you stay
    last night
8   Just the reason I ask you black gal : know your
    clothes ain't right
9   Now the little ??? black gal I been loving : she got
    teeth solid gold
10   That's the only black gal : that's got a mortgage on
    my soul
11   Now me and my black gal : walking down Main Street
12   She was *breaking* and bumming : every man she meet

Pick   2   Pickett, Charlie

    title: Let Me Squeeze Your Lemon
    place and date: New York, 3 Aug. 1937
    record numbers: (62487-A) De-7707 RBF RF-9

1   Now you got fruit on your tree : lemons on your
    shelf
2   You know loving mama : that you can't squeeze them
    all by yourself
3   I said please let me squeeze your lemon : while I'm
    in your lonesome town
4   Now let me squeeze your lemon baby : until my love
    come down
5   I says it make no difference baby : what your daddy
    don't allow
6   Let me squeeze your lemon mama : I mean anyhow
7   I say I come to your house : knocked on your door
8   You told me loving mama : that you couldn't use me
    no more
9   I says one two three four five : six seven eight
    nine ten
10   I would come and see you baby : but you really got
    too many men
11   I said now me and my baby : had a fuss last night
12   Will you let me tell you baby : what it was all
    about

Pick   3   Pickett, Charlie

      title: Down the Highway
      place and date: New York, 3 Aug. 1937
      record numbers: (62488-A) De-7707 RBF RF-202

1 Now I'm going to leave here walking : going down
   Highway Sixty-One
2 If I find my sweet mama : baby I believe we're going
   to have some fun
3 Oh well oh well : we're going to make everything all
   right
4 Now if I don't come in the morning : you know I will
   do just tomorrow night
5 Now the Sixty-One Highway : she only runs right by
   my door
6 Runs from Atlanta into Georgia : down into the Gulf
   of Mexico
7 Now I received a letter : some long-distance
   telegram
8 Now if I don't be home Sunday : ??? will be home ???

PooJ   1   Poor Jab (Memphis Jug Band)

      title: Whitewash Station Blues
      place and date: Memphis, 15 Sept. 1928
      record numbers: (47036-2) Vi-V38504 RBF RF-6

1 You can toot your whistle : blow your horn
2 The Memphis Jug Band : done been here and gone
3 Now if you want to get to heaven : I tell you what
   to do
4 You put on a sock : and boot and a shoe
5 You place a bottle of corn : in your right hand
6 That'll pass you right over : in the Promised Land
7 And if you meet the devil : he ask you how you do
8 I'm on my way to heaven : don't you want to go too
9 Know the other place : will do just as well
10 They call Whitewash Station : ten miles from hell
11 ??? mama : what's on your mind
12 You keep me worried : bothered all the time
13 Ain't got no stockings : ain't got no shoes
14 Know I've got : the Memphis Jug Band blues

PooJ   2   Poor Jab (Memphis Jug Band)

      title: Stealin' Stealin'
      place and date: Memphis, 15 Sept. 1928
      record numbers: (47037-2) Vi-V38504 RBF RF-1

1 Stealing stealing : pretty mama don't you tell on me
2 I'm stealing back : to my same old used-to-be
3 Now put your arms around me : like the circle around
   the sun
4 I want you to love me mama : like my easy rider done
5 If you don't believe I love you : look what a fool
   I've been
6 If you don't believe I'm sinking : look what a whole
   I'm in
7 The woman I'm loving : she's just my height and size
8 She's a married woman : come to see me sometime

PooJ   3   Poor Jab

      title: Come Along Little Children
      place and date: Richmond, Ind., 3 Aug. 1932
      record numbers: (18656) Ch-16654 Rt RL-307

1 Now some folks say : a preacher won't steal
2 I caught two : in my watermelon field
3 They was eating them watermelons : throwing away the
   rinds
4 They was *preaching* ??? : and stealing ???
5 You know I had a little dog : it didn't have no
   sense
6 He's always barking : at the pickets on the fence

PooJ   3   Poor Jab

7 Said a picket flew off : and hit him in the jaw
8 You ought to heard that dog : holler haw haw haw
9 Now when I die : you bury me deep
10 Place a jug of molasses : at my feet
11 Just put some ??? : in my hand
12 I'll *drop* my way : to the Promised Land

Pope   1   Pope, Jenny

      title: Whiskey Drinkin' Blues
      place and date: Memphis, c. 23 Sept. 1929
      record numbers: (M-193-) Vo-1438 His HLP-1

1 Have you ever woke up : with whiskey-drinking on
   your mind
2 You send away to that bootlegger : and you did not
   have a dime
3 It makes me mad makes me rage : almost sends me to
   my grave
4 I wonder : where is that bootlegger today
5 You's a mean old bootlegger : know you doing me
   wrong
6 I send for brandy : and you send me corn
7 I am going to the distillery : carry me a brand new
   rocking chair
8 I'm going to sit at the distillery : till the
   bootlegger pass by here
9 They arrested that bootlegger : gave him a solid
   year
10 And the guard told the prisoner : it ain't no
   whiskey-drinking here

Pope   2   Pope, Jenny

      title: Doggin' Me Around Blues
      place and date: Memphis, c. 23 Sept. 1929
      record numbers: (M-194-) Vo-1438 His HLP-1

1 I'm a stranger here : just blowed in your town
2 Just because I'm a stranger : I won't be dogged
   around
3 It's raining here : storming over on the sea
4 I ain't got nobody : here to take care of me
5 I wonder : do my man know I'm here
6 If he do : he sure don't feel my care
7 I been your dog : ever since I entered your door
8 I'm going to leave this town : I won't be dogged
   around no more
9 I been your dog : been your dog all my days
10 The reason I'm leaving you : I don't like your
   doggone ways

Pope   3   Pope, Jenny

      title: Bull Frog Blues
      place and date: Memphis, c. Feb. 1930
      record numbers: (MEM-757-A) Vo-1522 His HLP-15

1 Hey hey hey hey : bullfrog blues is really on my
   mind
2 They're all in my bedroom : drinking all my wine
3 Hey pretty papa hey pretty papa : I can't stand
   these bullfrog blues no more
4 They're all in my cabinet : hopping all over my
   clothes
5 I woke up this morning : to make a fire in the stove
6 Bullfrogs in the bread pan: *bacon and eggs ??? they
   go*
7 Hey Mr bullfrog hey I'm going to tell you all : I
   can't stand your jellyroll in here
8 You can go out in the back yard : I'll make a pallet
   there
9 I will make you a pallet : so you can jellyroll

Pope   3   Pope, Jenny

10   And you can cook a breakfast : right on my brand new
     stove

Pope   4   Pope, Jenny

        title: Tennessee Workhouse Blues
        place and date: Memphis, c. Feb. 1930
        record numbers: (MEM-758-B) Vo-1522 His HLP-15

1   This is that new workhouse : way out in Merlin
     Tennessee
2   That's where they take the prisoners : and never set
     them free
3   They carried my daddy to the workhouse : they put
     him down on the *lock*
4   Just because he's ??? prisoner : they had him on
     secret dock
5   He was charged with murder : but stealing was his
     crime
6   He stole my jelly : and had to serve his time
7   I went to a lawyer : I called him over the phone
8   Said listen me lawyer : when will my man be home
9   That workhouse workhouse : is way out on a lonesome
     road
10   I hate to see my daddy : carrying that heavy load

Pull   1   Pullum, Joe

        title: Black Gal What Makes Your Head So Hard?--
        No. 2
        place and date: San Antonio, 3 Apr. 1934
        record numbers: (82786-?) BB-B5592 Rt RL-327

1   I woke up this morning : couldn't even get out of my
     bed
2   I was just thinking about that black woman : and it
     almost killed me dead
3   She may be home with her mama : she's the one I only
     want
4   And when I find my black woman : Lord all *my bad
     days* are gone
5   Mmm : how my poor heart is aching for me
6   My black woman has quit me : I'm going back to
     Culver City
7   Black gal : what makes your head so hard
8   You got a head : just like some two-by-four in some
     lumber yard
9   And if I see you with another woman : I would rather
     kill myself

Rach   1   Rachel, James Yank

        title: Little Sarah
        place and date: Memphis, 26 Sept. 1929
        record numbers: (55597-2) Vi-V38595 Rt RL-310

1   And I got up this morning : a light all in my room
2   And I looked behind me : and I found my faro gone
3   If a man don't never study : oh you would never have
     no books
4   But you get to thinking way back : the way your baby
     used to do
5   I got a little faro : she weigh about ninety pounds
6   Now but her mama and papa : they sure don't allow me
     around
7   I'm going to sing this song baby : I ain't going to
     sing no more
8   I'm going to hang this mandolin under my shoulder :
     right down front street I'll go
9   I can hear that old train coming : oh it must be
     coming after me
10   And I'm going to slip right back home : to my same
     old used-to-be

Rach   2   Rachel, James Yank

        title: T-Bone Steak Blues
        place and date: Memphis, 2 Oct. 1929
        record numbers: (56336-2) Vi-V38595 Rt RL-310

1   Say you talking about your red ripe tomato : I'm
     crazy about my T-bone steak
2   Said I'm going to buy me a faro : to care my
     Cadillac Eight
3   I got the railroad blues : the boxcars on my mind
4   And the girl I'm loving : she sure done left this
     town
5   Say if I had wings : like a bullfrog on a pond
6   I would rise back here : right in sweet mama's arms
7   You know once ain't forever : you know baby two Lord
     ain't but twice
8   But you women all get a good man : you don't know
     how to treat him right
9   Say you mistreat me [now] mama : and that's the way
     you do
10   But you going to want me some of these mornings :
     and poor dad won't have you

Rach   3   Rachel, James Yank (Sleepy John Estes)

        title: Expressman Blues
        place and date: Memphis, 17 May 1930
        record numbers: (59934-) Vi-23318 Fwy FA-2953

1   I said expressman expressman Lord : you have parked
     your wagon wrong
2   You took and moved my good gal : when I was a long
     long way from home
3   But a woman make a man do things : and she knows
     darn well that's wrong
4   Lord that's why you hear Crow Jane : singing these
     lonesome songs
5   Said if you never if you never : hear me anymore
6   Lord you can remember one morning baby : when I
     walked up on your porch
7   Lord I'll sing this song : and ain't going to sing
     no more
8   I'm going to put this mandolin under my arm : to the
     ??? *cafe* I'll go

Rach   4   Rachel, James Yank (Sleepy John Estes)

        title: Sweet Mama
        place and date: Memphis, 30 May 1930
        record numbers: (62550) Vi-23318 Rt RL-329

1   I say you used to be sweet mama : but I ain't going
     to call you sweet no more
2   And every time I come to your house : there's a man
     standing in your door
3   I said I'm going up the country : where the ???
     cross the dog
4   If you don't see me tomorrow : you won't have no man
     at all
5   Baby if I had wings : like a bullfrog on a pond
6   I would ride right here : and land in sweet mama's
     arms
7   Lord said blues jumped a rabbit : run him for a
     solid mile
8   Lord that fool couldn't catch him : and he fall
     right down and cried
9   I said look a-here now baby : got something really
     worrying me
10   It had ??? : of my old-time used-to-be

Rach 5   Rachel, James Yank

    title: Squeaky Work Bench Blues
    place and date: New York, 6 Feb. 1934
    record numbers: (14792-2) Ba-33047 Yz L-1021

1 I can't love you baby : I'm going to tell what's
   this all about
2 It's that I don't begin to see you worry : hon'
   until I gets in the neighborhood of your house
3 You have old squeaky workbench : and your mattress
   is torn every which a-way
4 Baby and you come tell me to come and lay down : and
   I have not got no place to lay
5 I get my ??? boots nasty : from walking around on
   your dirty rug
6 Said I'd rather go by myself : and look to the good
   Lord above

Rach 6   Rachel, James Yank

    title: Gravel Road Woman
    place and date: New York, 6 Feb. 1934
    record numbers: (14793-2) Vo-02649 OJL-21

1 I don't want no skinny mama : I wants a woman she
   got on plenty of meat
2 She can walk all night long : babe you won't stop
   and eat
3 She won't cook me cook no breakfast : and she won't
   wash me no clothes
4 Well she won't do nothing : but walk up and down the
   gravel road
5 Baby it's dark babe dark at midnight : and the moon
   shine down like day
6 I'm going to find some woman : to come and blow all
   my blues away
7 I got up babe babe in a *slumber* : I put on my
   shoes and clothes
8 I'm going to try to find my woman : I know she's
   strolling babe on the road

Rain 1   Rainey, Ma Gertrude

    title: Bad Luck Blues
    place and date: Chicago, Dec. 1923
    record numbers: (1596-2) Pm-12081 BYG-529.078

1 Hey people : listen while I sing my news
2 I want to tell you people : all about my bad-luck
   blues
3 Did you ever wake up : just at the break of day
4 With your arms around the pillow : where your daddy
   used to lay
5 Lord Lord : look where the sun done gone
6 Hey Lord : there's something going on wrong
7 What's the use of living : can't get the man you
   love
8 You might as well die : give your soul to the man
   far above

Rain 2   Rainey, Ma Gertrude

    title: Bo-Weavil Blues
    place and date: Chicago, Dec. 1923
    record numbers: (1597-?) Pm-12080 BYG-529.078

1 Hey boll weevil : don't sing the blues no more
2 Boll weevil's here : boll weevil's everywhere you go
3 I'm a lone boll weevil : been out a great long time
4 I'm going to tell you people : the evil boll weevil
   loves *some vine*
5 I don't want no man : to put no sugar in my tea
6 That bug is so evil : I'm afraid it might poison me

Rain 3   Rainey, Ma Gertrude

    title: Barrel House Blues
    place and date: Chicago, Dec. 1923
    record numbers: (1598-2) Pm-12082 BYG-529.078

1 Got the barrelhousing blues : feeling awfully dry
2 I can't drink moonshine : because I'm afraid I'll
   die
3 Papa likes his sherry : mama likes her corn
4 Papa likes to shimmy : mama likes to *cole*
5 Papa likes his bourbon : mama likes her gin
6 Papa likes his outside women : mama likes the
   outside men

Rain 4   Rainey, Ma Gertrude

    title: Those All Night Long Blues
    place and date: Chicago, Dec. 1923
    record numbers: (1599-?) Pm-12081 BYG-529.078

1   I have ???ed : for many a week
2   Because my man and I : don't agree
3   There's no reason : why he should treat me this way
4   Because the way I worry : I will soon be old and
    grey
5   Don't want to do : nothing that's rough
6   I can't stand : to treat *men* tough
7   I just stay and suffer : sigh and cry all night long
8   Because the way I'm worried : Lordy it sure is wrong
9   With this one man : on my mind
10 Can't sleep a wink at night : for crying
11 All my worries : get renewed
12 And I suffer : with those all night blues

Rain 5   Rainey, Ma Gertrude

    title: Moonshine Blues
    place and date: Chicago, Dec. 1923
    record numbers: (1608-?) Pm-12083 BYG-529.078

1 I've been reeling and a-rocking : hounded like a
   hound
2 Catch the first train : that's running southbound
3 Boys I can't stand up : I can't sit down
4 The man I love : has done left town
5 I feel like screaming : I feel like crying
6 Lord I been mistreated : folks and I don't mind
   dying
7 I'm going home : I'm going to settle down
8 I'm going to stop : my running around

Rain 6   Rainey, Ma Gertrude

    title: Last Minute Blues
    place and date: Chicago, Dec. 1923
    record numbers: (1609-2) Pm-12080 BYG-529.078

1 Minutes seem like hours : hours seem like days
2 It seem like my daddy : won't stop his evil ways
3 Seem like every minute : is going to be my last
4 If I can't tell my future : I will tell my past
5 The brook runs into the river : river runs into the
   sea
6 If I don't run into daddy : somebody'll have to bury
   me
7 If anybody asks you : who wrote this lonesome song
8 Tell them you don't know the writer : but Ma Rainey
   put it on

Rain   7   Rainey, Ma Gertrude

        title: Southern Blues
        place and date: Chicago, Dec. 1923
        record numbers: (1612-2) Pm-12083 BYG-529.078

    1   House catches fire : ain't no water around
    2   Throw your trunk out the window : let it burn on
        down
    3   I went to the Gypsy : to have my fortune told
    4   He said doggone you girlie : doggone your bad-luck
        soul
    5   I turned around : went to the Gypsy next door
    6   She say you can get a man : anywhere you go
    7   Let me be your rag doll : until your China comes
    8   If he beats me ragging : he's got to rag it some

Rain   8   Rainey, Ma Gertrude

        title: Walking Blues
        place and date: Chicago, Dec. 1923
        record numbers: (1613-2) Pm-12082 BYG-529.078

    1   Woke up this morning : with my head bowed down
    2   I had that mean old feeling : I was in the wrong
        man's town
    3   Mailman's been here : but didn't leave no news
    4   That's the reason why : mama's got the walking blues
    5   Walked and walked : till I almost lost my mind
    6   I'm afraid to stop walking : because I might lose
        some time
    7   Short time to make it : and a long ways to go
    8   Trying to find the town : they call San Antonio
    9   Thought I'd rest babe : I couldn't hear no news
    10 I'll soon be there : because I've got the walking
        blues

Rain   9   Rainey, Ma Gertrude

        title: Lost Wandering Blues
        place and date: Chicago, c. Mar. 1924
        record numbers: (1698-2) Pm-12098 BYG-529.078

    1   I'm leaving this morning : with my clothes in my
        hand
    2   I won't stop to wandering : till I find my man
    3   I'm sitting here wondering : will a matchbox hold my
        clothes
    4   I've got a *sun to beat* : I'll be farther beyond
        the road
    5   I went up on the mountain : turned my face to the
        sky
    6   I heard the wind say : it said mama please don't die
    7   I turned around : looked into my right hand
    8   Well I looked there to see : if I was closer to my
        man
    9   Lord look a-yonder people : my love had been refused
    10 That's the reason why : mama's got the lost
        wandering blues

Rain   10   Rainey, Ma Gertrude

        title: Dream Blues
        place and date: Chicago, c. Mar. 1924
        record numbers: (1699-1) Pm-12098 BYG-529.078

    1   Had a dream last night : and the night before
    2   Going to get drunk now : I won't dream no more
    3   Lord I dreamed : my man didn't treat me right
    4   Packed my clothes in a ??? : and walked the streets
        all night
    5   Lord I saw my man : fall on his knees and cry
    6   Take me back mama : or else I'll die
    7   Lord I wonder : what am I to do
    8   When everybody : try to mistreat you
    9   My heart is aching : mama feel like crying

Rain   10   Rainey, Ma Gertrude

    10 Since I had that dream last night : mama don't mind
        dying

Rain   11   Rainey, Ma Gertrude

        title: Honey Where You Been So Long
        place and date: Chicago, c. Mar. 1924
        record numbers: (1701-2) Pm-12200 BYG-529.078

    1   My honey left me : he's gone away
    2   I've had the worried blues : all day
    3   My heart is aching : all for that man
    4   What makes me love him : I can't understand
    5   He'll soon be returning : and bad tidings he will
        bring
    6   Bad luck's *over* my house : ??? then begin to ???

Rain   12   Rainey, Ma Gertrude

        title: Ya-Da-Do
        place and date: Chicago, c. Mar. 1924
        record numbers: (1702-?) Pm-12257 BYG-529.078

    1   Every evening : about half past four
    2   Big piano playing : near my door

Rain   13   Rainey, Ma Gertrude

        title: Those Dogs of Mine
        place and date: Chicago, c. Mar. 1924
        record numbers: (1703-1) Pm-12215 BYG-529.078

    1   Oh Lord : these dogs of mine
    2   They sure do worry me : all the time
    3   The reason why : I don't know
    4   Sometimes I'm certain : it's the polio
    5   Lord : I beg to be excused
    6   I can't wear me : no *dark-toes* shoes

Rain   14   Rainey, Ma Gertrude

        title: Lucky Rock Blues
        place and date: Chicago, c. Mar. 1924
        record numbers: (1704-2) Pm-12215 BYG-529.078

    1   Going to New Orleans : to find that lucky rock
    2   *Find the* ??? : for this bad luck I've got
    3   I'm on my way : to find that lucky rock
    4   Just to ease my mind : of all this trouble I've got

Rain   15   Rainey, Ma Gertrude

        title: Jealous Hearted Blues
        place and date: New York, c. 15 Oct. 1924
        record numbers: (1924-2) Pm-12252 Mil MLP-2001

    1   You can have my money : everything I own
    2   But for God's sake : leave my man alone
    3   It takes a rocking chair to rock : a rubber ball to
        roll
    4   Takes a man I love : to satisfy my soul
    5   Yes I'm jealous jealous : jealous-hearted me
    6   Lord I'm just jealous : jealous as I can be
    7   Got a range in my kitchen : cooks nice and brown
    8   All I need is my man : to turn my damper down
    9   Going to buy me a bulldog : to watch me while I
        sleep
    10 To keep my man : from making his midnight creep

Rain 16   Rainey, Ma Gertrude

        title: Cell Bound Blues
        place and date: Chicago, c. Nov. 1924
        record numbers: (10001-2) Pm-12257 Mil MLP-2001

1   Hey jailor : tell me what have I done
2   You got me all bound in chains : because I killed
        that woman's son
3   I'm down in prison : all bound in chains
4   Cold and dark all around me : no one to go my bail
5   I've got a mother and father : they were never
        satisfied with me
6   Got a sister and brother : wonder do they think of
        poor me
7   I walked in my room : the other night
8   Some man walked in : and began to fight
9   I take my gun : in my right hand
10 Holy smokes : I don't know but I killed my man
11 When I did that : it crossed my head
12 First shot I fired : my man fell dead
13 The paper came out : and told the news
14 That's what I said : I got those cell bound blues

Rain 17   Rainey, Ma Gertrude

        title: Army Camp Harmony Blues
        place and date: Chicago, May 1925
        record numbers: (2136-1) Pm-12284 Mil MLP-2001

1   My man is leaving : crying won't make him stay
2   If crying do any good : I'd cry my poor self away
3   If I had wings : I'd fly all over the land
4   *When I look down* : I'd find my old-time man

Rain 18   Rainey, Ma Gertrude

        title: Explaining the Blues
        place and date: Chicago, May 1925
        record numbers: (2137-1) Pm-12284 Mil MLP-2001

1   Whole world would be forgived me : if I could just
        explain
2   The man I love has left me : because I called
        another man's name
3   Too sad to whisper : too broken-hearted to sing
4   *That mean crazy lover : the day I lost that real
        thing*
5   Explain why you left me : and tell me why you went
        away
6   I'll explain why I need you : and want you back
        today
7   I'm so alone without him : *ran away with some of
        the other bad news*
8   But I'll never be down-hearted : if I can explain
        these blues

Rain 19   Rainey, Ma Gertrude

        title: Rough and Tumble Blues
        place and date: Chicago, c. Aug. 1925
        record numbers: (2210-2) Pm-12311 Mil MLP-2001

1   I'm going to the Western Union : type the news all
        down the line
2   Because my man's on the Wabash : darling and I don't
        mind dying
3   My man is so good-looking : and his clothes fit him
        so cute
4   I cut off his mustache : and bought him a *Sunday*
        suit
5   A ??? little devil : got on my man's clothes
6   I wouldn't be so sore : hadn't've stole his
        drawers
7   ??? : I stepped in the door

Rain 19   Rainey, Ma Gertrude

8   He started *mauling* my man : ???ing down to the
        floor
9   *I got up* and killed three women : 'fore police got
        the news
10 Because my man's on the Wabash : with the rough and
        tumbling blues

Rain 20   Rainey, Ma Gertrude

        title: Night Time Blues
        place and date: Chicago, c. Aug. 1925
        record numbers: (2211-1) Pm-12303 Mil MLP-2001

1   Nighttime's falling : the day is almost dawned
2   My man leaves at midnight : don't come back till
        early morn
3   The night is dark and dreary : I can't see what to
        do
4   I wonder why he leaves me : to roar and cry the
        whole night through
5   Three o'clock in the morning : by the clock hanging
        on the wall
6   He used to come home at midnight : now he don't come
        home at all
7   When day starts to breaking : it seems to bring good
        news
8   But I'm just broken-hearted : trying to overcome
        these nighttime blues

Rain 21   Rainey, Ma Gertrude

        title: Four Day Honory Scat
        place and date: Chicago, c. Aug. 1925
        record numbers: (2213-1) Pm-12303 Mil MLP-2001

1   I have a man I can't control : I don't know what to
        do
2   My man left me two this morning : now he's trying to
        come back at noon
3   He got up and *packed his suit* : *said he was going
        along about nine*
4   I went to the fortuneteller to find my man : because
        he lays heavy on my mind
5   She said your man was on : that 'fore-day scat
6   And that's a different kind : of Maltese cat
7   Poor girl I know : your man has done you wrong
8   It's hard to tell : a man is long long gone
9   He left here riding : left on the Cannonball
10 He wasn't so handsome : and so long and tall
11 I want all you women : to spread the news
12 Want you to tell it : to who you choose

Rain 22   Rainey, Ma Gertrude

        title: Memphis Bound Blues
        place and date: Chicago, c. Aug. 1925
        record numbers: (2214-2) Pm-12311 Mil MLP-2001

1   You've got to drift to leave me : you're going to
        leave your home some day
2   You have got me ??? : and Memphis *is all I've got
        to say*
3   You can fly up high : you can ??? all alone
4   But when you get to love her : you got to come back
        to ???
5   Some *fool's* born with rickets : some *fool's* born
        with pain
6   But I'm here to tell you : when you leave me *all is
        the same*
7   I talk because I'm stubborn : I sing because I'm
        sick
8   My man is gone and left me : gone to Memphis
        Tennessee

Rain   23   Rainey, Ma Gertrude

        title: Slave to the Blues
        place and date: New York, Jan. 1926
        record numbers: (2369-2) Pm-12332 Mil MLP-2001

1   Ain't robbed no train : ain't done no hanging crime
2   It's that I'm a slave to the blues : even ??? that
    man of mine
3   Blues do tell me : do I have to die a slave
4   Do you hear me screaming : you're going to take me
    to my grave
5   If I could break these chains : and let my worried
    heart go free
6   Well it's too late now : the blues have made a slave
    of me
7   You see me raving : you hear me crying
8   Oh Lord : this wounded heart of mine
9   Folks I'm a-grieving : from my head to my shoes
10 I'm a good-hearted woman : but still I'm chained to
    the blues

Rain   24   Rainey, Ma Gertrude

        title: Bessemer Bound Blues
        place and date: New York, Jan. 1926
        record numbers: (2373-2) Pm-12374 Mil MLP-2001

1   Woke up this morning : looking for my darn old shoes
2   Because mama's going home : singing the Bessemer
    blues
3   Apple sugar papa : how come you do me like you do
4   I've done everything you asked me : trying to get
    along with you
5   I went in the water : walked through ice and snow
6   But from now on papa : I won't be your dog no more
7   *Electric all right : and* light shine nice and
    bright
8   But I'd rather be in Memphis : reading by a candle
    light

Rain   25   Rainey, Ma Gertrude

        title: Oh My Babe Blues
        place and date: New York, Jan. 1926
        record numbers: (2374-1) Pm-12332 Jo SM-3098

1   Tell my dad : I'm going to leave my home
2   Now I'm going I'm going : and it won't be long
3   Tell my dad : I won't be home tonight
4   My heart aches : said I'm not treated right
5   Lordy Lord : have mercy on poor me
6   Give me somebody : to let my heart go free
7   I'm leaving now : I'm sorry we have to part
8   Because you like : to break my aching heart

Rain   26   Rainey, Ma Gertrude

        title: Down in the Basement
        place and date: Chicago, c. Aug. 1926
        record numbers: (2627-1) Pm-12395 Jo SM-3098

1   I've got a man : he had a hound
2   Chase everything : that's going around
3   When he plays : that high brown stuff
4   I cry brother : that's enough
5   So take me to the basement : that's as low as I can
    go
6   I want something lowdown : daddy want it nice and
    slow
7   I will shimmy : from A to Z
8   If you'll play : that thing for me

Rain   27   Rainey, Ma Gertrude

        title: Trust No Man
        place and date: Chicago, c. Aug. 1926
        record numbers: (2631-1) Pm-12395 Jo SM-3098

1   I want all you women : to listen to me
2   Don't trust your man : no further than your eyes can
    see
3   I trusted my man : with my best friend
4   But that was a bad bargain : in the end
5   He'll say that he loves you : and swear that it's
    true
6   The very next minute : he'll turn his back on you
7   Just feed your daddy : with a long-handled spoon
8   Keep showing you love him : morning night and noon
9   Sometimes your heart will ache : and almost bust
10 That's why : there's no daddy good enough to trust
11 He'll stay with you in the winter : whilst your
    money is long
12 Come out in the summer : you'll find your pig will
    be gone

Rain   28   Rainey, Ma Gertrude

        title: Gone Daddy Blues
        place and date: Chicago, c. Aug. 1927
        record numbers: (4691-2) Pm-12526 Mil MLP-2001

1   I'm going away : I'm going to stay
2   I'll find a man : I love some day
3   I got my ticket : clothes in my hand
4   Trying to find : that southbound man
5   I'm going to ride : till I find that southbound man
6   Going to keep a-riding : till I shake hands with my
    man
7   I'm going away : I'm going to stay
8   I'll come back : for my daddy some day
9   I'm going away : I'm going to stay
10 I long for my daddy : somewhere

Rain   29   Rainey, Ma Gertrude

        title: Misery Blues
        place and date: Chicago, c. Aug. 1927
        record numbers: (4707-1) Pm-12508 Fwy FJ-2802

1   I love my brownskin : indeed I do
2   But there was no use : *tell me thing or two*
3   I'm going to tell you : what I went and done
4   I give him all my money : just to have some fun
5   He told me that he loved me : loved me so
6   If I would marry him : I needn't to work no more
7   Now I'm grieving : almost dying
8   Just because I didn't know : that he was lying
9   I've got to go to work now : get another start
10 Work is the thing : that's breaking my heart

Rain   30   Rainey, Ma Gertrude

        title: Slow Driving Moan
        place and date: Chicago, c. Aug. 1927
        record numbers: (4709-1) Pm-12526 Mil MLP-2001

1   I rambled till I'm tired : I'm not satisfied
2   Don't find my man : going to ramble till I die
3   Got the slow-driving blues : blue as I can be
4   Don't play that band Mr : just play the blues for me

Rain   31   Rainey, Ma Gertrude

      title: Black Eye Blues
      place and date: Chicago, c. Sept. 1928
      record numbers: (20898-2) Pm-12963 Yz L-1039

1 Take all my money : blacken both my eyes
2 Give it to another man : come home and tell me lies

Rame   1   Ramey, Ben (Memphis Jug Band)

      title: I Can't Stand It
      place and date: Memphis, 17 Sept. 1929
      record numbers: (55529-1) Vi-V38551 Rt RL-322

1 Now what are you going to do : when your supper get
   like mine
2 Take a mouthful of sugar : and drink a bottle of
   turpentine
3 You know the womens in the alley : they are playing
   cooncan
4 They do a whole lot of funny things : us men really
   cannot understand
5 And I went to my window : you know that window was
   blocked
6 Yes and I went to my door : and that sure were
   locked
7 My good gal come in this morning : about half past
   four
8 I say where have you been mama : been out selling
   sweet jellyroll

Rame   2   Ramey, Ben (Memphis Jug Band)

      title: Tired of You Driving Me
      place and date: Memphis, 3 Oct. 1929
      record numbers: (56344) Vi V38586 Rt RL-337

1 I woke up this morning : the crying blues on my mind
2 I done got to the place baby : that I hardly know my
   right mind
3 I'm tired of you driving me : I mean baby all the
   time
4 And if you want me to love you : you sure got to
   take you time
5 And if you don't want me baby : you don't have to
   pay me no mind
6 Because I done got tired of you driving me : ???ing
   me all the time

Rame   3   Ramey, Ben (Memphis Jug Band)

      title: Cocaine Habit Blues
      place and date: Memphis, 17 May 1930
      record numbers: (59933-2) Vi-V38620 BC-2

1   Cocaine habit : is mighty bad
2   It's the worst old habit : that I ever had
3   I went to Mr Lehman : in a lope
4   Saw a sign on the window : says no more dope
5   If you don't believe : cocaine is good
6   Ask Alma Rose : down in Minglewood
7   I love my whiskey : and I love my gin
8   But the way I love my coke : is a doggone sin
9   Since cocaine : went out of style
10 You can catch them shooting needles : all the while
11 It takes a little coke : to give me ease
12 Strut your stuff : long as you please

Rang   1   Ranger, Jack

      title: T. P. Window Blues
      place and date: San Antonio, 28 June 1929
      record numbers: (402768) OK-8785 Rt RL-315

1   I was leaning in my window : looking in my baby's
   door
2   She packed her trunk this morning : didn't know she
   was fixing to go
3   Well the T P's running : smoke settling on the
   ground
4   After the train was gone : couldn't find my easy
   rider around
5   I ain't got me no more no more : no more baby now
6   I didn't know my old pretty mama : to run me crazy
   now
7   Engineer man engineer man : please turn your train
   around
8   I want to speak one word to my baby : tell her she
   can heist her window down
9   I was standing in my door : reason I hear the T P
   when she blows
10 Taking my baby away : she ain't coming here no more

RedN   1   Red Nelson

      title: Crying Mother Blues
      place and date: Chicago, 4 Feb. 1936
      record numbers: (90597-A) De-7171 Br-87.504

1   Dear mother dead and gone to glory : my old dad done
   strayed away
2   Only way to meet my mother : I'm going to have to
   change my lowdown ways
3   Nobody knows my troubles : but myself and the good
   Lord
4   I used to have a sweet woman to love me : now she
   treats me like a lowdown dog
5   Tombstone's my pillow : graveyard going to be my bed
6   Blue sky's going to be my blanket : and the pale
   moon going to be my spread
7   Black cat crawls late hours at midnight : nightmares
   ride till the break of day
8   What the use of loving some woman : some man done
   stole your love away
9   Stop your crying : do away with all your tears
10 If you can't stay with me mother : it must have been
   your time to leave from here

RedN   2   Red Nelson

      title: Sweetest Thing Born
      place and date: Chicago, 6 Feb. 1936
      record numbers: (90605-A) De-7155 Cor CP-58

1   Says a married woman : sweetest thing ever been born
2   She would be most sweet and true to me : if I could
   go to her home
3   Blues and trouble : two things I've had all my life
4   I never had so much trouble : till I fell in love
   with another man's wife
5   What's the use of getting sober : know you're going
   to be drunk again
6   What's the use of leaving your mama : know you're
   going to beg back home again
7   She's so evil : baby you know you can't clown
8   Because you can't never tell : when your husband is
   around
9   Tell me what's the matter mama : can't see no mail
10 Post office on fire : mailman in jail
11 I'm going to call you one morning : please don't
   forget that day
12 If you can't do like I tell you : mama go on your
   no-good way

ReedW   1   Reed, Willie

        title: Dreaming Blues
        place and date: Dallas, 8 Dec. 1928
        record numbers: (147600-2) Co-14407-D Yz L-1004

1   I'm going to leave you : but I'll be back some old
        day
2   I'm going to make you remember : how you drove me
        away
3   Girl I lay down dreaming : woman I woke up crying
4   Since my bird dog fly away : poor girl is on my mind
5   Have you ever been accused mama : ain't done nothing
        wrong
6   That's the cause today : many people leave their
        homes
7   Sometime I think : my babe too sweet to die
8   Then again I think Lord : she ought to be buried
        alive
9   Excuse me mama : for knocking at your room
10 If I can't be your sweeper : let me be your broom
11 I followed Corrina : long as I could see
12 And that man had my woman : Lord and the blues had
        me

ReedW   2   Reed, Willie

        title: Texas Blues
        place and date: Dallas, 8 Dec. 1928
        record numbers: (147601-1) Co-14407-D Yz L-1010

1   I'm going out in West Texas : where you hear the
        wild ox moan
2   Till it moans so bad : till it make me leave my home
3   Lord pretty mama : what's the matter now
4   You know if you didn't want me : why didn't you
        leave me back in town
5   I'm going way out in West Texas : just to lie in the
        ???
6   Then I'm coming back down to Dallas : to run these
        women wild
7   You can read your schoolbook : and book on down
8   You can read my letter : but you sure can't read my
        mind
9   You can't never tell : when your woman going to put
        you down
10 She got a smile on her face : and a heart packed
        full of frowns
11 Take me pretty mama : try me one more time
12 If I don't treat you better : I'll break my neck
        a-trying
13 Said I laid down last night : my mind was rambling
        around
14 Thinking about my lover : she had done put me down

ReedW   3   Reed, Willie

        title: Leavin' Home
        place and date: Dallas, 5 Dec. 1929
        record numbers: (149544-1) Co unissued His
            HLP-17

1   I'm going to leave you : leaving some old day
2   Don't you worry mama : because I was carried away
3   Don't never take no woman : for to be your friend
4   It will be death and destruction : *may* ought to be
        your end
5   I was just sitting here a-wondering mama : about my
        used-to-be
6   I can see my lover : Lord but she can't see me
7   How can I love you : and you gone both night and day
8   Girl that's the very reason : I'm bound to jail
        today

ReyJ   1   Reynolds, Blind Joe

        title: Outside Woman Blues
        place and date: Grafton, Wis., c. Feb. 1930
        record numbers: (L-144-3) Pm-12927 OJL-8

1   When you lose your money : please God don't lose
        your mind
2   And when you lose your woman : please don't fool
        with mine
3   I'm going to buy me a bulldog : watch my old lady
        whilst I sleep
4   Because women these days is so doggone crooked :
        till they make a 'fore-day creep
5   Tell you married men : how to keep your wives at
        home
6   Just do a job roll for the man : and try to carry
        your labour home
7   Tell you married women : how to keep your husbands
        at home
8   You want to take care of the man's labour : and let
        these single boys alone
9   You can't watch your wife : and your outside woman
        too
10 While you're off with your woman : your wife could
        be at home beating you doing buddy what you trying
        to do

ReyJ   2   Reynolds, Blind Joe

        title: Nehi Blues
        place and date: Grafton, Wis., c. Feb. 1930
        record numbers: (L-146-2) Pm-12927 OJL-11

1   Some girls wear short dresses : some of these
        married women wear them too
2   That's the reason : we single men Lord don't know
        what we wants to do
3   Wish the proper judge : would make these women let
        their dresses down
4   So there'd quit being so doggone much : of murdering
        in town
5   When they pass the law : pulling the short dress
        down
6   So we single men : can tell a married woman from a
        child
7   Let me tell you boys : what these knee-high dresses
        will do
8   Get you broke naked and hungry : boys then come down
        on you
9   All of you [young] women : sure Lord ought to be
        ashamed
10 Taking these old men's money : when they walking on
        walking canes
11 A old man ain't nothing : but a young woman's slave
12 They work hard all the time : trying to stay in
        these young men's ways

ReyW   1   Reynolds, Blind Willie

        title: Married Man Blues
        place and date: Memphis, 26 Nov. 1930
        record numbers: (64721-2) Vi-23258 Yz L-1009

1   When you lose your money : please don't lose your
        mind
2   When you lose your woman : please don't fool with
        mine
3   Tell you married men : how to keep your wives at
        home
4   Get you a job and roll for the man : and try to
        carry your labour home
5   Tell you married women : how to keep your husband at
        home
6   Take care of your husband's labour : and let these
        single boys alone
7   What make a single woman : crazy about a married man

ReyW   1   Reynolds, Blind Willie

8   Because he works all the time : he puts money in her
    hand
9   What make a married woman : so crazy about a single
    man
10 Because the husband might lay down and die : and
    leave the fellow to her hand
11 Let me tell you men : what those married women will
    do
12 She will get your money : she will cat-curl up to
    you
13 Tell you this men : ain't going to tell you nothing
    else
14 Man's a fool : if he thinks he's got a whole woman
    by himself

ReyW   2   Reynolds, Blind Willie

        title: Third Street Woman Blues
        place and date: Memphis, 26 Nov. 1930
        record numbers: (64724-2) Vi-23258 OJL-11

1   Mmm : come my Third Street woman now
2   But the way she treats me : that's the coldest stuff
    in town
3   I had so much chicken : till I heard her clucking in
    my sleep
4   Now it's don't like my 'taters : mama please don't
    dig so deep
5   She's a big fat mama : with the meat shaking on her
    bones
6   And every time she shake it : Lord a hustling woman
    lose her home
7   She got something : that the men call a stingaree
8   Four o'clock every morning : she turn it loose on me
9   Mmm : where my Third Street woman gone
10 Believe to my soul : she will hustle everywhere but
    home
11 If you can't do my rolling mama : you can't spend my
    change

RhoW   1   Rhodes, Walter

        title: The Crowing Rooster
        place and date: Memphis, 10 Dec. 1927
        record numbers: (145358-2) Co-14289-D Rt RL-334

1   Going to buy me a rooster : put him in my back door
2   See a stranger coming : he'll flap his wings and
    crow
3   What you want with a rooster : he won't crow 'fore
    day
4   What you want with a woman : won't do nothing she
    say
5   What you want with a hen : won't cackle when she lay
6   What you want with a man : won't do nothing he say
7   Going to take my picture : hang it up against the
    wall
8   And if I ask you what about it : daddy that's all
    that's all
9   I'll take my picture : put it in a frame
10 So if I die : you can see me just the same
11 I know my dog : anywhere I hear him bark
12 I can tell my baby : if I see her in the dark

RhoW   2   Rhodes, Walter

        title: Leaving Home Blues
        place and date: Memphis, 10 Dec. 1927
        record numbers: (145359-2) Co-14289-D Rt RL-334

1   Well I dreamt a dream : I never dreamt before
2   Dreamt my baby told me : that I couldn't be
    talking no more
3   I lay down happy : woke up this morning crying

RhoW   2   Rhodes, Walter

4   I didn't have no blues : but I was just dissatisfied
5   I know my baby : sure don't know if I'm here
6   Well if she did : she would surely feel my care
7   Well I wonder : will my suitcase hold my clothes
8   I ain't got so many : but I got so far to go
9   Well my mama's dead : and my papa went to sea
10 Oh the life I'm living : oh and it's killing me
11 Well you used to know me : but you just don't know
    me now
13 My mama told me : and papa told me too
14 Well the life you're living : honey'll be the death
    of you

RichM   1   Richardson, Mooch

        title: T and T Blues
        place and date: Memphis, 13 Feb. 1928
        record numbers: (400213-B) OK-8554 Mam S-3803

1   Will you iron my jumper : yes and starch my overalls
2   Lord if I miss the Two-Nineteen : I'm surely can't
    catch the Cannonball
3   Well a brownskin woman : sure can get anything I got
4   But a jet-black woman I got a letter from : throw it
    in my back yard
5   Well it's T for Texas Lord : I got a T for Tennessee
6   Know I got a T for the best girl I love : Lord she
    stay right in Memphis Tennessee
7   Well I'm going away brownskin : I ain't going to
    come back here before next fall
8   If I don't get me no good brown : I ain't coming
    back in this town at all
9   Well the sun is going down : got mighty lonesome
    here
10 But I ain't got me nobody : I'm sleeping every night
    just by myself

RichM   2   Richardson, Mooch

        title: Mooch Richardson's Low Down Barrel House
        Blues Part 1
        place and date: Memphis, 13 Feb. 1928
        record numbers: (400215-A) OK-8554 Mam S-3803

1   I got something : some people call it worse than
    blues
2   It must be : the lowdown dirty barrelhouse blues I
    got
3   I'd rather see you dead : straight down in your
    grave
4   To see you give another man : Lord my *roof* and
    plate
5   Know my faro got something : mens all call it
    stingaree
6   Reason I know it isn't : tell no lie she have rolled
    that same thing down on me
7   Well I went to the nation : Lord I thought I'd fall
    Lord and die
8   *Sitting by the* ??? Lord :

RichM   3   Richardson, Mooch

        title: Burying Ground Blues
        place and date: Memphis, 23 Mar. 1928
        record numbers: (400375-A) OK-8576 Mam S-3803

1   Well I went up on the mountain : give my horn a blow
2   Thought I hear my true lover : say yonder come my
    beau
3   Oh ten thousand people : was around her burying
    ground
4   For to hear that elder say : for the laying her body
    down

RichM   3   Richardson, Mooch

    5 I follow her all the way : down to the burying
       ground
    6 I come back to my home : I's about to overboard and
       drown
    7 Bad luck in my family : all done fell on me
    8 It made me think about : going way across the sea
    9 I asked my captain : for to give me his best pair of
       shoes
   10 For I'm barefoot I ain't got nothing to wear Lord :
       I don't know what to do
   11 He told me he had a hole in his side : I don't
       expect he would do
   12 Lord these ain't like the shoes I got on the gutter
       : hole right in the bottom

RobB   1   Robinson, Bob (The Hokum Boys)

        title: Selling That Stuff
        place and date: Chicago, c. Dec. 1928
        record numbers: (21035-3) Pm-12714 Riv RM-8803

    1 Aunt Jane gave a dance : and she had a crowd
    2 And she sold more whiskey : than the law allowed
    3 Aunt Jane stayed out : all night long
    4 Didn't go home : till the break of dawn
    5 Took Aunt Jane : to the county jail
    6 She didn't need nothing : to go her bail
    7 She sold some corn : and she sold some gin
    8 She sold it to the women : and she sold it to the
       men
    9 Uncle Jim went to jail : with a heavy load
   10 They gave him thirty days : on the county road
   11 Aunt Jane got a sister : and her name is Lil
   12 She used to sell stuff : and she sells it still

RobB   2   Robinson, Bob (The Hokum Boys)

        title: Beedle Um Bum
        place and date: Chicago, c. Dec. 1928
        record numbers: (21036-2) Pm-12714 Riv RM-8803

    1 It'll make a dumb man speak : make a lame man run
    2 Sure miss something : if you don't get some
    3 It ain't made small : and it ain't made wide
    4 It's just made up : in a medium size
    5 Now you don't have to hurry : you don't have to go
    6 You get a little taste : you'll want some more

RolW   1   Roland, Walter

        title: T Model Blues
        place and date: New York, 17 July 1933
        record numbers: (13552-1) Ba-32932 Yz L-1017

    1 Said it's mmm baby : mmm baby mmm
    2 Say you know you do not love me : like I say I love
       you
    3 Say you know these here women : sure do treat me
       mean
    4 You know I ask one for a drink of water : she give
       me gasoline
    5 Says mmm baby : you won't do nothing you say
    6 You know you told me you love me : but what about
       that man I seed you with the other day
    7 These here women what called theirselves a Cadillac
       : ought to be a T Model Ford
    8 You know they got the shape all right : but they
       can't carry no heavy load
    9 Says you know I'm going to sing this here verse now
       : ain't going to sing no more
   10 Because you know I'm got to go home and ??? my old
       lady : because she won't come back no more

RolW   2   Roland, Walter

        title: Dices' Blues
        place and date: New York, 30 July 1934
        record numbers: (15485-2) Ba-33343 RBF RF-12

    1 Yes you know dices oh dices : please don't three on
       me
    2 You know says I'm just as broke and hungry : as any
       gambler ought to be
    3 Says my woman give me money : just to play *good*
       jack
    4 I didn't win no money : but great God you know I
       played my hand
    5 Says I went down in Louisiana : says you know down
       on that farm
    6 If I win any money : sure going to bring it home
    7 Says you know I gambled yesterday : and I gambled
       again today
    8 But you know if I don't win tomorrow : I'm going to
       throw my cards away
    9 Says you know I'm going to gamble : because you know
       I gamble all the time
   10 But you know says I've got to win some money : so I
       can give it to that gal of mine

RolW   3   Roland, Walter

        title: Early in the Morning No. 2
        place and date: New York, 31 July 1934
        record numbers: (15495-2) Ba-33343 Yz L-1017

    1 Says me and my good girl : we had a falling out
    2 And I bet you men can tell me : what it's all about
    3 We fell out early in the morning : baby about the
       break of day
    4 And I turned over and hugged the pillow : where my
       baby used to lay
    5 I says go get your hat baby : let's go in the woods
    6 If you can't go now : please ma'am tell me when you
       could
    7 She say I go early in the morning : baby about the
       break of day
    8 Then I turn over and hug the pillow : where my baby
       used to lay
    9 You know I got me a woman now : they call her Aunt
       Kate
   10 I told her to come to my house tonight : about half
       past eight
   11 She said she'd be there early in the morning : baby
       about the break of day
   12 Then I turned over and hugged the pillow : where my
       baby used to lay
   13 You know a girl get twelve years old : she thinks
       she's grown
   14 You never can catch : that kind of girl at home
   15 Unless you go there early in the morning : baby
       about the break of day
   16 Then I turned over and hugged the pillow : where my
       baby used to lay
   17 I'm going to sing this verse now : ain't going to
       sing no more
   18 I want to see my good girl : and I think I'll better
       go
   19 Before it get early in the morning : baby about the
       break of day
   20 Then I turn over and hug the pillow : where my baby
       used to lay

RolW   4   Roland, Walter

        title: Big Mama
        place and date: New York, 2 Aug. 1934
        record numbers: (15520-2) Ba-33282 RBF RF-12

    1 She got them great big legs : she got the walking
       size

RolW   4   Roland, Walter

2 And every time she leave me : you know it makes me
   cry
3 Every time she calls me : you know she makes me mad
4 But I ain't never told her : about the man she had
5 You know she make me [awful] mad : when she calls my
   name
6 But you know I never told her : she could not shake
   that thing

RolW   5   Roland, Walter

   title: Every Morning Blues
   place and date: New York, 2 Aug. 1934
   record numbers: (15521-2) Ba-33282 BC-7

1 Says every morning every morning : I wakes with the
   rising sun
2 Says won't you run here pretty mama : see what your
   man have done
3 I said take me back baby : I won't be bad no more
4 Says I give you my money : if you let that other man
   go
5 I said don't take my money : then try to dog me
   around
6 Because if you do : I'm going to tear you playhouse
   down
7 Says I ain't going to give you no more money : ain't
   going to let you do me wrong
8 For you would take my money : then you will slip on
   home

RolW   6   Roland, Walter

   title: 45 Pistol Blues
   place and date: New York, 14 Mar. 1935
   record numbers: (17081-2) ARC-6-03-61 BC-7

1 I'm going over to Third Alley : Lord but I'm going
   to carry my forty-five
2 Because you know ain't many men : goes there and
   comes back alive
3 They will shoot you and cut you : Lord they will
   knock you down
4 And you can ask anybody : ain't that the baddest
   place in town
5 Mens carry thirty-eights : womens carry their razors
   too
6 And you know you better not start nothing : know
   they'll make away with you
7 Says I ain't going to Third Alley no more : unless I
   change my mind
8 Because you know I done got shot once over there :
   Lord it's about three or four times

RolW   7   Roland, Walter

   title: Penniless Blues
   place and date: New York, 20 Mar. 1935
   record numbers: (17153-2) Ba-33461 Yz L-1017

1 I been blue all night : what is I going to do
2 You know the reason I'm that a-way : Lord I'm broke
   and hungry too
3 You know my woman left me : Lord when I wasn't
   feeling well
4 You know said living with that woman : Lord it is
   just like living in hell
5 I ain't got no money : not a penny can I show
6 And you know folks that's the reason : Lord that I'm
   worried so
7 You know I let that woman tote my money : Lord in a
   jomo sack
8 And you know it's going to be some hell raised :
   Lord if she don't bring some of my money back

RupO   1   Rupert, Ollie

   title: I Raised My Window and Looked at the
   Risin' Sun
   place and date: Memphis, 28 Feb. 1927
   record numbers: (37963-2) Vi-20577 Rt RL-323

1 Lord early one morning : just about the break of day
2 A passenger train : carried my man away
3 I raised my window : looked at the rising sun
4 Nobody else can love me : just like my good man done
5 I'm standing on the railroad : looking north and
   south
6 I couldn't see my good man : who done put me out
7 Far down the railroad : far as I could see
8 Look like I can see my good man : coming back to me
9 Now papa : what you want me to do
10 I did everything in this world : trying to get along
   with you
11 When I had you pretty papa : you was blind and could
   not see
12 When I quit you pretty papa : don't bring your blues
   to me
13 Have you ever been accused : when you ain't done
   nothing wrong
14 It's a hard-driving papa : just as sure as you born

RupO   2   Rupert, Ollie

   title: Ain't Goin' to Be Your Low Down Dog
   place and date: Memphis, 28 Feb. 1927
   record numbers: (37964-2) Vi-20577 Rt RL-323

1 I'm going to buy me a mansion : out on Bunker Hill
2 Where I can get my whiskey : get it right from the
   still
3 Out on Bunker Hill : where the peoples have their
   fun
4 Where they lay out on the green grass : and look up
   at the sun
5 I been your dog : every since I been your gal
6 You know I love you pretty papa : love you each and
   everywhere
7 Now pretty papa : what you want me to do
8 I did everything in this world : trying to get along
   with you
9 Going to write a letter : going to mail it in the
   air
10 When the north wind blows : blows news everywhere

Scha   1   Schaffer, Ed (Shreveport Home Wreckers)

   title: Fence Breakin' Blues
   place and date: Memphis, 21 May 1930
   record numbers: (59965-2) Vi-23275 Yz L-1026

1 Lord I'm going to start a-rambling : ain't going to
   stop mama from raising sand
2 Lord I'm going to thrill my baby : just like I ain't
   got no sense
3 Tell me baby : what's the matter now
4 Oh you trying to leave me : and you don't know how
5 Mmm : babe will come back home to you
6 Oh I'm coming right back babe : now that child's
   done roamed
7 Lord I don't know what to do baby : I can't get
   along with you
8 Now you may treat me right babe : that's all I can
   do

Scha   2   Schaffer, Ed (Shreveport Home Wreckers)

        title: Home Wreckin' Blues
        place and date: Memphis, 21 May 1930
        record numbers: (59966-2) Vi-23275 Rt RL-313

1   Oh tell me baby : the way back to your town
2   The reason I'm asking : because I got to go
3   Mmm : what's the matter now
4   My good girl done quit me : sure have got to go
5   Mmm : ain't going to sing no more
6   I'm going to leave from here baby : ain't coming
    back no more

ScotS   1   Scott, Sonny

        title: Red Cross Blues
        place and date: New York, 18 July 1933
        record numbers: (13572-1) Vo-25012 Rt RL-325

1   Let me tell you : what the what the Red Cross people
    will do
2   ??? *on King Street* : down on Third Avenue
3   I told them no : baby I don't want to go
4   You know I can't go down the hill : but I've got to
    go to the Red Cross store
5   Go to the Red Cross in the morning babe : go up
    there at night
6   Want me to tell the Red Cross : stop off day and
    night
7   Now my girl told me this morning : that she done
    collared a job
8   She going to take care of me : while the times was
    hard
9   And I told her yes : great God now I won't have to
    go
10 Because I can't go down the hill : you know I go to
    the Red Cross store
11 I works on the mountain : till my shirt got soaking
    wet
12 I don't want no foolishness : about my Red Cross
    check
13 Well I saw two women : they was arguing on the
    street
14 They asked me I go down to the Red Cross store : to
    get them to give me something to eat
15 And I told her yes : great God and you better go
16 Because I can't take you down the hill : but I'll
    show you to the Red Cross store

Scru   1   Scruggs, Irene

        title: My Back to the Wall
        place and date: Richmond, Ind., 30 Aug. 1930
        record numbers: (16975-A) Ge-7296 Yz L-1026

1   Everybody is screaming trouble : times ain't like
    they used to be
2   You can hardly hold your man : your job is uncertain
    guarantee
3   Well hard luck had me running : now my back is
    turned to the wall
4   But no matter what you say : a good woman never
    falls
5   Well you talk about drunken women : the kind that
    walks the streets all night
6   But that's the only kind of woman : that you men are
    going to treat right
7   So don't be no idle woman : don't be no sand-foot
    clown
8   If your man is double-crossing : don't you start to
    running around
9   Now I'll tell you the reason : I don't like a single
    man much
10 Well a single man's all right : but he ain't got
    that married man's touch

Shad   1   Shade, Will (Memphis Jug Band)

        title: Sometimes I Think I Love You
        place and date: Chicago, 9 June 1927
        record numbers: (38657-1) Vi-20809 OJL-19

1   Hey sometime I think I love you : then again I don't
2   Sometime I think I'll quit you : mama then again I
    won't
3   Says I beat it for you baby : when I needed shoes on
    my feet
4   All I know that she was doing partner : making her
    'fore-day creep
5   Hey baby : what do you want your papa to do
6   Want for me to beg rob and steal : bring it all home
    to you

Shad   2   Shade, Will (Memphis Jug Band)

        title: Memphis Boy--Blues
        place and date: Chicago, 9 June 1927
        record numbers: (38659-1) Vi-20809 Rt RL-337

1   Going out west partner : going to marry me an Indian
    squaw
2   That dirty big chief Indian : Lord can be my
    father-in-law
3   Say I'm a poor boy partner : and I ain't got no
    relation here
4   Say I ain't got no good woman : partner for to feel
    my care
5   Hey pretty mama : honey what you got on your mind
6   Lord I ain't going to stay with no woman : Lord no
    great long time

Shad   3   Shade, Will (Memphis Jug Band)

        title: I Packed My Suitcase, Started to the
        Train
        place and date: Atlanta, 19 Oct. 1927
        record numbers: (40312-1) Vi-21412 Rt RL-311

1   Hey black folks is evil : do anything that you want
    to do
2   *So long as I can get* ??? : *get back out of you*
3   I did more for you baby : mama in the rain and snow
4   But I'm sick and tired now baby : you say you don't
    want me no more
5   I packed my suitcase : Lord I started to the train
6   I wouldn't hurt so bad mama : but you had another
    man just the same

Shad   4   Shade, Will (Memphis Jug Band)

        title: State of Tennessee
        place and date: Atlanta, 19 Oct. 1927
        record numbers: (40313-2) Vi-21185 Rt RL-322

1   I got a voice like a radio : it broadcasts
    everywhere
2   Now if you can find the wild woman : boy by
    broadcasting in the air
3   I got a new way of spelling : dear old state of
    Tennessee
4   Double E double R : double E double N O P

Shad   5   Shade, Will (Memphis Jug Band)

        title: Kansas City Blues
        place and date: Atlanta, 19 Oct. 1927
        record numbers: (40315-1) Vi-21185 Rt RL-307

1   Boy I got three high yellows : one black and brown
2   High yellow quit me : black ain't going to throw me
    down

Shad   5   Shade, Will (Memphis Jug Band)

3 And you can always tell : when a woman want to play
4 It don't make any difference : in a ???
5 Hey mama mama : where you stay last night
6 Your hair's all wrinkled : that they beating you
   right

Shad   6   Shade, Will (Memphis Jug Band)

     title: Evergreen Money Blues
     place and date: Memphis, 1 Feb. 1928
     record numbers: (41818-2) Vi-21657 Rt RL-310

1 I been drinking all night long baby : mama I ain't
   going to drink no more
2 My good gal said if you drink any more corn liquor :
   how she don't want me no more
3 I'll pack your suitcase mama : I will throw it over
   the fence
4 I allow you don't need no telling baby : mama
   because you got plenty of sense
5 I told you stay away from my window baby : mama
   don't knock at my old back door
6 I allow you don't need no telling mama : babe
   because you already know

Shad   7   Shade, Will (Memphis Jug Band)

     title: She Stays Out All Night Long
     place and date: Memphis, 13 Feb. 1928
     record numbers: (41891-1) Vi unissued RCA
        INT-1175

1 Lord I told my old lady : no longer than week before
   last
2 *I told* when I staying all night long baby : mama
   it's done come *to pass*
3 How do you think a poor man feels : one he loves
   stay out all night long
4 Oh Lord he's rolling and he's tumbling : know he
   just can't sleep alone
5 How you think a poor man feels : one he loves stays
   out both night and day
6 Just like a hobo on a freight train : haven't a
   decent meal today

Shad   8   Shade, Will (Memphis Jug Band)

     title: She Stays Out All Night Long
     place and date: Memphis, 13 Feb. 1928
     record numbers: (41891-2) Vi-21524 Rt RL-322

1 I told my old lady : no longer than the week before
   last
2 *I told* when I'm staying all night long mama : Lord
   it's going to the *pass*
3 How can a poor man sleep : Lord when the one he
   loves stays out all night long
4 Now Lord he's rolling and he's tumbling : know he
   just can't sleep alone
5 Lord how can a poor man feel : one he loves stays
   out all night long

Shad   9   Shade, Will (Memphis Jug Band)

     title: A Black Woman Is Like a Black Snake
     place and date: Memphis, 11 Sept. 1928
     record numbers: (47010-2) Vi-V38015 Rt RL-322

1 A black woman is like a black snake : she will
   strike and run
2 ??? : *to give his dollar fun*
3 Now I wouldn't marry a black woman : I'll tell you
   the reason why

Shad   9   Shade, Will (Memphis Jug Band)

4 Because a black girl's evil : ???

Shad   10   Shade, Will (Memphis Jug Band)

     title: On the Road Again
     place and date: Memphis, 11 Sept. 1928
     record numbers: (47011-1) Vi-V38015 OJL-19

1 I wouldn't want a black woman : tell you the reason
   why
2 Black woman's evil : do things on the sly
3 You look for your supper : to be good and hot
4 The nigger put a neckbone : in the pot
5 I went to my window : my window was stuck
6 I went to my door : my door was locked
7 I stepped right back : I shook my head
8 A big black nigger : in my folding bed
9 I shot through the window : I broke the glass
10 I never seen a nigger : run so fast
11 Your friend come to your house : wife ask him to
   rest his hat
12 The next thing he'll want to know : where is your
   husband at
13 She says I don't know : he's gone and went to the
   'gin
14 Come on mama : let's get on the road again

Shad   11   Shade, Will (Memphis Jug Band)

     title: Whitewash Station Blues
     place and date: Memphis, 15 Sept. 1928
     record numbers: (47036-2) Vi-V38504 Rt RL-337

1 You can toot your whistle : blow your horn
2 The Memphis Jug Band : done been here and gone
3 Now if you want to get to heaven : I'll tell you
   what to do
4 You put on a sock : a boot and a shoe
5 You place a little corn : in your right hand
6 That'll pass you right over : in the Promised Land
7 And if you meet the devil : he ask you how you do
8 I'm on my way to heaven : don't you want to go too
9 Know there's a place : that do just as well
10 They call Whitewash Station : ten miles from hell
11 Lord mama : what's on your mind
12 You keep me worried : and bothered all the time
13 Ain't got no stockings : ain't got no shoes
14 Know I've got : the Memphis Jug Band blues

Shad   12   Shade, Will (Memphis Jug Band)

     title: Stealin' Stealin'
     place and date: Memphis, 15 Sept. 1928
     record numbers: (47037-2) Vi-V38504 Rt RL-337

1 Stealing stealing : pretty mama don't you tell on me
2 I'm stealing back : to my same old used-to-be
3 Now put your arms around me : like the circle around
   the sun
4 I want you to love me mama : like my easy rider done
5 If you don't believe I love you : look what a fool
   I've been
6 If you don't believe I'm sinking : look what a hole
   I'm in
7 The woman I'm loving : she's just my height and size
8 She's a married woman : come to see me sometime

Shad 13   Shade, Will

         title: Better Leave That Stuff Alone
         place and date: Memphis, 24 Sept. 1928
         record numbers: (47092-) Vi-21725 Mam S-3803

1 People across the water : they're crying for meat
      and bread
2 And the womens down on Beale Street : crying for
      that old canned heat every day
3 I give my woman a dollar : to get her something to
      eat
4 She spent a dime for neckbones : and ninety cents
      for that old canned heat
5 If your woman says she don't drink corn liquor :
      don't think she's nice and sweet
6 If she don't drink that old corn liquor : then your
      partner must drink the old canned heat
7 Now just look what a difference : a little money can
      buy
8 Before a woman spend fifty cents on corn liquor :
      she'll buy that bottle of canned heat on the sly
9 Canned heat is just like morphine : it crawls all
      through your bones
10 And if you keep on using canned heat mama : you soon
      get to the place you just can't leave it alone
11 When you catch your woman begging nickels and dimes
      : all up and down the street
12 She's only hustling them people : to get that stuff
      they call that old canned heat

Shad 14   Shade, Will (Memphis Jug Band)

         title: What's the Matter?
         place and date: Memphis, 17 Sept. 1929
         record numbers: (55530-2) Vi-V38551 Jo SM-3104

1 Now yonder comes baby : he's coming down the street
2 He going to knock you back : like Mr ???
3 There was old lady *Linus* : she was sitting on a
      rock
4 Had a forty-dollar razor : trying to shave that knot
5 Yes my mother told me : father told me too
6 Son that thing in Memphis : going to be the death of
      you
7 I'm going to chew my bacca : I'm going to spit my
      juice
8 I'm going to save my thing : for my particular use
9 Yes my *cola* lady rose : about half past four
10 Son you don't mean me no good : *I bet they* use you
      no more
11 I went down on the dike : about half past four
12 I seen two bullfrogs : doing the *cold down low*

Shad 15   Shade, Will (Memphis Jug Band)

         title: Feed Your Friend with a Long Handled
            Spoon
         place and date: Memphis, 27 Sept. 1929
         record numbers: (55598-1) Vi-V38578 Rt RL-311

1 Boy my mother always taught me : to learn to feed my
      friends with a long-handled spoon
2 She said son if you feed them with a short one :
      Lord they will soon lose friendship with you
3 Lord they will even laugh and grin in your face :
      Lord they don't mean you no good
4 And if you don't keep your eyes dead on them : Lord
      they will take your woman from you
5 Yes I'm going to taught my woman : don't never let a
      ??? at home
6 If you should ever let him get there baby : he'll
      give you more trouble than the day is long
7 I did something last winter : Lord I ain't going to
      do it no more
8 I quit a thousand dollar woman : *but it wasn't
      worth* ???

Shad 16   Shade, Will (Memphis Jug Band)

         title: I Can Beat You Plenty
         place and date: Memphis, 27 Sept. 1929
         record numbers: (55599-) Vi-V38586 Rt RL-337

1 Now if you ever go down south : go down in Dixieland
2 Don't forget : the Memphis Jug Band
3 You better hide : mama you better hide from me
4 I can beat you playing that hand : mama you tried to
      deal to me
5 I told my old lady : so long *as poker* last
6 If I gets on Beale Street : then mama things will
      come to pass
7 Now the preacher will come to your house : your wife
      will ask him to rest his hat
8 Next thing he want to know : lady where is your
      husband at
9 She say I don't know : I think he gone to jail
10 Oh well it's come on mama : and let me go his bail
11 Going to ask that black gal : won't you give me some
12 Said she told me to wait : until tomorrow come
13 Will tomorrow come : before I change my mind
14 And I looked around : her man was standing around
15 I'm going on ??? : I'm going to raise my hand
16 I am looking for the woman : that ain't got no man

Shad 17   Shade, Will (Memphis Jug Band)

         title: Taking Your Place
         place and date: Memphis, 3 Oct. 1929
         record numbers: (56343) Vi-23347 Jo SM-3104

1 Now tell me baby : how come you do me this a-way
2 Oh you go off to stay in the morning : and you stays
      all day
3 I love you baby : I didn't know that you would do me
      this a-way
4 How how can I love you mama : when you goes on the
      street always
5 Now you done drove me baby : until you drove me away
6 Now someone has done something mama : about to take
      your place

Shad 18   Shade, Will (Memphis Jug Band)

         title: Jim Strainer
         place and date: Memphis, 21 May 1930
         record numbers: (59961-2) Vi-23421 Rt RL-337

1 Oh Jim Strainer told Lula : on a Friday night
2 Lula if I catch you with the Willie : Lula I'm going
      to steal you life
3 Oh roll Mr hearseman : Mr hearseman roll slow
4 I want to see the last of poor Lula : Mr hearseman
      before you go
5 I followed poor Lula : Lord to that burying ground
6 I stood and watched the graveyard diggers : ease
      poor Lula down
7 I never have seen : Lord such a sight before
8 When Jim Strainer killed poor Lula : it was on that
      barroom floor
9 Lord poor Willie left here laughing : poor Jim left
      here crying
10 Willie got fifteen years : poor Jim got ninety-nine
11 I'm singing this tune : I ain't going to [play,
      pick] it no more
12 Jim Strainer killed poor Lula : I'm booked out and
      bound to go

Shad   19   Shade, Will (Memphis Jug Band)

      title: Mary Anna Cut Off
      place and date: Chicago, 6 Nov. 1934
      record numbers: (C-780-2) OK-8960 Jo SM-3104

1 I'm going Mary Anna : I'm riding that old engineer
2 When I come by : sweet babe will ???
3 Going to start walking : I've even got a new bottle
   of booze
4 Ain't going to stop walking : until I lose those
   Mary Anna blues
5 Engineer blow his whistle : and the fireman ring his
   bell
6 She poked her head out the window : daddy fare you
   well
7 She's a long tall woman : she's got teeth they shine
   like gold
8 Only woman in Mary Anna : done got a mortgage on my
   soul
9 Going to Mary Anna : if I have to ride the rods
10 I'm going to see that black gal : boys so help me
   God

Shad   20   Shade, Will (Memphis Jug Band)

      title: Take Your Fingers Off It
      place and date: Chicago, 7 Nov. 1934
      record numbers: (C-793-) Vo-03175 Jo SM-3104

1 Sometimes I walk : with my ???
2 I wouldn't stay here : but I can't take off
3 I'm going to tell everybody : in the neighborhood
4 I got a gal : who treats me good
5 ??? : ???
6 I'm going : I'm getting loose
7 Old Aunt Anna : long and tall
8 Her feets in the kitchen : her head's in the hall

Shad   21   Shade, Will (Memphis Jug Band)

      title: She Done Sold It Out
      place and date: Chicago, 7 Nov. 1934
      record numbers: (C-800-1) OK-8963 RBF RF-6

1 You know I had a gal : she run a java shop
2 I asked her how about it : not a crust in that shop
3 You know a man walked in : say have you any eggs
4 Say I'll sell you some meat : if you furnish your
   bread
5 Now the butcher's in the market : they begin to pout
6 She sold all their meat : and the butchers could not
   sell out
7 You know they taken me 'fore the judge : the judge
   asked me what is your name
8 Cooncan Suzie : and my mother was to blame
9 You know the judge said little girl : you know
   you're rather bold
10 You can sell me some meat : just before you go
11 I'm going to the races : see my pony run
12 I believe I can find something : just begun

Shaw   1   Shaw, Allen (Hattie Hart)

      title: Coldest Stuff in Town
      place and date: New York, 14 Sept. 1934
      record numbers: (15952-) Vo-02821 Yz L-1021

1 Hattie Hattie Hattie : what have you done to me
2 I believe to my soul : you got a doggone stingaree
3 My name is Rex : I lives down the west
4 Don't want to be tangled up : in that nest
5 Another drink Hattie : pass the bottle around
6 Because that jive you and Willie B's shooting :
   coldest stuff in town

Shaw   2   Shaw, Allen

      title: I Couldn't Help It
      place and date: New York, 17 Sept. 1934
      record numbers: (15967-1) Vo-02844 OJL-21

1 Well I got up this morning : feeling bad
2 Thinking about the times : that I once have had
3 Well it ain't but the one thing : can grieve my mind
4 All of these women : ain't nar' one mine
5 Well I whips my woman : with a singletree
6 You might've heard her holler : don't you murder me
7 Mama told me : papa told me too
8 Never let a woman : make a fool of you
9 Well I woke up this morning : feeling blue
10 Thinking about : no other one but you
11 Well mama told me : papa too
12 The way you got : it's going to be the ruin of you

Shaw   3   Shaw, Allen

      title: Moanin' the Blues
      place and date: New York, 18 Sept. 1934
      record numbers: (15978-1) Vo-02844 Yz L-1002

1 When I woke up this morning : mama's feeling bad
2 Got to thinking : about the time I once have had
3 Now if you don't want me : why don't you tell me so
4 I can get a woman : anywhere I go
5 Lord I asked the judge : what should be my fine
6 Said eleven twenty-nine : and fifty dollar fine
7 Yes I asked the judge : to be easy as you can
8 That's all I want : you to send me from the pen
9 Ever since : my mother has been dead
10 Been trouble : since I have jumped and caught my
   head
12 Crying mmm : don't nobody know

Shor   1   Short, Jaydee

      title: Telephone Arguin' Blues
      place and date: Grafton, Wis., c. 1 June 1930
      record numbers: (L-456-1) Pm-13043 OJL-11

1 There's so many people : arguing on the telegram
2 This thought have run through my head : just like a
   stone in sand
3 Hello Central : please give me five oh nine
4 I just want to talk : to that old-time gal of mine
5 Hey arguing : arguing everywhere
6 I can't get no message : over the phone nowhere I go
7 Mmm baby : when can I speak to you
8 If you don't talk to me soon : baby I don't know
   what I'm going to do
9 I picked up the receiver : I could not get a word
10 I want to talk to my home : from this sad New York
   land
11 I'm asking you a question : mama asking you very
   clear
12 And if *all things true* : man I'm going to leave on
   the ???
13 Mmm ain't seen my baby : in six long months today
14 Some woman love I used to have : gone seen my babe
   some day

Shor   2   Short, Jaydee

      title: Lonesome Swamp Rattlesnake
      place and date: Grafton, Wis., c. 1 June 1930
      record numbers: (L-468-1) Pm-13043 OJL-11

1 Way lonesome : out in some swamp I know
2 Well the lonesome rattlesnake : just creeped up to
   my door
3 You ought to heard my baby hollering : daddy won't
   you come home

4   Better be on your way : the rattlesnake's about to take your home
5   That's all right baby : I won't leave you here no more
6   For that creeping rattlesnake : done crawled up to my door
7   Walking along : and ain't doing a thing
8   I met a rattlesnake : oh baby at last
9   I can't travel honey : night or day
10 Lord these rattlesnakes traveling : won't let me get away
11 Creeping rattlesnakes : done crawled around my bed
12 And it loved my woman : hey man it done fell dead
13 I love my baby : and I know for sure
14 But these creeping rattlesnakes : done crawled up to my door
15 Going to sing this song : and I ain't going to sing no more
16 For that creeping rattlesnake : done crawled up to my door
17 Have you ever been lonely : honey and feel so blue
18 When the rattlesnake crawl : there ain't nobody can tell you what to do

Shor   3   Short, Jaydee

title: Snake Doctor Blues
place and date: New York, 14 Mar. 1932
record numbers: (11474-) Vo-1704 Yz L-1003

1   I'm a snake doctor man : everybody's trying to find out my name
2   And when I fly by easy : mama I'm going to fly low low distant land
3   I am a snake doctor : gang of womens everywhere I go
4   And when I get to flying sometime : I can see a gang of women standing out in the door
5   I'm going to fly by easy : man you know I ain't going to fly very low
6   What I got in these sacks on my back man : you don't know honey know
7   I ain't got many crooks in my bag : as the dyingest snake can crawl
8   I puts up a solid foundation mens : and you know it don't never fall
9   I'm a snake doctor man : got my medicine I say in my bag
10 I mean to be a real snake doctor man : and you know I don't mean to be no quack
11 Lord I know many of you mens wondering : what the snake doctor man got in his hand
12 He's got roots and herbs : steals a woman man everywhere he land

Shor   4   Short, Jaydee

title: Barefoot Blues
place and date: New York, 14 Mar. 1932
record numbers: (11475-) Vo-1704 Yz L-1003

1   Let's get stomp barefoot mama : and get drunk and run
2   I don't feel like running with you mama : but I just feel like having my fun
3   You are a long-ways traveler : long ways from your home
4   Spending all my money for whiskey and getting drunk : mama you don't know how you carry on
5   I work hard daily daily : mama trying to make a good home for you
6   Lord you do things to your good man : mama can make you feel so blue
7   In a few more days now mama : your good man going to be going away

8   You going to miss that hard-working man : you going to need his help some day
9   I work hard daily daily : bring you home my pay
10 I can't see how you have ??? : mama treat a good man this a-way
11 Now I believe I'll go mama : don't feel welcome here
12 You're a no-good woman : you don't feel in your hard-working man's care

Shor   5   Short, Jaydee

title: Grand Daddy Blues
place and date: New York, 14 Mar. 1932
record numbers: (11479-A) Vo-1708 Yz L-1018

1   Now please Mr granddaddy : don't crawl up and down my wall
2   You running so quick and dangerous : that I won't have no woman at all
3   It was early this morning : I was lying out on my floor
4   I was keeping daily watch on my wall : so that granddaddy won't crawl in my house no more
5   If that granddaddy crawls : boy you sure be in my shape some old day
6   You won't have no true-loving woman : for to pass your troubles away
7   When you get bad luck in your home : there's a few men know just how you feel
8   It takes a real good woman : for that *thirty-five year old soul to heal*
9   I get wicked lonesome sometimes : in a dark room by myself
10 The reason I feel that way mama : I ain't got nobody to feel my care

Simp   1   Simpson, Coletha

title: Down South Blues
place and date: Chicago, c. 16 Apr. 1929
record numbers: (C-3299) Br-7112 His HLP-1

1   I'm going to write down home : tell mama to send for me
2   I'm broke and disgusted : with every man I see
3   I was nice I was kind : as a poor girl could be
4   *Men are rather buy* kindness : you with every woman you see
5   I feel like cocking : my pistol in your face
6   I want to make the graveyard : be your resting place
7   They tell me : the graveyard is a lonesome nasty place
8   I want to lay my man down : smile right in his face
9   Now never think : you got a man all by yourself
10 He's sleeping with you : but he's loving somebody else

SimsH   1   Sims, Henry

title: Farrell Blues
place and date: Grafton, Wis., c. Nov. 1929
record numbers: (L-45-1) Pm-12912 OJL-8

1   I'm going to Farrell : so I can have my fun
2   Going to get me a gal now : so I can have my fun
3   I think I heard : that Riverside whistle blow
4   And I ain't going to stop walking : till I get to my rider's door
5   Farrell blues mama : sure don't worry me
6   It's all I want : just to do what a poor man do
7   Blues come to me : just like a dream
8   The blues *so* ??? : don't worry me
9   Oh mama : what have I done to you
10 The blues go away : I am going too

SimsH 2   Sims, Henry

        title: Tell Me Man Blues
        place and date: Grafton, Wis., c. Dec. 1929
        record numbers: (L-65-1) Pm-12940 OJL-2

1 Tell me man : which way the rising sun
2 It rise in the east : and go down in the west
3 I want to see you : go with the rising sun
4 So I can always tell : when the sun is going down
5 When I go : please don't talk after me
6 Because I'm going : where to my suposed-to-be
7 Tell me man : what you got on your mind
8 You keep me worried : and bothered all the time
9 You may want to see me : look little and cute
10 I'm going to get me : a khaki suit

Slue   1   Sluefoot Joe

        title: Tootin' Out Blues
        place and date: Long Island City, c. Apr. 1929
        record numbers: (490-A) QRS-R7086 His HLP-17

1 You used to be my sugar : but you ain't sweet no
     more
2 You got another joker : hanging around your door
3 I know my baby : thinks the world and all of me
4 Because every time she grins : she turns her light
     on me
5 Talking about your [rider, woman] : but you just
     ought to see mamlish mine
6 She's a long tall woman : and she tooting out behind
7 She ain't so good-looking : she ain't got no great
     long mamlish hair
8 She ain't got no gold teeth : you can follow her
     anywhere
9 She stood on the corner : between Twenty-Fifth and
     Main
10 You know a blind man saw her : and a dumb man called
     her name
11 The dumb man asked her : said who is your regular be
12 And then the blind man told her : said you sure look
     good to me

Slue   2   Sluefoot Joe

        title: Shouting Baby Blues
        place and date: Long Island City, c. Apr. 1929
        record numbers: (   ) QRS-R7086 His HLP-17

1 I know my baby : she going to jump and shout
2 When the train rolls up : and I come walking out
3 I wouldn't have a rooster : he won't crow for day
4 And I wouldn't have a hen : won't cackle when she
     lay
5 I wouldn't have a cook : wouldn't cook three meals a
     day
6 I wouldn't have a woman : if she couldn't do what I
     say
7 Lord I seen her at the station : and I seen her on
     the road
8 And I'm sitting here wondering : will a matchbox
     hold my clothes
9 When I leave town : my people started crying
10 Oh hollering and screaming : where that long-gone
     man of mine

SmiA   1   Smith, . . . (Smith and Harper)

        title: Insurance Policy Blues
        place and date: Augusta, Ga., 26 or 27 June 1936
        record numbers: (AUG-126-3) ARC-6-10-61 Rt
          RL-334

1 I said hey hey insurance man : quit knocking on my
     door

SmiA   1   Smith, . . . (Smith and Harper)

2 Because I'm four months behind : and you ought to
     know I ain't going to sell that old insurance no
     more
3 Well the last time I seed you : I give you a five
     dollar bill
4 And the next time I see you : you was running three
     or four whiskey stills
5 That's why I said please : please stop knocking on
     my door
6 Because I'm going to enjoy my simple straight life :
     and I ain't going to sell that old insurance no
     more
7 Well you know you didn't even see me : when I was
     lying sick on my bed
8 You haven't done no ways : like that old policy read

SmiB   1   Smith, Bessie

        title: Down Hearted Blues
        place and date: New York, 16 Feb. 1923
        record numbers: (80863-5) Co-A3844 Co CL-855

1 Gee but it's hard to love someone : when that
     someone don't love you
2 I'm so disgusted heart-broken too : I've got those
     down-hearted blues
3 Once I was crazy about a man : he mistreated me all
     the time
4 The next man I get has got to promise me : to be
     mine all mine
5 Trouble trouble : I've had it all my days
6 It seem like trouble : going to follow me to my
     grave
7 I ain't never loved : but three men in my life
8 My father my brother : the man that wrecked my life
9 It may be a week : it may be a month or two
10 But the day you quit me honey : it's coming home to
     you
11 I've got the world in a jug : the stopper's in my
     hand
12 I'm going to hold it : until you men come under my
     command

SmiB   2   Smith, Bessie

        title: Jail-House Blues
        place and date: New York, 21 Sept. 1923
        record numbers: (81226-2) Co-A4001 Co CL-855

1 Thirty days in jail : with my back turned to the
     wall
2 Look here Mr jail-keeper : put another gal in my
     stall
3 I don't mind being in jail : but I got to stay there
     so long so long
4 When every friend I had : is done shook hands and
     gone
5 You better stop your man : from tickling me under my
     chin
6 Because if he keeps on tickling : I'm sure going to
     beg him on in
7 Good morning blues : blues how do you do
8 Say I just come here : to have a few words with you

SmiB   3   Smith, Bessie

        title: Ticket Agent Ease Your Window Down
        place and date: New York, 5 Apr. 1924
        record numbers: (81670-2) Co-14025-D Co CL-855

1 Ticket agent : ease your window down
2 Because my man's done quit me : and tried to leave
     this town
3 I'd rather see : this whole world sloppy drunk

4   Than to see my man : starting in to pack his trunk
5   If he don't want me : he had no right to stall
6   I can get more men : than a passenger train can haul
7   He stole my money : and he pawned my clothes
8   And which a-way my daddy went : the Gypsy only knows
9   I hate a man : that don't play fair and square
10 Because you can get a crooked daddy : most anywhere

SmiB   4   Smith, Bessie

title: Weeping Willow Blues
place and date: New York, 26 Sept. 1924
record numbers: (140062-2) Co-14042-D Co CL-856

1   I went down to the river : sat beneath a willow tree
2   The blues dropped on those willow leaves : and it
    rolled right down on me
3   I went up on the mountain : high as any gal could
    stand
4   And looked down on that engine : that took away my
    loving man
5   I heard the whistle blowing : the fireman ring the
    bell
6   They taking away that willow tree : that give me
    this weeping spell
7   When you broken-hearted : and your man is out of
    town
8   Go to the river : take a chair and sit down
9   And if he don't come back to you : I tell you what
    to do
10 Just jump right overboard : because he ain't no more
    to you
11 Folks I love my man : I kiss him morning noon and
    night
12 I wash his clothes and keep him clean : and try to
    treat him right
13 Now he's gone and left me : after all I tried to do
14 The way he treats me girls : he'll do the same thing
    to you

SmiB   5   Smith, Bessie

title: The St. Louis Blues
place and date: New York, 14 Jan. 1925
record numbers: (140241-1) Co-14064-D Co CL-855

1   I hate to see : the evening sun go down
2   It makes me think : on on my last go-round
3   Feeling tomorrow : like I feel today
4   I'll pack my grip : and make my get-away
5   St Louis woman : wears diamond ring
6   Pulls a man around : by her apron strings
7   Wasn't for powder : and this store-bought hair
8   The man I love : wouldn't go nowhere

SmiB   6   Smith, Bessie

title: Reckless Blues
place and date: New York, 14 Jan. 1925
record numbers: (140242-1) Co-14056-D Co CL-855

1   When I was young : nothing but a child
2   All you men : tried to drive me wild
3   Now : I'm growing old
4   And I got what it takes : to get all of you men told
5   My mama says I'm reckless : my daddy says I'm wild
6   I ain't good-looking : but I'm somebody's angel
    child
7   Come in pretty papa : mama wants some loving I vow
8   Come in pretty papa : mama wants some loving right
    now

title: Sobbin' Hearted Blues
place and date: New York, 14 Jan. 1925
record numbers: (140249-2) Co-14056-D Co CL-855

1   You treated me wrong : I treated you right
2   I worked for you : both day and night
3   You brag to women : that I was your fool
4   So now : I got them sobbing-hearted blues
5   The sun's going to shine : in my back door some day
6   It's true I love you : but I won't take mistreatment
    anymore
7   All I want is your picture : it must be in a frame
8   When you go : I can see you just the same
9   I'm going to start walking : because I got a wooden
    pair of shoes
10 Going to keep on walking : until I lose these
    sobbing-hearted blues

SmiB   8   Smith, Bessie

title: Cold In Hand Blues
place and date: New York, 14 Jan. 1925
record numbers: (140250-2) Co-14064-D Co CL-855

1   Now I've tried hard : to treat him kind
2   But it seems to me : his love is gone blind
3   The man I've got : must have lost his mind
4   The way he quits me : I can't understand
5   I'm going to find myself : another man
6   Because the one I've got : have done gone cold in
    hand

SmiB   9   Smith, Bessie

title: You've Been a Good Old Wagon
place and date: New York, 14 Jan. 1925
record numbers: (140251-1) Co-14079-D Co CL-855

1   Look a-here daddy : I want to tell you please get
    out of my sight
2   I'm playing quits now : right from this very night
3   You've have your day : don't stand around and frown
4   You've been a good old wagon : daddy but you done
    broke down
5   Now you better go to the blacksmith's shop : and get
    yourself overhauled
6   There ain't nothing about you : to make a good woman
    fall
7   Nobody wants a baby : when a real man can be found
8   You've been a good old wagon : daddy but you done
    broke down
9   When the sun is shining : it's time to make hay
10 *I ??? operate* : you can't make that wagon pay
11 When you were in your prime : you loved to run
    around
12 You've been a good old wagon : honey but you done
    broke down
13 There's no need to cry : and make a big joke
14 This man has taught me more about loving : than you
    will ever know
15 He is the king of loving : this man deserve a crown
16 He's a good old wagon : daddy and he ain't broke
    down

SmiB   10   Smith, Bessie

title: The Yellow Dog Blues
place and date: New York, 6 May 1925
record numbers: (140586-2) Co-14075-D Co CL-857

1   Ever since Miss Suzie Johnson : lost her Jockey Lee
2   There's been much excitement : and more to be
3   You can hear her moaning : moaning night and morn
4   She's wondering : where her easy rider's gone

SmiB 11   Smith, Bessie

    title: Nashville Women's Blues
    place and date: New York, 26 May 1925
    record numbers: (140625-2) Co-14090-D Co CL-855

1 Folks up north : you all have heard the blues
2 But this is the one : you like to hear the news
3 If you go down there : you have no time to lose
4 Just go uptown : and buy a new pair of shoes
5 Folks down there : they drinks a lots of booze
6 You can ??? : just what you choose
7 Down there : they strut their stuff
8 They way they strut : is really no bluff

SmiB 12   Smith, Bessie

    title: J. C. Holmes Blues
    place and date: New York, 27 May 1925
    record numbers: (140629-2) Co-14095-D Co CL-855

1 Listen people : if you want to hear
2 A story told : about a brave engineer
3 J C Holmes : was the rider's name
4 *A heavy weight woman : with a hearty fate*
5 J C said : with a smile so fine
6 Woman gets tired : of one man all the time
7 Get two or three : if you have to hide
8 If the train go and leave : you got a mule to ride
9 In the second cabin : set Miss Alice Bry
10 Want to ride : with Mr J C or die
11 I ain't good-looking : and I don't dress fine
12 But I'm a rambling woman : with a rambling mind
13 Just then : the conductor hollered all aboard
14 And the porter said : we've got a load
15 Look a-here son : we ought to been gone
16 I feel like riding : if it's all night long
17 J C said : just before he died
18 Two more roads : he wanted to ride
19 Everybody wondered : what road it could be
20 He said the Southern Pacific : and the Santa Fe
21 J C said : I don't feel right
22 I saw my gal : with a man last night
23 Soon as I get : enough steam just right
24 I been mistreated : and I don't mind dying

SmiB 13   Smith, Bessie

    title: I Ain't Goin' to Play Second Fiddle
    place and date: New York, 27 May 1925
    record numbers: (140630-1) Co-14090-D Co CL-855

1 Let me tell you daddy : mama ain't going to sit and
     grieve
2 Pack up your duff : and get ready to leave
3 I stood your foolishness : long enough
4 So now : I'm going to call your bluff
5 On certain things : I'm going to call your hand
6 So now daddy : here's my plan
7 I ain't going to play no second fiddle : I'm used to
     playing lead
8 You must think that I am blind : you been cheating
     me all the time
9 I've gone to your house : the other night
10 Caught you and your good gal : having a fight
11 I caught you : with your good-time vamp
12 So now papa : I'm going to put out your lamp
13 Now papa : I ain't sore
14 You ain't going to mess up : with me no more
15 I'm going to play : with another key
16 Then you're going : to hang your head and weep

SmiB 14   Smith, Bessie

    title: Jazzbo Brown from Memphis Town
    place and date: New York, 18 Mar. 1926
    record numbers: (141819-2) Co-14133-D Co CL-856

1 Don't you start no crowing : lay your money down
2 I've got mine on Jazzbo : that Memphis clarinet
     clown
3 He ain't got no equal : nowhere in this land
4 So let me tell you people : about this Memphis man
5 He ain't seen no music school : he can't read a note
6 But he's the playingest fool : on that Memphis boat
7 When he wraps his big fat lips : around that doggone
     horn
8 ??? : Lord carrying on
9 He can moan and he can groan : I ain't fooling you
10 There ain't nothing on that horn : that old Jazz
     can't do

SmiB 15   Smith, Bessie

    title: The Gin House Blues
    place and date: New York, 18 Mar. 1926
    record numbers: (141820-3) Co-14158-D Co CL-856

1 I'm going to the gin house : when the whistle blows
2 My trouble come like rain : ??? *and cold*
3 I'm going to the gin house : stay there by myself
4 I mean to drown my sorrows : about sweet somebody
     else
5 I'll make one trip there : to see can I ease my mind
6 And if I do : I'm going to make it my last time
7 To hold her man : when these gals have got so many
     different ways
8 I mean to watch my man : don't care what these other
     gals say
9 Because these gin house blues : is camping around my
     door
10 I want him to drive them off : so they won't come
     back no more

SmiB 16   Smith, Bessie

    title: Baby Doll
    place and date: New York, 4 May 1926
    record numbers: (142147-2) Co-14147-D Co CL-857

1 I went to see the doctor the other day : he said I
     was well as well could be
2 But I says doctor you don't know : really what is
     worrying me
3 I want to be somebody's babydoll : so I can get my
     loving all the the time
4 I want to be somebody's babydoll : to ease my mind
5 He can be ugly : he can be black
6 So long as he can eagle rock : and ball the jack
7 Lord I went to the Gypsy : to get my fortune told
8 She say you in hard luck Bessie : doggone your
     bad-luck soul

SmiB 17   Smith, Bessie

    title: Lost Your Head Blues
    place and date: New York, 4 May 1926
    record numbers: (142149-2) Co-14158-D Co CL-857

1 I was with you baby : when you didn't have a dime
2 Now since you got plenty of money : you have throwed
     your good gal down
3 Once ain't for always : two ain't for twice
4 When you get a good gal : you better treat her nice
5 When you were lonesome : I tried to treat you kind
6 But since you got money : it's done changed your
     mind
7 I'm going to leave baby : ain't going to say goodbye

SmiB   17   Smith, Bessie

    8 But I'll write you : and tell you the reason why
    9 Days are lonesome : nights are [so] long
   10 I'm a good old gal : but I've just been treated
        wrong

SmiB   18   Smith, Bessie

        title: One and Two Blues
        place and date: New York, 26 Oct. 1926
        record numbers: (142876-2) Co-14172-D Co CL-857

    1 If you want me to love you : *keep much*
    2 Let mama : feel that money touch
    3 Quit messing around : you hear what I say
    4 Started to bringing : eight hours a day
    5 If you must be a rat : here's the fact
    6 Be a long-tailed one : have plenty of jack

SmiB   19   Smith, Bessie

        title: Young Woman's Blues
        place and date: New York, 26 Oct. 1926
        record numbers: (142878-3) Co-14179-D Co CL-857

    1 Woke up this morning : when the chickens was crowing
        for day
    2 *Turned* on the right side of my pillow : my man had
        gone away
    3 By his pillow : he left a note
    4 Reading I'm sorry Jane : you got my goat
    5 No time to marry : no time to settle down
    6 I'm a young woman : and ain't done running around
    7 Some people call me a hobo : some call me a bum
    8 Nobody knows my name : nobody knows what I've done
    9 I'm as good : as any woman in your town
   10 I ain't no high yellow : I'm a *deep killer* brown
   11 I ain't going to marry : ain't going to settle down
   12 I'm going to drink good moonshine : and run these
        browns down
   13 See that long lonesome road : don't you know it's
        got to end
   14 And I'm a good woman : and I can get plenty of men

SmiB   20   Smith, Bessie

        title: Preachin' the Blues
        place and date: New York, 17 Feb. 1927
        record numbers: (143490-2) Co-14195-D Co CL-858

    1 Because just a little spirit : of the blues tonight
    2 Let me tell you girls : if your man ain't treating
        you right
    3 Let me tell you : I don't mean no wrong
    4 I will learn you something : if you listen to this
        song
    5 I ain't here : to try to save your soul
    6 Just want to teach you : how to save your good
        jellyroll
    7 Going on down the line : a little further now
    8 There's : many a poor woman down
    9 Read on down : to Chapter Nine
   10 Woman must learn : how to take their time
   11 Read on down : to Chapter Ten
   12 Taking other women's men : you are doing a sin
   13 Lord one old sister : by the name of sister Green
   14 Jumped up and done a shimmy : you ain't never seen

SmiB   21   Smith, Bessie

        title: Back Water Blues
        place and date: New York, 17 Feb. 1927
        record numbers: (143491-1) Co-14195-D Co CL-858

    1 When it rained five days : and the skies turned dark
        as night
    2 Then trouble taken place : in the lowlands at night
    3 I woke up this morning : can't even get out of my
        door
    4 There's enough trouble : to make a poor girl wonder
        where she want to go
    5 Then they rowed a little boat : about five miles
        across the pond
    6 I packed all my clothes throwed them in : and they
        rolled me along
    7 When it thunders and lightning : and the wind begin
        to blow
    8 There's thousands of people : ain't got no place to
        go
    9 Then I went and stood : up on some high old lonesome
        hill
   10 And looked down on the house : where I used to live
   11 Backwater blues : done caused me to pack up my
        things and go
   12 Because my house fell down : and I can't live there
        no more
   13 Mmm : I can't move no more
   14 There ain't no place : for a poor old girl to go

SmiB   22   Smith, Bessie

        title: After You've Gone
        place and date: New York, 2 Mar. 1927
        record numbers: (143567-2) Co-14197-D Co CL-857

    1 Now listen honey : while I say
    2 How can you tell me : that you're going away
    3 You feel blue : you feel sad
    4 You'll miss the best pal : you ever had

SmiB   23   Smith, Bessie

        title: Trombone Cholly
        place and date: New York, 3 Mar. 1927
        record numbers: (143575-3) Co-14232-D Co CL-858

    1 If Gabriel knowed : how you could blow
    2 He'd let you lead : his band I know
    3 You ain't seen : such shaking hips
    4 Like when that horn : is to your lips
    5 And he would break : a leg I know
    6 A-doing the Charleston : while you blow

SmiB   24   Smith, Bessie

        title: Send Me to the 'Lectric Chair
        place and date: New York, 3 Mar. 1927
        record numbers: (143576-2) Co-14209-D Co CL-858

    1 Judge judge please Mr judge : send me to the
        electric chair
    2 Judge judge good Mr judge : let me go away from here
    3 I want to take a journey : to the devil down below
    4 I done killed my man : I want to reap just what I
        sow
    5 Judge judge hear me judge : send me to the electric
        chair
    6 Judge judge send me there judge : I love him so dear
    7 I cut him with my ??? : I kicked him in the side
    8 I stood there laughing over him : while he wobbled
        around and died
    9 Judge judge sweet me judge : send me to the electric
        chair

10 Judge judge good kind judge : burn me because I
    don't care
11 I don't want no bonded man : to go my bail
12 I don't want : to spend no ninety-ninety years in
    jail

        title: Mean Old Bed Bug Blues
        place and date: New York, 27 Sept. 1927
        record numbers: (144796-3) Co-14250-D Fwy
        FJ-2802

1   Yes bedbugs sure is evil : they don't mean me no
    good
2   Thinks he's a woodpecker : and I'm a chunk of wood
3   When I lay down at night : I wonder how can a poor
    girl sleep
4   When some is holding my hands : others eating my
    feet
5   Bedbugs big as a jackass : will bite you and stand
    and grin
6   Will drink all the *bedbug* ??? : and turn around
    and bite you again
7   Got myself a wishbone : bedbugs done got my goat
8   Got myself a wishbone : wish they cut their own
    doggone throats

        title: Empty Bed Blues--Part ?
        place and date: New York, 20 Mar. 1928
        record numbers: (14578?-?) Co-14312-D Co CL-858

1   I woke up this morning : with an awful aching head
2   My new man had left me : just a room and an empty
    bed
3   Bought me a coffee grinder : got the best one I
    could find
4   So he could grind my coffee : because he had a brand
    new grind
5   He's a deep-sea diver : with a stroke that can't go
    wrong
6   He can touch the bottom : and his wind holds out so
    long
7   He knows how to thrill me : and he thrills me night
    and day
8   He's got a new way of loving : almost takes my
    breath away
9   Lord he's got the sweetest something : and I told my
    gal friend Lou
10 By the way she's raving : she must have gone and
    tried it too

        title: Poor Man's Blues
        place and date: New York, 24 Aug. 1928
        record numbers: (146895-1) Co-14399-D Co CL-856

1   Mr rich man rich man : open up you heart and mind
2   Give a poor man a chance : help stop these hard hard
    times
3   While you living in your mansion : you don't know
    what hard times means
4   A workingman's wife is starving : your wife is
    living like a queen
5   Please listen to my pleading : because I can't stand
    these hard times long
6   They'll make an honest man : do things that you know
    is wrong
7   Poor man fought all the battles : poor man would
    fight again today

8   He would do anything you ask him : in the name of
    the U S A
9   Now the war is over : poor man must live the same as
    you
10 If it wasn't for the poor man : Mr rich man what
    would you do

        title: Me and My Gin
        place and date: New York, 25 Aug. 1928
        record numbers: (146897-3) Co-14384-D Co CL-856

1   Stay away from me : because I'm in my sin
2   If this place gets raided : it's me and my gin
3   Don't try me nobody : because you never will win
4   I'll fight the army and navy : just me and my gin
5   Any bootlegger : sure is a pal of mine
6   Because a good old bottle of gin : will get it all
    the time
7   When I'm feeling high : ain't nothing I won't do
8   Keep me full of liquor : and I'll sure be nice to
    you
9   I don't want no clothes : and I don't need no bed
10 I don't want no pork chop : just give me gin instead

        title: Nobody Knows You When You're Down and Out
        place and date: New York, 15 May 1929
        record numbers: (148534-3) Co-14451-D Co CL-856

1   Once I lived the life : of a millionaire
2   Spending my money : I didn't care
3   I carried my friends : out for a good time
4   Buying bootleg liquor : champagne and wine
5   When I begin : to fall so low
6   I didn't have a friend : and no place to go
7   So if I ever get my hands : on a dollar again
8   I'm going to hold on to it : till them eagles grin
9   It's mighty strange : without a doubt
10 Nobody knows you : when you down and out
11 Mmm : I done fell so low
12 Nobody wants me : around their door

        title: St. Louis Blues--Part ?
        place and date: New York, c. Aug. 1929
        record numbers: (NY-??-) Ci-J1016 or 17 Jo
        SM-3098

1   I hate to see : that evening sun go down
2   For my baby : he's done left this town
3   Feeling tomorrow : like I feel today
4   I'll pack my grip : and make my get-away
5   St Louis woman : with her diamond rings
6   Pulls my man around : by her apron strings
7   Wasn't for powder : and this store-bought hair
8   That man I love : he wouldn't go nowhere

        title: Blue Spirit Blues
        place and date: New York, 11 Oct. 1929
        record numbers: (149134-3) Co-14527-D Co CL-858

1   Had a dream last night : that I was dead
2   Evil spirits : all around my bed
3   The devil came : and grabbed my hand
4   Took me way down : to that red-hot land
5   Mean blues spirits : stuck their forks in me
6   Made me moan and groan : in misery

SmiB   31   Smith, Bessie

7   Fairies and dragons : spitting out blue flames
8   Showing their teeth : for they was glad I came
9   Demons : with their eyelash dripping blood
10 Dragging sinnners : to their brimstone flood
11 This is hell I cried : cried with all my might
12 Oh my soul : I can't bear the sight
13 Start running : because it is my *cup*
14 Run so fast : till someone woke me up

SmiB   32   Smith, Bessie

        title: Black Mountain Blues
        place and date: New York, 22 July 1930
        record numbers: (150658-2) Co-14554-D Co CL-856

1   Back in Black Mountain : a child will smack your
    face
2   Babies crying for liquor : and all the birds sing
    bass
3   Black Mountain people : are bad as they can be
4   They uses gunpowder : just to sweeten their tea
5   On this Black Mountain : can't keep a man in jail
6   If the jury finds them guilty : the judge'll go
    their bail
7   Had a man in Black Mountain : sweetest man in town
8   He met a city gal : and he throwed me down
9   I'm bound for Black Mountain : me and my razor and
    my gun
10 I'm going to shoot him if he stands still : and cut
    him if he run
11 Down in Black Mountain : they all shoots quick and
    straight
12 The bullet'll get you : if you starts a-dodging too
    late
13 Got the devil in my soul : and I'm full of bad booze
14 I'm out here for trouble : I've got the Black
    Mountain blues

SmiB   33   Smith, Bessie

        title: Long Old Road
        place and date: New York, 11 June 1931
        record numbers: (151595-3) Co-14663-D Co CL-858

1   It's a long old road : but I'm going to find the end
2   And when I get there : I'm going to shake hands with
    a friend
3   On the side of the road : I sat underneath a tree
4   Nobody knows : the thoughts that came over me
5   Weeping and crying : tears falling on the ground
6   When I got to the end : I was so worried down
7   He took me back baby : and I tried it again
8   I got to make it : I've got to find the end
9   You can't trust nobody : you might as well be alone
10 Found my long lost friend : and I might as well
    stayed at home

SmiB   34   Smith, Bessie

        title: Shipwreck Blues
        place and date: New York, 11 June 1931
        record numbers: (151597-3) Co-14663-D Co CL-858

1   Captain : tell your men to get on board
2   Cast your sail : just pull into another shore
3   I'm dreary in mind : and I'm so worried in heart
4   All the best friends : sure has got to part
5   Blow your whistle captain : so your men will know
    what to do
6   When a woman gets dreary : ain't no telling what she
    won't do
7   It's cloudy outdoors : as can be
8   That's the time : I need my good man with me
9   It's raining : and it's storming on the sea

SmiB   34   Smith, Bessie

10 I feel like : somebody has shipwrecked poor me

SmiB   35   Smith, Bessie

        title: Do Your Duty
        place and date: New York, 24 Nov. 1933
        record numbers: (152577-2) OK-8945 Co CL-856

1   I heard you say you didn't love me baby : *you say
    you heard* Mrs Brown
2   I don't believe a word she said : she's the lyingest
    woman in town
3   If you make your own bed hard : that's the way it
    lies
4   If I'm tired of sleeping by myself : you too dumb to
    realize

SmiB   36   Smith, Bessie

        title: Gimme a Pigfoot
        place and date: New York, 24 Nov. 1933
        record numbers: (152578-2) OK-8949 Co CL-856

1   Up in Harlem : every Saturday night
2   When the high browns get together : it's just too
    tight
3   They all congregates there : in an all night strut
4   And what they do : is tut tut tut
5   Old Hannah Brown : from cross town
6   Gets full of corn : and starts breaking them down
7   Check all your razors : and your guns
8   We going to be arrested : when the wagon comes
9   Check all your razors : and your guns
10 Do the shim-sham-shimmy : till the rising sun

SmiB   37   Smith, Bessie

        title: Take Me for a Buggy Ride
        place and date: New York, 24 Nov. 1933
        record numbers: (152579-2) OK-8949 Co CL-856

1   Daddy you really knows your stuff : when you take me
    for a buggy ride
2   I like you when you got your habits on : you can
    shift a gear with so much pride
3   I gets a funny feeling : when you gaze into my eyes
4   You give me such a thrill : you make my thermometer
    rise
5   Daddy you as sweet as you can be : when you take me
    for a buggy ride
6   When you get me down upon your knee : and ask me to
    be your bride
7   When you hug and kiss me : it makes me feel fine
8   I gets this funny feeling : up and down my spine
9   Your loving ain't so *fordy* : in the park
10 But you a loving *cold* creature : in the dark
11 You ain't so hot : what can it be
12 What makes me say : daddy take all of me
13 You always ready : every time that I call
14 What I like about you : you never stall
15 You ain't no creature : you a good old soul
16 You done sent salvation : to my very soul

SmiB   38   Smith, Bessie

        title: I'm Down in the Dumps
        place and date: New York, 24 Nov. 1933
        record numbers: (152580-2) OK-8945 Co CL-856

1   My man's got something : he gives me such a thrill
2   Every time he smiles at me : I can't keep my body
    still
3   I done cried so much : look like I got the mumps

SmiB 38   Smith, Bessie

4   I can't keep from worrying : because I'm down in the
    dumps
5   I had a nightmare last night : when I lay down
6   When I woke up this morning : my sweet man couldn't
    be found
7   I'm going down to the river : into it I'm going to
    jump
8   Can't keep from worrying : because I'm down in the
    dumps
9   Someone knocked on my door : last night when I was
    asleep
10 I thought it was that sweet man of mine : making his
    'fore-day creep
11 'Twas nothing but my landlord : a great big chump
12 Stay away from my door Mr landlord : because I'm
    down in the dumps
13 When I woke up : my pillow was wet with tears
14 Just one day from that man of mine : seem like a
    thousand years
15 But I'm going to straighten up : *straight as a
    answer come*
16 Ain't no use of telling me that lie : because I'm
    down in the dumps
17 I'm twenty-five years old : that ain't no maid
18 I got plenty of vim and vitality : I'm sure that I
    can make the grade
19 I'm always like a tiger : I'm ready to jump
20 I need a whole lots of loving : because I'm down in
    the dumps

SmiBM 1   Smith, Bessie Mae

        title: St. Louis Daddy
        place and date: Grafton, Wis., c. Dec. 1929
        record numbers: (L-78-?) Pm-12922 OJL-20

1   I hate to leave St Louis : and I tried so hard to
    stay
2   But the meanest treatment : is driving me away
3   You don't mean me no good : I can tell by the way
    you do
4   Now you can't be mine : every womans in St Louis too
5   Bad luck in St Louis : and it all fell on [poor] me
6   And these bad-luck rattlesnakes : won't let my good
    man be
7   I gave you clothes and money : and put shoes on your
    feet
8   Now you's the sheik of this town now : won't keep
    you off the streets
9   You done drove me from St Louis daddy : how much
    more can I stand
10 Now I'm going to Detroit : and find me an angel man

SmiBM 2   Smith, Bessie Mae

        title: Sugar Man Blues--Part 1
        place and date: Chicago, 19 Sept. 1930
        record numbers: (C-6167-) Vo-1559 His HLP-2

1   Sugar man sugar man : please come back to me
2   You know I love you : and I cannot let you be
3   Love you sweet man : do anything you say
4   Sweet daddy sweet daddy : don't treat me this a-way
5   You got that sweet kind of sugar : make a good woman
    lose her mind
6   If you take me back sweet daddy : I'll treat you so
    nice and kind
7   I'm so wild about your sugar : don't know what to do
8   It's that granulated sugar : ain't nobody got it but
    you
9   My coffee must be sugared in the morning : my tea
    late at night
10 When I don't get my sugar : babe I don't feel just
    right
11 If you see my sugar : tell him to hurry home

SmiBM 2   Smith, Bessie Mae

12 I ain't had nothing sweet : since my sugar been gone

SmiBM 3   Smith, Bessie Mae

        title: Sugar Man Blues--Part 2
        place and date: Chicago, 19 Sept. 1930
        record numbers: (C-6168-) Vo-1559 His HLP-2

1   Sugar man sugar man : you got the best sugar in town
2   Please don't let some other woman : tear your sugar
    barrel down
3   Every time you leave me : I hang my head and cry
4   If you don't want me baby : please tell me the
    reason why
5   Blues fell down on me : just like drops of rain
6   You give your lump of sugar to another woman : and
    don't give me a grain
7   I'm going to tell you something baby : want you to
    keep it to yourself
8   If you don't give me all your sugar : you won't give
    it to no one else
9   Mmm : want my sugar right now
10 Lord I want my sugar : just to *have my* sugar *and
    how*

SmiC 1   Smith, Clara

        title: I Got Everything a Woman Needs
        place and date: New York, 28 June 1923
        record numbers: (81059-6) Co-A3943 VJM VLP-15

1   I've got everything that a woman needs : to make a
    good man fall
2   I know just what to do : to back them in my stall
3   Once inside : I'll treat them kind of rough
4   Then I'll show them how : I can do my stuff

SmiC 2   Smith, Clara

        title: Every Woman's Blues
        place and date: New York, 28 June 1923
        record numbers: (81060-5) Co-A3943 VJM VLP-15

1   I'm so worried : down-hearted in mind
2   My brown keeps me worried : all the time
3   I love my daddy : honest and true
4   Seems like others look better to him : than I do
5   I haven't the heart to tell him : to his face
6   That some other good brown : has taken his place
7   Don't never let : no one man worry your mind
8   Just keep you four and five : *messed* up all the
    time
9   You can read my letters : but you sure can't read my
    mind
10 When you think I'm crazy about you : I'm leaving you
    all the time
11 Well there ain't no love : there ain't no getting
    along
12 My brown treat me so mean : sometime don't know
    right from wrong

SmiC 3   Smith, Clara

        title: Down South Blues
        place and date: New York, 27 July 1923
        record numbers: (81151-3) Co-A3961 VJM VLP-15

1   I'm going to the station : and catch the fastest
    train that goes
2   I'm going back south : where the weather suits my
    clothes
3   Because my mama told me : and my daddy told me too

SmiC   3   Smith, Clara

4   Don't go north : and let them men make a fool out of
     you
5   Because their love's like water : it turns off and
     on
6   Time you think you've got them : it turned off and
     gone
7   I'm going back south : if I wear out ninety-nine
     pair of shoes
8   Because I'm broke-down-hearted : got those
     down-south blues

SmiC   4   Smith, Clara

         title: All Night Blues
         place and date: New York, 27 July 1923
         record numbers: (81153-3) Co-A3966 VJM VLP-15

1   All night blues : ever ever on my mind
2   I've got those all night blues : feel like catching
     some old train and flying
3   I felt so low : don't know what to do
4   Ain't got nobody : to tell my troubles to
5   All night blues : ever ever on my mind
6   All night blues : feel like catching some disease
     and dying
7   I'm feeling blue : don't know what to do
8   Ain't got nobody : to tell my troubles to

SmiC   5   Smith, Clara

         title: Play It a Long Time Papa
         place and date: New York, 27 July 1923
         record numbers: (81154-2) Co-A3966 VJM VLP-15

1   Play it a long time papa : your mama's feeling blue
2   Do it a long time papa : I don't love no one but you
3   When you come on : beat that thing
4   That you have come : to have to plink

SmiC   6   Smith, Clara

         title: I Want My Sweet Daddy Now
         place and date: New York, 31 Aug. 1923
         record numbers: (81183-1) Co-A3991 VJM VLP-15

1   Folks I'll tell : that he's not my regular man
2   But he loves me better : than my regular can
3   Early in the morning : late at night
4   He gives me plenty loving : treats his mama right

SmiC   7   Smith, Clara

         title: I Never Miss My Sunshine
         place and date: New York, 7 Sept. 1923
         record numbers: (81202-2) Co-A4000 VJM VLP-15

1   You said you want to leave me : at the door
2   I've been disappointed : many times before
3   I'm going up on the mountain : to watch the sinking
     sun
4   Ain't found nobody else to love me : like my loving
     daddy done

SmiC   8   Smith, Clara

         title: Don't Never Tell Nobody
         place and date: New York, 1 Oct. 1923
         record numbers: (81198-4) Co-13002-D VJM VLP-15

1   Don't never tell nobody : what your perfect good man
     can do

SmiC   8   Smith, Clara

2   You just get them anxious : to try some of his good
     points too

SmiC   9   Smith, Clara

         title: Kansas City Man Blues
         place and date: New York, 2 Oct. 1923
         record numbers: (81222-6) Co-12-D VJM VLP-15

1   Soon I will be : Kansas City bound
2   When I get back : I will turn things upside down
3   Because it's Kansas City : where I long to be
4   I've got a Kansas City man : a-waiting there for me
5   He's got white teeth : and two pretty gold crowns
6   He's got *torro* hair : he's a coffee-colored brown
7   Women crying murder : I ain't raised my hand
8   It's all on account of : taking one woman's man

SmiC   10   Smith, Clara

         title: Uncle Sam Blues
         place and date: New York, 2 Oct. 1923
         record numbers: (81253-2) Co-12-D VJM VLP-15

1   Let me tell you postman : what the army have done to
     me
2   It took my husband my good man : come back and got
     my used-to-be
3   Uncle Sam is so bad : he walks so doggone cute
4   He took my daddy out of his ??? : put him in a khaki
     suit
5   Going to sit down and write a letter : to my Uncle
     Sam
6   Tell him that war is over : please send me back my
     man
7   Uncle Sam has told me : that things are ??? around
8   He took all the booze away : and my good brown from
     town

SmiC   11   Smith, Clara

         title: It Won't Be Long Now
         place and date: New York, 11 Jan. 1924
         record numbers: (81476-1) Co-14006-D VJM VLP-16

1   Some day you'll want me : and it won't be long
2   Then you'll be sorry : you ever done me wrong
3   You'll miss my kindness : most everywhere
4   No one to love you : no one to care
5   There'll be no sunshine : always rain
6   Then you going to want me back : once again
7   Then you'll remember : Miss Smith's old song
8   Some day you'll want me : and it won't be long

SmiC   12   Smith, Clara

         title: Hot Papa
         place and date: New York, 11 Jan. 1924
         record numbers: (81477-3) Co-14006-D VJM VLP-16

1   Hot papa : don't keep me waiting so long
2   Hot papa : you know you're treating me wrong
3   You had better come : and hurry home
4   I'm getting tired : of being alone
5   You better not do : just what I think
6   If you *don't know* : between each drink
7   Hot papa : you are driving me mad
8   Hot papa : you are making me bad
9   Now you better do right : stay out of my flat
10   I'm just carrying a brick : for you a brickbat
11   Now your ninety-nine degrees : would be just cool
12   If you were trying : to play me for a fool

SmiC 13   Smith, Clara

       title: I'm Gonna Tear Your Playhouse Down
       place and date: New York, 18 Jan. 1924
       record numbers: (81495-1) Co-14013-D VJM VLP-16

1   You only had : a boot and a shoe
2   Until : I fell in love with you
3   They will think : the world is coming to an end
4   It will only be the end : of one of my trifling men
5   Don't you say you won't : because you surely will
6   Because mama's going to stop you : with a *blue
      steel bill*

SmiC 14   Smith, Clara

       title: I Don't Love Nobody
       place and date: New York, 18 Jan. 1924
       record numbers: (81496-1) Co-14016-D VJM VLP-16

1   I don't want nobody : I want the world to know
2   When I'm with a fellow : it's strictly for making
      dough
3   I'll leave a fellow standing : till his money's gone
4   And tell him that he's nothing : but a pure
      greenhorn
5   I had a fellow take me : all around the town
6   And if he ask to kiss me : I would knock him down

SmiC 15   Smith, Clara

       title: Good Looking Papa Blues
       place and date: New York, 29 Jan. 1924
       record numbers: (81508-1) Co-14026-D VJM VLP-16

1   Oh good-looking papa : where have you been so long
2   Oh dough-spreading papa : you got your habits on
3   When you went away : you didn't have a thing
4   Now you come back : with clothes and diamond rings
5   You went west : and bought a beautiful home
6   You are looking good : as sure as you're born
7   You were sweet papa : without a doubt
8   But there is nothing doing : what you are thinking
      about

SmiC 16   Smith, Clara

       title: You Don't Know My Mind
       place and date: New York, 29 Jan. 1924
       record numbers: (81509-1) Co-14013-D VJM VLP-16

1   I went to the race track : my man *on derby* won
2   Give the money to another gal : and wouldn't give me
      none
3   You don't know : you don't know my mind
4   When you see me laughing : laughing to keep from
      crying
5   I said now papa : can you stand to see me cry
6   He said yes woman : I could stand to see you die
7   Fed my daddy : with plenty of jellyroll
8   Pull the shoes off my feet : let me out in the cold

SmiC 17   Smith, Clara

       title: My Doggone Lazy Man
       place and date: New York, 31 Jan. 1924
       record numbers: (81512-2) Co-14016-D VJM VLP-16

1   He ain't worth the salt : that goes in his bread
2   He is one third living : and three third dead
3   He hangs his britches : down on the floor
4   And wears his shoes and socks : ???
5   When the preacher doing : the hands in hands
6   The fool sat there : too tired to stand

SmiC 18   Smith, Clara

       title: 31st Street Blues
       place and date: New York, 31 Jan. 1924
       record numbers: (81514-2) Co-14009-D VJM VLP-16

1   Railroad take me back : got the Thirty-First Street
      blues
2   Please don't jump the track : I ain't got no time to
      lose
3   Can't get nothing : while roving around
4   But it's all gravy : in my home town
5   Ashes to ashes : dust to dust
6   New York don't get me : Chicago must

SmiC 19   Smith, Clara

       title: War Horse Mama
       place and date: New York, 10 Apr. 1924
       record numbers: (81683-2) Co-14021-D VJM VLP-16

1   War horse papa : how come you do me like you do
2   War horse papa : you can't be true
3   War horse papa : that's seven going to ride in a
      hack
4   War horse papa : but six is coming back
5   War horse papa : I'm too good a girl ???
6   War horse papa : you know you can't be true

SmiC 20   Smith, Clara

       title: Mean Papa, Turn in Your Key
       place and date: New York, 17 Apr. 1924
       record numbers: (81697-2) Co-14022-D VJM VLP-16

1   Mean papa turn in your key : because you don't live
      here no more
2   Mean papa just let me be : stay away from my door
3   *She can cheat murder* : ???
4   But you just cheat : away a beautiful home
5   I'm leaving town : I sure don't want to go
6   I think there'll be trouble : and I had better go

SmiC 21   Smith, Clara

       title: The Clearing House Blues
       place and date: New York, 17 Apr. 1924
       record numbers: (81698-2) Co-14019-D VJM VLP-17

1   It seems to me : as if I'm all broke down
2   Since I lost all my change : I lost my sealskin
      brown

SmiC 22   Smith, Clara

       title: Don't Advertise Your Man
       place and date: New York, 23 Apr. 1924
       record numbers: (81722-1) Co-14026-D VJM VLP-17

1   Your head will hang low : and your heart will ache
2   You are fattening a frog : for a vampire snake
3   Rave about the things : your loving man can do
4   Some other woman : sure to take him away from you

SmiC 23   Smith, Clara

       title: Back Woods Blues
       place and date: New York, 30 Apr. 1924
       record numbers: (81694-4) Co-14022-D VJM VLP-17

1   Got the backwoods blues : but I don't want to go
      back home
2   Got the blues so bad : for the place that I came
      from

SmiC   23   Smith, Clara

3   Ought to see my beau : but it's way too far
4   To ride in a ??? : ???
5   Got the backwoods blues : for the place way down in
    'Bam
6   Got the blues : but I'm going to stay here where I
    am
7   Going to stay right here : just where I'm at
8   Where there ain't no grinning : and snatching off my
    hat
9   Got the backwoods blues : for the folks I left down
    home
10 I got the blues : for them poor old folks alone
12 Yes I'm going down there : I'm going to stay

SmiC   24   Smith, Clara

        title: Deep Blue Sea Blues
        place and date: New York, 19 Aug. 1924
        record numbers: (81931-3) Co-14034-D VJM VLP-17

1   My man's on the ocean : bobbing up and down
2   He belongs to Uncle Sam : but he's always on my mind
3   I've got the blues : for the deep blue sea
4   Nothing but a *tear* : can satisfy me
5   No automobile : can change my mind
6   I feel like catching : a airplane and flying
7   When I hear : that whistle blow
8   I know : the ship is near ashore
9   Ain't but one man in this world : that can satisfy
    me
10 That's the man that keeps rocking : on the deep blue
    sea

SmiC   25   Smith, Clara

        title: Texas Moaner Blues
        place and date: New York, 19 Aug. 1924
        record numbers: (81932-1) Co-14034-D VJM VLP-17

1   I was born in Texas : but I didn't stay
2   A cruel little daddy : throwed me right away
3   I brought my man here : tried to treat him right
4   Started fighting over a woman : stayed out every day
    and night
5   What's the use of trying : I said trying trying to
    be kind
6   When the one you love : haven't got you on his mind
7   I stood at the station I said station : saw my man
    leaving town
8   When that man quit me : that's what brought me down
9   Talk about Texas I mean Texas : Texas people are
    your friends
10 When one don't want you : the other one will take
    you in

SmiC   26   Smith, Clara

        title: Basement Blues
        place and date: New York, 20 Sept. 1924
        record numbers: (140052-1) Co-14039-D VJM VLP-17

1   The man I love : got lowdown ways for two
2   That's why I'm *hanging* : and I'm lowdown too
3   He ain't no orchard : and I ain't trying to be
4   And you can't make : no orchard out of me
5   Every day : I get as low as a *coat*
6   For my home ain't here : it's further down the road
7   In ??? Mississippi : where my folks are at
8   And colored folks don't live : much lower down than
    that
9   My papa's name is low : with a zero if you please
10 And he can kiss my mammy : without bending his knees
11 So please keep your *alley* : take the air if you
    please

SmiC   26   Smith, Clara

12 But my eye is at the ??? : in the basement blues

SmiC   27   Smith, Clara

        title: Mama's Gone Goodbye
        place and date: New York, 20 Sept. 1924
        record numbers: (140053-4) Co-14039-D VJM VLP-17

1   For years you dog me around : but now is the time
2   To walk up and tell you : what's on my mind
3   I'm going to get me a daddy : to treat me right
4   One who will come home : and sleep every night
5   There's a fire in my range : bakes nice and brown
6   All I need is some good daddy : turn my damper down

SmiC   28   Smith, Clara

        title: Freight Train Blues
        place and date: New York, 30 Sept. 1924
        record numbers: (140064-3) Co-14041-D VJM VLP-17

1   I hate to hear : that engine blow boo hoo
2   Every time I hear it blowing : I feel like riding
    too
3   Got the freight train blues : I've got boxcars on my
    mind
4   Going to leave this town : because my man is so
    unkind
5   I'm going away : just to wear you off my mind
6   And I may be gone : for a doggone long long time
7   I asked the brakeman : let me ride the blinds
8   The brakeman said : Clara you know this train ain't
    mine
9   When a woman gets the blues : she goes to her room
    and hides
10 When a man gets the blues : he catches a freight
    train and rides

SmiC   29   Smith, Clara

        title: Done Sold My Soul to the Devil
        place and date: New York, 30 Sept. 1924
        record numbers: (140076-3) Co-14041-D VJM VLP-17

1   He trails me like a bloodhound : he's quicker than a
    snake
2   He follows right behind me : every crooked turn I
    make
3   I'm stubborn and I'm hateful : I'd die before I'd
    run
4   I'd drink carbolic acid : and I'd poke a gatling gun
5   I live down in the valley : right by a hornets' nest
6   Where lions bears and tigers : all come to take
    their rest

SmiC   30   Smith, Clara

        title: Death Letter Blues
        place and date: New York, 15 Oct. 1924
        record numbers: (140108-1) Co-14045-D VJM VLP-17

1   I received a letter : that my man was dying
2   I caught the first train : and went back home
    a-flying
3   He wasn't dead : but he was slowly dying
4   And just to think of him : I just can't keep from
    crying
5   I followed my daddy : to the burying ground
6   I watched the pallbearers : slowly let him down
7   That was the last time : I saw my daddy's face
8   Mama loves you sweet papa : but I just can't take
    your place

SmiC   31   Smith, Clara

    title: Prescription for the Blues
    place and date: New York, 15 Oct. 1924
    record numbers: (140109-1) Co-14045-D VJM VLP-17

1 All day long I'm worried : all night long I'm blue
2 I'm so awfully lonesome : I don't know what to do
3 So I ask the doctor : see if you can find
4 Something in your practice : to pacify my mind
5 Let me tell you doctor : why I'm in misery
6 Once I had a love : he went away from me
7 Been to see the Gypsy : hoodoo doctors too
8 Shook their heads and told me : nothing they could
     do
9 Like a little baby : all day long I cry
10 And if you can't cure me : I'm just as sure to die
11 Give me something poison : doctor won't you please
12 Then I'll sign a paper : died with heart disease

SmiC   32   Smith, Clara

    title: Steel Drivin' Man
    place and date: New York, 16 Dec. 1924
    record numbers: (140181-2) Co-14053-D VJM VLP-17

1 Steel-driving Sam : steel-driving man of mine
2 He works on the railroad : making that railroad tie
3 There ain't nobody : who lives in 'Bam
4 Who can make a hammer ring : like my man Sam
5 He swings a mean hammer : just as sure as you are
     born
6 Because he can't drive steel : with a doggone horn
7 Steel-driving Sam : steel-driving man of mine
8 He works on the railroad : on that old Southern line
9 He wouldn't know his name : printed on a wall
10 In boxcar letters : that's as long as he is tall
11 But steel-driving Sam : steel-driving man of mine
12 He works on the railroad : daylight-savings time

SmiC   33   Smith, Clara

    title: He's Mine, All Mine
    place and date: New York, 16 Dec. 1924
    record numbers: (140182-1) Co-14053-D VJM VLP-17

1 He works all day : with all his might
2 And brings me his money : every Saturday night
3 He don't talk much : he's a hard-boiled man
4 But I keep him eating : right out of my hand
5 He digs in a ditch : full of mud and slime
6 And when it ain't raining : he's making back time
7 He eats his supper : throws his clothes on the floor
8 And he's up every morning : at half past four

SmiC   34   Smith, Clara

    title: Broken Busted Blues
    place and date: New York, 7 Jan. 1925
    record numbers: (140227-2) Co-14062-D CC-32

1 I've got those broken busted blues : I feel bad
2 I've got those can't be trusted blues : gee I'm sad

SmiC   35   Smith, Clara

    title: Shipwrecked Blues
    place and date: New York, 3 Apr. 1925
    record numbers: (140491-1) Co-14077-D CC-32

1 Oh the gale is raging : and my ship without a sail
2 If the wind keeps on a-blowing : I won't be left to
     tell the tale
3 Oh the ship is sinking : and the line in such a mess

SmiC   35   Smith, Clara

4 And my crew is done deserted : I got to stick here
     to the last
5 Oh I don't mind drowning : but the water is so cold
6 If I must leave this good world : I want to leave it
     brave and bold
7 Mama's shipwrecked shipwrecked : she ain't got no
     time to lose
8 Lord if someone don't save me : I'll go down singing
     the shipwreck blues

SmiC   36   Smith, Clara

    title: Court House Blues
    place and date: New York, 3 Apr. 1925
    record numbers: (140492-1) Co-14073-D CC-32

1 I give him beer : then a glass of ale
2 For in this time tomorrow : I'll be laying in the
     county jail
3 Three months in jail : ain't no long long time
4 The man I love : he made ninety-nine
5 The jurymen sit all night : ??? from eight to three
6 And the verdict was : let the poor gal go free
7 I sit in the courthouse : with my face hid in my
     hands
8 And it all on account : of one trifling man

SmiC   37   Smith, Clara

    title: My John Blues
    place and date: New York, 3 Apr. 1925
    record numbers: (140493-1) Co-14077-D CC-32

1 You take a southbound *regular* : you ride my weary
     blues away
2 Because my heart is getting weaker : and I'm sinking
     lower and lower every day
3 To find myself a blue steel : I mean a blue steel
     blade
4 If I find her with my John : I'll slice and I'll cut
     and send her to her grave

SmiE   1   Smith, Eithel

    title: Jelly Roll Mill
    place and date: Richmond, Ind., 22 Sept. 1932
    record numbers: (18804) Ch-16613 Riv RM-8819

1 I sold some jelly : to a man named Will
2 Oh by all means : I had a jellyroll mill
3 Jellyroll every morning : jellyroll at night
4 He couldn't get my jelly : want to fuss and fight
5 I just come here : to get you told
6 Don't let him catch you : messing with my jellyroll
7 Let me tell you one thing : about sweet jellyroll
8 You can tell that jelly : and it's never been sold
9 I'll tell you one thing : about the jellyroll mill
10 If you have to have jelly : you won't have to steal

SmiIv   1   Smith, Ivy

    title: Sad and Blue
    place and date: Chicago, c. Jan. 1927
    record numbers: (4089-1) Pm-12447 His HLP-2

1 I'm going to write : my man today
2 Because I'm getting tired : of this lowdown place
3 Going to stay : I'll be all night long
4 You know daddy : you treated your little mama wrong
5 You got to stop : your running around
6 If you come home : and your mama can't be found
7 Don't start your mama : to slipping out on you

SmiIv   1   Smith, Ivy

8   Because when I start slipping : I'll make you sad
     and blue

SmiIv   2   Smith, Ivy

     title: Third Alley Blues
     place and date: Chicago, c. Jan. 1927
     record numbers: (4094-1) Pm-12447 His HLP-2

1   I just want to get back : to Birmingham
2   I got a gang in Third Alley : don't know where I am
3   I'd rather be in Third Alley : without a dime
4   Than to be in Chicago : simply wasting my time
5   I'm going to Third Alley : and bring my rider home
6   Because these women in Third Alley : won't let my
     rider alone

SmiJ   1   Smith, J. T. Funny Paper

     title: Howling Wolf Blues--No. 1
     place and date: Chicago, 19 Sept. 1930
     record numbers: (C-6404-A) Vo-1558 Yz L-1031

1   I am the wolf that everybody been trying to find out
     : where in the world I prowl
2   Nobody ever gets a chance to see me : but they all
     hear me when I howl
3   Know I howl to my baby : with her mother standing by
     her side
4   And that's the reason I'm howling : I'm-a-trying to
     be satisfied
5   I even howled for you baby : when you was down and
     couldn't stand up on your feet
6   Now you walk by the lone wolf : and act like you
     don't want to see
7   What made you quit me : I love you as I did three
     years ago
8   Take me back and I'll quit prowling : and I won't
     ever howl no more
9   Now the preacher told me that God will forgive a
     black man : most anything he do
10   I ain't black but I'm dark-complexioned : look like
     He ought to forgive me too
11   [Look, seem] like God don't treat me : like I'm a
     human kind
12   Seem like he wants me to be a prowler : and a
     howling wolf all the time

SmiJ   2   Smith, J. T. Funny Paper

     title: Howling Wolf Blues--No. 2
     place and date: Chicago, 19 Sept. 1930
     record numbers: (C-6405-A) Vo-1558 Yz L-1031

1   Baby here I am : down on my bended knees
2   Ask you to take me back and forgive me : do that for
     me if you please
3   Now when you hear me howling mama : I mean howling
     at your door
4   Come on and give me what I want mama : then you
     won't hear me howl no more
5   Ever since you quit me mama : I ain't wanted nobody
     else
6   For I'd rather be with nobody : than I'd rather be
     howling by myself
7   Now I done howled and howled : until I [wore, made]
     my tonsils sore
8   And when I howl this time mama : I never will howl
     no more
9   Now here I am in Chicago : doing the best I can
10   If I hear from my baby : I'll act the fool and go
     howling back south again
11   Mmm : mama listen at me howl

SmiJ   2   Smith, J. T. Funny Paper

12   Watch the roads dark as night mama : and you liable
     to see me prowl

SmiJ   3   Smith, J. T. Funny Paper

     title: Good Coffee Blues
     place and date: Chicago, c. 20 Sept. 1930
     record numbers: (C-6409-) Vo-1590 Yz L-1031

1   I heard you say this morning mama : that your head
     was throbbing through and through
2   Come on let me make you some coffee : let me show
     you what my coffee will do
3   Pull off your high shoes mama : lay down on the bed
4   I won't be but a few minutes : before I'll kill that
     old headache dead
5   Don't rush take your time : let it go down easy and
     slow
6   Then when you have headache again : come back to me
     baby and I'll give you some more
7   But I make coffee so good : it will make you bite
     your tongue
8   Been all over the world grinding coffee mama : come
     on let me grind you some
9   Now when your friends want coffee : please send all
     your friends to me
10   I swear I'll give them good coffee : and won't give
     them no rotten tea

SmiJ   4   Smith, J. T. Funny Paper (Magnolia Harris)

     title: Mama's Quittin' and Leavin'--Part 1
     place and date: Chicago, c. late Dec. 1930
     record numbers: (C-7100-) Vo-1602 Yz L-1031

1   Talking about changing men : mama you been saying
     that stuff all over town
2   But I'm liable to take my forty-five : mama and turn
     you upside down
3   Mama when I talk to you : God above know I don't
     mean no harm
4   But it's just because I love you : and I'm trying to
     teach you right from wrong
5   Mama it ain't no need of leaving me : because you're
     going to be mistreated by someone else
6   And rather than see someone else mistreat you : I'd
     rather keep you and mistreat you myself

SmiJ   5   Smith, J. T. Funny Paper (Magnolia Harris)

     title: Mama's Quittin' and Leavin'--Part 2
     place and date: Chicago, c. late Dec. 1930
     record numbers: (C-7101-) Vo-1602 Yz L-1031

1   When you drinking you talk too much mama : forgive
     me if you please
2   I love you and always will mama : I'm down on my
     bended knees
3   I know the reason I can't keep you mama : I taken
     you from my bosom friend
4   I can feel rested God knows I can : I know you going
     to take him right back again
5   Baby please don't baby please don't : I mean please
     don't go
6   Here's one thing : that you don't know
7   Baby come on and sit down and talk to me : and give
     me one more try
8   And you can do just as you please : and I'll act
     just like some mother's child

SmiJ 6   Smith, J. T. Funny Paper (Dessa Foster)

    title: Tell It to the Judge No. 1
    place and date: Chicago, c. 28 Jan. 1931
    record numbers: (C-7238-A) Me-M12117 Yz L-1031

1 Now you can lose your temper : but please don't lose
   your head
2 I'm going to search this shack this morning : come
   on and hear this search warrant read
3 Last time I searched this shack : you know I found
   half a pint of gin
4 Now what's the meaning of all this here liquor :
   call the wagon because I'm going to run you in
5 You've had lots of breaks : but here's what I'm
   going to tell you before you go
6 You better get on your knees and ask for mercy :
   because the judge giving breaks no more

SmiJ 7   Smith, J. T. Funny Paper (Dessa Foster)

    title: Tell It to the Judge No. 2
    place and date: Chicago, c. 28 Jan. 1931
    record numbers: (C-7239-?) Me-M12117 Yz L-1031

1 They got you charged with having liquor : now tell
   me what is your plea
2 You know I been giving you a-many break : but the
   break this morning belongs to me
3 Well you's a pretty good woman : and living in a
   nice neighborhood
4 But I think one hundred and costs : and thirty days
   in Bridewell will do you good
5 Don't get back at me Betty : because I'm liable to
   change my mind
6 And change your sentence from the Bridewell : send
   you to the pen for ninety-nine

SmiJ 8   Smith, J. T. Funny Paper

    title: Honey Blues
    place and date: Chicago, c. Mar. 1931
    record numbers: (VO-126-) Vo-1633 Yz L-1031

1 Come and kiss me honey babe : before I go
2 I'm going to take a ride : on the T and O
3 Goodbye honey : if you call that gone
4 I'm going to take a ride : in my high brown's arms
5 Me and my baby : we don't get along so well
6 She ain't working : have a chance to raise so much
   hell
7 You know the prettiest girl : that ever I seen
8 Was standing on Frank Street : in New Orleans
9 You know it's often said : and I've done found out
10 I ain't got but one thing : women crazy about
11 Monkey got his tail : caught up on the streetcar
   line honey
12 Didn't think about his tail : till I started
   twisting mine honey
13 Run back to the track : laid his head on a rail
14 And lose his head : about a little piece of tail

SmiJ 9   Smith, J. T. Funny Paper

    title: Corn Whiskey Blues
    place and date: Chicago, c. Mar. 1931
    record numbers: (VO-127-) Vo-1633 Yz L-1031

1 Now bring me that bottle : and let's have another
   drink of booze
2 Because I can feel something coming : and it seems
   something like the blues
3 I can tell when [I've got the blues, the blues is
   coming] : I can't help but feel so lowdown
4 Then I want to get drunk : and pitch a bugger all
   over town

SmiJ 9   Smith, J. T. Funny Paper

5 When I start drinking I'm mean and hateful : and I
   won't treat nobody right
6 I just keeps on walking : looking for places where
   they fuss and fight
7 I'm going to keep on drinking : until I find me a
   good corn friend
8 And when I can't find good corn : I'll drink
   moonshine again
9 I've got a girl in Texas : she lives four miles from
   town
10 And on account of moonshine : her people don't allow
   me around

SmiJ 10   Smith, J. T. Funny Paper

    title: County Jail Blues
    place and date: Chicago, c. Mar. 1931
    record numbers: (VO-132-A) Vo-1679 Yz L-1031

1 Here I am judge this morning : and here is my
   forty-five
2 I shot my woman on the corner : and I don't know
   whether she's dead or alive
3 Judge don't ask me no questions : about how our
   trouble began
4 Just have it printed in your paper : a little
   trouble between women and men
5 Mmm : oh Lord I heard that old judge say ninety-nine
6 And it's one thing I wished I had this morning :
   that's that forty-five of mine
7 I'm going to lay down in jail : like I used to lie
   down in Calumet
8 May be a good luck to you : because I haven't forgot
   you yet

SmiJ 11   Smith, J. T. Funny Paper

    title: Hungry Wolf
    place and date: Chicago, c. Apr. 1931
    record numbers: (VO-165-A) Vo-1655 Yz L-1031

1 I'm that hungry wolf : and the ground is where I dug
   my cave
2 I leave prowling just at dawn : and get back in the
   morning just a while before day
3 I stroll through dark places : threatening to do my
   part
4 With blood in my eye : and malice in my heart
5 In places I used to go : I ain't been there I been
   blowed out by the wind
6 I did think one more time : that I just about come
   to my end
7 I can howl like a wolf : and I can bark just like a
   dog
8 I can prowl and do good : because I sleeps in a
   hollow log
9 Most times when I get hungry : I'm like a [drunk]
   man acting a clown
10 Then my eyes start to jumping : then I'm dangerous
   as a doggone lion
11 You gobblers keep on gobbling : you roosters watch
   your setting hen
12 Old wolf is hungry now I'm going to do most 'napping
   : than I done since God knows when

SmiJ 12   Smith, J. T. Funny Paper

    title: Hoppin' Toad Frog
    place and date: Chicago, c. Apr. 1931
    record numbers: (VO-166-A) Vo-1655 Yz L-1031

1 I'm harmless as I can be : I stays out of all
   people's way

SmiJ 12   Smith, J. T. Funny Paper

2   I'm just a little old toad : I'm going to hop back
    to my home some day
3   I've hop down in your basement : don't mean to harm
    a single soul
4   I shake all of your ashes : then shovel you in some
    brand new coal
5   I don't have no friend : by myself I'm always on the
    road
6   Just let me hop you one time mama : and you'll keep
    me for your little old toad
7   Mom would you let a poor little old toad frog : hop
    down in your water pond
8   I'd dive down and come right out : and I won't stay
    in your water long
9   But I know for myself : and your front yard is where
    I get my load
10 Way you talk you like my hopping : why don't you
    keep me for your little toad
11 Mama do you know one thing : your water tank is just
    deep enough
12 I can dive down to the bottom : and take my time and
    tread right back up

SmiJ 13   Smith, J. T. Funny Paper

    title: Fool's Blues
    place and date: Chicago, c. Apr. 1931
    record numbers: (VO-167-A) Vo-1674 Yz L-1010

1   Some people tell me : God takes care of old folks
    and fools
2   But since I been born : he must a-have changed his
    rules
3   I used to ask a question : then answer that question
    myself
4   About when I was born : wonder was there any more
    mercy left
5   Look like here of late : I've been crying both day
    and night
6   Everybody talks about me : and nobody don't treat me
    right
7   You know until six months ago : I hadn't prayed a
    prayer since God knows when
8   Now I'm asking God every day : to please forgive me
    for my sin
9   You know this must be the devil I'm serving : I know
    it can't be Jesus Christ
10 Because I asked him to save me : and look like he's
    trying to take my life
11 My health is gone now : and left me with the
    sickness blues
12 People it don't seem like to me : that God takes
    care of old folks and fools

SmiJ 14   Smith, J. T. Funny Paper

    title: Seven Sisters Blues--Part 1
    place and date: Chicago, c. Apr. 1931
    record numbers: (VO-168-A) Vo-1641 Yz L-1031

1   They tell me seven sisters in New Orleans : they can
    really fix a man up right
2   And I'm headed for New Orleans Louisiana : I'm
    traveling both day and night
3   I hear them say : the oldest sister look like she's
    just twenty-one
4   And said she can look right in your eyes : and tell
    you exactly what you want done
5   They tell me they been hung : been bled and been
    crucified
6   But I just want enough help : to stand on the water
    and rule the tide
7   It's bound to be seven sisters : because I've heard
    it by everybody else

SmiJ 14   Smith, J. T. Funny Paper

8   Of course I'd love to take their word : but I'd
    rather go and see for myself
9   When I leave the seven sisters : I'm piling stones
    all around
10 And go to my baby and tell her : there's another
    seven-sister man in town
11 Good morning seven sisters : just thought I'd come
    down and see
12 Will you build me up where I'm torn down : and make
    me strong where I'm weak

SmiJ 15   Smith, J. T. Funny Paper

    title: Seven Sisters Blues--Part 2
    place and date: Chicago, c. Apr. 1931
    record numbers: (VO-169-A) Vo-1641 Yz L-1031

1   I went to New Orleans Louisiana : just on account of
    something I heard
2   The seven sisters told me everything I wanted to
    know : and they wouldn't let me speak a word
3   Now it's Sarah Minnie Bertha : Holly Dolly Betty and
    Jane
4   You can't know them seven sisters apart : because
    they all looks just the same
5   The seven sisters sent me away happy : around the
    corner I met another little girl
6   She looked at me and smiled : and said go devil and
    destroy the world
7   Seven times you hear the seven sisters : will visit
    me [all] in my sleep
8   And they said I won't have no more trouble : and
    said I'll live twelve days in a week
9   Boy go down in Louisiana : and get the lead right
    out of your bean
10 If seven sisters can't do anything in Louisiana :
    bet you'll have to go to New Orleans

SmiJ 16   Smith, J. T. Funny Paper

    title: Before Long
    place and date: Chicago, c. Apr. 1931
    record numbers: (VO-170-A) Vo-1674 Rt RL-312

1   When I had money baby : you was good to me
2   But now I'm broke and hungry : and you cruel as you
    can be
3   Last night you called me : a lowdown dirty name
4   Woke up Monday morning : and done the same old thing
5   It won't be long : before God will bring his day
6   Give me my shirt and tie baby : and I'll get on my
    way
7   You in good health now baby : and good and strong
8   But before long baby : you'll be down to skin and
    bone
9   I'm going now baby : kiss me goodbye
10 I know you don't love me baby : and I don't see how
    you cry
11 Reason I'm leaving you : you dog me all the time
12 Look like it *do you good somebody* : the day they
    saw me crying

SmiL 1   Smith, Laura

    title: Gonna Put You Right in Jail
    place and date: New York, c. early Feb. 1927
    record numbers: (7074-2) Ba-1977 VJM VLP-40

1   Since you gone : and got so rough
2   I won't stand : for that caveman stuff

SmiL   2   Smith, Laura

        title: Don't You Leave Me Here
        place and date: New York, c. Mar. 1927
        record numbers: (7130-2) Ba-1977 VJM VLP-40

 1 Don't you leave me here : a good gal I've been
 2 If you ain't coming back sweet papa : leave a dime
      for gin
 3 You can dog me around : baby I don't care
 4 But here's a thing I got to say : just quit me if
      you dare
 5 The boat's up the river : and it ain't coming down
 6 But I believe to my soul : my man is Alabama bound
 7 If you buy your ticket : papa you better buy two
 8 Because if you try to leave me here : the way will
      sure get you
 9 So if you got a bad man : and he won't do right
10 Take a chair and break it over his doggone head :
      and walk the streets all night

SmiM   1   Smith, Mamie

        title: Jenny's Ball
        place and date: New York, 19 Feb. 1931
        record numbers: (404852-A) OK-8915 Sw S-1240

 1 There's a man in town : who's called the ladies'
      lover now
 2 Keeps his pockets full of mirrors : he's the pup's
      bow-wow
 3 He went into a cabaret : to see Miss Jenny dance
 4 Jenny stepped right up : and said you have no chance
 5 There'll be no doings here : before you pay
 6 No dancing prancing : until the break of day
 7 I know there's lots of girlies : you may charm
 8 And long to hold them : close up right in your arms
 9 But here's a lesson : that was taught to me
10 You cannot eat and sleep : on mirth and glee
11 Goodbye : and please don't call at all
12 There'll be no preachers : at Miss Jenny's ball

SmiSi 1   Smith, Six Cylinder

        title: Oh Oh Lonesome Blues
        place and date: Grafton, Wis., c. Mar. 1930
        record numbers: (L-213-1) Pm-12968 Yz L-1004

 1 If I had wings baby : just like a morning dove
 2 I'd heist my wings baby : out to the brown I love
 3 She left this morning : she's border bound today
 4 I hate the mean old Gypsy : carried my brown away
 5 Oh oh oh oh oh : oh oh oh oh oh oh
 6 That is why you hear me : moan these lonesome blues
 7 One thing in creation : I sure can't understand
 8 That's why : Chicago women want every woman's man
 9 Ooh : ooh
10 That's why you hear me : ??? these lowdown blues
11 Ooh : ooh
12 That is why you hear me : singing these lonesome
      blues

SmiSi 2   Smith, Six Cylinder

        title: Pennsylvania Woman Blues
        place and date: Grafton, Wis., c. Mar. 1930
        record numbers: (L-214-2) Pm-12968 Yz L-1004

 1 Working in the steel mills baby : handling ???
 2 Pennsylvania women : think that old man cannot do
 3 I think I heard : that steel mill whistle blow
 4 She blowed just like : she ain't going no more
 5 I'm going away baby : won't be back till fall
 6 If I win any money : won't be back at all
 7 Pennsylvania women : got hearts like solid stone

SmiSi 2   Smith, Six Cylinder

 8 Well they're so doggone evil : break up every
      woman's home

SmiT   1   Smith, Trixie

        title: I Don't Know and I Don't Care Blues
        place and date: New York, c. May 1924
        record numbers: (1766-1) Pm-12208 CC-29

 1 I don't know and I don't care : where my loving
      daddy's gone
 2 He should have gone long ago : I'd like to know what
      he's waiting on
 3 If you love a man : he'll treat you like a dog
 4 If you don't : he'll hop around you like a frog
 5 I ain't seen the man : that I can't stand to lose
 6 Because I keep : the don't know and don't care blues

SmiT   2   Smith, Trixie

        title: Freight Train Blues
        place and date: New York, c. May 1924
        record numbers: (1767-1) Pm-12211 CC-29

 1 I hate to hear : that engine blow boo hoo
 2 Every time I hear it blowing : I feel like riding
      too
 3 Got the freight train blues : got boxcars on my mind
 4 I'm going to leave this town : because my man is so
      unkind
 5 I'm going away : just to wear you off my mind
 6 And I may be gone honey : for a doggone long long
      time
 7 I asked the brakeman : to let me ride the blinds
 8 The brakeman said little girlie : you know this
      train ain't mine
 9 When a woman gets the blues : she goes to her room
      and hides
10 But when a man gets the : he catches a freight train
      and rides

SmiT   3   Smith, Trixie

        title: Sorrowful Blues
        place and date: New York, c. May 1924
        record numbers: (1780-2) Pm-12208 CC-29

 1 If you catch me stealing : I don't mean no harm
 2 It's a mark in my family : it must be carried on
 3 I got nineteen men : and I want one more
 4 When I get that one more : I'll let that nineteen go
 5 I'm going to tell you daddy : like the Chinaman told
      the Jew
 6 If you don't likee me : I sure don't likee you
 7 It's hard to love : another woman's man
 8 You can't get him when you want him : you got to
      catch him when you can
 9 Have you ever seen peaches : grow on a sweet potato
      vine
10 Just step in my back yard : and take a peep at mine

SmiT   4   Smith, Trixie

        title: Don't Shake It No More
        place and date: New York, c. June 1924
        record numbers: (1807-2) Pm-12211 CC-29

 1 Shimmy-shee-wobble : babe that's all
 2 Every time you start to shake it : everybody starts
      to fall
 3 And if you do it mama : do it slow
 4 Just shake it around and around : don't shake it no
      more

SmiT   5   Smith, Trixie

        title: Praying Blues
        place and date: New York, Sept. 1924
        record numbers: (1886-2) Pm-12232 CC-29

1   Folks you don't know : half the trouble I've seen
2   Nobody knows : but the good Lord and me
3   Lord Lord : kindly hear my plea
4   Please send me a man : that wants nobody else but me
5   Lord Lord : I ain't got a friend
6   One man is in jail : the other one is in the pen

SmiT   6   Smith, Trixie

        title: Ride Jockey Ride
        place and date: New York, Dec. 1924
        record numbers: (1977-?) Pm-12245 CC-29

1   I got a jockey : riding for me
2   He mounts his saddle : so differently
3   The way he rides : is a shame
4   If he don't bring it home : he's not to blame
5   Get that hump : in your back
6   Wave your whip : and make it crack

SmiT   7   Smith, Trixie

        title: Choo Choo Blues
        place and date: New York, Dec. 1924
        record numbers: (1978-3) Pm-12245 CC-29

1   The sound of a train : fills my heart with misery
2   Since a choo choo train : took my man away from me
3   I went to the station : but I got there too doggone
    late
4   The last train was leaving : the boxcars were filled
    with freight
5   Northern men are splendid : they will treat you
    mighty fine
6   But when it comes to loving : I'll take a down-home
    man for mine
7   I got the choo choo blues : because my man's in
    Dixieland today
8   I'm going back to Dixie : if I have to crawl all the
    way

SmiT   8   Smith, Trixie

        title: You've Got to Beat Me to Keep Me
        place and date: New York, c. Feb. 1925
        record numbers: (2015-2) Pm-12256 CC-29

1   Beat me up for breakfast : knock me down for tea
2   Black my eye for supper : then you're pleasing me
3   Come down in my kitchen : *leave off instant and*
4   Beat me to a frazzle : with your skillets pots and
    pans

SmiT   9   Smith, Trixie

        title: Mining Camp Blues
        place and date: New York, c. Feb. 1925
        record numbers: (2016-1) Pm-12256 CC-29

1   Once I had a daddy : and he worked down in a hole
2   Digging and a-hauling : hauling that Birmingham coal
3   Many times I wondered : when they put my daddy down
4   Will he come back to me : will they leave him in the
    ground
5   Something like the pitcher : that they sent down in
    the well
6   Wondering will they break it : Lordy Lordy who can
    tell

SmiT   9   Smith, Trixie

7   It was late one evening : I was standing at that
    mine
8   Foreman said : my daddy had gone down for his last
    last time
9   How he was a coal miner : from his hat down to his
    shoes
10 And I'm nearly dying : with these mining camp blues

SmiT   10   Smith, Trixie

        title: The World's Jazz Crazy and So Am I
        place and date: New York, Mar. 1925
        record numbers: (2063-2) Pm-12262 CC-29

1   Jazz them : everybody jazz them now
2   My pretty papa : he don't know how
3   All night long : the band kept us awake
4   So we could jazz away : until daybreak
5   I like the motion : that my daddy has
6   For everyone likes : the real good jazz
7   Oh jazz them jazz them : play it all night
8   The world's jazz crazy : Lord and so am I

SmiT   11   Smith, Trixie

        title: Railroad Blues
        place and date: New York, Mar. 1925
        record numbers: (2064-2) Pm-12262 CC-29

1   Now if the train fails on the track : I'm Alabama
    bound
2   Don't you hear that train coming : I'm Alabama bound
3   Now the train went by : with my papa on the inside
4   Now I couldn't do nothing : but hang my head and cry
5   Did you ever take a trip : on the Seaboard line
6   Because if you ride that train : it will satisfy
    your mind
7   I got the railroad blues : I want to see my home
    town
8   And if the Seaboard God bless : I'm Alabama bound

SmiT   12   Smith, Trixie

        title: He Likes It Slow
        place and date: New York, c. Dec. 1925
        record numbers: (2363-?) Pm-12336 Jo SM-3098

1   Lord he likes it slow : when he goes to dance
2   He likes it slow : when he goes to France
3   Just like a snail : that man of mine
4   He never likes to hurry : he takes his time
5   And when he calls me : praying's no use
6   He always got : them lowdown blues

SmiT   13   Smith, Trixie

        title: Black Bottom Hop
        place and date: New York, c. Dec. 1925
        record numbers: (2364-1) Pm-12336 CC-29

1   First you get over *town* : ???
2   Do the Black Bottom : ???
3   Walk up to your baby : twist and turn
4   Get in a shape : like a fishing worm
5   Do the *bo bo* : ???
6   Turn out the lights : *cut out your* ???
7   Now they'll have ??? steaks : alligator pie
8   Pickled *eels* feet : and jambalaya
9   Bullfrog legs : with onion sauce
10 ??? stew : to kick it off
11 Fried hot tomales : with yellow rice
12 ??? crabs : and lemon ice
13 Throw it in the creek : ???

SmiT 13   Smith, Trixie

14 Strut your stuff : you dancing fool
15 Red-hot mama : *eggs hard-boiled*
16 They'll break up the dance : with a battle royal

SmiT 14   Smith, Trixie

     title: Love Me Like You Used To
     place and date: New York, c. Dec. 1925
     record numbers: (2365-?) Pm-12330 CC-29

1   Please come back and love me like you used to : I
     think about you every day
2   You reap just what you sow in the sweet by-and-by :
     and be sorry that you went away
3   Oh baby I'm crazy : almost dead
4   I wish I had you here : to hold my aching head

SmiT 15   Smith, Trixie

     title: Freight Train Blues
     place and date: New York, 26 May 1938
     record numbers: (63866-A) De-7489 Cor CP-58

1   I hate to hear : that freight train blow boo hoo
2   Every time I hear it blowing: I feel like riding too
3   I asked the brakeman : to let me ride the blinds
4   He said little girlie : you know this train ain't
     mine
5   Oh it's a mean old fireman : cruel old engineer
6   It was a mean old train : that took my man away from
     here
7   I've got the freight train blues : but I'm too darn
     mean to cry
8   I'm going to love that man : till the day he dies
9   There's three trains ready : but none ain't going my
     way
10 But the sun's going to shine : in my back door some
     day

SmiT 16   Smith, Trixie

     title: No Good Man
     place and date: New York, 14 June 1939
     record numbers: (65815-A) De-7617 AH-158

1   I'm one woman : who can't use a no-good man
2   Because a man like him : is only good for a one
     night stand
3   Now I'm a red-hot chick : just *puffing* out with
     flame and youth
4   It takes a real hip man : to make me tell the truth
5   He's got to get it in the groove : and get a new
     technique
6   I'm tired of old style loving : a modern man I'm
     forced to seek
7   My first name's Trixie : the last has never been
     told
8   I've been chasing pigmeat : since I was nine days
     old
9   [Now there ain't but, there's only] two people in
     this world : I can't stand
10 That's a two-faced woman : and a lying man

Span 1   Spand, Charlie

     title: Good Gal
     place and date: Richmond, Ind., 17 Aug. 1929
     record numbers: (15453) Pm-12817 Yz L-1015

1   You wonder why : I treat you so
2   You should have : sense enough to know
3   You may say : that I'm changing fast
4   But good things in life : don't never last

Span 1   Spand, Charlie

5   You used to treat me : like a dog
6   But now I learned : to hop from broad to broad
7   Once I couldn't stand : to see you cry
8   But I feel all the same : mama if you die
9   I might as well : to tell you the facts
10 I got a new gal : she's tight like that

Span 2   Spand, Charlie

     title: Back to the Woods Blues
     place and date: Richmond, Ind., 17 Aug. 1929
     record numbers: (15456) Pm-12817 Yz L-1015

1   I woke up this morning : clock was striking four
2   And my baby told me : pack your things and go
3   I'm going to pack my suitcase : and move back to the
     woods
4   It's nobody here : that means me any good
5   Just as sure as the good Lord : sits in the heaven
     above
6   Now your life ain't all pleasure : unless you be
     with that one you love
7   I'm going to the river : sit right on the ground
8   Now if my heart strikes sorrow : my tears come
     rolling down
9   Now she's little and she's low : right down on the
     ground
10 Now this the reason I love her : she ain't no
     hand-me-down
11 Mmm : ain't going to sing no more
12 Now my train is waiting : baby and I got to go

Spar 1   Sparks, Milton

     title: Erie Train Blues
     place and date: Chicago, 28 July 1935
     record numbers: (91445) BB-B6529 BC-6

1   Lord I hate to hear : that Erie train whistle when
     he blow
2   It give me a feeling : that I never had before
3   Mmm : that Erie's got my baby gone
4   That the reason why people : you hear me sing this
     moan
5   The Erie : I swear it ain't *coming* back
6   That train come and stole my baby people : swear it
     won't bring her back

Spau 1   Spaulding, Henry

     title: Cairo Blues
     place and date: Chicago, c. 6 May 1929
     record numbers: (C-3449-) Br-7085 Yz L-1003

1   Cairo : Cairo is my baby's home
2   Going where my Cairo baby lives : won't be long
3   Mmm : mmm
4   Mmm : won't be here long
5   Women in Cairo : will treat you [nice and] kind of
     strange
6   Get you rider : and take you off that thing
7   Kick you and knife you : beat you and cut you too
8   *When you through* : ???
9   Cairo : Cairo is my baby's home
10 I'm going home : and I swear and it won't be long

Spau 2   Spaulding, Henry

     title: Biddle Street Blues
     place and date: Chicago, c. 6 May 1929
     record numbers: (C-3450-) Br-7085 OJL-20

1   Say some strange something : is easing down on me

Spau   2   Spaulding, Henry

2   Because my best baby has quit me : and the world she
        cared for me
3   Now will you please be kind babe : let me speak just
        one more time
4   Because I have something to tell you baby : will
        ease your trouble in mind
5   Now I'm going back to Biddle Street : try and wear
        you off my mind
6   Because I have another woman on Biddle Street : will
        treat me nice and kind
7   Biddle Street Biddle Street now : is only twenty-six
        blocks long
8   And the women on Biddle Street : just won't leave me
        alone
9   That's why I'm going back to Biddle Street : I swear
        it won't be long
10 Because I know my baby's there : she will take my
        loving on

Spec   1   Speckled Red

        title: House Dance Blues
        place and date: Memphis, 22 Sept. 1929
        record numbers: (M-184-) Br-7137 OJL-20

1   Let me tell you people : some of the grandest news
2   Everybody's talking : about those house-dance blues
3   Police and detectives : will declare by surprise
4   They caught some wind of this : Lord in a dive
5   House-dance blues boys : *still got in the drink*
6   When you hear the judge : call your name
7   *Eleven twenty-two* thirty days : is your fine
8   Now ain't that enough : to change the colored
        people's mind
9   ??? : ???
10 *Doubt* if her could pay for her : all the time
11 Tell him not to *slip* so much : and pay your fine
12 You got to go to Cincy : to make your time
13 Razor man : going to take your name
14 Shave you up and down : put you on the ??? chain
15 You can go to house dance : stay home if you choose
16 You go to house dance : you catch them house-dance
        blues
17 I'm going and I'm going : crying ain't going to make
        me stay
18 The more that you cry : more fars I go away
19 May be tomorrow : may be a year or two
20 You mistreat me babe : it's coming home to you
21 Mama told me : pop told me too
22 Don't you let no woman : be the death of you
23 Cigarettes and ??? strong whiskey : is my crave
24 Son your ??? women : going to carry me to my grave
25 You told me that you loved me : to give my poor
        heart ease
26 Soon as my back was turned : you love just who you
        please
27 You mistreat me now mama : without a cause
28 I'm going away to leave you : and ain't coming back
        here at all

SpiS   1   Spivey, Sweet Pease

        title: Double Dozens
        place and date: Chicago, 12 Aug. 1936
        record numbers: (90787-C) De-7204 AH-158

1   Now you think : you are smart
2   But you really : ain't worth a
3   When I first met you : I thought I fell in good luck
4   Now I know : you ain't worth a
5   You want me to be humble to you : as a lamb
6   I wouldn't mind doing : you ain't worth a
7   I don't want no man : laying around on the grass
8   All you want to do : is just sit on your
9   I'm leaving you baby : fare you well

SpiS   1   Spivey, Sweet Pease

10 Now your D P aching : just go to

SpiV   1   Spivey, Victoria

        title: Arkansas Road Blues
        place and date: St. Louis, 27 Apr. 1927
        record numbers: (80768-B) OK-8481 Spi LP-2001

1   I ain't going to travel : this big road all by
        myself
2   If I don't take my baby : I sure want to have nobody
        else
3   When he were arrested : and put in that mean old
        jail
4   I were the only person : to try and go his bail
5   Ooh : baby why didn't you let me go
6   Daddy if you don't want me : had a-plenty more

SpiV   2   Spivey, Victoria

        title: The Alligator Pond Went Dry
        place and date: St. Louis, 27 Apr. 1927
        record numbers: (80769-B) OK-8481 Spi LP-2001

1   Now old Mr alligator : he got way back
2   He say look out children : I'm going to *float on*
        my back
3   Now old Mr alligator : he got real hot
4   He said we going to have this function : whether
        there's a-water or not
5   Now if you don't believe what I'm saying : ask old
        alligator Jack
6   Wasn't a drop of water in the pond : a-when he got
        back

SpiV   3   Spivey, Victoria

        title: Murder in the First Degree
        place and date: New York, 1 Nov. 1927
        record numbers: (81596-B) OK-8581 Spi LP-2001

1   Well I'm laying here in this jailhouse : scared as
        any fool can be
2   I believe they're going to hang me : from what my
        lawyer said to me
3   My man got running around : with a woman he know I
        can't stand
4   Add one notch on my gun : and the world's rid of one
        trifling man
5   I scrubbed them pots and kettles : I washed and
        ironed the white folks clothes
6   And he got it like I made it : I killed him judge
        and that's all I know
7   I said I ain't done nothing : but kill a man what
        belong to me
8   And here they got me charged : with murder in the
        first degree

SpiV   4   Spivey, Victoria

        title: My Handy Man
        place and date: New York, 12 Sept. 1928
        record numbers: (401114-B) OK-8615 Sw S-1240

1   Whoever said : a good man hard to find
2   Positively absolutely : sure was blind
3   He threads my needle : creams my wheat
4   Heats my heater : chops my meat
5   For everything : he's got a scheme
6   I like the way : he whips my cream
7   Sometimes he's up : before the dawn
8   Busy working : on my lawn
9   My ice don't seem : to melt away

SpiV   4   Spivey, Victoria

10   I get a fresh piece : every day

SpiV   5   Spivey, Victoria

        title: Organ Grinder Blues
        place and date: New York, 12 Sept. 1928
        record numbers: (401115-A) OK unissued Spi
          LP-2001

1   Organ grinder organ grinder : organ grinder play
       that melody
2   Take your organ : and grind some more for me
3   Grind it north grind it north : grind it north and
       grind it east and west
4   When you grind it slow : I like it the best
5   Organ grinder organ grinder : you don't have to pass
       your hat no more
6   You're the grinder : I've been waiting for
7   Organ grinder organ grinder : your sweet music seems
       to ease my mind
8   It's not your organ : but the way you grind
9   Organ grinder organ grinder : organ grinder don't
       tell me you're through
10   If you are tired : let mama grind awhile for you

SpiV   6   Spivey, Victoria

        title: Organ Grinder Blues
        place and date: New York, 12 Sept. 1928
        record numbers: (401115-C) OK-8615 Sw S-1240

1   Organ grinder organ grinder : organ grinder play
       that melody
2   Shake your organ : and grind some more for me
3   Grind it north grind it north : grind it north and
       grind it east and west
4   When you grind it so : I like it the best
5   Organ grinder organ grinder : you don't have to tip
       your hat no more
6   You're the grinder : I've been waiting for
7   Organ grinder organ grinder : your sweet music seems
       to ease my mind
8   It's not your organ : but it's the way you grind
9   Organ grinder organ grinder : organ grinder don't
       tell me you're through
10   If you are done : let mama grind awhile for you

SpiV   7   Spivey, Victoria

        title: New Black Snake Blues--Part 1
        place and date: New York, 13 Oct. 1928
        record numbers: (401222-A) OK-8626 Spi LP-2001

1   In my path lay a black snake : about eight or nine
       inches long
2   Got my ax and mean to kill him : before he sucks my
       rider's tongue
3   Ooh : wonder if my black snake will come back home
4   Wonder if he's got another woman : Lord since he
       been gone

SpiV   8   Spivey, Victoria

        title: How Do You Do It That Way?
        place and date: New York, 10 July 1929
        record numbers: (402526-A) OK-8713 Spi LP-2001

1   Oh when the river runs : flowers are blooming in May
2   And if you get good business : how do you do it that
       way
3   Streetwalking women : they are happy and gay
4   But I'm never happy : how do you get that way
5   Now they can come and go : to and fro every day

SpiV   8   Spivey, Victoria

6   But I can't make them like me : how do you do it
       that way
7   And when the rooster and the hen : go to the barn to
       play
8   Oh the hen had chickens : how do they do it that way

SpiV   9   Spivey, Victoria

        title: Telephoning the Blues
        place and date: New York, 1 Oct. 1929
        record numbers: (56735-1) Vi-V38546 Spi LP-2001

1   Hello there Central : please give me my best man
2   Well I gave you the right number : gee I can't
       understand
3   Ooh : there must be somebody there
4   Central Central : tell me what's that I hear
5   Lord : could that be another woman there
6   So start a-walking the floor : wring my hands and
       pulling my hair
7   Ooh : Central won't you let me know
8   Know that I can get a daddy : most any place I go
9   Oh Central Central : I've been telephoning the blues
10   Central Central : please give me good news
11   I've been phoning phoning : I've been telephoning
       all night long
12   Bet you fifty to one hundred : something is going on
       wrong

SpiV   10   Spivey, Victoria

        title: Don't Trust Nobody Blues
        place and date: Chicago, 20 Mar. 1931
        record numbers: (VO-150-) Vo-1640 Spi LP-2001

1   I don't trust nobody : but the good Lord above
2   And outside of my mother : there's nobody else I
       love
3   Now they will love you and fool you : make you spend
       all your dough
4   After they get what they want : why they don't like
       you no more
5   So-called friends : all that they do
6   Waiting for a chance : to double-cross you
7   Mmm : this ain't no place for me
8   Well I'm going up the country : I mean across the
       deep blue sea
9   Oh friendship ain't no good : that's why I'm hitting
       that long long trail
10   Because they fool with my money : mama don't mind
       going to jail
11   Here I lay here after midnight : drinking my poor
       self to sleep
12   While that lowdown man of mine : is trying to make
       his 'fore-day creep

SpiV   11   Spivey, Victoria

        title: Black Snake Swing
        place and date: Chicago, 7 July 1936
        record numbers: (90785-A) De-7203 AH-58

1   That is some black snake : trying to get the best of
       me
2   But I'm too good a woman : you just wait and see
3   Because oh : I ain't coming here no more
4   Black snake's in my house : black snake's all around
       my door
5   And it's no use to worry : baby about the days being
       long
6   Now black snake got the best dough : and you sure
       can't roll him on
7   Oh : I can't stay there no more

SpiV   11   Spivey, Victoria

8   My black snake is gone : and my poor heart is aching
    me so
9   I don't care what you say : don't you come here no
    more
10 Don't you crawl in my window : don't you creep in my
    door
11 Oh : I don't want you no more
12 Mmm : baby you really made me sore

SpiV   12   Spivey, Victoria

        title: I'll Never Fall in Love Again
        place and date: Chicago, 7 July 1936
        record numbers: (90789-A) De-7203 Spi LP-2001

1   Say I feel myself : falling again
2   In the same hole : that I once was in

SpiV   13   Spivey, Victoria

        title: T. B.'s Got Me Blues
        place and date: Chicago, 7 July 1936
        record numbers: (90790-A) De-7222 Spi LP-2001

1   T B's got me : all my friends done throwed me down
2   But they treated me so nice : when I was up able to
    run around
3   Ooh : my poor lungs are hurting me so
4   I don't get no peace or comfort : no matter where I
    go
5   Lord : my good man don't want me no more
6   Well I wished I was dead : and in the land I'm
    doomed to go

SpiV   14   Spivey, Victoria

        title: I Can't Last Long
        place and date: Chicago, 20 Aug. 1936
        record numbers: (C-1450-2) Vo-03314 Spi LP-2001

1   Lonesome lonesome : yes I'm sinking sinking sinking
    down below my grave
2   Done had a good time : but my how I done paid
3   Because the rising sun : ain't going to shine no
    more
4   Well it's dark and dreary : no matter where I go
5   For the lights in my room : even refuse to shine
6   If my baby don't come back : I know I'll be doing
    time
7   Because ooh : I can't stand no more
8   Well he quit me for my best friend : and don't come
    to see me no more
9   Tell all my good friends : because I know I can't
    last long
10 Please don't you wait : for I'll be dead and gone

SpiV   15   Spivey, Victoria

        title: Detroit Moan
        place and date: Chicago, 15 Oct. 1936
        record numbers: (C-1568-?) Vo unissued Spi
        LP-2001

1   Detroit's a cold cold place : and I ain't got a dime
    to my name
2   I would go to the poorhouse : but Lord you know I'm
    ashamed
3   I been walking Hastings Street : nobody seems to
    treat me right
4   I can make it in the daytime : but Lord these cold
    cold nights
5   Well I'm tired of eating chile : and I can't eat
    beans no more

SpiV   15   Spivey, Victoria

6   People it hurts my feelings : Lord from door to door
7   I've got to leave Detroit : if I have to flag Number
    Ninety-Four
8   And if I ever get back home : I ain't never coming
    to Detroit no more

Spru   1   Spruell, Freddie

        title: Milk Cow Blues
        place and date: Chicago, 25 June 1926
        record numbers: (9793-A) OK-8422 Yz L-1038

1   Listen to my story now : please listen to my song
2   Can you imagine how I feel now : have mercy my real
    milkcow gone
3   She's a full-blood Jersey : I'm going to tell you
    boys the way I know
4   ??? for my milkcow : I don't care where my Jersey go
5   I been on thirty fields : listens boys I been on
    thirty-nine
6   I rambled the whole South Side down : trying to find
    this real milkcow of mine
7   Say my bed [seem lonely, is lonesome] : my pillow
    now it sure do
8   I wake up out of the midnight : I really have those
    milkcow blues
9   Mmm : baby listen hoo hoo hoo
10 Say you look in my face now : run and tell them I
    got those milkcow blues
11 Listen hey : sugar listen hey hey hey
12 Can't you imagine how I feel now : I done told my
    real milkcow bye bye

Spru   2   Spruell, Freddie

        title: Muddy Water Blues
        place and date: Chicago, 17 Nov. 1926
        record numbers: (9908-A) OK-8422 Mam S-3802

1   I know you heard the story : listen now people I
    know the song
2   I mean I drink muddy water : I mean sugar now the
    whole night long
3   I'd rather drink muddy water : rather sleep in a
    real hollow log
4   Baby now before I'd stay with you : let you treat me
    like your driving dog
5   Now daddy daddy daddy listen : turn your lights down
    low
6   I got something good to tell you : she *holler*
    daddy just before you go
7   Put your hat on my dresser : put your shoes daddy
    now under my bed
8   You yearn for my pillow daddy : just to hold your
    little old worried head
9   Listen mmm : baby now how long how long
10 I mean I'd rather drink muddy water baby : because
    you know you sure have done me wrong
11 I'd rather drink muddy water : I'd rather wade in
    muddy water too
12 Now before I'd stay with you : and take these
    lowdown dirty things you do

Spru   3   Spruell, Freddie

        title: Way Back Down Home
        place and date: Chicago, 17 Nov. 1926
        record numbers: (9909-A) OK-8422 Mam S-3802

1   I went to the Western Union : just to send up a
    telephone
2   I heard a fellow say in Memphis : I really mean I
    was dragged down home

252

Spru   3   Spruell, Freddie

3 Some people say that I'm right now : and some say
   I'm wrong
4 You know I can't help but to study : when I really
   think about what it's like down home
5 I mean I'm used to drinking : and I'm used to seeing
   a great good time
6 Things happen way back down home now : they I
   declare they sure run across my mind
7 Now the ticket agent she told me : when the Western
   Union message give me my number wrong
8 You sure can get your number : but you can't go hear
   my words back down home
9 Tell me now what's the matter : now darling
   something must a-be going on wrong
10 I'd just like to get another ??? : I really mean now
   from way back down home
11 Crying hey listen operator now : don't you tell me
   wrong
12 I must've didn't have the right number : when I went
   to the Western Union to the telephone

Spru   4   Spruell, Freddie

    title: Tom Cat Blues
    place and date: Chicago, c. July 1928
    record numbers: (20727-2) Pm-12665 His HLP-17

1 It was late last night : I tried so hard to sleep
2 When a mean old tomcat : started his midnight creep
3 Tomcat's in my window : tomcat's all around my door
4 I never heard so much moaning and whining : in my
   life before
5 I don't trust the tomcat : he's got such an evil eye
6 He's sneaking and mistreating : die if that ain't no
   lie
7 A tomcat man : is trying to break up my home
8 That's why it makes me mad : when I hear a tomcat
   moan
9 Oh Mr tomcat : get somebody of your own
10 For you will lose your nine lives : if you don't let
   my baby alone

Spru   5   Spruell, Freddie

    title: Low-Down Mississippi Bottom Man
    place and date: Chicago, c. July 1928
    record numbers: (20728-1) Pm-12665 Mam S-3802

1 In the lowlands of Mississippi : that's where I was
   born
2 Way down in the sunny South : lowlands raise cotton
   and corn
3 Oh way down in the Delta : that's where I long to be
4 There's a Delta Bottom woman : who is sure going
   crazy over me
5 I'm looking for a lowdown woman : who's looking for
   a lowdown man
6 Ain't nobody in town : get no lowdowner I can
7 I likes lowdown music : I like to barrelhouse get
   drunk too
8 I'm just a lowdown man : always feeling lowdown and
   blue

Spru   6   Spruell, Freddie

    title: 4A Highway
    place and date: Chicago, 12 Apr. 1935
    record numbers: (85782-) BB-B5995 Mam S-3802

1 My baby woke me up this morning : she told me she's
   Joliet bound
2 She want to find Four-A Highway : that's the main
   Highway out of town

Spru   6   Spruell, Freddie

3 She wouldn't even talk with me : wouldn't even have
   a word to say
4 She asking all her friends around now : where she
   find number Four-A highway
5 Number Four-A Highway : that's the main highway out
   of town
6 And she leave out on that highway : I'm sure going
   to trail my baby down
7 I feel like taking my suitcase : setting down on the
   side of that lonesome highway
8 If she leave there between nine and midnight : I'll
   overtake her just before day
9 If I had my machine : I wouldn't worry about leaving
   town
10 I'd get on that Four-A Highway : and God knows I'd
   roll that highway down

Spru   7   Spruell, Freddie

    title: Don't Cry Baby
    place and date: Chicago, 12 Apr. 1935
    record numbers: (85783-) BB-B6025 Mam S-3802

1 Don't worry baby : daddy been here so long
2 I don't want you worrying all about me : because you
   know Freddie's coming back home
3 Don't cry baby : daddy be home some day
4 You know good and well when I left you baby : I did
   not leave to stay
5 She cried all last night : my baby cried all the
   night before
6 I'm going back home to my baby : so she won't have
   to cry no more
7 Don't worry baby : don't you weep and moan
8 Don't you be no ways uneasy about me : some day I'm
   coming back home
9 Baby baby : you understand what I say
10 Don't you worry nothing about me : because I'm
   coming back home some day

Spru   8   Spruell, Freddie

    title: Your Man Is Gone
    place and date: Chicago, 12 Apr. 1935
    record numbers: (85784-) BB-B6025 Mam S-3802

1 I feel like taking my suitcase : sitting down by
   that railroad side
2 If I ever get killed baby : don't tell nobody how I
   died
3 Baby please don't tell my mother : please don't let
   my sister know
4 Sure as you appreciate my death baby : will you
   please hang crepe on your door
5 When you walk into the undertaker : look over on
   your right-hand side
6 You can ask the undertakers about me : they may tell
   you how I died
7 Baby baby don't you worry : sugar don't you weep and
   moan
8 You may know about *bad luck* baby : that your Fred
   is dead and gone
9 Buy me some flowers : see how they put my body away
10 You can tell all your friends around baby : you
   heard the last word I had to say
11 When [you, they] go to the cemetery : they begin to
   lower my body down
12 You know that's the last of my good man : because
   they putting him down in the cold cold ground

253

Spru   9   Spruell, Freddie

       title: Let's Go Riding
       place and date: Chicago, 12 Apr. 1935
       record numbers: (85785-) BB-B6261 OJL-18

1   Now come on girl : let's go out and have some fun
2   Want to go out riding : I can tell you how it's done
3   We can go out : and have a very good time
4   I'll tell you all about it : now bear it in mind
5   Want to go riding : don't have to go far
6   You fix the blow-outs : I'll drive the car
7   Dum dee da : dee da do
8   Now explain it to me : tell me would you like to go
9   I have told you that I would explain it to you : how
       it's done
10 Now when you let me go out riding : and have some
       fun
11 Now in case you want to go : now let me know
12 Here now tell me : would you really like to go
13 Now if you want to go with me riding : we could
       really have some fun
14 If you buy the hot dogs : I got the buns
15 Now tell me now : can't you go
16 Now listen would you explain it to me : and tell me
       did you know
17 Now you don't have to worry : we ain't so old
18 Now if you got the line : I got the pole
19 Now tell me dear : don't you know
20 We can go out for a good time : would you like to go
21 Now if you will just tell me brown : to know
22 Tell me : would you like to go
23 Now you don't have to worry : about being gone so
       long
24 Now we going to have a good time : we'll take a
       blanket along
25 Soap and towels : included too
26 No telling what goes on : when you don't take that
       with you
27 Now it's tell me dear : what you mean to do
28 I'll go out riding : if you will too
29 Now come on baby : we'll go out and have some really
       fun
30 I told you you get the hot dogs : I'll get the buns
31 Well dear : that's what I mean to say
32 I want you to go out riding with me : and have a
       good time today

Spru   10   Spruell, Freddie

       title: Mr. Freddie's Kokomo Blues
       place and date: Chicago, 12 Apr. 1935
       record numbers: (85786-) BB-B5995 Mam S-3802

1   Won't you come on baby come on baby : let's go back
       to Kokomo
2   That's a small town in Western Michigan : tell daddy
       don't you want to go
3   Now these women around Chicago is crazy : hollering
       about the times so hard
4   And the women in Kokomo baby : they drinking liquor
       from real *costly* bar
5   Why don't you come on baby come on : and let's go
       back to Kokomo
6   Yes I'm leaving here tomorrow morning : tell me baby
       don't you want to go
7   Kokomo's about the best city : I declare that I ever
       saw
8   You can break them down both night and day : and
       won't be worried and bothered with no law
9   Now I tell you all about that city : I declare it
       ain't a great large town
10 But everywhere you go in Kokomo baby : you find the
       women there breaking them down
11 Said now Mary had a little lamb : I mean his fleece
       was white as snow
12 Mary take that little lamb with her : to most every
       place that she go

Spru   10   Spruell, Freddie

13 She went down to the depot agent : they give her a
       ticket back to Kokomo
14 Depot agent look down at Mary's lamb : said Mary I
       declare your lamb can't go
15 She *lied* just come on baby come on : I declare I'm
       going back to Kokomo
16 Why don't you come on baby come on : listen tell me
       don't you want to go
17 I will buy you a ticket baby : only cost us nineteen
       seventy-five
18 When that train leaves tomorrow morning : I want to
       catch that morning train and ride

Stev   1   Stevens, Vol (Memphis Jug Band)

       title: Beale Street Mess Around
       place and date: Atlanta, 20 Oct. 1927
       record numbers: (40320-1) Vi-21066 Rt RL-322

1   Woke up early this morning : blues around my bed
2   And the ??? : running everywhere
3   I can sit right here : think a thousand miles away
4   I was thinking about : that brownskin woman of mine
5   I'm going to blow this town : honey it won't be long
6   And I'm going to be dead : before I go back here no
       more
7   And I'm going for the summer : won't be back till
       fall
8   If I don't get no better treatment : go back here no
       more
9   And it's one of these mornings : honey it won't be
       long
10 You going to look for me : I'll be a thousand miles
       away
11 You can take these blues : and lay them on your
       shelf
12 ??? : sing them to yourself

Stev   2   Stevens, Vol (Memphis Jug Band)

       title: I'll See You in the Spring When the Birds
         Begin to Sing
       place and date: Atlanta, 20 Oct. 1927
       record numbers: (40321-1) Vi-21066 Rt RL-322

1   And I'm going away : just to wear you off my mind
2   You keep me troubled : honey all the time

Stev   3   Stevens, Vol

       title: Vol Stevens Blues
       place and date: Atlanta, 20 Oct. 1927
       record numbers: (40324-1) Vi-21356 OJL-21

1   Woke up early this morning : feeling awful low
2   And the blues they had me : *running up the wall*
3   You can read my letter : you sure can't read my mind
4   You think I love you : better change your mind
5   Said my mother told me : my dear old father too
6   Said I used to love some : *faro out of town*
7   If I had a-listened : what my mother say
8   I'd have been at home : with a *black-haired* ???
9   Now a brownskin woman : always on my mind
10 She keeps me troubled : worried all the time
11 You can take these blues : and lay them on your
       shelf
12 Get blue tomorrow : sing them for yourself

Stev   4   Stevens, Vol

        title: Baby Got the Rickets
        place and date: Atlanta, 20 Oct. 1927
        record numbers: (40325-1) Vi-21356 OJL-19

1   And it's one of these mornings : honey and it won't
    be long
2   Going to catch the *knocker* : down on *Maple* Hill
3   Got the rickets got the rickets : and my baby got
    the Mobile blues
4   ??? : wear you off my mind
5   And the girl I love : just went and broke my heart
6   And I'm going away : wear you off my mind
7   You can take these blues : and hang them on your
    shelf
8   ??? tomorrow : sing them to yourself

Stev   5   Stevens, Vol (Memphis Jug Band)

        title: Coal Oil Blues
        place and date: Memphis, 13 Feb. 1928
        record numbers: (41888-2) Vi-21278 OJL-4

1   Woke up early early this morning : got out of my bed
2   And the blues had started : climbing up the bed
3   If you ever been been down : you know just how I
    feel
5   Woke up early early this morning : with the blues
    all around my bed
6   And the blues they tell me : crying man oh man
7   Oh the preacher in the pulpit : he laid his Bible
    down
8   And the members in the corner : singing Alabama
    bound
9   ??? Coal-Oil Johnny : sure was a-born in hell
10 Papa *preacher* thought : he sure was a-born in born
11 I'm going to leave this town : honey and it won't be
    long
12 And I'm going to be at the depot : blow back hell or
    home
13 If I feel tomorrow : just like I feel right now
14 Before the rising sun come : sure won't *scarcely
    know*

Stev   6   Stevens, Vol (Memphis Jug Band)

        title: Papa Long Blues
        place and date: Memphis, 13 Feb. 1928
        record numbers: (41889-2) Vi-21278 Rt RL-322

1   Woke up early this morning : blues all around my bed
2   And the blues ain't there : they easing everywhere
3   If I feel tomorrow : like I feel right now
4   Going to pack my suitcase : get me down the road
    somewhere
5   And I'm going I'm going : your crying won't make me
    stay
6   And I won't be there : just won't blow back anymore
7   If I feel tomorrow : like I feel right now
8   Going to ride till sundown : tomorrow catch me
    there
9   And it's one of these mornings : honey it won't be
    long
10 You will call for me : and I'll be a thousand miles
    from home

Stev   7   Stevens, Vol (Memphis Jug Band)

        title: Aunt Caroline Dyer Blues
        place and date: Memphis, 29 May 1930
        record numbers: (62541-) Vi-23347 Jo SM-3104

1   I'm going to Newport News : just to see Aunt
    Caroline Dyer

Stev   7   Stevens, Vol (Memphis Jug Band)

2   She's the fortunetelling woman : oh Lord and she
    don't tell no lies
3   I'm going to Newport News : just to pass ??? on the
    doggone day
4   Because bad luck and hard work : oh Lord sure don't
    agree with me
5   Aunt Caroline Dyer she told me : son you don't have
    to feel so rough
6   I'm going to pick you up a mojo : oh Lord so you can
    strut your stuff
7   Aunt Caroline Dyer she told me : son these women
    they don't mean you no good
8   Said take my advice : and don't bother with none in
    your neighborhood
9   I am leaving in the morning : I don't want no one to
    feel blue
10 I'm going back to Newport News : and do what Aunt
    Caroline Dyer told me to do

Stev   8   Stevens, Vol (Memphis Jug Band)

        title: Stonewall Blues
        place and date: Memphis, 29 May 1930
        record numbers: (62542-) BB-B5675 BC-2

1   Tell me mailman : I can't get no news
2   Know by that baby : I'm bound to have those
    stonewall blues
3   I called my good gal : my tongue was too weak to
    talk
4   Go where she was : but my feet were too weak to walk
5   Seem like I can hear : my good gal's voice in the
    air
6   Said daddy I have a man ??? : and you have no rights
    in there
7   Oh you ever get in jail : boy and you have no
    friends
8   Feel just like Daniel : when they throwed him in
    that lion's den
9   My good gal wrote a letter : how do you reckon it
    read
10 Come home little daddy : your father's might near
    dead
11 How can I come home baby : with these tall rock
    walls over my head
12 Know by that baby : got no one to hold my aching
    head
13 Oh where were you : when the clock struck five 'fore
    day
14 Down in that old foundry : trying to roll my cares
    away

Stok   1   Stokes, Frank

        title: You Shall
        place and date: Chicago, c. Aug. 1927
        record numbers: (4771-3) Pm-12518 Rt RL-308

1   Oh well it's our Father : who art in heaven
2   The preacher owed me ten dollars : he paid me seven
3   Thy kingdom come : Thy will be done
4   If I hadn't took the seven Lord : I wouldn't have
    gotten none
5   Oh well some folks say : that a preacher won't steal
6   I caught about eleven : in the watermelon field
7   Just a-cutting and a-slicing : got to tearing up the
    vine
8   They's eating and talking : most all the time
9   Oh well you see a preacher : lay behind the log
10 A hand on the trigger : got his eye on the hog
11 The hog said mmm : the gun said zip
12 Jumped on the hog : with all his grip
13 Now when I first went over : to Memphis Tennessee
14 I was crazy about the preachers : as I could be
15 I went out on the front porch : a-walking about

255

Stok   1   Stokes, Frank

16 Invite the preacher over : to my house
17 He washed his face : he combed his head
18 And next thing he want to do : was slip in my bed
19 I caught him by the head : man kicked him out the
    door
20 Don't allow my preacher : at my house no more

Stok   2   Stokes, Frank

        title: Sweet to Mama
        place and date: Chicago, c. Aug. 1927
        record numbers: (4773-1) Pm-12531 Rt RL-308

1   Lord I woke up this morning : with the blues all
    around my baby's bed
2   I turned my face to the wall : baby these are the
    words I said
3   Lordy it's sweet to mama : now mama where you stay
    last night
4   Because your clothes all wrinkled : mama and your
    hair sure ain't fixed up right
5   Lord it's two drops of water : Lord and one or two
    grains of sand
6   Now babe the blues ain't nothing : but a woman want
    to see her man
7   Lord it's two pretty steamers : Lord they running
    along side by side
8   And now you know my good gal : I can't keep her
    satisfied
9   Lord my mama told me : Lord when I was a child
10 You having good times now : you have trouble after
    awhile
11 If I just had a-listened : to just what my mama said
12 I would have been at home : trying to live good and
    ???
13 Lord when you see the spider : Lord a-running up and
    down the wall
14 He must be going somewhere : great God to try and
    have his ashes hauled
15 I said a-weeping Mary : now Mary don't you weep no
    more
16 And now stop and take your time : and do your work
    everywhere you go

Stok   3   Stokes, Frank

        title: Half Cup of Tea
        place and date: Chicago, c. Aug. 1927
        record numbers: (4774-2) Pm-12531 Rt RL-308

1   Hey : what do you want your man to do
2   Said I rob and steal : and make everything for you
3   Well now for my breakfast : give me half a cup of
    tea
4   About half past nine : sing the same old song to me
5   Now : I ain't going to work for you no more
6   Every time I work for you : *carried* from door to
    door
7   Well now your wife get ??? : and don't want to stay
    at home
8   Find another one walking : let the front-door gal
    alone
9   Hey : something's really worrying me
10 It's not my best *filly* : but it's the gal I'd like
    to see
11 I say sometime I feel : like I'm going away from
    home
12 Men don't like my peaches : they sure can't leave me
    alone
13 Hey : mama what's the matter now
14 *Every midnight dream in the world* : and I don't
    know how
15 And I feel like hollering : murder in the first
    degree

Stok   3   Stokes, Frank

16 You didn't have no business gal : starting to deal
    with me
17 I : ain't going to stay with you no more
18 Every time I stay with you : *carried* from door to
    door

Stok   4   Stokes, Frank

        title: Beale Town Bound
        place and date: Chicago, c. Aug. 1927
        record numbers: (4775-2) Pm-12576 Rt RL-308

1   Said I'm [leaving mama, going away] : I'm going to
    leave you now
2   Every time I think : I think I'm downtown
3   Yeah listen mama : what I'm about to say to you
4   Ain't a thing to the world mama : that I want you to
    do
5   If the blues get away from me mama : I'm going back
    home with you
6   Every time I see you : I think about the things I
    want to do
7   And I'm going I'm going mama : what you want me to
    bring you back
8   Mama think about the things in the world : that your
    good friends have
9   I'm going to the workhouse : set out on the floor
10 And if the times don't get better : I ain't going
    back home no more
11 And I feel like hollering : murder in the first
    degree
12 You didn't have no business mama : starting this
    deal with me

Stok   5   Stokes, Frank

        title: Last Go Round
        place and date: Chicago, c. Aug. 1927
        record numbers: (4777-1) Pm-12591 Bio BLP-12041

1   Hey listen at me mama : don't be all night
2   I know something : suit your appetite
3   Yeah don't know nothing : meet my gal somewhere
4   And I won't be : when you meet me there
5   Oh when you meet me baby : go good and slow
6   I take my time baby : where I go
7   Now don't you think I know : my baby love me so
8   She make five dollars : and she give me four
9   She takes it to town : and she walks it about
10 And she treats me nice : around her house

Stok   6   Stokes, Frank

        title: You Shall
        place and date: Chicago, c. Sept. 1927
        record numbers: (20043-2) Pm-12518 Bio BLP-12041

1   Oh well it's our Father : who art in heaven
2   The preacher owed me ten dollars : he paid me seven
3   Thy kingdom come : Thy will be done
4   If I hadn't took the seven Lord : I wouldn't have
    gotten none
5   Oh well some folks say : that a preacher won't steal
6   I caught about eleven : in the watermelon field
7   Just a-cutting and a-slicing : got to tearing up the
    vine
8   They's eating and talking : most all the time
9   Oh well you see a preacher : laying behind the log
10 A hand on the trigger : got his eye on the hog
11 The hog said mmm : the gun said zip
12 Jumped on the hog : with all his grip
13 Now when I first went over : to Memphis Tennessee
14 I was crazy about preachers : as I could be
15 I went out on the front porch : a-walking about

256

16 Invite the preacher : over to my house
17 He washed his face : he combed his head
18 And the next thing he wanted to do : was slip in my
    bed
19 I caught him by the head : man kicked him out the
    door
20 Don't allow my preacher : at my house no more

Stok   7   Stokes, Frank

        title: Its a Good Thing
        place and date: Chicago, c. Sept. 1927
        record numbers: (20044-2) Pm-12518 Bio BLP-12041

1   Now when I was young : in my prime
2   *Pick these* different women : all the time
3   I had a woman : God her name was Lucy
4   God almighty devil : what that woman wouldn't do
5   Another woman : God her name Henrietta
6   Talk to six straight men : say she knows no better
7   Another woman : God her name was Mattie
8   She's a-slipping and a-stalling : in some dark alley
9   Another woman : God her name was Jenny
10 Talked to white folks black folks : she wouldn't
    give a penny
11 Another woman : God her name was Mae
12 A white man only : got every day
13 I knocked Mae down : I stomped in her face
14 Half her trouble : must have ???
15 I went to the workhouse : to work out my time
16 And the same doggone woman : on my mind
17 In time I got out : I drunk a little gin
18 I goed right back : to Mae's house again
19 By time I got in the house : getting ready to have a
    little fun
20 Made me come back *about* : I gotten more than one
21 Now let me tell you a little something : don't you
    raise no fuss
22 Boys these young women : want to do their stuff
23 From their legs and from their ankles : and on to
    their knees
24 *Trying to ??? devilment* : as they can be
25 While you're out man : trying to ???
26 She's a-winking and a-blinking : at another man
27 You get out at night : you peeping through a crack
28 I wonder how long : before my husband gets back
29 Your husband get back : you ready to have a little
    fun
30 Before you get out of sight : he got more than one
31 And now I'm getting old : Lord my head's getting
    grey
32 Lord I'm not bow-legged : but I walks that way
33 I *claim to see the oldest rat* : of the *barge*
34 I known about the women : long before I got grown
35 But some in the daytime : some at night
36 How in the world : can you treat any living man
    right
37 Any time you get out : you're ready to ???
38 Turn around and slipping down : jumping in your bed
39 He jumped in your bed : he begin to have a little
    fun
40 Anything you want to know : got a little *lunch*
    done
41 A little *lunch* done : from three to four
42 Have to *turn down* : before your old man go
43 You may be brownskin : you color may be black
44 What I say about you women : I won't take it back
45 I get drunk : love to have my fun
46 But all the darn women : got more than one

        title: Mr. Crump Don't Like It
        place and date: Chicago, c. Sept. 1927
        record numbers: (20045-1) Pm-12552 OJL-21

1   If Mr Crump don't like it : he ain't going to have
    it here
2   No barrelhouse women : God and drinking no beer
3   I saw the Baptist sister jump up : and began to
    shout
4   But I'm so glad : that that whiskey vote is out
5   I saw the Methodist sister jumped up : and they had
    a fit
6   She was doggone sorry : *weren't* king corn *here*
7   I saw the Presbyterian sister turn around : and
    began to grin
8   Lord I believe I'll start out : to barrelhousing
    again
9   I saw the deacon look around : sister why in the
    world don't you hush
10 I'd rather see you get drunk : than wear this
    hubbard skirt
11 You don't like my peaches : don't shake my tree
12 Don't like my fruit : let my orange juice be

Stok   9   Stokes, Frank

        title: Blues in D
        place and date: Chicago, c. Sept. 1927
        record numbers: (20048-2) Pm-12552 Bio BLP-12041

1   And I'm going and I'm going : and your crying won't
    make me stay
2   Baby the more you cry : the further you drive me
    away
3   And I'm leaving baby : what you want me to bring you
    back
4   Mama dream of what I'm leaving : something that your
    good gal like
5   Hey hey : mama what's the matter now
6   I would be your ??? : but I don't know how
7   Take me in your arms mama : and rock me good and
    slow
8   So I can take my time : and do my work everywhere I
    go
9   Now you can tell a good man : looking in his face
10 ??? shoulders : nice and cute through the waist

Stok   10   Stokes, Frank

        title: Downtown Blues
        place and date: Memphis, 1 Feb. 1928
        record numbers: (41822-1) Vi-21272 BC-5

1   Hey listen mama : the world is done gone away
2   I'm got a bad-luck deal : give me trouble every day
3   And I'm going I'm going : pin up black tape on your
    door
4   Tell your man ain't dead : just ain't coming to your
    house no more
5   And I'm going downtown : going to stay around there
    till dark
6   I don't want no trouble : don't want you to drive
    off
7   Now when you lay down at night : lit out early try
    to take your rest
8   You'll get a couple phone calls : wake up and try to
    do your best
9   I'm got a gal in the country : I'm got two that
    stays in town
10 Reason I can fill it so careful : because nar' of
    them don't throw me down

Stok   11   Stokes, Frank

        title: Downtown Blues
        place and date: Memphis, 1 Feb. 1928
        record numbers: (41822-2) Vi unissued His HLP-31

 1 Hey listen mama : the world is done gone away
 2 I got a bad-luck deal : give me trouble every day
 3 And I'm going I'm going : pin up black crepe on your
    door
 4 Tell your man ain't dead : just ain't coming to your
    house no more
 5 And I'm going downtown : going to stay around there
    till dawn
 6 And I want no trouble : don't want you to drive me
    home
 7 Now when you lay down at night : lit out early try
    to take your rest
 8 You'll get a couple phone calls : wake up and try to
    do your best
 9 I got a gal in the country : got two that stays in
    town
10 The reason I can *fill it* so careful : because man
    don't know me there

Stok   12   Stokes, Frank

        title: Bedtime Blues
        place and date: Memphis, 1 Feb. 1928
        record numbers: (41825-1) Vi-21272 Rt RL-308

 1 Now when you lay down at night : call your good
    friend by name
 2 You don't like my *teepee* : you sure can't make my
    ???
 3 And I looked at the sun : and the sun was shining
    warm
 4 You never miss your good gal : till you caught your
    train and gone
 5 And you stood and cried : what you want me to say to
    you
 6 I want you to think about the things baby : that me
    and you used to do
 7 Honey run here baby : let's join our good hands
 8 I been in trouble some place : gal ever since I been
    your man
 9 If the blues don't quit me : I'll stay drunk every
    day
10 The last time I seen you : trying to make your
    get-away

Stok   13   Stokes, Frank

        title: What's the Matter Blues
        place and date: Memphis, 1 Feb. 1928
        record numbers: (41826-1) Vi-V38531 Yz L-1002

 1 Oh now I wonder what's the matter : I can't rest at
    night
 2 A good woman that I'm loving : done took my appetite
 3 And she quit me she left me : to sing this song
 4 You never miss your friend : till you caught your
    train and gone
 5 And I'm going downtown : going to stay right there
    till fall
 6 Don't get the gal I want : I don't want no girl at
    all
 7 Say you talk about Sally : talk about Sally Lou
 8 Well the woman that I'm crazy about : she knows just
    what to do
 9 What's the matter now baby : that I could not treat
    you kind
10 You give me a bad-luck deal : kept something on my
    mind

Stok   14   Stokes, Frank

        title: Mistreatin' Blues
        place and date: Memphis, 27 Aug. 1928
        record numbers: (45419-1) Vi-21672 Rt RL-308

 1 Now you mistreat me : oh baby drove me from your
    door
 2 Oh but the Good Book say : mama you got to reap just
    what you sow
 3 Well if you don't want me : well mama you don't have
    to *run no salt*
 4 I can find more good girls : than a passenger train
    can haul
 5 I ain't going by your color : or woman neither by
    your good hair
 6 Oh but the dreams that you give me : baby call me
    from anywhere
 7 Now you may be brownskin : and your hair weren't too
    long
 8 If you mistreat me woman : you sure God lost your
    home
 9 And I'm going to the Gypsy : have my good gal's
    fortune told
10 She got a pocket full of green : and back her
    mouth's up full of gold
11 And it's wonder what the reason : now baby I can't
    rest at night
12 For the gal that I'm crazy about : have took my
    appetite

Stok   15   Stokes, Frank

        title: It Won't Be Long Now
        place and date: Memphis, 27 Aug. 1928
        record numbers: (45420-2) Vi-21672 Rt RL-307

 1 One of these mornings : mama and it won't be long
 2 Before you miss your good man : rolling in your arms
 3 I'm going I'm going mama : what you want me to bring
    you back
 4 Mama think what I'm carrying away : something that
    your good gal likes
 5 I don't want no gravy mama : when the gravy get cold
 6 Don't want no bad-luck woman : ain't got no place to
    go
 7 You miss your baby : rolling in your arms
 8 But if you don't come to see me : count the days I'm
    gone
 9 And I'm going I'm going : put a black tape on your
    door
10 For your man ain't dead : just ain't coming here no
    more
11 Now when you lay down at night : lay down early try
    to take your rest
12 You get a call before down : wake up and try to do
    your best

Stok   16   Stokes, Frank

        title: Nehi Mama Blues
        place and date: Memphis, 27 Aug. 1928
        record numbers: (45421-2) Vi-21738 Rt RL-308

 1 White man take the blues : he walk to the river and
    sit down
 2 If the blues get too heavy : he'll jump overboard
    and drown
 3 Now it's east and west : north and south
 4 Why the Nehi women : have done turned me out
 5 So they can eagle rock me they can talk me : about
    the things that I used to do
 6 I got the Nehi blues mama : don't know what in the
    world to do
 7 Well now T for Texas : T for Tennessee
 8 M is for mighty bad weather : boys she stole away
    from me

Stok   16   Stokes, Frank

 9 Now down North Third Street : the corner of Beale
10 Where the Nehi women : have got a terrible *steal*
11 Now papa got to singing : my folks got to crying
12 For Nehi women : stays on my mind
13 Now little batch of posies : laid on my door
14 The Nehi women keep me : everywhere I go

Stok   17   Stokes, Frank

     title: Stomp that Thing
     place and date: Memphis, 28 Aug. 1928
     record numbers: (45426-2) Vi-21738 Rt RL-308

 1 Now my song's gotten tight : they won't treat me
     right
 2 Try to keep good drinking whiskey : out of my sight
 3 Now I'm a lonely guy : following the browns
 4 I think about the times : since I left town
 5 Bring around the bottle stopper : let's bottle some
     beer
 6 The town done got : too dry around here
 7 Now stomp it in the summertime : you needn't wait
     till fall
 8 Don't stomp it right : you needn't stomp it at all
 9 Now mama said one thing : my papa said the same
10 Stomping that thing : is about to change my name

Stok   18   Stokes, Frank

     title: Take Me Back
     place and date: Memphis, 30 Aug. 1928
     record numbers: (45454-2) Vi-V38531 Yz L-1008

 1 Now what I mean : by treating you right
 2 I'll bring you my money : every Saturday night
 3 Now that old girl : that stayed in town
 4 Called me *booze* : and turned me around
 5 Now if you love me mama : you'll treat me right
 6 You'll bring me that money : every Saturday night
 7 Now if you will mama : take me back
 8 I'll be good : as any man can act

Stok   19   Stokes, Frank

     title: How Long?
     place and date: Memphis, 30 Aug. 1928
     record numbers: (45455-1) Vi-V38512 BC-6

 1 I never never never : can forget that day
 3 If you see my baby baby baby : tell her to hurry
     home
 5 Now listen at me mama mama : why did you let me go
 7 Well I hate the train train : that carried my baby
     away
 9 Now listen at me baby baby : everything all right
     with me
11 I never never : baby I can't see anymore
13 When you called me baby : how long how long
14 I ain't had no loving : how long how long
15 I ain't had no good feeling : how long how long
16 And I'm on my way babe : how long how long
17 Oh look here baby : how long how long
18 I ain't had no loving : how long how long
19 And left me standing : how long how long
20 I ain't had no loving : how long how long
21 When you called me baby : how long how long
22 I ain't had no loving : since my baby gone
23 Oh look here baby : how long how long
24 I ain't had no loving : since my baby gone
25 Oh run here baby : how long how long
26 I ain't had no loving : since my baby gone

Stok   20   Stokes, Frank

     title: Ain't Going to Do Like I Used to Do
     place and date: Chicago, c. Mar. 1929
     record numbers: (21229-2) Pm-12774 Rt RL-308

 1 I : ain't going to do like I used to do
 2 I'm going to stand right here : do the same old
     thing to you
 3 Hey listen mama : if you will treat me right
 4 I will be good to you : I won't mistreat you no time
 5 Now if you love me baby : I'll treat you good and
     kind
 6 I will start being nice : and keep you on my mind

Stok   21   Stokes, Frank

     title: Hunting Blues
     place and date: Chicago, c. Mar. 1929
     record numbers: (21234-1) Pm-12774 Rt RL-333

 1 Said I went out hunting : hunting all *night and
     day*
 2 When I got home : my gal was gone away
 3 Says that's all right : I'll see you again
 5 Now if you let me baby : I will treat you so good
     and kind
 6 Now you mistreat me : when you leave trouble in my
     mind
 7 If you feel like : your good gal just quit you in
     the *long*
 8 Then you'll set right here : play and begin to sing
     this song

Stok   22   Stokes, Frank

     title: South Memphis Blues
     place and date: Memphis, 23 Sept. 1929
     record numbers: (55573-2) Vi-V38548 Rt RL-308

 1 I don't want you to weep mama : I don't want you to
     moan
 2 But I'm so glad : now made me leave my home
 3 When I was down in Mississippi : having troubles of
     my own
 4 But I done got satisfied : South Memphis is my home
 5 Mmm : mama what's the matter now
 6 I would take you to South Memphis : mama but I don't
     know how
 7 I've been so true mama : and I want you to do
 8 Before I'll take you to South Memphis : I going bid
     you adieu

Stok   23   Stokes, Frank

     title: Bunker Hill Blues
     place and date: Memphis, 23 Sept. 1929
     record numbers: (55574-1) Vi-V38548 Rt RL-308

 1 Now old Bunker Hill : place that I [long, wants] to
     stay
 2 Where I can have a good time : ??? every day
 3 *Hey them* Mississippi mama : and you look all right
     to me
 4 I'm just crazy about your good looks : as any poor
     man can be
 5 And the people on Bunker Hill : look at me sing this
     song
 6 Say that's papa Frank Stokes : he sure got *worried
     on*
 7 I'm going to take me a *ladder* : I mean ??? *light*
     I see
 8 Mama that's all right : you're sweet enough for me
 9 I'm going to talk to some day : talk to you for
     myself

Stok   23   Stokes, Frank

   10   If you don't treat me right mama : you can't *treat*
        nobody else

Stok   24   Stokes, Frank

        title: Right Now Blues
        place and date: Memphis, 25 Sept. 1929
        record numbers: (55584-2) Vi-V38589 Yz L-1018

    1   Right now's the time : mama for you to change your
        mind
    2   You give me bad luck dear mama : you trouble me all
        the time
    3   Now I told mama listen : if you be good
    4   Give everything in this world mama : that a man ever
        could
    5   Sometime I think I will : then again I think I won't
    6   Sometime I think I like my good gal : again I think
        I don't
    7   Now listen at me mama : mama if you'll only be kind
    8   I do everything mama : to try to satisfy your mind

Stok   25   Stokes, Frank

        title: Shiney Town Blues
        place and date: Memphis, 25 Sept. 1929
        record numbers: (55591-1) Vi-V38589 RBF RF-202

    1   I ain't no rounder : but I stays at home
    2   If you don't like my treatment : you sure can leave
        me alone
    3   Babe it's some day : you'll come to be my friend
    4   Then we will be all right : be back on the road
        again
    5   Tell me cloudy weather : the sun refuse to shine
    6   And I'll take my home : back in shiny town
    7   I love you baby : the best way in my life
    8   Ain't nothing that separate from me : for you to be
        my wife

Stok   26   Stokes, Frank

        title: Frank Stoke's Dream
        place and date: Memphis, 30 Sept. 1929
        record numbers: (56305-2) Vi-23411 Yz L-1008

    1   And I'm going I'm going : and your crying won't make
        me stay
    2   Because the more you cry gal : the further you drive
        me away
    3   When I leave your house : pin up black crepe on your
        door
    4   Tell your man ain't dead : he ain't coming back here
        no more
    5   Ever dream that you lucky : and wake up cold in hand
    6   I wouldn't *hand her* my last dollar : to give your
        ???ing man
    7   Take me in your arms : rock me good and slow
    8   Know you hear them Frank Stokes blues : anywhere on
        earth you go
    9   And I'm leaving you mama : this is the last time
        I'll ever go
   10   When the Frank Stokes blues come around : I got a
        place to go

Stok   27   Stokes, Frank

        title: Memphis Rounders Blues
        place and date: Memphis, 30 Sept. 1929
        record numbers: (56306-2) Vi-23411 Rt RL-308

    1   Now what makes Memphis women : love a rounder so

Stok   27   Stokes, Frank

    2   Because he takes his time : doing the work
        everywhere he goes
    3   I don't drink whiskey : but I'm crazy about my wine
    4   If you take my good gal : I give you trouble all the
        time
    5   There's only four places in Memphis : that I'd like
        to go
    6   Where I could have a good time : and do my work
        everywhere I go
    7   Throwed up my hands : clasped them 'fore the sun
    8   I might take my time : with the work that I once
        have done
    9   Then I'm going to sing this verse : and I wasn't
        going to sing no more
   10   Know if you hear me doing any singing : I'll be
        standing around my door

Ston   1   Stone, Joe

        title: It's Hard Time
        place and date: Chicago, 2 Aug. 1933
        record numbers: (76837-) BB-B5169 Yz L-1030

    1   And it's hard time here : hard time everywhere
    3   I went down to the factory : where I worked three
        year
    4   And the bossman told me : man I ain't hiring here
    5   Now we have a little city : that they call *down in
        Baltimore*
    6   Times have got so hard : people ain't got no place
        to go
    7   Don't the moon look pretty : shining down through
        the trees
    8   I can see my fair brown : swear to God that she
        can't see me
    9   Car rolled this morning : I was lying out on my own
   10   Lord I didn't have no train fare baby : didn't have
        no place to go
   11   I'm going to send a trunk : babe I ain't going to
        send no more
   12   Because my baby keep on coming : baby and I believe
        that I better go
   13   Indeed I hate to hear : my faro call my name
   14   She don't call so lonesome : but she calls *my name*

Ston   2   Stone, Joe

        title: Back Door Blues
        place and date: Chicago, 2 Aug. 1933
        record numbers: (76838-) BB-B5169 Yz L-1030

    1   I'm going to buy me a little red rooster mama : put
        it in my back door
    2   So when a *trixie* be passing by : he will flap his
        little wings and crow
    3   I'm going to buy me a bulldog : because my pistol is
        number forty-one
    4   I'm going to shoot you if you stand still : mama I
        got a doggone dog to catch you if you run
    5   Catch a *day boat* at the freight yard : I'm going
        back to New Orleans
    6   Because honey I only want a mama : seems just like a
        country dream
    7   Sure to be buried in the river mama : than to be
        buried in a hollow log
    8   Because I got a no-good faro : and she treat me just
        like a dog
    9   Said I'm leave this time mama : please don't hang
        none that crepe on my door
   10   Because I won't be dead : but I ain't coming back
        here no more
   11   ??? : good as any man can be
   12   And I wonder why mama : that you can't get along
        with me

Stov   1   Stovepipe No. 1

        title: Court Street Blues
        place and date: St. Louis, 25 Apr. 1927
        record numbers: (80749-A) OK-8514 Fly LP-103

1   Thought I'd get me a picket : off a graveyard fence
2   Going to beat you brownskin : till you learn some
    sense
3   Hey : what's the matter now
4   Say you trying to flip with me : honey and you don't
    know how
5   I'm leaving here : ain't coming back till fall
6   If the blues overtake me : I ain't coming back at
    all
7   Tell me brownskin : what is on your mind
8   Reason I asks you browny : you about to run me blind

Stov   2   Stovepipe No. 1

        title: A Woman Gets Tired of the Same Man All
        the Time
        place and date: St. Louis, 26 Apr. 1927
        record numbers: (80748-A) OK-8514 Rt RL-310

1   Oh a woman gets tired I mean real tired : of the
    same man all the time
2   Oh the way my wife been *attracting* of late : she's
    about to make me lose my mind
3   When I'm out on my wagon : try to sell a little coal
4   Oh well she's around the corner : *oozing* sweet
    jellyroll

Stov   3   Stovepipe No. 1

        title: Bed Slats
        place and date: St. Louis, 26 Apr. 1927
        record numbers: (80760-B) OK-8543 His HLP-4

1   And I went upstairs : about four o'clock
2   I rapped on my door : and my door was locked
3   I peeped through transom : and my gal was gone
4   I caught another mule : kicking in my stall
5   I had a gal : and her name was *Leese*
6   Every time *I clasp her* : she would holler police
7   She cooked them biscuits : she cooked them brown
8   *Her pancakes were black* : when she turned them
    around
9   I told my gal : the week before last
10 I had to *take these canned beans* : most too fast
11 I went to the river : take my rocking chair
12 The blues overtake me : rock away from here
13 And I told my gal : the week before last
14 The gait she's carrying me : is most too fast

SykR   1   Sykes, Roosevelt

        title: 44 Blues
        place and date: New York, 14 June 1929
        record numbers: (402451-A) OK-8702 His HLP-5

1   And now I walked all night long : with my forty-four
    in my hand
2   I was looking for my woman : found her with another
    man
3   Lord I wore my forty-four so long : Lord it made my
    shoulder sore
4   After I do what I want to : ain't going to wear my
    forty-four no more
5   Lord my baby say : she heard the forty-four whistle
    blow
6   Lord it sound just like : ain't going to blow this
    horn no more
7   Lord I got a little cabin : Lord it's number
    forty-four

SykR   1   Sykes, Roosevelt

8   Lord I wake up every morning : the world be
    scratching on my door

SykR   2   Sykes, Roosevelt

        title: All My Money Gone Blues
        place and date: New York, 14 June 1929
        record numbers: (402452-A) OK-8727 Yz L-1033

1   All my money gone : and there ain't no more to say
2   Now you know I got to do something : baby that is
    not right
3   People you could not blame me : when all I gots been
    torn
4   A no-good woman mistreat me : she taken all my money
    and gone
5   Now this world is in a tangle : everybody singing
    this song
6   I ain't got a friend in the world : and all my
    money's gone
7   Now I believe I believe : I am on my last go-round
8   Have all my money gone : I feel myself sinking down

SykR   3   Sykes, Roosevelt

        title: The Way I Feel Blues
        place and date: New York, 14 June 1929
        record numbers: (402453-B) OK-8727 Yz L-1033

1   Hey : I know you don't know the way I feel
2   Lord you treats me : just like my heart is made of
    steel
3   My baby : don't see why I *pone thee* no more
4   Lord I believe to my soul : that she's got the man
    next door
5   I woke up this morning : just as sick as I could be
6   Now nothing but these blues : almost killing poor me
7   I spoke hard words to my mother : even to my dear
    old dad too
8   Which I wouldn't have spoken : if it hadn't've been
    for you
9   Since we been apart : my life don't seem the same
10 Lord it breaks my heart : to hear the *work-hard*
    Miss so-and-so's name

SykR   4   Sykes, Roosevelt

        title: Fire Detective Blues
        place and date: Richmond, Ind., 7 Sept. 1929
        record numbers: (15557) Pm-12827 Riv RM-8819

1   My house burning down : the firemen are taking their
    time
2   Please Mr fire detective : won't you save this old
    cabin of mine
3   I spent my money : looking to be happy some day
4   Now my house burning down : I ain't got no place to
    stay
5   That fire detective : don't mean me no good
6   Let my house burn into ashes : didn't leave me one
    stick of wood
7   Sat baby : won't you please write to me
8   I'm just as lonesome : as a young man can be
9   My house burned down : didn't leave me a doggone
    thing
10 Reason why it worries me : to hear that fire bell
    ring

SykR   5   Sykes, Roosevelt

    title: Single Tree Blues
    place and date: Richmond, Ind., 7 Sept. 1929
    record numbers: (15563) Pm-12827 Riv RM-8819

1 Hit my woman : with a singletree
2 You might've heard her hollering : daddy don't you
   murder me
3 Going to shoot you mama : going to cut you too
4 Lord on account : of the old way you do
5 Been sick and down babe : I'm getting up again
6 Mmm : but *I'm blowed in the wind*
7 Going away mama : coming here no more
8 You know you shout at me : you throwed my trunk
   outdoor
9 She's a good old gal : she do mess around
10 She ain't there : she's all over town

SykR   6   Sykes, Roosevelt

    title: Skeet and Garret
    place and date: Chicago, 16 Nov. 1929
    record numbers: (403312-A) OK-8749 Yz L-1033

1 Got me accused for murder : and stealing was my
   crime
2 Lord it was all on account : of me stealing a
   woman's mind
3 I wrote my baby a letter : she send me a telegram
4 She said daddy the reason I love you : you got ways
   just like a lamb
5 She got a head like a switch-engine : and her feet
   just like a teddy bear
6 She dipping her Skeet and Garret : and spitting it
   everywhere
7 Lord I'd rather be in the woods mama : Lord in a
   lion's den
8 Than to be here in this town mama : Lord and deceive
   her men
9 Good night blues : why don't you let me sleep
10 You been following me : around this whole week

SykR   7   Sykes, Roosevelt

    title: Lost All I Had Blues
    place and date: Chicago, 16 Nov. 1929
    record numbers: (403322-A) OK-8819 RBF RF-12

1 I woke up this morning : thousand things on my mind
2 Lord I thought about my troubles : could not keep
   from crying
3 I turned around : looked toward the sky
4 I said if these blues don't kill me : then I wasn't
   born to die
5 I lost all I had : everything I had to lose
6 I lost the one I love : I just can't lose these
   blues
7 And if I stay here : I'll be blue all the time
8 If I don't go crazy : then I will lose my mind

SykR   8   Sykes, Roosevelt

    title: Poor Boy Blues
    place and date: Chicago, 16 Nov. 1929
    record numbers: (403323-A) OK-8787 Yz L-1033

1 Lord I'm a poor boy : I'm going to and fro
2 What's on my mind : don't nobody know
3 Lord I am disgusted : and heart-broken too
4 So I went back to my mama : nothing else I can do
5 Poor boy poor boy : ain't got no friends at all
6 Lord I'm just like a rat : running from stall to
   stall
7 Lord : have mercy on me please

SykR   8   Sykes, Roosevelt

8 Lord I just want you : give this poor boy's heart
   some ease

SykR   9   Sykes, Roosevelt

    title: Kelly's 44 Blues
    place and date: Cincinnati, 12 June 1930
    record numbers: (62904-2) Vi-V38608 Yz L-1033

1 Lord I say good morning Mr pawnshop man : as I
   walked in his door
2 I says I feel bad this morning : and I really wants
   my forty-four
3 Lord I was at a party last night : I was out there
   till about half past two
4 I'm going back out there tonight : I'm out to have
   some shooting to do
5 Lord the policeman walked around me : they walked
   around me both night and day
6 When they know I got my forty-four : they won't have
   a word to say
7 Then I made up in my mind : and I [really, simply]
   don't care how I go
8 Before I'll be mistreated : I'm going to shoot my
   forty-four

SykR   10   Sykes, Roosevelt

    title: 3 6 and 9
    place and date: Grafton, Wis., c. Aug. 1930
    record numbers: (L-449-2) Pm-13004 Riv RM-8819

1 Well hello there old gal : you sure looks fine
2 All I hate you for : that three six and nine
3 Say no more : and I'll look for you down about half
   past nine
4 And I want you to bring along : that girl of mine
5 You know down here : where you got your steak
   potatoes and tea
6 If you act right : you get your gravy free
7 Well she's all right : a good old kid
8 But she ain't the gal : a man should be worried with
9 She's a fine kid too : *believe in your big time*
10 But ain't one thing about you : full of that three
   six and nine
11 Say who was that guy : you had with you last night
12 Fine old boy : he was tight

SykR   11   Sykes, Roosevelt

    title: We Can Sell that Thing
    place and date: Grafton, Wis., c. Aug. 1930
    record numbers: (L-450-2) Pm-13004 Riv RM-8819

1 There you was : down in then *lees*
2 Didn't have nothing : but a limburger cheese
3 It may be just as good : just as good as gold
4 No mess around it : and let it get too old
5 You go away : and you stays all day
6 When you come back : you smells in a different way
7 Well I know something : that I won't say
8 Tell me : why do you smell that old way
9 But I can't tell you : because you don't know
10 People talking : everywhere I go
11 Wind blow at night : and the wind blows in the day
12 Don't it smell : when it blowing your way

SykR   12   Sykes, Roosevelt

    title: No Good Woman Blues
    place and date: Chicago, 3 Nov. 1930
    record numbers: (C-6475-A) Me-M12086 Yz L-1033

1   I don't want no woman : partner that wants every man
    in town
2   Know she ain't no good : she will tear your
    reputation down
3   I went to my woman's house : just to sit down and
    talk awhile
4   Her husband come in with his shotgun : and he run me
    for a solid mile
5   When I got home partner : I didn't have time to
    [fasten, lock] my back gate
6   I thought he was still behind me : and I didn't
    hesitate
7   I won't try no mule : that don't know gee from haw
8   I don't want no woman : she just soon as say yes as
    to say no
9   Turn your light out mama : and [I want you to] pull
    you curtains down
10 I'm going to fill you car with gasoline : and meet
    you going downtown

SykR   13   Sykes, Roosevelt

    title: As True As I've Been to You
    place and date: Louisville, 9 June 1931
    record numbers: (69403-1) Vi-23286 Yz L-1033

1   Now listen here babe : is that the way you intend to
    do
2   Mistreat me for another man : as true as I have been
    to you
3   You used to treat me like you loved me : I wonder
    why you changed your mind
4   You know I did the best I could : to treat you
    loving and kind
5   I'm going to see you babe : when you down and out
    like myself
6   You're going to work for Willie Kelly : and he'll
    work for somebody else
7   I'm going away to leave you : I know the men will be
    better if I do
8   Because as long as I'm around here : they can't get
    a fair break at you
9   I hate to go : and I'm really afraid to stay
10 But I won't be around here : mama and let you have
    your way

SykR   14   Sykes, Roosevelt

    title: Hard Luck Man Blues
    place and date: Louisville, 9 June 1931
    record numbers: (69404-) Vi-23320 Yz L-1033

1   My babe my babe : she don't do no way to comfort me
2   She know that ain't no way : for a sweet little wife
    to be
3   I'm in a worse fix now baby : than I ever been
    before
4   I'd rather be on the North Pole : living in the ice
    and snow
5   Last time my baby quit me : I say I didn't no more
    want her around
6   But every time I see her smiling face : my
    kind-hearted feeling come down
7   Love will make you do things : that you swear that
    you would not do
8   You know if you ever been in love : what I'm say
    ain't nothing strange to you
9   I'm a hard-luck man : just as hard-luck as I can be
10 If I didn't have good friends : I don't know what
    would become of me

SykR   15   Sykes, Roosevelt

    title: Mr. Sykes Blues
    place and date: Richmond, Ind., 22 Sept. 1932
    record numbers: (18801) Ch-16586 Yz L-1033

1   Mmm I done you wrong : but I won't do that no more
2   You taught me a lesson : about a Mr so-and-so
3   My babe come running : [with a, she had] marriage
    license in her hand
4   You say I ain't hardly got the heart to tell you :
    but I have got another man
5   I said bye bye : bye bye girl friend bye bye
6   I can't stay here and be happy : and I ain't going
    to even try
7   Mmm : you asked me [to, would I] try you again
8   I shook my head and said : you going out with my
    best friend
9   Oh yeah : oh yes oh yes I know
10 I found out you's no good mama : I think I better
    let you go
11 Mmm : you can't do that again
12 I'm watching everybody : I'm only watching my only
    best friend

SykR   16   Sykes, Roosevelt

    title: Highway 61 Blues
    place and date: Richmond, Ind., 22 Sept. 1932
    record numbers: (18802) Ch-16586 Yz L-1033

1   If you ever been to Memphis : you stop down in
    Hollywood
2   Lord the women out there : don't mean no one man no
    good
3   I'm leaving St Louis : I'm going out Grand Avenue
4   I got to go to Memphis : something over there that I
    want to do
5   When I hit Grand [Avenue] : look like my troubles
    just begun
6   Lord it breaks my heart : to sing about Highway
    Sixty-One
7   I felt so blue : while I was out on that lonely
    highway
8   I say I'm riding now : but maybe my trouble will end
    some sweet day
9   I can stand right here : look [down] on Beale Avenue
10 I can see everything : that pretty Miss so-and-so do
11 Oh listen kind mama : don't worry about your dad
    when I'm gone
12 You know I'm wild about your kind mama : I ain't
    going to do nothing wrong

Sylv   1   Sylvester, Hannah

    title: Midnight Blues
    place and date: New York, c. May 1923
    record numbers: (1407-?) Pm-12033 VJM VLP-40

1   Daddy daddy : please come back to me
2   *Sure my mouth* so down : as he can be
3   Left me at midnight : clock was striking twelve
4   To face this cruel world : world all by myself

Sylv   2   Sylvester, Hannah

    title: Down South Blues
    place and date: New York, c. 21 Sept. 1923
    record numbers: (70328) Pat-032007 VJM VLP-40

1   I have learned my lesson : believe me I am through
2   And folks I am not joking : when I sing these
    down-south blues
3   I'm going to the station : and get the fastest train
    that goes

Sylv   2   Sylvester, Hannah

4   I'm going back south : where the weather suits my
     clothes
5   Because my mama told me : and my daddy told me too
6   Don't go north : and let the men make a fool out of
     you
7   I have found out : it doesn't pay to love a northern
     man
8   Can't get them when you want them : catch them when
     you can
9   Because their love is like a faucet : it turns off
     and on
10   Time you think you've got it : it turns off and gone
11   I'm going back down south : if I wear out
     ninety-nine pair of shoes
12   Because I'm broken-hearted : got those down-south
     blues

Sylv   3   Sylvester, Hannah

        title: I Want My Sweet Daddy
        place and date: New York, c. 21 Sept. 1923
        record numbers: (70329) Pat-032007 VJM VLP-40

1   Every night : when I go to bed
2   I just weep in my ??? : across my head
3   I'm a-tell you : that he's not my regular man
4   But he loves me nicer : than my regular can
5   If you knew the man like I do : you would agree
6   That's the reason : why he makes a fool out of me

Tamp   1   Tampa Red

        title: Through Train Blues
        place and date: Chicago, c. May 1928
        record numbers: (20544-2) Pm-12685 Yz L-1039

1   I hate to hear : that through train blow boo hoo
2   Every time I hear it blowing : I feel like riding
     too
3   The woman I love : treat me so unkind
4   Going to pack my grip : and leave this lonesome town
5   I'm going away : just to wear you off my mind
6   And I may be gone baby : a doggone long long time
7   I'm going to grab me a freight train : ride until it
     stops
8   Ain't going to stay around here : and be no
     stumbling block

Tamp   2   Tampa Red

        title: It's Tight Like That
        place and date: Chicago, c. Sept. 1928
        record numbers: (   ) Vo-1216 His HLP-1

1   Listen here folks : I'm going to sing a little song
2   Don't get mad : we don't mean no harm
3   There was a little black rooster : met a little
     brown hen
4   Made a date at the barn : about half past ten
5   I went to see my gal : up across the hall
6   Found another mule : kicking in my stall
7   Now the gal I love : she's long and slim
8   When she whip it : it's too bad Jim
9   Now the rooster crowed : and the hen looked around
10   At the *bom bom diddly* : got to carry me into town
11   Mama had a little dog : and its name was Ball
12   And if you give him a little taste : he want it all
13   Uncle Bud and Aunt Jane : went to *take a pan hon*
14   Aunt Jane fell down : and Uncle Bud ???
15   If you see my gal : tell her to hurry home
16   I ain't had no sass : since she been gone
17   I wear my britches : up above my knees
18   Strut my jelly : with who I please
19   Uncle Bill came home : about half past ten

Tamp   2   Tampa Red

20   He see in the hole : but he couldn't get in
21   Me and my brother : was up in the loft
22   We was seeing a film : when they broke it off

Tamp   3   Tampa Red

        title: The Duck Yas-Yas-Yas
        place and date: Chicago, c. 16 May 1929
        record numbers: (C-3485-) Vo-1277 Yz L-1039

1   Mama bought a rooster : she thought it was a duck
2   She brought him to the table : with his legs
     straight up
3   In came the children : with a cup and a glass
4   To catch the liquor : from his yas yas yas
5   Babe oh babe : have you ever been to Spain
6   See those hoodoo women : shaking that thing
7   They got rings on their fingers : bells on their
     toes
8   What they got good babe : nobody knows
9   I'm going down : Market Street
10   Where the men and women : all do meet
11   That's where the men : do the Georgia rub
12   Women fall in line : with a big washtub
13   Me and my gal : walking down the street
14   She caught the rheumatism : in her feet
15   She stooped over : to pick some grass
16   And the same thing struck her : in the yas yas yas
17   You catch the train : you call Forty-Nine
18   Carries you down : to Caroline
19   You catch the train : you call Forty-Eight
20   Takes you right in : to the Golden Gate
21   You shake your shoulder : you shake them fast
22   You can't shake your shoulders : shake your yas yas
     yas
23   Drink some rooster soup : before going to bed
24   Wake up in the morning : find your own self dead
25   Down on Morgan : there's a good location
26   Right there : next to a gasoline station
27   That's where you'll get your car : oil and greased
28   Women crying honey : won't you come in please
29   I'm going to sing this verse : ain't going to sing
     no more
30   Somebody's knocking : on my door
31   The people upstairs : have gone to bed
32   I better stop that noise : before they crack my head

Tamp   4   Tampa Red

        title: What Is It That Tastes Like Gravy?
        place and date: Chicago, c. 14 June 1929
        record numbers: (C-3594-) Vo-1426 Yz L-1039

1   What is it tastes like gravy : boys I bet you don't
     know
2   Can you guess what tastes like gravy : it's tight if
     you really want to know
3   I taste it last night : the night before
4   If I keep this appetite : I'm going to taste it a
     little more
5   Now the gal that let me taste it : they put her in
     jail
6   But she didn't need nothing : to go her bail
7   Now if you don't know : I tell you who do
8   Just see Tampa Red : and his best gal too

Tamp   5   Tampa Red (Jim Jackson)

        title: Jim Jackson's Jamboree--Part I
        place and date: Memphis, 14 Oct. 1929
        record numbers: (M-203/4) Vo-1428 Yz L-1021

1   Nobody knows : old Memphis like I do

264

Tamp   5   Tampa Red (Jim Jackson)

2   The reason I know it : I rambled it through and
    through
3   Boys if you got a good woman : here's a lesson I'll
    give to you
4   Don't bring her to Memphis : Jim Jackson will take
    them away from you

Tamp   6   Tampa Red

        title: No Matter How She Done It
        place and date: New York, 3 Feb. 1932
        record numbers: (11210-A) Vo-1699 Yz L-1039

1   I know a gal : by the name of Marylou
2   She shook it so much : she had the German flu
3   The women don't like her : they call her Ida Mae
4   But the way the men love her : is a crying shame
5   I tell you people : what she done
6   She made a hit with Jack the Ripper : and the *only*
    one
7   You women don't have to worry : about your life
8   She made Jack the Ripper : throw away his knife
9   She shakes all over : when she walks
10 She made a blind man see : and a dumb man talk
11 The copper brought her in : she didn't need no bail
12 She shook it for the judge : and put the cop in jail

Tamp   7   Tampa Red

        title: Kingfish Blues
        place and date: Chicago, 22 Mar. 1934
        record numbers: (80385-1) BB-B5617 RCA LPV-518

1   Little minnows in the river : kingfish in the deep
    blue sea
2   Lord I got a gang of women : trying to get a chance
    with me
3   You may think it's all right : but baby doll can't
    you see
4   Now you know doggone well : you are getting out of
    place with me
5   I will play kingfish : if you act just like the
    minnows do
6   In case old Tampa Red should flutter : don't you be
    ashamed to shoo
7   Now I'm a kingfish papa : and I know what kind of
    bait to choose
8   That's why so many women : crying those kingfish
    blues

Tamp   8   Tampa Red

        title: Mean Mistreater Blues
        place and date: Chicago, 14 June 1934
        record numbers: (80604-1) BB-B5546 RCA LPV-518

1   You's a mean mistreating mama : and you don't mean
    me no good
2   But I don't blame you baby : I'd be the same way if
    I could
3   You say you going to leave me : well you say you
    going away
4   But that's all right baby : baby you'll come back
    home some day
5   Now you's a mean mistreater : and you mistreat me
    all the time
6   But that's all right baby : I won't pay that no mind
7   Can't you remember baby : when I knocked upon your
    door
8   You had the nerve to tell me : that you didn't want
    me no more
9   Boys ain't it lonesome : sleeping all by yourself
10 When the woman that you loving : is loving someone
    else

Tamp   9   Tampa Red

        title: Seminole Blues
        place and date: Aurora, Ill., 11 Oct. 1937
        record numbers: (014333-) BB-B7315 Yz L-1039

1   My baby's gone : won't be back no more
2   She left me this morning : she caught that Seminole
3   I got the blues so bad : it hurt my tongue to talk
4   I would follow my baby : but it hurt my feet to walk
5   She give me her love : even let me draw her pay
6   She was a real good woman : but unkindness drove her
    away
7   I got the Seminole blues : leaving on my mind
8   I'm going to find my baby : if I have to ride the
    blinds

TayC   1   Taylor, Charley

        title: Heavy Suitcase Blues
        place and date: Grafton, Wis., Mar. or Apr. 1930
        record numbers: (L-251-2) Pm-12967 Yz L-1028

1   Lord I'm so *blurred so blurred* : can't hardly
    stand to play those blues myself
2   That's the way I talk pretty mama : I don't have to
    beg nobody here
3   Now my suitcase is packed : and my trunk's all ready
    to go
4   And my suitcase is too heavy : to tote down that
    dusty road
5   Now my baby my baby my baby : now she always keep me
    feeling blue
6   I bet she's just like ??? : can't never tell what
    she's going to do
7   Baby baby baby baby : I mean you really know what's
    wrong
8   That's mistreat a poor boy : don't you know that's a
    very long way from home
9   Mmm : oh Lord Lord Lordy Lord
10 My suitcase is too heavy : to walk down that dusty
    road

TayC   2   Taylor, Charley

        title: Louisiana Bound
        place and date: Grafton, Wis., Mar. or Apr. 1930
        record numbers: (L-252-2) Pm-12967 Her H-205

1   Oh baby you know that I love you : that is the
    reason you treat me so unkind
2   I'm going to get me a good girl : just to wear you
    off my mind
3   Hon' I'm going down in Louisiana : baby just behind
    the sun
4   And when I come back pretty mama : all my good work
    will be done
5   Baby you treat me *so unkind* : you always keep me
    feeling blue
6   Lord I sometimes wonder : honey what you trying to
    do
7   Ooh : oh Lord Lord Lord Lord Lord
8   I want to be you man : and you want me to be your
    dog
9   And I'm leaving in the morning : and I'm leaving on
    the southbound train
10 And when I come back baby : I don't want you to call
    my name

Temp   1   Temple, Johnnie

        title: Big Boat Whistle
        place and date: Chicago, 14 May 1935
        record numbers: (C-986-B) Vo-03068 OJL-17

1   And I heard a mighty rumbling : and it [sound,
    looks] just like a passenger train
2   And I heard a sweet little woman : ooo Lord I hate
    to call her name
3   Well I would ask of you my darling : just so quiet
    so soft and low
4   Mmm it give me many heartache : baby ooo Lord as the
    mamas come and go
5   Mmm now if I could holler : like this big boat
    whistle blow
6   Mmm I would call my baby : baby ooo Lord off the
    killing floor
7   Mmm now if I had a headlight : even like on some
    passenger train
8   Well I would shine my light : ooo Lord in the ocean
    spring
9   Now when my hair begin to snowdrift : and my eyes
    all dimmer grow
10 Then I will lean upon some loved ones : ooo Lord in
    the valley baby I will go
11 Now your love I know is truthful : but the truest
    love grow cold
12 Now that's only this darling : ooo will you love me
    baby when I'm old

Temp   2   Temple, Johnnie

        title: The Evil Devil Blues
        place and date: Chicago, 14 May 1935
        record numbers: (C-987-) Vo-02987 Yz L-1038

1   I'd rather be dead : and in my horrible tomb
2   To hear my woman : some man done taken my room
3   I'd rather be the devil : to be that woman's man
5   The woman I love : she don't pay me no mind
6   Going to pack my things : going further down the
    line
7   I lay down last night : and I tried to take my rest
8   My mind got to rambling : like the wild geese from
    the west
9   The devil's evil : changed my baby's mind
11 You be my woman : I tell you what I'll do
12 I'll cut your kindling : I will build your fire
13 I'll tote your water : from the boggy bayou
15 The woman I love : I stole her from my best friend
16 Lord he got lucky : and stoled her back again

Temp   3   Temple, Johnnie

        title: Louise Louise Blues
        place and date: Chicago, 12 Nov. 1936
        record numbers: (90981-A) De-7244 Cor CP-58

1   Louise : is the sweetest gal I know
2   She made me walk from Chicago : to the Gulf of
    Mexico
3   Now look a-here Louise : what you trying to do
4   You trying to give some man my loving : and me too
5   Now you know Louise : baby that will never do
6   Now you know you can't love me : and love some other
    man too
7   Louise I believe : somebody baby is fishing in my
    pond
8   They catching all my perches : grinding up the bone
9   Louise : baby won't you hurry home
10 I ain't had no loving : oh since Louise been gone
11 Louise you know you got ways : like a rattlesnake in
    his coil
12 Every time you go to loving: I swear it's out of
    this world

Temp   3   Temple, Johnnie

13 Now Louise the big boat is up the river : on a bank
    of sand
14 If she don't strike deep water : I swear she'll
    never land

Temp   4   Temple, Johnnie

        title: So Lonely and Blue
        place and date: Chicago, 14 May 1937
        record numbers: (91247-A) De-7337 RBF RF-16

1   Baby I'm feeling so lonely : and I'm feeling so blue
2   I just sitting here thinking : what in the world has
    become of you
3   I had a gal : and her name was Lou
4   Great God almighty : that woman she wouldn't do
5   And I am feeling so lonely : and I'm feeling so blue
6   I'm wondering : what in the world baby has done
    become of you
7   You got ways : dragging my heart around
8   Some of these days baby : I'm going to leave this
    town
9   Then you will be sorry : that you treated me so
    lowdown
10 And you will be feeling so lonely : and you will be
    feeling so blue
11 Have you ever woke up in the morning : your bed
    going around and around
12 You know about that baby : you have done throwed me
    down

Temp   5   Temple, Johnnie

        title: New Louise Louise Blues
        place and date: Chicago, 14 May 1937
        record numbers: (91248-A) De-7337 RBF RF-16

1   Louise left me this morning : she never said a word
2   And she left me : about something that she heard
3   Louise : baby please hurry home
4   I ain't had no loving : since my Louise been gone
5   Louise got ways : like a rolling stone
6   When she leave a man : he have to grieve and moan
7   I got a gal named Yola : she treats me nice and kind
8   I don't care what she do : Louise is on my mind
9   Louise wasn't so good-looking : and her hair wasn't
    red
10 But she cooked my breakfast : brings it to my bed

TexT   1   Texas Tommy

        title: Jail Break Blues
        place and date: Dallas, c. 25 Oct. 1928
        record numbers: (DAL-689-A) Br-7044 Rt RL-312

1   The rising sun : will never catch me here
2   I've been in this jailhouse : for one solid year
3   The turnkey don't like me : that's why I have to
    steal
4   The rising sun : will never catch me here
5   I was reared as an orphan : never harmed a man
6   But I've been kicked and driven : Lord from hand to
    hand
7   It seems as if the world : is turning round and
    around
8   Every time that old jailor : takes a prisoner down
9   I'm going to get me a *stone* : and *roll from Mr
    Brown*
10 Get me some cold-hearted man : I'm jailhouse bound

ThoE   1   Thomas, Elvie

        title: Motherless Child Blues
        place and date: Grafton, Wis., c. Apr. 1930
        record numbers: (L-264-2) Pm-12977 OJL-2

1   My mother told me : just before she died
3   Oh daughter daughter : please don't be like me
4   To fall in love : with every man you see
5   But I did not listen : to what my mother said
6   That's the reason why : I'm sitting here in
       Hattiesburg
7   Baby now she's dead : and six feet in the ground
8   And I'm her child : and I'm drifting around
9   Do you remember the day : baby you drove me from
       your door
10 Go away from here woman : and don't come here no
       more
11 I walked away : and I wrang my hands and cried
12 Didn't have no blues : I couldn't be satisfied

ThoG   1   Thomas, George

        title: Fast Stuff Blues
        place and date: Grafton, Wis., c. Nov. 1929
        record numbers: (L-17-2) Pm-12826 Rt RL-340

1   I keep tough : I'm clean all the time
2   I can make any woman : make her change her mind
3   I know my baby : bound to love me some
4   She *cook all around me* : when my work day come
5   She got on the Central : got on the Santa Fe
6   That woman : keeps me busy as I can be
7   Ain't but the one thing : really worries my mind
8   That gal wants to run : the same race all the time
9   Me and my gal : really had some race
10 She got fast ways : and beat me to the winning place
11 When your heart starts beating : and your hands and
       feets get cold
12 You can't get a baby : because you most too old

ThoG   2   Thomas, George

        title: Don't Kill Him in Here
        place and date: Grafton, Wis., c. Nov. 1929
        record numbers: (L-18-2) Pm-12826 Rt RL-340

1   I went out last night folks : I meant to have some
       fun
2   When I start to spend my money : a man pulled a
       great big gun
3   I said excuse me Mr : I don't mean no harm
4   I thought the girl was a ??? : and lived out on the
       farm
5   Please Mr : please don't kill me in here
6   Because I'm the landlord : I've got to sell the beer
7   Well I'm a good fellow : I really spends my dough
8   Every time I buy a drink : I ask if you want some
       more
9   When I get drunk : will you take me to my Harlot
       Hill
10 And don't you take all my money : and please don't
       kill him in here

ThoH   1   Thomas, Henry

        title: Cottonfield Blues
        place and date: Chicago, c. early July 1927
        record numbers: (   ) Vo-1094 OJL-3

1   I'm going to Texas : have to ride the rods
2   Just show me the train : left out of that Mobile
       yard
3   If you see my mama : before I do
4   Don't tell her faro : what road I'm on

ThoH   1   Thomas, Henry

5   Now the boat's up the river : and she won't come
       down
6   I believe to my soul : great God she's water bound
7   I look to the east : and I look to the west
8   If she headed to the south : she's Alabama bound
9   Said one of these mornings : it won't be long
10 You going to call me : and I'll be gone

ThoH   2   Thomas, Henry

        title: Arkansas
        place and date: Chicago, c. early July 1927
        record numbers: (   ) Vo-1286 Rt RL-312

1   Oh little honey : don't you make me go
2   I'll get a job : *if you allow me to*
3   I am a rambling gambling man : I gamble in many
       towns
4   I rambled this wide world over : I rambled and
       traveled around
5   I had my ups and downs in life : and bitter times I
       saw
6   But I never knew what misery was : till I left old
       Arkansas
7   I started out one morning : to meet the early train
8   He says you better work for me : I asked old Liza
       Jane
9   I'll give you fifty cents today : ??? *on*
10 And *yesterday* ??? : *was filled with ice and snow*

ThoH   3   Thomas, Henry

        title: Bob McKinney
        place and date: Chicago, Oct. 1927
        record numbers: (   ) Vo-1138 OJL-3

1   One of these mornings : won't be long
2   You going to call me : I'll be gone
3   Oh make me a pallet : on your floor
4   Won't you make it : so your man'll never know
5   Yes I'm looking for that bully : lay me down
6   I'm looking for that bully : and that bully can't be
       found

ThoH   4   Thomas, Henry

        title: Shanty Blues
        place and date: Chicago, Oct. 1927
        record numbers: (   ) Vo-1139 OJL-3

1   I'm going to the nation : I ain't going to make no
       fuss
2   Show me the woman : anybody can trust
3   Ashes to ashes : *roll it into* dust
4   Show me that woman : anybody can trust

ThoH   5   Thomas, Henry

        title: Honey, Won't You Allow Me One More Chance
        place and date: Chicago, 7 Oct. 1927
        record numbers: (C-1220) Vo-1141 OJL-3

1   Honey allow me a-one more chance : I only I will
       treat you right
2   Honey won't you allow me a-one more chance : I won't
       stay out all night
3   Honey won't you allow me a-one more chance : I take
       you to the ball in France
4   One kind of favor I'll ask of you : just allow me
       just one more chance

ThoH   6   Thomas, Henry

    title: Run, Mollie, Run
    place and date: Chicago, 7 Oct. 1927
    record numbers: (C-1222) Vo-1141 OJL-3

1   Music in the kitchen : music in the hall
2   If you can't come Saturday night : you need not come
    at all
3   I went down to Huntsville : I did not go to stay
4   Just got there in good old time : to wear them ball
    and chain

ThoH   7   Thomas, Henry

    title: Bull Doze Blues
    place and date: Chicago, c. 13 June 1928
    record numbers: (C-1999-) Vo-1230 OJL-3

1   I'm going away babe : and it won't be long
3   Just sure as that train : leaves out of that Mobile
    yard
5   I'll shake your hand : tell your papa goodbye
7   I'm going back : ??? Tennessee
9   I'm going where : I never could fool you
11 If you don't believe I'm sinking : look what a hole
    I'm in
12 If you don't believe I'm sinking : look what a fool
    I've been

ThoH   8   Thomas, Henry

    title: Texas Worried Blues
    place and date: Chicago, c. 13 June 1928
    record numbers: (C-2002-) Vo-1249 OJL-3

1   I've got the worried blues : Lord I'm feeling bad
2   I've got no one: tell my troubles to
3   You can box me up : and send me to my ma
4   If my ma don't want me : send me to my pa
5   If my pa don't want me : send me to my girl
7   If my girl don't want me : cast me in the sea
8   So the fish and the whales : make a fuss all over me
9   I'm going to build me : a heaven of my own
10 I'm going to give : all good-time women a home
11 Get your hat and your coat : get shaking it all down
    the line
14 Now fare thee my honey : fare thee

ThoH   9   Thomas, Henry

    title: Don't Ease Me In
    place and date: Chicago, c. 13 June 1928
    record numbers: (   ) Vo-1197 OJL-3

1   Sometimes I walk : and sometimes I talk
2   I love you girl great God : *till my bluebird talk*
3   I beat my girl : with a singletree
4   ??? up *the winter* street mama : have a watch on me
5   I've got a girl : her name is Joan
6   She leaves here walking running fast : chocolate to
    the bone
7   I was standing on the corner : talking to my brown
8   I turned around sweet mama : I was workhouse bound
9   Girl I've got a girl : and she working hard
10 She got a dress she wear sweet mama : said it's pink
    and blue
11 She brings me coffee : and she bring me tea
12 She bring me everything : except the jailhouse key
13 They got a little town man : all the other men too
14 They got all the women coming down to the man : *I
    mean in Texas too*

ThoH   10   Thomas, Henry

    title: Texas Easy Street Blues
    place and date: Chicago, c. 13 June 1928
    record numbers: (   ) Vo-1197 OJL-3

1   Tell me mama : what's the matter now
3   I'm going back to Texas : [live, sit] on Easy Street
5   When you see me coming : don't call my name
7   When you see me coming : heist your window high
9   I got the Texas blues : blue as I can be
11 Tell me mama : what's the matter now
12 Got a black mule : *really* kicking in my stall
14 When you see me running : something going on wrong

ThoH   11   Thomas, Henry

    title: Charmin' Betsy
    place and date: Chicago, c. 7 Oct. 1929
    record numbers: (C-4621-) Vo-1468 Rt RL-315

1   I'm going around the mountain charming Betsy : going
    around the mountain to leave
2   If I never see you no more : do Lord remember me
3   The first time I see charming Betsy : she want
    everything that she see
4   Last time I seen charming Betsy : she's wearing the
    ball and chain
5   I went down to Huntsville town : I did not go to
    stay
6   I just got there to do time : to wear that ball and
    chain
7   Yellow gal rides in an automobile : brownskin do the
    same
8   Black gal rides in an old airship : but she riding
    just the same

ThoH   12   Thomas, Henry

    title: Don't Leave Me Here
    place and date: Chicago, c. 7 Oct. 1929
    record numbers: (C-4624) Vo-1443 Yz L-1004

1   I was standing on the corner : a-talking to my brown
2   I turned around sweet mama : I went across town
3   Says I've got a girl : and she working hard
4   She had a dress she wear loving babe : says it's
    pink and blue
5   She bring me coffee : and she bring me tea
6   She bring me everything : except the jailhouse key
7   Yes I'm going away : and it won't be long
8   Just sure as the train leaves out of the yard :
    she's Alabama bound
9   I'm going away : and it won't be long
10 *Just ease your train eleven days* : I'm Alabama
    bound
11 Says the boat's up the river : and she won't come
    down
12 I believe to my soul pretty mama : she's *water*
    bound
13 I look to the east : and I look to the west
14 If she heads to the South great God : she's Alabama
    bound

ThoHo   1   Thomas, Hociel

    title: Gambler's Dream
    place and date: Chicago, 11 Nov. 1925
    record numbers: (9471-A) OK-8289 Bio BLP-C6

1   I've traveled traveled : and I've seen
2   And I've had the blues : they call the gambler's
    dream
3   Many times many times : I have cried
4   Many times many times : I wish that I could die
5   Mama told me : father told me too

ThoHo 1   Thomas, Hociel

  6 Don't you let no gamblers : be the ruin of you

ThoHo 2   Thomas, Hociel

       title: Adam and Eve Had the Blues
       place and date: Chicago, 11 Nov. 1925
       record numbers: (9473-A) OK-8258 Bio BLP-C6

  1 Eve called Adam : and he got close to her side
  2 Here's the tree with fruit : and it will make us
     wise
  3 The Lord said to Adam : also said to Eve
  4 You two have bit some fruit : from that forbidden
     tree

ThoHo 3   Thomas, Hociel

       title: Put It Where I Can Get It
       place and date: Chicago, 11 Nov. 1925
       record numbers: (9474-A) OK-8258 Bio BLP-C6

  1 I got something at home : on my shelf
  2 If that ain't enough : I will get you something else
  3 Now if you want to sin : slide across to me
  4 I'll back my wagon : underneath your Christmas tree
  5 Listen sweet daddy : you know it's understood
  6 That every woman wants a man : that means her good

ThoHo 4   Thomas, Hociel

       title: I've Stopped My Man
       place and date: Chicago, 11 Nov. 1925
       record numbers: (9476-A) OK-8326 Bio BLP-C6

  1 I know you love me : daddy it's understood
  2 Daddy you know : your mama means you good
  3 I got something : that sure will bring him back
  4 My daddy loves the *ground* : where I *have been
     sat*
  5 I've got a feeling : that I want to be mean
  6 I can do my stuff : and I'm going to do it *clean*
  7 You can get rough : but I will sure *stand*
  8 I can tell the world : that now that you're my man
  9 You can get rough : but I will too
 10 *Since my mother* : put that thing on you

ThoHo 5   Thomas, Hociel

       title: Listen to Ma
       place and date: Chicago, 24 Feb. 1926
       record numbers: (9521-A) OK-8346 Bio BLP-C6

  1 I grow lonely : day by day
  2 For my mother : in every way
  3 She won't tell you : nothing wrong
  4 You're always welcome : in her home

ThoJ 1   Thomas, Jesse Babyface

       title: Blue Goose Blues
       place and date: Dallas, 10 Aug. 1929
       record numbers: (55326-2) Vi-V38555 Yz L-1032

  1 If I lose : I'm going get some more
  2 I'm a pretty good worker : got a good way to go
  3 I can do anything : anybody else can do
  4 Any kind of work : and gambling too
  5 I'm going back to chauffeuring : I've been *done it*
     for three years
  6 I can make any hill : without shifting my gears
  7 Going to take my buddy : my buddy's friend
  8 Pick more cotton : than a gin can gin

ThoJ 1   Thomas, Jesse Babyface

  9 If I lose : won't be nothing lost
 10 Just two bits : and what did it cost
 11 When you go : to Shreveport town
 12 You find Blue Goose : happen to carry you down

ThoJ 2   Thomas, Jesse Babyface

       title: No Good Woman Blues
       place and date: Dallas, 10 Aug. 1929
       record numbers: (55327-2) Vi-V38555 Yz L-1032

  1 What makes some women : when you treat them so nice
     and kind
  2 You can ask them for a favor : they don't even pay
     you no mind
  3 Just because you love them : and do anything they
     say
  4 They will love somebody else : and do you any way
  5 Hey they think they happy : and don't know what it's
     all about
  6 Maybe she will remember me : when her man has put
     her out
  7 You can hears I ain't got nobody : somebody come and
     get me
  8 I know you was blind pretty mama : baby but now you
     see
  9 I was good to you pretty mama : tried to please your
     mind
 10 Now you ain't got nobody : and a good man's hard to
     find

ThoR 1   Thomas, Ramblin'

       title: So Lonesome
       place and date: Chicago, c. Feb. 1928
       record numbers: (20334-2) Pm-12637 Yz L-1026

  1 I'm so lonesome lonesome : I don't know what to do
  2 If you don't have no good woman : you'd be lonesome
     too
  3 Lord I'm going up the country : baby and I can't
     carry you
  4 Because I got one up there : and I can't see how you
     all would do
  5 I wished I had a-listened : what my baby sister said
  6 Said stay home brother : please don't stray away
  7 Oh my mama told me : when I first left her door
  8 Said be careful in your traveling son : you got to
     reap just what you sow

ThoR 2   Thomas, Ramblin'

       title: Hard to Rule Woman Blues
       place and date: Chicago, c. Feb. 1928
       record numbers: (20335-3) Pm-12670 Bio BLP-12004

  1 I've got a girl : I wish I could keep her home at
     night
  2 She's always going off : on automobile rides
  3 She sleeps late every morning : I can't hardly get
     her woke
  4 She will wake up in one second : when she hears a
     car horn blow
  5 Some of these days : I'm going to be like Mr Henry
     Ford
  6 Going to have a car and a woman : running on every
     road
  7 If you ain't got a car : man a woman is hard to rule
  8 That's why : I got them automobile blues

ThoR   3   Thomas, Ramblin'

    title: Lock and Key Blues
    place and date: Chicago, c. Feb. 1928
    record numbers: (20336-3) Pm-12637 Yz L-1032

1 Springtime coming : and the grass all growing green
2 And my time has come : where the blues don't worry
  me
3 There's so many women : there's so many different
  kinds
4 When one quit me : it's sure to worry my mind
5 My mama give me a lock : and my papa give me the key
6 Then after I know how : to lock them blues up for me
7 I got northern women : I got southern women too
8 I ain't going to tell the northern women : what the
  southern women can do

ThoR   4   Thomas, Ramblin'

    title: Sawmill Moan
    place and date: Chicago, c. Feb. 1928
    record numbers: (20337-2) Pm-12616 Bio BLP-12004

1 Oh : hey hey hey hey
2 And I had them all night : and got them all again
  today
3 And I wish I had : my same old good girl back
4 Because that's the only one : that I ever did like
5 How can I love you : you stay out both night and day
6 How can I love you : you treat me most any way
7 I'm going to sing this time : and I ain't going to
  sing no more
8 Because my girl have called me : and I've got to go
9 If I don't go crazy : I'm sure going to lose my mind
10 Because I can't sleep for dreaming : sure can't stay
  woke for crying

ThoR   5   Thomas, Ramblin'

    title: No Baby Blues
    place and date: Chicago, c. Feb. 1928
    record numbers: (20338-1) Pm-12670 Bio BLP-12004

1 Hey no more baby : I ain't got no more baby now
2 Since I looked into it : I don't need no baby nohow
3 If you want me woman : better buy you a pair of
  overalls
4 Because when I leave town : I'm going to ride that
  Cannonball
5 If you get you one woman : you sure to get you two
6 Better get you twenty-four : so twelve won't worry
  you
7 I had a girl : she went out sailing on that sea
8 That poor child got drownded : sailing after me

ThoR   6   Thomas, Ramblin'

    title: Ramblin' Mind Blues
    place and date: Chicago, c. Feb. 1928
    record numbers: (20339-2) Pm-12616 Bio BLP-12004

1 And I lay down last night : tried to take my rest
2 And my mind got to rambling : like the wild geese in
  the west
3 I'm going to West Texas : won't be back till fall
4 If the blues overtake me : I won't be back at all
5 And I had one woman : would make a passenger train
  hop the rail
6 But now I got one : would make a tomcat heist its
  tail
7 Said I started to write : but I believe I'll go
  myself
8 Says a letter's too slow : and a telegram may get
  left

ThoR   7   Thomas, Ramblin'

    title: No Job Blues
    place and date: Chicago, c. Feb. 1928
    record numbers: (20343-2) Pm-12609 Bio BLP-12004

1 I been walking all day : and all night too
2 Because my meal ticket woman have quit me : and I
  can't find no work to do
3 I picking up the newspaper : and I looking in the
  ads
4 And the policeman came along : and he arrested me
  for vag
5 I said judge : judge what may be my fine
6 He said get your pick and shovel : and get deep down
  in mine
7 I'm a poor black prisoner : working in the ice and
  snow
8 I got to get me another meal ticket woman : so I
  won't have to work no more

ThoR   8   Thomas, Ramblin'

    title: Back Gnawing Blues
    place and date: Chicago, c. Feb. 1928
    record numbers: (20344-2) Pm-12609 Bio BLP-12004

1 I ain't never loved : but three womens in my life
2 My mother and my sister : and my partner's wife
3 My mama told me : when I was about twelve years old
4 Man you nothing but a backbiter : may God bless your
  soul
5 I'm going to tell all you women something : baby you
  might not like
6 I want to know : if I can bite your man in the back
7 You might risk me brother : but I will never risk
  you
8 If you allow me a chance : I will gnaw your backbone
  half in two

ThoR   9   Thomas, Ramblin'

    title: Jig Head Blues
    place and date: Chicago, c. Nov. 1928
    record numbers: (21017-4) Pm-12708 Bio BLP-12004

1 I stay drunk so much : I can't tell night from day
2 Because the woman I love : she treats me any way
3 I likes my whiskey : I likes my *swig and dip* too
4 When I can't get alcorub : denatured alcohol will do
5 Oh : whiskey's killing me
6 Because I drink so much : I can't hardly see

ThoR   10   Thomas, Ramblin'

    title: Hard Dallas Blues
    place and date: Chicago, c. Nov. 1928
    record numbers: (21018-2) Pm-12708 Bio BLP-12004

1 Go out to Santa Fe : my baby go down
2 I was took all of my clothes : and walk the streets
  in my morning gown
3 And before I would stand to see : my baby leave this
  town
4 I would beat the train to the crossing : and burn
  that doggone bridge down
5 And Dallas is hard : I don't care how you work
6 There will be somebody coming on your payday : to
  collect
7 Hey : don't never make Dallas your home
8 When you look for your friend : they will all be
  gone

ThoR   11   Thomas, Ramblin'

       title: Ramblin' Man
       place and date: Chicago, c. Nov. 1928
       record numbers: (21019-4) Pm-12722 Bio BLP-12004

1 I feel like rambling : rambling stays on my mind
2 And I ain't satisfied : unless I'm rambling all the
   time
3 Now you will wake up in the morning : and find me
   gone
4 Because I'm a rambling man : I can't stay at one
   place long
5 It's one day and one night : is long as I stay in
   one place
6 But I been in Chicago one week : because I like
   these Chicago ways
7 Lord I'm going to leave here walking : chance is
   that I may ride
8 Because I'm going to ramble : until the day that I
   die

ThoR   12   Thomas, Ramblin'

       title: Poor Boy Blues
       place and date: Chicago, c. Nov. 1928
       record numbers: (21020-4) Pm-12722 Bio BLP-12004

1 I was down in Louisiana : doing as I please
2 Now I'm in Texas : I got to work or leave
3 If your home in Louisiana : what you doing over here
4 Said my home ain't in Texas : and I sure don't care
5 I don't care : if the boat don't never land
6 I'd like to stay on the water : as long as any man
7 And my boat come a-rocking : just like a drunken man
8 And my home's on the water : and I sure don't like
   land

ThoR   13   Thomas, Ramblin'

       title: Good Time Blues
       place and date: Chicago, c. Nov. 1928
       record numbers: (21027-1) Pm-12752 Bio BLP-12004

1 I woke up this morning : I had the blues three
   different ways
2 I had one mind to stay here : and two to leave this
   place
3 I got one mind to stay here : got two to leave this
   place
4 If you find me tomorrow : you'll find me in the same
   old way
5 She's a *little old* woman : *so nice and clean* all
   the time
6 The only thing I hate : she ain't no woman of mine
7 And I'm worried now : but I won't be worried long
8 Because I got a letter this morning : my baby was
   coming back home

ThoR   14   Thomas, Ramblin'

       title: New Way of Living Blues
       place and date: Chicago, c. Nov. 1928
       record numbers: (21028-2) Pm-12752 Bio BLP-12004

1 I got a new way of living : everybody can catch on
2 Always gamble and steal : and don't collect nothing
   from home
3 I don't bum : and I sure God don't beg
4 I just keep my eyes open : and work my head
5 I never wanted no woman : that I could not get
6 Because I got a new way of living : it just won't
   quit
7 I've got a gang of women : I got my eyes on a gang
   of *four*
8 So if one wants to quit : I can turn her *go*

ThoZ   1   Thomkins, Jim

       title: Bedside Blues
       place and date: Memphis, c. early Feb. 1930
       record numbers: (MEM-780-) Br-7200 Rt RL-319

1   I ain't going to be : your lowdown dog no more
2   I'll get me a good gal : most any place I go
3   I walked all night long : my feet got soaking wet
4   And I haven't walked : up on my good gal yet
5   Well mama mama : what's the matter now
6   Trying to quit your daddy : honey and you don't know
    how
7   I'm going I'm going : and your crying won't make me
    stay
8   Honey the more you cry : the further I'm going away
9   I don't like no woman : got hair like drops of rain
10 Because the girl I like : got hair like a horse's
    mane
11 That's what my mother told me : just before she died
12 Son your trouble ain't now : but it sure be after a
    while
13 Well I fell down on my knees : and cried
14 I fell down : right by my mama's side
15 Well there's one more thing son : that I want you to
    do
16 And then these women : sure take care of you

ThpA   1   Thompson, Ashley (Gus Cannon)

       title: Minglewood Blues
       place and date: Memphis, 30 Jan. 1928
       record numbers: (41803-2) Vi-21267 Fwy FA-2953

1 Don't you never : let no woman rule your life
2 Says she keeps you worried : worried all the time
3 Don't you wish a *fair woman* : didn't have teeth
   like pearls
4 *So* after you're married : ???
5 Don't you never : let no woman rule your life
6 She keep you troubled : worried all the time
7 I got a letter mama : you ought to heard it read
8 Says you coming back baby : and I'll be almost dead

ThpE   1   Thompson, Edward

       title: Showers of Rain Blues
       place and date: New York, c. 23 Oct. 1929
       record numbers: (GEX-2411-A) Pm-13018 Yz L-1006

1   Don't mistreat me mama : because I'm your little
    wild
2   Because you must remember : you once have been a
    child
3   Mama never : drive a stranger from your door
4   He may be your best friend : baby you don't know
5   I love my brownie : don't care what she do
6   Some one of these days : she going to love me too
7   I went to the station : in a shower rain
8   I seen the brown I love : when she caught that
    lowdown train
9   Got up one of these mornings : looked down in the
    sea
10 What see the way them fishes : do the shivaree

ThpE   2   Thompson, Edward

       title: Florida Bound
       place and date: New York, c. 23 Oct. 1929
       record numbers: (GEX-2412) Pm-12873 Yz L-1006

1 I'm going to Florida : where I can have my fun
2 Babe I'll lay in the green grass : look up at the
   sun
3 Say Mr redcap porter : help me with my load
4 Before your steamboat captain : let me on board

ThpE 2   Thompson, Edward

5 Got a letter from my baby : bought me a piece of
   ground
6 You can't blame me for leaving : boy I'm Florida
   bound
7 It you home in Florida : what in the world you doing
   up here
8 I wonder where you be : this time another year
9 My mama told me : papa told me too
10 Don't you let them bell-bottom : make no fool of you

ThpE 3   Thompson, Edward

       title: Seven Sister Blues
       place and date: New York, c. 23 Oct. 1929
       record numbers: (GEX-2413) Pm-12873 Yz L-1006

1 Coal-black woman : fry no meat for me
2 You know black is evil : that gal may poison me
3 I got a new way of spelling : sweet old Tennessee
4 Double T double N : double T double S U Z
5 My girl rolled and tumbled : cried the whole night
   long
6 She received that message : that the man she loved
   was gone
7 Said my love's like water : it turns off and on
8 When you think I'm loving : I done took off and gone
9 When the death wagon rolled up : with the rumbling
   sound
10 Says I knowed by that : my gal was graveyard bound

ThpE 4   Thompson, Edward

       title: West Virginia Blues
       place and date: New York, c. 23 Oct. 1929
       record numbers: (GEX-2416-A) Pm-13018 Yz L-1006

1 On West Virginia : where the brown I love
2 Ain't nobody stop me : ??? *home*
3 I hate to see Lord : the evening sun go down
4 Lord it make me think : of my last go-round
5 My brownie caught me : this morning soon
6 Got to go so far : to get my loving done
7 She used to love me : she don't love me no more
8 Got another man : she don't love me no more
9 She used to rock me : in the morning soon
10 Got another man : she don't rock me no more
11 Coal-black dark : baby when I'm gone
12 Come with my money baby : where you been so long
13 See them peaches : hanging in the tree
14 Then you know : that brown going to be the death of
   me

Tore 1   Torey, George

       title: Married Woman Blues
       place and date: Birmingham, Ala., 2 Apr. 1937
       record numbers: (B-64-2) ARC-7-08-57 Yz L-1002

1 If you ever been mistreated : then you know how
   mistreated feels
2 Like a broke down engine : ain't got no driver-wheel
3 You can always tell : when your brown want to throw
   you down
4 She's always got business : on the other side of
   town
5 Well I started once to write : but I believe I'll go
   myself
6 Because a letter too slow : and a telegram may get
   lost
7 Wake up soon every morning : babe wear a rag all
   around her head
8 Every time you speak to her : she'll swear she
   nearly dead
9 Ever been down : then you know just how I feel

Tore 1   Torey, George

10 I feel like I ain't got no business here : somewhere
   on the sea
11 It's mighty hard : to be married woman's man
12 Can't see her when you want to : got to catch her
   just when you can
13 If you love a married woman : you going to always
   have the blues
14 Every time you want to see her : her husband want to
   see her too
15 Then now run here run here baby : set down on your
   daddy's knee
16 Because I done got drunk : and I'm blue as a poor
   man can be
17 Said well I went to the window : and I looked down
   on the ground
18 And my heart struck sorrow : and the tears come
   easing down

Tore 2   Torey, George

       title: Lonesome Man Blues
       place and date: Birmingham, Ala., 2 Apr. 1937
       record numbers: (B-65-1) ARC-7-08-57 Yz L-1002

1 Baby how long baby how long : *long* before you
   bring your *load* back home
2 Say well it won't be no longer : than you quit doing
   me wrong
3 Hey redcap porter : did my best woman ever get on
   board
4 Say I don't know the clothes : she had on
5 Just as sure as a bluebird : flies in the skies
   above
6 Say your life ain't no pleasure : unless you with
   that one you love
7 Then if I just had wings : then I'd fly just like
   Noah's dove
8 Then I would heist my wings :and fly and light on
   that woman I love
9 Well I went up on a mountain : taking a peep in that
   old deep blue sea
10 I said I spied that woman : put them things on me
11 Singing now hey how long : is you going to still
   [do, treat] me wrong
13 Said I woke up this morning : just about the dawn of
   day
14 Some man had my woman : and the worried blues had me

TowH 1   Townsend, Henry

       title: Henry's Worried Blues
       place and date: Chicago, 15 Nov. 1929
       record numbers: (403300-A) Co-14529-D Yz L-1030

1 My blues start in the morning : and they worries me
   the whole day long
2 They worries the poor man so bad : until I wished
   that I was dead and gone
3 And my baby she worries me : she worries me on every
   hand
4 How she worries the poor man : just because she can
5 Well it's bye bye baby : I ain't going to let you
   worry poor me no more
6 I'm going to get me another woman : babe I'm going
   to let you go
7 Mmm I've been asking for a favor : even I ask the
   good Lord above
8 I cried oh Lord listen : please send back the woman
   I love
9 Oh because she mistreat me : she mistreat me both
   night and day
10 Lord she mistreats the poor man : to pass the time
   away
11 Now babe I've been in trouble : forty-four nights
   and days

TowH   1   Townsend, Henry

12 But I got another woman now : drive my troubles away

TowH   2   Townsend, Henry

     title: Mistreated Blues
     place and date: Chicago, 15 Nov. 1929
     record numbers: (403301-A) Co-14491-D Yz L-1030

1 My baby mistreat me : night and day
2 Oh she mistreat the poor man : just to pass the
   doggone time away
3 And it's baby : baby what have I done went wrong
4 Lord you mistreat me baby : and drove me from my
   home
5 But I'm going now baby : and I won't be back no more
6 Ain't going to let you mistreat me : drive me away
   from your door
7 Well never mind never mind babe : I've got my
   [doggone] eyes on you
8 And some old day pretty baby : you'll do like I want
   you to do

TowH   3   Townsend, Henry

     title: Long Ago Blues
     place and date: Chicago, 15 Nov. 1929
     record numbers: (403302-?) Co-14529-D Yz L-1003

1 Mmm can't you remember baby : long long time ago
2 When you mistreated poor me : and drove me away from
   around your door
3 Mmm and I'm going back home now baby : and I ain't
   coming back here no more
4 I ain't going to let you drive me : babe away from
   around your door
5 Mmm when I first seen you baby : you were so nice
   and kind to me
6 And why you want to dog me : babe I swear I just
   can't see
7 Mmm I'm going down on the levee : and down on the
   levee where I'm going to stay
8 I'm going to stay down on the levee : babe until you
   change your ways

TowH   4   Townsend, Henry

     title: Poor Man Blues
     place and date: Chicago, 15 Nov. 1929
     record numbers: (403303-A) Co-14491-D Yz L-1030

1 And it's never mind never mind baby : I've got my
   doggone eyes on you
2 And some old day pretty baby : do like I want you to
   do
3 When I was sick and down : you drove me from your
   door
4 Now you know honey I was a poor man : sleeping out
   in the ice and snow
5 Yes baby I'm going to see you : when you baby do
   something I swear is wrong
6 When you mistreat me baby : I'm going to send you
   clear back home
7 That's all right for you babe : I even pawned my
   watch and ring
8 I done give you my money : I can give you most
   anything

TowH   5   Townsend, Henry

     title: Sick with the Blues
     place and date: possibly Chicago, 1933
     record numbers: (   ) record unknown Yz L-1030

1 People I've tried every doctor : every doctor in my
   neighborhood
2 But I haven't even found nar' doctor : is capable of
   doing my blues any good
3 You had better leave her alone : she don't mean a
   doggone thing
4 Ain't but the one thing that she's after : that is
   your doggone spending change
5 Yes the girl that I wants now : she wants to walk
   out of my door
6 She just left me worried : telling me she won't come
   back in my house no more
7 But I'm going to try my best to leave her : Lord I'm
   going to try to let her go
8 I'm going to try to find someone now : thinks the
   world and all of me
9 So bye bye bye : reason that I'm leaving you
10 Because I've already found out : that your love is
   not true

TowH   6   Townsend, Henry

     title: She's Got a Mean Disposition
     place and date: Chicaco, 25 Feb. 1935
     record numbers: (85494-1) BB-B5966 Yz L-1030

1 She got a mean disposition : and she got such a
   lowdown dirty way
2 I been a-hoping and trusting : that my babe would
   change some day
3 Many year I have traveled : yes I've traveled from
   door to door
4 You can't find no heaven : nowhere in the world that
   you go
5 You having a good time now : you like a fly while
   that country may
6 You having your time now : but you got to die some
   day
7 But you going to need me : you going to need my help
   I say
8 And you had better use me lover : just before I go
   away
9 Why can't I be happy : people like everybody else
10 I just sit around and worry : I worry my fool self

TowS   1   Townsend, Sam

     title: Lily Kimball Blues
     place and date: Atlanta, 17 Apr. 1930
     record numbers: (150259-2) Co-14571-D Yz L-1021

1 Tell me Lilly Kimball : what did you do to me
2 These Lilly Kimball blues : is nearly killing me
3 It's hard it's hard : but I suppose it's fair
4 These Lilly Kimball blues : won't let me rest
   nowhere
5 I love you Lilly Kimball : don't want no other one
6 Is it too late now : to make up for all I done
7 It's hard to love you Lilly : you love somebody else
8 I believe it's going to make me : grieve myself to
   death
9 I believe I'm going crazy : my mind I'm bound to
   lose
10 If I don't get over : these Lilly Kimball blues
11 When I'm blue : it's good to have you around
12 Because when you start loving : it bring my kindness
   down
13 I'm going to the river : tie my hands behind
14 And let that Tennessee water : satisfy my mind
15 Can't you see Lilly : I want you to understand
16 Take me back Lilly : I'll be a different man

TucB   1   Tucker, Bessie

        title: Bessie's Moan
        place and date: Memphis, 29 Aug. 1928
        record numbers: (45436-2) Vi-V38526 His HLP-4

1   Hey : hey hey hey hey
2   Because the man I'm loving : treats me so unkind
3   I woke up this morning : feeling mighty bad
4   I done lost my daddy : best man I ever had
5   It's your time now : be mine after a while
6   You know that you hurt me : daddy because I seen you
    smile
7   My mama's dead : papa throwed me away from home
8   My man don't want me : that's why I weep and moan
9   If you don't want me : please don't dog me around
10 Just like you found me : you can put me down

TucB   2   Tucker, Bessie

        title: Penitentiary
        place and date: Memphis, 29 Aug. 1928
        record numbers: (45441-2) Vi-V38526 Fwy FJ-2801

1   Aah ha ha : what's the matter with my man today
2   I ask him if he love me : Lord and he walked away
3   Penitentiary penitentiary : oh is going to be my
    home
4   Because my man he mistreated me : Lord he have done
    me wrong
5   The man that I'm a-loving : Lord he going get me
    killed
6   Because love is a proposition : that's got many a
    poor girl killed
7   I'll love you *a minute* : oh but you won't behave
8   You going to keep on *a-palling* : you going to wake
    up in your grave

TurnB   1   Turner, Buck

        title: Black Ace
        place and date: Chicago, 15 Feb. 1937
        record numbers: (61790-A) De-7281 Yz L-1026

1   I am the black ace : I'm the boss card in your hand
2   And I'll play for you mama : if you please let me be
    your man
3   Sometimes a black ace : never comes inside
4   But I'll play for you mama : if you please will
    treat me right
5   There's a little ace in the deck mama : *I'll lay
    forth and* tight
6   But I'll play for you mama : if you treat me right
7   If you don't want me mama : I said please sit here
    alone
8   Because I'll play for you mama : eee when the
    can-get-it's gone
9   I'll be your winner : in any game you please
10 And if you don't want me mama : please just let me
    stay
11 If you know you don't want me mama : you won't even
    say
12 That's all right mama : you going to need my help
    some day
13 I said please : mama please don't drive me away
14 Because I'd be a good fellow : mama if you would
    please let me stay

TurnB   2   Turner, Buck

        title: Christmas Time Blues
        place and date: Chicago, 15 Feb. 1937
        record numbers: (61793-A) De-7387 Rt RL-327

1   Santa Claus : what is you going to bring

TurnB   2   Turner, Buck

2   If you don't bring my baby : don't bring me a
    doggone thing
3   You know I love her Santa Claus : why don't you
    bring her home
4   If you bring her back to me : I'll never do her
    wrong
5   Oh Lord it's Christmas time : and I want to see old
    Santa Claus
6   I asked my baby would she come home Christmas : she
    said go see old Santa Claus
7   Oh please Santa Claus Santa Claus Santa Claus :
    Santa Claus my eyes is almost blind
8   I am looking for you Christmas morning : before I
    lose my mind
9   I'm going to buy me a shepherd dog : and keep him at
    my door
10 And teach him to follow my baby : everywhere she
    goes

TurnJ   1   Turner, Joe

        title: Blues on Central Avenue
        place and date: Los Angeles, 8 Sept. 1941
        record numbers: (DLA-2739-A) De-7889 Br-87.504

1   I'm in the land of sunshine : standing on Central
    Avenue
2   I was doing all right : till I fell in love with you
3   Never have so much fought babe : anywhere in my life
4   Till I fell in love with you : and found out you was
    somebody else's wife
5   Now I'm in love with you baby : and I'm feeling
    awful low
6   Now you know you was married : well why didn't you
    tell me so
7   You have your chance at love : now I'm going to
    leave you flat
8   I know that don't bother you baby : because you used
    to that
9   Now let's have one more drink baby: we'll say
    goodbye to me and you
10 I'll always remember : I met you on Central Avenue

UnkA   1   unknown artist (Kansas City Blues Strummers)

        title: String Band Blues
        place and date: probably Chicago, c. late July
        1926
        record numbers: (   ) Vo-1048 Rt RL-311

1   Oh tell me brownskin : what's the matter now
2   Trying to quit your daddy : and you don't know how
3   I ain't going to marry : ain't going to settle down
4   Going to stay single : till my mustache drags the
    ground
5   Are you going to tell me : what's the matter now
6   If you don't want me : hold up your right hand
7   I had a good gal : I stole her from my friend
8   But my buddy came looking : got her back again

UnkA   2   unknown artist (Memphis Jug Band)

        title: Snitchin' Gambler Blues
        place and date: Memphis, 1 Feb. 1928
        record numbers: (41817-2) Vi-21524 Rt RL-322

1   People in this town : Lord they ain't no friend to
    you
2   All they'll do to you people : go down and tell lies
    on poor you
3   If I only had me : ??? house of my own
4   I wouldn't allow snitching and a-gambling : people
    around my home

UnkA   2   unknown artist (Memphis Jug Band)

5   I hate a-snitching : worse than the good Lord hates
    sin
6   If they ever get me into trouble : soon on my way to
    the pen
7   If I only had me : a shelter of my own
8   I wouldn't allow snitching and gambling : people
    around my home
9   Now it's eighteen hundred : and it's ninety-one
10 That's when the snitching : was people Lordy just
    begun
11 Now it's eighteen hundred : and it's ninety-two
12 The snitches in town : Lord they just won't do
13 Now it's eighteen hundred : and it's ninety-three
14 I got arrested : off of Beale Street
15 I went before the judge : I said judge what is my
    fine
16 A hundred dollar fine : and two eleven ninety-nine
17 Now look a-here judge : can't you hold up off of
    that fine
18 He say go ahead on nigger : that ain't no good long
    time
19 Now it's eighteen hundred : and it's ninety-four
20 The white people load me : in the workhouse door
21 It's eighteen hundred : and it's ninety-five
22 This people in the town : don't do nothing but tell
    dirty lies
23 Oh it's eighteen hundred : and it's ninety-six
24 That's when the snitchers thought : all all their
    snitching was fixed
25 Nineteen hundred : and it's twenty-seven
26 The snitchers that done the snitching : is way into
    heaven
27 It's nineteen hundred : and it's twenty-eight
28 I left the snitchers : standing at the workhouse
    gate
29 Now it's nineteen hundred : and it's twenty-nine
30 I left all the snitching people : way behind

UnkA   3   unknown artist (George Bullet Williams)

        title: Touch Me Light Mama
        place and date: Chicago, c. May 1928
        record numbers: (20590-2) Pm-12680 OJL-2

1   Touch me light pretty mama : this may be your last
3   I went to the nation : from that dirty territor'
4   Going to find my good gal : honey nowhere I go
5   Woke up this morning : woke up before day
6   Woke up this morning : with the same thing on my
    mind
7   I believe to my soul mama : got to leave your town
8   I got no pretty mama : talk baby-talk to me
9   I went to the nation : from that dirty territor'
10 I couldn't find my good gal : honey nowhere I go
11 Going uptown mama : some whiskey *skey* for me
12 Because my good gal done quit me : sure can't feel
    no peace

UnkA   4   unknown artist (Memphis Jug Band)

    title: Sugar Pudding
    place and date: Memphis, 11 Sept. 1928
    record numbers: (47009-1) Vi-21740 Rt RL-337

1   I'm tired of the women : *the day she cook*
2   *She* ??? : that sugar pudding
3   *That* ??? : she's long and tall
4   She sits up there : from wall to wall
5   *Oh won't you ??? me the* : *you going to* ???
6   I'm talking about the ??? : ??? *your head*

UnkA   5   unknown artist (possibly Skip James)

        title: Throw Me Down
        place and date: place unknown, c. Oct. 1928
        record numbers: (20998-1) Pm unissued Bio
            BLP-12029

1   Hey you threw me down : and you threw me from my
    home
2   That's all right baby : you're going to miss the
    days I'm gone
3   I felt like falling : from the treetop to the ground
4   *Should have been* my old babe : and she was leaving
    town
5   It was dark and stormy : and the sun shining bright
    like day
6   Some day the storm going to come : going to blow
    these old worried blues away
7   I'm going to hang my hat baby : Lord in some old
    weeping willow tree
8   Ain't going to wear it no more : till these old
    blues stop worrying me

UnkA   6   unknown artist (Noah Lewis)

        title: Selling the Jelly
        place and date: Memphis, 28 Nov. 1930
        record numbers: (64738-) Vi-23319 OJL-19

1   I'm a jelly-selling woman : I sell it every day
2   These women don't like me : because I almost give it
    away
3   Two and a half a potful : five dollars a cup
4   Ten dollars to the *one* : have me to wrap it up
5   I'm not a cheap woman : I sell about every day
6   My jelly too expensive : you know I can't give it
    away
7   A good jelly-selling woman : is heard all over town
8   You going to get my jellyroll : won't have no time
    to frown
9   I sell jelly : sell it fresh and cold
10 Before you buy my jelly : ???

UnkA   7   unknown artist (Birmingham Jug Band)

        title: German Blues
        place and date: Atlanta, 11 Dec. 1930
        record numbers: (404677-B) OK-8856 OJL-4

1   I believe I'll go back to Germany : *and pay a
    deposit gold*
3   I'm going to get no one woman : staying out in the
    cold
5   If you're worried mama : you know just how I feel
7   Say wake up mama : the children done come home
10 Nobody been here : since your daddy left your home

UnkA   8   unknown artist (Birmingham Jug Band)

        title: The Wild Cat Squawl
        place and date: Atlanta, 11 Dec. 1930
        record numbers: (404680-A) OK-8908 BC-2

1   I went home last night : about half past four
2   Mr wildcat told me : didn't *pay* you no more
3   Went a-hunting last night : out in the woods
4   You ought to see wildcat : make my dog go good
5   Went home this morning : about the break of day
6   Ha baby : he's just staying away
7   There's one thing about a wild cat : that he'll do
8   He makes you holler : and he make a fool of you
9   Ever been in the country : rattle around the woods
10 You ought to hear Mrs wildcat : make her do good
11 Say wake up mama : hear your rooster crow
12 One at your window : one at your door

UnkA   9   unknown artist (Birmingham Jug Band)

    title: Gettin' Ready for Trial
    place and date: Atlanta, 11 Dec. 1930
    record numbers: (404682-C) OK-8856 OJL-4

1 Down in Alabama : we will have a trial
2 Those jury down there : don't stand no lie
3 Tell me big boy : let's start it again
4 You had no business : catching that white man's hen
5 Every morning : about half past nine
6 Old judge : going to have somebody's wine
7 Wake up mama : hear your rooster crow
8 One at your window : one at your door
9 Sister and brother : you needn't have cried
10 The kids in the school : are ready to write
11 Come on sister : let's start that thing
12 Old brother : stole that hen again
13 *Well I didn't have a nickel* : wouldn't pay me no
    fine
14 Get you a shovel : and go down in the mine
15 Don't want me mama : don't you tell no lies
16 Because the day you quit me : that's the day you die
17 Hey big boy : did you aim to run
18 If you start to fooling : I'll shoot with my gun

UnkA   10   unknown artist (Birmingham Jug Band)

    title: Giving It Away
    place and date: Atlanta, 11 Dec. 1930
    record numbers: (404683-A) OK-8908 OJL-19

1 Say I woke up this morning : about the break of day
2 I hugged the pillow : where you used to lay
3 Red rooster comes back : with her *hen nipped* up
4 Just can't so it : for to strut that stuff
5 Old Aunt Anna : she's long and slim
6 When start to shaking : it's too tight then
7 What did the rooster : say to the hen
8 Ain't seen my woman : in God knows when
9 Says nickel is a nickel : and a dime a dime
10 Got a house full of children : ain't nar' one mine
11 Mama got the rowboat : papa got the tug
12 Well sister got the whiskey : and brother got the
    jug
13 Wake up mama : hear the rooster crow
14 One at your window : one at your door
15 Says the rooster crow : and the hen walk around
16 I ain't seen my woman : since she leave this town

Vinc   1   Vincson, Walter

    title: Overtime Blues
    place and date: Memphis, c. 22 Sept. 1929
    record numbers: (M-178) Br-7141 Yz L-1007

1 I been working overtime baby : oh the sun got hot
2 Just put a block on me baby : turn me in your back
    yard
3 I been walking all night : when the sun refused to
    shine
4 And if I find her tonight : I'm going to really work
    her overtime
5 Sweet baby crying won't help you : praying won't do
    no good
6 That's when your *faro sheriff* quit you : done
    everything you could
7 The work ain't so hard baby : just the way you do
8 Remember the way you treat poor Walter : it's coming
    home to you
9 It'll be a day going after : need my help alone
10 That's when you'll call for poor Walter : but he
    won't be in your home

Vinc   2   Vincson, Walter (Mississippi Sheiks)

    title: Sitting on Top of the World
    place and date: Shreveport, La., 17 Feb. 1930
    record numbers: (403805-B) OK-8784 Mam S-3804

1 Was all the summer : and all the fall
2 Just trying to find : my little all and all
3 Was in the spring : one summer day
4 Just when she left me : she'd gone to stay
5 Needn't a-come here running : holding up your hands
6 Can get me a woman : quick as you can a man
7 It have been days : I didn't know your name
8 Why should I worry : and prayer in vain
9 Went to the station : down in the yard
10 Going to get me a freight train : works done got
    hard
11 The lonesome days : they have gone by
12 Why should you beg me : and say goodbye

Vinc   3   Vincson, Walter (Mississippi Sheiks)

    title: Stop and Listen Blues
    place and date: Shreveport, La., 17 Feb. 1930
    record numbers: (403806-A) OK-8807 Yz L-1007

1 Yes I'm *jailhouse* ??? : long old lonesome day
2 Trying to *scream like* ??? : these ??? same old
    ways
3 Crying smokes like lightning : *bells* that shine
    like gold
4 Crying I found my baby : laying on a cooling board
5 Don't the house look lonesome mama : rolling before
    your door
6 Crying she's gone *tell you Lord* : won't be back no
    more
7 Oh stop and listen : hear how the bell is toned
8 I had a sweet little faro : but she been and gone
9 Crying followed my baby : down to the burying ground
10 It was ??? : ??? all around

Vinc   4   Vincson, Walter (Mississippi Sheiks)

    title: Lonely One in this Town
    place and date: Shreveport, La., 17 Feb. 1930
    record numbers: (403807-B) OK-8784 Rt RL-316

1 Because I'm a stranger here : everybody turned their
    back on me
2 I believe I'll go right back : to grand old
    Tennessee

Vinc   5   Vincson, Walter (Mississippi Sheiks)

    title: Yodeling Fiddling Blues
    place and date: San Antonio, 12 June 1930
    record numbers: (404146-B) OK-8834 Mam S-3804

1 Out in San Antone Texas : a long long ways from home
2 I would love to live there : but I will be all and
    all
3 My babe says she don't want me : she's calling
    someone else on
4 I will have to learn : to live out here in San
    Antone
5 Boys learn to yodel : that's the way to win her home
6 Then you will be the only sheik : it is in San
    Antone
7 These yodeling blues : make a Texas woman leave her
    home
8 I see the way you going : you sure won't be here
    long

title: Your Good Man Caught the Train and Gone
place and date: Jackson, Miss., 15 Dec. 1930
record numbers: (404710-A) OK-8905 Mam S-3804

1 If you don't want me : won't you please tell me so
2 I can get a woman : anywhere I go
3 Just as sure as you hear me : sing you this lonesome
   song
4 Swear it ain't no loving : it ain't no getting along
5 You can treat me mean : mean as you can be
6 But there is coming a day : you will be longing for
   me
7 You will long for me : but I will be far away
8 And you will miss my loving : each night and day
9 I lay down last night : tried to take my rest
10 My mind begin to ramble : like wild geese in the
   west
11 When you get up in the morning : begin to sing this
   lonesome song
12 I had a good man : he caught the train and gone

Vinc   7   Vincson, Walter (Mississippi Sheiks)

title: Unhappy Blues
place and date: Jackson, Miss., 15 Dec. 1930
record numbers: (404712-B) OK-8859 Mam S-3804

1 I can't be contented : oh nowhere I be
2 No place I go to : seem like home to me
3 Everybody seem welcome : here and every place but me
4 That whiskey and women : caused me can't see no
   peace
5 I have laid in jail : with my face turned to the
   wall
6 It was judges and lawyers : says man you's the cause
   of it all
7 Every day is growing older : and the nights growing
   near
8 And some got six months : I have got a year
9 And I been happy so : that I wished I was dead and
   gone
10 For I'm so unhappy : out here on the county farm

Vinc   8   Vincson, Walter (Mississippi Sheiks)

title: Honey Babe Let the Deal Go Down
place and date: Jackson, Miss., 19 Dec. 1930
record numbers: (404782-B) OK-8885 Mam S-3804

1 Honey babe : please let my deal go down
2 We can get the money : walk on down through town
3 I'm a stranger to you : and you's a stranger to me
4 If you be my babe : how happy I will be
5 I've traveled : until traveled the whole world
   through
6 I ain't found a woman : looked as sweet to me as you
7 Now honey babe : you got me troubled in mind
8 You keep me worried : and bothered all the time
9 I ain't mean : I'm good as I can be
10 Tell me sweet baby : what fault you find on me

Vinc   9   Vincson, Walter (Mississippi Sheiks)

title: She Ain't No Good
place and date: Jackson, Miss., 19 Dec. 1930
record numbers: (404783-B) OK-8885 Mam S-3804

1 Some men likes their country girl : my girl lives in
   town
2 A town girl will be loving you : when the country
   girl is messing around
3 A town girl will get one man : and always treat him
   swell

4 But a country girl will get her ten men : and give
   them all hell
5 A yellow gal drinks her corn whiskey : and a
   brownskin do the same
6 A country girl *jewel brown mule* : but she's
   getting drunk just the same
7 I went to a country girl's house : and only one
   night I spent
8 I got up next morning and come back home : been
   running ever since

Vinc   10   Vincson, Walter (Mississippi Sheiks)

title: Ramrod Blues
place and date: Jackson, Miss., 19 Dec. 1930
record numbers: (404784-A) OK-8905 Mam S-3804

1 I wonder where is the ramrod : belongs to my gun
2 My brother's got one : but I can't use it none
3 What good is a house : without a back yard
4 What good is a gun : without a ramrod
5 I rammed my gun : every morning before day
6 When I woke up this morning : my ramrod was gone
   away
7 I took you baby : when you was hand to hand
8 Telling everybody : that I was your loving man
9 Now I'm down : times is hard
10 You want to : give some other girl your ramrod
11 Now how you think : that I can have my fun
12 When I ain't got the ramrod : belongs to my gun

Vinc   11   Vincson, Walter (Mississippi Sheiks)

title: Stop and Listen Blues No. 2
place and date: Jackson, Miss., 19 Dec. 1930
record numbers: (404785-?) OK-8859 Mam S-3804

1 When I left town this morning : I was on my way back
   home
2 I heard the church bells : making a lonesome sound
3 I stopped and listened : as the bells continued on
4 I know by that : it's somebody's dead and gone
5 When I got home : the peoples met me and said
6 Oh run here Walter : your sweet little faro's dead
7 When I got home : I was began to scream and cry
8 I thought my little baby : was too cute to die
9 I went to the churchhouse : cried at the door
10 I never will see : sweet babe ever anymore

Vinc   12   Vincson, Walter (Mississippi Sheiks)

title: Please Baby
place and date: Atlanta, 24 Oct. 1931
record numbers: (405007-1) OK-8922 Mam S-3804

1 Please baby please baby : won't you come back to
   your daddy one more time
2 Please baby please baby : when I get my money I will
   give you my last dime
3 When you left me baby : you left me feeling so blue
4 You know babe : I didn't love no one but you
5 Please baby please baby : won't you come back to
   your daddy one more time
6 I'm so blue baby I'm so blue baby : I can't sleep at
   night I can't hardly talk for crying
7 You know baby you know baby : you always forever on
   my mind
9 Since you been gone : I can't sleep at night
10 I go to take my meals : I can't eat a bite
11 Please baby please baby : won't you come back and
   leave that other man alone
12 Please baby please baby : I need you here to carry
   my loving on

Vinc 13   Vincson, Walter (Mississippi Sheiks)

    title: The World Is Going Wrong
    place and date: Atlanta, 24 Oct. 1931
    record numbers: (405009-1) Co-14660-D Mam S-3804

1 Strange things have happened : that never before
2 My baby told me : I would have to go
3 Feel bad this morning : ain't got no home
4 No use a-worrying : because the world's gone wrong
5 I told you baby : right to your head
6 If I don't leave you : I would have to kill you dead
7 I tried to be loving : and treat you kind
8 But it seems that now : I got no loving mind
9 If you have a woman : and she don't do kind
10 Pray to the good Lord : to get her off your mind
11 Said when you been good now : can't do no more
12 Just tell her nicely : there is a front door
13 Pack up my suitcase : give me my hat
14 No use asking me babe : because I'll never be back

Vinc 14   Vincson, Walter (Mississippi Sheiks)

    title: Shake Hands and Tell Me Goodbye
    place and date: Atlanta, 25 Oct. 1931
    record numbers: (405020-1) OK-8951 Mam S-3804

1 I don't want you no more sweet baby : shake hands
   and tell your daddy goodbye
2 I don't want you no more sweet baby : you didn't
   love me nohow
3 Last night : the night before
4 I saw another man : knocking on your door
5 I worked all the winter : the winter was tough
6 With another man : just a-strutting your stuff
7 I don't want you no more sweet baby : shake hands
   and tell your daddy goodbye
8 I'm leaving this town tomorrow : no use to sigh and
   cry
9 I was good when you were sick : and good when you
   were well
10 Know you can play : when you get in hell
11 I don't want you no more sweet baby : shake hands
   and tell your daddy goodbye
12 I done everything I could do : still you pass me by
13 I worked all the winter : in the chilly winds
14 You give your loving : to the other men

Vinc 15   Vincson, Walter (Mississippi Sheiks)

    title: I've Got Blood in My Eyes for You
    place and date: Atlanta, 25 Oct. 1931
    record numbers: (405023-1) Co-14660-D Mam S-3804

1 I was out this morning : feeling blue
2 I seed a good-looking girl : can I make love with
   you
3 Hey hey baby : I got blood in my eye for you
4 I've got blood in my eyes for you baby : I don't
   care what in this world you do
5 I went back home : put on my tie
6 Going to get that girl : that this money will buy
7 She looked at me : begin to smile
8 Hey hey man : can't you wait awhile
9 No no man : I can't wait
10 You got the money : and trying to break this date
11 I'm going to tell you something : going to tell you
   the facts
12 If you don't want me : give me my money back
13 It ain't no need : of getting rocks in your jaws
14 You ain't going to get : none of my Santa Claus

Vinc 16   Vincson, Walter (Mississippi Sheiks)

    title: The New Stop and Listen Blues
    place and date: Grafton, Wis., c. July 1932
    record numbers: (L-1551-3) Pm-13134 Yz L-1014

1 Lord I went to the graveyard : and I peeped down in
   her face
2 Crying ooo Lord : what a ooo lonesome place
3 Well the woman I'm loving : she's six feet in the
   clay
4 But the one I hate : I sees her every day
5 Well I went to the churchhouse : praying on my
   bended knees
6 Crying Lord help ooo : give me my ooo favor please
7 Well I went to the graveyard : held up my right hand
8 I asked the graveyard ooo : to show me the right man
9 Ain't it sad to say : but the fun's all over now
10 ??? : you didn't want ooo me nohow

Vinc 17   Vincson, Walter (Mississippi Sheiks)

    title: Go Away Woman
    place and date: Grafton, Wis., c. July 1932
    record numbers: (L-1554-1) Pm-13152 Bio
    BLP-12041

1 Last night : and the night before
2 Saw another man : knocking on your door
3 Oh go away woman : I can't use you no more
4 Now you's a dirty mistreater : I can't use you no
   more
5 *Last summer this time : and going ??? fall*
6 I ain't going to let you : latch on to me no more
7 I've always put a dollar : in your hand
8 Now you done your cooking : for some other man
9 Just like a lemon : is ??? *to me*
10 You always got me : feeling so blue

Vinc 18   Vincson, Walter (Mississippi Sheiks)

    title: New Shake that Thing
    place and date: Grafton, Wis., c. July 1932
    record numbers: (L-1555-2) Pm-13143 Bio
    BLP-12041

1 So cold up north : till the birds can't sing
2 The people down south : shaking that thing
3 I lay down last night : I was awful sick
4 I woke up this morning : she had my pocket picked
5 I went down to the station : up to the train
6 I couldn't buy no ticket : for shaking that thing
7 I went down to the railroad : I laid my head on the
   track
8 The train come along : and it broke my back

Vinc 19   Vincson, Walter (Mississippi Sheiks)

    title: Don't Wake It Up
    place and date: Grafton, Wis., c. July 1932
    record numbers: (L-1560-1) Pm-13152 Bio
    BLP-12041

1 Now the girl's got something : I don't know what it
   is
2 Every time you move it : Lord I can't be still
3 I may be right : I may be wrong
4 Can't get me some *birdhouse* : to hold on strong
5 She has good hair : her nails is neat
6 But when you take off her shoe : you can smell her
   stinking feet
7 Now some of these girls : will call you honey
8 But when you go to their house : it will smell
   mighty funny
9 I'm going to tell you something baby : I know it's
   just right

Vinc   19   Vincson, Walter (Mississippi Sheiks)

10 Get a bar of *T and D* : and take a bath tonight
11 She got up this morning : she looking mighty sweet
12 The mens all thought : she was something good to eat
13 Now some days I worry : some days I don't
14 You got something : that I sure Lord want
15 Well it ain't no use : to get rocks in your jaws
16 You ain't going to get : none of my *peppermint
        cloth*

Vinc   20   Vincson, Walter (Mississippi Sheiks)

        title: I'll Be Gone Long Gone
        place and date: Grafton, Wis., c. July 1932
        record numbers: (L-1565-1) Pm-13153 Bio
            BLP-12041

1   I beg you baby : to treat me right
2   Now I'm going to leave you honey : tomorrow night
3   I work hard baby : give you all my dough
4   Now you gone to act so funny : I'm bound to go
5   You may have men around your house : everywhere you
        be
6   But some day baby : you going to long for me
7   You going to be sorry : sorry to your heart
8. But some day baby : we'll have to part
9   There's no use to grieve : no use to cry
10 You sure miss your water honey : when your well go
        dry
11 You may be happy : everywhere you be
12 But some day baby : you'll long for me

Virg   1   Virgial, Otto

        title: Little Girl in Rome
        place and date: Chicago, 31 Oct. 1935
        record numbers: (96240-1) BB-B6213 Mam S-3802

1   I got a letter this morning : from that girl in Rome
2   Said she got something for me : she going to bring
        it back home
3   Said I'm going way away : to wear you off my mind
4   Because you keeps me worried : and bothered all the
        time
5   I got something to tell you : just before you go
6   It ain't nothing baby : turn your lamp down low
7   I went down the railroad : I looked down the tracks
8   Thought about my little good girl : come a-easing on
        back
9   Yon comes my baby : coming down the line
10 With her headlights just shining : like ??? all
        behind
11 Well I had one good girl : and she strayed away
12 I didn't think : my baby treat me this a-way
13 Now if I could holler : like some mountain jack
14 I would go on a mountain : call my baby back
15 Mama she caught the Southern : my daddy rode the
        blinds
16 He said baby can't quit me : ain't no need of you
        trying

Virg   2   Virgial, Otto

        title: Bad Notion Blues
        place and date: Chicago, 31 Oct. 1935
        record numbers: (96241-1) BB-B6213 Mam S-3802

1   Oh I woke up this morning : sure was feeling bad
2   *Don't know* about the good times : that I oh that I
        once have had
3   Oh I had a notion this morning : oh and I believe I
        will
4   Believe I'll make my home : way up on Dago Hill
5   Oh I believe I'll leave here : before it is too late
6   For my woman I love : she just won't wait

Virg   2   Virgial, Otto

7   Oh my mama she told me : ain't been no great long
        time
8   Oh one of these mornings :
9   Oh I'm going away way : to wear you off my mind
10 For you keep me worried : and bothered all the time
11 Oh Lord have mercy : on my worried soul
12 I wouldn't mistreat my woman : for to save nobody's
        soul

WalkA   1   Walker, Aaron T-Bone

        title: Trinity River Blues
        place and date: Dallas, 5 Dec. 1929
        record numbers: (149548-1) Co-14506-D Rt RL-327

1   That dirty Trinity River : sure have done me wrong
2   It came in my windows and doors : now all my bacon
        gone
3   Trinity River blues : keep me bothered all the time
4   I lose all my clothes baby : believe I'm going to
        lose my mind
5   They'll build a levee now : I have no more to worry
        about
6   If that river should happen to rise : won't have to
        move my things out
7   Trinity River rising : it came in my windows and
        doors
8   *If it wasn't for* ??? baby : honey it won't rise no
        more

WalkB   1   Walker, Uncle Bud

        title: Look Here Mama Blues
        place and date: Atlanta, 30 July 1928
        record numbers: (402008-A) OK-8828 Yz L-1018

1   I I want to tell you : what I know about you
3   I believe to my soul : my girl got a black cat bone
4   For when I leave : sure come creeping home
5   I wonder what's the matter : with my rider here
6   ??? *need my blues* : and drive me away from here
7   *I wear* those blues mama : when the sun goes down
8   I declare to God : I never take you down
9   I ain't going to stay here : mama and nowhere else
10 I'm going to live up in the country : buy me a
        rocking chair
11 Now look a-here mama : what you trying to do
12 I believe to my soul : you break my heart in two
13 It rained five days : *and all lay dark* with me
14 Oh let me tell you : what my used-to-be

WalkB   2   Walker, Uncle Bud

        title: Stand Up Suitcase Blues
        place and date: Atlanta, 30 July 1928
        record numbers: (402009-B) OK-8828 Yz L-1009

1   Hey mama : honey what's the matter now
2   How in the world to tell me : honey what's the
        matter now
3   I ain't going to stay [there, here] : mama [stay
        there] and nowhere else
4   Said I walked from noon : honey way up north
5   I got up this morning : crying mama I got to go
6   Said I wait for Soo Lord : honey by the depot
7   Hey hey hey : honey what's the matter now
8   Said *won't poor* tell me : honey what's the matter
        now
9   I was standing here early one [morning, evening] :
        right before my clothes
10 I ain't got so many : got so far to go
11 I want you to stand still suitcase : till I find my
        clothes
12 Said the suitcase rolling : Monday man I go

WalkB 2   Walker, Uncle Bud

13   I ain't going to stay here : wondering about my soul
14   Said a sideboard sent me : got to roll you know
15   I got one old rider : all in my mind
16   I got one in Tampa : Georgia she was bound
17   [Oh see, oh look a-here] rider : I can't [stay, be]
     here long
18   Said the sideboard tell you : got to *line my home*
19   Hey rider : honey what is on your mind
20   Said this sideboard Soo Lord : carry load of wine

WalkW 1   Walker, Willie

        title: South Carolina Rag
        place and date: Atlanta, 6 Dec. 1930
        record numbers: (151065-) Co-14578-D OJL-18

1   I asked her for a drink of water : she brought
     gasoline
2   Now listen to me : you doing me mighty mean
3   Talk about your girl boy : you ought to see mine
4   Ain't so pretty : but she sure do dress fine
5   Talk about your gal : ought to see mine
6   She is the sweetest : gal in town
7   Music man : ain't it grand
8   Play that thing boy : long as you can
9   Asked her for water : she bring me gasoline
10   Now let me tell you : ain't that mean
11   Talk about your brown : you ought to see mine
12   Ain't so pretty : but she's the sweetest in town

WallM 1   Wallace, Minnie

        title: Dirty Butter
        place and date: Memphis, 23 Sept. 1929
        record numbers: (55571-2) Vi-V38547 Rt RL-322

1   Old Aunt Dinah : she's a sister of the church
2   She takes a drink : she says it will not hurt
3   I met her one day : coming down Beale Street
4   She was so drunk : until she could not see
5   Some folks say : a preacher won't steal
6   I caught a preacher : in my watermelon field
7   He took that watermelon : off the vine
8   He was running : when I thought he was flying
9   Had me before the judge : about selling corn
10   He made me hate the day : that I ever was born
11   I turned my face : right to the wall
12   He said a hundred and ten : and costs that's all
13   I went to the ball : the other night
14   My man danced with a gal : her dress was too tight
15   She doing the shimmy-shee-wobble : right across the
     hall
16   She made a misstep : you might've seen her fall
17   Early one morning : about half past four
18   A big police : was knocking on my door
19   He had a glass of whiskey : right in his hand
20   He's full of whiskey : and take me to the Promised
     Land

WallM 2   Wallace, Minnie

        title: The Old Folks Started It
        place and date: Memphis, 23 Sept. 1929
        record numbers: (55572-2) Vi-V38547 OJL-21

1   Talks about your *miller* : *he's from shore to
     shore*
2   I give you the strut : show him *got the floor*
3   Ain't no use : for you women to always be in a rut
4   Just step up to your man : and do your wicked strut
5   A hundred dollar bill : will make a broke man
     slobber
6   A woman with a strut : will make a good man holler
7   Take a Greyhound to run it : it's a round bumpy road

WallM 2   Wallace, Minnie

8   Takes a married woman to strut it : satisfy my soul
9   Talks about your women : when you're ???
10   Your grandma done the strut : in your grandpa's
     shirt
11   Some of you men : when you're *scratching hoe*
12   Do *young* about your strutting : in your ???
13   Just as sure as *the little pea* : ain't *leaving in
     the land*
14   A woman with the strut : can always get a man

WallM 3   Wallace, Minnie

        title: The Cockeyed World
        place and date: Jackson, Miss., 12 Oct. 1935
        record numbers: (JAX-113-2) Vo-03106 Rt RL-321

1   I woke up this morning : feeling mighty sad
2   Was the worst old feeling : that I ever had
3   It's war in Ethiopia : and mama's feeling blue
4   I tell the cockeyed world : I don't know what to do
5   They say that Ethiopia : is a long way from here
6   They trying to steal my man : and hurry him over
     there
7   I love my man : tell the cockeyed world I do
8   It's coming the time : that he'll sure love me too
9   This old cockeyed world : will make your good man
     treat you mean
10   He will treat you : just like a poor girl he never
     seen
11   It's war in Ethiopia : and my man won't behave
12   I tell the cockeyed world : I'll spit in my baby's
     face
13   It's war in Ethiopia : baby please please behave
14   I tell the cockeyed world : I'll follow you to your
     grave

WallM 4   Wallace, Minnie

        title: Field Mouse Stomp
        place and date: Jackson, Miss., 12 Oct. 1935
        record numbers: (JAX-114-1) Vo-03106 Rt RL-321

1   Now use to think : that you are cute
2   You look like a monkey : in a baseball suit
3   You come in creeping : just like a louse
4   Got a face : like Mickey Mouse
5   No use you doing : your evil ways
6   ??? : you think I crave
7   You prance around : *to be up trip*
8   Only time to do : the *lind* snake hips
9   No use to think : that you are tough
10   Trying to be : too hard and rough

WallS 1   Wallace, Sippie

        title: Special Delivery Blues
        place and date: Chicago, 1 Mar. 1926
        record numbers: (9547-A) OK-8328 CC-32

1   My man packed his trunk : and said I'm going away
2   And I'll send you a special delivery : some old day
3   He said I'm leaving you baby : it almost breaks my
     heart
4   But remember the times : that the best of friends
     must part
5   I run to the window : as the train was passing by
6   Lord it give me the blues so bad : I thought that I
     would die
7   Hey Mr mailman : did you bring me any news
8   Because if you didn't : it will give me those
     special delivery blues

WallS 2 Wallace, Sippie

title: Jack O' Diamonds Blues
place and date: Chicago, 1 Mar. 1926
record numbers: (9548-A) OK-8328 CC-32

1 Jack of diamonds : you appear to be my friend
2 But gambling : is going to be our end
3 You stole all my money : and cut up all my clothes
4 And you keep me broke : and tried to put me
   out-of-doors
5 We have traveled : the whole round world through
6 There is nothing in this world : I found that
   pleases you
7 I love jack of diamonds : but he was a cruel man
8 He would play dice and cards : and his game was old
   cooncan

WallS 3 Wallace, Sippie

title: Bedroom Blues
place and date: Chicago, 20 Nov. 1926
record numbers: (9930-A) OK-8439 Sw S-1240

1 My room sure looks lonesome : since my good man been
   gone
2 I ain't got nobody : that I can call my own
3 I lay down last night : tried to take my rest
4 My mind got to traveling : like the wild goose in
   the west
5 I was thinking about my sweet daddy : I mean all
   night long
6 Because he left me here : in this old lonesome home
7 Lord I tried to cry : but my tears refused to fall
8 I was all alone : no one to love at all
9 I got the bedroom blues : because there's a bedroom
   in my home
10 I thinks about my sweet man : all night long

WallS 4 Wallace, Sippie

title: Dead Drunk Blues
place and date: Chicago, 6 May 1927
record numbers: (80837-A) OK-8499 Bio BLP-C6

1 Give me Houston : Dallas is not my crave
2 So when I'm dry : I can drink whiskey just made
3 Whiskey whiskey : is some folk's downfall
4 But if I don't drink whiskey : I ain't no good at
   all
5 Have you ever been drunk : slept in all of your
   clothes
6 And when you woke up : you found that you were out
   of dough
7 I'm going to get drunk : papa just one more time
8 Because when I'm drunk : nothing don't worry my mind

WallS 5 Wallace, Sippie

title: Have You Ever Been Down
place and date: Chicago, 6 May 1927
record numbers: (80838-A) OK-8499 Bio BLP-C6

1 If you ever been down : you know just how I feel
2 Like a tramp on the railroad : ain't got a decent
   meal
3 I'm a real good woman : but my man don't treat me
   right
4 He takes all my money : and stays out all night
5 I'm down today : but I won't be down always
6 Because the sun's going to shine : in my back door
   some day
7 It's one thing papa : I've decided to do
8 I'm going to find another papa : then I can't use
   you

WallS 6 Wallace, Sippie

title: Lazy Man Blues
place and date: Chicago, 6 May 1927
record numbers: (80839-B) OK-8470 CC-32

1 Wake up man : see how bright the sun does shine
2 Get up in that section gang : and bring me up
   sometime
3 Now he ain't got no teeth : and *beard* so low as
   your toe
4 Now you know man : you got to bring me up some dough
5 Now the meal in the barrel : is going fast
6 How long man : do you think the *powder laws* will
   last
7 Rip Van Winkle : slept for a long long time
8 But Rip Van Winkle : wasn't no man of mine
9 I don't want a man : that don't work every day
10 I want a man : that brings home his pay
11 So get out of that bed : man be on your way
12 You ramble all night : and you sleep all day
13 So now I'm cross : and man I'm feeling mad
14 Because you's the laziest man : that I ever had

WallS 7 Wallace, Sippie

title: The Flood Blues
place and date: Chicago, 6 May 1927
record numbers: (80840-B) OK-8470 Sw S-1240

1 I'm standing in this water : wishing I had a boat
2 The only way I see : is take my clothes and float
3 The water is rising : people fleeing for the hills
4 Lord the water will obey : if you just say be still
5 They sent out a law : for everybody to leave town
6 But when I got the news : I was high-water bound
7 They dynamite the levee : thought it might give us
   ease
8 But the water still rising : do you hear this plea
9 I called on the good Lord : and my man too
10 What else is there : for a poor girl to do

WasbS 1 Washboard Sam

title: Mama Don't Allow No. 1
place and date: Chicago, 20 June 1935
record numbers: (C-1022-B) Vo-03275 BC-10

1 Now we don't care : what the mama don't allow
2 We going to wiggle-wob : anyhow
3 Oh we don't care : what the mama don't allow
4 We going to do rough stuff : anyhow
5 Oh we don't care : what the mama don't allow
6 We going to boogly-woogly : anyhow
7 Oh we don't care : what the mama don't allow
8 We going to bee-bop : anyhow
9 We don't care : what the mama don't allow
10 Boy girls coming in here : anyhow
11 Oh we don't care : what the mama don't allow
12 We going to drink our whiskey : anyhow
13 Oh we don't care : what the mama don't allow
14 We going to play washboards : anyhow

WasbS 2 Washboard Sam

title: Jesse James Blues
place and date: Chicago, 20 June 1935
record numbers: (C-1023-B) Vo-03375 BC-10

1 I wonder if you going to mistreat me woman : good as
   I have been to you
2 It seems like you don't want me : no matter what I
   do
3 Did you get that letter : that I throwed in your
   back yard

281

WasbS 2   Washboard Sam

4   Now I would come to see you : but your girl friend
       got me barred
5   Now woman you must want me : to be like Jesse James
6   I got to kill some man : and rob some passenger
       train
7   I feel just like : snapping my pistol in your
       no-good face
8   Because you told me late last night : you stayed in
       another place
9   I'm going to shoot you woman : as long as my pistol
       will fire
10 Because this is Jesse James : and you should not
       tell him a lie

WasbS 3   Washboard Sam

       title: Mama Don't Allow No. 2
       place and date: Chicago, 3 July 1935
       record numbers: (C-1059-?) Vo-03375 RBF RF-202

1   Says we don't care : what mama don't allow
2   We going to show : our nickers anyhow
3   Says we don't care : what mama don't allow
4   We going to play : our guitars anyhow
5   Says we don't care : what mama don't allow
6   We going to strut our stuff : anyhow
7   Says we don't care : what the mama don't allow
8   We going to shake our shimmy : anyhow
9   Says we don't care : what mama don't allow
10 We going to break them down : anyhow
11 Says we don't care : what the mama don't allow
12 We going to easy-woodle : anyhow

WasbS 4   Washboard Sam

       title: Out with the Wrong Woman
       place and date: Chicago, 21 Dec. 1936
       record numbers: (01883-) BB-B6794 BC-10

1   I went to a party last night : I was dressed to kill
2   When the people found who I was dancing with : I
       guess they laughing still
3   I looked up at her face : I looked down at her feet
4   She was built like an automobile : but didn't have
       no rumble seat
5   Now I got her home with me : I got into bed
6   When she pulled off her dress : she says daddy cover
       up your head
7   I bought myself a bottle of booze : I went to drink
       it to myself
8   But when I turned it up to my head : here comes
       somebody else
9   I went to her place last night : I knocked upon the
       door
10 When that lady opened that door : I said I'll never
       do this no more

WasbS 5   Washboard Sam

       title: Come On In
       place and date: Chicago, 21 Dec. 1936
       record numbers: (01884-) BB-B6870 RBF RF-16

1   Sit right down : have some fun
2   My old lady out : on a all night run
3   I'll cook some meat : bake some bread
4   If you get sleepy : there's a great big bed
5   Take this liquor : take this wine
6   Let's get drunk : have a whopping good time
7   You can have some of that : have some of this
8   Have everything : in the doggone flat
9   I'm drunk and disorderly : and I don't care
10 Why don't you : put on your underwear

WasbS 6   Washboard Sam

       title: Big Woman
       place and date: Chicago, 21 Dec. 1936
       record numbers: (01885-) BB-B6870 BC-10

1   Got a little bitty mama : and a big mama too
2   My little bitty mama : don't treat me like my big
       mama do
3   Hey hey mama : don't be mean to me
4   Because don't you know baby : you and I can't agree
5   Hey hey mama : take your big legs off of me
6   If you had good sense : you'd be down in misery
7   Hey hey mama : let's go across town
8   Now didn't we have fun : but you big legs is holding
       me down
9   Hey hey mama : give me my shoes and clothes
10 I done found out : I can't satisfy your soul
11 There's a train at the station : and I'm ready to go
12 You'll never get a chance : to put your big legs on
       me no more

WasbS 7   Washboard Sam

       title: Back Door
       place and date: Aurora, Ill., 4 May 1937
       record numbers: (07616-) BB-B7001 BC-10

1   Oh tell me mama : who's that here awhile ago
2   Yes when I come in : who is that went out that back
       door
3   Now don't come here mama : I'm going to start to
       raising sand
4   You been out boogly-wooglying : that's something I
       can't understand
5   This is something : I never seen before
6   You broke down my bed : got a pallet on my floor
7   I had the windows nailed down : he couldn't get
       through
8   Had his hat in his hand : and his underwear too
9   So tell me baby : before I let you go
10 Yes when I come in : who's that went out that back
       door
11 He come by me running : but it likely he ain't got a
       chance
12 With one leg in his pants : and his shoes in his
       hand

WasbS 8   Washboard Sam

       title: We Gonna Move
       place and date: Aurora, Ill., 4 May 1937
       record numbers: (07617-) BB-B7001 BC-10

1   When I get you mama : we going to move on the
       outskirts of town
2   Because I don't want nobody : ooo always hanging
       around
3   Well the reason mama : I don't want you to stay here
4   I don't need no iceman : I'm going to get me a
       frigidaire
5   That's why : I'm going to move on the outskirts of
       town
6   Because sweet baby : I don't want no iceman hanging
       around
7   Well I'm going to heat with gas mama : and not with
       coal
8   I don't need no coalman : stopping and hauling coal
9   That's why : we going to move on the outskirts of
       town
10 Because I don't want no coalman : always hanging
       around
11 Well I'm going to bring my groceries mama : myself
       every day
12 If that don't beat the grocery boy : I know a way
13 That's what I'm going to do : when we move to the
       outskirts of town

WasbS 8   Washboard Sam

14 Because I don't want no delivery boy : always
    hanging around
15 Well it may be funny mama : as funny as can be
16 If we have any babies : I want them all to look like
    me

WasbS 9   Washboard Sam

    title: Low Down Woman
    place and date: Aurora, Ill., 4 May 1937
    record numbers: (07618-) BB-B7048 BC-10

1   Hey hey baby : why you acting so lowdown
2   Yeah all you do is drink moonshine : and clown all
    over town
3   You drink moonshine : I believe you smoke reefers
    too
4   Yeah because when you get drunk woman : you don't
    care what you do
5   You said you loved me : I found out you told a lie
6   When I started to tell you about your lowdown ways :
    you just hang your head and cry
7   You can always tell : when your woman going to act
    lowdown
8   Yeah she start drinking moonshine : and running with
    the lowest class in town
9   I'm going to buy me a pistol : shotgun and some
    shells
10 I'm going to stop these lowdown women : because I'm
    going to start to raising hell

WasbS 10   Washboard Sam

    title: Lowland Blues
    place and date: Aurora, Ill., 4 May 1937
    record numbers: (07620-) BB-B7096 BC-10

1   I wonder why : that southbound train don't run
2   Woman you don't need no telling : you know just what
    you done
3   I got my ticket : I'm holding it in my hand
4   I got a real good woman : but the poor fool don't
    understand
5   I'm a hard-working man : to be mistreated where I go
6   When I get down in the lowlands : I won't be
    mistreated no more
7   I'm going to Jackson : Greenwood is where I belong
8   Anywhere in Mississippi : is my native home
9   I'm just like my mother left me : I ain't got
    nothing at all
10 I'm just like a big mule baby : I ain't got no stall

WasbS 11   Washboard Sam

    title: I'm On My Way Blues
    place and date: Aurora, Ill., 4 May 1937
    record numbers: (07621-) BB-B7096 BC-10

1   I was standing on the corner : and I was wringing my
    hands
2   And up come a copper : and say he was a
    plain-clothes man
3   He carried me to the station : and put me in a cell
4   He said you stay there partner : until about twelve
5   The judge he passed the sentence : the clerk he
    wrote it down
6   I know by that baby : I was prison bound
7   Bye bye baby : I see you some sweet day
8   Yeah I was not a bad fellow : but the judge he sent
    me away
9   I'm going away baby : but I never will forget this
    day
10 Yeah the Good Book do tell you : ooo that crime do
    not pay

WasbS 12   Washboard Sam

    title: Bucket's Got a Hole in It
    place and date: Aurora, Ill., 16 June 1938
    record numbers: (020808-) BB-B7906 BC-2

1   When you walking down Thirty-First Street : you had
    better look around
2   The vice squad is on the beat : and you'll be
    jailhouse bound
3   I was standing on the corner : everything was going
    slow
4   Can't make no money : tricks ain't walking no more
5   Going to start a little racket : going to start it
    out right
6   Going to sell moonshine in the day : and sell the
    dope at night
7   Then if I can't make no money : going to catch the
    Santa Fe
8   Going to drink good liquor : and let all women be

WasbS 13   Washboard Sam

    title: Save It for Me
    place and date: Aurora, Ill., 16 June 1938
    record numbers: (020809-) BB-B7866 BC-10

1   You's a good-looking woman : pretty as you can be
2   Lot of mens running after you : you must save it for
    me
3   You can invite men to dinner : let them drink my
    wine
4   But now when it comes to loving you : that had
    better be mine
5   You can throw away my money : drive me to the W P A
6   If you want to keep breathing : don't give my loving
    away
7   Oh men do tell me : I'm a doggone fool
8   But if you save it for me : I'll work like a doggone
    mule
9   Here I come mama : tired and dirty as I can be
10 Just want to know mama : if you save it for me

WasbS 14   Washboard Sam

    title: Sophisticated Mama
    place and date: Aurora, Ill., 16 June 1938
    record numbers: (020814-) BB-B7780 BC-2

1   Sophisticated mama : don't turn your nose up at me
2   Don't try to be ritzy : you ain't what you seem to
    be
3   You think you knows all answers : ain't got nothing
    to learn
4   You don't want no man : if he ain't got money to
    burn
5   I'm going to read you mama : tell you what I think
    of you
6   You will do anything : that any other woman will do
7   You can't drink nothing : unless it's champagne or
    wine
8   But you would drink beer and like it : if you were
    the woman of mine
9   You like high-price dresses : and mmm steaks every
    day
10 If you belongs to me : you would eat hot dogs any
    time I say
11 I'm a barrelhouse man : ain't got no money to give
    you
12 Can't give you nothing but loving : and you'll have
    to make that do

WasbS 15   Washboard Sam

       title: Diggin' My Potatoes
       place and date: Chicago, 15 May 1939
       record numbers: (034797-) BB-B8211 BC-10

 1 Baby's digging my potatoes : tramping on my vines
 2 I have a special plan : resting on my mind
 3 I don't eat no cabbage sprouts : bring me solid head
 4 Go to call a wagon : if I find him in my bed
 5 Now she powdered her face : *Lord her* wavy hair
 6 Caught a taxicab : she's out across town somewhere
 7 Said my vine's coloured green : potatoes solid red
 8 Never found a bruised one : till I caught them in my
    bed

WasbS 16   Washboard Sam

       title: I'm Goin' to St. Louis
       place and date: Chicago, 5 Aug. 1940
       record numbers: (049370-) BB-B8569 BC-10

 1 Well trouble start this morning : at my front door
 2 When you say : you didn't want me no more
 3 I'm going to St Louis : to wear you off my mind
 4 You keep me worried : and bothered all the time
 5 I tried to treat you : nice and kind
 6 But you got to the place : you didn't pay me no mind
 7 You been drinking whiskey : and been drinking gin
 8 First thing you know : you will be drunk again
 9 I tried hard : all my life
10 But you wouldn't try : to treat me right

WasbS 17   Washboard Sam

       title: Yes I Got Your Woman
       place and date: Chicago, 5 Aug. 1940
       record numbers: (049374-) BB-B8599 RBF RF-16

 1 You been tooting your whistle : and you been blowing
    your horn
 2 Oh you been raising sand : about what's going on
 3 Yes I got your woman : and you say that you was
    through
 4 Yes I got your woman : so what in the world are you
    going to do
 5 I wasn't bothering your woman : but you had left her
    alone
 6 So if she flagged my train : I'm sure going to take
    her home
 7 Oh you've unfastened your pistol : you've been
    making your bogus play
 8 If you bother me about that woman : I'm going to put
    you in your grave
 9 Oh when you had that woman : you didn't treat her
    right
10 Oh she walked these blocks for you : both day and
    night

WasbS 18   Washboard Sam

       title: Life Is Just a Book
       place and date: Chicago, 26 June 1941
       record numbers: (064477-1) BB-B8909 RCA LPV-577

 1 Life is just a book : every day is a brand new page
 2 There is one thing I know : ooo well we have no more
    ???
 3 There was so many people : standing on the corner
    today
 4 They can't find no job : ooo well and no place to
    stay
 5 Now once I had money : could go most anywhere
 6 Wouldn't wear a shirt : after it tear
 7 Now my money's gone : done pawned all my clothes

WasbS 18   Washboard Sam

 8 And if I don't make some changes : I'll be sleeping
    outdoors
 9 So take it easy take it easy : Lord how can I rest
10 If you ain't a stone pony : ooo well hard times will
    bust your vest
11 Now since prices have went up : on meal and leg bone
12 There's been a-many person : hung their head and
    moan
13 But the reason : so many without a place to stay
14 Standing around : depending on the W P A

WasbS 19   Washboard Sam

       title: I'm Not the Lad
       place and date: Chicago, 26 June 1941
       record numbers: (064478-1) BB-B8878 RCA LPV-577

 1 You are the same girl : I met in nineteen hundred
    and four
 2 You have a nice line of jive : with a plow and a hoe
 3 We can be buddies : you are a good scout
 4 But the road you are traveling : is done played out
 5 Your game is so strong mama : yes your dice is too
    bad
 6 So find you another chump : ooo well mama because
    I'm not the lad
 7 When you get your money : don't be so tight
 8 You don't buy nothing but whiskey : from morning
    till night
 9 Just buy yourself : one good feed
10 And you won't have to : weight everything you need
11 You can't slice my meat : you can't make my bread
12 You can't say : you want to fix your bed
13 Now don't think because you're smart : because you
    lot of mouth
14 For the line you are carrying : is done played out
15 Now a nickel is a nickel : and a dime is a dime
16 You spend your money : and I'll spend mine
17 If you think you can boss me : and eat up my grub
18 You are a lying sweet woman : so get up and out of
    that mud

WasbS 20   Washboard Sam

       title: My Feet Jumped Salty
       place and date: Chicago, 26 June 1941
       record numbers: (064479-1) BB-B8844 RCA LPV-577

 1 Then the cow jumped salty : Lord because it was
    against her rule
 2 Now if you think that she likes it : ooo well you
    just a blackeyed fool
 3 The little game rooster : told the little guinea hen
 4 If I ever catch you squatting : around my nest again
 5 I will have to jump salty : Lord because it's really
    against my rule
 6 Now if you think that he likes it : ooo well you
    just a blackeyed fool
 7 Now two old womens : are running hand in hand
 8 One found out : the other one had a man
 9 Then that woman jumped salty : Lord because it was
    against her rule
10 Now if you think that she likes it : ooo well you
    just a blackeyed fool
11 I was chatting with a girl : in the wrong place
12 A man cocked a pistol : right in my face
13 Then my feet jumped salty : Lord because it was
    against his rule
14 Now if you think that I liked it : ooo well you just
    a blackeyed fool

WasbS 21   Washboard Sam

        title: Flying Crow Blues
        place and date: Chicago, 26 June 1941
        record numbers: (064480-1) BB-B8844 BC-10

1 Flying Crow leave Port Arthur : come to Shreveport
   to change her crew
2 She will take water at Texarkana : yes boys and keep
   on through
3 That Flying Crow whistle : sounds so lonesome and
   sad
4 Lord it broke my heart : and took the last woman I
   had
5 Two days I cried : three days I walked the streets
6 I couldn't find nobody : to give my poor heart
   relief
7 Now she's gone she's gone : with a red and green
   light behind
8 The red is for trouble : and the green is for my
   rambling mind

WasbS 22   Washboard Sam

        title: Levee Camp Blues
        place and date: Chicago, 26 June 1941
        record numbers: (064481-1) BB-B8909 BC-10

1 Says I worked in a leveecamp : just about a month
   ago
2 Says I wind so many wagons : it made my poor hands
   sore
3 We slept just like dogs : eat beans both night and
   day
4 But I never did know : just when we were due our pay
5 They had two shifts on day : and the same two shifts
   at night
6 But if a man weren't working : he can't treat his
   baby right
7 Electric lights going out : telephones is bogging
   down
8 I'm going to keep on winding : because I'm the best
   old winder in town

WasbS 23   Washboard Sam

        title: I'm Feeling Low Down
        place and date: Chicago, 26 June 1941
        record numbers: (064482-1) BB-B8878 RCA LPV-577

1 I've got the blues : I feel so lowdown
2 It's all about my baby : down in my old home town
3 She got really white teeth : and long black wavy
   hair
4 Yes I love my baby : because that stuff is really
   there
5 I'm going back home : and take the right-hand road
6 And I ain't going to stop : until I get in my baby's
   door
7 These home-town blues : have got me down in mind
8 Because I love my baby : *and there's such a good
   time*

WasbS 24   Washboard Sam

        title: Brown and Yellow Woman Blues
        place and date: Chicago, 26 June 1941
        record numbers: (064483-1) BB-B8937 RCA LPV-577

1 I'm going to get me a brownskin woman : Lord and let
   all the yellow ones go
2 You know a brownskin woman : ooo well is not a don't
   you know
3 Don't let no yellow woman : know Lord how much you
   really care

WasbS 24   Washboard Sam

4 She'll keep your mind upset : ooo well and won't be
   on the square
5 Now I am a free man : Lord and sleeping all alone
6 But I'm going to get me a brownskin : ooo Lord
   because the yellow one is gone
7 That no-good woman followed me here : Lord but the
   police took her away
8 I was so glad of that : ooo well I didn't like her
   lowdown ways

WasbS 25   Washboard Sam

        title: She Belongs to the Devil
        place and date: Chicago, 26 June 1941
        record numbers: (064484-1) BB-B8937 RCA LPV-577

1 She belongs to the devil : Lord I cried many a day
2 Yes that child is so wicked : ooo well who could
   change her ways
3 She could wink a mean eye : Lord she learned me to
   sing the blues
4 And she had a little secret : ooo Lord make a
   washboard have it too
5 Now when we both was young : on our way to school
6 We stopped under a shade-tree : laying in the cool
7 Babe oh babe oh babe : honey you should have a heart
8 Just remember this day : ooo Lord Lord and we will
   never part
9 Now I did not know the year : Lord neither the month
   she was born
10 Yes she belongs to the devil : ooo well she have
   wrecked a-many home

WasbS 26   Washboard Sam

        title: Let Me Play Your Vendor
        place and date: Chicago, 4 Nov. 1941
        record numbers: (070375-1) BB-B8967 RCA LPV-577

1 First time I heard your music : I was just sixteen
2 I couldn't understand all the records : because I
   was young and green
3 Now let me play your *sea bird* : yes mama one more
   time
4 Just let me play your vendor : your music sure
   sounds good to me
5 I work hard for my money : I spends it all away
6 You open your vendor at night : and keep it locked
   all day
7 I don't know what folks tell me : if it's true or
   not
8 They say your day or night records : are kind that
   were hot
9 Play with these thirty year old nickels : will fit
   your machine just right
10 I can't play it right now : I'll play it later on
   tonight

WasbS 27   Washboard Sam

        title: Gonna Hit the Highway
        place and date: Chicago, 4 Nov. 1941
        record numbers: (070377-1) BB-B8997 RCA LPV-577

1 I'm going to hit this old highway : catch the
   fastest thing I see
2 Because I want to see my baby : ooo Lord I believe
   my baby want to see me
3 I want to find my baby : I pray to the good Lord I
   don't fail
4 If I never find her : ooo Lord I'll be forever on
   her trail
5 I'm going to call up China : and telephone every
   town I know

WasbS 27   Washboard Sam

6   And if I don't find her in Shanghai : ooo Lord I'm
        going to look all over the Gulf of Mexico
7   She's the onliest woman I ever loved : I can't get
        her off my mind
8   Now I may not find her in the next twenty years :
        ooo Lord but I'll be forever trying

WasbS 28   Washboard Sam

        title: I've Been Treated Wrong
        place and date: Chicago, 4 Nov. 1941
        record numbers: (070378-1) BB-B9007 RBF RF-1

1   I don't know my real name : I don't know when I was
        born
2   The trouble I been having : seem like I was raised
        in a orphan's home
3   My mother died and left me : when I was only two
        years old
4   And the trouble I been having : the good Lord only
        knows
5   I been treated like an orphan : and been worked like
        a slave
6   And if I ever get my revenge : evilness will carry
        me to my grave
7   Now I been having trouble : ever since I been grown
8   I'm too old for the orphan : and too young for the
        old folks' home

WasbS 29   Washboard Sam

        title: Evil Blues
        place and date: Chicago, 4 Nov. 1941
        record numbers: (070379-1) BB-B8997 RCA LPV-577

1   Yes yes : worst feeling I ever had
2   These old evil blues : have treated me awful bad
3   I had the blues all night : I'll be glad when
        morning comes
4   I'm going to have a talk with some Gypsy : see what
        evil have I done
5   These old evil blues : have been following me all
        this week
6   I can't rest at midnight : and day I just can't
        sleep
7   Down in old Death Valley : tombstones and old dry
        bones
8   These old evil blues keep following me : Death
        Valley going to be my home

WasbS 30   Washboard Sam

        title: Get Down Brother
        place and date: Chicago, 4 Nov. 1941
        record numbers: (070380-1) BB-B9018 RCA LPV-577

1   Now listen here brother : you may can understand
2   I might would pimp a woman : but I will never pimp a
        man
3   So please get down big boy : man you big enough to
        walk
4   And when I tell you about a job : ooo Lord you say
        you don't want to talk
5   You said you would never work : as long as you was
        free
6   So brother because I'm working : why you pick on me
7   You come by my house : with a great long lie
8   You say hello friends : I'm just passing by
9   You came to stay a day : and you stayed a week
10 And when my wife asked you to do her a favor : you
        pretend you were asleep

WasbS 31   Washboard Sam

        title: Lover's Lane Blues
        place and date: Chicago, 4 Nov. 1941
        record numbers: (070381-1) BB-B9007 BC-10

1   My name is Washboard Sam : but many call me loving
        Joe
2   Listen to what I says : if you really wants to know
3   Oh baby : meet me down in Lover's Lane
4   I want you to sit and listen : ooo gal to my
        wonderful plan
5   Now baby I'm not a bad man : you know we ain't no
        kin
6   If you don't want to be my woman : we will still be
        friends
7   Now when we are talking : I want you to hold my hand
8   Look me in the eye : I think I can make you
        understand
9   Now ask the ladies in your neighborhood : about my
        plan
10 And they will all tell you : that loving Sam is the
        man

WasbS 32   Washboard Sam

        title: You Stole My Love
        place and date: Chicago, 4 Nov. 1941
        record numbers: (070382-1) BB-B9018 RCA LPV-577

1   Gal you stole my love : and you know that it was a
        crime
2   So go on and take the punishment : it's no worry of
        mine
3   I worried a long time ago : and you was as happy as
        you could be
4   So now it's your worry : I'm glad you have set me
        free
5   Now you know you had me your way : and I just
        couldn't turn around
6   But now things have turned : but I ain't going to
        let you down
7   So now we are even : and let's start over this very
        day
8   Everything I start : I want you to meet me halfway

WasbS 33   Washboard Sam

        title: I Laid My Cards on the Table
        place and date: Chicago, 31 July 1942
        record numbers: (074686-1) BB-34-0710 RCA
        LPV-577

1   I laid my cards on the table : still you wouldn't
        give me a break
2   But some day baby : you poor heart is sure going to
        ache
3   Baby you made my poor heart bleed : and then you
        said I ain't fit
4   And you have found someone else : and you want to
        call it quits
5   Baby some day baby : I know things are going to turn
6   And that one-sided love : is going to make your poor
        heart burn
7   And I will look out of my window : and see you on
        the street
8   And that load your poor heart will be carrying :
        will knock you off of your feet
9   Because you stayed away all summer : and didn't come
        home till fall
10 Now you are too late baby : because someone else in
        your stall

WasbS 34   Washboard Sam

    title: I Get the Blues at Bedtime
    place and date: Chicago, 31 July 1942
    record numbers: (074687-1) BB-34-0710 RCA
    LPV-577

1 I get the blues at bedtime : them things don't leave
   until day
2 And if I just had you in my arms : them blues would
   blow away
3 Now if you love me baby : try to keep me satisfied
4 And you will lower down your chariot : and let your
   poor daddy ride
5 Now if I could go back to China : and start my life
   brand new
6 I would tell the whole world : just what I would do
7 I wouldn't start to drinking and gambling : I
   wouldn't run around
8 I think I would get married : baby and I would
   settle down

WasbW 1   Washboard Walter

    title: Narrow Face Blues
    place and date: Grafton, Wis., c. Feb. 1930
    record numbers: (L-142-4) Pm-12954 Her H-205

1 You can talk about burnt liver : but narrow-face is
   the meat I crave
2 You can take a narrow-face : and lead a preacher to
   his grave
3 You sister will do anything : when he begins to
   preach and smile
4 You *bake grub* for your husband : to find those
   narrow-faced boys
5 Lordy Lordy : here's what I want you to do
6 Please deliver me : from these narrow-faced blues
7 Hey hey hey : listen to the brother moan
8 While the preacher and the sister : *love* those
   narrow-face *bones*
9 You'd be surprised to know : what the word of
   narrow-face means
10 But you see it ain't nothing : but a great big fat
   hen
11 Hey hey : what you want me to do
12 *Johnny* it with you : and eat those narrow-face too

WasbW 2   Washboard Walter

    title: Insurance Man Blues
    place and date: Grafton, Wis., c. Apr. 1930
    record numbers: (L-283-2) Pm-12954 Her H-205

1 Insurance man came this morning : and knocked on my
   door
2 I didn't have no money : and I told him not to come
   no more
3 I've taken awful sick : and I had to go to bed
4 I didn't have no money : to get a nurse to hold my
   head
5 You will need your insurance : no matter where you
   go
6 Don't never : drive an insurance man from your door
7 I will have my money : next time he comes around
8 And then I can call up : old Dr Brown
9 Money is so tight : I can't pay my insurance bill
10 Please Mr insurance man : trust me if you will
11 Insurance man turned around : and he looked me in
   the eye
12 And said *your death* won't credit you : when you
   get ready to die
13 Oh well it's Lordy Lordy : what am I to do
14 Ain't got no money : now my insurance is due

WashE 1   Washington, Elizabeth

    title: Garden of Joy--Blues
    place and date: Chicago, 6 June 1927
    record numbers: (38637-2) Vi-21126 OJL-4

1 Well take me down : and have a time
2 All I want : is [a bottle of, some more]

WashL 1   Washington, Louis

    title: Tallahassee Woman
    place and date: New York, 18 Jan. 1934
    record numbers: (14637-1) Ba-33105 Fly LP-103

1 When you get in Tallahassee : put your money down in
   your shoe
2 Tallahassee women : they sure put a *method* on you
3 Lord I'm going to Tallahassee : I got these
   Tallahassee blues
4 Yes these Tallahassee women : sure put a *method* on
   you
5 Yes I was walking down the street the other day : my
   Hattie on my mind
6 A woman walked with me baby : to buy me one drink of
   shine
7 I told her I'm going back to Tallahassee : I ain't
   got no money to spend
8 But I'll buy you one drink baby : when I see you
   again
9 Tell me ain't no need to worry : ain't no need to
   feel bad
10 The folks down in Tallahassee : make me spend all
   the money I ever had
11 Lord these Tallahassee women : they put a *method*
   on you
12 But I can tell you one thing : I got these
   Tallahassee blues
13 And I don't feel good : I don't feel bad
14 I never had a gal : like the one I have had
15 Now that was down in Tallahassee : where I had these
   Tallahassee blues
16 I got these blues so bad : don't know what in the
   world to do
17 When you go down in Smoky Hollow : put your money
   down in your shoe
18 Them Smoky Hollow women : sure put a *method* on you
19 Now I'm feeling so bad : I'm feeling so sad
20 I ain't had a drink so long : till I feeling so bad
21 Now I'm going I'm going to Tallahassee : got these
   Tallahassee blues
22 When you get in Tallahassee : your woman put a
   method on you

WashL 2   Washington, Louis

    title: Black Snake Blues
    place and date: New York, 24 Jan. 1934
    record numbers: (14676-1) Ba-33058 Rt RL-313

1 I'm crying oh : where in the world my black snake
   gone
2 I mean now some pretty mama : done [run, drove] my
   black snake home
3 Mama it must have been a bedbug : baby a chinch
   can't bite that hard
4 And I asked my baby for fifty cents : she said honey
   ain't a child in the yard
5 I'm crying mmm : black snake crawling all in my room
6 I mean some pretty mama : better come and get this
   black snake soon
7 Now mama that's all right : mama that's all right
   for you
8 I mean now that's all right pretty mama : most any
   old any old way you do
9 Now you don't know : you don't worry my mind

WashL 2 Washington, Louis

10 You keep your black snake worried : and want him
   most all the time
12 I'm crying oh now : black snake crawling all on my
   room

Wate 1 Waters, Ethel

       title: One Man Nan
       place and date: New York, c. Aug. 1921
       record numbers: (P-146-1) BS-2021 Bio BLP-12022

1 The very thought of Sam sinking : that's my *cup*
2 It's going to be my place : to pick him up

Wate 2 Waters, Ethel

       title: There'll Be Some Changes Made
       place and date: New York, c. Aug. 1921
       record numbers: (P-147-1) BS-2021 Bio BLP-12022

1 My walk will be different : my talk and my name
2 Nothing about me : is going to be the same
3 I'm going to change my long ??? : for a little short
  spat
4 I'm going to change my number : where I'm living at
5 Why there's a change in the weather : there's a
  change in the sea
6 But from now on : there'll be a change in me
7 I'm going to change my way of living : and that
  ain't no bluff
8 Why I'm thinking about changing : the way I got to
  strut my stuff

Wate 3 Waters, Ethel

       title: Georgia Blues
       place and date: New York, c. May 1922
       record numbers: (B) BS-14120 Bio BLP-12022

1 A certain party : that I know
2 Offered me a ticket : to Chicago
3 *Arty* wanted to marry me : way last spring
4 Even bought me : a great big diamond ring

Wate 4 Waters, Ethel

       title: That Da Da Strain
       place and date: New York, c. May 1922
       record numbers: (A) BS-14120 Bio BLP-12022

1 Have you heard it have you heard it : the da da
  swing
2 It will shake you : it will make you really go
  insane
3 Everybody : *is still obsessed*
4 Make you watch : your every step
5 Every ??? every ??? : starts to lay them down
6 Everybody when they heard it : starts to ???ing
  around
7 And I get crazy : as a loon
8 When everybody : hums this tune

Wate 5 Waters, Ethel

       title: At the New Jump Steady Ball
       place and date: New York, c. May 1922
       record numbers: (   ) BS-14128 Bio BLP-12022

1 Now the Jump-Steady Club : they gave a ball
2 And it was held : down at the new hope hall
3 All the bootleggers : in the town
4 Why they brought : that *stuff steady* along

Wate 5 Waters, Ethel

5 People came : from far and near
6 To taste the different mixtures : that they handled
  there
7 When the jazz band struck up : you'd be surprised
8 Everybody in the hall : was goo-goo eyed
9 They started serving : ??? wine
10 And everything : that was alcohol-lined
11 Chicago pop : and *lilac* ???
12 All kinds of pep tonic : went along with the jazz
13 Jamaica gin : to mix with turpentine
14 With black molasses : made it super fine
15 Extract of lemon : and ginger ale
16 Sweet patuni with shoe polish : and you're bound for
   jail
17 Night's awful hot : I was feeling fine
18 To tell the truth : I was out of my mind
19 But just before : I lost my head
20 I saw them : carry six men out dead
21 They walked out the window : in the air
22 They called for music : but no jazz band was there
23 Then everybody there : was ???
24 You could get paralyzed : for fifteen cents
25 Extract of lemon : with ginger ale
26 *Eat cake* with some raisins : and you're bound for
   jail

Wate 6 Waters, Ethel

       title: Oh, Joe, Play that Trombone
       place and date: New York, c. May 1922
       record numbers: (   ) BS-14128 Bio BLP-12022

1 It makes me crazy : when you blow it up high
2 And when you bring it down : and swing it side to
  side
3 Because when you start to jazz : I get a feeling
  from the start
4 That gives me such a *kicking and a twicking* :
  around my heart

Wate 7 Waters, Ethel

       title: Memphis Man
       place and date: New York, c. Mar. 1923
       record numbers: (564-1) BS-14146 Bio BLP-12022

1 Memphis man : comes knocking at the door
2 Knocks like : nobody ever knocked before
3 If you know your business : let him in
4 Because he's so different : when loving begins
5 Memphis man : the lovingest man I know
6 Loves you : like you never been loved before
7 Love you while he's talking : love you while he
  sings
8 Swing his arms and hands : and a few other things
9 Love you when he's working : love you when he slaves
10 He could write a book : on his loving ways

Wate 8 Waters, Ethel

       title: Midnight Blues
       place and date: New York, c. Mar. 1923
       record numbers: (565-2) BS-14146 Bio BLP-12022

1 Daddy daddy : please come back to me
2 Your mama's lonesome : as she can be
3 You left [me] at midnight : clock was striking
  twelve
4 To face this cruel world : well all by myself

288

Wate   9   Waters, Ethel

        title: You Can't Do What My Last Man Did
        place and date: New York, c. June 1923
        record numbers: (A) BS-14151 Bio BLP-12022

 1 You can't do : what my last man did
 2 Dog me around : and treat me like he did
 3 My last man : tried to drag me down
 4 But he was one good man : to have around
 5 But when the clock on the wall : strikes half past
    three
 6 I want all the things : you do for me
 7 Early this morning : you wanted to fight
 8 Because you heard : I cabareted last night
 9 Tried to take my money : and pawn my *flat*
10 Now you've worn the welcome : clean off my mat
11 Now that last cruel papa : he blacked my eye
12 Then left me alone : to sigh and cry

Wate   10   Waters, Ethel

        title: Ethel Sings 'Em
        place and date: New York, c. June 1923
        record numbers: (B) BS-14154 Bio BLP-12022

 1 It's getting so I can't sleep for dreaming : and I
    can't laugh for crying
 2 Because the man I love : is forever on my mind
 3 He puts candy in my hand : and he calls me his candy
    doll
 4 Then he looks at me and cries mama : I mean your
    sweet old girl
 5 It's so hard to love : another woman's man
 6 Because you can't get him when you want him : you've
    got to take him when you can
 7 Oh love is like a faucet : that turns off and on
 8 Because every time you think you've got it : papa
    it's turned off and gone
 9 Life is nothing but a jam : a constant jamboree
10 It jams everybody : now it's about to jam poor me

Wate   11   Waters, Ethel

        title: Craving Blues
        place and date: Chicago, c. Apr. 1924
        record numbers: (1742-2) Pm-12313 Bio BLP-12022

 1 Some people crave for loving : some people crave for
    gold
 2 But craving is just a habit : so I've been told
 3 I love my man : I'll tell the world I do
 4 As good as I've been : he ought to love me too
 5 But he keeps me worried : day and night
 6 When I want to love him : he wants to fuss and fight

WeaC   1   Weaver, Curley

        title: Sweet Patunia
        place and date: Atlanta, 26 Oct. 1928
        record numbers: (147304-2) Co-14386-D His HLP-32

 1 I've got a gal : lives down by the jail
 2 Sign on the door : sweet patuni for sale
 3 Lord I'm wild about my tuni : only thing I crave
 4 Oh sweet patuni : going to carry me to my grave
 5 I got up this morning : about half past four
 6 Big Bill *Johnny* : had his *'spenders* on the floor
 7 I got a gal : she's long and tall
 8 Every time she do the shimmy : I holler hot dog
 9 If I could holler : like a mountain jack
10 Go up on a mountain : bring my tuni back
11 Way back yonder : in one-oh-one
12 Baby had good tunis : but she couldn't get none

WeaC   2   Weaver, Curley

        title: No No Blues
        place and date: Atlanta, 26 Oct. 1928
        record numbers: (147305-2) Co-14386-D His HLP-32

 1 Got up this morning : my good gal was gone
 2 Stood by my bedside : long many long many morn
 3 Went down the street : I couldn't be satisfied
 4 Had the no no blues : just too mean just too mean to
    cry
 5 Take a mighty good woman : treat her good man wrong
 7 Ain't none of my business : but it sure ain't right
 8 Take another man's woman : walk the streets all walk
    the streets all night
 9 If I mistreat you : I sure don't mean no harm
10 I'm a motherless child : don't know right from don't
    know right from wrong
11 I'm a stranger here : just come in your town
12 If I ask for a favor : don't turn me don't turn me
    down
13 I'm long and tall : like a cannonball
14 Take a long tall fellow : make a good gal make a
    good gal squall
15 I ain't no gambler : I don't play no pool
16 I'm just a roller : jelly-baking jelly-baking fool
17 I'm a stranger here : I just come on this train
18 I long to hear : some gal call some gal call my name
19 My mama told me : papa told me too
20 Don't let no woman : make a fool out of make a fool
    out of you

WeaC   3   Weaver, Curley

        title: Sometime Mama
        place and date: Chicago, 23 Apr. 1935
        record numbers: (C-9939-B) Ch-50065 His HLP-31

 1 Sometime mama : you're good as good can be
 2 You changed your mind baby : trying to make a dog of
    me
 3 When I met you baby : you didn't have no sometime
    ways
 4 Now you done changed baby : trying to carry me to my
    grave
 5 Walked by you baby : everything seemed to be all
    right
 6 You ain't got a place now baby : won't even love me
    at night
 7 Now listen baby : what I'm going to say
 8 You going to get you another man : if you don't stop
    your sometime ways

WeaC   4   Weaver, Curley

        title: Oh Lawdy Mama
        place and date: Chicago, 23 Apr. 1935
        record numbers: (C-9940-A) Ch-50077 Rt RL-326

 1 Meet me down at the river : bring me my suit of
    clothes
 2 I ain't got so many : but I got buggish far to go
 3 Woman I love : woman I crave to see
 4 She in Cincinnati : won't even write to me
 5 Woman I love : got mouth chock full of good gold
 6 Every time she hug and kiss me : make my buggish
    blood run cold
 7 Woman I love : caught that Southern train
 8 Heart she left me here : heart full of aching pain
 9 Now tell me sweet woman : time the train come
    through your town
10 I just want to have : a talk with that teasing brown
11 One goes south at eight : one goes north at nine
12 I just want to have a talk : with that brown of mine
13 Woman I love : right down on the ground
14 She's a tailor-made mama : not no hand-me-down
15 Going away to leave you : crying won't make me stay

WeaC   4   Weaver, Curley

16   I may be back in June baby : may be back in first of
     May

WeaC   5   Weaver, Curley

     title: Two Faced Woman
     place and date: Chicago, 23 Apr. 1935
     record numbers: (C-9941-A) Ch-50065 His HLP-31

1   Two-faced woman : trying to see her two days at one
    time
2   Be mighty doggone careful : of nar' one of them days
    be mine
3   Every time I see you woman : got your glasses nice
    and clean
4   If I tell you you can't go out : you say I'm acting
    mean
5   You two-faced woman : wear glasses all the time
6   Long you wear them glasses : you can't be no woman
    of mine
7   You know you didn't want me : when you stuck your
    four eyes in my door
8   I done spent all my money : now tell me you don't
    want me no more

WeaC   6   Weaver, Curley

     title: Fried Pie Blues
     place and date: Chicago, 23 Apr. 1935
     record numbers: (C-9943-A) Ch-50077 Rt RL-326

1   I ain't going down baby : that long road by myself
2   If I can't carry you baby : carry somebody else
3   Can I wait around here baby : till your fried pie
    get done
4   If I have any money : I will buy me some
5   My baby baked me fresh biscuits : baked them nice
    and brown
6   What please me so well : she bake them with her
    damper down
7   My baby she got a mojo : trying to keep it hid
8   Papa Weaver got something : find that mojo with

WeaS   1   Weaver, Sylvester

     title: Can't Be Trusted Blues
     place and date: New York, 31 Aug. 1927
     record numbers: (81401-B) OK-8504 Yz L-1012

1   I don't love nobody : that's my policy
2   I'll tell the world : that nobody can get along with
    me
3   I can't be trusted : can't be satisfied
4   The men all know it : and pin their women to their
    side
5   I will sure backbite you : gnaw you to the bone
6   I don't mean maybe : I can't let women alone
7   Pull down your windows : and lock up all your doors
8   Got ways like the devil : papa's *sneaking* on all
    fours

Weld   1   Weldon, Will (Memphis Jug Band)

     title: Stingy Woman--Blues
     place and date: Memphis, 24 Feb. 1927
     record numbers: (37942-1) Vi-20552 Rt RL-322

1   And it's stingy woman : come and sit down on my knee
2   ??? *Lordy* : unless you going to care for me
3   And it's hey faro : tell me what's the matter now
4   And you trying to quit me : Lordy woman and you
    don't know how

Weld   2   Weldon, Will (Memphis Jug Band)

     title: Memphis Jug--Blues
     place and date: Memphis, 24 Feb. 1927
     record numbers: (37943-2) Vi-20576 Rt RL-322

1   Hey drop down drop down : mama like drops of rain
2   Lord every once in a while : I think I hear my baby
    call my name
3   Hey : I ain't going to change no more
4   Said get away from my window mama : don't knock at
    my back door
5   Says I ain't been your good man : since you been my
    ???
6   Now you want me to ??? : and I ain't ???
7   I stuck with you mama : when you did not have no man
    at all
8   Now baby must want me : for to be her lowdown dog
9   Lord I can stand right here partner : and look on
    Culligan Avenue
10 Lord I can see everything : that my easy roller do

Weld   3   Weldon, Will (Memphis Jug Band)

     title: Sunshine Blues
     place and date: Chicago, 9 June 1927
     record numbers: (38658-1) Vi-20781 Rt RL-322

1   I've got the worried blues : got nowhere to go
3   You can starch my jumper : iron my overalls
4   I'm going down to the station : catch that West
    Cannonball
5   And it's hurry sundown : let tomorrow come
6   And it may bring sunshine : and it may bring rain

Weld   4   Weldon, Will

     title: Turpentine Blues
     place and date: Atlanta, 20 Oct. 1927
     record numbers: (40322-2) Vi-21134 Yz L-1008

1   Going home in the morning : woman and I sure can't
    carry you
2   Ain't nothing else I learned : Lord a monkey-woman
    can do
3   I don't want no jet-black woman : Lord to cook no
    pie for me
4   Because black is evil : I guess she might poison me
5   Some men love high yellows : boy you give me my
    black or brown
6   Before your gal be with you : a yellow put you down
7   Said I wonder : would a poor matchbox hold my
    clothes
8   I ain't got so many : Lord I got so far to go
9   Going to wash my face : in the dear old Mexico
10 Going to eat my breakfast : thousand miles or more
11 Now what you going to do boy : when your trouble get
    like mine
12 Take you a mouthful of sugar : boy and drink a
    bottle of turpentine

Weld   5   Weldon, Will

     title: Hitch Me to Your Buggy and Drive Me Like
     a Mule
     place and date: Atlanta, 20 Oct. 1927
     record numbers: (40323-2) Vi-21134 OJL-21

1   You can hitch me to your buggy : babe drive me just
    like I was a mule
2   But I want you to understand woman : ain't nobody's
    fool
3   Boy I may be right Lord : boy I may be wrong
4   But my faro done come here baby : caught the train
    and gone

290

5   Going to buy me a bulldog : watch my baby while she
    sleeps
6   Going to keep my baby : from making her midnight
    creep
7   ??? said she loves me : boy I don't believe she told
    me the truth
8   Every time I put my hand on her : boy she really get
    on me

Weld   6   Weldon, Will (Memphis Jug Band)

        title: Peaches in the Springtime
        place and date: Memphis, 13 Feb. 1928
        record numbers: (41890-2) Vi-21657 Rt RL-311

1   Now you give me peaches in the springtime : apples
    in the fall
2   Can't get the gal I love : don't want none at all
3   The woman I'm loving : she ain't no gal of mine
4   She's a married woman : boy but comes to see me
    sometime
5   Now it's apples on the table : peaches on the shelf
6   Getting sick and tired : of sleeping by myself
7   I'm going to build me a castle : fifteen story high
8   So I can see my good gal : when she try and pass me
    by

Weld   7   Weldon, Will

        title: W. P. A. Blues
        place and date: Chicago, 12 Feb. 1936
        record numbers: (C-1256-1) Vo-03186 BC-7

1   Everybody's working in this town : and it's worrying
    me night and day
2   If that mean working too : have to work for the W P
    A
3   Well well the landlord come this morning : and he
    knocked on my door
4   He asked me : if I was going to pay my rent no more
5   He said you have to move : if you can't pay
6   And then he turned : and he walked slowly away
7   So I have to try : find me some other place to stay
8   That housewrecking crew's coming : from the W P A
9   Well well went to the relief station : and I didn't
    have a cent
10 If that's the only way you stand : you don't have to
    pay no rent
11 So when I got back home : they was tacking a notice
    on the door
12 This house is condemned : and you can't live there
    no more
13 So a notion struck me : I better be on my way
14 They're going to tear my house down : ooo that crew
    from the W P A
15 Well well I went out next morning : I put a lock on
    my door
16 I thought I would move : but I have no place to go
17 The real estate people : they all done got so
18 They don't rent : to no relief clients no more
19 So I know : have to walk the streets night and day
20 Because that wrecking crew's coming : ooo from that
    W P A
21 Well well a notion struck me : I'll try to stay a
    day or two
22 But I soon found out : that that wouldn't do
23 Early next morning : while I was laying in my bed
24 I heard a mighty rumbling : and the bricks come
    tumbling down on my head
25 So I had to start ducking and dodging : and be on my
    way
26 They was tearing my house down on me : ooo that crew
    from that W P A

        title: Blues Everywhere I Go
        place and date: Chicago, 2 Apr. 1936
        record numbers: (100323) BB-B6356 Rt RL-329

1   Well well it's blues : it's blues everywhere I go
2   Well well I'm going to find my good girl : ooo and I
    won't be blue no more
3   Well the blues in my house : from the roof to the
    ground
4   And the blues everywhere : because my good gal have
    left this town
5   Well well the blues in my room : I don't know right
    from wrong
6   Because the blues in my kitchen : my
    biscuit-roller's gone
7   Well well the blues in my mailbox : because I can't
    get no mail
8   And the blues in my bread box : because my bread is
    done gone stale
9   Well well so I've blues in my meal barrel : and the
    blues on my shelf
10 And the blues in my bed : because I'm sleeping by
    myself

Weld   9   Weldon, Will

        title: Somebody's Got to Go
        place and date: Chicago, 2 Apr. 1936
        record numbers: (100324) BB-B6356 Rt RL-329

1   Well well me and my woman : we can't get along no
    more
2   Well well I don't want you hanging around : ooo
    somebody sure have to go
3   Well well you been telling everybody : you been
    playing in luck
4   My wife cook me neckbones and beans : why'd you cook
    me chicken and duck
5   So somebody : somebody will have to go
6   Therefore I don't want you : ooo a-hanging around my
    house no more
7   Well well you said I was your friend : and a friend
    you sure did like
8   But as soon as I'm gone : you always bite me in the
    back
9   So I don't want you : hanging around my wife no more
10 Therefore I'm sorry buddy : ooo somebody will have
    to go
11 Well I come home in the evening : when my day's work
    is done
12 My bed is all turned up : and my supper's never done
13 So I don't want you : hanging around my home no more
14 Well well I'm sorry buddy : ooo someone will sure
    have to go
15 Well well so look a-here buddy : now don't get hard
16 Because somebody : can't go to the graveyard
17 And it may be me : and it may be you

Weld   10   Weldon, Will

        title: Red Hot Blues
        place and date: Chicago, 21 Oct. 1937
        record numbers: (C-2031-1) Vo-04066 CC-3

1   Hey get your partner : put on your dancing shoes
2   Then you can dance : to these red-hot blues
3   All you got to do : is just to swing and sway
4   When you're feeling low : just dance these blues
    away
5   I had so many women : I didn't know which one to
    choose
6   So my best gal's gone : I got those red-hot blues
7   There's some folks say : that the red-hot blues
    ain't bad
8   It must not have been : those red-hot blues they had

Weld   10   Weldon, Will

9   Had a red-hot mama : that I sure did hate to lose
10 But now she's gone : and I got those red-hot blues

Weld   11   Weldon, Will

title: Worried About that Woman
place and date: Chicago, 21 Oct. 1937
record numbers: (C-2032-1) Vo-04066 CC-3

1   And I get worried I worry : I worries all the time
2   For the gal I'm loving : she just won't treat me
    kind
3   I just lay in my bed : I smoke cigarettes all night
4   I just thinking about my gal : because she ain't
    doing me right
5   You know I'm worried : worried all the time
6   Yes I'm worried : because she don't treat me kind
7   Said I woke up this morning : I was feeling so bad
8   Thinking about the good times : that I once have had
9   You know I'm worried : worried all the time
10 Lord I love that women : she just won't treat me
    kind
11 Well there's something about that woman : that's
    worrying me all the time
12 She got men's shoes under her bed : and they ain't
    mine
13 I'm going to pack my suitcase : down the road I'll
    go
14 Because the good times I've had : I don't have no
    more

WelS   1   Welsh, Nolan

title: The Bridwell Blues
place and date: Chicago, 16 June 1926
record numbers: (9727-A) OK-8372 Fwy FJ-2802

1   I was standing on the corner : did not mean no harm
2   And the police came : took me by the arm
3   Now the prosecutor questioned me partner : the clerk
    he wrote it down
4   The judge say I'll give you one chance Nolan : but
    you would not leave this town
5   Now I got to leave Bridewell : fell down on my knees
6   Crying kill me jailor : jailor kill me please
7   They sent me to the stone quarry : I was standing in
    the door
8   I said don't do me this a-way people : you know I
    been here before

WelS   2   Welsh, Nolan

title: St. Peter Blues
place and date: Chicago, 16 June 1926
record numbers: (9728-A) OK-8372 CC-32

1   Mama mama : baby how can it be
2   Well you loves everybody baby : better than you do
    poor me
3   But some old day : some old [rainy, sunny] day
4   Oh the wind going to rise baby : blow my blues away
5   Chicken when I'm hungry : white lightning when I'm
    dry
6   And a real kind woman : ??? when I die
7   When I get to heaven : sit down in St Peter's chair
8   I'll say look a-here St Peter : you got any white
    lightning here

WelS   3   Welsh, Nolan

title: Dying Pickpocket Blues
place and date: Chicago, c. Jan. 1929
record numbers: (21098-3) Pm-12759 Yz L-1028

1   It was in New York City workhouse : *so they called
    big Sam for days*
2   It was in a dirty ditch there : where the dying
    pickpocket lay
3   And his buddy stood beside him : with his lowdown
    drooping head
4   Listen to the last words : that the dying pickpocket
    say
5   He said tell my [friends, brothers] back in Cincy :
    although I know she will feel blue
6   That I got *these stones on the hammer* : and I
    cannot pull it through
7   Although I'm going partner : going to a better land
8   I ain't going to pick no more pockets : I'm going to
    be a regular man
9   Although she has been a real pal : and she answers
    to all my calls
10 I've ruined her health : trying to spring me from
    this vault

Whea   1   Wheatstraw, Peetie

title: Mama's Advice
place and date: Chicago, 4 Nov. 1930
record numbers: (C-6487-A) Vo-1620 BC-4

1   Well well I loved my little girl : and I loved her
    for myself
2   Well now now I'll tell you now baby : I don't love
    nobody else
3   Mama now she told me : ooo mmm till I hold her head
    and cry
4   Well well well some of these women now : done made
    up their minds all the time
5   Crying sorry : sorry to my heart
6   Well now I'm so sorry : I lose my only child
7   Mama now she gone : crying fare farewell to thee
8   Well well didn't never have no baby : now to laugh
    and talk with me
9   Mmm I wonder : do my little girl knows I'm here
10 Well well well if she do : well well she sure don't
    feel my care

Whea   2   Wheatstraw, Peetie

title: Ain't It a Pity and a Shame
place and date: Chicago, 4 Nov. 1930
record numbers: (C-6488-A) Vo-1649 Say SDR-191

1   Well that a pity and a shame : ways the women treats
    the men
2   Well well some of them now will take your money :
    carry it and give it to another man
3   Lord I woke up this morning : when everything was
    still
4   Well well well I seen my little mama : as she come
    creeping up the hill
5   Mmm bring me my pistol : shotgun and some shells
6   Well well now I been mistreated : baby and I'm going
    to raise some hell
7   Well well well did you ever wake up mama : baby now
    between midnight and day
8   Oh with your head on your pillow : babe where your
    good man he once have lay
9   Well now my little girl she quit me : mama now now
    why did she run away

Whea   3   Wheatstraw, Peetie

        title: Don't Hang My Clothes on No Barbed Wire
               Line
        place and date: Chicago, 4 Nov. 1930
        record numbers: (C-6489-A) Vo-1649 Say SDR-191

1   I don't want my clothes : hung on that barbed wire
    line
2   Well well well I'm going go crazy : but baby I've
    got to now lose my mind
3   Well well well I want none of that sugar : mama
    sprinkled in my tea
4   Well I *plan supper with* any of these women : they
    are sweet enough for me
5   Well well well I can't use no gravy : mixed up in my
    rice
6   Well well well now the one I love : I believe she
    could mix it for me so nice
7   Mmm little girl got buggy : she throwed all of my
    clothes outdoors
8   Well well right now I wonder : will a shopping bag
    hold my clothes
9   Mmm wonder : do my little girl know where I am
10 Well well now I wonder do she know : that I'm fixing
    to beat it on back to 'Bam

Whea   4   Wheatstraw, Peetie

        title: C and A Blues
        place and date: Chicago, 6 Jan. 1931
        record numbers: (C-6891-A) Vo-1672 OJL-20

1   Well now let me tell you people : what the C and A
    will do for you
2   Well now it will take your little woman : then will
    holler back at you
3   Mmm hate to hear : C and A whistle blow
4   Mama now it blows so lonesome baby : honey because I
    want to go
5   Mmm few more days : few more nights alone
6   Baby then I'm going to pack my suitcase : honey now
    I will be gone
7   Well now when a woman takes the blues : she will
    hang her head and cry
8   Well now when a man takes the blues : please now he
    will catch him a train and ride
9   Mmm going to write me a letter : mama going to mail
    it in the air
10 Well well well going to send it up the country :
    mama now to see if my little girl there

Whea   5   Wheatstraw, Peetie

        title: Ice and Snow Blues
        place and date: Chicago, 28 Sept. 1931
        record numbers: (67567-1) BB-B5626 BC-4

1   This winter babe : going to be ice and snow
2   You know my little mama : going to be sleeping on
    your floor
3   Remember last winter : you drove me from your door
4   Now little mama : it was in the ice and snow
5   You left me baby : because I was cold in hand
6   You taken my money : and spent it on your other man
7   I did more for you : than you understand
8   You can tell by the bullet holes mama : now here in
    my hand
9   Now you pawned your pajamas : baby now you sold your
    clothes
10 And the ??? : didn't have no : baby have no place to
    go

Whea   6   Wheatstraw, Peetie

        title: Sleepless Nights Blues
        place and date: New York, 17 Mar. 1932
        record numbers: (11519-A) Vo-1727 Yz L-1030

1   Now let me tell you : how I'd like to see my baby
    now
2   I bet I'd want to see her : ooo Lord you don't know
    how
3   Well I know my little woman : she can't sleep at
    night
4   Well now she got it in her mind : that I'm ain't
    going to treat her right
5   Baby baby : you may look for me most any day
6   Well where does it matter : ooo I ain't going to
    scare her away
7   Now how would you feel : baby now if I come home
    today
8   You wouldn't have no time *with man-o* : to pass the
    time away
9   Ooo look for me tomorrow : I'll be home I'm sure
10 I want you to hug and kiss me baby : now when I come
    walking in your door

Whea   7   Wheatstraw, Peetie

        title: All Night Long Blues
        place and date: Chicago, 18 Aug. 1934
        record numbers: (C-9315-A) De-7082 AH-158

1   Stay out all night long : babe now to keep you off
    my mind
2   Well now you keep me worried baby : honey now and
    bothered all the time
3   Once was a good girl : they don't breed that way no
    more
4   And don't forget the day now little mama : babe now
    you drove me from your door
5   How do you feel : when you drive a good man from
    your door
6   Well well now you must stop look and listen : may be
    your best friend you don't know
7   What would you do : if you came walking to my door
8   Well then I will tell you baby : see now don't come
    here no more
9   Honey that's why that I tell you : don't drive a
    good man from your door
10 Well well now you may need his help some day baby :
    oh well well you don't know

Whea   8   Wheatstraw, Peetie

        title: Throw Me in the Alley
        place and date: Chicago, 24 Aug. 1934
        record numbers: (C-9351-) De-7018 Say SDR-191

1   *When I get low* : let's go down in the alley
2   Peetie Wheatstraw good people : going to put you all
    in the alley
3   Bye bye baby : what's the matter now
4   The way you treat me little mama : you don't mean me
    no good nohow

Whea   9   Wheatstraw, Peetie

        title: Doin' the Best I Can
        place and date: Chicago, 11 Sept. 1934
        record numbers: (C-9443-?) De-7007 Say SDR-191

1   When a man is out working : working hard all his
    life
2   Some lowdown rascal : always trying to steal his
    wife
3   I hate to hear : New York Central whistle blow

4 Every time she whistle : to the roundhouse I got to
   go
5 I don't know hardly : baby what to do
6 Don't want to hurt your feelings : either get mad at
   you
7 You got up this morning : with a rag around your
   head
8 Asked you to cook my breakfast : babe you went back
   to bed
9 Went out this morning : could not make no time
10 Didn't have no blues : but I was all worried in mind
11 I'm a hard-working man : and trying to do things
   just right
12 But my woman she *keeps that* on me : I ain't going
   to work tonight

Whea   10   Wheatstraw, Peetie

        title: The Rising Sun Blues
        place and date: Chicago, 25 Mar. 1935
        record numbers: (C-921-A) Vo-03066 Say SDR-191

1 Well now I lay down every morning : but I get up
   with the rising sun
2 Well then I asked my little woman : mmm well now
   hat evil have I done
3 She said she had gone away to leave me : [and I
   wondered] now why don't she stay away
4 Seems like now she ought to have it in her mind :
   ooo well well that I can get me a girl each and
   every day
5 That's why I say I lays down every morning : said I
   get up with the rising sun
6 And when I speak to my little woman : ooo well well
   seems like my troubles they have just begun
7 Well now remember this morning : how you told me to
   pack up my clothes and go
8 Well you said you'd rather see a rattlesnake : ooo
   well well now come crawling across your floor
9 Well now that don't worry me baby : I have it in my
   mind that I can go
10 Well then again after I'm gone : ooo please now
   don't bother with me no more

Whea   11   Wheatstraw, Peetie

        title: Letter Writing Blues
        place and date: Chicago, 26 Mar. 1935
        record numbers: (C-944-A) Vo-02978 Say SDR-191

1 If you move away : then I can write [me] a few line
2 Well now the last word you gave me : ooo well well
   it keeps me bothered all the time
3 Well now everything I do : well now I try to do it
   nice
4 But now I feel like all of these women : ooo well
   well now they're trying to take my life
5 All last night : I was all alone
6 Well my little woman she had quit me : ooo well well
   now I didn't have no happy home
7 Then again last night : I sat down and I weep and
   moan
8 Well I was thinking about my little woman : ooo well
   but she was again you know she was gone
9 Well there's no need to worry : *not for a while* to
   weep and moan
10 Because now you know your little girl : ooo well
   well now have caught the train and gone

        title: Cocktail Man Blues
        place and date: Chicago, 17 July 1935
        record numbers: (90173-A) De-7144 Say SDR-191

1 Good morning people : just got back from cocktail
   land
2 Well I find my little woman : ooo well we going to
   raise some cocktail sand
3 And I got up this morning : went down in old
   alleycan
4 Now the women there was hollering : ooo well here
   come that little cocktail man
5 Cry cocktails for two : baby that's all it can be
6 Now if you got plenty of cocktails : please save it
   all for me
7 I mix this cocktail with you : and you know started
   it all with a feather
8 Now won't you come here little mama : please now
   let's have a cocktail together
9 Well now I ain't no *farmer* : but I'll *watch your
   crop* the best I can
10 But now when it comes to mixing cocktails : ooo well
   here's the little cocktail man

Whea   13   Wheatstraw, Peetie

        title: King Spider Blues
        place and date: Chicago, 17 July 1935
        record numbers: (90174-A) De-7144 Say SDR-191

1 Let me be your king spider : I want to build my web
   on your wall
2 Then I want to catch your little flies : ooo well
   well now when they begin to fall
3 Want to tell you baby : like the fox done told the
   hen
4 I've got something good to tell you : ooo well well
   if you come rolling to my den
5 I'm a good web-builder : please let me build your
   web one time
6 Because now there ain't another spider : ooo well
   well can build a web like mine
7 When I start to make a web : now I crawl around and
   around
8 But now when I get it almost finished : ooo well
   well I crawl up and down
9 Catfish told the *jackfish* : ??? now *I bet she
   going to build*
10 And now the way that I feel this morning : ooo well
   really now I got to ???

Whea   14   Wheatstraw, Peetie

        title: Last Dime Blues
        place and date: Chicago, 20 July 1935
        record numbers: (C-1081-B) Vo-03444 Say SDR-191

1 I once have had money : but now I'm down to my last
   dime
2 Well now the woman I have : ooo well well she
   bothers me all the time
3 I works hard : just to get me a few dimes
4 Well now if you don't watch yourself : ooo well well
   that woman will keep you down all the time
5 That is why I say : don't give no woman your last
   dime
6 Well now you know she's just trouble on your hands :
   ooo well and keep you worried all the time
7 Now if you don't know what you will have to do : now
   don't get you a few dimes
8 Well well but I can tell you : ooo well faro always
   hollering for mine all the time
9 Now when a woman call you : and ask you for your
   last dime

Whea 14   Wheatstraw, Peetie

10 Well now don't be no fool : ooo well well and give
    it to her all the time

Whea 15   Wheatstraw, Peetie

        title: King of Spades
        place and date: Chicago, 20 July 1935
        record numbers: (C-1082-B) Vo-03066 Say SDR-191

1   I'm the king of spades : and the women takes on over
    me
2   Well now when I lay my racket : ooo well well now
    I'm as sweet as I can be
3   I am the king of spades : ain't been out in a great
    long time
4   But I will work for you little mama : ooo well well
    baby if you ain't got a dime
5   Let me be your dealer : I'm the best dealer in town
6   Then again I say heave to me baby : ooo well well
    and let your love come falling down
7   Ace of spades caught the jack : and the [ten, king]
    of spades caught the ten
8   Dealer cut one more time : ooo well well and I will
    bring your dollars in
9   Yes I'm the little black king of spades : and then
    again I always win
10 Then again I will scratch for you little mama : ooo
    well well like a rooster scratch for a hen

Whea 16   Wheatstraw, Peetie

        title: First and Last Blues
        place and date: Chicago, 13 Feb. 1936
        record numbers: (C-1257-2) Vo-03185 Say SDR-191

1   I'm just sitting here thinking : thinking about the
    first
2   But the Good Book is tell me : ooo well well that
    the first shall be the last
3   I had the blues : every time I see your face
4   Well there ain't no other one woman : ooo well well
    in this world can take her place
5   I can't help but remember : those days of long time
    ago
6   And then again I often wonder : ooo well well will
    they happen anymore
7   I am worried : and I just can't help myself
8   And the one little girl I love : ooo well well left
    me for somebody else
9   I don't be happy : if I just could hold her hand
10 And maybe people : ooo well well I could get her to
    understand

Whea 17   Wheatstraw, Peetie

        title: True Blue Woman
        place and date: Chicago, 13 Feb. 1936
        record numbers: (C-1258-1) Vo-03185 Say SDR-191

1   I know my babe : is bound to think of me
2   Ain't no way she can forget : ooo well as close as
    we used to be
3   She was by me : if I stayed up all night long
4   Well now you know I want you people : ooo well now
    to listen to my song
5   Sometimes I feel : like I would just soon to be dead
6   Since now I got no baby : ooo well now to hold my
    aching head
7   She done me dirty : but I loves her just the same
8   And it hurts my heart : ooo well if I hear another
    man call her name
9   I love my babe : no matter where she be
10 Then again you know I know my babe : ooo well now is
    bound to think of me

Whea 18   Wheatstraw, Peetie

        title: Sweet Home Blues
        place and date: Chicago, 13 Feb. 1936
        record numbers: (C-1261-2) Vo-03396 Say SDR-191

1   I was thinking about going home : I don't believe
    that I will go
2   I'm going to stay away a long time : ooo well well
    like I did once before
3   My baby will be glad to see me : come walking in her
    door
4   Ah but now remember : ooo well she will never see me
    anymore
5   Home is a happy place : if you can make it that way
6   Now if you can't keep a happy home : ooo well well
    will be the devil each and every day
7   I try to be good : every place I go
8   But now you know there will come a day : ooo well
    well I will have some place I know
9   Now if I go home : do you think that is the best
    place to be
10 Well then again then if I go home : ooo well now do
    you think she will be mean to me

Whea 19   Wheatstraw, Peetie

        title: Good Woman Blues
        place and date: Chicago, 13 Feb. 1936
        record numbers: (C-1262-1) Vo-03396 RBF RF-12

1   What makes me love you baby : she loved me when I
    was down
2   Well now she was nice and kind : ooo well well she
    did not dog me around
3   You know the most of the women : [will] listen to
    what people say
4   Well but now you know my babe : ooo well well she's
    just the other way
5   Well now she gave me money : and kept me nice and
    clean
6   Well now you know when I was down : ooo well my babe
    didn't treat me mean
7   Now I'm good to my baby : since I'm up on my feet
8   Well now I don't care : ooo well if I never see a
    woman on the street

Whea 20   Wheatstraw, Peetie

        title: Working Man
        place and date: New York, 18 Feb. 1936
        record numbers: (60506-A) De-7200 BC-4

1   I been up the line : been up the line
2   I couldn't find nothing : to pacify my mind
3   I laying on my bed : holding my aching head
4   I received a letter : the girl I love was dead
5   I rolled and I tumbled : from side to side
6   I was trying so hard : to be satisfied
7   They call me Peetie : the lucky man
8   But I wish : someone would give me a lucky hand
9   I'm going away to leave you : ain't going to tell
    you goodbye
10 And after I'm gone : please don't hang your head and
    cry
11 I have so much bad luck : baby I'm the bad-luck man
12 And I'm trying so hard : to do the best I can

Whea 21   Wheatstraw, Peetie

        title: Low Down Rascal
        place and date: New York, 18 Feb. 1936
        record numbers: (60507-A) De-7200 Say SDR-192

1   You's a lowdown rascal : just as mean as you can be

2   Lays around my house : ooo well well trying to take my wife from me
3   If I catch you around my house : you better jump in some country well
4   Well I'm going to take my old shotgun : ooo well well and I'm going to raise some country hell
5   If a man call you buddy : please don't take him for your friend
6   Well well he'll hang around your house : ooo well and tickle your woman's can
7   I work for my woman : she's so nice and sweet
8   Well seem like she fall in love : ooo well with every lowdown rascal she meets
9   You got that lowdown no-good rascal : said I'm going to let you be
10 But now when you get broke and hungry : ooo well well please now don't you worry me

Whea   22   Wheatstraw, Peetie

        title: When I Get My Bonus
        place and date: New York, 18 Feb. 1936
        record numbers: (60511-A) De-7159 Say SDR-192

1   When I was broke : didn't have a dime
2   You had your women : wouldn't pay me no mind
3   Then I will be : up on my feet again
4   I'm going drink my whiskey : and going to drink my gin
5   You told everybody : I didn't do nothing but lie
6   I wouldn't give you women : even time to die
7   You had your women : get yourself a glass
8   You can have a little drink : of your yas yas yas
9   Now I'm telling you women : about my army pay
10 You think you can get my money : that is going to be your D B A

Whea   23   Wheatstraw, Peetie

        title: Coon Can Shorty
        place and date: New York, 18 Feb. 1936
        record numbers: (60512-A) De-7159 Say SDR-192

1   Well now they call me Cooncan Shorty : the man from Cooncan Land
2   Well I know how to play the man : ooo well well the game they call cooncan
3   My dice won't pass : cards is the only game you see
4   And every chump in town : ooo well well seems to fall out on me
5   My babe give me money : Cooncan Shorty is my name
6   Oh before I lose her money : ooo well I must *spread due* to the ??? game
7   But some day my dice going to pass : and my money going to be on the wood
8   And every chump in town : ooo well well they ain't going to be no good
9   Some say they will coon the devil : if you chain him down
10 But now you know I got a chump : ooo well well if he come in this town

Whea   24   Wheatstraw, Peetie

        title: The First Shall Be the Last and the Last Shall Be First
        place and date: New York, 19 Feb. 1936
        record numbers: (60523-A) De-7167 Say SDR-192

1   Well now the first shall be the last : and the last shall be the first
2   Well now you know I was just sitting here thinking : ooo well well which woman treats me the worst

3   Well now you know the last woman I had : she was so doggone mean
4   Well now you know I asked her for water : ooo well well and she give me gasoline
5   Well now the first woman I had : she made me get [down] on my knees
6   And had the nerve to ask me : ooo well well if I liked limburger cheese
7   Well the [next] woman I had : she do nothing but fuss and fight
8   Well now you know that will make a barrelhouse man : ooo well well stay out each and every night
9   That is why I say the first shall be the last : and the last shall be the first
10 If I just could know : ooo well well now what woman treats me the worst

Whea   25   Wheatstraw, Peetie

        title: Deep Sea Love
        place and date: New York, 20 Feb. 1936
        record numbers: (60539-A) De-7167 Say SDR-192

1   I went home last night : and my honey doll was mad
2   Well I wonder what did I do : ooo well well now to make her feel so sad
3   Now don't you feel bad : when you are all alone
4   Your friends have turned on you : ooo well well then again your little girl has gone
5   Well I'm going to take my love : down to the deep blue sea
6   Then again I'm going to give it to someone : ooo well well that will give it back to me
7   Well now I'm going to call up in China : just to see if my little girl is there
8   Well now if she's not in China : ooo well I believe she's in East St Louis somewhere
9   Well baby : I don't believe I'll have no more to say
10 Because now you know your love done changed : ooo well well that I feel this a-way

Whea   26   Wheatstraw, Peetie

        title: Remember and Forget Blues
        place and date: Chicago, 8 Apr. 1936
        record numbers: (C-1351-2) Vo-03273 Say SDR-192

1   It's so easy to remember : and it's so hard to forget
2   The way my woman mistreats me : ooo well well I ain't got over it yet
3   When I was working people : she really had her sway
4   Because I gave her my money : ooo well well and she lived in a great big way
5   She didn't have no worry : didn't have a lick at a snake
6   She didn't even cook her meals : ooo well well I mean she really had got a break
7   Now I ain't got no money : no job can I find
8   She tells me that she loves me : ooo well well but she has changed her mind
9   Now I ain't got nobody : I done put my love up on my shelf
10 Since the woman I loved have deceived me : ooo well well now I don't want nobody else

Whea   27   Wheatstraw, Peetie

        title: Don't Take a Chance
        place and date: Chicago, 8 Apr. 1936
        record numbers: (C-1352-1) Vo-03348 Say SDR-192

1   It's a crime to take a chance : when you know you can get by

Whea   27   Wheatstraw, Peetie

2   It's better to take it easy : ooo well well than to
    take a chance and die
3   When you know you got a good gal : I mean one that
    will treat you right
4   One that will keep you when you're down : ooo well
    well and don't like to clown and fight
5   When she says she want loving : don't tell her that
    you too tired
6   Some other man might flag her train : ooo well well
    and she might let him ride
7   Don't take a chance about telling her : that you can
    get a new gal every day
8   Because she might walk out on you : ooo well well
    and make you prove what you say
9   Just as sure as the red light [says, means] stop :
    and the green light means go
10 It's a crime on taking a chance on losing her : ooo
    well well when you drive her from your door

Whea   28   Wheatstraw, Peetie

        title: Block and Tackle
        place and date: Chicago, 9 Apr. 1936
        record numbers: (C-1354-2) Vo-03348 Say SDR-192

1   My babe got a block and tackle : and I swear I can't
    get away
2   Every time I try to quit her : ooo well well I find
    myself going her way
3   I have a mind to ramble : I don't want to stay here
    another day
4   But I can't leave my baby people : ooo well well I
    must do just what she say
5   She put a block and tackle on me last night : when
    she was in my arms
6   She said daddy I don't want to hurt you : ooo well
    but I just mean but to keep you safe from harm
7   What she did to me people : ain't never been done
    before
8   But she really made me like it : ooo well well and I
    want to do it some more
9   Now boys when you love your baby : be careful about
    the way you do
10 But if you don't want your good gal : ooo well now
    she will put a block and tackle on you too

Whea   29   Wheatstraw, Peetie

        title: Cut Out Blues
        place and date: Chicago, 9 Apr. 1936
        record numbers: (C-1355-1) Vo-03444 Say SDR-191

1   I'm going to cut out my way of living : and I'm
    going to change my ways
2   Because I've got a funny feeling : ooo well and I
    believe it will shorten my days
3   I'm going to cut out moaning and groaning : about
    these no-good Janes
4   Ah they don't care nothing about you : ooo well well
    they just want you payday change
5   I'm going to cut out going to the station : gazing
    down the railroad track
6   Because them double-crossing woman left me : ooo
    well well and won't come back
7   I'm going to cut out playing policy : because my
    numbers just won't fall
8   Somebody done put jinx on me : ooo well and I can't
    have no luck at all
9   I'm going to cut out all my troubles : start my life
    over again
10 And when my *Toby* tells me : ooo well I'm going to
    cut in with some good Jane

Whea   30   Wheatstraw, Peetie

        title: When a Man Gets Down
        place and date: Chicago, 26 Oct. 1936
        record numbers: (90961-A) De-7243 Say SDR-192

1   When a man gets down : feel like he ain't got no
    friends at all
2   It seem like everybody want to knock him around :
    like he's an old ball
3   When it comes to women : he can't have no luck at
    all
4   They want to put a halter on him : ooo well and tie
    him up like a mule in his stall
5   When he go to his used-to-be woman : one he has give
    a real good time
6   Then again you know if he ask her for her salary :
    if she got a dollar she will swear that she ain't
    got a dime
7   When he walks in to see his old gang : with whom he
    used to drink
8   Well if he asks them for a little taste : ooo well
    they say oh that's just what you think
9   Now men when you're down : one thing you must do
10 When you get up : try to remember everybody that
    mistreated you

Whea   31   Wheatstraw, Peetie

        title: False Hearted Woman
        place and date: Chicago, 26 Oct. 1936
        record numbers: (90963-A) De-7243 Say SDR-192

1   Lying here in prison : longing to be free
2   A false-hearted woman : ooo well well is the
    downfall of me
3   She caused me to steal : all a workingman could save
4   Ah she nearly caused poor me : ooo well well to be
    in my grave
5   She turn her back on me : time I landed in jail
6   Ah well she wouldn't even write : ooo well well send
    poor me no mail
7   May bad luck overtake you : pile up on you in a heap
8   Well you are nothing but a crook : may around you
    now you know death may creep
9   Now I have got to be old : and just about turning
    grey
10 No other false-hearted woman : ooo well well can
    drive me this a-way

Whea   32   Wheatstraw, Peetie

        title: Crazy with the Blues
        place and date: Chicago, 26 Mar. 1937
        record numbers: (91150-A) De-7348 Cor CP-58

1   I wake up this morning : just crazy with the blues
2   I can't even tell : oh well well the difference in
    my shoes
3   I am just a crazy fool : I can't do a thing
4   I am just jumping around here : oh well well now
    like a monkey on the end of a string
5   I went downtown this morning : with my hat on upside
    down
6   The people looked at me : like they thought that I
    was a country clown
7   I heard somebody call me : it was the policeman on
    his beat
8   Well well now he just wanted to tell me : oh well
    well that I was driving on the wrong side of the
    street
9   Folks I keep on telling you : that I'm just a-crazy
    with the blues
10 I'm going to the railroad then to the river : oh
    well well but I don't know which one that I will
    choose

Whea   33   Wheatstraw, Peetie

       title: Peetie Wheatstraw Stomp
       place and date: Chicago, 26 Mar. 1937
       record numbers: (91152-A) De-7292 BC-4

1 Women all raving : about Peetie Wheatstraw in this
   land
2 He got some of these women now : going from hand to
   hand
3 Don't tell all the girls : what that Peetie
   Wheatstraw can do
4 That will cause suspicion now : you know they will
   try him too
5 If you want to see : the women that may clown
6 Just let that Peetie Wheatstraw : come into your
   town
7 I am Peetie Wheatstraw : the high sheriff from hell
8 The way I strut my stuff : ooo well now you never
   can tell

Whea   34   Wheatstraw, Peetie

       title: Peetie Wheatstraw Stomp No. 2
       place and date: Chicago, 26 Mar. 1937
       record numbers: (91153-) De-7391 BC-4

1 Everybody hollering : here come that Peetie
   Wheatstraw
2 New he's better known : by the devil's son-in-law
3 Everybody wondering : what that Peetie Wheatstraw do
4 Because every time you hear him : he coming out with
   something new
5 He makes some happy : some he make cry
6 Well now he make one old lady : go hang herself and
   die
7 *Now what I say* : save up your nickels and dimes
8 You can come up : and see me sometime

Whea   35   Wheatstraw, Peetie

       title: Crapshooter's Blues
       place and date: Chicago, 26 Mar. 1937
       record numbers: (91154-A) De-7292 Say SDR-192

1 My baby's a crapshooter : and she shoots them like a
   man
2 And ever since she's being shooting crap : ooo well
   well she's been going from hand to hand
3 Sometime she win : but the most time she lose
4 Boys now when she lose : ooo well well then I have
   the crapshooting blues
5 She told me to always bet : that the dice won't pass
6 But every time since I been betting that way : ooo
   well well I've been having a raggedy yas yas yas
7 Says I have been shooting craps : I can't win a cent
8 Well I can't win enough dough : ooo well well now to
   even pay my rent
9 I am telling all you crapshooters : now to let
   crapshooting go
10 Because now you will be stone barefooted : ooo well
   well then again and out of dough

Whea   36   Wheatstraw, Peetie

       title: Working on the Project
       place and date: Chicago, 30 Mar. 1937
       record numbers: (91164-A) De-7311 BC-4

1 I was working on the project : begging the relief
   for shoes
2 Because the rock and concrete : oh well well they's
   giving my feet the blues
3 Working on the project : with holes all in my
   clothes

Whea   36   Wheatstraw, Peetie

4 Trying to make me a dime : oh well well to keep the
   rent man from putting me outdoors
5 I am working on the project : trying to make both
   ends meet
6 But the payday is so long : oh well well until the
   grocery man won't let me eat
7 Working on the project : my gal's spending all my
   dough
8 Now I have waked up on her : oh well well and I
   won't be that weak no more
9 Working on the project : with payday three or four
   weeks away
10 Now how can you make ends meet : oh well well well
   when you can't get no pay

Whea   37   Wheatstraw, Peetie

       title: Sick Bed Blues
       place and date: Chicago, 2 Nov. 1937
       record numbers: (91317-A) De-7403 Say SDR-192

1 When I left [home] : my little girl was sick and in
   the bed
2 Now I know she wished that I was there : ooo well
   now to hold her aching head
3 She's on her sickbed : suffering with aches and
   pains
4 Now you know it hurts my heart : ooo well now when
   she calls my name
5 She rolls and she tumbles : now from side to side
6 Then again now you know all that I can do : ooo well
   now is start and hang my head and cry
7 Ain't it hard : now when you're all alone
8 I *never did mind though* : ooo well now when all
   your *gold* is gone

Whea   38   Wheatstraw, Peetie

       title: I'm Gonna Cut Out Everything
       place and date: Chicago, 2 Nov. 1937
       record numbers: (91320-A) De-7422 Say SDR-192

1 I have cut out my way of living : I have changed my
   ways
2 Because the funny feeling I had : ooo well now would
   let me live so many more days
3 I have cut out moaning and groaning : about the
   no-good Jane
4 Now I don't worry about it : ooo well well they'll
   never get my payday change
5 I have cut out going to the station : gazing down at
   the railroad track
6 Now it don't worry my mind : ooo well now I don't
   care if the woman never come back
7 I'm going to cut out playing policy : because my
   number just won't fall
8 I know somebody have put a jinx on me : ooo well now
   I know I won't have no luck at all
9 I have cut out all my troubles : and started my life
   over again
10 And if my money lasts me : ooo well I know I won't
   have to cut it with no-good Jane

Whea   39   Wheatstraw, Peetie

       title: Devilment Blues
       place and date: Chicago, 2 Nov. 1937
       record numbers: (91323-A) De-7422 Say SDR-192

1 Listen here baby : you got devilment on your mind
2 If you don't change your way : ooo well well you
   might die before your time
3 I know baby : you are doing the best you can

Whea 39   Wheatstraw, Peetie

4 Oh you're the married woman : ooo well well but you
   have your outside man
5 I can look in your eyes sweet mama : tell what's on
   your mind
6 You swear that you love me : ooo well well but you
   mistreats me all the time
7 There's one thing about you women : I just can't
   understand
8 If I take you away from your husbands : ooo well
   well you will leave me for another man

Whea 40   Wheatstraw, Peetie

      title: Shack Bully Stomp
      place and date: New York, 1 Apr. 1938
      record numbers: (63539-A) De-7479 BC-4

1 I used to play slow : but now I play it fast
2 Just to see the women : shake their yas yas yas
3 Now I am a man : that everybody knows
4 And you can see a crowd : everywhere he goes
5 Rambled and I rambled : till about the break of day
6 I think it's time now : I stop my rambling ways
7 My name is Peetie : I'm on the line you bet
8 I got something new : that I ain't never told you
   yet

Whea 41   Wheatstraw, Peetie

      title: Road Tramp Blues
      place and date: New York, 1 Apr. 1938
      record numbers: (63540-B) De-7589 BC-4

1 I have walked the lonesome road : till my feet is
   too sore to walk
2 I have begged scraps from the people : oh well well
   until my tongue is too stiff to talk
3 I'm going to tell you women something : that I
   really ain't going to do
4 That is give you women my labour : oh well well and
   my money too
5 Everybody can tell you people : that I ain't no lazy
   man
6 But I guess I'll have to go to the poorhouse : oh
   well well and do the best I can
7 I am what I am : and all I was born to be
8 And hard luck was in my family : oh well well and
   it's rolling down on me
9 When I get over my troubles : I'm going to bring my
   money down
10 And change my way of living : oh oh well well so I
   won't have to tramp around

Whea 42   Wheatstraw, Peetie

      title: Truckin' Thru' Traffic
      place and date: Chicago, 18 Oct. 1938
      record numbers: (91525-A) De-7529 Say SDR-192

1 Listen here man : don't talk about me
2 I'm trucking through traffic : don't you see
3 I'm trucking through traffic : fast as I can go
4 When I truck this time : I ain't going to truck no
   more
5 I'm trucking through traffic : trying to make you a
   dime
6 Tell everybody : you ain't no woman of mine
7 You got me trucking : through the ice and snow
8 Taking my money : and told me to go
9 When you're trucking out of traffic : it's very well
10 But now I'm trucking through traffic : it's a
   burning hell
11 You had me trucking through traffic : all over town
12 Taken my money : and then throwed me down

Whea 43   Wheatstraw, Peetie

      title: Sugar Mama
      place and date: Chicago, 18 Oct. 1938
      record numbers: (91529-A) De-7529 Say SDR-192

1 Sugar mama sugar mama : where did you get your sugar
   from
2 You must have got that sweet sugar : ooo well well
   from down on your man's sugar farm
3 You got fine sugar sugar mama : and it's going right
   to my head
4 And if you take it from me sugar mama : ooo well
   well I know I'll soon be dead
5 Everybody's bragging about your sugar sugar mama :
   and I'm almost going bragging too
6 And if I can't get that sugar mama : ooo well well I
   don't know what I will do
7 I can do without my coffee in the morning : but I
   must have my tea at night
8 But when I want that sweet sugar sugar mama : ooo
   well well I don't feel just right
9 That sugar you got sugar mama : is going from town
   to town
10 Everybody wants some of your sugar mama : ooo well
   well but please don't let them have more than four
   or five pounds

WhhR   1   Whistlin' Rufus

      title: Sweet Jelly Rollin'
      place and date: Chicago, 11 Dec. 1933
      record numbers: (77305-) BB-B5306 Rt RL-334

1 Listen here mama : don't you be so fast
2 Get in this bed : and give papa every pound of your
3 I like you baby : you're short like a duck
4 Ooo my soul baby : you sure can
5 I hear you call uh-uh Mr : baby why you too fast
6 You'll not cram all that meat : up in my little
7 I hear it said baby : you too slick
8 You'll not give me : all of that great big
9 Guess who's sneaking around here : sneaking in the
   grass
10 Trying your best : to sneak up on some woman's
11 Mama mama : who you quit
12 What's that *stone-hot* rat : over the head of
   papa's
13 In Dixieland : take my stand
14 Can't get the woman I want : I'm going to use my

WhiG   1   White, Georgia

      title: Pigmeat Blues
      place and date: Chicago, 12 May 1936
      record numbers: (90722-A) De-7209 AH-158

1 I know this is pigmeat : the kind that you won't
   regret
2 I've got something about this pigmeat : I ain't told
   you yet
3 I was born in the country : but daddy I was raised
   in town
4 There's nobody there : can beat me from my head on
   down
5 I ain't good-looking : I got no great long hair
6 But I don't have to worry : because I knows pigmeat
   anywhere
7 You can carry it to the mountain : it will be
   pigmeat there
8 *Register it poor on* China : *span* the test
   anywhere

299

WhiG   2   White, Georgia

    title: Walking the Street
    place and date: Chicago, 28 Jan. 1937
    record numbers: (91104-A) De-7277 AH-158

1 Stood on the corner : till my feet got soaking wet
2 These are the words I said : to each and every man I
   met
3 If you ain't got a dollar : give me a lousy dime
4 I've got to beg and steal : to please that man of
   mine
5 My feets all blistered : just from walking these
   lonesome streets
6 I've been walking all night : like a police on his
   beat
7 Wait a minute Mr Mr : give me a cigarette
8 Stop your calling me in : I've got what you should
   get
9 I've got these streetwalking blues : I ain't got no
   time to lose
10 I've got to make six dollars : just to buy my man a
   pair of shoes

WhiG   3   White, Georgia

    title: The Blues Ain't Nothin' But. . .???
    place and date: Chicago, 21 Oct. 1938
    record numbers: (91545-A) De-7562 Cor CP-58

1 Oh the blues ain't nothing : but a woman want to see
   her man
2 Because she wants some loving : you women will
   understand
3 Oh the blues ain't nothing : but a lowdown heart
   disease
4 Because loving your man : he's so hard to please
5 Oh the blues ain't nothing : but a woman loving a
   married man
6 Can't see him when she want to : got to see him when
   she can
7 Oh the blues ain't nothing : but a good woman
   feeling bad
8 Always down-hearted : blue disgusted and sad
9 Oh the blues ain't nothing : but a feeling that will
   get you down
10 Falling out with your man : you feel like leaving
   town

WhiJ   1   White, Joshua

    title: Welfare Blues
    place and date: New York, 6 Mar. 1934
    record numbers: (14902-2) Ba-33024 His HLP-22

1 The welfare helping people : each and every day
2 But the rent men have put me out : I ain't got no
   place to stay
3 I believe to my soul : I'm just a bad-luck man
4 Welfare's helping everybody : but don't give me no
   helping hand
5 I believe I'll go back south : cotton'll be a good
   price next year
6 I might as well be gone : I ain't doing nothing
   around here
7 Now the president's warning people : things will
   break some day
8 He say everything will be all right : you will have
   a place to stay
9 I believe I'll go back south : raise everything I
   need
10 If I don't make nothing off my cotton : boss will
   pay me for my seed

WhiJ   2   White, Joshua

    title: Stormy Weather No 1
    place and date: New York, 6 Mar. 1934
    record numbers: (14903-1) Ba-33024 His HLP-22

1 Lord it rained : it rained as far as I could see
2 *I wonder what water creature* : keep on crawling up
   on poor me
3 Like a fool : I gave everything I had for you to you
4 Now you've gone and left me : seems like the world
   is falling on through
5 People talk : I can hear them whisper everywhere I
   go
6 All my friends come to see me : and say well I told
   you so
7 What did I ever do : that made you leave so all
   alone
8 Since you've gone and left me : I do nothing but
   weep and moan
9 Every night I pray : for you to walk across my door
10 And I won't be worried : about these stormy weather
   blues no more

WhiW   1   White, Washington

    title: The Panama Limited
    place and date: Memphis, 26 May 1930
    record numbers: (59996-) Vi-23295 OJL-5

1 I ain't got nobody : take me to this train
2 Mmm : mmm
3 Fare you well : if I don't see you no more
4 Mmm : Lord Lord Lord Lord
5 I'm a motherless child : I'm a long ways from home
6 Mmm : mmm
7 This train I ride : it don't burn no coal
8 Mmm : mmm

WhiW   2   White, Washington

    title: Pinebluff Arkansas
    place and date: Chicago, 2 Sept. 1937
    record numbers: (C-1996-2) Vo-03711 Co C-30036

1 Ooo well I got a little woman : in Pinebluff
   Arkansas
2 She was the sweetest little woman : that you men
   most ever saw
3 Going to get up in the morning : baby with the
   rising sun
4 If the train don't run : going to be some walking
   done
5 My baby she called me : she called me up on the
   phone
6 She said daddy daddy : I don't see how come you
   don't hurry home
7 My baby says I'm tired : going to bed and moan
8 She said I ain't had no loving daddy : daddy since
   that you been gone
9 Well she said I'm tired : daddy of singing these
   lonesome songs
10 She *tired even* her daddy : I ain't even had you
   home
11 My baby said I'm tired : daddy hearing my best
   friend groan
12 She said I declare if you want me daddy : you better
   hurry home

WhiW   3   White, Washington

    title: Shake 'Em On Down
    place and date: Chicago, 2 Sept. 1937
    record numbers: (C-1997-1) Vo-03711 Co C-30036

1 Get your nightshirt mama : and your gown

WhiW   3   White, Washington

2 Baby before day : we going to shake them on down
3 *To much you daddy* : to be going away
4 Train leaving *Jackson* : some old rainy day
5 Fix my supper : and let go to bed
6 This white lightning : done gone to my head
7 I ain't been in Georgia babe : I been told
8 Georgia women : got the best jellyroll
9 See see mama : what you done done
10 Made me love you : now your man done come
11 Baby got something : don't know what it is
12 Made me drunker : than that old whiskey still

WhiW   4   White, Washington

      title: Black Train Blues
      place and date: Chicago, 7 Mar. 1940
      record numbers: (WC-2977-A) Vo-05588 Co C-30036

1 My heart is filled with pain : I believe I can't be
   trained
2 The woman I love : she had another man
3 Yon come the train : and I got no change
4 All I can do : just stand and wring my hands
5 I don't feel ashamed : standing and wringing my
   hands at the train
6 I ain't the first man : the train left cold in hand
7 Now the same big black train : that put me in a
   strain
8 I'll ride the train : keep the women from spending
   my change
9 I don't see nothing : but hands standing at the
   train
10 That's the same black train : that left me in this
   pain

WhiW   5   White, Washington

      title: Strange Place Blues
      place and date: Chicago, 7 Mar. 1940
      record numbers: (WC-2978-A) Vo-05526 Co C-30036

1 I'm a stranger at this place : and I'm looking for
   my mother's grave
2 Well it seems like to me : ooo well someone must
   stoled it away
3 I was at my mother's grave : when they put my mother
   away
4 And I can't find no one : ooo well to take her place
5 I thought after my mother was put away : I thought
   my wife would take her place
6 I show you difference in a mother and a wife : ooo
   well my wife done throwed me away
7 I wished I could find someone : to take my mother's
   place
8 If I can't find no one : ooo well you will find me
   in a grave
9 I'm standing on my mother's grave : and I wished I
   could see her face
10 I be glad when that day comes : ooo well when these
   blues drive me away

WhiW   6   White, Washington

      title: When Can I Change My Clothes
      place and date: Chicago, 7 Mar. 1940
      record numbers: (WC-2979-A) Vo-05489 Co C-30036

1 Never will forget the day : when they had me in
   Parchman jail
2 Would no one even come : and go my bail
3 So many days : I would be sitting down
4 I would be sitting down : looking down on my clothes
5 So many days : when the days would be cold
6 They would carry me out : in the rain and cold

WhiW   6   White, Washington

7 So many days : when the days would be cold
8 You could stand : and look at the convict tow
9 So many days : I would be walking down the road
10 I could hardly walk : with looking down on my
   clothes
11 Never will forget the day : when they taken my
   clothes
12 Taken my citizen's clothes : and throwed them away

WhiW   7   White, Washington

      title: Sleepy Man Blues
      place and date: Chicago, 7 Mar. 1940
      record numbers: (WC-2980-A) OK-05743 Co C-30036

1 When a man gets troubled in mind : he want to sleep
   all the time
2 He knows if he can sleep all the time : his trouble
   won't worry his mind
3 I'm feeling worried in mind : and I'm trying to keep
   from crying
4 I am standing into the sunshine : to keep from
   weaking down
5 I wonder what's the matter with my right mind : my
   mind keep me sleeping all the time
6 But when I had plenty money : my friends would come
   around
7 If I had my right mind : I would write my woman a
   few lines
8 I will do most anything : to keep from weaking down

WhiW   8   White, Washington

      title: Parchman Farm Blues
      place and date: Chicago, 7 Mar. 1940
      record numbers: (WC-2981-A) OK-05683 Co C-30036

1 Judge give me life this morning : down on Parchman
   Farm
2 I wouldn't hate it so bad : but I left my wife and
   my home
3 Oh goodbye wife : all you have done gone
4 But I hope some day : you will hear my lonesome song
5 Oh listen men : I don't mean no harm
6 If you want to do good : you better stay off of
   Parchman Farm
7 We goes to work in the morning : just the dawn of
   day
8 Just at the setting of the sun : that's when the
   work is done
9 I'm down on old Parchman Farm : I sure want to go
   back home
10 But I hope some day : I will overcome

WhiW   9   White, Washington

      title: Good Gin Blues
      place and date: Chicago, 7 Mar. 1940
      record numbers: (WC-2982-A) OK-05625 Co C-30036

1 Good morning friends : I want [me] a drink of gin
2 Because they told me this morning : revenue mens
   will be back again
3 Oh listen you men : don't you let them in
4 Well they might catch me : all with a pint of gin
5 Oh come in friends : and have a drink of gin
6 I know it is a sin : but I loves my good old gin
7 Oh come back friends : when I need my gin
8 Because I don't care nothing : about oh them revenue
   men

301

WhiW   10   White, Washington

    title: High Fever Blues
    place and date: Chicago, 8 Mar. 1940
    record numbers: (WC-2987-A) Vo-05489 Co C-30036

1   I'm taken down with the fever : and it won't let me
    sleep
2   It was about three o'clock : before he could let me
    be
3   I wish somebody : would come and drive my fever away
4   This fever I'm having : sure is in my way
5   The fever I'm having : sure is hard on a man
6   They don't allow my lover : come and shake my hand
7   Doctor get your fever gauge : and put it under my
    tongue
8   Doctor says all you need : your lover in your arms
9   I wants my lover : come and drive my fever away
10 Doctor said she do me more good in a day : than he
    would in all of his days

WhiW   11   White, Washington

    title: District Attorney Blues
    place and date: Chicago, 8 Mar. 1940
    record numbers: (WC-2988-A) OK-05683 Co C-30036

1   District attorney : sure is hard on a man
2   They will take a woman's man : and leave her cold in
    hand
3   The district attorney : sure is hard on a man
4   He has caused a-many men : to be in some distant
    land
5   District attorney : sure is hard on a man
6   He has caused so many women : to be cold in hand
7   The district attorney : sure is hard on a man
8   He ain't no woman : but he sure will take a woman's
    man
9   The district attorney : sure is hard on a man
10 He can *tell us where* : when he going to take a
    woman's man
11 A district attorney : sure is hard on a man
12 He taken me from my woman : caused her to have some
    other man

WhiW   12   White, Washington

    title: Fixin' to Die Blues
    place and date: Chicago, 8 Mar. 1940
    record numbers: (WC-2989-A) Vo-05588 Co C-30036

1   I'm looking funny in my eyes : and I believe I'm
    fixing to die
2   I know I was born to die : but I hate to leave my
    children crying
3   Just as sure as we live : sure we's born to die
4   I know I was born to die : but I hate to leave my
    children crying
5   Your mother treated me : like I was her baby child
6   That's why's I tried so hard : to come home to die
7   So many nights at the fireside : how my children's
    mother would cry
8   Because I told their mother : I had to say goodbye
9   Look over yonder : on the burying ground
10 Yon stand ten thousand : standing to see them let me
    down
11 Mother take my children back : before they let me
    down
12 And don't leave them screaming and crying : on the
    graveyard ground

WhiW   13   White, Washington

    title: Aberdeen Mississippi Blues
    place and date: Chicago, 8 Mar. 1940
    record numbers: (WC-2990-A) OK-05743 Co C-30036

1   I was over in Aberdeen : on my way to New Orleans
2   Them Aberdeen women told me : they will buy my
    gasoline
3   There's two little women : that I ain't never seen
4   These two little women : they's from New Orleans
5   I'm sitting down in Aberdeen : with New Orleans on
    my mind
6   Lord I believe them Aberdeen women : going to make
    me lose my mind
7   Aberdeen is my home : but the mens don't want me
    around
8   They know I will take these women : and take them
    out of town
9   Listen you Aberdeen women : you know I ain't got no
    dime
10 They been had the poor boy : all hobbled down

WhiW   14   White, Washington

    title: Bukka's Jitterbug Swing
    place and date: Chicago, 8 Mar. 1940
    record numbers: (WC-2991-A) OK-05743 Co C-30036

1   Hey come on you women : let's a-do the jitterbug
    swing
2   When you do the jitterbug swing : then you know you
    will be doing a thing
3   Hey : you women working on my nerves
4   Hey : you going to drive me in my blood
6   Hey : please ma'am don't say uh-uh

WhiW   15   White, Washington

    title: Special Stream Line
    place and date: Chicago, 8 Mar. 1940
    record numbers: (WC-2992-A) OK-05743 Co C-30036

1   Hey dad : I'm sorry to leave my home
2   Mmm : Lord Lord Lord Lord
3   Daddy it's all right : how you turn me down
4   Mmm : I ain't got a dime
5   Hey daddy : I don't want to leave
6   Mmm : I believe I'll lose my mind

Wigg   1   Wiggins, James Boodle It

    title: Evil Woman Blues
    place and date: Chicago, c. Feb. 1928
    record numbers: (20379-2) Pm-12662 Mil MLP-2018

1   I wake up every morning : with leaving on my mind
2   Because my mama's so evil : and she treats me so
    unkind
3   She left me last night : left me in the wrong
4   But my times come : baby it won't be long
5   My train is made up : ready to leave this town
6   You can think about your baby : when the sun goes
    down
7   Mr conductor man : I want to talk with you
8   I want to ride your train : from here to Bugaloo
9   I'm leaving this morning : I haven't got my fare
10 I want to see : if I can find my good gal there

Wigg   2   Wiggins, James Boodle It

        title: Forty-Four Blues
        place and date: Richmond, Ind., 12 Oct. 1929
        record numbers: (15768-A) Pm-12860 OJL-15

1   I walked on and on : with my forty-four in my hand
2   I was looking for my woman : involved with another
        man
3   I wore my forty-four so long : that it made my
        shoulder sore
4   And I will tell everybody : I ain't going to wear my
        forty-four no more
5   Now baby said to your daddy : Forty-Four whistle
        blow
6   It blow just like : it ain't going to blow no more
7   Now I got a little old Chevy : Lord number is
        forty-four
8   I wake up every morning : wolves sitting in my door

Wigg   3   Wiggins, James Boodle It

        title: Frisco Bound Blues
        place and date: Richmond, Ind., 12 Oct. 1929
        record numbers: (15769-A) Pm-12860 OJL-15

1   That Frisco train : runs a mile a minute
2   You're in that coach : I'm going to stay there in it
3   You can toot your whistle : you can ring your bell
4   I know you been running : by the way you smell
5   It's a boa constrictor : and a lemon stick
6   I wouldn't mind being with you : but my mama's sick
7   I would tell you what's the matter : but I done got
        scared
8   You got to waits till the night : when we go to bed
9   If you were sick : I wouldn't worry you
10 I wouldn't want you to do something : that you
        couldn't do
11 If you want it you can get it : and I ain't mad
12 You going to get something baby : that you never had
13 Look a-here you get mad : every time I call your
        name
14 I ain't never told you : you couldn't get that thing
15 I woke up this morning : about half past five
16 My baby turned over : and tried to cop a jive
17 I got something to tell you : going to make you mad
18 I got something for you : going to make you feel
        glad
19 Look a-here look a-here : what you want me to do
20 You knew my jelly : didn't die for you
21 I got something to tell you : is going to break your
        heart
22 Been together so long : now got to get apart

Wigg   4   Wiggins, James Boodle It

        title: Corrine Corrina Blues
        place and date: Grafton, Wis., c. Jan. 1930
        record numbers: (L-103-2) Pm-12916 Her H-205

1   Corrine Corinna : where you been so long
2   Ain't had no loving : since you been gone
3   Corrine Corinna : where'd you stay last night
4   Come in this morning : the sun was shining bright
5   I miss Corinna : way across the sea
6   It make no matter : she didn't care for me
7   Corrine Corinna : what are you going to do
8   Just a little bitty loving : can't your heart be
        true
9   I love Corinna : tell the world I do
10 Just a little bitty loving : let your love be true
11 Corrine Corinna : that old pal of mine
12 You left me walking the road : and then crying
13 Corrine Corinna : what's the matter now
14 You didn't write no letter : you didn't love me
        nohow
15 Goodbye Corinna : and it's fare thee well

Wigg   4   Wiggins, James Boodle It

16 When I'm coming back babe : can't nobody tell

Wigg   5   Wiggins, James Boodle It

        title: Gotta Shave 'Em Dry
        place and date: Grafton, Wis., c. Jan. 1930
        record numbers: (L-104-1) Pm-12916 Her H-205

1   Now if you be my sweet woman : tell you what I'm
        bound to do
2   Going to beg borrow and steal : bring all my money
        home to you
3   Babe I'd do anything for you : I do swear to God and
        you refuse to come
4   You know it's hard to bring water : ???
5   I ain't going to never tell nobody : what my mama
        done to me
6   She done made me crazy about her : now she's trying
        to quit poor me
7   Sweet woman I ain't going to stand no quitting : I
        ain't going to stand no jumping down
8   Before I let you quit me baby : I'm going to burn
        half Chicago down
9   Now the rooster crows in Italy : I heard him way
        down in France
10 The way she getting down these days : you know I
        ain't going to have a possible chance
11 Better get your crowing from the rooster : better
        get your eggs from a hen
12 You get your feathers from a robin : get your music
        from a wren
13 Now mama little mama : what's on your *ruddy* mind
14 Any time you feel superstitious : you know somebody
        riding your blinds
15 And it's mmm : something must be wrong
16 If I keep on worrying about you baby : you know I
        can't last long

Wilb   1   Wilber, Bill

        title: My Babe My Babe
        place and date: Chicago, 22 July 1935
        record numbers: (90198-A) Ch-50053 OJL-8

1   My babe my babe : sure is good to me
2   She tore up my troubles : broke up my misery
3   I can ask her for whiskey : she gives me cherry wine
4   So you wish your woman : would treat you good like
        mine
5   Her hair ain't curly : but it hang like horse's mane
6   Know you wish you had a woman : to treat you just
        the same
7   I can ask her for a nickel : she gives me ten and a
        dime
8   Know you wish you had a woman : to treat you just
        like mine
9   She got me out of jail : bought me a diamond ring
10 I ain't going to do nothing : but lay around and
        shake that thing
11 She calls me daddy : then she calls me sugar pie
12 I ain't going to do nothing : but lay down by her
        side
13 Now when she's dead : six feet in the clay
14 Won't have another woman : to treat me this a-way
15 Now goodbye goodbye : baby now fare you well
16 If I don't meet you in heaven : you know I'll meet
        you in hell
17 Now I'm leaving I'm leaving : leaving on the eagle
        wing
18 All don't see me : know can hear me sing
19 She had an old job : making four dollars a day
20 I didn't have to do nothing : but lay around and
        throw it away

Wilb   2   Wilber, Bill

        title: Greyhound Blues
        place and date: Chicago, 22 July 1935
        record numbers: (90199-A) Ch-50053 Rt RL-334

1   Going to catch me a Greyhound : going to leave here
        tonight
2   Woman I'm loving : won't treat me right
3   My mama was a killer : and my old daddy was a bear
4   She grab her daddy : she run anywhere
5   I had an old ??? : in the ??? camp
6   She didn't do nothing : but lay down with her man
7   She makes me coffee : throws my sugar on the floor
8   Say big boy : you got to go
9   I went to the governor : to buy one of his bands
10 Leave here boy : you don't understand
11 Called her this morning : about half past five
12 She turned over : cried like a child
13 A nickel is a nickel : and a dime is a dime
14 House full of children : ain't nar' one mine

WileG   1   Wiley, Geeshie (Elvie Thomas)

        title: Over to My House
        place and date: Grafton, Wis., c. Apr. 1930
        record numbers: (L-265-1) Pm-12977 Yz L-1018

1   Come around over to my house : ain't nobody here but
        me
2   I been listening for the last six months : and I
        could not see
3   Now you can shake you can break it : you can hang it
        on the wall
4   Throw it out the window : run and catch it 'fore it
        falls
5   I say you need not think : because you little and
        cute
6   I'm going to buy you : a ??? suit
7   Well now I was sitting in the parlor : just as dumb
        as a lamb
8   I wasn't too dumb : to hear the back door slam
9   I'm going to grab me a picket : off of my back fence
10 Going to whip your nappy head : until you learn some
        sense
11 I cried ashes to ashes : said sand to sand
12 Every married woman : got a back-door man

WileG   2   Wiley, Geeshie

        title: Eagles on a Half
        place and date: Grafton, Wis., c. Mar. 1931
        record numbers: (L-826-1) Pm-13074 Yz L-1001

1   It's a low it's a low low : lowdown dirty shame
2   I've got a brownskin man : but I'm scared to call
        his name
3   I said squat low papa : let your mama see
4   I want to see that old business : keeps on worrying
        me
5   I twisted and I tumbled : I rolled the whole night
        long
6   I didn't have no daddy : to hold me in his arms
7   I said get back rider : don't care how you lay
8   I want to tell you : I can't stay here till day
9   I say eagle's on a half Lord : baby In God We Trust
10 I love you daddy : want your dollar first

Wilk   1   Wilkins, Robert

        title: Jail House Blues
        place and date: Memphis, 8 Sept. 1928
        record numbers: (45499-) Vi-23379 Yz L-1002

1   Oh look like : I can see trouble in the air
2   But ain't only here friend : it trouble everywhere

Wilk   1   Wilkins, Robert

3   Now I wished I had listened : what my mother said
4   I wouldn't have been bound down : in this trouble
        today
5   I'm lying in jail : with my face turned to the wall
6   And that woman I'm loving : she was the cause of it
        all
7   Now the judge going to sentence me : and the clerk
        going to write it down
8   So they accuse me of stealing : I fixing to leave
        your town
9   I got something to tell you : just before I go
10 Getting out of trouble this time : woman I won't do
        wrong no more
11 Oh the judge going to give me : six months on the
        road
12 Woman I can't stand it : God in heaven do know it
13 But I don't mind going : I'm going and leave you
        here
14 These men going to mistreat you : God knows they
        don't care
15 Going to tell you this : just before I go
16 When I come back here woman : you going to have me
        some more

Wilk   2   Wilkins, Robert

        title: I Do Blues
        place and date: Memphis, 8 Sept. 1928
        record numbers: (47000-) Vi-23379 OJL-5

1   Oh woman I do : God knows I do
2   I do more for you : than any poor man can do
3   I done everything woman : but die for you
4   Want you to tell me : what more woman do you want me
        to do
5   Woman : I done done all I know to do
6   I done everything woman : but lay down and die for
        you
7   Now if you don't want me : give me your right hand
8   I'll go to my woman : and you can go to your man
9   You better come here woman : sit down on my knee
10 Oh and talk all night : tell poor Timmy what you
        please
11 Want you to tell me something : give my mind some
        ease
12 I can't be satisfied : woman and I can't be pleased
13 Because I'd rather be dead : buried on my face
14 Than to love you woman : you treat me this a-way
15 But I don't want nobody : baby don't want me
16 I'd rather be somewhere friends : buried on my knee
17 I got something to tell you : tell you before I go
18 Meet me down at the station : and kiss me before I
        go
19 Because I'm going up the country : coming here no
        more
20 Oh I love you woman : but you always treat me so
21 Is today the day : that you walked away
22 Oh you told me you was going : you was going to stay

Wilk   3   Wilkins, Robert

        title: That's No Way to Get Along
        place and date: Memphis, c. 23 Sept. 1929
        record numbers: (M-189-) Br-7125 OJL-5

1   I'm going home : sit down and tell my ma
2   And that's no way : for me to get along
3   These lowdown women mama : treated your poor son
        wrong
4   And that's no way : for him to get along
5   Treated me : like my poor heart was made of a rock
        of stone
6   And that's no way : for me to get along
7   That was enough : to make your son mama wished he's
        dead and gone

8   Because that's no way : got him to get along
9   I stood on the roadside : and cried alone by myself
10 And that's no way : for me to get along
11 Some train come along : and take me away from here
12 And that be no way : for me to get along

title: Alabama Blues
place and date: Memphis, c. 23 Sept. 1929
record numbers: (M-190-) Br-7205 Rt RL-333

1   I tell you girls : and I'm going to tell you now
2   If you don't want me : please don't dog me around
3   My home ain't here : it's in most any old town
5   I'm going up on the mountain : and look down in the sea
6   *Troubling* alligators : keeps doing that shivaree
7   Tell me friends : ever since that *pull in Jackson maid*
8   Kansas City Missouri : has been her regular trade
9   ??? : that is turning around and around
10 The churn-wheel knocking : friends I'm Alabama bound
11 My mama told me : and papa told me too
12 Say brownskin women son : going to be the death of you
13 I told mama last night friends : and papa the night before
14 If brownskin women kills me : mama let me go
15 When I leaves that time mama : I won't be back no more
17 I ain't coming back here : to worry your papa so
19 I walked off : and left my mother standing in the snow
20 She's crying to me son : please son don't you go

title: Long Train Blues
place and date: Memphis, c. 23 Sept. 1929
record numbers: (M-191-) Br-7205 Rt RL-333

1   She walked down in the yard : caught the longest train she seen
2   Say she ride she ride : till the blues lay off of me
3   It's a *bull* and a freight train : running side by side
4   They done stole my rider : and I guess they satisfied
5   *They roll* in the Delta : ??? *leaves and rye*
6   Know I feel just like : she said her last goodbye
7   Well she won't write : she won't telephone
8   Makes me believe to my soul : that my rider's cold dead gone
9   Well if I had wings : baby like Noah's dove
10 I would raise and fly : God knows where my lover was
11 I lay down at night : I can't sleep at all
12 All for lying there wondering : if there one rolling in her arms
13 Laid my head on my pillow : ???
14 Take it down ??? : I'm getting sick and about to die

title: Falling Down Blues
place and date: Memphis, c. 23 Sept. 1929
record numbers: (M-192-) Br-7125 Yz L-1002

1   I'm tired of standing : on the long lonesome road
2   Thinking about my baby : and got nowhere to go
3   It's far down the road : friend as I can see
4   See the woman I love : standing waving after me
5   I run to her friend : fell down at her knees
6   Crying take me back baby : God knows if you please

7   If you don't believe : girl I'll treat you right
8   Come and walk with me : down to my loving shack tonight
9   I'll certainly treat you : just like you was white
10 That don't satisfy you : girl I'll take your life
11 I love you girl : I will tell the world I do
12 And that's the reason : you treat me like you do
13 But go ahead : that will be all right for you
14 I will meet you some day : when you down in hard luck too

title: Nashville Stonewall Blues
place and date: Memphis, c. early Feb. 1930
record numbers: (MEM-740-A) Br-7168 Rt RL-307

1   I stayed in jail : it was thirty long days
2   And that woman said she loved me : I could not see her face
3   I looked out the window : saw the long chain man
4   Oh he's coming : to call us boys name by name
5   He's going to take me from here : to Nashville Tennessee
6   He's going to take me right back : boys where I used to be
7   I got a letter from home : reckon how it read
8   It read son come home to your mama : she's sick and nearly dead
9   I sat down and cried : and I screamed and squawled
10 Said how can I come home mama : I'm behind these walls
11 Every morning about four : boys might be half past
12 You ought to see me down the foundry : trying to do my best
13 Oh the judge he sentenced me : boys from five to ten
14 I get out I'm going to that woman : and I'll be right back again

title: Police Sergeant Blues
place and date: Memphis, c. early Feb. 1930
record numbers: (MEM-741-B) Br-7168 Rt RL-307

1   I'm going to tell you : baby tell you now
2   If you don't want me : you don't have to dog me around
3   Now look a-yonder : baby what I see
4   The police and a sergeant : they's a-coming after me
5   I am going to tell you : that I'm going to the station to ride
6   When you see me going : baby hang your head and cry
7   I am going to tell the judge : I know that I done wrong
8   You go and get some lawyers : to come and go my bond
9   I know the judge : is going to give me thirty long days
10 I made it up in my mind : baby to go and stay
11 I'm going outside : and work out my time
12 Because the girl I love : she's not got a dime

title: Get Away Blues
place and date: Memphis, c. early Feb. 1930
record numbers: (MEM-742-B) Br-7158 OJL-11

1   I walked down to the station : fold my troubled arms
2   We walked and asked the agent : has the train done gone
3   I looked down the track : I seed it in the bend
4   Walked bought me a ticket : oh for me and my friend
5   Told her come on woman : let us board this train

Wilk   9   Wilkins, Robert

    6   Right here : while we get away from your man
    7   Woman you just tell me : do you want to go
    8   I'll take you somewhere : you never been before
    9   Then I'll give you silver : give you paper and gold
   10   I'll give you anything : that'll satisfy your
        worried soul
   11   Woman if I don't love you : I don't love myself
   12   You did something to me : I ain't going to tell
        nobody else

Wilk   10   Wilkins, Robert

        title: I'll Go With Her Blues
        place and date: Memphis, c. early Feb. 1930
        record numbers: (MEM-743-) Br-7158 OJL-11

    1   I'll go with her I'll follow her I will : to her
        burying place
    2   Hang my head and cry friend I will : mmm as she pass
        away
    3   Up a-yonder she goes friend : please run try to call
        her back
    4   Because that sure was one woman : I did mmm love and
        like
    5   I believe I'll go home friend : and do this dress
        myself in black
    6   Show the world I wants her : but I can't mmm get her
        back
    7   Every time I hear : that lonesome mmm church bell
        ring
    8   Makes me think about that song : my baby used to
        sing

Wilk   11   Wilkins, Robert

        title: Dirty Deal Blues
        place and date: Jackson, Miss., 10 Oct. 1935
        record numbers: (JAX-104-) Vo-03223 BC-5

    1   Early one morning : baby something was on my mind
    2   I thinking about my welfare : and I just couldn't
        keep from crying
    3   Oh I cried one time : mama your daddy ain't going to
        cry no more
    4   Lord I made up in my mind pretty mama : honest great
        God let you go
    5   Goodbye pretty mama : oh baby fare thee well
    6   Lord I'm afraid to meet you : in that other world
        somewhere
    7   Oh baby I'm so glad : that this whole round world do
        know
    8   That every living creature : mmm reap just what they
        sow
    9   That's the reason why you hear me crying : Lord
        please have mercy on me
   10   Because I don't want my woman : mmm reap no bad seed
   11   That's the reason why I'm through telling her : ???
        about her dirty deal
   12   Please God ??? : make my woman reap righteous seed

Wilk   12   Wilkins, Robert

        title: New Stock Yard Blues
        place and date: Jackson, Miss., 10 Oct. 1935
        record numbers: (JAX-107-) Vo-03223 OJL-21

    1   Listen here men : what I've got to say
    2   Monday and Tuesday : is [Mr Owens's] auction day
    3   Get your money in your hand : and don't be long
    4   Can't buy from a better man : than Mr Owens
    5   He's a man that sells : he's a man that buys
    6   I bet you my life : he'll treat you right
    7   When you wake up Monday morning : with the stockyard
        blues

Wilk   12   Wilkins, Robert

    8   Come and talk to Mr Owens : about his good-looking
        mules
    9   I know he's good : I know he's nice and kind
   10   Have a talk with him : before you start to buying
   11   The Union Stockyards : is a good place to go
   12   Not for so much talk : but to spend your dough
   13   I want you to understand : every word I say
   14   Monday and Tuesday : is [Mr Owens's] auction day
   15   I want all of you men : to meet me there
   16   Speak to Mr Kelly : he's the auctioneer

Wilk   13   Wilkins, Robert

        title: Old Jim Canan's
        place and date: Jackson, Miss., 12 Oct. 1935
        record numbers: (JAX-117-) Vo unissued Yz
        L-1018

    1   I wished I was back : at old Jim Canan's
    2   I'd stand on the corner : and wave my hand
    3   And if you don't believe : that I'm a drinking man
    4   Just baby stop by here : with the ??? can
    5   I'm going uptown : buy me coke and beer
    6   Coming back : and tell you how these women is
    7   They drink their whiskey : drink their coke and gin
    8   When you don't play the dozens : they will ease you
        in
    9   The men and women : running hand and hand
   10   Going to and fro : to old Jim Canan's
   11   Drinking their whiskey : sniffing cocaine
   12   That's the reason why : I wished I was back at Jim
        Canan's

WillH   1   Williams, Henry

        title: Georgia Crawl
        place and date: Atlanta, 19 Apr. 1928
        record numbers: (146148-2) Co-14328-D Rt RL-316

    1   Run here papa : look at sis
    2   Out in the back yard : just shaking like this
    3   I can shake it east : shake it west
    4   Way down south : I can shake it best
    5   *Come in this house* gal : come here right now
    6   Out there trying to do the crawl : and you don't
        know how
    7   There's old Aunt Sally : old and grey
    8   Do the Georgia crawl : till she died away

WillH   2   Williams, Henry

        title: Lonesome Blues
        place and date: Atlanta, 19 Apr. 1928
        record numbers: (146149-2) Co-14328-D Fly LP-103

    1   Did you ever wake up lonesome : all by yourself
    2   And the one you love : off loving someone else
    3   I wrote these blues : I'm going to sing them as I
        feel
    4   And old Mr Eddie liking me singing them : I swear to
        goodness there's no one else to please
    5   I tell you people : I don't know your name
    6   But taking other men's women : I swear to God is a
        shame
    7   Ooh : look where the sun going down
    8   I ain't had no righteous woman : since my baby
        blowed this town

WillI 1   Williams, Jabo

       title: Polock Blues
       place and date: Grafton, Wis., c. May 1932
       record numbers: (L-1406-?) Pm-13130 Yz L-1028

1 Way down way down : way down in Polack Town
2 There the ??? polices : have teared my playhouse
   down
3 And I went to the pawnshop : and I lays my diamond
   down
4 Said give me some money : I'm going to Polack Town
5 I went to the ticket office : and I lays my money
   down
6 I said gives me my ticket : I'm going to Polack Town
7 I said to the ticket agent : ease your window down
8 I got my ticket : and I'm going to Polack Town
9 I spent all my days : way down in Polack Town
10 For womens and bad whiskey : have torn my playhouse
   down
11 Said they cook good cabbage : but they *called it*
   ???
12 Oh the best old cabbage : that a man most ever seen
13 Now I'm going down : going to ride the same old way
14 And *the luck of the fortune* mama : you may need me
   around some day

WillJ 1   Williams, Joe

       title: Little Leg Woman
       place and date: Chicago, 25 Feb. 1935
       record numbers: (85487-1) BB-B5900 Yz L-1038

1 Well look here mama : let your daddy see
2 You got something baby : worrying me
3 Well mama don't allow : no laying out all night long
4 Well well you know I'm a mind to : because my woman
   done done me wrong
5 Well big-leg woman : better keep your dresses down
6 You got me standing around : with my face full of
   frowns
7 Little leg woman : do just like a squirrel
8 Get up in the morning : *caught that* on the world
9 Drop your window woman : and down your blinds
10 Can't hear nothing : but your doggone best friend
   crying
11 One of these mornings : either late or soon
12 Some old joker boys : can have my room
13 Yeah mama don't allow : no oh laying out all night
   long
14 Well well the woman I'm loving : ooo ooo Lord she
   done done me wrong
15 Well I'll tell you women : how to keep your man at
   home
16 Lord you can squeeze his lemon woman : and roll him
   all night long
17 Sweetest peaches woman : don't grow on no tree
18 Sweetest honey : now come from no bee

WillJ 2   Williams, Joe

       title: Somebody's Been Borrowing that Stuff
       place and date: Chicago, 25 Feb. 1935
       record numbers: (85488-1) BB-B5900 RCA LPV-518

1 Look a-here judge : give me the lowest fine
2 I killed a man : about the stuff of mine
3 I don't mind : my gal running around
4 *Saving* there's more : of that stuff of mine
5 I got up this morning : feeling bad
6 Thinking about : that stuff I had
7 Want to keep : your daddy from crying
8 Save a little more : of that stuff of mine
9 You can arrest me judge : put me in the cell
10 Me and my gal : ain't doing very well
11 You can drink your whiskey : woman I may decline
12 Got to save : that stuff of mine

WillJ 2   Williams, Joe

13 When I was a little boy : running around
14 Kill every man : about the stuff of mine
15 I got a little gal : she lives way edge of town
16 Save me : all of that stuff of mine
17 I cried last night : all night before
18 Took my stuff : and I walked out your door
19 You can put on your dress gal : and run around
20 Swear I'll kill you : about that stuff of mine
21 Farewell baby : I'm doing very well
22 I am going : to raise some hell

WillJ 3   Williams, Joe

       title: 49 Highway Blues
       place and date: Chicago, 25 Feb. 1935
       record numbers: (85490-) BB-B5996 OJL-17

1 Well I'll get up in the morning : catch the Highway
   Forty-Nine
2 Well well I'm going to look for little Malvina : ooo
   man don't say she can't be found
3 I got a long tall woman : live on Highway Forty-Nine
4 Well well I get up in the morning : ooo Lord boys
   she's down on my mind
5 Malvina my sweet woman : she don't pay me no mind
6 You got poor Joe walking down woman : ooo Lord
   Highway Forty-Nine
7 [I'm going to, if I] get up in the morning Malvina :
   I believe I'll dust my bed
8 I'm going down Highway Forty-Nine : boys I'm going
   to be rocking to my head
9 If you ever get the blues : catch the Highway
   Forty-Nine
10 Well Malvina my sweet woman : ooo Lord boys she
   don't pay me no mind
11 Soon this morning boys : I may roll in Jackson town
12 I done got tired of laying around : walking that
   Highway Forty-Nine
13 I'm standing in Chicago mama : New Orleans on my
   mind
14 Malvina she's my sweet woman : she on Highway
   Forty-Nine

WillJ 4   Williams, Joe

       title: My Grey Pony
       place and date: Chicago, 25 Feb. 1935
       record numbers: (85491-) BB-B5948 RBF RF-14

1 I got me a pony Lord : and she already trained
2 When I get in my bed mama : baby tighten up on your
   reins
3 Well I got something to tell you : mama when I get a
   chance
4 Well I don't want to marry : baby just want to be
   your man
5 I got a brownskin woman : she don't pay me no mind
6 And I know you going to miss me : baby when I leave
   this town
7 And I know my woman : she going to scream and cry
8 When she gets that letter : baby Lord I pass my ???
9 I got me a grey pony : down in my pasture somewhere
10 I'm going to find my woman : baby in this world
   somewhere
11 Fare you well : may be tomorrow or today
12 I want you to know : babe I didn't come here to stay
13 I ain't got nobody : to talk baby-talk to me
14 Said my mama's getting old : Lord her hair done got
   grey
15 Lord my mama she got older : now her hair done got
   grey
16 Well well why break her heart : you know ooo Lord
   treat her this way

WillJ 5   Williams, Joe

    title: Stepfather Blues
    place and date: Chicago, 25 Feb. 1935
    record numbers: (85492-1) BB-B5996 OJL-17

1 When I was a little boy baby : about sixteen inches high
2 I had a mean stepfather : Lord he didn't want me to eat a bite
3 I've got a mean stepfather : and I know you have one too
4 And my mother dead and gone : nothing in this world that he will do
5 Well my mother she gone : and I hope she gone to stay
6 I have a mean stepfather : he done drove me away
7 When I was a little boy Lord : my stepfather didn't allow me around
8 He's a no-good weed mama : and the cows going to mow him down
9 Well [poor Joe, I'm] leaving this morning : my face is full of frowns
10 I got a mean stepfather : and my dear mother she don't allow me around
11 That's all right : may be home some day
12 My mean stepfather : he won't give me no place to lay
13 I am a little boy : [I'm crying all, I cried the whole] night long
14 My stepfather : he swears he done done me wrong
15 And before I'll be a dog mama : I'll leave my happy home
16 He's a no-good weed : and swear he done me wrong

WillJ 6   Williams, Joe

    title: Baby Please Don't Go
    place and date: Chicago, 31 Oct. 1935
    record numbers: (96244-1) BB-B6200 RCA INT-1087

1 Now baby please don't go : now baby please don't go
2 Baby please don't go back to New Orleans : and get your cold ice cream
3 I believe another man done gone : I believe another man done gone
4 I believe another man done gone to the county farm : now with his long chain on
5 Turn your lamp down low : turn your lamp down low
6 Turn your lamp down low I crying all night long : now baby please don't go
7 I beg you night before : I beg you night before
8 I beg you night before turn your lamp down low : now baby please don't go
9 I believe my baby done lied : I believe my baby done lied
10 I believe my baby she lied said she didn't have a man : now while I had my time
11 Before I'll be your dog : before I'll be your dog
12 Before I'll be your dog I'll pack my trunk this morning baby : *and take* the road *and gone*
13 I believe I'll leave you here : I believe I'll leave you here
14 I believe I'll leave you here because you got me way out here : and you don't feel my care
15 Now baby please don't go : now baby please don't go
16 Now baby please don't go back to New Orleans : you know I love you so
17 I believe you trying to leave me here : trying to leave your daddy here
18 Trying to leave your daddy here they got me way down here : and you don't feel my care

WillJ 7   Williams, Joe

    title: Wild Cow Blues
    place and date: Chicago, 31 Oct. 1935
    record numbers: (96246-1) BB-B6200 RCA INT-1087

1 Yeah I got up this morning : I was feeling awful bad
2 I was thinking about the good time mama : mmm Lord me and my baby once have had
3 Babe I woke up this morning : I looked down the road
4 I think I heard my wild cow mama : when she begin to low
5 If you see my wild cow buddy : please tell her [hurry, come back] home
6 Lord I ain't had no milk and butter : since my wild cow been gone
7 I'm going to the bottom : just to hear my wild cow moan
8 If she moans so lonesome : I'm going to bring my wild cow home
9 My wild cow got a horn : just long as your right arm
10 She yields so much milk and butter : I hate to see my wild cow leave home
11 It take a ??? to roll : and a rocking chair to rock
12 The girl I'm loving : she talk that old baby-talk
13 Lord I don't feel welcome : I say nowhere I go
14 Lord I said good girl I'm loving : she done drove me away from her door
15 You can read out your hymn book : you got your Bible too
16 Fall down on your knees : ask the good Lord to help you
17 Because you going to need : you going to need my help some day
18 You won't quit your running around woman : please quit your lowdown ways
19 Lord I went home at night : I looked out my door
20 There some other man had my wild cow : she could low
21 If you see my wild cow : please drive her back home
22 Lord I ain't had no milk and butter : since he stole my wild cow and gone
23 Now good morning : blues how do you do
24 I cried all night long Lordy : and I can't get along with you

WillJ 8   Williams, Joe

    title: I Know You Gonna Miss Me
    place and date: Aurora, Ill., 5 May 1937
    record numbers: (07661-1) BB-B7022 RCA INT-1087

1 Well I beg you baby : baby so long
2 Know you're going to miss me : when I'm dead and gone
3 Well I know she going to miss me : well when I'm dead and gone
4 I know you going to miss me baby : *oh poor boy will be* ???
5 When you hear me singing : mama this old lonesome song
6 Know you going to miss poor Joe : when I'm dead and gone
7 Went down to the station : went out on the track
8 Saw my baby leaving : couldn't call her back
9 Well I know that woman going to miss me : well when I'm dead and gone
10 I know you going to miss me baby : count the days I'm gone
11 Cried last night baby : all night before
12 Stop my way of living : and I won't have to cry no more
13 When I get down and out : sing this lonesome song
14 Swear you going to miss me woman : when I'm dead and gone
15 Cried last night mama : cried all night before
16 Going back home to my baby : won't have to cry no more

WillJ   9   Williams, Joe

       title: Rootin' Ground Hog
       place and date: Aurora, Ill., 5 May 1937
       record numbers: (07662-1) BB-B7065 RCA INT-1087

1 Well I'm a rooting ground hog : and I roots both
    nights and days
2 I want some good-looking mama to come here now :
    please drive these blues away
3 I went home last night babe : just about the break
    of day
4 I did grab the pillow : where my baby used to lay
5 I'm a rooting ground hog : *if I do ??? day*
6 Well look for poor Joe down north : ooo well I will
    be so far away
7 I'm a rooting ground hog : and I roots everywhere I
    go
8 I'm trying to keep my woman taking my loving :
    carrying it out handing it to Mr so-and-so
9 Let me tell you now women : just before I go
10 Give me back my money : I'll catch the train and go
11 I'm a rooting ground hog : and I root everywhere I
    go
12 Well my baby had the nerve to tell me : that she
    didn't want me no more
13 I'm a-leaving Chicago : ain't going to leave my baby
    no more
14 I'm that good rooting ground hog : I got a home
    anywhere I go
15 I woke up this morning : I looked down the line
16 Couldn't hear nothing : but my babe's train crying

WillJ   10   Williams, Joe

       title: Brother James
       place and date: Aurora, Ill., 5 May 1937
       record numbers: (07663-1) BB-B7022 RCA INT-1087

1 Brother James went out riding : riding in that
    twenty-nine Ford
2 That poor man was drinking bad whiskey : ooo well
    boys he sure going to lose his soul
3 Lord I went out in Greenville : looked down in
    brother James' face
4 I says sleep on brother James : I'll meet you
    Resurrection Day
5 Lord brother James died under surgery : and he
    didn't have the time to pray
6 I said goodbye brother James : ooo well I'll meet
    you Resurrection Day
7 Now he love sister Lottie : trying to save her
    wicked soul
8 She ain't going to drink no more whiskey : ooo well
    boys going to ride no twenty-nine Ford
9 I went to the graveyard : and I peeped down in
    brother James' face
10 Says you know you died drunk brother James : and you
    didn't have no time to pray
11 Farewell brother James : hope we will meet some day
12 I will be at the *official table* : ooo well when
    they send brother James *my way*

WillJ   11   Williams, Joe

       title: I Won't Be in Hard Luck No More
       place and date: Aurora, Ill., 5 May 1937
       record numbers: (07664-1) BB-B7065 RCA INT-1087

1 I said goodbye baby : oh yes I got to go
2 I don't want to be wearing mustache : ooo well
    mistreated for Mr so-and-so
3 I say the hard luck and trouble : every place I go
4 I believe somebody put bad luck on me : ooo well I
    believe now it's time to go
5 I had money baby : I even had friends for miles
    around

WillJ   11   Williams, Joe

6 Well all the money gone : ooo well and my friends
    cannot be found
7 I started down : I started down in Polack Town
8 Seem like the snitches and the police babe : trying
    to tear poor Joe's reputation down
9 Now you can hear me when I'm down : be the same way
    when I rise
10 I got a gal in East St Louis : she lives in Polack
    Town

WillJ   12   Williams, Joe

       title: Crawlin' King Snake
       place and date: Chicago, 27 Mar. 1941
       record numbers: (053989-2) BB-B8738 RCA INT-1087

1 Yes I'm a crawling king snake : baby I'm going to
    ??? all around your door
2 You had the nerve to tell me : ooo well well she
    didn't want me no more
3 You couldn't see me baby : passing by
4 Mama be your crawling king snake : till the day I
    die
5 I'm going to be your crawling king snake : I'm
    ???ing all around your door
6 You had the nerve to tell me : ooo well well you
    didn't want poor Joey no more
7 You couldn't see me baby : now when I was walking by
8 Might be your crawling king snake : mama if I have
    to die
9 I'm going back to Memphis : if I have to walk
10 I ain't got nobody in Chicago : talk that old
    baby-talk
11 Now I'm going back to St Louis : I'm going to sit
    right down
12 I'm going to throw my poison : on every pretty woman
    in town

WillJ   13   Williams, Joe

       title: I'm Getting Wild About Her
       place and date: Chicago, 27 Mar. 1941
       record numbers: (053990-1) BB-B8774 BC-6

1 Good morning judge : he done lowered the fine
2 Tell the man : about this stuff of mine
3 Baby : want to keep your daddy from crying
4 Save me a little more : of that stuff of mine
5 Now baby : don't be so fast
6 If you can't shimmy : shake your yas yas yas
7 I get drunk : walk streets all night
8 All you got to do : is treat your daddy right
9 All I want : is my regular right
10 *Treat me in the days* : and my loving every night
11 The lawyer told the judge : can you lower his fine
12 Tell the man : about the stuff of mine
13 Yeah baby : don't you be so rough
14 Daddy wild : about my heavy stuff

WillJ   14   Williams, Joe

       title: Peach Orchard Mama
       place and date: Chicago, 27 Mar. 1941
       record numbers: (053991-1) BB-B8774 RCA INT-1087

1 Peach orchard mama : you swore wasn't nobody going
    to use your peaches but me
2 Well you want Joe Williams to work in your orchard :
    well and I'll keep your orchard clean
3 You done got me to the place : I hate to see that
    evening sun go down
4 Well when I get up in the morning : ooo well peach
    orchard man she's on my mind

WillJ 14   Williams, Joe

5 Got a man to buy your groceries : and another joker
     to pay your rent
6 Well you got me working in your orchard : ooo well
     well and bring you every cent
7 Sometime she make me happy : then again she make me
     cry
8 Ever again I want a peach orchard mama : ooo well
     well wish to God that you would die

WillJ 15   Williams, Joe

       title: Meet Me Around the Corner
       place and date: Chicago, 27 Mar. 1941
       record numbers: (053992-1R) BB-B8738 RCA
         INT-1087

1 Meet me around the corner baby : bring my boots and
     shoes
2 My best woman done quit me : and I ain't got no time
     to lose
3 Now she low and she squatty : she right down on the
     ground
4 Every time she wobbles : she make my love came down
5 Lord the woman I'm loving : sleeping in her *ray*
6 Lord the one I hate : I can meet her every day
7 Please : don't give my baby no job
8 She's a married woman : and I don't allow her to
     work too hard
9 What you going to do : when they take your man to
     the war
10 Have to drink muddy water : sleep in a hollow log
11 Early one morning : just about the break of day
12 I hugged the pillow : where my baby used to lay
13 She ain't [very] good-looking : she got two teeth
     crowned with gold
14 Got a lien on her body : got a mortgage on her soul

WillJ 16   Williams, Joe

       title: Please Don't Go
       place and date: Chicago, 12 Dec. 1941
       record numbers: (070484-1) BB-B8969 RCA
         INT-1087

1 Now baby please don't go : baby please don't go
2 Baby please don't go back to New Orleans : you know
     I love you so
3 Turn your lamp down low : turn your lamp down low
4 Turn your lamp down low now baby all night long :
     baby please don't go
5 I believe another man done gone : I believe another
     man done gone
6 He left the county farm : he got them shackles on
7 Baby please don't go : baby please don't go
8 Baby please don't go back to New Orleans : get your
     cold ice cream
9 Before I'll be your dog : before I'll be your dog
10 I'll get you way down here : I'll make you walk a
     log
11 You got me way down here : you got me way down here
12 You got me way down here by Rolling Fork : you treat
     me like a dog
13 Don't call my name : don't call my name
14 Don't call my name you got me way down here :
     wearing the ball and chain

WillJ 17   Williams, Joe

       title: Highway 49
       place and date: Chicago, 12 Dec. 1941
       record numbers: (070485-1) BB-B9025 RBF RF-11

1 Well I'm going to get up in the morning : get to
     Highway Forty-Nine

WillJ 17   Williams, Joe

2 Well *about* my sweet woman : ooo well well she
     don't pay poor Joey no mind
3 Well if you ever had the blues : get to Highway
     Forty-Nine
4 Well *about* sweet woman : ooo well boys she trying
     to throw poor Joey down
5 [I'm going to wake, well I'm going to get] in the
     morning : I believe I'll dust my bed
6 Going down the Highway Forty-Nine : ooo well boys I
     be rocking to my head
7 Blues this morning : I'll be rolling in Jackson town
8 Lord I'm tired of laying around : ooo well boys on
     Highway Forty-Nine

WillJ 18   Williams, Joe

       title: Someday Baby
       place and date: Chicago, 12 Dec. 1941
       record numbers: (070486-1) BB-B9025 RBF RF-11

1 Don't care where you go : how long you stay
2 Lord it's good-time females : bring you back some
     day
3 Ain't but the one thing Sonny Boy : get Joey in the
     blues
4 I got on : my last pair of shoes
5 Yes I keep on betting : but the dice won't pass
6 You going to leave Chicago running : running most
     too fast
7 I liked everybody : in your neighborhood
8 You a no-good woman : you don't mean me no good
9 You can steal my chickens boy : you sure can't make
     them lay
10 You can steal my best woman : but you sure can't
     make her stay

WillJ 19   Williams, Joe

       title: Break 'Em On Down
       place and date: Chicago, 12 Dec. 1941
       record numbers: (070487-1) BB-B8969 BC-21

1 Yes I'm a gambling man : still gambling yet
2 Don't never get too rough boy : *one kill* won't lay
     them dead
3 Done got funny baby : funny as it can be
4 If you raise any kids : they all got to look like me
5 Take your sweet potato : *raise them at your home*
6 If you want a good woman : get you one that long and
     tall
7 Raised in the country : first in town
8 Your *good time* : all is mine
9 Breaking them down : all I crave
10 Breaking them down : might take me to my grave
11 Mama went to town : papa ain't here
12 Take them down boys : because you know this stuff is
     here

WillK 1   Williams, Joe

       title: I Want It Awful Bad
       place and date: Memphis, c. 24 Sept. 1929
       record numbers: (M-195-) Vo-1457 Rt RL-321

1 You get mad : someone call your name
2 You never did ??? : get that thing
3 You wore your dresses : above your knees
4 You sell your jelly : to who you please
5 I got something to ask you : I done got scared
6 I got to wait now : before I go to bed
7 I called you this morning : about half past one
8 You told me : that you was done
9 I called you this morning : about half past five
10 You turned over : cried like a child

WillK 1   Williams, Joe

11 I called you this morning : about half past six
12 You told me : you got it fixed
13 I got something to ask you : don't you get mad
14 I want you to give me something : I ain't never had
15 Look pretty mama : what you done done
16 You squeezed my lemon : caused my juice to run

WillK 2   Williams, Joe

    title: Mr. Devil Blues
    place and date: Memphis, c. 24 Sept. 1929
    record numbers: (M-196-) Vo-1457 Rt RL-321

1 Good morning Mr devil : I come here to chain you
  down
2 Every time I move : you got my rider down
3 You's a mean old devil : cause me to weep and moan
4 Cause me to leave my family : and my happy home
5 I brought my chain : to lock it around your waist
6 I don't care woman : who gets all in my way
7 I wouldn't have been here : had not been for you
8 Now you got me here now : this old way you do
9 I was at home : doing very well
10 Now you got me here now : and I'm catching hell
11 Now look Mr devil : see what you done done
12 You done wrecked my family : caused me to leave a
  happy home
13 I'm going to write a letter now : going to mail it
  in the air
14 I'm going to ask Dr Jesus : if the devil ever been
  there

WillK 3   Williams, Joe

    title: Get Your Head Trimmed Down
    place and date: Aurora, Ill., 17 June 1938
    record numbers: (020854-1) BB-B7719 RCA INT-1175

1 The wind begin to blow : and my baby begin to knock
  on my door
2 Yes you keep fooling around downtown : you going to
  get your head trimmed down
3 I know you got men friends : baby when I drive from
  your door
4 Because you keep on running around : you going to
  get your head trimmed down
5 Now it ain't no use you fooling around : trying to
  take that other woman's man
6 Well now you keep on fooling around : you going to
  get your head trimmed down
7 Now when I left *Granville* : I was on my way back
  to *Shoetown* Road
8 Yes I know you going to miss me baby : from knocking
  on your door
9 Now you begin to run from hand to hand : and you
  begin to run around
10 Well now you keep on running around baby : you going
  to get your head trimmed down

WillK 4   Williams, Joe

    title: Peach Orchard Mama
    place and date: Aurora, Ill., 17 June 1938
    record numbers: (020855-1) BB-B7770 RCA INT-1175

1 Peach orchard mama : you swore no one get your fruit
  but me
2 Whilst I'm working in your orchard : keeping your
  orchard free
3 You got a man to buy your groceries : another
  [joker, man] to pay your rent
4 Whilst ??? Sonny Boy working in your orchard :
  giving you every cent

WillK 4   Williams, Joe

5 Now you done got me so : I hate to see that evening
  sun go down
6 I wake up in the morning : peach orchard woman on my
  mind
7 Sometimes you make me happy : sometimes you make me
  cry
8 Now peach orchard mama since you been in trouble :
  you wish to God that I would die

WillS 1   Williamson, Sonny Boy

    title: Skinny Woman
    place and date: Aurora, Ill., 5 May 1937
    record numbers: (07654-) BB-B7012 BC-20

1 Lord I don't want no skinny woman : I want a a woman
  with a-plenty of meat
2 Now we can roll all night long : this woman won't
  have to stop and eat
3 Lord I've got so many women : that I I really don't
  know who I love
4 Now it seems like the girl I been crazy for :
  slipped away to the good Lord above
5 Lord I have the blues in the morning : blues is the
  first thing when I lay down at night
6 Now that's the reason my baby worries me : my baby
  she don't treat me right
7 Oh Lord ah she's gone she's gone : she's forever be
  on my mind
8 Now she was a sweet little woman : she just wouldn't
  be loving and kind

WillS 2   Williamson, Sonny Boy

    title: Collector Man Blues
    place and date: Aurora, Ill., 11 Nov. 1937
    record numbers: (016521-) BB-B7428 BC-3

1 Now go open the door : here comes the collector man
2 Well you can tell him I said come back tomorrow :
  because Sonny Boy ain't got a doggone thing
3 Tell him that I ain't got no money : now and he know
  I trying to ???
4 Well you tell him a man ain't got no money : can't
  hardly find a place to stand
5 Tell him but some day I'll have some money : now I
  want everybody to watch and see
6 Well now tell him that it's hard : to keep down you
  know a real good man like me
7 Tell him I know I'm down now : now but I won't be
  down always
8 Well now you can tell him watch and see old Sonny
  Boy getting some money : oh Lord know it's some of
  these days

WillS 3   Williamson, Sonny Boy

    title: Early in the Morning
    place and date: Aurora, Ill., 11 Nov. 1937
    record numbers: (016524-) BB-B7302 RCA INT-1175

1 Lord when a little girl become twelve years old :
  begin to think she's grown
2 Say you can never : catch that kind of little girl
  at home
3 But you have to go down early in the morning : baby
  about the break of day
4 Now you ought to see me grab the pillows : where my
  baby used to lay
5 Well I got a new woman : her name is Miss Katy
6 She told me to come to her house this morning : I
  got there about half past eight
7 I said look a-here woman : you fool too many men

8 I can't never come to see you in the evening : now I
   have to come to see you when I can
9 Well I said look a-here woman : I ain't going to
   fool around with you no more
10 I know you don't love me : you wild about Mr
   so-and-so

WillS 4   Williamson, Sonny Boy

        title: Project Highway
        place and date: Aurora, Ill., 11 Nov. 1937
        record numbers: (016525-) BB-B7302 RCA INT-1175

1 Well well well I've got to get some money : I wants
   to buy a V-Eight Ford
2 Well well I wants to ride this new highway : ooo
   that the project just completed in a week ago
3 Well I got to ride this new highway : Lord and I'm
   going to cross the Gulf of Mexico
4 Well well well then I ain't going to stop riding :
   well until I park in front of my baby's door
5 Well when my baby come out and see me : I know she's
   going to jump and shout
6 Well well well if that don't draw a crowd : ooo
   people going to know what all this racket about
7 Now when people gather around : now in front of my
   baby's door
8 Well well then I'm going to tell them don't get
   excited : ooo same ??? *bit* I was singing about
   before

WillS 5   Williamson, Sonny Boy

        title: Moonshine
        place and date: Aurora, Ill., 13 Mar. 1938
        record numbers: (020113-1) BB-B7603 RCA LPV-518

1 Now and it's moonshine : moonshine do harm to many
   men
2 Now that is the reason why : you ain't got to
   believe I'll make a change
3 Now moonshine will make you shoot dice : make a-you
   want to sing
4 Now when you go home : you can't change your wild
   rice
5 You been drinking moonshine : moonshine do harm to
   many men
6 Now that is the reason why : I'm I'll believe I'll
   make a change
7 Now moonshine will make you think : that the
   policeman is really delivery boy
8 Moonshine will make you think : that shoe polish is
   really children's play-toy
9 Now moonshine will make you go home : lay down
   across your bed
10 And your wife try to talk with you : you say you
   didn't hear a word she said
11 Now moonshine will make you just drunk : walk out in
   the street
12 Moonshine will make you curse out : most anybody you
   meet

WillS 6   Williamson, Sonny Boy

        title: Miss Louisa Blues
        place and date: Aurora, Ill., 13 Mar. 1938
        record numbers: (020114-) BB-B7576 RBF RF-14

1 Now ever since Louisa you been gone : my life don't
   seem the same
2 Now you know it really breaks my heart : to hear
   anybody call Miss Louisa's name
3 Now Miss Louisa she mistreated me : and she drove me
   from her door

4 Now that will be all right : Louisa you will have to
   reap just what you sow
5 Now Louisa you know : I have been Lord the very best
   that I could
6 Now listen if you don't treat me no better : Lord I
   sure do wish you would
7 Now but that will be all right : Louisa you will
   come back home some day
8 Now but I'm scared that when you get back : Louisa
   you ain't going to have no place to stay

WillS 7   Williamson, Sonny Boy

        title: Down South
        place and date: Aurora, Ill., 13 Mar. 1938
        record numbers: (020117-1) BB-B7665 RCA LPV-518

1 Lord I'm going back down south : man where the
   weather suits my clothes
2 Now I done fooled around in Chicago : and I done
   almost froze
3 Lord my baby my baby : she don't treat me good no
   more
4 Now I know the reason she don't love me : she's wild
   about Mr so-and-so
5 Now and I know my baby : and I know Miss Mary's
   going to scream now
6 Because my baby she didn't want me : to come way
   back up here nohow

WillS 8   Williamson, Sonny Boy

        title: Until My Love Come Down
        place and date: Aurora, Ill., 13 Mar. 1938
        record numbers: (020119-) BB-B7576 RBF RF-14

1 Now you got fruit on your tree : lemons on your
   shelf
2 But you know loving mama : that you can't squeeze
   them all yourself
3 Now I said please let me be your lemon-squeezer :
   now while I'm in your lonesome town
4 Now if you let me be your lemon-squeezer : Lord
   until my love comes down
5 Now it makes no difference baby : what your mama
   don't allow
6 Come on let me squeeze your lemon baby : I mean
   anyhow
7 I like your apples on your tree : I'm crazy about
   your peaches too
8 I'm crazy about your fruit baby : because you know
   just how to do
9 Now and it ain't but the one thing : baby now that
   it really makes me cry
10 I asked you about your lemons : baby and you ups and
   tells me a lie

WillS 9   Williamson, Sonny Boy

        title: Honey Bee Blues
        place and date: Aurora, Ill., 17 June 1938
        record numbers: (020842-1) BB-B7707 RCA INT-1088

1 I want you to come on baby : now and take a walk
   with me
2 Well then I assure you there's won't nothing bother
   you : I'll be your little honeybee
3 I will make you honey in the morning : now I will
   make you honey in the night
4 Now then I'll make you honey three times a day :
   baby if you would just treat me right
5 Well we will take a walk out in the park : now and
   sit down under some little shady tree

6 Well now you said that I was your baby : and that I
   could be your little honeybee
7 I want to hold you in my arms : baby and I want you
   to hug me tight
8 Now because you said that I was your little honeybee
   : and I could make your honey just right

WillS 10   Williamson, Sonny Boy

   title: Whiskey Headed Blues
   place and date: Aurora, Ill., 17 June 1938
   record numbers: (020844-1) BB-B7707 RCA INT-1088

1 Now you's a whiskey-headed woman : now and you stay
   drunk all the time
2 Now if you don't stop drinking : now I believe you
   going to lose your mind
3 Well now every time I see you : you's at some
   whiskey joint
4 Standing at the back door : asking for another half
   a pint
5 Because you's a whiskey-headed woman : now and you
   stay drunk all the time
6 Now if you don't stop drinking : I believe you going
   to go stone blind
7 Well now and I took you out of the street baby :
   when you didn't have no place to lay
8 You ain't acting nothing but a fool : dogging me
   around this a-way
9 Well now every time I meet you baby : you walking up
   and down the street
10 You grinning laughing and talking : with most every
   man you meet

WillS 11   Williamson, Sonny Boy

   title: Lord, Oh Lord Blues
   place and date: Aurora, Ill., 17 June 1938
   record numbers: (020845-1) BB-B7847 RCA INT-1088

1 Now I'm going away baby : just to wear you off my
   mind
2 Now and you keep me bothered : worried all the time
3 Now and sometimes I feel : like I'm going going away
   to stay
4 Well I get to thinking about my baby : I just as
   swear and I can't stay away
5 Now I want you to tell me baby : baby just what's
   getting wrong with you
6 Now and you don't treat me : nothing baby like you
   used to do

WillS 12   Williamson, Sonny Boy

   title: You Give an Account
   place and date: Aurora, Ill., 17 June 1938
   record numbers: (020846-) BB-B7756 BC-3

1 I'm going to tell you something : baby you can't do
2 You better take it kind of easy : I've got my eyes
   on you
3 If you got a good woman : and she won't treat you
   right
4 You beat her three times a day : and whip her a
   little at night
5 Now Mr depot agent : don't you make me cry
6 Did my baby stop here : did she keep on by
7 Now I want all you people : to gather around
8 My baby done left me : treat me like a hound
9 I told her I'd buy her a Chevrolet : say but she
   wanted a V-Eight Ford
10 She say she wanted something : would beat us all on
   the road
11 Now I waved my hands : she wouldn't pay me no mind

12 Way out on my door : she made a loving sign

WillS 13   Williamson, Sonny Boy

   title: Shannon Street Blues
   place and date: Aurora, Ill., 17 June 1938
   record numbers: (020847-1) BB-B7847 RCA INT-1088

1 I went down on Shannon Street : now to buy me some
   alcohol
2 I told them to fill it half full of water : but they
   didn't put in a drop at all
3 So I drunk my straight whiskey : Lord I staggered on
   up the street
4 Now but my head got so heavy : that my eyes couldn't
   even give a peep
5 Lady tells me papa papa : well you ain't no good at
   all
6 Now she say you don't make me happy : so long as you
   fool with this alcohol
7 Sometimes I tell her oh : lady this alcohol is
   killing me
8 Well now they told me if I didn't quit drinking : in
   some lonesome cemetery I would be
9 I said lazy baby won't you go riding : can I take
   you riding with me in my car
10 She said Sonny Boy I'm scared if you get a drink of
   whiskey : and I'm scared that we won't ride very
   far

WillS 14   Williamson, Sonny Boy

   title: You've Been Foolin' Round Town
   place and date: Aurora, Ill., 17 June 1938
   record numbers: (020848-1) BB-B7756 RCA INT-1088

1 I'm going to tell you something : keep it to
   yourself
2 Don't tell your kid-man : and nobody else
3 Told her come on go out : come go and get a quart of
   wine
4 You told me yeah : you think that was just fine
5 Well I will tell you one thing baby : that I can't
   do
6 I can't love you : and be your dog too
7 Well a-here's my hand : I'll mind you like a child
8 Can't I be : you man awhile
9 Well I got something to tell you : I ain't going to
   tell you no more
10 About fooling around : with Mr so-and-so
11 Now tell me baby : what you want me to do
12 Think I can love you : and be your dog too
13 Well fare you well baby : I ain't going to have no
   more to say
14 Marry Mr so-and-so : you can have your way

WillS 15   Williamson, Sonny Boy

   title: Deep Down in the Ground
   place and date: Aurora, Ill., 17 June 1938
   record numbers: (020849-1) BB-B7805 RCA INT-1088

1 You hear that rumbling : deep down in the ground
2 Now it must be the devil : you know turning my
   womens around
3 Stack of dollars : just as high as I am tall
4 Now if you be my baby : mama you can have them all
5 She's a great big woman : head right full of hair
6 I call her tailor-made : but them people they don't
   allow me there
7 Now here's my hand : if I never see you anymore
8 Well now I'm going to leave you alone : to go with
   your Mr so-and-so
9 Tell me baby : baby where did you stay last night

WillS 15   Williamson, Sonny Boy

10 Now with your hair all tangled : and your clothes
    ain't fitting you right

WillS 16   Williamson, Sonny Boy

        title: Number Five Blues
        place and date: Aurora, Ill., 17 Dec. 1938
        record numbers: (030848-1R) BB-B8010 RCA INT-108

1   Number Five Number Five : please bring my baby back
    to me
2   Now you's the meanest old train : Number Five that I
    ever seen
3   Now when my baby left me : my baby wouldn't even
    wave her hand
4   Well I know the reason she left me : because she was
    wild about some other man
5   Woman that will be all right : I know my baby ain't
    going to stay away
6   Well now she forever stays on my mind : people she
    the only woman I crave
7   Lord and I just looked on the almanac : Lord just to
    see when your birthday was going to be
8   Now then I believe that you must have been born in
    ??? : because you got changing ways with me
9   Now fare you well : baby yes I'm going away
10 Well I know you didn't love me : now I'm going to
    find me some other place to stay

WillS 17   Williamson, Sonny Boy

        title: Christmas Morning Blues
        place and date: Aurora, Ill., 17 Dec. 1938
        record numbers: (030849-1) BB-B8094 RCA INT-1088

1   Well it was on one Christmas morning : *T-bird's*
    Christmas coming back again
2   Well now I'm trying to hide my little woman : to
    keep her from running around with these other men
3   Now Santa Claus : I want you to bring my baby a lot
    of toys
4   Now I know my baby wants to have fun : now with
    these other little girls and boys
5   Santa Claus Santa Claus : can I get you to
    understand
6   Now that I want you to bring my baby one of these
    radios : and two or three of them little electric
    fans
7   I want Santa Claus to bring my baby one of these
    coats : I mean with that long fur hanging down
8   Now then I want her to be looking good : Lord when I
    drop by in her town
9   Now Santa Claus : Santa Claus can't you hear my
    lonesome cry
10 Well now be sure to do what I told you : Santa Claus
    before I tell you goodbye

WillS 18   Williamson, Sonny Boy

        title: Susie-Q
        place and date: Aurora, Ill., 17 Dec. 1938
        record numbers: (030850-1) BB-B7995 RCA INT-1088

1   Well now I knowed a family : lived down in the
    avenue
2   Old man Mose : and sister Sue
3   Well now I knowed the man : by the name of old man
    Mose
4   He got so happy : pull off all his clothes
5   Well I knowed a lady : by the name of sister Kate
6   Pulled off her clothes : in front of her front gate
7   Crying you step one step : then mess all around
8   You look up : then you look down

WillS 18   Williamson, Sonny Boy

9   Well now I know a girl : by the name of sister
    Louise
10 She jumped up : and danced with who she pleased
11 Now look a-here baby : now tell me what you going to
    do
12 You can't marry me : and somebody else too

WillS 19   Williamson, Sonny Boy

        title: Blue Bird Blues--Part 1
        place and date: Aurora, Ill., 17 Dec. 1938
        record numbers: (030851-1) BB-B7979 RCA INT-1088

1   Lord I wonder where is my bluebird : wonder where is
    my bluebird gone
2   Now and she left me this morning : people and I been
    looking for her all day long
3   Now my bluebird left me the other day : people and I
    ain't seen her since
4   Now then I believe she gone to Washington : you know
    to visit the president
5   Now if my bluebird don't come back : wonder what am
    I going to do
6   Now if my bluebird continue on to stay : I believe
    I'll move to Washington too
7   Now when my bluebird left : she put a note up in my
    door
8   Now she said I'm going to Washington : Sonny Boy and
    I don't want you no more
9   Oh now but that will be all right : maybe my
    bluebird will change her mind
10 Now because a good bluebird now babe : peoples I
    just do swear they's hard to find

WillS 20   Williamson, Sonny Boy

        title: Little Girl Blues
        place and date: Aurora, Ill., 17 Dec. 1938
        record numbers: (030852-1) BB-B8010 RCA INT-1088

1   Little girl little girl : I got something I want to
    say to you
2   Now it ain't none of your bad treatment : I just
    want to warn you about the old way you do
3   You just my little girl : and I love to hold you in
    my arms
4   Now and if you think about me baby : I swear you
    can't do nothing wrong
5   Tell me baby : baby who can your little man be
6   Lord I wouldn't keep on worrying : but I wonder if
    there any chance for me
7   Think about me when I'm gone : little girl think
    about me in your sleep
8   Well I think about how you used to love me : little
    girl nobody in this world but me
9   But that's all right : little girl trouble ain't
    going to last always
10 Well now you can treat me like a dog : but you'll be
    sorry you treated me this a-way
11 Fare you well : little girl if I never see you
    anymore
12 Well I said that I always love you : and Sonny Boy
    don't care where you go

WillS 21   Williamson, Sonny Boy

        title: Low Down Ways
        place and date: Aurora, Ill., 17 Dec. 1938
        record numbers: (030853-1) BB-B7979 RCA INT-1088

1   Now listen little baby : do you think I'm going to
    be your fool
2   I mean what you think baby : you want Sonny Boy to
    be your mule

3 Every time I meet you baby : walking up and down the street
4 You walk by me smiling : act like you don't want to speak
5 But *honest* little girl : I got tired of your lowdown dirty ways
6 Well now drinking whiskey and running around : little girl that's all you crave
7 Well then I give you my money : baby and you left me cold in hand
8 You took my money : you know you started to raising sand
9 You started to hitting bootlegging joint : and every whiskeyhouse you know
10 Riding up and down the street : you know with Mr so-and-so
11 Well now and I was going to buy you a ??? : I was going to buy you a Packard too
12 I was going to buy you a Cadillac : you know just to try to get along with you
13 I was going down to the jewelry store : and I was going to buy you a diamond ring
14 But now you won't treat me nice : and I ain't going to buy you a doggone thing
15 When I left my mother told me one thing : you know my father said the same
16 You running around with this little girl : son and that going to change your name
17 But I won't pay them no mind : but I continue to drink
18 But I don't never sit down one time : you know and just sit and think
19 But I got tired : of this little girl's lowdown dirty ways
20 Now when I leave her this time : I swear I'm going away to stay

WillS 22   Williamson, Sonny Boy

title: Goodbye Red
place and date: Aurora, Ill., 17 Dec. 1938
record numbers: (030854-1) BB-B7995 RCA INT-1088

1 Well goodbye Red : now ain't going to cry
2 Well I ain't going to frown : wouldn't tell you no lie
3 Well my little Red : she just don't know
4 Well now she say she love me : she wild about Mr so-and-so
5 Well I ain't going to worry : about the way you do
6 Well the way you treat me : coming back home to you
7 Well I ain't going to frown : I ain't going to make no noise
8 Well I ain't going to bring no *help* : and none of these ??? *toys*
9 Well I waved my hand : Red shook her head
10 Well I'm sick and tired : I reckon I'm going to bed
11 Now tell me Red : what you want me to do
12 Now do you think I can love you : and be your little dog too
13 Well after a while : be all over now
14 Now because didn't have nobody : to raise no sand nohow

WillS 23   Williamson, Sonny Boy

title: The Right Kind of Life
place and date: Aurora, Ill., 17 Dec. 1938
record numbers: (030855-1) BB-B8034 RCA INT-1088

1 Now I'm only twenty-four : I just declare I been married twice
2 Well now you people know by that : Lord that I ain't been living the right kind of life

3 Now my mother often sit down and talked with me : talked with me about being so wild
4 Well then she said I'm scared that women and whiskey : is going to be the ruin of my only child
5 Oh you know how boys and girls is nowadays : they won't pay their mother no mind
6 Well and when they go out and stay all night long : your mother's standing in her back door crying
7 Well but some day : some day people I'm going to change my mind
8 Well now I'm going to stop running at women : and staying drunk all the time
9 Oh now ain't it hard to have a home : a home and you can't go there no more
10 Now when this little woman that you been loving : have fell in love with Mr so-and-so

WillS 24   Williamson, Sonny Boy

title: Insurance Man Blues
place and date: Aurora, Ill., 17 Dec. 1938
record numbers: (030856-1) BB-B8034 RCA INT-1088

1 Every Monday morning : people the insurance man knocking on my door
2 Well now I tell him to come back on a Tuesday : because Sonny Boy haven't made no money you know
3 He said yeah but you haven't paid your insurance in two or three weeks : said Sonny Boy and your insurance have done ???
4 He said if you don't pay it by next Wednesday : I reckon I'll have to let your insurance ???
5 I said insurance man please don't turn me out : Lord and I ain't got nobody to bury me
6 Well now I said if you won't bury me : they'll throw my body in the deep blue sea
7 I say you know how times is nowadays : can't no one man find a job
8 I said I can't even take care of my wife and baby : and I'm mighty near to letting my family starve
9 I said please give me two more weeks : insurance man please do that for me
10 Well I say I don't live up north : my home is back down in Tennessee

WillS 25   Williamson, Sonny Boy

title: Rainy Day Blues
place and date: Aurora, Ill., 17 Dec. 1938
record numbers: (030857-1) BB-B8094 RCA INT-1088

1 Rainy day rainy day : you ought to hear my baby sing the blues
2 Now and she said she just walking around : just to tell these strange people the news
3 Now what's the use of loving : people and I don't see why I should
4 Now and you know the woman I'm loving : Lord and she don't mean me no good
5 Now but that will be all right now : my bad luck ain't going to last always
6 Now just because I'm down and out now : I'm going to see some old lucky day
7 Take care of my wife and my baby : tell them that I'll be back home some day
8 Now tell her that she ain't acting nothing but a fool : dogging me around this way
9 Lord sometime I go out walking : people go out [walking, talking] to myself
10 Now because my baby bes on my mind : and I don't be thinking about nobody else
11 Now I'm just as sure : just as sure as one and one is two
12 Now when I get my money : babe I'm going to be ???ing just like you

WillS 26   Williamson, Sonny Boy

    title: Bad Luck Blues
    place and date: Chicago, 21 July 1939
    record numbers: (040525-) BB-B8265 BC-3

1 Now did you hear about this bad luck : the bad luck
   happened just about six months ago
2 Now my cousin *Martin* got shot down : just as he
   was walking out the door
3 Now and he said please Mr : said please don't shoot
   me no more
4 He said because my breath is getting short : and my
   heart is beating awful slow
5 And *Martin* said I know I got some friends : I want
   someone to go and get my mother please
6 Said maybe she can help me with my troubles : people
   I'm in so much misery
7 And he said I hate to go leave my mother and father
   : I hate to go and leave my cousin Sonny Boy ???
8 Now but tell them if they be good they come to see
   me : people on Resurrection Day

WillS 27   Williamson, Sonny Boy

    title: T. B. Blues
    place and date: Chicago, 21 July 1939
    record numbers: (040532-) BB-B8333 BC-20

1 Now but ooh : T B's is killing me
2 Now I want my body buried : way down in Jackson
   Tennessee
3 Now when I was up on my feet : now I couldn't even
   walk down the street
4 For the women looking at me : from my head to my
   feet
5 I ain't going to buy you no more pretty dresses : I
   ain't going to even buy you no diamond rings
6 And I'm going to sell my V-Eight Ford : because I
   don't want a doggone thing
7 Well now my mother she said one thing : you know my
   father said the same
8 You keep on fooling around : Sonny Boy they going to
   change your name
9 Well now here I am here sick baby : you know and I'm
   I'm laying here in my bed
10 And now even won't none of my friends : come and
   even rub my aching head

WillS 28   Williamson, Sonny Boy

    title: Joe Louis and John Henry
    place and date: Chicago, 21 July 1939
    record numbers: (040535-) BB-B8403 BC-3

1 Well well I was sitting in Madison Square Gardens :
   now to just watch the big fight come through
2 Well well the right and left that Joe Louis was
   using : ooo well man give John Henry Louis' head
   the blues
3 Well that night I didn't have but fifty cents : I
   was in Jackson whooping with them women and men
4 Well well and I bet my fifty cents on Joe : ooo well
   in no time I won my fifty cents back again

WillS 29   Williamson, Sonny Boy

    title: Train Fare Blues
    place and date: Chicago, 17 May 1940
    record numbers: (049198-) BB-B8610 BC-20

1 Mama all that I want : Lord is just my train fare
   home
2 Well now I ain't got nobody to love me : out here in
   this great big old world alone

WillS 29   Williamson, Sonny Boy

3 Now baby if'n you wouldn't write me : look like you
   would send me a telegram
4 Look like I would kind of run across your mind :
   baby you would want to know just where I am
5 Now but I know you don't love me : baby you don't
   love me no more
6 I know the reason you don't love woman : because you
   is crazy about Mr so-and-so
7 Now it was a lowdown fireman : and that must have
   been a dirty engineer
8 Lord and they sure did treat me mean : because they
   taking my babe away from here

WillS 30   Williamson, Sonny Boy

    title: Welfare Store Blues
    place and date: Chicago, 17 May 1940
    record numbers: (053001-) BB-B8610 BC-3

1 Now me and my baby talked last night : and we talked
   for nearly an hour
2 She wanted me to go down to the welfare store : and
   a sack of that welfare flour
3 But I told her no : baby and I sure don't want to go
4 I say I'll do anything in the world for you : I
   don't want to go down to that welfare store
5 Now you need to go get you some real white man : you
   know to sign you a little note
6 Then get you a pair of them *keen-*toed shoes : and
   one of them old *peat-*back soldier coats
7 President Roosevelt said : them welfare people they
   going to treat everybody right
8 Says they give you a can of them beans : and a can
   or two of them old tripe
9 Lord now me and my baby we talked yesterday : and we
   talked in my back yard
10 She say I take care of you Sonny Boy : just as long
   as these times stay hard
11 And I told her yeah : baby and I sure won't have to
   go
12 I say and if you do that for me : I won't have to go
   down to that welfare store

WillS 31   Williamson, Sonny Boy

    title: My Little Machine
    place and date: Chicago, 17 May 1940
    record numbers: (053002-) BB-B8674 BC-3

1 Oh yes : something getting wrong with my little
   machine
2 Now she got a standard carburettor : my baby been
   burning bad gasoline
3 Now I'm going to do like an eagle : I'm going to fly
   up on the mountain top
4 Lord and I don't find my baby : it ain't no telling
   where I'll stop
5 Well I don't know baby : I don't know what to do
6 You know I don't want to hurt your feelings : baby
   even getting mad with you
7 Well I don't know baby : I don't know what to do
8 Baby you is so sweet : but you just won't be true

WillS 32   Williamson, Sonny Boy

    title: Western Union Man
    place and date: Chicago, 4 Apr. 1941
    record numbers: (064019-) BB-B8731 BC-3

1 Western Union man : please stop by my house today
2 I'm expecting a call from Miss *Laza* : I've got to
   hear from her right away

WillS 32   Williamson, Sonny Boy

3   Now the reason I ain't been getting no calls :
    people I'm going to tell you all what it's all
    about
4   They tell me Western Union man been getting drunk :
    he been leaving my calls at somebody else's house
5   Western Union man : please don't you lose your head
6   You know I'm expecting a call from Miss *Laza* : you
    know some of my people might be dead
7   I been sitting here waiting on the Western Union man
    : oh you know he usually comes along about eleven
    o'clock
8   I reckon he must have had trouble with his machine :
    or *the word* the roads oh they must be blocked
9   I believe I'll move up here in Chicago : I'm going
    to get that old Mr Western Union man's route
10 Now what's the use of me worrying about a Western
    Union man : when I have passenger plane flying
    right over my house

WillS 33   Williamson, Sonny Boy

      title: Big Apple Blues
      place and date: Chicago, 4 Apr. 1941
      record numbers: (064020-) BB-B8766 BC-20

1   I know you got some good apples : right down on Mr
    Rudolph's farm
2   Now I love you so much : baby I'd like to hold you
    in my arms
3   Now I want to get a truck-load of your apples : I
    want to peddle your apples up north
4   Now maybe I can keep them ??? till your wintertime :
    and we'll make them be little children's Santa
    Claus
5   Now my grandmother says she want to buy a bushel of
    your apples : she wants to make her some
    applesauce
6   Now I'd be delighted and pay for them : for I bet
    they would be on out of this world
7   Lord I can see your little apple : hanging way up in
    your little apple tree
8   Now you may like you love me so much : baby please
    drop one down for me
9   Now you know the rain washed away my cotton : people
    and the sun burned up my new ground corn
10 Now if somebody don't give me *any* something to eat
    pretty soon : I just as swear we won't be here
    long

WillS 34   Williamson, Sonny Boy

      title: My Baby Made a Change
      place and date: Chicago, 4 Apr. 1941
      record numbers: (064022-) BB-B8766 BC-20

1   Now peoples I believe : somebody oh somebody's
    changed that lock on my door
2   Now because this little key that I got : oh well
    well won't fit my little lock no more
3   Now my baby have changed her way of living : I mean
    she's changed all around
4   Because she even changed her house number : oh you
    know she done moved to another town
5   Oh now but that change that hurt me : oh somebody
    have changed that lock on my door
6   Oh now because this little key that I got : oh well
    well it won't fit in that little lock no more
7   Well now my baby have changed her way of dancing :
    oh she don't two-step no more
8   Oh she do that new dance you call jitterbug : oh man
    she jumps clear the floor
9   Oh now my mother she says one thing : my grandmother
    jumped up and said the same
10 Oh said you keep on fooling around Sonny Boy : says
    I swear one of them going to change your name

WillS 35   Williamson, Sonny Boy

      title: Shotgun Blues
      place and date: Chicago, 4 Apr. 1941
      record numbers: (064023-) BB-B8731 BC-3

1   You ought to heard my grandmother : when she got my
    grandfather told
2   She said get away from me man : I swear you done
    gotten too old
3   Now when my baby left me : you know she left me a
    mule to ride
4   Now when the train left the station : know my mule
    laid down and died
5   You know I sent my baby : you know a brand new
    twenty dollar bill
6   Now if that don't bring her back : I'm doggone sure
    my shotgun will
7   Now if I can't come in : let me sit down in front of
    your door
8   I'll leave so early in the morning : you know your
    real man won't never know
9   Mmm baby : I ain't going to sing to you no more
10 Now if you can stand to leave me : I'll try to love
    to see you go

WillS 36   Williamson, Sonny Boy

      title: Shady Grove Blues
      place and date: Chicago, 2 July 1941
      record numbers: (064492-) BB-B8914 BC-20

1   Now baby but I'll see you : baby in the spring
2   Just after the bluebirds : begin to sing
3   Now but maybe I won't see you : babe but until in
    the fall
4   And I know : you won't have no real regular man at
    all
5   Now but I believe I'll wait and see you : baby some
    old rainy day
6   Just after the mockingbird : come out to play
7   Now you going to keep on : baby you know fooling
    around
8   Oh you know the police : is going to run you clean
    out of town
9   Now tell me babe : what do you want me to do
10 I did everything I could baby : to try to get along
    with you
11 Go bring my shotgun : my *biskins* and shells
12 You know my woman she done quit me : and I'm going
    to start to raising hell

WillS 37   Williamson, Sonny Boy

      title: Sloppy Drunk Blues
      place and date: Chicago, 2 July 1941
      record numbers: (064493-) BB-B8822 BC-3

1   Now I would rather be sloppy drunk : oh than
    anything I know
2   Oh you know and another half a pint : woman you will
    see me go
3   Now my gal she done quit me : for somebody else
4   Now and I'm sloppy drunk again woman : sleeping all
    by myself
5   Now I would rather be sloppy drunk : sitting in the
    can
6   Now than to be out in Beale Street : running from
    the man
7   Because mmm : bring another half a pint
8   Now I believe I'll get drunk : babe I'm going to
    wreck this joint
9   Now and I love my moonshine whiskey : I tell the
    world I do
10 Now but I drinks my whiskey : to get along with you
11 Now I'm going to drink whilst I'm up babe : drink
    until I fall

317

WillS 37   Williamson, Sonny Boy

12 Now if you want me to stop drinking whiskey : you
    ain't talking about nothing at all

WillS 38   Williamson, Sonny Boy

    title: She Was a Dreamer
    place and date: Chicago, 2 July 1941
    record numbers: (064494-) BB-B8914 BC-20

1   Now my baby was a girl : she was sweet sixteen
2   Her mother wouldn't listen : to her dreams
3   I knowed she was a dreamer : she dreamed them old
    southern dreams
4   She was the dreamingest girl : the dreamingest girl
    I most ever seen
5   Well she knowed about loving : from kisses on down
6   She was the dreamingest girl : from miles around
7   Well now she dreamed I was kissing and hugging her :
    close to my breast
8   She told that much of the dream : but she wouldn't
    tell the rest
9   Well she dreamed that we was kissing : down by the
    mill
10 She dreamed that she had taken me : from the girl on
    the hill
11 Well she knowed about kissing : from hugging on down
12 She was the dreamingest girl : from miles around

WillS 39   Williamson, Sonny Boy

    title: You Got to Step Back
    place and date: Chicago, 2 July 1941
    record numbers: (064495-) BB-B8822 BC-20

1   Well I asked you woman : where did you stay last
    night
2   You said it wasn't none of my business : just since
    you treating me right
3   Now tell me baby : what you trying to do
4   You trying to love me : and some other man too
5   Well now look a-here woman : I got something to tell
    you can't do
6   You can't love me : and some other man too
7   Well now look a-here baby : I ain't going to be your
    dog no more
8   You try to fool me baby : like you did a long time
    ago
9   Now baby it ain't but the one thing : really give me
    the blues
10 When I ain't got no bottom : on my last pair of
    shoes

WillS 40   Williamson, Sonny Boy

    title: Ground Hog Blues
    place and date: Chicago, 11 Dec. 1941
    record numbers: (070143-) BB-B9031 BC-3

1   Now I'm just a walking ground hog : mama and I walks
    around in my den
2   Lord if I come out and see my shadow : John I
    believe I'll go back in
3   Lord I want some feeding mama : so I can hear a
    high sound
4   Says if you don't feed me baby : I believe I'll go
    back in the ground
5   Lord I want to hear some swinging music : I want to
    hear a Fats Waller sound
6   Now if I start to jitterbugging : I'll forget my
    hole down in the ground
7   Now and I need some petting baby : if you know what
    I mean
8   Now if you don't pet me baby : I believe I'll go
    back down in New Orleans

WillS 41   Williamson, Sonny Boy

    title: Black Panter Blues
    place and date: Chicago, 11 Dec. 1941
    record numbers: (070144-) BB-34-0701 BC-3

1   My baby thinks she's a black panther : she want to
    climb up in a tree and jump down
2   Now she wants to cut my throat : when ain't nobody
    else around
3   My baby thinks she's a black panther : now and she
    won't do me awhile
4   Now when she says something contrary : now she don't
    want me to do nothing but smile
5   Last night in my bed I found a black panther : must
    have been about forty-nine inches
6   You could hear me holler : man and I didn't have no
    time to swallow
7   In my bed I found a black panther : must have been
    forty-nine inches long
8   Now I went and got my shotgun and I started to kill
    it : but I thought my baby's been doing me wrong
9   My little brown thinks she's the rule : now because
    she always has her way
10 Now but some day she going to meet the lion : she
    ain't going to even have no place to stay

WillS 42   Williamson, Sonny Boy

    title: Broken Hearted Blues
    place and date: Chicago, 11 Dec. 1941
    record numbers: (070145-) BB-B9031 BC-20

1   Now I'm broke and I'm hungry : ragged and I'm dirty
    too
2   Now if I clean up pretty mama : can I stay all night
    with you
3   Now you remember way last fall : ooo they put me in
    the old *Brisby* jail
4   Now that done learned me a lesson : about shaking my
    pistol in these womenfolks' face
5   Now and if I can't come in : let me sit down in
    front of your door
6   Now I'll leave so early in the morning : that your
    real man won't never know
7   Now just let me be your little dog : baby until your
    big dog comes
8   Now when your big dog comes : I want you to tell him
    what your little dog done done

WillS 43   Williamson, Sonny Boy

    title: She Don't Love Me That Way
    place and date: Chicago, 11 Dec. 1941
    record numbers: (070146-) BB-34-0701 BC-3

1   Now I got something to tell you baby : you can't do
2   You can't love me : and some other man too
3   Now I met an old lady : with her face right to the
    ground
4   She's up in the front : but she's all broke down
    behind
5   Now if the river was whiskey : and I was a diving
    duck
6   I would dive on the bottom : never would come up
7   Now the sun is going to shine : in my back door some
    day
8   The wind going to rise : and blow my blues away
9   Now I got something baby : I want to say to you
10 Had enough of you bad treatment : I wonder the way
    you do
11 You made plenty of money : in nineteen twenty-two
12 You let these cats : make a fool of you

WillS 44   Williamson, Sonny Boy

      title: My Black Name Blues
      place and date: Chicago, 11 Dec. 1941
      record numbers: (070147-) BB-B8992 BC-3

1 Now I can hear my black name a-ringing : all up and
    down the line
2 Now I don't believe you love me : woman I believe
    I'm just trifling away my time
3 Well I had this blues before sunrise : oh with tears
    standing in my eyes
4 Now that make me have such a funny feeling : man a
    feeling I do despise
5 Now last night I was laying down dreaming : oh you
    know and I was dreaming all to myself
6 Now I was just thinking my woman didn't love me : I
    hope she ain't in love with nobody else

WillX   1   Willis, Ruth Mary

      title: Experience Blues
      place and date: Atlanta, 23 Oct. 1931
      record numbers: (151906-1) Co-14642-D Yz L-1037

1 I once loved a man : that didn't mean me no good
2 Wasn't any use stop loving : I couldn't see why I
    should
3 I woke up one morning : walking across the floor
4 I'm going away to leave you baby : I don't mean you
    no good no more
5 You didn't mean it baby : you hadn't no right to lie
6 So go baby go : and stay until you die
7 I'm talking about a man : a man by the name of John
8 He's the meanest man : that ever lived under the sun
9 What you see here Jenkins : just look what you done
    done
10 Lord you treat me : like my troubles have just begun
11 Lord you left me worried : that's why I'm all
    confused
12 That's why I'm singing : these old experience blues

WillX   2   Willis, Ruth Mary

      title: Painful Blues
      place and date: Atlanta, 23 Oct. 1931
      record numbers: (151907-1) Co-14642-D Yz L-1037

1 My heart is painful : I believe my blues are pouring
    down
2 I feel like sinking : six feet in the lonesome
    ground
3 My heart did pain : when my baby got on the train
4 My heart struck sorrow : it fell like drops of rain
5 I've got a baby : that keeps me feeling blue
6 He acts like the weather : I can't tell what he's
    going to do
7 Women don't let your man : treat like mine done for
    me
8 He had me almost crazy : as a doggone girl could be
9 Delano was a man : who could flag my train for a
    ride
10 He has me almost crazy : till I was satisfied

WillX   3   Willis, Ruth Mary

      title: Man of My Own
      place and date: New York, 17 Jan. 1933
      record numbers: (12920-1) Ba-32687 Yz L-1026

1 Now I went down Eighteenth Street : didn't have no
    hat
2 Asking all the women : where was my man at
3 I'm going to grab me a train : ride it till it stops
4 Not going to stay around here : and be a stumbling
    block

WillX   3   Willis, Ruth Mary

5 Woke up this morning : at the break of day
6 Looked on my pillow : where my man used to lay
7 My suitcase was packed : trunk's already home
8 So it won't be long : before your mama be gone
9 You caused my heart to weep : you caused it to moan
10 So why fetch me : no train I'm on

WilsL   1   Wilson, Leola B.

      title: Scoop It
      place and date: Chicago, c. Aug. 1926
      record numbers: (2607-4) Pm-12379 His HLP-1

1 Now you grab your partner : large or small
2 And dance her : around the hall
3 Big fat mama : and I can bend down low
4 Just see me do this scoop it : across the floor
5 I can get way back : in my knees

WilsL   2   Wilson, Leola B.

      title: Stevedore Man
      place and date: Chicago, c. Aug. 1926
      record numbers: (2616-1) Pm-12379 His HLP-1

1 Woke up this morning about half past nine : and I
    just could not keep from crying
2 I was worried about : that stevedore man of mine
3 It's raining and it's hailing : storming daddy on
    the sea
4 Now that's the onliest way : to keep my sweet daddy
    away from me
5 I went down to the station : and I could not keep
    from crying
6 Lord a train had my man : and it was fairly flying
7 I stole that sweet man of mine : stole him from my
    best friend
8 And that woman done got lucky : Lord and stoled her
    man back again

WilsL   3   Wilson, Leola B.

      title: Down the Country
      place and date: Chicago, c. Nov. 1926
      record numbers: (4012-2) Pm-12444 Bio BLP-12037

1 You ever wake up : just about the break of day
2 With your arms around the pillow : where Mr
    so-and-so used to lay
3 I'm going away baby : won't be back until fall
4 If I don't win no money : I won't be back at all
5 I heard you scratching : early in this room
6 If you don't think I'm leaving : count the days I'll
    be gone
7 If the river was liquor : and I was a duck
8 I would go to the bottom : and I would never come up
9 I'm leaving this town : I got on my last pair of
    shoes
10 Walking away from here : these old down the country
    blues

WilsL   4   Wilson, Leola B.

      title: Back Biting Bee Blues
      place and date: Chicago, c. Nov. 1926
      record numbers: (4013-2) Pm-12444 Bio BLP-12037

1 Early this morning : heard someone calling me
2 It was my baby : that black backbiting bee
3 Going to take my razor : cut my honeysuckle vine
4 Darn black bee : that stole that honey of mine
5 Rather have my head in alcohol : my body on some
    railroad track

WilsL   4   Wilson, Leola B.

6   Than have that black bee : bite me in my back
7   It's raining in my kitchen : lightning on my wall
8   I know by that : some mule is kicking in my stall

WilsW   1   Wilson, Kid Wesley (Leola B. Wilson)

        title: Scoop It
        place and date: Chicago, c. Aug. 1926
        record numbers: (2607-4) Pm-12379 His HLP-1

2   Scoop it : pretty mama for me

WilsW   2   Wilson, Kid Wesley (Leola B. Wilson)

        title: The Gin Done Done It
        place and date: New York, 5 Sept. 1929
        record numbers: (148977-?) Co-14463-D His HLP-5

1   Going to take my gal : to a social dance
2   But I didn't have no seat : in my pants
3   Give me four dollars : take me in
4   I took the four dollars : and I bought some gin
5   I tore my hair : and I walked the streets
6   I wanted to whip : everyone I meet
7   Along came John : who's my best friend
8   Cut his head : till it was a sin
9   I shot some craps : to my disgrace
10 I run everybody : out the place
11 Dice was loaded : made me sore
12 I left four hustlers : lying on the floor
13 I went to church : to do the holy roll
14 Grabbed me a sister : to convert her soul
15 Two minutes later : preacher came in
16 She stopped rolling with me : started rolling with
    him
17 I took my cow : to the doctor man
18 Something about her : I couldn't understand
19 I milked her good : about half past ten
20 Didn't give nothing : but a bucket of gin
21 I tore up : all my gal's good clothes
22 Didn't mean to do it : the good Lord knows
23 My landlady : is a good old soul
24 I even took : some of her sweet jellyroll
25 I went downtown : about half past four
26 Stoled two hot dogs : from a butcher store
27 Got locked up : judge he said
28 Take six months : to clear your head
29 The jailhouse steps : was slick as glass
30 I tried to run away : got shot in my yas
31 Yes I told my gal : to bring me bail
32 Get some money : if she have to sell a little coal

WilsW   3   Wilson, Kid Wesley (Leola B. Wilson)

        title: Do It Right
        place and date: New York, 5 Sept. 1929
        record numbers: (148978-3) Co-14463-D His HLP-5

1   When your gal gets old : she wants to be alone
2   You left a little work : undone at home
3   Whenever you do it : whatever you should
4   Just do your best : to do it good
5   When you have a fight : and you didn't win
6   Buy a shotgun : start over again
7   If you gal come home : she's feeling tight
8   She wants some loving : that very night
9   If you feeling bad : because you're on the shelf
10 Get some rope : go hang yourself
11 If your gal need money : how bad you feel
12 Go get some money : if you have to steal
13 If your wife leave home : every time you do
14 Somebody outside : knows more than you
15 When your pal buy your gal : a Coca-Cola
16 You can bet your life : he's playing her victrola

WilsW   3   Wilson, Kid Wesley (Leola B. Wilson)

17 The elephant said : when he swallowed the cat
18 Got a mouthful of kitty : and it's tight like that

WooH   1   Woods, Hosea (Gus Cannon)

        title: Fourth and Beale
        place and date: Chicago, c. 12 Sept. 1929
        record numbers: (C-4338-) Br-7138 His HLP-15

1   And it's hey mama : I'm going to leave your town
2   I ain't got no man : to put my arms around
3   Oh did you get my letter : throwed in your back yard
4   I wanted to see you mama : but your good man had me
    barred
5   You caught me with a woman : I caught you with a man
6   Baby if I see you regular : mama see me when you can
7   I'm going to Memphis : stop on Fourth and Beale
8   If I can't find Roberta : I hope to find Lucille

WooH   2   Woods, Hosea (Gus Cannon)

        title: Last Chance Blues
        place and date: Memphis, 1 Oct. 1929
        record numbers: (56316-) Vi-V38593 Her H-205

1   I said hey baby : I give you your last chance
2   *All you do to wear my jacket* : but you want to
    wear my pants
3   Oh baby : what's the matter now
4   You just a trifling woman : don't mean me no good
    nohow
5   Said I give you my money baby : but that don't do no
    good
6   I bring her supper while you working : that's just
    what I do
7   I said hey : what am I going to do
8   I done everything baby : can't get along with you

WooH   3   Woods, Hosea (Gus Cannon)

        title: The Rooster's Crowing Blues
        place and date: Memphis, 3 Oct. 1929
        record numbers: (56340-) Vi-V38593 Her H-205

1   And hey what makes a rooster : crow at the break of
    day
2   That's to let the rounder know : the workingman is
    on his way
3   Hey : he is on his way
4   That's to let the rounder know : the workingman is
    on his way
5   I used to be a lover : baby in my younger days
6   Now I'm old and feeble : but I still got my loving
    ways
7   Hey : in my younger days
8   Now I'm old and feeble : I still got my loving ways
9   I tell you partner : I ain't got a friend
10 They'll take your baby from you : *just like ???
    hen*

WooH   4   Woods, Hosea (Gus Cannon)

        title: Wolf River Blues
        place and date: Memphis, 24 Nov. 1930
        record numbers: (64709-) Vi-23272 OJL-19

1   Says I left Memphis : went down the Macon Road
2   The Wolf River : sit down on the *road*
3   Cried Wolf River Wolf River : sure is deep and wide
4   I want to cross the river : go down the other side
5   So long so long : Wolf River so long
6   Lord I need somebody : hear me sing this song

WooH   5   Woods, Hosea (Gus Cannon)

    title: Prison Wall Blues
    place and date: Memphis, 28 Nov. 1930
    record numbers: (64747) Vi-23272 Rt RL-329

1 When they bring you : through that gate
2 You wish you hadn't a-done it : but it's just too late
3 You might as well laugh : ??? you fall
4 Now hollering won't get you nothing : behind the wall
5 The prison wall blues : keep rolling across my mind
6 I can't get parole : wish *like* the governor would quit my time
7 I once was lost : but now I'm found
8 I'd leave this place running : but I'm scared of them flop-eared hounds
9 This is the highest fence I ever saw : in my life I can't climb
10 This fence will make a high yellow girl turn dark : it make a weak-eyed man go blind
11 When I leave these walls : I'll be running ??? *a speed*
12 You see the bottom of my feet so many times : you think I'm on my knees

WooO   1   Woods, Oscar

    title: Evil Hearted Woman
    place and date: New Orleans, 21 Mar. 1936
    record numbers: (60847-) De-7904 Yz L-1026

1 I had an evil-hearted woman : she mistreated me all the time
2 She went away and left me : but she's forever on my mind
3 I done her wrong : and I can't deny myself
4 Lord I can't love her : and she loving somebody else
5 Let me tell you people : what she told me one sunny day
6 She said I love you daddy : I can't stand your lowdown ways
7 Early one morning : about the break of day
8 She told me daddy daddy : I'm going to let you have your way
9 I get lonesome : around here by myself
10 Thinking about you Jesse : you have been with someone else

WooO   2   Woods, Oscar

    title: Lone Wolf Blues
    place and date: New Orleans, 21 Mar. 1936
    record numbers: (60848-A) De-7219 Cor CP-58

1 Lord my mother told me : when I was quite a child
2 That the life that you are living : will kill you after a while
3 I just began to realize : the things my mother said
4 Since I been down here : and been mistreated this a-way
5 I never loved no one woman : hope to God I never will
6 All the attracting women : will get some good man killed
7 Now I ain't no monkey : and I sure can't climb no tree
8 And I ain't going to let no woman : make no monkey out of me
9 Now I sent my baby : a brand new twenty dollar bill
10 If that don't bring her : I know my shotgun will

WooO   3   Woods, Oscar

    title: Don't Sell It--Don't Give It Away
    place and date: New Orleans, 21 Mar. 1936
    record numbers: (60849-) De-7219 Yz L-1032

1 Says it was early one morning : about the break of day
2 Don't you hear me crying : won't you listen what I say
3 Early one morning : baby about the break of day
4 Well she told me not to sell it : papa don't you give it away
5 I said yes baby yes : then I said no baby no
6 I sold some jelly : I sure won't sell no more
7 Now you know you didn't want me : why did you so
8 Don't you hear me crying : little on and on
9 You know you didn't want me : baby why did you so
10 I can get more women : than a passenger train can haul
11 Now she told me not to sell it : don't you give it away
12 Don't you hear me crying : don't you listen what I say
13 She told me not to sell it : papa don't you give it away
14 You ought to keep that jelly : until Judgment Day
15 I said yes baby yes : then I said no baby no
16 I got a brand new gal : and I don't want you no more

WooO   4   Woods, Oscar

    title: Don't Sell It
    place and date: San Antonio, 30 Oct. 1937
    record numbers: (SA-2845-1) Vo-03906 Yz L-1015

1 It was early one morning : about the break of day
2 Don't you hear me crying : won't you lead me where to stay
3 Early one morning : baby about the break of day
4 She told me not to sell it : papa don't you give it away
5 I said yes baby yes : then I said no baby no
6 I sold some jelly : I sure won't sell no more
7 Now you know you didn't want me : why did you stall
8 Don't you hear me crying : little all and all
9 You know you didn't want me : baby why did you stall
10 I can get more women : than a passenger train can haul

Yate   1   Yates, Blind Richard

    title: I'm Gonna Moan My Blues Away
    place and date: New York, c. 9 Apr. 1927
    record numbers: (GEX-577-A) Ge-6104 His HLP-1

1 I went to the Gypsy : to have my fortune told
2 And the Gypsy told me : doggone my hard-luck soul
3 Then I turned right around : went to the next door
4 And the Gypsy told me : I have a woman every place I go
5 I got a brown in the bottom : one up on the hill
6 Now when one don't love me : I know the other one will
8 I done moaned I done groaned : moaned my blues away

Yate   2   Yates, Blind Richard

    title: Sore Bunion Blues
    place and date: New York, c. 9 Apr. 1927
    record numbers: (GEX-578-A) Ge-6104 His HLP-1

1 Told the shoe man : give me a size fourteen
2 My poor bunions : they are hard to me
3 Bunions bunions : won't you hear my plea
4 Stop your aching : let my poor feet be

5 Going to see : old Dr *fojo* bones
6 Let him start : to working on my buns

Concordance Index of Titles

ABERDEEN (1)
    WhiW 13   Aberdeen Mississippi Blues
ABOUT ['BOUT] (13)
    ChatB 8   Tellin' You 'Bout It
    ColFL 2   Wild About My Loving
    Este 39   Tell Me About It
    JackJ 2   I'm Wild About My Lovin'
    JefB 71   Bootin' Me 'Bout
    JohLo 14   I'm Nuts About that Gal
    McCoJ 4   I'm Wild About My Stuff
    MemM   3   I'm Talking About You
    MemM 14   I'm Talking About You--No. 2
    Nick   1   Everybody's Talking About Sadie Green
    Pick   1   Crazy 'Bout My Black Gal
    Weld 11   Worried About that Woman
    WillJ 13   I'm Getting Wild About Her
ACCOUNT (1)
    WillS 12   You Give an Account
ACE (1)
    TurnB 1   Black Ace
ACROSS (1)
    Blak 21   Walkin' Across the Country
ACT (2)
    BradT 3   Please Don't Act that Way
    Nick   3   It Won't Act Right
ACTIN' (1)
    JonE   2   Mean Actin' Mama
ACTIONS (1)
    ArnK 34   Your Ways and Actions
ADAM (2)
    BradT 1   Adam and Eve
    ThoHo 2   Adam and Eve Had the Blues
ADVERTISE (1)
    SmiC 22   Don't Advertise Your Man
ADVICE (2)
    ChatB 19   Bo Carter's Advice
    Whea   1   Mama's Advice
AFTER (2)
    MemM 23   After While Blues
    SmiB 22   After You've Gone
AGAIN (5)
    ChatB 25   Let's Get Drunk Again
    DaviW 6   Sloppy Drunk Again
    JohLo 27   Laplegged Drunk Again
    Shad 10   On the Road Again
    SpiV 12   I'll Never Fall in Love Again
AGENT (4)
    Este 34   Special Agent
    LewN   4   Ticket Agent Blues
    McTW 33   Ticket Agent Blues
    SmiB   3   Ticket Agent Ease Your Window Down
AGO (1)
    TowH   3   Long Ago Blues
AIN'T (20)   [see also 'TAIN'T]
    BogL   7   They Ain't Walking No More
    BogL 11   Tricks Ain't Working No More
    DaveC 1   I Ain't No Ice Man
    DaviW 2   That Stuff You Sell Ain't No Good
    Este 20   I Ain't Gonna Be Worried No More
    Glov   3   I Ain't Giving Nobody None
    Hurt   2   Ain't No Tellin'
    JackC 20   Your Baby Ain't Sweet Like Mine
    JohK   1   Lady, Your Clock Ain't Right
    JohLo 17   Hard Time Ain't Gone No Where
    JohLo 19   It Ain't What You Usta Be
    JohLo 24   I Ain't Gonna Be Your Fool
    McCoJ 26   Hallelujah Joe Ain't Preachin' No More
    MemM 25   Ain't No Use Trying to Tell On Me
    RupO   2   Ain't Goin' to Be Your Low Down Dog
    SmiB 13   I Ain't Goin' to Play Second Fiddle
    Stok 20   Ain't Going to Do Like I Used to Do
    Vinc   9   She Ain't No Good
    Whea   2   Ain't It a Pity and a Shame
    WhiG   3   The Blues Ain't Nothin' But. . . .???
AIRPLANE (1)
    Este 26   Airplane Blues
AIRY (1)
    JackC 2   Airy Man Blues

ALABAMA (6)
    BirB   2   Alabama Blues--Part 1
    BirB   3   Alabama Blues--Part 2
    CarrL 7   Alabama Woman Blues
    JackC 10   I'm Alabama Bound
    Patt   9   Going to Move to Alabama
    Wilk   4   Alabama Blues
ALBERTA (1)
    Ledb   7   Alberta
ALL (19)
    CarrL 2   Gettin' All Wet
    ChatB 14   All Around Man
    Este 18   I Wanta Tear It All the Time
    Gill 13   It's All Over Now
    JackC 16   All I Want Is a Spoonful
    JohLo 8   I'm So Tired of Living All Alone
    JohLs 1   All Night Long Blues
    JohM   1   If I Let You Get Away With It Once You'll Do
               It All of the Time
    Ledb   5   Honey, I'm All Out and Down
    Mann   1   The Blues Is All Wrong
    Rain   4   Those All Night Long Blues
    Shad   7   She Stays Out All Night Long
    Shad   8   She Stays Out All Night Long
    SmiC   4   All Night Blues
    SmiC 33   He's Mine, All Mine
    Stov   2   A Woman Gets Tired of the Same Man All the
               Time
    SykR   2   All My Money Gone Blues
    SykR   7   Lost All I Had Blues
    Whea   7   All Night Long Blues
ALLEY (5)
    BogL   9   Alley Boogie
    BogL 22   Down in Boogie Alley
    BrowR 1   James Alley Blues
    SmiIv 2   Third Alley Blues
    Whea   8   Throw Me in the Alley
ALLIGATOR ['GATOR] (2)
    JohM   2   When a 'Gator Holler, Folk Say It's a Sign of
               Rain
    SpiV   2   The Alligator Pond Went Dry
ALLOW (3)
    ThoH   5   Honey, Won't You Allow Me One More Chance?
    WasbS 1   Mama Don't Allow No. 1
    WasbS 3   Mama Don't Allow No. 2
ALONE (4)
    Brac   2   Left Alone Blues
    JohLo 8   I'm So Tired of Living All Alone
    Luca   5   Leave My Man Alone
    Shad 13   Better Leave That Stuff Alone
ALONG (3)
    Gill   5   I'll Get Along Somehow
    PooJ   3   Come Along Little Children
    Wilk   3   That's No Way to Get Along
ALRIGHT (1)
    McCoJ 1   That Will Be Alright
AM (2)
    AleT 10   I Am Calling Blues
    SmiT 10   The World's Jazz Crazy and So Am I
AMBULANCE (1)
    HarZ   2   Oh Ambulance Man
ANGEL (1)
    BogL 10   Black Angel Blues
ANNA (1)
    Shad 19   Mary Anna Cut Off
ANNIE (1)
    ArnK 10   Black Annie
ANOTHER (1)
    JohE   3   Can't Make Another Day
ANTS (1)
    ChatB 4   Ants in My Pants
ANY (1)
    JamS   8   If You Haven't Got Any Hay Get on Down the
               Road
ANYBODY (1)
    JonM   6   Anybody Here Want to Try My Cabbage
APPLE (1)
    WillS 33   Big Apple Blues

ARE (1) [see also WATCHA]
    ChatB 21 Your Biscuits Are Big Enough for Me
ARGUIN' (1)
    Shor   1 Telephone Arguin' Blues
ARKANSAS (3)
    SpiV   1 Arkansas Road Blues
    ThoH   2 Arkansas
    WhiW   2 Pinebluff Arkansas
ARMY (1)
    Rain 17 Army Camp Harmony Blues
AROUND (8) [see also ROUND]
    Blak   5 Come On Boys Let's Do that Messin' Around
    CarrL 20 Take a Walk Around the Corner
    ChatB 14 All Around Man
    JonJ   1 Monkeyin' Around
    McTW   9 Come On Around to My House Mama
    Pope   2 Doggin' Me Around Blues
    Stev   1 Beale Street Mess Around
    WillJ 15 Meet Me Around the Corner
ARRANGEMENT (1)
    ChatB 29 Arrangement for Me--Blues
ASH (1)
    JackC 26 Ash Tray Blues
ASHES (1)
    DaviW 16 Ashes in My Whiskey
ATLANTA (4)
    CollC 2 Atlanta Blues
    Gran   2 Lonesome Atlanta Blues
    HicR 21 Atlanta Moan
    McTW   7 Atlanta Strut
ATTORNEY (1)
    WhiW 11 District Attorney Blues
AUNT (1)
    Stev   7 Aunt Caroline Dyer Blues
AVALON (1)
    Hurt   3 Avalon Blues
AVENUE (2)
    DayW   1 Central Avenue Blues
    TurnJ 1 Blues on Central Avenue
AWAY (14)
    Beam   3 Goin' Away Blues
    Beam   4 Going Away Blues
    CamC   1 Goin' Away Blues
    Howe   9 Away from Home
    JackC 5 I Got What It Takes But It Breaks My Heart to
              Give It Away
    JohM   1 If I Let You Get Away With It Once You'll Do
              It All of the Time
    McCoC 2 That Lonesome Train Took My Baby Away
    McTW 11 Drive Away Blues
    MemM 32 You Can't Give It Away
    UnkA 10 Giving It Away
    Vinc 17 Go Away Woman
    Wilk   9 Get Away Blues
    WooO   3 Don't Sell It--Don't Give It Away
    Yate   1 I'm Gonna Moan My Blues Away
AWFUL (4)
    AleT 14 Awful Moaning Blues--Part 1
    AleT 15 Awful Moaning Blues--Part 2
    Hawk   5 Awful Fix Blues
    WillK 1 I Want It Awful Bad
AWHILE [WHILE] (2)
    DaviW 27 Just Want to Talk Awhile
    MemM 23 After While Blues
B AND O (1)
    McTW 28 B and O Blues No. 2
BABE (4)
    Rain 25 Oh My Babe Blues
    Vinc   8 Honey Babe Let the Deal Go Down
    Wilb   1 My Babe My Babe
BABY (30)
    BakW   6 Rag Baby
    BrowB 1 Nobody But My Baby Is Getting My Love
    ChatB 30 My Baby
    ChatL 3 Please Baby
    DaviW 25 New Come Back Baby
    DayT   1 Goin' Back to My Baby
    Este 13 Someday Baby Blues
    FulB   4 Bye Bye Baby Blues

BABY (cont.)
    HilK   5 Tell Me Baby
    JackC 20 Your Baby Ain't Sweet Like Mine
    JackC 28 Baby Please Loan Me Your Heart
    JefB 68 That Crawlin' Baby Blues
    JohLo 12 Baby Please Don't Leave Me No More
    JonL   7 Bye Bye Baby Blues
    Ledb   8 Baby, Don't You Love Me No More?
    LofW   2 My Mean Baby Blues
    McCl   2 Baby, Don't You Want to Go?
    McCoC 2 That Lonesome Train Took My Baby Away
    MartC 1 Farewell to You Baby
    MemM 39 My Baby Don't Want Me No More
    PetW   3 My Baby Left Me
    Slue   2 Shouting Baby Blues
    SmiB 16 Baby Doll
    Spru   7 Don't Cry Baby
    Stev   4 Baby Got the Rickets
    ThoR   5 No Baby Blues
    Vinc 12 Please Baby
    WillJ 6 Baby Please Don't Go
    WillJ 18 Someday Baby
    WillS 34 My Baby Made a Change
BABY'S (2)
    McCl   6 My Baby's Doggin' Me
    McTW 26 My Baby's Gone
BACK (33)
    ArnK   7 Back Door Blues
    ArnK 33 Back on the Job
    BelE   5 Carry It Right Back Home
    Blacw 9 Back Door Blues
    DaviW 25 New Come Back Baby
    DayT   1 Goin' Back to My Baby
    Este 29 Easin' Back to Tennessee
    Hawk   4 Snatch It Back Blues
    HicR 10 Hurry and Bring It Back Home
    JackC 13 Take Me Back Blues
    JefB   8 Beggin' Back
    JohJo 1 I'm Going Back Home
    JonB   1 Back Door Blues
    JonM 11 You May Go, But You'll Come Back Some Day
    JonM 18 I'm a Back Bitin' Mama
    KelJ   4 Believe I'll Go Back Home
    McCoJ 2 Goin' Back to Texas
    McCoJ 17 Going Back Home
    MemM   1 Goin' Back to Texas
    MemM   5 I'm Going Back Home
    Nick   4 Going Back to Memphis
    Nick   6 You May Leave But This Will Bring You Back
    Scru   1 My Back to the Wall
    SmiB 21 Back Water Blues
    SmiC 23 Back Woods Blues
    Span   2 Back to the Woods Blues
    Spru   3 Way Back Down Home
    Stok 18 Take Me Back
    Ston   2 Back Door Blues
    ThoR   8 Back Gnawing Blues
    WasbS 7 Back Door
    WillS 39 You Got to Step Back
    WilsL 4 Back Biting Bee Blues
BACKWATER (1)
    JohLo 29 South Bound Backwater
BAD (14)
    ArnK 38 Bad Luck Blues
    BakW   4 Bad Luck Moan
    Bare 10 Bad Boy
    Blak 10 Bad Feeling Blues
    DaviM 2 Too Black Bad
    Doyl   4 Bad in Mind Blues
    GibC 12 Bad Luck Dice
    Gill 11 It Looks Bad for You
    JefB 17 Bad Luck Blues
    LewN   6 Bad Luck's My Buddy
    Rain   1 Bad Luck Blues
    Virg   2 Bad Notion Blues
    WillK 1 I Want It Awful Bad
    WillS 26 Bad Luck Blues
BADLY (1)
    MartC 2 Badly Mistreated Man

BAKER (1)
  CarrL 36   Bread Baker
BAKERSHOP (1)
  JefB 65   Bakershop Blues
BAKING (1)
  BogL 13   Baking Powder Blues
BALKY (1)
  JefB 37   Balky Mule Blues
BALL (8)
  BracM 2   Cherry Ball
  FulB 11   Three Ball Blues
  Howe   8   Ball and Chain Blues
  JamS   3   Cherry Ball Blues
  McCoJ 6   Cherry Ball Blues
  McTW 14   Razor Ball
  SmiM   1   Jenny's Ball
  Wate   5   At the New Jump Steady Ball
BAMALONG (1)
  BaxJ   1   Bamalong Blues
BAND (1)
  UnkA   1   String Band Blues
BANKER'S (1)
  BigB   9   The Banker's Blues
BANTY (1)
  Patt   5   Banty Rooster Blues
BARBECUE (2)
  BogL 23   Barbecue Bess
  HicR   1   Barbecue Blues
BARBED (1)
  Whea   3   Don't Hang My Clothes on No Barbed Wire Line
BAREFOOT (2)
  Bare   8   Barefoot Bill's Hard Luck Blues
  Shor   4   Barefoot Blues
BARREL (7)
  CarrL 23   Barrel House Woman
  CarrL 24   Barrel House Woman No. 2
  Gait   1   Georgia Barrel House
  JohJa 1   Barrel of Whiskey Blues
  JohMa 1   Barrel House Flat Blues
  Rain   3   Barrel House Blues
  RichM 2   Mooch Richardson's Low Down Barrel House Blues
                Part 1
BARRELHOUSE (1)
  MemM 27   Drunken Barrelhouse Blues
BASEMENT (3)
  BigB   1   Down in the Basement Blues
  Rain 26   Down in the Basement
  SmiC 26   Basement Blues
BE (25)
  ArnK 18   I'll Be Up Some Day
  BigB   6   I Can't Be Satisfied
  BogL 19   Tired as I Can Be
  CollS 8   It Won't Be Long
  DaviW 23   Why Shouldn't I Be Blue
  Este 20   I Ain't Gonna Be Worried No More
  Hurt   6   Got the Blues Can't Be Satisfied
  JohEb 1   Be My Kid Blues
  JohLo 19   It Ain't What You Usta Be
  JohLo 24   I Ain't Gonna Be Your Fool
  McCoJ 1   That Will Be Alright
  McCoJ 15   Someday I'll Be in the Clay
  MartD 2   What You Was You Used to Be
  MemM 38   It's Hard to Be Mistreated
  MooA   2   It Wouldn't Be So Hard
  Patt   6   It Won't Be Long
  RupO   2   Ain't Goin' to Be Your Low Down Dog
  SmiC 11   It Won't Be Long Now
  Stok 15   It Won't Be Long Now
  Vinc 20   I'll Be Gone Long Gone
  Wate   2   There'll Be Some Changes Made
  WeaS   1   Can't Be Trusted Blues
  Whea 24   The First Shall Be the Last and the Last Shall
                Be First
  WillJ 11   I Won't Be in Hard Luck No More
BEALE (3)
  Stev   1   Beale Street Mess Around
  Stok   4   Beale Town Bound
  WooH   1   Fourth and Beale

BEAM (1)
  JohBi 1   Sun Beam Blues
BEANS (2)
  ArnK 26   Red Beans and Rice
  ChatB 7   Beans
BEAR (1)
  JefB 25   Teddy Bear Blues
BEAT (4)
  GibC   1   Beat You Doing It
  McCoJ 10   Beat It Right
  Shad 16   I Can Beat You Plenty
  SmiT   8   You've Got to Beat Me to Keep Me
BED (8)
  Cann   3   Feather Bed
  JefB 43   Competition Bed Blues
  JefB 61   Bed Springs Blues
  KelJ   6   Cold Iron Bed
  SmiB 25   Mean Old Bed Bug Blues
  SmiB 26   Empty Bed Blues--Part ?
  Stov   3   Bed Slats
  Whea 37   Sick Bed Blues
BEDBUG (1)
  LewF   7   Mean Old Bedbug Blues
BEDROOM (1)
  WallS 3   Bedroom Blues
BEDSIDE (1)
  ThoZ   1   Bedside Blues
BEDTIME (2)
  Stok 12   Bedtime Blues
  WasbS 34   I Get the Blues at Bedtime
BEE (6)
  ChatB 1   I'm an Old Bumble Bee
  MemM   4   Bumble Bee
  MemM   6   Bumble Bee Blues
  MemM 13   New Bumble Bee
  WillS 9   Honey Bee Blues
  WilsL 4   Back Biting Bee Blues
BEEDLE (1)
  RobB   2   Beedle Um Bum
BEEN (11)
  ChatB 24   Who's Been Here?
  DorsT 12   Been Mistreated Blues
  Este 14   Who's Been Tellin' You Buddy Brown Blues
  FulB 10   Somebody's Been Talkin'
  Rain 11   Honey Where You Been So Long
  SmiB   9   You've Been a Good Old Wagon
  SykR 13   As True As I've Been to You
  WallS 5   Have You Ever Been Down
  WasbS 28   I've Been Treated Wrong
  WillJ 2   Somebody's Been Borrowing that Stuff
  WillS 14   You've Been Foolin' Round Town
BEER (1)
  ChatP 1   Beer Drinking Woman
BEFORE ['FO, FO'] (4)
  CarrL 19   Blues Before Sunrise
  HicR   7   'Fo Day Creep
  McTW   3   Mama, 'Tain't Long Fo' Day
  SmiJ 16   Before Long
BEGGAR (1)
  JonM 20   Never Drive a Beggar from Your Door
BEGGIN' (1)
  JefB   8   Beggin' Back
BEGIN (1)
  Stev   2   I'll See You in the Spring When the Birds
                Begin to Sing
BEING (3)
  GibC   3   Tired of Being Mistreated Part 1
  GibC   4   Tired of Being Mistreated Part 2
  GibC   7   I'm Tired of Being Mistreated
BELIEVE (4)
  CarrL 25   I Believe I'll Make a Change
  ChatP 7   I Believe I'll Settle Down
  JohR   3   I Believe I'll Dust My Broom
  KelJ   4   Believe I'll Go Back Home
BELL (2)
  DickT 1   Death Bell Blues
  McTW 32   Bell Street Blues
BELLS (2)
  JorL   1   Church Bells Blues

BELLS (cont.)
JorL   2   Church Bells Blues
BELONGS (2)
JackC 22   She Belongs to Me Blues
WasbS 25   She Belongs to the Devil
BENCH (1)
Rach   5   Squeaky Work Bench Blues
BENDED (1)
HilK   3   Down on My Bended Knee
BERTHA (1)
PetW   2   Bertha Lee Blues
BESS (1)
BogL   23   Barbecue Bess
BESSEMER (1)
Rain   24   Bessemer Bound Blues
BESSIE'S (1)
TucB   1   Bessie's Moan
BEST (1)
Whea   9   Doin' the Best I Can
BETSY (1)
ThoH   11   Charmin' Betsy
BETTER (2)
AleT   17   Seen Better Days
Shad   13   Better Leave That Stuff Alone
BETTY (1)
KelJ   7   Betty Sue Blues
BIDDLE (1)
Spau   2   Biddle Street Blues
BIG (18)
ArnK   16   Big Leg Mama
ArnK   28   Big Ship Blues
Bare   3   Big Rock Jail
BigB   10   Big Bill Blues
CarrL 27   Big Four Blues
ChatB 21   Your Biscuits Are Big Enough for Me
DelaM   1   Down the Big Road Blues
FulB   7   Big House Bound
Hurt   4   Big Leg Blues
JefB   60   Big Night Blues
JohTo   2   Big Road Blues
JohTo   8   Big Fat Mama Blues
JorC   3   Big Four Blues
LewF   5   Big Chief Blues
RolW   4   Big Mama
Temp   1   Big Boat Whistle
WasbS   6   Big Woman
WillS 33   Big Apple Blues
BILL (2)
BennW   1   Railroad Bill
BigB   10   Big Bill Blues
BILLIKEN'S (1)
DayT   3   Billiken's Weary Blues
BILL'S (1)
Bare   8   Barefoot Bill's Hard Luck Blues
BILLY (1)
Byrd   1   Billy Goat Blues
BIRD (2)
Patt   21   Bird Nest Bound
WillS 19   Blue Bird Blues--Part 1
BIRDS (1)
Stev   2   I'll See You in the Spring When the Birds
            Begin to Sing
BISCUITS (1)
ChatB 21   Your Biscuits Are Big Enough for Me
BITING [BITIN'] (2)
JonM   18   I'm a Back Bitin' Mama
WilsL   4   Back Biting Bee Blues
BLACK (45)
ArnK   4   Old Black Cat Blues
ArnK   10   Black Annie
BelA   3   Shake It, Black Bottom
Blak   8   Black Dog Blues
BogL   10   Black Angel Blues
Bond   2   Black Gal Swing
Crud   1   Black Pony Blues
DaviM   2   Too Black Bad
Este   4   Black Mattie Blues
Este   10   My Black Gal Blues
EvanJ   3   Down in Black Bottom

BLACK (cont.)
HicR   14   Black Skunk Blues
Hous   1   My Black Mama--Part 1
Hous   2   My Black Mama--Part 2
JefB   5   Black Horse Blues
JefB   11   That Black Snake Moan
JefB   18   Black Snake Moan
JefB   26   Black Snake Dream Blues
JefB   58   That Black Snake Moan No. 2
JohLo 10   New Black Snake Blues--Part 1
JohTo 10   Black Mare Blues
Ledb   6   New Black Snake Moan
LewF   14   Black Gypsy Blues
LitS   1   Black Cat Swing
McCl   14   Black Minnie
McPB   1   Down in Black Bottom
MemM   35   Black Cat Blues
MooAl   1   Black and Evil Blues
MooAl   7   Black Evil Blues
MooM   1   Black Hearse Blues
Patt   18   Mean Black Moan
Pick   1   Crazy 'Bout My Black Gal
Pull   1   Black Gal What Makes Your Head So Hard?--No. 2
Rain   31   Black Eye Blues
Shad   9   A Black Woman Is Like a Black Snake
SmiB   32   Black Mountain Blues
SmiT   13   Black Bottom Hop
SpiV   7   New Black Snake Blues--Part 1
SpiV   11   Black Snake Swing
TurnB   1   Black Ace
WashL   2   Black Snake Blues
WhiW   4   Black Train Blues
WillS 41   Black Panter Blues
WillS 44   My Black Name Blues
BLAKE'S (1)
Blak   4   Blake's Worried Blues
BLIND (4)
HicR   8   Blind Pig Blues
JefB   33   Blind Lemon's Penitentiary Blues
Ledb   13   My Friend Blind Lemon
MartS   1   Blind Man Blues
BLOCK (1)
Whea   28   Block and Tackle
BLOOD (1)
Vinc   15   I've Got Blood in My Eyes for You
BLUE (18)
Blacw   6   Blue Day Blues
CoxI   4   Blue Kentucky Blues
DaviW 23   Why Shouldn't I Be Blue
Hurt   7   Blue Harvest Blues
JohLo   6   Blue Ghost Blues
JohLo 22   Friendless and Blue
JohLo 28   Blue Ghost Blues
Lock   1   Little Boy Blue
McCl   18   Deep Blue Sea Blues
MartD   1   Feelin' Blue
NelsT   1   Blue Coat Blues
SmiB   31   Blue Spirit Blues
SmiC   24   Deep Blue Sea Blues
SmiIv   1   Sad and Blue
Temp   4   So Lonely and Blue
ThoJ   1   Blue Goose Blues
Whea   17   True Blue Woman
WillS 19   Blue Bird Blues--Part 1
BLUEBIRD (1)
McCl   23   Bluebird Blues
BLUES (1107)
Aker   1   Cottonfield Blues--Part 1
Aker   2   Cottonfield Blues--Part 2
Aker   3   Dough Roller Blues
Aker   4   Jumpin' and Shoutin' Blues
AleT   1   Long Lonesome Day Blues
AleT   2   Corn-Bread Blues
AleT   3   Section Gang Blues
AleT   4   Levee Camp Moan Blues
AleT   5   Yellow Girl Blues
AleT   6   No More Woman Blues
AleT   8   Work Ox Blues
AleT   10   I Am Calling Blues

AleT	11	Double Crossing Blues
AleT	12	Ninety-Eight Degree Blues
AleT	13	Water Bound Blues
AleT	14	Awful Moaning Blues--Part 1
AleT	15	Awful Moaning Blues--Part 2
AleT	18	Frost Texas Tornado Blues
AleT	19	Easy Rider Blues
Amos	1	C and O Blues
AndeJ	1	Free Woman Blues
AndeJ	2	I. C. Blues
ArnK	1	Rainy Night Blues
ArnK	2	Milk Cow Blues
ArnK	3	Old Original Kokomo Blues
ArnK	4	Old Black Cat Blues
ArnK	5	Sissy Man Blues
ArnK	6	Front Door Blues
ArnK	7	Back Door Blues
ArnK	9	Slop Jar Blues
ArnK	11	Southern Railroad Blues
ArnK	14	Policy Wheel Blues
ArnK	17	Milk Cow Blues--No. 4
ArnK	23	Wild Water Blues
ArnK	24	Laugh and Grin Blues
ArnK	28	Big Ship Blues
ArnK	29	Buddie Brown Blues
ArnK	30	Rocky Road Blues
ArnK	31	Head Cuttin' Blues
ArnK	32	Broke Man Blues
ArnK	37	Midnight Blues
ArnK	38	Bad Luck Blues
ArnK	39	Kid Man Blues
BaiK	1	Mississippi Bottom Blues
BaiK	2	Rowdy Blues
BakW	1	Mama, Don't Rush Me Blues
BakW	2	No No Blues
BakW	3	Weak-Minded Blues
BakW	5	Crooked Woman Blues
BakW	7	Weak-Minded Blues
BakW	8	Sweet Patunia Blues
Bare	1	My Crime Blues
Bare	2	Snigglin' Blues
Bare	7	Squabblin' Blues
Bare	8	Barefoot Bill's Hard Luck Blues
Batt	2	Highway No. 61 Blues
BaxJ	1	Bamalong Blues
BaxJ	2	K. C. Railroad Blues
Beam	1	Wayward Girl Blues
Beam	2	Rolling Log Blues
Beam	3	Goin' Away Blues
Beam	4	Going Away Blues
Beam	5	Rollin' Log Blues
BelA	1	Hopeless Blues
BelA	2	Every Woman Blues
BelE	1	Mamlish Blues
BelE	2	Ham Bone Blues
BelE	3	Mean Conductor Blues
BelE	4	Frisco Whistle Blues
BennW	2	Real Estate Blues
BigB	1	Down in the Basement Blues
BigB	2	Starvation Blues
BigB	8	Pussy Cat Blues
BigB	9	The Banker's Blues
BigB	10	Big Bill Blues
BigB	13	Bull Cow Blues
BigB	16	Mississippi River Blues
BigB	17	C and A Blues
BirB	1	Mill Man Blues
BirB	2	Alabama Blues--Part 1
BirB	3	Alabama Blues--Part 2
Bird	1	Gas Man Blues
BlaAB	1	Sugarland Blues
BlaAL	1	Rock Island Blues
BlaAL	2	Gravel Camp Blues
BlaAL	3	Corn Liquor Blues
Blacw	1	Kokomo Blues
Blacw	2	Penal Farm Blues
Blacw	3	Trouble Blues--Part 1
Blacw	4	Trouble Blues--Part 2

Blacw	5	Rambling Blues
Blacw	6	Blue Day Blues
Blacw	7	Down South Blues
Blacw	8	Hard Time Blues
Blacw	9	Back Door Blues
Blacw	10	No Good Woman Blues
Blak	1	Early Morning Blues
Blak	2	Early Morning Blues
Blak	4	Blake's Worried Blues
Blak	7	Stonewall Street Blues
Blak	8	Black Dog Blues
Blak	9	One Time Blues
Blak	10	Bad Feeling Blues
Blak	11	Brownskin Mama Blues
Blak	12	Hard Road Blues
Blak	13	Hey Hey Daddy Blues
Blak	14	You Gonna Quit Me Blues
Blak	16	Doggin' Me Mama Blues
Blak	18	No Dough Blues
Blak	19	Bootleg Rum Dum Blues
Blak	20	Panther Squall Blues
Blak	22	Search Warrant Blues
Blak	23	Notoriety Woman Blues
Blak	25	Poker Woman Blues
Blak	28	Hookworm Blues
Blak	30	Too Tight Blues No. 2
Blak	31	Police Dog Blues
Blak	33	Playing Policy Blues
Blak	34	Righteous Blues
Blak	35	Rope Stretchin' Blues--Part 1
Blak	36	Rope Stretchin' Blues--Part 2
Blak	37	Depression's Gone from Me Blues
BliN	1	Sundown Blues
BliP	1	Coal River Blues
BliP	2	Fourteenth Street Blues
BogL	2	Levee Blues
BogL	3	Jim Tampa Blues
BogL	4	Coffee Grindin' Blues
BogL	5	Pot Hound Blues
BogL	8	Sloppy Drunk Blues
BogL	10	Black Angel Blues
BogL	12	T N and O Blues
BogL	13	Baking Powder Blues
BogL	15	Lonesome Midnight Blues
BogL	25	Man Stealer Blues
BogL	26	Stew Meat Blues
BogL	27	Skin Game Blues
Bond	1	Weary Worried Blues
Bond	3	80 Highway Blues
BoyG	1	Never Mind Blues
Brac	1	Saturday Blues
Brac	2	Left Alone Blues
Brac	3	Leavin' Town Blues
Brac	4	My Brown Mama Blues
Brac	5	Trouble-Hearted Blues
Brac	6	Trouble-Hearted Blues
Brac	7	The Four Day Blues
Brac	8	Woman Woman Blues
Brac	9	Suitcase Full of Blues
Brac	10	Bust Up Blues
BradT	2	Pack Up Your Trunk Blues
BradT	4	Four Day Blues
BradT	5	Window Pane Blues
BrowI	1	Titanic Blues
BrowI	2	Preacher Blues
BrowI	3	Nut Factory Blues
BrowR	1	James Alley Blues
BrowV	1	M and O Blues
BrowV	2	Future Blues
BryL	1	Dentist Chair Blues--Part 1
BryL	2	Dentist Chair Blues--Part 2
ButlS	3	Poor Boy Blues
ButlS	4	Jefferson County Blues
Byrd	1	Billy Goat Blues
Byrd	2	Old Timbrook Blues
Cali	1	Fare Thee Well Blues
Cali	2	Traveling Mama Blues
Call	1	Lazy Woman's Blues

CamB	1	Dice's Blues
CamB	2	Shotgun Blues
CamB	3	Starvation Farm Blues
CamC	1	Goin' Away Blues
CamG	1	Wandering Blues
CamG	2	Robbin' and Stealin' Blues
Cann	2	Heart Breakin' Blues
Cann	4	Last Chance Blues
CarrL	1	Naptown Blues
CarrL	5	Sloppy Drunk Blues
CarrL	7	Alabama Woman Blues
CarrL	8	Low Down Dog Blues
CarrL	9	New How Long How Long Blues--Part 2
CarrL	12	I Keep the Blues
CarrL	13	Midnight Hour Blues
CarrL	16	Corn Licker Blues
CarrL	18	Shady Lane Blues
CarrL	19	Blues Before Sunrise
CarrL	22	Southbound Blues
CarrL	27	Big Four Blues
CarrL	32	Good Woman Blues
CarrL	33	Hustler's Blues
CarrL	34	Eleven Twenty-Nine Blues
CarrL	37	Tight Time Blues
CarrL	41	Suicide Blues
CartG	1	Rising River Blues
CartG	2	Hot Jelly Roll Blues
CartS	1	Don't Leave Me Blues
ChatB	11	Howlin' Tom Cat Blues
ChatB	12	I Get the Blues
ChatB	13	Rolling Blues
ChatB	15	Dinner Blues
ChatB	16	Cigarette Blues
ChatB	17	Pussy Cat Blues
ChatB	29	Arrangement for Me--Blues
ChatB	31	Policy Blues
ChatP	3	Grinder Man Blues
ChatP	4	Empty Room Blues
ChatP	13	Whiskey and Gin Blues
Chur	1	Number Nine Blues
Chur	2	Pneumatic Blues
ClayJ	2	State of Tennessee Blues
ClayJ	3	Bob Lee Junior Blues
Clev	1	Goin' to Leave You Blues
ColeK	1	Hard Hearted Mama Blues
ColeK	2	Niagara Fall Blues
ColFB	1	Sing Song Blues
ColFJ	1	Man Trouble Blues
ColFJ	5	Coffee Grinder Blues
ColFJ	6	Man Trouble Blues
ColFL	1	Old Rock Island Blues
CollC	1	Walking Blues
CollC	2	Atlanta Blues
CollS	1	The Jail House Blues
CollS	3	Yellow Dog Blues
CollS	4	Loving Lady Blues
CollS	5	Riverside Blues
CollS	6	Hesitation Blues
CollS	7	Midnight Special Blues
CollS	10	Lonesome Road Blues
CookR	1	Dollar Blues
CoxI	1	Ida Cox's Lawdy, Lawdy Blues
CoxI	2	Wild Women Don't Have the Blues
CoxI	3	Misery Blues
CoxI	4	Blue Kentucky Blues
CoxI	5	Long Distance Blues
CoxI	6	Southern Woman's Blues
CoxI	7	Lonesome Blues
CoxI	8	Coffin Blues
CoxI	9	Rambling Blues
CoxI	10	Worn Down Daddy Blues
Crud	1	Black Pony Blues
Crud	2	Death Valley Blues
Crud	4	Mean Old 'Frisco Blues
Curr	1	Fat Mouth Blues
Dadd	1	Sundown Blues
Dadd	2	Stove Pipe Blues
Dadd	3	Tuxedo Blues

DanJ	2	Ninety-Nine Year Blues
Darb	1	Lawdy Lawdy Worried Blues
Darb	2	Deceiving Blues
DaviC	1	Elm Street Woman Blues
DaviW	1	M. and O. Blues
DaviW	3	Howling Wind Blues
DaviW	4	M. and O. Blues No. 3
DaviW	5	L and N Blues
DaviW	8	Sad and Lonesome Blues
DaviW	9	Minute Man Blues--Part 1
DaviW	10	Minute Man Blues--Part 2
DaviW	12	Root Man Blues
DayT	2	Elm Street Blues
DayT	3	Billiken's Weary Blues
DayW	1	Central Avenue Blues
DayW	2	Sunrise Blues
DelaM	1	Down the Big Road Blues
DelaM	2	Tallahatchie River Blues
DickP	2	Little Rock Blues
DickT	1	Death Bell Blues
DickT	2	Happy Blues
DickT	3	Labor Blues
DorsT	1	Grievin' Me Blues
DorsT	2	Broke Man's Blues
DorsT	3	Pig Meat Blues
DorsT	4	Second-Hand Woman Blues
DorsT	5	Maybe It's the Blues
DorsT	6	Levee Bound Blues
DorsT	8	Terrible Operation Blues
DorsT	9	Terrible Operation Blues
DorsT	12	Been Mistreated Blues
Doyl	1	Hard Scufflin' Blues
Doyl	3	Renewed Love Blues
Doyl	4	Bad in Mind Blues
EdwF	1	Terraplane Blues
Este	3	Diving Duck Blues
Este	4	Black Mattie Blues
Este	5	Milk Cow Blues
Este	6	Street Car Blues
Este	8	Poor John Blues
Este	10	My Black Gal Blues
Este	11	Down South Blues
Este	13	Someday Baby Blues
Este	14	Who's Been Tellin' You Buddy Brown Blues
Este	15	Married Woman Blues
Este	19	Vernita Blues
Este	22	Need More Blues
Este	23	Jack and Jill Blues
Este	25	Hobo Jungle Blues
Este	26	Airplane Blues
Este	28	Liquor Store Blues
Este	30	Fire Department Blues
Este	32	New Someday Blues
Este	33	Brownsville Blues
Este	35	Mailman Blues
Este	38	Jailhouse Blues
Este	42	Lawyer Clark Blues
Este	43	Little Laura Blues
Este	44	Working Man Blues
EvanJ	4	Shook It This Morning Blues
FloN	1	Jacksonville Blues
FloN	2	Midnight Weeping Blues
FoxJ	1	The Worried Man Blues
FoxJ	2	The Moanin' Blues
FulB	4	Bye Bye Baby Blues
FulB	5	Pistol Snapper Blues
FulB	11	Three Ball Blues
FulB	12	Good Feeling Blues
FulB	13	Crooked Woman Blues
FulB	14	Bus Rider Blues
FulB	16	Thousand Women Blues
GibB	2	Nothing But the Blues
GibC	2	Whiskey Moan Blues
GibC	8	Ice and Snow Blues
GibC	10	Drayman Blues
GibC	14	Hard-Headed Blues
GibC	15	Blues Without a Dime
GibC	17	Jive Me Blues

GibC	18	Brooklyn Blues
GibC	19	Society Blues
Gill	7	Keyhole Blues
Gill	9	Riley Springs Blues
Glaz	1	Rollin' Mama Blues
Glaz	2	Lonesome Day Blues
Glov	4	Gas Man Blues
Gran	1	Nappy Head Blues
Gran	2	Lonesome Atlanta Blues
Grav	1	New York Blues
GreLi	9	Country Boy Blues
Gros	1	Hard Luck Blues
Hann	1	Freakish Man Blues
Hard	1	California Desert Blues
HarO	1	Waking Blues
HarW	2	Bull Frog Blues
HarW	3	Hot Time Blues
HarY	1	Hop Head Blues
HarY	2	Iggly Oggly Blues
HarZ	1	Memphis Yo Yo Blues
Hawk	1	Shaggy Dog Blues
Hawk	2	Number Three Blues
Hawk	3	Jailhouse Fire Blues
Hawk	4	Snatch It Back Blues
Hawk	5	Awful Fix Blues
Hawk	6	How Come Mama Blues
Hawk	7	Voice Throwin' Blues
HayeN	1	Violin Blues
HendB	1	Lead Hearted Blues
HendK	1	West End Blues
HendK	2	St. Louis Blues
HenrH	1	Low Down Hound Blues
HenrL	1	Low Down Despondent Blues
HicR	1	Barbecue Blues
HicR	2	Cloudy Sky Blues
HicR	5	Motherless Chile Blues
HicR	6	Crooked Woman Blues
HicR	8	Blind Pig Blues
HicR	11	Ease It to Me Blues
HicR	12	She's Gone Blues
HicR	13	California Blues
HicR	14	Black Skunk Blues
HicR	18	Yo-Yo Blues No. 2
HilB	1	Low Land Blues
HilB	2	Kid Man Blues
HilB	3	Pleadin' for the Blues
HilB	4	Pratt City Blues
HilB	5	Lovesick Blues
HilB	6	Lonesome Weary Blues
HilK	1	Whoopee Blues
HilK	2	Whoopee Blues
HilSy	1	Cryin' for the Blues
HilSy	2	Needin' My Woman Blues
Hite	1	Graveyard Dream Blues
Hite	2	Mason-Dixon Blues
Hogg	1	Family Trouble Blues
HollT	1	Stamp Blues
Hous	3	Preachin' the Blues--Part 1
Hous	4	Preachin' the Blues--Part 2
Hous	5	Dry Spell Blues--Part 1
Hous	6	Dry Spell Blues--Part 2
Howe	1	Coal Man Blues
Howe	2	Tishamingo Blues
Howe	3	Too Tight Blues
Howe	5	Skin Game Blues
Howe	7	Low Down Rounder Blues
Howe	8	Ball and Chain Blues
Hull	2	France Blues
Hull	3	Two Little Tommies Blues
Hurt	3	Avalon Blues
Hurt	4	Big Leg Blues
Hurt	5	Candy Man Blues
Hurt	6	Got the Blues Can't Be Satisfied
Hurt	7	Blue Harvest Blues
JackC	1	Papa's Lawdy Lawdy Blues
JackC	2	Airy Man Blues
JackC	3	Salty Dog Blues
JackC	7	Coffee Pot Blues

JackC	9	The Faking Blues
JackC	12	Hot Papa Blues
JackC	13	Take Me Back Blues
JackC	15	Maxwell Street Blues
JackC	17	Texas Blues
JackC	18	Butter and Egg Man Blues
JackC	21	Fat Mouth Blues
JackC	22	She Belongs to Me Blues
JackC	23	Coal Man Blues
JackC	26	Ash Tray Blues
JackC	27	Jungle Man Blues
JackJ	1	Bootlegging Blues
JackJ	5	Hesitation Blues
JackJ	6	St. Louis Blues
JamJ	3	Lonesome Day Blues
JamS	2	Cypress Grove Blues
JamS	3	Cherry Ball Blues
JamS	4	Hard Time Killin' Floor Blues
JamS	5	Special Rider Blues
JamS	6	Little Cow and Calf Is Gonna Die Blues
JamS	7	22-20 Blues
JefB	1	Got the Blues
JefB	2	Long Lonesome Blues
JefB	3	Booster Blues
JefB	4	Dry Southern Blues
JefB	5	Black Horse Blues
JefB	6	Corinna Blues
JefB	7	Chock House Blues
JefB	9	Old Rounders Blues
JefB	10	Stocking Feet Blues
JefB	12	Wartime Blues
JefB	15	Booger Rooger Blues
JefB	16	Rabbit Foot Blues
JefB	17	Bad Luck Blues
JefB	19	Match Box Blues
JefB	20	Easy Rider Blues
JefB	21	Match Box Blues
JefB	22	Match Box Blues
JefB	23	Rising High Water Blues
JefB	24	Right of Way Blues
JefB	25	Teddy Bear Blues
JefB	26	Black Snake Dream Blues
JefB	27	Struck Sorrow Blues
JefB	28	Rambler Blues
JefB	29	Chinch Bug Blues
JefB	32	Lonesome House Blues
JefB	33	Blind Lemon's Penitentiary Blues
JefB	34	'Lectric Chair Blues
JefB	35	Lemon's Worried Blues
JefB	36	Mean Jumper Blues
JefB	37	Balky Mule Blues
JefB	38	Change My Luck Blues
JefB	39	Prison Cell Blues
JefB	42	Low Down Mojo Blues
JefB	43	Competition Bed Blues
JefB	44	Sad News Blues
JefB	46	Lock Step Blues
JefB	47	Hangman's Blues
JefB	48	Christmas Eve Blues
JefB	49	Happy New Year Blues
JefB	50	Maltese Cat Blues
JefB	51	D B Blues
JefB	53	Dynamite Blues
JefB	54	Oil Well Blues
JefB	55	Tin Cup Blues
JefB	56	Empty House Blues
JefB	57	Saturday Night Spender Blues
JefB	60	Big Night Blues
JefB	61	Bed Springs Blues
JefB	62	Yo Yo Blues
JefB	64	Southern Woman Blues
JefB	65	Bakershop Blues
JefB	66	Pneumonia Blues
JefB	68	That Crawlin' Baby Blues
JefB	69	Fence Breakin' Yellin' Blues
JefB	70	Cat Man Blues
JohAl	1	Miss Meal Cramp Blues
JohBi	1	Sun Beam Blues

JohBi	2	Interurban Blues
JohBi	3	Frisco Blues
JohBi	4	Wild Jack Blues
JohBu	1	Undertaker Blues
JohE	1	Nickel's Worth of Liver Blues
JohE	2	Good Chib Blues
JohE	4	Honeydripper Blues
JohEb	1	Be My Kid Blues
JohEb	2	Sobbin' Woman Blues
JohJa	1	Barrel of Whiskey Blues
JohK	2	Wrong Woman Blues
JohLe	1	Candy Blues
JohLo	1	Mr. Johnson's Blues
JohLo	2	Falling Rain Blues
JohLo	4	St. Louis Cyclone Blues
JohLo	5	Life Saver Blues
JohLo	6	Blue Ghost Blues
JohLo	10	New Black Snake Blues--Part 1
JohLo	15	Racketeers Blues
JohLo	18	Flood Water Blues
JohLo	23	Devil's Got the Blues
JohLo	26	New Falling Rain Blues
JohLo	28	Blue Ghost Blues
JohLo	30	Crowin' Rooster Blues
JohLs	1	All Night Long Blues
JohMa	1	Barrel House Flat Blues
JohMa	2	Key to the Mountain Blues
JohMa	3	Rattlesnake Blues
JohMa	4	Mary Johnson Blues
JohR	1	Kind Hearted Woman Blues
JohR	2	Kind Hearted Woman Blues
JohR	9	Terraplane Blues
JohR	10	Phonograph Blues
JohR	11	32-20 Blues
JohR	13	Dead Shrimp Blues
JohR	14	Cross Road Blues
JohR	15	Walkin' Blues
JohR	17	Preachin' Blues
JohR	18	Preachin' Blues
JohR	29	Me and the Devil Blues
JohR	30	Stop Breakin' Down Blues
JohR	31	Traveling Riverside Blues
JohR	32	Honeymoon Blues
JohR	35	Milkcow's Calf Blues
JohR	36	Milkcow's Calf Blues
JohT	1	J. C. Johnson's Blues
JohTo	1	Cool Drink of Water Blues
JohTo	2	Big Road Blues
JohTo	3	Bye-Bye Blues
JohTo	4	Maggie Campbell Blues
JohTo	5	Canned Heat Blues
JohTo	6	Lonesome Home Blues
JohTo	7	Lonesome Home Blues
JohTo	8	Big Fat Mama Blues
JohTo	9	Lonesome Home Blues
JohTo	10	Black Mare Blues
JonAn	1	Trixie Blues
JonB	1	Back Door Blues
JonB	2	Leavenworth Prison Blues
JonCo	1	Sweet Mama Blues
JonCo	2	Texas and Pacific Blues
JonJ	2	Southern Sea Blues
JonL	1	New Two Sixteen Blues
JonL	2	Two String Blues
JonL	3	Rolled From Side to Side Blues
JonL	4	Hurry Blues
JonL	5	Little Hat Blues
JonL	6	Corpus Blues
JonL	7	Bye Bye Baby Blues
JonL	8	Cross the Water Blues
JonL	9	Cherry Street Blues
JonM	2	Jealous Mama Blues
JonM	3	Box Car Blues
JonM	4	Western Union Blues
JonM	5	Poor House Blues
JonM	7	Thunderstorm Blues
JonM	9	Screamin' the Blues
JonM	10	Good Time Flat Blues

JonM	13	Dangerous Blues
JonM	14	Suicide Blues
JonM	15	Undertaker's Blues
JonM	16	North Bound Blues
JonM	19	Dallas Blues
JonM	21	Single Woman's Blues
JorC	1	Stack O' Dollars Blues
JorC	3	Big Four Blues
JorC	4	Raidin' Squad Blues
JorC	5	Hunkie Tunkie Blues
JorC	6	Gasoline Blues
JorC	9	Tight Haired Mama Blues
JorL	1	Church Bells Blues
JorL	2	Church Bells Blues
JorL	3	Cocaine Blues
KelE	1	Poole County Blues
KelJ	1	Highway No. 61 Blues
KelJ	2	Highway No. 61 Blues No. 2
KelJ	5	Ko-ko-mo Blues
KelJ	7	Betty Sue Blues
KelJ	8	Flower Blues
KelJ	9	Men Fooler Blues
KidS	1	Short Hair Blues
King	2	Rising Sun Blues
King	3	Sweet Potato Blues
Kyle	1	Kyle's Worried Blues
Lask	2	Teasin' Brown Blues
Ledb	3	Packin' Trunk Blues
Ledb	9	Death Letter Blues--Part 1
Ledb	10	Death Letter Blues--Part 2
Ledb	12	Red River Blues
Ledb	16	Match Box Blues
Ledb	18	T. B. Woman Blues
LeeB	1	Mind Reader Blues
LewF	2	Mr. Furry's Blues
LewF	4	Good Looking Girl Blues
LewF	5	Big Chief Blues
LewF	6	Falling Down Blues
LewF	7	Mean Old Bedbug Blues
LewF	8	Why Don't You Come Home Blues
LewF	9	Furry's Blues
LewF	12	Dry Land Blues
LewF	13	Judge Harsh Blues
LewF	14	Black Gypsy Blues
LewF	15	Creeper's Blues
LewN	1	Viola Lee Blues
LewN	3	Pretty Mama Blues
LewN	4	Ticket Agent Blues
LewN	5	New Minglewood Blues
Linc	1	Jealous Hearted Blues
Linc	2	Hard Luck Blues
Linc	3	Mojoe Blues
Linc	7	Doodle Hole Blues
Lint	1	Pretty Mama Blues
LofC	1	Monkey Man Blues
LofC	4	Change My Mind Blues
LofW	1	Jake Leg Blues
LofW	2	My Mean Baby Blues
LofW	3	Dark Road Blues
Luca	1	Pussy Cat Blues
Luca	4	Double Trouble Blues
McCl	11	Katy Mae Blues
McCl	15	Elsie Blues
McCl	16	Cross Cut Saw Blues
McCl	18	Deep Blue Sea Blues
McCl	21	Mozelle Blues
McCl	22	Mr. So and So Blues
McCl	23	Bluebird Blues
McClu	1	Prisoner's Blues
McCoC	1	Last Time Blues
McCoJ	5	My Mary Blues
McCoJ	6	Cherry Ball Blues
McCoJ	8	Pile Drivin' Blues
McCoJ	11	Preachers Blues
McCoJ	16	Evil Devil Woman Blues
McCoJ	22	Southern Blues
McCoR	2	Friar's Point Blues
McCoW	1	Central Tracks Blues

McFa	1	People People Blues
McFaB	1	I Got to Go Blues
MackA	1	West End Blues
MackA	2	Wicked Daddy Blues
McMu	2	De Kalb Chain Blues
McPB	2	My Dream Blues
McPB	3	Whiskey Man Blues
McTW	1	Writin' Paper Blues
McTW	2	Stole Rider Blues
McTW	4	Mr. McTell Got the Blues
McTW	5	Three Women Blues
McTW	6	Statesboro Blues
McTW	8	Travelin' Blues
McTW	11	Drive Away Blues
McTW	12	Love-Changing Blues
McTW	16	Broke Down Engine Blues
McTW	18	Scarey Day Blues
McTW	20	Rollin' Mama Blues
McTW	21	Searching the Desert for the Blues
McTW	27	Death Cell Blues
McTW	28	B and O Blues No. 2
McTW	29	Weary Hearted Blues
McTW	32	Bell Street Blues
McTW	33	Ticket Agent Blues
Mann	1	The Blues Is All Wrong
MartC	4	Joe Louis Blues
MartS	1	Blind Man Blues
MartS	2	Death Sting Me Blues
MartS	3	Mistreating Man Blues
MemM	6	Bumble Bee Blues
MemM	7	Meningitis Blues
MemM	10	Memphis Minnie-Jitis Blues
MemM	11	Plymouth Rock Blues
MemM	16	Grandpa and Grandma Blues
MemM	17	Garage Fire Blues
MemM	19	North Memphis Blues
MemM	21	Crazy Cryin' Blues
MemM	23	After While Blues
MemM	26	Stinging Snake Blues
MemM	27	Drunken Barrelhouse Blues
MemM	29	Chickasaw Train Blues
MemM	35	Black Cat Blues
MemM	40	Lonesome Shark Blues
MemM	42	Boy Friend Blues
MemM	45	Me and My Chauffeur Blues
MileL	1	Shootin' Star Blues
MillL	1	Dead Drunk Blues
MissM	2	It's Cold in China Blues
MontE	1	The Woman I Love Blues
MontE	2	Pleading Blues
MontE	3	Vicksburg Blues No. 2
MontE	6	Vicksburg Blues--Part 3
MontE	7	Out West Blues
MontE	8	Leaving Town Blues
MontE	9	West Texas Blues
MontE	10	Never Go Wrong Blues
MontE	11	Mistreatin' Woman Blues
MooAl	1	Black and Evil Blues
MooAl	2	Prison Blues
MooAl	3	My Man Blues
MooAl	4	Broadway St. Woman Blues
MooAl	5	Lonesome Dream Blues
MooAl	6	Kid Man Blues
MooAl	7	Black Evil Blues
MooM	1	Black Hearse Blues
MooM	2	Scandal Blues
MooP	1	Bug Juice Blues
MooR	1	Staggering Blues
MooR	2	Ha-Ha Blues
MooR	3	School Girl Blues
MooR	4	Stranger Blues
MooR	5	Mad Dog Blues
MooW	2	Midnight Blues
MossB	2	Hard Road Blues
NelsR	2	Dyin' Rider Blues
NelsT	1	Blue Coat Blues
Newb	3	Shelby County Workhouse Blues
Newb	4	Hambone Willie's Dreamy-Eyed Woman's Blues

BLUES (cont.)

Newb	5	Roll and Tumble Blues
Nick	2	Cave Man Blues
Nobl	1	The Seminole Blues
Oden	2	Sitting Down Thinking Blues
OweG	1	Kentucky Blues
OweM	1	Texas Blues
Palm	1	Broke Man Blues
Patt	1	Mississippi Bo Weavil Blues
Patt	2	Screamin' and Hollerin' Blues
Patt	3	Down the Dirt Road Blues
Patt	4	Pony Blues
Patt	5	Banty Rooster Blues
Patt	7	Pea Vine Blues
Patt	8	Tom Rushen Blues
Patt	11	Green River Blues
Patt	12	Hammer Blues
Patt	17	Rattlesnake Blues
Patt	19	Dry Well Blues
Patt	22	Jersey Bull Blues
Patt	23	High Sheriff Blues
Patt	24	Stone Pony Blues
Patt	25	34 Blues
Patt	27	Revenue Man Blues
PerkG	1	No Easy Rider Blues
Pett	1	Two Time Blues
Pett	2	Out on Santa Fe--Blues
Pett	3	Good Boy Blues
PetW	1	Catfish Blues
PetW	2	Bertha Lee Blues
PetW	4	Cotton Pickin' Blues
PooJ	1	Whitewash Station Blues
Pope	1	Whiskey Drinkin' Blues
Pope	2	Doggin' Me Around Blues
Pope	3	Bull Frog Blues
Pope	4	Tennessee Workhouse Blues
Rach	2	T-Bone Steak Blues
Rach	3	Expressman Blues
Rach	5	Squeaky Work Bench Blues
Rain	1	Bad Luck Blues
Rain	2	Bo-Weavil Blues
Rain	3	Barrel House Blues
Rain	4	Those All Night Long Blues
Rain	5	Moonshine Blues
Rain	6	Last Minute Blues
Rain	7	Southern Blues
Rain	8	Walking Blues
Rain	9	Lost Wandering Blues
Rain	10	Dream Blues
Rain	14	Lucky Rock Blues
Rain	15	Jealous Hearted Blues
Rain	16	Cell Bound Blues
Rain	17	Army Camp Harmony Blues
Rain	18	Explaining the Blues
Rain	19	Rough and Tumble Blues
Rain	20	Night Time Blues
Rain	22	Memphis Bound Blues
Rain	23	Slave to the Blues
Rain	24	Bessemer Bound Blues
Rain	25	Oh My Babe Blues
Rain	28	Gone Daddy Blues
Rain	29	Misery Blues
Rain	31	Black Eye Blues
Rame	3	Cocaine Habit Blues
Rang	1	T. P. Window Blues
RedN	1	Crying Mother Blues
ReedW	1	Dreaming Blues
ReedW	2	Texas Blues
ReyJ	1	Outside Woman Blues
ReyJ	2	Nehi Blues
ReyW	1	Married Man Blues
ReyW	2	Third Street Woman Blues
RhoW	2	Leaving Home Blues
RichM	1	T and T Blues
RichM	2	Mooch Richardson's Low Down Barrel House Blues Part 1
RichM	3	Burying Ground Blues
RolW	1	T Model Blues
RolW	2	Dices' Blues

RolW	5	Every Morning Blues
RolW	6	45 Pistol Blues
RolW	7	Penniless Blues
Scha	1	Fence Breakin' Blues
Scha	2	Home Wreckin' Blues
ScotS	1	Red Cross Blues
Shad	2	Memphis Boy--Blues
Shad	5	Kansas City Blues
Shad	6	Evergreen Money Blues
Shad	11	Whitewash Station Blues
Shaw	3	Moanin' the Blues
Shor	1	Telephone Arguin' Blues
Shor	3	Snake Doctor Blues
Shor	4	Barefoot Blues
Shor	5	Grand Daddy Blues
Simp	1	Down South Blues
SimsH	1	Farrell Blues
SimsH	2	Tell Me Man Blues
Slue	1	Tootin' Out Blues
Slue	2	Shouting Baby Blues
SmiA	1	Insurance Policy Blues
SmiB	1	Down Hearted Blues
SmiB	2	Jail-House Blues
SmiB	4	Weeping Willow Blues
SmiB	5	The St. Louis Blues
SmiB	6	Reckless Blues
SmiB	7	Sobbin' Hearted Blues
SmiB	8	Cold In Hand Blues
SmiB	10	The Yellow Dog Blues
SmiB	11	Nashville Women's Blues
SmiB	12	J. C. Holmes Blues
SmiB	15	The Gin House Blues
SmiB	17	Lost Your Head Blues
SmiB	18	One and Two Blues
SmiB	19	Young Woman's Blues
SmiB	20	Preachin' the Blues
SmiB	21	Back Water Blues
SmiB	25	Mean Old Bed Bug Blues
SmiB	26	Empty Bed Blues--Part ?
SmiB	27	Poor Man's Blues
SmiB	30	St. Louis Blues--Part ?
SmiB	31	Blue Spirit Blues
SmiB	32	Black Mountain Blues
SmiB	34	Shipwreck Blues
SmiBM	2	Sugar Man Blues--Part 1
SmiBM	3	Sugar Man Blues--Part 2
SmiC	2	Every Woman's Blues
SmiC	3	Down South Blues
SmiC	4	All Night Blues
SmiC	9	Kansas City Man Blues
SmiC	10	Uncle Sam Blues
SmiC	15	Good Looking Papa Blues
SmiC	18	31st Street Blues
SmiC	21	The Clearing House Blues
SmiC	23	Back Woods Blues
SmiC	24	Deep Blue Sea Blues
SmiC	25	Texas Moaner Blues
SmiC	26	Basement Blues
SmiC	28	Freight Train Blues
SmiC	30	Death Letter Blues
SmiC	31	Prescription for the Blues
SmiC	34	Broken Busted Blues
SmiC	35	Shipwrecked Blues
SmiC	36	Court House Blues
SmiC	37	My John Blues
SmiIv	2	Third Alley Blues
SmiJ	1	Howling Wolf Blues--No. 1
SmiJ	2	Howling Wolf Blues--No. 2
SmiJ	3	Good Coffee Blues
SmiJ	8	Honey Blues
SmiJ	9	Corn Whiskey Blues
SmiJ	10	County Jail Blues
SmiJ	13	Fool's Blues
SmiJ	14	Seven Sisters Blues--Part 1
SmiJ	15	Seven Sisters Blues--Part 2
SmiSi	1	Oh Oh Lonesome Blues
SmiSi	2	Pennsylvania Woman Blues
SmiT	1	I Don't Know and I Don't Care Blues

SmiT	2	Freight Train Blues
SmiT	3	Sorrowful Blues
SmiT	5	Praying Blues
SmiT	7	Choo Choo Blues
SmiT	9	Mining Camp Blues
SmiT	11	Railroad Blues
SmiT	15	Freight Train Blues
Span	2	Back to the Woods Blues
Spar	1	Erie Train Blues
Spau	1	Cairo Blues
Spau	2	Biddle Street Blues
Spec	1	House Dance Blues
SpiV	1	Arkansas Road Blues
SpiV	5	Organ Grinder Blues
SpiV	6	Organ Grinder Blues
SpiV	7	New Black Snake Blues--Part 1
SpiV	9	Telephoning the Blues
SpiV	10	Don't Trust Nobody Blues
SpiV	13	T. B.'s Got Me Blues
Spru	1	Milk Cow Blues
Spru	2	Muddy Water Blues
Spru	4	Tom Cat Blues
Spru	10	Mr. Freddie's Kokomo Blues
Stev	3	Vol Stevens Blues
Stev	5	Coal Oil Blues
Stev	6	Papa Long Blues
Stev	7	Aunt Caroline Dyer Blues
Stev	8	Stonewall Blues
Stok	9	Blues in D
Stok	10	Downtown Blues
Stok	11	Downtown Blues
Stok	12	Bedtime Blues
Stok	13	What's the Matter Blues
Stok	14	Mistreatin' Blues
Stok	16	Nehi Mama Blues
Stok	21	Hunting Blues
Stok	22	South Memphis Blues
Stok	23	Bunker Hill Blues
Stok	24	Right Now Blues
Stok	25	Shiney Town Blues
Stok	27	Memphis Rounders Blues
Ston	2	Back Door Blues
Stov	1	Court Street Blues
SykR	1	44 Blues
SykR	2	All My Money Gone Blues
SykR	3	The Way I Feel Blues
SykR	4	Fire Detective Blues
SykR	5	Single Tree Blues
SykR	7	Lost All I Had Blues
SykR	8	Poor Boy Blues
SykR	9	Kelly's 44 Blues
SykR	12	No Good Woman Blues
SykR	14	Hard Luck Man Blues
SykR	15	Mr. Sykes Blues
SykR	16	Highway 61 Blues
Sylv	1	Midnight Blues
Sylv	2	Down South Blues
Tamp	1	Through Train Blues
Tamp	7	Kingfish Blues
Tamp	8	Mean Mistreater Blues
Tamp	9	Seminole Blues
TayC	1	Heavy Suitcase Blues
Temp	2	The Evil Devil Blues
Temp	3	Louise Louise Blues
Temp	5	New Louise Louise Blues
TexT	1	Jail Break Blues
ThoE	1	Motherless Child Blues
ThoG	1	Fast Stuff Blues
ThoH	1	Cottonfield Blues
ThoH	4	Shanty Blues
ThoH	7	Bull Doze Blues
ThoH	8	Texas Worried Blues
ThoH	10	Texas Easy Street Blues
ThoHo	2	Adam and Eve Had the Blues
ThoJ	1	Blue Goose Blues
ThoJ	2	No Good Woman Blues
ThoR	2	Hard to Rule Woman Blues
ThoR	3	Lock and Key Blues

ThoR	5	No Baby Blues
ThoR	6	Ramblin' Mind Blues
ThoR	7	No Job Blues
ThoR	8	Back Gnawing Blues
ThoR	9	Jig Head Blues
ThoR	10	Hard Dallas Blues
ThoR	12	Poor Boy Blues
ThoR	13	Good Time Blues
ThoR	14	New Way of Living Blues
ThoZ	1	Bedside Blues
ThpA	1	Minglewood Blues
ThpE	1	Showers of Rain Blues
ThpE	3	Seven Sister Blues
ThpE	4	West Virginia Blues
Tore	1	Married Woman Blues
Tore	2	Lonesome Man Blues
TowH	1	Henry's Worried Blues
TowH	2	Mistreated Blues
TowH	3	Long Ago Blues
TowH	4	Poor Man Blues
TowH	5	Sick with the Blues
TowS	1	Lily Kimball Blues
TurnB	2	Christmas Time Blues
TurnJ	1	Blues on Central Avenue
UnkA	1	String Band Blues
UnkA	2	Snitchin' Gambler Blues
UnkA	7	German Blues
Vinc	1	Overtime Blues
Vinc	3	Stop and Listen Blues
Vinc	5	Yodeling Fiddling Blues
Vinc	7	Unhappy Blues
Vinc	10	Ramrod Blues
Vinc	11	Stop and Listen Blues No. 2
Vinc	16	The New Stop and Listen Blues
Virg	2	Bad Notion Blues
WalkA	1	Trinity River Blues
WalkB	1	Look Here Mama Blues
WalkB	2	Stand Up Suitcase Blues
WallS	1	Special Delivery Blues
WallS	2	Jack O' Diamonds Blues
WallS	3	Bedroom Blues
WallS	4	Dead Drunk Blues
WallS	6	Lazy Man Blues
WallS	7	The Flood Blues
WasbS	2	Jesse James Blues
WasbS	10	Lowland Blues
WasbS	11	I'm On My Way Blues
WasbS	21	Flying Crow Blues
WasbS	22	Levee Camp Blues
WasbS	24	Brown and Yellow Woman Blues
WasbS	29	Evil Blues
WasbS	31	Lover's Lane Blues
WasbS	34	I Get the Blues at Bedtime
WasbW	1	Narrow Face Blues
WasbW	2	Insurance Man Blues
WashE	1	Garden of Joy--Blues
WashL	2	Black Snake Blues
Wate	3	Georgia Blues
Wate	8	Midnight Blues
Wate	11	Craving Blues
WeaC	2	No No Blues
WeaC	6	Fried Pie Blues
WeaS	1	Can't Be Trusted Blues
Weld	1	Stingy Woman--Blues
Weld	2	Memphis Jug--Blues
Weld	3	Sunshine Blues
Weld	4	Turpentine Blues
Weld	7	W. P. A. Blues
Weld	8	Blues Everywhere I Go
Weld	10	Red Hot Blues
WelS	1	The Bridwell Blues
WelS	2	St. Peter Blues
WelS	3	Dying Pickpocket Blues
Whea	4	C and A Blues
Whea	5	Ice and Snow Blues
Whea	6	Sleepless Nights Blues
Whea	7	All Night Long Blues
Whea	10	The Rising Sun Blues

Whea	11	Letter Writing Blues
Whea	12	Cocktail Man Blues
Whea	13	King Spider Blues
Whea	14	Last Dime Blues
Whea	16	First and Last Blues
Whea	18	Sweet Home Blues
Whea	19	Good Woman Blues
Whea	26	Remember and Forget Blues
Whea	29	Cut Out Blues
Whea	32	Crazy with the Blues
Whea	35	Crapshooter's Blues
Whea	37	Sick Bed Blues
Whea	39	Devilment Blues
Whea	41	Road Tramp Blues
WhiG	1	Pigmeat Blues
WhiG	3	The Blues Ain't Nothin' But. . .???
WhiJ	1	Welfare Blues
WhiW	4	Black Train Blues
WhiW	5	Strange Place Blues
WhiW	7	Sleepy Man Blues
WhiW	8	Parchman Farm Blues
WhiW	9	Good Gin Blues
WhiW	10	High Fever Blues
WhiW	11	District Attorney Blues
WhiW	12	Fixin' to Die Blues
WhiW	13	Aberdeen Mississippi Blues
Wigg	1	Evil Woman Blues
Wigg	2	Forty-Four Blues
Wigg	3	Frisco Bound Blues
Wigg	4	Corrine Corrina Blues
Wilb	2	Greyhound Blues
Wilk	1	Jail House Blues
Wilk	2	I Do Blues
Wilk	4	Alabama Blues
Wilk	5	Long Train Blues
Wilk	6	Falling Down Blues
Wilk	7	Nashville Stonewall Blues
Wilk	8	Police Sergeant Blues
Wilk	9	Get Away Blues
Wilk	10	I'll Go With Her Blues
Wilk	11	Dirty Deal Blues
Wilk	12	New Stock Yard Blues
WillH	2	Lonesome Blues
WillI	1	Polock Blues
WillJ	3	49 Highway Blues
WillJ	5	Stepfather Blues
WillJ	7	Wild Cow Blues
WillK	2	Mr. Devil Blues
WillS	2	Collector Man Blues
WillS	6	Miss Louisa Blues
WillS	9	Honey Bee Blues
WillS	10	Whiskey Headed Blues
WillS	11	Lord, Oh Lord Blues
WillS	13	Shannon Street Blues
WillS	16	Number Five Blues
WillS	17	Christmas Morning Blues
WillS	19	Blue Bird Blues--Part 1
WillS	20	Little Girl Blues
WillS	24	Insurance Man Blues
WillS	25	Rainy Day Blues
WillS	26	Bad Luck Blues
WillS	27	T. B. Blues
WillS	29	Train Fare Blues
WillS	30	Welfare Store Blues
WillS	33	Big Apple Blues
WillS	35	Shotgun Blues
WillS	36	Shady Grove Blues
WillS	37	Sloppy Drunk Blues
WillS	40	Ground Hog Blues
WillS	41	Black Panter Blues
WillS	42	Broken Hearted Blues
WillS	44	My Black Name Blues
WillX	1	Experience Blues
WillX	2	Painful Blues
WilsL	4	Back Biting Bee Blues
WooH	2	Last Chance Blues
WooH	3	The Rooster's Crowing Blues
WooH	4	Wolf River Blues

BLUES (cont.)
WooH   5   Prison Wall Blues
WooO   2   Lone Wolf Blues
Yate   1   I'm Gonna Moan My Blues Away
Yate   2   Sore Bunion Blues
BO (7)
CarrL 26   Bo Bo Stomp
ChatB 6   Bo Carter Special
ChatB 19   Bo Carter's Advice
FulB   3   Stealing Bo-Hog
Patt   1   Mississippi Bo Weavil Blues
Rain   2   Bo-Weavil Blues
BOAT (1)
Temp   1   Big Boat Whistle
BOB (2)
ClayJ 3   Bob Lee Junior Blues
ThoH   3   Bob McKinney
BONE (2)
BelE   2   Ham Bone Blues
HicR   9   Chocolate to the Bone
BONES (1)
McCl 10   Down to Skin and Bones
BONUS (1)
Whea 22   When I Get My Bonus
BOODIE (1)
Burs   3   Boodie Bum Bum
BOODLE-DE-BUM (1)
CovB   2   Boodle-De-Bum Bum
BOOGAN (1)
BogL 16   My Man Is Boogan Me
BOOGER (1)
JefB 15   Booger Rooger Blues
BOOGIE (4)
BogL   9   Alley Boogie
BogL 22   Down in Boogie Alley
Ezel   1   Pitchin' Boogie
McCoJ 25   We Gonna Pitch a Boogie Woogie
BOOK (1)
WasbS 18   Life Is Just a Book
BOOSTER (1)
JefB   3   Booster Blues
BOOTIN' (2)
ArnK 12   Busy Bootin'
JefB 71   Bootin' Me 'Bout
BOOTLEG (1)
Blak 19   Bootleg Rum Dum Blues
BOOTLEGGING (1)
JackJ 1   Bootlegging Blues
BORN (1)
RedN   2   Sweetest Thing Born
BORROWING (1)
WillJ 2   Somebody's Been Borrowing that Stuff
BOTHERIN' (1)
McCoJ 7   Botherin' that Thing
BOTTOM (6)
BaiK   1   Mississippi Bottom Blues
BelA   3   Shake It, Black Bottom
EvanJ 3   Down in Black Bottom
McPB   1   Down in Black Bottom
SmiT 13   Black Bottom Hop
Spru   5   Low-Down Mississippi Bottom Man
BOUND (17)
AleT 13   Water Bound Blues
Blak   6   Tampa Bound
Blak 32   Georgia Bound
DorsT 6   Levee Bound Blues
FulB   7   Big House Bound
JackC 10   I'm Alabama Bound
JackC 19   Up the Way Bound
JonM 16   North Bound Blues
McCoJ 14   Joliet Bound
Patt 21   Bird Nest Bound
Rain 16   Cell Bound Blues
Rain 22   Memphis Bound Blues
Rain 24   Bessemer Bound Blues
Stok   4   Beale Town Bound
TayC   2   Louisiana Bound
ThpE   2   Florida Bound
Wigg   3   Frisco Bound Blues

BOX (5)
JefB 19   Match Box Blues
JefB 21   Match Box Blues
JefB 22   Match Box Blues
JonM   3   Box Car Blues
Ledb 16   Match Box Blues
BOY (11)
Bare 10   Bad Boy
ButlS 3   Poor Boy Blues
Cann   1   Poor Boy, Long Ways from Home
GreLi 9   Country Boy Blues
HicR   3   Poor Boy a Long Ways from Home
Lock   1   Little Boy Blue
MemM 42   Boy Friend Blues
Pett   3   Good Boy Blues
Shad   2   Memphis Boy--Blues
SykR   8   Poor Boy Blues
ThoR 12   Poor Boy Blues
BOYS (1)
Blak   5   Come On Boys Let's Do that Messin' Around
BREAD (2)
AleT   2   Corn-Bread Blues
CarrL 36   Bread Baker
BREAK (2)
TexT   1   Jail Break Blues
WillJ 19   Break 'Em On Down
BREAKDOWN (1)
Linc   5   Country Breakdown
BREAKIN' (4)
Cann   2   Heart Breakin' Blues
JefB 69   Fence Breakin' Yellin' Blues
JohR 30   Stop Breakin' Down Blues
Scha   1   Fence Breakin' Blues
BREAKS (2)
JackC 5   I Got What It Takes But It Breaks My Heart to
             Give It Away
McCoJ 3   When the Levee Breaks
BRIDGE (1)
Este 21   Floating Bridge
BRIDWELL (1)
WelS   1   The Bridwell Blues
BRING (2)
HicR 10   Hurry and Bring It Back Home
Nick   6   You May Leave But This Will Bring You Back
BROAD (1)
JohLo 16   Man Killing Broad
BROADWAY (1)
MooAl 4   Broadway St. Woman Blues
BROKE (7)
ArnK 32   Broke Man Blues
ClaL   1   Broke Down Engine
DorsT 2   Broke Man's Blues
JefB 13   Broke and Hungry
McTW 16   Broke Down Engine Blues
McTW 25   Broke Down Engine
Palm   1   Broke Man Blues
BROKEN (4)
CarrL 30   Broken-Hearted Man
Este   2   Broken-Hearted, Ragged and Dirty Too
SmiC 34   Broken Busted Blues
WillS 42   Broken Hearted Blues
BROOKLYN (1)
GibC 18   Brooklyn Blues
BROOM (1)
JohR   3   I Believe I'll Dust My Broom
BROTHER (2)
WasbS 30   Get Down Brother
WillJ 10   Brother James
BROWN (9)
ArnK 29   Buddie Brown Blues
Brac   4   My Brown Mama Blues
ButlS 2   You Can't Keep No Brown
Este 14   Who's Been Tellin' You Buddy Brown Blues
Lask   2   Teasin' Brown Blues
LofC   2   Brown Skin Girls
McCl   1   Brown Skin Girl
SmiB 14   Jazzbo Brown from Memphis Town
WasbS 24   Brown and Yellow Woman Blues

BROWNSKIN (3)
  Blak 11 Brownskin Mama Blues
  Hull   1 Gang of Brownskin Women
  JefB 30 Deceitful Brownskin Woman
BROWNSVILLE (1)
  Este 33 Brownsville Blues
BUCKET'S (1)
  WasbS 12 Bucket's Got a Hole in It
BUDDY [BUDDIE] (4)
  ArnK 29 Buddie Brown Blues
  Este 14 Who's Been Tellin' You Buddy Brown Blues
  Gill 12 Me and My Buddy
  LewN   6 Bad Luck's My Buddy
BUG (3)
  JefB 29 Chinch Bug Blues
  MooP   1 Bug Juice Blues
  SmiB 25 Mean Old Bed Bug Blues
BUGGY (2)
  SmiB 37 Take Me for a Buggy Ride
  Weld   5 Hitch Me to Your Buggy and Drive Me Like a
            Mule
BUILT (1)
  Darb   3 Built Right on the Ground
BUKKA'S (1)
  WhiW 14 Bukka's Jitterbug Swing
BULL (6)
  BigB 13 Bull Cow Blues
  HarW   2 Bull Frog Blues
  Ledb 20 Bull Cow
  Patt 22 Jersey Bull Blues
  Pope   3 Bull Frog Blues
  ThoH   7 Bull Doze Blues
BULLY (1)
  Whea 40 Shack Bully Stomp
BUM (4)
  Burs   3 Boodie Bum Bum
  CovB   2 Boodle-De-Bum Bum
  RobB   2 Beedle Um Bum
BUMBLE (4)
  ChatB 1 I'm an Old Bumble Bee
  MemM   4 Bumble Bee
  MemM   6 Bumble Bee Blues
  MemM 13 New Bumble Bee
BUNION (1)
  Yate   2 Sore Bunion Blues
BUNKER (1)
  Stok 23 Bunker Hill Blues
BURYING (1)
  RichM 3 Burying Ground Blues
BUS (1)
  FulB 14 Bus Rider Blues
BUSINESS (1)
  Hurt   1 Nobody's Dirty Business
BUST (1)
  Brac 10 Bust Up Blues
BUSTED (1)
  SmiC 34 Broken Busted Blues
BUSY (1)
  ArnK 12 Busy Bootin'
BUTTER (2)
  JackC 18 Butter and Egg Man Blues
  WallM 1 Dirty Butter
BYE BYE (3) [see also GOODBYE]
  FulB   4 Bye Bye Baby Blues
  JohTo 3 Bye-Bye Blues
  JonL   7 Bye Bye Baby Blues
C AND A (2)
  BigB 17 C and A Blues
  Whea   4 C and A Blues
C AND O (1)
  Amos   1 C and O Blues
C. C. (1)
  Ledb   4 C. C. Rider
CABBAGE (1)
  JonM   6 Anybody Here Want to Try My Cabbage
CAIRO (1)
  Spau   1 Cairo Blues
CALF (3)
  JamS   6 Little Cow and Calf Is Gonna Die Blues

CALF (cont.)
  JohR 35 Milkcow's Calf Blues
  JohR 36 Milkcow's Calf Blues
CALIFORNIA (2)
  Hard   1 California Desert Blues
  HicR 13 California Blues
CALL (1)
  DaviW 20 Call Your Name
CALLED (3)
  BogL 18 I Hate that Train Called the M. and O.
  McCoJ 9 I Called You This Morning
  MemM 15 I Called You This Morning
CALLING [CALLIN'] (2)
  AleT 10 I Am Calling Blues
  JaxF   4 Callin' Corrine
CAMP (6)
  AleT   4 Levee Camp Moan Blues
  BlaAL 2 Gravel Camp Blues
  GibC 13 Levee Camp Moan
  Rain 17 Army Camp Harmony Blues
  SmiT   9 Mining Camp Blues
  WasbS 22 Levee Camp Blues
CAMPBELL (1)
  JohTo 4 Maggie Campbell Blues
CAN (14)
  BogL 19 Tired as I Can Be
  CarrL 10 What More Can I Do?
  DaviW 13 I Can Tell By the Way You Smell
  GreLi 10 How Can I Go On?
  JaxF   3 She Can Love So Good
  King   4 I Can Deal Worry
  McTW 15 Southern Can Is Mine
  McTW 30 Southern Can Mama
  Shad 16 I Can Beat You Plenty
  SykR 11 We Can Sell that Thing
  ThoHo 3 Put It Where I Can Get It
  Whea   9 Doin' the Best I Can
  Whea 23 Coon Can Shorty
  WhiW   6 When Can I Change My Clothes
CANAN'S (1)
  Wilk 13 Old Jim Canan's
CANDY (2)
  Hurt   5 Candy Man Blues
  JohLe 1 Candy Blues
CANNED (1)
  JohTo 5 Canned Heat Blues
CAN'T (12)
  BigB   6 I Can't Be Satisfied
  ButlS 2 You Can't Keep No Brown
  DaviW 21 Can't See Your Face
  Hurt   6 Got the Blues Can't Be Satisfied
  JohE   3 Can't Make Another Day
  JohLo 3 Sweet Woman You Can't Go Wrong
  McCl 17 You Can't Read My Mind
  MemM 32 You Can't Give It Away
  Rame   1 I Can't Stand It
  SpiV 14 I Can't Last Long
  Wate   9 You Can't Do What My Last Man Did
  WeaS   1 Can't Be Trusted Blues
CAR (2)
  Este   6 Street Car Blues
  JonM   3 Box Car Blues
CARDS (1)
  WasbS 33 I Laid My Cards on the Table
CARE (3)
  BelA   4 I Don't Care Who Gets What I Don't Want
  MossB 1 Daddy Don't Care
  SmiT   1 I Don't Know and I Don't Care Blues
CAROLINA (1)
  WalkW 1 South Carolina Rag
CAROLINE (1)
  Stev   7 Aunt Caroline Dyer Blues
CARRY (2)
  BelE   5 Carry It Right Back Home
  BigB 19 Good Liquor Gonna Carry Me Down
CARTER (1)
  ChatB 6 Bo Carter Special
CARTER'S (1)
  ChatB 19 Bo Carter's Advice

337

CASEY (1)
JamJ   2   Southern Casey Jones
CAT (12)
ArnK   4   Old Black Cat Blues
BigB   8   Pussy Cat Blues
Bunn   2   Pattin' Dat Cat
ChatB 11   Howlin' Tom Cat Blues
ChatB 17   Pussy Cat Blues
JefB 50   Maltese Cat Blues
JefB 70   Cat Man Blues
LitS   1   Black Cat Swing
Luca   1   Pussy Cat Blues
MemM 35   Black Cat Blues
Spru   4   Tom Cat Blues
UnkA   8   The Wild Cat Squawl
CATFISH (1)
PetW   1   Catfish Blues
CATS (1)
JackC 4   The Cats Got the Measles
CAUGHT (2)
ChatP 15   Caught the Old Coon at Last
Vinc   6   Your Good Man Caught the Train and Gone
CAVE (1)
Nick   2   Cave Man Blues
CELL (3)
JefB 39   Prison Cell Blues
McTW 27   Death Cell Blues
Rain 16   Cell Bound Blues
CENTRAL (3)
DayW   1   Central Avenue Blues
McCoW 1   Central Tracks Blues
TurnJ 1   Blues on Central Avenue
CHAIN (3)
Howe   8   Ball and Chain Blues
Linc   6   Chain Gang Trouble
McMu   2   De Kalb Chain Blues
CHAIR (4)
BryL   1   Dentist Chair Blues--Part 1
BryL   2   Dentist Chair Blues--Part 2
JefB 34   'Lectric Chair Blues
SmiB 24   Send Me to the 'Lectric Chair
CHANCE (4)
Cann   4   Last Chance Blues
ThoH   5   Honey, Won't You Allow Me One More Chance?
Whea 27   Don't Take a Chance
WooH   2   Last Chance Blues
CHANGE (6)
CarrL 25   I Believe I'll Make a Change
Este 27   Everybody Oughta Make a Change
JefB 38   Change My Luck Blues
LofC   4   Change My Mind Blues
WhiW   6   When Can I Change My Clothes
WillS 34   My Baby Made a Change
CHANGES (1)
Wate   2   There'll Be Some Changes Made
CHANGING (1)
McTW 12   Love-Changing Blues
CHARLIE [CHOLLY] (2)
ArnK 20   Mister Charlie
SmiB 23   Trombone Cholly
CHARMIN' (1)
ThoH 11   Charmin' Betsy
CHAUFFEUR (1)
MemM 45   Me and My Chauffeur Blues
CHERRY (4)
BracM 2   Cherry Ball
JamS   3   Cherry Ball Blues
JonL   9   Cherry Street Blues
McCoJ 6   Cherry Ball Blues
CHIB (1)
JohE   2   Good Chib Blues
CHICAGO (1)
JohR   4   Sweet Home Chicago
CHICKASAW (1)
MemM 29   Chickasaw Train Blues
CHIEF (1)
LewF   5   Big Chief Blues
CHILD [CHILE] (2)
HicR   5   Motherless Chile Blues

CHILD [CHILE] (cont.)
ThoE   1   Motherless Child Blues
CHILDREN (1)
PooJ   3   Come Along Little Children
CHINA (1)
MissM 2   It's Cold in China Blues
CHINCH (1)
JefB 29   Chinch Bug Blues
CHOCK (1)
JefB   7   Chock House Blues
CHOCOLATE (1)
HicR   9   Chocolate to the Bone
CHOO (1)
SmiT   7   Choo Choo Blues
CHRISTMAS (3)
JefB 48   Christmas Eve Blues
TurnB 2   Christmas Time Blues
WillS 17   Christmas Morning Blues
CHURCH (2)
JorL   1   Church Bells Blues
JorL   2   Church Bells Blues
CIGARETTE (1)
ChatB 16   Cigarette Blues
CITY (4)
HilB   4   Pratt City Blues
Ledb 11   Kansas City Papa
Shad   5   Kansas City Blues
SmiC   9   Kansas City Man Blues
CLARK (1)
Este 42   Lawyer Clark Blues
CLAY (1)
McCoJ 15   Someday I'll Be in the Clay
CLEAN (3)
Este 31   Clean Up at Home
JorC   2   Keep It Clean
JorC   7   Keep It Clean--No. 2
CLEARING (1)
SmiC 21   The Clearing House Blues
CLOCK (1)
JohK   1   Lady, Your Clock Ain't Right
CLOTHES (2)
Whea   3   Don't Hang My Clothes on No Barbed Wire Line
WhiW   6   When Can I Change My Clothes
CLOUDY (1)
HicR   2   Cloudy Sky Blues
COAL (5)
BliP   1   Coal River Blues
Howe   1   Coal Man Blues
JackC 23   Coal Man Blues
JamF   1   Poor Coal Passer
Stev   5   Coal Oil Blues
COAT (1)
NelsT 1   Blue Coat Blues
COCAINE (2)
JorL   3   Cocaine Blues
Rame   3   Cocaine Habit Blues
COCKEYED (1)
WallM 3   The Cockeyed World
COCKTAIL (1)
Whea 12   Cocktail Man Blues
COFFEE (4)
BogL   4   Coffee Grindin' Blues
ColFJ 5   Coffee Grinder Blues
JackC 7   Coffee Pot Blues
SmiJ   3   Good Coffee Blues
COFFIN (1)
CoxI   8   Coffin Blues
COLD (5)
Gill 17   Woke Up Cold in Hand
KelJ   6   Cold Iron Bed
McTW 34   Cold Winter Day
MissM 2   It's Cold in China Blues
SmiB   8   Cold In Hand Blues
COLDEST (2)
HarZ   4   Coldest Stuff in Town
Shaw   1   Coldest Stuff in Town
COLLECTOR (1)
WillS 2   Collector Man Blues

338

```
COME (14)
   Blak    5   Come On Boys Let's Do that Messin' Around
   DaviW  25   New Come Back Baby
   DorsT  13   Come On In
   Este   37   Mary Come On Home
   Hawk    6   How Come Mama Blues
   HendB   2   Let Your Love Come Down
   JaxF    2   Come On, Mama, Do That Dance
   JohR    8   Come On in My Kitchen
   JonM   11   You May Go, But You'll Come Back Some Day
   LewF    8   Why Don't You Come Home Blues
   McTW    9   Come On Around to My House Mama
   PooJ    3   Come Along Little Children
   WasbS   5   Come On In
   WillS   8   Until My Love Come Down
COMPETITION (1)
   JefB   43   Competition Bed Blues
CONDUCTOR (2)
   BelE    3   Mean Conductor Blues
   BigB   11   Mr. Conductor Man
CONSTRUCTION (2)
   EdwJ    1   Construction Gang
   EdwS    1   Construction Gang
COOKIE (1)
   CarrL   3   Papa Wants a Cookie
COOL (1)
   JohTo   1   Cool Drink of Water Blues
COON (3)
   ChatP  15   Caught the Old Coon at Last
   OweG    2   The Coon Crap Game
   Whea   23   Coon Can Shorty
CORN (4)
   AleT    2   Corn-Bread Blues
   BlaAL   3   Corn Liquor Blues
   CarrL  16   Corn Licker Blues
   SmiJ    9   Corn Whiskey Blues
CORNER (2)
   CarrL  20   Take a Walk Around the Corner
   WillJ  15   Meet Me Around the Corner
CORPUS (1)
   JonL    6   Corpus Blues
CORRINA [CORINNA] (2)
   JefB    6   Corinna Blues
   Wigg    4   Corrine Corrina Blues
CORRINE (2)
   JaxF    4   Callin' Corrine
   Wigg    4   Corrine Corrina Blues
COTTON (1)
   PetW    4   Cotton Pickin' Blues
COTTONFIELD (3)
   Aker    1   Cottonfield Blues--Part 1
   Aker    2   Cottonfield Blues--Part 2
   ThoH    1   Cottonfield Blues
COULD (1)
   Newb    1   She Could Toodle-Oo
COULDN'T (2)
   JorC   10   I Couldn't Stay Here
   Shaw    2   I Couldn't Help It
COUNTRY (7)
   Batt    1   Country Woman
   Blak   21   Walkin' Across the Country
   ChatB  28   Country Fool
   East    3   Green Country Gal
   GreLi   9   Country Boy Blues
   Linc    5   Country Breakdown
   WilsL   3   Down the Country
COUNTY (4)
   ButlS   4   Jefferson County Blues
   KelE    1   Poole County Blues
   Newb    3   Shelby County Workhouse Blues
   SmiJ   10   County Jail Blues
COURT (2)
   SmiC   36   Court House Blues
   Stov    1   Court Street Blues
COW (10)
   ArnK    2   Milk Cow Blues
   ArnK   17   Milk Cow Blues--No. 4
   BigB   13   Bull Cow Blues
   ChatB  22   Sue Cow

COW (cont.)
   Este    5   Milk Cow Blues
   JamS    6   Little Cow and Calf Is Gonna Die Blues
   Ledb   20   Bull Cow
   MemM   22   Soo Cow Soo
   Spru    1   Milk Cow Blues
   WillJ   7   Wild Cow Blues
COX'S (1)
   CoxI    1   Ida Cox's Lawdy, Lawdy Blues
CRAMP (1)
   JohAl   1   Miss Meal Cramp Blues
CRAP (1)
   OweG    2   The Coon Crap Game
CRAPSHOOTER'S (1)
   Whea   35   Crapshooter's Blues
CRAVE (1)
   Lacy    2   Ham Hound Crave
CRAVING (1)
   Wate   11   Craving Blues
CRAWL (1)
   WillH   1   Georgia Crawl
CRAWLIN' (2)
   JefB   68   That Crawlin' Baby Blues
   WillJ  12   Crawlin' King Snake
CRAZY (5)
   McTW   31   Runnin' Me Crazy
   MemM   21   Crazy Cryin' Blues
   Pick    1   Crazy 'Bout My Black Gal
   SmiT   10   The World's Jazz Crazy and So Am I
   Whea   32   Crazy with the Blues
CREEP (1)
   HicR    7   'Fo Day Creep
CREEPER'S (1)
   LewF   15   Creeper's Blues
CRIME (1)
   Bare    1   My Crime Blues
CROOKED (3)
   BakW    5   Crooked Woman Blues
   FulB   13   Crooked Woman Blues
   HicR    6   Crooked Woman Blues
CROSS (4)
   JohR   14   Cross Road Blues
   JonL    8   Cross the Water Blues
   McCl   16   Cross Cut Saw Blues
   ScotS   1   Red Cross Blues
CROSSING (1)
   AleT   11   Double Crossing Blues
CROW (2)
   BlaAI   1   The Flying Crow
   WasbS  21   Flying Crow Blues
CROWING [CROWIN'] (3)
   JohLo  30   Crowin' Rooster Blues
   RhoW    1   The Crowing Rooster
   WooH    3   The Rooster's Crowing Blues
CRUMP (1)
   Stok    8   Mr. Crump Don't Like It
CRY (1)
   Spru    7   Don't Cry Baby
CRYING [CRYIN'] (5)
   CarrL  29   You Left Me Crying
   HilSy   1   Cryin' for the Blues
   McCl   20   It's a Cryin' Pity
   MemM   21   Crazy Cryin' Blues
   RedN    1   Crying Mother Blues
CUP (2)
   JefB   55   Tin Cup Blues
   Stok    3   Half Cup of Tea
CURLY (1)
   Este    1   The Girl I Love, She Got Long Curly Hair
CUT (5)
   LeeX    1   Macon Georgia Cut-Out
   McCl   16   Cross Cut Saw Blues
   Shad   19   Mary Anna Cut Off
   Whea   29   Cut Out Blues
   Whea   38   I'm Gonna Cut Out Everything
CUTTIN' (1)
   ArnK   31   Head Cuttin' Blues
CYCLONE (1)
   JohLo   4   St. Louis Cyclone Blues
```

CYPRESS (1)
  JamS   2 Cypress Grove Blues
D (1)
  Stok   9 Blues in D
D B (1)
  JefB   51 D B Blues
DA (2)
  Wate   4 That Da Da Strain
DADDY (17)
  Blak   13 Hey Hey Daddy Blues
  BogL   24 Jump Steady Daddy
  ChatB   2 Ram Rod Daddy
  CoxI   10 Worn Down Daddy Blues
  DickP   1 Twelve Pound Daddy
  FulB   1 I'm a Rattlesnakin' Daddy
  Glov   1 Shake It Daddy
  HarZ   3 I Let My Daddy Do That
  JorC   8 You Run and Tell Your Daddy
  McCoJ 24 My Daddy Was a Movin' Man
  MackA   2 Wicked Daddy Blues
  MossB   1 Daddy Don't Care
  Rain   28 Gone Daddy Blues
  Shor   5 Grand Daddy Blues
  SmiBM   1 St. Louis Daddy
  SmiC   6 I Want My Sweet Daddy Now
  Sylv   3 I Want My Sweet Daddy
DALLAS (2)
  JonM   19 Dallas Blues
  ThoR   10 Hard Dallas Blues
DANCE (2)
  JaxF   2 Come On, Mama, Do That Dance
  Spec   1 House Dance Blues
DANGEROUS (1)
  JonM   13 Dangerous Blues
DARK (2)
  LofW   3 Dark Road Blues
  Patt   13 When Your Way Gets Dark
DARLIN' (1)
  Nick   5 Got a Letter from My Darlin'
DAY (20)
  AleT   1 Long Lonesome Day Blues
  ArnK   18 I'll Be Up Some Day
  Blacw   6 Blue Day Blues
  BogL   14 You Got to Die Some Day
  Brac   7 The Four Day Blues
  BracM   4 I'll Overcome Some Day
  BradT   4 Four Day Blues
  CarrL   6 Four Day Rider
  ChatB 26 Some Day
  Glaz   2 Lonesome Day Blues
  HicR   7 'Fo Day Creep
  JamJ   3 Lonesome Day Blues
  JohE   3 Can't Make Another Day
  JohR   19 If I Had Possession Over Judgment Day
  JonM   11 You May Go, But You'll Come Back Some Day
  McTW   3 Mama, 'Tain't Long Fo' Day
  McTW   18 Scarey Day Blues
  McTW   34 Cold Winter Day
  Rain   21 Four Day Honory Scat
  WillS 25 Rainy Day Blues
DAYS (2)
  AleT   17 Seen Better Days
  MemM   44 In My Girlish Days
DE KALB (1)
  McMu   2 De Kalb Chain Blues
DEAD (4)
  HilK   4 The Gone Dead Train
  JohR   13 Dead Shrimp Blues
  MillL   1 Dead Drunk Blues
  WallS   4 Dead Drunk Blues
DEAL (5)
  JohR   16 Last Fair Deal Gone Down
  King   4 I Can Deal Worry
  MartC   5 Let's Have a New Deal
  Vinc   8 Honey Babe Let the Deal Go Down
  Wilk   11 Dirty Deal Blues
DEATH (7)
  Crud   2 Death Valley Blues
  DickT   1 Death Bell Blues

DEATH (cont.)
  Ledb   9 Death Letter Blues--Part 1
  Ledb   10 Death Letter Blues--Part 2
  McTW   27 Death Cell Blues
  MartS   2 Death Sting Me Blues
  SmiC   30 Death Letter Blues
DECEITFUL (1)
  JefB   30 Deceitful Brownskin Woman
DECEIVING (1)
  Darb   2 Deceiving Blues
DEEP (4)
  McCl   18 Deep Blue Sea Blues
  SmiC   24 Deep Blue Sea Blues
  Whea   25 Deep Sea Love
  WillS 15 Deep Down in the Ground
DEGREE (2)
  AleT   12 Ninety-Eight Degree Blues
  SpiV   3 Murder in the First Degree
DELIVERY (1)
  WallS   1 Special Delivery Blues
DEN (1)
  CollS   2 Devil in the Lion's Den
DENTIST (2)
  BryL   1 Dentist Chair Blues--Part 1
  BryL   2 Dentist Chair Blues--Part 2
DENY (1)
  HicR   4 Easy Rider Don't Deny My Name
DEPARTMENT (1)
  Este   30 Fire Department Blues
DEPRESSION'S (1)
  Blak   37 Depression's Gone from Me Blues
DESERT (2)
  Hard   1 California Desert Blues
  McTW   21 Searching the Desert for the Blues
DESPLAINES (1)
  JackC 25 Sheik of Desplaines Street
DESPONDENT (1)
  HenrL   1 Low Down Despondent Blues
DETECTIVE (1)
  SykR   4 Fire Detective Blues
DETROIT (1)
  SpiV   15 Detroit Moan
DEVIL (10)
  ChatB 27 Old Devil
  CollS   2 Devil in the Lion's Den
  JamS   1 Devil Got My Woman
  JohR   29 Me and the Devil Blues
  McCoJ 16 Evil Devil Woman Blues
  Patt   10 Devil Sent the Rain
  SmiC   29 Done Sold My Soul to the Devil
  Temp   2 The Evil Devil Blues
  WasbS 25 She Belongs to the Devil
  WillK   2 Mr. Devil Blues
DEVILMENT (1)
  Whea   39 Devilment Blues
DEVIL'S (1)
  JohLo 23 Devil's Got the Blues
DIAMONDS (1)
  WallS   2 Jack O' Diamonds Blues
DICE (1)
  GibC   12 Bad Luck Dice
DICE'S [DICES'] (2)
  CamB   1 Dice's Blues
  RolW   2 Dices' Blues
DID (3)
  DorsT 10 Where Did You Stay Last Night?
  Luca   2 Where Did You Stay Last Night?
  Wate   9 You Can't Do What My Last Man Did
DIDDIE (2)
  Blak   29 Diddie Wa Diddie
DIDN'T (1)
  GreLi 11 If I Didn't Love You
DIE (4)
  BogL   14 You Got to Die Some Day
  JamS   6 Little Cow and Calf Is Gonna Die Blues
  MoraH   1 Root Hog or Die
  WhiW   12 Fixin' to Die Blues
DIG (1)
  BigB   21 I've Got to Dig You

DIGGIN' (1)
  WasbS 15   Diggin' My Potatoes
DIME (3)
  ChatP 11   Maybe I'll Loan You a Dime
  GibC   15   Blues Without a Dime
  Whea   14   Last Dime Blues
DINNER (1)
  ChatB 15   Dinner Blues
DIRT (1)
  Patt   3   Down the Dirt Road Blues
DIRTY (8)
  Este   2   Broken-Hearted, Ragged and Dirty Too
  Hurt   1   Nobody's Dirty Business
  JorC   12   Don't Put Your Dirty Hands on Me
  MemM   12   New Dirty Dozens
  MemM   31   Dirty Mother For You
  NelsR   1   Gettin' Dirty Just Shakin' that Thing
  WallM   1   Dirty Butter
  Wilk   11   Dirty Deal Blues
DISPOSITION (1)
  TowH   6   She's Got a Mean Disposition
DISTANCE (2)
  CoxI   5   Long Distance Blues
  JefB   67   Long Distance Moan
DISTRICT (1)
  WhiW   11   District Attorney Blues
DIVING (1)
  Este   3   Diving Duck Blues
DO (22)
  BigB   5   Skoodle Do Do
  BigB   7   Skoodle Do Do
  Blak   5   Come On Boys Let's Do that Messin' Around
  CarrL 10   What More Can I Do?
  CollS   9   Do That Thing
  Este   41   You Shouldn't Do That
  GreLi   6   Why Don't You Do Right?
  HarZ   3   I Let My Daddy Do That
  JaxF   2   Come On, Mama, Do That Dance
  JohLi   1   Never Let Your Left Hand Know What Your Right
              Hand Do
  JohM   1   If I Let You Get Away With It Once You'll Do
              It All of the Time
  McCoJ 21   What You Gonna Do?
  SmiB   35   Do Your Duty
  SpiV   8   How Do You Do It That Way?
  Stok   20   Ain't Going to Do Like I Used to Do
  Wate   9   You Can't Do What My Last Man Did
  Wilk   2   I Do Blues
  WilsW   3   Do It Right
DOCTOR (1)
  Shor   3   Snake Doctor Blues
DOG (11)
  ArnK   22   Salty Dog
  Blak   8   Black Dog Blues
  Blak   31   Police Dog Blues
  CarrL   8   Low Down Dog Blues
  CollS   3   Yellow Dog Blues
  CollS 11   New Salty Dog
  Hawk   1   Shaggy Dog Blues
  JackC   3   Salty Dog Blues
  MooR   5   Mad Dog Blues
  RupO   2   Ain't Goin' to Be Your Low Down Dog
  SmiB   10   The Yellow Dog Blues
DOGGIN' (3)
  Blak   16   Doggin' Me Mama Blues
  McCl   6   My Baby's Doggin' Me
  Pope   2   Doggin' Me Around Blues
DOGGONE (1)
  SmiC   17   My Doggone Lazy Man
DOGS (1)
  Rain   13   Those Dogs of Mine
DOING [DOIN'] (6)
  Blak   26   Doing a Stretch
  Este   7   Watcha Doin'?
  GibC   1   Beat You Doing It
  HicR   22   Doin' the Scraunch
  Howe   4   Doin' Wrong
  Whea   9   Doin' the Best I Can

DOLL (1)
  SmiB   16   Baby Doll
DOLLAR (3)
  CookR   1   Dollar Blues
  FulB   15   You Got to Have Your Dollar
  HenrH   2   My Silver Dollar Mama
DOLLARS (2)
  Este   9   Stack O' Dollars
  JorC   1   Stack O' Dollars Blues
DONE (9)
  BigB   14   How You Want It Done?
  GreLi   2   What Have I Done?
  JorL   4   My Gal's Done Quit Me
  Lask   1   How You Want Your Rollin' Done
  Shad   21   She Done Sold It Out
  SmiC   29   Done Sold My Soul to the Devil
  Tamp   6   No Matter How She Done It
  WilsW   2   The Gin Done Done It
DON'T (53)
  BakW   1   Mama, Don't Rush Me Blues
  Bare   5   I Don't Like That
  BelA   4   I Don't Care Who Gets What I Don't Want
  BradT   3   Please Don't Act that Way
  CartS   1   Don't Leave Me Blues
  ChatP   2   You Don't Mean Me No Good
  CoxI   2   Wild Women Don't Have the Blues
  DaviW 22   Please Don't Mistreat Me
  DaviW 26   Don't You Want to Go
  GibC   9   Don't Put That Thing On Me
  GreLi   6   Why Don't You Do Right?
  HicR   4   Easy Rider Don't Deny My Name
  Hull   4   Don't You Leave Me Here
  Hull   5   Mama You Don't Know How
  JackC 14   Mama, Don't You Think I Know?
  JohJo   2   Don't Want No Woman
  JohLo 12   Baby Please Don't Leave Me No More
  JorC   12   Don't Put Your Dirty Hands on Me
  Ledb   8   Baby, Don't You Love Me No More?
  LewF   8   Why Don't You Come Home Blues
  LofC   3   I Don't Know
  McCl   2   Baby, Don't You Want to Go?
  MemM   8   Don't Want No Woman
  MemM   20   I Don't Want that Junk Outa You
  MemM   39   My Baby Don't Want Me No More
  MontE   4   Mama You Don't Mean Me No Good
  MossB   1   Daddy Don't Care
  SmiC   8   Don't Never Tell Nobody
  SmiC   14   I Don't Love Nobody
  SmiC   16   You Don't Know My Mind
  SmiC   22   Don't Advertise Your Man
  SmiL   2   Don't You Leave Me Here
  SmiT   1   I Don't Know and I Don't Care Blues
  SmiT   4   Don't Shake It No More
  SpiV   10   Don't Trust Nobody Blues
  Spru   7   Don't Cry Baby
  Stok   8   Mr. Crump Don't Like It
  ThoG   2   Don't Kill Him in Here
  ThoH   9   Don't Ease Me In
  ThoH   12   Don't Leave Me Here
  Vinc   19   Don't Wake It Up
  WasbS   1   Mama Don't Allow No. 1
  WasbS   2   Mama Don't Allow No. 2
  Whea   3   Don't Hang My Clothes on No Barbed Wire Line
  Whea   27   Don't Take a Chance
  WillJ   6   Baby Please Don't Go
  WillJ 16   Please Don't Go
  WillS 43   She Don't Love Me That Way
  WooO   3   Don't Sell It--Don't Give It Away
  WooO   4   Don't Sell It
DOODLE (1)
  Linc   7   Doodle Hole Blues
DOOR (11)
  ArnK   6   Front Door Blues
  ArnK   7   Back Door Blues
  ArnK   35   Tired of Runnin' from Door to Door
  Blacw   9   Back Door Blues
  BracM   1   You Scolded Me and Drove Me from Your Door
  JonB   1   Back Door Blues
  JonM   20   Never Drive a Beggar from Your Door

DOOR (cont.)
```
Linc    4  My Wife Drove Me From the Door
Ston    2  Back Door Blues
WasbS   7  Back Door
```
DOUBLE (4)
```
AleT   11  Double Crossing Blues
ChatB  20  Double Up in a Knot
Luca    4  Double Trouble Blues
SpiS    1  Double Dozens
```
DOUGH (2)
```
Aker    3  Dough Roller Blues
Blak   18  No Dough Blues
```
DOWN (72)
```
ArnK   27  Set Down Gal
BigB    1  Down in the Basement Blues
BigB   19  Good Liquor Gonna Carry Me Down
Blacw   7  Down South Blues
Blak   24  Low Down Loving Gal
BogL   22  Down in Boogie Alley
CarrL   8  Low Down Dog Blues
CarrL  15  Hurry Down Sunshine
ChatB  23  Shake 'Em On Down
ChatP   7  I Believe I'll Settle Down
ClaL    1  Broke Down Engine
ClaL    2  Down in Tennessee
CoxI   10  Worn Down Daddy Blues
DelaM   1  Down the Big Road Blues
Este   11  Down South Blues
Este   16  Drop Down Mama
Este   40  Drop Down
EvanJ   3  Down in Black Bottom
HendB   2  Let Your Love Come Down
HenrH   1  Low Down Hound Blues
HenrL   1  Low Down Despondent Blues
HilK    3  Down on My Bended Knee
Howe    7  Low Down Rounder Blues
JamS    8  If You Haven't Got Any Hay Get on Down the
             Road
JefB   42  Low Down Mojo Blues
JohLo   9  Way Down That Lonesome Road
JohR   16  Last Fair Deal Gone Down
JohR   30  Stop Breakin' Down Blues
Ledb    5  Honey, I'm All Out and Down
LeeX    2  Nobody Knows You When You're Down and Out
LewF    6  Falling Down Blues
McCl   10  Down to Skin and Bones
McCl   13  Drop Down Mama
McPB    1  Down in Black Bottom
McTW   16  Broke Down Engine Blues
McTW   17  Stomp Down Rider
McTW   25  Broke Down Engine
Oden    2  Sitting Down Thinking Blues
Oden    3  Going Down Slow
Patt    3  Down the Dirt Road Blues
Patt   20  Moon Going Down
Pick    3  Down the Highway
Rain   26  Down in the Basement
RichM   2  Mooch Richardson's Low Down Barrel House Blues
             Part 1
RupO    2  Ain't Goin' to Be Your Low Down Dog
Simp    1  Down South Blues
SmiB    1  Down Hearted Blues
SmiB    3  Ticket Agent Ease Your Window Down
SmiB   29  Nobody Knows You When You're Down and Out
SmiB   38  I'm Down in the Dumps
SmiC    3  Down South Blues
SmiC   13  I'm Gonna Tear Your Playhouse Down
Spru    3  Way Back Down Home
Spru    5  Low-Down Mississippi Bottom Man
Sylv    2  Down South Blues
UnkA    5  Throw Me Down
Vinc    8  Honey Babe Let the Deal Go Down
WallS   5  Have You Ever Been Down
WasbS   9  Low Down Woman
WasbS  23  I'm Feeling Low Down
WasbS  30  Get Down Brother
Whea   21  Low Down Rascal
Whea   30  When a Man Gets Down
WhiW    3  Shake 'Em On Down
```

DOWN (cont.)
```
Wilk    6  Falling Down Blues
WillJ  19  Break 'Em On Down
WillK   3  Get Your Head Trimmed Down
WillS   7  Down South
WillS   8  Until My Love Come Down
WillS  15  Deep Down in the Ground
WillS  21  Low Down Ways
WilsL   3  Down the Country
```
DOWNTOWN (2)
```
Stok   10  Downtown Blues
Stok   11  Downtown Blues
```
DOZE (1)
```
ThoH    7  Bull Doze Blues
```
DOZENS (2)
```
MemM   12  New Dirty Dozens
SpiS    1  Double Dozens
```
DRAWING (1)
```
Este   36  Time Is Drawing Near
```
DRAYMAN (1)
```
GibC   10  Drayman Blues
```
DREAM (8)
```
HarX    1  Lonesome Midnight Dream
Hite    1  Graveyard Dream Blues
JefB   26  Black Snake Dream Blues
McPB    2  My Dream Blues
MooAl   5  Lonesome Dream Blues
Rain   10  Dream Blues
Stok   26  Frank Stoke's Dream
ThoHo   1  Gambler's Dream
```
DREAMER (1)
```
WillS  38  She Was a Dreamer
```
DREAMING (1)
```
ReedW   1  Dreaming Blues
```
DREAMY (1)
```
Newb    4  Hambone Willie's Dreamy-Eyed Woman's Blues
```
DRINK (2)
```
Gill   15  You Drink Too Much Whiskey
JohTo   1  Cool Drink of Water Blues
```
DRINKING [DRINKIN'] (2)
```
ChatP   1  Beer Drinking Woman
Pope    1  Whiskey Drinkin' Blues
```
DRIPPING (1)
```
MooP    2  Honey Dripping Papa
```
DRIVE (3)
```
JonM   20  Never Drive a Beggar from Your Door
McTW   11  Drive Away Blues
Weld    5  Hitch Me to Your Buggy and Drive Me Like a
             Mule
```
DRIVING [DRIVIN'] (4)
```
McCoJ   8  Pile Drivin' Blues
Rain   30  Slow Driving Moan
Rame    2  Tired of You Driving Me
SmiC   32  Steel Drivin' Man
```
DROP (4)
```
Este   16  Drop Down Mama
Este   40  Drop Down
JackC  11  Drop that Sack
McCl   13  Drop Down Mama
```
DROVE (2)
```
BracM   1  You Scolded Me and Drove Me from Your Door
Linc    4  My Wife Drove Me From the Door
```
DRUNK (8)
```
BogL    8  Sloppy Drunk Blues
CarrL   5  Sloppy Drunk Blues
ChatB  25  Let's Get Drunk Again
DaviW   6  Sloppy Drunk Again
JohLo  27  Laplegged Drunk Again
MillL   1  Dead Drunk Blues
WallS   4  Dead Drunk Blues
WillS  37  Sloppy Drunk Blues
```
DRUNKARD'S (1)
```
JonCo   3  Drunkard's Special
```
DRUNKEN (3)
```
JohR   27  Drunken Hearted Man
JohR   28  Drunken Hearted Man
MemM   27  Drunken Barrelhouse Blues
```
DRY (9)
```
ArnK   36  My Well Is Dry
```

DRY (cont.)
    Hous   5   Dry Spell Blues--Part 1
    Hous   6   Dry Spell Blues--Part 2
    JackC   6   Shave Em Dry
    JefB   4   Dry Southern Blues
    LewF   12   Dry Land Blues
    Patt   19   Dry Well Blues
    SpiV   2   The Alligator Pond Went Dry
    Wigg   5   Gotta Shave 'Em Dry
DUCK (2)
    Este   3   Diving Duck Blues
    Tamp   3   The Duck Yas-Yas-Yas
DUM (1)
    Blak   19   Bootleg Rum Dum Blues
DUMPS (1)
    SmiB   38   I'm Down in the Dumps
DUST (1)
    JohR   3   I Believe I'll Dust My Broom
DUTY (1)
    SmiB   35   Do Your Duty
DYER (1)
    Stev   7   Aunt Caroline Dyer Blues
DYING [DYIN'] (2)
    NelsR   2   Dyin' Rider Blues
    WelS   3   Dying Pickpocket Blues
DYNAMITE (1)
    JefB   53   Dynamite Blues
EAGLE (2)
    BigB   3   Eagle Riding Papa
    JefB   52   Eagle Eyed Mama
EAGLES (1)
    WileG   2   Eagles on a Half
EARLY (5)
    Blak   1   Early Morning Blues
    Blak   2   Early Morning Blues
    JonM   12   Early Every Morn'
    RolW   3   Early in the Morning No. 2
    WillS   3   Early in the Morning
EASE (3)
    HicR   11   Ease It to Me Blues
    SmiB   3   Ticket Agent Ease Your Window Down
    ThoH   9   Don't Ease Me In
EASIN' (1)
    Este   29   Easin' Back to Tennessee
EASY (5)
    AleT   19   Easy Rider Blues
    HicR   4   Easy Rider Don't Deny My Name
    JefB   20   Easy Rider Blues
    PerkG   1   No Easy Rider Blues
    ThoH   10   Texas Easy Street Blues
EGG (1)
    JackC 18   Butter and Egg Man Blues
EIGHTY (1)
    Bond   3   80 Highway Blues
ELDER'S (1)
    JonCo   4   The Elder's He's My Man
ELECTRIC [see 'LECTRIC]
ELEVEN (1)
    CarrL 34   Eleven Twenty-Nine Blues
ELM (2)
    DaviC   1   Elm Street Woman Blues
    DayT   2   Elm Street Blues
ELSE (1)
    Gill   10   I Got Somebody Else
ELSIE (1)
    McCl   15   Elsie Blues
'EM [EM] (6)   [see also THEM]
    ChatB 23   Shake 'Em On Down
    JackC   6   Shave Em Dry
    Wate   10   Ethel Sings 'Em
    WhiW   3   Shake 'Em On Down
    Wigg   5   Gotta Shave 'Em Dry
    WillJ 19   Break 'Em On Down
EMPTY (3)
    ChatP   4   Empty Room Blues
    JefB   56   Empty House Blues
    SmiB   26   Empty Bed Blues--Part ?
END (2)
    HendK   1   West End Blues

END (cont.)
    MackA   1   West End Blues
ENGINE (3)
    ClaL   1   Broke Down Engine
    McTW   16   Broke Down Engine Blues
    McTW   25   Broke Down Engine
ENOUGH (1)
    ChatB 21   Your Biscuits Are Big Enough for Me
ERIE (1)
    Spar   1   Erie Train Blues
ESTATE (1)
    BennW   2   Real Estate Blues
ETHEL (1)
    Wate   10   Ethel Sings 'Em
EVE (3)
    BradT   1   Adam and Eve
    JefB   48   Christmas Eve Blues
    ThoHo   2   Adam and Eve Had the Blues
EVER (2)
    HendK   3   Have You Ever Felt That Way?
    WallS   5   Have You Ever Been Down
EVERGREEN (1)
    Shad   6   Evergreen Money Blues
EVERY (4)
    BelA   2   Every Woman Blues
    JonM   12   Early Every Morn'
    RolW   5   Every Morning Blues
    SmiC   2   Every Woman's Blues
EVERYBODY (1)
    Este   27   Everybody Oughta Make a Change
EVERYBODY'S (1)
    Nick   1   Everybody's Talking About Sadie Green
EVERYTHING (2)
    SmiC   1   I Got Everything a Woman Needs
    Whea   38   I'm Gonna Cut Out Everything
EVERYWHERE (3)
    Patt   15   High Water Everywhere--Part I
    Patt   16   High Water Everywhere--Part II
    Weld   8   Blues Everywhere I Go
EVIL (8)
    CarrL 31   Evil-Hearted Woman
    McCoJ 16   Evil Devil Woman Blues
    MooAl   1   Black and Evil Blues
    MooAl   7   Black Evil Blues
    Temp   2   The Evil Devil Blues
    WasbS 29   Evil Blues
    Wigg   1   Evil Woman Blues
    WooO   1   Evil Hearted Woman
EXPERIENCE (1)
    WillX   1   Experience Blues
EXPLAINING (1)
    Rain   18   Explaining the Blues
EXPRESSMAN (1)
    Rach   3   Expressman Blues
EYE (1)
    Rain   31   Black Eye Blues
EYED (2)
    JefB   52   Eagle Eyed Mama
    Newb   4   Hambone Willie's Dreamy-Eyed Woman's Blues
EYES (1)
    Vinc   15   I've Got Blood in My Eyes for You
FACE (2)
    DaviW 21   Can't See Your Face
    WasbW   1   Narrow Face Blues
FACED (1)
    WeaC   5   Two Faced Woman
FACTORY (1)
    BrowI   3   Nut Factory Blues
FAIR (1)
    JohR   16   Last Fair Deal Gone Down
FAKING (1)
    JackC   9   The Faking Blues
FALL (3)
    ColeK   2   Niagara Fall Blues
    JohLo 11   When You Fall For Someone That's Not Your Own
    SpiV   12   I'll Never Fall in Love Again
FALLING (4)
    JohLo   2   Falling Rain Blues
    JohLo 26   New Falling Rain Blues

FALLING (cont.)
  LewF   6   Falling Down Blues
  Wilk   6   Falling Down Blues
FALSE (1)
  Whea 31   False Hearted Woman
FAMILY (1)
  Hogg   1   Family Trouble Blues
FARE (2)
  Cali   1   Fare Thee Well Blues
  WillS 29   Train Fare Blues
FAREWELL (1)
  MartC 1   Farewell to You Baby
FARM (4)
  BigB   4   Grandma's Farm
  Blacw 2   Penal Farm Blues
  CamB   3   Starvation Farm Blues
  WhiW   8   Parchman Farm Blues
FARRELL (1)
  SimsH 1   Farrell Blues
FAST (1)
  ThoG   1   Fast Stuff Blues
FAT (3)
  Curr   1   Fat Mouth Blues
  JackC 21   Fat Mouth Blues
  JohTo 8   Big Fat Mama Blues
FEATHER (1)
  Cann   3   Feather Bed
FEED (1)
  Shad 15   Feed Your Friend with a Long Handled Spoon
FEEL (1)
  SykR   3   The Way I Feel Blues
FEELING [FEELIN'] (5)
  Blak 10   Bad Feeling Blues
  FulB 12   Good Feeling Blues
  MartD 1   Feelin' Blue
  McCl 12   Love with a Feeling
  WasbS 23   I'm Feeling Low Down
FEET (2)
  JefB 10   Stocking Feet Blues
  WasbS 20   My Feet Jumped Salty
FELT (1)
  HendK 3   Have You Ever Felt That Way?
FENCE (2)
  JefB 69   Fence Breakin' Yellin' Blues
  Scha   1   Fence Breakin' Blues
FEVER (1)
  WhiW 10   High Fever Blues
FIDDLE (1)
  SmiB 13   I Ain't Goin' to Play Second Fiddle
FIDDLING (1)
  Vinc   5   Yodeling Fiddling Blues
FIELD (1)
  WallM 4   Field Mouse Stomp
FIFTEEN (1)
  HilR   1   I Had a Gal for the Last Fifteen Years
FIFTY-ONE [see NO. 51]
FIGHT (1)
  CovB   1   It's a Fight Like That
FIGHTIN' (1)
  Blak 27   Fightin' the Jug
FINGERS (1)
  Shad 20   Take Your Fingers Off It
FIRE (4)
  Este 30   Fire Department Blues
  Hawk   3   Jailhouse Fire Blues
  MemM 17   Garage Fire Blues
  SykR   4   Fire Detective Blues
FIRST (5)
  MontE 5   The First Time I Met You
  SpiV   3   Murder in the First Degree
  Whea 16   First and Last Blues
  Whea 24   The First Shall Be the Last and the Last Shall
             Be First
FISHY (1)
  JohLo 20   Something Fishy
FIVE (1)
  WillS 16   Number Five Blues
FIX (3)
  DorsT 11   Fix It

FIX (cont.)
  Hawk   5   Awful Fix Blues
  Luca   3   Fix It
FIXED (1)
  HendR 1   Get It Fixed
FIXIN' (1)
  WhiW 12   Fixin' to Die Blues
FLAT (2)
  JohMa 1   Barrel House Flat Blues
  JonM 10   Good Time Flat Blues
FLOATING (1)
  Este 21   Floating Bridge
FLOOD (2)
  JohLo 18   Flood Water Blues
  WallS 7   The Flood Blues
FLOOR (1)
  JamS   4   Hard Time Killin' Floor Blues
FLORIDA (1)
  ThpE   2   Florida Bound
FLOWER (1)
  KelJ   8   Flower Blues
FLUSHING (1)
  JonM   1   Four Flushing Papa
FLY (2)
  HicR 20   The Spider and the Fly
  JonE   1   Katy Fly
FLYING (2)
  BlaAl 1   The Flying Crow
  WasbS 21   Flying Crow Blues
FOLK (1)
  JohM   2   When a 'Gator Holler, Folk Say It's a Sign of
             Rain
FOLKS (1)
  WallM 2   The Old Folks Started It
FOOL (4)
  BelE   6   She's a Fool Gal
  ChatB 28   Country Fool
  GreLi 12   If I'm a Fool
  JohLo 24   I Ain't Gonna Be Your Fool
FOOLER (1)
  KelJ   9   Men Fooler Blues
FOOLIN' (1)
  WillS 14   You've Been Foolin' Round Town
FOOL'S (1)
  SmiJ 13   Fool's Blues
FOOT (1)
  JefB 16   Rabbit Foot Blues
FORD (1)
  GibB   1   I've Got Ford Movements in My Hips
FORGET (1)
  Whea 26   Remember and Forget Blues
FORTY-FIVE (1)
  RolW   6   45 Pistol Blues
FORTY-FOUR [44] (3)
  SykR   1   44 Blues
  SykR   9   Kelly's 44 Blues
  Wigg   2   Forty-Four Blues
FORTY-NINE (2)
  WillJ 3   49 Highway Blues
  WillJ 17   Highway 49
FOUR [4A] (9)
  Brac   7   The Four Day Blues
  BradT 4   Four Day Blues
  CarrL 6   Four Day Rider
  CarrL 27   Big Four Blues
  JohR 22   From Four Until Late
  JonM   1   Four Flushing Papa
  JorC   3   Big Four Blues
  Rain 21   Four Day Honory Scat
  Spru   6   4A Highway
FOURTEENTH (1)
  BliP   2   Fourteenth Street Blues
FOURTH (1)
  WooH   1   Fourth and Beale
FRANCE (1)
  Hull   2   France Blues
FRANK (1)
  Stok 26   Frank Stoke's Dream

```
FREAKISH (1)                              GANG (cont.)
  Hann  1  Freakish Man Blues               EdwJ  1  Construction Gang
FREDDIE'S (1)                               EdwS  1  Construction Gang
  Spru 10  Mr. Freddie's Kokomo Blues        Hull  1  Gang of Brownskin Women
FREE (1)                                    Linc  6  Chain Gang Trouble
  AndeJ 1  Free Woman Blues              GARAGE (1)
FREEZE (1)                                  MemM 17  Garage Fire Blues
  HicR 15  Freeze to Me Mama            GARBAGE (1)
FREIGHT (3)                                 McCoJ 23  The Garbage Man
  SmiC 28  Freight Train Blues          GARDEN (1)
  SmiT  2  Freight Train Blues             WashE 1  Garden of Joy--Blues
  SmiT 15  Freight Train Blues          GAS (2)
FRIAR'S (1)                                 Bird  1  Gas Man Blues
  McCoR 2  Friar's Point Blues             Glov  4  Gas Man Blues
FRIED (1)                                GASOLINE (1)
  WeaC  6  Fried Pie Blues                 JorC  6  Gasoline Blues
FRIEND (7)                               GEE (1)
  ColeJ 1  Mistreated the Only Friend You Had   DorsT 7  Gee, But It's Hard
  Este 24  Poor Man's Friend            GEORGE (1)
  JohR  7  When You Get a Good Friend      Ledb 15  Shorty George
  JonM 22  Never Tell a Woman Friend    GEORGIA (8)
  Ledb 13  My Friend Blind Lemon           Blak 32  Georgia Bound
  MemM 42  Boy Friend Blues                BogL  6  My Georgia Grind
  Shad 15  Feed Your Friend with a Long Handled Spoon   Gait 1  Georgia Barrel House
FRIENDLESS (1)                              LeeX  1  Macon Georgia Cut-Out
  JohLo 22 Friendless and Blue             McTW 19  Georgia Rag
'FRISCO [FRISCO] (5)                        MemM  9  Georgia Skin
  BelE  4  Frisco Whistle Blues            Wate  3  Georgia Blues
  Crud  4  Mean Old 'Frisco Blues          WillH 1  Georgia Crawl
  JohBi 3  Frisco Blues                 GERMAN (1)
  MemM  2  'Frisco Town                    UnkA  7  German Blues
  Wigg  3  Frisco Bound Blues           GERMANY (1)
FROG (3)                                    LewN  2  Going to Germany
  HarW  2  Bull Frog Blues              GET (19)
  Pope  3  Bull Frog Blues                 AleT 16  When You Get to Thinking
  SmiJ 12  Hoppin' Toad Frog               Barn  2  If You Want a Good Woman--Get One Long and
FRONT (1)                                                   Tall
  ArnK  6  Front Door Blues                ChatB 12 I Get the Blues
FROST (1)                                   ChatB 25 Let's Get Drunk Again
  AleT 18  Frost Texas Tornado Blues       Crud  3  If I Get Lucky
FRYING (1)                                  EdwF  2  We Got to Get Together
  CartM 1  I Want Plenty of Grease in My Frying Pan   Gill 2  I'm Gonna Get It
FULL (1)                                    Gill  5  I'll Get Along Somehow
  Brac  9  Suitcase Full of Blues          HendR 1  Get It Fixed
FURNITURE (1)                               JamS  8  If You Haven't Got Any Hay Get on Down the
  McCli 1  Furniture Man                                Road
FURRY'S (2)                                 JohM  1  If I Let You Get Away With It Once You'll Do
  LewF  2  Mr. Furry's Blues                            It All of the Time
  LewF  9  Furry's Blues                   JohR  7  When You Get a Good Friend
FUTURE (1)                                  ThoHo 3  Put It Where I Can Get It
  BrowV 2  Future Blues                    WasbS 30 Get Down Brother
GAL (15)  [see also GIRL]                   WasbS 34 I Get the Blues at Bedtime
  ArnK 27  Set Down Gal                    Whea 22  When I Get My Bonus
  Barn  1  My Gal Treats Me Mean           Wilk  3  That's No Way to Get Along
  BelE  6  She's a Fool Gal                Wilk  9  Get Away Blues
  Blak 24  Low Down Loving Gal             WillK 3  Get Your Head Trimmed Down
  Bond  2  Black Gal Swing              GETS (4)
  BracM 3  Stered Gal                      BelA  4  I Don't Care Who Gets What I Don't Want
  ChatP 8  Jasper's Gal                    Patt  2  When Your Way Gets Dark
  East  3  Green Country Gal               Stov  2  A Woman Gets Tired of the Same Man All the
  Este 10  My Black Gal Blues                           Time
  HilR  1  I Had a Gal for the Last Fifteen Years   Whea 30 When a Man Gets Down
  JohLo 14 I'm Nuts About that Gal      GETTING [GETTIN'] (5)
  MooW  1  One Way Gal                     BrowB 1  Nobody But My Baby Is Getting My Love
  Pick  1  Crazy 'Bout My Black Gal        CarrL 2  Gettin' All Wet
  Pull  1  Black Gal What Makes Your Head So Hard?--No. 2   NelsR 1 Gettin' Dirty Just Shakin' that Thing
  Span  1  Good Gal                        UnkA  9  Gettin' Ready for Trial
GAL'S (1)                                   WillJ 13 I'm Getting Wild About Her
  JorL  4  My Gal's Done Quit Me        GHOST (2)
GAMBLER (1)                                 JohLo 6  Blue Ghost Blues
  UnkA  2  Snitchin' Gambler Blues         JohLo 28 Blue Ghost Blues
GAMBLER'S (1)                            GIMME (1)  [see also GIVE]
  ThoHo 1  Gambler's Dream                 SmiB 36  Gimme a Pigfoot
GAME (3)                                 GIN (5)
  BogL 27  Skin Game Blues                 ChatP 13 Whiskey and Gin Blues
  Howe  5  Skin Game Blues                 SmiB 15  The Gin House Blues
  OweG  2  The Coon Crap Game              SmiB 28  Me and My Gin
GANG (5)                                    WhiW  9  Good Gin Blues
  AleT  3  Section Gang Blues              WilsW 2  The Gin Done Done It
```

GIRL (10)   [see also GAL]
    AleT   5   Yellow Girl Blues
    Beam   1   Wayward Girl Blues
    ChatB 18   The Ins and Outs of My Girl
    Este   1   The Girl I Love, She Got Long Curly Hair
    LewF   4   Good Looking Girl Blues
    McCl   1   Brown Skin Girl
    McCl   5   My Little Girl
    MooR   3   School Girl Blues
    Virg   1   Little Girl in Rome
    WillS 20   Little Girl Blues
GIRLISH (1)
    MemM 44   In My Girlish Days
GIRLS (1)
    LofC   2   Brown Skin Girls
GIVE (6)   [see also GIMME]
    GreLi 3   Give Your Mama One Smile
    JackC 5   I Got What It Takes But It Breaks My Heart to
               Give It Away
    MemM 32   You Can't Give It Away
    MemM 36   Man You Won't Give Me No Money
    WillS 12   You Give an Account
    WooO   3   Don't Sell It--Don't Give It Away
GIVING (2)
    Glov   3   I Ain't Giving Nobody None
    UnkA 10   Giving It Away
GLAD (1)
    Dean   1   I'm So Glad I'm Twenty-One Years Old Today
GNAWING (1)
    ThoR   8   Back Gnawing Blues
GO (20)
    ColFJ 4   Save Your Money--Let These Women Go
    DaviW 26   Don't You Want to Go
    FulB   9   Step It Up and Go
    Gill   3   Let Her Go
    GreLi 10   How Can I Go On?
    JohLo 3   Sweet Woman You Can't Go Wrong
    JonM 11   You May Go, But You'll Come Back Some Day
    KelJ   4   Believe I'll Go Back Home
    McCl   2   Baby, Don't You Want to Go?
    McFaB 1   I Got to Go Blues
    MontE 10   Never Go Wrong Blues
    Spru   9   Let's Go Riding
    Stok   5   Last Go Round
    Vinc   8   Honey Babe Let the Deal Go Down
    Vinc 17   Go Away Woman
    Weld   8   Blues Everywhere I Go
    Weld   9   Somebody's Got to Go
    Wilk 10   I'll Go With Her Blues
    WillJ 6   Baby Please Don't Go
    WillJ 16   Please Don't Go
GOAT (1)
    Byrd   1   Billy Goat Blues
GOING [GOIN'] (20)
    Beam   3   Goin' Away Blues
    Beam   4   Going Away Blues
    CamC   1   Goin' Away Blues
    Clev   1   Goin' to Leave You Blues
    DayT   1   Goin' Back to My Baby
    JohJo 1   I'm Going Back Home
    LewN   2   Going to Germany
    McCoJ 2   Goin' Back to Texas
    McCoJ 17   Going Back Home
    MemM   1   Goin' Back to Texas
    MemM   5   I'm Going Back Home
    Nick   4   Going Back to Memphis
    Oden   3   Going Down Slow
    Patt   9   Going to Move to Alabama
    Patt 20   Moon Going Down
    RupO   2   Ain't Goin' to Be Your Low Down Dog
    SmiB 13   I Ain't Goin' to Play Second Fiddle
    Stok 20   Ain't Going to Do Like I Used to Do
    Vinc 13   The World Is Going Wrong
    WasbS 16   I'm Goin' to St. Louis
GONE (19)
    Blak 37   Depression's Gone from Me Blues
    CarrL 21   My Woman's Gone Wrong
    HicR 12   She's Gone Blues
    HilK   4   The Gone Dead Train

GONE (cont.)
    JackJ 3   This Mornin' She Was Gone
    JackJ 4   This Mornin' She Was Gone
    JohLi 2   You'll Never Miss Your Jelly Till Your Jelly
               Rollers Gone
    JohLo 17   Hard Time Ain't Gone No Where
    JohR 16   Last Fair Deal Gone Down
    McCoJ 13   My Wash Woman's Gone
    McTW 26   My Baby's Gone
    Rain 28   Gone Daddy Blues
    SmiB 22   After You've Gone
    SmiC 27   Mama's Gone Goodbye
    Spru   8   Your Man Is Gone
    SykR   2   All My Money Gone Blues
    Vinc   6   Your Good Man Caught the Train and Gone
    Vinc 20   I'll Be Gone Long Gone
GONNA (20)   [see also GOING]
    BigB 19   Good Liquor Gonna Carry Me Down
    Blak 14   You Gonna Quit Me Blues
    ChatB 3   The Law Gonna Step on You
    ChatP 14   You Gonna Worry Too
    Dool   1   Gonna Tip Out Tonight
    Este 20   I Ain't Gonna Be Worried No More
    Gill   2   I'm Gonna Get It
    Gill 16   I'm Gonna Leave You on the Outskirts of Town
    JamS   6   Little Cow and Calf Is Gonna Die Blues
    JohLo 24   I Ain't Gonna Be Your Fool
    McCoJ 19   Something Gonna Happen to You
    McCoJ 21   What You Gonna Do?
    McCoJ 25   We Gonna Pitch a Boogie Woogie
    SmiC 13   I'm Gonna Tear Your Playhouse Down
    SmiL   1   Gonna Put You Right in Jail
    WasbS 8   We Gonna Move
    WasbS 27   Gonna Hit the Highway
    Whea 38   I'm Gonna Cut Out Everything
    WillJ 8   I Know You Gonna Miss Me
    Yate   1   I'm Gonna Moan My Blues Away
GOOD (35)
    Barn   2   If You Want a Good Woman--Get One Long and
               Tall
    BigB 19   Good Liquor Gonna Carry Me Down
    Blacw 10   No Good Woman Blues
    Burs   2   I Got Good Taters
    CarrL 32   Good Woman Blues
    ChatP 2   You Don't Mean Me No Good
    ColFJ 2   No More Good Water
    DaviW 2   That Stuff You Sell Ain't No Good
    FulB 12   Good Feeling Blues
    JaxF   2   She Can Love So Good
    JohE   2   Good Chib Blues
    JohR   7   When You Get a Good Friend
    JonM 10   Good Time Flat Blues
    JonM 23   The Man I Love Is Oh So Good
    LewF   4   Good Looking Girl Blues
    McCl   4   She's Just Good Huggin' Size
    McCl   7   She's a Good Looking Mama
    McTW 23   It's a Good Little Thing
    MartC 3   Good Morning, Judge
    MemM 24   Where Is My Good Man
    MontE 4   Mama You Don't Mean Me No Good
    Pett   3   Good Boy Blues
    SmiB   9   You've Been a Good Old Wagon
    SmiC 15   Good Looking Papa Blues
    SmiJ   3   Good Coffee Blues
    SmiT 16   No Good Man
    Span   1   Good Gal
    Stok   7   Its a Good Thing
    SykR 12   No Good Woman Blues
    ThoJ   2   No Good Woman Blues
    ThoR 13   Good Time Blues
    Vinc   6   Your Good Man Caught the Train and Gone
    Vinc   9   She Ain't No Good
    Whea 19   Good Woman Blues
    WhiW   9   Good Gin Blues
GOODBYE (4)   [see also BYE-BYE]
    Blak 17   Goodbye Mama Moan
    SmiC 27   Mama's Gone Goodbye
    Vinc 14   Shake Hands and Tell Me Goodbye
    WillS 22   Goodbye Red

GOOSE (1)
  ThoJ   1   Blue Goose Blues
GOT [GOTTA] (39)
  Bare   6   She's Got a Nice Line
  BigB 21   I've Got to Dig You
  BogL 14   You Got to Die Some Day
  Burs   2   I Got Good Taters
  CarrL 35   You've Got Me Grieving
  ChatP   9   You Got to Help Me Some
  EdwF   2   We Got to Get Together
  Este   1   The Girl I Love, She Got Long Curly Hair
  FulB   8   You've Got Something There
  FulB 15   You Got to Have Your Dollar
  GibB   1   I've Got Ford Movements in My Hips
  Gill   6   Got to Reap What You Sow
  Gill 10   I Got Somebody Else
  HicR 19   We Sure Got Hard Times Now
  Hurt   6   Got the Blues Can't Be Satisfied
  JackC   4   The Cats Got the Measles
  JackC   5   I Got What It Takes But It Breaks My Heart to
                    Give It Away
  JamS   1   Devil Got My Woman
  JamS   8   If You Haven't Got Any Hay Get on Down the
                    Road
  JefB   1   Got the Blues
  JohLo 23   Devil's Got the Blues
  JorC 11   Got Your Water On
  McCoJ 18   You Got to Move--Part 1
  McFaB   1   I Got to Go Blues
  McTW   4   Mr. McTell Got the Blues
  MemM 28   You Got to Move--Part I
  Nick   5   Got a Letter from My Darlin'
  Nick   9   You Got Me Rollin'
  SmiC   1   I Got Everything a Woman Needs
  SmiT   8   You've Got to Beat Me to Keep Me
  SpiV 13   T. B.'s Got Me Blues
  Stev   4   Baby Got the Rickets
  TowH   6   She's Got a Mean Disposition
  Vinc 15   I've Got Blood in My Eyes for You
  WasbS 12   Bucket's Got a Hole in It
  WasbS 17   Yes I Got Your Woman
  Weld   9   Somebody's Got to Go
  Wigg   5   Gotta Shave 'Em Dry
  WillS 39   You Got to Step Back
GOVERNMENT (1)
  Este 17   Government Money
GRAND (1)
  Shor   5   Grand Daddy Blues
GRANDMA (1)
  MemM 16   Grandpa and Grandma Blues
GRANDMA'S (1)
  BigB   4   Grandma's Farm
GRANDPA (1)
  MemM 16   Grandpa and Grandma Blues
GRAVEL (2)
  BlaAL   2   Gravel Camp Blues
  Rach   6   Gravel Road Woman
GRAVEYARD (1)
  Hite   1   Graveyard Dream Blues
GRAVY (3)
  King   1   What's That Tastes Like Gravy
  MossB   3   Gravy Server
  Tamp   4   What Is It That Tastes Like Gravy?
GREASE (1)
  CartM   1   I Want Plenty of Grease in My Frying Pan
GREAT (1)
  ChatP   5   I See My Great Mistake
GREEN (4)
  East   3   Green Country Gal
  LewF 10   I Will Turn Your Money Green
  Nick   1   Everybody's Talking About Sadie Green
  Patt 11   Green River Blues
GREY (1)
  WillJ   4   My Grey Pony
GREYHOUND (1)
  Wilb   2   Greyhound Blues
GRIEF (1)
  Doyl   2   Grief Will Kill You

GRIEVING [GRIEVIN'] (2)
  CarrL 35   You've Got Me Grieving
  DorsT   1   Grievin' Me Blues
GRIN (1)
  ArnK 24   Laugh and Grin Blues
GRIND (1)
  BogL   6   My Georgia Grind
GRINDER (4)
  ChatP   3   Grinder Man Blues
  ColFJ   5   Coffee Grinder Blues
  SpiV   5   Organ Grinder Blues
  SpiV   6   Organ Grinder Blues
GRINDIN' (1)
  BogL   4   Coffee Grindin' Blues
GROAN (1)
  Lacy   1   Mississippi Jail House Groan
GROCERIES (1)
  McFa   2   Groceries on the Shelf
GROUND (5)
  Darb   3   Built Right on the Ground
  RichM   3   Burying Ground Blues
  WillJ   9   Rootin' Ground Hog
  WillS 15   Deep Down in the Ground
  WillS 40   Ground Hog Blues
GROVE (2)
  JamS   2   Cypress Grove Blues
  WillS 36   Shady Grove Blues
GUITAR (2)
  Bras   1   Guitar Rag
  McCl 19   I'm a Guitar King
GYPSY (1)
  LewF 14   Black Gypsy Blues
HABIT (1)
  Rame   3   Cocaine Habit Blues
HAD (6)
  BigB 22   When I Had Money
  ColeJ   1   Mistreated the Only Friend You Had
  HilR   1   I Had a Gal for the Last Fifteen Years
  JohR 19   If I Had Possession Over Judgment Day
  SykR   7   Lost All I Had Blues
  ThoHo   2   Adam and Eve Had the Blues
HA-HA (1)
  MooR   2   Ha-Ha Blues
HAIR (2)
  Este   1   The Girl I Love, She Got Long Curly Hair
  KidS   1   Short Hair Blues
HAIRED (1)
  JorC   9   Tight Haired Mama Blues
HALF (2)
  Stok   3   Half Cup of Tea
  WileG   2   Eagles on a Half
HALLELUJAH (1)
  McCoJ 26   Hallelujah Joe Ain't Preachin' No More
HAM (2)
  BelE   2   Ham Bone Blues
  Lacy   2   Ham Hound Crave
HAMBONE (1)
  Newb   4   Hambone Willie's Dreamy-Eyed Woman's Blues
HAMMER (1)
  Patt 12   Hammer Blues
HAND (5)
  DorsT   4   Second-Hand Woman Blues
  Gill 17   Woke Up Cold in Hand
  JohLi   1   Never Let Your Left Hand Know What Your Right
                    Hand Do
  SmiB   8   Cold In Hand Blues
HANDLED (1)
  Shad 15   Feed Your Friend with a Long Handled Spoon
HANDS (3)
  BigB 18   Keep Your Hands Off Her
  JorC 12   Don't Put Your Dirty Hands on Me
  Vinc 14   Shake Hands and Tell Me Goodbye
HANDY (2)
  LewAr   1   Miss Handy Hanks
  SpiV   4   My Handy Man
HANG (1)
  Whea   3   Don't Hang My Clothes on No Barbed Wire Line
HANGMAN'S (1)
  JefB 47   Hangman's Blues

HANKS (1)
  LewAr 1 Miss Handy Hanks
HAPPEN (1)
  McCoJ 19 Something Gonna Happen to You
HAPPY (2)
  DickT 2 Happy Blues
  JefB 49 Happy New Year Blues
HARD (23)
  Bare   8 Barefoot Bill's Hard Luck Blues
  Blacw 8 Hard Time Blues
  Blak 12 Hard Road Blues
  CarrL 28 Hard Hearted Papa
  ColeK 1 Hard Hearted Mama Blues
  DorsT 7 Gee, But It's Hard
  Doyl   1 Hard Scufflin' Blues
  GibC 14 Hard-Headed Blues
  Gros   1 Hard Luck Blues
  HicR 19 We Sure Got Hard Times Now
  JamS   4 Hard Time Killin' Floor Blues
  JohLo 17 Hard Time Ain't Gone No Where
  Linc   2 Hard Luck Blues
  MemM 38 It's Hard to Be Mistreated
  MemM 43 It's Hard to Please My Man
  MooA   2 It Wouldn't Be So Hard
  MossB 2 Hard Road Blues
  Pull   1 Black Gal What Makes Your Head So Hard?--No. 2
  Ston   1 It's Hard Time
  SykR 14 Hard Luck Man Blues
  ThoR   2 Hard to Rule Woman Blues
  ThoR 10 Hard Dallas Blues
  WillJ 11 I Won't Be in Hard Luck No More
HARMONY (1)
  Rain 17 Army Camp Harmony Blues
HARSH (1)
  LewF 13 Judge Harsh Blues
HARVEST (1)
  Hurt   7 Blue Harvest Blues
HAT (1)
  JonL   5 Little Hat Blues
HATE (1)
  BogL 18 I Hate that Train Called the M. and O.
HAVE (7)
  CoxI   2 Wild Women Don't Have the Blues
  FulB 15 You Got to Have Your Dollar
  GreLi 2 What Have I Done?
  HendK 3 Have You Ever Felt That Way?
  MartC 5 Let's Have a New Deal
  Oden   1 I Have Made Up My Mind
  WallS 5 Have You Ever Been Down
HAVEN'T (1)
  JamS   8 If You Haven't Got Any Hay Get on Down the
            Road
HAY (1)
  JamS   8 If You Haven't Got Any Hay Get on Down the
            Road
HE (3)
  EdwJ   2 He Likes It Slow
  EdwS   2 He Likes It Slow
  SmiT 12 He Likes It Slow
HEAD (8)
  ArnK 31 Head Cuttin' Blues
  Gran   1 Nappy Head Blues
  HarY   1 Hop Head Blues
  McCl   8 Whiskey Head Man
  Pull   1 Black Gal What Makes Your Head So Hard?--No. 2
  SmiB 17 Lost Your Head Blues
  ThoR   9 Jig Head Blues
  WillK 3 Get Your Head Trimmed Down
HEADED (2)
  GibC 14 Hard-Headed Blues
  WillS 10 Whiskey Headed Blues
HEARSE (1)
  MooM   1 Black Hearse Blues
HEART (4)
  Cann   2 Heart Breakin' Blues
  JackC 5 I Got What It Takes But It Breaks My Heart to
            Give It Away
  JackC 28 Baby Please Loan Me Your Heart
  Patt 14 Heart Like Railroad Steel

HEARTED (20)
  Brac   5 Trouble-Hearted Blues
  Brac   6 Trouble-Hearted Blues
  CarrL 28 Hard Hearted Papa
  CarrL 30 Broken-Hearted Man
  CarrL 31 Evil-Hearted Woman
  ColeK 1 Hard Hearted Mama Blues
  Este   2 Broken-Hearted, Ragged and Dirty Too
  HendB 1 Lead Hearted Blues
  JohR   1 Kind Hearted Woman Blues
  JohR   2 Kind Hearted Woman Blues
  JohR 27 Drunken Hearted Man
  JohR 28 Drunken Hearted Man
  Linc   1 Jealous Hearted Blues
  McTW 29 Weary Hearted Blues
  Rain 15 Jealous Hearted Blues
  SmiB   1 Down Hearted Blues
  SmiB   7 Sobbin' Hearted Blues
  Whea 31 False Hearted Woman
  WillS 42 Broken Hearted Blues
  WooO   1 Evil Hearted Woman
HEAT (1)
  JohTo 5 Canned Heat Blues
HEATED (1)
  JaxF   1 It's Heated
HEAVY (1)
  TayC   1 Heavy Suitcase Blues
HELL (1)
  JohR 23 Hell Hound on My Trail
HELP (2)
  ChatP 9 You Got to Help Me Some
  Shaw   2 I Couldn't Help It
HENRY (1)
  WillS 28 Joe Louis and John Henry
HENRY'S (1)
  TowH   1 Henry's Worried Blues
HER (4)
  BigB 18 Keep Your Hands Off Her
  Gill   3 Let Her Go
  Wilk 10 I'll Go With Her Blues
  WillJ 13 I'm Getting Wild About Her
HERE (8)
  ChatB 24 Who's Been Here?
  Hull   4 Don't You Leave Me Here
  JonM   6 Anybody Here Want to Try My Cabbage
  JorC 10 I Couldn't Stay Here
  SmiL   2 Don't You Leave Me Here
  ThoG   2 Don't Kill Him in Here
  ThoH 12 Don't Leave Me Here
  WalkB 1 Look Here Mama Blues
HE'S (3)
  JonCo 4 The Elder's He's My Man
  MemM 34 He's in the Ring
  SmiC 33 He's Mine, All Mine
HESITATION (2)
  CollS 6 Hesitation Blues
  JackJ 5 Hesitation Blues
HEY (2)
  Blak 13 Hey Hey Daddy Blues
HIGH (6)
  ButlS 1 Some Screamed High Yellow
  JefB 23 Rising High Water Blues
  Patt 15 High Water Everywhere--Part I
  Patt 16 High Water Everywhere--Part II
  Patt 23 High Sheriff Blues
  WhiW 10 High Fever Blues
HIGHWAY (14)
  Batt   2 Highway No. 61 Blues
  BigB 23 Key to the Highway
  Bond   3 80 Highway Blues
  Gill   8 Key to the Highway
  KelJ   1 Highway No. 61 Blues
  KelJ   2 Highway No. 61 Blues No. 2
  McCl   3 New Highway No. 51
  Pick   3 Down the Highway
  Spru   6 4A Highway
  SykR 16 Highway 61 Blues
  WasbS 27 Gonna Hit the Highway
  WillJ 3 49 Highway Blues

HIGHWAY (cont.)
WillJ 17 Highway 49
WillS   4 Project Highway
HILL (1)
Stok   23 Bunker Hill Blues
HIM (1)
ThoG   2 Don't Kill Him in Here
HIPS (1)
GibB   1 I've Got Ford Movements in My Hips
HIT (1)
WasbS 27 Gonna Hit the Highway
HITCH (1)
Weld   5 Hitch Me to Your Buggy and Drive Me Like a
              Mule
HOBO (1)
Este   25 Hobo Jungle Blues
HOCK (1)
CookR   2 Hock My Shoes
HOG (4)
FulB   3 Stealing Bo-Hog
MoraH   1 Root Hog or Die
WillJ   9 Rootin' Ground Hog
WillS 40 Ground Hog Blues
HOLD (1)
CarrL 17 Hold Them Puppies
HOLE (2)
Linc   7 Doodle Hole Blues
WasbS 12 Bucket's Got a Hole in It
HOLLER (1)
JohM   2 When a 'Gator Holler, Folk Say It's a Sign of
              Rain
HOLLERIN' (1)
Patt   2 Screamin' and Hollerin' Blues
HOLMES (1)
SmiB   12 J. C. Holmes Blues
HOME (23)
BelE   5 Carry It Right Back Home
Cann   1 Poor Boy, Long Ways from Home
Este   31 Clean Up at Home
Este   37 Mary Come On Home
Gill   14 One Letter Home
HicR   3 Poor Boy a Long Ways from Home
HicR   10 Hurry and Bring It Back Home
Howe   9 Away from Home
JohJo   1 I'm Going Back Home
JohLs   2 Long Way from Home
JohR   4 Sweet Home Chicago
JohTo   6 Lonesome Home Blues
JohTo   7 Lonesome Home Blues
JohTo   9 Lonesome Home Blues
KelJ   4 Believe I'll Go Back Home
LewF   8 Why Don't You Come Home Blues
McCoJ 17 Going Back Home
MemM   5 I'm Going Back Home
ReedW   3 Leavin' Home
RhoW   2 Leaving Home Blues
Scha   2 Home Wreckin' Blues
Spru   3 Way Back Down Home
Whea   18 Sweet Home Blues
HONEY (8)
ChatB 32 Honey
Ledb   5 Honey, I'm All Out and Down
MooP   2 Honey Dripping Papa
Rain   11 Honey Where You Been So Long
SmiJ   8 Honey Blues
ThoH   5 Honey, Won't You Allow Me One More Chance?
Vinc   8 Honey Babe Let the Deal Go Down
WillS   9 Honey Bee Blues
HONEYDRIPPER (1)
JohE   4 Honeydripper Blues
HONEYMOON (1)
JohR   32 Honeymoon Blues
HONORY (1)
Rain   21 Four Day Honory Scat
HOOKWORM (1)
Blak   28 Hookworm Blues
HOP (2)
HarY   1 Hop Head Blues
SmiT   13 Black Bottom Hop

HOPELESS (1)
BelA   1 Hopeless Blues
HOPPIN' (1)
SmiJ   12 Hoppin' Toad Frog
HORSE (2)
JefB   5 Black Horse Blues
SmiC   19 War Horse Mama
HOT (7)
CartG   2 Hot Jelly Roll Blues
DaviM   1 It's Red Hot
HarW   3 Hot Time Blues
JackC 12 Hot Papa Blues
JohR   12 They're Red Hot
SmiC   12 Hot Papa
Weld   10 Red Hot Blues
HOUND (4)
BogL   5 Pot Hound Blues
HenrH   1 Low Down Hound Blues
JohR   23 Hell Hound on My Trail
Lacy   2 Ham Hound Crave
HOUR (1)
CarrL 13 Midnight Hour Blues
HOUSE (22)
CarrL 23 Barrel House Woman
CarrL 24 Barrel House Woman No. 2
CollS   1 The Jail House Blues
FulB   7 Big House Bound
Gait   1 Georgia Barrel House
JefB   7 Chock House Blues
JefB   32 Lonesome House Blues
JefB   56 Empty House Blues
JohLi   3 House Rent Scuffle
JohMa   1 Barrel House Flat Blues
JonM   5 Poor House Blues
Lacy   1 Mississippi Jail House Groan
McTW   9 Come On Around to My House Mama
Rain   3 Barrel House Blues
RichM   2 Mooch Richardson's Low Down Barrel House Blues
              Part 1
SmiB   2 Jail-House Blues
SmiB   15 The Gin House Blues
SmiC   21 The Clearing House Blues
SmiC   36 Court House Blues
Spec   1 House Dance Blues
WileG   1 Over to My House
Wilk   1 Jail House Blues
HOW (12)
BigB   14 How You Want It Done?
CarrL   9 New How Long How Long Blues--Part 2
GreLi 10 How Can I Go On?
Hawk   6 How Come Mama Blues
Hull   5 Mama You Don't Know How
JefB   45 How Long How Long
Lask   1 How You Want Your Rollin' Done
SpiV   8 How Do You Do It That Way?
Stok   19 How Long?
Tamp   6 No Matter How She Done It
HOWLING [HOWLIN'] (4)
ChatB 11 Howlin' Tom Cat Blues
DaviW   3 Howling Wind Blues
SmiJ   1 Howling Wolf Blues--No. 1
SmiJ   2 Howling Wolf Blues--No. 2
HUGGIN' (1)
McCl   4 She's Just Good Huggin' Size
HUGHE'S (1)
Ledb   14 Mr. Hughe's Town
HUNGRY (2)
JefB   13 Broke and Hungry
SmiJ   11 Hungry Wolf
HUNKIE (1)
JorC   5 Hunkie Tunkie Blues
HUNTING (1)
Stok   21 Hunting Blues
HUNTSVILLE (1)
EvanJ   1 New Huntsville Jail
HURRY (3)
CarrL 15 Hurry Down Sunshine
HicR   10 Hurry and Bring It Back Home
JonL   4 Hurry Blues

HUSTLER'S (1)
  CarrL 33 Hustler's Blues
I (86)
  AleT 10 I Am Calling Blues
  Bare   5 I Don't Like That
  BelA   4 I Don't Care Who Gets What I Don't Want
  BigB   6 I Can't Be Satisfied
  BigB 22 When I Had Money
  Blacm 3 I Whipped My Woman With a Single Tree
  BogL 18 I Hate that Train Called the M. and O.
  BogL 19 Tired as I Can Be
  Burs   2 I Got Good Taters
  CarrL 10 What More Can I Do?
  CarrL 12 I Keep the Blues
  CarrL 25 I Believe I'll Make a Change
  CartM 1 I Want Plenty of Grease in My Frying Pan
  ChatB 5 I Want You To Know
  ChatB 12 I Get the Blues
  ChatP 5 I See My Great Mistake
  ChatP 7 I Believe I'll Settle Down
  ChatP 12 Me, Myself, and I
  ClayJ 1 I Packed My Suitcase, Started to the Train
  Crud   3 If I Get Lucky
  DaveC 1 I Ain't No Ice Man
  DaviW 13 I Can Tell By the Way You Smell
  DaviW 23 Why Shouldn't I Be Blue
  Este   1 The Girl I Love, She Got Long Curly Hair
  Este 18 I Wanta Tear It All the Time
  Este 20 I Ain't Gonna Be Worried No More
  Gill 10 I Got Somebody Else
  Glov   3 I Ain't Giving Nobody None
  GreLi 2 What Have I Done?
  GreLi 10 How Can I Go On?
  GreLi 11 If I Didn't Love You
  HarZ   3 I Let My Daddy Do That
  HilR   1 I Had a Gal for the Last Fifteen Years
  JackC 5 I Got What It Takes But It Breaks My Heart to
            Give It Away
  JackC 14 Mama, Don't You Think I Know?
  JackC 16 All I Want Is a Spoonful
  JohLo 24 I Ain't Gonna Be Your Fool
  JohM   1 If I Let You Get Away With It Once You'll Do
            It All of the Time
  JohR   3 I Believe I'll Dust My Broom
  JohR 19 If I Had Possession Over Judgment Day
  JonM   8 If I Lose, Let Me Lose
  JonM 23 The Man I Love Is Oh So Good
  JorC 10 I Couldn't Stay Here
  King   4 I Can Deal Worry
  LewF 10 I Will Turn Your Money Green
  LofC   3 I Don't Know
  McCoJ 9 I Called You This Morning
  McFaB 1 I Got to Go Blues
  MemM 15 I Called You This Morning
  MemM 20 I Don't Want that Junk Outa You
  MontE 1 The Woman I Love Blues
  MontE 5 The First Time I Met You
  Oden   1 I Have Made Up My Mind
  Rame   1 I Can't Stand It
  RupO   1 I Raised My Window and Looked at the Risin'
            Sun
  Shad   1 Sometimes I Think I Love You
  Shad   3 I Packed My Suitcase, Started to the Train
  Shad 16 I Can Beat You Plenty
  Shaw   2 I Couldn't Help It
  SmiB 13 I Ain't Goin' to Play Second Fiddle
  SmiC   1 I Got Everything a Woman Needs
  SmiC   6 I Want My Sweet Daddy Now
  SmiC   7 I Never Miss My Sunshine
  SmiC 14 I Don't Love Nobody
  SmiT   1 I Don't Know and I Don't Care Blues
  SmiT 10 The World's Jazz Crazy and So Am I
  SpiV 14 I Can't Last Long
  Stok 20 Ain't Going to Do Like I Used to Do
  SykR   3 The Way I Feel Blues
  SykR   7 Lost All I Had Blues
  Sylv   3 I Want My Sweet Daddy
  ThoHo 3 Put It Where I Can Get It
  WasbS 17 Yes I Got Your Woman

I (cont.)
  WasbS 33 I Laid My Cards on the Table
  WasbS 34 I Get the Blues at Bedtime
  Weld   8 Blues Everywhere I Go
  Whea   9 Doin' the Best I Can
  Whea 22 When I Get My Bonus
  WhiW   6 When Can I Change My Clothes
  Wilk   2 I Do Blues
  WillJ 8 I Know You Gonna Miss Me
  WillJ 11 I Won't Be in Hard Luck No More
  WillK 1 I Want It Awful Bad
I. C. (1)
  AndeJ 2 I. C. Blues
ICE (3)
  DaveC 1 I Ain't No Ice Man
  GibC   8 Ice and Snow Blues
  Whea   5 Ice and Snow Blues
IDA (1)
  CoxI   1 Ida Cox's Lawdy, Lawdy Blues
IF (9)
  Barn   2 If You Want a Good Woman--Get One Long and
            Tall
  Crud   3 If I Get Lucky
  DorsT 14 If You Want Me to Love You
  GreLi 11 If I Didn't Love You
  GreLi 12 If I'm a Fool
  JamS   8 If You Haven't Got Any Hay Get on Down the
            Road
  JohM   1 If I Let You Get Away With It Once You'll Do
            It All of the Time
  JohR 19 If I Had Possession Over Judgment Day
  JonM   8 If I Lose, Let Me Lose
IGGLY (1)
  HarY   2 Iggly Oggly Blues
I'LL (13)
  ArnK 18 I'll Be Up Some Day
  BracM 4 I'll Overcome Some Day
  CarrL 25 I Believe I'll Make a Change
  ChatP 7 I Believe I'll Settle Down
  ChatP 11 Maybe I'll Loan You a Dime
  Gill   5 I'll Get Along Somehow
  JohR   3 I Believe I'll Dust My Broom
  KelJ   4 Believe I'll Go Back Home
  McCoJ 15 Someday I'll Be in the Clay
  SpiV 12 I'll Never Fall in Love Again
  Stev   2 I'll See You in the Spring When the Birds
            Begin to Sing
  Vinc 20 I'll Be Gone Long Gone
  Wilk 10 I'll Go With Her Blues
I'M (36)
  ChatB 1 I'm an Old Bumble Bee
  CollS 13 I'm Sitting on Top of the World
  Dean   1 I'm So Glad I'm Twenty-One Years Old Today
  East   2 I'm Waitin' On You
  FulB   1 I'm a Rattlesnakin' Daddy
  GibC   7 I'm Tired of Being Mistreated
  Gill   2 I'm Gonna Get It
  Gill 16 I'm Gonna Leave You on the Outskirts of Town
  GreLi 12 If I'm a Fool
  GreLi 13 I'm Wasting My Time on You
  HarW   1 I'm Leavin' Town
  JackC 10 I'm Alabama Bound
  JackJ 2 I'm Wild About My Lovin'
  JohJo 1 I'm Going Back Home
  JohLo 8 I'm So Tired of Living All Alone
  JohLo 14 I'm Nuts About that Gal
  JohLo 21 I'm Nuts Over You
  JohR 21 I'm a Steady Rollin Man
  JonM 18 I'm a Back Bitin' Mama
  JonM 24 I'm a Real Kind Mama
  Ledb   5 Honey, I'm All Out and Down
  McCl 19 I'm a Guitar King
  McCoJ 4 I'm Wild About My Stuff
  MemM   3 I'm Talking About You
  MemM   5 I'm Going Back Home
  MemM 14 I'm Talking About You--No. 2
  SmiB 38 I'm Down in the Dumps
  SmiC 13 I'm Gonna Tear Your Playhouse Down
  WasbS 11 I'm On My Way Blues

I'M (cont.)
WasbS 16   I'm Goin' to St. Louis
WasbS 19   I'm Not the Lad
WasbS 23   I'm Feeling Low Down
Whea 38   I'm Gonna Cut Out Everything
WillJ 13   I'm Getting Wild About Her
Yate   1   I'm Gonna Moan My Blues Away

INS (1)
ChatB 18   The Ins and Outs of My Girl

INSURANCE (3)
SmiA   1   Insurance Policy Blues
WasbW 2   Insurance Man Blues
WillS 24   Insurance Man Blues

INTERURBAN (1)
JohBi 2   Interurban Blues

IRON (2)
BogL 17   Pig Iron Sally
KelJ   6   Cold Iron Bed

IS (17)
ArnK 36   My Well Is Dry
BogL 16   My Man Is Boogan Me
BrowB 1   Nobody But My Baby Is Getting My Love
CollS 14   My Road Is Rough and Rocky
DaviW 15   Moonlight Is My Spread
Este 36   Time Is Drawing Near
JackC 16   All I Want Is a Spoonful
JamS   6   Little Cow and Calf Is Gonna Die Blues
JonM 23   The Man I Love Is Oh So Good
McTW 15   Southern Can Is Mine
Mann   1   The Blues Is All Wrong
MemM 24   Where Is My Good Man
Shad   9   A Black Woman Is Like a Black Snake
Spru   8   Your Man Is Gone
Tamp   4   What Is It That Tastes Like Gravy?
Vinc 13   The World Is Going Wrong
WasbS 18   Life Is Just a Book

ISLAND (2)
BlaAL 1   Rock Island Blues
ColFL 1   Old Rock Island Blues

IT (70)
BelA   3   Shake It, Black Bottom
BelE   5   Carry It Right Back Home
BigB 14   How You Want It Done?
ChatB 8   Tellin' You 'Bout It
CollS 8   It Won't Be Long
DorsT 11   Fix It
EdwJ   2   He Likes It Slow
EdwS   2   He Likes It Slow
Este 18   I Wanta Tear It All the Time
Este 39   Tell Me About It
EvanJ 4   Shook It This Morning Blues
FosD   1   Tell It to the Judge No. 1
FosD   2   Tell It to the Judge No. 2
FulB   9   Step It Up and Go
GibC   1   Beat You Doing It
GibC 20   She Rolls It Slow
Gill   2   I'm Gonna Get It
Gill 11   It Looks Bad for You
Glov   1   Shake It Daddy
Hawk   4   Snatch It Back Blues
HendR 1   Get It Fixed
HicR 10   Hurry and Bring It Back Home
HicR 11   Ease It to Me Blues
JackC 5   I Got What It Takes But It Breaks My Heart to
             Give It Away
JohLo 19   It Ain't What You Usta Be
JohM   1   If I Let You Get Away With It Once You'll Do
             It All of the Time
JorC   2   Keep It Clean
JorC   7   Keep It Clean--No. 2
Luca   3   Fix It
McCoJ 10   Beat It Right
McTW 22   Warm It Up to Me
MemM 30   Squat It
MemM 32   You Can't Give It Away
MooA   2   It Wouldn't Be So Hard
Nick   3   It Won't Act Right
Patt   6   It Won't Be Long
Rame   1   I Can't Stand It

IT (cont.)
Shad 20   Take Your Fingers Off It
Shad 21   She Done Sold It Out
Shaw   2   I Couldn't Help It
SmiC   5   Play It a Long Time Papa
SmiC 11   It Won't Be Long Now
SmiJ   6   Tell It to the Judge No. 1
SmiJ   7   Tell It to the Judge No. 2
SmiT   4   Don't Shake It No More
SmiT 12   He Likes It Slow
SpiV   8   How Do You Do It That Way?
Stok   8   Mr. Crump Don't Like It
Stok 15   It Won't Be Long Now
Tamp   4   What Is It That Tastes Like Gravy?
Tamp   6   No Matter How She Done It
ThoHo 3   Put It Where I Can Get It
UnkA 10   Giving It Away
Vinc 19   Don't Wake It Up
WallM 2   The Old Folks Started It
WasbS 12   Bucket's Got a Hole in It
WasbS 13   Save It for Me
Whea   2   Ain't It a Pity and a Shame
WillK 1   I Want It Awful Bad
WilsL 1   Scoop It
WilsW 1   Scoop It
WilsW 2   The Gin Done Done It
WilsW 3   Do It Right
WooO   3   Don't Sell It--Don't Give It Away
WooO   4   Don't Sell It

IT'S (18)
Bunn   1   It's Sweet Like So
CarrL 40   It's Too Short
ChatL 1   It's a Pain to Me
CovB   1   It's a Fight Like That
DaviM 1   It's Red Hot
DorsT 5   Maybe It's the Blues
DorsT 7   Gee, But It's Hard
Gill 13   It's All Over Now
JaxF   1   It's Heated
JohM   2   When a 'Gator Holler, Folk Say It's a Sign of
             Rain
McCl 20   It's a Cryin' Pity
McTW 23   It's a Good Little Thing
MemM 38   It's Hard to Be Mistreated
MemM 43   It's Hard to Please My Man
MissM 2   It's Cold in China Blues
Stok   7   Its a Good Thing
Ston   1   It's Hard Time
Tamp   2   It's Tight Like That

I'VE (6)
BigB 21   I've Got to Dig You
GibB   1   I've Got Ford Movements in My Hips
SykR 13   As True As I've Been to You
ThoHo 4   I've Stopped My Man
Vinc 15   I've Got Blood in My Eyes for You
WasbS 28   I've Been Treated Wrong

J. C. (2)
JohT   1   J. C. Johnson's Blues
SmiB 12   J. C. Holmes Blues

JACK (3)
Este 23   Jack and Jill Blues
JohBi 4   Wild Jack Blues
WallS 2   Jack O' Diamonds Blues

JACKET (1)
Ledb 17   Yellow Jacket

JACKSON'S (1)
Tamp   5   Jim Jackson's Jamboree--Part I

JACKSONVILLE (2)
DaviW 17   Jacksonville--Part 2
FloN   1   Jacksonville Blues

JAIL (9)
Bare   3   Big Rock Jail
CollS 1   The Jail House Blues
EvanJ 1   New Huntsville Jail
Lacy   1   Mississippi Jail House Groan
SmiB   2   Jail-House Blues
SmiJ 10   County Jail Blues
SmiL   1   Gonna Put You Right in Jail
TexT   1   Jail Break Blues

JAIL (cont.)
  Wilk   1 Jail House Blues
JAILHOUSE (2)
  Este 38 Jailhouse Blues
  Hawk   3 Jailhouse Fire Blues
JAKE (1)
  LofW   1 Jake Leg Blues
JAMBOREE (1)
  Tamp   5 Jim Jackson's Jamboree--Part I
JAMES (3)
  BrowR 1 James Alley Blues
  WasbS 2 Jesse James Blues
  WillJ 10 Brother James
JAR (1)
  ArnK   9 Slop Jar Blues
JASPER'S (1)
  ChatP 8 Jasper's Gal
JAZZ (1)
  SmiT 10 The World's Jazz Crazy and So Am I
JAZZBO (1)
  SmiB 14 Jazzbo Brown from Memphis Town
JEALOUS (3)
  JonM   2 Jealous Mama Blues
  Linc   1 Jealous Hearted Blues
  Rain 15 Jealous Hearted Blues
JEFFERSON (1)
  ButlS 4 Jefferson County Blues
JELLY (2)
  JohLi 2 You'll Never Miss Your Jelly Till Your Jelly
           Rollers Gone
  UnkA   6 Selling the Jelly
JELLY ROLL [JELLYROLL] (3)
  CartG 2 Hot Jelly Roll Blues
  LewF   1 Jellyroll
  SmiE   1 Jelly Roll Mill
JELLY ROLLERS (1)
  JohLi 2 You'll Never Miss Your Jelly Till Your Jelly
           Rollers Gone
JELLY ROLLIN' (1)
  WhhR   1 Sweet Jelly Rollin'
JENNY'S (1)
  SmiM   1 Jenny's Ball
JERSEY (1)
  Patt 22 Jersey Bull Blues
JESSE (1)
  WasbS 2 Jesse James Blues
JIG (1)
  ThoR   9 Jig Head Blues
JILL (1)
  Este 23 Jack and Jill Blues
JIM (4)
  BogL   3 Jim Tampa Blues
  Shad 18 Jim Strainer
  Tamp   5 Jim Jackson's Jamboree--Part I
  Wilk 13 Old Jim Canan's
JITTERBUG (1)
  WhiW 14 Bukka's Jitterbug Swing
JIVE (1)
  GibC 17 Jive Me Blues
JOB (2)
  ArnK 33 Back on the Job
  ThoR   7 No Job Blues
JOCKEY (1)
  SmiT   6 Ride Jockey Ride
JOE (4)
  McCoJ 26 Hallelujah Joe Ain't Preachin' No More
  MartC 4 Joe Louis Blues
  Wate   6 Oh, Joe, Play that Trombone
  WillS 28 Joe Louis and John Henry
JOHN (3)
  Este   8 Poor John Blues
  SmiC 37 My John Blues
  WillS 28 Joe Louis and John Henry
JOHNSON (2)
  JohLo 25 Mr. Johnson Swing
  JohMa 4 Mary Johnson Blues
JOHNSON'S (2)
  JohLo 1 Mr. Johnson's Blues
  JohT   1 J. C. Johnson's Blues

JOLIET (1)
  McCoJ 14 Joliet Bound
JONES (1)
  JamJ   2 Southern Casey Jones
JOY (1)
  WashE 1 Garden of Joy--Blues
JUDGE (6)
  FosD   1 Tell It to the Judge No. 1
  FosD   2 Tell It to the Judge No. 2
  LewF 13 Judge Harsh Blues
  MartC 3 Good Morning, Judge
  SmiJ   6 Tell It to the Judge No. 1
  SmiJ   7 Tell It to the Judge No. 2
JUDGMENT (1)
  JohR 19 If I Had Possession Over Judgment Day
JUG (3)
  Blak 27 Fightin' the Jug
  CarrL 11 Papa Wants to Knock a Jug
  Weld   2 Memphis Jug--Blues
JUICE (1)
  MooP   1 Bug Juice Blues
JUMP (2)
  BogL 24 Jump Steady Daddy
  Wate   5 At the New Jump Steady Ball
JUMPED (2)
  CrawR 1 My Man Jumped Salty on Me
  WasbS 20 My Feet Jumped Salty
JUMPER (1)
  JefB 36 Mean Jumper Blues
JUMPIN' (1)
  Aker   4 Jumpin' and Shoutin' Blues
JUNGLE (2)
  Este 25 Hobo Jungle Blues
  JackC 27 Jungle Man Blues
JUNIOR (1)
  ClayJ 3 Bob Lee Junior Blues
JUNK (1)
  MemM 20 I Don't Want that Junk Outa You
JUST (6)
  DaviW 27 Just Want to Talk Awhile
  GreLi 1 Just Rockin'
  JohLo 13 Sam, You're Just a Rat
  McCl   4 She's Just Good Huggin' Size
  NelsR 1 Gettin' Dirty Just Shakin' that Thing
  WasbS 18 Life Is Just a Book
K. C. (3)
  BaxJ   2 K. C. Railroad Blues
  Blacm 1 K. C. Moan
  Blacm 2 K. C. Moan
KANSAS (3)
  Ledb 11 Kansas City Papa
  Shad   5 Kansas City Blues
  SmiC   9 Kansas City Man Blues
KATY (2)
  JonE   1 Katy Fly
  McCl 11 Katy Mae Blues
KEEP (7)
  BigB 18 Keep Your Hands Off Her
  ButlS 2 You Can't Keep No Brown
  CarrL 12 I Keep the Blues
  GibC 16 Keep Your Windows Pinned
  JorC   2 Keep It Clean
  JorC   7 Keep It Clean--No. 2
  SmiT   8 You've Got to Beat Me to Keep Me
KELLY'S (1)
  SykR   9 Kelly's 44 Blues
KENTUCKY (2)
  CoxI   4 Blue Kentucky Blues
  OweG   1 Kentucky Blues
KEY (5)
  BigB 23 Key to the Highway
  Gill   8 Key to the Highway
  JohMa 2 Key to the Mountain Blues
  SmiC 20 Mean Papa, Turn in Your Key
  ThoR   3 Lock and Key Blues
KEYHOLE (1)
  Gill   7 Keyhole Blues
KID (4)
  ArnK 39 Kid Man Blues

KID (cont.)
```
  HilB    2   Kid Man Blues
  JohEb   1   Be My Kid Blues
  MooAl   6   Kid Man Blues
```
KILL (2)
```
  Doyl    2   Grief Will Kill You
  ThoG    2   Don't Kill Him in Here
```
KILLING [KILLIN'] (2)
```
  JamS    4   Hard Time Killin' Floor Blues
  JohLo  16   Man Killing Broad
```
KIMBALL (1)
```
  TowS    1   Lily Kimball Blues
```
KIND (7)
```
  ChatP  10   Two of a Kind
  Gill    4   She Won't Treat Me Kind
  JohR    1   Kind Hearted Woman Blues
  JohR    2   Kind Hearted Woman Blues
  JonM   24   I'm a Real Kind Mama
  McTW   10   Kind Mama
  WillS  23   The Right Kind of Life
```
KING (4)
```
  McCl   19   I'm a Guitar King
  Whea   13   King Spider Blues
  Whea   15   King of Spades
  WillJ  12   Crawlin' King Snake
```
KINGFISH (1)
```
  Tamp    7   Kingfish Blues
```
KITCHEN (1)
```
  JohR    8   Come On in My Kitchen
```
KNEE (1)
```
  HilK    3   Down on My Bended Knee
```
KNOCK (1)
```
  CarrL  11   Papa Wants to Knock a Jug
```
KNOCKIN' (1)
```
  GreLi   5   Knockin' Myself Out
```
KNOT (1)
```
  ChatB  20   Double Up in a Knot
```
KNOW (8)
```
  ChatB   5   I Want You To Know
  Hull    5   Mama You Don't Know How
  JackC  14   Mama, Don't You Think I Know?
  JohLi   1   Never Let Your Left Hand Know What Your Right
                 Hand Do
  LofC    3   I Don't Know
  SmiC   16   You Don't Know My Mind
  SmiT    1   I Don't Know and I Don't Care Blues
  WillJ   8   I Know You Gonna Miss Me
```
KNOWS (3)
```
  LeeX    2   Nobody Knows You When You're Down and Out
  Newb    2   Nobody Knows
  SmiB   29   Nobody Knows You When You're Down and Out
```
KOKOMO [KO-KO-MO] (4)
```
  ArnK    3   Old Original Kokomo Blues
  Blacw   1   Kokomo Blues
  KelJ    5   Ko-ko-mo Blues
  Spru   10   Mr. Freddie's Kokomo Blues
```
KYLE'S (1)
```
  Kyle    1   Kyle's Worried Blues
```
L AND N (1)
```
  DaviW   5   L and N Blues
```
LABOR (1)
```
  DickT   3   Labor Blues
```
LAD (1)
```
  WasbS  19   I'm Not the Lad
```
LADY (2)
```
  CollS   4   Loving Lady Blues
  JohK    1   Lady, Your Clock Ain't Right
```
LAID (1)
```
  WasbS  33   I Laid My Cards on the Table
```
LAND (3)
```
  HilB    1   Low Land Blues
  JohLo   7   Low Land Moan
  LewF   12   Dry Land Blues
```
LANE (2)
```
  CarrL  18   Shady Lane Blues
  WasbS  31   Lover's Lane Blues
```
LAPLEGGED (1)
```
  JohLo  27   Laplegged Drunk Again
```

LAST (16)
```
  Cann    4   Last Chance Blues
  ChatP  15   Caught the Old Coon at Last
  DorsT  10   Where Did You Stay Last Night?
  HilR    1   I Had a Gal for the Last Fifteen Years
  JohR   16   Last Fair Deal Gone Down
  Luca    2   Where Did You Stay Last Night?
  McCoC   1   Last Time Blues
  Rain    6   Last Minute Blues
  SpiV   14   I Can't Last Long
  Stok    5   Last Go Round
  Wate    9   You Can't Do What My Last Man Did
  Whea   14   Last Dime Blues
  Whea   16   First and Last Blues
  Whea   24   The First Shall Be the Last and the Last Shall
                 Be First
  WooH    2   Last Chance Blues
```
LASTIN' (1)
```
  JefB   40   Long Lastin' Lovin'
```
LATE (1)
```
  JohR   22   From Four Until Late
```
LAUGH (1)
```
  ArnK   24   Laugh and Grin Blues
```
LAUGHING (1)
```
  Gill    1   You're Laughing Now
```
LAURA (1)
```
  Este   43   Little Laura Blues
```
LAW (1)
```
  ChatB   3   The Law Gonna Step on You
```
LAWDY (7)
```
  CoxI    1   Ida Cox's Lawdy, Lawdy Blues
  Darb    1   Lawdy Lawdy Worried Blues
  JackC   1   Papa's Lawdy Lawdy Blues
  WeaC    4   Oh Lawdy Mama
```
LAWYER (1)
```
  Este   42   Lawyer Clark Blues
```
LAZY (3)
```
  Call    1   Lazy Woman's Blues
  SmiC   17   My Doggone Lazy Man
  WallS   6   Lazy Man Blues
```
LEAD (1)
```
  HendB   1   Lead Hearted Blues
```
LEAVE (10)
```
  CartS   1   Don't Leave Me Blues
  Clev    1   Goin' to Leave You Blues
  Gill   16   I'm Gonna Leave You on the Outskirts of Town
  Hull    4   Don't You Leave Me Here
  JohLo  12   Baby Please Don't Leave Me No More
  Luca    5   Leave My Man Alone
  Nick    6   You May Leave But This Will Bring You Back
  Shad   13   Better Leave That Stuff Alone
  SmiL    1   Don't You Leave Me Here
  ThoH   12   Don't Leave Me Here
```
LEAVENWORTH (1)
```
  JonB    2   Leavenworth Prison Blues
```
LEAVING [LEAVIN'] (9)
```
  Brac    3   Leavin' Town Blues
  HarM    1   Mama's Quittin' and Leavin'--Part 1
  HarM    2   Mama's Quittin' and Leavin'--Part 2
  HarW    1   I'm Leavin' Town
  MontE   8   Leaving Town Blues
  ReedW   3   Leavin' Home
  RhoW    2   Leaving Home Blues
  SmiJ    4   Mama's Quittin' and Leavin'--Part 1
  SmiJ    5   Mama's Quittin' and Leavin'--Part 2
```
'LECTRIC (2)
```
  JefB   34   'Lectric Chair Blues
  SmiB   24   Send Me to the 'Lectric Chair
```
LEE (3)
```
  ClayJ   3   Bob Lee Junior Blues
  LewN    1   Viola Lee Blues
  PetW    2   Bertha Lee Blues
```
LEFT (4)
```
  Brac    2   Left Alone Blues
  CarrL  29   You Left Me Crying
  JohLi   1   Never Let Your Left Hand Know What Your Right
                 Hand Do
  PetW    3   My Baby Left Me
```

LEG (4)
ArnK   16   Big Leg Mama
Hurt   4   Big Leg Blues
LofW   1   Jake Leg Blues
WillJ   1   Little Leg Woman
LEMON (3)
ChatB 10   Let Me Roll Your Lemon
Ledb   13   My Friend Blind Lemon
Pick   2   Let Me Squeeze Your Lemon
LEMON'S (2)
JefB   33   Blind Lemon's Penitentiary Blues
JefB   35   Lemon's Worried Blues
LEND (1)
ChatP 16   Lend Me Your Love
LET (13)
ArnK   13   Let Your Money Talk
ChatB 10   Let Me Roll Your Lemon
ColFJ   4   Save Your Money--Let These Women Go
DaviW 19   Let Me in Your Saddle
Gill   3   Let Her Go
HarZ   3   I Let My Daddy Do That
HendB   2   Let Your Love Come Down
JohLi   1   Never Let Your Left Hand Know What Your Right
            Hand Do
JohM   1   If I Let You Get Away With It Once You'll Do
            It All of the Time
JonM   8   If I Lose, Let Me Lose
Pick   2   Let Me Squeeze Your Lemon
Vinc   8   Honey Babe Let the Deal Go Down
WasbS 26   Let Me Play Your Vendor
LET'S (4)
Blak   5   Come On Boys Let's Do that Messin' Around
ChatB 25   Let's Get Drunk Again
MartC   5   Let's Have a New Deal
Spru   9   Let's Go Riding
LETTER (6)
Gill   14   One Letter Home
Ledb   9   Death Letter Blues--Part 1
Ledb   10   Death Letter Blues--Part 2
Nick   5   Got a Letter from My Darlin'
SmiC   30   Death Letter Blues
Whea   11   Letter Writing Blues
LEVEE (6)
AleT   4   Levee Camp Moan Blues
BogL   2   Levee Blues
DorsT   6   Levee Bound Blues
GibC   13   Levee Camp Moan
McCoJ   3   When the Levee Breaks
WasbS 22   Levee Camp Blues
LICKER (1)   [see also LIQUOR]
CarrL 16   Corn Licker Blues
LIFE (3)
JohLo   5   Life Saver Blues
WasbS 18   Life Is Just a Book
WillS 23   The Right Kind of Life
LIGHT (1)
UnkA   3   Touch Me Light Mama
LIKE (14)
Bare   5   I Don't Like That
Bunn   1   It's Sweet Like So
CovB   1   It's a Fight Like That
HarO   2   You'll Like My Loving
JackC 20   Your Baby Ain't Sweet Like Mine
King   1   What's That Tastes Like Gravy
Patt   14   Heart Like Railroad Steel
Shad   9   A Black Woman Is Like a Black Snake
SmiT   14   Love Me Like You Used To
Stok   8   Mr. Crump Don't Like It
Stok   20   Ain't Going to Do Like I Used to Do
Tamp   2   It's Tight Like That
Tamp   4   What Is It That Tastes Like Gravy?
Weld   5   Hitch Me to Your Buggy and Drive Me Like a
            Mule
LIKES (3)
EdwJ   2   He Likes It Slow
EdwS   2   He Likes It Slow
SmiT   12   He Likes It Slow
LILY (1)
TowS   1   Lily Kimball Blues

LIMITED (1)
WhiW   1   The Panama Limited
LINE (3)
Bare   6   She's Got a Nice Line
Whea   3   Don't Hang My Clothes on No Barbed Wire Line
WhiW   15   Special Stream Line
LION'S (1)
Col1S   2   Devil in the Lion's Den
LIQUOR (3)   [see also LICKER]
BigB   19   Good Liquor Gonna Carry Me Down
BlaAL   3   Corn Liquor Blues
Este   28   Liquor Store Blues
LISTEN (6)
ArnK   15   Stop Look and Listen
McMu   1   Wait and Listen
ThoHo   5   Listen to Ma
Vinc   3   Stop and Listen Blues
Vinc   11   Stop and Listen Blues No. 2
Vinc   16   The New Stop and Listen Blues
LITTLE (17)
DickP   2   Little Rock Blues
Este   43   Little Laura Blues
Hull   3   Two Little Tommies Blues
JamS   6   Little Cow and Calf Is Gonna Die Blues
JohR   24   Little Queen of Spades
JohR   25   Little Queen of Spades
JonL   5   Little Hat Blues
Lock   1   Little Boy Blue
Lock   2   Take a Little Walk with Me
McCl   5   My Little Girl
McTW   23   It's a Good Little Thing
PooJ   3   Come Along Little Children
Rach   1   Little Sarah
Virg   1   Little Girl in Rome
WillJ   1   Little Leg Woman
WillS 20   Little Girl Blues
WillS 31   My Little Machine
LIVER (1)
JohE   1   Nickel's Worth of Liver Blues
LIVING (2)
JohLo   8   I'm So Tired of Living All Alone
ThoR   14   New Way of Living Blues
LOAN (2)
ChatP 11   Maybe I'll Loan You a Dime
JackC 28   Baby Please Loan Me Your Heart
LOCK (2)
JefB   46   Lock Step Blues
ThoR   3   Lock and Key Blues
LOG (3)
AleT   7   Sittin' on a Log
Beam   2   Rolling Log Blues
Beam   5   Rollin' Log Blues
LONE (1)
WooO   2   Lone Wolf Blues
LONELY (2)
Temp   4   So Lonely and Blue
Vinc   4   Lonely One in this Town
LONESOME (26)
AleT   1   Long Lonesome Day Blues
BogL   15   Lonesome Midnight Blues
Call   2   Lonesome Lovesick
Col1S 10   Lonesome Road Blues
CoxI   7   Lonesome Blues
DaviW   7   Travelin' this Lonesome Road
DaviW   8   Sad and Lonesome Blues
Glaz   2   Lonesome Day Blues
Gran   2   Lonesome Atlanta Blues
HarX   7   Lonesome Midnight Dream
HilB   6   Lonesome Weary Blues
JamJ   3   Lonesome Day Blues
JefB   2   Long Lonesome Blues
JefB   32   Lonesome House Blues
JohLo   9   Way Down That Lonesome Road
JohTo   6   Lonesome Home Blues
JohTo   7   Lonesome Home Blues
JohTo   9   Lonesome Home Blues
McCoC   2   That Lonesome Train Took My Baby Away
MemM   40   Lonesome Shark Blues
MooAl   5   Lonesome Dream Blues

LONESOME (cont.)
Shor   2   Lonesome Swamp Rattlesnake
SmiSi   1   Oh Oh Lonesome Blues
ThoR   1   So Lonesome
Tore   2   Lonesome Man Blues
WillH   2   Lonesome Blues
LONG (37)
AleT   1   Long Lonesome Day Blues
ArnK   21   Long and Tall
Barn   2   If You Want a Good Woman--Get One Long and
             Tall
BigB   15   Long Tall Mama
Cann   1   Poor Boy, Long Ways from Home
CarrL   9   New How Long How Long Blues--Part 2
CollS   8   It Won't Be Long
CoxI   5   Long Distance Blues
Este   1   The Girl I Love, She Got Long Curly Hair
HicR   3   Poor Boy a Long Ways from Home
JefB   '2   Long Lonesome Blues
JefB   40   Long Lastin' Lovin'
JefB   45   How Long How Long
JefB   67   Long Distance Moan
JohLs   1   All Night Long Blues
JohLs   2   Long Way from Home
McTW   3   Mama, 'Tain't Long Fo' Day
Patt   6   It Won't Be Long
Rain   4   Those All Night Long Blues
Rain   11   Honey Where You Been So Long
Shad   7   She Stays Out All Night Long
Shad   8   She Stays Out All Night Long
Shad   15   Feed Your Friend with a Long Handled Spoon
SmiB   33   Long Old Road
SmiC   5   Play It a Long Time Papa
SmiC   11   It Won't Be Long Now
SmiJ   16   Before Long
SpiV   14   I Can't Last Long
Stev   6   Papa Long Blues
Stok   15   It Won't Be Long Now
Stok   19   How Long?
TowH   3   Long Ago Blues
Vinc   20   I'll Be Gone Long Gone
Whea   7   All Night Long Blues
Wilk   5   Long Train Blues
LONGING (1)
CarrL   38   Longing for My Sugar
LOOK (2)
ArnK   15   Stop Look and Listen
WalkB   1   Look Here Mama Blues
LOOKED (1)
RupO   1   I Raised My Window and Looked at the Risin'
             Sun
LOOKING (3)
LewF   4   Good Looking Girl Blues
McCl   7   She's a Good Looking Mama
SmiC   15   Good Looking Papa Blues
LOOKS (1)
Gill   11   It Looks Bad for You
LORD (2)
WillS   11   Lord, Oh Lord Blues
LORDY   [see LAWDY]
LOSE (2)
JonM   8   If I Lose, Let Me Lose
LOST (3)
Rain   9   Lost Wandering Blues
SmiB   17   Lost Your Head Blues
SykR   7   Lost All I Had Blues
LOUIS (2)
MartC   4   Joe Louis Blues
WillS   28   Joe Louis and John Henry
LOUISA (1)
WillS   6   Miss Louisa Blues
LOUISE (5)
EdwT   1   Louise
Temp   3   Louise Louise Blues
Temp   5   New Louise Louise Blues
LOUISIANA (1)
TayC   2   Louisiana Bound
LOVE (27)
BrowB   1   Nobody But My Baby Is Getting My Love

LOVE (cont.)
ChatP   16   Lend Me Your Love
DorsT   14   If You Want Me to Love You
Doyl   3   Renewed Love Blues
Este   1   The Girl I Love, She Got Long Curly Hair
GreLi   7   Love Me
GreLi   8   What's the Matter with Love?
GreLi   11   If I Didn't Love You
HendB   2   Let Your Love Come Down
HendK   4   Mushy Love
JaxF   3   She Can Love So Good
JohR   33   Love in Vain
JohR   34   Love in Vain
JonM   23   The Man I Love Is Oh So Good
Ledb   8   Baby, Don't You Love Me No More?
McCl   12   Love with a Feeling
McTW   12   Love-Changing Blues
MontE   1   The Woman I Love Blues
Patt   26   Love My Stuff
Shad   1   Sometimes I Think I Love You
SmiC   14   I Don't Love Nobody
SmiT   14   Love Me Like You Used To
SpiV   12   I'll Never Fall in Love Again
WasbS   32   You Stole My Love
Whea   25   Deep Sea Love
WillS   8   Until My Love Come Down
WillS   43   She Don't Love Me That Way
LOVER'S (1)
WasbS   31   Lover's Lane Blues
LOVESICK (2)
Call   2   Lonesome Lovesick
HilB   5   Lovesick Blues
LOVING [LOVIN'] (6)
Blak   24   Low Down Loving Gal
ColFL   2   Wild About My Loving
CollS   4   Loving Lady Blues
HarO   2   You'll Like My Loving
JackJ   2   I'm Wild About My Lovin'
JefB   40   Long Lastin' Lovin'
LOW (15)
Blak   24   Low Down Loving Gal
CarrL   8   Low Down Dog Blues
HenrH   1   Low Down Hound Blues
HenrL   1   Low Down Despondent Blues
HilB   1   Low Land Blues
Howe   7   Low Down Rounder Blues
JefB   42   Low Down Mojo Blues
JohLo   7   Low Land Moan
RichM   2   Mooch Richardson's Low Down Barrel House Blues
             Part 1
RupO   2   Ain't Goin' to Be Your Low Down Dog
Spru   5   Low-Down Mississippi Bottom Man
WasbS   9   Low Down Woman
WasbS   23   I'm Feeling Low Down
Whea   21   Low Down Rascal
WillS   21   Low Down Ways
LOWLAND (1)   [see also LOW LAND]
WasbS   10   Lowland Blues
LUCK (13)
ArnK   38   Bad Luck Blues
BakW   4   Bad Luck Moan
Bare   8   Barefoot Bill's Hard Luck Blues
GibC   12   Bad Luck Dice
Gros   1   Hard Luck Blues
JefB   17   Bad Luck Blues
JefB   38   Change My Luck Blues
Linc   2   Hard Luck Blues
McCoR   1   Tough Luck
Rain   1   Bad Luck Blues
SykR   14   Hard Luck Man Blues
WillJ   11   I Won't Be in Hard Luck No More
WillS   26   Bad Luck Blues
LUCK'S (1)
LewN   6   Bad Luck's My Buddy
LUCKY (2)
Crud   3   If I Get Lucky
Rain   14   Lucky Rock Blues
M. AND O. (3)
BogL   18   I Hate that Train Called the M. and O.

M. AND O. (cont.)
```
  BrowV  1   M and O Blues
  DaviW  1   M. and O. Blues
  DaviW  4   M. and O. Blues No. 3
```
MA (1)
```
  ThoHo  5   Listen to Ma
```
MA'AM (1)
```
  Howe   6   Please Ma'am
```
MACHINE (1)
```
  WillS 31   My Little Machine
```
MACON (1)
```
  LeeX   1   Macon Georgia Cut-Out
```
MAD (1)
```
  MooR   5   Mad Dog Blues
```
MADE (3)
```
  Oden   1   I Have Made Up My Mind
  Wate   2   There'll Be Some Changes Made
  WillS 34   My Baby Made a Change
```
MAE (1)
```
  McCl  11   Katy Mae Blues
```
MAGGIE (1)
```
  JohTo  4   Maggie Campbell Blues
```
MAILMAN (1)
```
  Este  35   Mailman Blues
```
MAKE (3)
```
  CarrL 25   I Believe I'll Make a Change
  Este  27   Everybody Oughta Make a Change
  JohE   3   Can't Make Another Day
```
MAKES (1)
```
  Pull   1   Black Gal What Makes Your Head So Hard?--No. 2
```
MALTED (1)
```
  JohR  26   Malted Milk
```
MALTESE (1)
```
  JefB  50   Maltese Cat Blues
```
MAMA [MAMMA] (65)
```
  ArnK  16   Big Leg Mama
  BakW   1   Mama, Don't Rush Me Blues
  BigB  15   Long Tall Mama
  Blak  11   Brownskin Mama Blues
  Blak  16   Doggin' Me Mama Blues
  Blak  17   Goodbye Mama Moan
  Brac   4   My Brown Mama Blues
  Cali   2   Traveling Mama Blues
  CarrL 14   Mean Mistreater Mama
  ColeK  1   Hard Hearted Mama Blues
  ColFJ  3   Mistreatin' Mama
  CollS 12   Slow Mama Slow
  DanJ   1   My Mama Was a Sailor
  Este  16   Drop Down Mama
  FulB   2   Rag, Mama, Rag
  Glaz   1   Rollin' Mama Blues
  Glov   2   Pig Meat Mama
  GreLi  3   Give Your Mama One Smile
  Hawk   6   How Come Mama Blues
  HenrH      My Silver Dollar Mama
  HicR  15   Freeze to Me Mama
  Hous   1   My Black Mama--Part 1
  Hous   2   My Black Mama--Part 2
  Hull   5   Mama You Don't Know How
  JackC 14   Mama, Don't You Think I Know?
  JaxF   2   Come On, Mama, Do That Dance
  JefB  41   Piney Woods Money Mama
  JefB  52   Eagle Eyed Mama
  JefB  59   Peach Orchard Mama
  JohTo  8   Big Fat Mama Blues
  JonCo  1   Sweet Mama Blues
  JonE   2   Mean Actin' Mama
  JonM   2   Jealous Mama Blues
  JonM  17   Mamma
  JonM  18   I'm a Back Bitin' Mama
  JonM  24   I'm a Real Kind Mama
  JorC   9   Tight Haired Mama Blues
  LewF  11   Mistreatin' Mama
  LewN   3   Pretty Mama Blues
  Lint   1   Pretty Mama Blues
  McCl   7   She's a Good Looking Mama
  McCl   9   New Sugar Mama
  McCl  13   Drop Down Mama
  McTW   3   Mama, 'Tain't Long Fo' Day
```
MAMA [MAMMA] (cont.)
```
  McTW   9   Come On Around to My House Mama
  McTW  10   Kind Mama
  McTW  20   Rollin' Mama Blues
  McTW  24   Savannah Mama
  McTW  30   Southern Can Mama
  MontE  4   Mama You Don't Mean Me No Good
  Rach   4   Sweet Mama
  RolW   4   Big Mama
  SmiC  19   War Horse Mama
  Stok   2   Sweet to Mama
  Stok  16   Nehi Mama Blues
  UnkA   3   Touch Me Light Mama
  WalkB  1   Look Here Mama Blues
  WasbS  1   Mama Don't Allow No. 1
  WasbS  3   Mama Don't Allow No. 2
  WasbS 14   Sophisticated Mama
  WeaC   3   Sometime Mama
  WeaC   4   Oh Lawdy Mama
  Whea  43   Sugar Mama
  WillJ 14   Peach Orchard Mama
  WillK  4   Peach Orchard Mama
```
MAMA'S (6)
```
  HarM   1   Mama's Quittin' and Leavin'--Part 1
  HarM   2   Mama's Quittin' and Leavin'--Part 2
  SmiC  27   Mama's Gone Goodbye
  SmiJ   4   Mama's Quittin' and Leavin'--Part 1
  SmiJ   5   Mama's Quittin' and Leavin'--Part 2
  Whea   1   Mama's Advice
```
MAMLISH (1)
```
  BelE   1   Mamlish Blues
```
MAN (98)
```
  ArnK   5   Sissy Man Blues
  ArnK  32   Broke Man Blues
  ArnK  39   Kid Man Blues
  BigB  11   Mr. Conductor Man
  BigB  20   Rustlin' Man
  BirB   1   Mill Man Blues
  Bird   1   Gas Man Blues
  BogL  16   My Man Is Boogan Me
  BogL  20   Sweet Man, Sweet Man
  BogL  25   Man Stealer Blues
  BrowI  4   Skin Man
  CarrL 30   Broken-Hearted Man
  ChatB 14   All Around Man
  ChatP  3   Grinder Man Blues
  ColFJ  1   Man Trouble Blues
  ColFJ  6   Man Trouble Blues
  CoxI  11   You Stole My Man
  CrawR  1   My Man Jumped Salty on Me
  DaveC  1   I Ain't No Ice Man
  DaviW  9   Minute Man Blues--Part 1
  DaviW 10   Minute Man Blues--Part 2
  DaviW 12   Root Man Blues
  Este  44   Working Man Blues
  FoxJ   1   The Worried Man Blues
  Glov   4   Gas Man Blues
  GreLi  4   My Mellow Man
  Gros   2   Strange Man
  Hann   1   Freakish Man Blues
  HarZ   2   Oh Ambulance Man
  HilB   2   Kid Man Blues
  Howe   1   Coal Man Blues
  Hurt   5   Candy Man Blues
  JackC  2   Airy Man Blues
  JackC 18   Butter and Egg Man Blues
  JackC 23   Coal Man Blues
  JackC 27   Jungle Man Blues
  JefB  70   Cat Man Blues
  JohLo 16   Man Killing Broad
  JohR  21   I'm a Steady Rollin Man
  JohR  27   Drunken Hearted Man
  JohR  28   Drunken Hearted Man
  JonCo  4   The Elder's He's My Man
  JonM  23   The Man I Love Is Oh So Good
  LofC   1   Monkey Man Blues
  Luca   5   Leave My Man Alone
  McCl   8   Whiskey Head Man
  McCli  1   Furniture Man
```

MAN (cont.)

McCoJ	23	The Garbage Man
McCoJ	24	My Daddy Was a Movin' Man
McPB	3	Whiskey Man Blues
MartC	2	Badly Mistreated Man
MartS	1	Blind Man Blues
MartS	3	Mistreating Man Blues
MasM	1	Molly Man
MasM	2	Shrimp Man
MemM	24	Where Is My Good Man
MemM	36	Man You Won't Give Me No Money
MemM	43	It's Hard to Please My Man
MooAl	3	My Man Blues
MooAl	6	Kid Man Blues
Nick	2	Cave Man Blues
Palm	1	Broke Man Blues
Patt	27	Revenue Man Blues
Rain	27	Trust No Man
ReyW	1	Married Man Blues
SimsH	2	Tell Me Man Blues
SmiBM	2	Sugar Man Blues--Part 1
SmiBM	3	Sugar Man Blues--Part 2
SmiC	9	Kansas City Man Blues
SmiC	17	My Doggone Lazy Man
SmiC	22	Don't Advertise Your Man
SmiC	32	Steel Drivin' Man
SmiT	16	No Good Man
SpiV	4	My Handy Man
Spru	5	Low-Down Mississippi Bottom Man
Spru	8	Your Man Is Gone
Stov	2	A Woman Gets Tired of the Same Man All the Time
SykR	14	Hard Luck Man Blues
ThoHo	4	I've Stopped My Man
ThoR	11	Ramblin' Man
Tore	2	Lonesome Man Blues
TowH	4	Poor Man Blues
Vinc	6	Your Good Man Caught the Train and Gone
WallS	6	Lazy Man Blues
WasbW	2	Insurance Man Blues
Wate	1	One Man Nan
Wate	7	Memphis Man
Wate	9	You Can't Do What My Last Man Did
Whea	12	Cocktail Man Blues
Whea	20	Working Man
Whea	30	When a Man Gets Down
WhiW	7	Sleepy Man Blues
WillS	2	Collector Man Blues
WillS	24	Insurance Man Blues
WillS	32	Western Union Man
WillX	3	Man of My Own
WilsL	2	Stevedore Man

MAN'S (3)

DorsT	2	Broke Man's Blues
Este	24	Poor Man's Friend
SmiB	27	Poor Man's Blues

MARE (1)

JohTo	10	Black Mare Blues

MARRIED (3)

Este	15	Married Woman Blues
ReyW	1	Married Man Blues
Tore	1	Married Woman Blues

MARY (4)

Este	37	Mary Come On Home
JohMa	4	Mary Johnson Blues
McCoJ	5	My Mary Blues
Shad	19	Mary Anna Cut Off

MASON-DIXON (1)

Hite	2	Mason-Dixon Blues

MATCH (4)

JefB	19	Match Box Blues
JefB	21	Match Box Blues
JefB	22	Match Box Blues
Ledb	16	Match Box Blues

MATTER (5)

GreLi	8	What's the Matter with Love?
MemM	18	What's the Matter with the Mill?
Shad	14	What's the Matter?
Stok	13	What's the Matter Blues

MATTER (cont.)

Tamp	6	No Matter How She Done It

MATTIE (2)

Este	4	Black Mattie Blues
McCoJ	12	Shake Mattie

MAXWELL (1)

JackC	15	Maxwell Street Blues

MAY (2)

JonM	11	You May Go, But You'll Come Back Some Day
Nick	6	You May Leave But This Will Bring You Back

MAYBE (2)

ChatP	11	Maybe I'll Loan You a Dime
DorsT	5	Maybe It's the Blues

MCKINNEY (1)

ThoH	3	Bob McKinney

MCTELL (1)

McTW	4	Mr. McTell Got the Blues

ME (90) [see also GIMME]

BakW	1	Mama, Don't Rush Me Blues
Barn	1	My Gal Treats Me Mean
BigB	19	Good Liquor Gonna Carry Me Down
Blak	14	You Gonna Quit Me Blues
Blak	16	Doggin' Me Mama Blues
Blak	37	Depression's Gone from Me Blues
BogL	16	My Man Is Boogan Me
Brac	11	Pay Me No Mind
BracM	1	You Scolded Me and Drove Me from Your Door
CarrL	29	You Left Me Crying
CarrL	35	You've Got Me Grieving
CartS	1	Don't Leave Me Blues
ChatB	10	Let Me Roll Your Lemon
ChatB	21	Your Biscuits Are Big Enough for Me
ChatB	29	Arrangement for Me--Blues
ChatL	1	It's a Pain to Me
ChatP	2	You Don't Mean Me No Good
ChatP	9	You Got to Help Me Some
ChatP	12	Me, Myself, and I
ChatP	16	Lend Me Your Love
CrawR	1	My Man Jumped Salty on Me
DaveJ	1	Save Me Some
DaviW	19	Let Me in Your Saddle
DaviW	22	Please Don't Mistreat Me
DorsT	1	Grievin' Me Blues
DorsT	14	If You Want Me to Love You
Este	39	Tell Me About It
GibC	9	Don't Put That Thing On Me
GibC	17	Jive Me Blues
Gill	4	She Won't Treat Me Kind
Gill	12	Me and My Buddy
GreLi	7	Love Me
HicR	11	Ease It to Me Blues
HicR	15	Freeze to Me Mama
HicR	16	Me and My Whiskey
HilK	5	Tell Me Baby
Hull	4	Don't You Leave Me Here
JackC	13	Take Me Back Blues
JackC	22	She Belongs to Me Blues
JackC	28	Baby Please Loan Me Your Heart
JefB	71	Bootin' Me 'Bout
JohLo	12	Baby Please Don't Leave Me No More
JohR	29	Me and the Devil Blues
JonM	8	If I Lose, Let Me Lose
JorC	12	Don't Put Your Dirty Hands on Me
JorL	4	My Gal's Done Quit Me
Ledb	8	Baby, Don't You Love Me No More?
Linc	4	My Wife Drove Me From the Door
Lock	2	Take a Little Walk with Me
McCl	6	My Baby's Doggin' Me
McTW	22	Warm It Up to Me
McTW	31	Runnin' Me Crazy
MartS	2	Death Sting Me Blues
MemM	25	Ain't No Use Trying to Tell On Me
MemM	36	Man You Won't Give Me No Money
MemM	39	My Baby Don't Want Me No More
MemM	45	Me and My Chauffeur Blues
MontE	4	Mama You Don't Mean Me No Good
Nick	9	You Got Me Rollin'
OweM	2	Try Me One More Time
Patt	28	Poor Me

ME (cont.)
PetW	3	My Baby Left Me
Pick	2	Let Me Squeeze Your Lemon
Pope	2	Doggin' Me Around Blues
Rame	2	Tired of You Driving Me
SimsH	2	Tell Me Man Blues
SmiB	24	Send Me to the 'Lectric Chair
SmiB	28	Me and My Gin
SmiB	37	Take Me for a Buggy Ride
SmiL	2	Don't You Leave Me Here
SmiT	8	You've Got to Beat Me to Keep Me
SmiT	14	Love Me Like You Used To
SpiV	13	T. B.'s Got Me Blues
Stok	18	Take Me Back
ThoH	5	Honey, Won't You Allow Me One More Chance?
ThoH	9	Don't Ease Me In
ThoH	12	Don't Leave Me Here
UnkA	3	Touch Me Light Mama
UnkA	5	Throw Me Down
Vinc	14	Shake Hands and Tell Me Goodbye
WasbS	13	Save It for Me
WasbS	26	Let Me Play Your Vendor
Weld	5	Hitch Me to Your Buggy and Drive Me Like a Mule
Whea	8	Throw Me in the Alley
WillJ	8	I Know You Gonna Miss Me
WillJ	15	Meet Me Around the Corner
WillS	43	She Don't Love Me That Way

MEAL (1)
| JohAl | 1 | Miss Meal Cramp Blues |

MEAN (16)
ArnK	25	Mean Old Twister
Barn	1	My Gal Treats Me Mean
BelE	3	Mean Conductor Blues
CarrL	14	Mean Mistreater Mama
ChatP	2	You Don't Mean Me No Good
Crud	4	Mean Old 'Frisco Blues
JefB	36	Mean Jumper Blues
JonE	2	Mean Actin' Mama
LewF	7	Mean Old Bedbug Blues
LofW	2	My Mean Baby Blues
MontE	4	Mama You Don't Mean Me No Good
Patt	18	Mean Black Moan
SmiB	25	Mean Old Bed Bug Blues
SmiC	20	Mean Papa, Turn in Your Key
Tamp	8	Mean Mistreater Blues
TowH	6	She's Got a Mean Disposition

MEASLES (1)
| JackC | 4 | The Cats Got the Measles |

MEAT (4)
BogL	26	Stew Meat Blues
DorsT	3	Pig Meat Blues
Glov	2	Pig Meat Mama
Ledb	19	Pig Meat Papa

MEET (1)
| WillJ | 15 | Meet Me Around the Corner |

MELLOW (1)
| GreLi | 4 | My Mellow Man |

MEMPHIS (12)
CarrL	4	Memphis Town
HarZ	1	Memphis Yo Yo Blues
MemM	10	Memphis Minnie-Jitis Blues
MemM	19	North Memphis Blues
Nick	4	Going Back to Memphis
Rain	22	Memphis Bound Blues
Shad	2	Memphis Boy--Blues
SmiB	14	Jazzbo Brown from Memphis Town
Stok	22	South Memphis Blues
Stok	27	Memphis Rounders Blues
Wate	7	Memphis Man
Weld	2	Memphis Jug--Blues

MEN (1)
| KelJ | 9 | Men Fooler Blues |

MENINGITIS (1)
| MemM | 7 | Meningitis Blues |

MESS (1)
| Stev | 1 | Beale Street Mess Around |

MESSIN' (1)
| Blak | 5 | Come On Boys Let's Do that Messin' Around |

MET (1)
| MontE | 5 | The First Time I Met You |

MIDNIGHT (9)
ArnK	37	Midnight Blues
BogL	15	Lonesome Midnight Blues
CarrL	13	Midnight Hour Blues
CollS	7	Midnight Special Blues
FloN	2	Midnight Weeping Blues
HarX	1	Lonesome Midnight Dream
MooW	2	Midnight Blues
Sylv	1	Midnight Blues
Wate	8	Midnight Blues

MILK (5)
ArnK	2	Milk Cow Blues
ArnK	17	Milk Cow Blues--No. 4
Este	5	Milk Cow Blues
JohR	26	Malted Milk
Spru	1	Milk Cow Blues

MILKCOW'S (2)
| JohR | 35 | Milkcow's Calf Blues |
| JohR | 36 | Milkcow's Calf Blues |

MILL (3)
BirB	1	Mill Man Blues
MemM	18	What's the Matter with the Mill?
SmiE	1	Jelly Roll Mill

MIND (12)
BigB	12	Worrying You Off My Mind--Part 1
BoyG	1	Never Mind Blues
Brac	11	Pay Me No Mind
Doyl	4	Bad in Mind Blues
JohR	5	Ramblin' On My Mind
JohR	6	Ramblin' On My Mind
LeeB	1	Mind Reader Blues
LofC	4	Change My Mind Blues
McCl	17	You Can't Read My Mind
Oden	1	I Have Made Up My Mind
SmiC	16	You Don't Know My Mind
ThoR	6	Ramblin' Mind Blues

MINDED (2)
| BakW | 3 | Weak-Minded Blues |
| BakW | 7 | Weak-Minded Blues |

MINE (5)
JackC	20	Your Baby Ain't Sweet Like Mine
McTW	15	Southern Can Is Mine
Rain	13	Those Dogs of Mine
SmiC	33	He's Mine, All Mine

MINGLEWOOD (2)
| LewN | 5 | New Minglewood Blues |
| ThpA | 1 | Minglewood Blues |

MINING (1)
| SmiT | 9 | Mining Camp Blues |

MINNIE (1)
| McCl | 14 | Black Minnie |

MINNIE-JITIS (1)
| MemM | 10 | Memphis Minnie-Jitis Blues |

MINUTE (3)
DaviW	9	Minute Man Blues--Part 1
DaviW	10	Minute Man Blues--Part 2
Rain	6	Last Minute Blues

MISERY (2)
| CoxI | 3 | Misery Blues |
| Rain | 29 | Misery Blues |

MISS (6)
JohAl	1	Miss Meal Cramp Blues
JohLi	2	You'll Never Miss Your Jelly Till Your Jelly Rollers Gone
LewAr	1	Miss Handy Hanks
SmiC	7	I Never Miss My Sunshine
WillJ	8	I Know You Gonna Miss Me
WillS	6	Miss Louisa Blues

MISSISSIPPI (7)
BaiK	1	Mississippi Bottom Blues
BigB	16	Mississippi River Blues
Lacy	1	Mississippi Jail House Groan
MissM	1	Mississippi Moan
Patt	1	Mississippi Bo Weavil Blues
Spru	5	Low-Down Mississippi Bottom Man
WhiW	13	Aberdeen Mississippi Blues

MISTAKE (1)
  ChatP   5   I See My Great Mistake
MISTREAT (1)
  DaviW 22   Please Don't Mistreat Me
MISTREATED (8)
  ColeJ   1   Mistreated the Only Friend You Had
  DorsT 12   Been Mistreated Blues
  GibC   3   Tired of Being Mistreated Part 1
  GibC   4   Tired of Being Mistreated Part 2
  GibC   7   I'm Tired of Being Mistreated
  MartC   2   Badly Mistreated Man
  MemM   38   It's Hard to Be Mistreated
  TowH   2   Mistreated Blues
MISTREATER (2)
  CarrL 14   Mean Mistreater Mama
  Tamp   8   Mean Mistreater Blues
MISTREATING [MISTREATIN'] (5)
  ColFJ   3   Mistreatin' Mama
  LewF   11   Mistreatin' Mama
  MartS   3   Mistreating Man Blues
  MontE 11   Mistreatin' Woman Blues
  Stok   14   Mistreatin' Blues
MOAN (24)
  AleT   4   Levee Camp Moan Blues
  BakW   4   Bad Luck Moan
  Blacm   1   K. C. Moan
  Blacm   2   K. C. Moan
  Blak   17   Goodbye Mama Moan
  GibC   2   Whiskey Moan Blues
  GibC   6   Sunshine Moan
  GibC   13   Levee Camp Moan
  HicR   21   Atlanta Moan
  JefB   11   That Black Snake Moan
  JefB   18   Black Snake Moan
  JefB   58   That Black Snake Moan No. 2
  JefB   63   Mosquito Moan
  JefB   67   Long Distance Moan
  JohLo   7   Low Land Moan
  Ledb   6   New Black Snake Moan
  LewF   3   Sweet Papa Moan
  MissM   1   Mississippi Moan
  Patt   18   Mean Black Moan
  Rain   30   Slow Driving Moan
  SpiV   15   Detroit Moan
  ThoR   4   Sawmill Moan
  TucB   1   Bessie's Moan
  Yate   1   I'm Gonna Moan My Blues Away
MOANER (1)
  SmiC   25   Texas Moaner Blues
MOANING [MOANIN'] (4)
  AleT   14   Awful Moaning Blues--Part 1
  AleT   15   Awful Moaning Blues--Part 2
  FoxJ   2   The Moanin' Blues
  Shaw   3   Moanin' the Blues
MODEL (1)
  RolW   1   T Model Blues
MOJO [MOJOE] (2)
  JefB   42   Low Down Mojo Blues
  Linc   3   Mojoe Blues
MOLLIE (1)
  ThoH   6   Run, Mollie, Run
MOLLY (1)
  MasM   1   Molly Man
MONEY (9)
  ArnK   13   Let Your Money Talk
  BigB   22   When I Had Money
  ColFJ   4   Save Your Money--Let These Women Go
  Este   17   Government Money
  JefB   41   Piney Woods Money Mama
  LewF   10   I Will Turn Your Money Green
  MemM   36   Man You Won't Give Me No Money
  Shad   6   Evergreen Money Blues
  SykR   2   All My Money Gone Blues
MONKEY (1)
  LofC   1   Monkey Man Blues
MONKEYIN' (1)
  JonJ   1   Monkeyin' Around

MOOCH (1)
  RichM   2   Mooch Richardson's Low Down Barrel House Blues
                Part 1
MOON (2)
  JohLs   4   By the Moon and Stars
  Patt   20   Moon Going Down
MOONLIGHT (1)
  DaviW 15   Moonlight Is My Spread
MOONSHINE (3)
  MemM   37   Moonshine
  Rain   5   Moonshine Blues
  WillS   5   Moonshine
MORE (16)
  AleT   6   No More Woman Blues
  Bare   9   One More Time
  BogL   7   They Ain't Walking No More
  BogL   11   Tricks Ain't Working No More
  CarrL 10   What More Can I Do?
  ColFJ   2   No More Good Water
  Este   20   I Ain't Gonna Be Worried No More
  Este   22   Need More Blues
  JohLo 12   Baby Please Don't Leave Me No More
  Ledb   8   Baby, Don't You Love Me No More?
  McCoJ 26   Hallelujah Joe Ain't Preachin' No More
  MemM   39   My Baby Don't Want Me No More
  OweM   2   Try Me One More Time
  SmiT   4   Don't Shake It No More
  ThoH   5   Honey, Won't You Allow Me One More Chance?
  WillJ 11   I Won't Be in Hard Luck No More
MORN' (1)
  JonM   12   Early Every Morn'
MORNING [MORNIN'] (12)
  Blak   1   Early Morning Blues
  Blak   2   Early Morning Blues
  EvanJ   4   Shook It This Morning Blues
  JackJ   3   This Mornin' She Was Gone
  JackJ   4   This Mornin' She Was Gone
  McCoJ   9   I Called You This Morning
  MartC   3   Good Morning, Judge
  MemM   15   I Called You This Morning
  RolW   3   Early in the Morning No. 2
  RolW   5   Every Morning Blues
  WillS   3   Early in the Morning
  WillS 17   Christmas Morning Blues
MOSQUITO (1)
  JefB   63   Mosquito Moan
MOTHER (2)
  MemM   31   Dirty Mother For You
  RedN   1   Crying Mother Blues
MOTHERLESS (2)
  HicR   5   Motherless Chile Blues
  ThoE   1   Motherless Child Blues
MOUNTAIN (2)
  JohMa   2   Key to the Mountain Blues
  SmiB   32   Black Mountain Blues
MOUSE (1)
  WallM   4   Field Mouse Stomp
MOUTH (2)
  Curr   1   Fat Mouth Blues
  JackC 21   Fat Mouth Blues
MOVE (5)
  McCoJ 18   You Got to Move--Part 1
  MemM   28   You Got to Move--Part I
  Nick   7   Move that Thing
  Patt   9   Going to Move to Alabama
  WasbS   8   We Gonna Move
MOVEMENTS (1)
  GibB   1   I've Got Ford Movements in My Hips
MOVIN' (1)
  McCoJ 24   My Daddy Was a Movin' Man
MOZELLE (1)
  McCl   21   Mozelle Blues
MR. [MISTER] (12)
  ArnK   20   Mister Charlie
  BigB   11   Mr. Conductor Man
  JohLo   1   Mr. Johnson's Blues
  JohLo 25   Mr. Johnson Swing
  Ledb   14   Mr. Hughe's Town
  LewF   2   Mr. Furry's Blues

MR. [MISTER] (cont.)
McCl 22 Mr. So and So Blues
McTW   4 Mr. McTell Got the Blues
Spru 10 Mr. Freddie's Kokomo Blues
Stok   8 Mr. Crump Don't Like It
SykR 15 Mr. Sykes Blues
WillK 2 Mr. Devil Blues
MUCH (1)
Gill 15 You Drink Too Much Whiskey
MUDDY (1)
Spru   2 Muddy Water Blues
MULE (2)
JefB 37 Balky Mule Blues
Weld   5 Hitch Me to Your Buggy and Drive Me Like a
          Mule
MURDER (1)
SpiV   3 Murder in the First Degree
MUSHY (1)
HendK 4 Mushy Love
MY (118)
ArnK 36 My Well Is Dry
Bare   1 My Crime Blues
Barn   1 My Gal Treats Me Mean
BigB 12 Worrying You Off My Mind--Part 1
Blacm 3 I Whipped My Woman With a Single Tree
BogL   6 My Georgia Grind
BogL 16 My Man Is Boogan Me
Brac   4 My Brown Mama Blues
BrowB 1 Nobody But My Baby Is Getting My Love
CarrL 21 My Woman's Gone Wrong
CarrL 38 Longing for My Sugar
CartM 1 I Want Plenty of Grease in My Frying Pan
ChatB 4 Ants in My Pants
ChatB 18 The Ins and Outs of My Girl
ChatB 30 My Baby
ChatP 5 I See My Great Mistake
ClayJ 1 I Packed My Suitcase, Started to the Train
ColFL 2 Wild About My Loving
CollS 14 My Road Is Rough and Rocky
CookR 2 Hock My Shoes
CoxI 11 You Stole My Man
CrawR 1 My Man Jumped Salty on Me
DanJ   1 My Mama Was a Sailor
DaviW 15 Moonlight Is My Spread
DaviW 16 Ashes in My Whiskey
DayT   1 Goin' Back to My Baby
Este 10 My Black Gal Blues
GibB   1 I've Got Ford Movements in My Hips
Gill 12 Me and My Buddy
GreLi 4 My Mellow Man
GreLi 13 I'm Wasting My Time on You
HarO   2 You'll Like My Loving
HarZ   3 I Let My Daddy Do That
HenrH 2 My Silver Dollar Mama
HicR   4 Easy Rider Don't Deny My Name
HicR 16 Me and My Whiskey
HilK   3 Down on My Bended Knee
HilSy 2 Needin' My Woman Blues
Hous   1 My Black Mama--Part 1
Hous   2 My Black Mama--Part 2
JackC 5 I Got What It Takes But It Breaks My Heart to
          Give It Away
JackJ 2 I'm Wild About My Lovin'
JamS   1 Devil Got My Woman
JefB 38 Change My Luck Blues
JohEb 1 Be My Kid Blues
JohR   3 I Believe I'll Dust My Broom
JohR   5 Ramblin' On My Mind
JohR   6 Ramblin' On My Mind
JohR   8 Come On in My Kitchen
JohR 20 Stone in My Passway
JohR 23 Hell Hound on My Trail
JonCo 4 The Elder's He's My Man
JonM   6 Anybody Here Want to Try My Cabbage
JorL   4 My Gal's Done Quit Me
Ledb 13 My Friend Blind Lemon
LewN   6 Bad Luck's My Buddy
Linc   4 My Wife Drove Me From the Door
LofC   4 Change My Mind Blues

MY (cont.)
LofW   2 My Mean Baby Blues
Luca   5 Leave My Man Alone
McCl   5 My Little Girl
McCl   6 My Baby's Doggin' Me
McCl 17 You Can't Read My Mind
McCoC 2 That Lonesome Train Took My Baby Away
McCoJ 4 I'm Wild About My Stuff
McCoJ 5 My Mary Blues
McCoJ 13 My Wash Woman's Gone
McCoJ 24 My Daddy Was a Movin' Man
McPB   2 My Dream Blues
McTW   9 Come On Around to My House Mama
McTW 26 My Baby's Gone
MemM 24 Where Is My Good Man
MemM 39 My Baby Don't Want Me No More
MemM 43 It's Hard to Please My Man
MemM 44 In My Girlish Days
MemM 45 Me and My Chauffeur Blues
MooAl 3 My Man Blues
Nick   5 Got a Letter from My Darlin'
Oden   1 I Have Made Up My Mind
Patt 26 Love My Stuff
PetW   3 My Baby Left Me
Pick   1 Crazy 'Bout My Black Gal
Rain 25 Oh My Babe Blues
RupO   1 I Raised My Window and Looked at the Risin'
          Sun
Scru   1 My Back to the Wall
Shad   3 I Packed My Suitcase, Started to the Train
SmiB 28 Me and My Gin
SmiC   6 I Want My Sweet Daddy Now
SmiC   7 I Never Miss My Sunshine
SmiC 16 You Don't Know My Mind
SmiC 17 My Doggone Lazy Man
SmiC 29 Done Sold My Soul to the Devil
SmiC 37 My John Blues
SpiV   4 My Handy Man
SykR   2 All My Money Gone Blues
Sylv   3 I Want My Sweet Daddy
ThoHo 4 I've Stopped My Man
Vinc 15 I've Got Blood in My Eyes for You
WasbS 11 I'm On My Way Blues
WasbS 15 Diggin' My Potatoes
WasbS 20 My Feet Jumped Salty
WasbS 32 You Stole My Love
WasbS 33 I Laid My Cards on the Table
Wate   9 You Can't Do What My Last Man Did
Whea   3 Don't Hang My Clothes on No Barbed Wire Line
Whea 22 When I Get My Bonus
WhiW   6 When Can I Change My Clothes
Wilb   1 My Babe My Babe
WileG 1 Over to My House
WillJ 4 My Grey Pony
WillS 8 Until My Love Come Down
WillS 31 My Little Machine
WillS 34 My Baby Made a Change
WillS 44 My Black Name Blues
WillX 3 Man of My Own
Yate   1 I'm Gonna Moan My Blues Away
MYSELF (3)
ChatP 12 Me, Myself, and I
GreLi 5 Knockin' Myself Out
McTW 13 Talking to Myself
NAME (3)
DaviW 20 Call Your Name
HicR   4 Easy Rider Don't Deny My Name
WillS 44 My Black Name Blues
NAN (1)
Wate   1 One Man Nan
NAPPY (1)
Gran   1 Nappy Head Blues
NAPTOWN (1)
CarrL 1 Naptown Blues
NARROW (1)
WasbW 1 Narrow Face Blues
NASHVILLE (2)
SmiB 11 Nashville Women's Blues
Wilk   7 Nashville Stonewall Blues

```
NEAR (1)
    Este  36   Time Is Drawing Near
NEED (2)
    DaviW 18   Think You Need a Shot
    Este  22   Need More Blues
NEEDIN' (1)
    HilSy  2   Needin' My Woman Blues
NEEDS (1)
    SmiC   1   I Got Everything a Woman Needs
NEHI (2)
    ReyJ   2   Nehi Blues
    Stok  16   Nehi Mama Blues
NEST (1)
    Patt  21   Bird Nest Bound
NEVER (9)
    BoyG   1   Never Mind Blues
    JohLi  1   Never Let Your Left Hand Know What Your Right
               Hand Do
    JohLi  2   You'll Never Miss Your Jelly Till Your Jelly
               Rollers Gone
    JonM  20   Never Drive a Beggar from Your Door
    JonM  22   Never Tell a Woman Friend
    MontE 10   Never Go Wrong Blues
    SmiC   7   I Never Miss My Sunshine
    SmiC   8   Don't Never Tell Nobody
    SpiV  12   I'll Never Fall in Love Again
NEW (25)
    CarrL  9   New How Long How Long Blues--Part 2
    ChatL  2   New Sittin' On Top of the World
    CollS 11   New Salty Dog
    DaviW 25   New Come Back Baby
    Este  32   New Someday Blues
    EvanJ  1   New Huntsville Jail
    Grav   1   New York Blues
    JefB  49   Happy New Year Blues
    JohLo 10   New Black Snake Blues--Part 1
    JohLo 26   New Falling Rain Blues
    JonL   1   New Two Sixteen Blues
    Ledb   6   New Black Snake Moan
    LewN   5   New Minglewood Blues
    McCl   3   New Highway No. 51
    McCl   9   New Sugar Mama
    MartC  5   Let's Have a New Deal
    MemM  12   New Dirty Dozens
    MemM  13   New Bumble Bee
    SpiV   7   New Black Snake Blues--Part 1
    Temp   5   New Louise Louise Blues
    ThoR  14   New Way of Living Blues
    Vinc  16   The New Stop and Listen Blues
    Vinc  18   New Shake that Thing
    Wate   5   At the New Jump Steady Ball
    Wilk  12   New Stock Yard Blues
NEWS (1)
    JefB  44   Sad News Blues
NEXT (1)
    JohAl  2   Next Week Sometime
NIAGARA (1)
    ColeK  2   Niagara Fall Blues
NICE (1)
    Bare   6   She's Got a Nice Line
NICKEL (1)
    East   1   No Woman No Nickel
NICKEL'S (1)
    JohE   1   Nickel's Worth of Liver Blues
NIGHT (12)
    ArnK   1   Rainy Night Blues
    DorsT 10   Where Did You Stay Last Night?
    JefB  57   Saturday Night Spender Blues
    JefB  60   Big Night Blues
    JohLs  1   All Night Long Blues
    Luca   2   Where Did You Stay Last Night?
    Rain   4   Those All Night Long Blues
    Rain  20   Night Time Blues
    Shad   7   She Stays Out All Night Long
    Shad   8   She Stays Out All Night Long
    SmiC   4   All Night Blues
    Whea   7   All Night Long Blues
NIGHTS (1)
    Whea   6   Sleepless Nights Blues

NINE [9] (2)
    Chur   1   Number Nine Blues
    SykR  10   3 6 and 9
NINETY-EIGHT (1)
    AleT  12   Ninety-Eight Degree Blues
NINETY-NINE (1)
    DanJ   2   Ninety-Nine Year Blues
NO (42)
    AleT   6   No More Woman Blues
    BakW   2   No No Blues
    Blacw 10   No Good Woman Blues
    Blak  18   No Dough Blues
    BogL   7   They Ain't Walking No More
    BogL  11   Tricks Ain't Working No More
    Brac  11   Pay Me No Mind
    ButlS  2   You Can't Keep No Brown
    ChatP  2   You Don't Mean Me No Good
    ColFJ  2   No More Good Water
    DaveC  1   I Ain't No Ice Man
    DaviW  2   That Stuff You Sell Ain't No Good
    East   1   No Woman No Nickel
    Este  20   I Ain't Gonna Be Worried No More
    Hurt   2   Ain't No Tellin'
    JohJo  2   Don't Want No Woman
    JohLo 12   Baby Please Don't Leave Me No More
    JohLo 17   Hard Time Ain't Gone No Where
    Ledb   8   Baby, Don't You Love Me No More?
    McCoJ 26   Hallelujah Joe Ain't Preachin' No More
    MemM   8   Don't Want No Woman
    MemM  25   Ain't No Use Trying to Tell On Me
    MemM  36   Man You Won't Give Me No Money
    MemM  39   My Baby Don't Want Me No More
    MontE  4   Mama You Don't Mean Me No Good
    PerkG  1   No Easy Rider Blues
    Rain  27   Trust No Man
    SmiT   4   Don't Shake It No More
    SmiT  16   No Good Man
    SykR  12   No Good Woman Blues
    Tamp   6   No Matter How She Done It
    ThoJ   2   No Good Woman Blues
    ThoR   5   No Baby Blues
    ThoR   7   No Job Blues
    Vinc   9   She Ain't No Good
    WeaC   2   No No Blues
    Whea   3   Don't Hang My Clothes on No Barbed Wire Line
    Wilk   3   That's No Way to Get Along
    WillJ 11   I Won't Be in Hard Luck No More
NO. 1 (5)
    FosD   1   Tell It to the Judge No. 1
    SmiJ   1   Howling Wolf Blues--No. 1
    SmiJ   6   Tell It to the Judge No. 1
    WasbS  1   Mama Don't Allow No. 1
    WhiJ   2   Stormy Weather No. 1
NO. 2 (17)
    Blak  30   Too Tight Blues No. 2
    CarrL 24   Barrel House Woman No. 2
    FosD   2   Tell It to the Judge No. 2
    HicR  18   Yo-Yo Blues No. 2
    JefB  58   That Black Snake Moan No. 2
    JorC   7   Keep It Clean--No. 2
    KelJ   2   Highway No. 61 Blues No. 2
    McTW  28   B and O Blues No. 2
    MemM  14   I'm Talking About You--No. 2
    MontE  3   Vicksburg Blues No. 2
    Pull   1   Black Gal What Makes Your Head So Hard?--No. 2
    RolW   4   Early in the Morning No. 2
    SmiJ   2   Howling Wolf Blues--No. 2
    SmiJ   7   Tell It to the Judge No. 2
    Vinc  11   Stop and Listen Blues No. 2
    WasbS  3   Mama Don't Allow No. 2
    Whea  34   Peetie Wheatstraw Stomp No. 2
NO. 3 (1)
    DaviW  4   M. and O. Blues No. 3
NO. 4 (1)
    ArnK  17   Milk Cow Blues--No. 4
NO. 51 (1)
    McCl   3   New Highway No. 51
NO. 61 (3)
    Batt   2   Highway No. 61 Blues
```

NO. 61 (cont.)
    KelJ   1   Highway No. 61 Blues
    KelJ   2   Highway No. 61 Blues No. 2
NOBODY (8)
    BrowB   1   Nobody But My Baby Is Getting My Love
    Glov   3   I Ain't Giving Nobody None
    LeeX   2   Nobody Knows You When You're Down and Out
    Newb   2   Nobody Knows
    SmiB   29   Nobody Knows You When You're Down and Out
    SmiC   8   Don't Never Tell Nobody
    SmiC   14   I Don't Love Nobody
    SpiV   10   Don't Trust Nobody Blues
NOBODY'S (1)
    Hurt   1   Nobody's Dirty Business
NONE (1)
    Glov   3   I Ain't Giving Nobody None
NORTH (2)
    JonM   16   North Bound Blues
    MemM   19   North Memphis Blues
NOT (2)
    JohLo 11   When You Fall For Someone That's Not Your Own
    WasbS 19   I'm Not the Lad
NOTHING [NOTHIN'] (3)
    GibB   2   Nothing But the Blues
    MemM   41   Nothin in Rambling
    WhiG   3   The Blues Ain't Nothin' But. . .???
NOTION (1)
    Virg   2   Bad Notion Blues
NOTORIETY (1)
    Blak   23   Notoriety Woman Blues
NOW (8)
    Bare   4   From Now On
    Gill   1   You're Laughing Now
    Gill   13   It's All Over Now
    HicR   19   We Sure Got Hard Times Now
    SmiC   6   I Want My Sweet Daddy Now
    SmiC   11   It Won't Be Long Now
    Stok   15   It Won't Be Long Now
    Stok   24   Right Now Blues
NUMBER (3) [see also NO.]
    Chur   1   Number Nine Blues
    Hawk   2   Number Three Blues
    WilS   16   Number Five Blues
NUT (1)
    BrowI   3   Nut Factory Blues
NUTS (2)
    JohLo 14   I'm Nuts About that Gal
    JohLo 21   I'm Nuts Over You
OFF (4)
    BigB   12   Worrying You Off My Mind--Part 1
    BigB   18   Keep Your Hands Off Her
    Shad   19   Mary Anna Cut Off
    Shad   20   Take Your Fingers Off It
OGGLY (1)
    HarY   2   Iggly Oggly Blues
OH (9)
    HarZ   2   Oh Ambulance Man
    JonM   23   The Man I Love Is Oh So Good
    McCoJ 20   Oh Red
    Rain   25   Oh My Babe Blues
    SmiSi   1   Oh Oh Lonesome Blues
    Wate   6   Oh, Joe, Play that Trombone
    WeaC   4   Oh Lawdy Mama
    WilS   11   Lord, Oh Lord Blues
OIL (2)
    JefB   54   Oil Well Blues
    Stev   5   Coal Oil Blues
OLD (19)
    ArnK   3   Old Original Kokomo Blues
    ArnK   4   Old Black Cat Blues
    ArnK   25   Mean Old Twister
    Byrd   2   Old Timbrook Blues
    ChatB   1   I'm an Old Bumble Bee
    ChatB 27   Old Devil
    ChatP   6   Old Taylor
    ChatP 15   Caught the Old Coon at Last
    ColFL   1   Old Rock Island Blues
    Crud   4   Mean Old 'Frisco Blues
    Dean   1   I'm So Glad I'm Twenty-One Years Old Today

OLD (cont.)
    GibC   11   Old Time Rider
    JefB   9   Old Rounders Blues
    LewF   7   Mean Old Bedbug Blues
    SmiB   9   You've Been a Good Old Wagon
    SmiB   25   Mean Old Bed Bug Blues
    SmiB   33   Long Old Road
    WallM   2   The Old Folks Started It
    Wilk   13   Old Jim Canan's
ONCE (1)
    JohM   1   If I Let You Get Away With It Once You'll Do
                It All of the Time
ONE (11)
    Bare   9   One More Time
    Barn   2   If You Want a Good Woman--Get One Long and
                Tall
    Blak   9   One Time Blues
    Gill   14   One Letter Home
    GreLi   3   Give Your Mama One Smile
    MooW   1   One Way Gal
    OweM   2   Try Me One More Time
    SmiB   18   One and Two Blues
    ThoH   5   Honey, Won't You Allow Me One More Chance?
    Vinc   4   Lonely One in this Town
    Wate   1   One Man Nan
ONLY (2)
    ColeJ   1   Mistreated the Only Friend You Had
    DaviW 24   The Only Woman
OPERATION (2)
    DorsT   8   Terrible Operation Blues
    DorsT   9   Terrible Operation Blues
ORCHARD (3)
    JefB   59   Peach Orchard Mama
    WillJ 14   Peach Orchard Mama
    WillK   4   Peach Orchard Mama
ORGAN (2)
    SpiV   5   Organ Grinder Blues
    SpiV   6   Organ Grinder Blues
ORIGINAL (1)
    ArnK   3   Old Original Kokomo Blues
OUGHTA (1)
    Este   27   Everybody Oughta Make a Change
OUT [OUTA] (16)
    Dool   1   Gonna Tip Out Tonight
    GreLi   5   Knockin' Myself Out
    Ledb   5   Honey, I'm All Out and Down
    LeeX   1   Macon Georgia Cut-Out
    LeeX   2   Nobody Knows You When You're Down and Out
    MemM   20   I Don't Want that Junk Outa You
    MontE   7   Out West Blues
    Pett   2   Out on Santa Fe--Blues
    Shad   7   She Stays Out All Night Long
    Shad   8   She Stays Out All Night Long
    Shad   21   She Done Sold It Out
    Slue   1   Tootin' Out Blues
    SmiB   29   Nobody Knows You When You're Down and Out
    WasbS   4   Out with the Wrong Woman
    Whea   29   Cut Out Blues
    Whea   38   I'm Gonna Cut Out Everything
OUTS (1)
    ChatB 18   The Ins and Outs of My Girl
OUTSIDE (1)
    ReyJ   1   Outside Woman Blues
OUTSKIRTS (1)
    Gill   16   I'm Gonna Leave You on the Outskirts of Town
OVER (4)
    Gill   13   It's All Over Now
    JohLo 21   I'm Nuts Over You
    JohR   19   If I Had Possession Over Judgment Day
    WileG   1   Over to My House
OVERCOME (1)
    BracM   4   I'll Overcome Some Day
OVERTIME (1)
    Vinc   1   Overtime Blues
OWN (2)
    JohLo 11   When You Fall For Someone That's Not Your Own
    WillX   3   Man of My Own
OX (1)
    AleT   8   Work Ox Blues

PIGFOOT (1)
   SmiB 36 Gimme a Pigfoot
PIGMEAT (1) [see also PIG MEAT]
   WhiG   1 Pigmeat Blues
PILE (1)
   McCoJ 8 Pile Drivin' Blues
PINEBLUFF (1)
   WhiW   2 Pinebluff Arkansas
PINEY (1)
   JefB 41 Piney Woods Money Mama
PINNED (1)
   GibC 16 Keep Your Windows Pinned
PIPE (1)
   Dadd   2 Stove Pipe Blues
PISTOL (3)
   CarrL 39 Shinin' Pistol
   FulB   5 Pistol Snapper Blues
   RolW   6 45 Pistol Blues
PITCH (1)
   McCoJ 25 We Gonna Pitch a Boogie Woogie
PITCHIN' (1)
   Ezel   1 Pitchin' Boogie
PITY (2)
   McCl 20 It's a Cryin' Pity
   Whea   2 Ain't It a Pity and a Shame
PLACE (2)
   Shad 17 Taking Your Place
   WhiW   5 Strange Place Blues
PLAY (4)
   SmiB 13 I Ain't Goin' to Play Second Fiddle
   SmiC   5 Play It a Long Time Papa
   WasbS 26 Let Me Play Your Vendor
   Wate   6 Oh, Joe, Play that Trombone
PLAYHOUSE (1)
   SmiC 13 I'm Gonna Tear Your Playhouse Down
PLAYING (1)
   Blak 33 Playing Policy Blues
PLEADING [PLEADIN'] (2)
   HilB   3 Pleadin' for the Blues
   MontE 2 Pleading Blues
PLEASE (10)
   BradT 3 Please Don't Act that Way
   ChatL 3 Please Baby
   DaviW 22 Please Don't Mistreat Me
   Howe   6 Please Ma'am
   JackC 28 Baby Please Loan Me Your Heart
   JohLo 12 Baby Please Don't Leave Me No More
   MemM 43 It's Hard to Please My Man
   Vinc 12 Please Baby
   WillJ 6 Baby Please Don't Go
   WillJ 16 Please Don't Go
PLENTY (2)
   CartM 1 I Want Plenty of Grease in My Frying Pan
   Shad 16 I Can Beat You Plenty
PLUS (1)
   Ande   1 Thirty-Eight and Plus
PLYMOUTH (1)
   MemM 11 Plymouth Rock Blues
PNEUMATIC (1)
   Chur   2 Pneumatic Blues
PNEUMONIA (1)
   JefB 66 Pneumonia Blues
POINT (1)
   McCoR 2 Friar's Point Blues
POKER (1)
   Blak 25 Poker Woman Blues
POLICE (2)
   Blak 31 Police Dog Blues
   Wilk   8 Police Sergeant Blues
POLICY (4)
   ArnK 14 Policy Wheel Blues
   Blak 33 Playing Policy Blues
   ChatB 31 Policy Blues
   SmiA   1 Insurance Policy Blues
POLOCK (1)
   WillI 1 Polock Blues
POND (1)
   SpiV   2 The Alligator Pond Went Dry

PONY (4)
   Crud   1 Black Pony Blues
   Patt   4 Pony Blues
   Patt 24 Stone Pony Blues
   WillJ 4 My Grey Pony
POOLE (1)
   KelE   1 Poole County Blues
POOR (12)
   ButlS 3 Poor Boy Blues
   Cann   1 Poor Boy, Long Ways from Home
   Este   8 Poor John Blues
   Este 24 Poor Man's Friend
   HicR   3 Poor Boy a Long Ways from Home
   JamF   1 Poor Coal Passer
   JonM   5 Poor House Blues
   Patt 28 Poor Me
   SmiB 27 Poor Man's Blues
   SykR   8 Poor Boy Blues
   ThoR 12 Poor Boy Blues
   TowH   4 Poor Man Blues
POSSESSION (1)
   JohR 19 If I Had Possession Over Judgment Day
POT (2)
   BogL   5 Pot Hound Blues
   JackC 7 Coffee Pot Blues
POTATO (1)
   King   3 Sweet Potato Blues
POTATOES (1) [see also TATERS]
   WasbS 15 Diggin' My Potatoes
POUND (1)
   DickP 1 Twelve Pound Daddy
POWDER (1)
   BogL 13 Baking Powder Blues
PRATT (1)
   HilB   4 Pratt City Blues
PRAYING (1)
   SmiT   5 Praying Blues
PREACHER (1)
   BrowI 2 Preacher Blues
PREACHERS (1)
   McCoJ 11 Preachers Blues
PREACHIN' (6)
   Hous   3 Preachin' the Blues--Part 1
   Hous   4 Preachin' the Blues--Part 2
   JohR 17 Preachin' Blues
   JohR 18 Preachin' Blues
   McCoJ 26 Hallelujah Joe Ain't Preachin' No More
   SmiB 20 Preachin' the Blues
PRESCRIPTION (1)
   SmiC 31 Prescription for the Blues
PRETTY (2)
   LewN   3 Pretty Mama Blues
   Lint   1 Pretty Mama Blues
PRISON (4)
   JefB 39 Prison Cell Blues
   JonB   2 Leavenworth Prison Blues
   MooAl 2 Prison Blues
   WooH   5 Prison Wall Blues
PRISONER'S (1)
   McClu 1 Prisoner's Blues
PROJECT (2)
   Whea 36 Working on the Project
   WillS 4 Project Highway
PUDDING (1)
   UnkA   4 Sugar Pudding
PUPPIES (1)
   CarrL 17 Hold Them Puppies
PUSSY (3)
   BigB   8 Pussy Cat Blues
   ChatB 17 Pussy Cat Blues
   Luca   1 Pussy Cat Blues
PUT (4)
   GibC   9 Don't Put That Thing On Me
   JorC 12 Don't Put Your Dirty Hands on Me
   SmiL   1 Gonna Put You Right in Jail
   ThoHo 3 Put It Where I Can Get It
QUEEN (2)
   JohR 24 Little Queen of Spades
   JohR 25 Little Queen of Spades

QUIT (2)
   Blak 14 You Gonna Quit Me Blues
   JorL   4 My Gal's Done Quit Me
QUITTIN' (4)
   HarM   1 Mama's Quittin' and Leavin'--Part 1
   HarM   2 Mama's Quittin' and Leavin'--Part 2
   SmiJ   4 Mama's Quittin' and Leavin'--Part 1
   SmiJ   5 Mama's Quittin' and Leavin'--Part 2
RABBIT (1)
   JefB 16 Rabbit Foot Blues
RACKETEERS (1)
   JohLo 15 Racketeers Blues
RAG (8)
   BakW   6 Rag Baby
   Blak 15 Wabash Rag
   Bras   1 Guitar Rag
   FulB   2 Rag, Mama, Rag
   FulB   6 Piccolo Rag
   McTW 19 Georgia Rag
   WalkW 1 South Carolina Rag
RAGGED (1)
   Este   2 Broken-Hearted, Ragged and Dirty Too
RAIDIN' (1)
   JorC   4 Raidin' Squad Blues
RAILROAD (5)
   ArnK 11 Southern Railroad Blues
   BaxJ   2 K. C. Railroad Blues
   BennW 1 Railroad Bill
   Patt 14 Heart Like Railroad Steel
   SmiT 11 Railroad Blues
RAIN (5)
   JohLo 2 Falling Rain Blues
   JohLo 26 New Falling Rain Blues
   JohM   2 When a 'Gator Holler, Folk Say It's a Sign of
             Rain
   Patt 10 Devil Sent the Rain
   ThpE   1 Showers of Rain Blues
RAINY (2)
   ArnK   1 Rainy Night Blues
   WillS 25 Rainy Day Blues
RAISED (1)
   RupO   1 I Raised My Window and Looked at the Risin'
             Sun
RAM (1)
   ChatB 2 Ram Rod Daddy
RAMBLER (1)
   JefB 28 Rambler Blues
RAMBLIN' (4)
   JohR   5 Ramblin' On My Mind
   JohR   6 Ramblin' On My Mind
   ThoR   6 Ramblin' Mind Blues
   ThoR 11 Ramblin' Man
RAMBLING (4)
   Blacw 5 Rambling Blues
   CoxI   9 Rambling Blues
   GibC   5 Stop Your Rambling
   MemM 41 Nothin in Rambling
RAMROD (1) [see also RAM ROD]
   Vinc 10 Ramrod Blues
RASCAL (1)
   Whea 21 Low Down Rascal
RAT (1)
   JohLo 13 Sam, You're Just a Rat
RATTLESNAKE (3)
   JohMa 3 Rattlesnake Blues
   Patt 17 Rattlesnake Blues
   Shor   2 Lonesome Swamp Rattlesnake
RATTLESNAKIN' (1)
   FulB   1 I'm a Rattlesnakin' Daddy
RAZOR (1)
   McTW 14 Razor Ball
REACHIN' (1)
   MemM 33 Reachin' Pete
READ (1)
   McCl 17 You Can't Read My Mind
READER (1)
   LeeB   1 Mind Reader Blues
READY (1)
   UnkA   9 Gettin' Ready for Trial

REAL (2)
   BennW 2 Real Estate Blues
   JonM 24 I'm a Real Kind Mama
REAP (1)
   Gill   6 Got to Reap What You Sow
RECKLESS (2)
   BogL 21 Reckless Woman
   SmiB   6 Reckless Blues
RED (9)
   ArnK 26 Red Beans and Rice
   DaviM 1 It's Red Hot
   JohR 12 They're Red Hot
   KelJ   3 Red Ripe Tomatoes
   Ledb 12 Red River Blues
   McCoJ 20 Oh Red
   ScotS 1 Red Cross Blues
   Weld 10 Red Hot Blues
   WillS 22 Goodbye Red
REMEMBER (1)
   Whea 26 Remember and Forget Blues
RENEWED (1)
   Doyl   3 Renewed Love Blues
RENT (1)
   JohLi 3 House Rent Scuffle
REVENUE (1)
   Patt 27 Revenue Man Blues
RICE (1)
   ArnK 26 Red Beans and Rice
RICHARDSON'S (1)
   RichM 2 Mooch Richardson's Low Down Barrel House Blues
             Part 1
RICKETS (1)
   Stev   4 Baby Got the Rickets
RIDE (3)
   SmiB 37 Take Me for a Buggy Ride
   SmiT   6 Ride Jockey Ride
RIDER (12)
   AleT 19 Easy Rider Blues
   CarrL 6 Four Day Rider
   FulB 14 Bus Rider Blues
   GibC 11 Old Time Rider
   HicR   4 Easy Rider Don't Deny My Name
   JamS   5 Special Rider Blues
   JefB 20 Easy Rider Blues
   Ledb   4 C. C. Rider
   McTW   2 Stole Rider Blues
   McTW 17 Stomp Down Rider
   NelsR 2 Dyin' Rider Blues
   PerkG 1 No Easy Rider Blues
RIDING (2)
   BigB   3 Eagle Riding Papa
   Spru   9 Let's Go Riding
RIGHT (12)
   BelE   5 Carry It Right Back Home
   Darb   3 Built Right on the Ground
   GreLi 6 Why Don't You Do Right?
   JefB 24 Right of Way Blues
   JohK   1 Lady, Your Clock Ain't Right
   JohLi 1 Never Let Your Left Hand Know What Your Right
             Hand Do
   McCoJ 10 Beat It Right
   Nick   3 It Won't Act Right
   SmiL   1 Gonna Put You Right in Jail
   Stok 24 Right Now Blues
   WillS 23 The Right Kind of Life
   WilsW 3 Do It Right
RIGHTEOUS (1)
   Blak 34 Righteous Blues
RILEY (1)
   Gill   9 Riley Springs Blues
RING (1)
   MemM 34 He's in the Ring
RIPE (1)
   KelJ   3 Red Ripe Tomatoes
RISING [RISIN'] (6)
   AleT   9 The Risin' Sun
   CartG 1 Rising River Blues
   JefB 23 Rising High Water Blues
   King   2 Rising Sun Blues

RISING [RISIN'] (cont.)
　RupO　1　I Raised My Window and Looked at the Risin'
　　　　　　　Sun
　Whea　10　The Rising Sun Blues
RIVER (8)
　BigB　16　Mississippi River Blues
　BliP　1　Coal River Blues
　CartG　1　Rising River Blues
　DelaM　2　Tallahatchie River Blues
　Ledb　12　Red River Blues
　Patt　11　Green River Blues
　WalkA　1　Trinity River Blues
　WooH　4　Wolf River Blues
RIVERSIDE (2)
　CollS　5　Riverside Blues
　JohR　31　Traveling Riverside Blues
ROAD (18)
　ArnK　30　Rocky Road Blues
　Blak　12　Hard Road Blues
　CollS　10　Lonesome Road Blues
　CollS　14　My Road Is Rough and Rocky
　DaviW　7　Travelin' this Lonesome Road
　DelaM　1　Down the Big Road Blues
　JamS　8　If You Haven't Got Any Hay Get on Down the
　　　　　　　Road
　JohLo　9　Way Down That Lonesome Road
　JohR　14　Cross Road Blues
　JohTo　2　Big Road Blues
　LofW　3　Dark Road Blues
　MossB　2　Hard Road Blues
　Patt　3　Down the Dirt Road Blues
　Rach　6　Gravel Road Woman
　Shad　10　On the Road Again
　SmiB　33　Long Old Road
　SpiV　1　Arkansas Road Blues
　Whea　41　Road Tramp Blues
ROBBIN' (1)
　CamG　2　Robbin' and Stealin' Blues
ROBERTA (2)
　Ledb　1　Roberta--Part 1
　Ledb　2　Roberta--Part 2
ROCK (6)
　Bare　3　Big Rock Jail
　BlaAL　1　Rock Island Blues
　ColFL　1　Old Rock Island Blues
　DickP　2　Little Rock Blues
　MemM　11　Plymouth Rock Blues
　Rain　14　Lucky Rock Blues
ROCKIN' (1)
　GreLi　1　Just Rockin'
ROCKY (2)
　ArnK　30　Rocky Road Blues
　CollS　14　My Road Is Rough and Rocky
ROD (1)
　ChatB　2　Ram Rod Daddy
ROLL (2)
　ChatB　10　Let Me Roll Your Lemon
　Newb　5　Roll and Tumble Blues
ROLLED (1)
　JonL　3　Rolled From Side to Side Blues
ROLLER (1)
　Aker　3　Dough Roller Blues
ROLLING [ROLLIN'] (8)
　Beam　2　Rolling Log Blues
　Beam　5　Rollin' Log Blues
　ChatB　13　Rolling Blues
　Glaz　1　Rollin' Mama Blues
　JohR　21　I'm a Steady Rollin Man
　Lask　1　How You Want Your Rollin' Done
　McTW　20　Rollin' Mama Blues
　Nick　9　You Got Me Rollin'
ROLLS (1)
　GibC　20　She Rolls It Slow
ROLLS-ROYCE (1)
　List　1　Rolls-Royce Papa
ROME (1)
　Virg　1　Little Girl in Rome
ROOGER (1)
　JefB　15　Booger Rooger Blues

ROOM (1)
　ChatP　4　Empty Room Blues
ROOSTER (3)
　JohLo　30　Crowin' Rooster Blues
　Patt　5　Banty Rooster Blues
　RhoW　1　The Crowing Rooster
ROOSTER'S (1)
　WooH　3　The Rooster's Crowing Blues
ROOT (2)
　DaviW　12　Root Man Blues
　MoraH　1　Root Hog or Die
ROOTIN' (1)
　WillJ　9　Rootin' Ground Hog
ROPE (2)
　Blak　35　Rope Stretchin' Blues--Part 1
　Blak　36　Rope Stretchin' Blues--Part 2
ROUGH (2)
　CollS　14　My Road Is Rough and Rocky
　Rain　19　Rough and Tumble Blues
ROUND (4)　[see also AROUND]
　Nick　8　Round and Round
　Stok　5　Last Go Round
　WillS　14　You've Been Foolin' Round Town
ROUNDER (1)
　Howe　7　Low Down Rounder Blues
ROUNDERS (2)
　JefB　9　Old Rounders Blues
　Stok　27　Memphis Rounders Blues
ROWDY (1)
　BaiK　2　Rowdy Blues
RULE (1)
　ThoR　2　Hard to Rule Woman Blues
RUM (1)
　Blak　19　Bootleg Rum Dum Blues
RUN (3)
　JorC　8　You Run and Tell Your Daddy
　ThoH　6　Run, Mollie, Run
RUNNIN' (2)
　ArnK　35　Tired of Runnin' from Door to Door
　McTW　31　Runnin' Me Crazy
RUSH (1)
　BakW　1　Mama, Don't Rush Me Blues
RUSHEN (1)
　Patt　8　Tom Rushen Blues
RUSTLIN' (1)
　BigB　20　Rustlin' Man
SACK (1)
　JackC　11　Drop that Sack
SAD (3)
　DaviW　8　Sad and Lonesome Blues
　JefB　44　Sad News Blues
　SmiIv　1　Sad and Blue
SADDLE (1)
　DaviW　19　Let Me in Your Saddle
SADIE (1)
　Nick　1　Everybody's Talking About Sadie Green
SAILOR (1)
　DanJ　1　My Mama Was a Sailor
SAINT　[see ST.]
SALES (1)
　ChatB　9　Sales Tax
SALLY (1)
　BogL　17　Pig Iron Sally
SALTY (5)
　ArnK　22　Salty Dog
　CollS　11　New Salty Dog
　CrawR　1　My Man Jumped Salty on Me
　JackC　3　Salty Dog Blues
　WasbS　20　My Feet Jumped Salty
SAM (2)
　JohLo　13　Sam, You're Just a Rat
　SmiC　10　Uncle Sam Blues
SAME (1)
　Stov　2　A Woman Gets Tired of the Same Man All the
　　　　　　　Time
SAN FRANCISCO　[see 'FRISCO]
SANTA CLAUS (1)
　DaviW　14　Santa Claus

SHELF (1)
   McFa   2   Groceries on the Shelf
SHERIFF (1)
   Patt   23   High Sheriff Blues
SHE'S (6)
   Bare   6   She's Got a Nice Line
   BelE   6   She's a Fool Gal
   HicR   12   She's Gone Blues
   McCl   4   She's Just Good Huggin' Size
   McCl   7   She's a Good Looking Mama
   TowH   6   She's Got a Mean Disposition
SHIM (1)
   KelE   2   Shim Shamming
SHINEY (1)
   Stok   25   Shiney Town Blues
SHININ' (1)
   CarrL   39   Shinin' Pistol
SHIP (1)
   ArnK   28   Big Ship Blues
SHIPWRECK (1)
   SmiB   34   Shipwreck Blues
SHIPWRECKED (1)
   SmiC   35   Shipwrecked Blues
SHOES (1)
   CookR   2   Hock My Shoes
SHOOK (1)
   EvanJ   4   Shook It This Morning Blues
SHOOTIN' (1)
   MileL   1   Shootin' Star Blues
SHORT (2)
   CarrL   40   It's Too Short
   KidS   1   Short Hair Blues
SHORTY (2)
   Ledb   15   Shorty George
   Whea   23   Coon Can Shorty
SHOT (1)
   DaviW   18   Think You Need a Shot
SHOTGUN (2)
   CamB   2   Shotgun Blues
   WillS   35   Shotgun Blues
SHOULDN'T (2)
   DaviW   23   Why Shouldn't I Be Blue
   Este   41   You Shouldn't Do That
SHOUTING [SHOUTIN'] (2)
   Aker   4   Jumpin' and Shoutin' Blues
   Slue   2   Shouting Baby Blues
SHOWERS (1)
   ThpE   1   Showers of Rain Blues
SHRIMP (2)
   JohR   13   Dead Shrimp Blues
   MasM   2   Shrimp Man
SHUCKIN' (1)
   JefB   14   Shuckin' Sugar
SICK (2)
   TowH   5   Sick with the Blues
   Whea   37   Sick Bed Blues
SIDE (2)
   JonL   3   Rolled From Side to Side Blues
SIGN (1)
   JohM   2   When a 'Gator Holler, Folk Say It's a Sign of
                  Rain
SILVER (1)
   HenrH   2   My Silver Dollar Mama
SING (2)
   ColFB   1   Sing Song Blues
   Stev   2   I'll See You in the Spring When the Birds
                  Begin to Sing
SINGLE (3)
   Blacm   3   I Whipped My Woman With a Single Tree
   JonM   21   Single Woman's Blues
   SykR   5   Single Tree Blues
SINGS (1)
   Wate   10   Ethel Sings 'Em
SISSY (1)
   ArnK   5   Sissy Man Blues
SISTER (1)
   ThpE   3   Seven Sister Blues
SISTERS (2)
   SmiJ   14   Seven Sisters Blues--Part 1

SISTERS (cont.)
   SmiJ   15   Seven Sisters Blues--Part 2
SITTING [SITTIN'] (6)
   AleT   7   Sittin' on a Log
   ChatL   2   New Sittin' On Top of the World
   CollS   13   I'm Sitting on Top of the World
   EvanJ   2   Sitting on Top of the World
   Oden   2   Sitting Down Thinking Blues
   Vinc   2   Sitting on Top of the World
SIX (1)
   SykR   10   3 6 and 9
SIXTEEN (2)
   DaviW   11   Sweet Sixteen
   JonL   1   New Two Sixteen Blues
SIXTY-ONE (1) [see also NO. 61]
   SykR   16   Highway 61 Blues
SIZE (1)
   McCl   4   She's Just Good Huggin' Size
SKEET AND GARRET (1)
   SykR   6   Skeet and Garret
SKIN (7)
   BogL   27   Skin Game Blues
   BrowI   4   Skin Man
   Howe   5   Skin Game Blues
   LofC   2   Brown Skin Girls
   McCl   1   Brown Skin Girl
   McCl   10   Down to Skin and Bones
   MemM   9   Georgia Skin
SKINNY (1)
   WillS   1   Skinny Woman
SKOO (1)
   JackC   24   Skoodle Um Skoo
SKOODLE (3)
   BigB   5   Skoodle Do Do
   BigB   7   Skoodle Do Do
   JackC   24   Skoodle Um Skoo
SKUNK (1)
   HicR   14   Black Skunk Blues
SKY (1)
   HicR   2   Cloudy Sky Blues
SLATS (1)
   Stov   3   Bed Slats
SLAVE (1)
   Rain   23   Slave to the Blues
SLEEPLESS (1)
   Whea   6   Sleepless Nights Blues
SLEEPY (1)
   WhiW   7   Sleepy Man Blues
SLOP (1)
   ArnK   9   Slop Jar Blues
SLOPPY (4)
   BogL   8   Sloppy Drunk Blues
   CarrL   5   Sloppy Drunk Blues
   DaviW   6   Sloppy Drunk Again
   WillS   37   Sloppy Drunk Blues
SLOW (8)
   CollS   12   Slow Mama Slow
   EdwJ   2   He Likes It Slow
   EdwS   2   He Likes It Slow
   GibC   20   She Rolls It Slow
   Oden   3   Going Down Slow
   Rain   30   Slow Driving Moan
   SmiT   12   He Likes It Slow
SMELL (1)
   DaviW   13   I Can Tell By the Way You Smell
SMILE (1)
   GreLi   3   Give Your Mama One Smile
SNAKE (13)
   JefB   11   That Black Snake Moan
   JefB   18   Black Snake Moan
   JefB   26   Black Snake Dream Blues
   JefB   58   That Black Snake Moan No. 2
   JohLo   10   New Black Snake Blues--Part 1
   Ledb   6   New Black Snake Moan
   MemM   26   Stinging Snake Blues
   Shad   9   A Black Woman Is Like a Black Snake
   Shor   3   Snake Doctor Blues
   SpiV   7   New Black Snake Blues--Part 1
   SpiV   11   Black Snake Swing

SNAKE (cont.)
    WashL   2   Black Snake Blues
    WillJ 12   Crawlin' King Snake
SNAPPER (1)
    FulB   5   Pistol Snapper Blues
SNATCH (1)
    Hawk   4   Snatch It Back Blues
SNIGGLIN' (1)
    Bare   2   Snigglin' Blues
SNITCHIN' (1)
    UnkA   2   Snitchin' Gambler Blues
SNOW (2)
    GibC   8   Ice and Snow Blues
    Whea   5   Ice and Snow Blues
SO (13)
    Bunn   1   It's Sweet Like So
    Dean   1   I'm So Glad I'm Twenty-One Years Old Today
    JaxF   3   She Can Love So Good
    JohLo   8   I'm So Tired of Living All Alone
    JonM   23   The Man I Love Is Oh So Good
    McCl   22   Mr. So and So Blues
    MooA   2   It Wouldn't Be So Hard
    Pull   1   Black Gal What Makes Your Head So Hard?--No. 2
    Rain   11   Honey Where You Been So Long
    SmiT   10   The World's Jazz Crazy and So Am I
    Temp   4   So Lonely and Blue
    ThoR   1   So Lonesome
SOBBIN' (2)
    JohEb   2   Sobbin' Woman Blues
    SmiB   7   Sobbin' Hearted Blues
SOCIETY (1)
    GibC   19   Society Blues
SOLD (2)
    Shad   21   She Done Sold It Out
    SmiC   29   Done Sold My Soul to the Devil
SOME (9)
    ArnK   18   I'll Be Up Some Day
    BogL   14   You Got to Die Some Day
    BracM   4   I'll Overcome Some Day
    ButlS   1   Some Screamed High Yellow
    ChatB 26   Some Day
    ChatP   9   You Got to Help Me Some
    DaveJ   1   Save Me Some
    JonM   11   You May Go, But You'll Come Back Some Day
    Wate   2   There'll Be Some Changes Made
SOMEBODY (1)
    Gill   10   I Got Somebody Else
SOMEBODY'S (3)
    FulB   10   Somebody's Been Talkin'
    Weld   9   Somebody's Got to Go
    WillJ   2   Somebody's Been Borrowing that Stuff
SOMEDAY (4)   [see also SOME DAY]
    Este   13   Someday Baby Blues
    Este   32   New Someday Blues
    McCoJ 15   Someday I'll Be in the Clay
    WillJ 18   Someday Baby
SOMEHOW (1)
    Gill   5   I'll Get Along Somehow
SOMEONE (1)
    JohLo 11   When You Fall For Someone That's Not Your Own
SOMETHING (3)
    FulB   8   You've Got Something There
    JohLo 20   Something Fishy
    McCoJ 19   Something Gonna Happen to You
SOMETIME (2)
    JohAl   2   Next Week Sometime
    WeaC   3   Sometime Mama
SOMETIMES (1)
    Shad   1   Sometimes I Think I Love You
SONG (1)
    ColFB   1   Sing Song Blues
SOO (2)   [see also SUE]
    MemM   22   Soo Cow Soo
SOPHISTICATED (1)
    WasbS 14   Sophisticated Mama
SORE (1)
    Yate   2   Sore Bunion Blues
SORROW (1)
    JefB   27   Struck Sorrow Blues

SORROWFUL (1)
    SmiT   3   Sorrowful Blues
SOUL (1)
    SmiC   29   Done Sold My Soul to the Devil
SOUTH (8)
    Blacw   7   Down South Blues
    Este   11   Down South Blues
    Simp   1   Down South Blues
    SmiC   3   Down South Blues
    Stok   22   South Memphis Blues
    Sylv   2   Down South Blues
    WalkW   1   South Carolina Rag
    WillS   7   Down South
SOUTHBOUND [SOUTH BOUND] (2)
    CarrL 22   Southbound Blues
    JohLo 29   South Bound Backwater
SOUTHERN (10)
    ArnK   11   Southern Railroad Blues
    CoxI   6   Southern Woman's Blues
    JamJ   2   Southern Casey Jones
    JefB   4   Dry Southern Blues
    JefB   64   Southern Woman Blues
    JonJ   2   Southern Sea Blues
    McCoJ 22   Southern Blues
    McTW   15   Southern Can Is Mine
    McTW   30   Southern Can Mama
    Rain   7   Southern Blues
SOW (1)
    Gill   6   Got to Reap What You Sow
SPADES (3)
    JohR   24   Little Queen of Spades
    JohR   25   Little Queen of Spades
    Whea   15   King of Spades
SPECIAL (9)
    ChatB   6   Bo Carter Special
    CollS   7   Midnight Special Blues
    Este   34   Special Agent
    JamS   5   Special Rider Blues
    JefB   31   Sunshine Special
    JonCo   3   Drunkard's Special
    MillS   1   Sunshine Special
    WallS   1   Special Delivery Blues
    WhiW   15   Special Stream Line
SPELL (2)
    Hous   5   Dry Spell Blues--Part 1
    Hous   6   Dry Spell Blues--Part 2
SPENDER (1)
    JefB   57   Saturday Night Spender Blues
SPIDER (2)
    HicR   20   The Spider and the Fly
    Whea   13   King Spider Blues
SPIRIT (1)
    SmiB   31   Blue Spirit Blues
SPOON (1)
    Shad   15   Feed Your Friend with a Long Handled Spoon
SPOONFUL (1)
    JackC 16   All I Want Is a Spoonful
SPREAD (1)
    DaviW 15   Moonlight Is My Spread
SPRING (1)
    Stev   2   I'll See You in the Spring When the Birds
                 Begin to Sing
SPRINGS (2)
    Gill   9   Riley Springs Blues
    JefB   61   Bed Springs Blues
SPRINGTIME (1)
    Weld   6   Peaches in the Springtime
SQUABBLIN' (1)
    Bare   7   Squabblin' Blues
SQUAD (1)
    JorC   4   Raidin' Squad Blues
SQUAT (1)
    MemM   30   Squat It
SQUAWL [SQUALL] (2)
    Blak   20   Panther Squall Blues
    UnkA   8   The Wild Cat Squawl
SQUEAKY (1)
    Rach   5   Squeaky Work Bench Blues

369

```
SQUEEZE (1)                                    STING (1)
   Pick   2   Let Me Squeeze Your Lemon           MartS  2   Death Sting Me Blues
ST. LOUIS (7)                                  STINGING (1)
   HendK  2   St. Louis Blues                     MemM  26   Stinging Snake Blues
   JackJ  6   St. Louis Blues                  STINGY (1)
   JohLo  4   St. Louis Cyclone Blues             Weld   1   Stingy Woman--Blues
   SmiB   5   The St. Louis Blues              STOCK (1)
   SmiB  30   St. Louis Blues--Part ?             Wilk  12   New Stock Yard Blues
   SmiBM  1   St. Louis Daddy                  STOCKING (1)
   WasbS 16   I'm Goin' to St. Louis              JefB  10   Stocking Feet Blues
ST. PETER (1)                                  STOKE'S (1)
   WelS   2   St. Peter Blues                     Stok  26   Frank Stoke's Dream
STACK (2)                                      STOLE (3)
   Este   9   Stack O' Dollars                    CoxI  11   You Stole My Man
   JorC   1   Stack O' Dollars Blues              McTW   2   Stole Rider Blues
STAGGERING (1)                                    WasbS 32   You Stole My Love
   MooR   1   Staggering Blues                 STOMP (7)
STAMP (1)                                         CarrL 26   Bo Bo Stomp
   HollT  1   Stamp Blues                         McTW  17   Stomp Down Rider
STAND (2)                                         Stok  17   Stomp that Thing
   Rame   1   I Can't Stand It                    WallM  4   Field Mouse Stomp
   WalkB  2   Stand Up Suitcase Blues             Whea  33   Peetie Wheatstraw Stomp
STAR (1)                                          Whea  34   Peetie Wheatstraw Stomp No. 2
   MileL  1   Shootin' Star Blues                 Whea  40   Shack Bully Stomp
STARS (1)                                      STONE (2)
   JohLs  4   By the Moon and Stars               JohR  20   Stone in My Passway
STARTED (3)                                       Patt  24   Stone Pony Blues
   ClayJ  1   I Packed My Suitcase, Started to the Train    STONEWALL (3)
   Shad   3   I Packed My Suitcase, Started to the Train       Blak   7   Stonewall Street Blues
   WallM  2   The Old Folks Started It            Stev   8   Stonewall Blues
STARVATION (2)                                    Wilk   7   Nashville Stonewall Blues
   BigB   2   Starvation Blues                 STOP (7)
   CamB   3   Starvation Farm Blues               ArnK  15   Stop Look and Listen
STATE (2)                                         Este  12   Stop That Thing
   ClayJ  2   State of Tennessee Blues            GibC   5   Stop Your Rambling
   Shad   4   State of Tennessee                  JohR  30   Stop Breakin' Down Blues
STATESBORO (1)                                    Vinc   3   Stop and Listen Blues
   McTW   6   Statesboro Blues                    Vinc  11   Stop and Listen Blues No. 2
STATION (2)                                       Vinc  16   The New Stop and Listen Blues
   PooJ   1   Whitewash Station Blues          STOPPED (1)
   Shad  11   Whitewash Station Blues             ThoHo  4   I've Stopped My Man
STAY (3)                                       STORE (2)
   DorsT 10   Where Did You Stay Last Night?      Este  28   Liquor Store Blues
   JorC  10   I Couldn't Stay Here                WillS 30   Welfare Store Blues
   Luca   2   Where Did You Stay Last Night?   STORMY (1)
STAYS (2)                                         WhiJ   2   Stormy Weather No. 1
   Shad   7   She Stays Out All Night Long     STOVE (1)
   Shad   8   She Stays Out All Night Long        Dadd   2   Stove Pipe Blues
STEADY (3)                                     STRAIN (1)
   BogL  24   Jump Steady Daddy                   Wate   4   That Da Da Strain
   JohR  21   I'm a Steady Rollin Man          STRAINER (1)
   Wate   5   At the New Jump Steady Ball         Shad  18   Jim Strainer
STEAK (1)                                      STRANGE (2)
   Rach   2   T-Bone Steak Blues                  Gros   2   Strange Man
STEALER (1)                                       WhiW   5   Strange Place Blues
   BogL  25   Man Stealer Blues                STRANGER (1)
STEALING [STEALIN'] (6)                           MooR   4   Stranger Blues
   CamG   2   Robbin' and Stealin' Blues       STREAM (1)
   FulB   3   Stealing Bo-Hog                     WhiW  15   Special Stream Line
   PooJ   2   Stealin' Stealin'                STREAMLINE (1)
   Shad  12   Stealin' Stealin'                   LofC   5   Streamline Train
STEEL (2)                                      STREET [ST.] (19)
   Patt  14   Heart Like Railroad Steel           Blak   7   Stonewall Street Blues
   SmiC  32   Steel Drivin' Man                   BliP   2   Fourteenth Street Blues
STEP (4)                                          DaviC  1   Elm Street Woman Blues
   ChatB  3   The Law Gonna Step on You           DayT   2   Elm Street Blues
   FulB   9   Step It Up and Go                   Este   6   Street Car Blues
   JefB  46   Lock Step Blues                     JackC 15   Maxwell Street Blues
   WillS 39   You Got to Step Back                JackC 25   Sheik of Desplaines Street
STEPFATHER (1)                                    JonL   9   Cherry Street Blues
   WillJ  5   Stepfather Blues                    McTW  32   Bell Street Blues
STERED (1)                                        MooAl  4   Broadway St. Woman Blues
   BracM  3   Stered Gal                          NelsS  1   Street Walkin'
STEVEDORE (1)                                     ReyW   2   Third Street Woman Blues
   WilsL  2   Stevedore Man                       SmiC  18   31st Street Blues
STEVENS (1)                                       Spau   2   Biddle Street Blues
   Stev   3   Vol Stevens Blues                   Stev   1   Beale Street Mess Around
STEW (1)                                          Stov   1   Court Street Blues
   BogL  26   Stew Meat Blues                     ThoH  10   Texas Easy Street Blues
```

STREET [ST.] (cont.)
      WhiG   2 Walking the Street
      WillS 13 Shannon Street Blues
STRETCH (1)
      Blak   26 Doing a Stretch
STRETCHIN' (2)
      Blak   35 Rope Stretchin' Blues--Part 1
      Blak   36 Rope Stretchin' Blues--Part 2
STRING (2)
      JonL   2 Two String Blues
      UnkA   1 String Band Blues
STRUCK (1)
      JefB   27 Struck Sorrow Blues
STRUT (1)
      McTW   7 Atlanta Strut
STUFF (9)
      DaviW   2 That Stuff You Sell Ain't No Good
      HarZ   4 Coldest Stuff in Town
      McCoJ   4 I'm Wild About My Stuff
      Patt   26 Love My Stuff
      RobB   1 Selling That Stuff
      Shad   13 Better Leave That Stuff Alone
      Shaw   1 Coldest Stuff in Town
      ThoG   1 Fast Stuff Blues
      WillJ   2 Somebody's Been Borrowing that Stuff
SUE (2) [see also SOO]
      ChatB 22 Sue Cow
      KelJ   7 Betty Sue Blues
SUGAR (7)
      CarrL 38 Longing for My Sugar
      JefB   14 Shuckin' Sugar
      McCl   9 New Sugar Mama
      SmiBM   2 Sugar Man Blues--Part 1
      SmiBM   3 Sugar Man Blues--Part 2
      UnkA   4 Sugar Pudding
      Whea   43 Sugar Mama
SUGARLAND (1)
      BlaAB   1 Sugarland Blues
SUICIDE (2)
      CarrL 41 Suicide Blues
      JonM   14 Suicide Blues
SUITCASE (5)
      Brac   9 Suitcase Full of Blues
      ClayJ   1 I Packed My Suitcase, Started to the Train
      Shad   3 I Packed My Suitcase, Started to the Train
      TayC   1 Heavy Suitcase Blues
      WalkB   2 Stand Up Suitcase Blues
SUN (5)
      AleT   9 The Risin' Sun
      JohBi   1 Sun Beam Blues
      King   2 Rising Sun Blues
      RupO   1 I Raised My Window and Looked at the Risin'
                     Sun
      Whea   10 The Rising Sun Blues
SUNDOWN (2)
      BliN   1 Sundown Blues
      Dadd   1 Sundown Blues
SUNRISE (2)
      CarrL 19 Blues Before Sunrise
      DayW   2 Sunrise Blues
SUNSHINE (6)
      CarrL 15 Hurry Down Sunshine
      GibC   6 Sunshine Moan
      JefB   31 Sunshine Special
      MillS   1 Sunshine Special
      SmiC   7 I Never Miss My Sunshine
      Weld   3 Sunshine Blues
SURE (1)
      HicR   19 We Sure Got Hard Times Now
SUSIE-Q (1)
      WillS 18 Susie-Q
SWAMP (1)
      Shor   2 Lonesome Swamp Rattlesnake
SWEET (20)
      BakW   8 Sweet Patunia Blues
      BogL   1 Sweet Patunia
      BogL   20 Sweet Man, Sweet Man
      Bunn   1 It's Sweet Like So
      DaviW 11 Sweet Sixteen

SWEET (cont.)
      JackC 20 Your Baby Ain't Sweet Like Mine
      JamJ   1 Sweet Patuni
      JohLo   3 Sweet Woman You Can't Go Wrong
      JohR   4 Sweet Home Chicago
      JonCo   1 Sweet Mama Blues
      King   3 Sweet Potato Blues
      LewF   3 Sweet Papa Moan
      Rach   4 Sweet Mama
      SmiC   6 I Want My Sweet Daddy Now
      Stok   2 Sweet to Mama
      Sylv   3 I Want My Sweet Daddy
      WeaC   1 Sweet Patunia
      Whea   18 Sweet Home Blues
      WhhR   1 Sweet Jelly Rollin'
SWEETEST (1)
      RedN   2 Sweetest Thing Born
SWING (5)
      Bond   2 Black Gal Swing
      JohLo 25 Mr. Johnson Swing
      LitS   1 Black Cat Swing
      SpiV   11 Black Snake Swing
      WhiW   14 Bukka's Jitterbug Swing
SYKES (1)
      SykR   15 Mr. Sykes Blues
T (1)
      RolW   1 T Model Blues
T AND T (1)
      RichM   1 T and T Blues
T-BONE (1)
      Rach   2 T-Bone Steak Blues
T N AND O (1)
      BogL   12 T N and O Blues
T. B. (2)
      Ledb   18 T. B. Woman Blues
      WillS 27 T. B. Blues
T. B.'S (1)
      SpiV   13 T. B.'s Got Me Blues
T. P. (1)
      Rang   1 T. P. Window Blues
TABLE (1)
      WasbS 33 I Laid My Cards on the Table
TACKLE (1)
      Whea   28 Block and Tackle
'TAIN'T (1) [see also AIN'T]
      McTW   3 Mama, 'Tain't Long Fo' Day
TAKE (7)
      CarrL 20 Take a Walk Around the Corner
      JackC 13 Take Me Back Blues
      Lock   2 Take a Little Walk with Me
      Shad   20 Take Your Fingers Off It
      SmiB   37 Take Me for a Buggy Ride
      Stok   18 Take Me Back
      Whea   27 Don't Take a Chance
TAKES (1)
      JackC   5 I Got What It Takes But It Breaks My Heart to
                     Give It Away
TAKING (1)
      Shad   17 Taking Your Place
TALK (2)
      ArnK   13 Let Your Money Talk
      DaviW 27 Just Want to Talk Awhile
TALKING [TALKIN'] (5)
      FulB   10 Somebody's Been Talkin'
      McTW   13 Talking to Myself
      MemM   3 I'm Talking About You
      MemM   14 I'm Talking About You--No. 2
      Nick   1 Everybody's Talking About Sadie Green
TALL (3)
      ArnK   21 Long and Tall
      Barn   2 If You Want a Good Woman--Get One Long and
                     Tall
      BigB   15 Long Tall Mama
TALLAHASSEE (1)
      WashL   1 Tallahassee Woman
TALLAHATCHIE (1)
      DelaM   2 Tallahatchie River Blues
TAMPA (2)
      Blak   6 Tampa Bound

371

TAMPA (cont.)
    BogL   3   Jim Tampa Blues
TAPPIN' (1)
    Burs   1   Tappin' that Thing
TASTES (2)
    King   1   What's That Tastes Like Gravy
    Tamp   4   What Is It That Tastes Like Gravy?
TATERS (1) [see also POTATOES]
    Burs   2   I Got Good Taters
TAX (1)
    ChatB   9   Sales Tax
TAYLOR (1)
    ChatP   6   Old Taylor
TEA (1)
    Stok   3   Half Cup of Tea
TEAR (2)
    Este   18   I Wanta Tear It All the Time
    SmiC   13   I'm Gonna Tear Your Playhouse Down
TEASIN' (1)
    Lask   2   Teasin' Brown Blues
TEDDY (1)
    JefB   25   Teddy Bear Blues
TELEPHONE (1)
    Shor   1   Telephone Arguin' Blues
TELEPHONING (1)
    SpiV   9   Telephoning the Blues
TELL (13)
    DaviW 13   I Can Tell By the Way You Smell
    Este   39   Tell Me About It
    FosD   1   Tell It to the Judge No. 1
    FosD   2   Tell It to the Judge No. 2
    HilK   5   Tell Me Baby
    JonM   22   Never Tell a Woman Friend
    JorC   8   You Run and Tell Your Daddy
    MemM   25   Ain't No Use Trying to Tell On Me
    SimsH   2   Tell Me Man Blues
    SmiC   8   Don't Never Tell Nobody
    SmiJ   6   Tell It to the Judge No. 1
    SmiJ   7   Tell It to the Judge No. 2
    Vinc   14   Shake Hands and Tell Me Goodbye
TELLIN' (3)
    ChatB   8   Tellin' You 'Bout It
    Este   14   Who's Been Tellin' You Buddy Brown Blues
    Hurt   2   Ain't No Tellin'
TENNESSEE (5)
    ClaL   2   Down in Tennessee
    ClayJ   2   State of Tennessee Blues
    Este   29   Easin' Back to Tennessee
    Pope   4   Tennessee Workhouse Blues
    Shad   4   State of Tennessee
TERRAPLANE (2)
    EdwF   1   Terraplane Blues
    JohR   9   Terraplane Blues
TERRIBLE (2)
    DorsT   8   Terrible Operation Blues
    DorsT   9   Terrible Operation Blues
TEXAS (12)
    AleT   18   Frost Texas Tornado Blues
    JackC 17   Texas Blues
    JonCo   2   Texas and Pacific Blues
    McCoJ   2   Goin' Back to Texas
    MemM   1   Goin' Back to Texas
    MontE   9   West Texas Blues
    MooA   1   West Texas Woman
    OweM   1   Texas Blues
    ReedW   2   Texas Blues
    SmiC   25   Texas Moaner Blues
    ThoH   8   Texas Worried Blues
    ThoH   10   Texas Easy Street Blues
THEE (1)
    Cali   1   Fare Thee Well Blues
THEM (1) [see also 'EM]
    CarrL 17   Hold Them Puppies
THERE (1)
    FulB   8   You've Got Something There
THERE'LL (1)
    Wate   2   There'll Be Some Changes Made
THEY (1)
    BogL   7   They Ain't Walking No More

THEY'RE (1)
    JohR   12   They're Red Hot
THING (16)
    ArnK   19   Shake That Thing
    Burs   1   Tappin' that Thing
    CollS   9   Do That Thing
    Este   12   Stop That Thing
    GibC   9   Don't Put That Thing On Me
    JackC   8   Shake That Thing
    McCoJ   7   Botherin' that Thing
    Macon   1   Wringing that Thing
    McTW   23   It's a Good Little Thing
    NelsR   1   Gettin' Dirty Just Shakin' that Thing
    Nick   7   Move that Thing
    RedN   2   Sweetest Thing Born
    Stok   7   Its a Good Thing
    Stok   17   Stomp that Thing
    SykR   11   We Can Sell that Thing
    Vinc   18   New Shake that Thing
THINK (3)
    DaviW 18   Think You Need a Shot
    JackC 14   Mama, Don't You Think I Know?
    Shad   1   Sometimes I Think I Love You
THINKING (2)
    AleT   16   When You Get to Thinking
    Oden   2   Sitting Down Thinking Blues
THIRD (2)
    ReyW   2   Third Street Woman Blues
    SmiIv   2   Third Alley Blues
THIRTY-EIGHT (1)
    Ande   1   Thirty-Eight and Plus
THIRTY-FIRST (1)
    SmiC   18   31st Street Blues
THIRTY-FOUR (1)
    Patt   25   34 Blues
THIRTY-TWO (1)
    JohR   11   32-20 Blues
THOUSAND (1)
    FulB   16   Thousand Women Blues
THREE [3] (4)
    FulB   11   Three Ball Blues
    Hawk   2   Number Three Blues
    McTW   5   Three Women Blues
    SykR   10   3 6 and 9
THROUGH [THRU'] (2)
    Tamp   1   Through Train Blues
    Whea   42   Truckin' Thru' Traffic
THROW (2)
    UnkA   5   Throw Me Down
    Whea   8   Throw Me in the Alley
THROWIN' (1)
    Hawk   7   Voice Throwin' Blues
THUNDERSTORM (1)
    JonM   7   Thunderstorm Blues
TICKET (3)
    LewN   4   Ticket Agent Blues
    McTW   33   Ticket Agent Blues
    SmiB   3   Ticket Agent Ease Your Window Down
TIGHT (6)
    Blak   3   Too Tight
    Blak   30   Too Tight Blues No. 2
    CarrL 37   Tight Time Blues
    Howe   3   Too Tight Blues
    JorC   9   Tight Haired Mama Blues
    Tamp   2   It's Tight Like That
TILL (1) [see also UNTIL]
    JohLi   2   You'll Never Miss Your Jelly Till Your Jelly
                    Rollers Gone
TIMBROOK (1)
    Byrd   2   Old Timbrook Blues
TIME (24)
    Bare   9   One More Time
    Blacw   8   Hard Time Blues
    Blak   9   One Time Blues
    CarrL 37   Tight Time Blues
    Este   18   I Wanta Tear It All the Time
    Este   36   Time Is Drawing Near
    GibC   11   Old Time Rider
    GreLi 13   I'm Wasting My Time on You

TIME (cont.)
```
HarW     3   Hot Time Blues
JamS     4   Hard Time Killin' Floor Blues
JohLo   17   Hard Time Ain't Gone No Where
JohM     1   If I Let You Get Away With It Once You'll Do
             It All of the Time
JonM    10   Good Time Flat Blues
McCoC    1   Last Time Blues
McTW    35   Your Time to Worry
MontE    5   The First Time I Met You
OweM     2   Try Me One More Time
Pett     1   Two Time Blues
Rain    20   Night Time Blues
SmiC     5   Play It a Long Time Papa
Ston     1   It's Hard Time
Stov     2   A Woman Gets Tired of the Same Man All the
             Time
ThoR    13   Good Time Blues
TurnB    2   Christmas Time Blues
```
TIMES (1)
```
HicR    19   We Sure Got Hard Times Now
```
TIN (1)
```
JefB    55   Tin Cup Blues
```
TIP (1)
```
Dool     1   Gonna Tip Out Tonight
```
TIRED (8)
```
ArnK    35   Tired of Runnin' from Door to Door
BogL    19   Tired as I Can Be
GibC     3   Tired of Being Mistreated Part 1
GibC     4   Tired of Being Mistreated Part 2
GibC     7   I'm Tired of Being Mistreated
JohLo    8   I'm So Tired of Living All Alone
Rame     2   Tired of You Driving Me
Stov     2   A Woman Gets Tired of the Same Man All the
             Time
```
TISHAMINGO (1)
```
Howe     2   Tishamingo Blues
```
TITANIC (1)
```
BrowI    1   Titanic Blues
```
TOAD (1)
```
SmiJ    12   Hoppin' Toad Frog
```
TODAY (1)
```
Dean     1   I'm So Glad I'm Twenty-One Years Old Today
```
TOGETHER (1)
```
EdwF     2   We Got to Get Together
```
TOM (3)
```
ChatB   11   Howlin' Tom Cat Blues
Patt     8   Tom Rushen Blues
Spru     4   Tom Cat Blues
```
TOMALE [see MOLLY]
TOMATOES (1)
```
KelJ     3   Red Ripe Tomatoes
```
TOMMIES (1)
```
Hull     3   Two Little Tommies Blues
```
TONIGHT (1)
```
Dool     1   Gonna Tip Out Tonight
```
TOO (8)
```
Blak     3   Too Tight
Blak    30   Too Tight Blues No. 2
CarrL   40   It's Too Short
ChatP   14   You Gonna Worry Too
DaviM    2   Too Black Bad
Este     2   Broken-Hearted, Ragged and Dirty Too
Gill    15   You Drink Too Much Whiskey
Howe     3   Too Tight Blues
```
TOODLE-OO (1)
```
Newb     1   She Could Toodle-Oo
```
TOOK (1)
```
McCoC    2   That Lonesome Train Took My Baby Away
```
TOOTIN' (1)
```
Slue     1   Tootin' Out Blues
```
TOP (4)
```
ChatL    2   New Sittin' On Top of the World
CollS   13   I'm Sitting on Top of the World
EvanJ    2   Sitting on Top of the World
Vinc     2   Sitting on Top of the World
```
TORNADO (1)
```
AleT    18   Frost Texas Tornado Blues
```

TOUCH (1)
```
UnkA     3   Touch Me Light Mama
```
TOUGH (1)
```
McCoR    1   Tough Luck
```
TOWN (14)
```
Brac     3   Leavin' Town Blues
CarrL    4   Memphis Town
Gill    16   I'm Gonna Leave You on the Outskirts of Town
HarW     1   I'm Leavin' Town
HarZ     4   Coldest Stuff in Town
Ledb    14   Mr. Hughe's Town
MemM     2   'Frisco Town
MontE    8   Leaving Town Blues
Shaw     1   Coldest Stuff in Town
SmiB    14   Jazzbo Brown from Memphis Town
Stok     4   Beale Town Bound
Stok    25   Shiney Town Blues
Vinc     4   Lonely One in this Town
WillS   14   You've Been Foolin' Round Town
```
TRACKS (1)
```
McCoW    1   Central Tracks Blues
```
TRAFFIC (1)
```
Whea    42   Truckin' Thru' Traffic
```
TRAIL (1)
```
JohR    23   Hell Hound on My Trail
```
TRAIN (16)
```
BogL    18   I Hate that Train Called the M. and O.
ClayJ    1   I Packed My Suitcase, Started to the Train
HilK     4   The Gone Dead Train
LofC     5   Streamline Train
McCoC    2   That Lonesome Train Took My Baby Away
MemM    29   Chickasaw Train Blues
Shad     3   I Packed My Suitcase, Started to the Train
SmiC    28   Freight Train Blues
SmiT     2   Freight Train Blues
SmiT    15   Freight Train Blues
Spar     1   Erie Train Blues
Tamp     1   Through Train Blues
Vinc     6   Your Good Man Caught the Train and Gone
WhiW     4   Black Train Blues
Wilk     5   Long Train Blues
WillS   29   Train Fare Blues
```
TRAMP (1)
```
Whea    41   Road Tramp Blues
```
TRAVELING [TRAVELIN'] (4)
```
Cali     2   Traveling Mama Blues
DaviW    7   Travelin' this Lonesome Road
JohR    31   Traveling Riverside Blues
McTW     8   Travelin' Blues
```
TRAY (1)
```
JackC   26   Ash Tray Blues
```
TREAT (1)
```
Gill     4   She Won't Treat Me Kind
```
TREATED (1)
```
WasbS   28   I've Been Treated Wrong
```
TREATS (1)
```
Barn     1   My Gal Treats Me Mean
```
TREE (2)
```
Blacm    3   I Whipped My Woman With a Single Tree
SykR     5   Single Tree Blues
```
TRIAL (1)
```
UnkA     9   Gettin' Ready for Trial
```
TRICKS (1)
```
BogL    11   Tricks Ain't Working No More
```
TRIMMED (1)
```
WillK    3   Get Your Head Trimmed Down
```
TRINITY (1)
```
WalkA    1   Trinity River Blues
```
TRIXIE (1)
```
JonAn    1   Trixie Blues
```
TROMBONE (2)
```
SmiB    23   Trombone Cholly
Wate     6   Oh, Joe, Play that Trombone
```
TROUBLE (9)
```
Blacw    3   Trouble Blues--Part 1
Blacw    4   Trouble Blues--Part 2
Brac     5   Trouble-Hearted Blues
Brac     6   Trouble-Hearted Blues
ColFJ    1   Man Trouble Blues
```

TROUBLE (cont.)
    ColFJ   6   Man Trouble Blues
    Hogg   1   Family Trouble Blues
    Linc   6   Chain Gang Trouble
    Luca   4   Double Trouble Blues
TRUCKIN' (1)
    Whea   42   Truckin' Thru' Traffic
TRUE (2)
    SykR   13   As True As I've Been to You
    Whea   17   True Blue Woman
TRUNK (2)
    BradT   2   Pack Up Your Trunk Blues
    Ledb   3   Packin' Trunk Blues
TRUST (2)
    Rain   27   Trust No Man
    SpiV   10   Don't Trust Nobody Blues
TRUSTED (1)
    WeaS   1   Can't Be Trusted Blues
TRY (2)
    JonM   6   Anybody Here Want to Try My Cabbage
    OweM   2   Try Me One More Time
TRYING (1)
    MemM   25   Ain't No Use Trying to Tell On Me
TUMBLE (2)
    Newb   5   Roll and Tumble Blues
    Rain   19   Rough and Tumble Blues
TUNKIE (1)
    JorC   5   Hunkie Tunkie Blues
TURN (2)
    LewF   10   I Will Turn Your Money Green
    SmiC   20   Mean Papa, Turn in Your Key
TURPENTINE (1)
    Weld   4   Turpentine Blues
TUXEDO (1)
    Dadd   3   Tuxedo Blues
TWELVE (1)
    DickP   1   Twelve Pound Daddy
TWELVES (1)
    ArnK   8   The Twelves
TWENTY (2)
    JamS   7   22-20 Blues
    JohR   11   32-20 Blues
TWENTY-NINE (1)
    CarrL 34   Eleven Twenty-Nine Blues
TWENTY-ONE (1)
    Dean   1   I'm So Glad I'm Twenty-One Years Old Today
TWENTY-TWO (1)
    JamS   7   22-20 Blues
TWISTER (1)
    ArnK   25   Mean Old Twister
TWO (7)
    ChatP 10   Two of a Kind
    Hull   3   Two Little Tommies Blues
    JonL   1   New Two Sixteen Blues
    JonL   2   Two String Blues
    Pett   1   Two Time Blues
    SmiB   18   One and Two Blues
    WeaC   5   Two Faced Woman
UM (2)
    JackC 24   Skoodle Um Skoo
    RobB   2   Beedle Um Bum
UNCLE (1)
    SmiC   10   Uncle Sam Blues
UNDERTAKER (1)
    JohBu   1   Undertaker Blues
UNDERTAKER'S (1)
    JonM   15   Undertaker's Blues
UNHAPPY (1)
    Vinc   7   Unhappy Blues
UNION (2)
    JonM   4   Western Union Blues
    WillS 32   Western Union Man
UNTIL (2) [see also TILL]
    JohR   22   From Four Until Late
    WillS   8   Until My Love Come Down
UP (12)
    ArnK   18   I'll Be Up Some Day
    Brac   10   Bust Up Blues
    BradT   2   Pack Up Your Trunk Blues

UP (cont.)
    ChatB 20   Double Up in a Knot
    Este   31   Clean Up at Home
    FulB   9   Step It Up and Go
    Gill   17   Woke Up Cold in Hand
    JackC 19   Up the Way Bound
    McTW   22   Warm It Up to Me
    Oden   1   I Have Made Up My Mind
    Vinc   19   Don't Wake It Up
    WalkB   2   Stand Up Suitcase Blues
USE (1)
    MemM   25   Ain't No Use Trying to Tell On Me
USED [USTA] (4)
    JohLo 19   It Ain't What You Usta Be
    MartD   2   What You Was You Used to Be
    SmiT   14   Love Me Like You Used To
    Stok   20   Ain't Going to Do Like I Used to Do
VAIN (2)
    JohR   33   Love in Vain
    JohR   34   Love in Vain
VALLEY (1)
    Crud   2   Death Valley Blues
VENDOR (1)
    WasbS 26   Let Me Play Your Vendor
VERNITA (1)
    Este   19   Vernita Blues
VICKSBURG (2)
    MontE   3   Vicksburg Blues No. 2
    MontE   6   Vicksburg Blues--Part 3
VINE (1)
    Patt   7   Pea Vine Blues
VIOLA (1)
    LewN   1   Viola Lee Blues
VIOLIN (1)
    HayeN   1   Violin Blues
VIRGINIA (1)
    ThpE   4   West Virginia Blues
VOICE (1)
    Hawk   7   Voice Throwin' Blues
VOL (2)
    Stev   3   Vol Stevens Blues
W. P. A. (1)
    Weld   7   W. P. A. Blues
WA (1)
    Blak   29   Diddie Wa Diddie
WABASH (1)
    Blak   15   Wabash Rag
WAGON (1)
    SmiB   9   You've Been a Good Old Wagon
WAIT (1)
    McMu   1   Wait and Listen
WAITIN' (1)
    East   2   I'm Waitin' On You
WAKE (1)
    Vinc   19   Don't Wake It Up
WAKING (1)
    HarO   1   Waking Blues
WALK (2)
    CarrL 20   Take a Walk Around the Corner
    Lock   2   Take a Little Walk with Me
WALKING [WALKIN'] (7)
    Blak   21   Walkin' Across the Country
    BogL   7   They Ain't Walking No More
    CollC   1   Walking Blues
    JohR   15   Walkin' Blues
    NelsS   1   Street Walkin'
    Rain   8   Walking Blues
    WhiG   2   Walking the Street
WALL (3)
    JohLs   3   On the Wall
    Scru   1   My Back to the Wall
    WooH   5   Prison Wall Blues
WANDERING (2)
    CamG   1   Wandering Blues
    Rain   9   Lost Wandering Blues
WANT [WANTA] (20)
    Barn   2   If You Want a Good Woman--Get One Long and
                    Tall
    BelA   4   I Don't Care Who Gets What I Don't Want

WANT [WANTA] (cont.)
BigB 14 How You Want It Done?
CartM 1 I Want Plenty of Grease in My Frying Pan
ChatB 5 I Want You To Know
DaviW 26 Don't You Want to Go
DaviW 27 Just Want to Talk Awhile
DorsT 14 If You Want Me to Love You
Este 18 I Wanta Tear It All the Time
JackC 16 All I Want Is a Spoonful
JohJo 2 Don't Want No Woman
JonM 6 Anybody Here Want to Try My Cabbage
Lask 1 How You Want Your Rollin' Done
McCl 2 Baby, Don't You Want to Go?
MemM 8 Don't Want No Woman
MemM 20 I Don't Want that Junk Outa You
MemM 39 My Baby Don't Want Me No More
SmiC 6 I Want My Sweet Daddy Now
Sylv 3 I Want My Sweet Daddy
WillK 1 I Want It Awful Bad
WANTS (2)
CarrL 3 Papa Wants a Cookie
CarrL 11 Papa Wants to Knock a Jug
WAR (1)
SmiC 19 War Horse Mama
WARM (1)
McTW 22 Warm It Up to Me
WARRANT (1)
Blak 22 Search Warrant Blues
WARTIME (1)
JefB 12 Wartime Blues
WAS (6)
DanJ 1 My Mama Was a Sailor
JackJ 3 This Mornin' She Was Gone
JackJ 4 This Mornin' She Was Gone
McCoJ 24 My Daddy Was a Movin' Man
MartD 2 What You Was You Used to Be
WillS 38 She Was a Dreamer
WASH (1)
McCoJ 13 My Wash Woman's Gone
WASTING (1)
GreLi 13 I'm Wasting My Time on You
WATCHA (1)
Este 7 Watcha Doin'?
WATER (12)
AleT 13 Water Bound Blues
ArnK 23 Wild Water Blues
ColFJ 2 No More Good Water
JefB 23 Rising High Water Blues
JohLo 18 Flood Water Blues
JohTo 1 Cool Drink of Water Blues
JonL 8 Cross the Water Blues
JorC 11 Got Your Water On
Patt 15 High Water Everywhere--Part I
Patt 16 High Water Everywhere--Part II
SmiB 21 Back Water Blues
Spru 2 Muddy Water Blues
WAY (16)
BradT 3 Please Don't Act that Way
DaviW 13 I Can Tell By the Way You Smell
HendK 3 Have You Ever Felt That Way?
JackC 19 Up the Way Bound
JefB 24 Right of Way Blues
JohLo 9 Way Down That Lonesome Road
JohLs 2 Long Way from Home
MooW 1 One Way Gal
Patt 13 When Your Way Gets Dark
SpiV 8 How Do You Do It That Way?
Spru 3 Way Back Down Home
SykR 3 The Way I Feel Blues
ThoR 14 New Way of Living Blues
WasbS 11 I'm On My Way Blues
Wilk 3 That's No Way to Get Along
WillS 43 She Don't Love Me That Way
WAYS (4)
ArnK 34 Your Ways and Actions
Cann 1 Poor Boy, Long Ways from Home
HicR 3 Poor Boy a Long Ways from Home
WillS 21 Low Down Ways

WAYWARD (1)
Beam 1 Wayward Girl Blues
WE (5)
EdwF 2 We Got to Get Together
HicR 19 We Sure Got Hard Times Now
McCoJ 25 We Gonna Pitch a Boogie Woogie
SykR 11 We Can Sell that Thing
WasbS 8 We Gonna Move
WEAK (2)
BakW 3 Weak-Minded Blues
BakW 7 Weak-Minded Blues
WEARY (4)
Bond 1 Weary Worried Blues
DayT 3 Billiken's Weary Blues
HilB 6 Lonesome Weary Blues
McTW 29 Weary Hearted Blues
WEATHER (1)
WhiJ 2 Stormy Weather No. 1
WEAVIL (2)
Patt 1 Mississippi Bo Weavil Blues
Rain 2 Bo-Weavil Blues
WEEK (1)
JohAl 2 Next Week Sometime
WEEPING (2)
FloN 2 Midnight Weeping Blues
SmiB 4 Weeping Willow Blues
WELFARE (2)
WhiJ 1 Welfare Blues
WillS 30 Welfare Store Blues
WELL (4)
ArnK 36 My Well Is Dry
Cali 1 Fare Thee Well Blues
JefB 54 Oil Well Blues
Patt 19 Dry Well Blues
WENT (1)
SpiV 2 The Alligator Pond Went Dry
WEST (6)
HendK 1 West End Blues
MackA 1 West End Blues
MontE 7 Out West Blues
MontE 9 West Texas Blues
MooA 1 West Texas Woman
ThpE 4 West Virginia Blues
WESTERN (2)
JonM 4 Western Union Blues
WillS 32 Western Union Man
WET (1)
CarrL 2 Gettin' All Wet
WHAT (12) [see also WATCHA]
BelA 4 I Don't Care Who Gets What I Don't Want
CarrL 10 What More Can I Do?
Gill 6 Got to Reap What You Sow
GreLi 4 What Have I Done?
JackC 5 I Got What It Takes But It Breaks My Heart to
        Give It Away
JohLi 1 Never Let Your Left Hand Know What Your Right
        Hand Do
JohLo 19 It Ain't What You Usta Be
McCoJ 21 What You Gonna Do?
MartD 2 What You Was You Used to Be
Pull 1 Black Gal What Makes Your Head So Hard?--No. 2
Tamp 4 What Is It That Tastes Like Gravy?
Wate 9 You Can't Do What My Last Man Did
WHAT'S (5)
GreLi 8 What's the Matter with Love?
King 1 What's That Tastes Like Gravy
MemM 18 What's the Matter with the Mill?
Shad 14 What's the Matter?
Stok 13 What's the Matter Blues
WHEATSTRAW (2)
Whea 33 Peetie Wheatstraw Stomp
Whea 34 Peetie Wheatstraw Stomp No. 2
WHEEL (1)
ArnK 14 Policy Wheel Blues
WHEN (13)
AleT 16 When You Get to Thinking
BigB 22 When I Had Money
JohLo 11 When You Fall For Someone That's Not Your Own

WHEN (cont.)
JohM   2   When a 'Gator Holler, Folk Say It's a Sign of
           Rain
JohR   7   When You Get a Good Friend
LeeX   2   Nobody Knows You When You're Down and Out
McCoJ 3   When the Levee Breaks
Patt 13   When Your Way Gets Dark
SmiB 29   Nobody Knows You When You're Down and Out
Stev   2   I'll See You in the Spring When the Birds
           Begin to Sing
Whea 22   When I Get My Bonus
Whea 30   When a Man Gets Down
WhiW   6   When Can I Change My Clothes
WHERE (6)
DorsT 10   Where Did You Stay Last Night?
JohLo 17   Hard Time Ain't Gone No Where
Luca   2   Where Did You Stay Last Night?
MemM 24   Where Is My Good Man
Rain 11   Honey Where You Been So Long
ThoHo 3   Put It Where I Can Get It
WHIPPED (1)
Blacm 3   I Whipped My Woman With a Single Tree
WHISKEY (11)
ChatP 13   Whiskey and Gin Blues
DaviW 16   Ashes in My Whiskey
GibC   2   Whiskey Moan Blues
Gill 15   You Drink Too Much Whiskey
HicR 16   Me and My Whiskey
JohJa 1   Barrel of Whiskey Blues
McCl   8   Whiskey Head Man
McPB   3   Whiskey Man Blues
Pope   1   Whiskey Drinkin' Blues
SmiJ   9   Corn Whiskey Blues
WillS 10   Whiskey Headed Blues
WHISTLE (2)
BelE   4   Frisco Whistle Blues
Temp   1   Big Boat Whistle
WHITEWASH (2)
PooJ   1   Whitewash Station Blues
Shad 11   Whitewash Station Blues
WHO (1)
BelA   4   I Don't Care Who Gets What I Don't Want
WHOOPEE (2)
HilK   1   Whoopee Blues
HilK   2   Whoopee Blues
WHO'S (2)
ChatB 24   Who's Been Here?
Este 14   Who's Been Tellin' You Buddy Brown Blues
WHY (3)
DaviW 23   Why Shouldn't I Be Blue
GreLi 6   Why Don't You Do Right?
LewF   8   Why Don't You Come Home Blues
WICKED (1)
MackA 2   Wicked Daddy Blues
WIFE (1)
Linc   4   My Wife Drove Me From the Door
WILD (9)
ArnK 23   Wild Water Blues
ColFL 2   Wild About My Loving
CoxI   2   Wild Women Don't Have the Blues
JackJ 2   I'm Wild About My Lovin'
JohBi 4   Wild Jack Blues
McCoJ 4   I'm Wild About My Stuff
UnkA   8   The Wild Cat Squawl
WillJ 7   Wild Cow Blues
WillJ 13   I'm Getting Wild About Her
WILL (4)
Doyl   2   Grief Will Kill You
LewF 10   I Will Turn Your Money Green
McCoJ 1   That Will Be Alright
Nick   6   You May Leave But This Will Bring You Back
WILLIE'S (1)
Newb   4   Hambone Willie's Dreamy-Eyed Woman's Blues
WILLOW (1)
SmiB   4   Weeping Willow Blues
WIND (1)
DaviW 3   Howling Wind Blues
WINDOW (4)
BradT 5   Window Pane Blues

WINDOW (cont.)
Rang   1   T. P. Window Blues
RupO   1   I Raised My Window and Looked at the Risin'
           Sun
SmiB   3   Ticket Agent Ease Your Window Down
WINDOWS (1)
GibC 16   Keep Your Windows Pinned
WINTER (1)
McTW 34   Cold Winter Day
WIRE (1)
Whea   3   Don't Hang My Clothes on No Barbed Wire Line
WITHOUT (1)
GibC 15   Blues Without a Dime
WOKE (1)
Gill 17   Woke Up Cold in Hand
WOLF (5)
SmiJ   1   Howling Wolf Blues--No. 1
SmiJ   2   Howling Wolf Blues--No. 2
SmiJ 11   Hungry Wolf
WooH   4   Wolf River Blues
WooO   2   Lone Wolf Blues
WOMAN (72)
AleT   6   No More Woman Blues
AndeJ 1   Free Woman Blues
BakW   5   Crooked Woman Blues
Barn   2   If You Want a Good Woman--Get One Long and
           Tall
Batt   1   Country Woman
BelA   2   Every Woman Blues
Blacm 3   I Whipped My Woman With a Single Tree
Blacw 10   No Good Woman Blues
Blak 23   Notoriety Woman Blues
Blak 25   Poker Woman Blues
BogL 21   Reckless Woman
Brac   8   Woman Woman Blues
CarrL 7   Alabama Woman Blues
CarrL 23   Barrel House Woman
CarrL 24   Barrel House Woman No. 2
CarrL 31   Evil-Hearted Woman
CarrL 32   Good Woman Blues
ChatP 1   Beer Drinking Woman
DaviC 1   Elm Street Woman Blues
DaviW 24   The Only Woman
DorsT 4   Second-Hand Woman Blues
East   1   No Woman No Nickel
Este 15   Married Woman Blues
FulB 13   Crooked Woman Blues
HicR   6   Crooked Woman Blues
HilSy 2   Needin' My Woman Blues
JamS   1   Devil Got My Woman
JefB 30   Deceitful Brownskin Woman
JefB 64   Southern Woman Blues
JohEb 2   Sobbin' Woman Blues
JohJo 2   Don't Want No Woman
JohK   2   Wrong Woman Blues
JohLo 3   Sweet Woman You Can't Go Wrong
JohR   1   Kind Hearted Woman Blues
JohR   2   Kind Hearted Woman Blues
JonM 22   Never Tell a Woman Friend
Ledb 18   T. B. Woman Blues
McCoJ 16   Evil Devil Woman Blues
MemM   8   Don't Want No Woman
MontE 1   The Woman I Love Blues
MontE 11   Mistreatin' Woman Blues
MooA   1   West Texas Woman
MooAl 4   Broadway St. Woman Blues
Rach   6   Gravel Road Woman
ReyJ   1   Outside Woman Blues
ReyW   2   Third Street Woman Blues
Shad   9   A Black Woman Is Like a Black Snake
SmiC   1   I Got Everything a Woman Needs
SmiSi 2   Pennsylvania Woman Blues
Stov   2   A Woman Gets Tired of the Same Man All the
           Time
SykR 12   No Good Woman Blues
ThoJ   2   No Good Woman Blues
ThoR   2   Hard to Rule Woman Blues
Tore   1   Married Woman Blues
Vinc 17   Go Away Woman

YOU (cont.)
ColeJ	1	Mistreated the Only Friend You Had
CoxI	11	You Stole My Man
DaviW	2	That Stuff You Sell Ain't No Good
DaviW	13	I Can Tell By the Way You Smell
DaviW	18	Think You Need a Shot
DaviW	26	Don't You Want to Go
DorsT	10	Where Did You Stay Last Night?
DorsT	14	If You Want Me to Love You
Doyl	2	Grief Will Kill You
East	2	I'm Waitin' On You
Este	14	Who's Been Tellin' You Buddy Brown Blues
Este	41	You Shouldn't Do That
FulB	15	You Got to Have Your Dollar
GibC	1	Beat You Doing It
Gill	6	Got to Reap What You Sow
Gill	11	It Looks Bad for You
Gill	15	You Drink Too Much Whiskey
Gill	16	I'm Gonna Leave You on the Outskirts of Town
GreLi	6	Why Don't You Do Right?
GreLi	11	If I Didn't Love You
GreLi	13	I'm Wasting My Time on You
HendK	3	Have You Ever Felt That Way?
Hull	4	Don't You Leave Me Here
Hull	5	Mama You Don't Know How
JackC	14	Mama, Don't You Think I Know?
JamS	8	If You Haven't Got Any Hay Get on Down the Road
JohLo	3	Sweet Woman You Can't Go Wrong
JohLo	11	When You Fall For Someone That's Not Your Own
JohLo	19	It Ain't What You Usta Be
JohLo	21	I'm Nuts Over You
JohM	1	If I Let You Get Away With It Once You'll Do It All of the Time
JohR	7	When You Get a Good Friend
JonM	11	You May Go, But You'll Come Back Some Day
JorC	8	You Run and Tell Your Daddy
Lask	1	How You Want Your Rollin' Done
Ledb	8	Baby, Don't You Love Me No More?
LeeX	2	Nobody Knows You When You're Down and Out
LewF	8	Why Don't You Come Home Blues
Luca	2	Where Did You Stay Last Night?
McCl	2	Baby, Don't You Want to Go?
McCl	17	You Can't Read My Mind
McCoJ	9	I Called You This Morning
McCoJ	18	You Got to Move--Part 1
McCoJ	19	Something Gonna Happen to You
McCoJ	21	What You Gonna Do?
MartC	1	Farewell to You Baby
MartD	2	What You Was You Used to Be
MemM	3	I'm Talking About You
MemM	14	I'm Talking About You--No. 2
MemM	15	I Called You This Morning
MemM	20	I Don't Want that Junk Outa You
MemM	28	You Got to Move--Part I
MemM	31	Dirty Mother For You
MemM	32	You Can't Give It Away
MemM	36	Man You Won't Give Me No Money
MontE	4	Mama You Don't Mean Me No Good
MontE	5	The First Time I Met You
Nick	6	You May Leave But This Will Bring You Back
Nick	9	You Got Me Rollin'
Rain	11	Honey Where You Been So Long
Rame	2	Tired of You Driving Me
Shad	1	Sometimes I Think I Love You
Shad	16	I Can Beat You Plenty
SmiB	29	Nobody Knows You When You're Down and Out
SmiC	16	You Don't Know My Mind
SmiL	1	Gonna Put You Right in Jail
SmiL	2	Don't You Leave Me Here
SmiT	14	Love Me Like You Used To
SpiV	8	How Do You Do It That Way?
Stev	2	I'll See You in the Spring When the Birds Begin to Sing
Stok	1	You Shall
Stok	6	You Shall
SykR	13	As True As I've Been to You
ThoH	5	Honey, Won't You Allow Me One More Chance?
Vinc	15	I've Got Blood in My Eyes for You

YOU (cont.)
WallS	5	Have You Ever Been Down
WasbS	32	You Stole My Love
Wate	9	You Can't Do What My Last Man Did
WillJ	8	I Know You Gonna Miss Me
WillS	12	You Give an Account
WillS	39	You Got to Step Back

YOU'LL (4)
HarO	2	You'll Like My Loving
JohLi	2	You'll Never Miss Your Jelly Till Your Jelly Rollers Gone
JohM	1	If I Let You Get Away With It Once You'll Do It All of the Time
JonM	11	You May Go, But You'll Come Back Some Day

YOUNG (1)
SmiB	19	Young Woman's Blues

YOUR (52)
ArnK	13	Let Your Money Talk
ArnK	34	Your Ways and Actions
BigB	18	Keep Your Hands Off Her
BracM	1	You Scolded Me and Drove Me from Your Door
BradT	2	Pack Up Your Trunk Blues
ChatB	10	Let Me Roll Your Lemon
ChatB	21	Your Biscuits Are Big Enough for Me
ChatP	16	Lend Me Your Love
ColFJ	4	Save Your Money--Let These Women Go
DaviW	19	Let Me in Your Saddle
DaviW	20	Call Your Name
DaviW	21	Can't See Your Face
FulB	15	You Got to Have Your Dollar
GibC	5	Stop Your Rambling
GibC	16	Keep Your Windows Pinned
GreLi	3	Give Your Mama One Smile
HendB	2	Let Your Love Come Down
JackC	20	Your Baby Ain't Sweet Like Mine
JackC	28	Baby Please Loan Me Your Heart
JohK	1	Lady, Your Clock Ain't Right
JohLi	1	Never Let Your Left Hand Know What Your Right Hand Do
JohLi	2	You'll Never Miss Your Jelly Till Your Jelly Rollers Gone
JohLo	11	When You Fall For Someone That's Not Your Own
JohLo	24	I Ain't Gonna Be Your Fool
JonM	20	Never Drive a Beggar from Your Door
JorC	8	You Run and Tell Your Daddy
JorC	11	Got Your Water On
JorC	12	Don't Put Your Dirty Hands on Me
Lask	1	How You Want Your Rollin' Done
LewF	10	I Will Turn Your Money Green
McTW	35	Your Time to Worry
Patt	13	When Your Way Gets Dark
Pick	2	Let Me Squeeze Your Lemon
Pull	1	Black Gal What Makes Your Head So Hard?--No. 2
RupO	2	Ain't Goin' to Be Your Low Down Dog
Shad	15	Feed Your Friend with a Long Handled Spoon
Shad	17	Taking Your Place
Shad	20	Take Your Fingers Off It
SmiB	3	Ticket Agent Ease Your Window Down
SmiB	17	Lost Your Head Blues
SmiB	35	Do Your Duty
SmiC	13	I'm Gonna Tear Your Playhouse Down
SmiC	20	Mean Papa, Turn in Your Key
SmiC	22	Don't Advertise Your Man
Spru	8	Your Man Is Gone
Vinc	6	Your Good Man Caught the Train and Gone
WasbS	17	Yes I Got Your Woman
WasbS	26	Let Me Play Your Vendor
Weld	5	Hitch Me to Your Buggy and Drive Me Like a Mule
WillK	3	Get Your Head Trimmed Down

YOU'RE (4)
Gill	1	You're Laughing Now
JohLo	13	Sam, You're Just a Rat
LeeX	2	Nobody Knows You When You're Down and Out
SmiB	29	Nobody Knows You When You're Down and Out

YOU'VE (6)
CarrL	35	You've Got Me Grieving
FulB	8	You've Got Something There
SmiB	9	You've Been a Good Old Wagon

```
YOU'VE (cont.)
  SmiB  22  After You've Gone
  SmiT   8  You've Got to Beat Me to Keep Me
  WillS 14  You've Been Foolin' Round Town
YO-YO [YO YO] (3)
  HarZ   1  Memphis Yo Yo Blues
  HicR  18  Yo-Yo Blues No. 2
  JefB  62  Yo Yo Blues
??? (1)
  WhiG   3  The Blues Ain't Nothin' But. . .???
```